Note to Students

Accounting is a stimulating and rewarding field of study. To be successful, professionals in all areas of business, such as finance, production, marketing, personnel, and general management, must have an understanding of accounting. In addition, men and women whose careers are in nonbusiness areas often use their knowledge of accounting to perform their duties more effectively.

As you begin your study of accounting, you may find the following suggestions helpful:

- Read the learning objectives before you begin studying a chapter.
- Scan the chapter to get a feel for the material before you begin a detailed reading of the chapter.
- Briefly review the Glossary of Key Terms in the Chapter Review section to familiarize yourself with the terminology that will be emphasized in the chapter.
- As you read each chapter, you may wish to underline or highlight points that are important. Also, you should pay special attention to key terms that are identified in color when they are first defined in the chapter.
- After reading the chapter, carefully study the Chapter Review, giving special attention to the following items:

Key Points. The Key Points are summarized by learning objectives. You should be able to perform each of the learning objectives. If you cannot perform a learning objective, review the section of the chapter where it is discussed and illustrated.

Glossary of Key Terms. You should be able to define each key term. If you cannot, refer to the section of the chapter where the term is first presented and discussed.

Self-Examination Questions. Answer each of the self-examination questions. Check your answers by referring to the end of the chapter for the correct response and explanation.

Illustrative Problem. Study the illustrative problem and its suggested solution. Each illustrative problem applies the chapter's concepts and principles to a problem situation. If you have difficulty understanding the illustrative problem, refer to the section of the chapter where the applicable concepts and principles are discussed and illustrated.

- Work all assigned homework. In many cases, the homework is related to specific chapter illustrations, and you may find it helpful to review the relevant chapter sections before you begin a homework assignment.
- Take notes during class lectures and discussions. Pay special attention to the topics covered by your instructor in class.
- In reviewing for examinations, keep in mind those topics that your instructor has emphasized, and review your class notes and the text.
- If you feel you need additional aid, you will find the Study Guides that accompany this textbook helpful. The Study Guides can be ordered from South-Western Publishing Co. by your college or university bookstore.

Accounting Principles

SEVENTEENTH EDITION

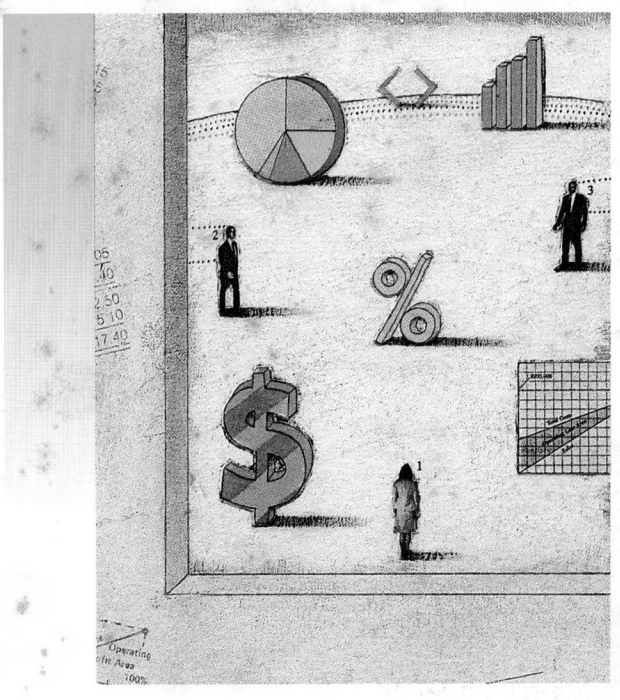

PHILIP E. FESS
Ph.D., C.P.A.
Professor Emeritus of Accountancy
University of Illinois, Champaign-Urbana

CARL S. WARREN
Ph.D., C.P.A., C.M.A., C.I.A.
Professor of Accounting
University of Georgia, Athens

Consulting Editor
JAMES M. REEVE
Ph.D., C.P.A.
Professor of Accounting
University of Tennessee, Knoxville

COLLEGE DIVISION South-Western Publishing Co.

Cincinnati Ohio

Publisher: Mark Hubble
Senior Developmental Editor: Ken Martin
Developmental Editor: Mary Draper
Production Editor II: Leslie Kauffman
Production Editor I: Malvine Litten
Designer: Craig LaGesse Ramsdell
Cover and Internal Illustrator: David Lesh
Internal Art: Rick Moore
Marketing Manager: Randy Haubner

AB70RA
Copyright © 1993
by South-Western Publishing Co.
Cincinnati, Ohio

Library of Congress Cataloging-in-Publication Data

Fess, Philip E.
    Accounting principles/Philip E. Fess, Carl S. Warren.
  —17th ed.
        p.   cm.
    Includes bibliographical references and index.
    ISBN 0-538-81850-6
      1. Accounting   I. Warren, Carl S.   II. Title.
HF5635.F386   1993
657—dc20   92-31633
                                                  CIP

ISBN 0-538-81850-6

1 2 3 4 5 6 7 D 8 7 6 5 4 3 2

Printed in the United States of America

Preface

As the leading text in the market, ACCOUNTING PRINCIPLES builds a solid foundation of basic accounting concepts and principles. Now, the 17th Edition opens the window to a full view of insightful accounting applications and innovative classroom supplements. Our text provides a fresh new perspective on a rapidly changing accounting environment. You'll find unique new features and interesting changes, based on recommendations by the Accounting Education Change Commission, extensive feedback from current users, independent reviews by numerous scholars and educators, and market research that included focus groups and questionnaires. Take a look at the features that make accounting even more intriguing and more fun to teach and learn.

STUDENT CONNECTIONS TO THE BUSINESS WORLD

"You and Accounting." This new feature at the beginning of each chapter relates students' personal experience to the chapter's topic. Students are more motivated to study the chapter when they begin to appreciate the relevance of the accounting and business topics presented.

Enrichment Material. Excerpts from *The Journal of Accountancy, The Wall Street Journal, Business Week, Forbes,* or other well-known business periodicals appear in each chapter to enrich students' learning experience by providing real-world information relevant to the topics in the chapter.

Real-World Examples. Real-world business examples, many taken directly from annual reports of companies such as J. C. Penney Co. and General Electric Co., provide students with a taste of the world of accounting. These examples, integrated throughout the text, add concrete meaning to concepts and principles that might otherwise appear abstract. Throughout the text, numerous citations from *Accounting Trends & Techniques* indicate the frequency with which alternative accounting presentations and methods are used in the real world.

 REAL WORLD FOCUS Each chapter includes at least one discussion question requiring students to interpret and respond to real-world business situations. Some chapters also include a real-world exercise. These questions and exercises are based on actual business data from Maytag Corporation, Tandy Corporation, and other companies.

Ethics. Students are introduced to ethics in accounting in Chapter 1. Ethics in management accounting is emphasized in Chapter 21. An **Ethics Discussion Case** at the end of the Discussion Questions in each chapter presents a scenario to stimulate student discussion of ethical dilemmas in today's business environment. **Videos** developed for the classroom dramatize selected ethics cases. Students can find the codes of professional conduct of the American Institute of Certified Public Accountants and the Institute of Management Accountants in an appendix at the end of the text for easy reference.

CONTEMPORARY COVERAGE

The New Manufacturing Environment. The managerial accounting chapters, beginning with Chapter 21, include the concepts and terminology related to the new manufacturing environment. For example, Chapter 21 discusses just-in-time manufacturing (JIT), the importance of total quality control (TQC), and computer-integrated manufacturing (CIM). Traditional and just-in-time manufacturing systems are compared in an appendix to Chapter 21.

Activity-based costing (ABC) is first discussed in the job order costing chapter (Chapter 22). A detailed discussion and illustration of ABC is presented in an appendix to the process costing chapter (Chapter 23).

Chapters 22 and 23 now include a discussion of the importance of cost allocation, using activity drivers. Cost allocation bases for manufacturing overhead, other than direct labor, are frequently used in the chapter illustrations and in the end-of-chapter exercises and problems. However, some examples of the use of direct-labor-based cost allo-

cation have been retained, since they are still relevant for labor-intensive manufacturing enterprises.

Cost-Volume-Profit Analysis. The cost-volume-profit analysis discussion in Chapter 24 begins with a brief discussion of cost behavior and cost estimation. The remainder of the chapter uses the contribution margin approach to cost-volume-profit analysis. This approach is useful for a variety of managerial decision-making needs. A new appendix, with exercises and problems, provides an in-depth discussion of variable costing.

Responsibility Accounting. The discussion in Chapter 26 now emphasizes the departmental margin approach to responsibility accounting. This approach is consistent with the emphasis in the cost-volume-profit chapter.

Capital Investment Analysis. The discussion of capital investment analysis in Chapter 28 includes considerations related to the new manufacturing environment and the importance of qualitative factors in such an analysis.

Perpetual Inventory Systems. Perpetual inventory systems are initially discussed in Chapter 5, with the introduction to merchandise transactions. This discussion continues in Chapter 6, where a work sheet and financial statements in a perpetual inventory system are illustrated. The discussion of cost flow assumptions (such as lifo and fifo) related to perpetual inventory systems is in Chapter 10. At this point, students are better able to handle the complexities of the physical flow of inventory and cost flows.

Internal Control. The discussion in Chapter 7 incorporates new examples of internal controls that students might encounter in their own experiences and in their future work environment. Similarly, internal controls are emphasized in Chapters 8–12. In each of these chapters, internal control exercises have been added.

Statement of Cash Flows. Chapter 19 now includes both the indirect and direct methods of preparing the cash flows from operating activities section of the statement of cash flows. The indirect method is presented first, since this method is used by 97% of the companies surveyed in the 45th Edition of *Accounting Trends & Techniques*. In addition, companies using the direct method must reconcile operating income with cash flows from operating activities, using the format of the indirect method. Thus, an understanding of the indirect method facilitates the discussion of the direct method. Work sheets that can be used for both methods are presented in an appendix to the chapter. End-of-chapter discussion questions, exercises, and problems are included for both methods.

International Accounting. The globalization of business and the impact on accounting are first recognized in the "Evolution of Accounting." Also, numerous references to companies that engage in international business, such as Hershey Foods Corporation and Toys "R" Us, Inc., are cited throughout the text. In addition, Chapter 18 covers accounting for international transactions. International competition is discussed in Chapter 21 in the context of trends in manufacturing and service industries.

SKILLS-ORIENTED FEATURES FOR TOMORROW'S BUSINESS LEADERS

These new end-of-chapter exercises challenge students to analyze and discover what is wrong with a financial statement, a report, or a management decision. They are ideal for a stimulating learning activity in the classroom.

SHARPEN YOUR COMMUNICATION SKILLS ► Several questions, exercises, problems, and the mini-case at the end of each chapter provide an opportunity for students to respond in an oral or written form. These assignments are designed to help students develop their ability to communicate effectively in an accounting and business environment. Additional writing assignments and some guidelines for using these assignments are provided in the *Instructor's Manual* that accompanies the text.

Mini-Cases. Each chapter contains a Mini-Case that simulates a real-world business situation. The Mini-Cases require students to use higher levels of cognitive learning and assist in summarizing chapter concepts. They can also be used as a group learning activity. Selected Mini-Cases are presented on **video** for an exciting classroom presentation.

Computer Applications. Students may use the **Solutions Software** to solve selected problems through Chapter 23, including the comprehensive

problems. The computer instructions for each of these problems, which involve a general ledger, are now included in the text, following the manual instructions. The instructions are identified by the symbol at the left. Students may also use the software to solve 5 practice sets.

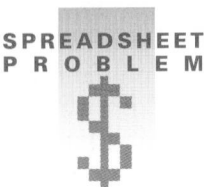

Spreadsheet Template Diskettes may also be used for solving selected exercises and problems. These diskettes include a spreadsheet tutorial and "what if" analysis for problems identified, through Chapter 28, by the symbol at the left.

PRACTICAL PEDAGOGICAL IMPROVEMENTS

Revision of the Accounting Cycle Chapters. This edition continues to reinforce the accounting cycle by presenting it twice—once for a service enterprise (in Chapters 1–4) and once for a merchandising enterprise (in Chapters 5–6). This basic presentation gives students a clear understanding of the accounting process and helps them develop the analytical thinking skills that are essential for success in the accounting principles course. To assist students in understanding the step-by-step process of preparing a work sheet, **acetate overlays** are used in Chapter 4.

Chapter 1 continues to introduce and illustrate the **statement of cash flows** as one of the basic financial statements. However, students are not required to prepare a statement of cash flows until Chapter 19.

Chapter 3 now presents the matching concept and all four basic types of adjusting entries. The discussion of recording prepaid expenses initially as expenses and unearned revenues initially as revenues is presented in **Appendix C**, which includes exercises. **Reversing entries** are covered in an appendix to Chapter 4.

New Continuing Illustration of the Accounting Cycle. A continuing illustration in Chapters 1 through 6 covers the accounting cycle for a service enterprise and a merchandising enterprise. In Chapters 1–4, the enterprise offers computer consulting services. In Chapters 5–6, the enterprise becomes a merchandising enterprise that sells microcomputers and related software. This continuity facilitates student understanding and enables students to correlate the concepts and principles introduced in these chapters.

Sole Proprietorship and Corporation Forms of Organization. The first 13 chapters use the sole proprietorship form of organization. This simplifies the discussion of basic accounting concepts and principles in the first accounting course. Accounting for the corporation form of organization is introduced in Chapter 15.

Use of Color. Extensive use of color throughout the text and captivating illustrations opening all the chapters draw students into the text. In addition, the chart below indicates how color is used to consistently highlight the material in the text.

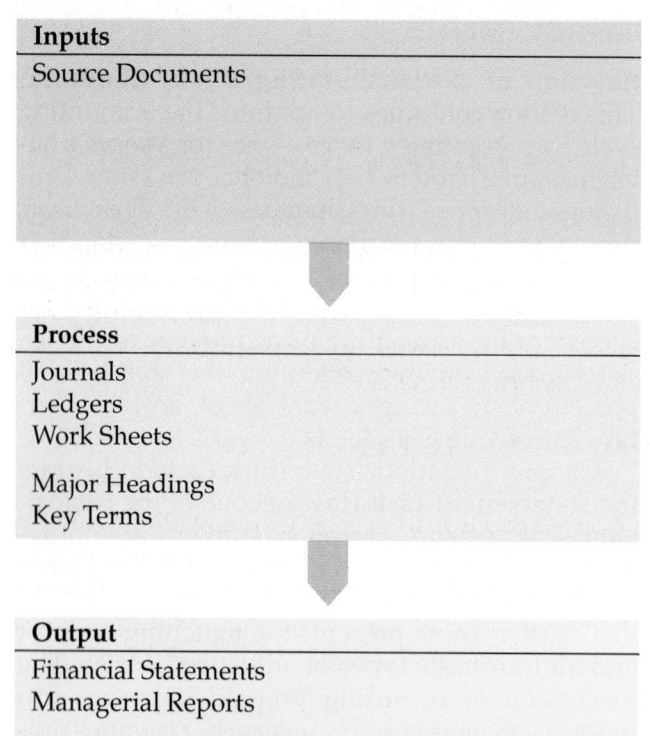

Inputs
Source Documents

Process
Journals
Ledgers
Work Sheets
Major Headings
Key Terms

Output
Financial Statements
Managerial Reports

Technology for Classroom and Student Use. State-of-the-art technology supports a multimedia package for capturing the attention of visually-oriented students. A **Video Laser Disk** provides easy, instant access to videos, software, transparencies, and illustrations. The **Hyper-Graphics** software enhances class lectures with graphics, color, and animation. In addition, a series of **videos** for classroom or student use reinforce accounting concepts and add the reality of the business world.

Learning Objectives. Revised to emphasize students' learning goals and actions, the learning objectives focus directly on the *action* objectives of studying each chapter.

- Each chapter begins with a listing of the learning objectives, providing a framework for the presentation of the chapter material.

- Each learning objective is repeated in the margin next to the start of the discussion to which the objective relates.

- The learning objectives are tied into the chapter review.

- All end-of-chapter exercises and problems are identified by learning objective.

Readability. To enhance clarity and understandability, the readability level of each chapter was analyzed, using a professional software program. In addition to revisions, an informal writing style and the active voice are used to enliven the text discussion of accounting issues.

Glossary. A new glossary at the end of each chapter defines each key term. The learning objective number follows the definition to indicate where the term was discussed in the chapter. The key terms also appear in a complete glossary at the end of the text.

Classification of Accounts. A classification of the accounts on the financial statements, including the normal account balance, is presented on the inside back cover for students' use when reading the text and solving end-of-chapter materials.

Accounting for Merchandising Enterprises. The two-chapter format for discussing merchandising enterprises (Chapters 5 and 6) now begins by presenting comparative income statements for service and merchandising enterprises. Differences between the two types of statements are then used as a basis for discussing merchandise transactions and financial statements for merchandising enterprises.

Special Journals. The presentation of special journals in Chapter 7 now begins with the less complex sales journal and the cash receipts journal, followed by the purchases journal and the cash payments journal. In addition, this chapter includes a new section on adapting special journals to the unique aspects of a business enterprise.

Partnerships. The partnership chapter (Chapter 14) now presents the bonus method rather than the goodwill method of recording the admission of a new partner. In addition, the discussion of partnership liquidation has been simplified.

Accounting for Bonds Payable. The coverage of bonds payable has been simplified in Chapter 17. The chapter first presents the amortization of bond discounts and premiums using the straight-line method. This enables students to grasp the essential concepts involved in amortizing discounts and premiums before the chapter introduces the more complex effective interest rate method. In addition, this flexible presentation allows instructors who wish to omit the effective interest rate method to easily do so without interrupting the flow of the material.

ILLUSTRATIVE PROBLEM Each chapter review includes a problem and solution that are similar to a possible homework assignment. Students can build confidence in their abilities to apply a chapter's concepts and principles by reviewing this problem.

Self-Examination Questions. Each chapter review also includes a set of multiple-choice questions on the basic concepts of the chapter. Students can answer these questions and compare their answers with the correct ones provided at the end of the chapter. The explanations of both the correct and the incorrect answers are a subtle yet effective learning tool.

End-of-Chapter Materials. The end-of-chapter questions, ethics cases, exercises, "What's Wrong With This?" exercises, problems, mini-cases, and comprehensive problems were carefully written and revised by the authors to be both practical and comprehensive. To ensure their accuracy, all end-of-chapter materials and related supplementary items were verified and proofed by the editorial staff and independent resources.

A **"B" Problem** is now included for each **"A" Problem** in the text. These problems increase the variety and volume of assignment materials and give instructors a wide choice of subject matter and range of difficulty.

Six **Comprehensive Problems**—at the end of Chapters 3, 6, 7, 12, 17, and 20—integrate and summarize the concepts and principles of several chapters. Instructors may assign these problems as mini practice sets for students to complete manually. As an alternative, these problems can be worked with the Solutions Software.

Check Figures. Check figures at the end of the text assist students in checking end-of-chapter problems. Agreement with the check figures indicates that a significant portion of the solution is basically correct.

SUPPLEMENTARY MATERIALS

ACCOUNTING PRINCIPLES is part of a well-integrated educational package that includes materials designed for use by both the student and the instructor. These materials are carefully prepared and reviewed to maintain consistency and high quality throughout.

Available to Instructors

Annotated Edition. In addition to the text material for students, the unique instructor's edition contains points of emphasis, points of interest, teaching suggestions, discussion points, in-class exercises, real-world notes, and check figures.

Solutions Manuals. These manuals contain solutions to all end-of-chapter materials, including the discussion questions, ethics cases, exercises, "What's Wrong With This?" exercises, problems, mini-cases, and comprehensive problems.

Instructor's Manual, prepared by Donna Chadwick of Sinclair Community College. Extensively rewritten, this manual provides suggestions for cooperative learning activities and additional examples and illustrations for use in the classroom. Transparency masters for classroom use are also included.

Spreadsheet Applications. These template diskettes are used with Lotus® 1-2-3[1] or Microsoft® Excel[2]. They are complimentary to instructors at educational institutions that adopt this text.

Solutions Transparencies. Transparencies of solutions to all exercises and problems, including the comprehensive problems, are available.

Teaching Transparencies. New teaching transparencies go beyond the text and add visual impact to the class lecture.

Videos. Six videotapes assist in classroom presentations. Part Opener videos show the real-world relevance of the material to be studied. Some of these Part Opener videos include interviews with executives, who highlight the importance of the accounting material to be covered. A set of new Instructional Videos and Illustrative Problem videos may be used to review the key points of each chapter. Selected Ethics Cases and Mini-Cases are dramatized on video. *Setting the Stage* includes 24 brief role-play segments that bring the world of financial accounting to life. *Luca Pacioli: Unsung Hero of the Renaissance* is a 25-minute documentary on the life of the father of accounting.

Video Laser Disk. The video laser disk is the ultimate multi-media approach to classroom presentations. Its flexibility and ease of use make it a dynamic tool for instructors.

Test Bank, prepared by Anita Hope of Tarrant County Junior College—Northeast. A collection of more than 2,700 problems, multiple-choice questions, and true or false questions, accompanied by solutions, is available in both printed and microcomputer **(MicroSWAT III and MicroSWAT FAST)** versions. The microcomputer versions are available in both IBM®[3] and Macintosh® formats.[4]

The Test Bank questions test three levels of learning—ability to recall key terms or key facts, computational ability, and analytical ability. Each question or problem is identified with its level of difficulty as well as the chapter's learning objective. Individual items may be selected for short quizzes, periodic exams, or final exams. The number of questions and problems provides variety from year to year and from class section to class section. The printed version of the Test Bank also contains illustrative Achievement Tests and solutions.

Keys for Practice Sets. Each key is a complete solution for its corresponding practice set.

HyperGraphics, revised by Dan Biagi of Walla Walla Community College. This instructional delivery system uses a microcomputer, a liquid crystal device (LCD), an overhead projector, and a hand-held remote control device. In addition, the Spreadsheet Template problems can be accessed through this software. An Instructor's Manual explains how to install and use the program. The addition of response pads allows students to interact in the presentation.

Available to Students

Solutions Software, prepared by Dale H. Klooster and Warren W. Allen of Educational Technical Systems. This general ledger program is tailored specifically to ACCOUNTING PRINCIPLES. It may be used with the IBM® PC, IBM® PS/2, the Tandy® 1000[5], and the Macintosh® microcomputers.

---

[1] Lotus and 1-2-3 are registered trademarks of the Lotus Development Corporation. Any reference to Lotus or 1-2-3 refers to this footnote.
[2] Microsoft is a registered trademark of Microsoft Corporation.
[3] IBM is a registered trademark of International Business Machines Corporation. Any reference to the IBM Personal Computer or the IBM Personal System/2 refers to this footnote.
[4] Macintosh is a registered trademark of McIntosh Laboratory, Inc., and is used by Apple Computer, Inc., with its express permission.
[5] Tandy 1000 is a registered trademark of the Radio Shack Division of Tandy Corporation. Any reference to the Tandy 1000 microcomputer refers to this footnote.

Working Papers. Appropriate printed forms for completing end-of-chapter problems and mini-cases are available in bound volumes. The first volume for use with Chapters 1–14 and the second volume for use with Chapters 14–28 are preprinted for working specific problems. The third volume for use with Chapters 1–28 is a set of blank forms that students may use to work exercises and problems.

Study Guides, prepared by James A. Heintz of the University of Connecticut and Carl S. Warren. Designed to assist in comprehending the concepts and principles presented in the text, these publications are printed in two volumes (one for Chapters 1–14 and one for Chapters 14–28). They include an outline for each chapter as well as brief objective questions and problems. Solutions to the questions and problems are at the back of the Study Guide. The Study Guides also contain quiz and test hints to help students focus on their review of material. The first Study Guide now features a **Continuing Problem, prepared by George Heyman of Oakton Community College.** This problem in Chapters 2–6 covers the accounting cycle for a single company.

Financial Accounting and Managerial Accounting Tutors, prepared by Thomas P. Lawler of SUNY College at Geneseo. These interactive computerized tutorials provide step-by-step explanations and examples for students' review of accounting principles.

Student Reference Card. This reference card provides students with a quick review of basic accounting facts, such as the rules of debit and credit and the break-even point formula.

Practice Sets. Six practice sets offer a variety of options for synthesizing and reinforcing the text's coverage.

- **Sally's Holiday Cleaning, prepared by L. L. Price of Pierce College,** is a sole proprietorship service enterprise that uses a general journal.

- **Columbia River Nursery, prepared by Dan Biagi of Walla Walla Community College,** is a merchandising sole proprietorship that uses special journals.

- **Key Systems, prepared by Edward E. Stumpf of Fullerton College,** is a merchandising sole proprietorship that uses a voucher system and a payroll register.

- **First Designs Inc., prepared by Edward Krohn of Miami-Dade Community College—South,** is a departmentalized merchandising corporation.

- **Highpoint Solar Inc., prepared by Alice Sineath of Forsyth Technical College,** is a manufacturing corporation that uses a job order cost system.

- **SEMO Sporting Goods Supply Inc., prepared by Deborah F. Beard and Stephen C. DelVecchio of Southeast Missouri State University and John A. Elfrink of Ferris State University,** requires the preparation of correcting entries and financial statements for a wholesaling corporation.

Integrated Accounting: IBM, 4e, and Integrated Accounting: Macintosh, prepared by Dale H. Klooster and Warren W. Allen, are stand-alone, automated accounting packages intended for a first course in microcomputer accounting. Completion time for each is approximately 45–55 hours.

Electronic Spreadsheet Applications for Accounting Principles, Financial Accounting, and Managerial Accounting, prepared by Gaylord N. Smith of Albion College, are supplemental text-workbooks with template diskettes that include accounting applications and a Lotus 1-2-3 tutorial. Each text-workbook requires approximately 20–25 hours for completion.

Writing for Accountants, by Aletha Hendrickson of the University of Maryland, is a handbook that emphasizes written and oral communication skills.

Ethical Issues in the Practice of Accounting, by W. Steve Albrecht of Brigham Young University, provides students with background material to stimulate discussions of ethics and increase students' awareness of ethical dilemmas faced by accountants.

Understanding Financial Statements, by Gus Gordon of the University of Southern Mississippi, develops an understanding of accounting statements, without the use of debits and credits.

x

ACKNOWLEDGMENTS

Throughout the textbook, relevant professional statements of the Financial Accounting Standards Board (including FASB Statement Nos. 105 and 107), the Institute of Management Accountants, and other authoritative publications are discussed, quoted, paraphrased, or footnoted. We are indebted to the American Accounting Association, the American Institute of Certified Public Accountants, the Financial Accounting Standards Board, and the Institute of Management Accountants for material from their publications.

In writing the 17th Edition, we received extensive feedback from users of previous editions as well as those who had not used our text. We are most grateful for this input, and we continue to welcome your comments and suggestions.

Faculty from the following schools provided comments that were useful to us as we began the revision process:

Alvin Community College
Austin Community College
Austin Peay State University
Bellarmine College
Bergen Community College
Brookdale Community College
Broward Community College
Bryant College
Central Connecticut State University
Central Wesleyan College
Cerritos College
Chicago State University
Cisco Junior College
College of DuPage
Cuesta College
CUNY Borough of Manhattan Community College
Dean Junior College
Foothill College
Galveston College
Georgetown College
Glendale Community College
Golden West College
Howard College
Hudson Valley Community College
Jamestown College
Johnson and Wales University
Joliet Junior College
Kearney State College
Los Angeles Pierce College
Manchester Community College
McLennan Community College
Middlesex County College
Moraine Valley Community College
Navarro College
Northeastern (OK) State University
Northeastern Oklahoma A & M College
Northeast Louisiana University
Northern Essex Community College
Northwestern (LA) State University
Orange Coast College
Palm Beach Community College
Palomar College
Pasadena City College
Quincy College
Raritan Valley Community College
Riverside Community College
Salem State College
Sam Houston State University
San Antonio College
Sante Fe Community College
School of the Ozarks College
Sinclair Community College
South Plains College
Southwest Texas State University
St. Philips College
Suffolk County Community College
SUNY College of Technology at Farmingdale
Tarrant County Junior College—Northeast
Texas Southmost College
Trinity Valley Community College
Troy State University
University of Georgia
University of Illinois
University of Mississippi
University of Northern Iowa
University of Rhode Island
University of Southwestern Louisiana
University of Tennessee—Martin
Westchester Community College
Xavier (OH) University
York College of Pennsylvania

The following faculty reviewed manuscript for the 17th Edition and provided helpful comments:

Karen Adamson
Central Washington University

Jamshid Bassieri
Cuesta College

Steve Carter
North Harris County College

Donna Chadwick
Sinclair Community College

Wayne D. Claflin
St. Clair County Community College

Ken Coffey
Johnson County Community College

William D. Cooper
North Carolina A & T University

Sue Counte
Moraine Valley Community College

Robert H. Cox
Edison State Community College

Larry Eaton
Gateway Technical College

Estelle Faier
Metropolitan Community College

William E. Faulk
Northwestern Michigan College

Carl J. Fisher
Foothill College

Edward Fratentaro
Orange Coast College

Ann Gregory
South Plains College

Tim Helton
Joliet Junior College

George Heyman
Oakton Community College

Anita Hope
Tarrant County Junior College—Northeast

James Lentz
Moraine Valley Community College

Larry F. Lofton
Hinds Community College

Gregory K. Lowry
Fort Valley State College

Daniel Luna
Raritan Valley Community College

Patrick McNabb
Ferris State University

Cynthia Middleton
University of Arkansas at Monticello

Greg Mostyn
Mission College

Susan Murphy
Monroe Community College

Terry J. Nunley
University of North Carolina at Charlotte

Alan Ransom
Cypress College

Robert Reas
Sinclair Community College

S. Gunter Samuelson
Suffolk County Community College

Jeanette Sanfillippo
Maryville University

James K. Smith
Baker College

John Uzzo
Northeastern (OK) State University

Joe Williams
Itawamba Community College

Comments from the following faculty were useful in revising the managerial chapters of the textbook:

Linda Bamber
University of Georgia

Shrirish B. Seth
California State University—Fullerton

Mark Frigo
DePaul University

Frank Selto
University of Colorado

David Keys
Northern Illinois University

Earl Kay Stice
Rice University

C. J. McNair
Babson College

We also received useful comments from the following faculty:

Richard Ahrens
Los Angeles Pierce College

Judith Kizzie
Clinton Community College

Lee Baker
Alvin Community College

Jack Klett
Indian River Community College

Hugh Bishop
Del Mar College

Mary Lisko
Augusta College

Craig Christopherson
Richland College

Paul Morgan
Gulf Coast Community College

Carol Collinsworth
Texas Southmost College

Jack Newman
Daytona Beach Community College

Sid Davidson
Foothill College

Alfred Partington
Los Angeles Pierce College

Sam Dean
Macon College

J. C. Randolph
Austin Community College

Larry Dennis
North Georgia College

William Rencher
Seminole Community College

Donald Green
SUNY College of Technology at Farmingdale

Don Sampson
Foothill College

Martha Halling
Daytona Beach Community College

William E. Smith
Xavier (OH) University

Erika Heider
Portland Community College

Pam Strysick
Broward Community College

Joan H. Holloway
Palm Beach Junior College—North

Kenneth Sylvester
Seminole Community College

David Keys
Macon College

Henry VanNoy
Los Angeles Pierce College

The following faculty reviewed manuscript to verify the accuracy of solutions:

Pamela Anglin
Navarro College

Donald MacGilvra
Shoreline Community College

Linda Benz
Jefferson Community College

William Phipps
Vernon Regional Junior College

Donald Brunner
Spokane Falls Community College

Jim Puthoff
Sinclair Community College

Brenda Hester
Volunteer State Community College

Donald Whisler
Spokane Falls Community College

Comments from the following faculty were useful in revising the Solutions Software:

Paul Concilio
McLennan Community College

John R. Stewart
University of Northern Colorado

Charles A. Konkol
University of Wisconsin—Milwaukee

We especially thank James M. Reeve of the University of Tennessee for his contributions to the managerial chapters of the text. We are also grateful to Linda Johnson of Northern Illinois University for reviewing the income tax material.

Finally, we deeply express our appreciation to the South-Western staff—editorial, production, art, advertising, marketing, and sales—for their input and assistance in helping us offer you this refreshing view of accounting.

Philip E. Fess

Carl S. Warren

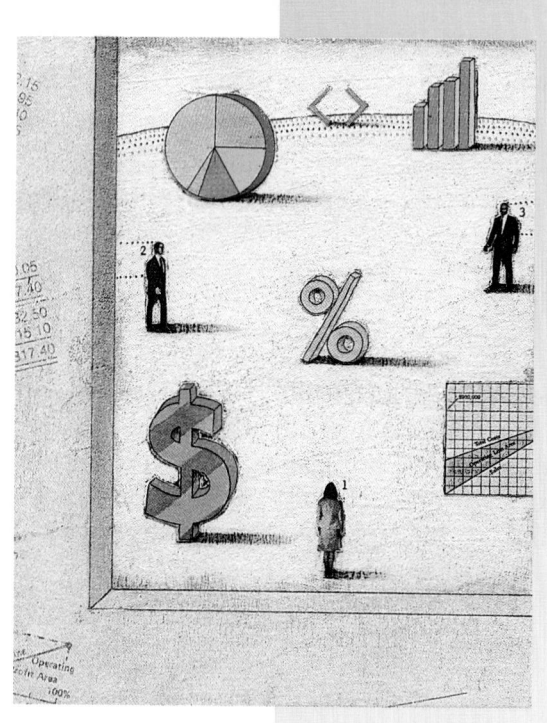

Accounting Principles

PHILIP E. FESS

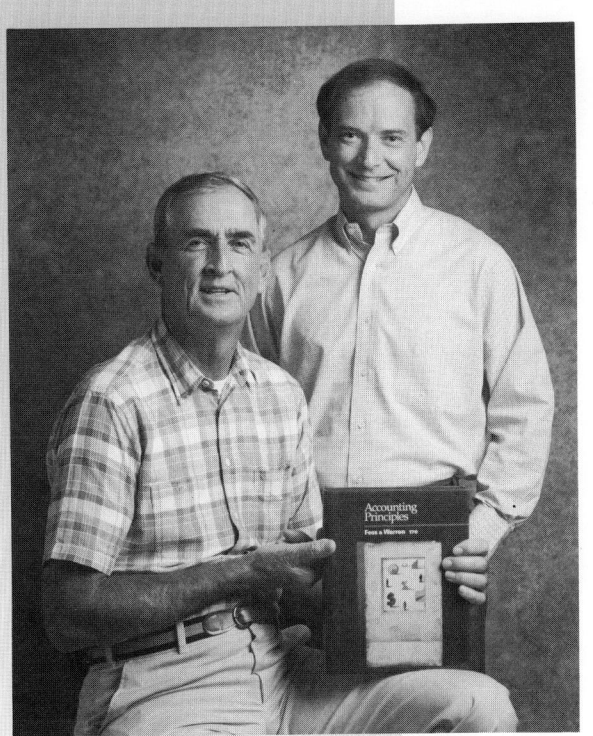

Professor Philip E. Fess (seated) is the Arthur Andersen & Co. Alumni Professor of Accountancy Emeritus at the University of Illinois, Champaign-Urbana. Professor Fess received his PhD from the University of Illinois and has been involved in textbook writing for over twenty-five years. In addition to having more than 30 years of teaching experience, he has won numerous teaching awards, including the University of Illinois, College of Commerce Alumni Association Excellence in Teaching Award and the Illinois CPA Society Educator of the Year Award.

Professor Fess is a CPA and a member of the American Institute of CPAs, the Illinois Society of CPAs, and the American Accounting Association. He has served many professional associations in a variety of ways, including a term as a member of the Auditing Standards Board, editorial advisor to the *Journal of Accountancy*, and chairperson of the American Accounting Association Committee on CPA Examinations. Professor Fess has written more than 100 books and articles, which have appeared in such journals as the *Journal of Accountancy*, the *Accounting Review*, the *CPA Journal*, and *Management Accounting*. He has also served as an expert witness before the U.S. Tax Court and as a member of the Cost Advisory Panel for the Secretary of the Air Force.

Professor Fess and his wife, Suzanne, have three daughters: Linda, who is an Assistant Professor of Accountancy at Northern Illinois University; Ginny, who is a CPA and is employed by Solar Turbine Co.; and Martha, who is also a CPA and is attending law school at the University of San Diego. Professor Fess's hobby is tennis, and he has represented the United States in international tennis competition.

CARL S. WARREN

Professor Carl S. Warren (standing) is the Arthur Andersen & Co. Alumni Professor of Accounting at the J.M. Tull School of Accounting at the University of Georgia, Athens. Professor Warren received his PhD from Michigan State University in 1973 and has taught accounting at the University of Iowa, Michigan State University, the University of Chicago, and the University of Georgia. He has received teaching awards from three different student organizations at the University of Georgia.

Professor Warren is a CPA and CMA. He received a Georgia Gold Key Award and a Certificate of Honorable Mention for his scores on the CPA examination. He received a Certificate of Distinguished Performance for his scores on the CMA examination. Professor Warren is also a Certified Internal Auditor (CIA) and Certified Fraud Examiner (CFE).

Professor Warren is a member of the American Institute of CPAs, the Georgia Society of CPAs, the Institute of Management Accountants, the Institute of Internal Auditors, the American Accounting Association, the Georgia Association of Accounting Educators, the National Association of Fraud Examiners, and the Financial Executives Institute. Professor Warren has served on numerous professional committees and editorial boards, including a term as a member of the Board of Examiners of the American Institute of CPAs. He has written eleven textbooks and numerous articles in such journals as the *Journal of Accountancy*, the *Accounting Review*, the *Journal of Accounting Research*, the *CPA Journal*, *Cost and Management*, and *Managerial Planning*.

Professor Warren resides in Athens, Georgia, with his wife, Sharon, and two children. His daughter, Stephanie, attends Wake Forest University and his son, Jeffrey, is a junior in high school. Professor Warren's hobbies include golf, racquetball, and fishing.

Brief Contents

Contents

Key Systems
This set is available with business documents and a narrative of transactions. The set provides practice in accounting for a merchandising sole proprietorship that uses a voucher system.

First Designs Inc.
This set is available with transactions in narrative form. The set provides practice in accounting for a merchandising corporation that operates a departmentalized business.

SEMO Sporting Goods Supply Inc.
This set requires the preparation of correcting entries and financial statements for a wholesaling corporation.

Highpoint Solar Inc.
This set is available with transactions in narrative form. The set provides practice in accounting for a manufacturing corporation that uses a job order cost system.

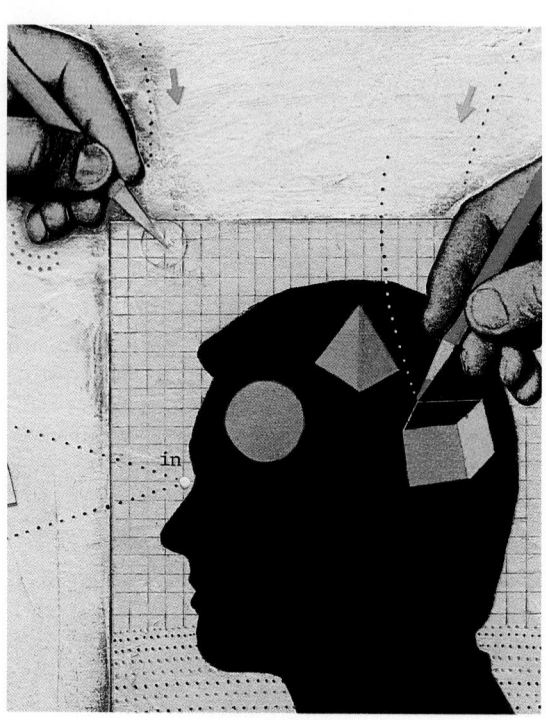

Introduction: Evolution of Accounting

Over the years, the evolution of accounting has been similar to that of other professions, such as medicine and law. These professions continually change as society and the needs of society change. In recent years, for example, the practice of medicine has changed significantly with the invention and use of lasers. Likewise, the practice of law has changed to reflect new specializations, such as environmental law.

The objective of this introduction is to make you aware of how accounting has evolved. This awareness will help you understand the role and the importance of accounting in society and in your everyday life.

EARLY ACCOUNTING

Just as you may keep a record of the money you spend, people throughout history have maintained records of their business activities. Some of these records were clay tablets that indicated the payment of wages in Babylon around 3600 B.C. Record keeping also existed in ancient Egypt and in the Greek city-states. Some of the earliest English records were compiled by William the Conqueror in the eleventh century. These early accounting records included only some of the financial activities of an entity. A systematic recording of all activities of an entity developed later in response to the needs of the commercial republics of Italy.

DOUBLE-ENTRY SYSTEM

How did the early recording of financial activities evolve into a system of accounting? The basic system of accounting, which is still used today, was invented by Luca Pacioli, a Franciscan monk. Pacioli was a mathematician who taught in various universities in Perugia, Naples, Pisa, and Florence. He was a close friend of Leonardo da Vinci, with whom he collaborated on a mathematics book. Pacioli wrote the text and da Vinci drew the illustrations.

Pacioli invented what is known as the *double-entry system of accounting*. A description of the double-entry system was first published in Italy in 1494. This system was strongly influenced by the financial needs of the Venetian merchants. Goethe, the German poet, novelist, and scientist, described the double-entry system as "one of the most beautiful inventions of the human spirit, and every good businessman should use it in his economic undertakings."[1]

What is so special about the double-entry system? It is unique because it records financial activities in such a way that an equilibrium is created within the records. For example, assume that you borrow $1,000 from a bank. Within a double-entry system, the loan is recorded as $1,000 of cash received, and at the same time, an obligation is recorded for the eventual repayment of the $1,000. Each of the $1,000 amounts is balanced by the other. In a complex business environment, in which an entity may be involved in thousands of transactions daily, this balancing is a valuable control that ensures the accuracy of the recording process.

In spite of the enormous changes in business operations and their complexity since 1494, the basic elements of the double-entry system have remained virtually unchanged. This is a lasting tribute to the significance of Pacioli's invention and his contribution to society.

INDUSTRIAL REVOLUTION

In addition to the invention of the double-entry system, other major events significantly influenced the evolution of accounting. One such event was the Industrial Revolution. The Industrial Revolution occurred in England from the mid-eighteenth to the mid-nineteenth centuries. It changed the method of producing marketable goods from a handicraft method to a factory system.

How did the Industrial Revolution change accounting? The Industrial Revolution affected accounting because managers of factories needed to know the cost of producing their products. These costs were used for such purposes as monitoring manufacturing processes and setting selling prices. For a small number of individually handcrafted products, costs were fairly easy to determine. However, determining costs for the manufacture of a large volume of machine-made products was much more difficult.

The field of cost accounting developed to meet this need for accurate and timely estimates of manufacturing costs. Cost accounting focuses on recording costs and providing management with reports on the costs of operations. Even today, the field of cost accounting is undergoing major changes as accountants attempt to more accurately record and estimate on a timely basis the costs of manufacturing processes.

CORPORATE ORGANIZATION

As you might expect, the Industrial Revolution created a demand for large amounts of money or capital to build factories and purchase machinery. To meet this need for capital, the corporate form of organization was developed.

The corporate form of organization was first established in England in 1845. It soon spread rapidly to the United States, which became one of the world's leading industrial nations shortly after the Civil War. In the United States, large amounts of capital were essential for the development of new industries, such as steel, transportation, mining, electric power, and communications. As in England, the corporation was the primary vehicle for raising the capital that was needed.

How does the corporate form of organization raise capital? If you answered "by issuing stock," you are correct. Corporate ownership is divided into shares of stock that can be readily transferred. The stockholders of a corporation normally do not exercise direct control over the operations of the corporation. The management of the corporation runs day-to-day operations, and the stockholders only

---

[1] Goethe, Johann Wolfgang von, *Samtliche Werke*, edited by Edward von der Hellen (Stuttgart and Berlin: J. G. Cotta, 1902-07), Vol. XVII, p. 37.

indirectly control the corporation through the election of a board of directors. The board of directors sets general policies and selects the officers who actively manage the corporation.

So how did the corporate form of organization affect accounting? The corporate form affected the evolution of accounting because the stockholders needed information about how well management was running the corporation. Since stockholders are not directly involved in day-to-day operations, they must rely on accounting reports in evaluating management's performance. These reports created additional demands upon accounting.

As corporations grew larger, the number of individuals and institutions relying on accounting reports increased. Potential shareholders and creditors needed information. Government agencies required information for purposes of taxation and regulation. Employees, union representatives, and customers requested information to judge the stability and profitability of corporations. Thus, largely due to the use of the corporate form of organization, accounting had to expand from serving the needs of a few owners to a public role of meeting the needs of a variety of interested parties.

PUBLIC ACCOUNTING

The corporate form of organization also created a need for an independent review or audit of reports prepared by the corporation's management. This audit was necessary to provide some assurance to users of the information that the reports were reliable. This audit function, called the *attest function,* was responsible for the development and growth of the public accounting profession. Unlike private accountants who work for a specific business entity, public accountants are self-employed. In this sense, they are independent of the enterprises whose reports they audit.

All states currently provide for the regulation and licensing of certified public accountants (CPAs). In 1944, fifty years after the enactment of the first CPA law, there were approximately 25,000 CPAs in the United States. During the next four decades, the number increased tenfold. Currently the number exceeds 300,000 and is continuing to increase.

Although auditing is still a major service offered by CPAs, much of their time is also spent assisting in the planning and controlling of clients' operations. Such consulting services have increased dramatically in recent years. Today, consulting services are a major part of the practice of many public accounting firms.

INCOME TAX

All of us are affected by income taxes. Since income taxes are based upon records of financial activities, the development of the income tax significantly affected the evolution of accounting, as you might expect.

The development of the federal income tax was made possible by the Sixteenth Amendment to the Constitution of the United States. The first federal income tax law was passed by the United States Congress in 1913. Currently, all business enterprises organized as corporations or partnerships, as well as many individuals and organizations, are required to file income tax returns. To meet this requirement properly, filers must maintain adequate financial records. Because of the complexity of the tax laws and regulations, more and more organizations and individuals depend upon accountants. In addition to preparing tax returns, accountants advise clients on how to minimize their taxes.

GOVERNMENT INFLUENCE

Local, state, and federal governments also have had a significant influence on the evolution of accounting. Current accounting systems must record and report financial data for a variety of governmental laws and regulations.

You are probably aware of some examples of such laws and regulations at the local, state, and federal levels. At the local level, commissions and boards levy property and sales taxes based upon accounting data. At the state level, public service commissions often approve utility rates. Such rate-making processes use and analyze accounting data. At the federal level, in addition to the income tax, the Social Security and Medicare laws require accounting record keeping and reporting by almost all businesses and many individuals.

ACCOUNTING'S FUTURE

As the preceding paragraphs emphasize, accounting touches all our lives in one way or another. Accounting data are essential to the functioning of modern society. As society changes, so too will accounting change. Although long-range predictions are risky, there are two areas of accounting that are rapidly evolving and will likely be seeing significant change in the future. These areas are international accounting and socioeconomic accounting.

International Accounting

As discussed, accounting changes to meet the needs of society. As a result, accounting rules and regulations differ significantly among countries, each of which has unique cultural and societal needs. These differences create major accounting problems when a firm has foreign operations in more than one country. In such cases, the firm must adapt its accounting system for the rules and regulations of each country. This increases the costs of recording accounting data and preparing accounting reports. Also, there is potential for confusing the users of accounting reports. To overcome these problems, the accounting profession is seeking to develop uniform international accounting standards.

Socioeconomic Accounting

Accounting traditionally focuses on recording and reporting financial activities of business enterprises or other specific entities. Recently, there has been a suggestion that accounting should also record and report the impact of organizations on society. This area of accounting is called socioeconomic accounting.

As socioeconomic accounting has evolved, three main areas have been identified for study. The first area is recording and reporting the impact of various organizations on matters that affect the overall quality of life in society. The second area is recording and reporting the impact of government programs on achieving specific social objectives. The third area is recording and reporting the impact of corporate social performance. Corporate social performance refers to the corporation's responsibilities in such areas as water and air pollution, conservation of natural resources, and equal employment practices.

The concept of socioeconomic accounting is relatively simple as a theory. However, additional study and research are needed before socioeconomic costs and benefits of various activities can be recorded and reported. For example, the overall impact of a public utility's proposal to build a nuclear power plant is difficult to measure, record, and report.

DO YOU USE ACCOUNTING?

As this introduction suggests, we all use accounting to some degree. For some of us, accounting involves recording checks in our checkbooks. For others, it may involve preparing our tax returns. As you begin your study of accounting, keep in mind the importance of accounting to your everyday life as well as its importance for your business career.

Part 1

Basic Structure of Accounting

You and Accounting

How much are you worth? In financial terms, the first step in answering this question is to determine what you own. For example, if you own a car costing $12,000, your financial worth includes your $12,000 car. However, if you have a $10,000 loan outstanding on the car, your financial worth is only $2,000 ($12,000 − $10,000). Your financial worth may help you to answer the question: "Can I afford to buy a new car?"

Managers of business enterprises must answer questions similar to these on a day-to-day basis. For example, a manager of a chain of pizza restaurants must decide whether to acquire delivery cars. The financial worth of the pizza restaurants may be a major factor in determining whether the cars can be acquired. Also, the financial worth of the restaurants may determine whether a loan can be obtained to finance the purchase of the cars.

This chapter discusses the accounting framework by which business enterprises gather and report economic data. These data are then used in making decisions such as the one described above. You may also apply the concepts described in this chapter to your personal finances. For example, these concepts can be used to determine your financial worth.

Chapter 1
Accounting Principles and Practices

LEARNING OBJECTIVES
After studying this chapter, you should be able to:

Objective 1
Define accounting as an information system.

Objective 2
Describe the profession of accounting and list its specialized fields.

Objective 3
Summarize the development of accounting principles and relate them to practice.

Objective 4
List the characteristics of a business transaction.

Objective 5
State the accounting equation and define each element of the equation.

Objective 6
Explain how business transactions can be stated in terms of the resulting changes in the three basic elements of the accounting equation.

Objective 7
Describe the financial statements of a sole proprietorship and explain how they interrelate.

Accounting provides and interprets economic data for economic units within society. These economic units include profit enterprises and not-for-profit entities, such as churches, government agencies, and charities. In addition, accounting provides information for individual persons and family units. Regardless of the type of economic unit, accounting must provide economic data that are reliable and accurate.

The primary focus of this text is business enterprises organized for profit. Accountants for such enterprises must have a thorough understanding of accounting in order to process, interpret, and communicate economic data. Many others directly involved in the enterprise's activities also come in contact with accounting. For example, individuals engaged in such areas of business as finance, production, marketing, personnel, and general management must have an understanding of accounting. In addition, the importance of understanding accounting is not limited to those directly involved in managing a business. For example, an engineer in designing a product may consider the costs of alternate manufacturing processes. Likewise, lawyers use accounting data in tax cases and in settling lawsuits.

ACCOUNTING AS AN INFORMATION SYSTEM

Objective 1
Define accounting as an
information system.

Accounting plays an important role in our economic and social system. The decisions made by individuals, businesses, governments, and other entities determine the use of the nation's scarce resources. The goal of accounting is to record, report, and interpret economic data for use by decision makers.

Accounting[1] is often called the "language of business." Accounting can be viewed as an information system that provides essential information about the economic activities of an entity to various individuals or groups. Accounting information is composed primarily of economic data about business activities.

Accounting provides the conceptual framework for gathering economic data and the language for reporting these data to various users. Investors in a business enterprise need information about its financial status and its future prospects. Bankers and creditors evaluate the financial condition of a business and assess the risks before making loans. Government agencies are concerned with the financial activities of business organizations for taxation and regulation. Employees and their unions are also interested in the condition and profit potential of the company that hires them. In directing the operations of a company, management depends upon and uses accounting data.

The process of using accounting to provide information to users is illustrated in Exhibit 1. First, user groups are identified and their information needs determined. These needs determine which economic data are recorded by the accounting system. Finally, accounting reports are prepared summarizing the information for users. For example, to evaluate their investments, investors need information on the financial condition and results of operations of enterprises. Although the information for one group of users may differ from another, accounting can provide each group with useful information.

Exhibit 1
Accounting as a Provider of
Information to Users

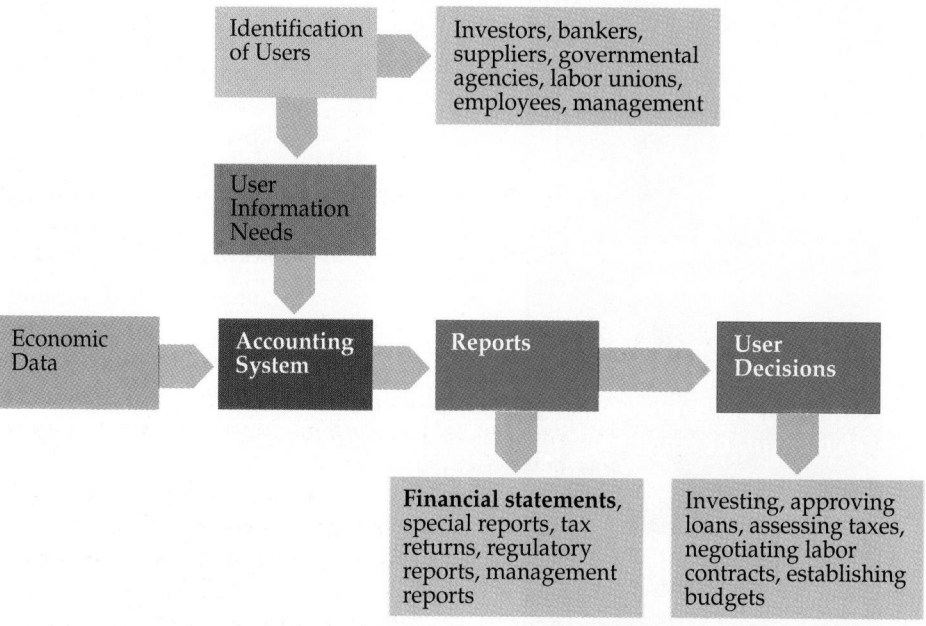

PROFESSION OF ACCOUNTING

Objective 2
Describe the profession of
accounting and list its
specialized fields.

The profession of accounting has grown rapidly during the current century. The career opportunities in accounting and the number of accountants have both increased. The increase in number, size, and complexity of business enterprises has

[1] A glossary of terms appears at the end of each chapter. A complete glossary is included at the end of the text. The terms included in each glossary are printed in color the first time they are defined in the text.

increased the demand for accounting services. In addition, new laws and regulations have also created a demand for accounting.

Employment opportunities in the profession of accountancy are expected to continue to grow and expand. In a report prepared by the U.S. Department of Labor, the accounting profession is projected to increase by 39.8% between the late 1980s and the year 2000.[2]

Accountants are engaged in either (1) private accounting or (2) public accounting. Accountants employed by a business firm or not-for-profit organization are said to be engaged in **private accounting.** Accountants and their staff who provide services on a fee basis are said to be engaged in **public accounting.**

Experience in private and public accounting has long been recognized as excellent training for top management positions. Many positions in industry and in state and federal agencies are held by individuals with education and experience in accounting. For example, in its 1990 Special Bonus Issue on "The Corporate Elite," *Business Week* reported that 31% of the chief executives of the 1,000 largest public corporations followed a finance-accounting career path. Merchandising-marketing was the career path for 27%, and engineering-technical was the career path for 22% of the chief executives.

Private Accounting

The scope of activities and duties of private accountants varies widely. Private accountants are frequently called management accountants. If they are employed by a manufacturing concern, they may be called industrial or cost accountants. Various state and federal agencies and other not-for-profit agencies also employ accountants.

The Institute of Certified Management Accountants, an affiliate of the Institute of Management Accountants (IMA), sponsors the **Certified Management Accountant (CMA)** program. The CMA certificate is evidence of competence in management accounting. To become a CMA, a college degree, two years of experience in management accounting, and successful completion of a two-day examination are required. Continuing professional education is required for renewal of the CMA certificate.

The Institute of Internal Auditors sponsors a similar program for internal auditors. Internal auditors are accountants who review the accounting and operating procedures prescribed by their firms. Accountants who specialize in internal auditing may be granted the **Certified Internal Auditor (CIA)** certificate.

Public Accounting

In public accounting, an accountant may practice as an individual or as a member of a public accounting firm. Public accountants who have met a state's education, experience, and examination requirements may become **Certified Public Accountants (CPAs).**

The requirements for obtaining the CPA certificate differ among the various states.[3] All states require a college education in accounting. In addition, a candidate must pass a two-day examination prepared by the American Institute of Certified Public Accountants (AICPA). Most states do not permit individuals to practice as CPAs until they have had from one to three years' experience in public accounting. Some states, however, accept similar employment in private accounting as equivalent experience.

All states require CPAs to obtain continuing professional education. CPAs who do not comply may lose their certificates and their right to practice. Although the details of this requirement may vary, most states require at least forty hours of continuing education per year.

[2] U.S. Department of Labor, Bureau of Labor Statistics, *Occupational Projections and Training Data: 1991 Edition* (Washington: U.S. Government Printing Office), April 1991.
[3] Information on a state's requirements is available from that state's Board of Accountancy.

Professional Ethics for Accountants

Ethics are moral principles that guide the conduct of individuals, whether they are acting alone or as members of a profession or business. Individuals may differ on what is "right" or "wrong" in a given situation. However, proper ethical conduct implies a duty beyond that of law to act in the interests of society. The essence of ethical conduct is the sacrifice of one's well-being for the benefit of society. The sacrificing of one's well-being for the benefit of others not only promotes self-worth, but is often good business. For example, a business that ignores the public welfare and pollutes the environment may find itself the focus of lawsuits and customer boycotts. Likewise, an automobile manufacturer that fails to correct a safety defect to save costs may later lose sales from the loss of consumer confidence.

Accountants in both private and public practice have developed standards to guide them in the conduct of their practices.[4] The Institute of Management Accountants (IMA) has prepared **standards of ethical conduct** to guide management accountants in serving their employers, their profession, and the public. As stated in these standards, management accountants have a responsibility to:[5]

1. Maintain an appropriate level of professional competence.
2. Refrain from disclosing confidential information.
3. Avoid conflicts of interest.
4. Communicate information fairly and objectively.

The American Institute of Certified Public Accountants (AICPA) has also developed standards to guide its members. The purpose of these standards, called **codes of professional conduct** or **codes of professional ethics**, is to instill public confidence in the public accounting profession. The standards require CPAs to:[6]

1. Exercise sensitive professional and moral judgments.
2. Act in a way that will serve the public interest, honor the public trust, and demonstrate commitment to professionalism.
3. Perform all professional responsibilities with integrity.
4. Maintain objectivity and be free of conflicts of interest.
5. Observe the profession's technical and ethical standards and continually improve competency.
6. Determine the scope and nature of professional services according to ethical standards.

The AICPA and state societies of CPAs can revoke a CPA's membership in their organizations for violations of the code of professional conduct. A State Board of Accountancy, the Securities and Exchange Commission (SEC), or other regulatory agencies may revoke or limit the CPA's ability to practice. This combination of review by the AICPA, state societies of CPAs, the SEC, and other regulatory agencies encourages ethical behavior by CPAs.

Codes of professional conduct change as society changes. However, ethical conduct is more than simply conforming to written standards of professional behavior. In a true sense, ethical conduct requires a personal commitment to honorable behavior.

---

[4] An ethics discussion case is provided at the end of each chapter to focus attention on meaningful ethical situations that accountants often face in practice.

[5] The text of the *Standards of Ethical Conduct For Management Accountants* (Institute of Management Accountants: Montvale, New Jersey, 1992) is reproduced in Appendix B.

[6] The text of the *Code of Professional Conduct* (American Institute of Certified Public Accountants: New York, 1992) is reproduced in Appendix B.

Ethics in American Business

In October, 1987, Touche Ross (now Deloitte & Touche) conducted a survey of 1,107 directors and top executives of corporations with $500 million or more in annual sales, deans of business schools, and members of Congress, seeking their opinions on ethics in American business. The survey's many interesting findings included the following:

- The United States has higher standards of business ethics than any other country in the world. Ethical standards are also considered high in the United Kingdom, Canada, Switzerland, and Germany, which respondents ranked in that order, followed by Japan.
- An enterprise actually strengthens its competitive position by maintaining high ethical standards.
- The four professions with the highest standards are clergy, accountants, teachers, and engineers, in that

order. The ethical standards of business people as a professional group are well regarded, particularly by bankers and accountants.

- A vast majority of the respondents believe that American business is ethical.
- Though respondents believe almost unanimously that the business community is troubled by ethical problems, they are very far from seeing a wholesale breakdown in American business ethics. Indeed, compared to 100 years ago, during the age of the robber barons, business ethics are definitely better today.
- Legislation is the least effective way of encouraging ethical business behavior. Rather, the adoption of business codes of ethics is the most effective way. Indeed, the main reason for high ethical standards in a profession is that profession's own standards and accreditation.

Source: *Ethics in American Business*, Touche Ross, January 1988.

Specialized Accounting Fields

Specialized fields in accounting have evolved as a result of technology advances and economic growth. The most important accounting fields are described in the following paragraphs.

Financial accounting is concerned with the recording of economic data for a business enterprise or other economic unit and the periodic preparation of reports from such records. The reports provide useful information for managers, owners, creditors, governmental agencies, and the public. Financial accountants use rules of accounting, termed **generally accepted accounting principles (GAAP)**. Business enterprises must employ these principles in preparing reports for use by their stockholders and the investing public. These rules ensure that accounting reports for different companies may be compared. The ability to compare company reports is essential if resources are to be divided efficiently among business organizations.

Auditing is a field of activity involving an independent review of the accounting records. In conducting an audit, CPAs examine the records supporting the financial reports of an enterprise. Based upon this examination, CPAs provide an opinion on the fairness of the financial reports. An important element of evaluating "fairness" is agreement with generally accepted accounting principles. Many companies also employ a staff of internal auditors who determine if the operating units of a company are following management's policies and procedures.

Management accounting, often called **managerial accounting**, uses both historical and estimated data to aid management in running day-to-day operations and in planning future operations. The management accountant is often concerned with identifying alternative courses of action and preparing reports evaluating each alternative. For example, the accountant may aid the company treasurer in preparing alternate plans for future financing.

In recent years, CPAs have realized that their training and experience uniquely qualify them to advise management. This rapidly growing field of specialization by CPAs is called *management advisory services*.

Cost accounting focuses on the estimation and control of costs. It is concerned mainly with the costs of manufacturing activities and manufactured products. In addition, an important duty of the cost accountant is to record and explain cost data, both actual and prospective. Management uses these data in planning and controlling operations.

Tax accounting involves preparing tax returns and analyzing possible tax results of proposed decisions. Accountants in this field must be familiar with the tax statutes affecting their employer or clients. In addition, tax accountants must keep up to date on tax regulations and court decisions on tax cases.

Accounting systems is the special field concerned with the design and use of procedures for recording and reporting economic data. The systems accountant must design procedures to safeguard business properties and provide for an efficient information flow. Knowledge of data processing methods, including computer hardware and software, is required.

International accounting focuses on the special issues related to international trade. Because businesses of all sizes sell and buy goods in world markets, this field of accounting is increasing in importance. Accountants in this area must understand the influences of various countries' customs, laws, and taxation on business.

Not-for-profit accounting specializes in recording, reporting, and planning operations of federal, state, and other government agencies. In addition, other not-for-profit agencies, such as churches, charities, and educational institutions, employ accountants. Not-for-profit accounting focuses on adherence to restrictions and other standards required by law, organizations, or individual donors.

Social accounting is a new field of accounting. There are demands on the accounting profession to measure the social costs and benefits of various actions. For example, accountants in this field might measure and evaluate the environmental impact of acid rain. Other accountants might analyze and evaluate the use of welfare funds in a large city or the use of federal and state lands.

Accounting instruction provides a career for dedicated individuals to share their knowledge of and experience in accounting with their students. In addition to teaching and advising students, accounting instructors often perform research and write articles to expand accounting knowledge. They often actively participate in professional organizations. Many instructors maintain part-time accounting practices or consulting services.

There is some overlap among the various fields, and accountants are often experts in several fields. In addition, there may be further specialization within a field. For example, an auditor may become an expert in a single type of business such as retailing or banking. A tax accountant might become a specialist in oil- and gas-producing companies.

PRINCIPLES AND PRACTICE

Objective 3
Summarize the development of accounting principles and relate them to practice.

In accounting, as in the physical sciences, change is never-ending. Professional accountants, educators, and accounting organizations such as the AICPA constantly seek answers to accounting issues facing business. Authoritative accounting pronouncements are issued by such bodies as the **Financial Accounting Standards Board (FASB).** It is from research, accepted accounting practices, and pronouncements of authoritative bodies that generally accepted accounting principles evolve. These principles form the basis for accounting practice.

In this chapter and throughout this text, accounting principles and concepts are emphasized. It is through this emphasis on the "why" of accounting as well as the "how" that the full significance of accounting can best be understood.

Business Entity Concept

The business entity concept is based on applying accounting to individual economic units in society, such as a business enterprise. The business entity concept requires that the first step in the practice of accounting is to identify the economic unit for which economic data are required. The data for the entity can then be recorded and analyzed and periodic reports prepared. A business entity could be identified as an individual, a not-for-profit organization such as a church, or an enterprise such as a real estate agency.

This textbook focuses on accounting concepts and principles for profit-making businesses. Such businesses are normally organized as sole proprietorships, partnerships, or corporations. A **sole proprietorship** is owned by one individual. A **partnership** is owned by two or more individuals. A **corporation** is organized under state or federal statutes as a separate legal entity. The ownership of a corporation is divided into shares of stock. The sole proprietorship is the most common business form. However, corporations receive over 90% of the total dollars of business receipts. These facts are shown in Exhibit 2.

Exhibit 2
Profit-Making Businesses

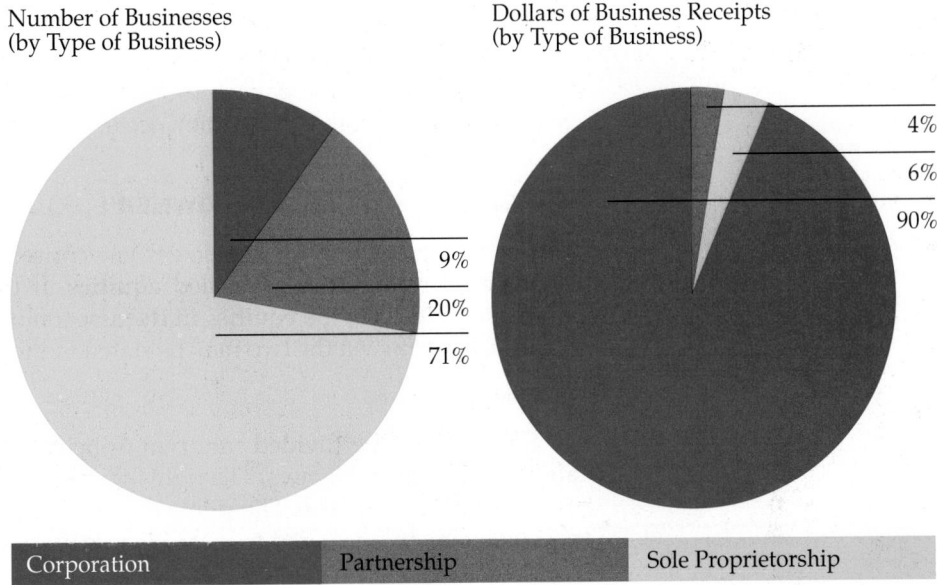

Number of Businesses
(by Type of Business)

Dollars of Business Receipts
(by Type of Business)

4%
6%
90%

9%
20%
71%

Corporation | Partnership | Sole Proprietorship

Source: U.S. Bureau of the Census, *Statistical Abstract of the United States*: 1991 (111th edition) Washington, DC.

The Cost Principle

The properties and services bought by a business are recorded using the **cost principle.** The cost principle requires that the actual cost of a property or service be entered into the accounting records. For example, if a building is bought for $150,000, that is the amount entered into the buyer's accounting records. The seller may have been asking $170,000 for the building up to the time of the sale. The buyer may have initially offered $130,000 for the building. The building may have been assessed at $125,000 for property tax purposes, and the buyer may have received an offer of $175,000 for the building the day after it was acquired. These latter amounts have no effect on the accounting records because they did not result in an exchange. *The exchange price, or cost, of $150,000 is the amount used in the accounting records for the building.*

Continuing the illustration, the $175,000 offer received by the buyer the day after the building was acquired indicates that it was a bargain purchase at $150,000. To use $175,000 in the accounting records, however, would record an illusory or unrealized profit. If, after buying the building, the buyer *should* accept the offer and sell the building for $175,000, a profit of $25,000 would then be realized and recorded. The new owner would record $175,000 as the cost of the building.

The use of cost in recording properties and services acquired is a basic concept of accounting. In exchanges between buyer and seller, both try to get the best price. Only the final amount agreed upon is objective enough for accounting purposes. If the amounts for which properties were recorded were constantly revised upward and downward based on offers, appraisals, and opinions, accounting reports would soon become unstable and unreliable.

BUSINESS TRANSACTIONS

Objective 4
List the characteristics of a
business transaction.

A **business transaction** is the occurrence of an exchange or an economic event that must be recorded by an entity. For example, the payment of a monthly telephone bill of $68 or the acquisition of land and a building for $210,000 are business transactions.

The first transaction is relatively simple: a payment of money in exchange for a service. The purchase of a building and the land on which it is situated is a more complex transaction. The total price agreed upon must be divided between the land and the building. In addition, the agreement usually provides for spreading the payment of a large part of the price over a period of years. The agreement may also require the payment of interest on the unpaid balance.

A business transaction may lead to an event or a condition that results in another transaction. For example, the purchase of $1,750 of merchandise on credit will be followed later by the payment to the creditor. Each time a portion of the merchandise is sold, another transaction occurs. Each of these events must be recorded.

ASSETS, LIABILITIES, AND OWNER'S EQUITY

Objective 5
State the accounting equation
and define each element of the
equation.

The properties owned by a business enterprise are called **assets.** The rights or claims to the properties are called **equities.** If the assets owned by a business amount to $100,000, the equities in the assets must also amount to $100,000. The relationship between the two may be stated in the form of an equation, as follows:

Assets = Equities

Equities may be divided into two principal types: (1) the rights of creditors and (2) the rights of owners. The rights of creditors represent debts of the business and are called **liabilities.** The rights of the owners are called **owner's equity.** The equation may be expanded to include these two types of equities, as follows:

Assets = Liabilities + Owner's Equity

The preceding equation is known as the **accounting equation.** It is usual to place "Liabilities" before "Owner's Equity" in the accounting equation because creditors have first rights to the assets. The claim of the owners is sometimes given greater emphasis by transposing liabilities to the other side of the equation, yielding:

Assets – Liabilities = Owner's Equity

TRANSACTIONS AND THE ACCOUNTING EQUATION

Objective 6
Explain how business
transactions can be stated in
terms of the resulting changes in
the three basic elements of the
accounting equation.

All business transactions can be stated in terms of changes in the three elements of the accounting equation. The effect of these changes on the accounting equation can be shown by studying some typical transactions. For example, assume that on November 1, 1993, Jere King begins a sole proprietorship to be known as Computer King. Using Jere's knowledge of microcomputers, the business will offer computer consulting services for a fee. Each transaction or group of similar transactions during the first month of operations is described. The effects of the transaction on the accounting equation are then shown.

Transaction a. King's first transaction is to deposit $15,000 in a bank account in the name of Computer King. The effect of this transaction is to increase the asset (cash), on the left side of the equation, by $15,000. To balance the equation, the owner's equity on the right side of the equation is increased by the same amount. The equity of the owner is referred to by using the owner's name and "Capital," such as "Jere King, Capital." The effect of this transaction on Jere King's accounting equation is shown below.

Assets		*Owner's Equity*	
Cash	=	Jere King, Capital	
a. 15,000		15,000	Investment

Note that the equation relates only to the business enterprise. King's personal assets, such as a home or personal bank account, and personal liabilities are excluded from the equation. The business is treated as a separate entity, with cash of $15,000 and owner's equity of $15,000.

Transaction b. Computer King's next transaction is to purchase land for $10,000 cash. The land is located near a shopping mall that contains three microcomputer stores. Computer King's current plans are to rent equipment and office space near the shopping mall for several months. If the business is a success, a building will be built on the land.

The purchase of the land changes the makeup of the assets but does not change the total assets. The items in the equation prior to this transaction and the effect of the transaction are shown below. The new amounts or *balances* of the items are also shown.

	Assets			Owner's Equity
	Cash +	Land	=	Jere King, Capital
	15,000			15,000
b.	−10,000	+10,000		
Bal.	5,000	10,000		15,000

Transaction c. During the month, Computer King purchases supplies for $1,350 from a supplier, agreeing to pay in the near future. This type of transaction is called a purchase *on account*. The liability created is termed an **account payable.** Items such as supplies that will be used in the business in the future are called **prepaid expenses,** which are assets.

In actual practice, each purchase would be treated as a separate transaction. However, to simplify this example, the purchases are treated as a group. The effect is to increase assets and liabilities by $1,350, as follows:

	Assets				Liabilities +	Owner's Equity
	Cash +	Supplies +	Land	=	Accounts Payable	Jere King, Capital
Bal.	5,000		10,000			15,000
c.		+1,350			+1,350	
Bal.	5,000	1,350	10,000		1,350	15,000

Transaction d. During the month, $950 is paid to creditors on account, thereby reducing both assets and liabilities. The effect on the equation is as follows:

	Assets				Liabilities +	Owner's Equity
	Cash +	Supplies +	Land	=	Accounts Payable +	Jere King, Capital
Bal.	5,000	1,350	10,000		1,350	15,000
d.	−950				−950	
Bal.	4,050	1,350	10,000		400	15,000

Transaction e. The amount charged to customers for goods or services sold to them is called **revenue.** Special terms may be used for certain kinds of revenue, such as *sales* for the sale of merchandise. Revenue from providing services is called *fees earned*. For example, a physician would record fees earned for services to patients. Other examples of revenue terms include *rent earned* for the use of real estate or other property, and *fares earned* for an airline.

The amount of revenue earned during a period is measured by the amount of assets received from customers for the goods sold or services rendered to them. The objective of earning revenue through business operations is to increase owner's equity. Thus, the effect of revenue on the accounting equation is to increase assets and increase owner's equity.

During its first month of operations, Computer King earns fees of $7,500, receiving the amount in cash. The total effect of these transactions is to increase cash and the owner's equity by $7,500. The effect on the accounting equation is as follows:

		Assets			Liabilities +	Owner's Equity	
	Cash +	Supplies +	Land		Accounts Payable +	Jere King, Capital	
Bal.	4,050	1,350	10,000		400	15,000	
e.	+7,500					+7,500	Fees earned
Bal.	11,550	1,350	10,000		400	22,500	

Instead of requiring the payment of cash at the time services are provided or goods are sold, a business may accept payment at a later date. Such revenues are called **fees on account** or **sales on account**. In such cases the firm has an **account receivable**, which is a claim against the customer. An account receivable is an asset, and the revenue is earned as if cash had been received. When customers pay their accounts, there is an exchange of one asset for another. Cash is increased and Accounts Receivable is decreased.

Transaction f. The amount of assets or services used in the process of earning revenue is called **expense**. Expenses include supplies used, wages of employees, and other assets and services used in operating the business. The effect of expenses on owner's equity is the opposite of the effect of revenues. Expenses decrease assets and decrease owner's equity.

For Computer King, the expenses paid during the month were as follows: wages, $2,125; rent, $800; utilities, $450; miscellaneous, $275. Miscellaneous expenses include small amounts paid for such items as postage due, coffee, and newspaper and magazine purchases. The effect of this group of transactions is to reduce cash and to reduce owner's equity, as follows:

		Assets			Liabilities +	Owner's Equity	
	Cash +	Supplies +	Land		Accounts Payable +	Jere King, Capital	
Bal.	11,550	1,350	10,000		400	22,500	
f.	−3,650					−2,125	Wages expense
						− 800	Rent expense
						− 450	Utilities expense
						− 275	Misc. expense
Bal.	7,900	1,350	10,000		400	18,850	

Transaction g. At the end of the month, it is determined that the cost of the supplies on hand is $550. The remainder of the supplies ($1,350−$550) were used in the operations of the business. This decrease of $800 in supplies and owner's equity is shown as follows:

		Assets			Liabilities +	Owner's Equity	
	Cash +	Supplies +	Land		Accounts Payable +	Jere King, Capital	
Bal.	7,900	1,350	10,000		400	18,850	
g.		−800				− 800	Supplies expense
Bal.	7,900	550	10,000		400	18,050	

Transaction h. At the end of the month, Jere King withdraws $2,000 in cash from the business for personal use. This transaction is the exact opposite of an investment in the business by the owner. Cash and owner's equity are decreased. The cash payment is not a business expense but a withdrawal of a part of the owner's equity. The effect of the $2,000 withdrawal is shown as follows:

	Assets			Liabilities +	Owner's Equity
	Cash +	Supplies +	Land	Accounts Payable +	Jere King, Capital
Bal.	7,900	550	10,000	400	18,050
h.	−2,000				−2,000 Withdrawal
Bal.	5,900	550	10,000	400	16,050

Summary. The transactions of Computer King are summarized as follows. The transactions are identified by letter, and the balance of each item is shown after each transaction.

	Assets			=	Liabilities +	Owner's Equity	
	Cash +	Supplies +	Land		Accounts Payable +	Jere King, Capital	
a.	+ 15,000					+ 15,000	Investment
b.	− 10,000		+10,000				
Bal.	5,000		10,000			15,000	
c.		+ 1,350			+1,350		
Bal.	5,000	1,350	10,000		1,350	15,000	
d.	− 950				− 950		
Bal.	4,050	1,350	10,000		400	15,000	
e.	+ 7,500					+ 7,500	Fees earned
Bal.	11,550	1,350	10,000		400	22,500	
f.	− 3,650					− 2,125	Wages expense
						− 800	Rent expense
						− 450	Utilities expense
						− 275	Misc. expense
Bal.	7,900	1,350	10,000		400	18,850	
g.		− 800				− 800	Supplies expense
Bal.	7,900	550	10,000		400	18,050	
h.	− 2,000					− 2,000	Withdrawal
Bal.	5,900	550	10,000		400	16,050	

The following comments, which apply to all types of businesses, should be noted:

1. The effect of every transaction can be stated in terms of increases and/or decreases in one or more of the accounting equation elements.
2. The two sides of the accounting equation are always equal.
3. The owner's equity is increased by amounts invested by the owner and is decreased by withdrawals by the owner. In addition, owner's equity is increased by revenues and is decreased by expenses. The effect of these four types of transactions on owner's equity is illustrated in Exhibit 3.

Exhibit 3
Effect of Transactions on Owner's Equity

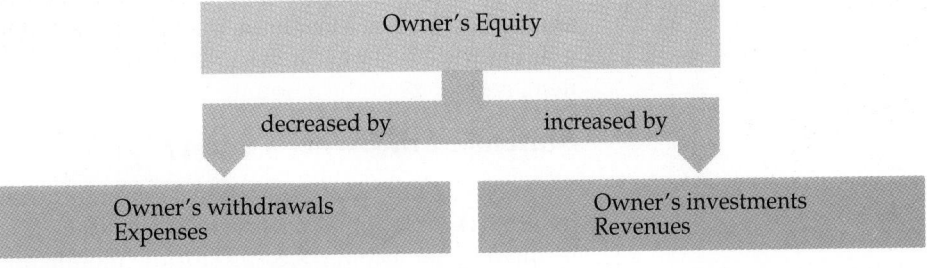

FINANCIAL STATEMENTS

Objective 7
Describe the financial statements of a sole proprietorship and explain how they interrelate.

After transactions have been recorded and summarized, reports are prepared for users. The accounting reports that provide this information are called **financial statements**. The principal financial statements of a sole proprietorship are the income statement, the statement of owner's equity, the balance sheet, and the statement of cash flows. The nature of the data presented in each statement is as follows:

Income statement—A summary of the revenue and the expenses of a business entity *for a specific period of time*, such as a month or a year.

Statement of owner's equity—A summary of the changes in the owner's equity of a business entity that have occurred *during a specific period of time*, such as a month or a year.

Balance sheet—A list of the assets, liabilities, and owner's equity of a business entity *as of a specific date*, usually at the close of the last day of a month or a year.

Statement of cash flows—A summary of the cash receipts and cash payments of a business entity *for a specific period of time*, such as a month or a year.

The basic features of the four statements and their interrelationships are illustrated in Exhibit 4. The data for the statements were taken from the summary of transactions of Computer King.

All financial statements should be identified by the name of the business, the title of the statement, and the *date* or *period of time*. The data presented in the income statement, the statement of owner's equity, and the statement of cash flows are for a period of time. The data presented in the balance sheet are for a specific date.

The use of indentions, captions, dollar signs, and rulings in the financial statements should be noted. They aid the reader by emphasizing the sections of the statements.

Income Statement

The excess of the revenue over the expenses incurred in earning the revenue is called **net income** or **net profit**. If the expenses of the enterprise exceed the revenue, the excess is a **net loss.** It is impractical to determine the exact amount of expense for each revenue transaction. Therefore, the net income or the net loss is reported for a period of time, such as a month or a year, rather than for each revenue transaction.

The net income (or net loss) is determined using a **matching** process involving two steps. First, revenue is recorded during the period. Second, expenses used in generating the revenue are **matched** against the revenue to determine the net income or the net loss. Generally, the revenue for providing a service is recorded after the service has been provided to the customer. The expenses incurred in generating revenue during a period are then recorded and are thus matched against the revenue.

The effects of revenue earned and expenses incurred during the month for Computer King were shown in the equation as increases and decreases in owner's equity. The revenue, expenses, and net income of $3,050 are reported in the income statement in Exhibit 4.

The order in which the expenses are listed in the income statement varies among businesses. A common method used is to list them in the order of size, beginning with the larger items. Miscellaneous expense is usually shown as the last item, regardless of the amount.

Statement of Owner's Equity

Three types of transactions affected owner's equity for Computer King during the month: (1) the original investment of $15,000, (2) the revenue and expenses that resulted in net income of $3,050 for the month, and (3) a withdrawal of $2,000 by the owner. This information is presented in the statement of owner's equity in Exhibit 4. The statement of owner's equity serves as a link between the balance sheet and the income statement.

Since Computer King had been in operation for only one month, it had no owner's equity at the beginning of November. For December and the following periods, however, there would normally be a beginning balance. This beginning balance would be reported on the statement of owner's equity. To illustrate,

Exhibit 4
Financial Statements

Computer King
Income Statement
For Month Ended November 30, 1993

Fees earned		$7 500 00
Operating expenses:		
Wages expense	$2 125 00	
Rent expense	800 00	
Supplies expense	800 00	
Utilities expense	450 00	
Miscellaneous expense	275 00	
Total operating expenses		4 450 00
Net income		$3 050 00

Computer King
Statement of Owner's Equity
For Month Ended November 30, 1993

Investment on November 1, 1993		$15 000 00
Net income for November	$3 050 00	
Less withdrawals	2 000 00	
Increase in owner's equity		1 050 00
Jere King, capital, November 30, 1993		$16 050 00

Computer King
Balance Sheet
November 30, 1993

Assets		
Cash		$ 5 900 00
Supplies		550 00
Land		10 000 00
Total assets		$16 450 00
Liabilities		
Accounts payable		$ 400 00
Owner's Equity		
Jere King, capital		16 050 00
Total liabilities and owner's equity		$16 450 00

Computer King
Statement of Cash Flows
For Month Ended November 30, 1993

Cash flows from operating activities:		
Cash received from customers	$ 7 500 00	
Deduct cash payments for expenses and		
payments to creditors	4 600 00	
Net cash flow from operating activities		$ 2 900 00
Cash flows from investing activities:		
Cash payments for acquisition of land		(10 000 00)
Cash flows from financing activities:		
Cash received as owner's investment	$15 000 00	
Deduct cash withdrawal by owner	2 000 00	
Net cash flow from financing activities		13 000 00
Net cash flow and Nov. 30, 1993 cash balance		$ 5 900 00

assume that Computer King reported net income of $4,075, and the owner withdrew $2,000 during December. The statement of owner's equity for Computer King for December is shown below.

Computer King Statement of Owner's Equity For Month Ended December 31, 1993		
Jere King, capital, December 1, 1993		$16 0 5 0 00
Net income for the month	$4 0 7 5 00	
Less withdrawals	2 0 0 0 00	
Increase in owner's equity		2 0 7 5 00
Jere King, capital, December 31, 1993		$18 1 2 5 00

Balance Sheet

The amounts of Computer King's assets, liabilities, and owner's equity at the end of November appear on the last line of Computer King's summary of transactions. Minor rearrangements of these data and the addition of a heading yield the balance sheet shown in Exhibit 4. This form of balance sheet, with the liability and owner's equity sections presented below the asset section, is called the **report form.** An alternative form of balance sheet is illustrated in a later chapter.

The asset section of the balance sheet begins with cash. Cash is followed by receivables, supplies, prepaid insurance, and other assets. The assets are normally presented in the order that they will be converted into cash or used in operations. The assets of a more permanent nature, such as land, buildings, and equipment, are listed in that order.

In the liabilities and owner's equity sections of the balance sheet, the liabilities are presented first, followed by owner's equity. In the balance sheet in Exhibit 4, accounts payable is the only liability. When there are two or more categories of liabilities, each should be listed and the total amount of liabilities presented as shown below.

Liabilities		
Accounts payable	$12,900	
Wages payable	2,570	
Total liabilities		$15,470

Statement of Cash Flows

The statement of cash flows in Exhibit 4 consists of three sections: (1) operating activities, (2) investing activities, and (3) financing activities. Each of these sections is briefly described below.

Cash flow from operating activities. This section reports a summary of cash receipts and cash payments from operations. The net cash flow from operating activities will normally differ from the amount of net income for the period. This difference occurs because revenues and expenses may not be recorded at the same time that cash is received from customers and cash is paid to creditors.[7]

Cash flow from investing activities. This section reports the cash transactions for the acquisition and sale of relatively long-term or permanent-type assets.

Cash flow from financing activities. This section reports the cash transactions related to cash investments by the owner, borrowings, and cash withdrawals by the owner.

The preparation of the statement of cash flows requires an understanding of concepts that have not been discussed in this chapter. Therefore, the preparation of the statement of cash flows is described and illustrated in a later chapter.

---

[7] The reconciliation of net income with cash flow from operating activities requires an understanding of concepts and principles discussed in other chapters. Therefore, this reconciliation is discussed in a later chapter.

CHAPTER REVIEW

Key Points

Objective 1. Define accounting as an information system.

Accounting is defined as an information system that provides essential information about the economic activities of an entity to various individuals or groups. The goal of accounting is to record, report, and interpret economic data for use by decision makers. Accounting is often called the "language of business."

Objective 2. Describe the profession of accounting and list its specialized fields.

The profession of accounting consists of (1) private accounting or (2) public accounting. Accountants in both private and public accounting must adhere to codes of professional ethics.

Specialized fields in accounting have evolved as a result of technological advances and economic growth. The most important accounting fields are financial accounting, auditing, management accounting, cost accounting, tax accounting, accounting systems, international accounting, not-for-profit accounting, social accounting, and accounting instruction.

Objective 3. Summarize the development of accounting principles and relate them to practice.

Generally accepted accounting principles have evolved to form a basis for accounting practice. The Financial Accounting Standards Board issues authoritative pronouncements on accounting principles.

The business entity concept is based on applying accounting to individual economic units in society. Profit-making businesses are normally organized as sole proprietorships, partnerships, or corporations.

The cost principle requires that properties and services bought by a business be recorded in terms of actual cost.

Objective 4. List the characteristics of a business transaction.

A business transaction is the occurrence of an economic event or a condition that must be recorded. Business transactions may lead to an event or a condition that results in another transaction.

Objective 5. State the accounting equation and define each element of the equation.

The properties owned by a business and the rights or claims to properties may be stated in the form of an equation, as follows: Assets = Equities. The expansion of the equation to give recognition to two basic types of equities yields the accounting equation: Assets = Liabilities + Owner's Equity.

Objective 6. Explain how business transactions can be stated in terms of the resulting changes in the three basic elements of the accounting equation.

All transactions can be stated in terms of the resulting change in one or more of the three elements of the accounting equation. That is, the effect of every transaction can be stated in terms of increases and/or decreases in one or more of these elements, with the equality of the two sides of the equation maintained.

Objective 7. Describe the financial statements of a sole proprietorship and explain how they interrelate.

The principal financial statements of a sole proprietorship are the income statement, the statement of owner's equity, the balance sheet, and the statement of cash flows. The income statement reports a net income or net loss for the period, which also appears on the statement of owner's equity. The ending owner's capital reported on the statement of owner's equity is also reported on the balance sheet. The ending cash balance is reported on the balance sheet and the statement of cash flows.

Glossary of Key Terms

Accounting. An information system that provides essential information about the economic activities of an entity to various individuals or groups. **Objective 1**

Accounting equation. The expression of the relationship between assets, liabilities, and owner's equity; most commonly stated as Assets = Liabilities + Owner's Equity. **Objective 5**

Account payable. A liability created by a purchase made on credit. **Objective 6**

Account receivable. A claim against a customer for services rendered or goods sold on credit. **Objective 6**

Assets. Properties owned by a business enterprise. **Objective 5**

Balance sheet. A financial statement listing the assets, liabilities, and owner's equity of a business entity as of a specific date. **Objective 7**

Business entity concept. The concept that accounting applies to individual economic units and that each unit is separate and distinct from the persons who supply its assets. **Objective 3**

Business transaction. The occurrence of an exchange or an economic event that must be recorded in the accounting records. **Objective 4**

Corporation. A separate legal entity that is organized in accordance with state or federal statutes and in which ownership is divided into shares of stock. **Objective 3**

Cost principle. The principle that the monetary record for properties and services purchased by a business should be maintained in terms of actual cost. **Objective 3**

Equities. The rights or claims to the properties of a business enterprise. **Objective 5**

Expense. The amount of assets or services used in the process of earning revenue. **Objective 6**

Financial Accounting Standards Board (FASB). An authoritative body for the development of accounting principles. **Objective 3**

Generally accepted accounting principles (GAAP). Generally accepted guidelines for the preparation of financial statements. **Objective 2**

Income statement. A summary of the revenues and expenses of a business entity for a specific period of time. **Objective 7**

Liabilities. Debts of a business enterprise. **Objective 5**

Matching. The concept that expenses incurred in generating revenue should be matched against the revenue in determining the net income or net loss for the period. **Objective 7**

Net income. The final figure in the income statement when revenues exceed expenses. **Objective 7**

Net loss. The final figure in the income statement when expenses exceed revenues. **Objective 7**

Owner's equity. The rights of the owners in a business enterprise. **Objective 5**

Partnership. An unincorporated business owned by two or more individuals. **Objective 3**

Prepaid expenses. Purchased commodities or services that have not been used up at the end of an accounting period. **Objective 6**

Private accounting. The profession whose members are accountants employed by a business firm or not-for-profit organization. **Objective 2**

Public accounting. The profession whose members render accounting services on a fee basis. **Objective 2**

Report form. The form of balance sheet with the liability and owner's equity sections presented below the asset section. **Objective 7**

Revenue. The gross increase in owner's equity as a result of business and professional activities that earn income. **Objective 6**

Sole proprietorship. An unincorporated business owned by one individual. **Objective 3**

Statement of cash flows. A summary of the major cash receipts and cash payments for a period. **Objective 7**

Statement of owner's equity. A summary of the changes in the owner's equity of a business entity that have occurred during a specific period of time. **Objective 7**

Self-Examination Questions
Answers at end of chapter.

1. A profit-making business that is a separate legal entity and in which ownership is divided into shares of stock is known as a:
   A. sole proprietorship   C. partnership
   B. single proprietorship   D. corporation

2. The properties owned by a business enterprise are called:
   A. assets   C. the accounting equation
   B. liabilities   D. owner's equity

3. A list of assets, liabilities, and owner's equity of a business entity as of a specific date is:
   A. a balance sheet   C. a statement of owner's equity
   B. an income statement   D. a statement of cash flows

4. If total assets increased $20,000 during a period of time and total liabilities increased $12,000 during the same period, the amount and direction (increase or decrease) of the period's change in owner's equity is:
   A. $32,000 increase   C. $8,000 increase
   B. $32,000 decrease   D. $8,000 decrease

5. If revenue was $45,000, expenses were $37,500, and the owner's withdrawals were $10,000, the amount of net income or net loss would be:
   A. $45,000 net income   C. $37,500 net loss
   B. $7,500 net income   D. $2,500 net loss

ILLUSTRATIVE PROBLEM

On October 1 of the current year, the assets and liabilities of E. F. Nelson, Attorney-at-Law, are as follows: Cash, $1,000; Accounts Receivable, $2,200; Supplies, $850; Land, $11,450; Accounts Payable, $2,030. E. F. Nelson, Attorney-at-Law, is a sole proprietorship owned and operated by E. F. Nelson. Currently, office space and office equipment are being rented, pending the construction of an office complex on land purchased last year. Business transactions during October are summarized as follows:

   a. Received cash from clients for services, $4,928.
   b. Paid creditors on account, $1,755.
   c. Received cash from E. F. Nelson as an additional investment, $3,700.
   d. Paid office rent for the month, $1,200.
   e. Charged clients for legal services on account, $1,025.
   f. Purchased office supplies on account, $245.
   g. Received cash from clients on account, $2,000.
   h. Received invoice for paralegal services from Legal Aid Inc. for October (to be paid on November 10), $1,635.
   i. Paid the following: wages expense, $850; answering service expense, $250; utilities expense, $325; miscellaneous expense, $75.
   j. Determined that the cost of office supplies used during the month was $115.

ILLUSTRATIVE PROBLEM ILLUSTRATIVE PROBLEM ILLUSTRATIVE PROBLEM ILLUSTRATIVE PROBLEM

Instructions

1. Determine the amount of owner's equity (E. F. Nelson's capital) as of October 1 of the current year.
2. State the assets, liabilities, and owner's equity as of October 1 in equation form similar to that shown in this chapter. In tabular form below the equation, indicate the increases and decreases resulting from each transaction and the new balances after each transaction. Explain the nature of each increase and decrease in owner's equity by an appropriate notation at the right of the amount.
3. Prepare (a) an income statement for October, (b) a statement of owner's equity for October, and (c) a balance sheet as of October 31.

Solution

1. Assets – Liabilities = Owner's Equity (E. F. Nelson, capital)
   $15,500 – $2,030 = Owner's Equity (E. F. Nelson, capital)
   $13,470 = Owner's Equity (E. F. Nelson, capital)

2.

	Cash +	Accounts Receivable +	Supplies +	Land =	Accounts Payable +	E. F. Nelson, Capital	
	Assets				**= Liabilities + Owner's Equity**		
Bal.	1,000	2,200	850	11,450	2,030	13,470	
a.	+4,928					+ 4,928	Fees earned
Bal.	5,928	2,200	850	11,450	2,030	18,398	
b.	–1,755				–1,755		
Bal.	4,173	2,200	850	11,450	275	18,398	
c.	+3,700					+ 3,700	Investment
Bal.	7,873	2,200	850	11,450	275	22,098	
d.	–1,200					– 1,200	Rent expense
Bal.	6,673	2,200	850	11,450	275	20,898	
e.		+1,025				+ 1,025	Fees earned
Bal.	6,673	3,225	850	11,450	275	21,923	
f.			+ 245		+ 245		
Bal.	6,673	3,225	1,095	11,450	520	21,923	
g.	+2,000	–2,000					
Bal.	8,673	1,225	1,095	11,450	520	21,923	
h.					+1,635	– 1,635	Paralegal exp.
Bal.	8,673	1,225	1,095	11,450	2,155	20,288	
i.	–1,500					– 850	Wages expense
						– 250	Answ. svc. exp.
						– 325	Utilities exp.
						– 75	Misc. exp.
Bal.	7,173	1,225	1,095	11,450	2,155	18,788	
j.			– 115			– 115	Supplies exp.
Bal.	7,173	1,225	980	11,450	2,155	18,673	

3. a.

E. F. Nelson, Attorney-at-Law		
Income Statement		
For Month Ended October 31, 19—		
Fees earned		$5 9 5 3 00
Operating expenses:		
Paralegal expense	$1 6 3 5 00	
Rent expense	1 2 0 0 00	
Wages expense	8 5 0 00	
Utilities expense	3 2 5 00	
Answering service expense	2 5 0 00	
Supplies expense	1 1 5 00	
Miscellaneous expense	7 5 00	
Total operating expenses		4 4 5 0 00
Net income		$1 5 0 3 00

3. b.

E. F. Nelson, Attorney-at-Law				
Statement of Owner's Equity				
For Month Ended October 31, 19—				
E. F. Nelson, capital, October 1, 19—			$13 4 7 0 00	
Additional investment by owner	$3 7 0 0 00			
Net income for the month	1 5 0 3 00			
Increase in owner's equity			5 2 0 3 00	
E. F. Nelson, capital, October 31, 19—			$18 6 7 3 00	

3. c.

E. F. Nelson, Attorney-at-Law		
Balance Sheet		
October 31, 19—		
Assets		
Cash		$ 7 1 7 3 00
Accounts receivable		1 2 2 5 00
Supplies		9 8 0 00
Land		11 4 5 0 00
Total assets		$20 8 2 8 00
Liabilities		
Accounts payable		$ 2 1 5 5 00
Owner's Equity		
E. F. Nelson, capital		18 6 7 3 00
Total liabilities and owner's equity		$20 8 2 8 00

DISCUSSION QUESTIONS

1. Name some of the categories of individuals and institutions who use accounting information.
2. Distinguish between private accounting and public accounting.
3. Describe in general terms the requirements that an individual must meet for (a) the CMA certificate and (b) the CPA certificate.
4. What are ethics?
5. Name some of the specialized fields in accounting.
6. How are generally accepted accounting principles (GAAP) established?
7. Identify each of the following abbreviations:
   a. AICPA
   b. CIA
   c. CMA
   d. CPA
   e. FASB
   f. GAAP
8. a. Name the three principal forms of profit-making business organizations.
   b. Which of these forms is identified with the greatest number of businesses?
   c. Which of these forms is the dominant form in terms of dollars of business activity?
9. What is meant by the cost principle?
10. On February 8, Allen Delivery Service extended an offer of $90,000 for land that had been priced for sale at $100,000. On February 20, Allen Delivery Service accepted the seller's counteroffer of $95,000. At what amount should the land be recorded by Allen Delivery Service?

11. a. Land with an assessed value of $60,000 for property tax purposes is acquired by a business enterprise for $75,000. At what amount should the land be recorded by the purchaser? *$75,000*

    b. Ten years later the plot of land in (a) has an assessed value of $110,000 and the business enterprise receives an offer of $150,000 for it. Should the monetary amount assigned to the land in the business records now be increased and, if so, by what amount? *NO, STILL WORTH $75,000*

    c. Assuming that the land acquired in (a) was sold for $175,000, (1) how much would the owner's equity increase, and (2) at what amount would the purchaser record the land?

12. a. If the assets owned by a business enterprise total $250,000, what is the amount of the equities of the enterprise?

    b. What are the two principal types of equities?

13. Name the three elements of the accounting equation.

14. a. An enterprise has assets of $210,000 and liabilities of $145,000. What is the amount of its owner's equity?

    b. An enterprise has assets of $450,000 and owner's equity of $200,000. What is the total amount of its liabilities?

    c. An enterprise has liabilities of $400,000 and owner's equity of $150,000. What is the total amount of its assets?

15. Describe how the following business transactions affect the three elements of the accounting equation.

    a. Invested cash in the business.

    b. Received cash for services performed.

    c. Purchased supplies for cash.

    d. Paid for utilities used in the business.

    e. Purchased supplies on account.

16. a. A vacant lot acquired for $50,000, on which there is a balance owed of $35,000, is sold for $65,000 in cash. What is the effect of the sale on the total amount of the seller's (1) assets, (2) liabilities, and (3) owner's equity?

    b. After receiving the $65,000 cash in (a), the seller pays the $35,000 owed. What is the effect of the payment on the total amount of the seller's (1) assets, (2) liabilities, and (3) owner's equity?

17. Operations of a service enterprise for a particular month are summarized as follows:
Services sold: on account, $15,000; for cash, $80,000. *95,000*
Expenses incurred: on account, $46,000; for cash, $35,000. *81,000*   *14,000*
What was the amount of the enterprise's (a) revenue, (b) expenses, and (c) net income?

18. Describe the difference between an account receivable and an account payable.

19. A business enterprise had revenues of $112,000 and operating expenses of $120,000. Did the enterprise (a) incur a net loss or (b) realize a net income?

20. A business enterprise had revenues of $202,500 and operating expenses of $170,000. Did the enterprise (a) incur a net loss or (b) realize a net income?

21. Name the two types of transactions that increase the owner's equity of a sole proprietorship.

22. Indicate whether each of the following types of transactions will (a) increase owner's equity or (b) decrease owner's equity:

    1. owner's investments

    2. revenues

    3. expenses

    4. owner's withdrawals

23. List a sole proprietorship's four major financial statements illustrated in this chapter, and briefly describe the nature of the information provided by each.

24. Indicate whether the data in each of the following financial statements (a) cover a period of time or (b) are for a specific date:

    1. balance sheet

    2. income statement

    3. statement of owner's equity

    4. statement of cash flows

25. What particular item of financial or operating data appears on (a) both the income statement and the statement of owner's equity, and (b) both the balance sheet and the statement of owner's equity?

26. House of Vision had owner's equity of $260,000 at the beginning of the period. At the end of the period, the company had total assets of $345,000 and total liabilities of

$95,000. (a) What was the net income or net loss for the period, assuming no additional investments or withdrawals? (b) What was the net income or net loss for the period, assuming a withdrawal of $30,000 had occurred during the period?

27. Name the three types of activities reported in the statement of cash flows.
28. Indicate whether each of the following activities would be reported on the statement of cash flows as (a) an operating activity, (b) an investing activity, or (c) a financing activity:
    1. cash received as owner's investment
    2. cash paid for land
    3. cash received from fees earned
    4. cash paid for expenses

 29. The 1991 annual report of Sears, Roebuck and Co. reported total assets of $106,434.8 million and total liabilities of $91,246.6 million on December 31, 1991. What was the owner's equity at December 31, 1991?

ETHICS DISCUSSION CASE

Joan Kelley, president of Kelley Enterprises, applied for a $100,000 loan from Pioneer National Bank. The bank requested financial statements from Kelley Enterprises as a basis for granting the loan. Joan Kelley has told her accountant to provide the bank with a balance sheet. Joan Kelley has decided to omit the other financial statements because there was a net loss during the past year.

SHARPEN YOUR COMMUNICATION SKILLS ▶ Discuss whether Joan Kelley is behaving in an ethical manner by omitting some of the financial statements.

EXERCISES

EXERCISE 1-1
PROFESSIONAL ETHICS
Objective 2

SHARPEN YOUR COMMUNICATION SKILLS

A fertilizer manufacturing company wants to relocate in Collier County. A 13-year-old report from a fired researcher at the company says the company's product is releasing toxic by-products. The company has suppressed that report. A second report commissioned by the company shows there is no problem with the fertilizer.

Should the company's chief executive officer reveal the context of the unfavorable report in discussions with Collier County representatives? Discuss.

Source: "Business Leaders Ponder Ethical Questions," *Naples Daily News*, May 12, 1991, p. 1E.

EXERCISE 1-2
ACCOUNTING EQUATION
Objective 5

Determine the missing amount for each of the following:

	Assets	=	Liabilities	+	Owner's Equity
a.	X	=	$15,500	+	$21,500
b.	$62,750	=	X	+	30,000
c.	57,000	=	19,000	+	X

EXERCISE 1-3
ASSET, LIABILITY, OWNER'S EQUITY ITEMS
Objective 6

Indicate whether each of the following represents (1) an asset, (2) a liability, or (3) owner's equity:

a. accounts payable   d. land
b. cash   e. supplies
c. fees earned   f. wages expense

EXERCISE 1-4
TRANSACTIONS
Objective 6

The following selected transactions were completed by Cavin Delivery Service during August:
1. Received cash from owner as additional investment, $15,000.
2. Paid rent for August, $2,500.
3. Billed customers for delivery services on account, $2,900.
4. Received cash from cash customers, $3,250.
5. Paid advertising expense, $625.
6. Purchased supplies for cash, $750.
7. Received cash from customers on account, $700.
8. Paid creditors on account, $550.
9. Determined that $575 of supplies had been used during the month.
10. Paid cash to owner for personal use, $2,000.

Indicate the effect of each transaction on the accounting equation by listing the numbers identifying the transactions, (1) through (10), in a vertical column, and inserting at the right of each number the appropriate letter from the following list:

a. Increase in one asset, decrease in another asset.
b. Increase in an asset, increase in a liability.
c. Increase in an asset, increase in owner's equity.
d. Decrease in an asset, decrease in a liability.
e. Decrease in an asset, decrease in owner's equity.

EXERCISE 1-5
NATURE OF
TRANSACTIONS
Objective 6

Carmine Darby is engaged in a service business. Summary financial data for July are presented in equation form as follows. Each line designated by a number indicates the effect of a transaction on the equation. Each increase and decrease in owner's equity, except transaction (5), affects net income.

	Cash	+ Supplies	+ Land	= Liabilities	+ Owner's Equity
Bal.	4,500	750	15,000	3,750	16,500
1.	+9,000				+9,000
2.	–3,250				–3,250
3.	–2,300			–2,300	
4.		+600		+ 600	
5.	–1,950				–1,950
6.	–4,000		+4,000		
7.		–680			– 680
Bal.	2,000	670	19,000	2,050	19,620

a. Describe each transaction.
b. What is the amount of net decrease in cash during the month?
c. What is the amount of net increase in owner's equity during the month?
d. What is the amount of the net income for the month?
e. How much of the net income for the month was retained in the business?

EXERCISE 1-6
NET INCOME AND
OWNER'S WITHDRAWALS
Objective 7

The income statement of a sole proprietorship for the month of October indicates a net income of $35,000. During the same period the owner withdrew $36,000 in cash from the business for personal use.

SHARPEN YOUR ▶
COMMUNICATION SKILLS

Would it be correct to say that the owner incurred a net loss of $1,000 during the month? Discuss.

EXERCISE 1-7
NET INCOME AND
OWNER'S EQUITY FOR
FOUR ENTERPRISES
Objective 7

Four different sole proprietorships, A, B, C, and D, show the same balance sheet data at the beginning and end of a year. These data, exclusive of the amount of owner's equity, are summarized as follows:

	Total Assets	Total Liabilities
Beginning of the year	$525,000	$190,000
End of the year	620,000	265,000

On the basis of the above data and the following additional information for the year, determine the net income (or loss) of each company for the year. (*Suggestion:* First determine the amount of increase or decrease in owner's equity during the year.)

Company A: The owner had made no additional investments in the business and had made no withdrawals from the business.
Company B: The owner had made no additional investments in the business but had withdrawn $40,000.
Company C: The owner had made an additional investment of $50,000 but had made no withdrawals.
Company D: The owner had made an additional investment of $50,000 and had withdrawn $40,000.

EXERCISE 1-8
BALANCE SHEET ITEMS
Objective 7

From the following list of selected items taken from the records of A-1 Appliance Service as of a specific date, identify those that would appear on the balance sheet:

1. Accounts Payable   6. Supplies
2. Cash   7. Supplies Expense
3. Fees Earned   8. Utilities Expense
4. Land   9. Wages Expense
5. Jack Neff, Capital   10. Wages Payable

EXERCISE 1-9
INCOME STATEMENT ITEMS
Objective 7

Based on the data presented in Exercise 1-8, identify those items that would appear on the income statement.

EXERCISE 1-10
STATEMENT OF OWNER'S EQUITY
Objective 7

Financial information related to Joan Benny Company, a sole proprietorship, for the month ended September 30, 1993, is as follows:

Net income for September	$ 4,750
Joan Benny's withdrawals during September	3,000
Joan Benny, capital, September 1, 1993	39,950

Prepare a statement of owner's equity for the month ended September 30, 1993.

EXERCISE 1-11
INCOME STATEMENT
Objective 7

Chavez Services was organized on June 1. A summary of the revenue and expense transactions for June are as follows:

Fees earned	$5,400
Wages expense	1,700
Miscellaneous expense	50
Rent expense	900
Supplies expense	250

Prepare an income statement for the month ended June 30.

EXERCISE 1-12
MISSING AMOUNTS FROM BALANCE SHEET AND INCOME STATEMENT DATA
Objective 7

One item is omitted in each of the following summaries of balance sheet and income statement data for four different sole proprietorships, I, II, III, and IV.

	I	II	III	IV
Beginning of the year:				
Assets	$270,000	$70,000	$90,000	(d)
Liabilities	160,000	35,000	76,000	$22,750
End of the year:				
Assets	315,000	95,000	94,000	79,000
Liabilities	185,000	25,000	87,000	52,000
During the year:				
Additional investment in the business	(a)	12,000	5,000	20,000
Withdrawals from the business	20,000	18,000	(c)	23,000
Revenue	87,750	(b)	88,100	99,000
Expenses	72,750	32,000	89,600	78,000

Determine the amounts of the missing items, identifying them by letter. (*Suggestion:* First determine the amount of increase or decrease in owner's equity during the year.)

EXERCISE 1-13
BALANCE SHEETS; NET INCOME
Objective 7

Financial information related to the sole proprietorship of L. Keaton Interiors for May and June of the current year is as follows:

	May 31, 19—	June 30, 19—
Accounts Payable	$ 7,720	$ 9,900
Accounts Receivable	10,300	13,400
Leon Keaton, Capital	?	?
Cash	10,150	12,050
Supplies	975	750

a. Prepare balance sheets for L. Keaton Interiors as of May 31 and as of June 30 of the current year.
b. Determine the amount of net income for June, assuming that the owner had made no additional investments or withdrawals during the month.
c. Determine the amount of net income for June, assuming that the owner had made no additional investments and had withdrawn $4,000 during the month.

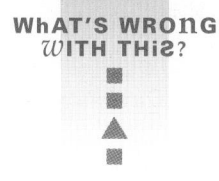

WhAT'S WRONG
WITH THiS?

How many errors can you find in the following financial statements for Cox Realty, pre-pared after the first month of operations?

COX REALTY
Income Statement
For Month Ended June 30, 19—

Sales commissions		$6 1 0 0 00
Operating expenses:		
Office salaries expense	$2 1 5 0 00	
Rent expense	1 8 0 0 00	
Automobile expense	4 0 0 00	
Supplies expense	1 2 5 00	
Miscellaneous expense	2 5 0 00	
Total operating expenses		4 7 2 5 00
Net income		$1 3 7 5 00

Statement of Owner's Equity
June 30, 19—

Investment during the month		$ 7 5 0 0 00
Net income for the month	$1 8 7 5 00	
Plus withdrawals	1 5 0 0 00	
Increase in owner's equity		3 3 7 5 00
Carol Cox, capital, June 30, 19—		$10 8 7 5 00

Balance Sheet
June 30, 19—

Assets		
Cash		$ 7 2 5 0 00
Accounts payable		2 0 0 00
Total assets		$ 7 4 5 0 00
Liabilities		
Supplies		$ 3 2 5 00
Owner's Equity		
Carol Cox, capital		10 8 7 5 00
Total liabilities and owner's equity		$11 2 0 0 00

PROBLEMS

Series A

PROBLEM 1-1A
TRANSACTIONS
Objective 6

Ruth Ruhl established a sole proprietorship on April 1 of the current year and completed the following transactions during April:

   a. Opened a business bank account with a deposit of $8,000.
   b. Paid rent on office and equipment for the month, $4, 000.
   c. Purchased supplies (stationery, stamps, pencils, etc.) on account, $1,950.
   d. Received cash from fees earned, $2,500.
   e. Paid creditors on account, $975.
   f. Billed customers for fees earned, $2,250.
   g. Paid automobile expenses (including rental charges) for month, $980, and miscella-neous expenses, $775.
   h. Paid office salaries, $1,500.
   i. Determined that the cost of supplies on hand was $925; therefore, the cost of supplies used was $1,025.
   j. Withdrew cash for personal use, $1,200.

Instructions

1. Indicate the effect of each transaction and the balances after each transaction, using the following tabular headings:

Assets	=	Liabilities	+	Owner's Equity
Cash + Accounts Receivable + Supplies	=	Accounts Payable +		Ruth Ruhl, Capital

By appropriate notations at the right of each change, indicate the nature of each increase and decrease in owner's equity.

SHARPEN YOUR COMMUNICATION SKILLS ▶

2. Briefly explain why the owner's investment and revenues increased owner's equity, while withdrawals and expenses decreased owner's equity.

PROBLEM 1-2A
FINANCIAL STATEMENTS
Objective 7

Following are the amounts of the assets and liabilities of Pelican Travel, a sole proprietorship, at October 31, 1994, the end of the current year, and its revenue and expenses for the year ended on that date. The items are listed in alphabetical order. The capital of Jim Rudd, owner, was $4,500 on November 1, 1993, the beginning of the current year. During the current year Rudd withdrew $25,000.

Accounts payable	$ 210
Cash	6,500
Miscellaneous expense	1,750
Rent expense	24,000
Fees earned	84,530
Supplies	865
Supplies expense	1,125
Utilities expense	4,500
Wages expense	25,500

Instructions

1. Prepare an income statement for the current year ended October 31, 1994.
2. Prepare a statement of owner's equity for the current year ended October 31, 1994.
3. Prepare a balance sheet as of October 31, 1994.

PROBLEM 1-3A
FINANCIAL STATEMENTS
Objective 7

Mary Hall established Mary Hall Services on April 1 of the current year. The effect of each transaction and the balances after each transaction for April are as follows:

	Assets			=	Liabilities + Owner's Equity			
		Accounts			Accounts	Mary Hall,		
	Cash +	Receivable +	Supplies	=	Payable +	Capital		
a.	+5,000					+5,000		Investment
b.	−1,800					−1,800		Rent expense
Bal.	3,200					3,200		
c.			+725		+725			
Bal.	3,200		725		725	3,200		
d.	− 225				−225			
Bal.	2,975		725		500	3,200		
e.	+3,750					+3,750		Fees earned
Bal.	6,725		725		500	6,950		
f.	−1,600					−1,250		Auto expense
						− 350		Misc. expense
Bal.	5,125		725		500	5,350		
g.	−1,900					−1,900		Salaries expense
Bal.	3,225		725		500	3,450		
h.			−450			− 450		Supplies expense
Bal.	3,225		275		500	3,000		
i.		+4,350				+4,350		Fees earned
Bal.	3,225	4,350	275		500	7,350		
j.	−2,000					−2,000		Withdrawal
Bal.	1,225	4,350	275		500	5,350		

Instructions

1. Prepare an income statement for the month ended April 30.
2. Prepare a statement of owner's equity for the month ended April 30.
3. Prepare a balance sheet as of April 30.

PROBLEM 1-4A
TRANSACTIONS;
FINANCIAL STATEMENTS
Objectives 6, 7

On August 1 of the current year, Doris Lusk established a sole proprietorship under the name Lusk Realty. Lusk completed the following transactions during the month of August:

  a. Opened a business bank account with a deposit of $7,500.
  b. Paid rent on office and equipment for the month, $4,100.
  c. Purchased supplies (stationery, stamps, pencils, etc.) on account, $750.
  d. Paid creditor on account, $500.
  e. Earned sales commissions, receiving cash, $14,100.
  f. Withdrew cash for personal use, $3,000.
  g. Paid automobile expenses (including rental charge) for month, $1,900, and miscellaneous expenses, $350.
  h. Paid office salaries, $4,150.
  i. Determined that the cost of supplies used was $550.

Instructions

1. Indicate the effect of each transaction and the balances after each transaction, using the following tabular headings:

Assets	=	Liabilities	+	Owner'sEquity
Cash + Supplies	=	Accounts Payable	+	Doris Lusk, Capital

By appropriate notations at the right of each change, indicate the nature of each increase and decrease in owner's equity.

2. Prepare an income statement for August, a statement of owner's equity for August, and a balance sheet as of August 31.

PROBLEM 1-5A
TRANSACTIONS;
FINANCIAL STATEMENTS
Objectives 6, 7

Guy Dry Cleaners is a sole proprietorship owned and operated by Karen Guy. Currently, a building and equipment are being rented, pending expansion to new facilities. The actual work of dry cleaning is done by another company at wholesale rates. The assets and the liabilities of the business on May 1 of the current year are as follows: Cash, $6,250; Accounts Receivable, $12,100; Supplies, $900; Land, $25,000; Accounts Payable, $7,800. Business transactions during May are summarized as follows:

  a. Received cash from cash customers for dry cleaning sales, $10,750.
  b. Paid rent for the month, $2,000.
  c. Purchased supplies on account, $820.
  d. Paid creditors on account, $7,800.
  e. Charged customers for dry cleaning sales on account, $6,920.
  f. Received monthly invoice for dry cleaning expense for May (to be paid on June 10), $7,700.
  g. Paid the following: wages expense, $2,400; truck expense, $1,580; utilities expense, $960; miscellaneous expense, $630.
  h. Received cash from customers on account, $8,100.
  i. Determined the cost of supplies used during the month, $970.

Instructions

1. Determine the amount of Karen Guy's capital as of May 1 of the current year.
2. State the assets, liabilities, and owner's equity as of May 1 in equation form similar to that shown in this chapter. In tabular form below the equation, indicate increases and decreases resulting from each transaction and the new balances after each transaction. Explain the nature of each increase and decrease in owner's equity by an appropriate notation at the right of the amount.
3. Prepare (a) an income statement for May, (b) a statement of owner's equity for May, and (c) a balance sheet as of May 31.

PROBLEM 1-6A
FINANCIAL STATEMENTS
Objective 7

Following are the amounts of the assets and liabilities of Graf Services, a sole proprietorship, at December 31, the end of the current year, and its revenue and expenses for the year ended on that date. The capital of Tom Graf, owner, was $20,450 at January 1, the beginning of the current year, and the owner withdrew $30,000 during the current year.

Cash	$ 7,200
Accounts receivable	21,000
Supplies	2,750
Accounts payable	3,100
Wages payable	1,500
Fees earned	99,250
Wages expense	29,700
Rent expense	12,000
Utilities expense	8,100
Supplies expense	4,800
Taxes expense	4,500
Advertising expense	3,000
Miscellaneous expense	1,250

Instructions

1. Prepare an income statement for the current year ended December 31.
2. Prepare a statement of owner's equity for the current year ended December 31.
3. Prepare a balance sheet as of December 31 of the current year.

Series B

PROBLEM 1-1B
TRANSACTIONS
Objective 6

David Key established a sole proprietorship on October 1 of the current year and completed the following transactions during October:

a. Opened a business bank account with a deposit of $5,000.
b. Paid rent on office and equipment for the month, $2,500.
c. Purchased supplies on account, $850.
d. Paid creditors on account, $625.
e. Received cash from fees earned, $3,250.
f. Paid automobile expenses for month, $780, and miscellaneous expenses, $250.
g. Paid office salaries, $1,500.
h. Determined that the cost of supplies on hand was $275; therefore, the cost of supplies used was $575.
i. Billed customers for fees earned, $2,350.
j. Withdrew cash for personal use, $1,000.

Instructions

1. Indicate the effect of each transaction and the balances after each transaction, using the following tabular headings:

Assets	=	*Liabilities*	+	*Owner's Equity*
Cash + Accounts Receivable + Supplies	=	Accounts Payable +		David Key, Capital

By appropriate notations at the right of each change, indicate the nature of each increase and decrease in owner's equity.

2. Briefly explain why the owner's investment and revenues increased owner's equity, while withdrawals and expenses decreased owner's equity.

SHARPEN YOUR ►
COMMUNICATION SKILLS

PROBLEM 1-2B
FINANCIAL STATEMENTS
Objective 7

Following are the amounts of the assets and liabilities of Cole Travel Service, a sole proprietorship, at June 30, 1994, the end of the current year, and its revenue and expenses for the year ended on that date. The capital of E. F. Cole, owner, was $5,400 at July 1, 1993, the beginning of the current year, and the owner withdrew $18,000 during the current year.

Cash	$ 6,125
Supplies	675
Accounts payable	1,100
Fees earned	68,775
Wages expense	24,900
Rent expense	9,900
Utilities expense	8,500
Supplies expense	4,550
Taxes expense	1,800
Miscellaneous expense	825

Instructions

1. Prepare an income statement for the current year ended June 30, 1994.
2 Prepare a statement of owner's equity for the current year ended June 30, 1994.
3. Prepare a balance sheet as of June 30, 1994.

PROBLEM 1-3B
FINANCIAL STATEMENTS
Objective 7

Jack Hyde established Jack Hyde Services on July 1 of the current year. The effect of each transaction and the balances after each transaction for July are as follows:

	Cash +	Accounts Receivable +	Supplies	=	Accounts Payable +	Jack Hyde, Capital	
a.	+2,500					+2,500	Investment
b.	−2,000					−2,000	Rent expense
Bal.	500					500	
c.			+550		+550		
Bal.	500		550		550	500	
d.	+5,000					+5,000	Fees earned
Bal.	5,500		550		550	5,500	
e.	− 250				−250		
Bal.	5,250		550		300	5,500	
f.		+1,750				+1,750	Fees earned
Bal.	5,250	1,750	550		300	7,250	
g.	−1,155					− 780	Auto expense
						− 375	Misc. expense
Bal.	4,095	1,750	550		300	6,095	
h.	−1,000					−1,000	Salaries expense
Bal.	3,095	1,750	550		300	5,095	
i.			−125			− 125	Supplies expense
Bal.	3,095	1,750	425		300	4,970	
j.	−1,200					−1,200	Withdrawal
Bal.	1,895	1,750	425		300	3,770	

Instructions

1. Prepare an income statement for the month ended July 31.
2. Prepare a statement of owner's equity for the month ended July 31.
3. Prepare a balance sheet as of July 31.

PROBLEM 1-4B
TRANSACTIONS;
FINANCIAL STATEMENTS
Objectives 6, 7

On July 1 of the current year, Leo Egan established a sole proprietorship under the name Egan Realty. Egan completed the following transactions during the month of July:

a. Opened a business bank account with a deposit of $5,000.
b. Paid rent on office and equipment for the month, $3,600.
c. Purchased supplies (stationery, stamps, pencils, etc.) on account, $825.
d. Paid creditor on account, $500.
e. Earned sales commissions, receiving cash, $11,100.
f. Withdrew cash for personal use, $2,000.
g. Paid automobile expenses (including rental charge) for month, $900, and miscellaneous expenses, $550.
h. Paid office salaries, $2,950.
i. Determined that the cost of supplies used was $425.

Instructions

1. Indicate the effect of each transaction and the balances after each transaction, using the following tabular headings:

Assets	=	Liabilities	+	Owner's Equity
Cash + Supplies	=	Accounts Payable +		Leo Egan, Capital

By appropriate notations at the right of each change, indicate the nature of each increase and decrease in owner's equity.
2. Prepare an income statement for July, a statement of owner's equity for July, and a balance sheet as of July 31.

PROBLEM 1-5B
TRANSACTIONS;
FINANCIAL STATEMENTS
Objectives 6, 7

Guy Dry Cleaners is a sole proprietorship owned and operated by Karen Guy. Currently, a building and equipment are being rented, pending expansion to new facilities. The actual work of dry cleaning is done by another company at wholesale rates. The assets and the liabilities of the business on June 1 of the current year are as follows: Cash, $5,400; Accounts Receivable, $6,750; Supplies, $560; Land, $10,000; Accounts Payable, $3,880. Business transactions during June are summarized as follows:

a. Paid rent for the month, $1,450.
b. Charged customers for dry cleaning sales on account, $7,150.
c. Paid creditors on account, $1,680.
d. Purchased supplies on account, $310.
e. Received cash from cash customers for dry cleaning sales, $3,600.
f. Received cash from customers on account, $3,750.
g. Received monthly invoice for dry cleaning expense for June (to be paid on July 10), $3,400.
h. Paid the following: wages expense, $1,800; truck expense, $725; utilities expense, $510; miscellaneous expense, $190.
i. Determined the cost of supplies used during the month, $570.

Instructions

1. Determine the amount of Karen Guy's capital as of June 1 of the current year.
2. State the assets, liabilities, and owner's equity as of June 1 in equation form similar to that shown in this chapter. In tabular form below the equation, indicate increases and decreases resulting from each transaction and the new balances after each transaction. Explain the nature of each increase and decrease in owner's equity by an appropriate notation at the right of the amount.
3. Prepare (a) an income statement for June, (b) a statement of owner's equity for June, and (c) a balance sheet as of June 30.

PROBLEM 1-6B
FINANCIAL STATEMENTS
Objective 7

Following are the amounts of the assets and liabilities of Bennett Consultants, a sole proprietorship, at July 31, 1994, the end of the current year, and its revenue and expenses for the year ended on that date. The items are listed in alphabetical order. The capital of Bob Bennett, owner, was $157,890 on August 1, 1993, the beginning of the current year. During the current year, the owner withdrew $50,000.

Accounts payable	$ 78,000
Accounts receivable	69,750
Advertising expense	30,000
Cash	64,515
Fees earned	827,500
Land	150,000
Miscellaneous expense	8,125
Rent expense	165,000
Supplies	6,250
Supplies expense	19,750
Taxes expense	33,500
Utilities expense	65,750
Wages expense	412,000
Wages payable	11,250

Instructions

1. Prepare an income statement for the current year ended July 31, 1994.
2. Prepare a statement of owner's equity for the current year ended July 31, 1994.
3. Prepare a balance sheet as of July 31, 1994.

MINI-CASE 1 VINES TENNIS SERVICES

Ana Gage, a junior in college, has been seeking ways to earn extra spending money. As an active sports enthusiast, Ana plays tennis regularly at the Vines Tennis Club, where her family has a membership. The president of the club recently approached Ana with the proposal that she manage the club's tennis courts on weekends. Ana's primary duty would be to supervise the operation of the club's four indoor and six outdoor courts, including court reservations.

In return for her services, the club would pay Ana $60 per weekend, plus Ana could keep whatever she earned from lessons and the fees from the use of the ball machine. The club and Ana agreed to a one-month trial, after which both would consider an arrangement for the remaining two years of Ana's college career. On this basis, Ana organized Vines Tennis Services. During September, Ana managed the tennis courts and entered into the following transactions:

a. Opened a business account by depositing $300.
b. Paid $150 for tennis supplies (practice tennis balls, etc.).
c. Paid $75 for the rental of video tape equipment to be used in offering lessons during September.
d. Arranged for the rental of two ball machines during September for $100. Paid $50 in advance, with the remaining $50 due October 1.
e. Received $950 for lessons given during September.
f. Received $150 in fees from the use of the ball machines during September.
g. Paid $300 for salaries of part-time employees who answered the telephone and took reservations while Ana was giving lessons.

h. Paid $75 for miscellaneous expenses.
i. Received $240 from the club for managing the tennis courts during September.
j. Determined that supplies on hand at the end of the month totaled $80.
k. Withdrew $600 for personal use on September 30.

As a friend and accounting student, you have been asked by Ana to aid her in assessing the venture.

Instructions:

1. Indicate the effect of each transaction and the balances after each transaction, using the following tabular headings:

Assets	Liabilities	+ Owner's Equity
Cash + Supplies	= Accounts Payable +	A. Gage, Capital

2. Prepare an income statement for September.
3. Prepare a statement of owner's equity for September.
4. Prepare a balance sheet as of September 30.
5. a. Assume that Ana Gage could earn $8 per hour working 20 hours per weekend as a waitress. Evaluate which of the two alternatives, working as a waitress or operating Vines Tennis Services, would provide Ana with the most income per month.
   b. ▮▮▮▮ ‣ Discuss any other factors that you believe Ana should consider before discussing a long-term arrangement with Vines Tennis Club.

ANSWERS TO SELF-EXAMINATION QUESTIONS

1. **D** A corporation, organized in accordance with state or federal statutes, is a separate legal entity in which ownership is divided into shares of stock (answer D). A sole proprietorship, sometimes called a single proprietorship (answers A and B), is an unincorporated business enterprise owned by one individual. A partnership (answer C) is an unincorporated business enterprise owned by two or more individuals.

2. **A** The properties owned by a business enterprise are called assets (answer A). The debts of the business are called liabilities (answer B), and the equity of the owners is called owner's equity (answer D). The relationship between assets, liabilities, and owner's equity is expressed as the accounting equation (answer C).

3. **A** The balance sheet is a listing of the assets, liabilities, and owner's equity of a business entity at a specific date (answer A). The income statement (answer B) is a summary of the revenue and expenses of a business entity for a specific period of time. The statement of owner's equity (answer C) summarizes the changes in owner's equity for a sole proprietorship or partnership during a specific pe-

riod of time. The statement of cash flows (answer D) summarizes the cash receipts and cash payments for a specific period of time.

4. **C** The accounting equation is:

Assets = Liabilities + Owner's Equity

Therefore, if assets increased by $20,000 and liabilities increased by $12,000, owner's equity must have increased by $8,000 (answer C), as indicated in the following computation:

$$\text{Assets} = \text{Liabilities} + \text{Owner's Equity}$$
$$\$20,000 = \$12,000 + \text{Owner's Equity}$$
$$\$20,000 - \$12,000 = \text{Owner's Equity}$$
$$\$ 8,000 = \text{Owner's Equity}$$

5. **B** Net income is the excess of revenue over expenses, or $7,500 (answer B). If expenses exceed revenue, the difference is a net loss. Withdrawals by the owner are the opposite of the owner's investing in the business and do not affect the amount of net income or net loss.

You and Accounting

Rico's Pizzeria is hiring students part-time to deliver pizzas. If you are hired, you will be using your own car. You will be paid $.20 per mile for each mile driven plus $5.00 an hour and tips. If your car has a standard odometer, how would you determine the number of miles driven each day delivering pizzas?

One method would be to record the reading of the odometer before work and then at quitting time. The difference would be the miles driven. For example, if the odometer read 56,743 at the start of work and 56,889 at the end of work, the miles driven would be 146 miles. However, this method is subject to error if you copy down the wrong odometer reading or make a math error. Is there a better method that would be more efficient and less subject to error?

If your car has a trip odometer, you could set the trip odometer to zero when you begin work and simply read it at the end of work for the miles driven. You could also check the accuracy of the trip odometer by recording the standard odometer readings as described in the preceding paragraph. If the estimates of the miles driven agreed, you could be confident that you are being paid for the actual miles driven.

In running a business, managers need to have information readily available for making decisions. For example, a manager needs to know how much cash is available, how much has been spent, and what services have been provided customers. In addition, the accounting system should provide a check on the accuracy of the recording process. This chapter discusses methods used to record data so that information is readily available for management's use. In addition, methods of checking the accuracy of the recording process are presented.

Chapter 2
Accounting Systems for Recording Business Transactions

LEARNING OBJECTIVES
After studying this chapter, you should be able to:

Objective 1
Explain the purpose of an account.

Objective 2
Prepare a chart of accounts for a service enterprise.

Objective 3
Explain the characteristics of an account.

Objective 4
List the rules of debit and credit and the normal balances of accounts.

Objective 5
Journalize and post transactions, using a two-column journal and a standard (four-column) account in the ledger.

Objective 6
Prepare a trial balance and explain how it can be used to discover errors.

Objective 7
Discover errors in recording transactions and correct them.

Basic concepts, principles, and methods of recording transactions were presented in Chapter 1. The preparation of financial statements summarizing the effects of transactions on an enterprise was also illustrated.

This chapter describes additional concepts, principles, forms, and methods used to initially record transactions. The chapter also discusses how errors may occur and how they are detected by the accounting process. Finally, methods of correcting errors are presented.

PURPOSE OF AN ACCOUNT

Objective 1
Explain the purpose of an account.

Transactions can be recorded by the use of the accounting equation, Assets = Liabilities + Owner's Equity. Although transactions can be analyzed and recorded in this way, such a format is not practical for actual accounting systems.

Accounting systems provide information on business transactions for use by management in directing operations and in preparing financial statements. This information is gathered by keeping a separate record of the effects of transactions on each item that appears on the financial statements. For example, since cash appears on the balance sheet, a separate record of the increases and decreases in cash is kept. Likewise, a separate record of increases and decreases is kept for supplies, land, accounts payable, and the other balance sheet items. Similar records would be kept for income statement items, such as fees earned, wages expense, and rent expense.

The record of the increases and decreases in individual financial statement items is called an **account.** A group of accounts for a business entity is a **ledger.**

CHART OF ACCOUNTS

Objective 2
Prepare a chart of accounts for a service enterprise.

To determine the number of accounts that are needed in its ledger, a company must analyze its expected operations and volume of business. In addition, the extent to which reports are needed for taxes, managerial decisions, and credit purposes must be considered. For example, an enterprise that expects to hire several employees for a variety of jobs may set up separate accounts for executive salaries, office salaries, sales salaries, and wages expense. For another enterprise, one wages expense account may be adequate.

The system of accounts that make up a ledger is called a **chart of accounts.** In a chart of accounts, the accounts are normally listed in the order in which they appear in the financial statements. The balance sheet accounts are usually listed first, in the order of assets, liabilities, and owner's equity. The income statement accounts are then listed in the order of revenues and expenses. Each of these major account classifications is briefly described below.

Assets are physical items (tangible) or rights (intangible) that have value and that are owned by the business entity. Examples of tangible assets include cash, accounts receivable, supplies, prepaid expenses (such as insurance), buildings, equipment, and land. An example of an intangible asset is patent rights.

Liabilities are debts owed to outsiders (creditors). Liabilities are often identified on the balance sheet by titles that include the word *payable*. Examples of liabilities include accounts payable, notes payable, and wages payable. Revenue received in advance, such as magazine subscriptions received by a publisher or tuition received by a college, is also classified as a liability. Revenue received in advance is often called *unearned* revenue.

Owner's equity is the claim against the assets of the business after the total liabilities are deducted. For a sole proprietorship, the owner's equity on the balance sheet is represented by the balance of the owner's *capital* account. A **drawing** account represents the amount of withdrawals made by the owner of a sole proprietorship.

Revenues are increases in owner's equity as a result of the rendering of services or the selling of products to customers. Examples of revenues include fees earned, fares earned, commissions revenue, rent income, and interest income.

Assets used up or services consumed in the process of generating revenues are **expenses.** Examples of typical expenses include wages expense, rent expense, utilities expense, supplies expense, interest expense, and miscellaneous expense.

The accounts in an enterprise's chart of accounts are numbered to permit indexing and for use as references. Although accounts in the ledger may be numbered in order as in the pages of this book, a flexible system of indexing is desirable. Such a system has the advantage of allowing the later addition of new accounts in their proper order without affecting other account numbers. For example, the chart of accounts in Exhibit 1 does not include all of Computer King's accounts. Additional accounts will be introduced in later chapters.

In the chart of accounts in Exhibit 1, each account number has two digits. The first digit indicates the major classification of the ledger in which the account is located. Accounts beginning with 1 represent assets; 2, liabilities; 3, owner's equity; 4, revenue; and 5, expenses. The second digit indicates the location of the account within its class. For a large enterprise with many departments or operations, it is common for each account number to have four or more digits.

Exhibit 1
Chart of Accounts for Computer King

Balance Sheet Accounts	Income Statement Accounts
1. Assets	4. Revenue
11 Cash	41 Fees Earned
12 Accounts Receivable	5. Expenses
14 Supplies	51 Wages Expense
15 Prepaid Insurance	52 Rent Expense
17 Land	54 Utilities Expense
18 Office Equipment	55 Supplies Expense
2. Liabilities	59 Miscellaneous Expense
21 Accounts Payable	
23 Unearned Rent	
3. Owner's Equity	
31 Jere King, Capital	
32 Jere King, Drawing	

CHARACTERISTICS OF AN ACCOUNT

Objective 3
Explain the characteristics of an account.

The simplest form of an account has three parts. First, each account has a title, which is the name of the item recorded in the account. Second, each account has a space for recording increases in the amount of the item, in terms of money. Third, each account has a space for recording decreases in the amount of the item, also in monetary terms. The account form presented below is called a **T account** because it is similar to the letter T.

Title
Left side	Right side
debit	*credit*

The left side of the account is called the **debit** side and the right side is called the **credit** side.[1] Amounts entered on the left side of an account, regardless of the account title, are called **debits** to the account. When debits are entered in an account, the account is said to be **debited**. Amounts entered on the right side of an account are called **credits**, and the account is said to be **credited**. Debits and credits are sometimes abbreviated as *Dr.* and *Cr.*

In the cash account shown below, receipts of cash during a period of time have been listed vertically on the debit side of the account. The cash payments for the same period have been listed in similar fashion on the credit side of the account. If at any time the total of cash receipts to date is needed, the entries on the debit side of the account may be added. A memorandum total, $10,950 in the account presented below, may be inserted below the last debit. The figures should be small or identified in some other way to avoid mistaking the amount for an additional debit.[2] The total of the cash payments, $6,850 in the example, may be inserted on the credit side in a similar manner. Subtraction of the smaller sum from the larger, $10,950 – $6,850, yields the amount of cash on hand. This amount is called the **balance of the account.** The cash account in the example has a balance of $4,100. This amount may be inserted next to the total of the debit column, which identifies it as

[1] The terms debit and credit are derived from the Latin *debere* and *credere*.
[2] These figures may be written in pencil, and this procedure is sometimes called *pencil footing*.

a **debit balance**. If a balance sheet were to be prepared at this time, cash of $4,100 would be reported.

		Cash	
	3,750		850
	4,300		1,400
	2,900		700
4,100	*10,950*		2,900
			1,000
			6,850

RECORDING TRANSACTIONS IN ACCOUNTS

Objective 4
List the rules of debit and credit and the normal balances of accounts.

The recording of transactions in accounts and the relationship of the accounts to the financial statements are discussed in this section.

Balance Sheet Accounts

Balance sheet accounts consist of the accounts that make up the enterprise's assets, liabilities, and owner's equity. The manner of recording transactions in these accounts and their relationship to the balance sheet are presented using the Computer King transactions from Chapter 1.

Jere King's first transaction (a) was to deposit $15,000 in a bank account in the name of Computer King. After the deposit, the balance sheet for the business is as follows:

Computer King
Balance Sheet
November 1, 1993

Assets		Owner's Equity	
Cash	$15,000	Jere King, capital	$15,000

Every business transaction affects a minimum of two accounts. The effect of the above transaction on accounts in the ledger is a $15,000 debit to Cash and a $15,000 credit to Jere King, Capital. This information is initially entered in a record called a **journal.** In the journal, the data are stated in a formal manner. The title of the account to be debited is listed first, followed by the amount to be debited. The title of the account to be credited is listed below and to the right of the debit, followed by the amount to be credited. This process of recording a transaction in the journal is called **journalizing.** The form of presentation is called a **journal entry**, as shown below.

Entry a. | Cash   15,000
     Jere King, Capital   15,000

The data in the journal entry are transferred to the proper accounts by a process known as **posting.** The accounts after posting the above journal entry appear as follows:

Cash		Jere King, Capital	
15,000			15,000

The amount of the asset, which is reported on the left side of the account form of balance sheet, is posted to the left (debit) side of Cash. The owner's equity in the business, which is reported on the right side of the balance sheet, is posted to the right (credit) side of Jere King, Capital. When other assets are acquired, the increases will also be recorded as debits to the proper asset accounts. As owner's equity is increased or liabilities are incurred, their increases will be recorded as credits.

After opening the checking account, Computer King bought land for $10,000, paying cash. The effect of this transaction is to increase one asset account and decrease another. The transaction can be expressed as a $10,000 increase (debit) to Land, and a $10,000 decrease (credit) to Cash. The journal entry for this transaction is shown below.

Entry b.   Land   10,000
               Cash   10,000

After the journal entry for transaction (b) has been posted, the accounts of Computer King appear as follows:

Cash		Land		Jere King, Capital	
15,000	10,000	10,000			15,000

In transaction (c), Jere King purchased supplies on account for $1,350. The effect of this transaction is to increase an asset account and increase a liability account. The transaction can be expressed as a $1,350 increase (debit) to Supplies and a $1,350 increase (credit) to Accounts Payable. The journal entry for this transaction is shown below.

Entry c.   Supplies   1,350
               Accounts Payable   1,350

Journal entries are normally posted to the accounts at periodic intervals. To simplify the discussion, journal entry (c) and the remaining journal entries for Computer King will be posted to the accounts later.

In transaction (d), Computer King paid creditors on account, $950. The effect of this transaction is to decrease a liability account and decrease an asset account. The transaction can be expressed as a $950 decrease (debit) to Accounts Payable and a $950 decrease (credit) to Cash. The journal entry for this transaction is shown below.

Entry d.   Accounts Payable   950
               Cash   950

In the preceding examples, observe that the left side of asset accounts is used for recording increases and the right side is used for recording decreases. Also observe that the right side of liability and owner's equity accounts is used to record increases. It naturally follows that the left side of such accounts is used to record decreases. The left side of all accounts, whether asset, liability, or owner's equity, is the debit side and the right side is the credit side. Thus, a debit may be either an increase or a decrease, depending on the account affected. A credit may likewise be either an increase or a decrease, depending on the account. The general rules of debit and credit for balance sheet accounts may therefore be stated as follows:

	Debit	Credit
Asset accounts	Increase (+)	Decrease (−)
Liability accounts	Decrease (−)	Increase (+)
Owner's equity accounts (capital)	Decrease (−)	Increase (+)

The rules of debit and credit may also be stated in relationship to the accounting equation, as shown below.

Balance Sheet Accounts

ASSETS Asset Accounts		LIABILITIES Liability Accounts	
Debit for increases	Credit for decreases	Debit for decreases	Credit for increases
		OWNER'S EQUITY Owner's Equity Accounts	
		Debit for decreases	Credit for increases

Income Statement Accounts

The rules of debit and credit for revenue and expense accounts are based upon how these accounts affect owner's equity. Revenue increases owner's equity. Just as increases in owner's equity are recorded as credits, increases in revenues are recorded as credits. Expenses decrease owner's equity. Just as decreases in owner's equity are recorded as debits, increases in expense accounts are recorded as debits.

Computer King's transactions (e), (f), and (g) illustrate the rules of debit and credit for revenue and expense accounts. In transaction (e), Computer King received fees of $7,500 from customers for services. The effect of this transaction is to increase an asset account and increase a revenue account. The transaction can be expressed as a $7,500 increase (debit) to Cash and a $7,500 increase (credit) to Fees Earned. The journal entry for this transaction is shown below.

Entry e.   Cash   7,500
                 Fees Earned   7,500

Computer King paid various expenses in transaction (f): wages, $2,125; rent, $800; utilities, $450; miscellaneous, $275. The effect of this transaction is to increase various expense accounts and decrease an asset account. The journal entry for transaction (f) is shown below.

Entry f.   Wages Expense   2,125
                 Rent Expense   800
                 Utilities Expense   450
                 Miscellaneous Expense   275
                     Cash   3,650

An entry of two or more debits or two or more credits is called a **compound journal entry**. Regardless of the number of accounts, the sum of the debits is always equal to the sum of the credits in a journal entry. This equality of debit and credit for each transaction is inherent in the accounting equation: Assets = Liabilities + Owner's Equity. It is also because of this double equality that the system is known as **double-entry accounting.**

Transaction (g) records the amount of supplies used in the operations during the month. The effect of this transaction is to increase an expense account and decrease an asset account. The journal entry for transaction (g) is shown below.

Entry g.   Supplies Expense   800
                 Supplies   800

The general rules of debit and credit for income statement accounts may be stated as follows:

	Debit	Credit
Revenue accounts	Decrease (–)	Increase (+)
Expense accounts	Increase (+)	Decrease (–)

The rules of debit and credit for income statement accounts may also be summarized in relationship to the owner's equity in the accounting equation, as shown below.

Income Statement Accounts			
Debit for decreases in owner's equity		*Credit for increases in owner's equity*	
Expense Accounts		Revenue Accounts	
Debit for increases	Credit for decreases	Debit for decreases	Credit for increases

Withdrawals by the Owner

The owner of a sole proprietorship may from time to time withdraw cash from the business for personal use. This practice is common if the owner devotes full time to the business. In this case, the business may be the owner's main source of income. Such withdrawals have the effect of decreasing owner's equity. Just as decreases in owner's equity are recorded as debits, withdrawals are recorded as debits. Withdrawals are debited to an account with the owner's name followed by Drawing or Personal. Debits to the drawing account are normally thought of as increasing drawings rather than as decreasing owner's equity.

In transaction (h), Jere King withdrew $2,000 in cash from Computer King for personal use. The effect of this transaction is to increase the drawing account and decrease the cash account. The journal entry for transaction (h) is shown below.

Entry h.   Jere King, Drawing   2,000
                 Cash   2,000

Normal Balances of Accounts

The sum of the increases recorded in an account is usually equal to or greater than the sum of the decreases recorded in the account. For this reason, the normal balances of all accounts are positive rather than negative. For example, the total debits (increases) in an asset account will ordinarily be greater than the total credits (decreases). Thus, asset accounts normally have debit balances.

The rules of debit and credit and the normal balances of the various types of accounts are summarized as follows:

	Increase (Normal Balance)	*Decrease*
Balance sheet accounts:		
Asset	**Debit**	Credit
Liability	**Credit**	Debit
Owner's Equity:		
Capital	**Credit**	Debit
Drawing	**Debit**	Credit
Income statement accounts:		
Revenue	**Credit**	Debit
Expense	**Debit**	Credit

When an account that normally has a debit balance actually has a credit balance, or vice versa, it is an indication of a possible error or of an unusual situation. For example, a credit balance in the office equipment account could result only from an error. On the other hand, a debit balance in an accounts payable account could result from an overpayment.

Taking the Human Spirit into Account

Double-entry bookkeeping is one of the most beautiful discoveries of the human spirit. . . . It came from the same spirit which produced the systems of Galileo and Newton and the subject matter of modern physics and chemistry. By the same means, it organizes perceptions into a system, and one can

characterize it as the first Cosmos constructed purely on the basis of mechanistic thought. . . . Without too much difficulty, we can recognize in double-entry bookkeeping the ideas of gravitation, of the circulation of the blood and of the conservation of matter.

Source: From the novel, *Wilhelm Meister's Lehrjahre (Apprenticeship)*, written in 1795-6 by the German poet Johann Wolfgang von Goethe, translated by the German political economist Werner Sombart (1863-1941)

JOURNALS AND ACCOUNTS

Objective 5
Journalize and post transactions, using a two-column journal and a standard (four-column) account in the ledger.

The flow of accounting data from the time a transaction occurs to its recording in the ledger is shown below.

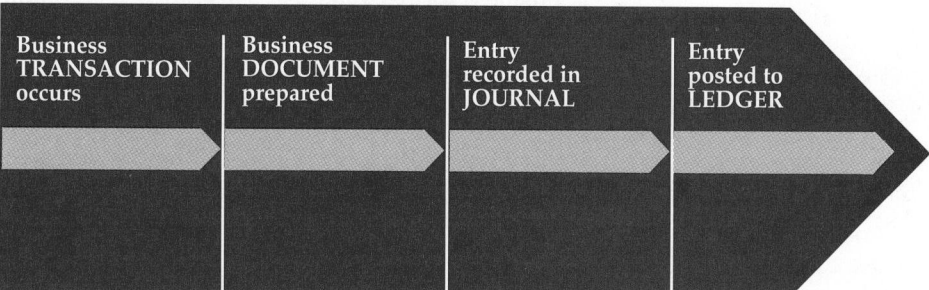

| Business TRANSACTION occurs | Business DOCUMENT prepared | Entry recorded in JOURNAL | Entry posted to LEDGER |

The initial record of each transaction or group of like transactions is a business document. For example, an invoice is a business document for the purchase of supplies. A billing statement is a business document for fees earned for providing services. On the basis of a business document, transactions are recorded in the journal. The amounts of the debits and the credits in the journal are periodically posted to the accounts in the ledger. The use of a two-column journal, a standard (four-column) account, and posting from the journal to standard ledger accounts are described below.

Two-Column Journal

The basic nature of a journal entry was presented earlier when debits and credits were introduced. There is great variety in the design of journals and the number of journals that may be used by an enterprise. A business may use a single all-purpose two-column journal, or it may use several multicolumn journals. Multicolumn journals are normally restricted to a single type of transaction, such as receipts of cash.[3]

Before a transaction is entered in a two-column journal, it should be analyzed using the following steps:

1. Determine whether an asset, a liability, owner's equity, revenue, or expense is affected.

[3] Examples of multicolumn journals are presented in a later chapter.

2. Determine whether the affected asset, liability, owner's equity, revenue, or expense increases or decreases.
3. Determine whether the effect of the transaction should be recorded as a debit or as a credit in an asset, liability, owner's equity, revenue, or expense account.

The results of such analyses can be illustrated by the $15,000 received by Computer King on November 1 as the initial investment in the business. The asset cash increases and therefore Cash should be debited for $15,000. The owner's equity account, Jere King, Capital, also increases and therefore should be credited for $15,000. The two-column journal in which the transaction has been recorded is shown below.

	JOURNAL			PAGE 1
DATE	DESCRIPTION	POST. REF.	DEBIT	CREDIT
1993 Nov. 1	Cash		15 0 0 0 00	
	Jere King, Capital			15 0 0 0 00
	Investment in business.			

The process of recording a transaction in a two-column journal is as follows:

1. Record the date:
   a. Insert the year only at the top of the Date column of each page. The only exception to this rule is when the year changes. In this case, insert the new year for the first transaction of the year wherever it occurs on the journal page.
   b. Insert the month only on the first line of the Date column of each page, except when the month changes. In this case, insert the new month for the first transaction of the month wherever it occurs on the journal page.
   c. Insert the day in the Date column on the first line used for each transaction, regardless of the number of transactions during the day.
2. Record the debit:
   Insert the title of the account to be debited next to the left margin of the Description column. Enter the amount of the debit in the Debit column.
3. Record the credit:
   Insert the title of the account to be credited below the account debited, indented several spaces. Enter the amount of the credit in the Credit column.
4. Write an explanation:
   Brief explanations may be written below each entry. Some accountants prefer that the explanation be omitted if the nature of the transaction is obvious. It is also acceptable to omit an explanation of a complex transaction if a reference to the related business document is indicated.

All transactions are recorded only in terms of debits and credits to specific accounts. The titles used in the entries should be the *same* as the titles of the accounts in the chart of accounts and ledger. For example, supplies purchased should be entered as a debit to *Supplies*, not to *Supplies Purchased*. Likewise, cash received should be entered as a debit to *Cash*, not to *Cash Received*.

Each journal entry is usually followed by a blank line to clearly separate each entry from the next. This avoids confusion and errors in reading the journal. The Posting Reference (Post. Ref.) column is not used until the debits and credits are posted to the accounts in the ledger.

Standard (Four-Column) Account

The T account form clearly separates debit entries and credit entries. It is because of this feature that the T form is often used to introduce the concept of an account. However, the T account is inadequate for use in most accounting systems. In practice, the T account is usually replaced with the standard four-column account. A four-column form is shown in Exhibit 2.

ACCOUNT *Cash*						ACCOUNT NO. *11*	
DATE	ITEM	POST. REF.	DEBIT	CREDIT	BALANCE		
					DEBIT	CREDIT	
1993 Nov. 1		1	15 0 0 0 00		15 0 0 0 00		
5		1		10 0 0 0 00	5 0 0 0 00		
16		1		9 5 0 00	4 0 5 0 00		
18		1	7 5 0 0 00		11 5 5 0 00		
30		1		3 6 5 0 00	7 9 0 0 00		
30		1		2 0 0 0 00	5 9 0 0 00		

The primary benefits of the standard account form are listed below.

1. Only a single date column is required, with each debit and credit listed in the order in which it occurred.
2. The balance of an account and its nature (debit or credit) is obvious.
3. The adjacent debit and credit columns make it easier to examine the data in the account.

Posting

The debits and credits for each journal entry are posted in the order that they occur in the journal. The posting of a debit journal entry or a credit journal entry to an account in the ledger is performed as follows:

1. Record the date and the amount of the entry in the account.
2. Insert the number of the journal page in the Posting Reference (Post. Ref.) column of the account.
3. Insert the ledger account number in the Posting Reference (Post. Ref.) column of the journal.

These procedures are shown in Exhibit 3 for the posting of a debit to the cash account and a credit to the owner's capital account.

JOURNAL					PAGE 1
DATE	DESCRIPTION	POST. REF.	DEBIT	CREDIT	
1993 Nov. 1	Cash	11	15 0 0 0 00		1
	Jere King, Capital	31		15 0 0 0 00	2
	Investment in business.				3

LEDGER

ACCOUNT *Cash*					ACCOUNT NO. *11*	
DATE	ITEM	POST. REF.	DEBIT	CREDIT	BALANCE	
					DEBIT	CREDIT
1993 Nov. 1		1	15 0 0 0 00		15 0 0 0 00	

ACCOUNT *Jere King, Capital*					ACCOUNT NO. *31*	
DATE	ITEM	POST. REF.	DEBIT	CREDIT	BALANCE	
					DEBIT	CREDIT
1993 Nov. 1		1		15 0 0 0 00		15 0 0 0 00

When the standard account is used in a computerized accounting system, the balance of an account is inserted in the proper column after each posting. The account balance is thus readily available. The same procedure may be followed when the posting is done manually. In these cases, such as the accounts shown in Exhibits 2 and 3, *running balances* in the accounts are maintained.

An alternative is to postpone the computation of balances until all postings for the month have been completed. When this is done, only the final month-end balance is inserted in the appropriate balance column.

Illustration of Journalizing and Posting

To illustrate the journalizing and posting process, the November and December transactions for Computer King will be used. Computer King's transactions for November were presented in Chapter 1. The journal entries for these transactions are listed below. The date of each entry has been inserted. The November entries for Computer King have been posted to the ledger in Exhibit 4.

JOURNAL   PAGE 1

		DATE		DESCRIPTION	POST. REF.	DEBIT	CREDIT	
Entry a.	1	1993 Nov.	1	Cash	11	15 0 0 0 00		1
	2			Jere King, Capital	31		15 0 0 0 00	2
	3							3
Entry b.	4		5	Land	17	10 0 0 0 00		4
	5			Cash	11		10 0 0 0 00	5
	6							6
Entry c.	7		10	Supplies	14	1 3 5 0 00		7
	8			Accounts Payable	21		1 3 5 0 00	8
	9							9
Entry d.	10		16	Accounts Payable	21	9 5 0 00		10
	11			Cash	11		9 5 0 00	11
	12							12
Entry e.	13		18	Cash	11	7 5 0 0 00		13
	14			Fees Earned	41		7 5 0 0 00	14
	15							15
Entry f.	16		30	Wages Expense	51	2 1 2 5 00		16
	17			Rent Expense	52	8 0 0 00		17
	18			Utilities Expense	54	4 5 0 00		18
	19			Miscellaneous Expense	59	2 7 5 00		19
	20			Cash	11		3 6 5 0 00	20
	21							21
Entry g.	22		30	Supplies Expense	55	8 0 0 00		22
	23			Supplies	14		8 0 0 00	23
	24							24
Entry h.	25		30	Jere King, Drawing	32	2 0 0 0 00		25
	26			Cash	11		2 0 0 0 00	26
	27							27
	28							28
	29							29
	30							30
	31							31
	32							32

To further illustrate the journalizing and posting process, the December transactions for Computer King will be used. To simplify and reduce repetition, some of the December transactions are stated in summary form. For example, cash received for services is normally recorded on a daily basis. In this example, however, only summary totals are recorded at the middle and end of the month. Likewise, all fees earned on account during December are recorded at the middle and end of the month. In practice, each fee earned is recorded separately.

Dec. 1. Computer King paid a premium of $2,400 for a comprehensive insurance policy covering liability, theft, and fire. The policy covers a two-year period.

Analysis: Advance payments of expenses such as insurance are prepaid expenses, which are assets. For Computer King, the asset acquired for the cash payment is insurance protection for twenty-four months. The asset Prepaid Insurance increases and is debited for $2,400. The asset Cash decreases and is credited for $2,400.

JOURNAL　　PAGE 2

	DATE		DESCRIPTION	POST. REF.	DEBIT	CREDIT	
1	1993 Dec.	1	Prepaid Insurance	15	2 4 0 0 00		1
2			Cash	11		2 4 0 0 00	2

Dec. 1. Computer King paid rent for December, $800. The company from which Computer King rented its store space in November now requires the payment of rent on the 1st of each month, rather than at the end of the month.

Analysis: Similar to the advance payment of the insurance premium in the preceding transaction, the advance payment of rent is an asset. However, the asset prepaid insurance will not completely expire for 24 months, while the asset prepaid rent will expire in one month. When an asset that is purchased will be used up in a short period of time, such as a month, it is normal to debit an expense account initially. This avoids having to transfer the balance from an asset account (Prepaid Rent) to an expense account (Rent Expense) at the end of the month. Thus, when the rent for December is prepaid at the beginning of the month, Rent Expense is debited for $800 and Cash is credited for $800.

3							3
4		1	Rent Expense	52	8 0 0 00		4
5			Cash	11		8 0 0 00	5

Dec. 1. Computer King received an offer from a local retailer to rent the land purchased on November 5th. The retailer plans to use the land as a parking lot for its employees and customers. Computer King agreed to rent the land for three months, payable in advance. Computer King received $360 for three months' rent beginning December 1st.

Analysis: By agreeing to rent the land and accepting the $360, Computer King has incurred an obligation (liability) to the retailer. This obligation is to make the land available for use for three months and not to interfere with its use. The liability created by receiving the revenue in advance is called **unearned revenue**. Thus, the $360 received is an increase in an asset and is debited to Cash. The liability account Unearned Rent increases and is credited for $360. As time passes, the unearned rent liability will decrease and will become revenue.

6							6
7		1	Cash	11	3 6 0 00		7
8			Unearned Rent	23		3 6 0 00	8

Dec. 4. Purchased office equipment on account from Executive Supply Co. for $1,800.

Analysis: The asset account Office Equipment increases and is therefore debited for $1,800. The liability account Accounts Payable increases and is credited for $1,800.

9					9
10	4	Office Equipment	18	1 8 0 0 00	10
11		Accounts Payable	21	1 8 0 0 00	11

Dec. 6. Paid $180 for a newspaper advertisement.

Analysis: An expense increases and is debited for $180. The asset Cash decreases and is credited for $180. Expense items that are expected to be minor in amount are normally included as part of the miscellaneous expense. Thus, Miscellaneous Expense is debited for $180.

12					12
13	6	Miscellaneous Expense	59	1 8 0 00	13
14		Cash	11	1 8 0 00	14

Dec. 11. Paid creditors $400.

Analysis: This payment decreases the liability account Accounts Payable, which is debited for $400. Cash also decreases and is credited for $400.

15					15
16	11	Accounts Payable	21	4 0 0 00	16
17		Cash	11	4 0 0 00	17

Dec. 13. Paid receptionist and part-time assistant $950 for two weeks' wages.

Analysis: This transaction is similar to the December 6th transaction, where an expense account is increased and Cash is decreased. Thus, Wages Expense is debited for $950 and Cash is credited for $950.

18					18
19	13	Wages Expense	51	9 5 0 00	19
20		Cash	11	9 5 0 00	20

Dec. 16. Received $3,100 from fees earned for the first half of December.

Analysis: Cash increases and is debited for $3,100. The revenue account Fees Earned increases and is credited for $3,100.

21					21
22	16	Cash	11	3 1 0 0 00	22
23		Fees Earned	41	3 1 0 0 00	23

Dec. 16.   Fees earned on account totaled $1,750 for the first half of December.

Analysis: When an enterprise agrees that payment for services provided or goods sold can be accepted at another date, the firm has an **account receivable**, which is a claim against the customer. The account receivable is an asset, and the revenue is earned even though no cash has been received. Thus, Accounts Receivable increases and is debited for $1,750. The revenue account Fees Earned increases and is credited for $1,750.

24																24
25	16	Accounts Receivable		12	1	7	5	0	00							25
26		Fees Earned		41							1	7	5	0	00	26

Dec. 20.   Paid $900 to Executive Supply Co. in partial payment of the $1,800 debt owed from the December 4 transaction.

Analysis: Similar to transaction of December 11.

27																27
28	20	Accounts Payable		21		9	0	0	00							28
29		Cash		11								9	0	0	00	29

Dec. 21.   Received $650 from customers in payment of their accounts.

Analysis: When customers pay amounts owed for services that have previously been billed, one asset increases and another asset decreases. Thus, Cash is debited for $650, and Accounts Receivable is credited for $650.

30																30
31	21	Cash		11		6	5	0	00							31
32		Accounts Receivable		12								6	5	0	00	32

Dec. 23.   Paid $1,450 for supplies.

Analysis: The asset account Supplies increases and is debited for $1,450. The asset account Cash decreases and is credited for $1,450.

33																33
34	23	Supplies		14	1	4	5	0	00							34
35		Cash		11							1	4	5	0	00	35

Dec. 27.   Paid receptionist and part-time assistant $1,200 for two weeks' wages.

Analysis: Similar to transaction of December 13.

37																37
38	27	Wages Expense		51	1	2	0	0	00							38
39		Cash		11							1	2	0	0	00	39
40																40
41																41

Dec. 31. Paid $310 telephone bill for the month.

Analysis: Similar to transaction of December 6. The expense account Utilities Expense is debited for $310 and Cash is credited for $310.

	DATE		DESCRIPTION	POST. REF.	DEBIT	CREDIT	
1	1993 Dec.	31	Utilities Expense	54	3 1 0 00		1
2			Cash	11		3 1 0 00	2

JOURNAL — PAGE 3

Dec. 31. Paid $225 electric bill for the month.

Analysis: Similar to the preceding transaction.

3							3
4		31	Utilities Expense	54	2 2 5 00		4
5			Cash	11		2 2 5 00	5

Dec. 31. Received $2,870 from fees earned for the second half of December.

Analysis: Similar to transaction of December 16.

6							6
7		31	Cash	11	2 8 7 0 00		7
8			Fees Earned	41		2 8 7 0 00	8

Dec. 31 Fees earned on account totaled $1,120 for the second half of December.

Analysis: Similar to transaction of December 16.

9							9
10		31	Accounts Receivable	12	1 1 2 0 00		10
11			Fees Earned	41		1 1 2 0 00	11

Dec. 31. Jere King withdrew $2,000 for personal use.

Analysis: The transaction resulted in an increase in the amount of withdrawals by the owner and is recorded by a $2,000 debit to Jere King, Drawing. The decrease in business cash is recorded by a $2,000 credit to Cash.

12							12
13		31	Jere King, Drawing	32	2 0 0 0 00		13
14			Cash	11		2 0 0 0 00	14
15							15
16							16
17							17
18							18

After all the entries for the month have been posted, the ledger will appear as shown in Exhibit 4. In practice, each account would appear on a separate page in the ledger. Tracing each entry from the journal to the accounts in the ledger illustrates the posting process.

Exhibit 4
Ledger—Computer King

ACCOUNT *Cash*   **ACCOUNT NO.** *11*

DATE	ITEM	POST. REF.	DEBIT	CREDIT	BALANCE DEBIT	BALANCE CREDIT
1993 Nov. 1		1	15 000 00		15 000 00	
5		1		10 000 00	5 000 00	
16		1		950 00	4 050 00	
18		1	7 500 00		11 550 00	
30		1		3 650 00	7 900 00	
30		1		2 000 00	5 900 00	
Dec. 1		2		2 400 00	3 500 00	
1		2		800 00	2 700 00	
1		2	360 00		3 060 00	
6		2		180 00	2 880 00	
11		2		400 00	2 480 00	
13		2		950 00	1 530 00	
16		2	3 100 00		4 630 00	
20		2		900 00	3 730 00	
21		2	650 00		4 380 00	
23		2		1 450 00	2 930 00	
27		2		1 200 00	1 730 00	
31		3		310 00	1 420 00	
31		3		225 00	1 195 00	
31		3	2 870 00		4 065 00	
31		3		2 000 00	2 065 00	

ACCOUNT *Accounts Receivable*   **ACCOUNT NO.** *12*

DATE	ITEM	POST. REF.	DEBIT	CREDIT	BALANCE DEBIT	BALANCE CREDIT
1993 Dec. 16		2	1 750 00		1 750 00	
21		2		650 00	1 100 00	
31		3	1 120 00		2 220 00	

ACCOUNT *Supplies*   **ACCOUNT NO.** *14*

DATE	ITEM	POST. REF.	DEBIT	CREDIT	BALANCE DEBIT	BALANCE CREDIT
1993 Nov. 10		1	1 350 00		1 350 00	
30		1		800 00	550 00	
Dec. 23		2	1 450 00		2 000 00	

ACCOUNT *Prepaid Insurance*   **ACCOUNT NO.** *15*

DATE		ITEM	POST. REF.	DEBIT	CREDIT	BALANCE	
						DEBIT	CREDIT
1993 Dec	1		2	2 40 0 00		2 40 0 00	

ACCOUNT *Land*   **ACCOUNT NO.** *17*

DATE		ITEM	POST. REF.	DEBIT	CREDIT	BALANCE	
						DEBIT	CREDIT
1993 Nov.	5		1	10 00 0 00		10 00 0 00	

ACCOUNT *Office Equipment*   **ACCOUNT NO.** *18*

DATE		ITEM	POST. REF.	DEBIT	CREDIT	BALANCE	
						DEBIT	CREDIT
1993 Dec.	4		2	1 80 0 00		1 80 0 00	

ACCOUNT *Accounts Payable*   **ACCOUNT NO.** *21*

DATE		ITEM	POST. REF.	DEBIT	CREDIT	BALANCE	
						DEBIT	CREDIT
1993 Nov.	10		1		1 35 0 00		1 35 0 00
	16		1	95 0 00			40 0 00
Dec.	4		2		1 80 0 00		2 20 0 00
	11		2	40 0 00			1 80 0 00
	20		2	90 0 00			90 0 00

ACCOUNT *Unearned Rent*   **ACCOUNT NO.** *23*

DATE		ITEM	POST. REF.	DEBIT	CREDIT	BALANCE	
						DEBIT	CREDIT
1993 Dec	1		2		3 60 0 00		3 60 0 00

ACCOUNT *Jere King, Capital*   **ACCOUNT NO.** *31*

DATE		ITEM	POST. REF.	DEBIT	CREDIT	BALANCE	
						DEBIT	CREDIT
1993 Nov	1		1		15 00 0 00		15 00 0 00

ACCOUNT *Jere King, Drawing*   **ACCOUNT NO.** *32*

DATE		ITEM	POST. REF.	DEBIT	CREDIT	BALANCE	
						DEBIT	CREDIT
1993 Nov.	30		1	2 00 0 00		2 00 0 00	
Dec.	31		3	2 00 0 00		4 00 0 00	

ACCOUNT *Fees Earned*   ACCOUNT NO. *41*

DATE		ITEM	POST. REF.	DEBIT	CREDIT	BALANCE	
						DEBIT	CREDIT
1993 Nov.	18		1		7 5 0 0 00		7 5 0 0 00
Dec.	16		2		3 1 0 0 00		10 6 0 0 00
	16		2		1 7 5 0 00		12 3 5 0 00
	31		3		2 8 7 0 00		15 2 2 0 00
	31		3		1 1 2 0 00		16 3 4 0 00

ACCOUNT *Wages Expense*   ACCOUNT NO. *51*

DATE		ITEM	POST. REF.	DEBIT	CREDIT	BALANCE	
						DEBIT	CREDIT
1993 Nov.	30		1	2 1 2 5 00		2 1 2 5 00	
Dec.	13		2	9 5 0 00		3 0 7 5 00	
	27		2	1 2 0 0 00		4 2 7 5 00	

ACCOUNT *Rent Expense*   ACCOUNT NO. *52*

DATE		ITEM	POST. REF.	DEBIT	CREDIT	BALANCE	
						DEBIT	CREDIT
1993 Nov.	30		1	8 0 0 00		8 0 0 00	
Dec.	1		2	8 0 0 00		1 6 0 0 00	

ACCOUNT *Utilities Expense*   ACCOUNT NO. *54*

DATE		ITEM	POST. REF.	DEBIT	CREDIT	BALANCE	
						DEBIT	CREDIT
1993 Nov.	30		1	4 5 0 00		4 5 0 00	
Dec.	31		3	3 1 0 00		7 6 0 00	
	31		3	2 2 5 00		9 8 5 00	

ACCOUNT *Supplies Expense*   ACCOUNT NO. *55*

DATE		ITEM	POST. REF.	DEBIT	CREDIT	BALANCE	
						DEBIT	CREDIT
1993 Nov.	30		1	8 0 0 00		8 0 0 00	

ACCOUNT *Miscellaneous Expense*   ACCOUNT NO. *59*

DATE		ITEM	POST. REF.	DEBIT	CREDIT	BALANCE	
						DEBIT	CREDIT
1993 Nov.	30		1	2 7 5 00		2 7 5 00	
Dec.	6		2	1 8 0 00		4 5 5 00	

TRIAL BALANCE

Objective 6
Prepare a trial balance and
explain how it can be used to
discover errors.

The equality of debits and credits in the ledger should be proved at the end of each
accounting period, if not more often. Such a proof, which is called a **trial balance**,
may be in the form of a computer printout or in the form shown in Exhibit 5.[4]

Exhibit 5
Trial Balance

Computer King		
Trial Balance		
December 31, 1993		
Cash	2 0 6 5 00	
Accounts Receivable	2 2 2 0 00	
Supplies	2 0 0 0 00	
Prepaid Insurance	2 4 0 0 00	
Land	10 0 0 0 00	
Office Equipment	1 8 0 0 00	
Accounts Payable		9 0 0 00
Unearned Rent		3 6 0 00
Jere King, Capital		15 0 0 0 00
Jere King, Drawing	4 0 0 0 00	
Fees Earned		16 3 4 0 00
Wages Expense	4 2 7 5 00	
Rent Expense	1 6 0 0 00	
Utilities Expense	9 8 5 00	
Supplies Expense	8 0 0 00	
Miscellaneous Expense	4 5 5 00	
	32 6 0 0 00	32 6 0 0 00

The first step in preparing the trial balance is to determine the balance of each
account in the ledger. When the standard account form is used, the balance of each
account appears in the balance column on the same line as the last posting to the
account.

The trial balance does not provide complete proof of the accuracy of the ledger.
It indicates only that the debits and the credits are equal. This proof is of value,
however, because errors often affect the equality of debits and credits. If the two
totals of a trial balance are not equal, an error has occurred. Procedures for discovering and correcting errors are discussed in the remainder of this chapter.

DISCOVERY AND CORRECTION OF ERRORS

Objective 7
Discover errors in recording
transactions and correct them.

Errors will sometimes occur in journalizing and posting transactions. The following paragraphs describe and illustrate how errors may be discovered and corrected.

Discovery of Errors

The trial balance is one of the principal means for discovering errors in the ledger.
However, it indicates *only* that the debits and credits are equal. If the two totals of
the trial balance are not equal, it is probably due to one or more of the following
types of errors:

---

[4] A trial balance is not a formal statement, but is used by the accountant to verify the accuracy of the accounting records. Thus, financial statement captions, subtotals, and dollar signs are normally omitted from a trial
balance.

1. Error in preparing the trial balance, such as:
    a. One of the columns of the trial balance was incorrectly added.
    b. The amount of an account balance was incorrectly recorded on the trial balance.
    c. A debit balance was recorded on the trial balance as a credit, or vice versa, or a balance was omitted entirely.
2. Error in determining the account balances, such as:
    a. A balance was incorrectly computed.
    b. A balance was entered in the wrong balance column.
3. Error in recording a transaction in the ledger, such as:
    a. An erroneous amount was posted to the account.
    b. A debit entry was posted as a credit, or vice versa.
    c. A debit or a credit posting was omitted.

Among the types of errors that will *not* cause an inequality in the trial balance totals are the following:

1. Failure to record a transaction or to post a transaction.
2. Recording the same erroneous amount for both the debit and the credit parts of a transaction.
3. Recording the same transaction more than once.
4. Posting a part of a transaction correctly as a debit or credit but to the wrong account.

It is obvious that care should be used in recording transactions in the journal and in posting to the accounts. The need for accuracy in determining account balances and reporting them on the trial balance is equally obvious.

Errors in the accounts may be discovered in various ways: (1) by audit procedures, (2) by chance, or (3) by looking at the trial balance. If the two trial balance totals are not equal, the amount of the difference between the totals should be determined before searching for the error.

The amount of the difference between the two totals of a trial balance sometimes gives a clue as to the nature of the error or where it occurred. For example, a difference of 10, 100, or 1,000 between two totals is often the result of an error in addition. A difference between totals can also be due to the omission of a debit or a credit posting. If the difference is divisible evenly by 2, the error may be due to the posting of a debit as a credit, or vice versa. For example, if the debit total is $20,640 and the credit total is $20,236, the difference of $404 may indicate that a credit posting of $404 was omitted or that a credit of $202 was incorrectly posted as a debit.

Two other common types of errors are known as transpositions and slides. A **transposition** is the erroneous rearrangement of digits, such as writing $542 as $452 or $524. In a **slide**, the entire number is erroneously moved one or more spaces to the right or the left, such as writing $542.00 as $54.20 or $5,420.00. If an error of either type has occurred and there are no other errors, the difference between the two trial balance totals can be evenly divided by 9.

A search for a trial balance difference along the lines suggested by the preceding paragraphs will often find the error. If it does not, the steps in the accounting process must be retraced, beginning with the last step and working back to the entries in the journal. Usually, errors causing the trial balance totals to be unequal will be discovered before all of the steps are retraced. While there are no standard rules for searching for errors, the steps presented below are usually followed:

1. Prove the accuracy of the trial balance totals by re-adding the columns.
2. Compare the listings in the trial balance with the balances shown in the ledger. Make certain that no accounts have been omitted.
3. Recompute the balance of each account in the ledger.

4. Trace the postings in the ledger back to the journal. Place a small check mark beside each item in the ledger and also in the journal. If the error is not found, examine each account to see if there is an entry without a check mark. Do the same with the entries in the journal.
5. Prove the equality of the debits and the credits in the journal.

Correction of Errors

When errors in journalizing and posting transactions are discovered, the procedures used to correct them vary according to the nature of the error and when the error is discovered. These procedures are discussed in the following paragraphs.

An error in an account title or amount in the journal may be discovered before the entry is posted. In this case, the correction may be made by drawing a line through the error and inserting the correct title or amount directly above. If there is any chance of questions arising later, the person responsible may initial the correction.

To illustrate, assume that a purchase of office equipment for cash was incorrectly journalized as a $12,500 debit to Supplies. The credit was correctly journalized as a $12,500 credit to Accounts Payable. If the journal entry has not been posted to the ledger, then the correction may be made as follows:

| | | JOURNAL | | | PAGE 30 |

	DATE		DESCRIPTION	POST. REF.	DEBIT	CREDIT	
1	1994 May	5	Office Equipment ~~Supplies~~	cw	12 5 0 0 00		1
2			Accounts Payable			12 5 0 0 00	2
3							3
4							4
5							5
6							6
7							7
8							8

An entry in the journal may be prepared correctly, but may be incorrectly posted to the account. In this case, the incorrect posting may be corrected by drawing a line through the error and posting the item correctly. As indicated above, if there is any chance of questions arising later, the person responsible may initial the correction.

To illustrate, a debit of $12,500 for office equipment was incorrectly posted as a $1,250 debit in the account presented below.

ACCOUNT *Office Equipment*						ACCOUNT NO. *18*	
DATE	ITEM	POST. REF.	DEBIT	CREDIT	BALANCE		
					DEBIT	CREDIT	
1994 May 5		cw 30	12 5 0 0 00 ~~1 2 5 0 00~~		12 5 0 0 00 ~~1 2 5 0 00~~		

An incorrect account title may appear in a journal entry and the error may not be discovered until after posting is completed. In this case, it is best to journalize and post a correcting entry. To illustrate, assume that a purchase of office equipment was incorrectly journalized and posted as a $12,500 debit to Supplies. The credit was correctly journalized and posted as a $12,500 credit to Accounts Payable. Before a correcting entry is made, it is best to determine (1) the debit(s) and credit(s) of the entry in which the error occurred and (2) the debit(s) and credit(s) that should have been recorded. T accounts may be helpful in making this analysis, as in the following example:

Entry in which error occurred:

Supplies		Accounts Payable	
12,500			12,500

Entry that should have been recorded:

Office Equipment		Accounts Payable	
12,500			12,500

Comparison of the two sets of T accounts shows that the incorrect debit of $12,500 to Supplies may be corrected by a $12,500 credit to Supplies and a debit of $12,500 to Office Equipment. The following correcting entry is then journalized and posted:

	DATE		DESCRIPTION	POST. REF.	DEBIT	CREDIT	
			JOURNAL			PAGE 30	
1	1994 May	31	Office Equipment	18	12 5 0 0 00		1
2			Supplies	14		12 5 0 0 00	2
3			To correct erroneous				3
4			debit to Supplies on May 5.				4
5			See invoice from Bell				5
6			Office Equipment Co. *cw*				6
7							7
8							8
9							9
10							10
11							11
12							12
13							13
14							14
15							15
16							16

The preceding procedures for correction of errors are summarized in Exhibit 6.

Exhibit 6
Procedures for Correcting Errors

Error	Correction Procedure
Journal entry incorrect, but not posted.	Draw line through the error and insert correct title or amount.
Journal entry correct, but posted incorrectly.	Draw line through the error and post correctly.
Journal entry incorrect and posted.	Journalize and post a correcting entry.

CHAPTER REVIEW

Key Points

Objective 1. Explain the purpose of an account.
The purpose of an account is to record individual transactions. A group of accounts is called a ledger.

Objective 2. Prepare a chart of accounts for a service enterprise.
In preparing a chart of accounts, the accounts are numbered and listed in the order in which they appear in the balance sheet and the income statement.

Objective 3. Explain the characteristics of an account.
The simplest form of an account, a T account, has three parts. First, each account has a title, which is the name of the item recorded in the account. Second, each account has a left side, called the debit side. Third, each account has a right side, called the credit side. Amounts entered on the left side of an account, regardless of the account title, are called debits to the account. Amounts entered on the right side of an account are called credits. Periodically, the debits and the credits in an account are summed and the balance of the account is determined.

Objective 4. List the rules of debit and credit and the normal balances of accounts.
The rules of debit and credit and normal account balances are summarized in the following table:

	Increase (Normal Balance)	*Decrease*
Balance sheet accounts:		
Asset	**Debit**	Credit
Liability	**Credit**	Debit
Owner's Equity:		
Capital	**Credit**	Debit
Drawing	**Debit**	Credit
Income statement accounts:		
Revenue	**Credit**	Debit
Expense	**Debit**	Credit

General rules of debit and credit have been established for recording increases or decreases to asset, liability, owner's equity, revenue, expense, and drawing accounts. Each transaction is recorded so that the sum of the debits is always equal to the sum of the credits.

Transactions are initially entered in a record called a journal. The data in the journal entry are transferred to the proper accounts by a process known as posting.

The sum of the increases recorded in an account is usually equal to or greater than the sum of the decreases recorded in the account. For this reason, the normal balance of an account is indicated by the side of the account (debit or credit) that receives the increases.

Objective 5. Journalize and post transactions, using a two-column journal and a standard (four-column) account in the ledger.
A two-column journal with a debit column and a credit column is used for recording initial transactions in an accounting system. In practice, the T account is usually replaced with the standard four-column account. Journal entries are periodically posted to the accounts.

Objective 6. Prepare a trial balance and explain how it can be used to discover errors.
A trial balance is prepared by listing the accounts from the ledger and their balances. If the two totals of a trial balance are not equal, an error has occurred.

Objective 7. Discover errors in recording transactions and correct them.
Errors may be discovered (1) by audit procedures, (2) by chance, or (3) by looking at the trial balance. The procedures for correcting errors are summarized in Exhibit 6.

Glossary of Key Terms

Account. The form used to record additions and deductions for each individual asset, liability, owner's equity, revenue, and expense. **Objective 1**

Assets. Physical items (tangible) or rights (intangible) that have value and that are owned by the business entity. **Objective 2**

Balance of the account. The amount of difference between the debits and the credits that have been entered into an account. **Objective 3**

Chart of accounts. The system of accounts that make up the ledger for a business enterprise. **Objective 2**

Credit. (1) The right side of an account; (2) the amount entered on the right side of an account; (3) to enter an amount on the right side of an account. **Objective 3**

Debit. (1) The left side of an account; (2) the amount entered on the left side of an account; (3) to enter an amount on the left side of an account. **Objective 3**

Double-entry accounting. A system for recording transactions, based on recording increases and decreases in accounts so that debits always equal credits. **Objective 4**

Drawing. The amount of withdrawals made by the owner of a sole proprietorship. **Objective 2**

Expenses. Assets used up or services consumed in the process of generating revenues. **Objective 2**

Journal. The initial record in which the effects of a transaction on accounts are recorded. **Objective 4**

Journalizing. The process of recording a transaction in a journal. **Objective 4**

Ledger. The group of accounts used by an enterprise. **Objective 1**

Liabilities. Debts owed to outsiders (creditors). **Objective 2**

Owner's equity. The claim of owners against the assets of the business after the total liabilities are deducted. **Objective 2**

Posting. The process of transferring debits and credits from a journal to the accounts. **Objective 4**

Revenues. Increases in owner's equity as a result of providing services or selling products to customers. **Objective 2**

Slide. The erroneous movement of all digits in a number, one or more spaces to the right or the left, such as writing $542 as $5,420. **Objective 7**

T account. A form of account resembling the letter T. **Objective 3**

Transposition. The erroneous arrangement of digits in a number, such as writing $542 as $524. **Objective 7**

Trial balance. A summary listing of the balances and the titles of the accounts in the ledger. **Objective 6**

Self-Examination Questions

Answers at end of chapter.

1. A debit may signify:
   - A. an increase in an asset account
   - B. a decrease in an asset account
   - C. an increase in a liability account
   - D. an increase in the owner's capital account

2. The type of account with a normal credit balance is:
   - A. an asset
   - B. a drawing
   - C. a revenue
   - D. an expense

3. A debit balance in which of the following accounts would indicate an error?
   - A. Accounts Receivable
   - B. Cash
   - C. Fees Earned
   - D. Miscellaneous Expense

4. The receipt of cash from customers in payment of their accounts would be recorded by a:
   - A. debit to Cash; credit to Accounts Receivable
   - B. debit to Accounts Receivable; credit to Cash
   - C. debit to Cash; credit to Accounts Payable
   - D. debit to Accounts Payable; credit to Cash

5. The form listing the balances and the titles of the accounts in the ledger on a given date is the:
   - A. income statement
   - B. balance sheet
   - C. statement of owner's equity
   - D. trial balance

ILLUSTRATIVE PROBLEM

Judy K. Schmidt, M.D., has been practicing as a pediatrician for three years. During June, she completed the following transactions in her practice of pediatrics:

June 1. Paid office rent for June, $600.

2. Purchased equipment on account, $2,100.

5. Received cash on account from patients, $4,150.

8. Purchased X-ray film and other supplies on account, $145.

9. One of the items of equipment purchased on June 2 was defective. It was returned with the permission of the supplier, who agreed to reduce the account for the amount charged for the item, $125.

12. Paid cash to creditors on account, $1,250.

16. Sold X-ray film to another doctor at cost, receiving cash, $63. (Record the credit in the supplies account.)

17. Paid cash for renewal of a 2-year property insurance policy, $370.

20. Discovered that the balances of the cash account and of the accounts payable account as of June 1 were overstated by $50. A payment of that amount to a creditor in May had not been recorded. Journalize the $50 payment as of June 20.

23. Paid cash for laboratory analyses, $245.

27. Paid cash from business bank account for personal and family expenses, $1,250.

30. Recorded the cash received in payment of services (on a cash basis) to patients during June, $1,720.

30. Paid salaries of receptionist and nurses, $1,725.

30. Paid gas and electricity expense, $157.

30. Paid water expense, $29.

30. Recorded fees charged to patients on account for services performed in June, $4,145.

30. Paid telephone expense, $74.

30. Paid miscellaneous expenses, $132.

Schmidt's account titles, numbers, and balances as of June 1 (all normal balances) are listed as follows: Cash, 11, $3,123; Accounts Receivable, 12, $6,725; Supplies, 13, $290; Prepaid Insurance, 14, $365; Equipment, 18, $19,745; Accounts Payable, 22, $765; Judy K. Schmidt, Capital, 31, $29,483; Judy K. Schmidt, Drawing, 32; Professional Fees, 41; Salary Expense, 51; Rent Expense, 53; Laboratory Expense, 55; Utilities Expense, 56; Miscellaneous Expense, 59.

ILLUSTRATIVE PROBLEM ILLUSTRATIVE PROBLEM ILLUSTRATIVE PROBLEM ILLUSTRATIVE PROBLEM ILLUSTRATIVE PROBLEM

Instructions

1. Open a ledger of standard four-column accounts for Dr. Schmidt as of June 1 of the current year. Enter the balances in the appropriate balance columns and place a check mark (✓) in the posting reference column. (It is advisable to verify the equality of the debit and credit balances in the ledger before proceeding with the next instruction.)
2. Journalize each transaction in a two-column journal.
3. Post the journal to the ledger, extending the month-end balances to the appropriate balance columns after each posting.
4. Prepare a trial balance as of June 30.

Solution

2. and 3.

	DATE		DESCRIPTION	POST. REF.	DEBIT	CREDIT	
1	19-- June	1	Rent Expense	53	6 0 0 00		1
2			Cash	11		6 0 0 00	2
3							3
4		2	Equipment	18	2 1 0 0 00		4
5			Accounts Payable	22		2 1 0 0 00	5
6							6
7		5	Cash	11	4 1 5 0 00		7
8			Accounts Receivable	12		4 1 5 0 00	8
9							9
10		8	Supplies	13	1 4 5 00		10
11			Accounts Payable	22		1 4 5 00	11
12							12
13		9	Accounts Payable	22	1 2 5 00		13
14			Equipment	18		1 2 5 00	14
15							15
16		12	Accounts Payable	22	1 2 5 0 00		16
17			Cash	11		1 2 5 0 00	17
18							18
19		16	Cash	11	6 3 00		19
20			Supplies	13		6 3 00	20
21							21
22		17	Prepaid Insurance	14	3 7 0 00		22
23			Cash	11		3 7 0 00	23
24							24
25		20	Accounts Payable	22	5 0 00		25
26			Cash	11		5 0 00	26
27							27
28		23	Laboratory Expense	55	2 4 5 00		28
29			Cash	11		2 4 5 00	29
30							30
31		27	Judy K. Schmidt, Drawing	32	1 2 5 0 00		31
32			Cash	11		1 2 5 0 00	32
33							33
34		30	Cash	11	1 7 2 0 00		34
35			Professional Fees	41		1 7 2 0 00	35
36							36

JOURNAL   PAGE 27

JOURNAL   PAGE 28

	DATE	DESCRIPTION	POST. REF.	DEBIT	CREDIT	
1	30	Salary Expense	51	1 7 2 5 00		1
2		Cash	11		1 7 2 5 00	2
3						3
4	30	Utilities Expense	56	1 5 7 00		4
5		Cash	11		1 5 7 00	5
6						6
7	30	Utilities Expense	56	2 9 00		7
8		Cash	11		2 9 00	8
9						9
10	30	Accounts Receivable	12	4 1 4 5 00		10
11		Professional Fees	41		4 1 4 5 00	11
12						12
13	30	Utilities Expense	56	7 4 00		13
14		Cash	11		7 4 00	14
15						15
16	30	Miscellaneous Expense	59	1 3 2 00		16
17		Cash	11		1 3 2 00	17

1. and 3.

ACCOUNT Cash   ACCOUNT NO. 11

DATE		ITEM	POST. REF.	DEBIT	CREDIT	BALANCE DEBIT	BALANCE CREDIT
19-- June	1	Balance	√			3 1 2 3 00	
	1		27		6 0 0 00	2 5 2 3 00	
	5		27	4 1 5 0 00		6 6 7 3 00	
	12		27		1 2 5 0 00	5 4 2 3 00	
	16		27	6 3 00		5 4 8 6 00	
	17		27		3 7 0 00	5 1 1 6 00	
	20		27		5 0 00	5 0 6 6 00	
	23		27		2 4 5 00	4 8 2 1 00	
	27		27		1 2 5 0 00	3 5 7 1 00	
	30		27	1 7 2 0 00		5 2 9 1 00	
	30		28		1 7 2 5 00	3 5 6 6 00	
	30		28		1 5 7 00	3 4 0 9 00	
	30		28		2 9 00	3 3 8 0 00	
	30		28		7 4 00	3 3 0 6 00	
	30		28		1 3 2 00	3 1 7 4 00	

ACCOUNT Accounts Receivable   ACCOUNT NO. 12

DATE		ITEM	POST. REF.	DEBIT	CREDIT	BALANCE DEBIT	BALANCE CREDIT
19-- June	1	Balance	√			6 7 2 5 00	
	5		27		4 1 5 0 00	2 5 7 5 00	
	30		28	4 1 4 5 00		6 7 2 0 00	

ACCOUNT *Supplies*   ACCOUNT NO. 13

DATE		ITEM	POST. REF.	DEBIT	CREDIT	BALANCE	
						DEBIT	CREDIT
19-- June	1	Balance	√			2 9 0 00	
	8		27	1 4 5 00		4 3 5 00	
	16		27		6 3 00	3 7 2 00	

ACCOUNT *Prepaid Insurance*   ACCOUNT NO. 14

DATE		ITEM	POST. REF.	DEBIT	CREDIT	BALANCE	
						DEBIT	CREDIT
19-- June	1	Balance	√			3 6 5 00	
	17		27	3 7 0 00		7 3 5 00	

ACCOUNT *Equipment*   ACCOUNT NO. 18

DATE		ITEM	POST. REF.	DEBIT	CREDIT	BALANCE	
						DEBIT	CREDIT
19-- June	1	Balance	√			19 7 4 5 00	
	2		27	2 1 0 0 00		21 8 4 5 00	
	9		27		1 2 5 00	21 7 2 0 00	

ACCOUNT *Accounts Payable*   ACCOUNT NO. 22

DATE		ITEM	POST. REF.	DEBIT	CREDIT	BALANCE	
						DEBIT	CREDIT
19-- June	1	Balance	√				7 6 5 00
	2		27		2 1 0 0 00		2 8 6 5 00
	8		27		1 4 5 00		3 0 1 0 00
	9		27	1 2 5 00			2 8 8 5 00
	12		27	1 2 5 0 00			1 6 3 5 00
	20		27	5 0 00			1 5 8 5 00

ACCOUNT *Judy K. Schmidt, Capital*   ACCOUNT NO. 31

DATE		ITEM	POST. REF.	DEBIT	CREDIT	BALANCE	
						DEBIT	CREDIT
19-- June	1	Balance	√				29 4 8 3 00

ACCOUNT *Judy K. Schmidt, Drawing*   ACCOUNT NO. 32

DATE		ITEM	POST. REF.	DEBIT	CREDIT	BALANCE	
						DEBIT	CREDIT
19-- June	27		27	1 2 5 0 00			1 2 5 0 00

ACCOUNT *Professional Fees*   ACCOUNT NO. *41*

DATE		ITEM	POST. REF.	DEBIT	CREDIT	BALANCE	
						DEBIT	CREDIT
19-- June	30		27		1 7 2 0 00		1 7 2 0 00
	30		28		4 1 4 5 00		5 8 6 5 00

ACCOUNT *Salary Expense*   ACCOUNT NO. *51*

DATE		ITEM	POST. REF.	DEBIT	CREDIT	BALANCE	
						DEBIT	CREDIT
19-- June	30		28	1 7 2 5 00		1 7 2 5 00	

ACCOUNT *Rent Expense*   ACCOUNT NO. *53*

DATE		ITEM	POST. REF.	DEBIT	CREDIT	BALANCE	
						DEBIT	CREDIT
19-- June	1		27	6 0 0 00		6 0 0 00	

ACCOUNT *Laboratory Expense*   ACCOUNT NO. *55*

DATE		ITEM	POST. REF.	DEBIT	CREDIT	BALANCE	
						DEBIT	CREDIT
19-- June	23		27	2 4 5 00		2 4 5 00	

ACCOUNT *Utilities Expense*   ACCOUNT NO. *56*

DATE		ITEM	POST. REF.	DEBIT	CREDIT	BALANCE	
						DEBIT	CREDIT
19-- June	30		28	1 5 7 00		1 5 7 00	
	30		28	2 9 00		1 8 6 00	
	30		28	7 4 00		2 6 0 00	

ACCOUNT *Miscellaneous Expense*   ACCOUNT NO. *59*

DATE		ITEM	POST. REF.	DEBIT	CREDIT	BALANCE	
						DEBIT	CREDIT
19-- June	30		28	1 3 2 00		1 3 2 00	

4.

Judy K. Schmidt, M.D. Trial Balance June 30, 19—				
Cash		3 1 7 4 00		
Accounts Receivable		6 7 2 0 00		
Supplies		3 7 2 00		
Prepaid Insurance		7 3 5 00		
Equipment		21 7 2 0 00		
Accounts Payable				1 5 8 5 00
Judy K. Schmidt, Capital				29 4 8 3 00
Judy K. Schmidt, Drawing		1 2 5 0 00		
Professional Fees				5 8 6 5 00
Salary Expense		1 7 2 5 00		
Rent Expense		6 0 0 00		
Laboratory Expense		2 4 5 00		
Utilities Expense		2 6 0 00		
Miscellaneous Expense		1 3 2 00		
		36 9 3 3 00		36 9 3 3 00

DISCUSSION QUESTIONS

1. What is an account?
2. Differentiate between an account and a ledger.
3. What is the name of the listing of accounts in the ledger?
4. Describe in general terms the sequence of accounts in the ledger.
5. Do the terms debit and credit signify increase or decrease, or may they signify either? Explain.
6. What is the name of the record in which a transaction is initially entered?
7. Define posting.
8. Indicate whether each of the following is recorded by a debit or by a credit: (a) increase in an asset account, (b) decrease in a liability account, (c) increase in a revenue account.
9. Explain why the rules of debit and credit are the same for liability accounts and owner's equity accounts.
10. What is the effect (increase or decrease) of debits to expense accounts (a) in terms of owner's equity and (b) in terms of expense?
11. What is the effect (increase or decrease) of credits to revenue accounts (a) in terms of owner's equity and (b) in terms of revenue?
12. Identify each of the following accounts as asset, liability, owner's equity, revenue, or expense, and state in each case whether the normal balance is a debit or a credit. If the account is an owner's equity account, also state whether it is capital or drawing.

a. Accounts Payable	f. Accounts Receivable
b. Equipment	g. Fees Earned
c. Salary Expense	h. Susan Parker, Capital
d. Susan Parker, Drawing	i. Supplies
e. Cash	j. Rent Expense

13. On June 1 the accounts payable account had a normal balance of $11,725. During June the account was debited for a total of $13,500 and credited for a total of $14,000. (a) What was the balance of the account on June 30? (b) Was the balance in (a) a debit or a credit?
14. Liebrandt Company adheres to a policy of depositing all cash receipts in a bank account and making all payments by check. The cash account as of June 30 has a credit balance of $575 and there is no undeposited cash on hand. (a) Assuming that there were no errors in journalizing or posting, what is the explanation of this unusual balance? (b) Is the $575 credit balance in the cash account an asset, a liability, owner's equity, a revenue, or an expense?

15. During the month, a business enterprise has a substantial number of transactions affecting each of the following accounts. State for each account whether it is likely to have (a) debit entries only, (b) credit entries only, or (c) both debit and credit entries.

    1. Fees Earned   5. Ann Redus, Drawing
    2. Cash   6. Accounts Receivable
    3. Miscellaneous Expense   7. Supplies Expense
    4. Accounts Payable

16. Rearrange the following in proper sequence: (a) entry posted to ledger, (b) business transaction occurs, (c) entry recorded in journal, (d) business document prepared.

17. Describe the three procedures required to post the credit portion of the following journal entry (Fees Earned is account no. 41):

	DATE		DESCRIPTION	POST. REF.	DEBIT	CREDIT	
			JOURNAL			PAGE 32	
1	1993 June	11	Accounts Receivable	12	8 7 5 00		1
2			Fees Earned			8 7 5 00	2
3							3

18. In examining an entry that has been recorded in the journal, what indicates that the entry has been posted to the accounts?

19. Justice Company performed services in June for a specific customer and the fee was $6,200. Payment was received in the following July. (a) Was the revenue earned in June or July? (b) What accounts should be debited and credited in (1) June and (2) July?

20. a. Describe the form known as a trial balance.
    b. What proof is provided by a trial balance?

21. If the two totals of a trial balance are equal, does it mean that there are no errors in the accounting records? Explain.

22. When a trial balance is prepared, an account balance of $36,750 is listed as $3,675 and an account balance of $4,500 is listed as $5,400. Identify the transposition and the slide.

23. When a purchase of supplies of $690 for cash was recorded, both the debit and the credit were journalized and posted as $960. (a) Would this error cause the trial balance to be out of balance? (b) Would the answer be the same if the $690 entry had been journalized correctly, but the debit to Cash had been posted as $960?

24. Indicate which of the following errors, each considered individually, would cause the trial balance totals to be unequal:
    a. A payment of $950 to a creditor was posted as a debit of $950 to Accounts Payable and a debit of $950 to Cash.
    b. A withdrawal of $2,000 by the owner was journalized and posted as a debit of $200 to Salary Expense and a credit of $200 to Cash.
    c. A payment of $5,000 for equipment purchased was posted as a debit of $5,000 to Equipment and a credit of $50,000 to Cash.
    d. A receipt of $500 from an account receivable was journalized and posted as a debit of $500 to Cash and a credit of $500 to Sales.
    e. A fee of $2,500 earned and due from a client was not debited to Accounts Receivable or credited to a revenue account, because the cash had not been received.

25. How is a correction made when an error in an account title or amount in the journal is discovered before the entry is posted?

26. In journalizing and posting the entry to record the purchase of supplies on account, the accounts receivable account was credited in error. What is the preferred procedure to correct the error?

REAL WORLD FOCUS
27. A business reported $75,094,500 and $8,271,100 of net revenues and net income respectively for the past year. Early in the current year, suspicions that the business had recorded revenues too early led to an investigation. The investigation disclosed that $418,000 of revenues applicable to the current year had been recorded in the past year. Determine (a) the corrected net income for the past year and (b) the percent error in the reported net income for the past year. (Adapted from annual report of Matrix Science Corporation.)

ETHICS DISCUSSION CASE

At the end of the current month, Ted Beam prepared a trial balance for Ace Services. The credit side of the trial balance exceeds the debit side by a significant amount. Ted has decided to add the difference to the balance of the miscellaneous expense account in order to complete the preparation of the current month's financial statements by a 5 o'clock deadline. Ted will look for the difference next week when there is more time.

SHARPEN YOUR COMMUNICATION SKILLS

Discuss whether Ted Beam is behaving in an ethical manner.

EXERCISES

EXERCISE 2-1
CHART OF ACCOUNTS
Objective 2

RB Co. is a newly organized enterprise. The list of accounts to be opened in the general ledger is as follows:

Accounts Payable	Miscellaneous Expense
Accounts Receivable	Prepaid Insurance
R. Bailey, Capital	Rent Expense
R. Bailey, Drawing	Supplies
Cash	Supplies Expense
Equipment	Unearned Rent
Fees Earned	Wages Expense

List the accounts in the order in which they should appear in the ledger of RB Co. and assign account numbers. Each account number is to have two digits: the first digit is to indicate the major classification ("1" for assets, etc.), and the second digit is to identify the specific account within each major classification ("11" for Cash, etc.).

EXERCISE 2-2
IDENTIFY TRANSACTIONS
Objectives 3, 4

The nine transactions recorded by Gross Services during June, its first month of operations, are indicated in the following T accounts:

Cash				Accounts Receivable				Supplies			
(1)	15,000	(2)	1,500	(5)	12,500	(7)	8,500	(2)	1,500	(9)	450
(7)	8,500	(3)	3,950								
		(4)	3,725								
		(6)	5,000								
		(8)	2,500								

Equipment				Accounts Payable				Debra Gross, Capital			
(3)	13,950			(6)	5,000	(3)	10,000			(1)	15,000

Debra Gross, Drawing				Service Revenue				Operating Expenses			
(8)	2,500					(5)	12,500	(4)	3,725		
								(9)	450		

Indicate for each debit and each credit: (a) whether an asset, liability, capital, drawing, revenue, or expense account was affected and (b) whether the account was increased (+) or decreased (−). Answers should be presented in the following form (transaction (1) is given as an example):

	Account Debited		*Account Credited*	
Transaction	*Type*	*Effect*	*Type*	*Effect*
(1)	asset	+	capital	+

EXERCISE 2-3
TRIAL BALANCE
Objective 6

Based upon the data presented in Exercise 2-2, prepare a trial balance, listing the accounts in their proper order.

EXERCISE 2-4
CAPITAL ACCOUNT
BALANCE
Objective 3

As of January 1, Donna Drabeck, Capital had a credit balance of $20,000. During the year, the owner's withdrawals totaled $18,000 and the business incurred a net loss of $6,000. There were no additional investments in the business.

a. Calculate the balance of Donna Drabeck, Capital as of the end of the year.

▶ **SHARPEN YOUR**
COMMUNICATION SKILLS

b. Assuming that there have been no recording errors, will the balance sheet prepared at December 31 balance? Explain.

EXERCISE 2-5
CASH ACCOUNT BALANCE
Objective 3

During the month, a business received $897,500 in cash and paid out $890,000 in cash.

▶ **SHARPEN YOUR**
COMMUNICATION SKILLS

a. Do the data indicate that the business earned $7,500 during the month? Explain.

b. If the balance of the cash account was $32,500 at the beginning of the month, what was the cash balance at the end of the month?

EXERCISE 2-6
ACCOUNT BALANCES
Objective 3

a. On July 1 the cash account balance was $12,750. During July, cash receipts totaled $26,000 and the July 31 balance was $14,000. Determine the cash payments made during July.

b. On July 1 the accounts receivable account balance was $19,900. During July, $21,000 was received from customers on account. If the July 31 balance was $22,500, determine the fees billed to customers on account during July.

c. During July, $30,500 was paid to creditors on account and purchases on account were $27,700. If the July 31 balance of Accounts Payable was $25,000, determine the account balance on July 1.

EXERCISE 2-7
TRANSACTIONS
Objectives 4, 5

Rago Company has the following accounts in its ledger: Cash; Accounts Receivable; Supplies; Office Equipment; Accounts Payable; Joseph Rago, Capital; Joseph Rago, Drawing; Fees Earned; Rent Expense; Advertising Expense; Utilities Expense; Miscellaneous Expense.

Journalize the following selected transactions, completed during May of the current year, in a two-column journal:

May 1. Paid rent for the month, $1,500.
     3. Paid cash for supplies, $270.
     5. Paid advertising expense, $350.
     5. Purchased office equipment on account, $4,200.
     8. Received cash from customers on account, $5,600.
    12. Paid creditor on account, $2,150.
    15. Withdrew cash for personal use, $1,800.
    25. Paid cash for repairs to office equipment, $90.
    27. Paid telephone bill for the month, $195.
    29. Fees earned and billed to customers for the month, $9,150.
    31. Paid electricity bill for the month, $430.

EXERCISE 2-8
TRANSACTIONS AND
T ACCOUNTS
Objectives 3, 4, 5

The following selected transactions were completed during November of the current year:

1. Purchased supplies on account, $720.
2. Billed customers for fees earned, $2,210.
3. Received cash from customers on account, $1,100.
4. Paid creditors on account, $500.

SPREADSHEET
PROBLEM

a. Journalize the foregoing transactions in a two-column journal, using the appropriate number to identify the transactions.

b. Post the entries prepared in (a) to the following T accounts: Cash, Supplies, Accounts Receivable, Accounts Payable, Fees Earned. To the left of each amount posted in the accounts, place the appropriate number to identify the transactions.

EXERCISE 2-9
TRIAL BALANCE
Objective 6

The accounts in the ledger of Pogue Company as of August 31 of the current year are listed in alphabetical order as follows. All accounts have normal balances. The balance of the cash account has been intentionally omitted.

Accounts Payable	$ 19,710	Notes Payable	$ 25,000
Accounts Receivable	20,500	Prepaid Insurance	3,150
Cash	?	Rent Expense	48,000
R. Pogue, Capital	120,290	Wages Expense	190,000
R. Pogue, Drawing	28,000	Supplies	4,100
Fees Earned	325,000	Supplies Expense	5,900
Insurance Expense	5,000	Unearned Rent	10,000
Land	125,000	Utilities Expense	41,500
Miscellaneous Expense	9,900		

Prepare a trial balance, listing the accounts in their proper order and inserting the missing figure for cash.

EXERCISE 2-10
ERRORS IN TRIAL BALANCE
Objective 6

The following preliminary trial balance of Brett Carpet Services does not balance:

Brett Carpet Services
Trial Balance
December 31, 19—

Cash	43,000	
Accounts Receivable	16,200	
Prepaid Insurance		3,300
Equipment	4,500	
Accounts Payable		10,050
Unearned Rent		480
Fran Brett, Capital	61,250	
Fran Brett, Drawing		24,000
Service Revenue		64,940
Wages Expense		33,400
Advertising Expense	5,200	
Miscellaneous Expense		1,380
	130,150	137,550

When the ledger and other records are reviewed, you discover the following: (1) the debits and credits in the cash account total $43,000 and $37,300, respectively; (2) a billing of $800 to a customer on account was not posted to the accounts receivable account; (3) a payment of $2,100 made to a creditor on account was not posted to the accounts payable account; (4) the balance of the unearned rent account is $840; (5) the correct balance of the equipment account is $45,000; and (6) each account has a normal balance. Prepare a corrected trial balance.

EXERCISE 2-11
EFFECT OF ERRORS ON TRIAL BALANCE
Objective 6

The following errors occurred in posting from a two-column journal:

1. A credit of $150 to Cash was posted as $510.
2. A debit of $1,000 to Cash was posted to Wages Expense.
3. A debit of $750 to Supplies was posted twice.
4. A credit of $500 to Accounts Payable was posted as a debit.
5. An entry debiting Accounts Receivable and crediting Fees Earned for $4,000 was not posted.
6. A debit of $750 to Wages Expense was posted as $570.
7. A credit of $1,730 to Accounts Receivable was not posted.

Considering each case individually (i.e., assuming that no other errors had occurred), indicate: (a) by "yes" or "no" whether the trial balance would be out of balance; (b) if answer to (a) is "yes," the amount by which the trial balance totals would differ; and (c) the column of the trial balance that would have the larger total. Answers should be presented in the following form (error (1) is given as an example):

Error	(a) Out of Balance	(b) Difference	(c) Larger Total
(1)	yes	$360	credit

EXERCISE 2-12
ENTRIES TO CORRECT
ERRORS
Objective 7

A number of errors in journalizing and posting transactions are described as follows:

a. A $500 purchase of supplies on account was recorded as a debit to Cash and a credit to Accounts Payable.

b. A withdrawal by A. C. Boyle, owner, of $2,500 was recorded as a debit to Miscellaneous Expense and a credit to Cash.

c. Rent of $800 paid for the current month was recorded as a debit to Supplies Expense and a credit to Cash.

Journalize the entries to correct the errors.

WhAT'S WROnG WITH THiƨ?

■
■
▲
■

How many errors can you find in the following trial balance? All accounts have normal balances.

Mason Company
Trial Balance
For Month Ended October 31, 19—

Cash	4,010	
Accounts Receivable		14,400
Prepaid Insurance	2,400	
Equipment	41,200	
Accounts Payable	5,850	
Salaries Payable		750
Ann Mason, Capital		49,600
Ann Mason, Drawing		9,000
Service Revenue	37,900	
Salary Expense	18,400	
Advertising Expense	4,200	
Miscellaneous Expense	490	
	94,100	94,100

PROBLEMS

Series A

PROBLEM 2-1A
ENTRIES INTO T ACCOUNTS
AND TRIAL BALANCE
Objectives 3, 4, 6

Lisa Kent, architect, opened an office on February 1 of the current year. During the month, she completed the following transactions connected with her professional practice:

a. Transferred cash from a personal bank account to an account to be used for the business, $10,000.

b. Paid February rent for office and workroom, $1,500.

c. Purchased used automobile for $9,500, paying $2,500 cash and giving a non-interest-bearing note for the remainder.

d. Purchased office and drafting room equipment on account, $6,000.

e. Paid cash for supplies, $900.

f. Paid cash for insurance policies, $850.

g. Received cash from client for plans delivered, $2,100.

h. Paid cash for miscellaneous services, $75.

i. Paid cash to creditors on account, $3,000.

j. Paid installment due on note payable, $400.

k. Received invoice for blueprint service, due in March, $110.

l. Recorded fee earned on plans delivered, payment to be made in March, $3,150.

m. Paid salary of assistant, $1,250.

n. Paid gas, oil, and repairs on automobile for February, $115.

Instructions

1. Record the foregoing transactions directly in the following T accounts, without journalizing: Cash; Accounts Receivable; Supplies; Prepaid Insurance; Automobiles; Equip-

ment; Notes Payable; Accounts Payable; Lisa Kent, Capital; Professional Fees; Rent Expense; Salary Expense; Automobile Expense; Blueprint Expense; Miscellaneous Expense. To the left of the amount entered in the accounts, place the appropriate letter to identify the transaction.

2. Determine the balances of the T accounts having two or more debits or credits. A memorandum balance should be inserted in accounts having both debits and credits, in the manner illustrated in the chapter. For accounts with entries on one side only (such as Professional Fees), there is no need to insert the memorandum balance in the item column. For accounts containing only a single debit and a single credit (such as Notes Payable), the memorandum balance should be inserted in the appropriate item column. Accounts containing a single entry only (such as Prepaid Insurance) do not need a memorandum balance.

3. Prepare a trial balance for Lisa Kent, Architect, as of February 28 of the current year.

PROBLEM 2-2A
JOURNAL ENTRIES AND
TRIAL BALANCE
Objectives 3, 4, 6

On July 1 of the current year, Janet Lopes established Lopes Realty, which completed the following transactions during July:

   a. Janet Lopes transferred cash from her personal bank account to an account to be used for the business, $5,000.
   b. Paid rent on office and equipment for the month, $3,000.
   c. Purchased supplies on account, $4,500.
   d. Paid creditor on account, $2,900.
   e. Earned sales commissions, receiving cash, $29,750.
   f. Paid automobile expenses (including rental charge) for month, $2,900, and miscellaneous expenses, $1,950.
   g. Paid office salaries, $8,000.
   h. Determined that the cost of supplies used was $1,325.
   i. Withdrew cash for personal use, $5,000.

Instructions

1. Journalize entries for transactions (a) through (i), using the following account titles: Cash; Supplies; Accounts Payable; Janet Lopes, Capital; Janet Lopes, Drawing; Sales Commissions; Office Salaries Expense; Rent Expense; Automobile Expense; Supplies Expense; Miscellaneous Expense.

2. Prepare T accounts, using the account titles in (1). Post the journal entries to these accounts, placing the appropriate letter to the left of each amount to identify the transactions. Determine the account balances, after all posting is complete, for all accounts having two or more debits or credits. A memorandum balance should also be inserted in accounts having both debits and credits, in the manner illustrated in the chapter. For accounts with entries on one side only, there is no need to insert a memorandum balance in the item column. For accounts containing only a single debit and a single credit, the memorandum balance should be inserted in the appropriate item column.

3. Prepare a trial balance as of July 31, 19—.

4. Determine the following:
   a. Amount of total revenue recorded in the ledger.
   b. Amount of total expenses recorded in the ledger.
   c. Amount of net income for July.

**SOLUTIONS
SOFTWARE**

Instructions for Solving Problem 2-2A Using Solutions Software

1. Load opening balances.
2. Set the run date to July 31 of the current year and enter your name.
3. Select the General Journal Entries option and key the journal entries. Use July 31 as the date of each transaction. Leave the reference field blank. (Note: To review the chart of accounts, select F-1.)
4. Display a journal entries report.
5. Display a detailed general ledger.
6. Display a trial balance.
7. Display an income statement.
8. Display a statement of owner's equity.
9. Display a balance sheet.
10. Save your data file to disk.
11. End the session.

PROBLEM 2-3A
JOURNAL ENTRIES AND
TRIAL BALANCE
Objectives 4, 5, 6

On June 5 of the current year, Tom Morgan established a sole proprietorship to be known as Morgan Decorators. During the remainder of the month, Morgan completed the following business transactions:

June 5. Morgan transferred cash from a personal bank account to an account to be used for the business, $15,000.
      5. Paid rent for period of June 5 to end of month, $950.
      7. Purchased office equipment on account, $6,250.
      8. Purchased a used truck for $15,000, paying $7,500 cash and giving a note payable for the remainder.
     10. Purchased supplies for cash, $525.
     12. Received cash for job completed, $600.
     15. Paid wages of employees, $800.
     20. Paid premiums on property and casualty insurance, $725.
     22. Recorded jobs completed on account and sent invoices to customers, $1,950.
     24. Received an invoice for truck expenses, to be paid in July, $310.
     26. Received cash for job completed, $650. This job had not been recorded previously.
     28. Purchased supplies on account, $190.
     29. Paid utilities expense, $390.
     29. Paid miscellaneous expenses, $95.
     30. Received cash from customers on account, $1,300.
     30. Paid wages of employees, $1,200.
     30. Paid creditor a portion of the amount owed for equipment purchased on June 7, $2,500.
     30. Withdrew cash for personal use, $2,000.

Instructions

1. Journalize each transaction in a two-column journal, referring to the following chart of accounts in selecting the accounts to be debited and credited. (Do not insert the account numbers in the journal at this time.)

11 Cash	41 Fees Earned
12 Accounts Receivable	51 Wages Expense
13 Supplies	53 Rent Expense
14 Prepaid Insurance	54 Utilities Expense
16 Equipment	55 Truck Expense
18 Truck	59 Miscellaneous Expense
21 Notes Payable	
22 Accounts Payable	
31 Tom Morgan, Capital	
32 Tom Morgan, Drawing	

2. Post the journal to a ledger of four-column accounts, inserting appropriate posting references as each item is posted. Extend the balances to the appropriate balance columns after each transaction is posted.
3. Prepare a trial balance for Morgan Decorators as of June 30.

SOLUTIONS
SOFTWARE

Instructions for Solving Problem 2-3A Using Solutions Software

1. Load opening balances.
2. Set the run date to June 30 of the current year and enter your name.
3. Select the General Journal Entries option and key the journal entries. Leave the reference field blank. (Note: To review the chart of accounts, select F-1.)
4. Display a journal entries report.
5. Display a detailed general ledger.
6. Display a trial balance.
7. Display an income statement.
8. Display a statement of owner's equity.
9. Display a balance sheet.
10. Save your data file to disk.
11. End the session.

PROBLEM 2-4A
JOURNAL ENTRIES AND
TRIAL BALANCE
Objectives 4, 5, 6

Frank Saul, M.D., completed the following transactions in the practice of his profession during June of the current year:

June 1. Paid office rent for June, $2,000.
2. Purchased equipment on account, $10,500.
3. Purchased X-ray film and other supplies on account, $725.
6. Received cash on account from patients, $10,025.
6. Paid cash to creditors on account, $5,240.
8. Sold X-ray film to another doctor at cost, receiving cash, $75. (Record the credit in the supplies account.)
10. Paid cash for renewal of property insurance policy, $495.
15. Paid cash for laboratory analyses, $395.
20. Discovered that the balance of the cash account was understated and the accounts receivable account was overstated as of June 1 by $100. A cash receipt of that amount on account from a patient in May had not been recorded. Journalized the $100 receipt as of June 20.
24. One of the items of equipment purchased on June 2 was defective. It was returned with the permission of the supplier, who agreed to reduce the account for the amount charged for the item, $550.
26. Paid cash from business bank account for personal and family expenses, $2,750.
30. Recorded fees charged to patients on account for services performed in June, $7,770.
30. Recorded the cash received in payment of services (on a cash basis) to patients during June, $9,610.
30. Paid salaries of receptionist and nurses, $4,050.
30. Paid miscellaneous expenses, $420.
30. Paid gas and electricity expense, $610.
30. Paid water expense, $130.
30. Paid telephone expense, $280.

Saul's chart of accounts and the balances of accounts as of June 1 (all normal balances) are as follows:

11	Cash	$ 5,075	41 Professional Fees	-0-
12	Accounts Receivable	15,110	51 Salary Expense	-0-
13	Supplies	1,140	53 Rent Expense	-0-
14	Prepaid Insurance	3,700	55 Utilities Expense	-0-
18	Equipment	52,200	56 Laboratory Expense	-0-
22	Accounts Payable	9,850	59 Miscellaneous Expense	-0-
31	Frank Saul, Capital	67,375		
32	Frank Saul, Drawing	-0-		

Instructions

1. Enter the June 1 account balances in the appropriate balance column of a four-column account. Place a check mark (√) in the posting reference column. (It is advisable to verify the equality of the debit and credit balances in the ledger before proceeding with the next instruction.)
2. Journalize each transaction in a two-column journal.
3. Post the journal to the ledger, extending the account balance to the appropriate balance column after each posting.
4. Prepare a trial balance as of June 30.
5. Assuming that the expenses that have not been recorded (such as supplies expense and insurance expense) total $2,950 for the month, determine the following amounts:
  a. Net income for the month of June.
  b. Increase or decrease in owner's equity during June.
  c. Owner's equity as of June 30.

PROBLEM 2-5A
JOURNAL ENTRIES AND
TRIAL BALANCE
Objectives 4, 5, 6

Lakeside Realty acts as an agent in buying, selling, renting, and managing real estate. The account balances at the end of March of the current year are as follows:

11 Cash	36,150	
12 Accounts Receivable	28,750	
13 Prepaid Insurance	1,100	
14 Office Supplies	715	
16 Land	-0-	
21 Accounts Payable		6,175
22 Notes Payable		-0-
31 J. J. Barr, Capital		40,840
32 J. J. Barr, Drawing	2,000	
41 Fees Earned		125,500
51 Salary and Commission Expense	92,100	
52 Rent Expense	4,500	
53 Advertising Expense	3,900	
54 Automobile Expense	2,750	
59 Miscellaneous Expense	550	
	172,515	172,515

The following business transactions were completed by Lakeside Realty during April of the current year:

April 1. Paid rent on office for month, $1,500.
    3. Purchased office supplies on account, $375.
    5. Paid insurance premiums, $1,650.
    7. Received cash from clients on account, $18,200.
   15. Paid salaries and commissions for the first half of the month, $16,650.
   15. Purchased land for a future building site for $55,000, paying $11,000 in cash and giving a note payable for the remainder.
   15. Recorded revenue earned and billed to clients during first half of month, $19,100.
   18. Paid creditors on account, $4,150.
   20. Returned a portion of the office supplies purchased on April 3, receiving full credit for their cost, $75.
   23. Received cash from clients on account, $16,700.
   24. Paid advertising expense, $1,550.
   27. Discovered an error in computing a commission; received cash from the salesperson for the overpayment, $350.
   28. Paid automobile expense (including rental charges for an automobile), $715.
   29. Paid miscellaneous expenses, $215.
   30. Recorded revenue earned and billed to clients during second half of the month, $16,300.
   30. Paid salaries and commissions for the second half of the month, $19,850.
   30. Withdrew cash for personal use, $2,000.

Instructions

1. Record the April 1 balance of each account in the appropriate balance column of a four-column account, write *Balance* in the item section, and place a check mark (√) in the posting reference column.
2. Journalize the transactions for April in a two-column journal.
3. Post to the ledger, extending the account balance to the appropriate balance column after each posting.
4. Prepare a trial balance of the ledger as of April 30.

If the working papers correlating with the textbook are not used, omit Problem 2-6A.

PROBLEM 2-6A
ERRORS IN TRIAL BALANCE
Objectives 6, 7

The following records of Donahue TV Repair are presented in the working papers:

Journal containing entries for the period March 1-31.
Ledger to which the March entries have been posted.
Preliminary trial balance as of March 31, which does not balance.

Locate the errors, supply the information requested, and prepare a corrected trial balance, proceeding in accordance with the following detailed instructions. The balances recorded in the accounts as of March 1 and the entries in the journal are correctly stated. If it is necessary to correct any posted amounts in the ledger, a line should be drawn through the erroneous figure and the correct amount inserted above. Corrections or notations may be inserted on the preliminary trial balance in any manner desired. It is not necessary to complete all of the instructions if equal trial balance totals can be obtained earlier. However, the requirements of instructions (6) and (7) should be completed in any event.

Instructions

1. Verify the totals of the preliminary trial balance, inserting the correct amounts in the schedule provided in the working papers.
2. Compute the difference between the trial balance totals.
3. Compare the listings in the trial balance with the balances appearing in the ledger and list the errors found in the space provided in the working papers.
4. Verify the accuracy of the balance of each account in the ledger and list the errors found in the space provided in the working papers.
5. Trace the postings in the ledger back to the journal, using small check marks to identify items traced. Correct any amounts in the ledger that may be necessitated by errors in posting and list the errors in the space provided in the working papers.
6. Journalize as of March 31 the payment of $125 for advertising expense. The bill had been paid on March 31 but was inadvertently omitted from the journal. Post to the ledger. (Revise any amounts necessitated by posting this entry.)
7. Prepare a new trial balance.

PROBLEM 2-7A
CORRECTED TRIAL
BALANCE
Objectives 6, 7

Bell Carpet Installation, a sole proprietorship, has the following trial balance as of August 31 of the current year:

Cash	4,400	
Accounts Receivable	6,400	
Supplies	1,010	
Prepaid Insurance	150	
Equipment	15,500	
Notes Payable		15,000
Accounts Payable		4,620
John Bell, Capital		15,300
John Bell, Drawing	7,000	
Fees Earned		49,980
Wages Expense	28,500	
Rent Expense	6,400	
Advertising Expense	3200	
Gas, Electricity, and Water Expense	3,150	
	72,830	84,900

The debit and credit totals are not equal as a result of the following errors:

a. The balance of cash was overstated by $500.
b. A cash receipt of $240 was posted as a debit to Cash of $420.
c. A debit of $1,000 for a withdrawal by the owner was posted as a credit to John Bell, Capital.
d. The balance of $3,200 in Advertising Expense was entered as $320 in the trial balance.
e. A debit of $725 to Accounts Receivable was not posted.
f. A return of $125 of defective supplies was erroneously posted as a $215 credit to Supplies.
g. The balance of Notes Payable was overstated by $5,000.
h. An insurance policy acquired at a cost of $200 was posted as a credit to Prepaid Insurance.
i. Miscellaneous Expense, with a balance of $945, was omitted from the trial balance.
j. A debit of $710 in Accounts Payable was overlooked when determining the balance of the account.

SPREADSHEET
PROBLEM

SHARPEN YOUR
COMMUNICATION SKILLS

Instructions

1. Prepare a corrected trial balance as of August 31 of the current year.
2. Does the fact that the trial balance in (1) is balanced mean that there are no errors in the accounts? Explain.

Series B

PROBLEM 2-1B
ENTRIES INTO T ACCOUNTS
AND TRIAL BALANCE
Objectives 3, 4, 6

Hector Cruz, architect, opened an office on November 1 of the current year. During the month, he completed the following transactions connected with his professional practice:

a. Transferred cash from a personal bank account to an account to be used for his business, $10,000.
b. Purchased used automobile for $14,300, paying $3,300 cash and giving a non-interest-bearing note for the remainder.
c. Paid November rent for office and workroom, $1,200.
d. Paid cash for supplies, $225.
e. Purchased office and drafting room equipment on account, $4,200.
f. Paid cash for insurance policies on automobile and equipment, $510.
g. Received cash from a client for plans delivered, $1,725.
h. Paid cash to creditors on account, $2,100.
i. Paid cash for miscellaneous expenses, $65.
j. Received invoice for blueprint service, due in following month, $75.
k. Recorded fee earned on plans delivered, payment to be made in December, $2,500.
l. Paid salary of assistant, $1,000.
m. Paid cash for miscellaneous expenses, $68.
n. Paid installment due on note payable, $300.
o. Paid gas, oil, and repairs on automobile for November, $70.

Instructions

1. Record the foregoing transactions directly in the following T accounts, without journalizing: Cash; Accounts Receivable; Supplies; Prepaid Insurance; Automobiles; Equipment; Notes Payable; Accounts Payable; Hector Cruz, Capital; Professional Fees; Rent Expense; Salary Expense; Automobile Expense; Blueprint Expense; Miscellaneous Expense. To the left of each amount entered in the accounts, place the appropriate letter to identify the transaction.
2. Determine the balances of the T accounts having two or more debits or credits. A memorandum balance should be inserted in accounts having both debits and credits, in the manner illustrated in the chapter. For accounts with entries on one side only (such as Professional Fees), there is no need to insert the memorandum balance in the item column. For accounts containing only a single debit and a single credit (such as Notes Payable), the memorandum balance should be inserted in the appropriate item column. Accounts containing a single entry only (such as Prepaid Insurance) do not need a memorandum balance.
3. Prepare a trial balance for Hector Cruz, Architect, as of November 30 of the current year.

PROBLEM 2-2B
JOURNAL ENTRIES AND
TRIAL BALANCE
Objectives 3, 4, 6

On July 1 of the current year, Rob Petrie established Midstate Realty, which completed the following transactions during the month:

a. Rob Petrie transferred cash from his personal bank account to an account to be used for the business, $15,000.
b. Paid rent on office and equipment for the month, $12,000.
c. Purchased supplies on account, $5,900.
d. Paid creditor on account, $4,000.
e. Earned sales commissions, receiving cash, $41,500.
f. Withdrew cash for personal use, $10,000.
g. Paid automobile expenses (including rental charge) for month, $3,900, and miscellaneous expenses, $1,950.
h. Paid office salaries, $10,000.
i. Determined that the cost of supplies used was $2,250.

Instructions

1. Journalize entries for transactions (a) through (i), using the following account titles: Cash; Supplies; Accounts Payable; Rob Petrie, Capital; Rob Petrie, Drawing; Sales Commissions; Rent Expense; Office Salaries Expense; Automobile Expense; Supplies Expense; Miscellaneous Expense.
2. Prepare T accounts, using the account titles in (1). Post the journal entries to these accounts, placing the appropriate letter to the left of each amount to identify the transactions. Determine the account balances, after all posting is complete, for all accounts having two or more debits or credits. A memorandum balance should be in-

serted in accounts having both debits and credits, in the manner illustrated in the chapter. For accounts with entries on one side only, there is no need to insert a memorandum balance in the item column. For accounts containing only a single debit and a single credit, the memorandum balance should be inserted in the appropriate item column.

3. Prepare a trial balance as of July 31, 19--.
4. Determine the following:
   a. Amount of total revenue recorded in the ledger.
   b. Amount of total expenses recorded in the ledger.
   c. Amount of net income for July.

SOLUTIONS SOFTWARE

Instructions for Solving Problem 2-2B Using Solutions Software

1. Load opening balances.
2. Set the run date to July 31 of the current year and enter your name.
3. Select the General Journal Entries option and key the journal entries. Use July 31 as the date of each transaction. Leave the reference field blank. (Note: To review the chart of accounts, select F-1.)
4. Display a journal entries report.
5. Display a detailed general ledger.
6. Display a trial balance.
7. Display an income statement.
8. Display a statement of owner's equity.
9. Display a balance sheet.
10. Save your data file to disk.
11. End the session.

PROBLEM 2-3B
JOURNAL ENTRIES AND
TRIAL BALANCE
Objectives 4, 5, 6

On July 10 of the current year, Jane Morse established a sole proprietorship to be known as Morse Decorators. During the remainder of the month, Morse completed the following business transactions:

July 10. Morse transferred cash from a personal bank account to an account to be used for the business, $10,000.
    10. Paid rent for period of July 10 to end of month, $600.
    11. Purchased a truck for $9,000, paying $3,000 cash and giving a note payable for the remainder.
    12. Purchased equipment on account, $1,700.
    14. Purchased supplies for cash, $885.
    14. Paid premiums on property and casualty insurance, $420.
    15. Received cash for job completed, $510.
    16. Purchased supplies on account, $240.
    17. Paid wages of employees, $600.
    21. Paid creditor for equipment purchased on July 12, $1,700.
    24. Recorded jobs completed on account and sent invoices to customers, $2,100.
    26. Received an invoice for truck expenses, to be paid in August, $225.
    26. Received cash for job completed, $1,050. This job had not been recorded previously.
    27. Paid utilities expense, $205.
    27. Paid miscellaneous expenses, $73.
    28. Received cash from customers on account, $1,420.
    31. Paid wages of employees, $1,350.
    31. Withdrew cash for personal use, $1,500.

Instructions

1. Journalize each transaction in a two-column journal, referring to the following chart of accounts in selecting the accounts to be debited and credited. (Do not insert the account numbers in the journal at this time.)

11 Cash	41 Fees Earned
12 Accounts Receivable	51 Wages Expense
13 Supplies	53 Rent Expense
14 Prepaid Insurance	54 Utilities Expense
16 Equipment	55 Truck Expense
18 Truck	59 Miscellaneous Expense
21 Notes Payable	
22 Accounts Payable	
31 Jane Morse, Capital	
32 Jane Morse, Drawing	

2. Post the journal to a ledger of four-column accounts, inserting appropriate posting references as each item is posted. Extend the balances to the appropriate balance columns after each transaction is posted.

3. Prepare a trial balance for Morse Decorators as of July 31.

SOLUTIONS
SOFTWARE

Instructions for Solving Problem 2-3B Using Solutions Software
1. Load opening balances.
2. Set the run date to July 31 of the current year and enter your name.
3. Select the General Journal Entries option and key the journal entries. Leave the reference field blank. (Note: To review the chart of accounts, select F-1.)
4. Display a journal entries report.
5. Display a detailed general ledger.
6. Display a trial balance.
7. Display an income statement.
8. Display a statement of owner's equity.
9. Display a balance sheet.
10. Save your data file to disk.
11. End the session.

PROBLEM 2-4B
JOURNAL ENTRIES AND
TRIAL BALANCE
Objectives 4, 5, 6

Chris Dunn, M.D., completed the following transactions in the practice of her profession during May of the current year:

May 1. Paid office rent for May, $2,100.
   2. Purchased equipment on account, $8,500.
   5. Purchased X-ray film and other supplies on account, $850.
   6. Received cash on account from patients, $8,925.
   7. Paid cash to creditors on account, $5,620.
  10. Sold X-ray film to another doctor at cost, receiving cash, $75. (Record the credit in the supplies account.)
  10. Paid cash for renewal of property insurance policy, $545.
  15. Paid cash for laboratory analyses, $345.
  20. Discovered that the balance of the cash account was understated and the accounts receivable account was overstated as of May 1 by $100. A cash receipt of that amount on account from a patient in April had not been recorded. Journalized the $100 receipt as of May 20.
  24. One of the items of equipment purchased on May 2 was defective. It was returned with the permission of the supplier, who agreed to reduce the account for the amount charged for the item, $250.
  26. Paid cash from business bank account for personal and family expenses, $2,200.
  28. Paid miscellaneous expenses, $420.
  30. Paid gas and electricity expense, $510.
  30. Paid water expense, $130.
  30. Paid telephone expense, $225.
  31. Recorded fees charged to patients on account for services performed in May, $8,200.
  31. Recorded the cash received in payment of services (on a cash basis) to patients during May, $9,910.
  31. Paid salaries of receptionist and nurses, $4,650.

Dunn's chart of accounts and the balances of accounts as of May 1 (all normal balances) are as follows:

11	Cash	$ 5,925	41	Professional Fees	-0-
12	Accounts Receivable	15,160	51	Salary Expense	-0-
13	Supplies	1,240	53	Rent Expense	-0-
14	Prepaid Insurance	3,500	55	Utilities Expense	-0-
18	Equipment	55,600	56	Laboratory Expense	-0-
22	Accounts Payable	9,850	59	Miscellaneous Expense	-0-
31	Chris Dunn, Capital	71,575			
32	Chris Dunn, Drawing	-0-			

Instructions
1. Enter the May 1 account balances in the appropriate balance column of a four-column account. Place a check mark (√) in the posting reference column. (It is advisable to verify

the equality of the debit and credit balances in the ledger before proceeding with the next instruction.)

2. Journalize each transaction in a two-column journal.
3. Post the journal to the ledger, extending the balances to the appropriate balance column after each posting.
4. Prepare a trial balance as of May 31.
5. Assuming that the expenses that have not been recorded (such as supplies expense and insurance expense) total $1,850 for the month, determine the following amounts:
   a. Net income for the month of May.
   b. Increase or decrease in owner's equity during May.
   c. Owner's equity as of May 31.

PROBLEM 2-5B
JOURNAL ENTRIES AND
TRIAL BALANCE
Objectives 4, 5, 6

Combs Realty acts as an agent in buying, selling, renting, and managing real estate. The account balances at the end of April of the current year are as follows:

11	Cash	39,500	
12	Accounts Receivable	28,600	
13	Prepaid Insurance	750	
14	Office Supplies	625	
16	Land	-0-	
21	Accounts Payable		9,250
22	Notes Payable		-0-
31	P. E. Combs, Capital		63,025
32	P. E. Combs, Drawing	20,000	
41	Fees Earned		157,750
51	Salary and Commission Expense	122,100	
52	Rent Expense	9,000	
53	Advertising Expense	4,900	
54	Automobile Expense	3,950	
59	Miscellaneous Expense	600	
		230,025	230,025

The following business transactions were completed by Combs Realty during May of the current year:

May 1. Paid rent on office for month, $2,500.
2. Purchased office supplies on account, $425.
3. Paid insurance premiums, $1,925.
9. Received cash from clients on account, $21,000.
15. Paid salaries and commissions for the first half of the month, $19,650.
15. Purchased land for a future building site for $50,000, paying $10,000 in cash and giving a note payable for the remainder.
15. Recorded revenue earned and billed to clients during first half of month, $20,900.
18. Paid creditors on account, $5,650.
20. Returned a portion of the office supplies purchased on May 2, receiving full credit for their cost, $50.
29. Received cash from clients on account, $19,200.
29. Paid advertising expense, $2,150.
29. Discovered an error in computing a commission; received cash from the salesperson for the overpayment, $500.
30. Paid automobile expense (including rental charges for an automobile), $850.
30. Paid miscellaneous expenses, $215.
31. Recorded revenue earned and billed to clients during the second half of the month, $19,300.
31. Paid salaries and commissions for the second half of the month, $19,850.
31. Withdrew cash for personal use, $10,000.

Instructions
1. Record the May 1 balance of each account in the appropriate balance column of a four-column account, write *Balance* in the item section, and place a check mark (√) in the posting reference column.
2. Journalize the transactions for May in a two-column journal.
3. Post to the ledger, extending the account balance to the appropriate balance column after each posting.
4. Prepare a trial balance of the ledger as of May 31.

If the working papers correlating with the textbook are not used, omit Problem 2-6B.

PROBLEM 2-6B
ERRORS IN TRIAL BALANCE
Objectives 6, 7

The following records of Donahue TV Repair are presented in the working papers:

> Journal containing entries for the period March 1-31.
> Ledger to which the March entries have been posted.
> Preliminary trial balance as of March 31, which does not balance.

Locate the errors, supply the information requested, and prepare a corrected trial balance, proceeding in accordance with the following detailed instructions. The balances recorded in the accounts as of March 1 and the entries in the journal are correctly stated. If it is necessary to correct any posted amounts in the ledger, a line should be drawn through the erroneous figure and the correct amount inserted above. Corrections or notations may be inserted on the preliminary trial balance in any manner desired. It is not necessary to complete all of the instructions if equal trial balance totals can be obtained earlier. However, the requirements of instructions (6) and (7) should be completed in any event.

Instructions
1. Verify the totals of the preliminary trial balance, inserting the correct amounts in the schedule provided in the working papers.
2. Compute the difference between the trial balance totals.
3. Compare the listings in the trial balance with the balances appearing in the ledger and list the errors found in the space provided in the working papers.
4. Verify the accuracy of the balance of each account in the ledger and list the errors found in the space provided in the working papers.
5. Trace the postings in the ledger back to the journal, using small check marks to identify items traced. Correct any amounts in the ledger that may be necessitated by errors in posting, and list the errors in the space provided in the working papers.
6. Journalize as of March 31 the payment of $160 for gas and electricity. The bill had been paid on March 31 but was inadvertently omitted from the journal. Post to the ledger. (Revise any amounts necessitated by posting this entry.)
7. Prepare a new trial balance.

PROBLEM 2-7B
CORRECTED TRIAL
BALANCE
Objectives 6, 7

Wells Photography, a sole proprietorship, has the following trial balance as of October 31 of the current year:

Cash	4,735	
Accounts Receivable	9,925	
Supplies	1,277	
Prepaid Insurance	330	
Equipment	12,500	
Notes Payable		5,000
Accounts Payable		3,025
Elaine Wells, Capital		12,490
Elaine Wells, Drawing	6,750	
Fees Earned		80,750
Wages Expense	48,150	
Rent Expense	750	
Advertising Expense	5,250	
Gas, Electricity, and Water Expense	3,150	
	92,817	101,265

SPREADSHEET
PROBLEM

The debit and credit totals are not equal as a result of the following errors:
a. The balance of cash was understated by $1,000.
b. A cash receipt of $540 was posted as a debit to Cash of $450.
c. A debit of $175 to Accounts Receivable was not posted.
d. A return of $252 of defective supplies was erroneously posted as a $225 credit to Supplies.
e. An insurance policy acquired at a cost of $310 was posted as a credit to Prepaid Insurance.
f. The balance of Notes Payable was understated by $2,500.
g. A credit of $75 in Accounts Payable was overlooked when the balance of the account was determined.
h. A debit of $750 for a withdrawal by the owner was posted as a credit to Elaine Wells, Capital.
i. The balance of $7,500 in Rent Expense was entered as $750 in the trial balance.
j. Miscellaneous Expense, with a balance of $915, was omitted from the trial balance.

Instructions

1. Prepare a corrected trial balance as of October 31 of the current year.

**SHARPEN YOUR
COMMUNICATION SKILLS** ►

2. Does the fact that the trial balance in (1) is balanced mean that there are no errors in the accounts? Explain.

MINI-CASE 2 PECK CADDY SERVICES

During June through August, Fran Peck is planning to manage and operate Peck Caddy Service at Flamingo Golf and Country Club. Fran will rent a small maintenance building from the country club for $100 per month and will offer caddy services, including cart rentals, to golfers. Fran has had no formal training in record keeping. During June, she kept notes of all receipts and expenses in a shoe box.

An examination of Fran's shoe box records for June revealed the following:

June 1. Withdrew $1,000 from personal bank account to be used to operate the caddy service.
1. Paid rent to Flamingo Golf and Country Club, $100.
2. Paid for golf supplies (practice balls, etc.), $190.
2. Paid miscellaneous expenses, $50.
3. Arranged for the rental of forty regular (pulling) golf carts and ten gasoline-driven carts for $1,000 per month. Paid $500 in advance, with the remaining $500 due June 20.
7. Purchased supplies, including gasoline, for the golf carts on account, $325. Flamingo Golf and Country Club has agreed to allow Fran to store the gasoline in one of its fuel tanks at no cost.
15. Cash receipts for June 1-15, $990.
15. For June 1-15, accepted IOUs from customers on account, $210.
15. Paid salary of part-time employees, $110.
17. Paid cash to creditors on account, $180.
20. Paid remaining rental on golf carts, $500.
22. Purchased supplies, including gasoline, on account, $280.

25. Received cash in payment of IOUs on account, $150.
28. Paid miscellaneous expenses, $60.
30. Cash receipts for June 16-30, $1,475.
30. For June 16-30, accepted IOUs from customers on account, $150.
30. Paid electricity (utilities) expense, $55.
30. Paid telephone (utilities) expense, $30.
30. Paid salary of part-time employees, $110.
30. Supplies on hand at the end of June, $170.

Fran has asked you several questions concerning her financial affairs to date, and she has asked you to assist with her record keeping and reporting of financial data.

Instructions:

1. To assist Fran with her record keeping, prepare a chart of accounts that would be appropriate for Peck Caddy Services.
2. Prepare an income statement for June in order to help Fran assess the profitability of Peck Caddy Services. For this purpose, the use of T accounts may be helpful in analyzing the effects of each of the June transactions.
3. Based on Fran's records of receipts and payments, calculate the amount of cash on hand on June 30. For this purpose, a T account for cash may be useful.
4. ■ ► A count of the cash on hand on June 30 totaled $420. Briefly discuss the possible causes of the difference between the amount of cash computed in (3) and the actual amount of cash on hand.

ANSWERS TO SELF-EXAMINATION QUESTIONS

1. **A** A debit may signify an increase in asset accounts (answer A) or a decrease in liability and owner's capital accounts. A credit may signify a decrease in asset accounts (answer B) or an increase in liability and owner's capital accounts (answers C and D).

2. **C** Liabili·y, capital, and revenue (answer C) accounts have normal credit balances. Asset (answer A), drawing (answer B), and expense (answer D) accounts have normal debit balances.

3. **C** Accounts Receivable (answer A), Cash (answer B), and Miscellaneous Expense (answer D) would all normally have debit balances. Fees Earned should normally have a credit balance. Hence, a debit balance in Fees Earned (answer C) would indicate an error in the recording process.

4. **A** The receipt of cash from customers on account increases the asset Cash and decreases the asset Accounts Receivable, as indicated by answer A. Answer B has the debit and credit reversed, and answers C and D involve transactions with creditors (accounts payable) and not customers (accounts receivable).

5. **D** The trial balance (answer D) is a listing of the balances and the titles of the accounts in the ledger on a given date, so that the equality of the debits and credits in the ledger can be verified. The income statement (answer A) is a summary of revenue and expenses for a period of time, the balance sheet (answer B) is a presentation of the assets, liabilities, and owner's equity on a given date, and the statement of owner's equity (answer C) is a summary of the changes in owner's equity for a period of time.

You and Accounting

Assume that you rented an apartment last month and signed a nine-month lease. When you signed the lease agreement, you were required to pay the final month's rent of $500.

You are now applying for a student loan at a local bank. The loan application requires a listing of all your assets. Should you list the $500 deposit as an asset?

The answer to this question is "yes." The deposit is an asset to you until you receive the use of the apartment in the ninth month.

A business enterprise faces similar accounting problems at the end of a period. A business must determine what assets, liabilities, and owner's equity should be reported on its balance sheet. It must also determine what revenues and expenses should be reported on its income statement. This chapter discusses concepts and procedures that a business would use in preparing its financial statements.

Chapter 3
The Matching Concept and the Adjusting Process

LEARNING OBJECTIVES
After studying this chapter, you should be able to:

Objective 1
Explain how the matching concept relates to the accrual basis of accounting.

Objective 2
Explain why adjustments are necessary and list the characteristics of adjusting entries.

Objective 3
Journalize entries for accounts requiring adjustment.

Objective 4
Enter adjustments on a work sheet and prepare an adjusted trial balance.

Transactions are recorded as they occur, as illustrated in Chapter 2. At the end of an accounting period, the ledger accounts must be analyzed and, if necessary, updated to ensure that revenues and expenses are properly matched. This matching concept ensures that the income statement fairly presents the results of operations for a period and the balance sheet fairly presents the financial condition at the end of the period.

This chapter describes the matching concept and how accounts are updated at the end of the accounting period. Accounts that normally require updating are described, and the journal entries necessary to update the accounts are illustrated. The chapter concludes with a discussion of the use of the work sheet in the adjustment process.

THE MATCHING CONCEPT

Revenues and expenses may be reported on the income statement, using either (1) the cash basis of accounting or (2) the accrual basis of accounting. When the cash basis is used, revenues are reported in the period in which cash is received and expenses are reported in the period in which cash is paid. For example, fees are recorded when cash is received from clients and wages expense is recorded when cash is paid to employees. The net income (or net loss) is the difference between the cash receipts (revenues) and the cash payments (expenses).

Small service enterprises that have few receivables and payables often use the cash basis of accounting. For example, accountants, attorneys, physicians, and real estate agents often use the cash basis. Also, most individuals use the cash basis of accounting in their personal financial records. For most businesses, however, the cash basis will not provide accurate financial statements for user needs. For this reason, the accrual basis will be emphasized in the remainder of this text.

When the accrual basis of accounting is used, revenues are reported in the period in which they are earned. Expenses are reported in the period in which they are incurred in producing revenues. For example, revenue is recorded as services are provided to customers. Cash may be received from customers at this time or at a later date if the services are provided on account. Likewise, wages expense is recorded in the period when the employees work and not when the cash is paid.

Generally accepted accounting principles require the use of the accrual basis. The accrual basis ensures that the expenses incurred are properly **matched** with the revenues they generate. In this way, the income statement will properly report the revenues earned, the expenses incurred, and the resulting income or loss for the period. The accounting principle that requires the matching of revenues and expenses is called the matching concept or **matching principle**.

The matching concept requires an analysis and updating of some accounts at the end of an accounting period. This process of analyzing and updating accounts in the ledger is called the adjusting process. The adjusting process is further described in the following paragraphs.

NATURE OF THE ADJUSTING PROCESS

At the end of an accounting period, many of the balances of accounts in the ledger can be reported, without change, in the financial statements. For example, the balance of the cash account is normally the amount reported on the balance sheet as the cash on hand at the end of the accounting period.

Some accounts in the ledger, however, require updating. For example, the balances listed for prepaid expenses are normally overstated because the use of these assets is not recorded on a day-to-day basis. The balance of the supplies account usually represents the cost of supplies at the beginning of the period plus the cost of supplies acquired during the period. The day-to-day use of supplies is not recorded, since to do so would require many entries with small amounts. In addition, the total amount of supplies is small relative to other assets, and managers usually do not require day-to-day information on the amount of supplies on hand.

Another example of a prepaid expense account that requires updating is Prepaid Insurance. The balance in Prepaid Insurance represents the beginning balance plus the cost of insurance policies acquired during the period. Journal entries are not made daily for the premiums as they expire. To make such entries would be costly and unnecessary.

The journal entries at the end of an accounting period to bring the accounts up to date and to properly match revenues and expenses are called adjusting entries. By their nature, *all adjusting entries affect at least one income statement account and one balance sheet account.* Thus, an adjusting entry will always involve a revenue or an expense account and an asset or a liability account.

Two basic classifications of items give rise to adjusting entries. The first class of items, deferrals, is created by recording a transaction in a way that delays or defers the recognition of an expense or a revenue. Deferrals may be either deferred expenses or deferred revenues, as described below.

Deferred expenses are items that have been initially recorded as assets but are expected to become expenses over time or through the normal operations of the enterprise. The supplies and prepaid insurance discussed in the preceding paragraphs are examples of deferred expenses. The supplies become an expense as they are used, and the prepaid insurance becomes an expense as time passes and the insurance expires. Deferred expenses are often called **prepaid expenses**.

Deferred revenues are items that have been initially recorded as liabilities but are expected to become revenues over time or through the normal operations of the enterprise. Examples of deferred revenues include tuition received by a college at the beginning of a term and magazine subscriptions received in advance by a publisher. The tuition is earned throughout the term as students attend class. The subscriptions are earned as the magazines are published and distributed. Deferred revenues are often called **unearned revenues**.

The second class of items that give rise to adjusting entries is accruals. Accruals are created by the failure to record an expense that has been incurred or a revenue that has been earned. Accruals may be either accrued expenses or accrued revenues, as described below.

Accrued expenses are expenses that have been incurred *but have not been recorded* in the accounts. Examples of accrued expenses include unrecorded wages owed to employees at the end of a period and unrecorded interest owed on loans. Accrued expenses are often called **accrued liabilities**.

Accrued revenues are revenues that have been earned *but have not been recorded* in the accounts. Examples of accrued revenues include unrecorded fees earned by an attorney or unrecorded commissions earned by a real estate agent. Accrued revenues are often called **accrued assets.**

The primary difference between deferrals and accruals is that deferrals have been recorded while accruals have not been recorded. The adjusting entries for deferrals and accruals are described and illustrated in the following paragraphs. These entries are based on the ledger of Computer King, as reported in the December 31 trial balance in Exhibit 1.

Exhibit 1
Unadjusted Trial Balance for Computer King

Computer King		
Trial Balance		
December 31, 1993		
Cash	2 0 6 5 00	
Accounts Receivable	2 2 2 0 00	
Supplies	2 0 0 0 00	
Prepaid Insurance	2 4 0 0 00	
Land	10 0 0 0 00	
Office Equipment	1 8 0 0 00	
Accounts Payable		9 0 0 00
Unearned Rent		3 6 0 00
Jere King, Capital		15 0 0 0 00
Jere King, Drawing	4 0 0 0 00	
Fees Earned		16 3 4 0 00
Wages Expense	4 2 7 5 00	
Rent Expense	1 6 0 0 00	
Utilities Expense	9 8 5 00	
Supplies Expense	8 0 0 00	
Miscellaneous Expense	4 5 5 00	
	32 6 0 0 00	32 6 0 0 00

An expanded chart of accounts for Computer King is shown in Exhibit 2. The additional accounts that will be used in this chapter are shown in color.

Exhibit 2
Expanded Chart of Accounts for Computer King

Balance Sheet Accounts	Income Statement Accounts
1. Assets	**4. Revenue**
11 Cash	41 Fees Earned
12 Accounts Receivable	42 Rent Income
14 Supplies	**5. Expenses**
15 Prepaid Insurance	51 Wages Expense
17 Land	52 Rent Expense
18 Office Equipment	53 Depreciation Expense
19 Accumulated Depreciation	54 Utilities Expense
2. Liabilities	55 Supplies Expense
21 Accounts Payable	56 Insurance Expense
22 Wages Payable	59 Miscellaneous Expense
23 Unearned Rent	
3. Owner's Equity	
31 Jere King, Capital	
32 Jere King, Drawing	

RECORDING ADJUSTING ENTRIES

Objective 3
Journalize entries for accounts requiring adjustment.

To simplify the examples of adjusting entries in the following paragraphs, T accounts are used. The balances reported on the trial balance for Computer King are identified in the T accounts. The adjusting entries are shown in color in the accounts.

Deferred Expenses (Prepaid Expenses)

The concept of adjusting the accounting records was introduced in Chapters 1 and 2 in the illustration for Computer King. In that illustration, supplies were purchased on November 10 (Transaction c). The supplies used during November were recorded on November 30 (Transaction g). In practice, this matching of revenues and expenses is part of the normal adjusting process that takes place only at the end of the accounting period.

The balance in Computer King's supplies account on December 31 is $2,000. Some of these supplies (computer diskettes, paper, envelopes, etc.) were used during December and some are still on hand. If either amount is known, the other can be readily determined. It is normally easier to determine the cost of the supplies on hand at the end of the month than it is to keep a record of those used daily. Assuming that the inventory of supplies on December 31 is $760, the amount to be transferred from the asset account to the expense account is $1,240, computed as follows:

Supplies available (balance of account)	$2,000
Supplies on hand (inventory)	760
Supplies used (amount of adjustment)	$1,240

As discussed in Chapter 2, increases in expense accounts are recorded as debits and decreases in asset accounts are recorded as credits. Hence, at the end of December, the supplies expense account should be debited for $1,240 and the supplies account should be credited for $1,240 to record the supplies used during December. The adjusting journal entry and T accounts for Supplies and Supplies Expense are as follows:

Supplies Expense	1,240	
Supplies		1,240

Supplies				Supplies Expense		
Bal.	2,000	Dec. 31	1,240	Bal.	800	
760				Dec. 31	1,240	
					2,040	

After the adjustment has been recorded and posted, the supplies account has a debit balance of $760. This balance represents an asset that will become an expense in a future period.

The debit balance of $2,400 in Computer King's prepaid insurance account represents a December 1 prepayment of insurance for 24 months. At the end of December, the insurance expense account should be increased (debited) and the prepaid insurance account should be decreased (credited) by $100, the insurance for one month. The adjusting journal entry and the T accounts for Prepaid Insurance and Insurance Expense are as follows:

Insurance Expense   100
    Prepaid Insurance   100

Prepaid Insurance				Insurance Expense	
Bal.	2,400	Dec. 31	100	Dec. 31	100
	2,300				

After the adjustment has been recorded and posted, the prepaid insurance account has a debit balance of $2,300. This balance represents an asset that will become an expense in future periods. The insurance expense account has a debit balance of $100, which is an expense of the current period.

If the preceding adjustments for supplies ($1,240) and insurance ($100) are not recorded, the financial statements prepared as of December 31 will be misstated. On the income statement, Supplies Expense and Insurance Expense would be understated by a total of $1,340 and net income would be overstated by $1,340. On the balance sheet, Supplies and Prepaid Insurance would be overstated by a total of $1,340. Since net income increases owner's equity, Jere King, Capital would also be overstated by $1,340 on the balance sheet. The effects of omitting these adjusting entries on the income statement and balance sheet are shown below.

	Amount of Misstatement
Income Statement	
Revenues correctly stated	$ xxx
Expenses understated by	(1,340)
Net income overstated by	$1,340
Balance Sheet	
Assets overstated by	$1,340
Liabilities correctly stated	$ xxx
Owner's equity overstated by	1,340
Total liabilities and owner's equity overstated by	$1,340

(1)   (2)

Arrows (1) and (2) indicate how omitting adjusting entries affects both the income statement and the balance sheet. Arrow (1) indicates the effects on the expenses and assets. Arrow (2) indicates the effect of the overstated net income on owner's equity. On the balance sheet, the assets and the total liabilities and owner's equity are misstated by the same amount.

Supplies and prepaid insurance are two examples of prepaid expenses that may require adjustment at the end of an accounting period. Other examples of prepaid expenses that may require adjustment are prepaid advertising and prepaid interest.

Prepayments of expenses are sometimes made at the beginning of the period during which they will be *entirely consumed*. On December 1, for example, Computer King paid rent of $800 for the month of December. On December 1, the rent payment represents the asset prepaid rent. The prepaid rent expires daily, and at the end of December the entire amount has become an expense (rent expense). In cases such as this, the initial payment is recorded as an expense rather than as an asset. During the month, the expense account debited will include an amount that represents an asset, but it will be entirely an expense at the end of the period. Thus, if the payment is recorded as a debit to Rent Expense, no adjusting entry is needed at the end of the period.[1]

Deferred Revenue (Unearned Revenue)

According to Computer King's trial balance on December 31, the balance in the unearned rent account is $360. This balance represents the receipt of three months' rent on December 1 for December, January, and February. At the end of December, the unearned rent account should be decreased by $120 (debited) and the rent income account should be increased by $120 (credited). The $120 represents the rental income for one month ($360 ÷ 3). The adjusting journal entry and T accounts are shown below.

Unearned Rent	120	
Rent Income		120

Unearned Rent				Rent Income		
Dec. 31	120	Bal.	360		Dec. 31	120
			240			

After the adjustment has been recorded and posted, the unearned rent account, which is a liability, has a credit balance of $240. This balance represents a deferral that will become revenue in a future period. The rent income account has a balance of $120, which is revenue of the current period.

If the preceding adjustment of unearned rent and rent income is not recorded, the financial statements prepared on December 31 will be misstated. On the income statement, Rent Income and the net income will be understated by $120. On the balance sheet, Unearned Rent will be overstated by $120, and Jere King, Capital will be understated by $120. The effects of omitting this adjusting entry are shown below.

	Amount of Misstatement
Income Statement	
Revenues understated by	$ (120)
Expenses correctly stated	xxx
Net income understated by	$ (120)
Balance Sheet	
Assets correctly stated	$ xxx
Liabilities overstated by	$ 120
Owner's equity understated by	(120)
Total liabilities and owner's equity correctly stated	$ xxx

The only unearned revenue for Computer King was unearned rent. Other examples of unearned revenue that may require adjustment include tuition received in advance by a school, an annual retainer fee received by an attorney, premiums received in advance by an insurance company, and amounts received in advance by an advertising firm for advertising services to be rendered in the future.[2]

---

[1] An alternative treatment of recording the cost of supplies, rent, and other prepayments of expenses is discussed in Appendix C.

[2] An alternative treatment of recording revenues received in advance is discussed in Appendix C.

Accrued Expenses (Accrued Liabilities)

Some types of services, such as insurance, are normally paid for *before* they are used. These prepayments are deferrals. Other types of services are paid for *after* the service has been performed. For example, wages expense accumulates or *accrues* hour by hour and day by day, but payment may be made only weekly, biweekly, or monthly. The amount of such an accrued but unpaid item at the end of the accounting period is both an expense and a liability. For this reason, such accruals are called **accrued expenses** or **accrued liabilities**. In the case of wages expense, if the last day of a pay period is not the last day of the accounting period, the accrued expense and the related liability must be recorded in the accounts by an adjusting entry. This adjusting entry is necessary so that expenses are matched to the period in which they were incurred.

At the end of December, accrued wages for Computer King were $250. This amount is an additional expense of December and is debited to the wages expense account. It is also a liability as of December 31 and is credited to Wages Payable. The adjusting journal entry and T accounts are shown below.

Wages Expense   250
    Wages Payable   250

	Wages Expense			Wages Payable	
Bal.	4,275			Dec. 31	250
Dec. 31	250				
	4,525				

After the adjustment has been recorded and posted, the debit balance of the wages expense account is $4,525, which is the wages expense for the two months, November and December. The credit balance of $250 in Wages Payable is the amount of the liability for wages owed as of December 31.

The accrual of the wages expense for Computer King is summarized in Exhibit 3. Note that Computer King paid wages of $950 on December 13 and $1,200 on December 27. These payments represent biweekly payroll payments made on alternate Fridays for the pay periods ending on those days. The wages of $250 earned for Monday and Tuesday, December 30 and 31, are accrued at December 31. The wages paid on January 10 totaled $1,275, which included the $250 accrued wages of December 31.

Exhibit 3
Accrued Wages

1. Wages are paid on the second and fourth Fridays for the two-week periods ending on those Fridays. The payments were $950 on December 13 and $1,200 on December 27.

2. The wages accrued for Monday and Tuesday, December 30 and 31, are $250.

3. Wages paid on Friday, January 10, total $1,275.

December

S	M	T	W	T	F	S	
1	2	3	4	5	6	7	Wages expense (paid), $950
8	9	10	11	12	13	14	
15	16	17	18	19	20	21	
22	23	24	25	26	27	28	Wages expense (paid), $1,200
29	30	31					

Wages expense (accrued), $250

January

S	M	T	W	T	F	S
			1	2	3	4
5	6	7	8	9	10	11

Wages expense (paid), $1,275

If the adjustment for wages ($250) is not recorded, the income statement for the period and the balance sheet as of December 31 will be misstated. On the income statement, Wages Expense will be understated by $250, and the net income will be overstated by $250. On the balance sheet, Wages Payable will be understated by $250, and Jere King, Capital will be overstated by $250. These effects of omitting the adjusting entry are shown below.

	Amount of Misstatement
Income Statement	
Revenues correctly stated	$ xxx
Expenses understated by	(250)
Net income overstated by	$ 250
Balance Sheet	
Assets correctly stated	$ xxx
Liabilities understated by	$(250)
Owner's equity overstated by	250
Total liabilities and	
owner's equity correctly stated	$ xxx

Accrued wages is an example of an accrued expense that must be recorded by an adjusting entry. Other accrued expenses include accrued interest on notes payable and accrued taxes.

Accrued Revenues (Accrued Assets)

All assets belonging to a business at the end of an accounting period and all revenue earned during a period should be recorded in the ledger. During an accounting period it is normal to record some revenues only when cash is received. Thus, at the end of an accounting period there may be items of revenue that have been earned *but have not been recorded.* In such cases, the amount of the revenue should be recorded by debiting an asset account and crediting a revenue account. Because of the dual nature of such accruals, they are called **accrued revenues** or **accrued assets**.

To illustrate, assume that Computer King signed an agreement with Dankner Co. on December 15. The agreement provides that Computer King will be on call to answer questions and render assistance to Dankner Co.'s employees concerning computer problems. The services provided will be billed to Dankner Co. on the fifteenth of each month at a rate of $20 per hour. As of December 31, Computer King had provided 25 hours of assistance to Dankner Co. Although the revenue of $500 (25 hours × $20) will be billed and collected in January, Computer King earned the revenue in December. The adjusting journal entry and T accounts to record the claim against the customer (an account receivable) and the revenue earned in December are shown below.

Accounts Receivable   500
   Fees Earned   500

Accounts Receivable				Fees Earned		
Bal.	2,220				Bal.	16,340
Dec. 31	500			Dec. 31		500
	2,720					16,840

If the adjustment for the accrued asset ($500) is not recorded, the income statement for the period and the balance sheet as of December 31 will be misstated. On the income statement, Fees Earned and the net income will be understated by $500. On the balance sheet, Accounts Receivable and Jere King, Capital will be understated by $500. These effects of omitting the adjusting entry are shown below.

	Amount of Misstatement
Income Statement	
Revenues understated by	(500)
Expenses correctly stated	xxx
Net income understated by	$(500)
Balance Sheet	
Assets understated by	$(500)
Liabilities correctly stated	$ xxx
Owner's equity understated by	(500)
Total liabilities and owner's equity understated by	$(500)

Accrued fees is an example of an accrued revenue that must be recorded by an adjusting entry to properly match revenues and expenses. Other accruals that would require similar treatment include accrued interest on notes receivable and accrued rent on property rented to others.

Plant Assets

Tangible assets that are owned by a business enterprise, are permanent or have a long life, and are used in the business are called **plant assets** or **fixed assets**. In a sense, plant assets are a type of long-term deferred expense. However, because of their nature and long life, they are discussed separately from other deferred expenses, such as supplies and prepaid insurance.

Computer King's plant assets include office equipment that is used much like the supplies are used to generate revenue. Unlike supplies, however, there is no visible reduction in the quantity of the equipment. Instead, as time passes, the equipment loses its ability to provide useful services. This decrease in usefulness is called *depreciation.*

All plant assets, except land, lose their usefulness. Any decrease in an asset used to generate revenue is an expense. However, it is difficult to objectively measure the decrease in usefulness of a plant asset. For this reason, **depreciation** in accounting is the systematic allocation of a plant asset's cost to expense. This allocation occurs over the asset's estimated life during which it is expected to generate revenue. Methods of computing depreciation are discussed and illustrated in a later chapter.

The adjusting entry to record depreciation is similar to the adjusting entry for supplies used, in which an expense account is debited and an asset account is credited. The account debited is a depreciation expense account. However, the asset account Office Equipment is not credited because both the original cost of a plant asset and the amount of depreciation recorded since its purchase are normally reported on the balance sheet. The account credited is an **accumulated depreciation account,** which is reported on the balance sheet as a deduction from the asset account. Accumulated depreciation accounts are called **contra accounts** or **contra asset accounts** because they are reported as deductions from the related asset accounts.

Normal titles for plant asset accounts and their related contra asset accounts are as follows:

Plant Asset	*Contra Asset*
Land	None—Land is not depreciated
Buildings	Accumulated Depreciation—Buildings
Equipment	Accumulated Depreciation—Equipment

The ledger could have a separate account for each of a number of buildings. Equipment may also be subdivided according to function, such as Delivery Equipment, Store Equipment, and Office Equipment, with a related accumulated depreciation account for each plant asset account.

The adjusting entry to record depreciation for December for Computer King is illustrated in the following journal entry and T accounts. The estimated amount of depreciation for the month is assumed to be $50.

Depreciation Expense   50
    Accumulated Depreciation—Office Equipment   50

Office Equipment		Accumulated Depreciation	
Bal.	1,800	Dec. 31	50

		Depreciation Expense	
Dec. 31	50		

The $50 increase in the accumulated depreciation account represents a subtraction from the $1,800 cost recorded in the related plant asset account. The difference between the two balances is the unexpired, undepreciated, or unallocated cost. This amount ($1,750) is called the book value of the asset. The book value may be presented on the balance sheet in the following manner:

Office equipment $1,800
    Less accumulated depreciation   50 $1,750

If the previous adjustment for depreciation ($50) is not recorded, the financial statements as of December 31 will be misstated. On the income statement, Depreciation Expense will be understated by $50, and the net income will be overstated by $50. On the balance sheet, the book value of the office equipment and Jere King, Capital will be overstated by $50. The effects of omitting the adjustment for depreciation are shown below.

	Amount of Misstatement
Income Statement	
Revenues correctly stated	$ xx
Expenses understated by	(50)
Net income overstated by	$ 50
Balance Sheet	
Assets overstated by	$ 50
Liabilities correctly stated	$ xx
Owner's equity overstated by	50
Total liabilities and	
owner's equity overstated by	$ 50

WORK SHEET

Objective 4
Enter adjustments on a work sheet and prepare an adjusted trial balance.

Before adjusting entries such as those described above can be prepared, the relevant data must be assembled. For example, the cost of supplies on hand and the wages accrued at the end of the period must be determined. Such data and analyses are summarized by accountants in **working papers**.

A working paper often used by accountants to summarize adjusting entries and assist in the preparation of the financial statements is the work sheet. The name of the business, the type of working paper (work sheet), and the period of time should be listed at the top of the work sheet, as shown in Exhibit 4. Such work sheets can be prepared quickly with the use of computer spreadsheet programs.

Trial Balance Columns

The trial balance discussed in Chapter 2 may be prepared directly on the work sheet. The work sheet in Exhibit 4 shows the trial balance for Computer King at December 31, 1993.

Exhibit 4
Work Sheet with Trial Balance Entered

Computer King
Work Sheet
For Two Months Ended December 31, 1993

	Trial Balance		Adjustments		Adjusted Trial Balance		Income Statement		Balance Sheet	
	Dr.	Cr.	Dr.	Cr.	Dr.	Cr.	Dr.	Cr.	Dr.	Cr.
Cash	2,065									
Accounts Receivable	2,220									
Supplies	2,000									
Prepaid Insurance	2,400									
Land	10,000									
Office Equipment	1,800									
Accounts Payable		900								
Unearned Rent		360								
Jere King, Capital		15,000								
Jere King, Drawing	4,000									
Fees Earned		16,340								
Wages Expense	4,275									
Rent Expense	1,600									
Utilities Expense	985									
Supplies Expense	800									
Miscellaneous Expense	455									
	32,600	32,600								

> The worksheet is used for assembling data and summarizing the effects of adjusting entries. It also aids in the preparation of financial statements.

Adjustments Columns

The adjustment data are entered on the work sheet in the Adjustments columns. Both the debit and the credit amounts are inserted for the proper accounts for each adjustment. Cross-referencing the debit and credit of each adjustment by letters is useful in reviewing the work sheet. It is also helpful when the adjusting entries are recorded in the journal.

The order in which the adjustments are entered on the work sheet is not important. Most accountants enter the adjustments in the order in which the data are assembled. If the titles of some of the accounts to be adjusted do not appear in the trial balance, they should be inserted in the Account Title column, below the trial balance totals, as needed. The adjustments for Computer King which were explained and illustrated earlier in the chapter have been entered on the work sheet in Exhibit 5.

Explanations for the entries in the Adjustments columns of the work sheet follow:

(a) **Supplies**. The supplies account has a debit balance of $2,000. The cost of the supplies on hand at the end of the period is $760. Therefore, the supplies expense for December is the difference between the two amounts, or $1,240. The adjustment is entered by writing (1) **$1,240** in the Adjustments Debit column on the same line as Supplies Expense and (2) **$1,240** in the Adjustments Credit column on the same line as Supplies.

Exhibit 5
Work Sheet with Trial Balance and Adjustments Entered

Computer King
Work Sheet
For Two Months Ended December 31, 1993

Account Title	Trial Balance Dr.	Trial Balance Cr.	Adjustments Dr.	Adjustments Cr.	Adjusted Trial Balance Dr.	Adjusted Trial Balance Cr.	Income Statement Dr.	Income Statement Cr.	Balance Sheet Dr.	Balance Sheet Cr.
Cash	2,065									
Accounts Receivable	2,220		(e) 500							
Supplies	2,000			(a)1,240						
Prepaid Insurance	2,400			(b) 100						
Land	10,000									
Office Equipment	1,800									
Accounts Payable		900								
Unearned Rent		360	(c) 120							
Jere King, Capital		15,000								
Jere King, Drawing	4,000									
Fees Earned		16,340		(e) 500						
Wages Expense	4,275		(d) 250							
Rent Expense	1,600									
Utilities Expense	985									
Supplies Expense	800		(a)1,240							
Miscellaneous Expense	455									
	32,600	32,600								
Insurance Expense			(b) 100							
Rent Income				(c) 120						
Wages Payable				(d) 250						
Depreciation Expense			(f) 50							
Accumulated Depreciation				(f) 50						
			2,260	2,260						

Accounts are added, as needed, to complete the adjustments.

(a) Supplies used, $1,240 ($2,000 – $760).
(b) Insurance expired, $100.
(c) Rent earned from amount received in advance, $120.
(d) Wages accrued but not paid, $250.
(e) Fees earned but not received, $500.
(f) Depreciation of office equipment, $50.

(b) **Prepaid Insurance**. The prepaid insurance account has a debit balance of $2,400, which represents the prepayment of insurance for 24 months beginning December 1. Thus, the insurance expense for December is $100 ($2,400 ÷ 24). The adjustment is entered by writing (1) Insurance Expense in the Account Title column, (2) $100 in the Adjustments Debit column on the same line as Insurance Expense and (3) $100 in the Adjustments Credit column on the same line as Prepaid Insurance.

(c) **Unearned Rent**. The unearned rent account has a credit balance of $360, which represents the receipt of three months' rent, beginning with December. Thus, the rent income for December is $120. The adjustment is entered by writing (1) $120 in the Adjustments Debit column on the same line as Unearned Rent, (2) Rent Income in the Account Title column, and (3) $120 in the Adjustments Credit column on the same line as Rent Income.

(d) **Wages**. Wages accrued but not paid at the end of December total $250. This amount is an increase in expenses and an increase in liabilities. The adjustment is entered by writing (1) $250 in the Adjustments Debit column on the same line as Wages Expense, (2) Wages Payable in the Account Title column, and (3) $250 in the Adjustments Credit column on the same line as Wages Payable.

(e) **Accrued Fees**. Fees accrued at the end of December but not recorded total $500. This amount is an increase in an asset and an increase in revenue. The adjustment is entered by writing (1) $500 in the Adjustments Debit column on the same line as Accounts Receivable and (2) $500 in the Adjustments Credit column on the same line as Fees Earned.

(f) **Depreciation**. Depreciation of the office equipment is $50 for December. The adjustment is entered by writing (1) Depreciation Expense in the Account Title column, (2) $50 in the Adjustments Debit column on the same line as Depreciation Expense, (3) Accumulated Depreciation in the Account Title column, and (4) $50 in the Adjustments Credit column on the same line as Accumulated Depreciation.

The Adjustments columns are totaled to verify the mathematical accuracy of the adjustment data. The total of the Debit column must equal the total of the Credit column.

Adjusted Trial Balance Columns

The data in the Trial Balance columns are added to or subtracted from the adjustments data and extended to the Adjusted Trial Balance columns, as shown on the work sheet in Exhibit 6. For example, the cash account is extended at its original

Exhibit 6
Work Sheet with Trial Balance, Adjustments,
and Adjusted Trial Balance Entered

Computer King
Work Sheet
For Two Months Ended December 31, 1993

Account Title	Trial Balance Dr.	Trial Balance Cr.	Adjustments Dr.	Adjustments Cr.	Adjusted Trial Balance Dr.	Adjusted Trial Balance Cr.	Income Statement Dr.	Income Statement Cr.	Balance Sheet Dr.	Balance Sheet Cr.
Cash	2,065				2,065					
Accounts Receivable	2,220		(e) 500		2,720					
Supplies	2,000			(a) 1,240	760					
Prepaid Insurance	2,400			(b) 100	2,300					
Land	10,000				10,000					
Office Equipment	1,800				1,800					
Accounts Payable		900				900				
Unearned Rent		360	(c) 120			240				
Jere King, Capital		15,000				15,000				
Jere King, Drawing	4,000				4,000					
Fees Earned		16,340		(e) 500		16,840				
Wages Expense	4,275		(d) 250		4,525					
Rent Expense	1,600				1,600					
Utilities Expense	985				985					
Supplies Expense	800		(a) 1,240		2,040					
Miscellaneous Expense	455				455					
	32,600	32,600								
Insurance Expense			(b) 100		100					
Rent Income				(c) 120		120				
Wages Payable				(d) 250		250				
Depreciation Expense			(f) 50		50					
Accumulated Depreciation				(f) 50		50				
			2,260	2,260	33,400	33,400				

> The adjusted trial balance amounts are determined by extending the trial balance amounts plus or minus the adjustments. For example, the Wages Expense debit of $4,525 is the trial balance amount of $4,275 plus the $250 adjustment debit.

amount of $2,065, since no adjustments affected Cash. Accounts Receivable has an initial balance of $2,220 and a debit adjustment (increase) of $500. The amount to be extended is the debit balance of $2,720. The same procedure is continued until all account balances have been extended to the Adjusted Trial Balance columns. The Debit and Credit columns are then totaled to verify the equality of the Debit and Credit columns.

Completion of the Work Sheet

The completion of the work sheet, including the use of the Income Statement and Balance Sheet columns, is described and illustrated in Chapter 4. The use of the work sheet in preparing financial statements and the journalizing and posting of the adjusting entries are also discussed in Chapter 4. Finally, the procedures necessary to prepare the accounting records for the next accounting period will be discussed.

CHAPTER REVIEW

Key Points

Objective 1. Explain how the matching concept relates to the accrual basis of accounting.
The accrual basis of accounting requires the use of an adjusting process at the end of the accounting period to match revenues and expenses properly. Revenues are reported in the period in which they are earned, and expenses are matched with the revenues they generate.

Objective 2. Explain why adjustments are necessary and list the characteristics of adjusting entries.
At the end of an accounting period, some of the amounts listed on the trial balance are not necessarily current balances. For example, amounts listed for prepaid expenses are normally overstated because the use of these assets has not been recorded on a daily basis. A delay of the recognition of an expense already paid or a revenue already received is called a deferral.

Some revenues and expenses related to a period may not be recorded at the end of the period, since these items are normally recorded only when cash has been received or paid. A revenue or expense that has not been paid or recorded is called an accrual.

The entries required at the end of an accounting period to bring accounts up to date and to ensure the proper matching of revenues and expenses are called adjusting entries. Adjusting entries require a debit or a credit to a revenue or an expense account and an offsetting debit or credit to an asset or a liability account.

Adjusting entries affect amounts reported in the income statement, the statement of owner's equity, and the balance sheet. Thus, if an adjusting entry is not recorded or incorrectly recorded, these financial statements will be incorrect (misstated).

Objective 3. Journalize entries for accounts requiring adjustment.
Adjusting entries illustrated in this chapter include deferred (prepaid) expenses, deferred (unearned) revenues, accrued expenses (accrued liabilities), and accrued revenues (accrued assets). In addition, the adjusting entry necessary to record depreciation on plant assets was illustrated.

Objective 4. Enter adjustments on a work sheet and prepare an adjusted trial balance.
The work sheet illustrated in this chapter has trial balance, adjustments, adjusted trial balance, income statement, and balance sheet columns. Adjustments are entered on the work sheet in the Adjustments columns. The adjustments are added to or subtracted from the trial balance amounts, and the resulting amounts are extended to the Adjusted Trial Balance columns. The Debit and Credit columns are then totaled to verify the equality of the Debit and Credit columns.

Glossary of Key Terms

Accruals. Expenses that have been incurred or revenues that have been earned, but have not been recorded. **Objective 2**

Accrual basis. Revenues are recognized in the period earned and expenses are recognized in the period incurred in the process of generating revenues. **Objective 1**

Accrued expenses. Expenses that have been incurred but not recorded in the accounts. Sometimes called accrued liabilities. **Objective 2**

Accrued revenues. Revenues that have been earned but not recorded in the accounts. Sometimes called accrued assets. **Objective 2**

Accumulated depreciation account. The contra asset account used to accumulate the depreciation recognized to date on plant assets. **Objective 3**

Adjusting entries. Entries required at the end of an accounting period to bring the ledger up to date. **Objective 2**

Adjusting process. The process of updating the accounts at the end of a period. **Objective 1**

Book value of the asset. The difference between the balance of a plant asset account and its related accumulated depreciation account. **Objective 3**

Cash basis. Revenue is recognized in the period cash is received, and expenses are recognized in the period cash is paid. **Objective 1**

Contra accounts. Accounts that are offset against other accounts. **Objective 3**

Deferrals. Delays in the recognition of expenses that have been incurred or revenues that have been received. **Objective 2**

Deferred expenses. Items that are initially recorded as assets but are expected to become expenses over time or through the normal operations of the enterprise. Sometimes called prepaid expenses. **Objective 2**

Deferred revenues. Items that are initially recorded as liabilities but are expected to become revenues over time or

through the normal operations of the enterprise. Sometimes called unearned revenues. **Objective 2**

Depreciation. In a general sense, the decrease in usefulness of plant assets other than land. In accounting, refers to the systematic allocation of a plant asset's cost to expense. **Objective 3**

Matching concept. The concept that all expenses incurred should be matched with the revenue they generate during a period of time. **Objective 1**

Plant assets. Tangible assets that are owned by a business enterprise, are permanent or have a long life, and are used in the business. **Objective 3**

Work sheet. A working paper used to summarize adjusting entries and assist in the preparation of financial statements. **Objective 4**

Self-Examination Questions
Answers at end of chapter.

1. Which of the following items represents a deferral?
   A. prepaid insurance
   B. wages payable
   C. fees earned
   D. accumulated depreciation

2. If the supplies account, before adjustment on May 31, indicated a balance of $2,250, and supplies on hand at May 31 totaled $950, the adjusting entry would be:
   A. debit Supplies, $950; credit Supplies Expense, $950
   B. debit Supplies, $1,300; credit Supplies Expense, $1,300
   C. debit Supplies Expense, $950; credit Supplies, $950
   D. debit Supplies Expense, $1,300; credit Supplies, $1,300

3. The balance in the unearned rent account for Jones Co. as of December 31 is $1,200. If Jones Co. failed to record the adjusting entry for $600 of rent earned during December, the effect on the balance sheet and income statement for December is:
   A. assets understated $600; net income overstated $600
   B. liabilities understated $600; net income understated $600

   C. liabilities overstated $600; net income understated $600
   D. liabilities overstated $600; net income overstated $600

4. If the estimated amount of depreciation on equipment for a period is $2,000, the adjusting entry to record depreciation would be:
   A. debit Depreciation Expense, $2,000; credit Equipment, $2,000
   B. debit Equipment, $2,000; credit Depreciation Expense, $2,000
   C. debit Depreciation Expense, $2,000; credit Accumulated Depreciation, $2,000
   D. debit Accumulated Depreciation, $2,000; credit Depreciation Expense, $2,000

5. If the equipment account has a balance of $22,500 and its accumulated depreciation account has a balance of $14,000, the book value of the equipment is:
   A. $36,500
   B. $22,500
   C. $14,000
   D. $8,500

ILLUSTRATIVE PROBLEM

Two years ago, K. L. Waters organized Star Realty as a sole proprietorship. At March 31, 1994, the end of the current year, the trial balance of Star Realty is as follows:

Cash	2,425	
Accounts Receivable	5,000	
Supplies	1,870	
Prepaid Insurance	620	
Office Equipment	32,650	
Accumulated Depreciation		9,700
Accounts Payable		925
Unearned Fees		1,250
K. L. Waters, Capital		20,930
K. L. Waters, Drawing	10,200	
Fees Earned		39,125
Wages Expense	12,415	
Rent Expense	3,600	
Utilities Expense	2,715	
Miscellaneous Expense	435	
	71,930	71,930

The data needed to determine year-end adjustments are as follows:

a. Supplies *on hand* at March 31, 1994	$ 480
b. Insurance premiums *expired* during the year	315
c. *Depreciation* on equipment during the year	1,950
d. Wages *accrued but not paid* at March 31, 1994	140
e. Accrued fees *earned but not recorded* at March 31, 1994	1,000
f. *Unearned fees* on March 31, 1994	750

Instructions

1. Enter the March 31, 1994 trial balance on a work sheet.
2. Using the adjustment data, enter the necessary adjustments on the work sheet.
3. Extend the adjustment data on the work sheet to the adjusted trial balance columns.

Solution

1, 2, 3

Star Realty
Work Sheet
For Year Ended March 31,1994

	ACCOUNT TITLE	TRIAL BALANCE DEBIT	TRIAL BALANCE CREDIT	ADJUSTMENTS DEBIT	ADJUSTMENTS CREDIT	ADJUSTED TRIAL BALANCE DEBIT	ADJUSTED TRIAL BALANCE CREDIT
1	Cash	2 4 2 5 00				2 4 2 5 00	
2	Accounts Receivable	5 0 0 0 00		(e)1 0 0 0 00		6 0 0 0 00	
3	Supplies	1 8 7 0 00			(a)1 3 9 0 00	4 8 0 00	
4	Prepaid Insurance	6 2 0 00			(b) 3 1 5 00	3 0 5 00	
5	Office Equipment	32 6 5 0 00				32 6 5 0 00	
6	Accumulated Depreciation	00	9 7 0 0 00		(c)1 9 5 0 00		11 6 5 0 00
7	Accounts Payable	00	9 2 5 00				9 2 5 00
8	Unearned Fees	00	1 2 5 0 00	(f) 5 0 0 00			7 5 0 00
9	K.L. Waters, Capital	00	20 9 3 0 00				20 9 3 0 00
10	K.L. Waters, Drawing	10 2 0 0 00				10 2 0 0 00	
11	Fees Earned		39 1 2 5 00		(e)1 0 0 0 00		40 6 2 5 00
12					(f) 5 0 0 00		
13	Wages Expense	12 4 1 5 00		(d) 1 4 0 00		12 5 5 5 00	
14	Rent Expense	3 6 0 0 00				3 6 0 0 00	
15	Utilities Expense	2 7 1 5 00				2 7 1 5 00	
16	Miscellaneous Expense	4 3 5 00				4 3 5 00	
17		71 9 3 0 00	71 9 3 0 00				
18	Supplies Expense			(a)1 3 9 0 00		1 3 9 0 00	
19	Insurance Expense			(b) 3 1 5 00		3 1 5 00	
20	Depreciation Expense			(c)1 9 5 0 00		1 9 5 0 00	
21	Wages Payable				(d) 1 4 0 00		1 4 0 00
22				5 2 9 5 00	5 2 9 5 00	75 0 2 0 00	75 0 2 0 00
23							
24							
25							
26							
27							
28							
29							
30							
31							
32							

ILLUSTRATIVE PROBLEM ILLUSTRATIVE PROBLEM ILLUSTRATIVE PROBLEM ILLUSTRATIVE PROBLEM

DISCUSSION QUESTIONS

1. How are revenues and expenses reported on the income statement under (a) the cash basis of accounting and (b) the accrual basis of accounting?
2. Fees for services provided are billed to a customer during 1993. The customer remits the amount owed in 1994. During which year would the revenues be reported on the income statement under (a) the cash basis? (b) the accrual basis?
3. Employees performed services in 1993 but the wages were not paid until 1994. During which year would the wages expense be reported on the income statement under (a) the cash basis? (b) the accrual basis?
4. Is the matching concept related to (a) the cash basis of accounting or (b) the accrual basis of accounting?
5. Is the balance listed for cash on the trial balance, before the accounts have been adjusted, the amount that should normally be reported on the balance sheet? Explain.
6. Is the balance listed for supplies on the trial balance, before the accounts have been adjusted, the amount that should normally be reported on the balance sheet? Explain.
7. Why are adjusting entries needed at the end of an accounting period?
8. What is the difference between *adjusting entries* and *correcting entries*?
9. Identify the five different categories of adjusting entries frequently required at the end of an accounting period.
10. If the effect of the credit portion of an adjusting entry is to increase the balance of a liability account, which of the following statements describes the effect of the debit portion of the entry?
    a. Increases the balance of a revenue account.
    b. Increases the balance of an expense account.
    c. Increases the balance of an asset account.
11. Does every adjusting entry have an effect on the determination of the amount of net income for a period? Explain.
12. What is the nature of the balance in the prepaid insurance account at the end of the accounting period (a) before adjustment? (b) after adjustment?
13. On May 1 of the current year, an enterprise paid the May rent on the building that it occupies. (a) Do the rights acquired at May 1 represent an asset or an expense? (b) What is the justification for debiting Rent Expense at the time of payment?
14. At December 31, the end of the first *month* of the year, the usual adjusting entry transferring supplies used to an expense account is inadvertently omitted. Which items will be incorrectly stated, because of the error, on (a) the income statement for the year and (b) the balance sheet as of December 31? Also indicate whether the items in error will be overstated or understated.
15. At the end of January, the first *month* of the year, the usual adjusting entry transferring rent earned to a revenue account from the unearned rent account was omitted. Which items will be incorrectly stated, because of the error, on (a) the income statement for January, (b) the statement of owner's equity for January, and (c) the balance sheet as of January 31? Also indicate whether the items in error will be overstated or understated.
16. Accrued salaries of $3,000 owed to employees for December 30 and 31 are not taken into consideration in preparing the financial statements for the year ended December 31. Which items will be erroneously stated, because of the error, on (a) the income statement for the year and (b) the balance sheet as of December 31? Also indicate whether the items in error will be overstated or understated.
17. Assume that the error in Question 16 was not corrected and that the $3,000 of accrued salaries was included in the first salary payment in January. Which items will be erroneously stated, because of failure to correct the initial error, on (a) the income statement for the month of January and (b) the balance sheet as of January 31?
18. The adjusting entry for accrued fees was omitted at December 31, the end of the current year. Which items will be in error, because of the omission, on (a) the income statement for the current year and (b) the balance sheet as of December 31? Also indicate whether the items in error will be overstated or understated.
19. What are plant assets?
20. What is depreciation?
21. In accounting for depreciation on equipment, what is the name of the account that would be referred to as a contra asset account?

22. (a) Explain the purpose of the two accounts: Depreciation Expense and Accumulated Depreciation. (b) What is the normal balance of each account? (c) Is it customary for the balances of the two accounts to be equal in amount? (d) In what financial statements, if any, will each account appear?

23. What term is applied to the difference between the balance in a plant asset account and its related accumulated depreciation account?

24. The adjusting entry for depreciation of equipment was omitted at December 31, the end of the current year. Which items will be in error, because of the omission, on (a) the income statement for the current year and (b) the balance sheet as of December 31? Also indicate whether the items in error will be overstated or understated.

25. Classify the following items as (a) deferred expense (prepaid expense), (b) deferred revenue (unearned revenue), (c) accrued expense (accrued liability), or (d) accrued revenue (accrued asset).
    (1) Utilities owed but not yet paid.
    (2) Fees received but not yet earned.
    (3) Salary owed but not yet paid.
    (4) A two-year premium paid on a fire insurance policy.
    (5) Fees earned but not yet received.
    (6) Taxes owed but payable in the following period.
    (7) Supplies on hand.
    (8) Tuition collected in advance by a university.

26. Identify each of the following accounts as (a) revenue, (b) expense, (c) asset, or (d) liability:
    (1) Rent Income
    (2) Wages Payable
    (3) Supplies Expense
    (4) Accounts Receivable
    (5) Supplies
    (6) Unearned Rent
    (7) Fees Earned
    (8) Wages Expense

27. What is a work sheet?

REAL W🌐RLD FOCUS   28. Campbell Soup Company reported *Plant Assets, at Cost* of $2,921.9 million and *Accumulated Depreciation* of $1,131.5 million at July 31, 1991, the end of the year. What was the book value of the plant assets at July 31, 1991?

REAL W🌐RLD FOCUS   29. The balance sheet for Tandy Corporation as of June 30, 1991, includes the following accrued expenses as liabilities:

Accrued payroll and bonuses $54,962,000
Accrued sales and payroll taxes   16,949,000
Accrued insurance   37,804,000
Accrued interest   12,148,000

The net income for Tandy Corporation for the year ended June 30, 1991, was $195,444,000. (a) If the accrued expenses had not been recorded at June 30, 1991, how much would net income have been misstated for the fiscal year ended June 30, 1991? (b) What is the percentage of the misstatement in (a) to the reported net income of $195,444,000?

ETHICS DISCUSSION CASE

Paul Martinez opened Martinez Real Estate, a small sole proprietorship, on January 11 of the current year. A CPA friend explained the accrual basis of reporting revenue and expenses, explained that it was the most widely used method, and suggested its use for Martinez Real Estate. Martinez decided that the accrual basis was too complicated and unnecessary for his business. He decided to use the cash basis because almost all expense and revenue transactions were in cash.

Discuss whether Paul Martinez behaved in an ethical manner by using the cash basis for reporting revenue and expenses.

SHARPEN YOUR ►
COMMUNICATION SKILLS

EXERCISES

EXERCISE 3-1
DETERMINATION OF PLANT
ASSET'S BOOK VALUE
Objective 3

The balance in the equipment account is $75,000 and the balance in the accumulated depreciation—equipment account is $25,000.

a. What is the book value of the equipment?

SHARPEN YOUR ►
COMMUNICATION SKILLS

b. Does the balance in the accumulated depreciation account mean that the equipment's loss of value is $25,000? Explain.

EXERCISE 3-2
ADJUSTING ENTRY FOR
SUPPLIES
Objective 3

The balance in the supplies account, before adjustment at the end of the year, is $3,725. Journalize the adjusting entry required if the amount of supplies on hand at the end of the year is $1,575.

EXERCISE 3-3
ADJUSTING ENTRIES FOR
PREPAID INSURANCE
Objective 3

The balance in the prepaid insurance account, before adjustment at the end of the year, is $8,650. Journalize the adjusting entry required under each of the following *alternatives* for determining the amount of the adjustment: (a) the amount of insurance expired during the year is $4,900; (b) the amount of unexpired insurance applicable to future periods is $3,750.

EXERCISE 3-4
ADJUSTING ENTRIES FOR
PREPAID INSURANCE
Objective 3

The prepaid insurance account had a balance of $4,750 at the beginning of the year. The account was debited for $5,150 for premiums on policies purchased during the year. Journalize the adjusting entry required at the end of the year for each of the following situations: (a) the amount of unexpired insurance applicable to future periods is $4,300; (b) the amount of insurance expired during the year is $5,100.

EXERCISE 3-5
ADJUSTING ENTRIES FOR
UNEARNED FEES
Objective 3

The balance in the unearned fees account, before adjustment at the end of the year, is $6,000. Journalize the adjusting entry required if the amount of unearned fees at the end of the year is $3,500.

EXERCISE 3-6
ADJUSTING ENTRIES FOR
ACCRUED SALARIES
Objective 3

A business enterprise pays weekly salaries of $15,000 on Friday for a five-day week ending on that day. Journalize the necessary adjusting entry at the end of the accounting period, assuming that the period ends (a) on Tuesday, (b) on Wednesday.

EXERCISE 3-7
ADJUSTING ENTRIES FOR
PREPAID AND ACCRUED
TAXES
Objective 3

A business enterprise was organized on March 1 of the current year. On March 2, the enterprise prepaid $9,600 to the city for taxes (license fees) for the *next* 12 months, and debited the prepaid taxes account. The same enterprise is also required to pay in January an annual tax (on property) for the *previous* calendar year. The estimated amount of the property tax for the current year is $12,600. (a) Journalize the two adjusting entries required to bring the accounts affected by the two taxes up to date as of December 31, the end of the current year. (b) What is the amount of tax expense for the current year?

EXERCISE 3-8
DETERMINE SUPPLIES
PURCHASED AND WAGES
PAID
Objective 3

Selected account balances at December 31, the end of the first year of operations after the adjusting entries have been posted, are shown in the following T accounts:

Supplies		Supplies Expense	
Bal. 750		Bal. 1,050	

Wages Payable		Wages Expense	
	Bal. 300	Bal. 11,900	

Determine (a) the amount of supplies purchased during the year and (b) the amount of wages paid during the year.

EXERCISE 3-9
ADJUSTING ENTRY FOR
ACCRUED FEES
Objective 3

At the end of the current year, $4,950 of fees have been earned but have not been billed to clients.

a. Journalize the adjusting entry to record the accrued fees.

b. If the cash basis rather than the accrual basis had been used, would an adjusting entry have been necessary? Explain.

EXERCISE 3-10
ADJUSTING ENTRIES FOR
UNEARNED AND ACCRUED
FEES
Objective 3

The balance in the unearned fees account, before adjustment at the end of the year, is $9,000. Of these fees, $6,500 have been earned. In addition, $3,750 of fees have been earned but have not been billed. Journalize the adjusting entries (a) to adjust the unearned fees account and (b) to record the accrued fees.

EXERCISE 3-11
ADJUSTING ENTRY FOR
DEPRECIATION
Objective 3

The estimated amount of depreciation on equipment for the current year is $420. Journalize the adjusting entry to record the depreciation.

EXERCISE 3-12
ADJUSTING ENTRIES FOR
DEPRECIATION; EFFECT OF
ERROR
Objective 3

On December 31, a business enterprise estimates depreciation on equipment used during the first year of operations to be $2,500. (a) Journalize the adjusting entry required as of December 31. (b) If the adjusting entry in (a) were omitted, which items would be erroneously stated on (1) the income statement for the year and (2) the balance sheet as of December 31?

EXERCISE 3-13
ADJUSTING ENTRIES FOR
SUPPLIES AND
DEPRECIATION
Objective 3

The balance in the supplies account, before adjustment at the end of the year, is $1,950. The amount of supplies on hand at the end of the year was determined to be $600. The estimated depreciation on equipment used during the year is $690. Journalize the adjusting entries required at the end of the year to recognize (a) supplies used during the year and (b) depreciation expense for the year.

WhAT'S WRONG WITH THi2?

The accountant for Lakeside Laundromat prepared the following portion of a work sheet. How many errors can you find in the accountant's work?

LAKESIDE LAUNDROMAT
Work Sheet
For Year Ended July 31, 1994

Account Title	Trial Balance Dr.	Trial Balance Cr.	Adjustments Dr.	Adjustments Cr.	Adjusted Trial Balance Dr.	Adjusted Trial Balance Cr.
Cash	7,790				7,790	
Laundry Supplies	4,750		(a) 2,910		7,660	
Prepaid Insurance	2,825			(b) 1,500	1,325	
Laundry Equipment		85,600				85,600
Accumulated Depreciation	55,700			(c) 5,720	61,420	
Accounts Payable		4,950				4,950
Alex Black, Capital		30,900				30,900
Alex Black, Drawing	18,000				18,000	
Laundry Revenue		76,900				76,900
Wages Expense	24,500		(d) 850		25,350	
Rent Expense	15,575				15,575	
Utilities Expense	8,500				8,500	
Miscellaneous Expense	910				910	
	138,550	198,350				
Laundry Supplies Expense			(a) 2,910		2,910	
Insurance Expense			(b) 1,500		1,500	
Depreciation Expense				(c) 5,720	5,720	
Wages Payable			(d) 850			850
			14,740	7,220	156,660	199,200

PROBLEMS

Series A

PROBLEM 3-1A
ADJUSTING ENTRIES
Objective 3

On December 31, the end of the current year, the following data were accumulated to assist the accountant in preparing the adjusting entries:

  a. The supplies account balance on December 31 is $1,450. The supplies on hand on December 31 are $695.
  b. The unearned rent account balance on December 31 is $2,700, representing the receipt of an advance payment on December 1 of three months' rent from tenants.
  c. Wages accrued but not paid at December 31 are $3,100.
  d. Fees accrued but unbilled at December 31 are $7,500.
  e. Depreciation on office equipment for the year is $550.

Instructions

1. Journalize the adjusting entries required at December 31.
2. Briefly explain the difference between adjusting entries and entries that would be made to correct errors.

SHARPEN YOUR COMMUNICATION SKILLS

PROBLEM 3-2A
ADJUSTING ENTRIES
Objective 3

Selected account balances before adjustment for Midstate Realty at December 31, the end of the current year, are shown below.

	Debits	Credits
Accounts Receivable	$11,250	
Supplies	3,600	
Prepaid Rent	26,000	
Equipment	42,500	
Accumulated Depreciation		$10,900
Wages Payable		—
Unearned Fees		6,000
Fees Earned		87,950
Wages Expense	29,400	
Rent Expense	—	
Depreciation Expense	—	
Supplies Expense	—	

Data needed for year-end adjustments are as follows:

a. Unbilled fees at December 31	$ 8,650
b. Supplies on hand at December 31	1,275
c. Rent expired during year	24,000
d. Depreciation on equipment during year	4,750
e. Unearned fees at December 31	2,350
f. Wages accrued but not paid at December 31	750

Instructions

Journalize the six adjusting entries required at December 31, based upon the data presented.

If the working papers correlating with the textbook are not used, omit Problem 3-3A.

PROBLEM 3-3A
ADJUSTING ENTRIES
Objectives 3, 4

A portion of the work sheet for J. L. Rhodes Services for the current year ending December 31 is presented in the working papers.

Instructions

1. Enter the data for the six adjustments in the two adjustments columns of the work sheet. (Although the sequence in which the accounts are analyzed is not important, it is suggested that the analysis begin with Cash and proceed downward in the order that the accounts are listed on the work sheet.) Cross-reference the debit and credit for each adjustment by letters. Total the adjustments columns after all adjustment data have been entered.

2. Assume that the adjusting entries were omitted for (a) supplies used and (b) accrued wages. Indicate the effect of each error, considered individually, on net income for the current year and assets, liabilities, and owner's equity at December 31. Record your answers by inserting the dollar amount in the appropriate spaces of the following table. Insert -0- if the error does not affect the item.

	Error (a)		Error (b)	
	Over-stated	Under-stated	Over-stated	Under-stated
1. Net income for the year would be	$	$	$	$
2. Assets at December 31 would be	$	$	$	$
3. Liabilities at December 31 would be	$	$	$	$
4. Owner's equity at December 31 would be	$	$	$	$

PROBLEM 3-4A
ADJUSTING ENTRIES
Objective 3

As of June 30, 1994, the end of the current year, the accountant for Hoover Company prepared a trial balance and an adjusted trial balance. The two trial balances are as follows:

Hoover Company
Trial Balance
June 30, 1994

	Unadjusted		Adjusted	
Cash	12,825		12,825	
Accounts Receivable	19,500		19,500	
Supplies	8,950		3,635	
Prepaid Insurance	3,750		1,250	
Equipment	92,150		92,150	
Accumulated Depreciation—Equipment		53,480		66,270
Automobiles	56,500		56,500	
Accumulated Depreciation—Automobiles		28,250		36,900
Accounts Payable		8,310		8,730
Salaries Payable		—		3,400
Unearned Service Fees		5,000		1,225
Mary Hoover, Capital		55,470		55,470
Mary Hoover, Drawing	18,600		18,600	
Service Fees Earned		261,200		264,975
Salary Expense	172,300		175,700	
Rent Expense	18,000		18,000	
Supplies Expense	—		5,315	
Depreciation Expense—Equipment	—		12,790	
Depreciation Expense—Automobiles	—		8,650	
Utilities Expense	4,700		5,120	
Taxes Expense	2,725		2,725	
Insurance Expense	—		2,500	
Miscellaneous Expense	1,710		1,710	
	411,710	411,710	436,970	436,970

**SPREADSHEET
PROBLEM**

Instructions
Journalize the seven entries that adjusted the accounts at June 30. None of the accounts were affected by more than one adjusting entry.

PROBLEM 3-5A
ADJUSTING ENTRIES
Objective 3

Carey Company prepared the following trial balance at the end of its first year of operations:

Carey Company
Trial Balance
June 30, 19—

Cash	3,150	
Accounts Receivable	1,500	
Supplies	800	
Equipment	7,900	
Accounts Payable		750
Unearned Fees		2,000
G. G. Carey, Capital		10,000
G. G. Carey, Drawing	15,000	
Fees Earned		35,750
Wages Expense	8,500	
Rent Expense	8,000	
Utilities Expense	2,750	
Miscellaneous Expense	900	
	48,500	48,500

In preparation for making the adjusting entries, the following data were assembled:

a. Fees earned but unbilled on June 30 were $2,550.
b. Supplies on hand on June 30 were $310.
c. Depreciation on equipment was estimated to be $1,100 for the year.
d. The balance in unearned fees represented the March 1 receipt in advance for services to be provided. Only $900 of the services were provided between March 1 and June 30.
e. Unpaid wages accrued on June 30 were $175.

Instructions
Journalize the adjusting entries necessary on June 30.

Instructions for Solving Problem 3-5A Using Solutions Software

SOLUTIONS SOFTWARE

1. Load opening balances.
2. Save the opening balances file to your drive and directory.
3. Set the run date to June 30 of the current year and enter your name.
4. Key the adjusting entries. Key ADJ.ENT. in the reference field.
5. Display the adjusting entries.
6. Display the financial statements.
7. Save your data file to disk.
8. End the session.

PROBLEM 3-6A
WORK SHEET AND
ADJUSTING ENTRIES
Objectives 3, 4

Elster Bowl prepared the following trial balance at December 31, the end of the current year:

Elster Bowl
Trial Balance
December 31, 19—

Cash	9,700	
Prepaid Insurance	3,400	
Supplies	1,950	
Land	50,000	
Building	141,500	
Accumulated Depreciation—Building		91,700
Equipment	90,100	
Accumulated Depreciation—Equipment		65,300
Accounts Payable		7,500
Unearned Rent		6,000
Cathy Elster, Capital		70,700
Cathy Elster, Drawing	20,000	
Bowling Revenue		218,400
Salaries and Wages Expense	80,200	
Utilities Expense	28,200	
Advertising Expense	19,000	
Repairs Expense	11,500	
Miscellaneous Expense	4,050	
	459,600	459,600

The data needed to determine year-end adjustments are as follows:

a. Unexpired insurance at December 31	$ 700
b. Supplies on hand at December 31	450
c. Depreciation of building for the year	1,620
d. Depreciation of equipment for the year	5,500
e. Rent unearned at December 31	2,000
f. Accrued salaries and wages at December 31	2,000

Instructions

SPREADSHEET PROBLEM

1. Enter the trial balance on a ten-column work sheet.
2. Enter the data for the six adjustments in the adjustments columns of the work sheet. Add additional accounts as needed.
3. Complete the adjusted trial balance columns in the work sheet.
4. On the basis of the adjustment data in the work sheet, journalize the adjusting entries.

SOLUTIONS
SOFTWARE

Instructions for Solving Problem 3-6A Using Solutions Software

1. Load opening balances.
2. Save the opening balances file to your drive and directory.
3. Set the run date to December 31 of the current year and enter your name.
4. Key the adjusting entries. Key ADJ.ENT. in the reference field.
5. Display the adjusting entries.
6. Display the financial statements.
7. Save your data file to disk.
8. End the session.

PROBLEM 3-7A
ADJUSTING ENTRIES AND
ERRORS
Objective 3

At the end of June, the first month of operations, the following selected data were taken from the financial statements:

Net income for June	$39,750
Total assets at June 30	89,700
Total liabilities at June 30	30,200
Total owner's equity at June 30	59,500

In preparing the financial statements, adjustments for the following data were overlooked:

a. Supplies used during June, $1,750.
b. Unbilled fees earned at June 30, $3,900.
c. Depreciation on equipment for June, $300.
d. Accrued wages at June 30, $2,500.

Instructions

1. Journalize the entries to record the omitted adjustments.
2. Determine the correct amount of net income for June and the total assets, liabilities, and owner's equity at June 30. In addition to indicating the corrected amounts, indicate the effect of each omitted adjustment by completing the following columnar table. Adjustment (a) is presented as an example.

	Net Income	Total Assets	Total Liabilities	Total Owner's Equity
Reported amounts	$39,750	$89,700	$30,200	$59,500
Corrections:				
Adjustment (a)	– 1,750	– 1,750	0	– 1,750
Adjustment (b)				
Adjustment (c)				
Adjustment (d)				
Corrected amounts				

Series B

PROBLEM 3-1B
ADJUSTING ENTRIES
Objective 3

On December 31, the end of the current year, the following data were accumulated to assist the accountant in preparing the adjusting entries:

a. Fees accrued but unbilled at December 31 are $8,250.
b. The supplies account balance on December 31 is $2,100. The supplies on hand on December 31 are $535.
c. Wages accrued but not paid at December 31 are $4,350.
d. The unearned rent account balance on December 31 is $3,000, representing the receipt of an advance payment on December 1 of three months' rent from tenants.
e. Depreciation on office equipment for the year is $600.

Instructions

1. Journalize the adjusting entries required at December 31.

SHARPEN YOUR
COMMUNICATION SKILLS

2. Briefly explain the difference between adjusting entries and entries that would be made to correct errors.

PROBLEM 3-2B
ADJUSTING ENTRIES
Objective 3

Selected account balances before adjustment for Centrex Realty at December 31, the end of the current year, are shown below.

	Debits	Credits
Accounts Receivable	$ 9,250	
Supplies	2,700	
Prepaid Rent	24,000	
Equipment	50,500	
Accumulated Depreciation		$16,900
Wages Payable		—
Unearned Fees		6,600
Fees Earned		89,850
Wages Expense	30,750	
Rent Expense	—	
Depreciation Expense	—	
Supplies Expense	—	

Data needed for year-end adjustments are as follows:

a. Supplies on hand at December 31	$ 750
b. Depreciation on equipment during year	4,950
c. Rent expired during year	18,000
d. Wages accrued but not paid at December 31	525
e. Unearned fees at December 31	2,250
f. Unbilled fees at December 31	4,750

Instructions
Journalize the six adjusting entries required at December 31, based upon the data presented.

PROBLEM 3-3B
ADJUSTING ENTRIES
Objective 3, 4

If the working papers correlating with the textbook are not used, omit Problem 3-3B.

A portion of the work sheet for J. L. Rhodes Services for the current year ending December 31 is presented in the working papers.

Instructions

1. Enter the data for the six adjustments in the two adjustments columns of the work sheet. (Although the sequence in which the accounts are analyzed is not important, it is suggested that the analysis begin with Cash and proceed downward in the order that the accounts are listed on the work sheet.) Cross-reference the debit and credit for each adjustment by letters. Total the adjustments columns after all adjustment data have been entered.
2. Assume that the adjusting entries were omitted for (a) insurance expired and (b) accrued service revenue. Indicate the effect of each error, considered individually, on net income for the current year and assets, liabilities, and owner's equity at December 31. Record your answers by inserting the dollar amount in the appropriate spaces of the following table. Insert -0- if the error does not affect the item.

	Error (a)		Error (b)	
	Over-stated	Under-stated	Over-stated	Under-stated
1. Net income for the year would be	$	$	$	$
2. Assets at December 31 would be	$	$	$	$
3. Liabilities at December 31 would be	$	$	$	$
4. Owner's equity at December 31 would be	$	$	$	$

PROBLEM 3-4B
ADJUSTING ENTRIES
Objective 3

As of December 31, the end of the current year, the accountant for Linke Company prepared a trial balance and an adjusted trial balance. The two trial balances are as follows:

Linke Company
Trial Balance
December 31, 19—

	Unadjusted		Adjusted	
Cash	19,750		19,750	
Accounts Receivable	10,400		10,400	
Supplies	9,880		3,460	
Prepaid Insurance	2,700		700	
Land	47,500		47,500	
Buildings	107,480		107,480	
Accumulated Depreciation—Buildings		79,600		84,400
Trucks	72,000		72,000	
Accumulated Depreciation—Trucks		32,800		50,900
Accounts Payable		8,920		9,520
Salaries Payable		—		1,450
Unearned Service Fees		7,500		920
Charles Linke, Capital		93,890		93,890
Charles Linke, Drawing	24,000		24,000	
Service Fees Earned		170,680		177,260
Salary Expense	81,200		82,650	
Depreciation Expense—Trucks	—		18,100	
Rent Expense	9,600		9,600	
Supplies Expense	—		6,420	
Utilities Expense	6,200		6,800	
Depreciation Expense—Buildings	—		4,800	
Taxes Expense	1,720		1,720	
Insurance Expense	—		2,000	
Miscellaneous Expense	960		960	
	393,390	393,390	418,340	418,340

Instructions

Journalize the seven entries that adjusted the accounts at December 31. None of the accounts were affected by more than one adjusting entry.

SPREADSHEET PROBLEM

PROBLEM 3-5B
ADJUSTING ENTRIES
Objective 3

Fuller Company prepared the following trial balance at the end of its first year of operations:

Fuller Company
Trial Balance
April 30, 19—

Cash	3,150	
Accounts Receivable	1,500	
Supplies	1,300	
Equipment	9,900	
Accounts Payable		750
Unearned Fees		2,000
Ann Fuller, Capital		14,500
Ann Fuller, Drawing	15,000	
Fees Earned		36,750
Wages Expense	9,500	
Rent Expense	9,000	
Utilities Expense	3,750	
Miscellaneous Expense	900	
	54,000	54,000

In preparation for making the adjusting entries, the following data were assembled:

a. Supplies on hand on April 30 were $310.
b. Fees earned but unbilled on April 30 were $3,025.

c. Depreciation on equipment was estimated to be $950 for the year.
d. Unpaid wages accrued on April 30 were $210.
e. The balance in unearned fees represented the March 1 receipt in advance for services to be provided. Only $800 of the services were provided between March 1 and April 30.

Instructions
Journalize the adjusting entries necessary on April 30.

Instructions for Solving Problem 3-5B Using Solutions Software

1. Load opening balances.
2. Save the opening balances file to your drive and directory.
3. Set the run date to April 30 of the current year and enter your name.
4. Key the adjusting entries. Key ADJ.ENT. in the reference field.
5. Display the adjusting entries.
6. Display the financial statements.
7. Save your data file to disk.
8. End the session.

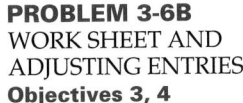

SOLUTIONS
SOFTWARE

PROBLEM 3-6B
WORK SHEET AND
ADJUSTING ENTRIES
Objectives 3, 4

Midtown Bowl prepared the following trial balance at December 31, the end of the current year:

Midtown Bowl
Trial Balance
December 31, 19—

Cash	10,200	
Prepaid Insurance	3,900	
Supplies	2,450	
Land	50,000	
Building	141,500	
Accumulated Depreciation—Building		95,700
Equipment	90,100	
Accumulated Depreciation—Equipment		65,300
Accounts Payable		7,500
Unearned Rent		4,000
John Fox, Capital		70,700
John Fox, Drawing	20,000	
Bowling Revenue		218,400
Salaries and Wages Expense	78,700	
Utilities Expense	28,200	
Advertising Expense	19,000	
Repairs Expense	13,500	
Miscellaneous Expense	4,050	
	461,600	461,600

The data needed to determine year-end adjustments are as follows:

a. Unexpired insurance at December 31 $ 825
b. Supplies on hand at December 31   450
c. Depreciation of building for the year   1,500
d. Depreciation of equipment for the year   5,500
e. Rent unearned at December 31   2,000
f. Accrued salaries and wages at December 31   1,900

SPREADSHEET PROBLEM

SOLUTIONS SOFTWARE

Instructions

1. Enter the trial balance on a ten-column work sheet.
2. Enter the data for the six adjustments in the adjustments columns of the work sheet. Add additional accounts as needed.
3. Complete the adjusted trial balance columns in the work sheet.
4. On the basis of the adjustment data in the work sheet, journalize the adjusting entries.

Instructions for Solving Problem 3-6B Using Solutions Software

1. Load opening balances.
2. Save the opening balances file to your drive and directory.
3. Set the run date to December 31 of the current year and enter your name.
4. Key the adjusting entries. Key ADJ.ENT. in the reference field.
5. Display the adjusting entries.
6. Display the financial statements.
7. Save your data file to disk.
8. End the session.

PROBLEM 3-7B
ADJUSTING ENTRIES AND ERRORS
Objective 3

At the end of July, the first month of operations, the following selected data were taken from the financial statements:

Net income for July	$ 60,500
Total assets at July 31	127,250
Total liabilities at July 31	46,500
Total owner's equity at July 31	80,750

In preparing the financial statements, adjustments for the following data were overlooked:

a. Unbilled fees earned at July 31, $5,900.
b. Supplies used during July, $3,100.
c. Depreciation on equipment for July, $1,300.
d. Accrued wages at July 31, $3,250.

Instructions

1. Journalize the entries to record the omitted adjustments.
2. Determine the correct amount of net income for July and the total assets, liabilities, and owner's equity at July 31. In addition to indicating the corrected amounts, indicate the effect of each omitted adjustment by completing the following columnar table. Adjustment (a) is presented as an example.

	Net Income	Total Assets	Total Liabilities	Total Owner's Equity
Reported amounts	$60,500	$127,250	$46,500	$80,750
Corrections:				
Adjustment (a)	+ 5,900	+ 5,900	0	+ 5,900
Adjustment (b)	_____	_____	_____	_____
Adjustment (c)	_____	_____	_____	_____
Adjustment (d)	_____	_____	_____	_____
Corrected amounts	══════	══════	══════	══════

MINI-CASE 3 A-1 TELEVISION REPAIR

Several years ago your father opened A-1 Television Repair. He made a small initial investment and added money from his personal bank account as needed. He withdrew money for living expenses at irregular intervals. As the business grew, he hired an assistant. He is now considering adding more employees, purchasing additional service trucks, and purchasing the building which he now rents. To secure funds for the expansion, your father submitted a loan application to the bank and included the most recent financial statements (shown at right) prepared from accounts maintained by a part-time bookkeeper.

After reviewing the financial statements, the loan officer at the bank asked your father if he used the accrual basis of accounting for revenues and expenses. Your father responded that he did and that is why he included an account for "Amounts Due from Customers." The loan officer then asked whether or not the accounts were adjusted prior to the preparation of the statements. Your father answered that they had not been adjusted.

Instructions:

1. ▬▬▶ Why do you think that the loan officer suspected that the accounts had not been adjusted prior to the preparation of the statements?
2. Indicate possible accounts that might need to be adjusted before an accurate set of financial statements could be prepared.

A-1 Television Repair
Income Statement
For the Year Ended December 31, 19—

Service revenue		$76,900
Less: Rent paid	$18,000	
Wages paid	16,500	
Supplies paid	7,000	
Utilities paid	3,100	
Insurance paid	3,000	
Miscellaneous payments	2,150	49,750
Net income		$27,150

A-1 Television Repair
Balance Sheet
December 31, 19—

Assets	
Cash	$ 3,750
Amounts due from customers	2,100
Truck	15,000
Total assets	$20,850
Equities	
Owner's capital	$20,850

ANSWERS TO SELF-EXAMINATION QUESTIONS

1. **A** A deferral is the delay in recording an expense already paid, such as prepaid insurance (answer A). Wages payable (answer B) is considered an accrued expense or accrued liability. Fees earned (answer C) is a revenue item. Accumulated depreciation (answer D) is a contra account to a plant asset.

2. **D** The balance in the supplies account, before adjustment, represents the amount of supplies available. From this amount ($2,250) is subtracted the amount of supplies on hand ($950) to determine the supplies used ($1,300). Since increases in expense accounts are recorded by debits and decreases in asset accounts are recorded by credits, answer D is the correct entry.

3. **C** The failure to record the adjusting entry debiting unearned rent, $600, and crediting rent income, $600, would have the effect of overstating liabilities by $600 and understating net income by $600 (answer C).

4. **C** Since increases in expense accounts (such as depreciation expense) are recorded by debits and it is customary to record the decreases in usefulness of plant assets as credits to accumulated depreciation accounts, answer C is the correct entry.

5. **D** The book value of a plant asset is the difference between the balance in the asset account and the balance in the related accumulated depreciation account, or $22,500 − $14,000, as indicated by answer D ($8,500).

You and Accounting

Most of us have ridden in a taxicab. When you get into a taxi, you tell the driver where you want to go, and the driver lowers the meter lever (flag) to start the meter running. At the end of the trip, the driver raises the meter lever, which stops the meter. You then pay the driver for the amount indicated on the meter. As the next passenger is picked up, the driver lowers the lever and the cycle starts all over again.

Business enterprises also go through a cycle of business activities. At the beginning of the cycle, management plans where it wants the business to go and begins the necessary actions to achieve its operating goals. Throughout the cycle, which is normally one year, the accountant records the operating activities (transactions) of the enterprise. At the end of the cycle, the accountant prepares financial statements, which summarize the operating activities for the year. The accountant then prepares the accounts for the recording of the operating activities in the next cycle. This chapter summarizes this accounting cycle for a business enterprise.

Chapter 4
Completion of the Accounting Cycle

LEARNING OBJECTIVES
After studying this chapter, you should be able to:

Objective 1
Prepare a work sheet.

Objective 2
Prepare financial statements from a work sheet.

Objective 3
Journalize and post the adjusting entries.

Objective 4
Journalize and post the closing entries and prepare a post-closing trial balance.

Objective 5
Explain what is meant by the fiscal year and the natural business year.

Objective 6
List the seven basic steps of the accounting cycle.

The matching concept and the adjusting process were described and illustrated in Chapter 3. The use of a work sheet to assist in the year-end procedures was also introduced in Chapter 3. This chapter completes the discussion of the use of the work sheet, including its use in preparing financial statements. In addition, journalizing and posting the adjusting entries is illustrated. Finally, the chapter concludes with a discussion of procedures for preparing the accounting records for the next accounting period.

WORK SHEET

Objective 1
Prepare a work sheet.

The use of a work sheet for assembling data and summarizing the effects of adjusting entries on the accounts was illustrated in Chapter 3. The December 31, 1994 trial balance for Computer King was prepared directly on the work sheet, as shown in Exhibit 1. The adjustments were then entered in the Adjustments Debit and Credit columns, and the Trial Balance amounts were extended through these columns to the Adjusted Trial Balance columns, as shown in the first transparency overlay (Exhibit 2). The following paragraphs describe how the extension of the Adjusted Trial Balance amounts to Income Statement and Balance Sheet columns can aid in the preparation of financial statements.

Income Statement and Balance Sheet Columns

The Income Statement Debit and Credit columns are directly to the right of the Adjusted Trial Balance columns in the work sheet. The Balance Sheet Debit and Credit columns are directly to the right of the Income Statement columns.

The work sheet may be expanded to include Statement of Owner's Equity columns. However, because of the few accounts affected (Capital and Drawing), separate columns for the statement of owner's equity are normally not included in the work sheet. Instead, the owner's equity accounts are extended to the Balance Sheet columns.

Completion of the Work Sheet

The work sheet is completed by extending the Adjusted Trial Balance amounts to the Income Statement and Balance Sheet columns. The amounts for assets, liabilities, owner's capital, and drawing are extended to the Balance Sheet columns. The amounts for revenues and expenses are extended to the Income Statement columns.

In the Computer King work sheet, the first account listed is Cash and the balance appearing in the Adjusted Trial Balance Debit column is $2,065. This amount should be extended to the proper column. Cash is an asset, it is listed on the balance sheet, and it has a debit balance. Thus, the $2,065 is extended to the Debit column of the Balance Sheet section. The $2,720 balance of Accounts Receivable is extended in similar fashion. The same procedure is continued until all account balances have been extended to the proper columns, as shown in the second transparency overlay (Exhibit 3). The balances of the capital and drawing accounts are extended to the Balance Sheet columns because this work sheet does not provide for separate Statement of Owner's Equity columns.

After all of the balances have been extended, each of the four statement columns is added, as shown in the third transparency overlay (Exhibit 4). The difference between the two Income Statement columns is the amount of the net income or the net loss for the period. Likewise, the difference between the two Balance Sheet columns is also the amount of the net income or net loss for the period.

If the Income Statement Credit column total (representing total revenue) is greater than the Income Statement Debit column total (representing total expenses), the difference is the net income. If the Income Statement Debit column total is greater than the Income Statement Credit column total, the difference is a net loss. For Computer King, the computation of net income is as follows:

Total of Credit column (revenues)	$16,960
Total of Debit column (expenses)	9,755
Net income (excess of revenues over expenses)	$ 7,205

As shown in Exhibit 4, the amount of the net income, $7,205, is inserted in the Income Statement Debit column and the Balance Sheet Credit column. The term *Net income* is inserted in the Account Title column. If there had been a net loss instead of net income, the amount would have been entered in the Income Statement Credit column and the Balance Sheet Debit column. The term *Net loss* would then be inserted in the Account Title column. Inserting the net income or net loss into the statement columns on the work sheet shows the effect of transferring the net balance of the revenue and expense accounts to the owner's capital account. Journalizing this transfer is discussed later in this chapter.

After the net income or net loss has been entered on the work sheet, each of the four statement columns is totaled. The totals of the two Income Statement columns must be equal. The totals of the two Balance Sheet columns must also be equal.

FINANCIAL STATEMENTS

Objective 2
Prepare financial statements from a work sheet.

The work sheet is an aid in preparing the income statement, the statement of owner's equity, and the balance sheet, which are presented in Exhibit 5. These financial statements for Computer King, prepared from the completed work sheet in Exhibit 4, are discussed in the following paragraphs. The basic form of the statements is similar to those presented in Chapter 1.

Income Statement

The income statement is normally prepared directly from the accounts listed in the work sheet. The order of the expenses may be changed, however. On the income statement, the expenses are normally presented in order of size, from largest to smallest.

Statement of Owner's Equity

The first item normally presented on the statement of owner's equity is the balance of the proprietor's capital account at the beginning of the period. On the work sheet, however, the amount listed as capital does not always represent the account balance at the beginning of the period. The proprietor may have invested additional assets in the business during the period. Hence, for the beginning balance and any additional investments, it is necessary to refer to the capital account in the ledger. The amount of net income (or net loss) and the amount of the drawings are then used to determine the ending capital account balance. The net income (or net loss) and the drawings amounts can be taken from the Balance Sheet columns of the work sheet.

The basic form of the statement of owner's equity is shown in Exhibit 5. For Computer King, the amount of drawings by the owner was less than the net income. If the owner's withdrawals had exceeded the net income, the order of the net income and the withdrawals would have been reversed. The difference between the two items would then be deducted from the beginning capital account balance. Other factors, such as additional investments or a net loss, also require some change in the form, as shown in the following example:

Allan Johnson, capital, January 1, 19—	$39,000	
Additional investment during the year	6,000	
Total		$45,000
Net loss for the year	$ 5,600	
Withdrawals	9,500	
Decrease in owner's equity		15,100
Allan Johnson, capital, December 31, 19—		$29,900

Exhibit 1
Work Sheet with Trial Balance Entered

Computer King
Work Sheet
For Two Months Ended December 31, 1993

Account Title	Trial Balance		Adjustments		Adjusted Trial Balance		Income Statement		Balance Sheet	
	Dr.	Cr.	Dr.	Cr.	Dr.	Cr.	Dr.	Cr.	Dr.	Cr.
Cash	2,065									
Accounts Receivable	2,220									
Supplies	2,000									
Prepaid Insurance	2,400									
Land	10,000									
Office Equipment	1,800									
Accounts Payable		900								
Unearned Rent		360								
Jere King, Capital		15,000								
Jere King, Drawing	4,000									
Fees Earned		16,340								
Wages Expense	4,275									
Rent Expense	1,600									
Utilities Expense	985									
Supplies Expense	800									
Miscellaneous Expense	455									
	32,600	32,600								

The work sheet is used for assembling data and summarizing the effects of adjusting entries. It also aids in the preparation of financial statements.

Exhibit 5
Financial Statements
Prepared from Work Sheet

Computer King
Income Statement
For Two Months Ended December 31, 1993

Fees earned	$16 8 4 0 00	
Rent income	1 2 0 00	
Total revenues		$16 9 6 0 00
Expenses:		
Wages expense	$ 4 5 2 5 00	
Supplies expense	2 0 4 0 00	
Rent expense	1 6 0 0 00	
Utilities expense	9 8 5 00	
Insurance expense	1 0 0 00	
Depreciation expense	5 0 00	
Miscellaneous expense	4 5 5 00	
Total expenses		9 7 5 5 00
Net income		$ 7 2 0 5 00

Computer King
Statement of Owner's Equity
For Two Months Ended December 31, 1993

Investment on November 1, 1993		$15 0 0 0 00
Net income for November and December	$ 7 2 0 5 00	
Less withdrawals	4 0 0 0 00	
Increase in owner's equity		3 2 0 5 00
Jere King, capital, December 31, 1993		$18 2 0 5 00

Computer King
Balance Sheet
December 31, 1993

Assets			
Current assets:			
Cash		$ 2 0 6 5 00	
Accounts receivable		2 7 2 0 00	
Supplies		7 6 0 00	
Prepaid insurance		2 3 0 0 00	
Total current assets			$ 7 8 4 5 00
Plant assets:			
Land		$10 0 0 0 00	
Office equipment	$1 8 0 0 00		
Less accumulated depreciation	5 0 00	1 7 5 0 00	
Total plant assets			11 7 5 0 00
Total assets			$19 5 9 5 00
Liabilities			
Current liabilities:			
Accounts payable		$ 9 0 0 00	
Wages payable		2 5 0 00	
Unearned rent		2 4 0 00	
Total liabilities			$ 1 3 9 0 00
Owner's Equity			
Jere King, capital			18 2 0 5 00
Total liabilities and owner's equity			$19 5 9 5 00

Balance Sheet

The balance sheet in Exhibit 5 was expanded by the addition of subsections for current assets, plant assets, and current liabilities. Such a balance sheet may sometimes be described as a *classified* balance sheet. Some of the sections and subsections that may be used in a balance sheet are described in the following paragraphs. Additional sections are introduced in later chapters.

ASSETS. Assets are commonly divided into classes for presentation on the balance sheet. Two of these classes are (1) current assets and (2) plant assets.

Current Assets. Cash and other assets that are expected to be converted to cash or sold or used up usually within one year or less, through the normal operations of the business, are called current assets. In addition to cash, the current assets usually owned by a service business are notes receivable and accounts receivable, and supplies and other prepaid expenses. Notes receivable and accounts receivable are current assets because they will usually be converted to cash within one year or less.

Notes receivable are written claims against debtors who promise to pay the amount of the note and possibly interest at an agreed rate to a specified person or bearer. Accounts receivable are also claims against debtors but are less formal than notes and do not provide for interest. Accounts receivable normally arise from providing services or selling merchandise on account.

Plant Assets. The plant assets section may also be described as **property, plant, and equipment**. Plant assets include equipment, machinery, buildings, and land. With the exception of land, such assets depreciate over a period of time, as discussed in Chapter 3. The cost, accumulated depreciation, and book value of each major type of plant asset is normally reported on the balance sheet.

LIABILITIES. Liabilities are debts of the business entity owed to outsiders (creditors). The two most common classes of liabilities are (1) current liabilities and (2) long-term liabilities.

Current Liabilities. Liabilities that will be due within a short time (usually one year or less) and that are to be paid out of current assets are called current liabilities. The most common liabilities in this group are notes payable and accounts payable. These liabilities are like their receivable counterparts, except that the debtor-creditor relationship is reversed. Other current liability accounts commonly found in the ledger are Wages Payable, Interest Payable, Taxes Payable, and Unearned Fees.

Long-Term Liabilities. Liabilities that will not be due for a long time (usually more than one year) are called long-term liabilities. If Computer King had long-term liabilities, they would be reported below the current liabilities. As long-term liabilities come due and are to be paid within one year, they are classified as current liabilities. If they are to be renewed rather than paid, they would continue to be classified as long-term. When an asset is pledged as security for a liability, the obligation may be called a *mortgage note payable* or a *mortgage payable*.

OWNER'S EQUITY. The owner's claim against the assets of the business entity is presented on the balance sheet below the liabilities section. The owner's equity is added to the total liabilities, and this total must be equal to the total assets.

JOURNALIZING AND POSTING ADJUSTING ENTRIES

Objective 3
Journalize and post the adjusting entries.

At the end of the accounting period, the adjustment data appearing in the work sheet are normally used to record the adjusting entries in the journal. After all the adjusting entries have been posted, the ledger is in agreement with the data reported on the financial statements. The adjusting entries are dated as of the last day of the period, even though they are usually recorded at a later date. Each entry may be supported by an explanation, but a caption above the first adjusting entry is acceptable.

The adjusting entries for Computer King are as follows. The accounts to which they have been posted appear in the ledger in Exhibit 7.

JOURNAL   PAGE 4

	DATE	DESCRIPTION	POST. REF.	DEBIT	CREDIT	
1		Adjusting Entries				1
2	1993 Dec. 31	Supplies expense	55	1 2 4 0 00		2
3		Supplies	14		1 2 4 0 00	3
4						4
5	31	Insurance expense	56	1 0 0 00		5
6		Prepaid Insurance	15		1 0 0 00	6
7						7
8	31	Unearned Rent	23	1 2 0 00		8
9		Rent Income	42		1 2 0 00	9
10						10
11	31	Wages Expense	51	2 5 0 00		11
12		Wages Payable	22		2 5 0 00	12
13						13
14	31	Accounts Receivable	12	5 0 0 00		14
15		Fees Earned	41		5 0 0 00	15
16						16
17	31	Depreciation Expense	53	5 0 00		17
18		Accumulated Depreciation—				18
19		Office Equipment	19		5 0 00	19

NATURE OF THE CLOSING PROCESS

Objective 4
Journalize and post the closing entries and prepare a post-closing trial balance.

At the end of an accounting period, the revenue and expense account balances are reported in the income statement. The expenses are deducted from revenues to determine the net income or net loss for the period. Since revenues and expenses are reported for each period, the balances of these accounts should be zero at the beginning of the next period. The zero balances allow the next period's revenues and expenses to be recorded separately from the preceding period. Because the balances of revenue and expense accounts are not carried forward, they are sometimes called **temporary accounts** or **nominal accounts**.

The balances of the accounts reported in the balance sheet are carried forward from year to year. Because of their permanent nature, balance sheet accounts are sometimes called **real accounts**.

At the end of an accounting period, the balance of the owner's drawing account is reported on the statement of owner's equity. The owner's withdrawals are deducted from the net income or added to the net loss for the period to determine the net increase or decrease in owner's equity. Since withdrawals are reported for each period, the balance of the owner's drawing account should be zero at the beginning of the next period. Thus, the owner's drawing account is also a temporary account, and its balance must be transferred to the owner's capital account at the end of the period.

Revenue, expense, and drawing account balances are transferred to the owner's capital account by a series of entries called **closing entries**. This transfer process is called the **closing process.**

Journalizing and Posting Closing Entries

A summarizing account is normally used for closing the revenue and expense account balances to the owner's capital account at the end of the period. Because the net of these account balances is the net income or net loss for the period, the summarizing account is called **Income Summary**. The balance in Income Summary is transferred to the owner's capital account.

Income Summary is used *only* at the end of the period. At the beginning of the closing process, Income Summary has no balance. During the closing process, Income Summary will be debited and credited for various amounts. At the end of the closing process, Income Summary will again have no balance. Because Income Summary has the effect of clearing the revenue and expense accounts of their balances, it is sometimes called a **clearing account.** Other titles used for this account include Revenue and Expense Summary, Profit and Loss Summary, and Income and Expense Summary.[1]

Four entries are required in order to close the temporary accounts of a sole proprietorship at the end of the period. These entries are as follows:

1. Each revenue account is debited for the amount of its balance, and Income Summary is credited for the total revenue.
2. Each expense account is credited for the amount of its balance, and Income Summary is debited for the total expense.
3. Income Summary is debited for the amount of its balance (net income), and the capital account is credited for the same amount. (The accounts debited and credited are reversed if there is a net loss.)
4. The drawing account is credited for the amount of its balance, and the capital account is debited for the same amount.

The account titles and balances needed in preparing the closing entries may be obtained from either the (1) work sheet, (2) income statement and statement of owner's equity, or (3) ledger. If a work sheet is used, the data for the first two entries appear in the Income Statement columns. The amount for the third entry is the net income or net loss appearing at the bottom of the work sheet. The drawing account balance appears in the Balance Sheet Debit column of the work sheet.

The closing entries for Computer King are as follows:

	DATE	DESCRIPTION	POST. REF.	DEBIT	CREDIT	
		JOURNAL			PAGE 5	
1		Closing Entries				1
2	1993 Dec. 31	Fees Earned	41	16 8 4 0 00		2
3		Rent Income	42	1 2 0 00		3
4		Income Summary	33		16 9 6 0 00	4
5						5
6	31	Income Summary	33	9 7 5 5 00		6
7		Wages Expense	51		4 5 2 5 00	7
8		Rent Expense	52		1 6 0 0 00	8
9		Depreciation Expense	53		5 0 00	9
10		Utilities Expense	54		9 8 5 00	10
11		Supplies Expense	55		2 0 4 0 00	11
12		Insurance Expense	56		1 0 0 00	12
13		Miscellaneous Expense	59		4 5 5 00	13

[1] It is possible to close the temporary accounts without using a clearing account. In this case, the balances of the revenue and expense accounts are debited directly to the owner's capital account.

	31	Income Summary	33	7 2 0 5 00		
15						15
16		Jere King, Capital	31		7 2 0 5 00	16
17						17
18	31	Jere King, Capital	31	4 0 0 0 00		18
19		Jere King, Drawing	32		4 0 0 0 00	19

A flowchart of the closing process for Computer King is shown in Exhibit 6. The balances in the accounts are those shown in the trial balance columns of the work sheet in Exhibit 1.

Exhibit 6
Flowchart of Closing Process for Computer King

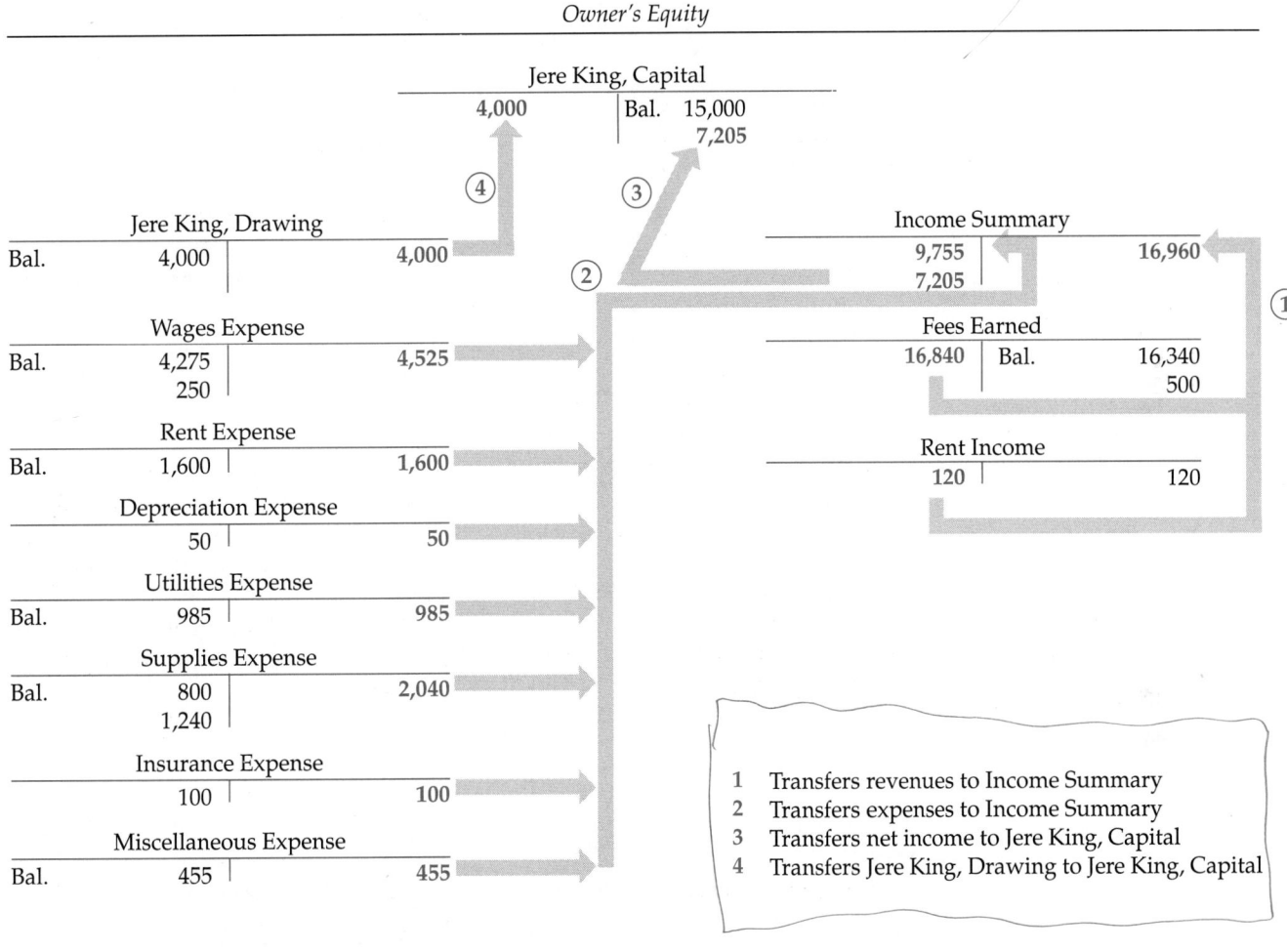

After the closing entries have been posted to the ledger, the balance in the capital account will agree with the amount reported on the statement of owner's equity and the balance sheet. In addition, the revenue, expense, and drawing accounts will have zero balances.

The ledger of Computer King after the adjusting and closing entries have been posted appears in Exhibit 7. Each posting of an adjusting entry and a closing entry is identified in the item section of the account as an aid. It is not necessary that this be done in actual practice.

After the entry to close an account has been posted, a line should be inserted in both Balance columns opposite the final entry. The next period's transactions for the revenue, expense, and drawing accounts will be posted directly below the closing entry.

Exhibit 7
Ledger for Computer King

ACCOUNT Cash   **ACCOUNT NO.** 11

DATE		ITEM	POST. REF.	DEBIT	CREDIT	BALANCE	
						DEBIT	CREDIT
1993 Nov.	1		1	15 0 0 0 00		15 0 0 0 00	
	5		1		10 0 0 0 00	5 0 0 0 00	
	16		1		9 5 0 00	4 0 5 0 00	
	18		1	7 5 0 0 00		11 5 5 0 00	
	30		1		3 6 5 0 00	7 9 0 0 00	
	30		1		2 0 0 0 00	5 9 0 0 00	
Dec.	1		2		2 4 0 0 00	3 5 0 0 00	
	1		2		8 0 0 00	2 7 0 0 00	
	1		2	3 6 0 00		3 0 6 0 00	
	6		2		1 8 0 00	2 8 8 0 00	
	11		2		4 0 0 00	2 4 8 0 00	
	13		2		9 5 0 00	1 5 3 0 00	
	16		2	3 1 0 0 00		4 6 3 0 00	
	20		2		9 0 0 00	3 7 3 0 00	
	21		2	6 5 0 00		4 3 8 0 00	
	23		2		1 4 5 0 00	2 9 3 0 00	
	27		2		1 2 0 0 00	1 7 3 0 00	
	31		3		3 1 0 00	1 4 2 0 00	
	31		3		2 2 5 00	1 1 9 5 00	
	31		3	2 8 7 0 00		4 0 6 5 00	
	31		3		2 0 0 0 00	2 0 6 5 00	

ACCOUNT Accounts Receivable   **ACCOUNT NO.** 12

DATE		ITEM	POST. REF.	DEBIT	CREDIT	BALANCE	
						DEBIT	CREDIT
1993 Dec.	16		2	1 7 5 0 00		1 7 5 0 00	
	21		2		6 5 0 00	1 1 0 0 00	
	31		3	1 1 2 0 00		2 2 2 0 00	
	31	Adjusting	4	5 0 0 00		2 7 2 0 00	

ACCOUNT Supplies   **ACCOUNT NO.** 14

DATE		ITEM	POST. REF.	DEBIT	CREDIT	BALANCE	
						DEBIT	CREDIT
1993 Nov.	10		1	1 3 5 0 00		1 3 5 0 00	
	30		1		8 0 0 00	5 5 0 00	
Dec.	23		2	1 4 5 0 00		2 0 0 0 00	
	31	Adjusting	4		1 2 4 0 00	7 6 0 00	

ACCOUNT Prepaid Insurance   **ACCOUNT NO.** 15

DATE		ITEM	POST. REF.	DEBIT	CREDIT	BALANCE	
						DEBIT	CREDIT
1993 Dec.	1		2	2 4 0 0 00		2 4 0 0 00	
	31	Adjusting	4		1 0 0 00	2 3 0 0 00	

Exhibit 7 (continued)
Ledger for Computer King

ACCOUNT Land   ACCOUNT NO. 17

DATE		ITEM	POST. REF.	DEBIT	CREDIT	BALANCE DEBIT	BALANCE CREDIT
1993 Nov.	5		1	10 0 0 0 00		10 0 0 0 00	

ACCOUNT Office Equipment   ACCOUNT NO. 18

DATE		ITEM	POST. REF.	DEBIT	CREDIT	BALANCE DEBIT	BALANCE CREDIT
1993 Dec.	4		2	1 8 0 0 00		1 8 0 0 00	

ACCOUNT Accumulated Depreciation   ACCOUNT NO. 19

DATE		ITEM	POST. REF.	DEBIT	CREDIT	BALANCE DEBIT	BALANCE CREDIT
1993 Dec.	31	Adjusting	4		5 0 00		5 0 00

ACCOUNT Accounts Payable   ACCOUNT NO. 21

DATE		ITEM	POST. REF.	DEBIT	CREDIT	BALANCE DEBIT	BALANCE CREDIT
1993 Nov.	10		1		1 3 5 0 00		1 3 5 0 00
	16		1	9 5 0 00			4 0 0 00
Dec.	4		2		1 8 0 0 00		2 2 0 0 00
	11		2	4 0 0 00			1 8 0 0 00
	20		2	9 0 0 00			9 0 0 00

ACCOUNT Wages Payable   ACCOUNT NO. 22

DATE		ITEM	POST. REF.	DEBIT	CREDIT	BALANCE DEBIT	BALANCE CREDIT
1993 Dec.	31	Adjusting	4		2 5 0 00		2 5 0 00

ACCOUNT Unearned Rent   ACCOUNT NO. 23

DATE		ITEM	POST. REF.	DEBIT	CREDIT	BALANCE DEBIT	BALANCE CREDIT
1993 Dec.	1		2		3 6 0 00		3 6 0 00
	31	Adjusting	4	1 2 0 00			2 4 0 00

ACCOUNT Jere King, Capital   ACCOUNT NO. 31

DATE		ITEM	POST. REF.	DEBIT	CREDIT	BALANCE DEBIT	BALANCE CREDIT
1993 Nov.	1		1		15 0 0 0 00		15 0 0 0 00
Dec.	31	Closing	5		7 2 0 5 00		22 2 0 5 00
	31	Closing	5	4 0 0 0 00			18 2 0 5 00

Exhibit 7 (continued)
Ledger for Computer King

ACCOUNT Jere King, Drawing   **ACCOUNT NO.** 32

DATE		ITEM	POST. REF.	DEBIT	CREDIT	BALANCE	
						DEBIT	CREDIT
1993 Nov.	30		1	2 0 0 0 00		2 0 0 0 00	
Dec.	31		3	2 0 0 0 00		4 0 0 0 00	
	31	Closing	5		4 0 0 0 00	—	—

ACCOUNT Income Summary   **ACCOUNT NO.** 33

DATE		ITEM	POST. REF.	DEBIT	CREDIT	BALANCE	
						DEBIT	CREDIT
1993 Dec.	31	Closing	5		16 9 6 0 00		16 9 6 0 00
	31	Closing	5	9 7 5 5 00			7 2 0 5 00
	31	Closing	5	7 2 0 5 00		—	—

ACCOUNT Fees Earned   **ACCOUNT NO.** 41

DATE		ITEM	POST. REF.	DEBIT	CREDIT	BALANCE	
						DEBIT	CREDIT
1993 Nov.	18		1		7 5 0 0 00	7 5 0 0 00	
Dec.	16		2		3 1 0 0 00	10 6 0 0 00	
	16		2		1 7 5 0 00	12 3 5 0 00	
	31		3		2 8 7 0 00	15 2 2 0 00	
	31		3		1 1 2 0 00	16 3 4 0 00	
	31	Adjusting	4		5 0 0 00	16 8 4 0 00	
	31	Closing	5	16 8 4 0 00		—	—

ACCOUNT Rent Income   **ACCOUNT NO.** 42

DATE		ITEM	POST. REF.	DEBIT	CREDIT	BALANCE	
						DEBIT	CREDIT
1993 Dec.	31	Adjusting	4		1 2 0 00		1 2 0 00
	31	Closing	5	1 2 0 00		—	—

ACCOUNT Wages Expense   **ACCOUNT NO.** 51

DATE		ITEM	POST. REF.	DEBIT	CREDIT	BALANCE	
						DEBIT	CREDIT
1993 Nov.	30		1	2 1 2 5 00		2 1 2 5 00	
Dec.	13		2	9 5 0 00		3 0 7 5 00	
	27		2	1 2 0 0 00		4 2 7 5 00	
	31	Adjusting	4	2 5 0 00		4 5 2 5 00	
	31	Closing	5		4 5 2 5 00	—	—

ACCOUNT Rent Expense   **ACCOUNT NO.** 52

DATE		ITEM	POST. REF.	DEBIT	CREDIT	BALANCE	
						DEBIT	CREDIT
1993 Nov.	30		1	8 0 0 00		8 0 0 00	
Dec.	1		2	8 0 0 00		1 6 0 0 00	
	31	Closing	5		1 6 0 0 00	—	—

Exhibit 7 (concluded)
Ledger for Computer King

ACCOUNT Depreciation Expense   ACCOUNT NO.53

DATE		ITEM	POST. REF.	DEBIT	CREDIT	BALANCE DEBIT	BALANCE CREDIT
Dec. 1993	31	Adjusting	4	5 0 00		5 0 00	
	31	Closing	5		5 0 00	—	—

ACCOUNT Utilities Expense   ACCOUNT NO. 54

DATE		ITEM	POST. REF.	DEBIT	CREDIT	BALANCE DEBIT	BALANCE CREDIT
Nov. 1993	30		1	4 5 0 00		4 5 0 00	
Dec.	31		3	3 1 0 00		7 6 0 00	
	31		3	2 2 5 00		9 8 5 00	
	31	Closing	5		9 8 5 00	—	—

ACCOUNT Supplies Expense   ACCOUNT NO. 55

DATE		ITEM	POST. REF.	DEBIT	CREDIT	BALANCE DEBIT	BALANCE CREDIT
Nov. 1993	30		1	8 0 0 00		8 0 0 00	
Dec.	31	Adjusting	4	1 2 4 0 00		2 0 4 0 00	
	31	Closing	5		2 0 4 0 00	—	—

ACCOUNT Insurance Expense   ACCOUNT NO. 56

DATE		ITEM	POST. REF.	DEBIT	CREDIT	BALANCE DEBIT	BALANCE CREDIT
Dec. 1993	31	Adjusting	4	1 0 0 00		1 0 0 00	
	31	Closing	5		1 0 0 00	—	—

ACCOUNT Miscellaneous Expense   ACCOUNT NO. 59

DATE		ITEM	POST. REF.	DEBIT	CREDIT	BALANCE DEBIT	BALANCE CREDIT
Nov. 1993	30		1	2 7 5 00		2 7 5 00	
Dec.	6		2	1 8 0 00		4 5 5 00	
	31	Closing	5		4 5 5 00	—	—

Post-Closing Trial Balance

The last accounting procedure for a period is to prepare a trial balance after the closing entries have been posted. The purpose of the **post-closing** (after closing) **trial balance** is to make sure that the ledger is in balance at the beginning of the next period. The accounts and amounts should agree exactly with the accounts and amounts listed on the balance sheet at the end of the period. The post-closing trial balance for Computer King is shown in Exhibit 8.

Exhibit 8
Post-Closing Trial Balance

Computer King Post-Closing Trial Balance December 31, 1993		
Cash	2 0 6 5 00	
Accounts Receivable	2 7 2 0 00	
Supplies	7 6 0 00	
Prepaid Insurance	2 3 0 0 00	
Land	10 0 0 0 00	
Office equipment	1 8 0 0 00	
Accumulated Depreciation		5 0 00
Accounts Payable		9 0 0 00
Wages Payable		2 5 0 00
Unearned Rent		2 4 0 00
Jere King, Capital		18 2 0 5 00
	19 6 4 5 00	19 6 4 5 00

Instead of preparing a formal post-closing trial balance, it is possible to list the accounts directly from the ledger, using a printing calculator or a computer. The calculator tape or computer printout, in effect, becomes the post-closing trial balance. Without such a tape or printout, there are no efficient means of determining the cause of an inequality of trial balance totals.

FISCAL YEAR

The maximum length of an accounting period is usually one year, which includes a complete cycle of business activities. Income, property taxes, and other financial reporting requirements are often based on yearly periods.

In the Computer King illustration, the length of the accounting period was for two months, November and December. Computer King began operations November 1, and a sole proprietorship, except in rare cases, is required by the federal income tax law to maintain the same accounting period as its owner. Since Jere King maintains a calendar-year accounting period for tax purposes, Computer King must also close its accounts on December 31, 1993. In future years, the financial statements for Computer King will be prepared for twelve months ending on December 31 each year.

The annual accounting period adopted by an enterprise is known as its **fiscal year**. Fiscal years begin with the first day of the month selected and end on the last day of the following twelfth month. The period most commonly used is the calendar year. Other periods are not unusual, especially for businesses organized as corporations. For example, an enterprise may adopt a fiscal year that ends when business activities have reached the lowest point in the enterprise's annual operating cycle. Such a fiscal year is called the **natural business year**.

The 1991 edition of *Accounting Trends & Techniques*, published by the American Institute of Certified Public Accountants, reported the following results of a survey of 600 industrial and merchandising companies concerning the month of their fiscal year end.

Percentage of companies with fiscal years ending in the month of:			
January	4%	July	3%
February	2	August	3
March	2	September	5
April	1	October	4
May	3	November	3
June	10	December	60

Closing the Books

Habit is a wonderful saver of mental effort. But too close adherence to habit in business limits efficiency by shutting off initiative.

This is particularly true in the adherence of general business to the habit of following a fixed date for closing the so-called "fiscal" year.

The best date for closing the books and preparing financial statements for the "fiscal" year is when business is in its most liquid condition—when bank loans and other liabilities are lowest, accounts receivable reduced, and, especially, when the inventory is at a minimum.

The most logical date for closing your "fiscal" year is that time when *your* business is logically over for the twelve months—when stocks are lowest—when prices are normal—when selling is not being forced—when you are not buying heavily—when profits can be most accurately determined—when your accounting department is not working nights, or your bank is not burdened with December 31st reports. In other words, close *your* books when *your* business is most naturally through with the rush of *your* year, when proper time and attention can be given, and your public accountants can serve you best.

Source: *Management and Administration* (May 1924), p. 503.

The financial history of a business enterprise may be shown by a series of balance sheets and income statements. If the life of a business enterprise is expressed by a line moving from left to right, the series of balance sheets and income statements may be graphed as follows:

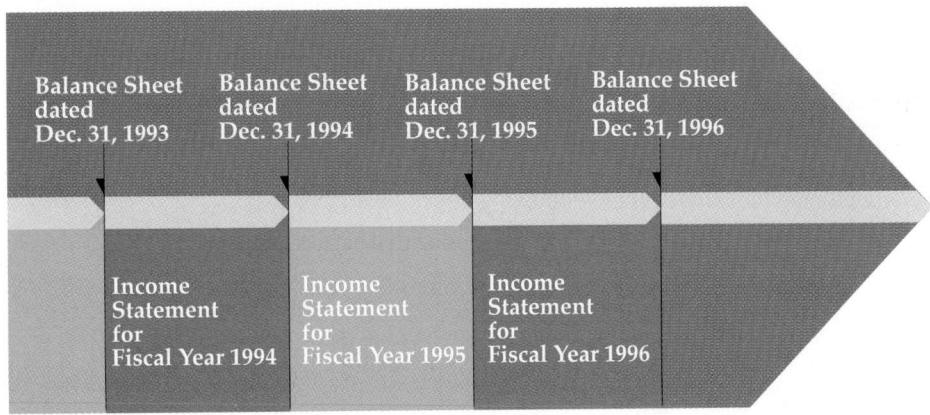

ACCOUNTING CYCLE

Objective 6
List the seven basic steps of the accounting cycle.

The primary accounting procedures of a fiscal period have been presented in this chapter and Chapters 2 and 3. This sequence of procedures is called the **accounting cycle**. It begins with the analysis and the journalizing of transactions and ends with the post-closing trial balance. The most important output of the accounting cycle is the financial statements.

An understanding of the steps of the accounting cycle is essential for further study of accounting. The following basic steps of the cycle are shown, by number, in the flowchart in Exhibit 9.

1. Transactions analyzed and recorded in journal.
2. Transactions posted to ledger.
3. Trial balance prepared, adjustment data assembled, and work sheet completed.
4. Financial statements prepared.
5. Adjusting entries journalized and posted to ledger.
6. Closing entries journalized and posted to ledger.
7. Post-closing trial balance prepared.

Exhibit 9
Accounting Cycle

1 Transactions analyzed and recorded in journal.
2 Transactions posted to ledger.
3 Trial balance prepared, adjustment data
   assembled, and work sheet completed.
4 Financial statements prepared.
5 Adjusting entries journalized and posted to ledger.
6 Closing entries journalized and posted to ledger.
7 Post-closing trial balance prepared.

Financial Statements

APPENDIX

REVERSING ENTRIES

Some of the adjusting entries recorded at the end of an accounting period have an important effect on otherwise routine transactions that occur in the following period. A typical example is accrued wages owed to employees at the end of a period. If there has been an adjusting entry for accrued wages expense, the first payment of wages in the following period will include the accrual. In the absence of some special provision, Wages Payable must be debited for the amount owed for the earlier period, and Wages Expense must be debited for the portion of the payroll that represents expense for the later period. However, an *optional* entry— the reversing entry—may be used to simplify the analysis and recording of this first payroll entry in a period. As the term implies, a **reversing entry** is the exact reverse of the adjusting entry to which it relates. The amounts and accounts are the same as the adjusting entry; the debits and credits are reversed.

The use of reversing entries will be illustrated using the data for Computer King's accrued wages, which were presented in Chapter 3. These data are summarized in Exhibit 10.

1. Wages are paid on the second and fourth Fridays for the two-week periods ending on those Fridays.

2. The wages accrued for Monday and Tuesday, December 30 and 31, are $250.

3. Wages paid on Friday, January 10, total $1,275.

The adjusting entry for the accrued wages of December 30 and 31 is as follows:

	Dec.	31	Wages Expense	51	2 5 0 00		
3							3
4			Wages Payable	22		2 5 0 00	4

After the adjusting entry has been posted, Wages Expense will have a debit balance of $4,525 ($4,275 + $250), and Wages Payable will have a credit balance of $250. After the closing process is completed, Wages Expense will have a zero balance and will be ready for entries in the next period. Wages Payable, on the other hand, has a balance of $250. Without the use of a reversing entry, it is necessary to record the $1,275 payroll on January 10 as a debit of $250 to Wages Payable, a debit of $1,025 to Wages Expense, and a credit of $1,275 to Cash. The employee who records this entry must refer to the prior period's adjusting entries to determine the amount of the debits to Wages Payable and Wages Expense.

Because the January 10th payroll is not recorded in the usual manner, there is a greater chance that an error may occur. This chance of error is reduced by recording a reversing entry as of the first day of the fiscal period. For example, the reversing entry for the accrued wages expense is as follows:

	1994						
3	Jan.	1	Wages Payable	22	2 5 0 00		3
4			Wages Expense	51		2 5 0 00	4

The reversing entry transfers the $250 liability from Wages Payable to the credit side of Wages Expense. The nature of the $250 is unchanged—it is still a liability. When the payroll is paid on January 10, Wages Expense is debited and Cash is credited for the entire amount of the payment, $1,275. After this entry is posted, Wages Expense has a debit balance of $1,025. This amount is the wages expense for the period January 1-10. The sequence of entries, including adjusting, closing, and reversing entries, is illustrated in the following accounts:

ACCOUNT Wages Payable						ACCOUNT NO. 22	
						BALANCE	
DATE	ITEM	POST. REF.	DEBIT	CREDIT		DEBIT	CREDIT
1993 Dec. 31	Adjusting	4		2 5 0 00			2 5 0 00
1994 Jan. 1	Reversing	6	2 5 0 00			—	—

ACCOUNT Wages Expense | | | | | | **ACCOUNT NO. 51**

DATE		ITEM	POST. REF.	DEBIT	CREDIT	BALANCE DEBIT	BALANCE CREDIT
1993 Nov.	30		1	2 1 2 5 00		2 1 2 5 00	
Dec.	13		2	9 5 0 00		3 0 7 5 00	
	27		2	1 2 0 0 00		4 2 7 5 00	
	31	Adjusting	4	2 5 0 00		4 5 2 5 00	
	31	Closing	5		4 5 2 5 00	—	—
1994 Jan.	1	Reversing	6		2 5 0 00		2 5 0 00
	10		6	1 2 7 5 00		1 0 2 5 00	

In addition to accrued expenses (accrued liabilities), reversing entries may be journalized for accrued revenues (accrued assets). For example, the following reversing entry could be recorded for Computer King's accrued fees earned:

4	1	Fees Earned	41	5 0 0 00	
5		Accounts Receivable	12		5 0 0 00

Reversing entries may also be journalized for prepaid expenses that are initially recorded as expenses and unearned revenues that are initially recorded as revenues. These situations are described and illustrated in Appendix C.

As mentioned, the use of reversing entries is optional. However, with the increased use of computerized accounting systems, data entry personnel may be inputting routine accounting entries. In such an environment, reversing entries may be useful, since these individuals may not recognize the impact of adjusting entries on the related transactions in the following period.

CHAPTER REVIEW

Key Points

Objective 1. Prepare a work sheet.
The work sheet is prepared by first entering a trial balance in the Trial Balance columns. The adjustments are then entered in the Adjustments Debit and Credit columns. The Trial Balance accounts plus or minus the adjustments are extended to the Adjusted Trial Balance columns. The work sheet is completed by extending the Adjusted Trial Balance amounts of assets, liabilities, owner's equity, and drawing to the Balance Sheet columns. The Adjusted Trial Balance amounts of revenues and expenses are extended to the Income Statement columns. The net income (or net loss) for the period is entered on the work sheet in the Income Statement Debit (or Credit) column and the Balance Sheet Credit (or Debit) column. Each of the four statement columns is then totaled.

Objective 2. Prepare financial statements from a work sheet.
The income statement is normally prepared directly from the accounts listed in the work sheet. On the income statement, the expenses are normally presented in the order of size, from largest to smallest.

The basic form of the statement of owner's equity is prepared by listing the beginning balance of owner's equity, adding net income and investments in the business during the period, and deducting the owner's withdrawals. The amount listed on the work sheet as the capital of a sole proprietor does not always represent the account balance at the beginning of the accounting period. The proprietor may have invested additional assets in the business during the period. Hence, for the beginning balance and any additional investments, it is necessary to refer to the capital account.

Various sections and subsections are often used in preparing a balance sheet. Two common classes of assets are current assets and plant assets. Cash and other assets that are normally expected to be converted to cash or sold or used up within one year or less are called current assets. Plant assets may also be called property, plant, and equipment. The cost, accumulated depreciation, and book value of each major type of plant asset is normally reported on the balance sheet.

Two common classes of liabilities are current liabilities and long-term liabilities. Liabilities that will be due within a short time (usually one year or less) and that are to be paid out of current assets are called current liabilities. Liabilities that will not be due for a long time (usually more than one year) are called long-term liabilities.

The owner's claim against the assets is presented below the liabilities section and added to the total liabilities. The total liabilities and total owner's equity must equal the total assets.

Objective 3. Journalize and post the adjusting entries.
At the end of the accounting period, the adjusting entries appearing in the work sheet are recorded in the journal and posted to the ledger. This brings the ledger into agreement with the data reported on the financial statements.

Objective 4. Journalize and post the closing entries and prepare a post-closing trial balance.
The four entries required in closing the temporary accounts of a sole proprietorship are:

1. Each revenue account is debited for the amount of its balance, and Income Summary is credited for the total revenue.
2. Each expense account is credited for the amount of its balance, and Income Summary is debited for the total expense.
3. Income Summary is debited for the amount of its balance (net income), and the capital account is credited for the same amount. (Debit and credit are reversed if there is a net loss.)

4. The drawing account is credited for the amount of its balance, and the capital account is debited for the same amount.

After the closing entries have been posted to the ledger, the balance in the capital account will agree with the amount reported on the statement of owner's equity and balance sheet. In addition, the revenue, expense, and drawing accounts will have zero balances.

The last step of the accounting cycle is to prepare a post-closing trial balance. The purpose of the post-closing trial balance is to make sure that the ledger is in balance at the beginning of the next period.

Objective 5. Explain what is meant by the fiscal year and the natural business year.
The annual accounting period adopted by an enterprise is known as its fiscal year. An enterprise may adopt a fiscal year that ends when business activities have reached the lowest point in the enterprise's annual operating cycle. Such a fiscal year is called the natural business year.

Objective 6. List the seven basic steps of the accounting cycle.
The basic steps of the accounting cycle are:

1. Transactions analyzed and recorded in a journal.
2. Transactions posted to the ledger.
3. Trial balance prepared, adjustment data assembled, and work sheet completed.
4. Financial statements prepared.
5. Adjusting entries journalized and posted to ledger.
6. Closing entries journalized and posted to ledger.
7. Post-closing trial balance prepared.

Glossary of Key Terms

Accounting cycle. The sequence of basic accounting procedures during a fiscal period. **Objective 6**

Closing entries. Entries necessary to eliminate the balances of temporary accounts in preparation for the following accounting period. **Objective 4**

Current assets. Cash or other assets that are expected to be converted to cash or sold or used up, usually within a year or less, through the normal operations of a business. **Objective 2**

Current liabilities. Liabilities that will be due within a short time (usually one year or less) and that are to be paid out of current assets. **Objective 2**

Fiscal year. The annual accounting period adopted by an enterprise. **Objective 5**

Income Summary. The account used in the closing process for transferring the revenue and expense accounts bal-

ances to the owner's capital account at the end of the period. **Objective 4**

Long-term liabilities. Liabilities that are not due for a long time (usually more than one year). **Objective 2**

Natural business year. A year that ends when a business's activities have reached the lowest point in its annual operating cycle. **Objective 5**

Nominal accounts. Revenue or expense accounts that are periodically closed to the income summary account; temporary owner's equity accounts. **Objective 4**

Post-closing trial balance. A trial balance prepared after all of the temporary accounts have been closed. **Objective 4**

Real accounts. Balance sheet accounts. **Objective 4**

Temporary accounts. Revenue or expense accounts that are periodically closed to the income summary account; nominal accounts. **Objective 4**

Self-Examination Questions
Answers at end of chapter.

1. Which of the following accounts would be extended from the Adjusted Trial Balance columns of the work sheet to the Balance Sheet columns?
   A. Utilities Expense   C. J. C. Smith, Drawing
   B. Rent Income   D. Miscellaneous Expense

2. Which of the following accounts would be classified as a current asset on the balance sheet?
   A. Office Equipment   C. Accumulated Depreciation
   B. Land   D. Accounts Receivable

3. Which of the following entries closes the owner's drawing account at the end of the period?
   A. Debit the drawing account, credit the income summary account.
   B. Debit the owner's capital account, credit the drawing account.
   C. Debit the income summary account, credit the drawing account.
   D. Debit the drawing account, credit the owner's capital account.

4. Which of the following accounts would not be closed to the income summary account at the end of a period?
   A. Fees Earned   C. Rent Expense
   B. Wages Expense   D. Accumulated Depreciation

5. Which of the following accounts would not be included in a post-closing trial balance?
   A. Cash   C. Accumulated Depreciation
   B. Fees Earned   D. J. C. Smith, Capital

ILLUSTRATIVE PROBLEM

Two years ago, K. L. Waters organized Star Realty as a sole proprietorship. At March 31, 1994, the end of the current fiscal year, the trial balance of Star Realty is as follows:

	Star Realty	
	Trial Balance	
	March 31, 1994	
Cash	2 4 2 5 00	
Accounts Receivable	5 0 0 0 00	
Supplies	1 8 7 0 00	
Prepaid Insurance	6 2 0 00	
Office Equipment	32 6 5 0 00	
Accumulated Depreciation		9 7 0 0 00
Accounts Payable		9 2 5 00
Unearned Fees		1 2 5 0 00
K. L. Waters, Capital		20 9 3 0 00
K. L. Waters, Drawing	10 2 0 0 00	
Fees Earned		39 1 2 5 00
Wages Expense	12 4 1 5 00	
Rent Expense	3 6 0 0 00	
Utilities Expense	2 7 1 5 00	
Miscellaneous Expense	4 3 5 00	
	71 9 3 0 00	71 9 3 0 00

The following adjustment data have been entered on the 10-column work sheet.

a. Supplies on hand at March 31, 1994, are $480.
b. Insurance premiums expired during the year are $315.
c. Depreciation of equipment during the year is $1,950.
d. Wages accrued but not paid at March 31, 1994, are $140.
e. Accrued fees earned but not recorded at March 31, 1994, are $1,000.
f. Unearned fees on March 31, 1994, are $750.

Instructions

1. Complete the 10-column work sheet.
2. Prepare an income statement, a statement of owner's equity (no additional investments were made during the year), and a balance sheet.
3. On the basis of the adjustment data in the work sheet, journalize the adjusting entries.
4. On the basis of the data in the work sheet, journalize the closing entries.

Solution

1.

Star Realty
Work Sheet
For Year Ended March 31, 1994

Account Title	Trial Balance Dr.	Trial Balance Cr.	Adjustments Dr.	Adjustments Cr.	Adjusted Trial Balance Dr.	Adjusted Trial Balance Cr.	Income Statement Dr.	Income Statement Cr.	Balance Sheet Dr.	Balance Sheet Cr.
Cash	2,425				2,425				2,425	
Accounts Receivable	5,000		(e) 1,000		6,000				6,000	
Supplies	1,870			(a) 1,390	480				480	
Prepaid Insurance	620			(b) 315	305				305	
Office Equipment	32,650				32,650				32,650	
Accumulated Depreciation		9,700		(c) 1,950		11,650				11,650
Accounts Payable		925				925				925
Unearned Fees		1,250	(f) 500			750				750
K.L. Waters, Capital		20,930				20,930				20,930
K.L. Waters, Drawing	10,200				10,200				10,200	
Fees Earned		39,125		(e) 1,000 (f) 500		40,625		40,625		
Wages Expense	12,415		(d) 140		12,555		12,555			
Rent Expense	3,600				3,600		3,600			
Utilities Expense	2,715				2,715		2,715			
Miscellaneous Expense	435				435		435			
	71,930	71,930								
Supplies Expense			(a) 1,390		1,390		1,390			
Insurance Expense			(b) 315		315		315			
Depreciation Expense			(c) 1,950		1,950		1,950			
Wages Payable				(d) 140		140				140
			5,295	5,295	75,020	75,020	22,960	40,625	52,060	34,395
Net income							17,665			17,665
							40,625	40,625	52,060	52,060

2.

Star Realty
Income Statement
For Year Ended March 31, 1994

Fees Earned			$40 625 00
Operating expenses:			
Wages expense	$12 555 00		
Rent expense	3 600 00		
Utilities expense	2 715 00		
Depreciation expense	1 950 00		
Supplies expense	1 390 00		
Insurance expense	315 00		
Miscellaneous expense	435 00		
Total operating expenses		22 960 00	
Net income		$17 665 00	

Star Realty
Statement of Owner's Equity
For Year Ended March 31, 1994

K. L. Waters, capital, April 1, 1993			$20 930 00
Net income for the year	$17 665 00		
Less withdrawals	10 200 00		
Increase in owner's equity		7 465 00	
K. L. Waters, capital, March 31, 1994			$28 395 00

Star Realty
Balance Sheet
March 31, 1994

Assets		
Current assets:		
Cash	$ 2 4 2 5 00	
Accounts receivable	6 0 0 0 00	
Supplies	4 8 0 00	
Prepaid insurance	3 0 5 00	
Total current assets		$ 9 2 1 0 00
Plant assets:		
Office equipment	$32 6 5 0 00	
Less accumulated depreciation	11 6 5 0 00	21 0 0 0 00
Total assets		$30 2 1 0 00
Liabilities		
Current liabilities:		
Accounts payable	$ 9 2 5 00	
Unearned fees	7 5 0 00	
Wages payable	1 4 0 00	
Total liabilities		$ 1 8 1 5 00
Owner's Equity		
K. L. Waters, capital		28 3 9 5 00
Total liabilities and owner's equity		$30 2 1 0 00

JOURNAL   PAGE

	DATE		DESCRIPTION	POST. REF.	DEBIT	CREDIT	
1			Adjusting Entries				1
2	1994 Mar.	31	Supplies Expense		1 3 9 0 00		2
3			Supplies			1 3 9 0 00	3
4							4
5		31	Insurance Expense		3 1 5 00		5
6			Prepaid Insurance			3 1 5 00	6
7							7
8		31	Depreciation Expense		1 9 5 0 00		8
9			Accumulated Depreciation			1 9 5 0 00	9
10							10
11		31	Wages Expense		1 4 0 00		11
12			Wages Payable			1 4 0 00	12
13							13
14		31	Accounts Receivable		1 0 0 0 00		14
15			Fees Earned			1 0 0 0 00	15
16							16
17		31	Unearned Fees		5 0 0 00		17
18			Fees Earned			5 0 0 00	18
19							19
20							20
21							21

ILLUSTRATIVE PROBLEM ILLUSTRATIVE PROBLEM ILLUSTRATIVE PROBLEM ILLUSTRATIVE PROBLEM

ILLUSTRATIVE PROBLEM ILLUSTRATIVE

	DATE		DESCRIPTION	POST. REF.	DEBIT	CREDIT	
			JOURNAL PAGE				
1			Closing Entries				1
2	1994 Mar.	31	Fees Earned		40 6 2 5 00		2
3			Income Summary			40 6 2 5 00	3
4							4
5		31	Income Summary		22 9 6 0 00		5
6			Wages Expense			12 5 5 5 00	6
7			Rent Expense			3 6 0 0 00	7
8			Utilities Expense			2 7 1 5 00	8
9			Miscellaneous Expense			4 3 5 00	9
10			Supplies Expense			1 3 9 0 00	10
11			Insurance Expense			3 1 5 00	11
12			Depreciation Expense			1 9 5 0 00	12
13							13
14		31	Income Summary		17 6 6 5 00		14
15			K. L. Waters, Capital			17 6 6 5 00	15
16							16
17		31	K. L. Waters, Capital		10 2 0 0 00		17
18			K. L. Waters, Drawing			10 2 0 0 00	18

DISCUSSION QUESTIONS

1. Is the work sheet a substitute for the financial statements? Discuss.
2. The balances for the accounts listed below appeared in the Adjusted Trial Balance columns of the work sheet. Indicate whether each balance should be extended to (a) the Income Statement columns or (b) the Balance Sheet columns.
   (1) Ann Blair, Drawing   (6) Unearned Fees
   (2) Fees Earned   (7) Utilities Expense
   (3) Accounts Payable   (8) Ann Blair, Capital
   (4) Wages Expense   (9) Accounts Receivable
   (5) Supplies   (10) Wages Payable
3. Balances for each of the following accounts appear in the Adjusted Trial Balance columns of the work sheet. Identify each as (a) asset, (b) liability, (c) revenue, or (d) expense.
   (1) Unearned Rent   (7) Accounts Receivable
   (2) Supplies   (8) Land
   (3) Salary Expense   (9) Fees Earned
   (4) Rent Income   (10) Supplies Expense
   (5) Prepaid Advertising   (11) Salary Payable
   (6) Insurance Expense   (12) Prepaid Insurance
4. In the Income Statement columns of the work sheet, the Debit column total is greater than the Credit column total before the amount for the net income or net loss has been included. Would the income statement report a net income or a net loss? Explain.
5. In the Balance Sheet columns of the work sheet for McReynolds Company for the current year, the Debit column total is $91,500 greater than the Credit column total before the amount for net income or net loss has been included. Would the income statement report a net income or a net loss? Explain.
6. Describe the nature of the assets that compose the following sections of a balance sheet: (a) current assets, (b) plant assets.
7. Identify each of the following as (a) a current asset or (b) a plant asset:
   (1) supplies   (4) accounts receivable
   (2) cash   (5) equipment
   (3) building   (6) land
8. What is the difference between a current liability and a long-term liability?

9. What type of accounts are referred to as temporary accounts?
10. Are adjusting and closing entries in the journal dated as of the last day of the fiscal period or as of the day the entries are actually made? Explain.
11. Why are closing entries required at the end of an accounting period?
12. What is the difference between adjusting entries and closing entries?
13. Describe the four entries that close the temporary accounts.
14. What type of accounts are closed by transferring their balances to Income Summary (a) as a debit, (b) as a credit?
15. To what account is the income summary account closed?
16. To what account is the drawing account closed?
17. From the following list, identify the accounts that should be closed to Income Summary at the end of the fiscal year:
    a. Accounts Payable
    b. Salaries Payable
    c. Fees Earned
    d. Salaries Expense
    e. Depreciation Expense—Buildings
    f. Supplies
    g. Equipment
    h. Supplies Expense
    i. B. W. Bowes, Capital
    j. B. W. Bowes, Drawing
    k. Land
    l. Accumulated Depreciation—Buildings
18. Which of the following accounts will usually appear in the post-closing trial balance?
    a. Accounts Receivable
    b. Accumulated Depreciation
    c. Cash
    d. Supplies
    e. Depreciation Expense
    f. Wages Payable
    g. Equipment
    h. Wages Expense
    i. S. D. Sands, Capital
    j. Fees Earned
    k. S. D. Sands, Drawing
19. What is the purpose of the post-closing trial balance?
20. What term is applied to the annual accounting period adopted by a business enterprise?
21. What is the natural business year?
22. Why might a department store select a fiscal year ending January 31, rather than a fiscal year ending December 31?
23. Rearrange the following steps in the accounting cycle in proper sequence:
    a. Adjusting entries journalized and posted to ledger.
    b. Post-closing trial balance prepared.
    c. Closing entries journalized and posted to ledger.
    d. Transactions analyzed and recorded in journal.
    e. Financial statements prepared.
    f. Trial balance prepared, adjustment data assembled, and work sheet completed.
    g. Transactions posted to ledger.

 REAL WORLD FOCUS

24. The fiscal years for several well-known companies were as follows:

Company	Fiscal Year Ending
K Mart	January 30
J.C. Penney	January 26
Zayre Corp.	January 26
Toys "R" Us, Inc.	February 3
Federated Department Stores	February 2
The Limited, Inc.	February 2

What general characteristic shared by these companies explains why they do not have fiscal years ending December 31?

ETHICS DISCUSSION CASE

McRee Company's fiscal year ends October 31. During the first week of November, McRee Company's accountant prepared the work sheet for the year ended October 31, 1994. After the financial statements were prepared, the accountant journalized and posted the adjusting and closing entries. The accountant dated the adjusting and closing entries October 31, 1994, even though the entries were actually prepared and entered on November 6, 1994.

Evaluate whether the accountant behaved in an ethical manner in dating the adjusting and closing entries October 31, 1994.

EXERCISES

EXERCISE 4-1
INCOME STATEMENT
Objective 2

The following account balances were taken from the Adjusted Trial Balance columns of the work sheet for A. D. Finney Company for the current fiscal year ended June 30:

Fees Earned	$92,500
Salaries Expense	37,100
Rent Expense	18,000
Utilities Expense	8,500
Supplies Expense	2,050
Miscellaneous Expense	1,750
Insurance Expense	1,500
Depreciation Expense	2,100

Prepare an income statement.

EXERCISE 4-2
INCOME STATEMENT; NET
LOSS
Objective 2

The following revenue and expense account balances were taken from the ledger of J. J. Henderson Co. after the accounts had been adjusted on October 31, the end of the current fiscal year:

Depreciation Expense	$ 4,000
Insurance Expense	3,900
Miscellaneous Expense	2,250
Rent Expense	24,000
Service Revenue	71,200
Supplies Expense	3,100
Utilities Expense	8,500
Wages Expense	26,750

Prepare an income statement.

EXERCISE 4-3
STATEMENT OF OWNER'S
EQUITY
Objective 2

Selected accounts from the ledger of Sampras Services, for the current fiscal year ended December 31, are as follows:

P. C. Sampras, Capital						P. C. Sampras, Drawing			
Dec. 31	30,000	Jan. 1	62,500	Mar. 31	7,500	Dec. 31	30,000		
		Dec. 31	40,250	June 30	7,500				
				Sep. 30	7,500				
				Dec. 31	7,500				

Income Summary			
Dec. 31	548,150	Dec. 31	588,400
31	40,250		

Prepare a statement of owner's equity for the year.

SPREADSHEET PROBLEM

EXERCISE 4-4
STATEMENT OF OWNER'S
EQUITY; NET LOSS
Objective 2

Selected accounts from the ledger of John Chang Co., for the current fiscal year ended March 31, are as follows:

John Chang, Capital						John Chang, Drawing			
Mar. 31	24,000	Apr. 1	60,500	June 30	6,000	Mar. 31	24,000		
31	10,500			Sep. 30	6,000				
				Dec. 31	6,000				
				Mar. 31	6,000				

Income Summary			
Mar. 31	623,400	Mar. 31	612,900
		31	10,500

Prepare a statement of owner's equity for the year.

EXERCISE 4-5
BALANCE SHEET
CLASSIFICATION
Objective 2

At the balance sheet date, a business enterprise owes a mortgage note payable of $250,000, the terms of which provide for monthly payments of $5,000.

SHARPEN YOUR ▶
COMMUNICATION SKILLS

Explain how the liability should be classified on the balance sheet.

EXERCISE 4-6
BALANCE SHEET
Objective 2

After all of the accounts have been closed on June 30, the end of the current fiscal year, the balances of selected accounts from the ledger of Leeds Company are as follows:

Accounts Payable	$12,750
Accounts Receivable	9,920
Accumulated Depreciation—Equipment	21,100
Robert Leeds, Capital	48,320
Cash	6,150
Equipment	60,600
Prepaid Insurance	3,100
Prepaid Rent	2,400
Salaries Payable	3,750
Supplies	4,750
Unearned Fees	1,000

Prepare a classified balance sheet.

EXERCISE 4-7
CLOSING ENTRIES
Objective 4

Prior to the completion of the closing process, Income Summary had total debits of $357,500 and total credits of $378,000.

SHARPEN YOUR ▶
COMMUNICATION SKILLS

Briefly explain the purpose served by the income summary account and the nature of the entries that resulted in the $357,500 and the $378,000.

EXERCISE 4-8
CLOSING ENTRIES
Objective 4

After all revenue and expense accounts have been closed at the end of the fiscal year, Income Summary has a debit of $795,500 and a credit of $867,500. At the same date, Wayne Ferrara, Capital has a credit balance of $99,500, and Wayne Ferrara, Drawing has a balance of $36,000. (a) Journalize the entries required to complete the closing of the accounts. (b) State the amount of Ferrara's capital at the end of the period.

EXERCISE 4-9
CLOSING ENTRIES
Objective 4

After the accounts have been adjusted at February 28, the end of the fiscal year, the following balances were taken from the ledger of Dunn Services:

L. M. Dunn, Capital	$27,250	Rent Expense	$ 9,000
L. M. Dunn, Drawing	20,000	Supplies Expense	5,500
Fees Earned	55,000	Miscellaneous Expense	2,000
Wages Expense	21,500		

Journalize the four entries required to close the accounts. (Use a compound journal entry to close the expense accounts.)

EXERCISE 4-10
POST-CLOSING TRIAL
BALANCE
Objective 4

The accountant prepared the following post-closing trial balance:

Parrish Machine Repairs
Post-Closing Trial Balance
July 31, 19—

Cash	8,500	
Accounts Receivable	11,250	
Supplies		900
Equipment		31,500
Accumulated Depreciation—Equipment	15,130	
Accounts Payable	6,250	
Salaries Payable		3,500
Unearned Rent	4,000	
Jane Parrish, Capital	23,270	
	68,400	35,900

Prepare a corrected post-closing trial balance. Assume that all accounts have normal balances and that the amounts shown are correct.

APPENDIX EXERCISE 4-11
ADJUSTING AND REVERSING ENTRIES

On the basis of the following data, journalize (a) the adjusting entries at December 31, 1993, the end of the current fiscal year, and (b) the reversing entries on January 1, 1994, the first day of the following year.

1. Sales salaries are uniformly $9,000 for a five-day workweek, ending on Friday. The last payday of the year was Friday, December 27.
2. Accrued fees earned but not recorded at December 31, $2,750.

APPENDIX EXERCISE 4-12
ENTRIES POSTED TO THE WAGES EXPENSE ACCOUNT

Portions of the wages expense account of an enterprise are as follows:

ACCOUNT   Wages Expense   ACCOUNT NO.   53

Date	Item	Post. Ref.	Dr.	Cr.	Balance Dr.	Balance Cr.
19—						
Jan. 2		24		1,400		1,400
6		24	7,000		5,600	
Dec. 27	(1)	51	7,500		245,500	
31	(2)	51	3,000		248,500	
31	(3)	52		248,500	—	—
19—						
Jan. 2	(4)	52		3,000		3,000

a. Indicate the nature of the entry (payment, adjusting, closing, reversing) from which each numbered posting was made.
b. Journalize the complete entry from which each numbered posting was made.

WhAT'S WRONG WITH THiS?

How many errors can you find in the following balance sheet?

Eastland Services
Balance Sheet
For Year Ended July 31, 1994

Assets

Current assets:
Cash	$ 6,170	
Accounts payable	5,390	
Supplies	590	
Prepaid insurance	845	
Land	20,000	
Total current assets		$ 32,995

Plant assets:
Building	$55,500		
Plus accumulated depreciation	23,525	$79,025	
Equipment	$28,250		
Plus accumulated depreciation	17,340	45,590	
Total plant assets			224,615
Total assets			$257,610

Liabilities

Current liabilities:
Accounts receivable	$ 5,390	
Net loss	15,500	
Total liabilities		$ 20,890

Owner's Equity
Wages payable	$ 975	
Paul Beck, capital	69,515	
Total capital		70,490
Total liabilities and owner's equity		$ 91,380

PROBLEMS

Series A

PROBLEM 4-1A
WORK SHEET AND
RELATED ITEMS
Objectives 1, 2, 3, 4

The trial balance of Suds Laundromat at July 31, 1994, the end of the current fiscal year, and the data needed to determine year-end adjustments are as follows:

Suds Laundromat
Trial Balance
July 31, 1994

Cash	6,290	
Laundry Supplies	3,850	
Prepaid Insurance	2,400	
Laundry Equipment	81,600	
Accumulated Depreciation		52,700
Accounts Payable		3,950
J. R. Barr, Capital		33,900
J. R. Barr, Drawing	16,600	
Laundry Revenue		66,900
Wages Expense	22,900	
Rent Expense	14,400	
Utilities Expense	8,500	
Miscellaneous Expense	910	
	157,450	157,450

a. Laundry supplies on hand at July 31 are $940.
b. Insurance premiums expired during the year are $1,500.
c. Depreciation of equipment during the year is $5,220.
d. Wages accrued but not paid at July 31 are $850.

Instructions

1. Record the trial balance on a ten-column work sheet and complete the work sheet.
2. Prepare an income statement, a statement of owner's equity (no additional investments were made during the year), and a balance sheet.
3. On the basis of the adjustment data in the work sheet, journalize the adjusting entries.
4. On the basis of the data in the work sheet, journalize the closing entries.

Instructions for Solving Problem 4-1A Using Solutions Software

1. Load opening balances.
2. Save the opening balances file to your drive and directory.
3. Set the run date to July 31, 1994, and enter your name.
4. Key the adjusting entries. Key ADJ.ENT. in the reference field.
5. Display the adjusting entries.
6. Display the financial statements.
7. Save a backup copy of your data file.
8. Perform period-end closing.
9. Display a post-closing trial balance.
10. Save your data file to disk.
11. End the session.

PROBLEM 4-2A
ADJUSTING AND CLOSING
ENTRIES; STATEMENT OF
OWNER'S EQUITY
Objectives 2, 3

On April 30, 1994, the end of the current fiscal year, the accountant for Riley Company prepared a trial balance, journalized and posted the adjusting entries, prepared an adjusted trial balance, prepared the financial statements, and completed the other procedures required at the end of the accounting cycle. The two trial balances as of April 30, one before adjustments and the other after adjustments, are as follows:

Riley Company
Trial Balance
April 30, 1994

	Unadjusted		Adjusted	
Cash	7,325		7,325	
Accounts Receivable	16,900		20,900	
Supplies	6,920		1,610	
Prepaid Insurance	1,275		350	
Equipment	69,750		69,750	
Accumulated Depreciation—Equipment		33,480		36,270
Accounts Payable		4,310		4,530
Salaries Payable		—		3,480
Taxes Payable		—		1,200
Unearned Rent		750		500
J. R. Riley, Capital		33,975		33,975
J. R. Riley, Drawing	18,300		18,300	
Service Fees Earned		181,200		185,200
Rent Income		—		250
Salary Expense	112,300		115,780	
Rent Expense	15,600		15,600	
Supplies Expense	—		5,310	
Depreciation Expense—Equipment	—		2,790	
Utilities Expense	2,720		2,940	
Taxes Expense	915		2,115	
Insurance Expense	—		925	
Miscellaneous Expense	1,710		1,710	
	253,715	253,715	265,405	265,405

SPREADSHEET
PROBLEM

SHARPEN YOUR
COMMUNICATION SKILLS ►

Instructions

1. Journalize the eight entries that were required to adjust the accounts at April 30. None of the accounts were affected by more than one adjusting entry.
2. Journalize the entries that were required to close the accounts at April 30.
3. Prepare a statement of owner's equity for the fiscal year ended April 30, 1994. There were no additional investments during the year.
4. If the balance of J. R. Riley, Drawing had been $75,000 instead of $18,300, what would the balance of J. R. Riley, Capital have been on April 30, 1994? Explain how this balance would be reported on the balance sheet.

If the working papers correlating with this textbook are not used, omit Problem 4-3A.

PROBLEM 4-3A
LEDGER ACCOUNTS AND
WORK SHEET AND
RELATED ITEMS
Objectives 1, 2, 3, 4

The ledger and trial balance of Salazar Company as of January 31, 1994, the end of the first month of its current fiscal year, are presented in the working papers.

Instructions

1. Complete the ten-column work sheet. Data needed to determine the necessary adjusting entries are as follows:
   a. Service revenue accrued at January 31 is $700.
   b. Supplies on hand at January 31 are $450.
   c. Insurance premiums expired during January are $80.
   d. Depreciation of the building during January is $110.
   e. Depreciation of equipment during January is $115.
   f. Unearned rent at January 31 is $100.
   g. Wages accrued at January 31 are $975.
2. Prepare an income statement, a statement of owner's equity, and a balance sheet. (Note: The owner made an additional investment during the period.)
3. Journalize and post the adjusting entries, inserting balances in the accounts affected.
4. Journalize and post the closing entries. Indicate closed accounts by inserting a line in both Balance columns opposite the closing entry.
5. Prepare a post-closing trial balance.

PROBLEM 4-4A
WORK SHEET AND
FINANCIAL STATEMENTS
Objectives 1, 2

Beacon Company prepared the following trial balance at June 30, 1994, the end of the current fiscal year:

Beacon Company
Trial Balance
June 30, 1994

Cash	11,500	
Accounts Receivable	12,500	
Prepaid Insurance	2,400	
Supplies	1,950	
Land	40,000	
Building	100,500	
Accumulated Depreciation—Building		81,700
Equipment	72,400	
Accumulated Depreciation—Equipment		63,800
Accounts Payable		6,100
Unearned Rent		1,500
Joan Marone, Capital		60,500
Joan Marone, Drawing	24,000	
Fees Revenue		161,200
Salaries and Wages Expense	60,200	
Advertising Expense	19,000	
Utilities Expense	18,200	
Repairs Expense	8,100	
Miscellaneous Expense	4,050	
	374,800	374,800

The data needed to determine year-end adjustments are as follows:

a. Accrued fees revenue at June 30 is $1,500.
b. Insurance expired during the year is $1,050.
c. Supplies on hand at June 30 are $450.
d. Depreciation of building for the year is $1,620.
e. Depreciation of equipment for the year is $5,160.
f. Accrued salaries and wages at June 30 are $1,950.
g. Unearned rent at June 30 is $500.

Instructions

1. Record the trial balance on a ten-column work sheet and complete the work sheet.
2. Prepare an income statement for the year ended June 30.
3. Prepare a statement of owner's equity for the year ended June 30. No additional investments were made during the year.
4. Prepare a balance sheet as of June 30.
5. Compute the percent of net income to total revenue for the year.

SOLUTIONS
SOFTWARE

Instructions for Solving Problem 4-4A Using Solutions Software

1. Load opening balances.
2. Save the opening balances file to your drive and directory.
3. Set the run date to June 30, 1994, and enter your name.
4. Key the adjusting entries. Key ADJ.ENT. in the reference field.
5. Display the adjusting entries.
6. Display the financial statements.
7. Save a backup copy of your data file.
8. Perform period-end closing.
9. Display a post-closing trial balance.
10. Save your data file to disk.
11. End the session.

PROBLEM 4-5A
LEDGER ACCOUNTS, WORK
SHEET, AND RELATED
ITEMS
Objectives 1, 2, 3, 4

The trial balance of Jordan Machine Repairs at July 31, 1994, the end of the current year, and the data needed to determine year-end adjustments are as follows:

Jordan Machine Repairs
Trial Balance
July 31, 1994

11	Cash	6,491	
13	Supplies	4,295	
14	Prepaid Insurance	1,735	
16	Equipment	30,650	
17	Accumulated Depreciation—Equipment		9,750
18	Trucks	23,300	
19	Accumulated Depreciation—Trucks		6,400
21	Accounts Payable		2,015
31	J. J. Jordan, Capital		30,426
32	J. J. Jordan, Drawing	18,000	
41	Service Revenue		89,950
51	Wages Expense	33,925	
53	Rent Expense	9,600	
55	Truck Expense	8,350	
59	Miscellaneous Expense	2,195	
		138,541	138,541

    a. Supplies on hand at July 31 are $302.
    b. Insurance premiums expired during year are $990.
    c. Depreciation of equipment during year is $3,380.
    d. Depreciation of trucks during year is $4,400.
    e. Wages accrued but not paid at July 31 are $693.

Instructions

1. For each account listed in the trial balance, enter the balance in the appropriate Balance column of a four-column account and place a check mark (✓) in the Posting Reference column.
2. Record the trial balance on a ten-column work sheet and complete the work sheet.
3. Prepare an income statement, a statement of owner's equity (no additional investments were made during the year), and a balance sheet.
4. Journalize and post the adjusting entries, inserting balances in the accounts affected. The following additional accounts from Jordan's chart of accounts should be used: Wages Payable, 22; Supplies Expense, 52; Depreciation Expense—Equipment, 54; Depreciation Expense—Trucks, 56; Insurance Expense, 57.
5. Journalize and post the closing entries. (Income Summary is account #33 in the chart of accounts.) Indicate closed accounts by inserting a line in both Balance columns opposite the closing entry.
6. Prepare a post-closing trial balance.

SOLUTIONS
SOFTWARE

Instructions for Solving Problem 4-5A Using Solutions Software

1. Load opening balances.
2. Save the opening balances file to your drive and directory.
3. Set the run date to July 31, 1994, and enter your name.
4. Key the adjusting entries. Key ADJ.ENT. in the reference field.
5. Display the adjusting entries.
6. Display the financial statements.
7. Save a backup copy of your data file.
8. Perform period-end closing.
9. Display a post-closing trial balance.
10. Save your data file to disk.
11. End the session.

Series B

PROBLEM 4-1B
WORK SHEET AND
RELATED ITEMS
Objectives 1, 2, 3, 4

The trial balance of E-Z Coin Laundry at October 31, 1994, the end of the current fiscal year, and the data needed to determine year-end adjustments are as follows:

E-Z Coin Laundry
Trial Balance
October 31, 1994

Cash	13,100	
Laundry Supplies	6,560	
Prepaid Insurance	2,750	
Laundry Equipment	84,100	
Accumulated Depreciation		45,200
Accounts Payable		6,100
Jan Marker, Capital		36,060
Jan Marker, Drawing	18,000	
Laundry Revenue		140,900
Wages Expense	51,400	
Rent Expense	36,000	
Utilities Expense	13,650	
Miscellaneous Expense	2,700	
	228,260	228,260

a. Laundry supplies on hand at October 31 are $3,050.
b. Insurance premiums expired during the year are $1,800.
c. Depreciation of equipment during the year is $4,600.
d. Wages accrued but not paid at October 31 are $1,750.

Instructions

1. Record the trial balance on a ten-column work sheet and complete the work sheet.
2. Prepare an income statement, a statement of owner's equity (no additional investments were made during the year), and a balance sheet.
3. On the basis of the adjustment data in the work sheet, journalize the adjusting entries.
4. On the basis of the data in the work sheet, journalize the closing entries.

Instructions for Solving Problem 4-1B Using Solutions Software

1. Load opening balances.
2. Save the opening balances file to your drive and directory.
3. Set the run date to October 31, 1994, and enter your name.
4. Key the adjusting entries. Key ADJ.ENT. in the reference field.
5. Display the adjusting entries.
6. Display the financial statements.
7. Save a backup copy of your data file.
8. Perform period-end closing.
9. Display a post-closing trial balance.
10. Save your data file to disk.
11. End the session.

PROBLEM 4-2B
ADJUSTING AND CLOSING
ENTRIES; STATEMENT OF
OWNER'S EQUITY
Objectives 2, 3

As of December 31, the end of the current fiscal year, the accountant for Furstner Company prepared a trial balance, journalized and posted the adjusting entries, prepared an adjusted trial balance, prepared the financial statements, and completed the other procedures required at the end of the accounting cycle. The two trial balances as of December 31, one before adjustments and the other after adjustments, follow on the next page:

Instructions

1. Journalize the nine entries that were required to adjust the accounts at December 31. None of the accounts were affected by more than one adjusting entry.
2. Journalize the entries that were required to close the accounts at December 31.

Continued

3. Prepare a statement of owner's equity for the fiscal year ended December 31. There were no additional investments during the year.

4. If the balance of C. C. Furstner, Drawing had been $200,000 instead of $21,000, what would the balance of C. C. Furstner, Capital have been on December 31? Explain how this balance would be reported on the balance sheet.

Furstner Company
Trial Balance
December 31, 19—

	Unadjusted		Adjusted	
Cash	13,650		13,650	
Accounts Receivable	10,380		13,960	
Supplies	9,750		3,330	
Prepaid Insurance	2,400		800	
Land	42,500		42,500	
Buildings	116,000		116,000	
Accumulated Depreciation—Buildings		77,600		82,400
Equipment	82,000		82,000	
Accumulated Depreciation—Equipment		32,800		50,900
Accounts Payable		7,120		7,520
Salaries Payable		—		1,450
Taxes Payable		—		920
Unearned Rent		900		600
C. C. Furstner, Capital		124,890		124,890
C. C. Furstner, Drawing	21,000		21,000	
Service Fees Earned		140,680		144,260
Rent Income		—		300
Salary Expense	71,200		72,650	
Depreciation Expense—Equipment	—		18,100	
Rent Expense	9,000		9,000	
Supplies Expense	—		6,420	
Utilities Expense	4,550		4,950	
Depreciation Expense—Buildings	—		4,800	
Taxes Expense	600		1,520	
Insurance Expense	—		1,600	
Miscellaneous Expense	960		960	
	383,990	383,990	413,240	413,240

If the working papers correlating with this textbook are not used, omit Problem 4-3B.

PROBLEM 4-3B
LEDGER ACCOUNTS AND
WORK SHEET AND
RELATED ITEMS
Objectives 1, 2, 3, 4

The ledger and trial balance of Salazar Company as of January 31, 1994, the end of the first month of its current fiscal year, are presented in the working papers.

Instructions

1. Complete the ten-column work sheet. Data needed to determine the necessary adjusting entries are as follows:
   a. Service revenue accrued at January 31 is $750.
   b. Supplies on hand at January 31 are $550.60.
   c. Insurance premiums expired during January are $72.50.
   d. Depreciation of the building during January is $125.
   e. Depreciation of equipment during January is $95.
   f. Unearned rent at January 31 is $100.
   g. Wages accrued but not paid at January 31 are $1,006.50.
2. Prepare an income statement, a statement of owner's equity, and a balance sheet. (Note: The owner made an additional investment during the period.)
3. Journalize and post the adjusting entries, inserting balances in the accounts affected.
4. Journalize and post the closing entries. Indicate closed accounts by inserting a line in both Balance columns opposite the closing entry. Insert the new balance of the capital account.
5. Prepare a post-closing trial balance.

PROBLEM 4-4B
WORK SHEET AND
FINANCIAL STATEMENTS
Objectives 1, 2

Willis Company prepared the following trial balance at June 30, 1994, the end of the current fiscal year:

Willis Company
Trial Balance
June 30, 1994

Cash	7,200	
Accounts Receivable	6,500	
Prepaid Insurance	3,400	
Supplies	1,950	
Land	50,000	
Building	137,500	
Accumulated Depreciation—Building		51,700
Equipment	90,100	
Accumulated Depreciation—Equipment		35,300
Accounts Payable		7,500
Unearned Rent		3,000
G. E. Willis, Capital		163,700
G. E. Willis, Drawing	20,000	
Fees Revenue		198,400
Salaries and Wages Expense	80,200	
Advertising Expense	28,200	
Utilities Expense	19,000	
Repairs Expense	11,500	
Miscellaneous Expense	4,050	
	459,600	459,600

The data needed to determine year-end adjustments are as follows:

a. Accrued fees revenue at June 30 are $1,200.
b. Insurance expired during the year is $2,700.
c. Supplies on hand at June 30 are $450.
d. Depreciation of building for the year is $1,620.
e. Depreciation of equipment for the year is $5,500.
f. Accrued salaries and wages at June 30 are $2,000.
g. Unearned rent at June 30 is $1,500.

Instructions

1. Record the trial balance on a ten-column work sheet and complete the work sheet.
2. Prepare an income statement for the year ended June 30.
3. Prepare a statement of owner's equity for the year ended June 30. No additional investments were made during the year.
4. Prepare a balance sheet as of June 30.
5. Compute the percent of net income to total revenue for the year.

SOLUTIONS
SOFTWARE

Instructions for Solving Problem 4-4B Using Solutions Software

1. Load opening balances.
2. Save the opening balances file to your drive and directory.
3. Set the run date to June 30, 1994, and enter your name.
4. Key the adjusting entries. Key ADJ.ENT. in the reference field.
5. Display the adjusting entries.
6. Display the financial statements.
7. Save a backup copy of your data file.
8. Perform period-end closing.
9. Display a post-closing trial balance.
10. Save your data file to disk.
11. End the session.

PROBLEM 4-5B
LEDGER ACCOUNTS, WORK
SHEET, AND RELATED
ITEMS
Objectives 1, 2, 3, 4

The trial balance of Lee Machine Repairs at December 31, 1994, the end of the current year, and the data needed to determine year-end adjustments are as follows:

Lee Machine Repairs
Trial Balance
December 31, 1994

11 Cash	6,825	
13 Supplies	4,820	
14 Prepaid Insurance	2,000	
16 Equipment	32,200	
17 Accumulated Depreciation—Equipment		9,050
18 Trucks	42,000	
19 Accumulated Depreciation—Trucks		27,100
21 Accounts Payable		4,015
31 S. T. Lee, Capital		25,800
32 S. T. Lee, Drawing	18,000	
41 Service Revenue		99,950
51 Wages Expense	37,925	
53 Rent Expense	9,600	
55 Truck Expense	9,350	
59 Miscellaneous Expense	3,195	
	165,915	165,915

   a. Supplies on hand at December 31 are $860.
   b. Insurance premiums expired during year are $1,050.
   c. Depreciation of equipment during year is $6,080.
   d. Depreciation of trucks during year is $5,500.
   e. Wages accrued but not paid at December 31 are $700.

Instructions

1. For each account listed in the trial balance, enter the balance in the appropriate Balance column of a four-column account and place a check mark (✓) in the Posting Reference column.
2. Record the trial balance on a ten-column work sheet and complete the work sheet.
3. Prepare an income statement, a statement of owner's equity (no additional investments were made during the year), and a balance sheet.
4. Journalize and post the adjusting entries, inserting balances in the accounts affected. The following additional accounts from Lee's chart of accounts should be used: Wages Payable, 22; Supplies Expense, 52; Depreciation Expense—Equipment, 54; Depreciation Expense—Trucks, 56; Insurance Expense, 57.
5. Journalize and post the closing entries. (Income Summary is account #33 in the chart of accounts.) Indicate closed accounts by inserting a line in both Balance columns opposite the closing entry.
6. Prepare a post-closing trial balance.

SOLUTIONS
SOFTWARE

Instructions for Solving Problem 4-5B Using Solutions Software

1. Load opening balances.
2. Save the opening balances file to your drive and directory.
3. Set the run date to December 31, 1994, and enter your name.
4. Key the adjusting entries. Key ADJ.ENT. in the reference field.
5. Display the adjusting entries.
6. Display the financial statements.
7. Save a backup copy of your data file.
8. Perform period-end closing.
9. Display a post-closing trial balance.
10. Save your data file to disk.
11. End the session.

MINI-CASE 4 NO-PEST

Assume that you recently accepted a position with the Second National Bank as an assistant loan officer. As one of your first duties, you have been assigned the responsibility of evaluating a loan request for $75,000 from No-Pest, a small sole proprietorship. In support of the loan application, Jean Wicks, owner, submitted the following "Statement of Accounts" (trial balance) for the first year of operations ended December 31, 1994:

No-Pest
Statement of Accounts
December 31, 1994

Cash	4,120	
Billings Due from Others	7,740	
Supplies (chemicals, etc.)	14,950	
Trucks	32,750	
Equipment	16,150	
Amounts Owed to Others		4,700
Investment in Business		47,500
Service Revenue		97,650
Wages Expense	60,100	
Utilities Expense	6,900	
Rent Expense	4,800	
Insurance Expense	1,400	
Other Expenses	940	
	149,850	149,850

Instructions:

1. ▪▪▪ ▸ Explain to Jean Wicks why a set of financial statements (income statement, statement of owner's equity, and balance sheet) would be useful to you in evaluating the loan request.

2. In discussing the "Statement of Accounts" with Jean Wicks, you discovered that the accounts had not been adjusted at December 31. Through analysis of the "Statement of Accounts," indicate possible adjusting entries that might be necessary before an accurate set of financial statements could be prepared.

3. Assuming that an accurate set of financial statements will be submitted by Jean Wicks in a few days, what other considerations or information would you require before making a decision on the loan request?

COMPREHENSIVE PROBLEM 1

For the past several years, Lance Fox has operated a consulting business from his home on a part-time basis. As of September 1, Fox decided to move to rented quarters and to devote full time to the business, which was to be known as Fox Consulting. Fox Consulting entered into the following transactions during September:

Sep. 1. The following assets were received from Lance Fox: cash, $6,000; accounts receivable, $1,000; supplies, $1,250; and office equipment, $6,200. There were no liabilities received.

2. Paid three months' rent on a lease rental contract, $2,400.

2. Paid the premiums on property and casualty insurance policies, $1,800.

4. Received cash from clients as an advance payment for services to be performed and recorded them as unearned fees, $2,500.

4. Purchased additional office equipment on account from Payne Company, $2,000.

6. Received cash from clients on account, $600.

9. Paid cash for a newspaper advertisement, $80.

11. Paid Payne Company for part of the debt incurred on September 4, $1,100.

12. Recorded services performed on account for the period September 1-12, $1,200.

13. Paid part-time receptionist for two weeks' salary, $400.

17. Recorded cash from cash clients for fees earned during the first half of September, $2,100.

17. Paid cash for supplies, $950.

20. Recorded services performed on account for the period September 13-20, $1,100.

24. Recorded cash from cash clients for fees earned for the period September 17-24, $1,850.

Sep. 27. Received cash from clients on account, $1,200.

     27. Paid part-time receptionist for two weeks' salary, $400.

     30. Paid telephone bill for September, $65.

     30. Paid electricity bill for September, $140.

     30. Recorded cash from cash clients for fees earned for the period September 25-30, $850.

     30. Recorded services performed on account for the remainder of September, $500.

     30. Fox withdrew $1,200 for personal use.

Instructions

1. Journalize each transaction in a two-column journal, referring to the following chart of accounts in selecting the accounts to be debited and credited. (Do not insert the account numbers in the journal at this time.)

11 Cash	41 Fees Earned
12 Accounts Receivable	51 Salary Expense
14 Supplies	52 Rent Expense
15 Prepaid Rent	53 Supplies Expense
16 Prepaid Insurance	54 Depreciation Expense
18 Office Equipment	55 Insurance Expense
19 Accumulated Depreciation	59 Miscellaneous Expense
21 Accounts Payable	
22 Salaries Payable	
23 Unearned Fees	
31 Lance Fox, Capital	
32 Lance Fox, Drawing	

2. Post the journal to a ledger of four-column accounts.
3. Prepare a trial balance as of September 30, on a ten-column work sheet, listing all the accounts in the order given in the ledger. Complete the work sheet, using the following adjustment data:
   a. Insurance expired during September is $250.
   b. Supplies on hand on September 30 are $1,420.
   c. Depreciation of office equipment for September is $750.
   d. Accrued receptionist salary on September 30 is $100.
   e. Rent expired during September is $800.
   f. Unearned fees on September 30 are $1,100.
4. Prepare an income statement, a statement of owner's equity, and a balance sheet.
5. Journalize and post the adjusting entries.
6. Journalize and post the closing entries. (Income Summary is account #33 in the chart of accounts.) Indicate closed accounts by inserting a line in both Balance columns opposite the closing entry.
7. Prepare a post-closing trial balance.

SOLUTIONS SOFTWARE

Instructions for Solving Comprehensive Problem 1 Using Solutions Software

1. Load opening balances.
2. Save the opening balances file to your drive and directory.
3. Set the run date to September 30 of the current year and enter your name.
4. Select the General Journal Entries option and key the journal entries. Leave the reference field blank. (Note: To review the chart of accounts, select F-1.)
5. Display a journal entries report.
6. Display a trial balance.
7. Key the adjusting entries. Key ADJ.ENT. in the reference field.
8. Display the adjusting entries.
9. Display the financial statements.
10. Save a backup copy of your data file.
11. Perform period-end closing.
12. Display a post-closing trial balance.
13. Save your data file to disk.
14. End the session.

ANSWERS TO SELF-EXAMINATION QUESTIONS

1. **C** The drawing account, J. C. Smith, Drawing (answer C) would be extended to the Balance Sheet columns of the work sheet. Utilities Expense (answer A), Rent Income (answer B), and Miscellaneous Expense (answer D) would all be extended to the Income Statement columns of the work sheet.

2. **D** Cash or other assets that are expected to be converted to cash or sold or used up within one year or less, through the normal operations of the business, are classified as current assets on the balance sheet. Accounts Receivable (answer D) is a current asset, since it will normally be converted to cash within one year. Office Equipment (answer A), Land (answer B), and Accumulated Depreciation (answer C) are all reported in the plant asset section of the balance sheet.

3. **B** The entry to close the owner's drawing account is to debit the owner's capital account and credit the drawing account (answer B).

4. **D** Since all revenue and expense accounts are closed at the end of the period, Fees Earned (answer A), Wages Expense (answer B), and Rent Expense (answer C) would all be closed to Income Summary. Accumulated Depreciation (answer D) is a contra asset account that is not closed.

5. **B** Since the post-closing trial balance includes only balance sheet accounts (all of the revenue, expense, and drawing accounts are closed), Cash (answer A), Accumulated Depreciation (answer C), and J. C. Smith, Capital (answer D) would appear on the post-closing trial balance. Fees Earned (answer B) is a temporary account that is closed prior to the preparation of the post-closing trial balance.

Part 2

Accounting for Merchandising Enterprises

You and Accounting

When you purchase merchandise at a store and pay cash, the clerk normally uses a cash register to record the sale. The cash register is designed to record the sale electronically or on a tape within the machine.

After the sale has been "rung up," the clerk provides you with a receipt similar to the one shown below.

```
                  INGLES #426
                  ATHENS GA

                                 10/02/92

   GROCERY                       2.99L
   GROCERY                       1.00L
   FZ FOOD                       1.29L
   SUBTOTAL                      5.28
   TAX                            .32
   TOTAL                         5.60

   CASH                         10.00

   CHANGE                        4.40

   # ITEMS      3


   THANK YOU C123 R03 T12:38
```

The receipt indicates the items purchased, the subtotal of the purchases, the sales tax, the total due, the amount of cash received, and the amount of change. In this example, three items were purchased totaling $5.28, sales tax of $.32 (6%) was charged, the total due was $5.60, the clerk was given $10.00, and change of $4.40 was received. The receipt also indicates that the sale was made by Store #426 of the Ingles chain located in Athens, Georgia. The date and time of the sale and other data used internally by the store are also indicated.

Chapter 5
Merchandising Transactions— Periodic Inventory Systems

The accounting for service enterprises was described and illustrated in preceding chapters. This chapter focuses on the accounting principles and concepts for merchandising enterprises, which purchase merchandise for sale to customers. It is this purchasing and selling of merchandise that makes the activities of merchandising enterprises different from the activities of service enterprises. This chapter discusses the accounting for purchases and sales of merchandise.

LEARNING OBJECTIVES
After studying this chapter, you should be able to:

Objective 1
Compare and contrast a service enterprise's income statement to a merchandising enterprise's income statement.

Objective 2
Journalize the entries for merchandise transactions, including:

a. Merchandise sales
b. Merchandise purchases
c. Merchandise transportation costs

Objective 3
Journalize the entries for merchandise transactions from both the buyer's and the seller's point of view.

Objective 4
Explain the differences between the periodic and perpetual inventory systems.

Objective 5
Prepare the cost of merchandise sold section of an income statement.

Objective 6
Prepare a chart of accounts for a merchandising enterprise.

INCOME STATEMENTS FOR MERCHANDISING ENTERPRISES

Objective 1
Compare and contrast a service enterprise's income statement to a merchandising enterprise's income statement.

The primary differences between a service enterprise and a merchandising enterprise relate to the revenue activities of the enterprises. These differences are highlighted in the following condensed income statements for each type of enterprise:

Service Enterprise		Merchandising Enterprise	
Fees earned	$XXX	Sales	$XXX
Operating expenses	XXX	Cost of merchandise sold	XXX
Net income	$XXX	Gross profit	$XXX
		Operating expenses	XXX
		Net income	$XXX

The revenue-generating activities of a service enterprise involve providing services to customers. On the income statement for a service enterprise, the revenues from services are reported as fees earned. The operating expenses incurred in providing the services are subtracted from the fees earned to arrive at net income.

In contrast, the revenue-generating activities of a merchandise enterprise involve the buying and selling of merchandise. A merchandising enterprise must first purchase merchandise to sell to its customers. When this merchandise is sold, the revenue is reported as sales, and its cost is recognized as an expense called the *cost of merchandise sold*. The cost of merchandise sold is subtracted from sales to arrive at *gross profit*. This amount is called gross profit because from it the operating expenses are deducted to arrive at net income. The transactions that affect these identifying features of the merchandising enterprise income statement—sales, cost of merchandise sold, and gross profit—are discussed in the remainder of this chapter.

Merchandise that is not sold at the end of an accounting period is called **merchandise inventory**. Merchandise inventory is reported as a current asset on the balance sheet of a merchandising enterprise. The reporting of merchandise inventory is discussed in more detail in the next chapter.

ACCOUNTING FOR SALES

Objective 2a
Journalize the entries for merchandise sales.

Merchandise sales are usually identified in the ledger as *Sales*. Sometimes an enterprise will use a more exact title, such as *Sales of Merchandise*.

A business may sell merchandise for cash. Cash sales are normally "rung up" (entered) on a cash register. At the end of the day, the sales are recorded as follows:

Jan. 3	Cash	1,800	
	Sales		1,800
	Cash sales for the day.		

Sales to customers who use bank credit cards (such as MasterCard and VISA) are usually treated as cash sales. The credit card receipts (slips) for these sales are deposited by the seller directly into the bank. The credit card slips, cash, and checks received for the sales make up the total deposit.

Normally, banks charge service fees for handling credit card sales. These service fees should be debited to an expense account. An entry at the end of a month to record the payment of service charges on bank credit card sales is shown below.

Jan. 31	Bank Credit Card Expense	48	
	Cash		48
	Service charges on bank credit card sales for the month.		

Sales may also be made by accepting a customer's nonbank credit card (such as American Express). These sales must be reported directly to the card company before cash is received. Therefore, such sales create a receivable with the card company. Before the card company pays cash, it normally deducts a service fee. For example, assume that nonbank credit card sales of $1,000 are made and reported to the card company on January 20. On January 27, the card company deducts a service fee of $50 and sends $950 to the seller. These transactions are recorded by the seller as follows:

Jan. 20	Accounts Receivable	1,000	
	Sales		1,000
	American Express credit		
	card sales.		
Jan. 27	Cash	950	
	Nonbank Credit Card Expense	50	
	Accounts Receivable		1,000
	Receipt of cash from American Express		
	for sales reported on January 20.		

A business may sell merchandise on account. Such sales result in a debit to Accounts Receivable and a credit to Sales. An example of an entry for a sale on account is shown below.

Jan. 12	Accounts Receivable	510	
	Sales		510
	Invoice No. 7172 to Sims Co.		

The Battle of Credit Cards

The decade of the 1990s is shaping up as the decade in which critical battles will be fought among the major credit card companies—Discover, VISA, MasterCard, and American Express. One particular area in which battle lines are being drawn is service fees. The following excerpts from an article in *Business Week* illustrate how pressures from VISA, MasterCard, and Discover have caused American Express (AmEx) to, in some cases, lower its service fees charged to retailers.

In mid-April . . . a group of Boston restaurants . . . staged a modern-day version of the Boston Tea Party. The eateries threatened to boycott American Express Co. cards and complained that the merchant fees it collects every time a diner charges a meal were too high. AmEx responded by shaving off half a percentage point from its 3.25% fee to larger restaurants that file their charge records electronically.

   Three weeks later . . . U-Haul's chief financial officer . . . fired off a letter to [American Express] . . . demanding a similar re-duction. Why should U-Haul, which rang up $88 million a year in AmEx charges, pay a higher fee than restaurants with only $10 million a year in AmEx charges? If U-Haul got the same break, it would save about half a million a year in fees. . . .

   . . . Like most merchants, U-Haul pays about one percentage point more if a customer uses an AmEx card rather than a VISA, Discover, or MasterCard. U-Haul is . . . talking to other card issuers about whether more patronage from their cardholders would make up for the loss of AmEx's. Says [a] U-Haul treasury analyst, "Will we lose business if we don't take the card? It's a guessing game."

   . . . Whatever the impact on American Express of the merchant uprising, there is no question that AmEx is suffering from white-hot competition in the credit-card business. . . . AmEx's overall strategy is to stress to merchants its upscale cardholders, who charge an average of $3,409 a year vs. VISA's $1,122 per card. . . .

Source: Lea Nathans Sprio, Geoffrey Smith, and Maria Shao, "AmEx Fights To Discourage Defectors," *Business Week* (July 1, 1991), pp. 56–58.

Sales Discounts

The terms of a sale are normally indicated on the **invoice** or **bill** that the seller sends to the buyer. An example of such an invoice is shown in Exhibit 1.

Exhibit 1
Invoice

Wallace   3800 Mission Street
Electronics   San Francisco, CA 94110-1732
Supply

Made in U.S.A.

SOLD TO	CUSTOMER'S ORDER NO. & DATE
Hollis Electric Company	412 Jan. 10, 1993
1277 Sixth Avenue	**REFER TO INVOICE NO.**
Los Angeles, CA 90019-2350	106-8

DATE SHIPPED	HOW SHIPPED AND ROUTE	TERMS	INVOICE DATE
Jan. 12, 1993	Western Trucking Co.	2/10, n/30	Jan.12,1993
FROM	**F.O.B.**	**PREPAID OR COLLECT ?**	
San Francisco	Los Angeles	Prepaid	

QUANTITY	DESCRIPTION	UNIT PRICE	AMOUNT
20	392E Monitors	75.00	1,500.00

FOR CUSTOMER'S USE ONLY
Calculations Checked _____ *W.M.L.* _____   Price Approved _____ *GP* _____

Material Received _____ *1-14* ____ 19 *93*   _____ *A.S.* _____   *Rec. C.* _____
                        Date   Signature   Title

Audited _____ *L.R.A.* _____   Final Approval _____

The terms agreed upon by the buyer and the seller as to when payments for merchandise are to be made are called the **credit terms.** If payment is required upon delivery, the terms are said to be *cash* or *net cash*. Otherwise, the buyer is allowed an amount of time, known as the **credit period**, in which to pay.

The credit period usually begins with the date of the sale as shown on the invoice. If payment is due within a stated number of days after the date of the invoice, such as 30 days, the terms are said to be *net 30 days*. These terms may be written as *n/30*.[1] If payment is due by the end of the month in which the sale was made, it may be written as *n/eom*.

As a means of encouraging payment before the end of the credit period, the seller may offer a discount to the buyer for the early payment of cash. For example, a seller may offer a buyer a 2% discount if payment is received within 10 days of the invoice date. If the buyer does not take the discount, the total amount is due within 30 days. These terms are expressed as *2/10, n/30* and are read as *2% discount if paid within 10 days, net amount due within 30 days*. The credit terms of 2/10, n/30 are summarized in Exhibit 2.

Exhibit 2
Credit Terms

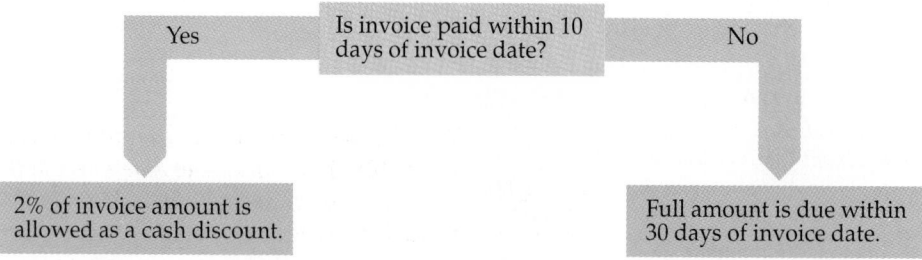

The seller refers to the discounts taken by the buyer for early payment of an invoice as **sales discounts**. They are recorded by debiting the sales discounts account. For example, if cash is received within the discount period (10 days) from the credit sale of $1,500, shown on the invoice in Exhibit 1, the transaction would be recorded as follows:

[1] The word *net* as used here does not have the usual meaning of a number after deductions have been subtracted, as in *net income*.

Jan. 22	Cash	1,470	
	Sales Discounts	30	
	Accounts Receivable		1,500
	Collection on Invoice No. 106-8 to		
	Hollis Electric Company, less discount.		

Sales discounts are considered to be a reduction in the amount initially recorded in Sales. In this sense, the balance of the sales discounts account is viewed as a contra (or offsetting) account to Sales.

Sales Returns and Allowances

Merchandise sold may be returned by the buyer **(sales return)**. In addition, the buyer may be allowed a reduction from the initial price at which the goods were sold because of defects or for other reasons **(sales allowance)**. If the return or allowance is for a sale on account, the seller usually gives the buyer a **credit memorandum**. This memorandum shows the amount and the reason for which the buyer's account receivable is to be credited. A credit memorandum is illustrated in Exhibit 3.

Exhibit 3
Credit Memorandum

The effect of a sales return or allowance is to reduce sales revenue and cash or accounts receivable. To reduce sales, the sales account could be debited. However, the balance of the sales account would then represent net sales for the period. Because of the loss in revenue and the related expense that may result from returns and allowances, management closely monitors the amount of returns and allowances. If it becomes too large, management may take appropriate action to reduce returns and allowances. For this reason, sales returns and allowances are recorded in a separate account entitled *Sales Returns and Allowances*. Because sales returns and allowances reduce the amount initially recorded in Sales, the sales returns and allowances account is a contra (or offsetting) account to Sales.

Sales Returns and Allowances is debited for the amount of the return or allowance. If the original sale is on account, Accounts Receivable is credited. For example, the credit memo presented above would be recorded by Creech Manufacturing Company as follows:

Jan. 13	Sales Returns and Allowances	225	
	Accounts Receivable		225
	Credit Memo No. 32.		

If a cash refund is made for merchandise returned or for an allowance, Sales Returns and Allowances is debited and Cash is credited.

Sales Taxes

Almost all states and many other taxing units levy a tax on sales of merchandise.[2] The liability for the sales tax is incurred at the time the sale is made.

At the time of a cash sale, the seller collects the sales tax. When a sale is made on account, the tax is charged to the buyer by debiting Accounts Receivable. The seller credits the sales account for only the amount of the sale and credits the tax to Sales Tax Payable. For example, a sale of $100 on account, subject to a tax of 6%, is recorded by the following entry:

Aug. 12	Accounts Receivable	106	
	Sales		100
	Sales Tax Payable		6
	Invoice No. 339.		

The amount of the sales tax that has been collected is normally paid to the taxing unit on a regular basis. An entry to record such a payment is shown below.

Sep. 15	Sales Tax Payable	2,900	
	Cash		2,900

ACCOUNTING FOR PURCHASES

Objective 2b
Journalize the entries for merchandise purchases.

Purchases of merchandise for resale are usually identified in the ledger as *Purchases*. A more exact account title could be used, such as *Purchases of Merchandise*, but the shorter title is more common.

When purchases are made for cash, the transaction could be recorded as follows:

Jan. 3	Purchases	2,510	
	Cash		2,510
	Purchases from supplier, Bowen Co.		

Most purchases of merchandise are made on account and are recorded as follows:

Jan. 4	Purchases	9,250	
	Accounts Payable		9,250
	Purchases from supplier,		
	Thomas Corporation.		

Purchases Discounts

Discounts taken by the buyer for early payment of an invoice are called **purchases discounts**. As discussed previously, these same discounts are *sales discounts* from the seller's point of view.

---

[2] Enterprises that purchase merchandise for resale to others are normally exempt from paying sales taxes on their purchases. Only *final* buyers of the merchandise normally pay sales taxes.

Purchases discounts are recorded by crediting the purchases discounts account. For example, the entries recorded by Hollis Electric Company for the invoice in Exhibit 1 and its payment at the end of the discount period are as follows:

Oct. 11	Purchases	1,500	
	Accounts Payable		1,500
	Invoice 106-8 from Wallace		
	Electronics Supply.		
Oct. 21	Accounts Payable	1,500	
	Cash		1,470
	Purchases Discounts		30
	Invoice 106-8 from Wallace		
	Electronics Supply.		

Purchases discounts are usually reported as a deduction from the amount initially recorded in Purchases. In this sense, the purchases discounts account is a contra (or offsetting) account to Purchases.

A buyer should normally pay on the last day of the credit period and take all available discounts, even if money must be borrowed to make the payment. For example, assume that Hollis Electric Company borrows money to pay the invoice for $1,500, with terms of 2/10, n/30, on October 21. The money is borrowed for the remaining 20 days of the credit period. If an annual interest rate of 12% and a 360-day year are assumed, the interest on the loan of $1,470 ($1,500 − $30) is $9.80 ($1,470 × 12% × 20/360). The net savings to Hollis Electric Company is $20.20, computed as follows:

Discount of 2% on $1,500	$30.00
Interest for 20 days at rate of 12% on $1,470	9.80
Savings from borrowing	$20.20

The approximate interest rate earned on taking a discount on a purchase with credit terms of 2/10, n/30 is 36%. As shown in the following calculation, this rate is estimated by annualizing 2% for 20 days.

$$2\% \times \frac{360 \text{ days}}{20 \text{ days}} = 2\% \times 18 = 36\%$$

In this example, as long as Hollis Electric Company can borrow the necessary amount at a rate of less than 36%, it should take advantage of the discount and pay within the discount period.

Purchases Returns and Allowances

When merchandise is returned (**purchases return**) or a price adjustment (**purchases allowance**) is requested, the buyer usually notifies the seller in writing. The details may be stated in a letter, or the buyer (debtor) may use a **debit memorandum** form. This form, shown in Exhibit 4, informs the seller (creditor) of the amount the buyer proposes to debit to the account payable due the seller. It also states the reasons for the return or the request for a price reduction.

The buyer may use a copy of the debit memorandum as the basis for an entry or may wait for confirmation from the seller. The seller confirms the return or allowance by issuing a **credit memorandum.** In either event, Accounts Payable must be debited and Purchases Returns and Allowances must be credited.[3] To il-

---

[3] Some businesses prefer to credit the purchases account. If this alternative is used, the balance of the purchases account will be a net amount—the total purchases less the total returns and allowances for the period.

Exhibit 4
Debit Memorandum

Thomas Company 2130 Washington St. Lexington, KY 40510	No. 18

DEBIT MEMORANDUM

TO	DATE
Power Electronics 1614 LaSalle Street Chicago, IL 60602-2391	July 7, 1993

WE DEBIT YOUR ACCOUNT AS FOLLOWS

5 No. 8241 Printer Covers, your Invoice No. 7291, are being returned via parcel post. Our order specified No. 825X.	@ 18.00	90.00

lustrate, the entry by Thomas Company to record the return of the merchandise indicated in the debit memo in Exhibit 4 is as follows:

July 7	Accounts Payable	90	
	Purchases Returns and Allowances		90
	Debit Memo No. 18.		

The purchases returns and allowances account is a deduction from the amount initially recorded in Purchases. Like Purchases Discounts, the purchases returns and allowances account is a contra (or offsetting) account to Purchases.

When a buyer returns merchandise or has been granted an allowance prior to the payment of the invoice, the amount of the debit memorandum is deducted from the invoice amount. The amount is deducted before the purchases discount is computed. For example, assume that the details related to the amount payable to Power Electronics Co., for which the debit memo in Exhibit 4 was issued, are as follows:

Invoice No. 7291 dated July 1 (terms 2/10, n/30)	$2,040
Debit Memo No. 18 dated July 7	90
Balance of account	$1,950
Discount (2% of $1,950)	39
Cash payment, July 11	$1,911

The cash payment is recorded by Thomas Company as follows:

July 11	Accounts Payable	1,950	
	Cash		1,911
	Purchases Discounts		39
	Payment of Invoice No. 7291 from Power Electronics Co., less Debit Memo No. 18.		

Trade Discounts

Many wholesalers of merchandise publish periodic catalogs that are used by buyers in ordering merchandise. Rather than updating their catalogs frequently, wholesalers publish price updates, which may involve large discounts from the list prices in their catalogs. In addition, sellers frequently offer certain classes of buyers, such as government agencies or buyers who order large quantities, special discounts called **trade discounts.**

Sellers and buyers do not normally record the list prices of merchandise and the related trade discounts in their accounts. For example, assume that a seller offers for sale an item with a list price of $1,000 and a 40% trade discount. The seller records the sale of the item at $600 [$1,000 less the trade discount of $400 ($1,000 × 40%)]. Likewise, the buyer records the purchase at $600. For accounting purposes, only the final price—$600 in this example—is important.

TRANSPORTATION COSTS

Objective 2c
Journalize the entries for merchandise transportation costs.

The terms of a sales agreement between a buyer and a seller should indicate when the ownership (title) of the merchandise passes to the buyer. The point at which the title of the merchandise passes to the buyer determines which party, the buyer or the seller, must pay the transportation costs.[4]

The ownership of the merchandise may pass to the buyer when the seller delivers the merchandise to the transportation company or freight carrier. In this case, the terms are said to be **FOB shipping point.** This shipping term means that the seller delivers the merchandise *free on board* to the shipping point. The buyer pays the transportation costs to the final destination.

The ownership of the merchandise may pass to the buyer when the merchandise is received by the buyer. In this case, the terms are said to be **FOB destination.** This shipping term means that the seller delivers the merchandise *free on board* to the buyer's final destination. The seller pays the transportation costs to the final destination.

Sometimes FOB shipping point and FOB destination are expressed in terms of the location at which the title to the merchandise passes to the buyer. For example, assume that a seller located in Philadelphia ships merchandise to a buyer located in Chicago. In this case, the terms FOB shipping point could be expressed as *FOB Philadelphia.* Likewise, the terms FOB destination could be expressed as *FOB Chicago.*

Shipping terms, the passage of title, and whether the buyer or seller is to pay the transportation costs are summarized below.

	FOB Shipping Point	FOB Destination
Ownership (title) passes to buyer when merchandise is	delivered to freight carrier	delivered to buyer
Transportation costs are paid by	buyer	seller

When merchandise is purchased on terms of FOB shipping point, the transportation costs paid by the buyer should be debited to Transportation In, Freight In, or a similarly titled account. The balance of the transportation in account should be added to net purchases in determining the total cost of merchandise purchased.[5]

---

[4] The passage of title also determines whether the buyer or seller must pay other costs, such as the cost of insurance while the merchandise is in transit.
[5] Some businesses prefer to debit the purchases account for transportation charges paid on merchandise purchased FOB shipping point. If this alternative is used, the balance of the purchases account will include the transportation costs borne by the buyer. The total cost of merchandise purchased will be the same as when a separate transportation in or freight in account is used.

When the terms of shipment are FOB destination, the amounts paid by the seller for delivery are debited to Transportation Out, Delivery Expense, or a similarly titled account. The total of such costs incurred during a period is reported on the seller's income statement as an expense.

As a convenience or courtesy to the buyer, the seller may prepay the transportation costs, even though the terms are FOB shipping point. The seller will then add the transportation costs to the invoice. The buyer will debit Transportation In for the transportation costs when the invoice is paid.

To illustrate, assume that on June 10, Bell Company sells merchandise to Cave Company on account, $900, terms FOB shipping point, 2/10, n/30. Bell Company pays the transportation costs of $50 and adds them to the invoice. The entries by Bell Company (the seller) are shown below.

June 10	Accounts Receivable	900	
	Sales		900
10	Accounts Receivable	50	
	Cash[6]		50

The entry by Cave Company (the buyer) on receipt of the invoice is shown below.

June 10	Purchases	900	
	Transportation In	50	
	Accounts Payable		950

If Cave Company pays the invoice within the discount period, the amount of the discount will be computed on the amount of the purchase rather than on the invoice total. For example, assume that Cave Company pays the amount due on the purchase of June 10 within 10 days. The amount of the discount and the amount of the payment are shown below.

Invoice from Bell Company, including		
prepaid transportation of $50		$950
Amount subject to discount	$900	
Rate of discount	2%	
Amount of purchases discount		18
Amount of payment		$932

Cave Company would record the payment as follows:

June 20	Accounts Payable	950	
	Cash		932
	Purchases Discounts		18

ILLUSTRATION OF ACCOUNTING FOR MERCHANDISE TRANSACTIONS

Objective 3
Journalize the entries for merchandise transactions from both the buyer's and the seller's point of view.

Each merchandising transaction, as described in the preceding paragraphs, affects a buyer and a seller. The following illustration summarizes the principles and concepts of accounting for merchandising transactions by presenting the entries that the seller and the buyer would record. In this example, the seller is Scully Company and the buyer is Burton Co.

---

[6] A company may use one freight carrier for all its shipments. In such cases, the company normally receives a monthly freight bill. If this were the case for Bell Company, Freight Payable (rather than Cash) would be credited for $50 on June 10. The freight would then be paid as part of the monthly bill.

	Scully Company (Seller)			Burton Co. (Buyer)		
July 1. Scully Company sold merchandise on account to Burton Co., $5,000, terms FOB destination, 2/10, n/30.	Accounts Receivable Sales	5,000	5,000	Purchases Accounts Payable	5,000	5,000
July 3. Scully Company paid transportation costs of $250 for delivery of merchandise sold to Burton Co. on July 1.	Transportation Out Cash	250	250	No entry.		
July 9. Scully Company issued Burton Co. a credit memorandum for merchandise returned, $1,000. The merchandise had been purchased by Burton Co. on account on July 1.	Sales Returns & Allowances Accounts Receivable	1,000	1,000	Accounts Payable Purchases Returns and Allowances	1,000	1,000
July 11. Scully Company received payment from Burton Co. for purchase of July 1, less discount and less return of July 9.	Cash Sales Discounts Accounts Receivable	3,920 80	4,000	Accounts Payable Purchases Discounts Cash	4,000	80 3,920
July 13. Scully Company sold merchandise on account to Burton Co., $12,000, terms FOB shipping point, 1/15, n/eom. Scully Company prepaid transportation costs of $500, which were added to the invoice.	Accounts Receivable Sales Accounts Receivable Cash	12,000 500	12,000 500	Purchases Transportation In Accounts Payable	12,000 500	12,500
July 28. Scully Company received payment from Burton Co. for purchase of July 13, less discount.	Cash Sales Discounts Accounts Receivable	12,380 120	12,500	Accounts Payable Purchases Discounts Cash	12,500	120 12,380
July 30. Scully Company sold merchandise on account to Burton Co., $7,500, terms FOB shipping point, 1/15, n/45.	Accounts Receivable Sales	7,500	7,500	Purchases Accounts Payable	7,500	7,500
July 31. Burton Co. paid transportation charges of $150 on July 30 purchase from Scully Company.	No entry.			Transportation In Cash	150	150

MERCHANDISE INVENTORY SYSTEMS

Objective 4
Explain the differences between the periodic and perpetual inventory systems.

There are two systems for accounting for merchandise held for sale: periodic and perpetual. In the **periodic inventory system**, the revenues from sales are recorded when sales are made. However, no attempt is made on the sale date to record the cost of the merchandise sold. A detailed listing of the merchandise on hand (called a **physical inventory** at the end of the accounting period is prepared. This physical inventory listing is used to determine (1) the cost of the merchandise sold during the period and (2) the cost of the inventory on hand at the end of the period. The periodic system, which has been used in the illustrations in this chapter, is used by many merchandising enterprises.

Under the **perpetual inventory system,** both the sales amount and the cost of merchandise sold amount are recorded when each item of merchandise is sold. In this manner, the amount of inventory on hand can always (perpetually) be determined from the accounting records. The perpetual system is discussed in the next chapter.

COST OF MERCHANDISE SOLD

Objective 5
Prepare the cost of merchandise sold section of an income statement.

Under the periodic inventory system, the cost of merchandise sold during a period is reported in a separate section in the income statement. For example, assume that on January 3, 1994, Computer King opened a merchandising outlet selling microcomputers and software. During 1994, Computer King purchased $340,000 of merchandise. The inventory at December 31, 1994, the end of the year, is $59,700. The cost of merchandise sold during 1994 is reported as follows:

Cost of merchandise sold:		
Purchases	$340,000	
Less merchandise inventory, December 31, 1994	59,700	
Cost of merchandise sold		$280,300

To continue the example, assume that during 1995 Computer King purchased additional merchandise of $521,980. Computer King also received credit for purchases returns and allowances of $9,100, took purchases discounts of $2,525, and paid transportation costs of $17,400. The purchases returns and allowances and the purchases discounts are deducted from the total purchases to yield the **net purchases.** The transportation costs are then added to the net purchases to yield the **cost of merchandise purchased.** These amounts are reported in the cost of merchandise sold section of Computer King's income statement for 1995 as follows:

Purchases		$521,980
Less: Purchases returns and allowances	$9,100	
Purchases discounts	2,525	11,625
Net purchases		$510,355
Add transportation in		17,400
Cost of merchandise purchased		$527,755

The ending inventory of Computer King on December 31, 1994, $59,700, becomes the beginning inventory for 1995. In the cost of merchandise sold section of the income statement for 1995, this beginning inventory is added to the cost of merchandise purchased to yield the **merchandise available for sale.** The ending inventory on December 31, 1995, $62,150, is then subtracted from the merchandise available for sale to yield the cost of merchandise sold. The cost of merchandise sold during 1995 is reported as follows:

Cost of merchandise sold:			
Merchandise inventory, January 1, 1995			$ 59,700
Purchases		$521,980	
Less: Purchases returns and allowances	$9,100		
Purchases discounts	2,525	11,625	
Net purchases		$510,355	
Add transportation in		17,400	
Cost of merchandise purchased			527,755
Merchandise available for sale			$587,455
Less merchandise inventory,			
December 31, 1995			62,150
Cost of merchandise sold			$525,305

The complete income statement as well as the statement of owner's equity and a balance sheet for a merchandising enterprise are illustrated in the next chapter. This discussion includes the use of a work sheet to prepare these financial statements.

CHART OF ACCOUNTS FOR A MERCHANDISING ENTERPRISE

Objective 6
Prepare a chart of accounts for a merchandising enterprise.

When Computer King opened a merchandising outlet selling microcomputers and software on January 1, 1994, it stopped providing consulting services. As a result of this change in the type of its transactions, Computer King's chart of accounts changed. A new chart of accounts for Computer King is shown in Exhibit 5. The accounts related to merchandising transactions are shown in color.

Exhibit 5
Chart of Accounts for Computer King, MerchandisingEnterprise

Balance Sheet Accounts	Income Statement Accounts
100 Assets	400 Revenues
110 Cash	410 Sales
111 Notes Receivable	411 Sales Returns and Allowances
112 Accounts Receivable	412 Sales Discounts
113 Interest Receivable	500 Expenses
115 Merchandise Inventory	510 Purchases
116 Office Supplies	511 Purchases Returns and Allowances
117 Prepaid Insurance	512 Purchases Discounts
120 Land	513 Transportation In
123 Store Equipment	520 Sales Salaries Expense
124 Accumulated Depreciation—	521 Advertising Expense
Store Equipment	522 Depreciation Expense—Store
125 Office Equipment	Equipment
126 Accumulated Depreciation—	529 Miscellaneous Selling Expense
Office Equipment	530 Office Salaries Expense
200 Liabilities	531 Rent Expense
210 Accounts Payable	532 Depreciation Expense—Office
211 Salaries Payable	Equipment
212 Unearned Rent	533 Insurance Expense
215 Notes Payable	534 Office Supplies Expense
300 Owner's Equity	539 Misc. Administrative Expense
310 Jere King, Capital	600 Other Income
311 Jere King, Drawing	610 Rent Income
312 Income Summary	611 Interest Income
	700 Other Expense
	710 Interest Expense

Computer King is now using 3-digit account numbers, which are assigned in a manner that permits the addition of new accounts as they are needed. The first digit indicates the major financial statement classification (1 for assets, 2 for liabilities, etc.). The second digit indicates the subclassification (11 for current assets, 21 for current liabilities, etc.). The third digit identifies the specific account (110 for Cash, 210 for Accounts Payable, etc.).

Computer King is using a more complex numbering system because it has a greater variety of transactions. As enterprises grow, the types of transactions and the complexities of transactions usually increase. For example, a rapidly growing enterprise may borrow funds to expand its operations by issuing notes payable. The enterprise may also accept notes receivable from major customers for sales of merchandise. Interest expense may be incurred on the notes payable, and interest income may be earned on the notes receivable. Thus, such transactions require the inclusion of Notes Receivable, Notes Payable, Interest Income, and Interest Expense in the chart of accounts.

The growth of an enterprise also creates a need for more detailed information for use in managing the enterprise. For example, a wages expense account may be adequate for managing a small service enterprise with one or two employees. However, a merchandising enterprise normally uses two or more payroll accounts, such as Sales Salaries Expense and Office Salaries Expense. Also, the chart of accounts for a merchandising enterprise normally classifies expenses as selling or administrative expenses.

The increase in the complexity of Computer King's transactions also increases the complexity of its financial statements. The financial statements for Computer King's operations as a merchandising enterprise are illustrated in the next chapter.

CHAPTER REVIEW

Key Points

Objective 1. Compare and contrast a service enterprise's income statement to a merchandising enterprise's income statement.

The primary differences between a service enterprise and a merchandising enterprise relate to the revenue activities of the enterprises. Merchandising enterprises purchase merchandise for selling to customers.

On a merchandise enterprise's income statement, revenue from selling merchandise is reported as sales. The cost of the merchandise sold is subtracted from sales to arrive at gross profit. The operating expenses are subtracted from gross profit to arrive at net income.

Merchandise inventory, which is merchandise not sold, is reported as a current asset on a merchandise enterprise's balance sheet.

Objective 2a. Journalize the entries for merchandise sales.

Sales of merchandise for cash or on account are recorded in the ledger as a credit to Sales. For sales of merchandise on account, the credit terms may allow sales discounts for early payment. Such discounts are recorded by the seller as a debit to Sales Discounts. Sales discounts are reported as a deduction from the amount initially recorded in Sales. Likewise, when merchandise is returned or a price adjustment is granted, the seller records the adjustment as a debit to Sales Returns and Allowances.

The liability for sales tax is incurred at the time the sale is made and is recorded by the seller as a credit to the sales tax payable account. When the amount of the sales tax is paid to the taxing unit, Sales Tax Payable is debited and Cash is credited.

Objective 2b. Journalize the entries for merchandise purchases.

Purchases of merchandise for cash or on account are recorded in the ledger as a debit to Purchases. For purchases of merchandise on account, the credit terms may allow cash discounts for early payment. Such discounts are recorded by the buyer as a credit to Purchases Discounts. Purchases discounts are reported as a deduction from the amount initially recorded in Purchases. Likewise, when merchandise is returned or a price adjustment is granted, the buyer records the adjustment as a credit to Purchases Returns and Allowances.

Many wholesalers offer trade discounts, which are discounts off the list prices of merchandise. Neither the seller nor the buyer normally records the list price and the trade discount.

Objective 2c. Journalize the entries for merchandise transportation costs.

When merchandise is shipped FOB shipping point, the buyer pays the transportation costs and debits either Transportation In or Freight In. When merchandise is shipped FOB destination, the seller pays the transportation costs and debits Transportation Out, Delivery Expense, or a similarly titled account. If the seller pays transportation costs as a convenience to the buyer, the seller debits Accounts Receivable for the amount of the costs.

Objective 3. Journalize the entries for merchandise transactions from both the buyer's and the seller's point of view.

The illustration in this chapter summarizes the principles and concepts of accounting for merchandising transactions by presenting the entries that the seller and the buyer would record.

Objective 4. Explain the differences between the periodic and perpetual inventory systems.

Under the periodic system of accounting for merchandise, no attempt is made to record the cost of merchandise sold until the end of the period. A detailed listing of the merchandise on hand (called a **physical inventory**) at the end of the accounting period is prepared. This physical inventory listing is used to determine (1) the cost of the merchandise sold during the period and (2) the cost of the inventory on hand at the end of the period.

Under the **perpetual system,** both the sales amount and the cost of merchandise sold amount are recorded when each item of merchandise is sold. In this manner, the amount of inventory on hand can always (perpetually) be determined from the accounting records.

Objective 5. Prepare the cost of merchandise sold section of an income statement.

In preparing the cost of merchandise sold section of an income statement under a periodic inventory system, purchases returns and allowances and purchases discounts are deducted from the total purchases to yield the net purchases. The transportation costs are then added to the net purchases to yield the cost of merchandise purchased. The beginning inventory is added to the cost of merchandise purchased to yield the merchandise available for sale. The ending inventory is subtracted from this amount to yield the cost of merchandise sold.

Objective 6. Prepare a chart of accounts for a merchandising enterprise.

The chart of accounts for a merchandising enterprise is more complex than that for a service enterprise and normally includes accounts such as Sales, Sales Discounts, Sales Returns and Allowances, Purchases, Purchases Discounts, Purchases Returns and Allowances, Advertising Expense, and Sales Salaries.

Glossary of Key Terms

Credit memorandum. The form issued by a seller to inform a buyer that a credit has been posted to the buyer's account receivable. **Objective 2a**

Debit memorandum. The form issued by a buyer to inform a seller that a debit has been posted to the seller's account payable. **Objective 2b**

FOB destination. Terms of agreement between buyer and seller whereby ownership passes when merchandise is received by the buyer, and the seller pays the transportation costs. **Objective 2c**

FOB shipping point. Terms of agreement between buyer and seller whereby ownership passes when merchandise is delivered to the freight carrier, and the buyer pays the transportation costs. **Objective 2c**

Invoice. The bill provided by the seller (who refers to it as a sales invoice) to a buyer (who refers to it as a purchase invoice) for items purchased. **Objective 2a**

Merchandise inventory. Merchandise on hand and available for sale to customers. **Objective 1**

Periodic inventory system. A system of inventory accounting in which only the revenue from sales is recorded each time a sale is made. The cost of merchandise on hand at the end of a period is determined by a detailed listing (physical inventory) of the merchandise on hand. **Objective 4**

Perpetual inventory system. A system of inventory accounting in which both the revenue from sales and the cost of merchandise sold are recorded each time a sale is made, so that the records continually disclose the amount of the inventory on hand. **Objective 4**

Physical inventory. The detailed listing of merchandise on hand. **Objective 4**

Purchases discounts. An available discount taken by a buyer for early payment of an invoice; a contra account to Purchases. **Objective 2b**

Purchases returns and allowances. Reductions in purchases, resulting from merchandise being returned to the seller or from the seller's reduction in the original purchase price; a contra account to Purchases. **Objective 2b**

Sales discounts. An available discount granted by a seller for early payment of an invoice; a contra account to Sales. **Objective 2a**

Sales returns and allowances. Reductions in sales, resulting from merchandise being returned by customers or from the seller's reduction in the original sales price; a contra account to Sales. **Objective 2a**

Trade discounts. Special discounts from published list prices, offered by sellers to certain classes of buyers. **Objective 2b**

Self-Examination Questions
Answers at end of chapter.

1. If merchandise purchased on account is returned, the buyer may inform the seller of the details by issuing:
   A. a debit memorandum   C. an invoice
   B. a credit memorandum   D. a bill

2. If merchandise is sold on account to a customer for $1,000, terms FOB shipping point, 1/10, n/30, and the seller prepays $50 in transportation costs, the amount of the discount for early payment would be:
   A. $0   C. $10.00
   B. $5.00   D. $10.50

3. Merchandise is sold on account to a customer for $1,000, terms FOB destination, 1/10, n/30. If the seller pays $50 in transportation costs and the customer returns $100 of the merchandise prior to payment, what is the amount of the discount for early payment?
   A. $0   C. $10.00
   B. $9.00   D. $10.50

4. Sorter Co. sells merchandise on account to Beecher Co., terms FOB shipping point. Sorter Co. pays the transportation costs and adds them to the invoice. The accounts debited by Sorter Co. (seller) and Beecher Co. (buyer) to record the transportation costs are, respectively:
   A. Transportation Out, Purchases
   B. Accounts Receivable, Accounts Payable
   C. Sales, Transportation In
   D. Accounts Receivable, Transportation In

5. For an enterprise using the periodic inventory system, which of the following is added in computing the cost of merchandise sold?
   A. purchases
   B. purchases discounts
   C. purchases returns and allowances
   D. merchandise inventory at the end of the period

ILLUSTRATIVE PROBLEM

MacBride Discount Stores entered into the following selected transactions during August of the current year:

Aug. 1.   Purchased merchandise on account, terms 2/10, n/30, FOB shipping point, $28,500.
    1.   Paid rent for August, $4,500.
    2.   Paid transportation charges on purchase of August 1, $1,180.

Aug. 5.   Purchased office supplies for cash, $600.

7.   Sold merchandise on account, terms 1/10, n/30, FOB destination, $12,400.

8.   Paid transportation charges on sale of August 7, $550.

11.   Paid for merchandise purchased on August 1, less discount.

12.   Received merchandise returned from sale of August 7, $3,200.

14.   Purchased merchandise on account, terms 4/15, n/30, FOB shipping point, $18,300, with prepaid transportation costs of $750 added to the invoice.

16.   Returned merchandise purchased on August 14, $5,200.

17.   Received cash on account from sale of August 7, less return and discount.

18.   Sold merchandise on account, terms 1/10, n/30, FOB shipping point, $8,800. Prepaid transportation costs for the customer's convenience, $250.

26.   Sold merchandise on bank credit cards, $3,700.

29.   Paid for merchandise purchased on August 14, less return and discount.

31.   Received cash on account from sale of August 18, $9,050.

Instructions

Journalize the entries to record the August transactions.

Solution

Aug. 1	Purchases	28,500	
	Accounts Payable		28,500
1	Rent Expense	4,500	
	Cash		4,500
2	Transportation In	1,180	
	Cash		1,180
5	Office Supplies	600	
	Cash		600
7	Accounts Receivable	12,400	
	Sales		12,400
8	Transportation Out	550	
	Cash		550
11	Accounts Payable	28,500	
	Purchases Discounts		570
	Cash		27,930
12	Sales Returns and Allowances	3,200	
	Accounts Receivable		3,200
14	Purchases	18,300	
	Transportation In	750	
	Accounts Payable		19,050
16	Accounts Payable	5,200	
	Purchases Returns and Allowances		5,200
17	Cash	9,108	
	Sales Discounts	92	
	Accounts Receivable		9,200
18	Accounts Receivable	8,800	
	Sales		8,800
18	Accounts Receivable	250	
	Cash		250
26	Cash	3,700	
	Sales		3,700
29	Accounts Payable	13,850	
	Purchases Discounts*		524
	Cash		13,326
	*($18,300 − $5,200) × 4% = $524		
31	Cash	9,050	
	Accounts Receivable		9,050

DISCUSSION QUESTIONS

1. What distinguishes a merchandising enterprise from a service enterprise?
2. What is gross profit?
3. If sales were $250,000 and the cost of merchandise sold was $175,000, what was the amount of the gross profit?
4. If sales were $410,000 and the gross profit was $150,000, what was the amount of the cost of merchandise sold?
5. Can a business enterprise earn a gross profit but incur a net loss? Explain.
6. What is the name of the account in which sales of merchandise are recorded?
7. How does the accounting for sales to customers using bank credit cards, such as MasterCard and VISA, differ from accounting for sales to customers using nonbank credit cards, such as American Express?
8. The credit period during which the buyer of merchandise is allowed to pay usually begins with what date?
9. Boggs Company ordered $1,000 of merchandise from Sherrill Company on June 1, terms 1/10, n/30. Although Sherrill Company shipped the merchandise on June 6, the merchandise was not received by Boggs Company until June 7. The invoice received with the merchandise was dated June 6. What is the last date Boggs Company could pay the invoice and still receive the discount?
10. What is the meaning of (a) 1/10, n/60; (b) n/30; (c) n/eom?
11. What is the term applied by the seller to discounts for early payment of an invoice?
12. What is the nature of a credit memorandum issued by the seller of merchandise?
13. What two contra accounts are normally used with the sales account?
14. After the amount due on a sale of $5,000, terms 1/10, n/eom, is received from a customer within the discount period, the seller consents to the return of the entire shipment. (a) What is the amount of the refund owed to the customer? (b) What accounts should be debited and credited by the seller to record the return and the refund?
15. The debits and credits for three related transactions are presented in the following T accounts. Describe each transaction.

	Cash			Sales Discount	
(3)	9,310		(3)	190	

	Accounts Receivable				Sales Returns and Allowances	
(1)	10,000	(2)	500	(2)	500	
		(3)	9,500			

	Sales	
	(1)	10,000

16. A sale of merchandise on account for $200 is subject to a 6% sales tax. (a) Should the sales tax be recorded at the time of sale or when payment is received? (b) What is the amount of the sale? (c) What is the amount debited to Accounts Receivable? (d) What is the title of the account to which the $12 is credited?
17. What is the name of the account in which purchases of merchandise are recorded?
18. What term is used by the buyer to refer to discounts taken for early payment of an invoice?
19. Indicate the account that would be debited for each of the following purchases by a grocery supermarket: (a) purchase of a computerized cash register, (b) purchase of a frozen foods display case, (c) purchase of a case of breakfast cereal, (d) purchase of office supplies.
20. Ames Company purchased merchandise on account from a supplier for $2,000, terms 1/10, n/30. Ames Company returned $500 of the merchandise and received full credit. (a) If Ames Company pays the invoice within the discount period, what is the amount of cash required for the payment? (b) What accounts are credited by Ames Company to record the return and the cash discount?

21. The debits and credits from four related transactions are presented in the following T
    accounts. (a) Describe each transaction. (b) What is the rate of the discount and on
    what amount was it computed?

Cash			Accounts Payable			
(2)	100		(3)	1,000	(1)	5,000
(4)	3,920		(4)	4,000		

Purchases			Purchases Discounts		
(1)	5,000			(4)	80

Transportation In			Purchases Returns and Allowances		
(2)	100			(3)	1,000

22. What is the nature of a debit memorandum issued by the buyer of merchandise?
23. Who bears the transportation costs when the terms of sale are (a) FOB shipping point,
    (b) FOB destination?
24. Merchandise is sold on account to a customer for $10,000, terms FOB shipping point,
    1/10, n/30. The seller paid the transportation costs of $250. Determine the following:
    (a) amount of the sale, (b) amount debited to Accounts Receivable, (c) amount of the
    discount for early payment, (d) amount due within the discount period.
25. A retailer is considering the purchase of 10 units of a specific item from either of two
    suppliers. Their offers are as follows:
    A: $500 a unit, total of $5,000, 2/10, n/30, plus transportation costs of $275.
    B: $520 a unit, total of $5,200, 1/10, n/30, no charge for transportation.
    Which of the two offers, A or B, yields the lower price?
26. If purchases during an accounting period totaled $610,000, transportation in was
    $5,500, purchases discounts were $7,000, and purchases returns and allowances were
    $20,000, what was the (a) net purchases, (b) cost of merchandise purchased?
27. What is the normal balance of the following accounts: (a) sales returns and allowances,
    (b) purchases discounts, (c) sales discounts, (d) transportation in, (e) purchases returns
    and allowances, (f) sales, (g) purchases?
28. In which type of system for accounting for merchandise held for sale is there no at-
    tempt to record the cost of merchandise sold until the end of the period, when a physi-
    cal inventory is taken?

REAL W🌐RLD FOCUS

29. It is not unusual for a customer to drive into some Texaco, Mobil, or BP gasoline sta-
    tions and discover that the cash price per gallon is 3 or 4 cents less than the credit price
    per gallon. As a result, many customers pay cash rather than use their credit cards.
    Why would a gasoline station owner establish such a policy?

ETHICS DISCUSSION CASE

On March 1, 1993, Katz Company purchased $5,000 of merchandise, terms 1/10, n/30,
from C. L. Allan Co. Even though the discount period had expired on March 15, 1993, Kay
Williams subtracted the discount of $50 when she processed the documents for payment by
the treasurer.

Discuss whether Kay Williams behaved in an ethical manner by subtracting the discount, even though the discount period had expired.

EXERCISES

EXERCISE 5-1
**DETERMINATION OF GROSS
PROFIT**
Objective 1

During the current year, merchandise is sold for $200,000 cash and for $375,000 on account.
The cost of the merchandise sold is $490,000.

a. What is the amount of the gross profit?

b. Will the income statement necessarily report a net income? Explain.

EXERCISE 5-2
CONDENSED INCOME
STATEMENT
Objective 1

The following data for the current year ended December 31 were taken from the accounting records of Bridges Company:

Cost of merchandise sold	$142,500
Operating expenses	50,000
Sales	210,000

Prepare an income statement for the year ended December 31.

EXERCISE 5-3
DETERMINATION OF
AMOUNTS TO BE PAID ON
INVOICES
Objective 2

Determine the amount to be paid in full settlement of each of the following invoices, assuming that credit for returns and allowances was received prior to payment and that all invoices were paid within the discount period.

	Merchandise	Transportation	Terms	Returns and Allowances
a.	$10,000	—	FOB destination, n/30	$ 500
b.	8,000	—	FOB destination, 2/10, n/30	—
c.	6,000	—	FOB shipping point, 1/10, n/30	1,000
d.	4,000	$90	FOB shipping point, 1/10, n/30	100
e.	2,000	50	FOB shipping point, 2/10, n/30	750

EXERCISE 5-4
SALES-RELATED
TRANSACTIONS,
INCLUDING THE USE OF
CREDIT CARDS
Objective 2

Journalize the entries for the following transactions:

a. Sold merchandise for cash, $12,500.
b. Sold merchandise on account, $10,000.
c. Sold merchandise to customers who used MasterCard and VISA, $4,750.
d. Sold merchandise to customers who used American Express, $3,100.
e. Paid an invoice from First National Bank for $250, representing a service fee for processing of MasterCard and VISA sales.
f. Received $2,910 from American Express Company after a $190 collection fee had been deducted.

EXERCISE 5-5
SALES TAX TRANSACTIONS
Objective 2

Journalize the entries to record the following selected transactions:

a. Sold $5,000 of merchandise on account, subject to a sales tax of 6%.
b. Paid $1,650 to the state sales tax department for taxes collected.

EXERCISE 5-6
SALES RETURNS AND
ALLOWANCES
Objective 2

During the year, sales returns and allowances totaled $89,950. The accountant recorded all the returns and allowances by debiting the sales account.

▌SHARPEN YOUR ►
COMMUNICATION SKILLS

Was the accountant's method of recording returns acceptable? Explain. In your explanation, include the advantages of using a sales returns and allowances account.

EXERCISE 5-7
SALES-RELATED
TRANSACTIONS
Objective 2

Journalize the entries for the following related transactions:

May 5. Sold merchandise to a customer for $10,000, terms FOB shipping point, 2/10, n/30.
     5. Paid the transportation charges of $120, debiting the amount to Accounts Receivable.
    10. Issued a credit memorandum for $1,000 to the customer for merchandise returned.
    15. Received a check for the amount due from the sale.

EXERCISE 5-8
SALES-RELATED
TRANSACTIONS
Objective 2

Curtis Company sells merchandise to FDF Co. on account, $7,500, FOB shipping point, 1/10, n/30. Curtis Company pays the transportation charges of $250 as a convenience to FDF Co. and adds it to the invoice. Curtis Company issues a credit memorandum for $500 for merchandise returned and subsequently receives the amount due within the discount period. Journalize Curtis Company's entries to record (a) the sale and the transportation costs, (b) the credit memorandum, and (c) the receipt of the check for the amount due.

EXERCISE 5-9
PURCHASE-RELATED
TRANSACTIONS
Objective 2

Based upon the data presented in Exercise 5-8, journalize FDF Co.'s entries to record (a) the purchase, including the transportation charges, (b) the return of the merchandise for credit, and (c) the payment of the invoice within the discount period.

EXERCISE 5-10
PURCHASE-RELATED
TRANSACTIONS
Objective 2

Leonard Co. purchases $6,000 of merchandise from a supplier on account, terms FOB shipping point, 1/10, n/30. The supplier adds transportation charges of $150 to the invoice. Leonard Co. returns some of the merchandise, receiving a credit memorandum for $500, and then pays the amount due within the discount period. Journalize Leonard Co.'s entries to record (a) the purchase, (b) the merchandise return, and (c) the payment.

EXERCISE 5-11
PURCHASE-RELATED
TRANSACTIONS
Objective 2

Journalize entries for the following related transactions of Drysdale Company:
a. Purchased $10,000 of merchandise from Craig Co. on account, terms 1/10, n/30.
b. Paid the amount owed on the invoice within the discount period.
c. Discovered that some of the merchandise was defective and returned items with an invoice price of $1,000, receiving credit.
d. Purchased $800 of merchandise from Craig Co. on account, terms 1/10, n/30.
e. Received a check for the balance owed from the return in (c), after deducting for the purchase in (d).

EXERCISE 5-12
SALES, PURCHASES, AND
SALES TAX
Objective 2

Journalize entries to record the following related transactions of Mattix Co.:
a. Purchased merchandise on account, $15,000, terms 1/10, n/30.
b. Sold $3,000 of merchandise on account, subject to a sales tax of 5%.
c. Paid the amount owed in (a) within the discount period.
d. Paid $2,100 to the state sales tax department for taxes collected.

EXERCISE 5-13
SAVINGS FROM TAKING
PURCHASES DISCOUNTS
Objective 2

On August 1, Stone Co. purchases $15,000 of merchandise, terms 1/10, n/30.
a. Determine the latest date that Stone Co. can make payment and take the cash discount.
b. Determine the latest date that Stone Co. can make payment under the credit terms.
c. If Stone Co. can borrow money at a 10% annual rate of interest, determine how much can be saved by borrowing to take advantage of the discount.

EXERCISE 5-14
IDENTIFY ITEMS MISSING IN
DETERMINING COST OF
MERCHANDISE SOLD
Objective 5

For (a) through (d), identify the items designated by "X."
a. Purchases - (X + X) = Net purchases.
b. Net purchases + X = Cost of merchandise purchased.
c. Merchandise inventory (beginning) + Cost of merchandise purchased = X.
d. Merchandise available for sale - X = Cost of merchandise sold.

EXERCISE 5-15
CHART OF ACCOUNTS
Objective 6

Kline Co. is a newly organized enterprise with the following list of accounts, arranged in alphabetical order:

Accounts Payable	Notes Payable (short-term)
Accounts Receivable	Notes Receivable (short-term)
Accumulated Depreciation—Office Equipment	Office Equipment
Accumulated Depreciation—Store Equipment	Office Salaries Expense
Advertising Expense	Office Supplies
Cash	Office Supplies Expense
Depreciation Expense—Office Equipment	Prepaid Insurance
Depreciation Expense—Store Equipment	Purchases
Income Summary	Purchases Returns and Allowances
Insurance Expense	Purchases Discounts
Interest Expense	Rent Expense
Interest Income	Salaries Payable
Interest Receivable	Sales
C. C. Kline, Capital	Sales Returns and Allowances
C. C. Kline, Drawing	Sales Discounts
Land	Sales Salaries Expense
Merchandise Inventory	Store Equipment
Miscellaneous Administrative Expense	Store Supplies
Miscellaneous Selling Expense	Store Supplies Expense
	Transportation In

Construct a chart of accounts, assigning account numbers and arranging the accounts in balance sheet and income statement order, as illustrated in Exhibit 5. Each account number is to be composed of three digits: the first digit is to indicate the major classification ("1" for assets, etc.), the second digit is to indicate the subclassification ("11" for current assets, etc.), and the third digit is to identify the specific account ("110" for Cash, etc.).

How many errors can you find in the following schedule of cost of merchandise sold for the current year ended December 31?

Cost of merchandise sold:

Merchandise inventory, December 31			$105,000
Purchases		$500,000	
Plus: Purchases returns and allowances	$12,500		
Purchases discounts	6,500	19,000	
Gross purchases		$519,000	
Less transportation in		2,400	
Cost of merchandise purchased			516,600
Merchandise available for sale			$621,600
Less merchandise inventory, January 1			111,300
Cost of merchandise sold			$510,300

PROBLEMS

Series A

PROBLEM 5-1A
SALES-RELATED
TRANSACTIONS
Objective 2

The following selected transactions were completed by Lawrence Supply Co., which sells primarily to wholesalers but occasionally sells to retail customers.

July 1. Sold merchandise on account to Griffin Company, $4,000, terms FOB destination, 2/10, n/30.
       1. Paid transportation costs of $95 on merchandise sold on July 1.
       2. Sold merchandise for $600 plus 5% sales tax to cash customers.
       3. Sold merchandise on account to Vance Co., $2,500, terms FOB shipping point, n/eom.
       5. Sold merchandise for $1,200 plus 5% sales tax to customers who used Master-Cards. Deposited credit card receipts into the bank.
       8. Sold merchandise on account to Vance Co., $1,500, terms FOB shipping point, n/eom.
      11. Received check for amount due from Griffin Company for sale on July 1.
      12. Sold merchandise to customers who used American Express cards, $3,500.
      13. Sold merchandise on account to Monroe Co., $6,500, terms FOB shipping point, 1/10, n/30.
      15. Issued credit memorandum for $500 to Monroe Co. for merchandise returned from sale on July 13.
      16. Sold merchandise on account to Davis Co., $10,000, terms FOB destination, 2/15, n/30.
      18. Sold merchandise on account to Braggs Company, $7,500, terms FOB shipping point, 1/10, n/30. Paid $85 for transportation costs and added them to the invoice.
      23. Received check for amount due from Monroe Co. for sale on July 13 less credit memorandum of July 15 and discount.
      24. Issued credit memorandum for $250 to Davis Co. for allowance for damaged merchandise sold on July 16.
      26. Received $9,410 from American Express for $10,000 of sales reported during the week of July 11–17.
      28. Received check for amount due from Braggs Company for sale of July 18.
      30. Received check for amount due from Vance Co. for sales of July 3 and July 8.
      31. Paid Ace Delivery Service $770 for merchandise delivered during July to local customers under shipping terms of FOB destination.
Aug. 4. Paid First National Bank $480 for service fees for handling MasterCard sales during July.
      10. Paid $875 to state sales tax division for taxes owed on July sales.
      15. Received check for amount due from Davis Co. for sale of July 16, less credit memorandum of July 24.

Instructions
Journalize entries to record the transactions of Lawrence Supply Co.

PROBLEM 5-2A
PURCHASE-RELATED
TRANSACTIONS
Objective 2

The following selected transactions were completed by Willis Company during July of the current year.

July 1. Purchased merchandise from Larkin Co., $4,800, terms FOB destination, n/30.
      3. Purchased merchandise from Toomes Co., $10,000, terms FOB shipping point, 1/10, n/eom. Prepaid transportation costs of $200 were added to the invoice.
      5. Purchased merchandise from Warwich Co., $5,000, terms FOB destination, 2/10, n/30.
      8. Issued debit memorandum for $1,000 to Warwich Co. for merchandise returned from purchase on July 5.
      13. Paid Toomes Co. for invoice of July 3, less discount.
      15. Paid Warwich Co. for invoice of July 5, less debit memorandum of July 8 and discount.
      18. Purchased merchandise from Astro Company, $8,250, terms FOB shipping point, n/eom.
      18. Paid transportation charges of $220 on July 18 purchase from Astro Company.
      19. Purchased merchandise from Hatcher Co., $4,500, terms FOB destination, 2/10, n/30.
      29. Paid Hatcher Co. for invoice of July 19, less discount.
      31. Paid Larkin Co. for invoice of July 1.
      31. Paid Astro Company for invoice of July 18.

Instructions
Journalize entries to record the transactions of Willis Company for July.

PROBLEM 5-3A
SALES-RELATED AND
PURCHASE-RELATED
TRANSACTIONS FOR
SELLER AND BUYER
Objectives 2, 3

The following selected transactions were completed during October between Sims Company and J. C. Power Co.

Oct. 4. Sims Company sold merchandise on account to J. C. Power Co., $10,000, terms FOB destination, 1/15, n/eom.
      4. Sims Company paid transportation costs of $600 for delivery of merchandise sold to J. C. Power Co. on October 4.
      10. Sims Company sold merchandise on account to J. C. Power Co., $15,000, terms FOB shipping point, n/eom.
      12. J. C. Power Co. returned merchandise purchased on account on October 4 from Sims Company, $2,000.
      14. J. C. Power Co. paid transportation charges of $1,200 on October 10 purchase from Sims Company.
      18. Sims Company sold merchandise on account to J. C. Power Co., $18,000, terms FOB shipping point, 2/10, n/30. Sims Company paid transportation costs of $1,500, which were added to the invoice.
      19. J. C. Power Co. paid Sims Company for purchase of October 4, less discount and less return of October 12.
      28. J. C. Power Co. paid Sims Company on account for purchase of October 18, less discount.
      31. J. C. Power Co. paid Sims Company on account for purchase of October 10.

Instructions
Journalize the October transactions for (1) Sims Company and (2) J. C. Power Co.

PROBLEM 5-4A
SALES-RELATED AND
PURCHASE-RELATED
TRANSACTIONS
Objective 2

The following were selected from among the transactions completed by Freeman Company during November of the current year

Nov. 3. Purchased office supplies for cash, $720.
      5. Purchased merchandise on account from Butler Co., list price $20,000, trade discount 37.5%, terms FOB destination, 1/10, n/30.
      6. Sold merchandise for cash, $2,950.
      7. Purchased merchandise on account from Mattox Co., $6,400, terms FOB shipping point, 2/10, n/30, with prepaid transportation costs of $190 added to the invoice.
      7. Returned merchandise purchased on November 5 from Butler Co., $2,500.
      11. Sold merchandise on account to Bowles Co., list price $2,250, trade discount 20%, terms 1/10, n/30.

Nov. 15. Paid Butler Co. on account for purchase of November 5, less return of November 7 and discount.

16. Sold merchandise on nonbank credit cards and reported accounts to the card company, $3,850.

17. Paid Mattox Co. on account for purchase of November 7, less discount.

19. Purchased merchandise for cash, $3,500.

21. Received cash on account from sale of November 11 to Bowles Co., less discount.

24. Sold merchandise on account to Clemons Co., $4,200, terms 1/10, n/30.

28. Received cash from card company for nonbank credit card sales of November 16, less $190 service fee.

30. Received merchandise returned by Clemons Co. from sale on November 24, $2,700.

Instructions

Journalize the transactions for Freeman Co.

SOLUTIONS SOFTWARE

Instructions for Solving Problem 5-4A Using Solutions Software

1. Load opening balances.
2. Save the opening balances file to your drive and directory.
3. Set the run date to November 30 of the current year and enter your name.
4. Select the General Journal Entries option and enter the journal entries. Leave the refer-reference field blank.
5. Display the journal entries.
6. Display a trial balance.
7. Key the adjusting entry for merchandise inventory. (The merchandise inventory on November 30 is $60,000.) Key ADJ.ENT. in the reference field.
8. Display the adjusting entry. Key ADJ.ENT. in the Reference Restriction area of the Selection Options screen.
9. Display the financial statements.
10. Save your data file to disk.
11. End the session.

PROBLEM 5-5A
SALES-RELATED AND PURCHASE-RELATED TRANSACTIONS, TRIAL BALANCE
Objective 2

The account balances at July 1 of the current year of Raleigh Company are as follows:

11	Cash	$ 15,540
12	Accounts Receivable	31,800
13	Merchandise Inventory	82,600
14	Prepaid Insurance	2,500
15	Store Supplies	1,700
21	Accounts Payable	28,300
31	C. Raleigh, Capital	105,840
32	C. Raleigh, Drawing	—
33	Income Summary	—
41	Sales	—
42	Sales Returns and Allowances	—
43	Sales Discounts	—
51	Purchases	—
52	Purchases Returns and Allowances	—
53	Purchases Discounts	—
54	Transportation In	—
55	Sales Salaries Expense	—
56	Advertising Expense	—
57	Store Supplies Expense	—
58	Miscellaneous Selling Expense	—
59	Office Salaries Expense	—
60	Rent Expense	—
61	Insurance Expense	—
62	Miscellaneous Administrative Expense	—

The following transactions were completed during July of the current year:

July 1. Paid rent for month, $2,500.
      3. Purchased merchandise on account, $11,200.
      5. Purchased merchandise on account, FOB shipping point, $18,600.
      8. Sold merchandise on account, $12,300.
      9. Paid transportation charges on the purchase on July 5, $450.
     10. Received $14,750 cash from customers on account, after discounts of $250 were deducted.
     11. Paid creditors $16,700 on account, after discounts of $280 had been deducted.
     14. Sold merchandise for cash, $9,500.
     15. Received merchandise returned on account, $800.
     16. Paid sales salaries of $3,400 and office salaries of $1,100.
     17. Paid creditors $12,750 on account, after discounts of $200 had been deducted.
     18. Received $9,500 cash from customers on account, after discounts of $120 had been deducted.
     21. Purchased merchandise on account, $15,200.
     22. Paid advertising expense, $3,000.
     23. Sold merchandise for cash, $8,100.
     24. Returned merchandise purchased on account, $6,800.
     25. Sold merchandise for cash, $4,600.
     28. Sold merchandise on account, $27,300.
     28. Refunded $350 cash on sales made for cash.
     29. Paid sales salaries of $2,800 and office salaries of $1,100.
     30. Paid creditors $10,900 on account, no discount.
     31. Received $12,500 cash from customers on account, no discount.

Instructions
1. Enter the July 1 balances in the appropriate balance column of a four-column account. Write *Balance* in the item section, and place a check mark (✓) in the Posting Reference column.
2. Journalize the transactions for July.
3. Post the journal to the ledger, extending the month-end balances to the appropriate balance columns after all posting is completed.
4. Prepare a trial balance of the ledger as of July 31.

SOLUTIONS
SOFTWARE

Instructions for Solving Problem 5-5A Using Solutions Software
1. Load opening balances.
2. Save the opening balances file to your drive and directory.
3. Set the run date to July 31 of the current year and enter your name.
4. Select the General Journal Entries option and enter the journal entries. Leave the reference field blank.
5. Display the journal entries.
6. Display a trial balance.
7. Key the adjusting entries, based on the following data:

Insurance expired on July 31	$ 500
Store supplies on hand on July 31	900
Merchandise inventory, July 31	86,600

    Key ADJ.ENT. in the reference field.
8. Display the adjusting entries. Key ADJ.ENT. in the Reference Restriction area of the Selection Options screen.
9. Display the financial statements.
10. Save your data file to disk.
11. End the session.

PROBLEM 5-6A
COST OF MERCHANDISE
SOLD AND RELATED ITEMS
Objective 5

The following data were extracted from the accounting records of C. L. Williams Company for the year ended April 30, 1994:

Merchandise Inventory, May 1, 1993	$115,000
Merchandise Inventory, April 30, 1994	125,000
Purchases	550,000
Purchases Returns and Allowances	4,500
Purchases Discounts	2,950
Sales	670,625
Transportation In	3,950

SPREADSHEET PROBLEM

$

SHARPEN YOUR COMMUNICATION SKILLS ►

Instructions

1. Prepare the cost of merchandise sold section of the income statement for the year ended April 30, 1994.
2. Determine the gross profit to be reported on the income statement for the year ended April 30, 1994.
3. What is the rate of gross profit to sales for the year ended April 30, 1994?
4. If the merchandise inventory on April 30, 1994, had been overstated by $20,000, what would be the effect of the error on the gross profit? Explain.

Series B

PROBLEM 5-1B
SALES-RELATED
TRANSACTIONS
Objective 2

The following selected transactions were completed by Buller Co., which sells primarily to wholesalers but occasionally sells to retail customers.

May 1. Sold merchandise on account to McGee Company, $12,000, terms FOB destination, 1/10, n/30.
   1. Paid transportation costs of $225 on merchandise sold on May 1.
   2. Sold merchandise for $700 plus 6% sales tax to cash customers.
   3. Sold merchandise on account to Boskie Co., $2,500, terms FOB shipping point, n/eom.
   5. Sold merchandise for $1,200 plus 6% sales tax to customers who used VISA Cards. Deposited credit card receipts into the bank.
   8. Sold merchandise on account to Boskie Co., $4,500, terms FOB shipping point, n/eom.
   11. Received check for amount due from McGee Company for sale on May 1.
   12. Sold merchandise to customers who used American Express cards, $2,500.
   13. Sold merchandise on account to Monroe Co., $6,500, terms FOB shipping point, 1/10, n/30.
   15. Issued credit memorandum for $500 to Monroe Co. for merchandise returned from sale on May 13.
   16. Sold merchandise on account to Felder Co., $5,000, terms FOB destination , 2/15, n/30.
   18. Sold merchandise on account to Stockton Company, $7,500, terms FOB shipping point, 1/10, n/30. Paid $110 for transportation costs and added them to the invoice.
   23. Received check for amount due from Monroe Co. for sale on May 13 less credit memorandum of May 15 and discount.
   24. Issued credit memorandum for $250 to Felder Co. for allowance for damaged merchandise sold on May 16.
   26. Received $7,410 from American Express for $8,000 of sales reported during the week of May 12-18.
   28. Received check for amount due from Stockton Company for sale of May 18.
   30. Received check for amount due from Boskie Co. for sales of May 3 and May 8.
   31. Paid Ace Delivery Service $670 for merchandise delivered during May to local customers under shipping terms of FOB destination .
June 4. Paid American National Bank $380 for service fees for handling MasterCard sales during May.
   10. Paid $375 to state sales tax division for taxes owed on May sales.
   15. Received check for amount due from Felder Co. for sale of May 16, less credit memorandum of May 24.

Instructions

Journalize entries to record the transactions of Buller Co.

PROBLEM 5-2B
PURCHASE-RELATED
TRANSACTIONS
Objective 2

The following selected transactions were completed by Wilton Company during May of the current year.

May 1. Purchased merchandise from Duncan Co., $5,750, terms FOB destination, n/30.
       3. Purchased merchandise from Darwin Co., $10,000, terms FOB shipping point, 2/10, n/eom. Prepaid transportation costs of $250 were added to the invoice.
       5. Purchased merchandise from Thompson Co., $5,000, terms FOB destination, 1/10, n/30.
       8. Issued debit memorandum for $1,000 to Thompson Co. for merchandise returned from purchase on May 5.
      13. Paid Darwin Co. for invoice of May 3, less discount.
      15. Paid Thompson Co. for invoice of May 5, less debit memorandum of May 8 and discount.
      18. Purchased merchandise from Moat Company, $8,250, terms FOB shipping point, n/eom.
      18. Paid transportation charges of $220 on May 18 purchase from Moat Company.
      19. Purchased merchandise from Hatcher Co., $7,500, terms FOB destination , 2/10, n/30.
      29. Paid Hatcher Co. for invoice of May 19, less discount.
      31. Paid Duncan Co. for invoice of May 1.
      31. Paid Moat Company for invoice of May 18.

Instructions
Journalize entries to record the transactions of Wilton Company for May.

PROBLEM 5-3B
SALES-RELATED AND
PURCHASE-RELATED
TRANSACTIONS FOR
SELLER AND BUYER
Objectives 2, 3

The following selected transactions were completed during April between Swalm Company and Parker Company:

Apr. 3. Swalm Company sold merchandise on account to Parker Company, $12,500, terms FOB shipping point, 2/10, n/30. Swalm Company paid transportation costs of $600, which were added to the invoice.
       8. Swalm Company sold merchandise on account to Parker Company, $16,000, terms FOB destination , 1/15, n/eom.
       8. Swalm Company paid transportation costs of $800 for delivery of merchandise sold to Parker Company on April 8.
      11. Parker Company returned merchandise purchased on account on April 8 from Swalm Company, $4,000.
      13. Parker Company paid Swalm Company for purchase of April 3, less discount.
      23. Parker Company paid Swalm Company for purchase of April 8, less discount and less return of April 11.
      24. Swalm Company sold merchandise on account to Parker Company, $8,000, terms FOB shipping point, n/eom.
      27. Parker Company paid transportation charges of $300 on April 24 purchase from Swalm Company.
      30. Parker Company paid Swalm Company on account for purchase of April 24.

Instructions
Journalize the April transactions for (1) Swalm Company and (2) Parker Company.

PROBLEM 5-4B
SALES-RELATED AND
PURCHASE-RELATED
TRANSACTIONS
Objective 2

The following were selected from among the transactions completed by Montrose Company during May of the current year:

May 3. Purchased merchandise on account from Floyd Co., list price $5,000, trade discount 20%, terms FOB shipping point, 2/10, n/30, with prepaid transportation costs of $120 added to the invoice.
       5. Purchased merchandise on account from Kramer Co., $8,500, terms FOB destination, 1/10, n/30.
       6. Sold merchandise on account to C. F. Howell Co., list price $4,000, trade discount 30%, terms 2/10, n/30.
       8. Purchased office supplies for cash, $650.
      10. Returned merchandise purchased on May 5 from Kramer Co., $1,300.
      13. Paid Floyd Co. on account for purchase of May 3, less discount.
      14. Purchased merchandise for cash, $10,500.

May 15. Paid Kramer Co. on account for purchase of May 5, less return of May 10 and discount.

16. Received cash on account from sale of May 6 to C. F. Howell Co., less discount.

19. Sold merchandise on nonbank credit cards and reported accounts to the card company, $2,450.

22. Sold merchandise on account to Comer Co., $3,480, terms 2/10, n/30.

24. Sold merchandise for cash, $4,350.

30. Received merchandise returned by Comer Co. from sale on May 22, $1,480.

28. Received cash from card company for nonbank credit card sales of May 19, less $140 service fee.

Instructions

Journalize the transactions for Montrose Co.

Instructions for Solving Problem 5-4B Using Solutions Software

1. Load opening balances.
2. Save the opening balances file to your drive and directory.
3. Set the run date to May 31 of the current year and enter your name.
4. Select the General Journal entries option and key the journal entries. Leave the reference field blank.
5. Display the journal entries.
6. Display a trial balance.
7. Key the adjusting entry for merchandise inventory. (The merchandise inventory on May 31 is $51,000.) Key ADJ.ENT. in the reference field.
8. Display the adjusting entry. Key ADJ.ENT. in the Reference Restriction area of the Selection Options screen.
9. Display the financial statements.
10. Save your data file to disk.
11. End the session.

PROBLEM 5-5B
SALES-RELATED AND
PURCHASE-RELATED
TRANSACTIONS, TRIAL
BALANCE
Objective 2

The account balances at June 1 of the current year of Evans Company are as follows:

11 Cash	$ 19,940
12 Accounts Receivable	32,350
13 Merchandise Inventory	79,600
14 Prepaid Insurance	4,050
15 Store Supplies	2,700
21 Accounts Payable	28,300
31 Art Evans, Capital	110,340
32 Art Evans, Drawing	—
33 Income Summary	—
41 Sales	—
42 Sales Returns and Allowances	—
43 Sales Discounts	—
51 Purchases	—
52 Purchases Returns and Allowances	—
53 Purchases Discounts	—
54 Transportation In	—
55 Sales Salaries Expense	—
56 Advertising Expense	—
57 Store Supplies Expense	—
58 Miscellaneous Selling Expense	—
59 Office Salaries Expense	—
60 Rent Expense	—
61 Insurance Expense	—
62 Miscellaneous Administrative Expense	—

The following transactions were completed during June of the current year:

June 1. Paid rent for month, $3,500.

2. Purchased merchandise on account, $12,500.

4. Purchased merchandise on account, FOB shipping point, $20,100.

7. Sold merchandise on account, $16,000.

9. Paid transportation charges on the purchase on June 4, $525.

June 10. Received $9,800 cash from customers on account, after discounts of $200 were deducted.
   11. Paid creditors $16,700 on account, after discounts of $280 had been deducted.
   14. Sold merchandise for cash, $9,500.
   15. Received merchandise returned on account, $800.
   16. Paid sales salaries of $3,950 and office salaries of $1,280.
   17. Paid creditors $12,740 on account, after discounts of $260 had been deducted.
   18. Received $14,700 cash from customers on account, after discounts of $300 had been deducted.
   21. Purchased merchandise on account, $15,200.
   22. Paid advertising expense, $4,250.
   23. Sold merchandise for cash, $11,600.
   24. Returned merchandise purchased on account, $2,200.
   25. Sold merchandise on account, $30,200.
   28. Sold merchandise for cash, $8,200.
   28. Refunded $350 cash on sales made for cash.
   29. Paid sales salaries of $3,800 and office salaries of $1,280.
   30. Paid creditors $10,900 on account, no discount.
   30. Received $12,500 cash from customers on account, no discount.

Instructions

1. Enter the June 1 balances in the appropriate balance column of a four-column account. Write *Balance* in the item section, and place a check mark (✓) in the Posting Reference column.
2. Journalize the transactions for June.
3. Post the journal to the ledger, extending the month-end balances to the appropriate balance columns after all posting is completed.
4. Prepare a trial balance of the ledger as of June 30.

SOLUTIONS
SOFTWARE

Instructions for Solving Problem 5-5B Using Solutions Software

1. Load opening balances.
2. Save the opening balances file to your drive and directory.
3. Set the run date to June 30 of the current year and enter your name.
4. Select the General Journal entries option and key the journal entries. Leave the reference field blank.
5. Display the journal entries.
6. Display a trial balance.
7. Key the adjusting entries, based on the following data:

Insurance expired on June 30	$ 405
Store supplies on hand on June 30	1,700
Merchandise inventory, June 30	82,900

   Key ADJ.ENT. in the reference field.
8. Display the adjusting entries. Key ADJ.ENT. in the Reference Restriction area of the Selection Options screen.
9. Display the financial statements.
10. Save your data file to disk.
11. End the session.

PROBLEM 5-6B
COST OF MERCHANDISE
SOLD AND RELATED ITEMS
Objective 5

The following data were extracted from the accounting records of Josie Lind Co. for the year ended December 31, 1993:

Merchandise Inventory, January 1, 1993	$ 92,500
Merchandise Inventory, December 31, 1993	85,650
Purchases	475,000
Purchases Returns and Allowances	7,250
Purchases Discounts	2,750
Sales	640,000
Transportation In	8,150

**SPREADSHEET
PROBLEM**

**SHARPEN YOUR
COMMUNICATION SKILLS** ►

Instructions

1. Prepare the cost of merchandise sold section of the income statement for the year ended December 31, 1993.
2. Determine the gross profit to be reported on the income statement for the year ended December 31, 1993.
3. What is the rate of gross profit to sales for the year ended December 31, 1993?
4. If the merchandise inventory on December 31, 1993, had been understated by $10,000, what would be the effect of the error on the gross profit? Explain.

MINI-CASE 5 VALLEY DISCOUNT STORES

For the past twenty years, your father has managed and operated Valley Discount Stores, a regional chain of retail stores. You have recently accepted a position with Valley Discount Stores. As a first assignment, you are to review the purchases and payments policies of the enterprise.

For your analysis, the treasurer has gathered the following data covering the past three years

	19X3	19X2	19X1
Purchases	$20,400,000	$18,200,000	$16,300,000
Purchases returns and allowances	204,000	136,500	81,500
Transportation in	591,600	564,200	489,000

After reviewing these data, you ask the treasurer why no purchases discounts are shown for the three-year period. The treasurer responds as follows:

Your father won't let us take purchases discounts. It doesn't make sense to me. The industry standard is 2/10, n/30. Your father always has believed in paying the bills on the final due date and not a day before. I've tried to convince him that we should take the discounts, but he won't budge.

The treasurer also indicates that the company has recently entered into a store expansion program that will likely create a cash shortage. Because of this situation, the company has negotiated a $500,000 line of credit with its bank at an interest rate of 11%.

Instructions:

1. Prepare an analysis indicating the net savings that could have been earned from taking all discounts for the past three years. Assume that discounts are available on all purchases. In addition, assume that Valley Discount Stores had sufficient cash to pay all invoices without borrowing and that the average rates at which the excess cash could have been invested in each of the past three years were as follows:

19X3	7%
19X2	7%
19X1	6%

(Hint: You should take into consideration the interest income Valley Discount Stores would have forgone by paying the invoices within the discount period.)

2. Assume that you are able to convince your father to use the new line of credit to pay all invoices within the discount period during 19X4. The net purchases for 19X4 are projected to increase 15% over the net purchases for 19X3. Compute the expected net savings for 19X4 by taking all the available purchases discounts.

3. ■■■ ► Based upon the purchase data for 19X3, 19X2, and 19X1, what other questions might you raise concerning purchases and payments policies?

ANSWERS TO SELF-EXAMINATION QUESTIONS

1. **A** A debit memorandum (answer A), issued by the buyer, indicates the amount the buyer proposes to debit to the accounts payable account. A credit memorandum (answer B), issued by the seller, indicates the amount the seller proposes to credit to the accounts receivable account. An invoice (answer C) or a bill (answer D), issued by the seller, indicates the amount and terms of the sale.

2. **C** The amount of discount for early payment is $10 (answer C), or 1% of $1,000. Although the $50 of transportation costs paid by the seller are debited to the customer's account, the customer is not entitled to a discount on that amount.

3. **B** The customer is entitled to a discount of $9 (answer B) for early payment. This amount is 1% of $900, which is the

sales price of $1,000 less the return of $100. The $50 of transportation costs is an expense of the seller.

4. **D** Since the terms of the sale are FOB shipping point, the transportation costs are the buyer's expense. The seller (Sorter Co.) adds the transportation costs to the invoice and debits Accounts Receivable, and the buyer (Beecher Co.) debits Transportation In (answer D).

5. **A** Purchases discounts (answer B), purchases returns and allowances (answer C), and merchandise inventory at the end of the period (answer D) are all subtracted from the sum of merchandise inventory at the beginning of the period and purchases (answer A) in determining the cost of merchandise sold.

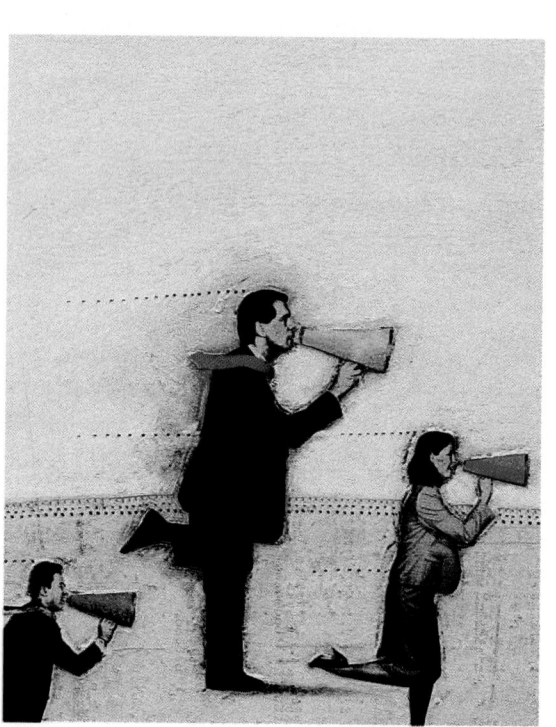

You and Accounting

Do you know the balance of your checking account? You probably keep a check register in which you record deposits to and withdrawals from your checking account. At any point in time, you can look up the balance to determine how much cash you have available to spend. In essence, you are maintaining a continuous or perpetual record of the amount of cash in your checking account. As discussed later in this chapter, businesses often maintain similar records for inventories.

Chapter 6
Financial Statements; Perpetual Inventory Systems

LEARNING OBJECTIVES
After studying this chapter, you should be able to:

Objective 1
List the year-end procedures for a merchandising enterprise.

Objective 2
Prepare a work sheet for a merchandising enterprise, using the periodic inventory system.

Objective 3
Prepare an income statement, a statement of owner's equity, and a balance sheet for a merchandising enterprise.

Objective 4
Journalize the adjusting entries for a merchandising enterprise.

Objective 5
Journalize the closing entries for a merchandising enterprise.

Objective 6
Explain when a perpetual inventory system is likely to be used by a merchandising enterprise.

Objective 7
Journalize the entries for merchandise transactions, using a perpetual inventory system.

Objective 8
Prepare a work sheet, prepare financial statements, and journalize the adjusting and closing entries for a merchandising enterprise using the perpetual inventory system.

Accounting for merchandising enterprises was introduced in Chapter 5. This discussion included the use of the periodic inventory system for recording sales and purchases transactions. In addition, the preparation of the cost of merchandise sold section of the income statement was described and illustrated.

This chapter completes the discussion of the accounting cycle for merchandising enterprises that use the periodic inventory system. The preparation of the work sheet, financial statements, adjusting entries, closing entries, and the post-closing trial balance for a merchandising enterprise are discussed. The chapter concludes with a discussion and illustration of the perpetual inventory system.

PERIODIC REPORTING FOR MERCHANDISING ENTERPRISES

Objective 1
List the year-end procedures for a merchandising enterprise.

At periodic intervals throughout the life of a business enterprise, operating data must be summarized and reported. Operating data are reported at least yearly for use by managers, owners, creditors, governmental agencies, and other interested persons. The assets, liabilities, and owner's equity on the last day of the fiscal period must also be reported. At the end of the period, the ledger must be updated through the use of adjusting entries. Finally, the accounts are prepared for recording transactions for the next period. The following sequence of end-of-period procedures is typical:

1. Prepare a trial balance of the ledger on a work sheet.
2. Review the accounts and gather the data required for the adjustments.
3. Insert the adjustments and complete the work sheet.
4. Prepare financial statements from the data in the work sheet.
5. Journalize the adjusting entries and post to the ledger.
6. Journalize the closing entries and post to the ledger.
7. Prepare a post-closing trial balance of the ledger.

The end-of-period procedures discussed in this chapter are similar to those discussed in Chapters 3 and 4. The major difference is that Chapters 3 and 4 focused on service enterprises, while this chapter focuses on merchandising enterprises.

We've Only Just Begun

It is important for the management of a retailer to look beyond the financial statements to the intangibles of sound operating philosophies. One company that has been highly successful in doing this is Wal-Mart. The following excerpts from an article in *Retail Control* describe some of the reasons for Wal-Mart's success.

. . . *Relentless innovation and remorseless boosterism delivered $21 billion of new market value to Wal-Mart's shareholders over the past five years. . . .*
. . . *[There] hasn't been much growth in discount retailing during the [recent] past . . . [but] Wal-Mart's earnings have grown at an average rate of 31 percent annually for the past five years. . . .*

. . . *[Wal-Mart] is fueled by values like self-respect, initiative, and belonging. Wal-Mart employees, called associates, "are constantly being challenged by one another and forced to laugh at themselves" . . . "They take pride in the fact that they are working to create perhaps the finest company in the world and their individual contributions are recognized."*
. . . *To fuel competition among department managers, Wal-Mart tracks each department's sales as a percentage of total sales for each store. . . . At this year's annual meeting, department managers who ranked No. 1 by this measure were honored. . . .*
. . . *"Wal-Mart is making a contribution . . . of a magnitude previously not dreamt of in business." And, says the company motto, "We've only just begun."*

Source: Gregory J. Millman, "These Companies Add Value for Shareholders," *Retail Control* (November 1991), pp. 16-18.

WORK SHEET FOR MERCHANDISING ENTERPRISES

Objective 2
Prepare a work sheet for a merchandising enterprise, using the periodic inventory system.

At the end of the accounting period, a work sheet may be used to assist in the preparation of adjusting entries, closing entries, and financial statements. Exhibit 1 illustrates a work sheet for a merchandising enterprise. In this work sheet, the trial balance differs slightly from trial balances presented earlier. All of the accounts, including accounts that have no balances, are listed in the order that they appear in the ledger.

The work sheet in Exhibit 1 for Computer King is for the year ended December 31, 1995. As mentioned at the end of Chapter 5, Computer King opened a retail store in January 1994. The account balances in Exhibit 1 reflect Computer King's second year of operations as a merchandising enterprise.

Exhibit 1
Work Sheet for Merchandising
Enterprise

Computer King
Work Sheet
For Year Ended December 31, 1995

Account Title	Trial Balance Dr.	Trial Balance Cr.	Adjustments Dr.	Adjustments Cr.	Adjusted Trial Balance Dr.	Adjusted Trial Balance Cr.	Income Statement Dr.	Income Statement Cr.	Balance Sheet Dr.	Balance Sheet Cr.
Cash	52,950				52,950				52,950	
Notes Receivable	40,000				40,000				40,000	
Accounts Receivable	60,880				60,880				60,880	
Interest Receivable			(a) 200		200				200	
Merchandise Inventory	59,700		(c) 62,150	(b) 59,700	62,150				62,150	
Office Supplies	1,090			(d) 610	480				480	
Prepaid Insurance	4,560			(e) 1,910	2,650				2,650	
Land	10,000				10,000				10,000	
Store Equipment	27,100				27,100				27,100	
Accum. Depr.—Store Equip.		2,600		(f) 3,100		5,700				5,700
Office Equipment	15,570				15,570				15,570	
Accum. Depr.—Office Equipment		2,230		(g) 2,490		4,720				4,720
Accounts Payable		22,420				22,420				22,420
Salaries Payable				(h) 1,140		1,140				1,140
Unearned Rent		2,400	(i) 600			1,800				1,800
Notes Payable (final payment, 2000)		25,000				25,000				25,000
Jere King, Capital		153,800				153,800				153,800
Jere King, Drawing	18,000				18,000				18,000	
Income Summary			(b) 59,700	(c) 62,150	59,700	62,150	59,700	62,150		
Sales		720,185				720,185		720,185		
Sales Returns and Allowances	6,140				6,140		6,140			
Sales Discounts	5,790				5,790		5,790			
Purchases	521,980				521,980		521,980			
Purchases Returns & Allowances		9,100				9,100		9,100		
Purchases Discounts		2,525				2,525		2,525		
Transportation In	17,400				17,400		17,400			
Sales Salaries Expense	59,250		(h) 780		60,030		60,030			
Advertising Expense	10,860				10,860		10,860			
Depr. Exp.—Store Equip.			(f) 3,100		3,100		3,100			
Miscellaneous Selling Expense	630				630		630			
Office Salaries Expense	20,660		(h) 360		21,020		21,020			
Rent Expense	8,100				8,100		8,100			
Depr. Ex.—Office Equip.			(g) 2,490		2,490		2,490			
Insurance Expense			(e) 1,910		1,910		1,910			
Office Supplies Expense			(d) 610		610		610			
Misc. Administrative Expense	760				760		760			
Rent Income				(i) 600		600		600		
Interest Income		3,600		(a) 200		3,800		3,800		
Interest Expense	2,440				2,440		2,440			
	943,860	943,860	131,900	131,900	1,012,940	1,012,940	722,960	798,360	289,980	214,580
Net Income							75,400			75,400
							798,360	798,360	289,980	289,980

(a) Interest earned but not received on notes receivable, $200.
(b) Beginning merchandise inventory, $59,700.
(c) Ending merchandise enventory, $62,150.
(d) Office supplies used, $610 ($1,090–$480).
(e) Insurance expired, $1,910.

(f) Depreciation of store equipment, $3,100.
(g) Depreciation of office equipment, $2,490.
(h) Salaries accrued but not paid (sales salaries, $780; office salaries, $360), $1,140.
(i) Rent earned from amount received in advance, $600.

The data needed for adjusting the accounts of Computer King are as follows:

Interest accrued on notes receivable on December 31, 1995		$ 200
Merchandise inventory on December 31, 1995		62,150
Office supplies on hand on December 31, 1995		480
Insurance expired during 1995		1,910
Depreciation during 1995 on: Store Equipment		3,100
Office equipment		2,490
Salaries accrued on December 31, 1995: Sales salaries	$780	
Office salaries	360	1,140
Rent income earned during 1995		600

There is no specific order in which the accounts in the work sheet need to be analyzed, the adjustment data assembled, and the adjusting entries made. However, time can normally be saved by selecting the accounts in the order in which they appear on the trial balance. Using this approach, the adjustment for accrued interest is listed first (entry (a) on the work sheet), followed by the adjustments for merchandise inventory (entries (b) and (c) on the work sheet), and so on. Except for merchandise inventory, all the adjustments on the work sheet have been discussed in previous chapters. The following paragraphs discuss the nature of the merchandise inventory adjustments and the completion of the work sheet.

Merchandise Inventory Adjustments

Under the periodic inventory system, a separate merchandise inventory account is maintained in the ledger. Throughout the accounting period, this account shows the inventory at the beginning of the period. As shown in the following cost of merchandise sold section of Computer King's income statement for 1995, the merchandise inventory on January 1, 1995, $59,700, is a part of the merchandise available for sale.

Cost of merchandise sold:			
Merchandise inventory, Jan. 1, 1995			$ 59,700
Purchases		$521,980	
Less: Purchases returns and allowances	$9,100		
Purchases discounts	2,525	11,625	
Net purchases		$510,355	
Add transportation in		17,400	
Cost of merchandise purchased			527,755
Merchandise available for sale			$587,455
Less merchandise inventory, Dec. 31, 1995			62,150
Cost of merchandise sold			$525,305

At the end of the period, the beginning inventory amount in the ledger is replaced with the ending inventory amount. To record this updating of the inventory account, two adjusting entries are used.[1] The first adjusting entry transfers the beginning inventory balance to Income Summary. This entry, shown below, has the effect of increasing cost of merchandise sold and decreasing net income.

Dec. 31	Income Summary	59,700	
	Merchandise Inventory		59,700

After the first adjusting entry has been recorded and posted, the balance of the merchandise inventory account is zero. The second adjusting entry records the cost of the merchandise on hand at the end of the period by debiting Merchandise Inventory. Since the merchandise inventory at December 31, 1995, $62,150, is subtracted from the cost of merchandise available for sale in determining the cost of merchandise sold, Income Summary is credited. This credit has the effect of decreasing the cost of merchandise available for sale during the period, $587,455, by the cost of the unsold merchandise. The second adjusting entry is shown below.

---

[1] Another method of updating the merchandise inventory account at the end of the period is called the *closing method*. This method is presented in Appendix D.

Dec. 31   Merchandise Inventory   62,150
              Income Summary   62,150

After the second adjusting entry has been recorded and posted, the balance of the merchandise inventory account is the amount of the ending inventory. The accounts for Merchandise Inventory and Income Summary after both entries have been posted would appear as follows, in T account form:

Merchandise Inventory

1995						
Jan.	1	Beginning inventory	59,700	Dec. 31 Beginning inventory	59,700
Dec.	31	Ending inventory	62,150		

Income Summary

Dec.	31	Beginning inventory	59,700	Dec. 31 Ending inventory	62,150

Completing the Work Sheet

After all of the necessary adjustments have been entered on the work sheet, the Adjustments columns are totaled to prove the equality of debits and credits. As illustrated in Chapters 3 and 4, the balances of the accounts in the Trial Balance columns and the amount of any adjustments are extended to the Adjusted Trial Balance columns.[2] The Adjusted Trial Balance columns are then totaled to prove the equality of debits and credits.

An exception to the usual practice of extending only account balances is Income Summary. Both the debit and credit amounts for Income Summary are extended to the Adjusted Trial Balance columns. Extending both amounts aids in the preparation of the income statement because the debit adjustment (the beginning inventory of $59,700) and the credit adjustment (the ending inventory of $62,150) are reported as part of the cost of merchandise sold.

The process of extending the balances, as adjusted, to the statement columns usually begins with Cash and moves down the work sheet, item by item. Note that the two merchandise inventory amounts in Income Summary are extended to the Income Statement columns. After all of the items have been extended to the statement columns, the four columns are totaled and the net income or net loss is determined. For Computer King, the difference between the credit and the debit columns of the Income Statement section is $75,400, the amount of the net income. The difference between the debit and the credit columns of the Balance Sheet section is also $75,400, which is the increase in owner's equity as a result of the net income. Agreement between the two balancing amounts is evidence of debit-credit equality and mathematical accuracy.

FINANCIAL STATEMENTS FOR MERCHANDISING ENTERPRISES

Objective 3
Prepare an income statement, a statement of owner's equity, and a balance sheet for a merchandising enterprise.

The basic financial statements for a merchandising enterprise are similar to those for a service enterprise. As discussed in Chapter 5, the income statements differ in the reporting of revenue, cost of merchandise sold, and gross profit. The balance sheets are similar, except that merchandise inventory is included as a current asset on the balance sheet of a merchandising enterprise. The statement of owner's equity and the statement of cash flows do not differ significantly for service and merchandising enterprises.

In the following paragraphs, the income statement, balance sheet, and statement of owner's equity for a merchandising enterprise are described and illustrated.[3] These statements are prepared from the work sheet for Computer King in Exhibit 1.

---

[2] Some accountants prefer to eliminate the Adjusted Trial Balance columns and to extend the adjusted account balances directly to the statement columns. Such a work sheet is often used if there are only a few adjustment items.

[3] Examples of financial statements are also presented in Appendix G, "Specimen Financial Statements."

Income Statement

There are two widely used forms for the income statement: multiple-step and single-step. The 1991 edition of *Accounting Trends & Techniques* reported that 64% of the 600 industrial and merchandising companies surveyed use the multiple-step form, while 36% use the single-step form.

MULTIPLE-STEP FORM. The multiple-step income statement contains several sections, subsections, and subtotals. The amount of detail presented in these sections varies from company to company. For example, instead of reporting gross sales, sales returns and allowances, and sales discounts, some companies just report net sales. Likewise, some companies report the cost of merchandise sold as a single item without reporting the details of purchases, purchases returns and allowances, purchases discounts, and transportation in.

The multiple-step income statement for Computer King is presented in Exhibit 2. The various sections of this income statement are discussed in the following paragraphs.

Revenue from Sales. The total amount charged customers for merchandise sold, for cash and on account, is reported in this section. Sales returns and allowances and sales discounts are deducted from this total to yield net sales.

Cost of Merchandise Sold. Chapter 5 described and illustrated the preparation of the cost of merchandise sold section. Other terms frequently used to describe this section are **cost of goods sold** and **cost of sales**.

Gross Profit. The excess of net sales over cost of merchandise sold is called gross profit. It is sometimes called **gross profit on sales** or **gross margin**.

Operating Expenses. Most merchandising enterprises classify operating expenses as either selling expenses or administrative expenses. However, depending upon the decision-making needs of managers and other users of the financial statements, other classifications could be used.

Expenses that are incurred directly in the selling of merchandise are selling expenses. They include such expenses as salespersons' salaries, store supplies used, depreciation of store equipment, and advertising.

Expenses incurred in the administration or general operations of the business are administrative expenses or **general expenses**. Examples of these expenses are office salaries, depreciation of office equipment, and office supplies used.

Expenses that are related to both administrative and selling functions may be divided between the two classifications. In small businesses, however, such expenses as rent, insurance, and taxes are commonly reported as administrative expenses. Transactions for small, infrequent expenses are often reported as Miscellaneous Selling Expense or Miscellaneous Administrative Expense.

Income from Operations. The excess of gross profit over total operating expenses is called income from operations or **operating income**. The relationships of income from operations to total assets and to net sales are important factors in judging the efficiency and profitability of operations. If operating expenses are greater than the gross profit, the excess is called a **loss from operations**.

Other Income and Other Expense. Revenue from sources other than the primary operating activity of a business is classified as other income or **nonoperating income**. In a merchandising enterprise, these items include income from interest, rent, dividends, and gains resulting from the sale of plant assets.

Expenses that cannot be traced directly to operations are identified as other expense or **nonoperating expense**. Interest expense that results from financing activities and losses incurred in the disposal of plant assets are examples of these items.

Exhibit 2
Multiple-Step Income Statement
for Merchandising Enterprise

Computer King
Income Statement
For Year Ended December 31, 1995

Revenue from sales:				
Sales			$720,185	
Less: Sales returns and allowances		$ 6,140		
Sales discounts		5,790	11,930	
Net Sales				$708,255
Cost of merchandise sold:				
Merchandise inventory				
January 1, 1995			$ 59,700	
Purchases		$521,980		
Less: Purchases returns and allowances	$9,100			
Purchases discounts	2,525	11,625		
Net purchases		$510,355		
Add transportation in		17,400		
Cost of merchandise purchased			527,755	
Merchandise available for sale			$587,455	
Less merchandise inventory,				
December 31, 1995			62,150	
Cost of merchandise sold				525,305
Gross profit				$182,950
Operating expenses:				
Selling expenses:				
Sales salaries expense		$ 60,030		
Advertising expense		10,860		
Depreciation expense—store equipment		3,100		
Miscellaneous selling expense		630		
Total selling expenses			$ 74,620	
Administrative expenses:				
Office salaries expense		$ 21,020		
Rent expense		8,100		
Depreciation expense—office equipment		2,490		
Insurance expense		1,910		
Office supplies expense		610		
Miscellaneous administrative expense		760		
Total administrative expenses			34,890	
Total operating expenses				109,510
Income from operations				$ 73,440
Other income:				
Interest income		$ 3,800		
Rent income		600		
Total other income			$ 4,400	
Other expense:				
Interest expense			2,440	1,960
Net income				$ 75,400

Other income and other expense are offset against each other on the income statement. If the total of other income exceeds the total of other expense, the difference is added to income from operations. If the reverse is true, the difference is subtracted from income from operations.

Net Income. The final figure on the income statement is called **net income** (or **net loss**). It is the net increase (or net decrease) in the owner's equity as a result of the period's profit-making activities.

SINGLE-STEP FORM. In the **single-step income statement**, the total of all expenses is deducted *in one step* from the total of all revenues. Such a statement is shown in Exhibit 3 for Computer King. The statement has been condensed to focus attention on its primary features. Such condensing is not essential for the single-step form.

Exhibit 3
Single-Step Income Statement for Merchandising Enterprise

Computer King
Income Statement
For Year Ended December 31, 1995

Revenues:		
Net sales		$708,255
Interest income		3,800
Rent income		600
Total revenues		$712,655
Expenses:		
Cost of merchandise sold	$525,305	
Selling expenses	74,620	
Administrative expenses	34,890	
Interest expense	2,440	
Total expenses		637,255
Net income		$ 75,400

The single-step form has the advantage of emphasizing total revenues and total expenses as the factors that determine net income. A criticism of the single-step form is that such amounts as gross profit and income from operations are not readily available for analysis.

Statement of Owner's Equity

The statement of owner's equity shows the changes to the beginning-of-the-period owner's capital as a result of the net income (or net loss) and additional investments in and withdrawals from the business. The statement of owner's equity for Computer King is shown in Exhibit 4.

Exhibit 4
Statement of Owner's Equity for Merchandising Enterprise

Computer King
Statement of Owner's Equity
For Year Ended December 31, 1995

Jere King, capital, January 1, 1995		$153,800
Net income for year	$75,400	
Less withdrawals	18,000	
Increase in owner's equity		57,400
Jere King, capital, December 31, 1995		$211,200

Balance Sheet

As discussed and illustrated in previous chapters, the balance sheet may be presented in a downward sequence in three sections. The total of the Assets section equals the combined total of the Liabilities and Owner's Equity sections. This form of balance sheet is called the **report form**. The balance sheet may also be presented with Assets on the left-hand side of the balance sheet and the Liabilities and Owner's Equity on the right-hand side. This form of the balance sheet is called the **account form**. The account form of balance sheet for Computer King is shown in Exhibit 5. In this balance sheet, note that merchandise inventory at the end of the period is reported as a current asset, and the current portion of the note payable is $5,000.

Exhibit 5 *Account Form of Balance Sheet*

Computer King
Balance Sheet
December 31, 1995

Assets			Liabilities		
Current assets:			Current liabilities:		
Cash	$ 52,950		Accounts payable	$ 22,420	
Notes receivable	40,000		Note payable (current		
Accounts receivable	60,880		portion)	5,000	
Interest receivable	200		Salaries payable	1,140	
Merchandise inventory	62,150		Unearned rent	1,800	
Office supplies	480		Total current liabilities		$ 30,360
Prepaid insurance	2,650		Long-term liabilities:		
Total current assets		$219,310	Note payable (final		
Plant assets:			payment, 2000)		20,000
Land	$ 10,000		Total liabilities		$ 50,360
Store equipment	$27,100				
Less accumulated depreciation	5,700	21,400			
Office equipment	$15,570			Owner's Equity	
Less accumulated depreciation	4,720	10,850			
Total plant assets		42,250	Jere King, Capital		211,200
Total assets		$261,560	Total liabilities and owner's equity		$261,560

ADJUSTING ENTRIES

Objective 4
Journalize the adjusting entries for a merchandising enterprise.

The analyses required to make the adjustments were completed during the process of preparing the work sheet. It is thus not necessary to refer to the basic data when the adjusting entries are journalized. After these entries have been posted, the balances of all asset, liability, revenue, and expense accounts equal the amounts reported in the financial statements. The adjusting entries for Computer King are as follows:

JOURNAL   PAGE 28

	DATE		DESCRIPTION	POST. REF.	DEBIT	CREDIT	
1			Adjusting Entries				1
2	1995 Dec.	31	Interest Receivable	113	2 0 0 00		2
3			Interest Income	611		2 0 0 00	3
4							4
5		31	Income Summary	312	59 7 0 0 00		5
6			Merchandise Inventory	115		59 7 0 0 00	6
7							7
8		31	Merchandise Inventory	115	62 1 5 0 00		8
9			Income Summary	312		62 1 5 0 00	9
10							10
11		31	Office Supplies Expense	534	6 1 0 00		11
12			Office Supplies	116		6 1 0 00	12
13							13
14		31	Insurance Expense	533	1 9 1 0 00		14
15			Prepaid Insurance	117		1 9 1 0 00	15
16							16
17		31	Depreciation Expense—Store Equip.	522	3 1 0 0 00		17
18			Accumulated Depr.—Store Equip.	124		3 1 0 0 00	18
19							19

	DATE	DESCRIPTION	POST. REF.	DEBIT	CREDIT	
20	31	Depreciation Expense—Office Equip.	532	2 4 9 0 00		20
21		Accumulated Depr.—Office Equip.	126		2 4 9 0 00	21
22						22
23	31	Sales Salaries Expense	520	7 8 0 00		23
24		Office Salaries Expense	530	3 6 0 00		24
25		Salaries Payable	211		1 1 4 0 00	25
26						26
27	31	Unearned Rent	212	6 0 0 00		27
28		Rent Income	610		6 0 0 00	28

CLOSING ENTRIES

Objective 5
Journalize the closing entries for a merchandising enterprise.

The closing entries are recorded in the journal immediately following the adjusting entries. The closing entries for Computer King are as follows:

JOURNAL   PAGE 29

	DATE	DESCRIPTION	POST. REF.	DEBIT	CREDIT	
1		Closing Entries				1
2	1995 Dec. 31	Sales	410	720 1 8 5 00		2
3		Purchases Returns and Allowances	511	9 1 0 0 00		3
4		Purchases Discounts	512	2 5 2 5 00		4
5		Rent Income	610	6 0 0 00		5
6		Interest Income	611	3 8 0 0 00		6
7		Income Summary	312		736 2 1 0 00	7
8						8
9	31	Income Summary	312	663 2 6 0 00		9
10		Sales Returns and Allowances	411		6 1 4 0 00	10
11		Sales Discounts	412		5 7 9 0 00	11
12		Purchases	510		521 9 8 0 00	12
13		Transportation In	513		17 4 0 0 00	13
14		Sales Salaries Expense	520		60 0 3 0 00	14
15		Advertising Expense	521		10 8 6 0 00	15
16		Depreciation Exp.—Store Equip.	522		3 1 0 0 00	16
17		Miscellaneous Selling Expense	529		6 3 0 00	17
18		Office Salaries Expense	530		21 0 2 0 00	18
19		Rent Expense	531		8 1 0 0 00	19
20		Depreciation Exp.—Office Equip.	532		2 4 9 0 00	20
21		Insurance Expense	533		1 9 1 0 00	21
22		Office Supplies Expense	534		6 1 0 00	22
23		Miscellaneous Administrative Exp.	539		7 6 0 00	23
24		Interest Expense	710		2 4 4 0 00	24
25						25
26	31	Income Summary	312	75 4 0 0 00		26
27		Jere King, Capital	310		75 4 0 0 00	27
28						28
29	31	Jere King, Capital	310	18 0 0 0 00		29
30		Jere King, Drawing	311		18 0 0 0 00	30
31						31

As discussed in Chapter 4, the effect of the closing entries is to clear all of the temporary owner's equity accounts of their balances, reducing them to zero. The first entry closes all income statement accounts with *credit* balances by transferring the total to the credit side of Income Summary. The second entry closes all income statement accounts with *debit* balances by transferring the total to the debit side of Income Summary. For a merchandising enterprise, the income statement accounts with credit balances include the revenue accounts and the contra purchases accounts. The income statement accounts with debit balances include the purchases and transportation in accounts and the contra sales accounts.

The balance of Income Summary, after the merchandise inventory adjustments and the first two closing entries have been posted, is the net income or net loss for the period. The third closing entry transfers this balance to Jere King, Capital. The income summary account after the merchandise inventory adjustments and the closing entries have been posted is as follows:

ACCOUNT	*Income Summary*				ACCOUNT NO. *312*	
DATE	ITEM	POST. REF.	DEBIT	CREDIT	BALANCE DEBIT	BALANCE CREDIT
1995 Dec. 31	Mer. inv., Jan. 1	28	59 7 0 0 00		59 7 0 0 00	
31	Mer. inv., Dec. 31	28		62 1 5 0 00		2 4 5 0 00
31	Revenue, etc.	29		736 2 1 0 00		738 6 6 0 00
31	Expense, etc.	29	663 2 6 0 00			75 4 0 0 00
31	Net income	29	75 4 0 0 00			

The fourth closing entry transfers the balance of Jere King, Drawing to Jere King, Capital. Thus, the effect of closing the temporary owner's equity accounts is a net increase or a net decrease in the owner's capital account. The owner's capital account and the asset, contra asset, and liability accounts are the only accounts with balances after the closing entries have been posted. To verify the debit-credit equality of the balances of these accounts, a post-closing trial balance is normally prepared. The account balances should be the same as the amounts appearing on the balance sheet in Exhibit 5.

USE OF PERPETUAL INVENTORY SYSTEMS

Objective 6
Explain when a perpetual inventory system is likely to be used by a merchandising enterprise.

The periodic inventory system of accounting for sales and purchases of merchandise was described and illustrated in the preceding paragraphs and in Chapter 5. Such a system is often used by a small retailer, such as a locally owned hardware store, which sells many different kinds of low-unit-cost merchandise.

In a perpetual inventory system, each transaction that affects inventory is recorded in an inventory account. Thus, the inventory records always (perpetually) disclose the amount of merchandise on hand. For many small businesses, such as the hardware store mentioned above, it is normally too costly to use such a system.

Large retailers will likely use computerized perpetual inventory systems. Such systems use bar codes, such as the one on the back of this textbook. An optical scanner reads the bar code and records purchases and sales. Examples of such retailers are K Mart, Sears, Wal-Mart, and the Winn-Dixie and Kroger grocery chains.

Manual perpetual inventory systems may be used by retailers that sell a relatively small number of high-unit-cost items, such as office equipment, automobiles, or jewelry. Such systems can be used at a relatively low cost.

MERCHANDISE TRANSACTIONS IN A PERPETUAL INVENTORY SYSTEM

Objective 7
Journalize the entries for merchandise transactions, using a perpetual inventory system.

In a perpetual inventory system, all increases and decreases related to merchandise are recorded directly in the merchandise inventory account. Thus, accounts for purchases, purchases returns and allowances, purchases discounts, and transportation in are not used. To illustrate the recording of merchandise transactions in a perpetual system, the following selected transactions for Taylor Co. are used. An explanation of how the transaction would have been recorded under a periodic system is also indicated.

June 5. Purchased $30,000 of merchandise on account from Owen Clothing, terms 2/10, n/30.

June 5 Merchandise Inventory   30,000
            Accounts Payable   30,000

Under the perpetual inventory system, purchases of merchandise are recorded in the merchandise inventory account. *Under the periodic inventory system, such purchases are recorded in the purchases account.*

June 8. Returned merchandise purchased on account from Owen Clothing on June 5, $500.

June 8 Accounts Payable   500
            Merchandise Inventory   500

Under the perpetual inventory system, the merchandise inventory account must be reduced by the cost of the merchandise returned. *Under the periodic inventory system, returns are recorded in the purchases returns and allowances account.*

June 15. Paid Owen Clothing for purchase of June 5 on account, less return of $500 and discount of $590 [($30,000−$500)×2%].

June 15 Accounts Payable   29,500
              Cash   28,910
              Merchandise Inventory   590

Under the perpetual inventory system, purchases discounts are recorded directly as a reduction in the cost of the merchandise inventory. *Under a periodic inventory system, purchases discounts are recorded in the purchases discounts account.*

June 18. Sold merchandise on account to Jones Co., $12,500, 1/10, n/30. The cost of the merchandise sold was $9,000.

June 18 Accounts Receivable   12,500
              Sales   12,500
      18 Cost of Merchandise Sold   9,000
              Merchandise Inventory   9,000

The entry to record the sale of $12,500 is the same under both the perpetual and periodic inventory systems. Under the perpetual inventory system, however, the cost of merchandise sold and the reduction in merchandise inventory are also recorded on the date of sale. *Under the periodic system, no attempt is made to record the cost of merchandise sold at the date of the sale.*

June 21. Received merchandise returned on account from Jones Co., $4,000. The cost of the merchandise returned was $2,800.

June 21	Sales Returns and Allowances	4,000	
	Accounts Receivable		4,000
	Merchandise Inventory	2,800	
	Cost of Merchandise Sold		2,800

The first entry to record the sales return is the same under both the perpetual and periodic inventory systems. Since the merchandise inventory records must be kept up to date in a perpetual inventory system, however, the cost of the merchandise returned must be added to the merchandise inventory account. The cost of the merchandise returned must also be credited to the cost of merchandise sold account, since this account was debited when the original sale was recorded. *Under the periodic system, no attempt is made to record the cost of merchandise returned at the date of the return.*

June 22. Purchased merchandise from Norcross Clothiers, $15,000, terms FOB shipping point, 2/15, n/30, with prepaid transportation charges of $750 added to the invoice.

| June 22 | Merchandise Inventory | 15,750 | |
| | Accounts Payable | | 15,750 |

This entry is similar to the June 5 entry for the purchase of merchandise. Since the transportation terms were FOB shipping point, the prepaid freight charges of $750 must be added to the invoice cost of $15,000. Under the perpetual inventory system, the total cost of the purchase of $15,750 must be debited to the merchandise inventory account. *Under the periodic system, the purchases account would be debited for $15,000 and the transportation in account would be debited for $750.*

June 28. Received $8,415 as payment on account from Jones Co., less return of June 21 and less discount of $85 [($12,500−$4,000)×1%].

June 28	Cash	8,415	
	Sales Discounts	85	
	Accounts Receivable		8,500

This entry is the same under both the perpetual and periodic inventory systems.

June 29. Received $19,600 from cash sales. The cost of the merchandise sold was $13,800.

June 29	Cash	19,600	
	Sales		19,600
	Cost of Mercandise Sold	13,800	
	Merchandise Inventory		13,800

The entry to record the sale of $19,600 is the same under both the perpetual and periodic inventory systems. Under the perpetual inventory system, however, the cost of merchandise sold and the reduction in merchandise inventory are also recorded on the date of sale. *Under the periodic system, no attempt is made to record the cost of merchandise sold at the date of the sale.*

The preceding entries for both the perpetual and periodic inventory systems are presented side by side in Exhibit 6.

Exhibit 6 *Comparison of Perpetual and Periodic Inventory Systems*

	Perpetual Inventory System			*Periodic Inventory System*		

June 5. Purchased $30,000 of merchandise on account from Owen Clothing, terms 2/10, n/30.	Merchandise Inventory
	    Accounts Payable
		30,000	30,000	Purchases
				    Accounts Payable
					30,000	30,000

June 8. Returned merchandise purchased on account from Owen Clothing on June 5, $500.	Accounts Payable
	    Merchandise Inventory
		500	500	Accounts Payable
				    Purchases Returns & Allowances
					500	500

June 15. Paid Owen Clothing for purchase of June 5 on account, less return of $500 and discount of $590 [($30,000–$500)× 2%].	Accounts Payable
	    Cash
	    Merchandise Inventory
		29,500	28,910
			590
				Accounts Payable
				    Cash
				    Purchases Discounts
					29,500	28,910
						590

June 18. Sold merchandise on account to Jones Co., $12,500, 1/10, n/30. The cost of the merchandise sold was $9,000.	Accounts Receivable
	    Sales
	
	Cost of Merchandise Sold
	    Merchandise Inventory
		12,500
		
		9,000
			12,500
			
			9,000
				Accounts Receivable
				    Sales
				
				No Entry. Adjusting entries are made at the end of the period for merchandise on hand and the cost of merchandise sold.
					12,500	12,500

June 21. Received merchandise returned on account from Jones Co., $4,000. The cost of the merchandise returned was $2,800.	Sales Returns & Allowances
	    Accounts Receivable
	
	Merchandise Inventory
	    Cost of Merchandise Sold
		4,000
		
		2,800
			4,000
			
			2,800
				Sales Returns & Allowances
				    Accounts Receivable
				
				No Entry. Adjusting entries are made at the end of the period for merchandise on hand and the cost of merchandise sold.
					4,000	4,000

June 22. Purchased merchandise from Norcross Clothiers, $15,000, terms FOB shipping point, 2/15, n/30, with prepaid transportation charges of $750 added to the invoice.	Merchandise Inventory
	    Accounts Payable
		15,750	15,750	Purchases
				Transportation In
				    Accounts Payable
					15,000
					750
						15,750

June 28. Received $8,415 as payment on account from Jones Co., less return of June 21 and less discount of $85 [($12,500–$4,000)× 1%].	Cash
	Sales Discounts
	    Accounts Receivable
		8,415
		85
			8,500	Cash
				Sales Discounts
				    Accounts Receivable
					8,415
					85
						8,500

June 29. Received $19,600 from cash sales. The cost of the merchandise sold was $13,800.	Cash
	    Sales
	
	Cost of Merchandise Sold
	    Merchandise Inventory
		19,600
		
		13,800
			19,600
			
			13,800
				Cash
				    Sales
				
				No Entry. Adjusting entries are made at the end of the period for merchandise on hand and the cost of merchandise sold.
					19,600	19,600

END-OF-PERIOD PROCEDURES IN A PERPETUAL INVENTORY SYSTEM

Objective 8
Prepare a work sheet, prepare financial statements, and journalize the adjusting and closing entries for a merchandising enterprise using the perpetual inventory system.

The end-of-period procedures are generally the same for the periodic and perpetual inventory systems. The differences in procedures for the two systems, which affect the work sheet, the income statement, the adjusting entries, and the closing entries, are discussed in the remainder of this chapter. The data for Computer King presented earlier in the chapter are used as the basis for illustration.

Work Sheet

The differences in the work sheet for a merchandising enterprise that uses the perpetual inventory system are highlighted in the work sheet for Computer King in Exhibit 7. As mentioned earlier, accounts for purchases, purchases returns and allowances, purchases discounts, and transportation in are not used in a perpetual inventory system. Transactions involving these items are recorded directly in the merchandise inventory account. The balance of the merchandise inventory account at the end of the period is the cost of merchandise on hand. Thus, on the work sheet in Exhibit 7, the merchandise inventory shown in the trial balance, $62,150, is extended directly to the Adjusted Trial Balance Debit column and the Balance Sheet Debit column. In contrast to the periodic system, *no adjusting entry is required for the beginning and ending merchandise inventories.*[4]

Exhibit 7
Perpetual Inventory
System—Work Sheet

Computer King
Work Sheet
For Year Ended December 31, 1995

Account Title	Trial Balance Dr.	Trial Balance Cr.	Adjustments Dr.	Adjustments Cr.	Adjusted Trial Balance Dr.	Adjusted Trial Balance Cr.	Income Statement Dr.	Income Statement Cr.	Balance Sheet Dr.	Balance Sheet Cr.
Cash	52,950				52,950				52,950	
Notes Receivable	40,000				40,000				40,000	
Accounts Receivable	60,880				60,880				60,880	
Interest Receivable			(a) 200		200				200	
Merchandise Inventory	62,150				62,150				62,150	
Office Supplies	1,090			(b) 610	480				480	
Sales		720,185				720,185		720,185		
Sales Returns and Allowances	6,140				6,140		6,140			
Sales Discounts	5,790				5,790		5,790			
Cost of Merchandise Sold	525,305				525,305		525,305			
Sales Salaries Expense	59,250		(f) 780		60,030		60,030			
Advertising Expense	10,860				10,860		10,860			
Rent Income				(g) 600		600		600		
Interest Income		3,600		(a) 200		3,800		3,800		
Interest Expense	2,440				2,440		2,440			
	932,235	932,235	10,050	10,050	939,165	939,165	649,185	724,585	289,980	214,580
Net Income							75,400			75,400
							724,585	724,585	289,980	289,980

Under a perpetual inventory system, the cost of merchandise sold is accumulated directly in a cost of merchandise sold account. The balance of this account in the trial balance of Computer King, $525,305, is extended directly to the Adjusted Trial Balance Debit column and the Income Statement Debit column.

---

[4] An adjusting entry may be required, however, if the physical inventory of merchandise at the end of the period differs from the perpetual inventory record. Such an entry is described and illustrated in a later chapter. This later chapter also discusses alternate methods of assigning costs to inventory quantities.

Only a portion of the work sheet for Computer King is shown in Exhibit 7. Accounts that are not shown do not differ from those same accounts in the work sheet in Exhibit 1. In comparing these work sheets, note that *the net income is the same under both the perpetual and periodic inventory systems.*

Financial Statements

The financial statements for Computer King are essentially the same under both the perpetual and periodic inventory systems. The major difference is that *the cost of merchandise sold is reported as a single amount in the income statement when the perpetual inventory system is used.*

Adjusting and Closing Entries

The adjusting entries are the same under both the perpetual and periodic inventory systems, except for merchandise inventory. As indicated above, no adjusting entries are necessary for merchandise inventory in a perpetual inventory system.

The closing entries differ under the perpetual inventory system in that the balance of the cost of merchandise sold account is closed to Income Summary. To illustrate, the closing entries under a perpetual inventory system for Computer King are shown below.

	DATE		DESCRIPTION	POST. REF.	DEBIT	CREDIT	
			JOURNAL			PAGE 29	
1			Closing Entries				1
2	1995 Dec.	31	Sales	410	720 1 8 5 00		2
3			Interest Income	611	3 8 0 0 00		3
4			Rent Income	610	6 0 0 00		4
5			Income Summary	312		724 5 8 5 00	5
6							6
7		31	Income Summary	312	649 1 8 5 00		7
8			Sales Returns and Allowances	411		6 1 4 0 00	8
9			Sales Discounts	412		5 7 9 0 00	9
10			Cost of Merchandise Sold	510		525 3 0 5 00	10
11			Sales Salaries Expense	520		60 0 3 0 00	11
12			Advertising Expense	521		10 8 6 0 00	12
13			Depreciation Exp.—Store Equip.	522		3 1 0 0 00	13
14			Miscellaneous Selling Expense	529		6 3 0 00	14
15			Office Salaries Expense	530		21 0 2 0 00	15
16			Rent Expense	531		8 1 0 0 00	16
17			Depreciation Expense—Office Equip.	532		2 4 9 0 00	17
18			Insurance Expense	533		1 9 1 0 00	18
19			Office Supplies Expense	534		6 1 0 00	19
20			Miscellaneous Administrative Exp.	539		7 6 0 00	20
21			Interest Expense	710		2 4 4 0 00	21
22							22
23		31	Income Summary	312	75 4 0 0 00		23
24			Jere King, Capital	310		75 4 0 0 00	24
25							25
26		31	Jere King, Capital	310	18 0 0 0 00		26
27			Jere King, Drawing	311		18 0 0 0 00	27
28							28

CHAPTER REVIEW

Key Points

Objective 1. List the year-end procedures for a merchandising enterprise.

The year-end procedures for a merchandising enterprise, which are similar to those for a service enterprise, are as follows:

1. Prepare a trial balance of the ledger on a work sheet.
2. Review the accounts and gather the data required for the adjustments.
3. Insert the adjustments and complete the work sheet.
4. Prepare financial statements from the data in the work sheet.
5. Journalize the adjusting entries and post to the ledger.
6. Journalize the closing entries and post to the ledger.
7. Prepare a post-closing trial balance of the ledger.

Objective 2. Prepare a work sheet for a merchandising enterprise, using the periodic inventory system.

The preparation of a work sheet for a merchandising enterprise is similar to that for a service enterprise, except for the merchandising inventory adjustments. Two adjusting entries are necessary in order to update the merchandise inventory account. Income Summary is debited and Merchandise Inventory is credited for the amount of the beginning inventory. Merchandise Inventory is debited and Income Summary is credited for the amount of the ending inventory. In the work sheet, both the debit and the credit in Income Summary are extended to the Adjusted Trial Balance columns and the Income Statement columns.

Objective 3. Prepare an income statement, a statement of owner's equity, and a balance sheet for a merchandising enterprise.

The income statement for a merchandising enterprise reports sales, cost of merchandise sold, and gross profit. The balance sheet reports merchandise inventory as a current asset.

There are two widely used forms for the income statement: multiple-step and single-step. The multiple-step income statement contains several sections, subsections, and subtotals. In the single-step income statement, the total of all expenses is deducted from the total of all revenues.

The balance sheet may be prepared using the report form or the account form. The report form lists assets, liabilities, and owner's equity in a downward sequence. The account form lists assets on the left-hand side and liabilities and owner's equity on the right-hand side of the statement.

Objective 4. Journalize the adjusting entries for a merchandising enterprise.

The adjusting entries, including those for merchandise inventory, are prepared for a merchandising enterprise from the work sheet Adjustments columns. After the adjusting entries have been posted, the balances of all asset, liability, revenue, and expense accounts equal the amounts reported in the financial statements.

Objective 5. Journalize the closing entries for a merchandising enterprise.

The first closing entry for a merchandise enterprise closes all income statement accounts with credit balances, which include revenue accounts and the contra purchases accounts. The second entry closes all income statement accounts with debit balances, which include the expense accounts and the contra sales accounts. The closing entries reduce the balances of all the temporary owner's equity accounts to zero.

Objective 6. Explain when a perpetual inventory system is likely to be used by a merchandising enterprise.

Large retailers with computerized accounting operations will likely use a perpetual inventory system. These retailers maintain their merchandise records electronically through the use of bar codes and optical scanners. Smaller retailers that sell a relatively small number of high-unit-cost items may use a manual perpetual inventory system.

Objective 7. Journalize the entries for merchandise transactions, using a perpetual inventory system.

In a perpetual inventory system, all increases and decreases related to merchandise are recorded directly in the merchandise inventory account. Thus, accounts for purchases, purchases returns and allowances, purchases discounts, and transporation in are not used. A cost of merchandise sold account is used to record the reduction in inventory when a sale occurs.

Objective 8. Prepare a work sheet, prepare financial statements, and journalize the adjusting and closing entries for a merchandising enterprise using the perpetual inventory system.

When preparing a work sheet for a merchandising enterprise that uses a perpetual inventory system, no adjusting entries are required for the beginning and ending inventories. This is because the balance of the merchandise inventory account at the end of the period is the cost of merchandise on hand. The balance of the cost of merchandise sold account, which appears on the work sheet, is reported in the income statement.

Glossary of Key Terms

Account form of balance sheet. A form of balance sheet with assets on the left-hand side and liabilities and owner's equity on the right-hand side. **Objective 3**

Administrative expenses. Expenses incurred in the administration or general operations of a business. **Objective 3**

Gross profit. The excess of net sales over the cost of merchandise sold. **Objective 3**

Income from operations. The excess of gross profit over total operating expenses. **Objective 3**

Multiple-step income statement. An income statement with several sections, subsections, and subtotals. **Objective 3**

Other expense. An expense that cannot be traced directly to operations. **Objective 3**

Other income. Revenue from sources other than the primary operating activity of a business. **Objective 3**

Report form of balance sheet. A form of balance sheet with the liabilities and owner's equity sections below the asset section. **Objective 3**

Selling expenses. Expenses incurred directly in the sale of merchandise. **Objective 3**

Single-step income statement. An income statement in which the total of all expenses is deducted in one step from the total of all revenues. **Objective 3**

Self-Examination Questions
Answers at end of chapter.

1. The income statement in which the total of all expenses is deducted from the total of all revenues is termed:
   A. multiple-step form
   B. single-step form
   C. account form
   D. report form

2. On a multiple-step income statement, the excess of net sales over the cost of merchandise sold is called:
   A. operating income
   B. income from operations
   C. gross profit
   D. net income

3. Which of the following expenses would normally be classified as *Other expense* on a multiple-step income statement?
   A. Depreciation expense—office equipment
   B. Sales salaries expense
   C. Insurance expense
   D. Interest expense

4. In a periodic inventory system, the entry to adjust the merchandise inventory account for the beginning inventory is:
   A. debit Merchandise Inventory, credit Income Summary
   B. debit Income Summary, credit Merchandise Inventory
   C. debit Cost of Merchandise Sold, credit Income Summary
   D. debit Income Summary, credit Purchases

5. Which of the following accounts would normally appear in the ledger of a merchandising enterprise that uses the perpetual inventory system?
   A. Transportation In
   B. Purchases
   C. Cost of Merchandise Sold
   D. Purchases Discounts

ILLUSTRATIVE PROBLEM

A work sheet for Hadley Co., shown on the next page, has been completed through the Adjustments columns.

Instructions

1. Complete the work sheet for Hadley Co.
2. Prepare a multiple-step income statement.
3. Prepare a statement of owner's equity.
4. Prepare an account form of balance sheet, assuming that the current portion of the note payable is $7,500.
5. Journalize the adjusting entries.
6. Journalize the closing entries.

Solution

1.

Hadley Co.
Work Sheet
For Year Ended October 31, 1994

Account Title	Trial Balance Dr.	Trial Balance Cr.	Adjustments Dr.	Adjustments Cr.	Adjusted Trial Balance Dr.	Adjusted Trial Balance Cr.	Income Statement Dr.	Income Statement Cr.	Balance Sheet Dr.	Balance Sheet Cr.
Cash	26,400				26,400				26,400	
Accounts Receivable	62,200				62,200				62,200	
Merchandise Inventory	141,300		(b)156,000	(a)141,300	156,000				156,000	
Prepaid Insurance	6,800			(c) 4,300	2,500				2,500	
Store Supplies	1,250			(d) 660	590				590	
Office Supplies	800			(e) 480	320				320	
Store Equipment	65,000				65,000				65,000	
Accum. Depr.—Store Equip.		20,100		(f) 5,850		25,950				25,950
Office Equipment	19,600				19,600				19,600	
Accum. Depr.—Office Equip.		8,100		(g) 2,160		10,260				10,260
Accounts Payable		36,400				36,400				36,400
Salaries Payable				(h) 2,700		2,700				2,700
Unearned Rent		1,000	(i) 500			500				500
Note Payable (final payment, 2004)		75,000				75,000				75,000
J. Hadley, Capital		112,420				112,420				112,420
J. Hadley, Drawing	8,000				8,000				8,000	
Income Summary			(a)141,300	(b)156,000	141,300	156,000	141,300	156,000		
Sales		540,000				540,000		540,000		
Sales Returns and Allowances	4,300				4,300		4,300			
Sales Discounts	2,500				2,500		2,500			
Purchases	360,000				360,000		360,000			
Purchases Returns and Allowances		9,000				9,000		9,000		
Purchases Discounts		4,680				4,680		4,680		
Transportation In	1,800				1,800		1,800			
Sales Salaries Expense	43,200		(h) 1,800		45,000		45,000			
Advertising Expense	15,000				15,000		15,000			
Depr. Exp.—Store Equip.			(f) 5,850		5,850		5,850			
Store Supplies Expense			(d) 660		660		660			
Miscellaneous Selling Expense	970				970		970			
Office Salaries Expense	30,000		(h) 900		30,900		30,900			
Rent Expense	8,500				8,500		8,500			
Insurance Expense			(c) 4,300		4,300		4,300			
Depr. Exp.—Office Equip.			(g) 2,160		2,160		2,160			
Office Supplies Expense			(e) 480		480		480			
Misc. Administrative Expense	830				830		830			
Rent Income				(i) 500		500		500		
Interest Expense	8,250				8,250		8,250			
	806,700	806,700	313,950	313,950	973,410	973,410	632,800	710,180	340,610	263,230
Net Income							77,380			77,380
							710,180	710,180	340,610	340,610

ILLUSTRATIVE PROBLEM ILLUSTRATIVE PROBLEM ILLUSTRATIVE PROBLEM ILLUSTRATIVE PROBLEM ILLUSTRATIVE PROBLEM

2.

Hadley Co. Income Statement For Year Ended October 31, 1994			
Revenue from sales:			
Sales		$540,000	
Less: Sales returns and allowances	$ 4,300		
Sales discounts	2,500	6,800	
Net sales			$533,200
Cost of merchandise sold:			
Merchandise inventory, November 1, 1993		$141,300	
Purchases	$360,000		
Less: Purchases returns and allowances	$9,000		
Purchases discounts	4,680	13,680	
Net purchases		$346,320	
Add transportation in		1,800	
Cost of merchandise purchased		348,120	
Merchandise available for sale		$489,420	
Less merchandise inventory, October 31, 1994		156,000	
Cost of merchandise sold			333,420
Gross profit			$199,780
Operating expenses:			
Selling expenses:			
Sales salaries expense	$ 45,000		
Advertising expense	15,000		
Depreciation expense—store equipment	5,850		
Store supplies expense	660		
Miscellaneous selling expense	970		
Total selling expenses		$ 67,480	
Administrative expenses:			
Office salaries expense	$ 30,900		
Rent expense	8,500		
Insurance expense	4,300		
Depreciation expense—office equipment	2,160		
Office supplies expense	480		
Miscellaneous administrative expense	830		
Total administrative expenses		47,170	
Total operating expenses			114,650
Income from operations			$ 85,130
Other income:			
Rent income		$ 500	
Other expense:			
Interest expense		8,250	7,750
Net income			$ 77,380

3.

Hadley Co. Statement of Owner's Equity For Year Ended October 31, 1994		
J. Hadley, capital, November 1, 1993		$112,420
Net income for the year	$77,380	
Less withdrawals	8,000	
Increase in owner's equity		69,380
J. Hadley, capital, October 31, 1994		$181,800

4.

Hadley Co.
Balance Sheet
October 31, 1994

Assets

Current assets:			
Cash		$ 26,400	
Accounts receivable		62,200	
Merchandise inventory		156,000	
Prepaid insurance		2,500	
Store supplies		590	
Office supplies		320	
Total current assets			$248,010
Plant assets:			
Store equipment	$65,000		
Less accumulated depreciation	25,950	$ 39,050	
Office equipment	$19,600		
Less accumulated depreciation	10,260	9,340	
Total plant assets			48,390
Total assets			$296,400

Liabilities

Current liabilities:		
Accounts payable	$ 36,400	
Note payable (current portion)	7,500	
Salaries payable	2,700	
Unearned rent	500	
Total current liabilities		$ 47,100
Long-term liabilities:		
Note payable (final payment, 2004)		67,500
Total liabilities		$114,600

Owner's Equity

J. Hadley, capital	181,800
Total liabilities and owner's equity	$296,400

5.

	DATE		DESCRIPTION	POST. REF.	DEBIT	CREDIT	
1			Adjusting Entries				1
2	1994 Oct.	31	Income Summary		141 3 0 0 00		2
3			Merchandise Inventory			141 3 0 0 00	3
4							4
5		31	Merchandise Inventory		156 0 0 0 00		5
6			Income Summary			156 0 0 0 00	6
7							7
8		31	Insurance Expense		4 3 0 0 00		8
9			Prepaid Insurance			4 3 0 0 00	9
10							10
11		31	Store Supplies Expense		6 6 0 00		11
12			Store Supplies			6 6 0 00	12
13							13
14		31	Office Supplies Expense		4 8 0 00		14
15			Office Supplies			4 8 0 00	15

15. What particular item of financial or operating data appears on (a) both the income statement and the statement of owner's equity, and (b) both the balance sheet and the statement of owner's equity?
16. Differentiate between the account form and the report form of balance sheet.
17. From the following list, identify the accounts that should be closed to Income Summary at the end of the fiscal year: (a) Accounts Receivable, (b) Land, (c) Purchases, (d) Purchases Returns and Allowances, (e) Sales, (f) Sales Discounts, (g) Supplies, (h) Supplies Expense, (i) Salaries Expense, (j) Salaries Payable.
18. Which of the following accounts in the ledger will ordinarily appear in the post-closing trial balance? (a) Accounts Payable, (b) Accumulated Depreciation, (c) Cash, (d) Jan Collins, Drawing, (e) Equipment, (f) Purchases Discounts, (g) Sales, (h) Salaries Expense.
19. In which of the following types of businesses would a perpetual inventory system ordinarily be used: (a) foreign luxury-car dealer, (b) small bakery, (c) large retailer with computerized accounting system that utilizes optional scanners to read bar-coded merchandise sold?

20. If a perpetual inventory system is used, what account is (a) debited to record purchases of merchandise and (b) credited to record the cost of merchandise sold?
21. Are adjusting entries required at the end of an accounting period for the beginning and ending merchandise inventories if the perpetual inventory system is used? Explain.
22. A recent trend in retailing is the establishment of warehouse clubs. These clubs, whose members pay a nominal yearly fee, offer name-brand merchandise at prices ranging from 20 to 40 percent below discount store prices. The Price Club, with projected annual sales of over $1 billion, is one of the leaders in this growing area of retailing. The following graph compares the gross profit as a percent of sales of The Price Club with that of K Mart Corp.:

Briefly discuss how The Price Club can remain profitable with a gross profit percentage less than one-half that of K Mart Corp.

ETHICS DISCUSSION CASE

D. L. McLain, president of McLain's Stores, has decided to use the single-step form rather than the multiple-step form for McLain's Stores' income statement for the year ended December 31.

Discuss whether D. L. McLain has behaved in an ethical manner by using the single-step income statement form rather than the multiple-step form.

4.

Hadley Co.	
Balance Sheet	
October 31, 1994	

Assets

Current assets:
Cash	$ 26,400	
Accounts receivable	62,200	
Merchandise inventory	156,000	
Prepaid insurance	2,500	
Store supplies	590	
Office supplies	320	
Total current assets		$248,010

Plant assets:
Store equipment	$65,000		
Less accumulated depreciation	25,950	$ 39,050	
Office equipment	$19,600		
Less accumulated depreciation	10,260	9,340	
Total plant assets			48,390
Total assets			$296,400

Liabilities

Current liabilities:
Accounts payable	$ 36,400	
Note payable (current portion)	7,500	
Salaries payable	2,700	
Unearned rent	500	
Total current liabilities		$ 47,100
Long-term liabilities:		
Note payable (final payment, 2004)		67,500
Total liabilities		$114,600

Owner's Equity

J. Hadley, capital		181,800
Total liabilities and owner's equity		$296,400

5.

	DATE		DESCRIPTION	POST. REF.	DEBIT	CREDIT	
1			Adjusting Entries				1
2	1994 Oct.	31	Income Summary		141 3 0 0 00		2
3			Merchandise Inventory			141 3 0 0 00	3
4							4
5		31	Merchandise Inventory		156 0 0 0 00		5
6			Income Summary			156 0 0 0 00	6
7							7
8		31	Insurance Expense		4 3 0 0 00		8
9			Prepaid Insurance			4 3 0 0 00	9
10							10
11		31	Store Supplies Expense		6 6 0 00		11
12			Store Supplies			6 6 0 00	12
13							13
14		31	Office Supplies Expense		4 8 0 00		14
15			Office Supplies			4 8 0 00	15

5. (cont.)

	DATE	DESCRIPTION	POST. REF.	DEBIT	CREDIT	
17	31	Depr. Expense—Store Equipment		5 8 5 0 00		17
18		Accumulated Depr.—Store Equip.			5 8 5 0 00	18
19						19
20	31	Depr. Expense—Office Equipment		2 1 6 0 00		20
21		Accumulated Depr.—Office Equip.			2 1 6 0 00	21
22						22
23	31	Sales Salaries Expense		1 8 0 0 00		23
24		Office Salaries Expense		9 0 0 00		24
25		Salaries Payable			2 7 0 0 00	25
26						26
27	31	Unearned Rent		5 0 0 00		27
28		Rent Income			5 0 0 00	28

6.

	DATE		DESCRIPTION	POST. REF.	DEBIT	CREDIT	
1			Closing Entries				1
2	Oct. 1994	31	Sales		540 0 0 0 00		2
3			Purchases Returns and Allowances		9 0 0 0 00		3
4			Purchases Discounts		4 6 8 0 00		4
5			Rent Income		5 0 0 00		5
6			Income Summary			554 1 8 0 00	6
7							7
8		31	Income Summary		491 5 0 0 00		8
9			Sales Returns and Allowances			4 3 0 0 00	9
10			Sales Discounts			2 5 0 0 00	10
11			Purchases			360 0 0 0 00	11
12			Transportation In			1 8 0 0 00	12
13			Sales Salaries Expense			45 0 0 0 00	13
14			Advertising Expense			15 0 0 0 00	14
15			Depr. Expense—Store Equipment			5 8 5 0 00	15
16			Store Supplies Expense			6 6 0 00	16
17			Miscellaneous Selling Expense			9 7 0 00	17
18			Office Salaries Expense			30 9 0 0 00	18
19			Rent Expense			8 5 0 0 00	19
20			Insurance Expense			4 3 0 0 00	20
21			Depr. Expense—Office Equipment			2 1 6 0 00	21
22			Office Supplies Expense			4 8 0 00	22
23			Miscellaneous Administrative Exp.			8 3 0 00	23
24			Interest Expense			8 2 5 0 00	24
25							25
26		31	Income Summary		77 3 8 0 00		26
27			J. Hadley, Capital			77 3 8 0 00	27
28							28
29		31	J. Hadley, Capital		8 0 0 0 00		29
30			J. Hadley, Drawing			8 0 0 0 00	30

DISCUSSION QUESTIONS

1. What is the name of the account in which unsold merchandise at the end of a period is recorded?
2. In a periodic inventory system, what account is used to remove from the merchandise inventory account the inventory at the beginning of the period and replace it with the amount representing the inventory at the end of the period?
3. The account Merchandise Inventory is listed at $195,000 in the Trial Balance columns of the work sheet at December 31, the end of the fiscal year. Which one of the following phrases describes the item correctly, assuming that a periodic inventory system is used?
   a. Inventory of merchandise at January 1, beginning of the year.
   b. Purchases of merchandise during the year.
   c. Merchandise available for sale during the year.
   d. Inventory of merchandise at December 31, end of the year.
   e. Cost of merchandise sold during the year.
4. The following data appear in a work sheet as of December 31, the end of the fiscal year, for a company that uses the periodic inventory system:

	Adjustments		Income Statement	
	Dr.	Cr.	Dr.	Cr.
Income Summary	(a) 205,000	(b) 187,500	205,000	187,500

   a. To what account was the $205,000 credited in adjustment (a)?
   b. To what account was the $187,500 debited in adjustment (b)?
   c. What was the amount of the merchandise inventory at January 1, the beginning of the fiscal year?
   d. What amount will be listed for merchandise inventory on the balance sheet at December 31, the end of the fiscal year?
   e. If the totals of the Income Statement columns of the work sheet are $1,550,000 debit and $1,675,000 credit, what is the amount of the net income for the year?

5. In which of the columns on a 10-column work sheet will the amount of the merchandise inventory at the end of the period appear if the periodic inventory system is used?
6. What are the two widely used forms for the income statement?
7. What is the primary characteristic of the multiple-step income statement?
8. For the fiscal year, sales were $1,250,000, sales discounts were $10,100, and sales returns and allowances were $40,000. What was the amount of net sales?
9. For the fiscal year, net sales were $995,000 and the cost of merchandise purchased was $695,000. Merchandise inventory at the beginning of the year was $110,000, and at the end of the year it was $90,000. Determine the following amounts:
   a. Merchandise available for sale.
   b. Cost of merchandise sold.
   c. Gross profit.
   d. Merchandise inventory listed on the balance sheet as of the end of the year.
10. Differentiate between selling expenses and administrative expenses.
11. The following expenses were incurred by a merchandising enterprise during the year. In which expense section of the income statement should each be reported: (a) selling, (b) administrative, or (c) other?
    (1) Interest expense on notes payable.
    (2) Salaries of office personnel.
    (3) Advertising expense.
    (4) Insurance expense on store equipment.
    (5) Rent expense on office building.
    (6) Depreciation expense on office equipment.
    (7) Office supplies used.
    (8) Salary of sales manager.
12. Differentiate between the multiple-step and the single-step forms of the income statement.
13. What major advantages and disadvantages does the single-step form of income statement have in comparison to the multiple-step statement?
14. What type of revenue is reported in the Other Income section of the multiple-step income statement?

15. What particular item of financial or operating data appears on (a) both the income statement and the statement of owner's equity, and (b) both the balance sheet and the statement of owner's equity?

16. Differentiate between the account form and the report form of balance sheet.

17. From the following list, identify the accounts that should be closed to Income Summary at the end of the fiscal year: (a) Accounts Receivable, (b) Land, (c) Purchases, (d) Purchases Returns and Allowances, (e) Sales, (f) Sales Discounts, (g) Supplies, (h) Supplies Expense, (i) Salaries Expense, (j) Salaries Payable.

18. Which of the following accounts in the ledger will ordinarily appear in the post-closing trial balance? (a) Accounts Payable, (b) Accumulated Depreciation, (c) Cash, (d) Jan Collins, Drawing, (e) Equipment, (f) Purchases Discounts, (g) Sales, (h) Salaries Expense.

19. In which of the following types of businesses would a perpetual inventory system ordinarily be used: (a) foreign luxury-car dealer, (b) small bakery, (c) large retailer with computerized accounting system that utilizes optional scanners to read bar-coded merchandise sold?

20. If a perpetual inventory system is used, what account is (a) debited to record purchases of merchandise and (b) credited to record the cost of merchandise sold?

21. Are adjusting entries required at the end of an accounting period for the beginning and ending merchandise inventories if the perpetual inventory system is used? Explain.

REAL W🌐RLD FOCUS

22. A recent trend in retailing is the establishment of warehouse clubs. These clubs, whose members pay a nominal yearly fee, offer name-brand merchandise at prices ranging from 20 to 40 percent below discount store prices. The Price Club, with projected annual sales of over $1 billion, is one of the leaders in this growing area of retailing. The following graph compares the gross profit as a percent of sales of The Price Club with that of K Mart Corp.:

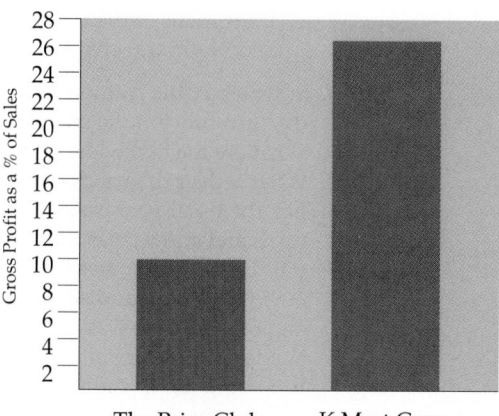

SHARPEN YOUR COMMUNICATION SKILLS ►

Briefly discuss how The Price Club can remain profitable with a gross profit percentage less than one-half that of K Mart Corp.

   ETHICS DISCUSSION CASE

D. L. McLain, president of McLain's Stores, has decided to use the single-step form rather than the multiple-step form for McLain's Stores' income statement for the year ended December 31.

SHARPEN YOUR COMMUNICATION SKILLS ►

Discuss whether D. L. McLain has behaved in an ethical manner by using the single-step income statement form rather than the multiple-step form.

EXERCISES

EXERCISE 6-1
MERCHANDISING
ADJUSTING ENTRIES
Objective 2

Data assembled for preparing the work sheet for T. C. Randall Co. for the fiscal year ended December 31, 1993, included the following:

Merchandise inventory as of January 1, 1993	$145,000
Merchandise inventory as of December 31, 1993	137,500

Journalize the two adjusting entries for merchandise inventory that would appear on the work sheet, assuming that the periodic inventory system is used.

EXERCISE 6-2
INCOME STATEMENT
THROUGH GROSS PROFIT
Objective 3

Selected data for Simone Company for the current year ended December 31 are as follows:

Merchandise inventory, January 1	$ 55,000
Merchandise inventory, December 31	57,500
Purchases	562,000
Purchases discounts	8,000
Purchases returns and allowances	15,500
Sales	705,000
Sales discounts	6,500
Sales returns and allowances	8,700
Transportation in	12,500

Prepare a multiple-step income statement through gross profit for Simone Company for the current year ended December 31.

EXERCISE 6-3
IDENTIFICATION OF ITEMS
MISSING FROM INCOME
STATEMENT
Objective 3

For (a) through (i), identify the items designated by "X."

a. Sales – (X + X) = Net sales
b. Purchases – (X + X) = Net purchases
c. Net purchases + X = Cost of merchandise purchased
d. Merchandise inventory (beginning) + cost of merchandise purchased = X
e. Merchandise available for sale – X = Cost of merchandise sold
f. Net sales – cost of merchandise sold = X
g. X + X = Operating expenses
h. Gross profit – operating expenses = X
i. Income from operations + X – X = Net income

EXERCISE 6-4
DETERMINATION OF
AMOUNTS FOR ITEMS
OMITTED FROM INCOME
STATEMENT
Objective 3

Three items are omitted in each of the following four lists of income statement data. Determine the amounts of the missing items, identifying them by letter.

Sales	$ (a)	$610,000	$990,000	$757,500
Sales returns and allowances	9,000	17,000	(g)	30,500
Sales discounts	3,000	8,000	10,000	(j)
Net sales	150,000	(d)	965,000	(k)
Beginning inventory	(b)	125,000	215,000	(l)
Cost of merchandise purchased	95,000	(e)	600,000	580,000
Ending inventory	30,000	105,000	(h)	135,000
Cost of merchandise sold	90,000	375,000	(i)	540,000
Gross profit	(c)	(f)	390,000	180,000

EXERCISE 6-5
SINGLE-STEP INCOME
STATEMENT
Objective 3

Summary operating data for Solar Products Company during the current year ended June 30, 1994, are as follows: cost of merchandise sold, $925,000; administrative expenses, $145,000; interest expense, $27,500; rent income, $30,000; net sales, $1,500,000; and selling expenses, $210,000. Prepare a single-step income statement.

EXERCISE 6-6
MULTIPLE-STEP INCOME
STATEMENT
Objective 3

Selected account titles and related amounts appearing in the Income Statement and Balance Sheet columns of the work sheet of Vincent Company for the year ended December 31 are listed in alphabetical order as follows:

Administrative Expenses	$ 79,500
Building	312,500
N. L. Vincent, Capital	300,000
Cash	58,500
N. L. Vincent, Drawing	60,000
Interest Expense	2,500
Merchandise Inventory (1/1)	225,000
Merchandise Inventory (12/31)	230,000
Notes Payable	25,000
Office Supplies	10,600
Purchases	850,000
Purchases Discounts	8,000
Purchases Returns and Allowances	12,000
Salaries Payable	4,220
Sales	1,275,000
Sales Discounts	10,200
Sales Returns and Allowances	34,300
Selling Expenses	132,700
Store Supplies	7,700
Transportation In	11,300

**SPREADSHEET
PROBLEM**

All selling expenses have been recorded in the account entitled *Selling Expenses*, and all administrative expenses have been recorded in the account entitled *Administrative Expenses*.

a. Prepare a multiple-step income statement for the year.

**SHARPEN YOUR
COMMUNICATION SKILLS**   ►

b. Compare the major advantages and disadvantages of the multiple-step and single-step forms of income statements .

EXERCISE 6-7
MERCHANDISE INVENTORY
ADJUSTMENTS AND
CLOSING ENTRIES
Objectives 4, 5

Based on the data presented in Exercise 6-6, journalize (a) the adjusting entries for merchandise inventory and (b) the closing entries.

EXERCISE 6-8
BALANCE SHEET ITEMS
Objective 3

From the following list of selected items taken from the records of J. M. Posey Company as of a specific date, identify those that would appear on the balance sheet:

a. J. M. Posey, Capital   f. Accounts Receivable
b. Cash   g. Sales
c. Salaries Expense   h. Purchases Discounts
d. Land   i. Supplies
e. Accounts Payable   j. Purchases

EXERCISE 6-9
SALES-RELATED
TRANSACTIONS—
PERPETUAL INVENTORY
SYSTEM
Objective 7

Coyles Co. sells merchandise to Westbury Co. on account, $6,900, terms 2/15, n/30. The cost of the merchandise sold is $3,900. Coyles Co. issues a credit memorandum for $750 for merchandise returned and subsequently receives the amount due within the discount period. The cost of the merchandise returned is $450. Assuming that Coyles Co. uses the perpetual inventory system, journalize Coyles Co.'s entries for (a) the sale, including the cost of the merchandise sold, (b) the credit memorandum, including the cost of the returned merchandise, and (c) the receipt of the check for the amount due from Westbury Co.

EXERCISE 6-10
PURCHASE-RELATED
TRANSACTIONS—
PERPETUAL INVENTORY
SYSTEM
Objective 7

Based upon the data presented in Exercise 6-9 and using the perpetual inventory system, journalize Westbury Co.'s entries for (a) the purchase, (b) the return of the merchandise for credit, and (c) the payment of the invoice within the discount period.

EXERCISE 6-11
CLOSING ENTRIES—
PERPETUAL INVENTORY
SYSTEM
Objective 8

Selected account titles and related amounts appearing in the Income Statement and Balance Sheet columns of the work sheet of Kelly Company for the year ended March 31 are listed in alphabetical order as follows:

Administrative Expenses	$ 42,300
Building	147,500
C. F. Kelly, Capital	200,590
Cash	30,200
Cost of Merchandise Sold	382,500
C. F. Kelly, Drawing	15,000
Interest Expense	3,600
Interest Income	5,000
Merchandise Inventory	112,000
Notes Payable	30,000
Office Supplies	6,200
Salaries Payable	2,810
Sales	637,500
Sales Discounts	11,200
Sales Returns and Allowances	21,750
Selling Expenses	95,600
Store Supplies	8,050

Journalize the closing entries, assuming that Kelly Company uses a perpetual inventory system.

WhAT'S WRONG WITH THI?

How many errors can you find in the following income statement?

Baxter Company
Income Statement
For Year Ended December 31, 19—

Revenue from sales:				
Sales			$1,200,000	
Add: Sales returns and allowances		$ 28,000		
Sales discounts		9,500	37,500	
Gross sales				$1,237,500
Cost of merchandise sold:				
Merchandise inventory, January 1, 19—			$ 200,000	
Purchases		$850,000		
Less: Purchases returns and allowances	$15,000			
Purchases discounts	10,000	25,000		
Cost of merchandise purchased		$825,000		
Add transportation in		6,300		
Net purchases			831,300	
Merchandise available for sale			$1,031,300	
Less merchandise inventory December 31, 19—			230,000	
Cost of merchandise sold				801,300
Income from operations				$ 436,200
Operating expenses:				
Selling expenses			$ 125,000	
Administrative expenses			87,200	
Total operating expenses				212,200
Gross profit				$ 224,000
Other expense:				
Interest expense				7,500
Net loss				$ 216,500

PROBLEMS

Series A

PROBLEM 6-1A
WORK SHEET FOR
MERCHANDISING
ENTERPRISE USING THE
PERIODIC INVENTORY
SYSTEM
Objective 2

The accounts in the ledger of Horwitz Company, with the unadjusted balances on April 30, the end of the current fiscal year, are as follows:

Cash	$ 19,750
Accounts Receivable	64,100
Merchandise Inventory	87,150
Prepaid Insurance	7,100
Store Supplies	5,450
Store Equipment	53,700
Accumulated Depreciation—Store Equipment	15,180
Accounts Payable	26,800
Salaries Payable	—
J. A. Horwitz, Capital	144,020
J. A. Horwitz, Drawing	15,000
Income Summary	—
Sales	562,200
Purchases	360,000
Sales Salaries Expense	46,500
Advertising Expense	15,800
Depreciation Expense—Store Equipment	—
Store Supplies Expense	—
Miscellaneous Selling Expense	2,750
Office Salaries Expense	30,000
Rent Expense	24,000
Heating and Lighting Expense	9,660
Taxes Expense	5,100
Insurance Expense	—
Miscellaneous Administrative Expense	2,140

The data needed for year-end adjustments on April 30 are as follows:

Merchandise inventory on April 30		$90,000
Insurance expired during the year		3,800
Store supplies on hand on April 30		1,750
Depreciation for the current year		11,500
Accrued salaries on April 30:		
Sales salaries	$1,600	
Office salaries	750	2,350

SPREADSHEET
PROBLEM

SOLUTIONS
SOFTWARE

Instructions

Prepare a work sheet for the fiscal year ended April 30, listing all of the accounts in the order given.

Instructions for Solving Problem 6-1A Using Solutions Software

1. Load opening balances.
2. Save the opening balances file to your drive and directory.
3. Set the run date to April 30 of the current year and enter your name.
4. Key the adjusting entries. Key ADJ.ENT. in the reference field.
5. Display the adjusting entries. Key ADJ.ENT. in the Reference Restriction area of the Selection Options screen.
6. Display the financial statements.
7. Save a backup copy of your data file.
8. Perform period-end closing.
9. Display a post-closing trial balance.
10. Save your data file to disk.
11. End the session.

PROBLEM 6-2A
MULTIPLE-STEP INCOME
STATEMENT AND REPORT
FORM OF BALANCE
SHEET—PERIODIC
INVENTORY SYSTEM
Objective 3

The following selected accounts and their normal balances appear in the Income Statement and Balance Sheet columns of the work sheet of Merz Company for the fiscal year ended January 31, 1994:

Cash	$ 39,000
Notes Receivable	120,000
Accounts Receivable	212,000
Merchandise Inventory, Feb. 1, 1993	125,000
Merchandise Inventory, Jan. 31, 1994	100,000
Office Supplies	5,600
Prepaid Insurance	3,400
Office Equipment	35,000
Accumulated Depreciation—Office Equipment	12,800
Store Equipment	72,000
Accumulated Depreciation—Store Equipment	24,200
Accounts Payable	45,600
Salaries Payable	2,400
Note Payable (final payment, 2004)	56,000
P. C. Merz, Capital	391,000
P. C. Merz, Drawing	15,000
Sales	1,400,000
Sales Returns and Allowances	12,100
Sales Discounts	11,900
Purchases	1,100,000
Purchases Returns and Allowances	24,600
Purchases Discounts	15,400
Transportation In	15,000
Sales Salaries Expense	123,200
Advertising Expense	22,800
Depreciation Expense—Store Equipment	6,400
Miscellaneous Selling Expense	1,600
Office Salaries Expense	31,150
Rent Expense	16,350
Depreciation Expense—Office Equipment	12,700
Insurance Expense	3,900
Office Supplies Expense	1,300
Miscellaneous Administrative Expense	1,600
Interest Income	21,000
Interest Expense	6,000

Instructions

1. Prepare a multiple-step income statement.
2. Prepare a statement of owner's equity.
3. Prepare a report form of balance sheet, assuming that the current portion of the note payable is $6,000.
4. Briefly explain (a) how multiple-step and single-step income statements differ and (b) how report form and account form balance sheets differ.

SHARPEN YOUR
COMMUNICATION SKILLS

PROBLEM 6-3A
SINGLE-STEP INCOME
STATEMENT AND
ACCOUNT FORM OF
BALANCE SHEET—
PERIODIC INVENTORY
SYSTEM
Objective 3

Selected accounts and related amounts for Merz Company for the fiscal year ended January 31, 1994, are presented in Problem 6-2A.

Instructions

1. Prepare a single-step income statement.
2. Prepare a statement of owner's equity.
3. Prepare an account form of balance sheet, assuming that the current portion of the note payable is $6,000.

PROBLEM 6-4A
WORK SHEET AND
STATEMENTS—PERIODIC
INVENTORY SYSTEM
Objective 3

SPREADSHEET
PROBLEM

PROBLEM 6-5A
ADJUSTING ENTRIES FROM
WORK SHEET—PERIODIC
INVENTORY SYSTEM
Objective 4

If the working papers correlating with this textbook are not used, omit Problem 6-4A.

A partially completed work sheet for Watson Company is presented in the working papers. All adjustments have been entered on the work sheet.

Instructions

1. Complete the work sheet for Watson Company.
2. Prepare a multiple-step income statement.
3. Prepare a statement of owner's equity.
4. Prepare an account form of balance sheet, assuming that the current portion of the note payable is $12,000.

A portion of the work sheet of Smoltz Co. for the current year ended October 31 is as follows:

Account Title	Income Statement		Balance Sheet	
	Debit	Credit	Debit	Credit
Cash			57,900	
Notes Receivable			25,000	
Accounts Receivable			122,500	
Interest Receivable			500	
Merchandise Inventory			335,000	
Prepaid Rent			3,000	
Prepaid Insurance			2,340	
Supplies			1,380	
Store Equipment			126,800	
Accumulated Depr.—Store Equipment				51,000
Office Equipment			44,520	
Accumulated Depr.—Office Equipment				35,000
Accounts Payable				115,600
Sales Salaries Payable				4,500
Note Payable				250,000
T. A. Smoltz, Capital				240,850
T. A. Smoltz, Drawing			43,200	
Income Summary	354,000	335,000		
Sales		1,020,000		
Sales Returns and Allowances	12,000			
Sales Discounts	8,500			
Purchases	617,720			
Purchases Returns and Allowances		14,650		
Purchases Discounts		8,140		
Transportation In	7,230			
Sales Salaries Expense	124,000			
Depreciation Expense—Store Equip.	16,460			
Supplies Expense	960			
Miscellaneous Selling Expense	3,800			
Office Salaries Expense	70,000			
Rent Expense	36,000			
Heating and Lighting Expense	21,750			
Insurance Expense	4,100			
Depreciation Expense—Office Equip.	5,180			
Miscellaneous Administrative Expense	2,900			
Interest Income		2,000		
Interest Expense	30,000			
	1,314,600	1,379,790	762,140	696,950

Instructions

From the partial work sheet, journalize the nine entries that appeared in the Adjustments columns. The only accounts affected by more than one adjusting entry were Merchandise Inventory and Income Summary. The balance in Prepaid Rent before adjustment was $39,000, representing 13 months' rent at $3,000 per month.

PROBLEM 6-6A
PREPARATION OF WORK
SHEET, FINANCIAL
STATEMENTS, AND
ADJUSTING AND CLOSING
ENTRIES—PERIODIC
INVENTORY SYSTEM
Objectives 2, 3, 4, 5

The accounts and their balances in the ledger of Gant Company on December 31 of the current year are as follows:

Cash	$ 68,175
Accounts Receivable	112,500
Merchandise Inventory	180,000
Prepaid Insurance	9,700
Store Supplies	4,250
Office Supplies	2,100
Store Equipment	112,000
Accumulated Depreciation—Store Equipment	40,300
Office Equipment	50,000
Accumulated Depreciation—Office Equipment	17,200
Accounts Payable	66,700
Salaries Payable	—
Unearned Rent	1,200
Note Payable (final payment, 2000)	105,000
R. L. Gant, Capital	220,510
R. L. Gant, Drawing	40,000
Income Summary	—
Sales	995,000
Sales Returns and Allowances	11,900
Sales Discounts	7,100
Purchases	635,000
Purchases Returns and Allowances	10,100
Purchases Discounts	4,900
Transportation In	6,200
Sales Salaries Expense	86,400
Advertising Expense	30,000
Depreciation Expense—Store Equipment	—
Store Supplies Expense	—
Miscellaneous Selling Expense	1,335
Office Salaries Expense	54,000
Rent Expense	36,000
Insurance Expense	—
Depreciation Expense—Office Equipment	—
Office Supplies Expense	—
Miscellaneous Administrative Expense	1,650
Rent Income	—
Interest Expense	12,600

The data needed for year-end adjustments on December 31 are as follows:

Merchandise inventory on December 31		$220,000
Insurance expired during the year		7,260
Supplies on hand on December 31:		
Store supplies		1,700
Office supplies		400
Depreciation for the year:		
Store equipment		9,500
Office equipment		4,800
Salaries payable on December 31:		
Sales salaries	$2,750	
Office salaries	1,150	3,900
Unearned rent on December 31		400

Instructions

1. Prepare a work sheet for the fiscal year ended December 31, listing all accounts in the order given.
2. Prepare a multiple-step income statement.
3. Prepare a statement of owner's equity.

Continued

4. Prepare a report form of balance sheet, assuming that the current portion of the note payable is $15,000.
5. Journalize the adjusting entries.
6. Journalize the closing entries.

PROBLEM 6-7A
SALES-RELATED AND
PURCHASE-RELATED
TRANSACTIONS—
PERPETUAL INVENTORY
SYSTEMS
Objective 7

The following were selected from among the transactions completed by Freeman Company during November of the current year. Freeman Company uses a perpetual inventory system.

Nov. 3. Purchased office supplies for cash, $120.
      5. Purchased merchandise on account from Butler Co., list price $20,000, trade discount 37.5%, terms FOB destination, 1/10, n/30.
      6. Sold merchandise for cash, $2,950. The cost of the merchandise sold was $1,450.
      7. Purchased merchandise on account from Mattox Co., $6,400, terms FOB shipping point, 2/10, n/30, with prepaid transportation costs of $190 added to the invoice.
      7. Returned merchandise purchased on November 5 from Butler Co., $2,500.
     11. Sold merchandise on account to Bowles Co., list price $2,250, trade discount 20%, terms 1/10, n/30. The cost of the merchandise sold was $880.
     15. Paid Butler Co. on account for purchase of November 5, less return of November 7 and discount.
     16. Sold merchandise on nonbank credit cards and reported accounts to the card company, $3,850. The cost of the merchandise sold was $1,900.
     17. Paid Mattox Co. on account for purchase of November 7, less discount.
     19. Purchased merchandise for cash, $3,500.
     21. Received cash on account from sale of November 11 to Bowles Co., less discount.
     24. Sold merchandise on account to Clemons Co., $4,200, terms 1/10, n/30. The cost of the merchandise sold was $2,025.
     28. Received cash from card company for nonbank credit card sales of November 16, less $190 service fee.
     30. Received merchandise returned by Clemons Co. from sale on November 24, $2,700. The cost of the returned merchandise was $1,310.

Instructions
Journalize the transactions.

SOLUTIONS
SOFTWARE

Instructions for Solving Problem 6-7A Using Solutions Software

1. Load opening balances.
2. Save the opening balances file to your drive and directory.
3. Set the run date to November 30 of the current year and enter your name.
4. Select the General Journal Entries option and key the journal entries. Leave the reference field blank. Note: To review the chart of accounts, select F-1.
5. Display a journal entries report.
6. Display a trial balance.
7. Key the adjusting entries, based on the following data:

   Insurance expired on November 30 $400
   Office supplies on hand on November 30   300

   Key ADJ.ENT. in the reference field.
8. Display the adjusting entries. Key ADJ.ENT. in the Reference Restriction area of the Selection Options screen.
9. Display the financial statements.
10. Save a backup copy of your data file.
11. Perform period-end closing.
12. Display a post-closing trial balance.
13. Save your data file to disk.
14. End the session.

PROBLEM 6-8A
WORK SHEET FOR
MERCHANDISING
ENTERPRISE USING THE
PERPETUAL INVENTORY
SYSTEM
Objective 8

The accounts in the ledger of Iyer Co., with the unadjusted balances on July 31, the end of the current fiscal year, are as follows:

Cash	$ 18,500
Notes Receivable	50,000
Accounts Receivable	53,340
Merchandise Inventory	80,000
Prepaid Insurance	4,200
Store Supplies	2,100
Store Equipment	154,200
Accumulated Depreciation—Store Equipment	84,600
Accounts Payable	32,000
Salaries Payable	—
Unearned Rent	7,600
C. A. Iyer, Capital	241,640
C. A. Iyer, Drawing	26,000
Sales	790,500
Cost of Merchandise Sold	474,300
Sales Salaries Expense	79,800
Advertising Expense	34,850
Depreciation Expense—Store Equipment	—
Store Supplies Expense	—
Miscellaneous Selling Expense	1,600
Office Salaries Expense	83,700
Rent Expense	45,000
Heating and Lighting Expense	37,400
Taxes Expense	7,850
Insurance Expense	—
Miscellaneous Administrative Expense	3,500
Rent Income	—

The data needed for year-end adjustments on July 31 are as follows:

Insurance expired during the year		$1,060
Store supplies on hand on July 31		820
Depreciation for the current year		9,300
Accrued salaries on July 31:		
Sales salaries	$1,500	
Office salaries	1,200	2,700
Rent income earned during the year		3,800

Instructions
Prepare a work sheet for the fiscal year ended July 31. List all accounts in the order given. Iyer Co. uses a perpetual inventory system.

**SOLUTIONS
SOFTWARE**

Instructions for Solving Problem 6-8A Using Solutions Software

1. Load opening balances.
2. Save the opening balances file to your drive and directory.
3. Set the run date to July 31 of the current year and enter your name.
4. Key the adjusting entries. Key ADJ.ENT. in the reference field.
5. Display the adjusting entries. Key ADJ.ENT. in the Reference Restriction area of the Selection Options screen.
6. Display the financial statements.
7. Save a backup copy of your data file.
8. Perform period-end closing.
9. Display a post-closing trial balance.
10. Save your data file to disk.
11. End the session.

PROBLEM 6-2B
MULTIPLE-STEP INCOME
STATEMENT AND REPORT
FORM OF BALANCE
SHEET—PERIODIC
INVENTORY SYSTEM
Objective 3

The following selected accounts and their normal balances appear in the Income Statement and Balance Sheet columns of the work sheet of Kilgore Company for the fiscal year ended November 30, 1994:

Cash	$ 105,000
Notes Receivable	50,000
Accounts Receivable	92,000
Merchandise Inventory, Dec. 1, 1993	90,000
Merchandise Inventory, Nov. 30, 1994	100,000
Office Supplies	1,600
Prepaid Insurance	6,800
Office Equipment	24,000
Accumulated Depreciation—Office Equipment	10,800
Store Equipment	40,500
Accumulated Depreciation—Store Equipment	18,900
Accounts Payable	32,000
Salaries Payable	1,700
Note Payable (final payment, 2004)	35,000
S. T. Kilgore, Capital	294,010
S. T. Kilgore, Drawing	25,000
Sales	1,000,000
Sales Returns and Allowances	9,000
Sales Discounts	8,500
Purchases	790,000
Purchases Returns and Allowances	16,200
Purchases Discounts	3,800
Transportation In	10,300
Sales Salaries Expense	88,000
Advertising Expense	16,300
Depreciation Expense—Store Equipment	4,600
Miscellaneous Selling Expense	1,000
Office Salaries Expense	30,900
Rent Expense	12,150
Depreciation Expense—Office Equipment	3,700
Insurance Expense	2,750
Office Supplies Expense	900
Miscellaneous Administrative Expense	1,150
Interest Income	5,400
Interest Expense	3,660

Instructions

1. Prepare a multiple-step income statement.
2. Prepare a statement of owner's equity.
3. Prepare a report form of balance sheet, assuming that the current portion of the note payable is $3,500.

SHARPEN YOUR
COMMUNICATION SKILLS ▶

4. Briefly explain (a) how multiple-step and single-step income statements differ and (b) how report form and account form balance sheets differ.

PROBLEM 6-3B
SINGLE-STEP INCOME
STATEMENT AND
ACCOUNT FORM OF
BALANCE SHEET—
PERIODIC INVENTORY
SYSTEM
Objective 3

Selected accounts and related amounts for Kilgore Company for the fiscal year ended November 30, 1994, are presented in Problem 6-2B.

Instructions

1. Prepare a single-step income statement.
2. Prepare a statement of owner's equity.
3. Prepare an account form of balance sheet, assuming that the current portion of the note payable is $3,500.

PROBLEM 6-8A
WORK SHEET FOR
MERCHANDISING
ENTERPRISE USING THE
PERPETUAL INVENTORY
SYSTEM
Objective 8

The accounts in the ledger of Iyer Co., with the unadjusted balances on July 31, the end of the current fiscal year, are as follows:

Cash	$ 18,500
Notes Receivable	50,000
Accounts Receivable	53,340
Merchandise Inventory	80,000
Prepaid Insurance	4,200
Store Supplies	2,100
Store Equipment	154,200
Accumulated Depreciation—Store Equipment	84,600
Accounts Payable	32,000
Salaries Payable	—
Unearned Rent	7,600
C. A. Iyer, Capital	241,640
C. A. Iyer, Drawing	26,000
Sales	790,500
Cost of Merchandise Sold	474,300
Sales Salaries Expense	79,800
Advertising Expense	34,850
Depreciation Expense—Store Equipment	—
Store Supplies Expense	—
Miscellaneous Selling Expense	1,600
Office Salaries Expense	83,700
Rent Expense	45,000
Heating and Lighting Expense	37,400
Taxes Expense	7,850
Insurance Expense	—
Miscellaneous Administrative Expense	3,500
Rent Income	—

The data needed for year-end adjustments on July 31 are as follows:

Insurance expired during the year		$1,060
Store supplies on hand on July 31		820
Depreciation for the current year		9,300
Accrued salaries on July 31:		
Sales salaries	$1,500	
Office salaries	1,200	2,700
Rent income earned during the year		3,800

Instructions

Prepare a work sheet for the fiscal year ended July 31. List all accounts in the order given. Iyer Co. uses a perpetual inventory system.

SOLUTIONS
SOFTWARE

Instructions for Solving Problem 6-8A Using Solutions Software

1. Load opening balances.
2. Save the opening balances file to your drive and directory.
3. Set the run date to July 31 of the current year and enter your name.
4. Key the adjusting entries. Key ADJ.ENT. in the reference field.
5. Display the adjusting entries. Key ADJ.ENT. in the Reference Restriction area of the Selection Options screen.
6. Display the financial statements.
7. Save a backup copy of your data file.
8. Perform period-end closing.
9. Display a post-closing trial balance.
10. Save your data file to disk.
11. End the session.

PROBLEM 6-9A
WORK SHEET, INCOME
STATEMENT AND CLOSING
ENTRIES—PERPETUAL
INVENTORY SYSTEM
Objective 8

Sycamore Co. uses a perpetual inventory system. A partially completed work sheet for Sycamore Co. for the current year ended April 30 is as follows:

Sycamore Co.
Work Sheet
For Year Ended April 30, 19—

	Trial Balance		Adjustments	
Account Title	Dr.	Cr.	Dr.	Cr.
Cash	28,500			
Accounts Receivable	88,300			
Merchandise Inventory	105,200			
Prepaid Insurance	11,500			(a) 6,900
Store Supplies	2,300			(b) 1,400
Office Supplies	1,500			(c) 900
Store Equipment	166,600			
Accum. Depr.—Store Equip.		68,000		(d) 8,100
Office Equipment	49,300			
Accum. Depr.—Office Equip.		12,000		(e) 3,000
Accounts Payable		29,500		
Salaries Payable				(f) 4,700
Unearned Rent		2,400	(g) 1,600	
Note Payable (due 1999)		100,000		
D. B. Sycamore, Capital		136,100		
D. B. Sycamore, Drawing	30,000			
Sales		760,000		
Sales Returns and Allowances	12,000			
Sales Discounts	7,500			
Cost of Merchandise Sold	456,300			
Sales Salaries Expense	64,000		(f) 3,500	
Advertising Expense	13,000			
Depr. Expense—Store Equip.			(d) 8,100	
Store Supplies Expense			(b) 1,400	
Misc. Selling Expense	4,400			
Office Salaries Expense	31,000		(f) 1,200	
Rent Expense	24,000			
Depr. Expense—Office Equip			(e) 3,000	
Insurance Expense			(a) 6,900	
Office Supplies Expense			(c) 900	
Misc. Administrative Expense	1,100			
Rent Income				(g) 1,600
Interest Expense	11,500			
	1,108,000	1,108,000	26,600	26,600

SPREADSHEET PROBLEM

SOLUTIONS SOFTWARE

Instructions

1. Complete the work sheet for Sycamore Co.
2. Prepare a single-step income statement for the year ended April 30.
3. Journalize the closing entries for Sycamore Co.

Instructions for Solving Problem 6-9A Using Solutions Software

1. Load opening balances.
2. Save the opening balances file to your drive and directory.
3. Set the run date to April 30 of the current year and enter your name.
4. Key the adjusting entries. Key ADJ.ENT. in the reference field.
5. Display the adjusting entries. Key ADJ.ENT. in the Reference Restriction area of the Selection Options screen.
6. Display the financial statements.
7. Save a backup copy of your data file.
8. Perform period-end closing.
9. Display a post-closing trial balance.
10. Save your data file to disk.
11. End the session.

Series B

PROBLEM 6-1B
WORK SHEET FOR
MERCHANDISING
ENTERPRISE USING THE
PERIODIC INVENTORY
SYSTEM
Objective 2

The accounts in the ledger of R. Fern Company, with the unadjusted balances on August 31, the end of the current fiscal year, are as follows:

Cash	$ 17,760
Accounts Receivable	53,340
Merchandise Inventory	121,400
Prepaid Insurance	2,480
Store Supplies	2,120
Store Equipment	166,200
Accumulated Depreciation—Store Equipment	84,600
Accounts Payable	32,000
Salaries Payable	—
R. Fern, Capital	199,550
R. Fern, Drawing	16,000
Income Summary	—
Sales	790,500
Purchases	513,700
Sales Salaries Expense	82,800
Advertising Expense	23,300
Depreciation Expense—Store Equipment	—
Store Supplies Expense	—
Miscellaneous Selling Expense	1,600
Office Salaries Expense	52,200
Rent Expense	25,000
Heating and Lighting Expense	17,400
Taxes Expense	7,850
Insurance Expense	—
Miscellaneous Administrative Expense	3,500

The data needed for year-end adjustments on August 31 are as follows:

Merchandise inventory on August 31		$100,000
Insurance expired during the year		1,560
Store supplies on hand on August 31		520
Depreciation for the current year		9,300
Accrued salaries on August 31:		
Sales salaries	$1,500	
Office salaries	1,200	2,700

SPREADSHEET PROBLEM

Instructions
Prepare a work sheet for the fiscal year ended August 31, listing all of the accounts in the order given.

Instructions for Solving Problem 6-1B Using Solutions Software

SOLUTIONS SOFTWARE

1. Load opening balances.
2. Save the opening balances file to your drive and directory.
3. Set the run date to August 31 of the current year and enter your name.
4. Key the adjusting entries. Key ADJ.ENT. in the reference field.
5. Display the adjusting entries. Key ADJ.ENT. in the Reference Restriction area of the Selection Options screen.
6. Display the financial statements.
7. Save a backup copy of your data file.
8. Perform period-end closing.
9. Display a post-closing trial balance.
10. Save your data file to disk.
11. End the session.

PROBLEM 6-2B
MULTIPLE-STEP INCOME
STATEMENT AND REPORT
FORM OF BALANCE
SHEET—PERIODIC
INVENTORY SYSTEM
Objective 3

The following selected accounts and their normal balances appear in the Income Statement and Balance Sheet columns of the work sheet of Kilgore Company for the fiscal year ended November 30, 1994:

Cash	$ 105,000
Notes Receivable	50,000
Accounts Receivable	92,000
Merchandise Inventory, Dec. 1, 1993	90,000
Merchandise Inventory, Nov. 30, 1994	100,000
Office Supplies	1,600
Prepaid Insurance	6,800
Office Equipment	24,000
Accumulated Depreciation—Office Equipment	10,800
Store Equipment	40,500
Accumulated Depreciation—Store Equipment	18,900
Accounts Payable	32,000
Salaries Payable	1,700
Note Payable (final payment, 2004)	35,000
S. T. Kilgore, Capital	294,010
S. T. Kilgore, Drawing	25,000
Sales	1,000,000
Sales Returns and Allowances	9,000
Sales Discounts	8,500
Purchases	790,000
Purchases Returns and Allowances	16,200
Purchases Discounts	3,800
Transportation In	10,300
Sales Salaries Expense	88,000
Advertising Expense	16,300
Depreciation Expense—Store Equipment	4,600
Miscellaneous Selling Expense	1,000
Office Salaries Expense	30,900
Rent Expense	12,150
Depreciation Expense—Office Equipment	3,700
Insurance Expense	2,750
Office Supplies Expense	900
Miscellaneous Administrative Expense	1,150
Interest Income	5,400
Interest Expense	3,660

Instructions

1. Prepare a multiple-step income statement.
2. Prepare a statement of owner's equity.
3. Prepare a report form of balance sheet, assuming that the current portion of the note payable is $3,500.

**SHARPEN YOUR
COMMUNICATION SKILLS**

4. Briefly explain (a) how multiple-step and single-step income statements differ and (b) how report form and account form balance sheets differ.

PROBLEM 6-3B
SINGLE-STEP INCOME
STATEMENT AND
ACCOUNT FORM OF
BALANCE SHEET—
PERIODIC INVENTORY
SYSTEM
Objective 3

Selected accounts and related amounts for Kilgore Company for the fiscal year ended November 30, 1994, are presented in Problem 6-2B.

Instructions

1. Prepare a single-step income statement.
2. Prepare a statement of owner's equity.
3. Prepare an account form of balance sheet, assuming that the current portion of the note payable is $3,500.

If the working papers correlating with this textbook are not used, omit Problem 6-4B.

PROBLEM 6-4B
WORK SHEET AND
STATEMENTS—PERIODIC
INVENTORY SYSTEM
Objective 3

A partially completed work sheet for Watson Company is presented in the working papers. All adjustments have been entered on the work sheet.

**SPREADSHEET
PROBLEM**

Instructions

1. Complete the worksheet for Watson Company.
2. Prepare a multiple-step income statement.
3. Prepare a statement of owner's equity.
4. Prepare an account form of balance sheet, assuming that the current portion of the note payable is $10,000.

PROBLEM 6-5B
ADJUSTING ENTRIES FROM
WORK SHEET—PERIODIC
INVENTORY SYSTEM
Objective 4

A portion of the work sheet of Sasser Company for the current year ended November 30 is as follows:

Account Title	Income Statement Debit	Income Statement Credit	Balance Sheet Debit	Balance Sheet Credit
Cash			62,650	
Notes Receivable			40,000	
Accounts Receivable			170,200	
Interest Receivable			600	
Merchandise Inventory			241,650	
Prepaid Rent			8,400	
Prepaid Insurance			17,200	
Supplies			3,360	
Store Equipment			87,750	
Accumulated Depr.—Store Equipment				33,490
Office Equipment			45,600	
Accumulated Depr.—Office Equip.				15,750
Accounts Payable				93,750
Sales Salaries Payable				4,500
Note Payable				180,000
W. B. Sasser, Capital				217,160
W. B. Sasser, Drawing			15,000	
Income Summary	260,500	241,650		
Sales		1,240,700		
Sales Returns and Allowances	31,400			
Sales Discounts	12,900			
Purchases	770,650			
Purchases Returns and Allowances		15,050		
Purchases Discounts		8,000		
Transportation In	12,100			
Sales Salaries Expense	120,750			
Depreciation Expense—Store Equip.	11,800			
Supplies Expense	2,040			
Miscellaneous Selling Expense	1,600			
Office Salaries Expense	50,300			
Rent Expense	33,600			
Heating and Lighting Expense	13,420			
Insurance Expense	11,500			
Depreciation Expense—Office Equip.	5,180			
Miscellaneous Administrative Exp.	1,900			
Interest Income		3,600		
Interest Expense	21,600			
	1,361,240	1,509,000	692,410	544,650

Instructions

From the partial work sheet, journalize the nine entries that appeared in the Adjustments columns. The only accounts affected by more than one adjusting entry were Merchandise Inventory and Income Summary. The balance in Prepaid Rent before adjustment was $42,000, representing 15 months' rent at $2,800 per month.

PROBLEM 6-6B
PREPARATION OF WORK
SHEET, FINANCIAL
STATEMENTS, AND
ADJUSTING AND CLOSING
ENTRIES—PERIODIC
INVENTORY SYSTEM
Objectives 2, 3, 4, 5

The accounts and their balances in the ledger of Dietz Company on December 31 of the current year are as follows:

Cash	$ 59,575
Accounts Receivable	116,100
Merchandise Inventory	180,000
Prepaid Insurance	10,600
Store Supplies	3,750
Office Supplies	1,700
Store Equipment	115,000
Accumulated Depreciation—Store Equipment	40,300
Office Equipment	52,000
Accumulated Depreciation—Office Equipment	17,200
Accounts Payable	66,700
Salaries Payable	—
Unearned Rent	1,200
Note Payable (final payment, 2000)	105,000
N. L. Dietz, Capital	220,510
N. L. Dietz, Drawing	40,000
Income Summary	—
Sales	997,500
Sales Returns and Allowances	15,500
Sales Discounts	6,000
Purchases	637,500
Purchases Returns and Allowances	11,500
Purchases Discounts	6,000
Transportation In	6,200
Sales Salaries Expense	86,400
Advertising Expense	29,450
Depreciation Expense—Store Equipment	—
Store Supplies Expense	—
Miscellaneous Selling Expense	1,885
Office Salaries Expense	60,000
Rent Expense	30,000
Insurance Expense	—
Depreciation Expense—Office Equipment	—
Office Supplies Expense	—
Miscellaneous Administrative Expense	1,650
Rent Income	—
Interest Expense	12,600

The data needed for year-end adjustments on December 31 are as follows:

Merchandise inventory on December 31		$220,000
Insurance expired during the year		6,760
Supplies on hand on December 31:		
Store supplies		1,800
Office supplies		500
Depreciation for the year:		
Store equipment		9,500
Office equipment		4,800
Salaries payable on December 31:		
Sales salaries	$3,050	
Office salaries	1,550	4,600
Unearned rent on December 31		400

Instructions

1. Prepare a work sheet for the fiscal year ended December 31, listing all accounts in the order given.
2. Prepare a multiple-step income statement.
3. Prepare a statement of owner's equity.
4. Prepare a report form of balance sheet, assuming that the current portion of the note payable is $15,000.
5. Journalize the adjusting entries.
6. Journalize the closing entries.

PROBLEM 6-7B
SALES-RELATED AND
PURCHASE-RELATED
TRANSACTIONS—
PERPETUAL INVENTORY
SYSTEM
Objective 7

The following were selected from among the transactions completed by Montrose Company during May of the current year. Montrose Company uses a perpetual inventory system.

May 3. Purchased merchandise on account from Floyd Co., list price $5,000, trade discount 20%, terms FOB shipping point, 2/10, n/30, with prepaid transportation costs of $120 added to the invoice.
5. Purchased merchandise on account from Kramer Co., $8,500, terms FOB destination, 1/10, n/30.
6. Sold merchandise on account to C. F. Howell Co., list price $4,000, trade discount 30%, terms 2/10, n/30. The cost of the merchandise sold was $1,125.
8. Purchased office supplies for cash, $150.
10. Returned merchandise purchased on May 5 from Kramer Co., $1,300.
13. Paid Floyd Co. on account for purchase of May 3, less discount.
14. Purchased merchandise for cash, $10,500.
15. Paid Kramer Co. on account for purchase of May 5, less return of May 10 and discount.
16. Received cash on account from sale of May 6 to C. F. Howell Co., less discount.
19. Sold merchandise on nonbank credit cards and reported accounts to the card company, $2,450. The cost of the merchandise sold was $980.
22. Sold merchandise on account to Comer Co., $3,480, terms 2/10, n/30. The cost of the merchandise sold was $1,400.
24. Sold merchandise for cash, $4,350. The cost of the merchandise sold was $1,750.
25. Received merchandise returned by Comer Co. from sale on May 22, $1,480. The cost of the returned merchandise was $600.
31. Received cash from card company for nonbank credit card sales of May 19, less $140 service fee.

Instructions
Journalize the transactions.

Instructions for Solving Problem 6-7B Using Solutions Software

1. Load opening balances.
2. Save the opening balances file to your drive and directory.
3. Set the run date to May 31 of the current year and enter your name.
4. Select the General Journal Entries option and enter the journal entries. Leave the reference field blank. Note: To review the chart of accounts, select F-1.
5. Display a journal entries report.
6. Display a trial balance.
7. Key the adjusting entries, based on the following data:

Insurance expired on May 31	$400
Office supplies on hand on May 31	300

Key ADJ.ENT. in the reference field.
8. Display the adjusting entries. Key ADJ.ENT. in the Reference Restriction area of the Selection Options screen.
9. Display the financial statements.
10. Save a backup copy of your data file.
11. Perform period-end closing.
12. Display a post-closing trial balance.
13. Save your data file to disk.
14. End the session.

PROBLEM 6-8B
WORK SHEET FOR
MERCHANDISING
ENTERPRISE USING THE
PERPETUAL INVENTORY
SYSTEM
Objective 8

The accounts in the ledger of Marden Company, with the unadjusted balances on June 30, the end of the current fiscal year, are as follows:

Cash	$ 15,100
Notes Receivable	50,000
Accounts Receivable	67,600
Merchandise Inventory	91,700
Prepaid Insurance	5,800
Store Supplies	4,950
Store Equipment	50,500
Accumulated Depreciation—Store Equipment	30,130
Accounts Payable	26,800
Salaries Payable	—
Unearned Rent	4,600
L. Marden, Capital	169,870
L. Marden, Drawing	15,000
Sales	600,500
Cost of Merchandise Sold	360,300
Sales Salaries Expense	61,500
Advertising Expense	25,800
Depreciation Expense—Store Equipment	—
Store Supplies Expense	—
Miscellaneous Selling Expense	3,750
Office Salaries Expense	39,000
Rent Expense	24,000
Heating and Lighting Expense	9,660
Taxes Expense	5,100
Insurance Expense	—
Miscellaneous Administrative Expense	2,140
Rent Income	—

The data needed for year-end adjustments on June 30 are as follows:

Insurance expired during the year		$ 3,800
Store supplies on hand on June 30		870
Depreciation for the current year		10,500
Accrued salaries on June 30:		
Sales salaries	$2,600	
Office salaries	1,650	4,250
Rent income earned during the year		3,800

Instructions

Prepare a work sheet for the fiscal year ended June 30. List all accounts in the order given. Marden Company uses a perpetual inventory system.

SOLUTIONS
SOFTWARE

Instructions for Solving Problem 6-8B Using Solutions Software

1. Load opening balances.
2. Save the opening balances file to your drive and directory.
3. Set the run date to June 30 of the current year and enter your name.
4. Key the adjusting entries. Key ADJ.ENT. in the reference field.
5. Display the adjusting entries. Key ADJ.ENT. in the Reference Restriction area of the Selection Options screen.
6. Display the financial statements.
7. Save a backup copy of your data file.
8. Perform period-end closing.
9. Display a post-closing trial balance.
10. Save your data file to disk.
11. End the session.

PROBLEM 6-9B
WORK SHEET, INCOME
STATEMENT, AND CLOSING
ENTRIES—PERPETUAL
INVENTORY SYSTEM
Objective 8

McNair Company uses a perpetual inventory system. A partially completed work sheet for McNair Company for the current year ended October 31 is as follows:

McNair Company
Work Sheet
For Year Ended October 31, 19—

Account Title	Trial Balance Dr.	Trial Balance Cr.	Adjustments Dr.	Adjustments Cr.
Cash	14,400			
Accounts Receivable	86,300			
Merchandise Inventory	108,400			
Prepaid Insurance	10,500			(a) 7,600
Store Supplies	3,800			(b) 2,200
Office Supplies	1,200			(c) 750
Store Equipment	159,600			
Accum. Depr.—Store Equip.		53,000		(d) 10,500
Office Equipment	47,300			
Accum. Depr.—Office Equip.		12,000		(e) 3,800
Accounts Payable		30,500		
Salaries Payable				(f) 4,100
Unearned Rent		2,400	(g) 1,600	
Note Payable (due 1999)		80,000		
A. C. McNair, Capital		149,200		
A. C. McNair, Drawing	29,000			
Sales		820,000		
Sales Returns and Allowances	7,000			
Sales Discounts	8,500			
Cost of Merchandise Sold	515,000			
Sales Salaries Expense	70,000		(f) 3,200	
Advertising Expense	28,000			
Depr. Expense—Store Equip.			(d) 10,500	
Store Supplies Expense			(b) 2,200	
Misc. Selling Expense	2,400			
Office Salaries Expense	35,000		(f) 900	
Rent Expense	10,000			
Depr. Expense—Office Equip.			(e) 3,800	
Insurance Expense			(a) 7,600	
Office Supplies Expense			(c) 750	
Misc. Administrative Expense	1,100			
Rent Income				(g) 1,600
Interest Expense	9,600			
	1,147,100	1,147,100	30,550	30,550

SPREADSHEET
PROBLEM

SOLUTIONS
SOFTWARE

Instructions

1. Complete the work sheet for McNair Company.
2. Prepare a single-step income statement for the year ended October 31.
3. Journalize the closing entries for McNair Company.

Instructions for Solving Problem 6-9B Using Solutions Software

1. Load opening balances.
2. Save the opening balances file to your drive and directory.
3. Set the run date to October 31 of the current year and enter your name.
4. Key the adjusting entries. Key ADJ.ENT. in the reference field.
5. Display the adjusting entries. Key ADJ.ENT. in the Reference Restriction area of the Selection Options screen.
6. Display the financial statements.
7. Save a backup copy of your data file.
8. Perform period-end closing.
9. Display a post-closing trial balance.
10. Save your data file to disk.
11. End the session.

MINI-CASE 6 BROOKS VIDEO COMPANY

Your sister operates Brooks Video Company, a videotape distributorship that is in its third year of operation. The firm's accountant, Helen Hill, recently resigned. Before leaving, she completed the work sheet for the year ended May 31, 1994, and recorded the necessary adjusting entries. From this work sheet, your sister prepared the following financial statements:

Brooks Video Company
Income Statement
For Year Ended May 31, 1994

Sales		$308,200
Less cost of merchandise sold:		
Purchases	$231,600	
Net increase in merchandise inventory	17,500	214,100
Gross profit		$ 94,100
Operating expenses:		
Salaries expense	$ 29,600	
Heat and lighting expense	5,750	
Insurance expense	4,050	
Depreciation expense—building	2,880	
Depreciation expense—office equipment	1,260	
Depreciation expense—store equipment	2,160	
Supplies expense	2,440	
Miscellaneous expense	1,620	
Transportation in	7,100	56,860
		$ 37,240
Selling expenses:		
Advertising expense	$ 6,940	
Transportation out	14,160	21,100
Income from operations		$ 16,140
Other income:		
Purchases discounts	$ 2,480	
Purchases returns and allowances	3,820	
Interest income	500	6,800
		$ 22,940
Other expenses:		
Sales returns	$ 1,200	
Owner's withdrawals	15,000	
Interest expense	6,000	22,200
Net income		$ 740

Brooks Video Company
Statement of Owner's Equity
For Year Ended May 31, 1994

D. Brooks, capital, June 1, 1993	$130,760
Net income for the year	740
D. Brooks, capital, May 31, 1994	$131,500

Brooks Video Company
Balance Sheet
May 31, 1994

Assets

Cash	$ 15,100
Merchandise inventory	62,300
Supplies	1,820
Prepaid insurance	1,680
Accounts receivable	25,600
Store equipment	12,800
Office equipment	6,300
Building	58,900
Land	30,000
Notes receivable	5,000
Total assets	$219,500

Liabilities and Owner's Equity

Accumulated depreciation—store equipment	$ 4,320
Accumulated depreciation—office equipment	2,520
Accumulated depreciation—building	5,760
Accounts payable	13,800
Salaries payable	1,600
Note payable—First National Bank (due in 2002)	60,000
D. Brooks, capital	131,500
Total liabilities and owner's equity	$219,500

As part of the existing loan agreement with First National Bank, Brooks Video Company must submit financial statements annually to the bank. In reviewing your sister's statements and supporting records before she submits the statements to the bank, you discover the following information:

Merchandise inventory:	
June 1, 1993	$44,800
May 31, 1994	62,300
Salaries expense:	
Sales salaries	20,200
Office salaries	9,400
Supplies expense:	
Store supplies	1,600
Office supplies	840
Miscellaneous expense:	
Selling	1,020
Administrative	600

Instructions:

1. Revise your sister's statements as necessary to conform to proper form for a multiple-step income statement, a statement of owner's equity, and a report form of balance sheet.

2. Prepare a projected single-step income statement for the year ending May 31, 1995, based upon the following data:

Your sister is considering a proposal to increase net income by offering sales discounts of 2/15, n/30, and by shipping all merchandise FOB shipping point. Currently, no sales discounts are allowed and merchandise is shipped FOB destination. It is estimated that these credit terms will increase net sales by 10%. The ratio of the cost of merchandise sold to net sales is 70% and is not expected to change under the proposed plan. All selling and administrative expenses are expected to remain unchanged, except for store supplies, miscellaneous selling, office supplies, and miscellaneous administrative expenses, which are expected to increase proportionately with increased net sales. The other income and other expense items will remain unchanged. The shipment of all merchandise FOB shipping point will eliminate all transportation out expenses.

3. a. ▇▇▶ Based upon the projected income statement in (2), would you recommend the implementation of the proposed changes?

   b. ▇▇▶ Describe any possible concerns you may have related to the proposed changes described in (2).

COMPREHENSIVE PROBLEM 2

Oliver Company is a merchandising enterprise that uses a periodic inventory system. The account balances for Oliver Company as of May 1, 1994 (unless otherwise indicated) are as follows:

110	Cash	$ 39,160
111	Notes Receivable	—
112	Accounts Receivable	60,220
113	Interest Receivable	—
115	Merchandise Inventory, June 1, 1993	123,900
116	Prepaid Insurance	3,750
117	Store Supplies	2,550
123	Store Equipment	44,300
124	Accumulated Depreciation	12,600
210	Accounts Payable	38,500
211	Salaries Payable	—
310	F. L. Oliver, Capital, June 1, 1993	173,270
311	F. L. Oliver, Drawing	4,500
312	Income Summary	—
410	Sales	741,600
411	Sales Returns and Allowances	13,600
412	Sales Discounts	5,200
510	Purchases	540,000
511	Purchases Returns and Allowances	21,600
512	Purchases Discounts	5,760
513	Transportation In	5,400
520	Sales Salaries Expense	74,400
521	Advertising Expense	18,000
522	Depreciation Expense	—
523	Store Supplies Expense	—
529	Miscellaneous Selling Expense	2,800
530	Office Salaries Expense	29,400
531	Rent Expense	24,500
532	Insurance Expense	—
539	Miscellaneous Administrative Expense	1,650
611	Interest Income	—

During May, the last month of the fiscal year, the following transactions were completed:

May 1. Paid rent for May, $2,500.
1. Received a $10,000 note receivable from a customer on account.
2. Purchased merchandise on account, terms 2/10, n/30, FOB shipping point, $22,000.
3. Paid transportation charges on purchase of May 2, $860.
4. Purchased merchandise on account, terms 1/10, n/30, FOB destination, $16,200.
5. Sold merchandise on account, terms 2/10, n/30, FOB shipping point, $8,500.
8. Received $14,900 cash from customers on account, no discount.
10. Sold merchandise for cash, $18,300.
11. Paid $12,800 to creditors on account, after discounts of $200 had been deducted.
12. Paid for merchandise purchased on May 2, less discount.
13. Received merchandise returned on sale of May 5, $1,000.
14. Paid advertising expense for last half of May, $2,000.
15. Received cash from sale of May 5, less return and discount.
18. Paid sales salaries of $1,500 and office salaries of $500.
18. Received $28,500 cash from customers on account, after discounts of $400 had been deducted.
19. Purchased merchandise for cash, $6,400.
19. Paid $13,150 to creditors on account, after discounts of $250 had been deducted.
20. Sold merchandise on account, terms 1/10, n/30, FOB shipping point, $16,000.
21. For the convenience of the customer, paid shipping charges on sale of May 20, $600.

May 21. Purchased merchandise on account, terms 1/10, n/30, FOB destination, $15,000.
   22. Paid for merchandise purchased on May 4.
   24. Returned damaged merchandise purchased on May 21, receiving credit from the seller, $3,000.
   25. Refunded cash on sales made for cash, $400.
   27. Paid sales salaries of $1,200 and office salaries of $400.
   28. Sold merchandise on account, terms 2/10, n/30, FOB shipping point, $24,700.
   29. Purchased store supplies for cash, $350.
   30. Received cash from sale of May 20, less discount, plus transportation paid on May 21.
   31. Paid for purchase of May 21, less return and discount.
   31. Sold merchandise on account, terms 2/10, n/30, FOB shipping point, $17,400.
   31. Purchased merchandise on account, terms 1/10, n/30, FOB destination, $19,700.

Instructions

1. Enter the balances of each of the accounts in the appropriate balance column of a four-column account. Write *Balance* in the item section, and place a check mark (✓) in the Posting Reference column.
2. Journalize the transactions for May.
3. Post the journal to the ledger, extending the month-end balances to the appropriate balance columns after all posting is completed.
4. Prepare a trial balance as of May 31 on a ten-column work sheet, listing all the accounts in the order given in the ledger. Complete the work sheet for the fiscal year ended May 31, using the following adjustment data:

   a. Interest accrued on notes receivable
      on May 31 $ 100
   b. Merchandise inventory on May 31   134,150
   c. Insurance expired during the year   2,250
   d. Store supplies on hand on May 31   750
   e. Depreciation for the current year   8,860
   f. Accrued salaries on May 31:
      Sales salaries $400
      Office salaries   140   540

5. Prepare a multiple-step income statement, a statement of owner's equity, and a report form of balance sheet.
6. Journalize and post the adjusting entries.
7. Journalize and post the closing entries. Indicate closed accounts by inserting a line in both balance columns opposite the closing entry. Insert the new balance in the owner's capital account.
8. Prepare a post-closing trial balance.

SOLUTIONS SOFTWARE

Instructions for Solving Comprehensive Problem 2 Using Solutions Software

1. Load opening balances.
2. Save the opening balances file to your drive and directory.
3. Set the run date to May 31 of the current year and enter your name.
4. Select the General Journal Entries option and key the journal entries. Leave the reference field blank. Note: To review the chart of accounts, select F-1.
5. Display a journal entries report.
6. Display a trial balance.
7. Key the adjusting entries. Key ADJ.ENT. in the reference field.
8. Display the adjusting entries. Key ADJ.ENT. in the Reference Restriction area of the Selection Options screen.
9. Display the financial statements.
10. Save a backup copy of your data file.
11. Perform period-end closing.
12. Display a post-closing trial balance.
13. Save your data file to disk.
14. End the session.

ANSWERS TO SELF-EXAMINATION QUESTIONS

1. **B** The single-step form of income statement (answer B) is so named because the total of all expenses is deducted in one step from the total of all revenues. The multiple-step form (answer A) includes numerous sections and subsections with several subtotals. The account form (answer C) and the report form (answer D) are two common forms of the balance sheet.

2. **C** Gross profit (answer C) is the excess of net sales over the cost of merchandise sold. Operating income (answer A) or income from operations (answer B) is the excess of gross profit over operating expenses. Net income (answer D) is the final figure on the income statement after all revenues and expenses have been reported.

3. **D** Expenses such as interest expense (answer D) that cannot be associated directly with operations are identified as *Other expense* or *nonoperating expense*. Depreciation expense—office equipment (answer A) is an administrative expense. Sales salaries expense (answer B) is a selling expense. Insurance expense (answer C) is a mixed expense with elements of both selling expense and administrative expense. For small businesses, insurance expense is usually reported as an administrative expense.

4. **B** To adjust the merchandise inventory account for the beginning inventory, Income Summary is debited and Merchandise Inventory is credited (answer B). To record the ending inventory in the merchandise inventory account, Merchandise Inventory is debited and Income Summary is credited (answer A). To close the Purchases account, Income Summary is debited and Purchases is credited (answer D).

5. **C** In a perpetual inventory system, Cost of Merchandise Sold (answer C) is debited for the cost of each sale. Transportation In (answer A), Purchases (answer B), and Purchases Discounts (answer D) are not used in a perpetual inventory system.

Part 3

Accounting Systems

You and Accounting

Most of you have a checking account at a bank. In order to keep track of the amount of cash in your account, you probably keep a record of each withdrawal, such as checks that you write, and each deposit. A transactions register provided by the bank may be used for this purpose. The typical transactions register, as shown below, has columns for the item or check number, the date, the description of the transaction, deductions (the check amount, for example), additions (the deposit amount, for example), and the balance.

		TRANSACTIONS REGISTER			
Item (Check) No.	Date	Description of Transaction	Deductions	Additions	Balance Forward 520.50
	1994				
342	May 9	To: Palmer Cablevision	45.20		45.20
		Cable TV Installation			475.30
343	May 10	To: Florida Power Co.	92.10		92.10
		Electric Bill			383.20
344	May 11	To: Dr. Carr	50.00		50.00
		Eye Examination			333.20
—	May 12	Cash withdrawal from ATM	100.00		100.00
		(Automatic Teller Machine)			233.20
—	May 15	Payroll Deposit		590.10	590.10
					823.30

The transactions register illustrated above is a type of special journal used by individuals. This chapter discusses common special journals used by business enterprises to record transactions. These special journals are discussed in relationship to the basic principles of accounting systems.

Chapter 7
Accounting Systems and Special Journals

229

LEARNING OBJECTIVES
After studying this chapter, you should be able to:

Objective 1
Describe the basic principles of accounting systems.

Objective 2
List the three phases of accounting systems installation and revision.

Objective 3
List, define, and give examples of the three elements of the internal control structure.

Objective 4
Journalize and post transactions, using subsidiary ledgers and the following special journals:

Sales journal
Cash receipts journal
Purchases journal
Cash payments journal

Objective 5
Describe and give examples of additional subsidiary ledgers and modified special journals.

Managers need information for use in planning and controlling the operations of a business enterprise. The accounting system of an enterprise provides this information, in addition to reports for external users, such as investors and creditors. This chapter discusses basic principles of accounting systems, including internal controls. In addition, basic principles of accounting systems design and implementation, including data processing methods, are discussed. The chapter concludes by describing and illustrating methods used by business enterprises to efficiently record transactions. These methods include the use of subsidiary ledgers and special journals.

PRINCIPLES OF ACCOUNTING SYSTEMS

Objective 1
Describe the basic principles of accounting systems.

The methods and procedures used by an enterprise to record and report financial data make up the accounting system. Accounting systems vary from business to business. For example, the accounting system for a not-for-profit hospital will differ significantly from the accounting system for a retailer. This variation is due to differences in management's information needs, the type and number of transactions to be recorded, and the information needs of external users of financial statements. However, there are a number of broad principles that apply to all systems.

Cost-Benefit Balance

An accounting system must be designed to meet the specific information needs of a business. However, providing information is costly. Thus, a major consideration in designing an accounting system is balancing the benefits against the cost of the information. In general, the benefits should be at least equal to the cost of producing the information.

Effective Reports

To be effective, the reports generated by an accounting system must be prepared in a timely, clear, and concise manner. When these reports are prepared, the needs and knowledge of the user should be considered. For example, managers may need a variety of detailed reports for planning and controlling operations on a daily or weekly basis. In contrast, regulatory agencies often require uniform reports at established intervals, such as quarterly or yearly.

Ability to Adapt to Future Needs

Businesses operate in a changing environment. This environment may include changes beyond the control of a business, such as new government regulations, changes in accounting principles, or changes in computer technology. An accounting system must be able to adapt to the changing needs for information in such an environment. For example, regulatory agencies such as the Securities and Exchange Commission and the Internal Revenue Service often change the information and reports they require of businesses.

Accounting systems reflect the organizational structure and the information needs of individuals within the business. As individuals or lines of authority and responsibility within a business change, the accounting system must also adapt and change. To be effective, the accounting system must support all levels of management.

Adequate Internal Controls

An accounting system provides information that management reports to owners, creditors, and other interested parties. In addition, the system should aid management in planning and controlling operations. The detailed policies and procedures used to direct operations, protect assets, and provide reasonable assurance that the business's objectives are achieved are called internal controls. The general principles for an adequate internal control structure are discussed later in this chapter.

ACCOUNTING SYSTEMS INSTALLATION AND REVISION

Objective 2
List the three phases of accounting systems installation and revision.

Designing and installing an accounting system for an enterprise requires a thorough knowledge of the enterprise's operations. In addition, accounting systems must be continually reviewed for possible revisions in order to keep pace with the changing information needs of enterprises. For example, some areas of the system, such as the types and design of forms and the number and titles of accounts, continually change as the enterprise grows and adapts to its environment. This process of installing or changing an accounting system is made up of three phases: (1) analysis, (2) design, and (3) implementation.

Systems Analysis

The goal of systems analysis is to determine information needs, the sources of such information, and weaknesses in the procedures and the data processing methods being used. In addition, the systems analyst should assess management's plans for changes in operations (volume, products, territories, etc.).

Systems analysis usually begins with a review of the organizational structure and the job descriptions of personnel. This review is followed by a study of the forms, records, procedures, processing methods, and reports used by the enterprise. The source of such information is usually the firm's *Systems Manual*.

Systems Design

Accounting systems are changed as a result of the kind of systems analysis described above. Such changes may involve only minor changes from the existing system, such as revision of a particular form and the related procedures and processing methods. In contrast, a complete revision of the entire system may be required.

Systems design requires the ability to evaluate alternative data processing methods. In addition, designing a system to meet the many information needs of a business enterprise at the lowest cost requires creativity and imagination.

Systems Implementation

The final phase of systems installation or revision is to carry out, or implement, the systems design. New or revised forms, records, procedures, and equipment must be installed, and any that are no longer useful must be withdrawn. All personnel responsible for operating the system must be carefully trained and supervised until the system is fully operational.

Major revisions of a system, such as changing from a centralized computer system to a decentralized, micro-computer-based data processing system, must be carefully planned. Managers must have reasonable assurance that the new system will provide complete and accurate information. Therefore, many companies implement new or revised systems in stages over a period of time. Weaknesses and conflicting or unnecessary elements in the design are easier to detect when the implementation is gradual rather than all at once. In addition, this approach reduces the chances that essential operating information will be unavailable during the systems implementation.

Another approach to new system implementation is to conduct a parallel test. In a parallel test, the old and new systems are run at the same time. The outputs of both systems are then compared. Parallel tests are costly, since two systems are being run. However, many managers believe this additional cost is worth the assurance that the new system is complete and accurate. In addition, this approach guarantees that essential operating information will be available from the old system if the new system does not function properly.

Accounting Systems, Profit Measurement, and Management

A Greek restaurant owner in Canada had his own system of accounting. He kept his accounts payable in a cigar box on the left-hand side of his cash register, his daily cash returns in the cash register, and his receipts for paid bills in another cigar box on the right.

When his youngest son graduated as an accountant, he was appalled by his father's primitive methods. "I don't know how you can run a business that way," he said. "How do you know what your profits are?"

"Well, son," the father replied, "when I got off the boat from Greece, I had nothing but the pants I was wearing. Today, your brother is a doctor. You are an accountant. Your sister is a speech therapist. Your mother and I have a nice car, a city house, and a country home. We have a good business, and everything is paid for. . . ."

"So, you add all that together, subtract the pants, and there's your profit!"

Source: Anonymous.

INTERNAL CONTROL STRUCTURE

Objective 3
List, define, and give examples of
each of the three elements of the
internal control structure.

The objective of an internal control structure is to provide assurance that an enterprise's goals and objectives are achieved. The internal control structure also exists to protect assets from theft or misuse. In a small business where it is possible for the owner-manager to supervise employees directly, the control structure may be very simple. As the number of employees and the complexities of an enterprise increase, it becomes more difficult for the owner-manager to supervise and control all phases of operations. As a result, more authority is delegated to employees. Managers, in turn, rely more on the internal control structure to motivate employees to act in a way that is consistent with the enterprise's goals and objectives. In such cases, the internal control structure can become very complex.

An **internal control structure** consists of an enterprise's (1) accounting system, (2) control environment, and (3) control procedures.[1] The basic principles underlying each of these three elements of internal control structure are briefly discussed in the following paragraphs.

The Accounting System

The accounting system is an integral part of the internal control structure of an enterprise. It provides management with data necessary to plan and direct operations. The principles of an effective accounting system were discussed earlier in this chapter.

The Control Environment

An enterprise's control environment is the overall attitude of management and employees about the importance of controls. One of the factors that influences the control environment of an enterprise is management's philosophy and operating style. A management that overemphasizes operating goals may indirectly encourage employees to overstate or misreport operating data. For example, one of the largest company frauds in history involved the Equity Funding Corporation of America. In the 1970s, this company recorded over $2 billion of fictitious insurance policies. One of the factors that contributed to this fraud was top management's overemphasis on improving operating results.

A management that often deviates from established control policies and procedures may also be indicating to employees that controls are not important. On the other hand, a management that emphasizes the importance of controls and encourages adherence to control policies will create an effective control environment.

Another factor that influences the control environment is the enterprise's organizational structure, which is the framework for planning and controlling operations. For example, a merchandising enterprise might organize each of its stores as relatively separate business units. Each store manager may be given full authority over pricing and other operating activities. In such a structure, each store manager would have the responsibility for establishing an effective control environment.

Personnel policies and procedures also affect the control environment. Personnel policies involve the hiring, training, evaluating, compensating, and promoting of employees. The human resource area also includes the development of job descriptions, employee codes of ethics, and conflict-of-interest policies. Such policies and procedures can enhance the internal control environment if they provide reasonable assurance that only competent, honest employees are hired and retained.

Control Procedures

Control procedures are those policies and procedures that management has established to provide reasonable assurance that enterprise goals will be achieved.

---

[1] *Statements on Auditing Standards, No. 55,* "Consideration of the Internal Control Structure in a Financial Statement Audit" (New York: American Institute of Certified Public Accountants, 1988).

Control procedures that can be integrated throughout the accounting system are briefly discussed in the following sections.

COMPETENT PERSONNEL, ROTATION OF DUTIES, AND MANDATORY VACATIONS. The successful operation of an accounting system requires procedures to ensure that people are able to perform the duties to which they are assigned. Hence, it is necessary that all accounting employees be adequately trained and supervised to perform their jobs. It may also be advisable to rotate clerical personnel periodically from job to job. In addition to increasing their understanding of the system, the knowledge that an employee's work may be performed by others encourages adherence to prescribed procedures. For nonclerical personnel such as managers, mandatory vacations normally are used rather than job rotations. During vacation periods, the relevant job responsibilities are performed by other managers.

Rotation of duties and mandatory vacations may prevent errors and fraud and may also lead to the detection of errors or fraud. For example, an accounts receivable clerk should be periodically rotated to another job or required to take a vacation. If the clerk steals customers' cash payments, the thefts will likely be discovered when a new clerk bills customers for amounts they have already paid.

ASSIGNMENT OF RESPONSIBILITY. If employees are to work efficiently, their responsibilities must be clearly defined. Control procedures should provide assurance that no overlapping or undefined areas of responsibility exist and that employees are held accountable for their responsibilities. For example, if a certain cash register is to be used by two or more salesclerks, the clerks should be assigned separate cash drawers and register keys. In this way, the clerks are held responsible for their individual cash drawers, and a daily proof of cash can be obtained for each clerk.

SEPARATION OF RESPONSIBILITIES FOR RELATED OPERATIONS. To decrease the possibility of inefficiency, errors, and fraud, responsibility for a sequence of related operations should be divided among two or more persons. For example, the responsibilities for purchasing, receiving, and paying for merchandise should be divided among three persons or departments. If one individual orders merchandise, verifies the receipt of the merchandise, and pays the supplier, the following abuses are possible:

1. Orders may be placed on the basis of friendship with a supplier, rather than on price, quality, and other objective factors.
2. The quantity and the quality of merchandise received may not be verified.
3. Merchandise may be stolen by the employee.
4. The validity and accuracy of invoices may be verified carelessly, thus causing the payment of false or inaccurate invoices.

The "checks and balances" provided by dividing responsibilities among various departments requires no duplication of effort. The business documents prepared as a result of the work of each department are designed to coordinate and support those prepared by the other departments.

SEPARATION OF ACCOUNTING, CUSTODY OF ASSETS, AND OPERATIONS. Control policies and procedures should establish the responsibilities for various business activities. To reduce the possibility of errors and fraud, the following functions should be separated:

1. Accounting for the enterprise's transactions.
2. Custody of the firm's assets.
3. Engaging in the enterprise's operating activities.

When these functions are separated, the accounting records serve as an independent check on the individuals who have custody of the assets and who engage in the business operations. For example, the employees entrusted with handling cash receipts from credit customers should not record cash receipts in the accounting records. To do so would allow employees to borrow or steal cash and hide the theft in the records. Likewise, if those engaged in operating activities also record the results of operations, they could distort the accounting reports to show favorable results. For example, a store manager whose year-end bonus is based upon operating profits might be tempted to record fictitious sales in order to receive a larger bonus.

PROOFS AND SECURITY MEASURES. Proofs and security measures should be used to safeguard business assets and ensure reliable accounting data. This control procedure applies to many different techniques, such as authorization, approval, and reconciliation procedures. For example, a control procedure might require reports to verify the receipt of all sales returns before credit is approved and granted to a customer. Other examples of control procedures include the use of bank accounts and other measures to ensure the safety of cash and other valuable documents. Using a cash register that displays the amount recorded for each sale and provides for the customer a printed receipt can be an effective part of the internal control structure.

Companies may obtain insurance to protect against losses from employee fraud. Such insurance, called a fidelity bond, normally requires background checks on all employees covered. If a claim is paid, insurance companies normally take legal action against the employees responsible. Such legal action tends to deter employee fraud and enhances the internal control structure.

INDEPENDENT REVIEW. To determine whether internal control procedures are being effectively applied, the control structure should be periodically reviewed and evaluated. In large businesses, internal auditors who are independent of operations normally have this responsibility. An example of the use of internal auditors for review of internal control procedures is described in the annual report of Rose's Stores Inc. as follows:

To meet its responsibilities with respect to financial information, management maintains and enforces internal accounting policies, procedures, and controls which are designed to provide reasonable assurance that assets are safeguarded and that transactions are properly recorded and executed in accordance with management's authorization. The concept of reasonable assurance is based on the recognition that the cost of controls should not exceed the expected benefits. Management maintains an internal audit function and an internal control function which are responsible for evaluating the adequacy and application of financial and operating controls and for testing compliance with Company policies and procedures.

Internal auditors should report any weaknesses and recommend changes to correct them. For example, a review of cash payments may disclose that invoices were not paid within the discount period, even though enough cash was available.

SUBSIDIARY LEDGERS AND SPECIAL JOURNALS

Objective 4
Journalize and post transactions, using subsidiary ledgers and the following special journals:

Sales journal
Cash receipts journal
Purchases journal
Cash payments journal

In preceding chapters, all transactions were manually recorded in a two-column journal. The journal entries were then posted individually to the accounts in the ledger. Such manual accounting systems are simple to use and easy to understand. Manually kept records may serve a business reasonably well when the amount of data collected, stored, and used by an enterprise, called its **database**, is relatively small. For a large retailer with a large database, however, manual processing is too costly and too time-consuming. For example, a large retailer such as J. C. Penney Co. has thousands of credit sale transactions with thousands of customers daily. Each credit sale requires an entry debiting Accounts Receivable and crediting Sales. In addition, a record of each customer's receivable must be kept.

When an enterprise has a large number of similar transactions, the use of a two-column journal is inefficient and impractical. In such cases, subsidiary ledgers and special journals are useful. In addition, the manual system can be supplemented or replaced by a computerized system. Although the following paragraphs illustrate the manual use of subsidiary ledgers and special journals, the basic principles apply in a computerized accounting system.

Subsidiary Ledgers

An accounting system should be designed to provide information on the amounts due from various customers (accounts receivable) and amounts owed to various creditors (accounts payable). A separate account for each customer and creditor could be added to the ledger. However, as the number of customers and creditors increases, the ledger becomes unwieldy when a separate account for each customer and creditor is included.

When there are a large number of individual accounts with a common characteristic, they can be grouped together in a separate ledger called a **subsidiary ledger.** The primary ledger, which contains all of the balance sheet and income statement accounts, is then called the general ledger. Each subsidiary ledger is represented in the general ledger by a summarizing account, called a **controlling account.** The sum of the balances of the accounts in a subsidiary ledger must equal the balance of the related controlling account. Thus, a subsidiary ledger can be thought of as a secondary ledger that supports a controlling account in the general ledger.

The individual accounts with customers are arranged in alphabetical order in a subsidiary ledger called the accounts receivable ledger or **customers ledger.** The controlling account in the general ledger that summarizes the debits and credits to the individual customer's accounts is Accounts Receivable. The individual accounts with creditors are arranged in alphabetical order in a subsidiary ledger called the accounts payable ledger or **creditors ledger.** The related controlling account in the general ledger is Accounts Payable. The relationship between the general ledger and these subsidiary ledgers is illustrated in Exhibit 1.

Exhibit 1
General Ledger and Subsidiary Ledgers

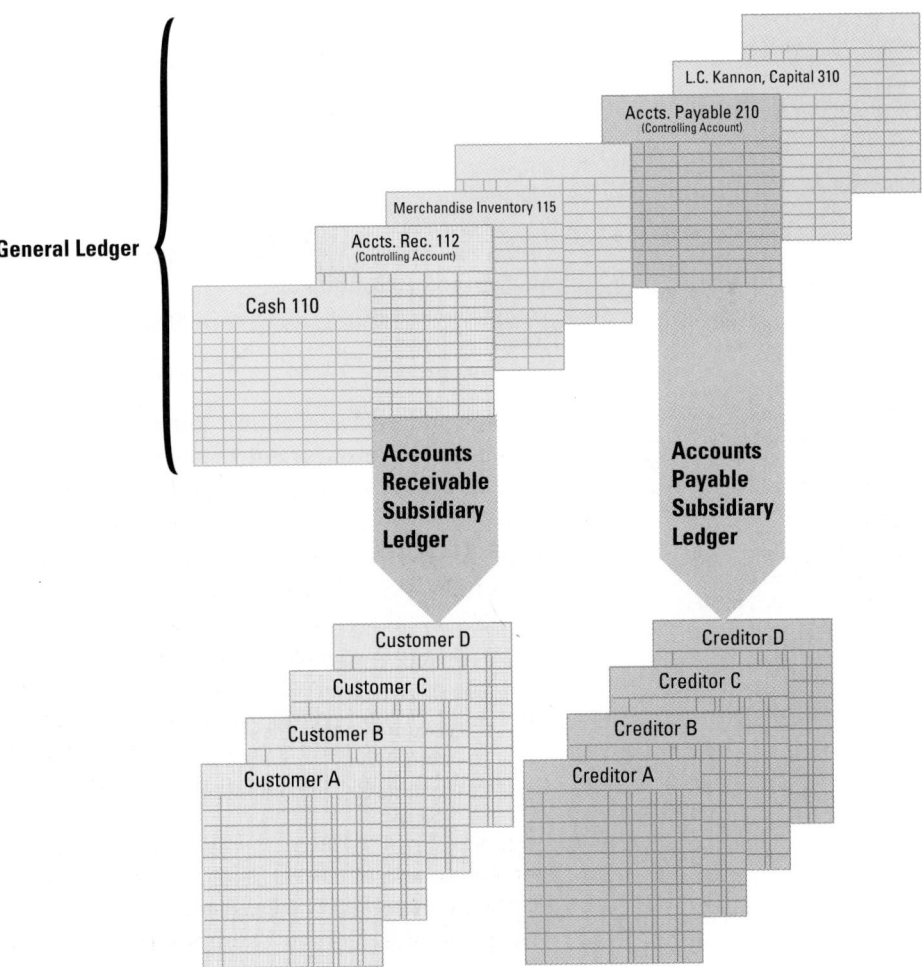

Special Journals

One method of processing data more efficiently in a manual accounting system is to expand the two-column journal to a multicolumn journal. Each column in a multicolumn journal is used only for recording transactions that affect a certain account. For example, a special column could be used only for recording debits to the cash account and another special column could be used only for recording credits to the cash account. The addition of the two special columns would eliminate the writing of *Cash* in the journal for every receipt and payment of cash. Also, there would be no need to post each individual debit and credit to the cash account. Instead, the *Cash Dr.* and *Cash Cr.* columns could be totaled periodically and only the totals posted. In a similar way, special columns could be added for recording credits to Sales, debits and credits to Accounts Receivable and Accounts Payable, and for other entries that are often repeated.

An all-purpose multicolumn journal may be adequate for a small business enterprise that has many transactions of a similar nature. However, a journal that has many columns for recording many different types of transactions is impractical for larger enterprises.

The next logical extension of the accounting system is to replace the single multicolumn journal with a number of **special journals**. Each special journal is designed to be used for recording a single kind of transaction that occurs frequently. For example, since most enterprises have many transactions in which cash is paid out, it is common practice to use a special journal for recording cash payments. Likewise, another special journal normally is used to record cash receipts.

The format and number of special journals that an enterprise uses depends upon the nature of the business. An enterprise that sells merchandise to customers on account might use a special journal designed for recording only credit sales. On the other hand, a business that does not give credit would have no need for such a journal. In other cases, record-keeping costs may be reduced by using sales and purchases documents as special journals.

The transactions that occur most often in a medium-size merchandising enterprise and the special journals in which they are recorded are as follows:

Sale of merchandise *on account*	**recorded in**	Sales journal
Receipt of cash from *any* source	**recorded in**	Cash receipts journal
Purchase of merchandise or other items *on account*	**recorded in**	Purchases journal
Payment of cash for *any* purpose	**recorded in**	Cash payments journal

The standard two-column journal, called the **general journal** or simply the **journal**, can be used for entries that do not fit into any of the special journals. For example, adjusting and closing entries are recorded in the general journal.

Sales Journal

The **sales journal** is only used for recording **sales of merchandise on account**. *Cash sales are recorded in the cash receipts journal.* To illustrate the efficiency of using a sales journal, consider the following sales transactions of Kannon Co., recorded in a general journal:

Oct.	2	Accounts Receivable—Barnes Co	9,350
		Sales	9,350
	3	Accounts Receivable—Standard Supply Co.	1,600
		Sales	1,600

~~~~~~

	27	Accounts Receivable—Standard Supply Co.	1,908
		Sales	1,908

If Kannon Co. had a total of 9 credit sales transactions during October, 18 account titles and amounts would be recorded. In addition, 27 postings must be made—9 postings to Accounts Receivable, 9 to the accounts receivable subsidiary ledger, and 9 to Sales. In contrast, these transactions could be recorded more efficiently in a sales journal, as shown in Exhibit 2.

Exhibit 2
Sales Journal After Posting

SALES JOURNAL

	DATE		INVOICE NO.	AMMOUNT DEBITED	POST. REF.	ACCTS. REC. DR. SALES CR.	
1	1994 Oct.	2	615	Barnes Co.	√	9 3 5 0 00	1
2		3	616	Standard Supply Co.	√	1 6 0 0 00	2
3		5	617	David T. Mattox	√	15 3 0 5 00	3
4		9	618	Barnes Co.	√	1 3 9 6 00	4
5		10	619	Adler Company	√	6 7 5 0 00	5
6		17	620	Hamilton Co.	√	7 8 5 0 00	6
7		23	621	Cooper & Co.	√	1 5 0 2 00	7
8		26	622	Tracy & Lee Co.	√	3 2 7 9 00	8
9		27	623	Standard Supply Co.	√	1 9 0 8 00	9
10		31				48 9 4 0 00	10
11						(113) (411)	11

The first sale recorded by Kannon Co. in October is to Barnes Co. for $9,350 (Invoice No. 615). Since the amount of the debit to Accounts Receivable is the same as the credit to Sales, only a single amount column is necessary. The date, invoice number, customer name, and amount are entered for each sale.

POSTING THE SALES JOURNAL. When sales on account are recorded in a sales journal, individual transactions are posted to customer accounts in the accounts receivable ledger. A single monthly total is posted to Accounts Receivable and Sales. The basic procedure of posting from a sales journal to an accounts receivable ledger and the general ledger is shown in Exhibit 3.

Exhibit 3
Flow of Data from Sales Journal to Ledgers

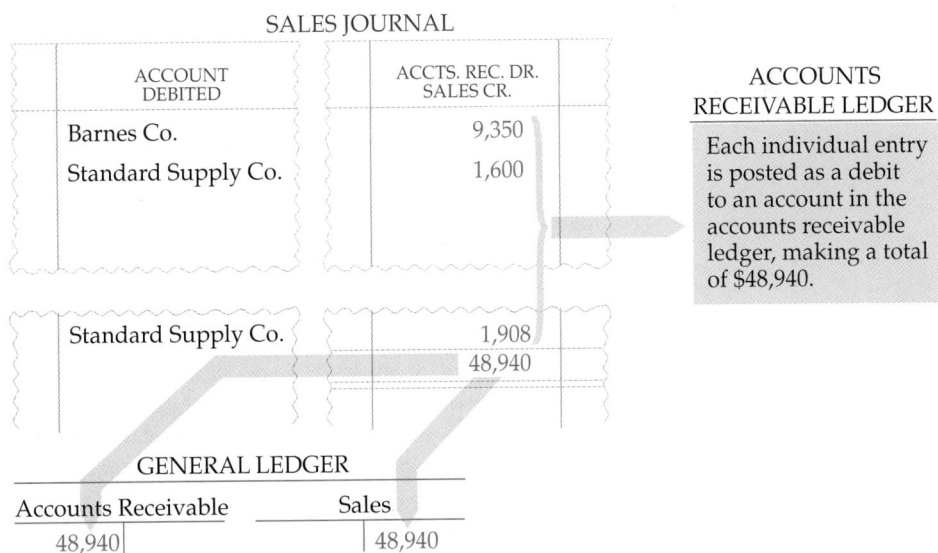

The individual amounts in Exhibit 3, such as the $9,350 debit to Barnes Co., are posted to the accounts receivable ledger. Since the balances in the customer accounts are usually debit balances, the three-column account form shown below is often used.

NAME   Barnes Co.

ADDRESS   9350 Ridge Ave., Los Angeles, CA 90048-3694

DATE		ITEM	POST. REF.	DEBIT	CREDIT	BALANCE
Sep. [1994]	25		S34	5 8 0 0 00		5 8 0 0 00
Oct.	2		S35	9 3 5 0 00		15 1 5 0 00

The source of the entries posted to the subsidiary ledger is indicated in the Posting Reference column of each account by inserting the letter *S* and the page number of the sales journal. A check mark (√) instead of a number is then inserted in the Posting Reference column of the sales journal, as shown in Exhibit 2.

The customer accounts in the subsidiary ledger are maintained in alphabetical order. They are usually not numbered because the order changes each time a new account is inserted or an old account is removed. If a customer's account has a credit balance, that fact should be indicated by an asterisk or parentheses in the Balance column. When an account's balance is zero, a line may be drawn in the Balance column.

At the end of each month, the amount column of the sales journal is totaled and ruled. This total is equal to the sum of the month's debits to the individual accounts in the subsidiary ledger. It is posted in the general ledger as a debit to Accounts Receivable and a credit to Sales, as shown below. The respective account numbers are then inserted below the total in the sales journal to indicate that the posting is completed, as shown in Exhibit 2.

ACCOUNT   *Accounts Receivable*   ACCOUNT NO.   113

DATE		ITEM	POST. REF.	DEBIT	CREDIT	BALANCE	
						DEBIT	CREDIT
Oct. [1994]	1	Balance	√	16 1 1 9 00		16 1 1 9 00	
	31		S35	48 9 4 0 00		64 8 0 9 00	

ACCOUNT   *Sales*   ACCOUNT NO.   411

DATE		ITEM	POST. REF.	DEBIT	CREDIT	BALANCE	
						DEBIT	CREDIT
Oct. [1994]	31		S35		48 9 4 0 00		48 9 4 0 00

SALES RETURNS AND ALLOWANCES. When merchandise sold is returned or a price adjustment is granted, an entry is made in the general journal. Sales returns are recorded in the general journal because they do not fit in any of the special journals. During October, Kannon Co. issued a credit memorandum and recorded the transaction in a two-column general journal, as shown below.

JOURNAL   PAGE 18

	DATE		DESCRIPTION	POST. REF.	DEBIT	CREDIT	
1	Oct. [1994]	13	Sales Returns and Allowances	412	2 5 0 00		1
2			Accounts Receivable—				2
3			Adler Company	113 √		2 5 0 00	3
4			Credit Memo No. 32				4

The debit portion of the entry is posted to Sales Returns and Allowances (No. 412) in the general ledger. The credit portion of the entry is posted to Accounts Receivable (No. 113) in the general ledger and also to the customer's account in the subsidiary ledger (√). At the time these entries are journalized, a diagonal line is drawn in the Posting Reference column to indicate the need for posting the credits to two different accounts. The account number and check mark are inserted at the time the entry is posted.

If a cash refund is made because of merchandise returned or for an allowance, Sales Returns and Allowances is debited and Cash is credited. Since this transaction involves the payment of cash, the entry would be recorded in the cash payments journal.

Cash Receipts Journal

All transactions that involve the receipt of cash are recorded in a **cash receipts journal**. Thus, the cash receipts journal has a special column entitled *Cash Dr.*, as shown in the cash receipts journal of Kannon Co. in Exhibit 4.

Exhibit 4
Cash Receipts Journal after Posting

CASH RECEIPTS JOURNAL — PAGE 14

	DATE	ACCOUNT CREDITED	POST. REF.	OTHER ACCOUNTS CR.	SALES CR.	ACCOUNTS REC. CR.	SALES DISCOUNTS DR.	CASH DR.	
1	1994 Oct. 2	Notes Receivable	112	2400 00				2544 00	1
2		Interest Income	812	144 00					2
3	5	Barnes Co.	√			5800 00	116 00	5684 00	3
4	6	Fogarty & Jacobs	√			2625 00		2625 00	4
5	7	Sales	√		3700 00			3700 00	5
6	10	David T. Mattox	√			600 00	12 00	588 00	6
7	13	Standard Supply Co.	√			1600 00	32 00	1568 00	7
8	14	Sales	√		1632 00			1632 00	8
9	17	Adler Company	√			6500 00	130 00	6370 00	9
10	19	Hamilton Co.	√			4865 00		4865 00	10
11	21	Sales	√		1920 00			1920 00	11
12	23	Purchases Returns and Allowances	512	86 00				86 00	12
13	24	Wallace Co.	√			2229 00		2229 00	13
14	27	Hamilton Co.	√			7850 00	157 00	7693 00	14
15	28	Sales	√		2086 00			2086 00	15
16	31	Sales	√		2423 00			2423 00	16
17	31			2630 00	11761 00	32069 00	447 00	46013 00	17
18				(√)	(411)	(113)	(413)	(111)	18

DO NOT POST

The kinds of transactions in which cash is received and how often they occur determine the titles of the other columns. In a typical merchandising business, the most frequent sources of cash receipts are likely to be cash sales and collections from customers on account. Thus, the cash receipts journal in Exhibit 4 also has special columns for Sales Cr., Accounts Receivable Cr., and Sales Discounts Dr.

ENTRIES IN THE CASH RECEIPTS JOURNAL. All transactions recorded in the cash receipts journal will involve an entry in the Cash Dr. column. For example, on October 2, Kannon Co. received cash of $2,544 and entered that amount in the Cash Dr. column.

The Sales Cr. column is used for recording sales of merchandise for cash. Each sale is normally recorded on a cash register. The cash register totals are accumulated and are recorded in the cash receipts journal daily, weekly, or at other regular intervals. For example, the entry of October 7 records weekly sales and cash receipts of $3,700. The total of the Sales Cr. column will be posted at the end of the month. Thus, a check mark is inserted in the Posting Reference column to indicate that the $3,700 item needs no further attention.

The Accounts Receivable Cr. column is used for recording credits to customer accounts for payments of invoices on account. If a cash discount is granted, it is recorded in the Sales Discounts Dr. column. To illustrate, cash was received on October 5 from Barnes Co. in payment of its account less a cash discount. Entries are made in the Cash Dr. column for $5,684, in the Sales Discounts Dr. column for $116, and in the Accounts Receivable Cr. column for $5,800.

The Other Accounts Cr. column is used for recording credits to any account for which there is no special credit column. For example, Kannon Co. received cash on October 2 in payment of an interest-bearing note. Since no special columns exist for Notes Receivable or Interest Income, Notes Receivable of $2,400 and Interest Income of $144 are entered in the Other Accounts Cr. column.

POSTING THE CASH RECEIPTS JOURNAL. The flow of data from the cash receipts journal to the ledgers of Kannon Co. is shown in Exhibit 5. At regular intervals, each amount in the Other Accounts Cr. column of the cash receipts journal is posted to the proper account in the general ledger. The posting is indicated by inserting the account number in the Posting Reference column of the cash receipts journal. The posting reference *CR* and the proper page number are inserted in the Posting Reference columns of the accounts.

Exhibit 5
Flow of Data from Cash Receipts Journal to Ledgers

CASH RECEIPTS JOURNAL

ACCOUNT CREDITED	P. R.	OTHER ACCOUNTS CR.	SALES CR.	ACCOUNTS RECEIVABLE CR.	SALES DISCOUNTS DR.	CASH DR.
Notes Receivable	112	2,400				2,544
Interest Income	812	144				
Barnes Co.	✓			5,800	116	5,684
Fogarty & Jacobs	✓			2,625		2,625
Sales	✓		3,700			3,700
David T. Mattox	✓			600	12	588
Sales	✓		2,423			2,423
		2,630	11,761	32,069	447	46,013

GENERAL LEDGER

ACCOUNTS RECEIVABLE LEDGER

Notes Receivable	Sales	Sales Discounts
2,400	11,761	447

Interest Income	Accounts Receivable	Cash
144	32,069	46,013

Each individual entry is posted as a credit to an account in the accounts receivable ledger, making a total of $32,069.

The amounts in the Accounts Receivable Cr. column are posted at regular intervals to the customer accounts in the accounts receivable ledger. These customers are identified in the Account Credited column of the cash receipts journal. The initials *CR* and the proper page number are inserted in the Posting Reference column of each customer's account. A check mark is placed in the Posting Reference column of the cash receipts journal to show that each amount has been posted. None of the individual amounts in the Sales Cr., Sales Discounts Dr., and Cash Dr. columns are posted separately.

At the end of the month, all of the amount columns are totaled and ruled. The equality of the debits and credits should then be verified. Because each amount in the Other Accounts Cr. column has been posted individually to a general ledger account, a check mark is inserted below the column total to indicate that no further action is needed. The totals of the other four columns are posted to the proper accounts in the general ledger, and their account numbers are inserted below the totals to show that the posting has been completed.

Accounts Receivable Control and Subsidiary Ledger

During October, the following postings were made to Accounts Receivable in the general ledger of Kannon Co.:

	Debits	
Oct. 31	Total sales on account (sales journal)	$48,940
	Credits	
Oct. 13	A sales return (general journal)	250
Oct. 31	Total cash received on account (cash receipts journal)	32,069

The accounts receivable controlling account is presented in Exhibit 6, and the subsidiary accounts receivable ledger of Kannon Co. is presented in Exhibit 7.

Exhibit 6
Accounts Receivable Account in the General Ledger at the End of the Month

ACCOUNT *Accounts Receivable*   ACCOUNT NO. *113*

DATE	ITEM	POST. REF.	DEBIT	CREDIT	BALANCE DEBIT	BALANCE CREDIT
1994 Oct. 1	Balance	√	16 1 1 9 00		16 1 1 9 00	
13		J18		2 5 0 00	15 8 6 9 00	
31		S35	48 9 4 0 00		64 8 0 9 00	
31		CR14		32 0 6 9 00	32 7 4 0 00	

Exhibit 7
Accounts Receivable Ledger at the End of the Month

ACCOUNTS RECEIVABLE LEDGER

NAME   Adler Company
ADDRESS   7608 Melton Ave, Los Angeles, CA 90025-3942

DATE	ITEM	POST. REF.	DEBIT	CREDIT	BALANCE
1994 Oct. 10		S35	6 7 5 0 00		6 7 5 0 00
13		J18		2 5 0 00	6 5 0 0 00
17		CR14		6 5 0 0 00	——

NAME   Barnes Co.
ADDRESS   9350 Ridge Ave., Los Angeles, CA 90048-3694

DATE	ITEM	POST. REF.	DEBIT	CREDIT	BALANCE
1994 Sep. 25		S34	5 8 0 0 00		5 8 0 0 00
Oct. 2		S35	9 3 5 0 00		15 1 5 0 00
5		CR14		5 8 0 0 00	9 3 5 0 00
9		S35	1 3 9 6 00		10 7 4 6 00

Exhibit 7 (concluded)
Accounts Receivable Ledger at the End of the Month

NAME Cooper & Co.
ADDRESS 650 Wilson, Portland, OR 97209-1406

DATE	ITEM	POST. REF.	DEBIT	CREDIT	BALANCE
1994 Oct. 23		S35	1 5 0 2 00		1 5 0 2 00

NAME Fogarty & Jacobs
ADDRESS 142 West 8th, Los Angeles, CA 90014-1225

DATE	ITEM	POST. REF.	DEBIT	CREDIT	BALANCE
1994 Sep. 17		S34	2 6 2 5 00		2 6 2 5 00
Oct. 6		CR14		2 6 2 5 00	——————

NAME Hamilton Co.
ADDRESS 5200 Charter Ave., San Francisco, CA 94110-1732

DATE	ITEM	POST. REF.	DEBIT	CREDIT	BALANCE
1994 Sep. 10		S33	4 8 6 5 00		4 8 6 5 00
Oct. 17		S35	7 8 5 0 00		12 7 1 5 00
19		CR14		4 8 6 5 00	7 8 5 0 00
27		CR14		7 8 5 0 00	——————

NAME David T. Mattox
ADDRESS 1200 Capital Ave., Sacramento, CA 95814-1048

DATE	ITEM	POST. REF.	DEBIT	CREDIT	BALANCE
1994 Sep. 30		S34	6 0 0 00		6 0 0 00
Oct. 5		S35	15 3 0 5 00		15 9 0 5 00
10		CR14		6 0 0 00	15 3 0 5 00

NAME Standard Supply Co.
ADDRESS 9554 W. Colorado Blvd., Pasadena, CA 91107-1318

DATE	ITEM	POST. REF.	DEBIT	CREDIT	BALANCE
1994 Oct. 3		S35	1 6 0 0 00		1 6 0 0 00
13		CR14		1 6 0 0 00	——————
27		S35	1 9 0 8 00		1 9 0 8 00

NAME Tracy & Lee Co.
ADDRESS 521 Scottsdale Blvd., Phoenix, AZ 85004-1100

DATE	ITEM	POST. REF.	DEBIT	CREDIT	BALANCE
1994 Oct. 26		S35	3 2 7 9 00		3 2 7 9 00

NAME Wallace Co.
ADDRESS 1004 Market St., Sacramento, CA 95814-1048

DATE	ITEM	POST. REF.	DEBIT	CREDIT	BALANCE
1994 Sep. 12		S34	2 2 2 9 00		2 2 2 9 00
Oct. 24		CR14		2 2 2 9 00	——————

After all posting has been completed for the month, the sum of the balances in the accounts receivable ledger should be compared with the balance of the accounts receivable account in the general ledger. If the controlling account and the subsidiary ledger do not agree, the error or errors must be located and corrected. The balances of the individual customer accounts may be summarized on a computer printout, or a schedule may be prepared, as shown below. The total of the schedule, $32,740, agrees with the balance of the accounts receivable account shown in Exhibit 6.

Kannon Co.	
Schedule of Accounts Receivable	
October 31, 1994	
Barnes Co.	$10,746
Cooper & Co.	1,502
David T. Mattox	15,305
Standard Supply Co.	1,908
Tracy & Lee Co.	3,279
Total accounts receivable	$32,740

Purchases Journal

The types of items purchased most often on account by a merchandising enterprise are:

1. Merchandise for resale to customers.
2. Supplies for use in the business.
3. Equipment and other plant assets.

The **purchases journal** should be designed to allow for the recording of **all items purchased on account**. *Cash purchases of items are recorded in the cash payments journal.* The form of a purchases journal used by Kannon Co. is shown in Exhibit 8.

Exhibit 8
Purchases Journal after Posting

PURCHASES JOURNAL   PAGE 19

	DATE	ACCOUNT CREDITED	POST. REF.	ACCOUNTS PAYABLE CR.	PURCHASES DR.	STORE SUPPLIES DR.	OFFICE SUPPLIES DR.	OTHER ACCOUNTS DR. ACCOUNT	POST. REF.	AMOUNT	
1	1994 Oct. 2	Video Co.	√	5 7 2 4 00	5 7 2 4 00						1
2	3	Marsh Co.	√	7 4 0 0 00	7 4 0 0 00						2
3	9	Parker Supply Co.	√	2 5 7 00		1 3 1 00	1 2 6 00				3
4	10	Beale Office									4
5		Equipment	√	5 0 0 0 00				Office Equipment	111	5 0 0 0 00	5
6	11	Marsh Co.	√	3 2 0 0 00	3 2 0 0 00						6
7	16	Dunlap Co.	√	3 5 9 3 00	3 5 9 3 00						7
8	17	Robinson Supply	√	1 5 0 0 00	1 5 0 0 00						8
9	20	Walton Co.	√	15 1 2 5 00				Store Equipment	121	15 1 2 5 00	9
10	23	Parker Supply Co.	√	1 3 2 00		7 5 00	5 7 00				10
11	27	Dunlap Co.	√	6 3 8 9 00	6 3 8 9 00						11
12	31			48 3 2 0 00	27 8 0 6 00	2 0 6 00	1 8 3 00			20 1 2 5 00	12
13				(2 1 1)	(5 1 1)	(1 1 5)	(1 1 6)			(√)	13

For each transaction recorded in the purchases journal, the credit is entered in the Accounts Payable Cr. column. The next three amount columns are used for recording debits to the accounts most often affected. Invoice amounts for merchandise purchased for sale to customers are recorded in the Purchases Dr. column. Likewise, purchases of store supplies and office supplies are entered in the

Store Supplies Dr. and Office Supplies Dr. columns. If supplies are purchased only once in a while, the two columns could be omitted from the journal.

The Other Accounts Dr. column is used to record purchases, on account, of any item for which there is not a special debit column. The title of the account to be debited is entered in the Account column and the amount is entered in the Amount column. A separate Posting Reference column is provided for this section of the purchases journal.

POSTING THE PURCHASES JOURNAL. The principles used in posting the purchases journal are similar to those used in posting the sales and cash receipts journals. The source of the entries posted to the subsidiary and general ledgers is indicated in the Posting Reference column of each account by inserting the letter *P* and the page number of the purchases journal, as shown below. A check mark (√) is inserted in the Posting Reference column of the purchases journal after each credit is posted to a creditor's account in the subsidiary accounts payable ledger.

NAME	Robinson Supply					
ADDRESS	3800 Mission Street, San Francisco, CA 94110-1732					

DATE	ITEM	POST. REF.	DEBIT	CREDIT	BALANCE
1994 Oct. 17		P19		1 5 0 0 00	1 5 0 0 00

The flow of data from the purchases journal of Kannon Co. to the ledgers is shown in Exhibit 9. At regular intervals, the amounts in the Other Accounts Dr. column of the purchases journal are posted to the accounts in the general ledger. As each amount is posted, the related general ledger account number is inserted in the Posting Reference column of the Other Accounts section.

Exhibit 9
Flow of Data from Purchases Journal to Ledgers

PURCHASES JOURNAL

ACCOUNT CREDITED	P. R.	ACCTS. PAYABLE CR.	PURCHASES DR.	STORE SUP. DR.	OFFICE SUP. DR.	OTHER ACCOUNTS DEBIT		
						ACCOUNT	P.R.	AMOUNT
Video Co.	✓	5,724	5,724					
Marsh Co.	✓	7,400	7,400					
Parker Supply Co.	✓	257		131	126			
Robinson Supply	✓	1,500	1,500					
Walton Co.	✓	15,125				Store Equip.	121	15,125
Parker Supply Co.	✓	132		75	57			
Dunlap Co.	✓	6,389	6,389					
		48,320	27,806	206	183			20,125

GENERAL LEDGER

Accounts Payable	Store Supplies	Office Supplies
48,320	206	183

Purchases	Store Equipment
27,806	15,125

ACCOUNTS PAYABLE LEDGER

Each individual entry is posted as a credit to an account in the accounts payable ledger, making a total of $48,320.

At the end of each month, the purchases journal is totaled and ruled, as shown in Exhibit 8. Before the totals are posted to the general ledger, the sum of the totals of the four debit columns should be compared with the total of the credit column to prove their equality.

The totals of the four special columns are posted to the appropriate general ledger accounts in the usual manner, with the related account numbers inserted below the columnar totals. Because each amount in the Other Accounts Dr. column was posted individually, a check mark is placed below the $20,125 total to show that no further action is needed.

PURCHASES RETURNS AND ALLOWANCES. When merchandise purchased is returned or a price adjustment is granted, an entry is made in the general journal. Purchases returns are recorded in the general journal because they do not fit in any of the special journals. To illustrate, assume that Kannon Co. issued a debit memorandum for a return of merchandise during October. The transaction may be recorded in a two-column general journal, as shown below.

	JOURNAL				PAGE 18
	DATE	DESCRIPTION	POST. REF.	DEBIT	CREDIT
17	Oct. 20	Accounts Payable—Dunlap Co.	211 √	1 0 0 00		17
18		Purchases Returns and Allowances	512		1 0 0 00	18
19		Debit Memo No. 20.				19
20						20
21						21

The debit portion of the entry is posted to Accounts Payable (No. 211) in the general ledger and to the creditor's account in the subsidiary ledger (√). At the time these entries are journalized, the need for posting the debits to two different accounts is indicated by drawing a diagonal line in the Posting Reference column. The account number and check mark are inserted at the time the entry is posted.

After the entry has been recorded, the memorandum is attached to the related unpaid invoice. If the invoice had been paid before the return or allowance was granted, a cash refund might be received.

If goods other than merchandise are returned or a price adjustment is granted, the account to which the goods were first debited should be credited. For example, if a purchase of office equipment is returned, the credit would be to Office Equipment rather than Purchases Returns and Allowances.

Cash Payments Journal

The special columns for the **cash payments journal** are determined in the same manner as for the sales, cash receipts, and purchases journals. The determining factors are the kinds of transactions to be recorded and how often they occur. It is necessary to have a Cash Cr. column. Payments to creditors on account happen often enough to require columns for Accounts Payable Dr. and Purchases Discounts Cr. The cash payments journal in Exhibit 10 has these three columns and an additional column for Other Accounts Dr.

All payments by Kannon Co. are made by check. As each transaction is recorded in the cash payments journal, the related check number is entered in the column at the right of the Date column. The check numbers are helpful in controlling cash payments, and they provide a useful cross-reference.

The Other Accounts Dr. column is used for recording debits to any account for which there is no special column. For example, Kannon Co. paid $1,275 on October 2 for a purchase of merchandise. The transaction was recorded by writing *Purchases* in the space provided and $1,275 in the Other Accounts Dr. and the Cash Cr. columns. The Posting Reference (511) was inserted at the time the debit was posted.

Exhibit 10
Cash Payments Journal after Posting

CASH PAYMENTS JOURNAL   PAGE 16

	DATE	CK. NO.	ACCOUNT DEBITED	POST. REF.	OTHER ACCOUNTS DR.		ACCOUNTS PAYABLE DR.		PURCHASES DISCOUNTS CR.		CASH CR.		
1	1994 Oct. 2	312	Purchases	511	1 2 7 5 00						1 2 7 5 00		1
2	4	313	Store Equipment	121	3 5 0 00						3 5 0 00		2
3	12	314	Marsh Co.	✓			7 4 0 0 00		7 4 00		7 3 2 6 00		3
4	12	315	Sales Salaries Exp.	611	2 5 6 0 00						2 5 6 0 00		4
5	12	316	Office Salaries Exp.	711	8 8 0 00						8 8 0 00		5
6	14	317	Misc. Admin. Exp.	719	5 6 00						5 6 00		6
7	16	318	Prepaid Insurance	117	9 8 4 00						9 8 4 00		7
8	20	319	Marsh Co.	✓			3 2 0 0 00		3 2 00		3 1 6 8 00		8
9	20	320	Heath Co.	✓			4 8 5 0 00				4 8 5 0 00		9
10	21	321	Sales Ret. & Allow.	412	4 6 2 00						4 6 2 00		10
11	23	322	Robinson Supply	✓			1 5 0 0 00		3 0 00		1 4 7 0 00		11
12	23	323	Video Co.	✓			7 6 0 0 00				7 6 0 0 00		12
13	23	324	Rent Expense	712	7 9 0 00						7 9 0 00		13
14	24	325	Walton Co.	✓			9 5 2 5 00				9 5 2 5 00		14
15	26	326	Sales Salaries Exp.	611	2 5 6 0 00						2 5 6 0 00		15
16	26	327	Office Salaries Exp.	711	8 8 0 00						8 8 0 00		16
17	26	328	Advertising Exp.	612	7 8 6 00						7 8 6 00		17
18	27	329	Misc. Selling Exp.	619	4 2 00						4 2 00		18
19	28	330	Office Equipment	123	9 0 0 00						9 0 0 00		19
20	31				12 5 2 5 00		34 0 7 5 00		1 3 6 00		46 4 6 4 00		20
21					(✓)		(2 1 1)		(5 1 3)		(1 1 1)		21
22													22
23													23
24													24
25													25

Debits to creditor accounts for invoices paid are recorded in the Accounts Payable Dr. column and credits for the amounts paid are recorded in the Cash Cr. column. If a discount is taken, the debit to the account payable will differ from the amount of the payment. Cash discounts taken on merchandise purchased for resale are recorded in the Purchases Discounts Cr. column.

The flow of data from the cash payments journal to the ledgers of Kannon Co. is shown in Exhibit 11. At frequent intervals during the month, the amounts entered in the Accounts Payable Dr. column are posted to the creditor accounts in the accounts payable ledger. After each posting, *CP* and the page number of the journal are inserted in the Posting Reference column of the account. A check mark is placed in the Posting Reference column of the cash payments journal to indicate that each amount has been posted.

The items in the Other Accounts Dr. column are also posted to the accounts in the general ledger at regular intervals. The posting is indicated by writing the account numbers in the Posting Reference column of the cash payments journal. At the end of the month, each of the amount columns in the cash payments journal is totaled. The sum of the two debit totals is compared with the sum of the two credit totals to determine their equality, and the journal is ruled.

A check mark is placed below the total of the Other Accounts Dr. column to indicate that it is not posted. When each of the totals of the other three columns is posted to a general ledger account, the account numbers are inserted below the column totals.

Exhibit 11
Flow of Data From Cash
Payments Journal to Ledgers

CASH PAYMENTS JOURNAL

ACCOUNT DEBITED	P. R.	OTHER ACCOUNTS DR.	ACCOUNTS PAYABLE DR.	PURCHASES DISCOUNTS CR.	CASH CR.
Purchases	511	1,275			1,275
Store Equipment	121	350			350
Marsh Co.	✓		7,400	74	7,326
Sales Salaries Expense	611	2,560			2,560
Misc. Selling Expense	619	42			42
Office Equipment	123	900			900
		12,525	34,075	136	46,464

GENERAL LEDGER

Other Accounts	Accounts Payable	Purchases Discounts	Cash
Each entry is posted separately to the appropriate account.	34,075	136	46,464

ACCOUNTS PAYABLE LEDGER

Each individual entry is posted as a debit to an account in the accounts payable ledger, making a total of $34,075.

Accounts Payable Control and Subsidiary Ledger

During October, the following postings were made to Accounts Payable in the general ledger of Kannon Co.:

	Credits to Accounts Payable	
Oct. 31	Total purchases on account (**purchases journal**)	$48,320
	Debits to Accounts Payable	
Oct. 20	A return of merchandise (**general journal**)	100
31	Total cash payments on account (**cash payments journal**)	34,075

The accounts payable controlling account of Kannon Co. as of October 31 is shown in Exhibit 12. The procedures for posting and balancing the accounts payable subsidiary ledger are similar to those for accounts receivable. Therefore, the accounts payable subsidiary ledger is not illustrated.

Exhibit 12
Accounts Payable Account in the
General Ledger at the End of the
Month

ACCOUNT Accounts Payable   ACCOUNT NO. 211

DATE		ITEM	POST. REF.	DEBIT	CREDIT	BALANCE DEBIT	BALANCE CREDIT
1994 Oct.	1	Balance	✓				21 9 7 5 00
	20		J18	1 0 0 00			21 8 7 5 00
	31		P19		48 3 2 0 00		70 1 9 5 00
	31		CP16	34 0 7 5 00			36 1 2 0 00

After all posting has been completed for the month, the sum of the balances in the accounts payable ledger should be compared with the balance of the accounts payable account in the general ledger. If the controlling account and the subsidiary ledger do not agree, the error or errors must be located and corrected. The balances of the individual creditor accounts may be summarized on a schedule, as shown below. The total of the schedule, $36,120, agrees with the balance of the accounts payable account shown in Exhibit 12.

Kannon Co. Schedule of Accounts Payable October 31, 1994	
Beale Office Equipment	$ 5,000
Dunlap Co.	9,882
Parker Supply Co.	389
Video Co.	5,724
Walton Co.	15,125
Total accounts payable	$36,120

ADAPTING ACCOUNTING SYSTEMS

Objective 5
Describe and give examples of additional subsidiary ledgers and modified special journals.

The preceding sections of this chapter illustrate subsidiary ledgers and special journals that are common for a medium-size merchandising enterprise. Many business enterprises use subsidiary ledgers for other accounts, in addition to Accounts Receivable and Accounts Payable. Also special journals are often adapted or modified in practice to meet the specific need of an enterprise.

Some examples of additional subsidiary ledgers and modified special journals are illustrated in the following paragraphs. Computerized accounting systems are also briefly described.

Additional Subsidiary Ledgers

Generally, subsidiary ledgers are used for accounts that consist of a large number of individual items, each of which has unique characteristics. For example, automobile dealerships keep subsidiary inventory ledgers of the automobiles they own and offer for sale. In a perpetual inventory system, the inventory records must be kept up to date at all times. This updating normally is accomplished by using a perpetual inventory subsidiary ledger.

If an enterprise has a large number of notes receivable or notes payable, a subsidiary ledger may be used to keep track of each note, its due date, and interest payment date. Such ledgers are similar to the accounts receivable and accounts payable subsidiary ledgers illustrated in this chapter.

Enterprises may also use a subsidiary equipment ledger to keep track of each item of equipment purchased, its cost, location, and other data. An example of such a subsidiary ledger is illustrated in a later chapter.

Modified Special Journals

Business enterprises may modify special journals by adding one or more columns for recording transactions that occur frequently. For example, retailers may collect sales taxes and then remit them periodically to the taxing authorities. Thus, the sales journal is often modified by adding a special column for Sales Taxes Payable, as shown below.

	DATE		INVOICE NO.	ACCOUNT DEBITED	POST. REF.	ACCTS. REC. DR.	SALES CR.	SALES TAXES PAYABLE	
	SALES JOURNAL							PAGE 40	
1	Nov.¹⁹⁹⁴	2	842	Litten Co.	✓	4 7 7 0 00	4 5 0 0 00	2 7 0 00	1
2		3	843	Kauffman Supply Co.	✓	1 1 6 6 00	1 1 0 0 00	6 6 00	2
4									4
5									5

Some other examples of how special journals may be modified for a variety of different types of business enterprises are described below.

Farm
The purchases journal may be modified to include columns for various types of seeds (corn, wheat), livestock (cows, hogs, sheep), fertilizer, and fuel.

Automobile Repair Shop
The sales journal may be modified to include columns for each major type of repair service. In addition, columns for warranty repairs, credit card charges, and sales taxes may be added.

Hospital
The cash receipts journal may be modified to include columns for receipts from patients on account, from Blue Cross/Blue Shield or other major insurance reimbursers, and Medicare.

Movie Theater
The cash receipts journal may be modified to include columns for revenues from admissions, gift certificates, and concession sales.

Restaurant
The purchases journal may be modified to include columns for food, linen, silverware and glassware, and kitchen supplies.

Regardless of how a special journal is modified, the basic principles and procedures discussed in this chapter apply. For example, special journals are normally totaled and ruled at periodic intervals. The totals of the debit and credit columns are then compared to verify their equality before the totals are posted to the general ledger accounts.

Computerized Accounting Systems

Many business enterprises use computers to process accounting data. These computers may be large computers or small microcomputers. Regardless of the size of the system, however, the concepts, methods, and procedures that have been described for a manual system also apply to computerized systems.

To illustrate how an *advanced* computerized system might operate, assume that a sales order has been accepted. The customer's identification code, the inventory code of the item sold, and any special instructions such as shipping terms are entered directly into the system. The system, in turn, generates a shipping document authorizing the release of the inventory from the warehouse, and a bill of lading, which contains the shipping instructions. When the item is removed from the warehouse, the bar code on the item is scanned, using an optical scanning device. The inventory code is thus entered directly into the system, which updates the perpetual inventory files. When the item is shipped, its bar code is again scanned, along with the bar code on the bill of lading identifying the carrier. Daily or at some other interval, the computer generates a customer invoice by referring to an approved price list for the item sold and posts directly to the customer's account. Monthly or at some other interval, the computer system generates a variety of reports, such as a report of sales backorders and sales by region.

The speed and accuracy of computerized accounting systems allow greater flexibility in the generation of reports for management's use. For example, the computerized system described above allows for up-to-date reporting of inventory quantities and other data. With such reports, managers can make more timely decisions.

A thorough understanding of the concepts and principles described in this chapter provides a solid foundation for applying these concepts in a computer environment. In addition, an understanding of manual accounting systems assists managers in recognizing the interrelationships that exist within accounting data and reports. This recognition, in turn, enables managers to better anticipate how decisions may affect operations and the financial statements and other reports of an enterprise.

CHAPTER REVIEW

Key Points

Objective 1. Describe the basic principles of accounting systems.

Although accounting systems vary from business to business, the following principles apply to all systems:

1. The cost of the information must be balanced against its benefits.
2. Reports must be prepared with the needs and the knowledge of the user considered.
3. The system must be able to adapt to changing needs.
4. Internal controls must be adequate.

Objective 2. List the three phases of accounting systems installation and revision.

The three phases of accounting system installation and revision are (1) analysis of information needs, (2) design of the system, and (3) implementation of the systems design.

Objective 3 List, define, and give examples of the three elements of the internal control structure.

The three elements of the internal control structure of an entity are (1) the accounting system, (2) the control environment, and (3) the control procedures. The accounting system provides the information needed by management to plan and direct operations in achieving enterprise goals. Procedures for recording transactions are part of the accounting system. The control environment is the overall attitude of management and employees about the importance of controls. The existence of employee codes of ethics and conflict-of-interest policies contributes to the effectiveness of a control environment. Control procedures are those policies and procedures that management has established to provide reasonable assurance that enterprise goals will be achieved. Control procedures include the rotation of duties and mandatory vacations.

Objective 4. Journalize and post transactions, using subsidiary ledgers and the following special journals: sales journal, cash receipts journal, purchases journal, and cash payments journal.

Subsidiary ledgers may be used to maintain separate records for each customer (the accounts receivable ledger) and creditor (the accounts payable ledger). When subsidiary ledgers are used, each subsidiary ledger is represented in the general ledger by a summarizing account, called a controlling account. The sum of the balances of the accounts in a subsidiary ledger must agree with the balance of the related controlling account.

Special journals may be used to reduce the processing time and expense of recording a large number of similar transactions. The sales journal is used to record the sale of merchandise on account. The cash receipts journal is used to record all receipts of cash. The purchases journal is used to record purchases of merchandise or other items on account. The cash payments journal is used to record all payments of cash. The two-column general journal is used for recording transactions that do not fit in any of the special journals. The use of each special journal and the accounts receivable and accounts payable subsidiary ledgers is illustrated in the chapter.

Objective 5. Describe and give examples of additional subsidiary ledgers and modified special journals.

Subsidiary ledgers may be maintained for a variety of accounts, such as inventories and plant assets, as well as accounts receivable and accounts payable. Special journals may be modified by adding columns in which to record frequently occurring transactions. For example, an additional column is often added to the sales journal for recording the collection of sales taxes payable.

Glossary of Key Terms

Accounting system. The methods and procedures used by an enterprise to record and report financial data for use by management and external users. **Objective 1**

Accounts payable ledger. The subsidiary ledger containing the individual accounts with suppliers (creditors). **Objective 4**

Accounts receivable ledger. The subsidiary ledger containing the individual accounts with customers (debtors). **Objective 4**

Cash payments journal. The journal in which all cash payments are recorded. **Objective 4**

Cash receipts journal. The journal in which all cash receipts are recorded. **Objective 4**

Controlling account. The account in the general ledger that summarizes the balances of the accounts in a subsidiary ledger. **Objective 4**

General journal. The two-column form used for entries that do not "fit" in any of the special journals. **Objective 4**

General ledger. The primary ledger, when used in conjunction with subsidiary ledgers, that contains all of the balance sheet and income statement accounts. **Objective 4**

Internal controls. The detailed policies and procedures used by an enterprise to direct operations and provide reasonable assurance that the enterprise objectives are achieved. **Objective 1**

Internal control structure. Consists of the following three elements: (1) the accounting system, (2) the control environment, and (3) the control procedures. **Objective 3**

Purchases journal. The journal in which all items purchased on account are recorded. **Objective 4**

Sales journal. The journal in which all sales of merchandise on account are recorded. **Objective 4**

Special journals. Journals designed to be used for recording a single type of transaction. **Objective 4**

Subsidiary ledger. A ledger containing individual accounts with a common characteristic. **Objective 4**

Self-Examination Questions
Answers at end of chapter.

1. The final phase of the revision of an accounting system that involves carrying out the proposals for changes in the system is called:
   A. systems analysis
   B. systems design
   C. systems implementation
   D. systems training

2. The detailed procedures used by management to direct operations so that enterprise goals can be achieved are called:
   A. internal controls
   B. systems analysis
   C. systems design
   D. systems implementation

3. A payment of cash for the purchase of merchandise should be recorded in the:
   A. purchases journal
   B. cash payments journal
   C. sales journal
   D. cash receipts journal

4. When there are a large number of individual accounts with a common characteristic, it is common to place them in a separate ledger called:
   A. a subsidiary ledger
   B. a creditors ledger
   C. an accounts payable ledger
   D. an accounts receivable ledger

5. The controlling account in the general ledger that summarizes the debits and credits to the individual customer accounts in the subsidiary ledger is entitled:
   A. Accounts Payable
   B. Accounts Receivable
   C. Sales
   D. Purchases

ILLUSTRATIVE PROBLEM

Selected transactions of O'Malley Co. for the month of May are as follows:

May
a.   1 Issued Check No. 1001 in payment of rent for May, $1,200.
b.   2 Purchased merchandise on account from McMillan Co., terms 2/10, n/30, FOB shipping point, $3,600.
c.   4 Issued Check No. 1003 in payment of transportation charges on the merchandise purchased on May 2, $320.
d.   8 Sold merchandise on account to Waller Co., Invoice No. 51, terms 1/10, n/eom, FOB shipping point, $4,500.
e.   9 Issued Check No. 1005 for office supplies purchased, $450.
f. 10 Received cash for office supplies sold to employees at cost, $120.
g. 11 Purchased office equipment on account from Fender Office Products, $15,000.
h. 12 Issued Credit Memorandum No. 801 for $400 to Waller Co. for merchandise returned.
i. 12 Issued Check No. 1010 in payment of the merchandise purchased from McMillan Co. on May 2, less discount, $3,528.

May

j.   16 Sold merchandise on account to Riese Co., Invoice No. 58, terms 1/10, n/30, FOB shipping point, $8,000.
k.   18 Received $4,059 from Waller Co. in payment of May 8 invoice, less return of May 12 and discount.
l.   20 Invested additional cash in the business, $10,000.
m.   23 Issued Credit Memorandum No. 802 for $220 to Riese Co. for a price adjustment on damaged merchandise sold on May 16.
n.   24 Sold merchandise on nonbank credit cards, $16,700.
o.   25 Sold merchandise for cash, $15,900.
p.   30 Issued Check No. 1040 for withdrawal of cash for personal use, $1,000.
q.   30 Issued Check No. 1041 in payment of electricity and water bills, $690.
r.   30 Issued Check No. 1042 in payment of office and sales salaries for May, $15,800.
s.   31 Journalized adjusting entries from the work sheet prepared for the fiscal year ended May 31.

O'Malley Co. maintains a sales journal, a cash receipts journal, a purchases journal, a cash payments journal, and a general journal. In addition, accounts receivable and accounts payable subsidiary ledgers are used.

Instructions

1. Indicate the journal in which each of the preceding transactions (a) through (s) would be recorded.
2. Indicate whether an account in the accounts receivable or accounts payable subsidiary ledgers would be affected for each of the preceding transactions.
3. Journalize transactions (b), (c), (d), (h), (i), and (k) in the appropriate journals.

Solution

1. Journal	*2. Subsidiary Ledger*
a. Cash payments journal	
b. Purchases journal	Accounts payable ledger
c. Cash payments journal	
d. Sales journal	Accounts receivable ledger
e. Cash payments journal	
f. Cash receipts journal	
g. Purchases journal	Accounts payable ledger
h. General journal	Accounts receivable ledger
i. Cash payment Journal	Accounts payable ledger
j. Sales journal	Accounts receivable ledger
k. Cash receipts journal	Accounts receivable ledger
l. Cash receipts journal	
m. General journal	Accounts receivable ledger
n. Sales journal	Accounts receivable ledger
o. Cash receipts journal	
p. Cash payments journal	
q. Cash payments journal	
r. Cash payments journal	
s. General journal	

3.

Transaction (b):

PURCHASES JOURNAL

DATE	ACCOUNT CREDITED	POST. REF.	ACCOUNTS PAYABLE CR.	PURCHASES DR.	STORE SUPPLIES DR.
May 2	McMillan Co.		3 6 0 0 00	3 6 0 0 00	

ILLUSTRATIVE PROBLEM ILLUSTRATIVE PROBLEM ILLUSTR

Transactions (c) and (i):

CASH PAYMENTS JOURNAL

DATE	CK. NO.	ACCOUNT DEBITED	POST. REF.	OTHER ACCOUNTS DR.	ACCOUNTS PAYABLE DR.	PURCHASES DISCOUNTS CR.	CASH CR.
May 4	1003	Transp. In		3 2 0 00			3 2 0 00
12	1010	McMillan Co.			3 6 0 0 00	7 2 00	3 5 2 8 00

Transaction (d):

SALES JOURNAL

DATE	INVOICE NO.	AMOUNT DEBITED	POST. REF.	ACCTS. REC. DR. SALES CR.
May 8	51	Waller Co.		4 5 0 0 00

Transaction (h):

GENERAL JOURNAL

DATE	DESCRIPTION	POST. REF.	DEBIT	CREDIT
May 12	Sales Returns and Allowances		4 0 0 00	
	Accounts Receivable—Waller Co.			4 0 0 00
	Credit Memo No. 801.			

Transaction (k):

CASH RECEIPTS JOURNAL

DATE	ACCOUNT CREDITED	POST. REF.	OTHER ACCOUNTS CR.	SALES CR.	ACCOUNTS REC. CR.	SALES DISCOUNTS DR.	CASH DR.
May 18	Waller Co.				4 1 0 0 00	4 1 00	4 0 5 9 00

DISCUSSION QUESTIONS

1. Why is the accounting system of an enterprise an information system?
2. What are internal controls?
3. What is the objective of systems analysis?
4. What is included in an enterprise's *Systems Manual?*
5. Name and describe the three elements of the internal control structure.
6. How does a policy of rotating clerical employees from job to job aid in strengthening the control procedures within the control environment?
7. Why should the responsibility for a sequence of related operations be divided among different persons?
8. Why should the employee who handles cash receipts not have the responsibility for maintaining the accounts receivable records?
9. Why should the employee who handles cash receipts not be responsible for approving sales returns and allowances?

10. In an attempt to improve operating efficiency, one employee was made responsible for all purchasing, receiving, and storing of merchandise. Is this organizational change wise from an internal control standpoint? Explain.

11. In an attempt to improve operating efficiency, one employee was made responsible for maintaining all personnel records, for timekeeping, for preparing payroll records, and for distributing payroll checks. Is this organizational change wise from an internal control standpoint? Explain.

12. The ticket seller at a movie theater doubles as a ticket taker for a few minutes each day while the ticket taker is on a break. Which control procedure of an enterprise's system of internal control is violated in this situation?

13. Why should the responsibility for maintaining the accounting records be separated from the responsibility for operations?

14. How can the use of a fidelity bond aid internal control?

15. How does a periodic review by internal auditors strengthen the internal control structure?

16. What is the term applied (a) to the ledger containing the individual customer accounts, and (b) to the single account summarizing accounts receivable?

17. What are the major advantages of the use of special journals?

18. Environmental Products Co. uses the special journals described in this chapter. Which journal will be used to record sales of merchandise (a) for cash, (b) on account?

19. In recording 250 sales of merchandise on account during a single month, how many times will it be necessary to write *Sales* (a) if each transaction, including sales, is recorded individually in a two-column general journal; (b) if each sale is recorded in a sales journal?

20. How many individual postings to Sales for the month would be needed in Question 19 if the procedure described in (a) had been used; if the procedure described in (b) had been used?

21. In posting the following general journal entry, the bookkeeper posted correctly to Vega's account but failed to post to the controlling account.

Mar. 5	Sales Returns and Allowances		402	995	
	Accounts Receivable—E. N. Vega	✓			995

(a) How will the error be discovered? (b) Describe the procedure that is designed to prevent oversights of this type.

22. As illustrated in this chapter, what does a check mark (✓) in the Posting Reference column of the cash receipts journal signify (a) when the account credited is an account receivable, (b) when the account credited is Sales?

23. Assuming the use of a two-column general journal, a sales journal, and a cash receipts journal as illustrated in this chapter, indicate the journal in which each of the following transactions should be recorded:
   a. Investment of additional cash in the business by the owner.
   b. Receipt of cash refund for an overcharge on a purchase of merchandise.
   c. Sale of merchandise for cash.
   d. Sale of merchandise on account.
   e. Receipt of cash from sale of office equipment.
   f. Receipt of cash on account from customer.
   g. Sale of office supplies on account, at cost, to a neighboring business.
   h. Issuance of credit memorandum to customer.
   i. Adjustment to record accrued salaries at the end of the year.
   j. Closing of the drawings account at the end of the year.

24. The following items were purchased on account by a retail hardware store. Indicate the account to which each purchase should be debited.
   a   Forty cans of cement block sealer
   b. Two dozen electric drills
   c. Three cash registers
   d. One gross of pads of sales tickets
   e. Ten stepladders
   f. Two display cases
   g. Two-year fire insurance policy on building
   h. One PC computer for office use
   i. Two kegs of nails

25. During the current month, the following errors occurred in recording transactions in the purchases journal or in posting therefrom:
    a. An invoice for $900 of merchandise from Hoffman Co. was recorded as having been received from Hoffer Co., another supplier.
    b. A credit of $840 to JPC Company was posted as $480 in the subsidiary ledger.
    c. An invoice for merchandise of $6,500 was recorded as $5,500.
    d. The Accounts Payable column of the purchases journal was overstated by $2,000.
    How will each error come to the bookkeeper's attention, other than by chance discovery?

26. The Accounts Payable and Cash columns in the cash payments journal were unknowingly overstated by $100 at the end of the month. (a) Assuming no other errors in recording or posting, will the error cause the trial balance totals to be unequal? (b) Will the creditors ledger agree with the accounts payable controlling account?

27. In recording a cash payment, the bookkeeper enters the correct amount of $1,000 in the Accounts Payable Dr. column and the correct amount of $990 in the Cash Cr. column, but omits the entry for Purchases Discounts. How will the error be found, other than by chance discovery?

28. Assuming the use of a two-column general journal, a purchases journal, and a cash payments journal as illustrated in this chapter, indicate the journal in which each of the following transactions should be recorded:
    a. Purchase of merchandise for cash.
    b. Purchase of office supplies on account.
    c. Payment of cash on account to creditor.
    d. Return of portion of merchandise purchased on account.
    e. Purchase of store equipment on account.
    f. Payment of cash for office supplies.

29. ITC Co. installed a perpetual inventory system. It also revised its sales journal to include two amount columns—one for the sales price and one for the cost price of the merchandise sold. (a) Indicate the general ledger accounts to be debited and credited for the column totals for (1) the sales price and (2) the cost price. (b) What two subsidiary ledgers will receive postings from the sales journal?

30. In the Equity Funding fraud, approximately $2 billion of insurance policies that were claimed to have been sold by the company were bogus. The bogus policies, which were supported by falsified policy applications, were listed along with real policies on Equity Funding's computer tapes (records). These computer tapes were kept in a separate room where they were easily accessible by Equity Funding personnel, including the computer programmers. In addition, computer programmers and other company personnel had access to the computer. What general weaknesses in Equity Funding's internal controls contributed to the occurrence and the size of the fraud?

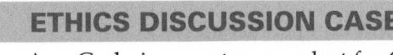

ETHICS DISCUSSION CASE

Ann Godwin, a systems analyst for Cardenas Co., is currently helping a neighbor set up an accounting system for a new business venture. Ann has agreed to set up the system for a fee of $1,000. In designing the new system, Ann has utilized several special journal and subsidiary ledger formats especially developed for Cardenas Co. by its public accountants.

Discuss whether Ann Godwin is behaving in an ethical manner.

SHARPEN YOUR COMMUNICATION SKILLS ►

EXERCISES

EXERCISE 7-1
INTERNAL CONTROLS
Objective 3

Susan Voltz has recently been hired as the manager of Lizzy's Deli. Lizzy's is a national chain of franchised delicatessens. During her first month as store manager, Susan encountered the following internal control situations:

a. Lizzy's has one cash register. Prior to Susan's joining the deli, each employee working on a shift would take a customer order, accept payment, and then prepare the order. Susan made one employee on each shift responsible for taking orders and accepting the customer's payment. Other employees prepare the orders.

b Since only one employee uses the cash register, that employee is responsible for counting the cash at the end of the shift and verifying that the cash in the drawer matches the amount of cash sales recorded by the cash register. Susan expects each cashier to balance the drawer to the penny **every** time—no exceptions.

c. Susan caught an employee putting a box of 100 single-serving bags of potato chips in his car. Not wanting to create a scene, Susan smiled and said, "I don't think you're putting those chips on the right shelf. Don't they belong inside the deli?" The employee returned the chips to the stockroom.

SHARPEN YOUR ►
COMMUNICATION SKILLS

State whether you agree or disagree with Susan's handling of each situation and explain your answer.

EXERCISE 7-2
INTERNAL CONTROLS
Objective 3

Fashions Now is a retail store specializing in women's clothing. The store has established a liberal return policy for the holiday season in order to encourage gift purchases. Any item purchased during November and December may be returned through January 31, with a receipt, for cash or exchange. If the customer does not have a receipt, cash will still be refunded for any item under $25. If the item is more than $25, a check is mailed to the customer.

Whenever an item is returned, a store clerk completes a return slip, which the customer signs. The return slip is placed in a special box. The store manager visits the return counter approximately once every two hours to authorize the return slips. Clerks are instructed to place the returned merchandise on the proper rack on the selling floor as soon as possible.

This year, returns at Fashions Now have reached an all-time high. There are a large number of returns under $25 without receipts.

SHARPEN YOUR ►
COMMUNICATION SKILLS
SHARPEN YOUR ►
COMMUNICATION SKILLS

a. How can sales clerks employed at Fashions Now use the store's return policy to steal money from the cash register?
b. 1. What internal control weaknesses do you see in the return policy that make cash thefts easier?
 2. Would issuing a store credit in place of a cash refund for all merchandise returned without a receipt reduce the possibility of theft? List some advantages and disadvantages of issuing a store credit in place of a cash refund.
 3. Assume that Fashions Now is committed to the current policy of issuing cash refunds without a receipt. What changes could be made in the store's procedures regarding customer refunds in order to improve internal control?

EXERCISE 7-3
IDENTIFICATION OF POSTINGS FROM SALES JOURNAL
Objective 4

Using the following sales journal for J. A. Bach Co., identify each of the posting references, indicated by a letter, as representing (1) a posting to a general ledger account, (2) a posting to a subsidiary ledger account, or (3) a posting to two general ledger accounts.

SALES JOURNAL

Date	Invoice No.	Account Debited	Post. Ref.	
19--				
Nov. 1	772	Environmental Safety Co.	(a)	$ 1,500
10	773	Greenberg Co.	(b)	795
20	774	Smith and Smith	(c)	1,100
27	775	Envirolab	(d)	640
30				$4,035
				(e)

EXERCISE 7-4
IDENTIFICATION OF POSTINGS FOR SALES RETURNS AND ALLOWANCES
Objective 4

The following entry for a sales return was entered in the general journal of J. A. Bach Co. Identify each of the posting references, indicated by a letter, as representing (1) a posting to a general ledger account, (2) a posting to a general ledger account and a subsidiary ledger account, or (3) a posting to a subsidiary ledger account.

JOURNAL

Date	Description	Post. Ref.	Debit	Credit
19--				
Nov. 21	Sales Returns and Allowances	(a)	500	
	Accounts Receivable—			
	Greenberg Co.	(b)		500
	Credit Memo. 117			

EXERCISE 7-5
ACCOUNTS RECEIVABLE
LEDGER
Objective 4

Based upon the data presented in Exercises 7-3 and 7-4, (a) set up a T account for Accounts Receivable and T accounts for the four accounts needed in the customers ledger, (b) post to the T accounts, (c) determine the balance in the accounts, if necessary, and (d) prepare a schedule of accounts receivable at November 30.

EXERCISE 7-6
IDENTIFICATION OF
TRANSACTIONS IN
ACCOUNTS RECEIVABLE
LEDGER
Objective 4

The debits and credits from three related transactions are presented in the following customer's account taken from the accounts receivable ledger:

NAME   Future Environmental Services
ADDRESS   1319 Main Street

Date	Item	Post. Ref.	Debit	Credit	Balance
19--					
Sep. 3		S50	5,000		5,000
9		J9		700	4,300
13		CR38		4,300	—

Describe each transaction and identify the source of each posting.

EXERCISE 7-7
IDENTIFICATION OF
POSTINGS FROM
PURCHASES JOURNAL
Objective 4

Using the following purchases journal, identify each of the posting references, indicated by a letter, as representing (1) a posting to a general ledger account, (2) a posting to a subsidiary ledger account, or (3) that no posting is required.

PURCHASES JOURNAL   Page 49

Date	Account Credited	Post. Ref.	Accounts Payable Cr.	Purchases Dr.	Store Supplies Dr.	Office Supplies Dr.	Other Accounts Dr. Account	Other Accounts Dr. Post. Ref.	Other Accounts Dr. Amount
19--									
June 4	Coastal Resource Management Co.	(a)	4,525	4,525					
6	Porter Supply Co.	(b)	3,000				Office Equipment	(c)	3,000
11	Baker Products	(d)	1,950		1,500	450			
13	Wilson and Wilson	(e)	6,800	6,800					
20	Cowen Auto Supply	(f)	3,775	3,775					
27	Porter Supply Co.	(g)	9,100				Store Equipment	(h)	9,100
30			29,150	15,100	1,500	450			12,100
			(i)	(j)	(k)	(l)			(m)

EXERCISE 7-8
IDENTIFICATION OF
POSTINGS FROM CASH
PAYMENTS JOURNAL
Objective 4

Using the following cash payments journal, identify each of the posting references, indicated by a letter, as representing (1) a posting to a general ledger account, (2) a posting to a subsidiary ledger account, or (3) that no posting is required.

CASH PAYMENTS JOURNAL   Page 46

Date	Ck. No.	Account Debited	Post Ref.	Other Accounts Dr.	Accounts Payable Dr.	Purchases Discounts Cr.	Cash Cr.
19--							
July 3	611	Aquatic Systems Co.	(a)		4,000	40	3,960
5	612	Sales Returns and Allowances	(b)	325			325
10	613	Purchases	(c)	3,200			3,200
17	614	Coe Bros.	(d)		2,500	50	2,450
20	615	Office Equipment	(e)	2,100			2,100
22	616	Advertising Expense	(f)	400			400
25	617	Office Supplies	(g)	250			250
27	618	Evans Co.	(h)		5,500	55	5,445
31	619	Salaries Expense	(i)	1,750			1,750
31				8,025	12,000	145	19,880
				(j)	(k)	(l)	(m)

EXERCISE 7-9
IDENTIFICATION OF
TRANSACTIONS IN
ACCOUNTS PAYABLE
LEDGER ACCOUNT
Objective 4

The debits and credits from three related transactions are presented in the following creditor's account taken from the accounts payable ledger:

NAME   Vera Cruz Co.
ADDRESS   1717 Kirby Street

Date	Item	Post. Ref.	Debit	Credit	Balance
19--					
July 6		P34		12,500	12,500
10		J10	500		12,000
16		CP37	12,000		—

Describe each transaction and identify the source of each posting.

EXERCISE 7-10
ERROR IN ACCOUNTS
PAYABLE LEDGER AND
SCHEDULE OF ACCOUNTS
PAYABLE
Objective 4

After Sypek Company had completed all postings for the month of October in the current year, the sum of the balances in the following accounts payable ledger did not agree with the balance of the appropriate controlling account in the general ledger.

NAME   C. D. Cali Co.
ADDRESS   1240 W. Main Street

Date	Item	Post. Ref.	Debit	Credit	Balance
19--					
Oct. 1	Balance	✓			4,750
10		CP22	4,750		—
17		P30		3,250	3,250
25		J7	250		2,000

NAME   Cutler and Powell
ADDRESS   717 Elm Street

Date	Item	Post. Ref.	Debit	Credit	Balance
19--					
Oct. 1	Balance	✓			6,100
18		CP23	6,100		—
29		P31		7,500	7,500

NAME   C. D. Greer and Son
ADDRESS   972 S. Tenth Street

Date	Item	Post. Ref.	Debit	Credit	Balance
19--					
Oct. 17		P30		3,750	3,750
27		P31		7,000	10,750

NAME   Taber Supply
ADDRESS   1170 Mattis Avenue

Date	Item	Post. Ref.	Debit	Credit	Balance
19--					
Oct. 1	Balance	✓			8,250
7		P30		4,900	13,050
12		J7	250		12,800
20		CP23	5,700		7,100

NAME   L. L. Weiss Co.
ADDRESS   915 E. Walnut Street

Date	Item	Post. Ref.	Debit	Credit	Balance
19--					
Oct. 5		P30		2,750	2,750

Assuming that the controlling account balance of $31,200 has been verified as correct, (a) determine the error(s) in the preceding accounts and (b) prepare a schedule of accounts payable from the corrected accounts payable subsidiary ledger.

EXERCISE 7-11
IDENTIFY POSTINGS FROM SPECIAL JOURNALS
Objective 4

Tracy Company makes most of its sales and purchases on credit. It uses the five journals described in this chapter (sales, cash receipts, purchases, cash payments, and general journals). Identify the journal most likely used in recording the postings for selected transactions indicated by letter in the following T accounts:

Cash			
a.	10,000	b.	8,750

Sales			
		i.	10,950
		j.	450

Purchases		
m.	6,500	
n.	725	

Accounts Receivable			
c.	10,950	d.	9,200
		e.	300

Sales Returns and Allowances	
k.	300

Purchases Returns and Allowances	
o.	250

Accounts Payable			
f.	7,600	h.	7,790
g.	250		

Sales Discounts	
l.	110

Purchases Discounts	
p.	195

EXERCISE 7-12
ENTRIES TO RECORD MEMORANDUMS AND CORRECTIONS OF ERRORS
Objective 4

Journalize the following transactions in a general journal:

July 5. Received credit memorandum for return of equipment purchased on account from Mathews Equipment Co. on July 1, $4,000.

8. Issued credit memorandum for return of merchandise sold on account to R. D. Sharp Co. on June 30, $900.

12. Issued debit memorandum for return of merchandise purchased on account from L. L. Linke Co. on July 7, $1,100.

19. Issued credit memorandum for allowance made to C. C. Palmer for defective merchandise sold on account on July 13, $220.

24. Corrected error of June 30 when a note received from JMB Co. for a $5,000 account receivable was not recorded.

WhAT'S WRONG WITH THiS?

The following cash receipts journal headings have been suggested for a small merchandising firm. How many errors can you find in the headings?

CASH RECEIPTS JOURNAL   PAGE

DATE	ACCOUNT CREDITED	POST. REF.	SALES CR.	ACCOUNTS REC. CR.	SALES DISCOUNTS CR.	OTHER ACCOUNTS DR.	CASH DR.

PROBLEMS

Series A

PROBLEM 7-1A
SALES JOURNAL; ACCOUNTS RECEIVABLE AND GENERAL LEDGERS
Objective 4

C. L. Wolfe Co. was established on May 20 of the current year. Its sales of merchandise on account and related returns and allowances during the remainder of the month are as follows. Terms of all sales were 1/10, n/30, FOB destination.

May 21. Sold merchandise on account to Boritz Co., Invoice No. 1, $1,200.

22. Sold merchandise on account to Stark Co., Invoice No. 2, $2,750.

24. Sold merchandise on account to Morris Co., Invoice No. 3, $3,175.

25. Issued Credit Memorandum No. 1 for $100 to Boritz Co. for merchandise returned.

27. Sold merchandise on account to C. D. Walters Co., Invoice No. 4, $2,500.

May 28. Sold merchandise on account to A. Udall Co., Invoice No. 5, $1,500.
    28. Issued Credit Memorandum No. 2 for $150 to Stark Co. for merchandise returned.
    30. Sold merchandise on account to Stark Co., Invoice No. 6, $2,925.
    30. Issued Credit Memorandum No. 3 for $75 to C. D. Walters Co. for damages to merchandise caused by faulty packing.
    31. Sold merchandise on account to Morris Co., Invoice No. 7, $995.

Instructions

1. Journalize the transactions for May, using a single-column sales journal and a two-column general journal. Post to the following customer accounts in the accounts receivable ledger and insert the balance immediately after recording each entry: Boritz Co.; Morris Co.; Stark Co.; A. Udall Co.; C. D. Walters Co.
2. Post the general journal and the sales journal to the following accounts in the general ledger, inserting the account balances only after the last postings:
   113 Accounts Receivable
   411 Sales
   412 Sales Returns and Allowances
3. a. What is the sum of the balances of the accounts in the subsidiary ledger at May 31?
   b. What is the balance of the controlling account at May 31?

SHARPEN YOUR COMMUNICATION SKILLS ▶

4. Assume that on June 1, C. L. Wolfe Co. decides to sell to retail as well as wholesale customers. Briefly explain how the sales journal may be modified to accomodate sales on account that require the collection of a state sales tax.

PROBLEM 7-2A
SALES AND CASH RECEIPTS
JOURNALS; ACCOUNTS
RECEIVABLE AND GENERAL
LEDGERS
Objective 4

If the working papers correlating with the textbook are not used, omit Problem 7-2A.
Three journals, the accounts receivable ledger, and portions of the general ledger of Unisac Co. are presented in the working papers. Sales invoices and credit memorandums were entered in the journals by an assistant. Terms of sales on account are 2/10, n/30, FOB shipping point. Transactions in which cash and notes receivable were received during July are as follows:

July   1. Received $5,880 from C. D. Martin Co. in payment of June 21 invoice less discount.
    3. Received $10,300 in payment of $10,000 note receivable and interest of $300.
       Post transactions of July 1, 2, and 6 to accounts receivable ledger.
    7. Received $6,370 from Janet Rowe Co. in payment of June 28 invoice less discount.
    8. Received $2,200 from R. C. Fellows Co. in payment of June 10 invoice, no discount.
       Post transactions of July 7, 8, 10, 12, and 15 to accounts receivable ledger.
    16. Cash sales for first half of July totaled $4,610.
    19. Received $1,000 refund for return of defective equipment purchased for cash in June.
    20. Received $2,842 from C. D. Martin Co. in payment of balance due on July 10 invoice less discount.
    22. Received $5,684 from R. C. Fellows Co. in payment of July 12 invoice less discount.
       Post transactions of July 17, 20, 22, and 23 to accounts receivable ledger.
    27. Received $40 for sale of office supplies at cost.
    31. Received $1,750 cash and a $2,500 note receivable from Ignacio and Co. in settlement of the balance due on the invoice of July 2, no discount. (Journalize the receipt of the note in the general journal.)
    31. Cash sales for the second half of July totaled $4,150.
       Post transactions of July 27, 28, 30, and 31 to accounts receivable ledger.

Instructions

1. Journalize the cash receipts in the cash receipts journal and the note in the general journal. Before journalizing a receipt of cash on account, determine the balance of the customer's account. Post the entries from the three journals, in date sequence, to the accounts receivable ledger in accordance with the instructions in the narrative of transactions. Insert the new balance after each posting to an account.
2. Post the appropriate individual entries from the cash receipts journal and the general journal to the general ledger.
3. Total each of the columns of the sales journal and the cash receipts journal and post the appropriate totals to the general ledger. Insert the balance of each account after the last posting.
4. Prepare a schedule of accounts receivable as of July 31 and compare the total with the balance of the controlling account.

PROBLEM 7-3A
SALES AND CASH RECEIPTS
JOURNALS; ACCOUNTS
RECEIVABLE AND GENERAL
LEDGERS
Objective 4

Transactions related to sales and cash receipts completed by Environmental Products of Collier County during the period June 15-30 of the current year are as follows. The terms of all sales on account are 2/10, n/30, FOB shipping point.

June 15. Issued Invoice No. 793 to Towers Co., $4,425.
       16. Received cash from F. G. Black Co. for the balance owed on its account less discount.
       19. Issued Invoice No. 794 to Halloway Co., $7,500.
       20. Issued Invoice No. 795 to Ross and Son, $2,975.
             Post all journals to the accounts receivable ledger.
       23. Received cash from Halloway Co. for the balance owed on June 15, no discount.
       24. Issued Credit Memorandum No. 35 to Towers Co., $275.
       24. Issued Invoice No. 796 to Halloway Co., $4,950.
       24. Received $1,560 in payment of a $1,500 note receivable and interest of $60.
             Post all journals to the accounts receivable ledger.
       25. Received cash from Towers Co. for the balance due on invoice of June 15 less discount.
       28. Received cash from Halloway Co. for invoice of June 19 less discount.
       28. Issued Invoice No. 797 to F. G. Black Co., $2,100.
       30. Issued Credit Memorandum No. 36 to F. G. Black Co., $250.
       30. Recorded cash sales for the second half of the month, $8,155.
             Post all journals to the accounts receivable ledger.

Instructions

1. Insert the following balances in the general ledger as of June 1:

111	Cash	$13,705
112	Notes Receivable	7,500
113	Accounts Receivable	15,975
411	Sales	—
412	Sales Returns and Allowances	—
413	Sales Discounts	—
811	Interest Income	—

2. Insert the following balances in the accounts receivable ledger as of June 15:

F. G. Black Co.	$8,900
Halloway Co.	9,825
Ross and Son	—
Towers Co.	—

3. In a single-column sales journal and a cash receipts journal similar to the ones illustrated in this chapter, insert *June 15 Total(s) Forwarded* on the left side of the first line of the journal. Insert a check mark (✓) in the Post. Ref. column, and the following dollar figures in the respective amount columns:

    Sales journal: 25,350
    Cash receipts journal: 3,467; 13,470; 22,600; 366; 39,171.

4. Using the two special journals and a two-column general journal, journalize the transactions for the remainder of June. Post to the accounts receivable ledger and insert the balances at the points indicated in the narrative of transactions. *Determine the balance in the customer's account before recording a cash receipt.*
5. Total each of the columns of the special journals and post the individual entries and totals to the general ledger. Insert account balances after the last posting.
6. Determine that the subsidiary ledger agrees with the controlling account in the general ledger.

**SOLUTIONS
SOFTWARE**

Instructions for Solving Problem 7-3A Using Solutions Software

1. Load opening balances.
2. Save the opening balances file to your drive and directory.
3. Set the run date to June 30 of the current year and enter your name.
4. Key the journal entries.
5. Display the journal entries.
6. Display a trial balance.
7. Save your data file to disk.
8. End the session.

PROBLEM 7-4A
PURCHASES AND
PURCHASES RETURNS,
ACCOUNTS PAYABLE
ACCOUNT, AND ACCOUNTS
PAYABLE LEDGER
Objective 4

Purchases on account and related returns and allowances completed by Chan and Son Sales during May of the current year are as follows:

May 1. Purchased merchandise on account from Yu Co., $6,150.50.
     4. Purchased merchandise on account from O'Grady Co., $9,250.
     5. Received a credit memorandum from Yu Co. for merchandise returned, $200.
     9. Purchased office supplies on account from Tyler Supply, $175.30.
    13. Purchased merchandise on account from Yu Co., $4,370.50.
    14. Purchased office equipment on account from Diamond Equipment Co., $5,500.
    17. Purchased merchandise on account from James Co., $3,100.
    19. Received a credit memorandum from Tyler Supply for office supplies returned, $22.50.
    20. Purchased merchandise on account from Craig Co., $1,130.30.
    24. Purchased store supplies on account from Tyler Supply, $325.
    27. Received a credit memorandum from O'Grady Co. as an allowance for damaged merchandise, $500.
    29. Purchased merchandise on account from James Co., $475.15.
    31. Purchased office supplies on account from Tyler Supply, $210.50.

Instructions

1. Insert the following balances in the general ledger as of May 1:

114	Store Supplies	$ 460.00
115	Office Supplies	327.40
122	Office Equipment	32,500.00
211	Accounts Payable	12,212.30
511	Purchases	89,917.40
512	Purchases Returns and Allowances	2,170.10

2. Insert the following balances in the accounts payable ledger as of May 1:

Craig Co.	$2,177.70
Diamond Equipment Co.	—
James Co.	4,550.25
O'Grady Co.	5,484.35
Tyler Supply	—
Yu Co.	—

3. Journalize the transactions for May, using a purchases journal similar to the one illustrated in this chapter and a two-column general journal. Post to the creditor accounts in the accounts payable ledger immediately after each entry.
4. Post the general journal and the purchases journal to the accounts in the general ledger.
5. a. What is the sum of the balances in the subsidiary ledger at May 31?
    b. What is the balance of the controlling account at May 31?

PROBLEM 7-5A
PURCHASES AND CASH
PAYMENTS JOURNALS;
ACCOUNTS PAYABLE AND
GENERAL LEDGERS
Objective 4

Fashion Clothiers Co. was established on June 16 of the current year. Transactions related to purchases, returns and allowances, and cash payments during the remainder of June are as follows:

June 16. Issued Check No. 1 in payment of rent for the remainder of June, $900 .
     16. Purchased office equipment on account from Harper Equipment Co., $7,250.
     16. Purchased merchandise on account from Hernandez Clothing Co., $15,500.
     17. Issued Check No. 2 in payment of store supplies, $410, and office supplies, $290.
     18. Purchased merchandise on account from Carter Clothing, $9,720.
     19. Purchased merchandise on account from Adams Co., $2,150.
     20. Received a credit memorandum from Carter Clothing for returned merchandise, $720.
          Post the journals to the accounts payable ledger.
     23. Issued Check No. 3 to Harper Equipment Co. in payment of invoice, $7,250.
     23. Received a credit memorandum from Adams Co. for defective merchandise, $465.
     24. Issued Check No. 4 to Hernandez Clothing Co. in payment of invoice of $15,500 less 1% discount.

June 25. Issued Check No. 5 to a cash customer for merchandise returned, $215.

26. Issued Check No. 6 to Carter Clothing in payment of the balance owed less 2% discount.

27. Purchased merchandise on account from Adams Co., $1,610.
Post the journals to the accounts payable ledger.

30. Purchased the following from Harper Equipment Co. on account: store supplies, $150; office supplies, $75; store equipment, $1,500.

30. Issued Check No. 7 to Adams Co. in payment of invoice of $2,150 less the credit of $465.

30. Purchased merchandise on account from Hernandez Clothing Co., $6,200.

30. Issued Check No. 8 in payment of sales salaries, $1,775.

30. Received a credit memorandum from Harper Equipment Co. for defect in office equipment, $75.
Post the journals to the accounts payable ledger.

SPREADSHEET
PROBLEM

Instructions

1. Journalize the transactions for June. Use a purchases journal and a cash payments journal, similar to those illustrated in this chapter, and a two-column general journal. Refer to the following partial chart of accounts:

111	Cash	412	Sales Returns and Allowances
116	Store Supplies	511	Purchases
117	Office Supplies	512	Purchases Returns and Allowances
121	Store Equipment	513	Purchases Discounts
123	Office Equipment	611	Sales Salaries Expense
211	Accounts Payable	712	Rent Expense

At the points indicated in the narrative of transactions, post to the following accounts in the accounts payable ledger:

Adams Co.	Harper Equipment Co.
Carter Clothing	Hernandez Clothing Co.

2. Post the individual entries (Other Accounts columns of the purchases journal and the cash payments journal; both columns of the general journal) to the appropriate general ledger accounts.

3. Total each of the columns of the purchases journal and the cash payments journal and post the appropriate totals to the general ledger. (Because the problem does not include transactions related to cash receipts, the cash account in the ledger will have a credit balance.)

4. Prepare a schedule of accounts payable.

PROBLEM 7-6A
ALL JOURNALS AND
GENERAL LEDGER; TRIAL
BALANCE
Objective 4

The transactions completed by Miles Company during July, the first month of the current fiscal year, were as follows:

July 1. Issued Check No. 610 for July rent, $1,400.

2. Purchased merchandise on account from Bidwell Co., $2,590.

3. Purchased equipment on account from Glass Equipment Co., $9,600.

5. Issued Invoice No. 940 to W. Cox Co., $1,700.

6. Received check for $2,772 from Powell Co. in payment of $2,800 invoice less 1% discount.

6. Issued Check No. 611 for miscellaneous selling expense, $310.

9. Received credit memorandum from Bidwell Co. for returned merchandise, $290.

9. Issued Invoice No. 941 to Collins Co., $8,500.

10. Issued Check No. 612 for $9,405 to Howell Co. in payment of $9,500 invoice less 1% discount.

10. Received check for $7,375 from Sax Manufacturing Co. in payment of $7,375 invoice, no discount.

10. Issued Check No. 613 to Bone Enterprises in payment of $2,120 invoice, no discount.

11. Issued Invoice No. 942 to Joy Co., $3,120.

11. Issued Check No. 614 for $705 to Porter Co. in payment of account, no discount.

12. Received check for $1,683 from W. Cox Co. in payment of $1,700 invoice less 1% discount.

July 13. Issued credit memorandum to Joy Co. for damaged merchandise, $320.

13. Issued Check No. 615 for $2,254 to Bidwell Co. in payment of $2,300 balance less 2% discount.

16. Issued Check No. 616 for $2,725 for cash purchase of merchandise.

16. Cash sales for July 1-16, $21,520.

17. Purchased merchandise on account from Bone Enterprises, $7,920.

18. Received check for return of merchandise that had been purchased for cash, $790.

18. Issued Check No. 617 for miscellaneous administrative expense, $238.

19. Purchased the following on account from Moore Supply Co.: store supplies, $248; office supplies, $197.

20. Issued Check No. 618 in payment of advertising expense, $1,850.

23. Issued Invoice No. 943 to Sax Manufacturing Co., $8,172.

24. Purchased the following on account from Howell Co.: merchandise, $5,127; store supplies, $292.

25. Issued Invoice No. 944 to Collins Co., $4,650.

25. Received check for $2,800 from Powell Co. in payment of $2,800 balance, no discount.

26. Issued Check No. 619 to Glass Equipment Co. in payment of $9,600 invoice of July 3, no discount.

27. Issued Check No. 620 to D. D. Miles as a personal withdrawal, $3,500.

30. Issued Check No. 621 for monthly salaries as follows: sales salaries, $9,100; office salaries, $3,800.

31. Cash sales for July 17-31, $18,150.

31. Issued Check No. 622 in payment of transportation charges for merchandise purchased during the month, $930.

Instructions

1. Enter the following account balances in the general ledger as of July 1:

111	Cash	$ 9,850
113	Accounts Receivable	12,975
114	Merchandise Inventory	35,500
115	Store Supplies	545
116	Office Supplies	360
117	Prepaid Insurance	2,100
121	Equipment	47,250
122	Accumulated Depreciation	22,250
211	Accounts Payable	13,530
311	D. D. Miles, Capital	72,800
312	D. D. Miles, Drawing	—
411	Sales	—
412	Sales Returns and Allowances	—
413	Sales Discounts	—
511	Purchases	—
512	Purchases Returns and Allowances	—
513	Purchases Discounts	—
514	Transportation In	—
611	Sales Salaries Expense	—
612	Advertising Expense	—
619	Miscellaneous Selling Expense	—
711	Office Salaries Expense	—
712	Rent Expense	—
719	Miscellaneous Administrative Expense	—

2. Journalize the transactions for July, using the following journals similar to those illustrated in this chapter: single-column sales journal, cash receipts journal, purchases journal, cash payments journal, and two-column general journal. The terms of all sales on account are FOB shipping point, 1/10, n/30. Assume that an assistant makes daily postings to the individual accounts in the accounts payable ledger and the accounts receivable ledger.

3. Post the appropriate individual entries to the general ledger.
4. Total each of the columns of the special journals and post the appropriate totals to the general ledger; insert the account balances.
5. Prepare a trial balance.
6. Verify the agreement of each subsidiary ledger with its controlling account. Balances of the accounts in the subsidiary ledgers as of July 31 are as follows:

Accounts receivable: 13,150; 8,172; 2,800
Accounts payable: 5,419; 7,920; 1,650

SOLUTIONS SOFTWARE

Instructions for Solving Problem 7-6A Using Solutions Software

1. Load opening balances.
2. Save the opening balances file to your drive and directory.
3. Set the run date to July 31 of the current year and enter your name.
4. Key the journal entries.
5. Display the journal entries.
6. Display a trial balance.
7. Save your data file to disk.
8. End the session.

PROBLEM 7-7A
SALES JOURNAL WITH SALES TAX PAYABLE COLUMN; ACCOUNTS RECEIVABLE AND GENERAL LEDGERS
Objective 5

Rivera Company was established on May 15 of the current year. Its sales of merchandise on account and related returns and allowances during the remainder of the month are as follows. Terms of all sales were 1/15, n/30, FOB shipping point. The sales tax was 5%.

May 18. Sold merchandise on account to JCM Co., Invoice No. 1, $1,500 plus sales tax of $75.
20. Sold merchandise on account to Reese Co., Invoice No. 2, $3,300 plus sales tax of $165.
22. Sold merchandise on account to Innis Co., Invoice No. 3, $3,600 plus sales tax of $180.
23. Issued Credit Memorandum No. 1 for $300 plus sales tax of $15 to JCM Co. for merchandise returned.
27. Sold merchandise on account to D. L. Victor Co., Invoice No. 4, $2,800 plus sales tax of $140.
28. Sold merchandise on account to Tyson Co., Invoice No. 5, $500 plus sales tax of $25.
28. Issued Credit Memorandum No. 2 for $100 plus sales tax of $5 to Reese Co. for merchandise returned.
30. Sold merchandise on account to Reese Co., Invoice No. 6, $1,800 plus sales tax of $90.
30. Issued Credit Memorandum No. 3 for $200 plus sales tax of $10 to D. L. Victor Co. for damages to merchandise caused by faulty packing.
31. Sold merchandise on account to Innis Co., Invoice No. 7, $2,500 plus sales tax of $125.

SPREADSHEET PROBLEM

Instructions

1. Journalize the transactions for May, using a three-column sales journal and a two-column general journal. Post to the following customer accounts in the accounts receivable ledger and insert the balance immediately after recording each entry: JCM Co.; Innis Co.; Reese Co.; Tyson Co.; D. L. Victor Co.
2. Post the general journal and the sales journal to the following accounts in the general ledger, inserting the account balances only after the last postings:

113   Accounts Receivable
215   Sales Tax Payable
411   Sales
412   Sales Returns and Allowances

3. a. What is the sum of the balances of the accounts in the subsidiary ledger at May 31?
   b. What is the balance of the controlling account at May 31?

Series B

PROBLEM 7-1B
SALES JOURNAL;
ACCOUNTS RECEIVABLE
AND GENERAL LEDGERS
Objective 4

Pronto Company was established on May 15 of the current year. Its sales of merchandise on account and related returns and allowances during the remainder of the month are as follows. Terms of all sales were 1/15, n/30, FOB shipping point.

May 18. Sold merchandise on account to JCM Co., Invoice No. 1, $1,500.
  20. Sold merchandise on account to Reese Co., Invoice No. 2, $3,250.
  22. Sold merchandise on account to Innis Co., Invoice No. 3, $3,375.
  23. Issued Credit Memorandum No. 1 for $250 to JCM Co. for merchandise returned.
  27. Sold merchandise on account to D. L. Victor Co., Invoice No. 4, $3,125.
  28. Sold merchandise on account to Tyson Co., Invoice No. 5, $500.
  28. Issued Credit Memorandum No. 2 for $150 to Reese Co. for merchandise returned.
  30. Sold merchandise on account to Reese Co., Invoice No. 6, $1,800.
  30. Issued Credit Memorandum No. 3 for $200 to D. L. Victor Co. for damages to merchandise caused by faulty packing .
  31. Sold merchandise on account to Innis Co., Invoice No. 7, $1,495.

Instructions

1. Journalize the transactions for May, using a single-column sales journal and a two-column general journal. Post to the following customers accounts in the accounts receivable ledger and insert the balance immediately after recording each entry: JCM Co.; Innis Co.; Reese Co.; Tyson Co.; D. L. Victor Co.

2. Post the general journal and the sales journal to the following accounts in the general ledger, inserting the account balances only after the last postings:

   113   Accounts Receivable
   411   Sales
   412   Sales Returns and Allowances

3. a. What is the sum of the balances of the accounts in the subsidiary ledger at May 31?
   b. What is the balance of the controlling account at May 31?

SHARPEN YOUR ►
COMMUNICATION SKILLS

4. Assume that on June 1, Pronto Company decides to sell to retail as well as wholesale customers. Briefly explain how the sales journal may be modified to accomodate sales on account that require the collection of a state sales tax.

If the working papers correlating with the textbook are not used, omit Problem 7-2B.

PROBLEM 7-2B
SALES AND CASH RECEIPTS
JOURNALS; ACCOUNTS
RECEIVABLE AND GENERAL
LEDGERS
Objective 4

Three journals, the accounts receivable ledger, and portions of the general ledger of Doran Co. are presented in the working papers. Sales invoices and credit memorandums were entered in the journals by an assistant. Terms of sales on account are 1/10, n/30, FOB shipping point. Transactions in which cash and notes receivable were received during July are as follows:

July   1. Received $5,940 from C. D. Martin Co. in payment of June 21 invoice less discount.
   3. Received $20,200 in payment of $20,000 note receivable and interest of $200.
      Post transactions of July 1, 2, and 6 to accounts receivable ledger.
   8. Received $6,435 from Janet Rowe Co. in payment of June 28 invoice less discount.
   10. Received $2,200 from R. C. Fellows Co. in payment of June 10 invoice, no discount.
   15. Cash sales for first half of July totaled $14,915.
      Post transactions of July 8, 10, 12, and 15 to accounts receivable ledger.
   19. Received $1,250 refund for return of defective equipment purchased for cash in June.
   20. Received $2,871 from C. D. Martin Co. in payment of balance due on July 10 invoice less discount.
   22. Received $5,742 from R. C. Fellows Co. in payment of July 12 invoice less discount.
      Post transactions of July 17, 20, 22, and 23 to accounts receivable ledger.
   28. Received $50 for sale of office supplies at cost.
   31. Received $1,750 cash and a $2,500 note receivable from Ignacio and Co. in settlement of the balance due on the invoice of July 2, no discount. (Journalize the receipt of the note in the general journal.)
   31. Cash sales for the second half of July totaled $16,100.
      Post transactions of July 27, 28, 30, and 31 to accounts receivable ledger.

Instructions

1. Journalize the cash receipts in the cash receipts journal and the note in the general journal. Before journalizing a receipt of cash on account, determine the balance of the customer's account. Post the entries from the three journals, in date sequence, to the accounts receivale ledger in accordance with the instructions in the narrative of transactions. Insert the new balance after each posting to an account.
2. Post the appropriate individual entries from the cash receipts journal and the general journal to the general ledger.
3. Total each of the columns of the sales journal and the cash receipts journal and post the appropriate totals to the general ledger. Insert the balance of each account after the last posting.
4. Prepare a schedule of accounts receivable as of July 31 and compare the total with the balance of the controlling account.

PROBLEM 7-3B
SALES AND CASH RECEIPTS
JOURNALS; ACCOUNTS
RECEIVABLE AND GENERAL
LEDGERS
Objective 4

Transactions related to sales and cash receipts completed by K. M. West Co. during the period June 15-30 of the current year are as follows. The terms of all sales on account are 1/10, n/30, FOB shipping point.

June 15. Issued Invoice No. 717 to Towers Co., $6,100.
  16. Received cash from F. G. Black Co. for the balance owed on its account less discount.
  17. Issued Invoice No. 718 to Halloway Co., $7,700.
  18. Issued Invoice No. 719 to Ross and Son, $2,600.
       Post all journals to the accounts receivable ledger.
  21. Received cash from Halloway Co. for the balance owed on June 15, no discount.
  22. Issued Credit Memorandum No. 55 to Towers Co., $200.
  24. Issued Invoice No. 720 to Halloway Co., $7,000.
  24. Received $1,050 in payment of a $1,000 note receivable and interest of $50.
       Post all journals to the accounts receivable ledger.
  25. Received cash from Towers Co. for the balance due on invoice of June 15 less discount.
  27. Received cash from Halloway Co. for invoice of June 17 less discount.
  29. Issued Invoice No. 721 to F. G. Black Co., $8,500.
  30. Recorded cash sales for the second half of the month, $11,750 .
  30. Issued Credit Memorandum No. 56 to F. G. Black Co., $150.
       Post all journals to the accounts receivable ledger.

Instructions

1. Insert the following balances in the general ledger as of June 1:

111	Cash	$13,705
112	Notes Receivable	7,500
113	Accounts Receivable	15,975
411	Sales	—
412	Sales Returns and Allowances	—
413	Sales Discounts	—
811	Interest Income	—

2. Insert the following balances in the accounts receivable ledger as of June 15:

F. G. Black Co.	$8,900
Halloway Co.	9,825
Ross and Son	—
Towers Co.	—

3. In a single-column sales journal and a cash receipts journal similar to the ones illustrated in this chapter, insert *June 15 Total(s) Forwarded* on the left side of the first line of the journal. Insert a check mark (√) in the Post. Ref. column, and the following dollar figures in the respective amount columns:

Sales journal: 25,350
Cash receipts journal: 3,467; 13,470; 22,600; 366; 39,171.

4. Using the two special journals and a two-column general journal, journalize the transactions for the remainder of June. Post to the accounts receivable ledger and insert the balances at the points indicated in the narrative of transactions. *Determine the balance in the customer's account before recording a cash receipt.*

5. Total each of the columns of the special journals and post the individual entries and totals to the general ledger. Insert account balances after the last posting.

6. Determine that the subsidiary ledger agrees with the controlling account in the general ledger.

SOLUTIONS SOFTWARE

Instructions for Solving Problem 7-3B Using Solutions Software

1. Load opening balances.
2. Save the opening balances file to your drive and directory.
3. Set the run date to June 30 of the current year and enter your name.
4. Key the journal entries.
5. Display the journal entries.
6. Display a trial balance.
7. Save your data file to disk.
8. End the session.

PROBLEM 7-4B
PURCHASES AND
PURCHASES RETURNS,
ACCOUNTS PAYABLE
ACCOUNT, AND ACCOUNTS
PAYABLE LEDGER
Objective 4

Purchases on account and related returns and allowances completed by Brooks Co. during May of the current year are as follows:

May 1. Purchased merchandise on account from Wong Co., $6,085.20.
    3. Purchased merchandise on account from Lane Co., $11,552.50.
    4. Received a credit memorandum from Wong Co. for merchandise returned, $200.
    8. Purchased office supplies on account from Tyler Supply, $175.30.
   12. Purchased merchandise on account from Wong Co., $4,060.50.
   13. Purchased office equipment on account from Gregg Equipment Co., $11,900.
   15. Purchased merchandise on account from James Co., $3,100.
   18. Received a credit memorandum from Tyler Supply for office supplies returned, $22.50.
   19. Purchased merchandise on account from Eber Co., $2,500.
   23. Purchased store supplies on account from Tyler Supply, $325.
   26. Received a credit memorandum from Lane Co. as an allowance for damaged merchandise, $500.
   26. Purchased merchandise on account from James Co., $475.15.
   30. Purchased office supplies on account from Tyler Supply, $375.10.

Instructions

1. Insert the following balances in the general ledger as of May 1:

114	Store Supplies	$ 603.50
115	Office Supplies	295.00
122	Office Equipment	29,700.00
211	Accounts Payable	11,855.10
511	Purchases	102,150.50
512	Purchases Returns and Allowances	3,050.25

2. Insert the following balances in the accounts payable ledger as of May 1:

Eber Co.	$3,150.00
Gregg Equipment Co.	—
James Co.	4,020.75
Lane Co.	4,684.35
Tyler Supply	—
Wong Co.	—

3. Journalize the transactions for May, using a purchases journal similar to the one illustrated in this chapter and a two-column general journal. Post to the creditor accounts in the accounts payable ledger immediately after each entry.

4. Post the general journal and the purchases journal to the accounts in the general ledger.

5. a. What is the sum of the balances in the subsidiary ledger at May 31?
    b. What is the balance of the controlling account at May 31?

PROBLEM 7-5B
PURCHASES AND CASH
PAYMENTS JOURNALS;
ACCOUNTS PAYABLE AND
GENERAL LEDGERS
Objective 4

Carr Co. was established on March 15 of the current year. Transactions related to purchases, returns and allowances, and cash payments during the remainder of March are as follows:

Mar. 16. Issued Check No. 1 in payment of rent for March, $1,000.
   16. Purchased store equipment on account from Harper Equipment Co., $9,900.
   17. Purchased merchandise on account from Carter Clothing, $3,250.
   18. Issued Check No. 2 in payment of store supplies, $140, and office supplies, $75.
   19. Purchased merchandise on account from Hernandez Clothing Co., $5,920.
   20. Purchased merchandise on account from Adams Co., $4,600.
   22. Received a credit memorandum from Hernandez Clothing Co. for returned merchandise, $220.
       Post the journals to the accounts payable ledger.
   24. Issued Check No. 3 to Harper Equipment Co. in payment of invoice, $9,900.
   25. Received a credit memorandum from Adams Co. for defective merchandise, $300.
   26. Issued Check No. 4 to Carter Clothing in payment of invoice of $3,250 less 2% discount.
   28. Issued Check No. 5 to a cash customer for merchandise returned, $65.
   28. Issued Check No. 6 to Hernandez Clothing Co. in payment of the balance owed less 2% discount.
   28. Purchased merchandise on account from Adams Co., $5,250.
       Post the journals to the accounts payable ledger.
   30. Purchased the following from Harper Equipment Co. on account: store supplies, $110; office supplies, $42; office equipment, $3,450.
   30. Issued Check No. 7 to Adams Co. in payment of invoice of $4,600 less the credit of $300 and 1% discount.
   30. Purchased merchandise on account from Carter Clothing, $1,200.
   31. Issued Check No. 8 in payment of store supplies, $170.
   31. Issued Check No. 9 in payment of sales salaries, $2,200.
   31. Received a credit memorandum from Harper Equipment Co. for defect in office equipment, $50.
       Post the journals to the accounts payable ledger.

SPREADSHEET
PROBLEM

Instructions

1. Journalize the transactions for March. Use a purchases journal and a cash payments journal, similar to those illustrated in this chapter, and a two-column general journal. Refer to the following partial chart of accounts:

111	Cash	412	Sales Returns and Allowances
116	Store Supplies	511	Purchases
117	Office Supplies	512	Purchases Returns and Allowances
121	Store Equipment	513	Purchases Discounts
123	Office Equipment	611	Sales Salaries Expense
211	Accounts Payable	712	Rent Expense

   At the points indicated in the narrative of transactions, post to the following accounts in the accounts payable ledger:

   Adams Co.   Harper Equipment Co.
   Carter Clothing   Hernandez Clothing Co.

2. Post the individual entries (Other Accounts columns of the purchases journal and the cash payments journal; both columns of the general journal) to the appropriate general ledger accounts.
3. Total each of the columns of the purchases journal and the cash payments journal and post the appropriate totals to the general ledger. (Because the problem does not include transactions related to cash receipts, the cash account in the ledger will have a credit balance.)
4. Prepare a schedule of accounts payable.

PROBLEM 7-6B
ALL JOURNALS AND
GENERAL LEDGER; TRIAL
BALANCE
Objective 4

The transactions completed by Miles Company during July, the first month of the current fiscal year, were as follows:

July 1. Issued Check No. 920 for July rent, $2,000.
   2. Purchased equipment on account from Mann Co., $7,500.
   2. Purchased merchandise on account from Evans Co., $4,250.
   3. Issued Invoice No. 832 to Black Co., $1,975.

July   7. Received check for $2,475 from Owens Co. in payment of $2,500 invoice less 1% discount.

   7. Issued Check No. 921 for miscellaneous selling expense, $190.

   7. Received credit memorandum from Evans Co. for returned merchandise, $250.

   8. Issued Invoice No. 833 to Kane Co., $5,000.

   9. Issued Check No. 922 for $9,310 to Frank Co. in payment of $9,500 invoice less 2% discount.

   9. Received check for $7,425 from Baker Manufacturing Co. in payment of $7,500 invoice less 1% discount.

  10. Issued Check No. 923 to Davis Enterprises in payment of $3,100 invoice, no discount.

  12. Issued Invoice No. 834 to Owens Co., $3,500.

  12. Issued Check No. 924 for $930 to Ross Co. in payment of account, no discount.

  12. Received check for $775 from Black Co. on account, no discount.

  14. Issued credit memorandum to Owens Co. for damaged merchandise, $500.

  15. Issued Check No. 925 for $3,920 to Evans Co. in payment of $4,000 balance less 2% discount.

  15. Issued Check No. 926 for $2,250 for cash purchase of merchandise.

  15. Cash sales for July 1-15, $23,750.

  18. Purchased merchandise on account from Davis Enterprises, $6,420.

  19. Received check for return of merchandise that had been purchased for cash, $90.

  19. Issued Check No. 927 for miscellaneous administrative expense, $145.

  21. Purchased the following on account from Cass Supply Co.: store supplies, $225; office supplies, $195.

  22. Issued Check No. 928 in payment of advertising expense, $945.

  23. Issued Invoice No. 835 to Baker Manufacturing Co., $1,950.

  24. Purchased the following on account from Frank Co.: merchandise, $4,170; store supplies, $130.

  25. Issued Invoice No. 836 to Jackson Co., $3,290.

  25. Received check for $2,970 from Owens Co. in payment of $3,000 balance less discount.

  29. Issued Check No. 929 for $7,500 to Mann Co. in payment of invoice of July 2, no discount.

  30. Issued Check No. 930 to D. D. Miles as a personal withdrawal, $3,000.

  31. Issued Check No. 931 for monthly salaries as follows: sales salaries, $11,100; office salaries, $4,500.

  31. Cash sales for July 16-31, $26,150.

  31. Issued Check No. 932 in payment of transportation charges for merchandise purchased during the month, $465.

Instructions

1. Enter the following account balances in the general ledger as of July 1:

111	Cash	$ 9,850
113	Accounts Receivable	12,975
114	Merchandise Inventory	35,500
115	Store Supplies	545
116	Office Supplies	360
117	Prepaid Insurance	2,100
121	Equipment	47,250
122	Accumulated Depreciation	22,250
211	Accounts Payable	13,530
311	D. D. Miles, Capital	72,800
312	D. D. Miles, Drawing	—
411	Sales	—
412	Sales Returns and Allowances	—
413	Sales Discounts	—

511	Purchases	—
512	Purchases Returns and Allowances	—
513	Purchases Discounts	—
514	Transportation In	—
611	Sales Salaries Expense	—
612	Advertising Expense	—
619	Miscellaneous Selling Expense	—
711	Office Salaries Expense	—
712	Rent Expense	—
719	Miscellaneous Administrative Expense	—

2. Journalize the transactions for July, using the following journals similar to those illustrated in this chapter: single-column sales journal, cash receipts journal, purchases journal, cash payments journal, and two-column general journal. The terms of all sales on account are FOB shipping point, 1/10, n/30. Assume that an assistant makes daily postings to the individual accounts in the accounts payable ledger and the accounts receivable ledger.
3. Post the appropriate individual entries to the general ledger.
4. Total each of the columns of the special journals and post the appropriate totals to the general ledger; insert the account balances.
5. Prepare a trial balance.
6. Verify the agreement of each subsidiary ledger with its controlling account. Balances of the accounts in the subsidiary ledgers as of July 31 are as follows:

Accounts receivable: 2,200; 1,975; 5,000; 1,950; 3,290
Accounts payable: 6,420; 420; 4,300

SOLUTIONS SOFTWARE

Instructions for Solving Problem 7-6B Using Solutions Software

1. Load opening balances.
2. Save the opening balances file to your drive and directory.
3. Set the run date to July 31 of the current year and enter your name.
4. Key the journal entries.
5. Display the journal entries.
6. Display a trial balance.
7. Save your data file to disk.
8. End the session.

PROBLEM 7-7B
SALES JOURNAL WITH
SALES TAX PAYABLE
COLUMN; ACCOUNTS
RECEIVABLE AND GENERAL
LEDGERS
Objective 5

HLC Company was established on May 15 of the current year. Its sales of merchandise on account and related returns and allowances during the remainder of the month are as follows. Terms of all sales were 1/15, n/30, FOB shipping point. The sales tax was 6% on all sales as well as sales returns and allowances.

May 21. Sold merchandise on account to Boritz Co., Invoice No. 1, $1,200 plus sales tax.
22. Sold merchandise on account to Stark Co., Invoice No. 2, $2,750 plus sales tax.
24. Sold merchandise on account to Morris Co., Invoice No. 3, $3,100 plus sales tax.
25. Issued Credit Memorandum No. 1 for $100 plus sales tax of $6 to Boritz Co. for merchandise returned.
27. Sold merchandise on account to C. D. Walters Co., Invoice No. 4, $2,500 plus sales tax.
28. Sold merchandise on account to A. Udall Co., Invoice No. 5, $1,500 plus sales tax.
28. Issued Credit Memorandum No. 2 for $150 plus sales tax of $9 to Stark Co. for merchandise returned.
30. Sold merchandise on account to Stark Co., Invoice No. 6, $2,900 plus sales tax.
30. Issued Credit Memorandum No. 3 for $200 plus sales tax of $12 to C. D. Walters Co. for damages to merchandise caused by faulty packing.
31. Sold merchandise on account to Morris Co., Invoice No. 7, $1,000 plus sales tax.

SPREADSHEET PROBLEM

Instructions

1. Journalize the transactions for May, using a three-column sales journal and a two-column general journal. Post to the following customer accounts in the accounts receivable ledger and insert the balance immediately after recording each entry: Boritz Co.; Morris Co.; Stark Co.; A. Udall Co.; C. D. Walters Co.

2. Post the general journal and the sales journal to the following accounts in the general ledger, inserting the account balances only after the last postings:

   113 Accounts Receivable
   215 Sales Tax Payable
   411 Sales
   412 Sales Returns and Allowances

3. a. What is the sum of the balances of the accounts in the subsidiary ledger at May 31?
   b. What is the balance of the controlling account at May 31?

MINI-CASE 7 CREATIVE JEWELERS

For the past few years, your aunt has operated a small jewelry store, Creative Jewelers. Its current annual revenues are approximately $450,000. Because the company's accountant has been taking more and more time each month to record all transactions in a two-column journal and to prepare the financial statements, your aunt is considering improving the company's accounting system by adding special journals and subsidiary ledgers. Your aunt has asked you to help her with this project. She has compiled the following information:

1.

Type of Transaction	Estimated Frequency per Month
Purchases of merchandise on account	200
Sales on account	175
Cash receipts from customers on account	150
Daily cash register summaries of cash sales	25
Purchases of merchandise for cash	20
Purchases of office supplies on account	5
Purchases of store supplies on account	5
Cash payments for utilities expenses	4
Cash purchases of office supplies	4
Cash purchases of store supplies	4

2. For merchandise purchases of high dollar-value items, Creative Jewelers issues notes payable at current interest rates to vendors. These notes are issued because many of the high-value items may not sell immediately and the issuance of the notes reduces the need to maintain large balances of cash or assets that can be readily converted to cash. Notes are issued for approximately 10% of the purchases on account.

3. All purchases discounts are taken when available.

4. A sales discount of 1/10, n/30 is offered to all credit customers.

5. A local sales tax of 6% is collected on all intrastate sales of merchandise.

6. Monthly financial statements are prepared.

Instructions:

1. ▉▉▉ ▸ Briefly discuss the circumstances under which special journals would be used in place of a two-column journal. Include in your answer your recommendations for Creative Jewelers' accounting system.

2. Assume that your aunt has decided to use a sales journal and a purchases journal. Design the format for each journal, giving special consideration to the needs of Creative Jewelers.

3. Which subsidiary ledgers would you recommend for Creative Jewelers?

COMPREHENSIVE PROBLEM 3

The transactions completed by Redman Supply Co. during January, the first month of the current fiscal year, were as follows:

Jan. 2. Issued Check No. 810 for January rent, $1,500.
      2. Purchased merchandise on account from Dane Co., $2,250.
      2. Purchased equipment on account from Lee Equipment Co., $3,700.
      3. Issued Invoice No. 942 to C. Block Co., $1,320.
      7. Received check for $2,744 from Nichols Co. in payment of $2,800 invoice less 2% discount.
      7. Issued Check No. 811 for miscellaneous selling expense, $205.
      8. Received credit memorandum from Dane Co. for merchandise returned to them, $150.

Jan. 8. Issued Invoice No. 943 to Jackson Co., $5,000.

9. Issued Check No. 812 for $9,310 to Easterly Co. in payment of $9,500 invoice less 2% discount.

9. Received check for $9,604 from Baker Manufacturing Co. in payment of $9,800 invoice less 2% discount.

10. Issued Check No. 813 to Collins Enterprises in payment of $2,120 invoice, no discount.

10. Issued Invoice No. 944 to Nichols Co., $3,225.

11. Issued Check No. 814 to Peak Co. in payment of account, $705, no discount.

12. Received check for $775 from C. Block Co. on account, no discount.

14. Issued credit memorandum to Nichols Co. for damaged merchandise, $225.

15. Issued Check No. 815 for $2,058 to Dane Co. in payment of $2,100 balance less 2% discount.

15. Issued Check No. 816 for $1,250 for cash purchase of merchandise.

15. Cash sales for January 2–15, $18,942.

17. Purchased merchandise on account from Collins Enterprises, $6,420.

18. Received check for return of merchandise that had been purchased for cash, $75.

18. Issued Check No. 817 for miscellaneous administrative expense, $130.

21. Purchased the following on account from Bunn Supply Co.: store supplies, $215; office supplies, $170.

22. Issued Check No. 818 in payment of advertising expense, $610.

23. Issued Invoice No. 945 to Baker Manufacturing Co., $1,950.

24. Purchased the following on account from Easterly Co.: merchandise, $3,125; store supplies, $110.

25. Issued Invoice No. 946 to Jackson Co., $3,290.

25. Received check for $2,940 from Nichols Co. in payment of $3,000 balance less 2% discount.

26. Issued Check No. 819 to Lee Equipment Co. in payment of $3,700 invoice of January 2, no discount.

29. Issued Check No. 820 for $2,500 for cash purchase of merchandise.

30. Issued Check No. 821 for monthly salaries as follows: sales salaries, $9,600; office salaries, $3,800.

31. Cash sales for January 16–31, $19,250.

31. Issued Check No. 822 for cash purchase of merchandise, $390.

Instructions

1. Enter the following account balances in the general ledger as of January 1:

111	Cash	$ 9,100
113	Accounts Receivable	16,200
114	Merchandise Inventory	31,500
115	Store Supplies	410
116	Office Supplies	225
117	Prepaid Insurance	2,100
121	Equipment	40,650
122	Accumulated Depreciation	12,350
211	Accounts Payable	12,325
311	D. L. Redman, Capital	75,510
411	Sales	—
412	Sales Returns and Allowances	—
413	Sales Discounts	—
511	Purchases	—
512	Purchases Returns and Allowances	—
513	Purchases Discounts	—
611	Sales Salaries Expense	—
612	Advertising Expense	—
619	Miscellaneous Selling Expense	—
711	Office Salaries Expense	—
712	Rent Expense	—
719	Miscellaneous Administrative Expense	—

2. Enter the following account balances in the accounts receivable ledger as of January 1:

Baker Manufacturing Co.	$9,800
C. Block Co.	775
Jackson Co.	—
Nichols Co.	2,800
Wilson and Son	2,825

3. Enter the following account balances in the accounts payable ledger as of January 1:

Bunn Supply Co.	—
Collins Enterprises	$2,120
Dane Co.	—
Easterly Co.	9,500
Lee Equipment Co.	—
Peak Co.	705

4. Journalize the transactions for January, using the following special journals similar to those illustrated in this chapter: single-column sales journal, cash receipts journal, purchases journal, cash payments journal, and a two-column general journal. The terms of all sales on account are 2/15, n/60, FOB shipping point. Post to the accounts receivable and accounts payable ledgers and insert the balances immediately after recording each entry.
5. Post the appropriate individual entries to the general ledger.
6. Add the columns of the special journals and post the appropriate totals to the general ledger; insert the account balances.
7. Prepare a trial balance.
8. Prepare schedules of accounts receivable and accounts payable as of January 31 and compare the total of each schedule with the balance of the appropriate controlling account.

Instructions for Solving Comprehensive Problem 3 Using Solutions Software

1. Load opening balances.
2. Save the opening balances file to your drive and directory.
3. Set the run date to January 31 of the current year and enter your name.
4. Key the journal entries.
5. Display the journal entries.
6. Display a trial balance.
7. Save your data file to disk.
8. End the session.

ANSWERS TO SELF-EXAMINATION QUESTIONS

1. **C** The task of revising an accounting system is composed of three phases. Systems analysis (answer A) is the initial phase involving the determination of the informational needs, sources of such information, and deficiencies in the procedures and data processing methods currently employed. Systems design (answer B) is the phase in which proposals for changes are developed. Systems implementation (answer C) is the final phase involving carrying out or implementing the proposals for changes. Systems training (answer D) is not a separate phase of revising an accounting system, but is considered part of the systems implementation.

2. **A** The policies and procedures established by an enterprise to provide reasonable assurance that the enterprise's goals will be achieved are called internal controls (answer A). The three phases of installing or changing an accounting system are (1) analysis (answer B), (2) design (answer C), and (3) implementation (answer D). Systems analysis is the determination of the informational needs, sources of such information, and deficiencies in the procedures and data processing methods presently used. Systems design refers to the design of a new system or change in the present system based on the systems analysis. The carrying out of proposals for the design of a system is called sys-

tems implementation.

3. **B** All payments of cash for any purpose are recorded in the cash payments journal (answer B). Only purchases of merchandise or other items on account are recorded in the purchases journal (answer A). All sales of merchandise on account are recorded in the sales journal (answer C), and all receipts of cash are recorded in the cash receipts journal (answer D).

4. **A** The general term used to describe the type of separate ledger that contains a substantial number of individual accounts with a common characteristic is a subsidiary ledger (answer A). The creditors ledger (answer B), sometimes called the accounts payable ledger (answer C), is a specific subsidiary ledger containing only individual accounts with creditors. Likewise, the accounts receivable ledger (answer D), also called the customers ledger, is a specific subsidiary ledger containing only individual accounts with customers.

5. **B** The controlling account for the customers ledger (the ledger that contains the individual accounts with customers) is Accounts Receivable (answer B). The accounts payable account (answer A) is the controlling account for the creditors ledger. There are no subsidiary ledgers for the sales (answer C) and purchases (answer D) accounts.

You and Accounting

When you receive the monthly statement for your checking account, you may simply accept the bank statement as correct. However, banks can make mistakes. For example, at the bottom right-hand corner of each check returned from the bank is a magnetic coding that has been entered by a bank clerk. This coding indicates the amount of the check. If the clerk enters the coding incorrectly, then the check will be processed for a wrong amount. To illustrate, the following check written for $25 was incorrectly processed as $250:

Ed Smith
1026 3rd Ave., So.
Lansing, Wisconsin 58241

7406

7/23 19 94   64-7088/2611

PAY TO THE ORDER OF   Jones C. $ 25 00/100

Twenty-Five and no/100   DOLLARS

FIRST FEDERAL
SAVINGS BANK
OF WISCONSIN
LANSING, WISCONSIN

FOR   Ed Smith

⑆261170889⑆ 04 33 503662⑈ 7406 ⑈000002 5000⑈

Not only can banks make errors, but so can you. To find both types of errors, the balance of your checking account should be brought into agreement, or reconciled, monthly with your bank statement balance. This chapter discusses how businesses reconcile their monthly bank statements as one feature of a system for accounting for and controlling cash. The basic techniques of reconciling a business bank account also apply to your individual checking account.

Chapter 8
Cash

LEARNING OBJECTIVES
After studying this chapter, you should be able to:

Objective 1
Prepare a bank reconciliation and journalize any necessary entries.

Objective 2
Summarize basic procedures for achieving internal control over cash receipts, including the use of cash change funds and the cash short and over account.

Objective 3
Summarize basic procedures for achieving control over cash payments, including the use of a voucher system, a discounts lost account, and a petty cash account.

Objective 4
Summarize how cash is presented in the balance sheet.

Objective 5
Define electronic funds transfer and give an example of how it is used to process cash transactions.

The qualities of a properly designed accounting system and the principles of internal control for directing operations have been discussed in preceding chapters. This chapter applies these principles to the design of systems for controlling cash and the accounting for cash transactions.

BANK RECONCILIATIONS AS A CONTROL OVER CASH

Objective 1
Prepare a bank reconciliation and
journalize any necessary entries.

Because of the ease with which money can be transferred, cash is the asset most likely to be diverted and used improperly by employees. In addition, many transactions either directly or indirectly affect the receipt or the payment of cash. It is therefore necessary to use special controls for safeguarding cash.

The Bank Account as a Tool for Controlling Cash

One of the main tools for controlling cash is the bank account. To maximize control over cash, all cash received should be deposited in a bank account. Likewise, all cash payments should be disbursed from a bank account. When such a system is strictly followed, there is a double record of cash—one by the business and the other by the bank. Thus, when the amount of cash recorded by the business is compared and reconciled with the amount of cash recorded by the bank, any errors and misuse or thefts may be detected.

The forms used by a business with a bank account are a signature card, deposit ticket, check, and record of checks drawn. These forms are described below.

SIGNATURE CARD. At the time an account is opened, a **signature card** is signed by each person authorized to sign checks written on the account. This card is used by the bank to verify the signatures on checks presented for payment. Also, at the time an account is opened, an identifying number is assigned to the account.

DEPOSIT TICKET. The details of a deposit are listed by the depositor on a printed form supplied by the bank. These **deposit tickets** may be prepared in duplicate. A copy of the deposit ticket is stamped or initialed by the bank's teller and given to the depositor as a receipt. Other types of receipts may also be used to give the depositor written proof of the date and the total amount of the deposit.

CHECK. A **check** is a written instrument signed by the depositor, ordering the bank to pay a sum of money to an individual or entity. There are three parties to a check—the drawer, the drawee, and the payee. The **drawer** is the one who signs the check, ordering payment by the bank. The **drawee** is the bank on which the check is drawn. The **payee** is the party to whom payment is to be made.

When checks are issued to pay bills, they are recorded as credits to Cash on the day issued. The credit to Cash is recorded even though the checks will not be presented by the payee to the drawer's bank until a later date. Likewise, when checks are received from customers, they are recorded as debits to Cash.

Check forms may be obtained in many styles. The name and the address of the depositor are often printed on each check. In addition, checks are normally prenumbered, so that they can easily be kept track of as an aid to internal control. Most banks use automatic sorting and posting equipment. This equipment requires that the bank's identification number and the depositor's account number be printed on each check. These numbers are usually printed along the lower margin in machine-readable magnetic ink. When the check is presented for payment, the amount for which it is drawn is inserted next to the account number, also in magnetic ink. A check that has been processed by a bank was illustrated earlier in this chapter.

RECORD OF CHECKS DRAWN. A record of the basic details of a check should be prepared at the time the check is written. A copy of each check written or a stub from which the check is detached may be used as the basis for recording transactions in the cash payments journal. A small booklet called a transactions register may also be used.

The invoice number or other data may be inserted in spaces provided on the check or on an attachment to the check. Normally, checks issued to a creditor on account are sent with a form that identifies the specific invoice that is being paid. The purpose of this form, sometimes called a **remittance advice**, is to make sure that proper credit is recorded in the accounts of the creditor. In this way, mistakes are less likely to occur. A check and remittance advice is shown in Exhibit 1.

Exhibit 1
Check and Remittance Advice

MONROE COMPANY

813 Greenwood Street   Detroit, MI 48206-4070

April 12 19 94

363

9-42
720

| Pay to the Order of | Hammond Office Products | $ 921.20 |

Nine hundred twenty-one 20/100------------------------------- Dollars

A **AMERICAN NATIONAL BANK**
NB **OF DETROIT**
DETROIT, MI 48201-2500   (313)933-8547   MEMBER FDIC

K. R Simons _____ Treasurer

Earl M. Hartman _____ Vice President

⑆072000423⑆ ⑈627042 363⑈

DETACH THIS PORTION BEFORE CASHING

Date	Description	Gross Amount	Deductions	Net Amount
4/12/94	Invoice No. 529482	940.00	18.80	921.20

MONROE COMPANY

Before depositing the check at the bank, the payee removes the remittance advice. The remittance advice may then be used by the payee as written proof of the details of the cash receipt.

Bank Statement

Banks usually maintain a record of all checking account transactions. A summary of all transactions, called a statement of account, is mailed to the depositor, usually once each month. Like any account with a customer or a creditor, the bank statement shows the beginning balance, additions, deductions, and the balance at the end of the period.

The depositor's checks received by the bank during the period may accompany the bank statement, arranged in the order of payment. The paid or canceled checks are perforated or stamped "Paid," together with the date of payment. Debit or credit memorandums describing other entries in the depositor's account may also be enclosed with the statement. For example, the bank may have debited the depositor's account for service charges or for deposited checks returned because of insufficient funds. It may have credited the account for receipts from notes receivable left for collection, for loans to the depositor, or for interest.[1] A typical bank statement is shown in Exhibit 2.

---

[1] Although interest-bearing checking accounts are common for individuals, Federal Reserve Regulation Q prohibits the paying of interest on corporate checking accounts.

Vouchers are normally prenumbered for control purposes. Each voucher provides space for the name and address of the creditor, the date, and a summary of the basic details of the supporting document. Such basic details in the voucher shown include the invoice number and the amount and terms of the invoice. One half of the back of the voucher is devoted to the account distribution and the other half to summaries of the voucher and the details of payment. Spaces are also provided for the signature or initials of certain employees.

A voucher must be prepared for every expenditure. A check may not be issued except in payment of a properly authorized voucher. Vouchers may be paid immediately after they are prepared or at a later date, depending upon the credit terms.

A voucher is normally prepared by the Accounting Department on the basis of an invoice or a memorandum that serves as support for the expenditure. A voucher is usually prepared only after the following steps have been completed and noted on the invoice:

1. The invoice is compared with a copy of the purchase order to verify quantities, prices, and terms.
2. The invoice is compared with the receiving report to verify receipt of the items billed.
3. The arithmetical accuracy of the invoice is proved.

After all data except details of payment have been inserted, the invoice or other supporting evidence is attached to the voucher. The voucher is then given to the proper official for approval.

VOUCHER REGISTER. After a voucher has been approved, it is recorded in a journal called a **voucher register**. The voucher register is similar to and replaces the purchases journal in a periodic inventory system. A typical voucher register is shown in Exhibit 4.

Vouchers are entered in a voucher register in numerical order. Each voucher is recorded as a credit to Accounts Payable (sometimes entitled Vouchers Payable) and as a debit to the account or accounts to be debited for the expenditure.

Exhibit 4
Voucher Register

Page 11   VOUCHER

Date	Vou. No.	Payee	Date Paid	Check No.	Accounts Payable Cr.	Purchases Dr.
19-						
July 1	451	Allied Mfg. Co.	7-8	863	450.00	450.00
1	452	Chavez Realtors	7-1	856	600.00	
2	453	Foster Publications	7-2	857	52. 50	
3	454	Benson Express Co.	7-3	859	36.80	24.20
3	455	Roberson's Supply Co.		*NOT PAID*	784.20	
3	456	Moore & Co.	7-11	866	1,236.00	1,236.00
6	457	J. L. Brown Co.	7-6	860	22.50	
6	458	Turner Co.		*NOT PAID*	395.30	395.30
				NOT PAID		
31	477	Central Motors			112.20	
31	478	Petty Cash	7-31	883	48.60	
31					15,551.60	11,640.30
					(212)	(511)

To determine the reasons for any differences in the balance of Cash in Bank and the ending cash balance shown on the bank statement, a bank reconciliation should be prepared. A **bank reconciliation** is divided into two sections. The first section begins with the cash balance according to the bank statement and ends with the adjusted balance. The second section begins with the cash balance according to the depositor's records and ends with the adjusted balance. The two amounts designated as the adjusted balance must be equal. The form and the content of the bank reconciliation are outlined as follows:

Cash balance according to **bank statement**			$XXX
Add:	Additions by depositor not on bank statement	$XX	
	Bank errors	XX	XX
			$XXX
Deduct:	Deductions by depositor not on bank statement	$XX	
	Bank errors	XX	XX
Adjusted balance			$XXX
Cash balance according to **depositor's records**			$XXX
Add:	Additions by bank not recorded by depositor	$XX	
	Depositor errors	XX	XX
			$XXX
Deduct:	Deductions by bank not recorded by depositor	$XX	
	Depositor errors	XX	XX
Adjusted balance			$XXX

The following steps are useful in finding the reconciling items and determining the adjusted balance of Cash in Bank:

1. Individual deposits listed on the bank statement are compared with unrecorded deposits appearing in the preceding period's reconciliation and with deposit receipts or other records of deposits. *Deposits not recorded by the bank are added to the balance according to the bank statement.*
2. Paid checks are compared with outstanding checks appearing on the preceding period's reconciliation and with checks listed in the cash payments journal. *Checks issued that have not been paid by the bank are outstanding and are deducted from the balance according to the bank statement.*
3. Bank credit memorandums are compared to entries in the cash receipts journal. For example, a bank would issue a credit memorandum for a note receivable and interest that it collected for a customer. *Credit memorandums that have not been recorded in the cash receipts journal are added to the balance according to the depositor's records.*
4. Bank debit memorandums are compared to entries in the cash payments journal. For example, a bank normally issues debit memorandums for service charges and check printing charges. A bank also issues debit memorandums for not-sufficient-funds checks. A **not-sufficient-funds (NSF) check** is a customer's check that was recorded and deposited but was not paid when it was presented to the customer's bank for payment. NSF checks are normally charged back to the customer's account receivable. *Debit memorandums that have not been recorded are deducted from the balance according to the depositor's records.*
5. Errors discovered during the preceding steps are listed separately on the reconciliation. For example, if an amount has been recorded incorrectly by the depositor, the amount of the error should be added to or deducted from the Cash in Bank balance. Similarly, errors by the bank should be added to or deducted from the cash balance according to the bank statement.

ILLUSTRATION OF BANK RECONCILIATION. The bank statement for Monroe Company in Exhibit 2 shows a balance of $3,359.78 as of July 31. The balance in Cash in Bank in Monroe Company's ledger as of the same date is $2,249.99. The following reconciling items are revealed by using the steps outlined above:

Deposit of July 31 not recorded on bank statement $ 816.20
Checks outstanding: No. 812, $1,061.00; No. 878, $435.39;
     No. 883, $48.60   1,544.99
Note plus interest of $8 collected by bank (credit memorandum),
     not recorded in cash receipts journal   408.00
Bank service charges (debit memorandum) not recorded in cash
     payments journal   18.00
Check No. 879 for $732.26 to Taylor Co. on account, recorded in
     cash payments journal as $723.26   9.00

    The bank reconciliation based on the bank statement and the reconciling items is as follows:

Monroe Company		
Bank Reconciliation		
July 31, 1994		
Cash balance according to bank statement		$3,359.78
Add deposit of July 31, not recorded by bank		816.20
		$4,175.98
Deduct outstanding checks:		
No. 812	$1,061.00	
No. 878	435.39	
No. 883	48.60	1,544.99
Adjusted balance		$2,630.99
Cash balance according to depositor's records		$2,249.99
Add note and interest collected by bank		408.00
		$2,657.99
Deduct: Bank service charges	$ 18.00	
Error in recording Check No. 879	9.00	27.00
Adjusted balance		$2,630.99

ENTRIES BASED ON BANK RECONCILIATION. No entries are necessary on the depositor's records as a result of the information included in the first section of the bank reconciliation. This section begins with the cash balance according to the bank statement. However, the bank should be notified of any errors that need to be corrected on its records.

    Any addition or deduction items in the second section of the bank reconciliation must be recorded in the depositor's accounts. This section begins with the cash balance according to the depositor's records. Entries should be made for bank memorandums not recorded by the depositor and any depositor's errors. These entries may be recorded in the appropriate special journals if posting for the month has not been completed, or they may be recorded in the general journal.

    The entries for Monroe Company, based on the bank reconciliation above, are as follows:

July 31	Cash in Bank	408	
	Notes Receivable		400
	Interest Income		8
	Note collected by bank.		
31	Miscellaneous Administrative Expense	18	
	Accounts Payable—Taylor Co.	9	
	Cash in Bank		27
	Bank service charges and error in recording		
	Check No. 879.		

After the above entries have been posted, Cash in Bank will have a debit balance of $2,630.99. This balance agrees with the adjusted cash balance shown on the bank reconciliation. It is the amount of cash available as of July 31 and the amount that would be reported on the balance sheet on that date.

IMPORTANCE OF BANK RECONCILIATION. The bank reconciliation is an important part of the system of internal control. It is a means of comparing recorded cash, as shown by the accounting records, with the amount of cash reported by the bank. It thus provides for finding and correcting errors and irregularities. To enhance internal control, the bank reconciliation should be prepared by an employee who does not take part in and record cash transactions with the bank. Without a proper separation of these duties, cash is more likely to be embezzled. For example, an employee who takes part in all of these duties could prepare an unauthorized check, omit it from the accounts, and cash it. To hide the theft, the employee could understate the amount of the outstanding checks on future bank reconciliations by the amount of the unauthorized check.

INTERNAL CONTROL OF CASH RECEIPTS

Objective 2
Summarize basic procedures for achieving internal control over cash receipts, including the use of cash change funds and the cash short and over account.

Retailers normally use special control procedures for safeguarding and handling the large volume of cash receipts. To protect cash from theft and misuse, a business enterprise must control cash from the time it is received until it can be deposited in a bank. Such procedures are called **protective controls**.

Procedures that are designed to detect theft or misuse of cash are called **detective controls**. In a sense, detective controls are also preventive in nature, since employees are less likely to steal or misuse cash if they know there is a good chance they will be detected.

Department stores and other retail businesses normally receive cash from two main sources: (1) over the counter from cash customers and (2) by mail from credit customers making payments on account. Cash is received over the counter when a customer pays cash for the purchase of merchandise. One of the most important controls to protect cash received in over-the-counter sales is a cash register. When the clerk (cashier) enters the amount of the sale, the cash register normally displays the amount to the customer. The customer can then verify the accuracy of the purchase, which serves as an additional control.

The recording of the sale in the cash register establishes the initial accountability for the cash received. Most cash registers are designed to record this initial data on paper tapes. In addition, most businesses prohibit cashiers from changing or otherwise altering the cash register tapes without the approval of a supervisor.

At the end of the day or work shift, the cashiers count the cash in their cash drawers and record the amounts on cash or sales memorandum forms. The cashiers' supervisor removes the cash register tapes on which total receipts were recorded. The supervisor counts the cash and compares the total with the memoranda and the tapes, noting any differences. Normally, the cash is then placed in a store safe until it can be deposited in the bank. The tapes and memorandums are forwarded to the Accounting Department, where they become the basis for entries in the cash receipts journal.

Cash is received in the mail when customers pay their bills. This cash is usually in the form of checks and money orders. Most companies' invoices are designed so that customers return a remittance advice with these payments. The employee who opens the incoming mail should initially compare the amount of cash received with the amount shown on the remittance advice. Any differences are noted. If a customer does not return a remittance advice, an employee prepares one on a form designed for such use. Like the cash register, this record of cash received establishes the initial accountability for the cash. It also helps ensure that the posting to the customer's account is accurate.

All cash received in the mail is sent to the Cashier's Department. An employee there combines it with the receipts from cash sales and prepares a bank deposit ticket. The remittance advices and their summary totals are delivered to the Accounting Department. An accounting clerk then prepares the entries in the cash receipts journal and posts to the customer accounts in the subsidiary ledger.

After the cash is deposited in the bank, the duplicate deposit tickets or other bank receipt forms are returned to the Accounting Department. An accounting clerk then compares the total amount deposited with the amount recorded as the cash receipt. This control helps ensure that all the cash is deposited and that no cash is lost or stolen on the way to the bank. Any shortages are thus promptly detected.

The separation of the duties of the Cashier's Department, which handles cash, and the Accounting Department, which records cash, is a preventive control. If Accounting Department employees both handled and recorded cash, an employee could steal cash and change the accounting records to hide the theft.

An important detective control for the handling of cash receipts is the use of a bank account and the bank reconciliation. Bank reconciliations are useful in detecting errors by both the bank and the business in recording cash receipts. Bank reconciliations may also be useful in detecting thefts of cash. For example, assume that an assistant store manager decides to borrow (take) cash from the daily deposits on the way to the bank. The assistant store manager then alters the daily deposit slip from the bank to show the amount of cash that should have been deposited. When the store manager prepares the bank reconciliation at the end of the month, the amount stolen will be evident because the daily deposits on the bank statement will not agree with the store's records. By preparing a bank reconciliation on a timely basis, the loss is detected before large amounts are stolen.

Cash Change Funds

Retail stores and other businesses that receive cash directly from customers must keep some currency and coins on hand in order to make change. This cash is recorded in a cash change fund account.

The cash change fund may be established by drawing a check for the required amount, debiting Cash on Hand, and crediting Cash in Bank. No additional charges or credits to the cash on hand account are necessary unless the amount of the fund is to be increased or decreased.

The cash on hand may be divided up among the various cash registers and drawers. The amount in each cash register or drawer is recorded for later use in reconciling cash sales for the day. The total amount of cash received during the day is deposited, and the original amount of the change fund is retained. The desired makeup of the fund is maintained by exchanging bills or coins at the bank.

Cash Short and Over

The amount of cash on hand at the end of each day should be the beginning amount of cash in each cash register plus the cash sales for the day. However, the amount of actual cash on hand at the end of the day often differs from this amount. This occurs because of errors in recording cash sales or errors in making change.

Differences in the amount of cash counted and the amount of cash in the records are normally recorded in an account entitled Cash Short and Over. A common method for handling entries in this account is to add two special columns to the cash receipts journal. All cash shortages are recorded in a Cash Short and Over Debit column. All cash overages are recorded in a Cash Short and Over Credit column. For example, the following entry records one day's cash sales, when the actual cash received is less than the amount indicated by the cash register tally:

Cash in Bank	4,577.60	
Cash Short and Over	3.16	
Sales		4,580.76

If there is a debit balance in the cash short and over account at the end of a period, it is an expense that may be included as a miscellaneous administrative expense in the income statement. If there is a credit balance, it is revenue that may be listed in the Other Income section. If the balance becomes larger than may be accounted for by minor errors in making change, management should take corrective measures.

INTERNAL CONTROL OF CASH PAYMENTS

Objective 3
Summarize basic procedures for achieving control over cash payments, including the use of a voucher system, a discounts lost account, and a petty cash account.

It is common practice for business enterprises to require that all payments of cash be made by check signed by an authorized individual. As an additional control, some firms require two signatures on all checks or on checks which are larger than a certain amount. It is also common to use a check protector, which imprints amounts on the check that are not easily removed or changed.

In a small business, an owner/manager may sign all checks based upon personal knowledge of all goods and services purchased. In large business enterprises, however, disbursing officials are seldom able to have such a complete knowledge of business transactions. In such enterprises, the issuance of purchase orders, inspection of goods received, and verification of invoices is divided among the employees of several departments. These activities must be coordinated with the final issuance of checks to creditors. One system used for this purpose is the voucher system.

Basic Features of the Voucher System

A **voucher system** is a set of methods and procedures for authorizing and recording liabilities and cash payments. A voucher system normally uses (1) vouchers, (2) a voucher register, (3) a file for unpaid vouchers, (4) a check register, and (5) a file for paid vouchers. As in all accounting systems, many differences in detail are possible. The following discussion refers to a medium-size merchandising enterprise with separate departments for purchasing, receiving, accounting, and disbursing.

VOUCHERS. The term voucher is widely used in accounting. In a general sense, a voucher is any document that serves as proof of authority to pay cash, such as an invoice approved for payment. A voucher may also be a document that serves as evidence that cash has been paid, such as a canceled check.

In a voucher system, a **voucher** is a special form on which is recorded relevant data about a liability and the details of its payment. A voucher form is shown in Exhibit 3.

Exhibit 3
Voucher

Vouchers are normally prenumbered for control purposes. Each voucher provides space for the name and address of the creditor, the date, and a summary of the basic details of the supporting document. Such basic details in the voucher shown include the invoice number and the amount and terms of the invoice. One half of the back of the voucher is devoted to the account distribution and the other half to summaries of the voucher and the details of payment. Spaces are also provided for the signature or initials of certain employees.

A voucher must be prepared for every expenditure. A check may not be issued except in payment of a properly authorized voucher. Vouchers may be paid immediately after they are prepared or at a later date, depending upon the credit terms.

A voucher is normally prepared by the Accounting Department on the basis of an invoice or a memorandum that serves as support for the expenditure. A voucher is usually prepared only after the following steps have been completed and noted on the invoice:

1. The invoice is compared with a copy of the purchase order to verify quantities, prices, and terms.
2. The invoice is compared with the receiving report to verify receipt of the items billed.
3. The arithmetical accuracy of the invoice is proved.

After all data except details of payment have been inserted, the invoice or other supporting evidence is attached to the voucher. The voucher is then given to the proper official for approval.

VOUCHER REGISTER. After a voucher has been approved, it is recorded in a journal called a **voucher register**. The voucher register is similar to and replaces the purchases journal in a periodic inventory system. A typical voucher register is shown in Exhibit 4.

Vouchers are entered in a voucher register in numerical order. Each voucher is recorded as a credit to Accounts Payable (sometimes entitled Vouchers Payable) and as a debit to the account or accounts to be debited for the expenditure.

Exhibit 4
Voucher Register

Page 11   VOUCHER

Date	Vou. No.	Payee	Date Paid	Check No.	Accounts Payable Cr.	Purchases Dr.
19-						
July 1	451	Allied Mfg. Co.	7-8	863	450.00	450.00
1	452	Chavez Realtors	7-1	856	600.00	
2	453	Foster Publications	7-2	857	52. 50	
3	454	Benson Express Co.	7-3	859 *NOT PAID*	36.80	24.20
3	455	Roberson's Supply Co.			784.20	
3	456	Moore & Co.	7-11	866	1,236.00	1,236.00
6	457	J. L. Brown Co.	7-6	860	22.50	
6	458	Turner Co.		*NOT PAID*	395.30	395.30
31	477	Central Motors		*NOT PAID*	112.20	
31	478	Petty Cash	7-31	883	48.60	
31					15,551.60	11,640.30
					(212)	(511)

When a voucher is paid, the date of payment and the number of the check are inserted in the proper columns in the voucher register. These notations provide a means of determining at any time the amount of an individual unpaid voucher or of the total amount of unpaid vouchers.

UNPAID VOUCHER FILE. After a voucher has been recorded in the voucher register, it is filed in an unpaid voucher file. The amount due on each voucher represents the credit balance of an account payable, and the voucher itself is like an individual account in a subsidiary accounts payable ledger. Accordingly, a separate subsidiary accounts payable ledger is not needed.

All voucher systems include procedures to ensure payment within the discount period or on the last day of the credit period. A simple but effective procedure is to file each voucher according to its payment date. The unpaid voucher file may be made up of a group of folders with numbers from 1 to 31, which represent the days of a month. Such a system brings to the attention of the disbursing official the vouchers that are to be paid on each day. It also provides management with a convenient means of predicting the amount of cash needed to pay creditors.

When a voucher is to be paid, it is removed from the unpaid voucher file and a check is issued in payment. The date, the number, and the amount of the check are listed on the back of the voucher. These data will be used later for recording the payment in the check register. Paid vouchers and supporting documents should be stamped *PAID* or otherwise canceled to prevent accidental or intentional reuse.

An exception to the general rule that vouchers be prepared for all expenditures may be made for bank charges shown by debit memorandums or notations on the bank statement. Such items as bank service charges and returned NSF (Not-Sufficient-Funds) checks are charged to the depositor's account directly by the bank. The bank may also charge the depositor's account for large expenditures such as the repayment of a loan. In this latter case, a supporting voucher may be prepared and the paid note attached as evidence of the obligation and its payment.

(REPLACES   PURCHASES   JOURNAL)

REGISTER							Page 11
Store Supplies Dr.	Adv. Exp. Dr.	Del. Exp. Dr.	Misc. Selling Exp. Dr.	Misc. Admin. Exp. Dr.	Other Accounts Dr. Account	Post. Ref.	Amount
					Rent Expense	712	600.00
	52.50						
		12.60					
34.20					Office Equipment	122	750.00
				22.50			
		112.20					
4.30		16.20	19.50	8.60			
59.80	176.40	286.10	48.30	64.90			3,275.80
(116)	(612)	(613)	(618)	(718)			(✓)

CHECK REGISTER. The payment of a voucher is recorded in a check register such as the one shown in Exhibit 5. The check register is a complete record of all checks. It is a modified form of the cash payments journal. For control purposes, all checks, including checks voided during preparation, are listed in sequential order in the check register. In this way, all checks can easily be accounted for on a periodic basis.

(handwritten: REPLACES CASH PAYMENTS JOURNAL)

Exhibit 5
Check Register

						CHECK REGISTER			Page 14

Date	Check No.	Payee	Vou. No.	Accounts Payable Dr.	Purchases Discounts Cr.	Cash in Bank Cr.	Bank Deposits	Bank Balance
19-								8,743.10
July 1	856	Chavez Realtors	452	600.00		600.00	1,240.30	9,383.40
2	857	Foster Publications	453	52.50		52.50		9,330.90
2	858	Hill and Davis	436	1,420.00	14.20	1,405.80	865.70	8,790.80
3	859	Benson Express Co.	454	36.80		36.80	942.20	9,696.20
30	879	Voided						
30	880	Stone & Co.	460	14.30		14.30		9,521.80
30	881	Evans Co.	448	1,015.00		1,015.00	765.50	9,272.30
31	882	Graham & Co.	469	830.00	16.60	813.40		8,458.90
31	883	Petty Cash	478	48.60		48.60	938.10	9,348.40
31				17,322.90 (212)	198.20 (513)	17,124.70 (111)		

(handwritten: PETTY CASH MONEY TAKEN FROM ACCOUNTS PAYABLE ACCOUNTS)

Each check issued is in payment of a voucher that has previously been recorded as an account payable in the voucher register. Each entry in the check register is a debit to Accounts Payable and a credit to Cash in Bank (and Purchases Discounts, when appropriate).

The memorandum columns for Bank Deposits and Bank Balance appearing in the check register are optional. They provide a convenient means of determining the amount of cash available.

When check forms with a remittance advice are prepared in duplicate, the copies retained may make up the check register. At the end of each month, summary totals can be obtained for Accounts Payable debit, Purchases Discounts credit, and Cash in Bank credit, and the entry recorded in the general journal.

PAID VOUCHER FILE. After payment, vouchers are usually filed in numerical order in a paid voucher file. They are then readily available for examination by employees needing information about a certain expenditure. Eventually the paid vouchers are destroyed according to the firm's policies concerning the retention of records.

THE VOUCHER SYSTEM, SPECIAL JOURNALS, AND SUBSIDIARY LEDGERS. The relationship of the voucher system and special journals and subsidiary ledgers discussed in preceding chapters is summarized below.

Special Journal		*Voucher System*
Purchases Journal	⟹	Voucher Register
Cash Payments Journal	⟹	Check Register

Subsidiary Ledger		
Accounts Payable Subsidiary Ledger	⟶	Unpaid Voucher File

THE VOUCHER SYSTEM AND MANAGEMENT. The voucher system not only provides effective accounting controls but also aids management in fulfilling their responsibilities. For example, the voucher system ensures that all payments are for valid liabilities. In addition, up-to-date information is always available for use in predicting future cash requirements. This in turn enables management to make the best use of cash resources. Invoices on which cash discounts are allowed are highlighted for payment within the discount period. Other invoices are highlighted for payment on the final day of the credit period. This aids management in maintaining a favorable credit standing. Borrowing can also be planned more accurately, with a savings in interest costs.

Purchases Discounts Lost

In earlier chapters, purchases of merchandise were recorded at the invoice price. Cash discounts taken were credited to the purchases discounts account at the time of payment. The balance of this account was reported on the income statement as a deduction from purchases.

To illustrate, if merchandise with an invoice price of $1,000 is subject to terms of 2/10, n/30, the cost of the merchandise is recorded initially at $1,000. If payment is made within the discount period, the discount of $20 reduces the cost to $980. If the invoice is not paid within the discount period, the cost of the merchandise remains $1,000.

The deduction of purchases discounts from purchases may be criticized on the grounds that the date of payment should not affect the cost of merchandise. The additional payment required beyond the discount period adds nothing to the value of the merchandise purchased.

The recording of purchases at the invoice price and recognizing purchases discounts at the time of payment may also be criticized because the cost of failing to take discounts is not measured. Well-managed enterprises pay invoices within a discount period. A failure to take a discount is viewed as an inefficiency.

To account for purchases discounts lost and to determine the cost of merchandise without regard to whether discounts are taken, purchases invoices may be recorded at their net amount. When this method is used, management assumes that all discounts will be taken. Any discounts not taken are then recorded in an expense account called *Discounts Lost*. The balance of this account represents the cost of failing to take cash discounts. If the balance is significant, management can take action to avoid losing discounts in the future.

To illustrate, using the same data as above, the invoice for $1,000 would be recorded as a debit to Purchases of $980 and a credit to Accounts Payable for $980. If the invoice is not paid until after the discount period has passed, the payment entry in general journal form would be as follows:

Accounts Payable	980	
Discounts Lost	20	
Cash in Bank		1,000

When the net method is used with the voucher system, all vouchers are prepared and recorded at the net amount. Any discount lost is noted on the related voucher and recorded in a special column in the check register when the voucher is paid.

Another advantage of the net method is that all merchandise purchased is recorded initially at the net price; hence, no later adjustments to cost are necessary. An objection, however, is that the amount reported as accounts payable in the balance sheet may be less than the amount needed to discharge the liability.

Petty Cash

In most businesses there is a frequent need for the payment of small amounts, such as for postage due or for small purchases of urgently needed supplies. Payment by check in such cases could result in unnecessary delay and expense. Yet,

Overpayments of Accounts Payable—Can It Happen?

The business of Howard Schultz & Associates (HS&A) is reviewing payments of accounts payable. HS&A scours its clients' books, looking for duplicate payments, failures to get promised discounts, and inaccurate calculations. Some of the findings that HS&A has discovered for its clients are listed below. The magnitude of these findings indicates the importance of strong controls over cash payments of accounts payable.

. . . *The typical amount recovered for a company amounts to about one-tenth of 1 percent of the total payments made to sup-*

pliers. That doesn't sound like much, but for a company with $250 million in payments, it would mean a recovery of about $250,000. . . .

The average [amount recovered is] more than $300,000 for [a] client. . . .

For . . . a "fast-growing major discount chain". . . HS&A recovered . . . $4.5 million. . . .

HS&A once discovered a quarter-million-dollar overpayment on a single order . . . [HS&A] even unearthed a double payment made to itself. The money was refunded immediately. . . .

Source: Thomas Buell, Jr., "Demand Grows for Auditor," *The Naples Daily News* (January 12, 1992), p. 14F.

these small payments may occur frequently enough to amount to a significant total amount. Thus, it is desirable to retain control over such payments. For this purpose, a special cash fund called a **petty cash fund** is used.

A petty cash fund is established by first estimating the amount of cash needed for disbursements from the fund during a period, such as a week or a month. If a voucher system is used, a voucher is prepared for this amount. The voucher is recorded in the voucher register as a debit to Petty Cash and a credit to Accounts Payable. The check drawn to pay the voucher is recorded in the check register as a debit to Accounts Payable and a credit to Cash in Bank.

The money obtained from cashing the check is placed in the custody of a specific employee who is authorized to disburse monies from the fund. Restrictions may also be placed on the maximum amount and the nature of fund disbursements. Each time monies are disbursed from the fund, the fund custodian records the essential details on a petty cash receipt form. In addition, the signature of the payee and the initials of the custodian of the fund are written on the form as proof of the payment. A typical petty cash receipt is illustrated in Exhibit 6.

Exhibit 6
Petty Cash Receipt

PETTY CASH RECEIPT

No. _____121_____   Date _____August 1, 1994_____

Paid to _____Metropolitan Times_____   Amount

For _____Daily newspaper_____   3 | 70

Charge to _____Miscellaneous Administrative Expense_____

Payment received:

_____S.O. Hall_____   Approved by _____N.E.R._____

A petty cash fund is normally replenished at periodic intervals or when it is depleted or reaches a minimum amount. When a petty cash fund is replenished, the accounts debited are determined by summarizing the petty cash receipts. If a voucher system is used, the voucher is recorded in the voucher register as a debit to the various expense and asset accounts and a credit to Accounts Payable. The check in payment of the voucher is recorded in the check register in the usual manner.

To illustrate the entries that would be made in accounting for petty cash, assume that a voucher system is used and that a petty cash fund of $100 is established on August 1. At the end of August, the petty cash receipts indicate expenditures for the following items: office supplies, $28; postage (office supplies), $22; store supplies, $35; and daily newspapers (miscellaneous administrative expense), $3.70. The entries in general journal form to establish and replenish the petty cash fund are as follows:

Aug. 1	Petty Cash	100.00	
	Accounts Payable		100.00
1	Accounts Payable	100.00	
	Cash in Bank		100.00
31	Office Supplies	50.00	
	Store Supplies	35.00	
	Miscellaneous Administrative Expense	3.70	
	Accounts Payable		88.70
31	Accounts Payable	88.70	
	Cash in Bank		88.70

[handwritten margin notes: ESTABLISH FUND; REPLENISH FUND]

Replenishing the petty cash fund restores it to its original amount of $100. Note that there is no entry in Petty Cash when the fund is replenished. Petty Cash is debited only when the fund is initially set up or when the permanent amount of the fund is increased or decreased at some later time.

Other Cash Funds

Cash funds may also be established to meet other special needs of a business. For example, money may be advanced for travel expenses as needed. Periodically, after expense reports have been received, the expenses are recorded and the fund is replenished. A similar procedure may be used to provide a cash operating fund for a sales office located in another city. The amount of the fund may be deposited in a local bank and the sales representative may be authorized to draw checks for payment of rent, salaries, and other operating expenses. Each month, the representative sends the invoices, bank statement, paid checks, bank reconciliation, and other business documents to the home office. The data are audited, the expenditures are recorded, and a replenishing check is returned for deposit in the local bank.

Like petty cash funds, disbursements from other cash funds are not recorded in the accounts until the funds are replenished. To bring the accounts up to date, such funds should always be replenished at the end of an accounting period. The amount of monies in these funds will then agree with the balances in the fund accounts. At the same time, the expenses and the assets for which payments have been made will be recorded in the proper period.

PRESENTATION OF CASH ON THE BALANCE SHEET

Objective 4
Summarize how cash is presented in the balance sheet.

Cash is the most liquid asset, and therefore it is listed as the first asset in the Current Assets section of the balance sheet. Most companies combine all their cash accounts and present only a single cash amount on the balance sheet.

A company may have cash in excess of its operating needs. In such cases, it may invest in highly liquid investments in order to earn interest. These investments are called **cash equivalents**.[3] Examples of cash equivalents include United States Treasury Bills, notes issued by major corporations (referred to as commercial paper), and money market funds. Companies that have invested excess cash

---

[3] To be classified as a cash equivalent, it is expected that the investment will be converted to cash within 90 days.

in cash equivalents usually report *Cash and cash equivalents* as one amount on the balance sheet.

Cash and cash equivalents normally do not require special disclosures in the notes to the financial statements. However, if the ability to withdraw cash is restricted, the restrictions should be disclosed. For example, companies with foreign operations often have cash deposits in foreign banks. These deposits may be subject to foreign laws that limit withdrawals to certain amounts. Such limitations should be disclosed in the notes to the financial statements.

A bank often requires a business to maintain in a bank account a minimum cash balance. Such a balance is called a **compensating balance**. This requirement is generally imposed by the bank as a part of a loan agreement or line of credit. A line of credit is a pre-approved amount the bank is willing to lend to a customer upon request. Compensating balance requirements should be disclosed in notes to the financial statements. An example of such a note is shown below for K Mart Corporation:

. . . In support of lines of credit, it is expected that compensating balances will be maintained on deposit with the banks, which will average 10% of the line to the extent that it is not in use and an additional 10% on the portion in use, whereas other lines require fees in lieu of compensating balances. . . .

CASH TRANSACTIONS AND ELECTRONIC FUNDS TRANSFER

Objective 5
Define electronic funds transfer and give an example of how it is used to process cash transactions.

Most cash transactions are in the form of currency or check. The broad principles discussed in earlier sections provide the basis for developing an effective system to control such cash transactions. However, the use of electronic funds transfer is changing the form in which many cash transactions are executed. This, in turn, affects the processing and controlling of cash transactions.

Electronic funds transfer (EFT) can be defined as a payment system that uses computerized electronic impulses rather than paper (money, checks, etc.) to effect a cash transaction. For example, a business may pay its employees by means of EFT. Under such a system, employees may authorize the deposit of their payroll checks directly in a checking account. For each pay period, the business's computer produces a payroll file with computer-sensitive notations for relevant payroll data. This file is transmitted over telephone lines to the banks indicated by the employees. The banks then credit each employee's account. Similar cash payments might be made for other authorized payments. The federal government currently processes several million social security checks through EFT.

EFT may also be used for retail sales. Through a point-of-sale (POS) system, a customer pays for goods at the time of purchase by presenting a plastic card. The card is used to transfer monies from the customer's checking account to the retailer's account at the bank.

Some companies are using EFT systems to process both cash payments and cash receipts. For example, General Electric Co. estimates that 40%–50% of its payments to creditors and its collections from customers are processed by EFT systems.

Studies have indicated that EFT systems generally reduce the cost of processing certain cash transactions and contribute to better control over cash receipts and cash payments. Offsetting these advantages are problems of protecting the privacy of information stored in computers and difficulties in documenting purchase and sale transactions.

Controlling EFT Systems

Many companies use EFT to transfer cash among various bank accounts, to make investments, and to pay vendors. Control weaknesses and some relatively simple steps to safeguard electronically transferred funds were described in a *Journal of Accountancy* article, as follows:

The key element in most EFT systems is the telephone. Once a . . . cash manager has established an EFT facility with a bank, he or she usually only needs to call the bank (or make contact through a computer hookup), identify himself and specify the dollar amount to be transferred from a particular account at the disbursing bank, as well as the account and bank to which funds are to be transferred. . . . As a result of these calls, hundreds of billions of dollars are transferred through the banking system every business day. . . .

When cash disbursements are made by written check, most companies' control procedures . . . [provide] reasonable assurance that cash disbursements . . . are being made [properly. When an EFT system is used] . . . several relatively inexpensive and easily implemented control procedures can be added to traditional controls to reduce the risk of losing funds during electronic transfers. . . .

- *Passwords. Companies should instruct banks not to accept transfer instructions from any caller who is unable to provide an established password. . . .*

- *Additional authorization. The vast majority of fund transfers by most companies are routine, such as transfers between their own bank accounts and transfers to investment accounts in the company's name. These reasonably could be considered relatively low risk, since funds never leave the company's accounts. Transfers to outside accounts, on the other hand, generally are much less frequent and obviously involve much higher risk.*

To minimize the risk of lost funds . . . additional authorizations [should be required] before unusual transfers are completed. . . .

- *After the transfer. The traditional bank account reconciliation process is an effective control except for the time lag involved. . . . To overcome this weakness, an ongoing reconciliation system can be used with EFTs. Banks should be instructed to provide the transaction advice for each fund transfer on a timely basis. . . .*

Transaction advices should be sent directly to a person not involved in the EFT process. This person should be instructed to match the advices on the day they are received with the internal cash receipt or disbursement records, as well as with required internal documentation. . . .

Source: Michael J. Fischer, "Electronic Funds Transfers: Controlling the Risk," *The Journal of Accountancy* (June 1988), pp. 130–134.

CHAPTER REVIEW

Key Points

Objective 1. Prepare a bank reconciliation and journalize any necessary entries.

The first section of the bank reconciliation begins with the cash balance according to the bank statement. This balance is adjusted for the depositor's changes in cash that do not appear on the bank statement and for any bank errors. The second section begins with the cash balance according to the depositor's records. This balance is adjusted for the bank's changes in cash that do not appear on the depositor's records and for any depositor errors. The adjusted balances for the two sections must be equal.

No entries are necessary on the depositor's records as a result of the information included in the first section of the bank reconciliation. However, the items in the second section must be journalized on the depositor's records.

Objective 2. Summarize basic procedures for achieving internal control over cash receipts, including the use of cash change funds and the cash short and over account.

To protect cash from theft and misuse, business enterprises use protective and detective controls. One of the most important controls to protect cash received in over-the-counter sales is a cash register. A remittance advice is a protective control for cash received through the mail. The separation of the duties of handling cash and recording cash is also a protective control.

Retail stores and other businesses that receive cash directly from customers must keep some currency and coins in a cash change fund in order to make change. Differences in the amount of cash counted and the amount of cash in the records are normally recorded in Cash Short and Over.

Objective 3. Summarize basic procedures for achieving control over cash payments, including the use of a voucher system, a discounts lost account, and a petty cash account.

A voucher system can assist in achieving control over cash payments. A voucher system is a set of methods and procedures for authorizing and recording liabilities and cash payments. A voucher system normally uses vouchers, a voucher register, a file for unpaid vouchers, a check register, and a file for paid vouchers.

Because of the importance of taking advantage of all purchases discounts, a business may use a separate account, called Discounts Lost, to account for any discounts not taken during the discount period. When this procedure is used with a voucher system, all vouchers are prepared and recorded at the net amount, assuming that the discount will be taken.

A petty cash fund may be used by a business to make small payments that occur frequently, for which payment by check would cause unnecessary delay and expense. The money in a petty cash fund is placed in the custody of a specific employee, who authorizes payments from the fund according to restrictions as to maximum amount and purpose. Periodically or when the amount of money in the fund is depleted or reduced to a minimum amount, the fund is replenished.

Objective 4. Summarize how cash is presented in the balance sheet.
Cash is listed as the first asset in the Current Assets section of the balance sheet. Companies that have invested excess cash in highly liquid investments usually report *Cash and cash equivalents* on the balance sheet.

Objective 5. Define electronic funds transfer and give an example of how it is used to process cash transactions.
Electronic funds transfer (EFT) is a payment system that uses computerized electronic impulses rather than paper (money, checks, etc.) to effect cash transactions. EFT may be used in processing cash payments and cash receipts and in processing retail sales.

Glossary of Key Terms

Bank reconciliation. The method of analysis that details the items that are responsible for the difference between the cash balance reported in the bank statement and the balance of the cash account in the ledger. **Objective 1**

Cash equivalents. Highly liquid investments that are usually reported on the balance sheet with cash. **Objective 4**

Check register. A modified form of the cash payments journal used to record all transactions paid by check. **Objective 3**

Electronic funds transfer (EFT). A payment system that uses computerized electronic impulses rather than paper (money, checks, etc.) to effect a cash transaction. **Objective 5**

Petty cash fund. A special cash fund used to pay relatively small amounts. **Objective 3**

Voucher. A document that serves as evidence of authority to pay cash. **Objective 3**

Voucher register. A modified form of the purchase journal, in which all vouchers are recorded. **Objective 3**

Voucher system. Records, methods, and procedures employed in verifying and recording liabilities and paying and recording cash payments. **Objective 3**

Self-Examination Questions
Answers at end of chapter.

1. In preparing a bank reconciliation, the amount of checks outstanding would be:
   A. added to the cash balance according to the bank statement
   B. deducted from the cash balance according to the bank statement
   C. added to the cash balance according to the depositor's records
   D. deducted from the cash balance according to the depositor's records

2. Journal entries based on the bank reconciliation are required for:
   A. additions to the cash balance according to the depositor's records
   B. deductions from the cash balance according to the depositor's records
   C. both A and B
   D. neither A nor B

3. The journal used to record liabilities when a voucher system is used is called:
   A. a voucher
   B. an unpaid voucher file
   C. a check register
   D. a voucher register

4. A voucher system is used and all vouchers for purchases are recorded at the net amount. When a purchase is made for $500 under terms 1/10, n/30:
   A. Purchases would be debited for $495
   B. Discounts Lost would be debited for $5 if the voucher is not paid within the discount period
   C. the discount lost would be reported as an expense on the income statement if the voucher is not paid until after the discount period has expired
   D. all of the above

5. A petty cash fund is:
   A. used to pay relatively small amounts
   B. established by estimating the amount of cash needed for disbursements of relatively small amounts during a specified period
   C. reimbursed when the amount of money in the fund is reduced to a predetermined minimum amount
   D. all of the above

ILLUSTRATIVE PROBLEM

The bank statement for Dunlap Company for April 30 indicates a balance of $10,443.11. Dunlap Company uses a voucher system in controlling cash payments. All cash receipts are deposited each evening in a night depository, after banking hours. The accounting records indicate the following summary data for cash receipts and payments for April:

CASH IN BANK ACCOUNT	
Balance as of April 1	$ 5,143.50
CASH RECEIPTS JOURNAL	
Total cash receipts for April	$28,971.60
CHECK REGISTER	
Total amount of checks issued in April	$26,060.85

Comparison of the bank statement and the accompanying canceled checks and memorandums with the records reveals the following reconciling items:

a. The bank had collected for Dunlap Company $912 on a note left for collection. The face of the note was $900.
b. A deposit of $1,852.21, representing receipts of April 30, had been made too late to appear on the bank statement.
c. Checks outstanding totaled $3,265.27.
d. A check drawn for $79 had been erroneously charged by the bank as $97.
e. A check for $10 returned with the statement had been recorded in the check register as $100. The check was for the payment of an obligation to Davis Equipment Company for the purchase of office supplies on account.
f. Bank service charges for April amounted to $8.20.

Instructions

1. Prepare a bank reconciliation for April.
2. Journalize the entries that should be made by Dunlap Company.

Solution

1.

Dunlap Company
Bank Reconciliation
April 30, 19—

Cash balance according to bank statement		$10,443.11
Add: Deposit of April 30 not recorded by bank	$1,852.21	
Bank error in charging check for $97 instead of $79	18.00	1,870.21
		$12,313.32
Deduct: Outstanding checks		3,265.27
Adjusted balance		$ 9,048.05
Cash balance according to depositor's records		$ 8,054.25*
Add: Proceeds of note collected by bank, including		
$12 interest	$ 912.00	
Error in recording check	90.00	1,002.00
		$ 9,056.25
Deduct: Bank service charges		8.20
Adjusted balance		$ 9,048.05

*$5,143.50 + $28,971.60 − $26,060.85

2.

Cash in Bank	1,002.00	
Notes Receivable		900.00
Interest Income		12.00
Accounts Payable		90.00
Miscellaneous Administrative Expense	8.20	
Cash in Bank		8.20

DISCUSSION QUESTIONS

1. Why is cash the asset that often warrants the most attention in the design of an effective internal control structure?
2. Distinguish between the drawer and the payee of a check.
3. What name is often given to the notification, attached to a check, that indicates the specific invoice being paid?
4. The balance of Cash in Bank is likely to differ from the cash balance reported by the bank statement. What two factors are likely to be responsible for the difference?
5. What is the purpose of preparing a bank reconciliation?
6. Do items reported on the bank statement as credits represent (a) additions made by the bank to the depositor's balance, or (b) deductions made by the bank from the depositor's balance?
7. What entry should be made if a check received from a customer and deposited is returned by the bank for lack of sufficient funds (an NSF check)?
8. Identify each of the following reconciling items as: (a) an addition to the cash balance according to the bank statement, (b) a deduction from the cash balance according to the bank statement, (c) an addition to the cash balance according to the depositor's records, or (d) a deduction from the cash balance according to the depositor's records. (None of the transactions reported by bank debit and credit memorandums have been recorded by the depositor.)
   (1) Check for $27 charged by bank as $72.
   (2) Check drawn by depositor for $90 but recorded as $900.
   (3) Outstanding checks, $8,515.50.
   (4) Deposit in transit, $3,279.12.
   (5) Note collected by bank, $5,200.00.
   (6) Check of a customer returned by bank to depositor because of insufficient funds, $212.50.
   (7) Bank service charges, $40.10.
9. Which of the reconciling items listed in Question 8 necessitate an entry in the depositor's accounts?
10. The procedures used for over-the-counter receipts are as follows: At the close of each day's business, the sales clerks count the cash in their respective cash drawers, after which they determine the amount recorded by the cash register and prepare the memorandum cash form, noting any discrepancies. An employee from the cashier's office counts the cash, compares the total with the memorandum, and takes the cash to the cashier's office. (a) Indicate the weak link in internal control. (b) How can the weakness be corrected?
11. The mailroom employees send all remittances and remittance advices to the cashier. The cashier deposits the cash in the bank and forwards the remittance advices and duplicate deposit slips to the Accounting Department. (a) Indicate the weak link in internal control in the handling of cash receipts. (b) How can the weakness be corrected?
12. The combined cash count of all cash registers at the close of business is $4 less than the cash sales indicated by the cash register tapes. (a) In what account is the cash shortage recorded? (b) Are cash shortages debited or credited to this account?
13. In which section of the income statement would a credit balance in Cash Short and Over be reported?
14. What is meant by the term *voucher* as applied to the voucher system?
15. Before a voucher for the purchase of merchandise is approved for payment, three documents should be compared to verify the accuracy of the liability. Name these three documents.
16. a. When the voucher system is used, is the accounts payable account in the general ledger a controlling account?
    b. Is there a subsidiary creditors ledger?
17. The controller approves all vouchers before they are submitted to the treasurer for payment. What procedure can the controller add to the system to ensure that the documents accompanying the vouchers and supporting the payments are not "reused" to support future vouchers improperly?
18. The accounting clerk pays all obligations by prenumbered checks. What are the strengths and weaknesses in the internal control over cash payments in this situation?

19. In what order are vouchers ordinarily filed (a) in the unpaid voucher file and (b) in the paid voucher file? Give reasons for the answers.

20. What are the advantages of recording purchases at the net amount?

21. Merchandise with an invoice price of $5,000 is purchased subject to terms of 2/10, n/30. Determine the cost of the merchandise according to each of the following systems:
   a. Discounts taken are treated as deductions from the invoice price.
      (1) The invoice is paid within the discount period.
      (2) The invoice is paid after the discount period has expired.
   b. Discounts allowable are treated as deductions from the invoice price, regardless of when payment is made.
      (1) The invoice is paid within the discount period.
      (2) The invoice is paid after the discount period has expired.

22. As a general rule, all cash payments should be made by check. Explain why some cash payments are made in coins and currency from a petty cash fund.

23. What account or accounts are debited when recording the voucher (a) establishing a petty cash fund and (b) replenishing a petty cash fund?

24. The petty cash account has a debit balance of $500. At the end of the accounting period, there is $93 in the petty cash fund, along with petty cash receipts totaling $407. Should the fund be replenished as of the last day of the period? Discuss.

25. a. What is meant by the term *cash equivalents*?
    b. How are cash equivalents reported in the financial statements?

26. a. What is meant by the term compensating balance as applied to the checking account of a firm?
    b. How is the compensating balance reported in the financial statements?

27. What is meant by *electronic funds transfer*?

 28. Between September 3 and September 22, seventeen prenumbered checks totaling $1,129,232.39 were forged and cashed on the accounts of Perini Corporation, a construction company based in the Boston suburb of Framingham. Perini Corporation kept its supply of blank prenumbered checks in an unlocked storeroom with items such as styrofoam coffee cups. Every clerk and secretary had access to this storeroom. It was later discovered that someone had apparently stolen two boxes of prenumbered checks. The numbers of the missing checks matched the numbers of the out-of-sequence checks cashed by the banks. What fundamental principle of control over cash was violated in this case?

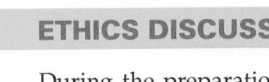

ETHICS DISCUSSION CASE

During the preparation of the bank reconciliation for Klaus Co., Jane Ellet, the assistant controller, discovered that Banco National Bank erroneously recorded a $700 check written by Klaus as $70. Jane has decided not to notify the bank, but to wait for the bank to detect the error. Jane plans to record the $630 error as Other Income if the bank fails to detect the error within the next three months.

Discuss whether Jane Ellet is behaving in an ethical manner.

EXERCISES

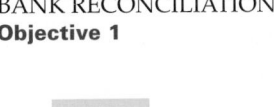

EXERCISE 8-1
BANK RECONCILIATION
Objective 1

The following data are accumulated for use in reconciling the bank account of C. C. Davidson Co. for February:

a. Cash balance according to the depositor's records at February 28, $5,530.20.

b. Cash balance according to the bank statement at February 28, $9,100.50.

c. Checks outstanding, $4,111.20.

d. Deposit in transit, not recorded by bank, $780.40.

e. A check for $140 in payment of a voucher was erroneously recorded in the check register as $410.

f. Bank debit memorandum for service charges, $30.50.

Prepare a bank reconciliation.

EXERCISE 8-2
ENTRIES FOR BANK
RECONCILIATION
Objective 1

Using the data presented in Exercise 8-1, journalize in general journal form the entry or entries that should be made by the depositor.

EXERCISE 8-3
ENTRIES FOR NOTE
COLLECTED BY BANK
Objective 1

Accompanying a bank statement for Cross Company is a credit memorandum for $5,075, representing the principal ($5,000) and interest ($75) on a note that had been collected by the bank. The depositor had been notified by the bank at the time of the collection, but had made no entries. In general journal form, journalize the entry that should be made by the depositor to bring the accounting records up to date.

EXERCISE 8-4
ENTRY FOR CASH SALES
Objective 2

The actual cash received from cash sales was $7,160.70, and the amount indicated by the cash register total was $7,155.20. Journalize the entry, in general journal form, to record the cash receipts and cash sales.

EXERCISE 8-5
EVALUATION OF INTERNAL
CONTROL OF CASH
Objectives 1, 2, 3

The following procedures were recently installed by Nero Company:

a. The bank reconciliation is prepared by the accountant.
b. Each cashier is assigned a separate cash register drawer, to which no other cashier has access.
c. All sales are rung up on the cash register and a receipt is given to the customer. All sales are recorded on a tape locked inside the cash register.
d. Checks received through the mail are given daily to the accounts receivable clerk for recording collections on account and for depositing in the bank.
e. At the end of a shift, each cashier counts the cash in his or her drawer, unlocks the tape, and compares the amount of cash with the amount on the tape to determine cash shortages and overages.
f. Vouchers and all supporting documents are perforated with a PAID designation after being paid by the treasurer.
g. Disbursements are made from the petty cash fund only after a petty cash receipt has been completed and signed by the payee.

Indicate whether each of the procedures of internal control over cash represents (1) a strength or (2) a weakness.

EXERCISE 8-6
INTERNAL CONTROL OVER
CASH RECEIPTS
Objective 2

Jeanette Jones works at the drive-through window of Bob's Burgers. Occasionally, when a drive-through customer orders, Jeanette fills the order and pockets the customer's money. She does not ring up the order on the cash register.

**SHARPEN YOUR ▶
COMMUNICATION SKILLS**

Identify the internal control weaknesses that exist at Bob's Burgers, and discuss what can be done to prevent this theft.

EXERCISE 8-7
PROCEDURES FOR
INTERNAL CONTROL OF
CASH PAYMENTS
Objective 3

H. L. Stricker Co. is a medium-size merchandising enterprise. When its current income statement was reviewed, it was noted that the amount of purchases discounts was disproportionately small in comparison with earlier periods. Further investigation revealed that in spite of a sufficient bank balance, a significant amount of available cash discounts had been lost because of failure to make timely payments. In addition, it was discovered that several purchases invoices had been paid twice.

**SHARPEN YOUR ▶
COMMUNICATION SKILLS**

Outline procedures for the payment of vendors' invoices, so that the possibilities of losing available cash discounts and of paying an invoice a second time will be minimized.

EXERCISE 8-8
INTERNAL CONTROL OVER
CASH PAYMENTS
Objective 3

NDT Company, a communications equipment manufacturer, recently fell victim to an embezzlement scheme masterminded by one of its employees. To understand the scheme, it is necessary to review NDT's procedures for the purchase of services.

The purchasing agent is responsible for ordering services (such as repairs to a photocopy machine or office cleaning) after receiving a service requisition from an authorized manager. However, since no tangible goods are delivered, a receiving report is not prepared. When the Accounting Department receives an invoice billing NDT for a service call, the accounts payable clerk calls the manager who requested the service in order to verify that it was performed.

The embezzlement scheme involves Rob Ryan, the manager of plant and facilities. Rob arranged for his uncle's company, Ralph's Industrial Supply and Service, to be placed on NDT's approved vendor list. Rob did not disclose the family relationship.

On several occasions, Rob would submit a requisition for services to be provided by Ralph's Industrial Supply and Service. However, the service requested was really not needed and it was never performed. Ralph would bill NDT for the service and then split the cash payment with Rob.

SHARPEN YOUR ►
COMMUNICATION SKILLS

Explain what changes should be made to NDT's procedures for ordering and paying for services in order to prevent such occurrences in the future.

EXERCISE 8-9
ENTRIES FOR VOUCHERS
AND CHECKS; PURCHASES
AT GROSS AMOUNT
Objective 3

Journalize in general journal form the following selected transactions, indicating above each entry the name of the register in which it should be recorded. Assume the use of a voucher register and a check register similar to those illustrated in this chapter. All invoices are recorded at invoice price.

May 1. Recorded Voucher No. 890 for $2,000, payable to Barr Co., for merchandise purchased, terms 1/10, n/30.
     5. Recorded Voucher No. 896 for $1,500, payable to T. A. Fox Co., for merchandise purchased, terms 2/10, n/30.
     14. Issued Check No. 875 in payment of Voucher No. 896.
     17. Recorded Voucher No. 920 for $2,500, payable to Ness Co., for merchandise purchased, terms 2/10, n/30.
     26. Issued Check No. 911 in payment of Voucher No. 920.
     30. Recorded Voucher No. 930 for $171.90 to replenish the petty cash fund for the following disbursements: store supplies, $67.50; office supplies, $41.25; miscellaneous administrative expense, $36.10; miscellaneous selling expense, $27.05.
     30. Issued Check No. 920 in payment of Voucher No. 930.
     31. Issued Check No. 921 in payment of Voucher No. 890.

EXERCISE 8-10
ENTRIES FOR PURCHASES
AT NET AMOUNT
Objective 3

Journalize in general journal form the following related transactions, assuming that invoices for items purchased are recorded at their net price after the allowable discount is deducted:

July 7. Voucher No. 419 is prepared for merchandise purchased from Tewkbery Co., $5,000, terms 1/10, n/30.
     15. Voucher No. 430 is prepared for merchandise purchased from Torre Co., $2,500, terms 2/10, n/30.
     25. Check No. 410 is issued in payment of Voucher No. 430.
Aug. 6. Check No. 423 is issued in payment of Voucher No. 419.

EXERCISE 8-11
PETTY CASH FUND ENTRIES
Objective 3

Journalize in general journal form the entries to record the following:

a. Voucher No. 5 is prepared to establish a petty cash fund of $150.
b. Check No. 4 is issued in payment of Voucher No. 5.
c. The amount of cash in the petty cash fund is now $17.30. Voucher No. 59 is prepared to replenish the fund, based on the following summary of petty cash receipts: office supplies, $52.15; miscellaneous selling expense, $50.60; miscellaneous administrative expense, $28.70. (Since the amount of the check to replenish the fund plus the balance in the fund do not equal $150, record the discrepancy in the cash short and over account.)
d. Check No. 55 is issued by the disbursing officer in payment of Voucher No. 59. The check is cashed and the money is placed in the fund.

EXERCISE 8-12
CASH CHANGE FUND
ENTRIES
Objective 3

Journalize in general journal form the following transactions:

a. Voucher No. 31 is prepared to establish a change fund of $500.
b. Check No. 25 is issued in payment of Voucher No. 31.
c. Cash sales for the day, according to the cash register tapes, were $4,655.30, and cash on hand is $5,156.50. A bank deposit ticket was prepared for $4,656.50.

How many errors can you find in the following bank reconciliation prepared as of the end of the current month?

Wright Company
Bank Reconciliation
For Month Ended April 30, 19—

Cash balance according to bank statement			$10,767.76
Add deposit of April 29, not recorded by bank			510.06
			$11,277.82
Deduct outstanding checks:			
No. 721		$ 345.95	
739		172.75	
743		359.60	
744		601.50	1,479.80
Adjusted balance			$ 9,801.02
Cash balance according to depositor's records			$ 7,491.32
Add: Proceeds of note collected by bank:			
Principal	$2,500.00		
Interest	75.00	$2,575.00	
Service charges		19.50	2,594.50
			$10,085.82
Deduct: Check returned because of insufficient funds		$ 266.80	
Error in recording April 15 deposit of $497			
as $479		18.00	284.80
Adjusted balance			$ 9,801.02

PROBLEMS

Series A

PROBLEM 8-1A
BANK RECONCILIATION
AND ENTRIES
Objective 1

The cash in bank account for A. C. Forrest Co. at June 30 of the current year indicated a balance of $20,100.30 after both the cash receipts journal and the check register for June had been posted. The bank statement indicated a balance of $31,016.30 on June 30. Comparison of the bank statement and the accompanying canceled checks and memorandums with the records revealed the following reconciling items:

a. Checks outstanding totaled $15,391.50.
b. A deposit of $6,917.75, representing receipts of June 30, had been made too late to appear on the bank statement.
c. The bank had collected $3,045 on a note left for collection. The face of the note was $2,900.
d. A check for $91 returned with the statement had been recorded erroneously in the check register as $19. The check was for the payment of an obligation to Leeco for the purchase of office equipment on account.
e. A check drawn for $55 had been erroneously charged by the bank as $550.
f. Bank service charges for June amounted to $35.75.

SPREADSHEET
PROBLEM

Instructions

1. Prepare a bank reconciliation.
2. Journalize the necessary entries in general journal form. The accounts have not been closed. The voucher system is used.

PROBLEM 8-2A
BANK RECONCILIATION
DETERMINED FROM
LISTINGS IN CHECK
REGISTER AND BANK
STATEMENT; RELATED
ENTRIES
Objective 1

Sorter Company uses the voucher system in controlling cash payments. All cash receipts are deposited each Wednesday and Friday in a night depository, after banking hours. The data required to reconcile the bank statement as of April 30 have been taken from various documents and records and are reproduced as follows. The sources of the data are printed in capital letters.

CASH IN BANK ACCOUNT:
  Balance as of April 1 $8,317.40

CASH RECEIPTS JOURNAL:
  Total of Cash in Bank Debit column for month of April   7,679.58

DUPLICATE DEPOSIT TICKETS:
  Date and amount of each deposit in April:

Date	Amount	Date	Amount	Date	Amount
April 1	$908.50	April 10	$896.61	April 22	$897.34
3	854.17	15	882.95	24	942.71
8	840.50	17	946.74	29	510.06

CHECK REGISTER:
  Number and amount of each check issued in April:

Check No.	Amount	Check No.	Amount	Check No.	Amount
740	$237.50	747	Void	754	$249.75
741	495.15	748	$450.90	755	172.75
742	501.90	749	640.13	756	113.95
743	671.30	750	376.77	757	907.95
744	506.88	751	299.37	758	359.60
745	117.25	752	537.01	759	601.50
746	298.66	753	380.95	760	486.39

Total amount of checks issued in April $ 8,405.66

APRIL BANK STATEMENT:
  Balance as of April 1 $ 8,447.20
  Deposits and other credits   10,502.77
  Checks and other debits   (8,082.21)
  Balance as of April 30 $10,867.76

Date and amount of each deposit in April:

Date	Amount	Date	Amount	Date	Amount
April 1	$690.25	April 9	$840.50	April 18	$964.74
2	908.50	11	896.61	23	897.34
4	854.17	16	882.95	25	942.71

CHECKS ACCOMPANYING APRIL BANK STATEMENT:
  Number and amount of each check, rearranged in numerical sequence:

Check No.	Amount	Check No.	Amount	Check No.	Amount
731	$162.15	744	$506.88	751	$299.37
738	251.40	745	117.25	752	537.01
739	60.55	746	298.66	753	380.95
740	237.50	748	450.90	754	249.75
741	495.15	749	640.13	756	113.95
742	501.90	750	376.77	757	907.95
743	671.30			760	486.39

BANK MEMORANDUMS ACCOMPANYING APRIL BANK STATEMENT:

Date	Description	Amount
April 9	Bank credit memo for note collected:	
	Principal	$2,500.00
	Interest	125.00
28	Bank debit memo for check returned because of insufficient funds	291.90
30	Bank debit memo for service charges	44.40

BANK RECONCILIATION FOR PRECEDING MONTH:

Sorter Company
Bank Reconciliation
March 31, 19—

Cash balance according to bank statement		$8,447.20
Add deposit for March 31, not recorded by bank		690.25
		$9,137.45
Deduct outstanding checks:		
No. 731	$162.15	
736	345.95	
738	251.40	
739	60.55	820.05
Adjusted balance		$8,317.40
Cash balance according to depositor's records		$8,352.50
Deduct service charges		35.10
Adjusted balance		$8,317.40

Instructions

1. Prepare a bank reconciliation as of April 30. If errors in recording deposits or checks are discovered, assume that the errors were made by the company. Assume that all deposits are from cash sales. All checks are in payment of vouchers.
2. Journalize the necessary entries in general journal form. The accounts have not been closed.
3. What is the amount of Cash in Bank that should appear on the balance sheet as of April 30?
4. Assume that in preparing the bank reconciliation, you note that a canceled check for $450 has been incorrectly recorded by the bank as $540. Briefly explain how the error would be included in the bank reconciliation and how it should be corrected.

SHARPEN YOUR COMMUNICATION SKILLS

PROBLEM 8-3A
VOUCHER AND CHECK REGISTERS; ACCOUNTS PAYABLE ACCOUNT; BANK RECONCILIATION
Objectives 1, 3

If the working papers correlating with the textbook are not used, omit Problem 8-3A.

Portions of the voucher register, check register, and accounts payable account of Midler Co. are presented in the working papers. Cash disbursements and other selected transactions completed during the period May 26–31 of the current year are described as follows:

May 26. Issued Check No. 754 to Lowe Co. in payment of Voucher No. 611 for $3,000, less cash discount of 2%.
26. Recorded Voucher No. 617, payable to Victor Co. for merchandise, $5,000, terms 2/10, n/30. (Purchases invoices are recorded at the invoice price.)
26. Recorded Voucher No. 618, payable to United Auto Insurance Co. for an insurance policy, $1,975.
26. Issued Check No. 755 in payment of Voucher No. 618.
27. Recorded Voucher No. 619, payable to Gleason Co. for merchandise, $2,250, terms 1/10, n/30.
27. Recorded Voucher No. 620 for $10,200, payable to Marine National Bank for note payable, $10,000, and interest, $200.
27. Issued Check No. 756 in payment of Voucher No. 620.
28. Recorded Voucher No. 621, payable to Lakewood Gazette for advertising for May, $630.
28. Issued Check No. 757 in payment of Voucher No. 621.
29. Recorded Voucher No. 622, payable to Petty Cash for $189.05, distributed as follows: office supplies, $57.40; advertising expense, $20.55; delivery expense, $40.10; miscellaneous selling expense, $31.95; miscellaneous administrative expense, $39.05.
29. Issued Check No. 758 in payment of Voucher No. 622.
31. Issued Check No. 759 to Marcus Co. in payment of Voucher No. 614 for $1,550, no discount.

After the journals are posted at the end of the month, the cash in bank account has a debit balance of $19,930. The bank statement indicates a May 31 balance of $23,565.10. A comparison of paid checks with the check register reveals that Check Nos. 755 and 759 are outstanding. Check No. 699 for $290, which appeared on the April reconciliation as outstanding, is still outstanding. Debit memorandums accompanying the bank statement indicate a charge of $150 for a check drawn by Ann Franks, a customer, which was returned because of insufficient funds, and $29.90 for service charges.

Instructions

1. Journalize the transactions for May 26–31 in the appropriate journals.
2. Total and rule the voucher register and the check register, and post totals to the accounts payable account. (*CR* may be used in the Posting Reference column of accounts to indicate postings from the check register.)
3. Complete the schedule of unpaid vouchers. (Compare the total with the balance of the accounts payable account as of May 31.)
4. Prepare a bank reconciliation and journalize any necessary entries.

PROBLEM 8-4A
TRANSACTIONS FOR PETTY CASH, ADVANCES TO SALESPERSONS FUND; CASH SHORT AND OVER
Objectives 2, 3

Crump Company has just adopted the policy of depositing all cash receipts in the bank and of making all payments by check in conjunction with the voucher system. The following transactions were selected from those completed in May of the current year:

May 2. Recorded Voucher No. 1 to establish a petty cash fund of $200 and a change fund of $500.
     2. Issued Check No. 419 in payment of Voucher No. 1.
     4. Recorded Voucher No. 5 to establish an advances to salespersons fund of $1,000.
     4. Issued Check No. 422 in payment of Voucher No. 5.
    17. The cash sales for the day, according to the cash register tapes, totaled $3,970.60. The combined count of all cash on hand (including the change fund) totaled $4,473.20.
    29. Recorded Voucher No. 44 to reimburse the petty cash fund for the following disbursements, each evidenced by a petty cash receipt:
        May 3. Store supplies, $21.50.
             5. Express charges on merchandise purchased, $16.00.
             8. Office supplies, $12.75.
            11. Office supplies, $9.20.
            17. Postage stamps, $52 (Office Supplies).
            19. Repair to office calculator, $37.50 (Miscellaneous Administrative Expense).
            22. Postage due on special delivery letter, $1.05 (Miscellaneous Administrative Expense).
            23. Express charges on merchandise purchased, $20.
            27. Office supplies, $11.10.
    29. Issued Check No. 452 in payment of Voucher No. 44.
    30. The cash sales for the day, according to the cash register tapes, totaled $4,055.50. The count of all cash on hand (including the change fund) totaled $4,551.60.
    31. Recorded Voucher No. 49 to replenish the advances to salespersons fund for the following expenditures for travel: Frank Abott, $212.50; Jeff Marlow, $356.50; Nancy Powell, $272.10.
    31. Issued Check No. 460 in payment of Voucher No. 49.

Instructions
Journalize the transactions in general journal form.

PROBLEM 8-5A
VOUCHER AND CHECK REGISTERS; ACCOUNTS PAYABLE ACCOUNT; SCHEDULE OF UNPAID VOUCHERS
Objective 3

Keller Company began business on May 21 of the current year. The following selected transactions were completed during the remainder of May:

May 22. Recorded Voucher No. 1, payable to Carr Co. for merchandise, $5,000, terms 1/10, n/30.
    22. Recorded Voucher No. 2, payable to Walter Company for office supplies, $250.
    23. Recorded Voucher No. 3, payable to Dwyer Co. for merchandise, $7,500, terms n/30.
    23. Issued Check No. 1 for $250 to Walter Company in payment of Voucher No. 2.
    25. Recorded Voucher No. 4, payable to Bunker Co. for store supplies, $490, terms cash.
    25. Issued Check No. 2 for $490 to Bunker Co. in payment of Voucher No. 4.
    27. Recorded Voucher No. 5, payable to Reese Co. for merchandise, $9,500, terms 1/10, n/30.

May 28. Recorded Voucher No. 6, payable to Andrews Office Equipment Co. for office equipment, $6,500, terms n/30.
　　30. Recorded Voucher No. 7, payable to Flash Express for transportation on merchandise purchases, $60.
　　30. Issued Check No. 3 for $60 to Flash Express in payment of Voucher No. 7.
　　31. Issued Check No. 4 to Carr Co. in payment of Voucher No. 1, less cash discount of 1%.

Instructions

1. Record the May vouchers in a voucher register similar to the one illustrated in this chapter, with the following amount columns: Accounts Payable Cr., Purchases Dr., Store Supplies Dr., Office Supplies Dr., and Other Accounts Dr. Purchases invoices are recorded at the gross amount.
2. Record the May checks in a check register similar to the one illustrated in this chapter, but omit the Bank Deposits and Balance columns. As each check is recorded in the check register, the date and check number should be inserted in the appropriate columns of the voucher register.
3. Total and rule the registers and post to a four-column ledger account for Accounts Payable, Account No. 211. (CR may be used in the Posting Reference column of the ledger account to indicate postings from the check register.)
4. Prepare a schedule of unpaid vouchers.

Instructions for Solving Problem 8-5A Using Solutions Software

1. Load opening balances.
2. Save the opening balances file to your drive and directory.
3. Set the run date to May 31 of the current year and enter your name.
4. Key the journal entries.
5. Display the journal entries.
6. Display a trial balance.
7. Save your data file to disk.
8. End the session.

S O L U T I O N S
S O F T W A R E

PROBLEM 8-6A
VOUCHER AND CHECK
REGISTERS; ACCOUNTS
PAYABLE ACCOUNT;
SCHEDULE OF UNPAID
VOUCHERS
Objective 3

Stanley Co. had the following vouchers in its unpaid voucher file at May 31 of the current year:

Due Date	Voucher No.	Creditor	Date of Invoice	Amount	Terms
June 3	714	Iris Co.	May 24	$3,000	1/10, n/30
June 12	696	Reese Co.	May 13	2,500	n/30
June 28	720	Horst Co.	May 29	1,750	n/30

The vouchers prepared and the checks issued during the month of June were as follows:

VOUCHERS

Date	Voucher No.	Payee	Amount	Terms	Account(s) Debited
June 1	723	Marshall Co.	$4,800	1/10, n/30	Purchases
2	724	LCS Co.	400	cash	Office supplies
6	725	Walls Co.	750	2/10, n/30	Purchases
7	726	Mann Supply	105	cash	Store supplies
9	727	Ramos Co.	1,250	2/10, n/30	Purchases
12	728	Ace Express	52	cash	Delivery expense
15	729	S&C Bank	7,140		Notes payable, $7,000 Interest expense, $140
18	730	Duncan Office Co.	2,250	n/30	Office equipment
19	731	Ross & Co.	950	2/10, n/30	Purchases
23	732	L. M. Carr Co.	2,200	cash	Store equipment
25	733	Thomas Co.	3,450	2/10, n/30	Purchases
30	734	Petty Cash	170		Store supplies, $55 Office supplies, $47 Misc. selling exp., $38 Misc. adm. exp., $30

CHECKS

Date	Check No.	Payee	Voucher Paid	Amount
June 2	690	LCS Co.	724	$ 400
3	691	Iris Co.	714	2,970
7	692	Mann Supply	726	105
11	693	Marshall Co.	723	4,752
12	694	Ace Express	728	52
12	695	Reese Co.	696	2,500
15	696	S&C Bank	729	7,140
16	697	Walls Co.	725	735
19	698	Ramos Co.	727	1,225
23	699	L. M. Carr Co.	732	2,200
28	700	Horst Co.	720	1,750
29	701	Ross & Co.	731	931
30	702	Petty Cash	734	170

SPREADSHEET PROBLEM

Instructions

1. Record the June 1 balance of $7,250 in a four-column ledger account for Accounts Payable, Account No. 205. Place a ✓ in the Posting Reference column.
2. Record the June vouchers in a voucher register similar to the one illustrated in this chapter, with the following amount columns: Accounts Payable Cr., Purchases Dr., Store Supplies Dr., Office Supplies Dr., and Other Accounts Dr. Purchases invoices are recorded at the gross amount.
3. Record the June checks in a check register similar to the one illustrated in this chapter, but omit the Bank Deposits and Balance columns. As each check is recorded in the check register, the date and check number should be inserted in the appropriate columns of the voucher register. (Assume that notations for payment of the May vouchers are made in the voucher register for May.)
4. Total and rule the registers and post to Accounts Payable. (CR may be used in the Posting Reference column of the ledger account to indicate postings from the check register.)
5. Prepare a schedule of unpaid vouchers.

SOLUTIONS SOFTWARE

Instructions for Solving Problem 8-6A Using Solutions Software

1. Load opening balances.
2. Save the opening balances file to your drive and directory.
3. Set the run date to June 30 of the current year and enter your name.
4. Key the journal entries.
5. Display the journal entries.
6. Display a trial balance.
7. Save your data file to disk.
8. End the session.

Series B

PROBLEM 8-1B
BANK RECONCILIATION
AND ENTRIES
Objective 1

The cash in bank account for R. O. Dibble Co. at May 31 of the current year indicated a balance of $14,460 after both the cash receipts journal and the check register for May had been posted. The bank statement indicated a balance of $19,391.40 on May 31. Comparison of the bank statement and the accompanying canceled checks and memorandums with the records revealed the following reconciling items:

a. Checks outstanding totaled $5,950.
b. A deposit of $4,215.50, representing receipts of May 31, had been made too late to appear on the bank statement.
c. The bank had collected $3,120 on a note left for collection. The face of the note was $3,000.
d. A check for $120 returned with the statement had been recorded erroneously in the check register as $210. The check was for the payment of an obligation to Buck & Co. for the purchase of office supplies on account.
e. A check drawn for $63 had been erroneously charged by the bank as $36.
f. Bank service charges for May amounted to $40.10.

**SPREADSHEET
PROBLEM**

PROBLEM 8-2B
BANK RECONCILIATION
DETERMINED FROM
LISTINGS IN CHECK
REGISTER AND BANK
STATEMENT; RELATED
ENTRIES
Objective 1

Instructions

1. Prepare a bank reconciliation.
2. Journalize the necessary entries in general journal form. The accounts have not been closed. The voucher system is used.

Rundle Company employs the voucher system in controlling cash payments. All cash receipts are deposited each Wednesday and Friday in a night depository, after banking hours. The data required to reconcile the bank statement as of July 31 have been taken from various documents and records and are reproduced as follows. The sources of the data are printed in capital letters.

CASH IN BANK ACCOUNT:
   Balance as of July 1 $9,578.00

CASH RECEIPTS JOURNAL:
   Total of Cash in Bank Debit column for month of July   6,232.60

DUPLICATE DEPOSIT TICKETS:
   Date and amount of each deposit in July:

Date	Amount	Date	Amount	Date	Amount
July 2	$619.50	July 12	$780.70	July 23	$731.45
5	701.80	16	600.10	26	601.50
9	819.24	19	701.26	30	677.05

CHECK REGISTER:
   Number and amount of each check issued in July:

Check No.	Amount	Check No.	Amount	Check No.	Amount
614	$243.50	621	$409.50	628	$737.70
615	650.10	622	Void	629	329.90
616	279.90	623	Void	630	882.80
617	395.50	624	707.01	631	981.56
618	535.40	625	658.63	632	62.40
619	220.10	626	550.03	633	310.08
620	238.87	627	318.73	634	103.30

   Total amount of checks issued in July: $8,615.01

JULY BANK STATEMENT:
   Balance as of July 1 $ 9,422.80
   Deposits and other credits   11,436.35
   Checks and other debits   (8,583.61)
   Balance as of April 30 $12,275.54

Date and amount of each deposit in July:

Date	Amount	Date	Amount	Date	Amount
July 1	$780.80	July 11	$819.24	July 21	$701.26
3	619.50	13	780.70	24	731.45
6	701.80	17	600.10	28	601.50

CHECKS ACCOMPANYING JULY BANK STATEMENT:
   Number and amount of each check, rearranged in numerical sequence:

Check No.	Amount	Check No.	Amount	Check No.	Amount
580	$310.10	618	$535.40	626	$550.03
612	92.50	619	230.10	627	318.73
613	137.50	620	238.87	629	329.90
614	243.50	621	409.50	630	882.80
615	650.10	624	707.01	631	981.56
616	279.90	625	658.63	632	62.40
617	395.50			633	310.08

BANK MEMORANDUMS ACCOMPANYING JULY BANK STATEMENT:

Date	Description	Amount
July 14	Bank credit memo for note collected:	
	Principal	$5,000.00
	Interest	100.00
20	Bank debit memo for check returned because of insufficient funds	225.40
31	Bank debit memo for service charges	34.10

BANK RECONCILIATION FOR PRECEDING MONTH:

Rundle Company
Bank Reconciliation
June 30, 19—

Cash balance according to bank statement		$ 9,422.80
Add deposit for June 30, not recorded by bank		780.80
		$10,203.60
Deduct outstanding checks:		
No. 580	$310.10	
602	85.50	
612	92.50	
613	137.50	625.60
Adjusted balance		$ 9,578.00
Cash balance according to depositor's records		$ 9,605.70
Deduct service charges		27.70
Adjusted balance		$ 9,578.00

Instructions

1. Prepare a bank reconciliation as of July 31. If errors in recording deposits or checks are discovered, assume that the errors were made by the company. Assume that all deposits are from cash sales. All checks are in payment of vouchers.
2. Journalize the necessary entries in general journal form. The accounts have not been closed.
3. What is the amount of Cash in Bank that should appear on the balance sheet as of July 31?

■ SHARPEN YOUR ►
COMMUNICATION SKILLS

4. Assume that in preparing the bank reconciliation, you note that a canceled check for $800 has been incorrectly recorded by the bank as $900. Briefly explain how the error would be included in the bank reconciliation and how it should be corrected.

If the working papers correlating with the textbook are not used, omit Problem 8-3B.

PROBLEM 8-3B
VOUCHER AND CHECK
REGISTERS; ACCOUNTS
PAYABLE ACCOUNT; BANK
RECONCILIATION
Objectives 1, 3

Portions of the voucher register, check register, and accounts payable account of Midler Co. are presented in the working papers. Cash disbursements and other selected transactions completed during the period May 26–31 of the current year are described as follows:

May 26. Recorded Voucher No. 635, payable to Fox Co. for merchandise, $10,000, terms 2/10, n/30. (Purchases invoices are recorded at the invoice price.)
26. Issued Check No. 616 to Booker Co. in payment of Voucher No. 623 for $3,000, less cash discount of 1%.
27. Recorded Voucher No. 636, payable to Acme Auto Insurance Co. for an insurance policy, $1,584.
27. Issued Check No. 617 in payment of Voucher No. 636.
27. Recorded Voucher No. 637, payable to Solo Co. for merchandise, $2,500, terms 1/10, n/30.
28. Recorded Voucher No. 638 for $4,200, payable to Castle National Bank for note payable, $4,000, and interest, $200.
28. Issued Check No. 618 in payment of Voucher No. 638.
28. Issued Check No. 619 to Henry Stevens Co. in payment of Voucher No. 631 for $1,550, less cash discount of 2%.
29. Recorded Voucher No. 639, payable to Royal News for advertising for May, $350.
29. Issued Check No. 620 in payment of Voucher No. 639.

May 31. Recorded Voucher No. 640, payable to Petty Cash for $179.90, distributed as follows: office supplies, $42.50; advertising expense, $31.45; delivery expense, $22.50; miscellaneous selling expense, $47.22; miscellaneous administrative expense, $36.23.
     31. Issued Check No. 621 in payment of Voucher No. 640.

After the journals are posted at the end of the month, the cash in bank account has a debit balance of $18,075.50. The bank statement indicates a May 31 balance of $21,443.50. A comparison of paid checks with the check register reveals that Check Nos. 617, 619, and 620 are outstanding. Check No. 600 for $375, which appeared on the April reconciliation as outstanding, is still outstanding. A debit memorandum accompanying the bank statement indicates a charge of $460 for a check drawn by Vernon Co., a customer, which was returned because of insufficient funds.

Instructions

1. Journalize the transactions for May 26–31 in the appropriate journals.
2. Total and rule the voucher register and the check register, and post totals to the accounts payable account. (CR may be used in the Posting Reference column of accounts to indicate postings from the check register.)
3. Complete the schedule of unpaid vouchers. (Compare the total with the balance of the accounts payable account as of May 31.)
4. Prepare a bank reconciliation and journalize any necessary entries.

PROBLEM 8-4B
TRANSACTIONS FOR PETTY
CASH, ADVANCES TO
SALESPERSONS FUND;
CASH SHORT AND OVER
Objectives 2, 3

Jordan Company has just adopted the policy of depositing all cash receipts in the bank and of making all payments by check in conjunction with the voucher system. The following transactions were selected from those completed in June of the current year:

June 1. Recorded Voucher No. 1 to establish a petty cash fund of $250 and a change fund of $500.
      1. Issued Check No. 699 in payment of Voucher No. 1.
      3. Recorded Voucher No. 5 to establish an advances to salespersons fund of $1,000.
      4. Issued Check No. 702 in payment of Voucher No. 5.
     15. The cash sales for the day, according to the cash register tapes, totaled $2,995.60. The combined count of all cash on hand (including the change fund) totaled $3,498.20.
     26. Recorded Voucher No. 38 to reimburse the petty cash fund for the following disbursements, each evidenced by a petty cash receipt:
         June 4. Store supplies, $26.50.
               6. Express charges on merchandise purchased, $15.50.
               8. Office supplies, $14.75.
               9. Office supplies, $9.20.
              12. Postage stamps, $52 (Office Supplies).
              16. Repair to adding machine, $29.50 (Miscellaneous Administrative Expense).
              20. Repair to typewriter, $31.50 (Miscellaneous Administrative Expense).
              22. Postage due on special delivery letter, $1.05 (Miscellaneous Administrative Expense).
              24. Express charges on merchandise purchased, $19.50.
     26. Issued Check No. 737 in payment of Voucher No. 38.
     30. The cash sales for the day, according to the cash register tapes, totaled $3,009.50. The count of all cash on hand (including the change fund) totaled $3,505.60.
     30. Recorded Voucher No. 43 to replenish the advances to salespersons fund for the following expenditures for travel: Susan Reeser, $219.50; Frank Sampson, $333.40; Alice Yates, $275.10.
     30. Issued Check No. 740 in payment of Voucher No. 43.

Instructions

Journalize the transactions in general journal form.

PROBLEM 8-5B
VOUCHER AND CHECK
REGISTERS; ACCOUNTS
PAYABLE ACCOUNT;
SCHEDULE OF UNPAID
VOUCHERS
Objective 3

Buckingham Company began business on June 20 of the current year. The following selected transactions were completed during the remainder of June:

June 21. Recorded Voucher No. 1, payable to Polk Co. for merchandise, $9,500, terms 1/10, n/30.
   22. Recorded Voucher No. 2, payable to Newton Supplies Co. for office supplies, $620.
   23. Recorded Voucher No. 3, payable to C. Masters and Son for merchandise, $5,100, terms n/30.
   23. Issued Check No. 1 for $620 to Newton Supplies Co. in payment of Voucher No. 2.
   25. Recorded Voucher No. 4, payable to Rudd Co. for store supplies, $375, terms cash.
   25. Issued Check No. 2 for $375 to Rudd Co. in payment of Voucher No. 4.
   27. Recorded Voucher No. 5, payable to Ramos Co. for merchandise, $4,500, terms 1/10, n/30.
   28. Recorded Voucher No. 6, payable to Hoffman Office Equipment Co. for office equipment, $6,500, terms n/30.
   29. Recorded Voucher No. 7, payable to Ace Express for transportation on merchandise purchases, $65.
   30. Issued Check No. 3 for $65 to Ace Express in payment of Voucher No. 7.
   30. Issued Check No. 4 to Polk Co. in payment of Voucher No. 1, less cash discount of 1%.

Instructions

1. Record the June vouchers in a voucher register similar to the one illustrated in this chapter, with the following amount columns: Accounts Payable Cr., Purchases Dr., Store Supplies Dr., Office Supplies Dr., and Other Accounts Dr. Purchases invoices are recorded at the gross amount.
2. Record the June checks in a check register similar to the one illustrated in this chapter, but omit the Bank Deposits and Balance columns. As each check is recorded in the check register, the date and check number should be inserted in the appropriate columns of the voucher register.
3. Total and rule the registers and post to a four-column ledger account for Accounts Payable, Account No. 211. (*CR* may be used in the Posting Reference column of the ledger account to indicate postings from the check register.)
4. Prepare a schedule of unpaid vouchers.

S O L U T I O N S
S O F T W A R E

Instructions for Solving Problem 8-5B Using Solutions Software

1. Load opening balances.
2. Save the opening balances file to your drive and directory.
3. Set the run date to June 30 of the current year and enter your name.
4. Key the journal entries.
5. Display the journal entries.
6. Display a trial balance.
7. Save your data file to disk.
8. End the session.

PROBLEM 8-6B
VOUCHER AND CHECK
REGISTERS; ACCOUNTS
PAYABLE ACCOUNT;
SCHEDULE OF UNPAID
VOUCHERS
Objective 3

Milner Clothiers had the following vouchers in its unpaid voucher file at May 31 of the current year:

Due Date	Voucher No.	Creditor	Date of Invoice	Amount	Terms
June 8	510	Down Co.	May 29	$9,000	1/10, n/30
June 10	498	RX Shoes	May 11	3,500	n/30
June 13	500	Hill Co.	May 14	4,750	n/30

The vouchers prepared and the checks issued during the month of June were as follows:

VOUCHERS

Date	Voucher No.	Payee	Amount	Terms	Account(s) Debited
June 3	518	Sheer Fashions	$ 9,500	cash	Purchases
4	519	R and M Supply	110	n/10	Store Supplies
5	520	Barr Co.	1,250	2/10, n/30	Purchases
8	521	C. C. Glass Co.	900	2/10, n/30	Purchases
13	522	Second National Bank	20,500		Notes payable, $20,000
					Interest expense, $500
15	523	Roberts Supply	13,950	n/30	Office equipment
20	524	Sax Printers	215	cash	Office supplies
22	525	Bach Sportswear	1,250	2/10, n/30	Purchases
25	526	The Blouse Shop	1,900	1/10, n/30	Purchases
28	527	Eastman Co.	550	n/30	Purchases
30	528	Parkhill Motors	30,000	cash	Delivery equipment
30	529	Petty Cash	175		Office supplies, $50
					Store supplies, $49
					Misc. selling exp., $39
					Misc. adm. exp., $37

CHECKS

Date	Check No.	Payee	Voucher Paid	Amount
June 3	390	Sheer Fashions	518	$ 9,500
8	391	Down Co.	510	8,910
10	392	RX Shoes	498	3,500
13	393	Hill Co.	500	4,750
13	394	Second National Bank	522	20,500
14	395	R and M Supply	519	110
15	396	Barr Co.	520	1,225
18	397	C. C. Glass Co.	521	882
20	398	Sax Printers	524	215
30	399	Parkhill Motors	528	30,000
30	400	Petty Cash	529	175

SPREADSHEET PROBLEM

Instructions

1. Record the June 1 balance of $17,250 in a four-column ledger account for Accounts Payable, Account No. 205. Place a ✔ in the Posting Reference column.
2. Record the June vouchers in a voucher register similar to the one illustrated in this chapter, with the following amount columns: Accounts Payable Cr., Purchases Dr., Store Supplies Dr., Office Supplies Dr., and Other Accounts Dr. Purchases invoices are recorded at the gross amount.
3. Record the June checks in a check register similar to the one illustrated in this chapter, but omit the Bank Deposits and Balance columns. As each check is recorded in the check register, the date and check number should be inserted in the appropriate columns of the voucher register. (Assume that notations for payment of the May vouchers are made in the voucher register for May.)
4. Total and rule the registers and post to Accounts Payable. (CR may be used in the Posting Reference column of the ledger account to indicate posting from the check register.)
5. Prepare a schedule of unpaid vouchers.

SOLUTIONS
SOFTWARE

Instructions for Solving Problem 8-6B Using Solutions Software

1. Load opening balances.
2. Save the opening balances file to your drive and directory.
3. Set the run date to June 30 of the current year and key your name.
4. Key the journal entries.
5. Display the journal entries.
6. Display a trial balance.
7. Save your data file to disk.
8. End the session.

MINI-CASE 8 CRIER & COMPANY

The records of Crier & Company indicate a July 31 cash in bank balance of $21,931.05, which includes undeposited receipts for July 30 and 31. The cash balance on the bank statement as of July 31 is $18,704.95. This balance includes a note of $5,000 plus $150 interest collected by the bank but not recorded in the cash receipts journal. Checks outstanding on July 31 were as follows: No. 470, $950.20; No. 479, $510; No. 490, $616.50; No. 996, $227.40; No. 997, $720; and No. 999, $351.50.

On July 3, the cashier resigned, effective at the end of the month. Before leaving on July 31, the cashier prepared the following bank reconciliation:

Cash balance per books, July 31		$21,931.05
Add outstanding checks:		
No. 996	$227.40	
997	720.00	
999	351.50	1,198.90
		$23,129.95
Less undeposited receipts		4,425.00
Cash balance per bank, July 31		$18,704.95
Deduct unrecorded note with interest		5,150.00
True cash, July 31		$13,554.95

Calculator Tape of Outstanding Checks

0.00	*
227.40	+
720.00	+
351.50	+
1,198.90	*

Subsequently, the owner of Crier & Company discovered that the cashier had stolen all undeposited receipts in excess of the $4,425 on hand on July 31. The owner, a close family friend, has asked your help in determining the amount that the former cashier has stolen.

Instructions:

1. Determine the amount the cashier stole from Crier & Company. Show your computations in good form.
2. How did the cashier attempt to conceal the theft?
3. a. ▪ ► Identify two major weaknesses in internal controls, which allowed the cashier to steal the undeposited cash receipts.
   b. ▪ ► Recommend improvements in internal controls, so that similar types of thefts of undeposited cash receipts can be prevented.

ANSWERS TO SELF-EXAMINATION QUESTIONS

1. **B** On any specific date, the cash in bank account in a depositor's ledger may not agree with the reciprocal account in the bank's ledger because of delays and/or errors by either party in recording transactions. The purpose of a bank reconciliation, therefore, is to determine the reasons for any differences between the two account balances. All errors should then be corrected by the depositor or the bank, as appropriate. In arriving at the adjusted (correct) cash balance according to the bank statement, outstanding checks must be deducted (answer B) to adjust for checks that have been written by the depositor but that have not yet been presented to the bank for payment.

2. **C** All reconciling items that are added to and deducted from the *cash balance according to the depositor's records* on the bank reconciliation (answer C) require that journal entries be made by the depositor to correct errors made in recording transactions or to bring the cash account up to date for delays in recording transactions.

3. **D** A voucher (answer A) is the form on which is recorded pertinent data about a liability. After a voucher is approved by the designated official, it is recorded in the voucher register (answer D). The voucher is filed in an unpaid vouchers file (answer B) until it is due for payment. It is then removed from the file and a check is issued in payment and an entry is made in the check register (answer C).

4. **D** A major advantage of recording purchases at the net amount (answer A) is that the cost of failing to take discounts is recorded in the accounts (answer B) and then reported as an expense on the income statement (answer C).

5. **D** To avoid the delay, annoyance, and expense that is associated with paying all obligations by check, relatively small amounts (answer A) are paid from a petty cash fund. The fund is established by estimating the amount of cash needed to pay these small amounts during a specified period (answer B), and it is then reimbursed when the amount of money in the fund is reduced to a predetermined minimum amount (answer C).

You and Accounting

At one time or another, most people borrow money in order to buy such items as a stereo system, a car, or a home. When you borrow money, the lender generally charges interest on the outstanding balance. For example, when you borrow money to buy a car, you must pay the lender interest on the money borrowed. This chapter describes and illustrates the computation of interest. This discussion will allow you to estimate the amount of interest you can expect to pay when you borrow money. In turn, this discussion will allow you to determine whether the lender is computing your interest accurately and truthfully according to the lending agreement.

Chapter 9
Receivables and Temporary Investments

For many businesses, the revenue from sales on account is one of the largest factors influencing the amount of net income. As credit is granted, the resulting receivables may represent a significant portion of the total current assets. This chapter discusses the accounting for such receivables as well as the accounting for notes receivable. As the receivables are collected, the cash is recorded and accounted for in the manner discussed in prior chapters. If the amount of cash on hand exceeds the business's immediate cash needs, the excess cash may be invested in securities until it is needed. This chapter concludes with a discussion of the accounting for such temporary investments.

LEARNING OBJECTIVES
After studying this chapter, you should be able to:

Objective 1
List the common classifications of receivables.

Objective 2
Summarize and provide examples of internal control procedures that apply to receivables.

Objective 3
State the accounting implications of promissory notes.

Objective 4
Journalize the entries for notes receivable transactions, including discounted notes receivable and dishonored notes receivable.

Objective 5
Name and describe two methods of accounting for uncollectible receivables.

Objective 6
Journalize the entries for the allowance method of accounting for uncollectibles, and estimate uncollectible receivables based on sales and on an analysis of receivables.

Objective 7
Journalize the entries for the direct write-off of uncollectible receivables.

Objective 8
Define temporary investments, give an example of two kinds of temporary investments, and explain how temporary investments are valued on the balance sheet.

Objective 9
Prepare the Current Assets section of a balance sheet that includes temporary investments and receivables.

CLASSIFICATIONS OF RECEIVABLES

Objective 1
List the common classifications
of receivables.

The term **receivables** includes all money claims against other entities, including people, business firms, and other organizations. Receivables are acquired by business enterprises in various kinds of transactions, the most common of which is the sale of merchandise or services on credit.

Credit may be granted on open account or on the basis of a formal instrument of credit, such as a promissory note. A promissory note, often simply called a **note**, is a written promise to pay a sum of money on demand or at a definite time. Notes are often used for credit periods of more than sixty days, such as an installment plan for equipment sales. Notes may also be used in settlement of an open account and in borrowing or lending money.

To the creditor, a claim supported by a note has some advantages over a claim in the form of an account receivable. By signing a note, the debtor recognizes the debt and agrees to pay it according to the terms listed. A note is therefore a stronger legal claim if there is court action. It is also more liquid than an open account because the holder can usually sell it more readily to a bank or other financial agency in exchange for cash.

The enterprise owning a note refers to it as a note receivable. If notes and accounts receivable originate from sales transactions, they are sometimes called **trade receivables**. Unless otherwise described, accounts and notes receivable may be assumed to have originated from credit sales in the usual course of business.

Other receivables include interest receivable, loans to officers or employees, and loans to affiliated companies. As an aid in classifying receivables properly on the balance sheet, a general ledger account should be maintained for each type of receivable. Subsidiary ledgers may also be maintained, as necessary.

All receivables that are expected to be realized in cash within a year are presented in the Current Assets section of the balance sheet. Those that are not currently collectible, such as long-term loans, should be listed under the caption *Investments* below the Current Assets section.

INTERNAL CONTROL OF RECEIVABLES

Objective 2
Summarize and provide
examples of internal control
procedures that apply to
receivables.

The principles of internal control discussed in prior chapters can be used to establish procedures to safeguard receivables. These controls include the separation of the business operations and the accounting for receivables. In this way, the accounting records can serve as an independent check on operations. Thus, the employee who handles the accounting for notes and accounts receivable should not be involved with the operating aspects of approving credit or collecting receivables. The separation of these functions reduces the possibility of errors and the misuse of funds.

To further illustrate the internal control principle of separating related operating functions, assume that salespersons have been given authority to approve credit. If the salespersons are paid salaries plus commissions, say 10% of sales, they can increase their commissions by approving poor credit risks. Thus, the credit approval function is normally assigned to an individual outside the sales area.

Within the accounting function, related functions should also be separated. In this way, the work of one employee serves as a check on the work of another employee. For example, the responsibilities for the accounts receivable subsidiary ledger and for the general ledger should be separated. The work of the accounts receivable clerk can be checked by comparing the total of the individual account balances in the subsidiary ledger with the balance of the accounts receivable controlling account that is maintained by the general ledger clerk. If one individual performed both functions, this control would be lacking.

For most businesses, the primary receivables are notes receivable and accounts receivable. Generally, notes receivable are recorded in a single general ledger account. If there are many notes, the general ledger account can be supported by a notes receivable register or a subsidiary ledger. The register would contain details of each note, such as the name of the maker, place of payment, amount, term, interest rate, and due date. Reference to the due date section directs attention to those notes that are due for payment. In this way, the maker of the note can be notified when the note is due, and the risk that the maker will overlook the due date is minimized.

Control over accounts receivable begins with the proper credit approval of the sale by an authorized company official. Procedures for granting credit should be developed by the credit department of the company. Likewise, procedures for authorizing adjustments of accounts receivable, such as for sales returns and allowances and sales discounts, should be developed. Collection procedures should also be established to ensure timely collection of accounts receivable and to minimize losses from uncollectible accounts.

CHARACTERISTICS OF NOTES RECEIVABLE

Objective 3
State the accounting implications of promissory notes.

As indicated earlier in the chapter, a note is a written promise to pay a sum of money on demand or at a definite time. As in the case of a check, it must be payable to the order of a certain person or firm or to the bearer. It must also be signed by the person or firm that makes the promise. The one to whose order the note is payable is called the **payee**, and the one making the promise is called the **maker**. The face amount of the note is called the **principal**. In the example in Exhibit 1, Pearland Company is the payee, Selig Company is the maker, and the principal is $2,500.

Exhibit 1
Promissory Note

$ 2,500.00	Fresno, California March 16 19 94

Ninety days _____ AFTER DATE __We__ PROMISE TO PAY TO

THE ORDER OF __Pearland Company_____

__Two thousand five hundred 00/100 - - - - - - - - - - -__ DOLLARS

PAYABLE AT __First National Bank_____

VALUE RECEIVED WITH INTEREST AT __10%__
NO. __14__ DUE __June 14, 1994__   *H.B. Lane*
                                    TREASURER, *SELIG COMPANY*

Notes have several characteristics that have accounting implications. These characteristics are described in the following paragraphs.

Due Date

The date a note is to be paid is called the **due date** or **maturity date**. The period of time between the issuance date and the due date of a short-term note may be stated in either days or months. When the term of a note is stated in days, the due date is the specified number of days after its issuance. To illustrate, the due date of the 90-day note in Exhibit 1 is determined as follows:

Term of the note		90
March (days)	31	
Date of note	16	15
Number of days remaining		75
April (days)		30
		45
May (days)		31
Due date, June		14

When the term of a note is stated as a certain number of months after the issuance date, the due date is determined by counting the number of months from the issuance date. Thus, a 3-month note dated June 5 would be due on September 5. In those cases in which there is no date in the month of maturity that corresponds to the issuance date, the due date becomes the last day of the month. For example, a 2-month note dated July 31 would be due on September 30.

Interest-Bearing Notes and Non-Interest-Bearing Notes

A note that specifies an interest rate for the period between the issuance date and the due date is called an **interest-bearing note**. A **non-interest-bearing note** does not specify an interest rate. The note in Exhibit 1 is an interest-bearing note.

Interest

Interest rates for interest-bearing notes are usually stated in terms of a period of one year, regardless of the actual period of time involved. Thus, the interest on $2,000 for one year at 12% is $240 (12% of $2,000); the interest on $2,000 for one-fourth of one year at 12% is $60 (1/4 of $240).

Notes covering a period of time longer than one year normally provide that the interest be paid semiannually, quarterly, or at some other stated interval. The time involved in business credit transactions is usually less than one year, and the interest provided for by a note is payable at the time the note is paid. In computing interest for a period of less than one year, agencies of the federal government use the actual number of days in the year. For example, 90 days is 90/365 of one year. The usual business practice is to use 360 days. Thus, 90 days is considered to be 90/360 of one year.

The basic formula for computing interest is as follows:

$$\text{Principal} \times \text{Rate} \times \text{Time} = \text{Interest}$$

To illustrate the use of the formula, the $62.50 interest for the $2,500, 90-day, 10% note in Exhibit 1 is computed as follows:

$$\$2,500 \times \frac{10}{100} \times \frac{90}{360} = \$62.50 \text{ interest}$$

One of the commonly used shortcut methods of computing interest is called the 60-day, 6% method. The 6% annual rate is converted to the effective rate of 1% for a 60-day period (60/360 of 6%). Accordingly, the interest on any amount for 60 days at 6% is determined by moving the decimal point in the principal two places to the left. For example, the interest on $1,500 at 6% for 60 days is $15. The amount obtained by moving the decimal point must be adjusted (1) for interest rates greater or less than 6% and (2) for periods of time greater or less than 60 days. For example, the interest on $1,500 at 6% for 90 days is $22.50 (90/60 of $15). The interest on $1,500 at 12% for 60 days is $30 (12/6 of $15).

When the term of a note is stated in months instead of in days, each month may be considered as being 1/12 of a year. Alternatively, the actual number of days in the term may be counted. For example, the interest on a 3-month note dated June 1 could be computed on the basis of 3/12 of a year or on the basis of 92/360 of a year. It is the usual business practice to use the first method, while banks usually charge interest for the exact number of days. To simplify, the usual business practice will be used in this text.

Maturity Value

The amount that is due at the maturity or due date is called the **maturity value**. The maturity value of a non-interest-bearing note is the face amount. The maturity value of an interest-bearing note is the sum of the face amount and the interest. In the note in Exhibit 1, the maturity value is $2,562.50 ($2,500 face amount plus $62.50 interest).

The Bobtailed Year

The practice of using the 360-day year for determining interest has a surprisingly significant effect on the economy as a whole. Both the background of the practice and its effect are described in the following excerpts from an article in *The Wall Street Journal*:

In 46 B.C., Julius Caesar proclaimed that a year would be pegged at 365 days, with an extra day added every fourth year. What was good enough for Caesar has been good enough for the rest of us ever since except for the nation's bankers.

A lot of bankers are using a 360-day year to compute the interest they charge to borrowers on commercial and corporate loans. This means, in effect, that they are collecting a smidgin more interest on these loans than their stated "annual" interest rates would indicate. . . .

Though only small amounts of money are involved in the difference between 365- and 360-day charges on any one loan, the nickels and dimes add up to an impressive pile. . . . [In fact, the overcharges that result from the use of the bobtailed year have been estimated to be at least $145 million a year.]

According to the bankers, use of the bobtailed year began before the widespread use of adding machines; clerks who had to do the computations with pencil and paper found it a lot easier to multiply and divide by 360 rather than 365 or 366. Since nobody seemed to care much, the 360-day base continued in use through the age of calculators and now is embedded in the banks' computer programs. "Converting our computers to a 365-day year would be a massive job", says one officer of a major bank.

Source: James F. Carberry, "365 Days May Have Been Good Enough For Caesar, But Lenders Find That 360 Provide More Profit," *The Wall Street Journal* (March 30, 1973).

ACCOUNTING FOR NOTES RECEIVABLE

Objective 4
Journalize the entries for notes receivable transactions, including discounted notes receivable and dishonored notes receivable.

The typical retail enterprise makes most of its sales for cash or on account. If the account of a customer becomes past due, the creditor may insist that the account be converted into a note. In this way, the debtor is given more time to make payment. Also, if the creditor needs more funds, the note may be endorsed and sold to a bank or other financial agency. Notes may also be received by retail firms that sell merchandise on long-term credit. For example, a dealer in household appliances may require a down payment at the time of sale and accept a note or a series of notes for the remainder. Such arrangements usually provide for monthly payments.

When a note is received from a customer to apply on account, the facts are recorded by debiting the notes receivable account and crediting Accounts Receivable. The accounts receivable subsidiary account of the customer from whom the note is received is also credited. To illustrate, assume that the account of Glenn Enterprises, which has a balance of $9,200, is past due. A 90-day, non-interest-bearing note for that amount, dated May 16, 1994, is accepted in settlement of the account. The note receivable is recorded at its face value, and the entry to record the transaction is as follows:

May 16	Notes Receivable	9,200	
	Accounts Receivable—Glenn Enterprises		9,200
	Received 90-day, non-interest-bearing note dated May 16, 1994.		

When the $9,200 due on the note is collected, the following entry is recorded in the cash receipts journal:

| Aug. 14 | Cash | 9,200 | |
| | Notes Receivable | | 9,200 |

Interest-Bearing Notes Receivable

If the note received from a customer on account is interest-bearing, interest must be recorded. For example, assume that a 30-day, 12% note dated November 21,

1994, is accepted in settlement of the account of W. A. Bunn Co., which has a balance of $6,000. The entry to record the transaction is as follows:

Nov. 21	Notes Receivable	6,000	
	Accounts Receivable—W. A. Bunn Co.		6,000
	Received 30-day, 12% note dated		
	November 21, 1994.		

At the time the note matures, the entry to record the receipt of $6,060 ($6,000 principal plus $60 interest) is as follows:

Dec. 21	Cash	6,060	
	Notes Receivable		6,000
	Interest Income		60

If an interest-bearing note matures in a later fiscal period, the interest accrued in the period in which the note is received must be recorded. For example, assume that a 90-day, 12% note dated December 1 is received from Crawford Company in settlement of its account, which has a balance of $4,000. The entry to record the receipt of the note is similar to the November 21 entry above. On December 31, the following adjusting entry is necessary to record the $40 interest earned for 30 days in December ($4,000 × 30/360 × 12/100):

| Dec. 31 | Interest Receivable | 40 | |
| | Interest Income | | 40 |

The interest income account is closed at December 31. The amount of interest income is reported in the Other Income section of the income statement for the year ended December 31, 1994.

Discounting Notes Receivable

Although it is not a common transaction, a company in need of cash may transfer its notes receivable to a bank by endorsement. The **discount** (interest) charged by the bank is computed on the maturity value of the note for the period that the bank must hold the note. This period, called the **discount period,** is the time that will pass between the date of the transfer and the due date of the note. The amount of the **proceeds** paid to the endorser is the excess of the maturity value over the discount.

For example, assume that a 90-day, 12% note receivable for $1,800, dated April 8, is discounted at the payee's bank on May 3 at the rate of 14%. The data used in determining the effect of the transaction are as follows:

Face value of note dated April 8	$1,800.00
Interest on note (90 days at 12%)	54.00
Maturity value of note due July 7	$1,854.00
Discount on maturity value (65 days from May 3 to July 7, at 14%)	46.87
Proceeds	$1,807.13

The same information is presented graphically in Exhibit 2. In reading the data, follow the direction of the arrows.

Exhibit 2
Diagram of Discounting a Note Receivable

The excess of the proceeds from discounting the note, $1,807.13, over its face value, $1,800, is recorded as interest income. The entry for the transaction, in general journal form, is as follows:

May 3	Cash	1,807.13	
	Notes Receivable		1,800.00
	Interest Income		7.13

The proceeds from discounting a note receivable may be less than the face value. When this situation occurs, the excess of the face value over the proceeds is recorded as interest expense. The length of the discount period and the difference between the interest rate and the discount rate determines whether interest expense or interest income will result from discounting.

Without a statement limiting responsibility, the endorser of a note is committed to paying the note if the maker defaults. Such potential obligations will become actual liabilities only if certain events occur in the future. These potential obligations are called **contingent liabilities**. Thus, the endorser of a note that has been discounted has a contingent liability until the due date. If the maker pays the promised amount at maturity, the contingent liability is removed without any action on the part of the endorser. If, on the other hand, the maker defaults and the endorser is notified according to legal requirements, the liability becomes an actual one.

Significant contingent liabilities should be disclosed on the balance sheet or in an accompanying note. Disclosure requirements for contingent liabilities are discussed and illustrated in a later chapter.

Dishonored Notes Receivable

If the maker of a note fails to pay the debt on the due date, the note is said to be *dishonored*. A **dishonored note receivable** is no longer negotiable. For this reason the holder usually transfers the claim, including any interest due, to the accounts receivable account. For example, assume that a $6,000, 30-day, 12% note received and recorded on November 21 has been dishonored at maturity. The entry to charge the note, including the interest, back to the customer's account is as follows:

Dec. 21	Accounts Receivable—W. A. Bunn Co.	6,060	
	Notes Receivable		6,000
	Interest Income		60
	Dishonored note and interest.		

If there had been some assurance that the maker would pay the note within a short time, action could be delayed until the matter is resolved. However, for future reference in extending credit, it may be desirable that the customer's account in the subsidiary ledger disclose the dishonor of the note.

When a discounted note receivable is dishonored, the holder usually notifies the endorser of that fact and asks for payment. If the request for payment and notification of dishonor are timely, the endorser is legally obligated to pay the amount due on the note. The entire amount paid to the holder by the endorser, including the interest, should be debited to the account receivable of the maker. For example, assume that the $1,800, 90-day, 12% note discounted on May 3 (Exhibit 2) is dishonored at maturity by the maker, Pryor & Co. The entry to record the payment by the endorser, in general journal form, is as follows:

| July 7 | Accounts Receivable—Pryor & Co. | 1,854 | |
| | Cash | | 1,854 |

In some cases, the holder of a dishonored note gives the endorser a notarized statement of the facts of the dishonor. The fee for this statement, known as a **protest fee**, is charged to the endorser, who in turn charges it to the maker of the note. For example, if the bank charges a protest fee of $12 in connection with the dishonored Pryor & Co. note, the entry to record the payment by the endorser is as follows:

| July 7 | Accounts Receivable—Pryor & Co. | 1,866 | |
| | Cash | | 1,866 |

UNCOLLECTIBLE RECEIVABLES

Objective 5
Name and describe two methods of accounting for uncollectible receivables.

Regardless of the care used in granting credit and the collection procedures used, a part of the claims from sales to customers on credit will normally not be collectible. The operating expense incurred because of the failure to collect receivables is called an expense or a loss from **uncollectible accounts, doubtful accounts,** or **bad debts.**[1]

There is no general rule for determining when an account or a note becomes uncollectible. The fact that a debtor fails to pay an account according to a sales contract or dishonors a note on the due date does not necessarily mean that the account will be uncollectible. Bankruptcy of the debtor is one of the most significant indications of partial or complete uncollectibility of a receivable. Other indications that an account may be uncollectible include the closing of the customer's business and the failure of repeated attempts to collect.

There are two methods of accounting for receivables that are believed to be uncollectible. The **allowance method** provides in advance for uncollectible receivables.[2] The other procedure, called the **direct write-off method** or **direct charge-off method**, recognizes the expense only when certain accounts are judged to be worthless.

ALLOWANCE METHOD OF ACCOUNTING FOR UNCOLLECTIBLES

Objective 6
Journalize the entries for the allowance method of accounting for uncollectibles, and estimate uncollectible receivables based on sales and on an analysis of receivables.

Most large business enterprises estimate currently the uncollectible portion of their trade receivables. The provision for future uncollectibility is made by an adjusting entry at the end of a fiscal period. As with all periodic adjustments, this entry serves two purposes. First, it provides for the reduction of the value of the receivables to the amount of cash expected to be realized in the future, called the **net realizable value.** Second, it matches the uncollectible expense of the current period with the related revenues of the period.

---

[1] If both notes and accounts are involved, both may be included in the expense account title, as in *Uncollectible Notes and Accounts Expense,* or *Uncollectible Receivables Expense.* Because of its wide usage and simplicity, *Uncollectible Accounts Expense* will be used in this text.
[2] The allowance method is not acceptable for determining the federal income tax of most taxpayers.

To illustrate the allowance method, assumed data for a new business firm, Richards Company, is used. The enterprise began business in August and chose to use the calendar year as its fiscal year. The accounts receivable account, shown below, has a balance of $105,000 at the end of the period.

ACCOUNT ACCOUNTS RECEIVABLE   ACCOUNT NO. 114

Date		Item	Post. Ref.	Debit	Credit	Balance Debit	Balance Credit
19—							
Aug.	31		S3	20,000		20,000	
Sep.	30		S6	25,000		45,000	
	30		CR4		15,000	30,000	
Oct.	31		S10	40,000		70,000	
	31		CR7		25,000	45,000	
Nov.	30		S13	38,000		83,000	
	30		CR10		23,000	60,000	
Dec.	31		S16	75,000		135,000	
	31		CR13		30,000	105,000	

Among the customer accounts making up the $105,000 balance in Accounts Receivable are a number of balances that are past due. No specific accounts are believed to be totally uncollectible at this time. However, it seems likely that some will be collected only in part and that others will become worthless. Based on a careful study, it is estimated that a total of $3,000 will eventually prove to be uncollectible. The net realizable value of the accounts receivable is therefore $102,000 ($105,000 – $3,000). The $3,000 reduction in value is the uncollectible accounts expense for the period.

Because the $3,000 reduction in accounts receivable is an estimate, it cannot be credited to specific customer accounts or to the accounts receivable controlling account. Instead, a contra asset account entitled Allowance for Doubtful Accounts is credited. The adjusting entry to record the expense and the reduction in the asset is as follows:

Page 4

	Adjusting Entry			
Dec. 31	Uncollectible Accounts Expense	717	3,000	
	Allowance for Doubtful Accounts	115		3,000

The two accounts to which the entry is posted are illustrated as follows:

ACCOUNT UNCOLLECTIBLE ACCOUNTS EXPENSE   ACCOUNT NO. 717

Date		Item	Post. Ref.	Debit	Credit	Balance Debit	Balance Credit
19—							
Dec.	31	Adjusting	J4	3,000		3,000	

ACCOUNT ALLOWANCE FOR DOUBTFUL ACCOUNTS   ACCOUNT NO. 115

Date		Item	Post. Ref.	Debit	Credit	Balance Debit	Balance Credit
19—							
Dec.	31	Adjusting	J4		3,000		3,000

The debit balance of $105,000 in Accounts Receivable is the amount of the total claims against customers on open account. The credit balance of $3,000 in Allowance for Doubtful Accounts is the amount to be deducted from Accounts Receivable to determine the net realizable value.

Uncollectible accounts expense is normally reported on the income statement as an administrative expense. This classification is used because the credit-granting and collection duties are the responsibilities of departments within the administrative area. At the end of the period, the $3,000 balance in Uncollectible Accounts Expense is closed to Income Summary.

The accounts receivable may be listed on the balance sheet at the net amount of $102,000, with a notation in parentheses showing the amount of the allowance. Alternately, the details may be presented as shown below in the Current Assets section of the balance sheet. When the allowance account includes provision for doubtful notes as well as accounts, it should be deducted from the total of Notes Receivable and Accounts Receivable.

Current assets:

Cash		$ 21,600
Accounts receivable	$105,000	
Less allowance for doubtful accounts	3,000	102,000

Write-Offs to the Allowance Account

When an account is believed to be uncollectible, it is written off against the allowance account as follows:

Jan. 21	Allowance for Doubtful Accounts	610	
	Accounts Receivable—John Parker		610
	To write off the uncollectible account.		

During the year, as accounts or portions of accounts are determined to be uncollectible, they are written off against Allowance for Doubtful Accounts. Authorization for write-offs should originate with the credit manager or other designated officer. The authorizations, which should be written, serve as support for the accounting entry.

The total amount written off against the allowance account during a period will rarely be equal to the amount in the account at the beginning of the period. The allowance account will have a credit balance at the end of the period if the write-offs during the period are less than the beginning balance. It will have a debit balance if the write-offs exceed the beginning balance. After the year-end adjusting entry is recorded, the allowance account will have a credit balance.

An account receivable that has been written off against the allowance account may later be collected. In such cases, the account should be reinstated by an entry that is the exact reverse of the write-off entry. For example, assume that the account of $610 written off in the preceding journal entry is later collected. The entry to reinstate the account would be as follows:

June 10	Accounts Receivable—John Parker	610	
	Allowance for Doubtful Accounts		610
	To reinstate account written		
	off earlier in the year.		

The cash received in payment would be recorded as a receipt on account as follows:

June 10	Cash	610	
	Accounts Receivable—John Parker		610

The two preceding entries can be combined. However, recording two separate entries in the customer's account, with proper notation, provides useful credit information.

Estimating Uncollectibles

The estimate of uncollectibles at the end of a fiscal period is based on past experience and forecasts of future business activity. When the general economic environment is favorable, the amount of the expense should normally be less than when the trend is in the opposite direction. The estimate of uncollectibles is usually based on either (1) the amount of sales for the period or (2) the amount and the age of the receivable accounts at the end of the period.

ESTIMATE BASED ON SALES. Accounts receivable are acquired as a result of sales on account. The amount of such sales during the year may therefore be used to estimate the amount of uncollectible accounts. The amount of this estimate is added to whatever balance exists in Allowance for Doubtful Accounts. For example, assume that the allowance account has a credit balance of $700 before adjustment. It is estimated from past experience that 1% of credit sales will be uncollectible. If credit sales for the period are $300,000, the adjusting entry for uncollectible accounts at the end of the period is as follows:

| Dec. 31 | Uncollectible Accounts Expense | 3,000 | |
| | Allowance for Doubtful Accounts | | 3,000 |

After the adjusting entry has been posted, the balance in the allowance account is $3,700. If there had been a debit balance of $200 in the allowance account before the year-end adjustment, the amount of the adjustment would still have been $3,000. The balance in the allowance account, after the adjusting entry has been posted, would be $2,800 ($3,000 – $200).

Instead of credit sales, total sales (including those made for cash) may be used in estimating the percentage of uncollectible accounts. Using total sales is less costly, since total sales is available in the sales account in the ledger. In contrast, a separate analysis may be required to determine credit sales. If the ratio of credit sales to cash sales does not change very much from year to year, estimates using total sales will be acceptable. In the above example, if 3/4 of 1% is used to estimate uncollectibles, based upon total sales of $400,000, the same estimate of $3,000 would result.

If the amount of write-offs is always greater or less than the amount provided by the adjusting entry, the percentage applied to the sales data should be revised. A new business enterprise, having no prior credit experience, may estimate uncollectible percentages using data from trade association journals and other industry publications.

The estimate-based-on-sales method of estimating the uncollectible accounts expense is widely used. Its advantages are that it is simple and it emphasizes the matching of uncollectible accounts expense with the related sales of the period.

ESTIMATE BASED ON ANALYSIS OF RECEIVABLES. The process of analyzing each account receivable in terms of the length of time it is past due is called aging the receivables. The base point for determining age is the due date of the account. The number and length of the time intervals used varies according to the credit terms granted to customers. An example of a typical aging of accounts receivable is shown in Exhibit 3.

Exhibit 3
Aging of Accounts Receivable

Customer	Balance	Not Due	Days Past Due					
			1-30	31-60	61-90	91-180	181-365	over 365
Ashby & Co.	$ 150			$ 150				
B. T. Barr	610					$ 350	$260	
Brock Co.	470	$ 470						
J. Zimmer Co.	160							160
Total	$86,300	$75,000	$4,000	$3,100	$1,900	$1,200	$800	$300

The aging schedule is completed by adding the columns to determine the total amount of receivables in each age group. A sliding scale of percentages, based on experience, is used to estimate the amount of uncollectibles in each group. The manner in which the data may be presented is shown in Exhibit 4.

Exhibit 4
Estimate of Uncollectible
Accounts

Age Interval	Balance	Estimated Uncollectible Accounts	
		Percent	Amount
Not due	$75,000	2%	$1,500
1–30 days past due	4,000	5	200
31–60 days past due	3,100	10	310
61–90 days past due	1,900	20	380
91–180 days past due	1,200	30	360
181–365 days past due	800	50	400
Over 365 days past due	300	80	240
Total	$86,300		$3,390

The estimate of uncollectible accounts is $3,390 in Exhibit 4. This amount is deducted from accounts receivable to yield the accounts receivable net realizable value. It is also the amount of the desired balance of the allowance account at the end of the period. The excess of this amount over the balance of the allowance account before adjustment is the amount of the uncollectible accounts expense for the period.

To continue the example, assume that the allowance account has a credit balance of $510 before adjustment. The amount to be added to this balance is therefore $2,880 ($3,390 – $510). The adjusting entry is as follows:

Dec. 31	Uncollectible Accounts Expense	2,880	
	Allowance for Doubtful Accounts		2,880

After the adjusting entry has been posted, the credit balance in the allowance account is $3,390, the desired amount. If there had been a debit balance of $300 in the allowance account before the year-end adjustment, the amount of the adjustment would have been $3,690 ($3,390 desired balance + $300 debit balance).

Estimations of uncollectible accounts expense based on an analysis of receivables are less common than estimations based on sales volume. The primary advantage of an analysis of receivables is that it emphasizes the current net realizable value of the receivables.

DIRECT WRITE-OFF METHOD OF ACCOUNTING FOR UNCOLLECTIBLES

Objective 7
Journalize the entries for the direct write-off of uncollectible receivables.

The allowance method illustrated in the preceding paragraphs emphasizes reporting uncollectible accounts expense in the period in which the sales occur. This emphasis on matching expenses with related revenue is the preferred

The Older It Gets

A properly designed accounting system should provide for the careful screening of credit, prompt reporting of delinquent accounts, and effective collection procedures for delinquent accounts. As illustrated in the following article from a public accounting firm's newsletter, collection success depends on quick collection efforts.

There is a direct relationship between the age of outstanding receivables and the chance of successfully collecting [them]. . . . [The] Commercial Law League of America published the following data showing the precise correlation between the age of the receivable and the chance of collection:

Period of Delinquency	Collection Likelihood
1 month	94%
2 months	85%
3 months	74%
6 months	48%
9 months	43%
1 year	27%
2 years	14%

Source: "The Older It Gets," *The Advisor* (Spring 1988), p. 2.

method of accounting for uncollectible receivables. However, there are situations in which it is impossible to estimate, with reasonable accuracy, the uncollectibles at the end of the period. Also, if an enterprise sells most of its goods or services on a cash basis, the amount of its expense from uncollectible accounts is usually small in relation to its revenue. The amount of its receivables at any time is also likely to represent a relatively small part of its total current assets. In such cases, it is acceptable to delay recognition of uncollectible expense until the accounts are determined to be worthless. Thus, under the direct write-off method, an allowance account and an adjusting entry are not needed at the end of the period. The entry to write off an account when it is determined to be uncollectible is as follows:

May 10	Uncollectible Accounts Expense	420	
	Accounts Receivable—D. L. Ross		420
	To write off uncollectible account.		

If an account that has been written off is collected later, the account should be reinstated. If the recovery is in the same period as the write-off, the earlier entry should be reversed to reinstate the account. For example, assume that the account written off in the May 10 entry is collected in November of the same fiscal year. The entry to reinstate the account is as follows:

Nov. 21	Accounts Receivable—D. L. Ross	420	
	Uncollectible Accounts Expense		420
	To reinstate account written off earlier in the year.		

The receipt of cash in payment of the reinstated amount is recorded in the usual manner. That is, Cash is debited and Accounts Receivable is credited.

When an account that has been written off is collected in a later fiscal year, it may be reinstated by debiting Accounts Receivable and crediting Uncollectible Accounts Expense. An alternative is to credit some other appropriately titled account, such as Recovery of Uncollectible Accounts Written Off. The credit balance in such an account at the end of the period may then be reported on the income statement as a deduction from Uncollectible Accounts Expense. In either case, only the net uncollectible expense is reported.

TEMPORARY INVESTMENTS

Objective 8
Define temporary investments,
give an example of two kinds of
temporary investments, and
explain how temporary
investments are valued on the
balance sheet.

A business may have excess cash that is not needed immediately for operations. Rather than allow this excess cash to be idle until it is needed, a business may invest all or a part of it in income-yielding securities. Since these investments can be quickly sold and converted to cash as needed, they are called **temporary investments** or **marketable securities**. Although such investments may be retained for a number of years, they continue to be classified as temporary, provided that two conditions are met. First, the securities are readily marketable and thus can be sold for cash at any time. Second, it is the intent of management to sell the securities at such time as the enterprise needs more cash for operations.

Temporary investments include investments in stocks and bonds. **Stocks** are equity securities issued by corporations. **Bonds** are debt securities issued by corporations and various government agencies. Stocks and bonds held as temporary investments are classified on the balance sheet as current assets. They may be listed after *Cash*, or they may be combined with cash and cash equivalents and described as *Cash, cash equivalents, and marketable securities*.

A temporary investment in a portfolio of debt securities is normally carried at cost. However, the **carrying amount** (also called **basis**) of a temporary investment in equity securities is the lower of its total cost or market value. The market value is determined at the date of the balance sheet.[3] The carrying amount is based on the comparison between the *total* cost and the *total* market value of the investment, not the cost and market price of *each item*. To illustrate, the following portfolio of temporary investments in equity securities is valued at the lower of the total cost ($690,000) or total market ($660,000):

Temporary Investment Portfolio	Cost	Market	Unrealized Gain (Loss)
Equity security A	$150,000	$100,000	$(50,000)
Equity security B	200,000	200,000	—
Equity security C	180,000	210,000	30,000
Equity security D	160,000	150,000	(10,000)
Total	$690,000	$660,000	$(30,000)

The above marketable equity securities are reported at a cost of $690,000 in the Current Assets section of the balance sheet in Exhibit 5. An allowance for decline to market value of $30,000 is subtracted to yield the carrying amount of $660,000. The unrealized loss of $30,000 is included in the determination of net income and reported as a separate item on the income statement.

If the total market value of the investment portfolio later rises, the unrealized loss is reversed and included in net income. It is reported separately in the Other Income section of the income statement, and the amount reported on the balance sheet is adjusted. However, the carrying value cannot exceed the original cost.[4]

---

[3] *Statement of Financial Accounting Standards, No. 12*, "Accounting for Certain Marketable Securities" (Stamford: Financial Accounting Standards Board, 1975), par. 8.
[4] The discussion of temporary investments in this chapter focuses on the concepts applicable to their presentations on the financial statements. Other aspects of accounting for investments, such as dividend income and interest income, are discussed in a later chapter.

TEMPORARY INVESTMENTS AND RECEIVABLES IN THE BALANCE SHEET

Objective 9
Prepare the Current Assets section of a balance sheet that includes temporary investments and receivables.

Temporary investments and all receivables that are expected to be realized in cash within a year are presented in the Current Assets section of the balance sheet. It is normal to list the assets in the order of their liquidity. This is the order in which they are expected to be converted to cash during normal operations. An example of the presentation of temporary investments and receivables is shown in the partial balance sheet for Pilar Enterprises in Exhibit 5.

Exhibit 5
Temporary Investments and Receivables in Balance Sheet

Pilar Enterprises Balance Sheet December 31, 19—		
Assets		
Current assets:		
Cash		$119,500
Marketable equity securities	$690,000	
Less allowance for decline to market	30,000	660,000
Notes receivable		250,000
Accounts receivable	$445,000	
Less allowance for doubtful accounts	15,000	430,000
Interest receivable		14,500

Disclosures related to temporary investments and receivables are presented either on the face of the financial statements or in the accompanying notes. Such disclosures include the market (fair) value of the temporary investments and receivables.[5] Generally, the market value of receivables approximates their carrying value. In addition, if unusual credit risks exist within the receivables, the nature of the risks should be disclosed. For example, if the majority of the receivables are due from one customer or are due from customers located in one area of the country or one industry, these facts should be disclosed.[6] An illustration of a credit risk disclosure taken from the 1991 financial statements of Deere & Company is shown below.

Credit receivables have significant concentrations of credit risk in the agricultural, industrial, lawn and grounds care, and recreational (non-Deere equipment) business sectors. At October 31, 1991 and 1990, the portions of credit receivables related to the agricultural equipment business were 60 percent and 56 percent, those related to the industrial equipment business were 12 percent and 14 percent, those related to the lawn and grounds care equipment business were seven percent and eight percent, and those related to the recreational equipment business were 21 percent and 22 percent, respectively. On a geographic basis, there is not a disproportionate concentration of credit risk in any area. . . .

---

[5] *Statement of Financial Accounting Standards, No. 107,* "Disclosures about Fair Value of Financial Instruments," (Norwalk: Financial Accounting Standards Board, 1991), par. 10.
[6] *Statement of Financial Accounting Standards, No. 105,* "Disclosure of Information about Financial Instruments with Off-Balance Sheet Risk and Financial Instruments with Concentrations of Credit Risk," (Norwalk: Financial Accounting Standards Board, 1990), par. 20, and *Statement of Financial Accounting Standards, No. 107, op. cit.,* par. 13.

CHAPTER REVIEW

Key Points

Objective 1. List the common classifications of receivables.

The common classes of receivables include accounts receivable and notes receivable. Accounts and notes receivable originating from sales transactions are called trade receivables.

Objective 2. Summarize and provide examples of internal control procedures that apply to receivables.

The internal controls that apply to receivables include the separation of responsibilities for related functions. In this way, the work of one employee can serve as a check on the work of another employee. Other controls are the use of subsidiary ledgers and authorization procedures for credit approval and adjustments of accounts.

Objective 3. State the accounting implications of promissory notes.

The accounting implications of a promissory note include the recognition of interest and the determination of the due date and the maturity value of the note. The basic formula for computing interest on a note is: Principal × Rate × Time = Interest. The due date is the date a note is to be paid, and the period of time between the issuance date and the due date is normally stated in either days or months. The maturity value of an interest-bearing note is the sum of the face amount and the interest. The maturity value of a non-interest-bearing note is the face value of the note.

Objective 4. Journalize the entries for notes receivable transactions, including discounted notes receivable and dishonored notes receivable.

A note received in settlement of an account receivable is recorded as a debit to Notes Receivable and a credit to Accounts Receivable. When a note matures, Cash is debited, Notes Receivable is credited, and Interest Income is credited for any interest. A note receivable may be discounted at a bank. In this case, Cash is debited for the proceeds, Notes Receivable is credited, and any interest income or interest expense is recorded.

If the maker of a note that has been discounted fails to pay the debt on the due date, the note is said to be dishonored. When the holder of a dishonored note has been paid by the endorser, the amount of the endorser's claim against the maker of the note is debited to an accounts receivable account.

Objective 5. Name and describe two methods of accounting for uncollectible receivables.

The two methods of accounting for uncollectible receivables are the allowance method and the direct write-off method. The allowance method provides in advance for uncollectible receivables. The direct write-off method recognizes the expense only when the account is judged to be uncollectible.

Objective 6. Journalize the entries for the allowance method of accounting for uncollectibles,

and estimate uncollectible receivables based on sales and on an analysis of receivables.

An adjusting entry made at the end of the fiscal period provides for (1) the reduction of the value of the receivables to the amount of cash expected to be realized from them in the future and (2) the allocation to the current period of the expected expense resulting from such reduction. The adjusting entry debits Uncollectible Accounts Expense and credits Allowance for Doubtful Accounts. When an account is believed to be uncollectible, it is written off against the allowance account.

When the estimate of uncollectibles is based upon the amount of sales for the fiscal period, the adjusting entry at the end of the period is made without regard to the balance of the allowance account. When the estimate of uncollectibles is based upon the amount and the age of the receivable accounts at the end of the period, the adjusting entry is recorded so that the balance of the allowance account will equal the estimated uncollectibles at the end of the period.

The allowance account, which will have a credit balance after the adjusting entry has been posted, is a contra asset account. The uncollectible accounts expense is generally reported on the income statement as an administrative expense.

Objective 7. Journalize the entries for the direct write-off of uncollectible receivables.

Under the direct write-off method, the entry to write off an account debits Uncollectible Accounts Expense and credits Accounts Receivable. Neither an allowance account nor an adjusting entry is needed at the end of the period.

Objective 8. Define temporary investments, give an example of two kinds of temporary investments, and explain how temporary investments are valued on the balance sheet.

Temporary investments are income-yielding securities that can be quickly sold and converted to cash. Such investments include stocks and bonds. Stocks are equity securities, and bonds are debt securities issued by corporations and various government agencies. A temporary investment in debt securities is normally carried at cost on the balance sheet. However, a temporary investment in equity securities must be carried at the lower of its total cost or total market value at the balance sheet date.

Objective 9. Prepare the Current Assets section of a balance sheet that includes temporary investments and receivables.

Temporary investments and all receivables that are expected to be realized in cash within a year are presented in the Current Assets section of the balance sheet. It is normal to list the assets in the order of their liquidity, which is the order in which they can be converted to cash in normal operations.

Glossary of Key Terms

Aging the receivables. The process of analyzing the accounts receivable and classifying them according to various age groupings, with the due date being the base point for determining age. **Objective 6**

Allowance method. A method of accounting for uncollectible receivables, whereby advance provision for the uncollectibles is made. **Objective 5**

Carrying amount. The amount at which a temporary investment is reported on the balance sheet; also called basis or book value. **Objective 8**

Contingent liabilities. Potential obligations that will materialize only if certain events occur in the future. **Objective 4**

Direct write-off method. A method of accounting for uncollectible receivables, whereby an expense is recognized only when specific accounts are judged to be uncollectible. **Objective 5**

Discount. The interest deducted from the maturity value of a note receivable. **Objective 4**

Dishonored note receivable. A note that the maker fails to pay on its due date. **Objective 4**

Marketable securities. Investments in securities that can be readily sold when cash is needed. **Objective 8**

Maturity value. The amount due at the maturity or due date of a note. **Objective 3**

Note receivable. A written promise to pay, representing an amount to be received by a business. **Objective 1**

Proceeds. The net amount available from discounting a note. **Objective 4**

Promissory note. A written promise to pay a sum in money on demand or at a definite time. **Objective 1**

Temporary investments. Investments in securities that can be readily sold when cash is needed. **Objective 8**

Self-Examination Questions
Answers at end of chapter.

1. What is the maturity value of a 90-day, 12% note for $10,000?
   A. $8,800   C. $10,300
   B. $10,000   D. $11,200

2. On June 16, an enterprise discounts a 60-day, 10% note receivable for $15,000, dated June 1, at the rate of 12%. The proceeds are:
   A. $15,000.00   C. $15,250.00
   B. $15,021.25   D. $15,478.75

3. At the end of the fiscal year, before the accounts are adjusted, Accounts Receivable has a balance of $200,000 and Allowance for Doubtful Accounts has a credit balance of $2,500. If the estimate of uncollectible accounts determined by aging the receivables is $8,500, the current provision to be made for uncollectible accounts expense is:
   A. $2,500   C. $8,500
   B. $6,000   D. $11,000

4. At the end of the fiscal year, Accounts Receivable has a balance of $100,000 and Allowance for Doubtful Accounts has a balance of $7,000. The expected net realizable value of the accounts receivable is:
   A. $7,000   C. $100,000
   B. $93,000   D. $107,000

5. Under what caption would a temporary investment in stock be reported in the balance sheet?
   A. Current assets   C. Investments
   B. Plant assets   D. Current liabilities

ILLUSTRATIVE PROBLEM

Rodriguez Company uses the allowance method of accounting for uncollectible accounts receivable. Selected transactions completed by Rodriguez Company are as follows:

Jan. 28. Sold merchandise on account to Lakeland Co., $10,000.
Mar.   1. Accepted a 60-day, 12% note for $10,000 from Lakeland Co. on account.
Apr. 11. Wrote off a $4,500 account from Exdel Co. as uncollectible.
      16. Loaned $7,500 cash to Thomas Glazer, receiving a 90-day, 14% note.
      30. Received the interest due from Lakeland Co. and a new 90-day, 14% note as a renewal of the loan. (Record both the debit and the credit to the notes receivable account.)
May   1. Discounted the note from Thomas Glazer at the First National Bank at 10%.
June 13. Reinstated the account of Exdel Co., written off on April 11, and received $4,500 in full payment.
July 15. Received notice from First National Bank that Thomas Glazer dishonored his note. Paid the bank the maturity value of the note plus a $20 protest fee.
      29. Received from Lakeland Co. the amount due on its note of April 30.

Aug. 14. Received from Thomas Glazer the amount owed on the dishonored note, plus interest for 30 days at 15%, computed on the maturity value of the note and the protest fee.

Dec. 16. Accepted a 60-day, 12% note for $6,000 from Harden Company on account.

31. It is estimated that 2% of the credit sales of $958,600 for the year ended December 31 will be uncollectible.

Instructions

1. Journalize the transactions in general journal form.
2. Journalize the adjusting entry to record the accrued interest on December 31.

Solution

1.

Jan. 28	Accounts Receivable—Lakeland Co.		10,000.00	
	Sales			10,000.00
Mar. 1	Notes Receivable—Lakeland Co.		10,000.00	
	Accounts Receivable—Lakeland Co.			10,000.00
Apr. 11	Allowance for Doubtful Accounts		4,500.00	
	Accounts Receivable—Exdel Co.			4,500.00
16	Notes Receivable—Thomas Glazer		7,500.00	
	Cash			7,500.00
30	Notes Receivable—Lakeland Co.		10,000.00	
	Cash		200.00	
	Notes Receivable—Lakeland Co.			10,000.00
	Interest Income			200.00
May 1	Cash		7,600.78	
	Notes Receivable—Thomas Glazer			7,500.00
	Interest Income			100.78

Face value	$7,500.00
Interest on note	
(90 days at 14%)	262.50
Maturity value	$7,762.50
Discount on maturity	
value (75 days at 10%)	161.72
Proceeds	$7,600.78

June 13	Accounts Receivable—Exdel Co.		4,500.00	
	Allowance for Doubtful Accounts			4,500.00
13	Cash		4,500.00	
	Accounts Receivable—Exdel Co.			4,500.00
July 15	Accounts Receivable—Thomas Glazer		7,782.50	
	Cash			7,782.50
29	Cash		10,350.00	
	Notes Receivable—Lakeland Co.			10,000.00
	Interest Income			350.00
Aug. 14	Cash		7,879.78	
	Accounts Receivable—Thomas Glazer			7,782.50
	Interest Income			97.28
	($7,782.50 × 15% × 30/360)			
Dec. 16	Notes Receivable—Harden Company		6,000.00	
	Accounts Receivable—Harden Company			6,000.00
31	Uncollectible Accounts Expense		19,172.00	
	Allowance for Doubtful Accounts			19,172.00

2.

Dec. 31	Interest Receivable		30.00	
	Interest Income			30.00
	($6,000 × 12% × 15/360)			

DISCUSSION QUESTIONS

1. For a business, what are the advantages of a note receivable in comparison to an account receivable?
2. What are trade receivables?
3. In what section of the balance sheet should a note receivable be listed if its term is (a) 90 days, (b) 5 years?
4. The accounts receivable clerk is also responsible for handling cash receipts. Which principle of internal control is violated in this situation?
5. Carey Company issued a promissory note to Stevens Company. (a) Who is the payee? (b) What is the title of the account used by Stevens Company in recording the note?
6. If a note provides for payment of principal of $10,000 and interest at the rate of 10%, will the interest amount to $1,000? Explain.
7. The following questions refer to a 90-day, 9% note for $5,000, dated May 1: (a) What is the face value of the note? (b) What is the amount of interest payable at maturity? (c) What is the maturity value of the note? (d) What is the due date of the note?
8. At the end of the fiscal year, an enterprise holds a $3,600, 10%, 90-day note receivable accepted from a customer thirty days earlier. What is the amount of interest accrued at the end of the fiscal year?
9. The payee of a 60-day, 9% note for $5,000, dated April 20, endorses it to a bank on May 10. The bank discounts the note at 10%, paying the endorser $5,018.61. Identify or determine the following as they relate to the note: (a) face value, (b) maturity value, (c) due date, (d) number of days in the discount period, (e) proceeds, (f) interest income or expense recorded by endorser, (g) amount payable to the bank if the maker defaults.
10. Arnould Co. received a 60-day note dated July 7 from a customer on account. Arnould Co. discounted the note at the bank on July 22. (a) Did Arnould Co. have a contingent liability on July 22 after the note was discounted? (b) If the answer in (a) is "yes," when does the contingent liability expire?
11. During the year, notes receivable of $150,000 were discounted at a bank by an enterprise. By the end of the year, $112,500 of these notes have matured. What is the amount of the endorser's contingent liability for notes receivable discounted at the end of the year?
12. The maker of a $6,000, 8%, 90-day note receivable failed to pay the note on the due date. What entry should be made in the accounts of the payee to record the dishonored note receivable?
13. A discounted note receivable is dishonored by the maker and the endorser pays the bank the face of the note, $8,000, the interest, $120, and a protest fee of $15. What entry should be made in the accounts of the endorser to record the payment?
14. The series of six transactions recorded in the following T accounts were related to a sale to a customer on account and receipt of the amount owed. Briefly describe each transaction.

Cash				Sales			
(4)	19,305	(5)	19,540	(2)	500	(1)	20,000
(6)	19,600						

Notes Receivable				Interest Income			
(3)	19,500	(4)	19,500			(6)	60

Accounts Receivable				Interest Expense			
(1)	20,000	(2)	500	(4)	195		
(5)	19,540	(3)	19,500				
		(6)	19,540				

15. Which of the two methods of accounting for uncollectible accounts provides for the recognition of the expense at the earlier date?
16. What kind of an account (asset, liability, etc.) is Allowance for Doubtful Accounts, and is its normal balance a debit or a credit?

17. Give the adjusting entry to increase Allowance for Doubtful Accounts by $5,900.

18. After the accounts are adjusted and closed at the end of the fiscal year, Accounts Receivable has a balance of $201,250 and Allowance for Doubtful Accounts has a balance of $12,250. (a) What is the expected net realizable value of the accounts receivable? (b) If an account receivable of $1,000 is written off against the allowance account, what will be the expected net realizable value of the accounts receivable after the write-off, assuming that no other changes in either account have occurred in the meantime?

19. A firm has consistently adjusted its allowance account at the end of the fiscal year by adding a fixed percent of the period's net sales on account. After five years, the balance in Allowance for Doubtful Accounts has become disproportionately large in relationship to the balance in Accounts Receivable. Give two possible explanations.

20. Evans Company has decided to write off the $750 balance of an account owed by a customer. Give the entry to record the write-off in the general ledger (a) assuming that the allowance method is used and (b) assuming that the direct write-off method is used.

21. Which of the two methods of estimating uncollectibles, when advance provision for uncollectible receivables is made, provides for the most accurate estimate of the current net realizable value of the receivables?

22. Under what caption should securities held as a temporary investment be reported on the balance sheet?

23. A company has two equity securities that it holds as a temporary investment. If they have a total cost of $210,000 and a fair market value of $202,750, at what amount should these securities be reported in the Current Assets section of the company's balance sheet?

REAL W●RLD FOCUS   24. Hilton Hotels Corporation owns and operates casinos at several of its hotels, located primarily in Nevada. At the end of a recent fiscal year, the following accounts and notes receivable were reported (in thousands):

Hotel accounts and notes receivable	$75,796
Less Allowance for doubtful accounts	3,256
	$72,540
Casino accounts receivable	$26,334
Less Allowance for doubtful accounts	6,654
	$19,680

(a) Compute the percentage of allowance for doubtful accounts to the gross hotel accounts and notes receivable for the end of the fiscal year. (b) Compute the percentage of the allowance for doubtful accounts to the gross casino accounts receivable for the end of the fiscal year. (c) Discuss possible reasons for the difference in the two ratios computed in (a) and (b).

ETHICS DISCUSSION CASE

Andrew Wilson, vice-president of operations for Palmer National Bank, has instructed the bank's computer programmer to program the bank's computers to calculate interest on depository accounts (payables) using the 365-day year and to calculate interest on loans (receivables) using the 360-day year.

Discuss whether Andrew Wilson is behaving in an ethical manner.

SHARPEN YOUR ▶
COMMUNICATION SKILLS

EXERCISES

EXERCISE 9-1
INTERNAL CONTROL
PROCEDURES
Objective 2

Simpson Carpet Company sells carpeting. Over 80% of all carpet sales are on credit. The following procedures are used by Simpson to process this large number of credit sales and the subsequent collections.

a. All credit sales to a first-time customer must be approved by the Credit Department. Salespersons will assist the customer in filling out a credit application, but an employee in the Credit Department is responsible for verifying employment and checking the customer's credit history before granting credit.

b. Simpson's standard credit period is 60 days. The Credit Department may approve an extension of this repayment period of up to one year. Whenever an extension is granted, the customer signs a promissory note. Up to 35% of the credit sales in any one year are for repayment periods exceeding 60 days.

c. Simpson maintains a subsidiary ledger in which all sales and receipts from customers on open account are recorded. A formal ledger is not maintained for customers who sign promissory notes. Simpson simply keeps a copy of each signed note in a file cabinet. These unpaid notes are filed by due date.

d. Simpson employs an accounts receivable clerk to oversee the accounts receivable subsidiary ledger. The clerk is responsible for recording customer credit sales (based on sales tickets), receiving cash from customers, giving customers credit for their payments in the subsidiary ledger, and handling all customer billing complaints.

e. The general ledger control account for Accounts Receivable is maintained by the General Accounting Department at Simpson. This department records total credit sales, based on credit sale information from the store's electronic cash register, and total customer receipts, based on the bank deposit slip.

■ SHARPEN YOUR ►
COMMUNICATION SKILLS

State whether each of these procedures is appropriate or inappropriate, considering the principles of internal control. If the procedure is inappropriate, state which internal control principle is violated.

EXERCISE 9-2
INTERNAL CONTROL
PROCEDURES
Objective 2

Rob Loude is the accounts receivable clerk at Milford Florists. As accounts receivable clerk, Rob is responsible for recording customer credit sales and receipts on credit accounts in the accounts receivable ledger. Entries to the general ledger are made by the store's chief accountant, based on appropriate documentation.

Recently, Rob made two errors in recording customer credit transactions. First of all, Rob posted a $50 receipt from John Redman to Kevin Reedman's account in the accounts receivable ledger. Secondly, Rob forgot to post a $250 credit sale, made to Kathy Haley, to the accounts receivable ledger.

■ SHARPEN YOUR ►
COMMUNICATION SKILLS

How will each of these errors be detected?

EXERCISE 9-3
DETERMINATION OF DUE
DATE AND INTEREST ON
NOTES
Objective 3

Determine the due date and the amount of interest due at maturity on the following notes:

Date of Note	Face Amount	Term of Note	Interest Rate
a. March 11	$ 5,000	30 days	9%
b. May 20	6,000	60 days	10%
c. May 30	10,000	75 days	12%
d. June 9	15,000	90 days	10%
e. July 11	17,500	120 days	12%

EXERCISE 9-4
ENTRIES FOR NOTES
RECEIVABLE
Objectives 3, 4

Wallace Company issued a 90-day, 9% note for $10,000, dated May 10, to Preston Company on account.

SPREADSHEET
PROBLEM

a. Determine the due date of the note.
b. Determine the maturity value of the note.
c. Journalize the entries, in general journal form, to record the following: (1) receipt of the note by the payee, and (2) receipt by the payee of payment of the note at maturity.

EXERCISE 9-5
ENTRIES FOR NOTE
RECEIVABLE, INCLUDING
YEAR-END ENTRIES
Objective 4

The following selected transactions were completed by Thompson Co. during the current year:

Dec. 1. Received from Barr Co., on account, a $10,000, 90-day, 12% note dated December 1.

31. Recorded an adjusting entry for accrued interest on the note of December 1.

31. Closed the interest income account. The only entry in this account originated from the December 31 adjustment.

Journalize the transactions in general journal form.

EXERCISE 9-6
DISCOUNTING NOTE
RECEIVABLE
Objective 4

Geraldi Co. holds a 120-day, 9% note for $20,000, dated March 20, that was received from a customer on account. On April 19, the note is discounted at the bank at the rate of 10%.

a. Determine the maturity value of the note.
b. Determine the number of days in the discount period.
c. Determine the amount of the discount.
d. Determine the amount of the proceeds.
e. Journalize the entry, in general journal form, to record the discounting of the note on April 19.

EXERCISE 9-7
ENTRIES FOR RECEIPT AND
DISCOUNTING OF NOTE
RECEIVABLE AND
DISHONORED NOTE
Objective 4

Journalize the following transactions, in general journal form, in the accounts of L. L. McLean Company:

Mar. 1. Received a $40,000, 60-day, 12% note dated March 1 from Sutcliffe Company on account.
      16. Discounted the note at First National Bank at 14%.
Apr. 30. The note is dishonored by Sutcliffe; paid the bank the amount due on the note, plus a protest fee of $50.
June 29. Received the amount due on the dishonored note plus interest for 60 days at 12% on the total amount charged to Sutcliffe Company on April 30.

EXERCISE 9-8
ENTRIES FOR RECEIPT AND
DISHONOR OF NOTES
RECEIVABLE
Objectives 4, 6

Journalize the following transactions, in general journal form, in the accounts of Sandburg Co.:

July 1. Received a $20,000, 30-day, 12% note dated July 1 from Grace Co. on account.
      10. Received a $12,000, 60-day, 12% note dated July 10 from O'Neil Co. on account.
      31. The note dated July 1 from Grace Co. is dishonored and the customer's account is charged for the note, including interest.
Sep. 9. The note dated July 10 from O'Neil Co. is dishonored and the customer's account is charged for the note, including interest.
Oct. 14. Cash is received for the amount due on the dishonored note dated July 1 plus interest for 75 days at 12% on the total amount debited to Grace Co. on July 31.
      30. Wrote off against the allowance account the amount charged to O'Neil Co. on September 9 for the dishonored note dated July 10.

EXERCISE 9-9
PROVISION FOR DOUBTFUL
ACCOUNTS
Objective 6

At the end of the current year, the accounts receivable account has a debit balance of $290,000, and net sales for the year total $3,100,000. Determine the amount of the adjusting entry to record the provision for doubtful accounts under each of the following assumptions:

a. The allowance account before adjustment has a credit balance of $1,750. (1) Uncollectible accounts expense is estimated at ½ of 1% of net sales. (2) Analysis of the accounts in the customers ledger indicates doubtful accounts of $16,000.
b. The allowance account before adjustment has a debit balance of $1,500. (1) Uncollectible accounts expense is estimated at ¾ of 1% of net sales. (2) Analysis of the accounts in the customers ledger indicates doubtful accounts of $20,000.

EXERCISE 9-10
ENTRIES FOR
UNCOLLECTIBLE
RECEIVABLES USING
ALLOWANCE METHOD
Objective 6

In general journal form, journalize the following transactions in the accounts of Loveday Company, which uses the allowance method of accounting for uncollectible receivables:

Feb. 9. Sold merchandise on account to B. C. Burr, $5,500.
Aug. 19. Received $2,500 from B. C. Burr and wrote off the remainder owed on the sale of February 9 as uncollectible.
Dec. 30. Reinstated the account of B. C. Burr that had been written off on August 19 and received $3,000 cash in full payment.

EXERCISE 9-11
ENTRIES FOR
UNCOLLECTIBLE
ACCOUNTS USING DIRECT
WRITE-OFF METHOD
Objective 7

In general journal form, journalize the following transactions in the accounts of Henderson and Co., which uses the direct write-off method of accounting for uncollectible receivables:

Jan. 11. Sold merchandise on account to John Lang, $3,000.
June 1. Received $2,000 from John Lang and wrote off the remainder owed on the sale of January 11 as uncollectible.
Dec. 10. Reinstated the account of John Lang that had been written off on June 1 and received $1,000 cash in full payment.

EXERCISE 9-12
TEMPORARY EQUITY
SECURITIES IN FINANCIAL
STATEMENTS
Objective 8

As of December 31 of the first year of operations, Knight Company has the following port-folio of temporary equity securities:

	Cost	Market
Security A	$65,500	$67,000
Security B	21,000	19,100
Security C	39,250	35,000
Security D	40,250	41,500

SHARPEN YOUR
COMMUNICATION SKILLS

Describe how the portfolio of temporary equity securities would affect the year-end bal-ance sheet and income statement of Knight Company.

WhAT'S WRONG
WITH THi2?

Can you find any errors in the following partial balance sheet?

Lane Company
Balance Sheet
December 31, 19—

Assets

Current assets:

Cash		$ 95,000
Marketable equity securities (cost)	$460,000	
Plus allowance for increase to market	30,000	490,000
Notes receivable		250,000
Accounts receivable	$445,000	
Plus allowance for doubtful accounts	15,000	460,000
Interest receivable		9,000

PROBLEMS

Series A

PROBLEM 9-1A
SALES, NOTES RECEIVABLE,
DISCOUNTING NOTES
RECEIVABLE
TRANSACTIONS
Objective 4

The following were selected from among the transactions completed by Gonzales Co. during the current year:

Jan. 15. Loaned $10,000 cash to Jose Montes, receiving a 90-day, 10% note.
Feb. 1. Sold merchandise on account to Bryant and Son, $6,000.
   20. Sold merchandise on account to C. D. Connors Co., $7,500.
Mar. 2. Received from C. D. Connors Co. the amount of the invoice of February 20, less 1% discount.
   3. Accepted a 60-day, 12% note for $6,000 from Bryant and Son on account.
Apr. 15. Received the interest due from Jose Montes and a new 90-day, 12% note as a re-newal of the loan of January 15. (Record both the debit and the credit to the notes receivable account.)
May 2. Received from Bryant and Son the amount due on the note of March 3.
July 10. Sold merchandise on account to Song Yu and Co., $30,000.
   14. Received from Jose Montes the amount due on his note of April 15.
Aug. 9. Accepted a 60-day, 12% note for $30,000 from Song Yu and Co. on account.
Sep. 8. Discounted the note from Song Yu and Co. at the American National Bank at 14%.
Oct. 8. Received notice from the American National Bank that Song Yu and Co. had dis-honored its note. Paid the bank the maturity value of the note.
   28. Received from Song Yu and Co. the amount owed on the dishonored note, plus interest for 20 days at 12% computed on the maturity value of the note.

Instructions
Journalize the transactions in general journal form.

Instructions for Solving Problem 9-1A Using Solutions Software

1. Load the opening balances.
2. Save the opening balances file to your drive and directory.
3. Set the run date to December 31 of the current year and enter your name.
4. Key the journal entries.
5. Display the journal entries.
6. Display a trial balance.
7. Save your data file to disk.
8. End the session.

PROBLEM 9-2A
DETAILS OF NOTES RECEIVABLE, INCLUDING DISCOUNTING
Objective 4

During the current fiscal year, Stone Co. received the following notes. Notes (1), (2), (3), and (4) were discounted on the dates and at the rates indicated.

	Date	Face Amount	Term	Interest Rate	Date Discounted	Discount Rate
1.	Oct. 1	$ 6,000	60 days	10%	Oct. 16	12%
2.	Oct. 11	10,000	30 days	12%	Oct. 21	14%
3.	Oct. 28	6,200	90 days	14%	Dec. 27	12%
4.	Nov. 8	8,000	60 days	12%	Nov. 23	16%
5.	Dec. 11	14,400	60 days	11%	—	—
6.	Dec. 26	18,000	30 days	12%	—	—

Instructions

1. Determine for each note (a) the due date and (b) the amount of interest due at maturity, identifying each note by number.
2. Determine for each of the first four notes (a) the maturity value, (b) the discount period, (c) the discount, (d) the proceeds, and (e) the interest income or interest expense, identifying each note by number.
3. Journalize, in general journal form, the entries to record the discounting of notes (2) and (4) at a bank.
4. Journalize the adjusting entry to record the accrued interest on Notes (5) and (6) on December 31.

PROBLEM 9-3A
NOTES RECEIVABLE ENTRIES
Objective 4

The following data relate to notes receivable and interest for Goldberg Co. (All notes are dated as of the day they are received.)

Apr.   1. Received a $7,500, 14%, 60-day note on account.
       11. Received a $30,000, 12%, 120-day note on account.
May. 16. Received a $24,000, 13%, 60-day note on account.
       21. Received a $12,000, 12%, 30-day note on account.
       31. Received $7,675 on note of April 1.
June 20. Received $12,120 on note of May 21.
       26. Received a $9,000, 12%, 30-day note on account.
July 15. Received $24,520 on note of May 16.
       26. Received $9,090 on note of June 26.
Aug.   9. Received $31,200 on note of April 11.

Instructions

Journalize entries in general journal form to record the transactions.

PROBLEM 9-4A
ENTRIES RELATED TO UNCOLLECTIBLE ACCOUNTS
Objective 6

The following transactions, adjusting entries, and closing entries were completed during the current fiscal year ended December 31:

Feb.   1. Received 75% of the $8,000 balance owed by Nixon Co., a bankrupt business, and wrote off the remainder as uncollectible.
May 17. Reinstated the account of Barbara Lyman, which had been written off in the preceding year as uncollectible. Journalized the receipt of $675 cash in full payment of Lyman's account.
June 9. Wrote off the $7,250 balance owed by Larkin Co., which has no assets.

Oct. 30. Reinstated the account of Viscano Co., which had been written off in the preceding year as uncollectible. Journalized the receipt of $2,500 cash in full payment of the account.

Dec. 31. Wrote off the following accounts as uncollectible (compound entry): Davis Co., $3,950; Nance Co., $4,600; Powell Distributors, $6,500; J. J. Stevens, $4,200.

31. Based on an analysis of the $695,000 of accounts receivable, it was estimated that $32,700 will be uncollectible. Journalized the adjusting entry.

31. Journalized the entry to close the appropriate account to Income Summary.

Instructions

1. Record the following January 1 credit balance in the account indicated:

115	Allowance for Doubtful Accounts	$29,050
313	Income Summary	—
718	Uncollectible Accounts Expense	—

2. Journalize in general journal form the transactions and the adjusting and closing entries described. After it has been journalized, post each entry to the three selected accounts affected and extend the new balances.

3. Determine the expected net realizable value of the accounts receivable as of December 31.

4. Assuming that, instead of basing the provision for uncollectible accounts on an analysis of receivables, the adjusting entry on December 31 had been based on an estimated loss of 3/4 of 1% of the net sales of $4,000,000 for the year, determine the following:

   a. Uncollectible accounts expense for the year.

   b. Balance in the allowance account after the adjustment of December 31.

   c. Expected net realizable value of the accounts receivable as of December 31.

PROBLEM 9-5A
COMPARISON OF TWO
METHODS OF
ACCOUNTING FOR
UNCOLLECTIBLE
RECEIVABLES
Objectives 6, 7

Lebaron Company has just completed its fourth year of operations. The direct write-off method of recording uncollectible accounts expense has been used during the entire period. Because of substantial increases in sales volume and amount of uncollectible accounts, the firm is considering the possibility of changing to the allowance method. Information is requested as to the effect that an annual provision of 1% of sales would have had on the amount of uncollectible accounts expense reported for each of the past four years. It is also considered desirable to know what the balance of Allowance for Doubtful Accounts would have been at the end of each year. The following data have been obtained from the accounts:

Year	Sales	Uncollectible Accounts Written Off	Year of Origin of Accounts Receivable Written Off as Uncollectible			
			1st	2d	3d	4th
1st	$400,000	$2,000	$2,000			
2d	600,000	2,950	1,500	$1,450		
3d	850,000	4,700	700	2,400	$1,600	
4th	900,000	6,000		1,900	2,500	$1,600

SPREADSHEET
PROBLEM

Instructions

1. Assemble the desired data, using the following columnar captions:

	Uncollectible Accounts Expense			Balance of Allowance Account, End of Year
Year	Expense Actually Reported	Expense Based on Estimate	Increase in Amount of Expense	

SHARPEN YOUR
COMMUNICATION SKILLS

2. Experience during the first four years of operations indicated that the receivables were either collected within two years or had to be written off as uncollectible. Does the estimate of 1% of sales appear to be reasonably close to the actual experience with uncollectible accounts originating during the first two years? Explain.

PROBLEM 9-6A
FINANCIAL STATEMENTS
Objective 9

The following data for Chen Company were selected from the ledger, after adjustment at December 31, the end of the current fiscal year:

Accounts payable	$ 26,100
Accounts receivable	57,500
Accumulated depreciation, building	175,000
Accumulated depreciation, office equipment	49,750
Administrative expenses	73,500
Allowance for decline to market of marketable equity securities	1,100
Allowance for doubtful accounts	1,500
Building	335,000
Cash	29,500
C. Chen, capital	455,900
C. Chen, drawing	60,000
Cost of merchandise sold	520,000
Interest income	6,100
Land	65,000
Marketable equity securities	60,000
Merchandise inventory	74,200
Notes receivable	40,000
Office equipment	79,750
Office supplies	5,600
Prepaid insurance	5,200
Salaries payable	2,900
Sales	805,000
Sales discounts	6,500
Selling expenses	110,500
Unrealized loss from decline to market of marketable equity securities	1,100

Instructions

1. Prepare an income statement in multiple-step form.
2. Prepare a statement of owner's equity.
3. Prepare a balance sheet in report form.

**SOLUTIONS
SOFTWARE**

Instructions for Solving Problem 9-6A Using Solutions Software

1. Load the opening balances.
2. Save the opening balances file to your drive and directory.
3. Set the run date to December 31 of the current year and enter your name.
4. Display a trial balance. (Use these account balances as the basis for the adjusting entries.)
5. Key the adjusting entries. Key ADJ.ENT. in the reference field. The data needed for year-end adjustments are as follows:
   a. Office supplies on hand, $5,600.
   b. Insurance expired, $1,500.
   c. Depreciation expense on building, $25,000.
   d. Depreciation expense on office equipment, $9,750.
   e. Uncollectible accounts expense, $1,000.
   f. Decline in market value of temporary investments, $1,100.
6. Display the adjusting entries. Key ADJ.ENT. in the Reference Restriction area of the Selection Options screen.
7. Display the financial statements.
8. Save a backup copy of your data file.
9. Perform period-end closing.
10. Display a post-closing trial balance.
11. Save your data file to disk.
12. End the session.

Series B

PROBLEM 9-1B
SALES, NOTES RECEIVABLE,
DISCOUNTING NOTES
RECEIVABLE
TRANSACTIONS
Objective 4

The following were selected from among the transactions completed by J. J. Borge Co. during the current year:

Jan. 31. Sold merchandise on account to Perras Co., $10,000.
Mar.   2. Accepted a 60-day, 12% note for $10,000 from Perras Co. on account.
May   1. Received from Perras Co. the amount due on the note of March 2.
June   1. Sold merchandise on account to Kohl's for $5,000.
        5. Loaned $9,000 cash to Frank Gary, receiving a 30-day, 14% note.
       11. Received from Kohl's the amount due on the invoice of June 1, less 2% discount.
July   5. Received the interest due from Frank Gary and a new 60-day, 14% note as a renewal of the loan of June 5. (Record both the debit and the credit to the notes receivable account.)
Sep.   3. Received from Frank Gary the amount due on his note of July 5.
        4. Sold merchandise on account to Alice Gow, $4,000.
Oct.   4. Accepted a 60-day, 12% note for $4,000 from Alice Gow on account.
Nov.   3. Discounted the note from Alice Gow at the Pelican National Bank at 10%.
Dec.   3. Received notice from Pelican National Bank that Alice Gow had dishonored her note. Paid the bank the maturity value of the note.
       18. Received from Alice Gow the amount owed on the dishonored note, plus interest for 15 days at 10% computed on the maturity value of the note.

Instructions

Journalize the transactions in general journal form.

SOLUTIONS SOFTWARE

Instructions for Solving Problem 9-1B Using Solutions Software

1. Load the opening balances.
2. Save the opening balances file to your drive and directory.
3. Set the run date to December 31 of the current year and enter your name.
4. Key the journal entries.
5. Display the journal entries.
6. Display a trial balance.
7. Save your data file to disk.
8. End the session.

PROBLEM 9-2B
DETAILS OF NOTES
RECEIVABLE, INCLUDING
DISCOUNTING
Objective 4

During the last six months of the current fiscal year, Brackett Co. received the following notes. Notes (1), (2), (3), and (4) were discounted on the dates and at the rates indicated.

	Date	Face Amount	Term	Interest Rate	Date Discounted	Discount Rate
1.	Mar. 1	$15,000	60 days	12%	Mar. 21	10%
2.	May 10	12,000	60 days	12%	May 20	15%
3.	July 11	30,000	90 days	10%	Aug. 10	12%
4.	Sep. 1	20,000	90 days	11%	Oct. 1	12%
5.	Dec. 11	18,000	60 days	12%	—	—
6.	Dec. 16	36,000	30 days	13%	—	—

SPREADSHEET PROBLEM

Instructions

1. Determine for each note (a) the due date and (b) the amount of interest due at maturity, identifying each note by number.
2. Determine for each of the first four notes (a) the maturity value, (b) the discount period, (c) the discount, (d) the proceeds, and (e) the interest income or interest expense, identifying each note by number.
3. Journalize, in general journal form, the entries to record the discounting of notes (2) and (3) at a bank.
4. Journalize the adjusting entry to record the accrued interest on Notes (5) and (6) on December 31.

PROBLEM 9-3B
NOTES RECEIVABLE
ENTRIES
Objective 4

The following data relate to notes receivable and interest for French Co. (All notes are dated as of the day they are received.)

Apr. 1. Received a $30,000, 12%, 60-day note on account.
     21. Received an $18,000, 14%, 90-day note on account.
May 16. Received a $12,000, 15%, 90-day note on account.
     21. Received a $10,800, 13%, 30-day note on account.
     31. Received $30,600 on note of April 1.
June 20. Received $10,917 on note of May 21.
     21. Received a $7,000, 12%, 30-day note on account.
July 20. Received $18,630 on note of April 21.
     21. Received $7,070 on note of June 21.
Aug. 14. Received $12,450 on note of May 16.

Instructions

Journalize entries in general journal form to record the transactions.

PROBLEM 9-4B
ENTRIES RELATED TO
UNCOLLECTIBLE
ACCOUNTS
Objective 6

The following transactions, adjusting entries, and closing entries were completed by Bradford Company during the current fiscal year ended December 31:

Feb. 1. Reinstated the account of Nancy Boyle, which had been written off in the preceding year as uncollectible. Journalized the receipt of $1,025 cash in full payment of Boyle's account.
     28. Wrote off the $8,500 balance owed by D'Arrigo Co., which is bankrupt.
May   7. Received 60% of the $5,000 balance owed by C. D. Clark Co., a bankrupt business, and wrote off the remainder as uncollectible.
July 29. Reinstated the account of Louis Jaeger, which had been written off two years earlier as uncollectible. Recorded the receipt of $625 cash in full payment.
Dec. 30. Wrote off the following accounts as uncollectible (compound entry): Boyd Co., $1,050; Engel Co., $1,760; Loach Furniture, $2,775; Briana Parker, $620.
Dec. 31. Based on an analysis of the $335,500 of accounts receivable, it was estimated that $15,200 will be uncollectible. Journalized the adjusting entry.
     31. Journalized the entry to close the appropriate account to Income Summary.

Instructions

1. Record the following January 1 credit balance in the account indicated:

115	Allowance for Doubtful Accounts	$17,955
313	Income Summary	—
718	Uncollectible Accounts Expense	—

2. Journalize in general journal form the transactions and the adjusting and closing entries described. After it has been journalized, post each entry to the three selected accounts affected and extend the new balances.
3. Determine the expected net realizable value of the accounts receivable as of December 31.
4. Assuming that, instead of basing the provision for uncollectible accounts on an analysis of receivables, the adjusting entry on December 31 had been based on an estimated loss of 1/2 of 1% of the net sales of $2,500,000 for the year, determine the following:
    a. Uncollectible accounts expense for the year.
    b. Balance in the allowance account after the adjustment of December 31.
    c. Expected net realizable value of the accounts receivable as of December 31.

PROBLEM 9-5B
COMPARISON OF TWO
METHODS OF
ACCOUNTING FOR
UNCOLLECTIBLE
RECEIVABLES
Objectives 6, 7

Lantz Company has just completed its fourth year of operations. The direct write-off method of recording uncollectible accounts expense has been used during the entire period. Because of substantial increases in sales volume and amount of uncollectible accounts, the firm is considering the possibility of changing to the allowance method. Information is requested as to the effect that an annual provision of 1% of sales would have had on the amount of uncollectible accounts expense reported for each of the past four years. It is also considered desirable to know what the balance of Allowance for Doubtful Accounts would have been at the end of each year. The following data have been obtained from the accounts:

Year	Sales	Uncollectible Accounts Written Off	Year of Origin of Accounts Receivable Written Off as Uncollectible			
			1st	2d	3d	4th
1st	$600,000	$2,600	$2,600			
2d	700,000	3,500	1,950	$1,550		
3d	850,000	7,600	1,200	3,400	$3,000	
4th	950,000	8,550		2,300	2,950	$3,300

SPREADSHEET PROBLEM

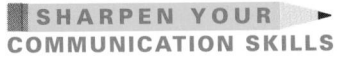

SHARPEN YOUR COMMUNICATION SKILLS

Instructions

1. Assemble the desired data, using the following columnar captions:

	Uncollectible Accounts Expense			Balance of
Year	Expense Actually Reported	Expense Based on Estimate	Increase in Amount of Expense	Allowance Account, End of Year

2. Experience during the first four years of operations indicated that the receivables were either collected within two years or had to be written off as uncollectible. Does the estimate of 1% of sales appear to be reasonably close to the actual experience with uncollectible accounts originating during the first two years? Explain.

PROBLEM 9-6B
FINANCIAL STATEMENTS
Objective 9

The following data for Landsburg Company were selected from the ledger, after adjustment at December 31, the end of the current fiscal year:

Accounts payable	$ 29,250
Accounts receivable	88,000
Accumulated depreciation, building	162,500
Accumulated depreciation, office equipment	47,250
Administrative expenses	82,250
Allowance for decline to market of marketable equity securities	2,400
Allowance for doubtful accounts	8,400
Building	363,000
Cash	40,500
Cost of merchandise sold	610,000
G. M. Landsburg, capital	603,400
G. M. Landsburg, drawing	75,000
Interest income	5,100
Land	80,000
Marketable equity securities	75,000
Merchandise inventory	95,100
Notes receivable	50,000
Office equipment	79,750
Office supplies	5,500
Prepaid insurance	7,000
Salaries payable	5,950
Sales	935,000
Sales discounts	8,500
Selling expenses	137,250
Unrealized loss from decline to market of marketable equity securities	2,400

Instructions

1. Prepare an income statement in multiple-step form.
2. Prepare a statement of owner's equity.
3. Prepare a balance sheet in report form.

SOLUTIONS SOFTWARE

Instructions for Solving Problem 9-6B Using Solutions Software

1. Load the opening balances.
2. Save the opening balances file to your drive and directory.
3. Set the run date to December 31 of the current year and enter your name.
4. Display a trial balance. (Use these account balances as the basis for the adjusting entries.)
5. Key the adjusting entries. Key ADJ.ENT. in the reference field. The data needed for year-end adjustments are as follows:
   a. Office supplies on hand, $5,500.
   b. Insurance expired, $1,500.
   c. Depreciation expense on building, $25,000.
   d. Depreciation expense on office equipment, $9,750.
   e. Uncollectible accounts expense, $5,000.
   f. Decline in market value of temporary investments, $2,400.
6. Display the adjusting entries. Key ADJ.ENT. in the Reference Restriction area of the Selection Options screen.
7. Display the financial statements.
8. Save a backup copy of your data file.
9. Perform period-end closing.
10. Display a post-closing trial balance.
11. Save your data file to disk.
12. End the session.

MINI-CASE 9 HARDING'S

For several years, sales have been on a "cash only" basis. On January 1, 1990, however, Harding's began offering credit on terms of n/30. The amount of the adjusting entry to record the estimated uncollectible receivables at the end of each year has been ½ of 1% of credit sales, which is the rate reported as the average for the industry. Credit sales and the year-end credit balances in Allowance for Doubtful Accounts for the past four years are as follows:

Year	Credit Sales	Allowance for Doubtful Accounts
1990	$6,000,000	$ 6,000
1991	6,700,000	10,000
1992	6,200,000	14,500
1993	5,500,000	19,500

Janet Harding, president of Harding's, is concerned that the method used to account for and write off uncollectible receivables is unsatisfactory. She has asked for your advice in the analysis of past operations in this area and for recommendations for change.

Instructions:

1. Determine the amount of (a) the addition to Allowance for Doubtful Accounts and (b) the accounts written off for each of the four years.
2. a. ▌▌▌ ‣ Advise Janet Harding as to whether the estimate of ½ of 1% of credit sales appears reasonable.
   b. ▌▌▌ ‣ Assume that after discussing (a) with Janet Harding, she asked you what action might be taken to determine what the balance of Allowance for Doubtful Accounts should be at December 31, 1993, and possible changes, if any, you might recommend in accounting for uncollectible receivables. How would you respond?

ANSWERS TO SELF-EXAMINATION QUESTIONS

1. **C** Maturity value is the amount that is due at the maturity or due date. The maturity value of $10,300 (answer C) is determined as follows:

Face amount of note	$10,000
Plus interest ($10,000 x 90/360 x 12/100)	300
Maturity value of note	$10,300

2. **B** The proceeds of $15,021.25 (answer B) are determined as follows:

Face value of note dated June 1	$15,000.00
Interest on note (60 days at 10%)	250.00
Maturity value of note due July 31	$15,250.00
Discount on maturity value (45 days, from June 16 to July 31, at 12%)	228.75
Proceeds	$15,021.25

3. **B** The estimate of uncollectible accounts, $8,500 (answer C), is the amount of the desired balance of Allowance for Doubtful Accounts after adjustment. The amount of the current provision to be made for uncollectible accounts expense is thus $6,000 (answer B), which is the amount that must be added to the Allowance for Doubtful Accounts credit balance of $2,500 (answer A), so that the account will have the desired balance of $8,500.

4. **B** The amount expected to be realized from accounts receivable is the balance of Accounts Receivable, $100,000, less the balance of Allowance for Doubtful Accounts, $7,000, or $93,000 (answer B).

5. **A** Securities held as temporary investments are classified on the balance sheet as current assets (answer A).

You and Accounting

Assume that you purchased a Sony Compact Disk (CD)/Receiver in June of last year. You planned on attaching three pairs of speakers to the system. Initially, however, you could afford only one pair of speakers, which cost $160. In August and October, you purchased the second and third pairs of speakers at higher prices. The pair of speakers bought in August cost $170, and the pair of speakers bought in October cost $180.

Over the holidays, you take the CD/Receiver and one pair of speakers home. Unfortunately, someone breaks into your dorm room and steals your other two pairs of speakers. Luckily, your parents' homeowners insurance policy will cover the theft, but the insurance company needs to know the cost of the speakers that were stolen.

All the speakers are identical. To respond to the insurance company, however, you will need to identify which pairs of speakers were stolen. Were they the first and second pairs, which cost a total of $330? Or were they the second and third pairs, which cost a total of $350? Whichever assumption you make may determine the amount that you receive from the insurance company.

Merchandise enterprises make similar assumptions when identical merchandise is purchased at different costs. At the end of a period, some of the merchandise will be on hand and some will have been sold. But which costs relate to the sold merchandise and which costs relate to the merchandise on hand? If you sell one pair of your speakers, what is the cost of those speakers? This chapter discusses this cost issue as well as other similar issues.

Chapter 10
Inventories

LEARNING OBJECTIVES
After studying this chapter, you should be able to:

Objective 1
Determine the effect of misstatements of inventory on the financial statements of the current period and the following period.

Objective 2
Summarize and provide examples of internal control procedures that apply to inventories.

Objective 3
List the procedures for determining the actual quantities in inventory.

Objective 4
Identify and list the costs included in inventory.

Objective 5
Compute the cost of inventory under the periodic inventory system, using the following costing methods:

First-in, first-out
Last-in, first-out
Average cost

Objective 6
Compute the cost of inventory under the perpetual inventory system, using the following costing methods:

First-in, first-out
Last-in, first-out

Objective 7
Compute the proper valuation of inventory at other than cost, using the lower-of-cost-or-market and net realizable value concepts.

Objective 8
Prepare a balance sheet presentation of merchandise inventory.

Objective 9
Estimate the cost of inventory, using the retail method and the gross profit method.

The buying and selling of merchandise is the primary activity in operating a wholesale or retail business. The sale of merchandise provides the major source of revenue for such enterprises. The cost of merchandise sold is often the largest deduction from sales in determining net income. Also, merchandise inventory is usually the largest current asset of such a firm. This chapter describes and illustrates several topics related to merchandise inventory. These include the effect of misstatements of inventory on the financial statements and the use of cost flow assumptions in determining the cost of inventory.

345

THE EFFECT OF ERRORS IN REPORTING INVENTORY

Objective 1
Determine the effect of misstatements of inventory on the financial statements of the current period and the following period.

The term **inventory** is used to indicate (1) merchandise held for sale in the normal course of business, and (2) materials in the process of production or held for production. This chapter discusses inventory of merchandise purchased for resale. Inventories of raw materials and partially processed materials of a manufacturing enterprise will be discussed in a later chapter.

For merchandising enterprises, inventory plays an important role in matching expired costs with revenues of the current period as well as the following period. Thus, any errors in reporting inventory affect the balance sheet and income statement, as discussed in the following paragraphs.

The Effect of Inventory on the Current Period's Statements

As was discussed in a previous chapter, the cost of merchandise available for sale during a period must be divided into two parts at the end of each period. The cost of the merchandise on hand at the end of the period is reported on the balance sheet as a current asset. The other part of the merchandise available for sale—the cost of the merchandise sold—is reported on the income statement as a deduction from the net sales to yield the gross profit.

An error in determining the amount of inventory at the end of a period will cause an equal misstatement of gross profit and net income. In addition, the amount of inventory and owner's equity reported in the balance sheet will also be misstated by the same amount.

The effects of understatements and overstatements of merchandise inventory at the end of a period are illustrated in the following three sets of condensed income statements and balance sheets. The first set of statements is based on a correct ending inventory of $20,000. The second set is based on an incorrect ending inventory of $12,000, which is an understatement of $8,000 ($20,000 − $12,000). The third set is based on an incorrect ending inventory of $27,000, which is an overstatement of $7,000 ($27,000 − $20,000). In all three cases, net sales are $200,000, merchandise available for sale is $140,000, and expenses are $55,000.

	Income Statement for the Year		Balance Sheet at End of Year	
1. Inventory at end of period correctly stated at $20,000.	Net sales	$200,000	Merchandise inventory	$ 20,000
	Cost of merchandise sold	120,000	Other assets	80,000
	Gross profit	$ 80,000	Total	$100,000
	Expenses	55,000	Liabilities	$ 30,000
	Net income	$ 25,000	Owner's equity	70,000
			Total	$100,000
2. Inventory at end of period incorrectly stated at $12,000; (understated by $8,000).	Net sales	$200,000	Merchandise inventory	$ 12,000
	Cost of merchandise sold	128,000	Other assets	80,000
	Gross profit	$ 72,000	Total	$ 92,000
	Expenses	55,000	Liabilities	$ 30,000
	Net income	$ 17,000	Owner's equity	62,000
			Total	$ 92,000
3. Inventory at end of period incorrectly stated at $27,000; (overstated by $7,000).	Net sales	$200,000	Merchandise inventory	$ 27,000
	Cost of merchandise sold	113,000	Other assets	80,000
	Gross profit	$ 87,000	Total	$107,000
	Expenses	55,000	Liabilities	$ 30,000
	Net income	$ 32,000	Owner's equity	77,000
			Total	$107,000

Although the total cost of merchandise available for sale was $140,000 in each of the preceding income statements, it was allocated in different ways. The variations in the allocation of the $140,000 to the ending inventory and the cost of merchandise sold are summarized as follows:

	Merchandise Available		
	Total	Inventory	Sold
1. Inventory correctly stated	$140,000	$20,000	$120,000
2. Inventory understated by $8,000	140,000	12,000	128,000
3. Inventory overstated by $7,000	140,000	27,000	113,000

The effect of the errors on net income, assets, and owner's equity is summarized below. This summary was developed by comparing the financial statements in 2 and 3 with the financial statements in 1.

	Net Income	Assets	Owner's Equity
2. Ending inventory understated $8,000	Understated $8,000	Understated $8,000	Understated $8,000
3. Ending inventory overstated $7,000	Overstated $7,000	Overstated $7,000	Overstated $7,000

The Effect of Inventory on the Following Period's Statements

The inventory at the end of one period becomes the inventory for the beginning of the following period. Thus, if the inventory is incorrectly stated at the end of one period, the net income of that period as well as the net income of the following period will be misstated. The amount of the two misstatements will be equal but will have opposite effects on net income. Thus, the effect on net income of an incorrectly stated inventory, if not corrected, is limited to the period of the error and the following period. At the end of this following period, assuming no additional errors, both the assets and the owner's equity will be correctly stated.

To illustrate, assume that the ending inventory for Period 1 was understated by $10,000, and no other errors occur. On the income statement, the gross profit (and net income) is understated for Period 1 and overstated for Period 2 by $10,000, as shown below.

	Period 1		Period 2	
	No Error	Error	Error	No Error
Net sales	$90,000	$90,000	$85,000	$85,000
Cost of merchandise sold:				
Beginning inventory	$25,000	$25,000	$20,000	$30,000
Purchases	70,000	70,000	65,000	65,000
Merchandise available for sale	$95,000	$95,000	$85,000	$95,000
Less ending inventory	30,000	20,000	28,000	28,000
Cost of merchandise sold	65,000	75,000	57,000	67,000
Gross profit	$25,000	$15,000	$28,000	$18,000

Understated $10,000   Overstated $10,000

In the above example, the $10,000 understatement of inventory at the end of Period 1 created an overstatement of the cost of merchandise sold and thus an understatement of gross profit by $10,000. On the balance sheet, merchandise inventory and owner's equity are also understated by $10,000. Because the ending inventory of Period 1 becomes the beginning inventory for Period 2, the cost of merchandise sold was understated and gross profit was overstated by $10,000 for Period 2. At the end of Period 2, merchandise inventory and owner's equity are correct.

Falsified Inventory and Income Inflate Company's Value

The importance of inventory to financial statements is recognized even by those who attempt to manipulate a company's statements in a fraudulent manner. One example of such inventory fraud is described in the following excerpt from an article in *The Wall Street Journal*:

Until last year, Crazy Eddie Inc. steadily recorded superb gains in sales and earnings, apparently because of rapid expansion of its electronics stores, adept sales-floor techniques and catchy commercials.

But the now-troubled company's latest court and regulatory filings suggest another element: a possible scheme by founder Eddie Antar and others to falsify inventory and profit reports. . . .

. . . Crazy Eddie says its former management—led by Mr. Antar—created "phantom" inventory and profits, then destroyed records in a cover-up. The purpose, the company says . . . was to "artificially inflate the net worth of the company" and the value of stock owned by Mr. Antar and others.

For instance, Crazy Eddie says the former management inflated the March 1987 inventory count at one warehouse by $10 million, by drafting phony count sheets and, among other things, improperly including $4 million in merchandise that was [recorded as] being returned to suppliers. Stores were also packed with unrecorded [purchases] prior to physical [inventory] counts. . . .

Source: Jeffrey A. Tannenbaum, "Filings by Crazy Eddie Suggest Founder Led Scheme to Inflate Company's Value," *The Wall Street Journal* (May 31, 1988), p. 28.

INTERNAL CONTROL OF INVENTORIES

Objective 2
Summarize and provide examples of internal control procedures that apply to inventories.

Because of the importance of inventory, an enterprise should have effective internal controls over its inventory. The objective of these controls over inventory is to ensure that the inventory is safeguarded and properly reported in the financial statements. As discussed in earlier chapters, internal controls can be either preventive or detective in nature. Types of preventive and detective controls over inventory are briefly discussed in the following paragraphs.

Internal controls for safeguarding inventory begin with developing and using security measures to protect the inventory from damage or employee theft. For example, inventory should be stored in a warehouse or other area to which access is restricted to authorized employees. The storage area should also be climate controlled to prevent damage to the inventory from heat or cold. Also, when the enterprise is not operating or the business is not open, the storage area should be locked.

To protect inventory from customer theft, retail enterprises often use such devices as two-way mirrors, cameras, and security guards. High-priced items are often displayed in locked cabinets, or they may be tagged so that an alarm is set off if the tagged merchandise is taken out of the store.

Other controls over inventory include using a voucher system similar to the one described in an earlier chapter. In such a system, the use of prenumbered receiving reports establishes the initial accountability for inventory. These receiving reports are reconciled to the initial purchase order and the vendor's invoice before the purchase is recorded in the voucher register. Also, requisition forms authorizing withdrawals of merchandise from storage can be used to control inventory.

The use of a perpetual inventory system for merchandise provides an effective means of control over inventory. The inventory of each type of merchandise is always readily available in a subsidiary **inventory ledger**. In addition, the subsidiary ledger can be an aid in maintaining inventory quantities at optimum levels. Frequent comparisons of balances with predetermined maximum and minimum levels allow for the timely reordering of merchandise and prevent the ordering of excess inventory.

To ensure the accuracy of the amount of inventory reported in the financial statements, the inventory should be counted periodically. This count is called a **physical inventory**. In a perpetual inventory system, the physical inventory should be compared to the recorded inventory in order to detect any shortages or possible thefts. The knowledge that a physical inventory will be taken also serves to deter (prevent) possible employee thefts or misuses of inventory.

DETERMINING ACTUAL QUANTITIES IN THE INVENTORY

Objective 3
List the procedures for determining the actual quantities in inventory.

The first step in the process of "taking" an inventory is to determine the quantity of each kind of merchandise owned by the enterprise. The specific procedures for determining inventory quantities and assembling the data differ among companies. A common practice is to use teams made up of two persons. One person counts, weighs, or otherwise determines the quantity, and the other lists the description and the quantity on inventory count sheets. The quantities indicated for high-cost items may be checked by a second count team during the inventory-taking process. It is also recommended that the second count team check quantities of other items selected at random from the inventory count sheets.

All of the merchandise owned by the business on the inventory date, and only such merchandise, should be included in the inventory. For merchandise in transit, the party (the seller or the buyer) who has title to the merchandise on the inventory date must be determined. To determine who has title, it may be necessary to examine purchases and sales invoices of the last few days of the current period and the first few days of the following period.

As discussed in a previous chapter, shipping terms are often helpful in determining when title passes. When goods are purchased or sold **FOB shipping point**, title usually passes to the buyer when the goods are shipped. When the terms are **FOB destination**, title usually does not pass to the buyer until the goods are delivered.

To illustrate, assume that merchandise purchased FOB shipping point is shipped by the seller on the last day of the buyer's fiscal period. The merchandise does not arrive until the following period and thus is not available for counting by the inventory crew. However, such merchandise should be included in the buyer's inventory because title has passed. A debit to Purchases and a credit to Accounts Payable should be recorded by the buyer as of the end of the current period.

Another example, although less common, further illustrates the importance of carefully examining transactions involving shipments of merchandise. Manufacturers sometimes ship merchandise to retailers who act as the manufacturer's agent when selling the merchandise. The manufacturer retains title until the goods are sold. Such merchandise is said to be shipped *on consignment* to the retailers. The unsold merchandise is a part of the manufacturer's (consignor's) inventory, even though the merchandise is in the hands of the retailers. Likewise, the consigned merchandise should not be included in the retailer's (consignee's) inventory.

THE COST OF INVENTORY

Objective 4
Identify and list the costs included in inventory.

The purchase price of merchandise is part of the cost of inventory. In addition, costs incurred in acquiring the merchandise, such as transportation, customs duties, and insurance against losses in transit, are normally included in the cost of inventory. However, some costs of acquiring merchandise, such as the salaries of Purchasing Department employees and other administrative costs, are not easily allocated to the inventory. Therefore, these costs are treated as operating expenses of the period.

If purchases discounts are treated as a deduction from purchases on the income statement, they should also be deducted from the purchase price of items in the inventory. If it is not possible to determine the exact amount of discount applicable to each inventory item, a pro rata amount of the total discount for the period may be deducted. For example, if net purchases are $200,000 and purchases discounts for the period are $3,000, the discounts are 1½% ($3,000 ÷ $200,000) of net purchases. If the inventory cost before considering the cash discounts is $30,000, the amount may be reduced by 1½%, or $450, to yield an inventory cost of $29,550.

INVENTORY COSTING METHODS UNDER A PERIODIC INVENTORY SYSTEM

Objective 5

Compute the cost of inventory under the periodic inventory system, using the following costing methods:

First-in, first-out
Last-in, first-out
Average cost

When the periodic inventory system is used, as discussed in an earlier chapter, only revenue is recorded each time a sale is made. No entry is made at the time of the sale to record the cost of the merchandise sold. At the end of the accounting period, a physical inventory is taken in order to determine the cost of the inventory on hand and the cost of the merchandise sold.

A major accounting issue arises in the use of the periodic system when identical units of a commodity are acquired at different unit costs during a period. In such cases, it is necessary to determine the unit costs of the items on hand at the end of the period. Likewise, the costs of the items sold during the period must be determined. For example, assume that three identical units of Commodity X were available for sale to customers during the fiscal year. One of these units was in the inventory at the beginning of the year, and the other two were purchased on March 4 and May 9. The costs per unit are as follows:

Commodity X		Units	Cost
Jan. 1	Inventory	1	$ 9
Mar. 4	Purchase	1	13
May 9	Purchase	1	14
Total		3	$36
	Average cost per unit		$12

During the year, two units of Commodity X were sold, leaving one unit in the inventory at the end of the year. If this unit can be identified with a specific purchase, the **specific identification method** can be used to determine the cost of the inventory. For example, if the unit in the inventory was purchased on March 4, the cost assigned to the unit is $13.

The specific identification method is not practical unless each unit can be identified as either sold or on hand. An automobile dealer, for example, may be able to use this method. For businesses that buy and sell units that are basically identical, however, a flow of costs must be assumed. That is, an assumption must be made as to which units were sold and which units are on hand. The three most common cost flow assumptions are as follows:

1. Cost flow is in the order in which the costs were incurred—first-in, first-out.
2. Cost flow is in the reverse order in which the costs were incurred—last-in, first-out.
3. Cost flow is an average of the costs.

The cost of the two units of Commodity X sold and the cost of the one unit on hand are shown below for each of the cost flow assumptions.

	Commodity X Costs		
	Units Available	Units Sold	Unit Remaining
1. In order in which costs were incurred (first-in, first out)	$36	–	($ 9+$13) = $14
2. In reverse order in which costs were incurred (last-in, first-out)	36	–	(14+ 13) = 9
3. In accordance with average costs	36	–	(12+ 12) = 12

These three assumptions of cost flows are the basis for the following widely used inventory costing methods:

1. **First-in, first-out (fifo)**
2. **Last-in, first-out (lifo)**
3. **Average cost**

The extent of the use of these three methods is indicated by the chart in Exhibit 1.

Exhibit 1
Inventory Costing Methods

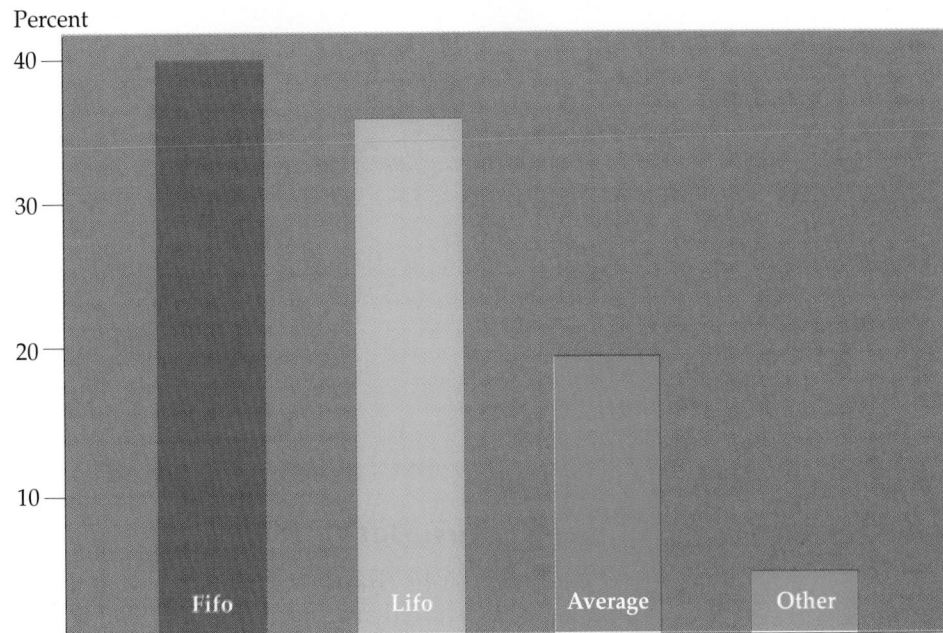

Source: *Accounting Trends & Techniques,* 45th ed. (New York: American Institute of Certified Public Accountants, 1991).

First-In, First-Out Method

When the **first-in, first-out (fifo) method** of costing inventory is used, costs are assumed to be charged against revenue in the order in which they were incurred. Hence the inventory remaining is assumed to be made up of the most recent costs. An example of the use of this method is based on the following data for a commodity:

Jan. 1	Inventory:	200 units at $ 9	$ 1,800
Mar. 10	Purchase:	300 units at 10	3,000
Sep. 21	Purchase:	400 units at 11	4,400
Nov. 18	Purchase:	100 units at 12	1,200
	Available for sale during year	1,000	$10,400

The physical count on December 31 shows that 300 units of the commodity are on hand. Using the fifo method, the cost of these units is determined as follows:

Most recent costs, Nov. 18:	100 units at $12	$1,200
Next most recent costs, Sep. 21:	200 units at 11	2,200
Inventory, Dec. 31:	300	$3,400

Deducting the inventory of $3,400 from the $10,400 of merchandise available for sale yields $7,000 as the cost of merchandise sold. The $7,000 cost of merchandise sold is made up of the earliest costs incurred for this commodity. The relationship of the inventory at December 31 and the cost of merchandise sold during the year is shown in Exhibit 2.

Most businesses dispose of goods in the order in which the goods are purchased. This would be especially true of perishables and goods whose styles or models often change. Thus, the fifo method is often consistent with the physical movement of merchandise in an enterprise. To the extent that this is the case, the fifo method provides results that are about the same as those obtained by identifying the specific costs of each item sold and in inventory.

Exhibit 2
First-In, First-Out Flow of Costs

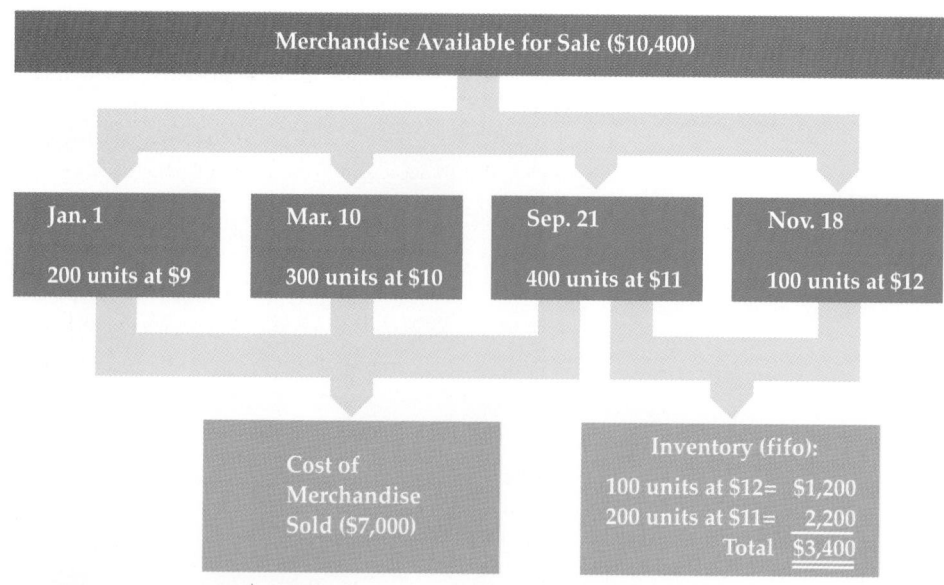

Last-In, First-Out Method

When the **last-in, first-out (lifo) method** of inventory costing is used, the most recent costs incurred are assumed to be matched against revenue. Hence the inventory remaining is assumed to be composed of the earliest costs. Based on the data in the fifo example, the cost of the 300 units of inventory is determined as follows:

Earliest costs, Jan. 1:	200 units at $ 9	$1,800
Next earliest costs, Mar. 10:	100 units at 10	1,000
Inventory, Dec. 31:	300	$2,800

Deducting the inventory of $2,800 from the $10,400 of merchandise available for sale yields $7,600 as the cost of merchandise sold. The $7,600 cost of merchandise sold is made up of the most recent costs incurred for this commodity. The relationship of the inventory at December 31 and the cost of merchandise sold during the year is shown in Exhibit 3.

Exhibit 3
Last-In, First-Out Flow of Costs

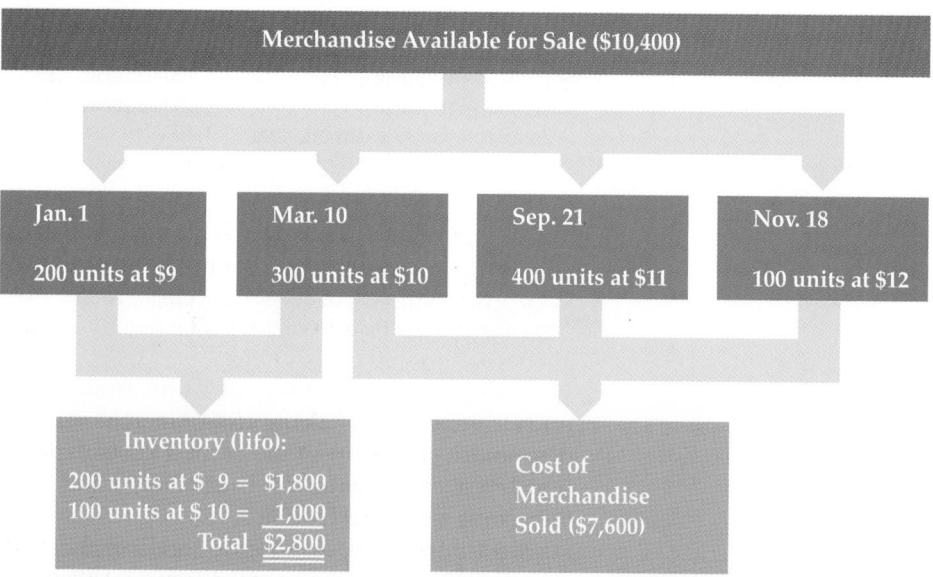

The use of the lifo method was originally limited to rare situations in which the units sold were taken from the most recently acquired goods. For tax reasons, its use has greatly increased during the past few decades. Lifo is now often used even when it does not represent the physical flow of goods.

Average Cost Method

The **average cost method** is sometimes called the **weighted average method.** When this method is used, costs are assumed to be matched against revenue according to an average of the unit costs of the goods sold. The same weighted average unit costs are used in determining the cost of the merchandise inventory at the end of the period. For businesses in which merchandise sales may be made up of various purchases of identical units, the average method approximates the physical flow of goods.

The weighted average unit cost is determined by dividing the total cost of the units of each commodity available for sale during the period by the related number of units of that commodity. Using the same cost data as in the fifo and lifo examples, the average cost of the 1,000 units, $10.40, and the cost of the 300 units in inventory, $3,120, are determined as follows:

Average unit cost: $10,400÷1,000 units = $10.40
Inventory, Dec. 31:   300 units at $10.40 = $3,120

Deducting the inventory of $3,120 from the $10,400 of merchandise available for sale yields $7,280 as the cost of merchandise sold.

Comparison of Inventory Costing Methods

For each of the three alternative methods of costing inventories under the periodic system, a different flow of costs is assumed. If the cost of units had remained stable, all three methods would have yielded the same results. Since prices do change, however, the three methods will normally yield different amounts for (1) the ending inventory, (2) the cost of the merchandise sold for the period, and (3) the gross profit (and net income) for the period. Using the examples presented above and assuming that net sales were $15,000, the following partial income statements indicate the effects of each method when prices are rising:

	First-In, First-Out		Average Cost		Last-In, First-Out	
Net sales		$15,000				$15,000
Cost of merchandise sold:						
Beginning inventory	$ 1,800		$ 1,800		$ 1,800	
Purchases	8,600		8,600		8,600	
Merchandise available for sale	$10,400		$10,400		$10,400	
Less ending inventory	3,400		3,120		2,800	
Cost of merchandise sold		7,000		7,280		7,600
Gross profit		$ 8,000		$ 7,720		$ 7,400

As shown in the income statements, the fifo method yielded the lowest amount for the cost of merchandise sold and the highest amount for gross profit (and net income). It also yielded the highest amount for the ending inventory. On the other hand, the lifo method yielded the highest amount for the cost of merchandise sold, the lowest amount for gross profit (and net income), and the lowest amount for ending inventory. The average cost method yielded results that were between those of fifo and lifo.

USE OF THE FIRST-IN, FIRST-OUT METHOD. When the fifo method is used, the costs of the units sold are assumed to be in the order in which they were incurred. During a period of inflation or rising prices, the earlier unit costs are lower than the more recent unit costs, as shown in the preceding fifo example. Much of the benefit of the larger amount of gross profit is lost, however, because the inventory must be replaced at ever higher prices. When the rate of inflation reaches double-digits, as it did during the 1970s, the larger gross profits that result from the fifo method are often called *inventory profits* or *illusory profits.*

In a period of deflation or declining prices, the effect described above is just the opposite. The fifo method, compared to the other methods, yields the lowest amount of gross profit. A major criticism of the fifo method is its tendency to pass through the effects of inflationary and deflationary trends to gross profit. An advantage of the fifo method, however, is that the balance sheet will report the ending merchandise inventory at an amount that is about the same as its current replacement cost.

USE OF THE LAST-IN, FIRST-OUT METHOD. When the lifo method is used during a period of inflation or rising prices, the results are opposite those of the other two methods. As shown in the preceding example, the lifo method will yield a lower amount of inventory at the end of the period, a higher amount of cost of merchandise sold, and a lower amount of gross profit than the other two methods. The reason for these effects is that the cost of the most recently acquired units most nearly approximates the cost of their replacement. In a period of inflation, the more recent unit costs are higher than the earlier unit costs. Thus, it can be argued that the lifo method more nearly matches current costs with current revenues. This latter point was one reason that Chrysler Corporation changed from the fifo method to the lifo method in the 1980s, as stated in the following footnote that accompanied Chrysler's financial statements:

Chrysler changed its method of accounting from first-in, first-out (fifo) to last-in, first-out (lifo) for substantially all of its domestic productive inventories. The change to lifo was made to more accurately match current costs with current revenues.

During periods of rising prices, the use of lifo offers a savings in income taxes. The income tax savings results because lifo reports the lowest amount of net income of the three methods. During the double-digit inflationary period of the 1970s, many businesses changed from fifo to lifo to take advantage of tax savings.

In a period of deflation or falling price levels, the effect described above is just the opposite. The lifo method yields the highest amount of gross profit. The major argument for using lifo is its tendency to minimize the effect of price trends on gross profit. A criticism of the use of lifo, however, is that the ending merchandise inventory on the balance sheet may be quite different from its current replacement cost. In such cases, however, the financial statements normally include a note that states the estimated difference between the lifo inventory and the inventory if fifo had been used. An example of such a note accompanied the 1991 statements of The Walgreen Co., as shown below.

Inventories are valued on a last-in, first-out (LIFO) cost basis. At August 31, 1991 and 1990, inventories would have been greater by $208,894,000 and $179,282,000 respectively, if they had been valued on a lower of first-in, first-out (FIFO) cost or market basis.

USE OF THE AVERAGE COST METHOD. The average cost method of inventory costing is, in a sense, a compromise between fifo and lifo. The effect of price trends is averaged in determining the cost of merchandise sold and the ending inventory. For a series of purchases, the average cost will be the same, regardless of the direction of price trends. For example, a complete reversal of the sequence of unit costs presented in the preceding illustration would not affect the reported cost of merchandise sold, gross profit, or ending inventory.

SELECTION OF AN INVENTORY COSTING METHOD. The preceding comparisons show the importance attached to the selection of the inventory costing method. Often enterprises apply one method to one class of inventory and a different method to another class. For example, a computer retailer might use the fifo method for its microcomputer inventory and the lifo method for software and other inventory. The method(s) used may also be changed for a valid reason. The effect of any change in method and the reason for the change should be disclosed in the financial statements for the period in which the change occurred.

Inflation and Adoption of LIFO

The effects of using lifo and some of the reasons that the method is adopted (or not adopted) by businesses were discussed in an article in *Management Accounting*. Some excerpts from that article follow.

... *The primary advantage of lifo is that in today's inflationary environment lifo defers (not avoids) income taxes by reducing income. The improved cash flow, then, can be profitably invested or used to reduce borrowings. ...*

In addition to deferring income taxes, though, lifo has a great deal of theoretical justification. By matching current costs against current sales, lifo produces a truer picture of income; that is, the quality of income produced by the use of lifo is higher because it more nearly approximates disposable income. ...

Even though the primary advantage of lifo—reduced tax payments—is a function of lower income, the negative earnings impact ironically continues to cloud corporate managers' deci- *sions about the adoption of lifo. Managers fear that lower reported earnings will [have unfavorable effects on the stock price, executive compensation contracts, and credit ratings. ...]*

Another concern about lifo commonly expressed by corporate managers is misstatement of the inventories on the lifo balance sheet. Particularly over a period of rapidly rising inventory quantities and prices, the use of lifo can lead to a valuation of inventories that is significantly less than current replacement cost. However, this misstatement can be mitigated by presenting inventories valued on a non-lifo basis and deducting the lifo valuation [allowance to reduce the balance sheet inventory to the lifo amount, as follows:]

Inventory	XXX
Less reduction to lifo cost	XXX
Total	XXX

Source: Clayton T. Rumble, "So You Still Have Not Adopted Lifo," *Management Accounting* (October 1983), pp. 59-67.

INVENTORY COSTING METHODS UNDER A PERPETUAL INVENTORY SYSTEM

Objective 6
Compute the cost of inventory under the perpetual inventory system, using the following costing methods:

First-in, first-out
Last-in, first-out

In contrast to the periodic system, all merchandise increases and decreases in a perpetual system are recorded in a manner similar to the recording of increases and decreases in cash. The merchandise inventory account at the beginning of an accounting period indicates the merchandise on hand on that date. Purchases are recorded by debiting Merchandise Inventory and crediting Cash or Accounts Payable. Sales are recorded in the sales account. On the date of each sale, the cost of the merchandise sold is recorded by debiting Cost of Merchandise Sold and crediting Merchandise Inventory. Thus, the merchandise inventory account constantly (perpetually) discloses the balance of merchandise on hand. At the end of the period, the balance in the merchandise inventory account is reported on the balance sheet, and the balance in the cost of merchandise sold account is reported on the income statement.

Unlike cash, which is uniform in nature, merchandise is normally a mixture of different kinds of goods with different costs. Thus, a subsidiary inventory ledger, with a separate account for each type of good, is normally maintained. The balances of these accounts are called the **book inventories** of the items on hand. Costs are normally assigned to units in a perpetual system inventory ledger by using one of the three costing methods discussed earlier in this chapter—fifo, lifo, or average cost. In the following paragraphs, the use of those methods in a perpetual system is discussed. The fifo and lifo methods are also illustrated using the following data for merchandise identified as Commodity 127B:

Commodity 127B		Units	Cost
Jan. 1	Inventory	10	$20
4	Sale	7	
10	Purchase	8	21
22	Sale	4	
28	Sale	2	
30	Purchase	10	22

First-In, First-Out Method

To illustrate the first-in, first-out method of cost flow in a perpetual inventory system, the inventory ledger account for Commodity 127B is shown in Exhibit 4. The number of units on hand after each transaction, together with total costs and unit costs, appear in the inventory section of the account.

Exhibit 4
Perpetual Inventory Account
(Fifo)

Commodity 127B

Date	Purchases Quantity	Unit Cost	Total Cost	Cost of Merchandise Sold Quantity	Unit Cost	Total Cost	Inventory Quantity	Unit Cost	Total Cost
Jan. 1							10	20	200
4				7	20	140	3	20	60
10	8	21	168				3	20	60
							8	21	168
22				3	20	60			
				1	21	21	7	21	147
28				2	21	42	5	21	105
30	10	22	220				5	21	105
							10	22	220

Note that after the 7 units of the commodity were sold on January 4, there was an inventory of 3 units at $20 each. The 8 units purchased on January 10 were acquired at a unit cost of $21, instead of $20. Therefore, the inventory after the January 10 purchase is reported on two lines—3 units at $20 each and 8 units at $21 each. Next, note that the $81 cost of the 4 units sold on January 22 is composed of the remaining 3 units at $20 each and 1 unit at $21. At this point, 7 units are in inventory at a cost of $21 per unit. The remainder of the illustration can be explained in a similar manner.

Last-In, First-Out Method

When the last-in, first-out method is used in a perpetual inventory system, the cost of the units sold is the cost of the most recent purchases. To illustrate, the ledger account for Commodity 127B, prepared on a lifo basis, is shown in Exhibit 5.

Exhibit 5
Perpetual Inventory Account
(Lifo)

Commodity 127B

Date	Purchases Quantity	Unit Cost	Total Cost	Cost of Merchandise Sold Quantity	Unit Cost	Total Cost	Inventory Quantity	Unit Cost	Total Cost
Jan. 1							10	20	200
4				7	20	140	3	20	60
10	8	21	168				3	20	60
							8	21	168
22				4	21	84	3	20	60
							4	21	84
28				2	21	42	3	20	60
							2	21	42
30	10	22	220				3	20	60
							2	21	42
							10	22	220

A comparison of the ledger accounts for the fifo perpetual system and the lifo perpetual system indicates that the accounts are the same through the January 10 purchase. Using the lifo perpetual system, however, the cost of the 4 units sold on January 22 is the cost of the units from the January 10 purchase ($21 per unit). The cost of the 7 units in inventory after the sale on January 22 is the cost of the 3 units remaining from the beginning inventory and the cost of the 4 units remaining from the January 10 purchase. The remainder of the lifo illustration can be explained in a similar manner.

When the lifo method is used, the inventory ledgers may be maintained in units only. The units are converted to dollars when the financial statements are prepared at the end of the period.

Average Cost Method

When the average cost method is used in a perpetual inventory system, an average unit cost for each type of commodity is computed each time a purchase is made, rather than at the end of the period. This unit cost is then used to determine the cost of each sale, until another purchase is made and a new average is computed. This averaging technique is called a **moving average**.[1]

Computerized Perpetual Inventory Systems

A perpetual inventory system may be maintained using manually kept records. However, such a system is often too costly and too time consuming for enterprises with a large number of inventory items and/or many purchase and sales transactions. In such cases, the record keeping is often computerized.

An example of the use of computers in maintaining perpetual inventory records for retail stores is described below.

1. The relevant details for each inventory item, such as a description, quantity, and unit size, are stored in an inventory record. The individual inventory records make up the computerized inventory ledger or master file.
2. Each time an item is purchased or returned by a customer, the inventory data are entered into the computer and stored. Hourly, daily, or at some other interval, the computerized inventory ledger (master file) is updated.
3. Each time an item is sold, a sales clerk passes an electronic wand (optical scanner) over the price tag attached to the merchandise. The electronic wand *reads* the magnetic code on the price tag. The inventory data provided in the magnetic code are immediately entered into the computer and stored. Periodically, these data are used to update the computerized inventory ledger (detailed inventory records).
4. After a physical inventory is taken, the inventory count data are entered into the computer. These data are compared with the current balances and a listing of the overages and shortages is printed. The inventory balances are then adjusted to the quantities determined by the physical count.

By entering additional data, the system described above can be extended to aid in maintaining inventory quantities at optimal levels. For example, data on the most economical quantity to be purchased in a single order and the minimum quantity to be maintained for each item can be entered into the computer records. The computer software is then programmed to compare these data with data on the book inventories. As necessary, the computer program begins the purchasing activity by preparing purchase orders.

---

[1] The inventory ledger in a perpetual system that uses the average cost method is illustrated in cost accounting texts.

The system can also be extended to aid in processing the related accounting transactions. For example, as cash sales are entered on an electronic cash register, the sales data are accumulated and used for the daily accounting entries. These entries debit Cash and credit Sales as well as debit Cost of Merchandise Sold and credit Merchandise Inventory.

VALUATION OF INVENTORY AT OTHER THAN COST

Objective 7
Compute the proper valuation of inventory at other than cost, using the lower-of-cost-or-market and net realizable value concepts.

As discussed earlier in the chapter, cost is the primary basis for the valuation of inventories. In some cases, however, inventory is valued at other than cost. Two such cases arise when (1) the cost of replacing items in inventory is below the recorded cost, and (2) the inventory is not salable at normal sales prices. This latter case may be due to imperfections, shop wear, style changes, or other causes.

Valuation at Lower of Cost or Market

If the cost of replacing an item in inventory is lower than the original purchase cost, the **lower-of-cost-or-market method** is used to value the inventory. *Market,* as used in the phrase *lower of cost or market*, is the cost to replace the merchandise on the inventory date. This market value is based on quantities normally purchased from the usual source of supply.

The lower-of-cost-or-market method provides two advantages. First, the gross profit (and net income) is reduced in the period in which the decline occurred. Second, an approximately normal gross profit will be realized during the period in which the item is later sold.

To illustrate, assume that merchandise with a unit cost of $70 has sold at $100 during the period, yielding a gross profit of $30 a unit, or 30% of sales. Assume also that at the end of the year, there is a single unit in the inventory and that its replacement cost has declined to $63. In such a case, it would be expected that the selling price would also decline, if it has not already done so. Assuming a reduction in the selling price to $90, the gross profit based on the replacement cost of $63 would be $27, which is also 30% of the selling price.

The valuation of the unit in the inventory at $63 reduces gross profit of the past period by $7 and permits a normal gross profit of $27 to be realized on its sale in the following period. If the unit had been valued at its original cost of $70, the gross profit determined for the past year would have been $7 greater. Likewise, the gross profit for the sale of the item in the following period would have been $7 less.

To apply the lower-of-cost-or-market method, the cost and the replacement cost can be determined for (1) each item in the inventory, (2) major classes or categories, or (3) the inventory as a whole. In practice, the cost and replacement cost of each item are usually determined. To illustrate, assume that there are 400 identical units of Commodity A in the inventory, each acquired at a unit cost of $10.25. If at the inventory date the item would cost $10.50 to replace, the cost price of $10.25 would be multiplied by 400 to determine the inventory value. On the other hand, if the item could be replaced at $9.50 a unit, the replacement cost of $9.50 would be used for valuation purposes. The table in Exhibit 6 illustrates one way of organizing inventory data in applying the lower-of-cost-or-market method to each inventory item.

Exhibit 6
Determination of Inventory at Lower of Cost or Market

Commodity	Inventory Quantity	Unit Cost Price	Unit Market Price	Total Cost	Total Lower of C or M
A	400	$10.25	$ 9.50	$ 4,100	$ 3,800
B	120	22.50	24.10	2,700	2,700
C	600	8.00	7.75	4,800	4,650
D	280	14.00	14.75	3,920	3,920
Total				$15,520	$15,070

Although accumulating the data for total cost is not necessary, as shown in Exhibit 6, it provides management with the amount of the reduction in inventory value caused by the decline in market prices. The amount of the market decline, $450 ($15,520–$15,070), may be reported as a separate item on the income statement. Otherwise, the market decline will be included in the cost of merchandise sold. Regardless, net income will be reduced by the amount of the market decline.

Valuation at Net Realizable Value

Obsolete, spoiled, or damaged merchandise and other merchandise that can be sold only at prices below cost should be valued at net realizable value. Net realizable value is the estimated selling price less any direct cost of disposal, such as sales commissions. For example, assume that damaged merchandise costing $1,000 can be sold for only $800, and direct selling expenses are estimated to be $150. This inventory should be valued at $650 ($800–$150), which is its net realizable value.

PRESENTATION OF MERCHANDISE INVENTORY ON THE BALANCE SHEET

Objective 8
Prepare a balance sheet presentation of merchandise inventory.

Merchandise inventory is usually presented in the Current Assets section of the balance sheet, following receivables. Both the method of determining the cost of the inventory (fifo, lifo, or average) and the method of valuing the inventory (cost, or lower of cost or market) should be shown. These details may be disclosed in parentheses on the balance sheet or in a footnote to the financial statements. An example of the use of parentheses is shown in Exhibit 7.

Exhibit 7
Merchandise Inventory on the Balance Sheet

Afro-Arts Company
Balance Sheet
December 31, 1994

Assets

Current assets:		
Cash		$ 19,400
Accounts receivable	$80,000	
Less allowance for doubtful accounts	3,000	77,000
Merchandise inventory—at lower of cost (first-in, first-out method) or market		216,300

It is not unusual for large enterprises with varied activities to use different costing methods for different segments of their inventories. The following note taken from the financial statements of Chrysler Corp. illustrates this:

INVENTORIES

Inventories are valued at the lower of cost or market. The cost of approximately 41 percent and 49 percent of inventories at December 31, 1991 and 1990, respectively is determined on a Last-In, First-Out (LIFO) basis. The balance of inventory cost is determined on a First-In, First-Out (FIFO) basis.

ESTIMATING INVENTORY COST

Objective 9
Estimate the cost of inventory, using the retail method and the gross profit method.

In practice, it may be necessary to know the amount of inventory when it is impractical to take a physical inventory or to maintain perpetual inventory records. For example, an enterprise that uses a periodic inventory system may need monthly income statements, but taking a physical inventory each month may be too costly. Also, when a disaster such as a fire has destroyed the inventory, an enterprise will need to determine the amount of the loss, but taking a physical inventory is impossible. In such cases, the inventory cost can be estimated by using (1) the retail method or (2) the gross profit method.

Retail Method of Inventory Costing

The retail inventory method of estimating inventory cost is based on the relationship of the cost of merchandise available for sale to the retail price of the same merchandise. This method is widely used by retail businesses, such as department stores. To use this method, as illustrated in Exhibit 8, the retail prices of all merchandise acquired are accumulated. Next, the inventory at retail is determined by deducting sales for the period from the retail price of the goods that were available for sale during the period. The estimate of the inventory cost is then calculated by multiplying the inventory at retail by the ratio of cost to selling (retail) price for the merchandise available for sale.

Exhibit 8
Determination of Inventory by
Retail Method

	Cost	Retail
Merchandise inventory, January 1	$19,400	$ 36,000
Purchases in January (net)	42,600	64,000
Merchandise available for sale	$62,000	$100,000
Ratio of cost to retail price: $\dfrac{\$62,000}{\$100,000} = 62\%$		
Sales for January (net)		70,000
Merchandise inventory, January 31, at retail		$ 30,000
Merchandise inventory, January 31, at estimated cost ($30,000×62%)		$ 18,600

In terms of the percent of cost to selling price, the *mix* of the items in the ending inventory is assumed to be the same as the entire stock of merchandise available for sale. In Exhibit 8, for example, it is unlikely that the retail price of every item was composed of exactly 62% cost and 38% gross profit. It is assumed, however, that the weighted average of the cost percentages of the merchandise in the inventory ($30,000) is the same as in the merchandise available for sale ($100,000). When the inventory is made up of different classes of merchandise with very different gross profit rates, the cost percentages and the inventory should be developed for each class of inventory.

One of the major advantages of the retail method is that it provides inventory figures for use in preparing monthly or quarterly statements. Department stores and similar merchandisers usually determine gross profit and operating income each month but take a physical inventory only once a year. In addition, a comparison of the estimated ending inventory with the physical ending inventory, both at retail prices, will help identify inventory shortages resulting from shoplifting and other causes. Management can then take appropriate actions.

The retail method can also be used with the periodic system when a physical inventory is taken at the end of the year. In such a case, the items counted are recorded on the inventory sheets at their retail (selling) prices instead of their cost prices. The physical inventory at selling price is then converted to cost by applying the ratio of cost to selling (retail) price for the merchandise available for sale.

To illustrate, assume that the data in Exhibit 8 are for an entire fiscal year rather than for only January. If the physical inventory taken at the end of the year totaled $29,000, priced at retail, it would be this amount rather than the $30,000 that would be converted to cost. Thus, the inventory at cost would be $17,980 ($29,000 × 62%) instead of $18,600 ($30,000 × 62%). The $17,980 would be used for the year-end financial statements and for income tax purposes.

Gross Profit Method of Estimating Inventories

The gross profit method of estimating inventories uses an estimate of the gross profit realized during the period to estimate the inventory at the end of the period. This estimate is usually based on the actual rate for the preceding year, adjusted for any changes made in the cost and sales prices during the current period. By using the rate of gross profit, the dollar amount of sales for a period can be divided into its two components: (1) gross profit and (2) cost of merchandise sold.

The latter amount may then be deducted from the cost of merchandise available for sale to yield the estimated cost of merchandise on hand.

Exhibit 9 illustrates the use of the gross profit method for estimating a company's inventory on January 31. In this example, the inventory on January 1 is assumed to be $57,000, the net purchases during the month are $180,000, and the net sales during the month are $250,000. In addition, the gross profit is estimated to be 30% of net sales.

Exhibit 9
Estimate of Inventory by Gross
Profit Method

Merchandise inventory, January 1		$ 57,000
Purchases in January (net)		180,000
Merchandise available for sale		$237,000
Sales in January (net)	$250,000	
Less estimated gross profit ($250,000 × 30%)	75,000	
Estimated cost of merchandise sold		175,000
Estimated merchandise inventory, January 31		$ 62,000

The gross profit method is useful for estimating inventories for monthly or quarterly financial statements. It is also useful in estimating the cost of merchandise destroyed by fire or other disaster.

CHAPTER REVIEW

Key Points

Objective 1. Determine the effect of misstatements of inventory on the financial statements of the current period and the following period.
An error in determining the amount of inventory at the end of a period will cause an equal misstatement of gross profit and net income. The effect on net income is limited to the period of the error and the following period. The amount of inventory reported for assets and the amount of owner's equity in the balance sheet will be misstated by the same amount in the period of the error. In the following period, the balance sheet will be correctly stated.

Objective 2. Summarize and provide examples of internal control procedures that apply to inventories.
Internal control procedures for inventories include those developed to protect the inventories from damage, employee theft, and customer theft. In addition, a physical inventory count should be taken periodically in order to detect shortages as well as to deter employee thefts.

Objective 3. List the procedures for determining the actual quantities in inventory.
The first step in "taking" an inventory is to count the merchandise on hand. Count teams are often made up of two persons—one who counts and the other who records the quantities and descriptions on inventory count sheets. A second count team may be used to check quantities of high-cost items and other items selected at random. Care must be used to include all merchandise in transit that is owned. Consigned merchandise should not be included in the consignee's inventory.

Objective 4. Identify and list the costs included in inventory.
The cost of merchandise inventory is made up of the purchase price and all costs incurred in acquiring the merchandise, including freight, customs duties, and insurance against losses in transit.

Objective 5. Compute the cost of inventory under the periodic inventory system, using the following costing methods: first-in, first-out; last-in, first-out; average cost.
The cost of inventory under the fifo method includes the cost of items purchased last. Costs are charged against revenue in the order in which they were incurred. The cost of inventory under the lifo method includes the cost of items purchased first. Costs are charged against revenue in the reverse order of occurrence. The average cost method uses a weighted average cost for determining inventory cost and amounts charged against revenue.

Objective 6. Compute the cost of inventory under the perpetual inventory system, using the following costing methods: first-in, first-out and last-in, first-out.
In a perpetual inventory system, the number of units and the cost of each type of merchandise are recorded in a subsidiary inventory ledger, with a separate account for each type of merchandise. Inventory costs and the amounts charged against revenue are illustrated, using the fifo and lifo methods.

Objective 7. Compute the proper valuation of inventory at other than cost, using the lower-of-cost-or-market and net realizable value concepts.
If the market price of an item of inventory is lower than its cost, the lower market price is used to compute the value of the item. Market price is the cost to replace the merchandise on the inventory date. It is possible to apply the lower of cost or market to each item in the inventory, to major classes or categories, or to the inventory as a whole.

Merchandise that can be sold only at prices below cost should be valued at net realizable value, which is the estimated selling price less any direct cost of disposal.

Objective 8. Prepare a balance sheet presentation of merchandise inventory.
Merchandise inventory is usually presented in the Current Assets section of the balance sheet, following receivables. Both the method of determining the cost of the inventory (fifo, lifo, or average) and the method of valuing the inventory (cost, or lower of cost or market) should be shown.

Objective 9. Estimate the cost of inventory, using the retail method and the gross profit method.
In using the retail method to estimate inventory, the retail prices of all merchandise acquired are accumulated. The inventory at retail is determined by deducting sales for the period from the retail price of the goods that were available for sale during the period. The inventory at retail is then converted to cost on the basis of the ratio of cost to selling (retail) price for the merchandise available for sale.

In using the gross profit method to estimate inventory, the estimated gross profit is deducted from the sales to determine the estimated cost of merchandise sold. This amount is then deducted from the cost of merchandise available for sale to determine the estimated ending inventory.

Glossary of Key Terms

Average cost method. The method of inventory costing that is based on the assumption that costs should be charged against revenue in accordance with the weighted average unit costs of the items sold. **Objective 5**

First-in, first-out (fifo) method. A method of inventory costing based on the assumption that the costs of merchandise sold should be charged against revenue in the order in which the costs were incurred. **Objective 5**

Gross profit method. A means of estimating inventory on hand, based on the relationship of gross profit to sales. **Objective 9**

Last-in, first-out (lifo) method. A method of inventory costing based on the assumption that the most recent merchandise costs incurred should be charged against revenue. **Objective 5**

Lower-of-cost-or-market method. A method of valuing inventory that reports the inventory at the lower of its cost or current market value (replacement cost). **Objective 7**

Net realizable value. The amount at which merchandise that can be sold only at prices below cost should be valued; determined as the estimated selling price less any direct costs of disposal. **Objective 7**

Physical inventory. The detailed listing of merchandise on hand. **Objective 2**

Retail inventory method. A method of inventory costing based on the relationship of the cost and the retail price of merchandise. **Objective 9**

Self-Examination Questions
Answers at end of chapter.

1. If the merchandise inventory at the end of the year is overstated by $7,500, the error will cause an:
   A. overstatement of cost of merchandise sold for the year by $7,500
   B. understatement of gross profit for the year by $7,500
   C. overstatement of net income for the year by $7,500
   D. understatement of net income for the year by $7,500

2. The inventory costing method that is based on the assumption that costs should be charged against revenue in the order in which they were incurred is:
   A. fifo
   B. lifo
   C. average cost
   D. perpetual inventory

3. The following units of a particular item were available for sale during the period:

Beginning inventory	40 units at $20
First purchase	50 units at $21
Second purchase	50 units at $22
Third purchase	50 units at $23

   What is the unit cost of the 35 units on hand at the end of the period, as determined under the periodic inventory system by the fifo costing method?
   A. $20
   B. $21
   C. $22
   D. $23

4. The following units of a particular item were purchased and sold during the period:

Beginning inventory	40 units at $20
First purchase	50 units at $21
Second purchase	50 units at $22
First sale	110 units
Third purchase	50 units at $23
Second sale	45 units

   What is the unit cost of the 35 units on hand at the end of the period, as determined under the perpetual inventory system by the lifo costing method?
   A. $20 and $23
   B. $20 and $21
   C. $20
   D. $23

5. If merchandise inventory is being valued at cost and the price level is steadily rising, the method of costing that will yield the highest net income is:
   A. lifo
   B. fifo
   C. average
   D. periodic

ILLUSTRATIVE PROBLEM

Stewart Co.'s beginning inventory and purchases during the fiscal year ended March 31, 1994, were as follows:

		Unit	Total Cost	Units Cost
April 1, 1993	Inventory	1,000	$50.00	$ 50,000
April 10, 1993	Purchase	1,200	52.50	63,000
May 30, 1993	Purchase	800	55.00	44,000
August 26, 1993	Purchase	2,000	56.00	112,000
October 15, 1993	Purchase	1,500	57.00	85,500
December 31, 1993	Purchase	700	58.00	40,600
January 18, 1994	Purchase	1,350	60.00	81,000
March 21, 1994	Purchase	450	62.00	27,900
Total		9,000		$504,000

Stewart Co. uses the periodic inventory system, and there are 3,200 units of inventory on March 31, 1994.

Instructions

1. Determine the cost of inventory on March 31, 1994, using each of the following inventory costing methods:
   a. first-in, first-out
   b. last-in, first-out
   c. average cost
2. Assume that during the fiscal year ended March 31, 1994, sales were $536,000 and the estimated gross profit rate was 40%. Estimate the ending inventory at March 31, 1994, using the gross profit method.

Solution

1. a. First-in, first-out method:

450	units at $62	$ 27,900
1,350	units at $60	81,000
700	units at $58	40,600
700	units at $57	39,900
3,200	units	$189,400

   b. Last-in, first-out method:

1,000	units at $50.00	$ 50,000
1,200	units at $52.50	63,000
800	units at $55.00	44,000
200	units at $56.00	11,200
3,200	units	$168,200

   c. Average cost method:

   Average cost per unit: $504,000 ÷ 9,000 units = $56
   Inventory, March 31, 1994:   3,200 units at $56 = $179,200

2.
Merchandise inventory, April 1, 1993		$ 50,000
Purchases (net), April 1, 1993–March 31, 1994		454,000
Merchandise available for sale		$504,000
Sales (net), April 1, 1993–March 31, 1994	$536,000	
Less estimated gross profit ($536,000×40%)	214,400	
Estimated cost of merchandise sold		321,600
Estimated merchandise inventory, March 31, 1994		$182,400

DISCUSSION QUESTIONS

1. Explain why an error in the inventory at the end of one period, unless corrected, will misstate the net income of two periods.
2. The merchandise inventory at the end of the year was inadvertently overstated by $10,000. (a) Did the error cause an overstatement or an understatement of the gross profit for the year? (b) Which items on the balance sheet at the end of the year were overstated or understated as a result of the error?
3. The $10,000 inventory error in Question 2 was not discovered, and the inventory at the end of the following year was correctly stated. (a) Will the earlier error cause an overstatement or an understatement of the gross profit for the following year? (b) Which items on the balance sheet at the end of the following year will be overstated or understated as a result of the error in the earlier year?
4. What security measures may be used by retailers to protect merchandise inventory from customer theft?
5. Which inventory system provides the more effective means of controlling inventories (perpetual or periodic)? Why?
6. Before inventory purchases are recorded, the receiving report should be reconciled to what documents?
7. What document should be presented by an employee requesting inventory items to be released from the company's warehouse?
8. Why is it important to periodically take a physical inventory if the perpetual system is used?
9. When does title to merchandise pass from the seller to the buyer if the terms of shipment are (a) FOB shipping point; (b) FOB destination?
10. Bradley Co. sold merchandise to Midland Company on December 31, FOB shipping point. If the merchandise is in transit on December 31, the end of the fiscal year, which company would report it in its financial statements? Explain.
11. A manufacturer shipped merchandise to a retailer on a consignment basis. If the merchandise is unsold at the end of the period, in whose inventory should the merchandise be included?
12. What are the two most widely used inventory costing methods?
13. Which of the three methods of inventory costing—fifo, lifo, or average cost—is based on the assumption that costs should be charged against revenue in the reverse order in which they were incurred?
14. Do the terms *fifo* and *lifo* refer to techniques used in determining quantities of the various classes of merchandise on hand? Explain.
15. Does the term *last-in* in the lifo method mean that the items in the inventory are assumed to be the most recent (last) acquisitions? Explain.
16. Under which method of cost flow are (a) the earliest costs assigned to inventory; (b) the most recent costs assigned to inventory; (c) average costs assigned to inventory?
17. The following units of a particular item were available for sale during the year:

    Beginning inventory　20 units at $50
    First purchase　　　　30 units at $54
    Second purchase　　　40 units at $65

    The firm uses the periodic system, and there are 15 units of the item on hand at the end of the year. What is the unit cost of the ending inventory according to (a) fifo, (b) lifo, (c) average cost?
18. If merchandise inventory is being valued at cost and the price level is steadily rising, which of the three methods of costing—fifo, lifo, or average cost—will yield (a) the highest inventory cost, (b) the lowest inventory cost, (c) the highest gross profit, (d) the lowest gross profit?
19. Which of the three methods of inventory costing—fifo, lifo, or average cost—will in general yield an inventory cost most nearly approximating current replacement cost?
20. If inventory is being valued at cost and the price level is steadily rising, which of the three methods of costing—fifo, lifo, or average cost—will yield the lowest annual income tax expense? Explain.
21. Can a company change its method of costing inventory? Explain.
22. What is the meaning of the term *book inventory*?
23. In the phrase *lower of cost or market*, what is meant by *market*?

24. The cost of a particular inventory item is $410, the current replacement cost is $400, and the selling price is $525. At what amount should the item be included in the inventory according to the lower-of-cost-or-market basis?

25. Because of imperfections, an item of merchandise cannot be sold at its normal selling price. How should this item be valued for financial statement purposes?

26. How is the method of determining the cost of the inventory and the method of valuing it disclosed in the financial statements?

27. An enterprise using the retail method of inventory costing determines that merchandise inventory at retail is $500,000. If the ratio of cost to retail price is 65%, what is the amount of inventory to be reported on the financial statements?

28. What uses can be made of the estimate of the cost of inventory determined by the gross profit method?

29. The following footnote was taken from the 1991 financial statements of The Walgreen Co.:

REAL WORLD FOCUS

Inventories are valued on a last-in, first-out (LIFO) cost basis. At August 31, 1991 and 1990, inventories would have been greater by $325,431,000 and $285,143,000 respectively, if they had been valued on a lower of first-in, first-out (FIFO) cost or market basis.

Additional data are as follows:

Earnings before income taxes, 1991	$311,944,000
Total lifo inventories, August 31, 1991	911,995,000

Based on the preceding data, determine (a) what the total inventories at August 31, 1991, would have been, using the fifo method, and (b) what the earnings before income taxes for the year ended August 31, 1991, would have been if fifo had been used instead of lifo.

ETHICS DISCUSSION CASE

Lemke Co. is experiencing a decrease in sales and operating income for the fiscal year ending December 31, 1993. Betty Arnett, controller of Lemke Co., has suggested that all orders received before the end of the fiscal year be shipped by midnight, December 31, 1993, even if the shipping department must work overtime. Since Lemke Co. ships all merchandise FOB shipping point, it would record all such shipments as sales for the year ending December 31, 1993, thereby offsetting some of the decreases in sales and operating income.

Discuss whether Betty Arnett is behaving in an ethical manner.

SHARPEN YOUR COMMUNICATION SKILLS

EXERCISES

EXERCISE 10-1
INTERNAL CONTROL OF INVENTORIES
Objective 2

Amis Hardware Store currently uses a periodic inventory system. Jim Amis, the owner, is considering the purchase of a computer system that would make it feasible to switch to a perpetual inventory system.

Jim is unhappy with the periodic inventory system because it does not provide timely information on inventory levels. Jim has noticed several occasions when the store runs out of good-selling items, while too many poor-selling items are on hand.

Jim is also concerned about lost sales while a physical inventory is being taken. Amis Hardware currently takes a physical inventory twice a year. In order to minimize distractions, the store is closed on the day inventory is taken. Jim believes closing the store is the only way to get an accurate inventory count.

SHARPEN YOUR COMMUNICATION SKILLS

Will switching to a perpetual inventory system strengthen Amis Hardware's control over inventory items? Will switching to a perpetual inventory system eliminate the need for a physical inventory count? Explain.

EXERCISE 10-2
INTERNAL CONTROL OF INVENTORIES
Objective 2

Govan Luggage Shop is a small retail establishment located in a large shopping mall. This shop has implemented the following procedures regarding inventory items:

a. Since the shop carries mostly high-quality, designer luggage, all inventory items are tagged with a control device that activates an alarm if a tagged item is removed from the store.

b. Since the display area of the store is limited, only a sample of each piece of luggage is kept on the selling floor. Whenever a customer selects a piece of luggage, the salesclerk gets the appropriate piece from the store's stockroom. Since all salesclerks need access to the stockroom, it is not locked. The stockroom is adjacent to the break room used by all mall employees.

c. Whenever Govan receives a shipment of new inventory, the items are taken directly to the stockroom. Govan's accountant uses the vendor's invoice to record the amount of inventory received.

SHARPEN YOUR COMMUNICATION SKILLS ▶ State whether each of these procedures is appropriate or inappropriate, considering the principles of internal control. If the procedure is inappropriate, state which internal control principle is violated.

EXERCISE 10-3
PERIODIC INVENTORY BY THREE METHODS
Objective 5

SPREADSHEET PROBLEM

The units of an item available for sale during the year were as follows:

Jan.	1	Inventory	40 units at $39
Apr.	4	Purchase	30 units at $40
July	20	Purchase	40 units at $42
Sep.	30	Purchase	30 units at $41

There are 45 units of the item in the physical inventory at December 31. The periodic inventory system is used. Determine the inventory cost by the (a) first-in, first-out method, (b) last-in, first-out method, (c) average cost method.

EXERCISE 10-4
PERIODIC INVENTORY BY THREE METHODS; COST OF MERCHANDISE SOLD
Objective 5

SPREADSHEET PROBLEM

The units of an item available for sale during the year were as follows:

Jan.	1	Inventory	15 units at $60
Mar.	4	Purchase	10 units at $62
June	7	Purchase	20 units at $65
Nov.	15	Purchase	15 units at $70

There are 20 units of the item in the physical inventory at December 31. The periodic inventory system is used. Determine the inventory cost and the cost of merchandise sold by three methods, presenting your answers in the following form:

	Cost	
Inventory Method	Merchandise Inventory	Merchandise Sold
a. First-in, first-out	$	$
b. Last-in, first-out		
c. Average cost		

EXERCISE 10-5
PERPETUAL INVENTORY USING FIFO
Objective 6

Beginning inventory, purchases, and sales data for Commodity E29 are as follows:

Jan.	1	Inventory	15 units at $45
	6	Sale	5 units
	9	Purchase	15 units at $47
	15	Sale	18 units
	22	Sale	3 units
	30	Purchase	10 units at $48

The enterprise maintains a perpetual inventory system, costing by the first-in, first-out method. Determine the cost of the merchandise sold in each sale and the inventory balance after each sale, presenting the data in the form illustrated in Exhibit 4.

EXERCISE 10-6
PERPETUAL INVENTORY USING LIFO
Objective 6

Beginning inventory, purchases, and sales data for Commodity A40 for May are as follows:

Inventory:		Purchases:	
May 1	30 units at $30	May 4	20 units at $31
Sales:		20	15 units at $32
May 11	15 units		
17	10 units		
27	10 units		

Assuming that the perpetual inventory system is used, costing by the lifo method, determine the cost of the inventory balance at May 31, presenting data in the form illustrated in Exhibit 5.

EXERCISE 10-7
LOWER-OF-COST-OR-
MARKET INVENTORY
Objective 7

On the basis of the following data, determine the value of the inventory at the lower of cost or market. Assemble the data in the form illustrated in Exhibit 6.

Commodity	Inventory Quantity	Unit Cost Price	Unit Market Price
43B	8	$340	$350
19H	17	110	105
33P	12	275	260
90R	35	60	65
45T	20	95	100

EXERCISE 10-8
MERCHANDISE INVENTORY
ON THE BALANCE SHEET
Objective 8

Based on the data in Exercise 10-7 and assuming that cost was determined by the fifo method, show how the merchandise inventory would appear on the balance sheet.

EXERCISE 10-9
RETAIL INVENTORY
METHOD
Objective 9

On the basis of the following data, estimate the cost of the merchandise inventory at June 30 by the retail method:

	Cost	Retail
June 1 Merchandise inventory	$244,500	$370,500
June 1–30 Purchases (net)	164,700	249,500
June 1–30 Sales (net)		259,000

EXERCISE 10-10
GROSS PROFIT INVENTORY
METHOD
Objective 9

The merchandise inventory was destroyed by fire on March 20. The following data were obtained from the accounting records:

Jan. 1	Merchandise inventory	$172,250
Jan. 1–March 20	Purchases (net)	212,250
	Sales (net)	380,000
	Estimated gross profit rate	40%

a. Estimate the cost of the merchandise destroyed.
b. Briefly describe the situations in which the gross profit method is useful.

SHARPEN YOUR
COMMUNICATION SKILLS

WHAT'S WRONG
WITH THIS?

During 1994, it was discovered that the merchandise inventory at the end of 1993 had been overstated by $50,000. Instead of correcting the error, the accountant decided to understate the ending inventory of 1994 by $50,000. The accountant reasoned that the two errors would balance each other and the error in 1993 would be balanced out by the error in 1994. Are there any flaws in the accountant's reasoning?

PROBLEMS
Series A

PROBLEM 10-1A
EFFECT OF INVENTORY
ERRORS; CORRECTED
INCOME STATEMENTS
Objective 1

Condensed versions of the income statements for Edwards Company for the past two fiscal years ended December 31 are as follows:

Edwards Company
Income Statements
For Years Ended December 31, 1994 and 1993

	1994		1993	
Net sales		$900,000		$850,000
Cost of merchandise sold:				
Inventory, January 1	$ 75,000		$ 70,000	
Cost of merchandise purchased	640,000		610,000	
Merchandise available for sale	$715,000		$680,000	
Less inventory, December 31	85,000		75,000	
Cost of merchandise sold		630,000		605,000
Gross profit		$270,000		$245,000
Operating expenses		190,000		185,000
Net income		$ 80,000		$ 60,000

SPREADSHEET PROBLEM

PROBLEM 10-2A
CORRECTIONS TO
INVENTORY; REVISED
INCOME STATEMENT
Objectives 1, 3

In late 1995, it was discovered that the merchandise inventory had been understated by $10,000 at December 31, 1993, and overstated by $10,000 at December 31, 1994.

Instructions

1. Prepare corrected income statements for each of the two years ended December 31, 1993 and 1994.
2. If the accounts are not corrected, (a) will the net income for the year ended December 31, 1995, be overstated or understated, and in what amount; (b) what items on the balance sheet at December 31, 1995, will be overstated or understated, and in what amount(s)?

The following preliminary income statement of Poole Enterprises was prepared *before the accounts were adjusted or closed* at the end of the fiscal year. The company uses the periodic inventory system.

Poole Enterprises
Income Statement
For Year Ended December 31, 19—

Sales (net)		$996,750
Cost of merchandise sold:		
Merchandise inventory, January 1, 19—	$190,000	
Purchases (net)	695,000	
Merchandise available for sale	$885,000	
Less merchandise inventory, December 31, 19—	205,000	
Cost of merchandise sold		680,000
Gross profit		$316,750
Operating expenses		202,250
Net income		$114,500

The following errors in the ledger and on the inventory sheets were discovered by the independent CPA retained to conduct the annual audit:

a. A number of errors were discovered in pricing inventory items, in extending amounts, and in footing inventory sheets. The net effect of the errors, exclusive of those described below, was to overstate by $3,500 the amount of the ending inventory on the income statement.
b. A purchases invoice for merchandise of $1,500, dated December 30, had been received and correctly recorded, but the merchandise was not received until January 3 and had not been included in the December 31 inventory. Title had passed to Poole Enterprises on December 30.
c. A purchases invoice for merchandise of $4,250, dated December 31, was not received until January 4 and had not been recorded by December 31. However, the merchandise, of which title had passed, had arrived and had been included in the December 31 inventory.
d. A sales order for $9,500, dated December 31, had been recorded as a sale on that date, but title did not pass to the buyer until shipment was made on January 3. The merchandise, which had cost $6,500, was excluded from the December 31 inventory.
e. A sales invoice for $1,250, dated December 30, had not been recorded. The merchandise was shipped on December 30, FOB shipping point, and its cost, $775, was excluded from the December 31 inventory.
f. An item of office equipment, received on December 27, was erroneously included in the December 31 merchandise inventory at its cost of $8,500. The invoice had been recorded correctly.

Instructions

1. Journalize the entries to correct the general ledger accounts as of December 31, inserting the identifying letters in the date column. All purchases and sales were made on account.
2. Determine the correct inventory for December 31, beginning your analysis with the $205,000 inventory shown on the preliminary income statement. Assemble the corrections in two groupings, "Additions" and "Deductions," allowing six lines for each group. Identify each correction by the appropriate letter.
3. Prepare a revised income statement.

PROBLEM 10-3A
PERIODIC INVENTORY BY
THREE METHODS
Objective 5

House of Television uses the periodic inventory system. Details regarding the inventory of television sets at January 1, purchases invoices during the year, and the inventory count at December 31 are summarized as follows:

Model	Inventory, January 1	1st	2d	3d	Inventory Count, December 31
B91	4 at $150	6 at $150	8 at $155	7 at $155	5
F10	3 at 210	3 at 215	5 at 213	4 at 225	3
H21	2 at 520	2 at 530	2 at 530	2 at 536	3
J39	6 at 520	8 at 531	4 at 549	6 at 542	8
P80	9 at 213	7 at 215	6 at 222	6 at 225	8
T15	6 at 305	3 at 310	3 at 316	4 at 321	5
V11	—	4 at 220	4 at 230	—	2

(Purchases Invoices span columns 1st, 2d, 3d)

Instructions

1. Determine the cost of the inventory on December 31 by the first-in, first-out method. Present data in columnar form, using the following headings:

Model	Quantity	Unit Cost	Total Cost

If the inventory of a particular model is composed of one entire purchase plus a portion of another purchase acquired at a different unit cost, use a separate line for each purchase.

2. Determine the cost of the inventory on December 31 by the last-in, first-out method, following the procedures indicated in (1).
3. Determine the cost of the inventory on December 31 by the average cost method, using the columnar headings indicated in (1).

SHARPEN YOUR COMMUNICATION SKILLS ►

4. Discuss which method (fifo or lifo) would be preferred for income tax purposes in periods of (a) rising prices and (b) declining prices.

PROBLEM 10-4A
FIFO AND LIFO PERPETUAL
INVENTORY
Objective 6

The beginning inventory of Commodity 37D and data on purchases and sales for a three-month period are as follows:

Date		Transaction	Number of Units	Per Unit	Total
April	1	Inventory	9	$220	$1,980
	5	Purchase	25	225	5,625
	12	Sale	10	300	3,000
	22	Sale	6	300	1,800
May	4	Purchase	10	230	2,300
	6	Sale	8	310	2,480
	21	Sale	5	310	1,550
	28	Purchase	15	235	3,525
June	5	Sale	9	315	2,835
	13	Sale	10	315	3,150
	19	Purchase	10	240	2,400
	26	Sale	8	320	2,560

Instructions

1. Record the inventory, purchases, and cost of merchandise sold data in a perpetual inventory record similar to the one illustrated in Exhibit 4, using the first-in, first-out method.
2. Determine the total sales and the total cost of Commodity 37D sold for the period. Journalize the entries in the sales and cost of merchandise sold accounts. Assume that all sales were on account.
3. Determine the gross profit from sales of Commodity 37D for the period.
4. Record the inventory, purchases, and cost of merchandise sold data in a perpetual inventory record similar to the one illustrated in Exhibit 5, using the last-in, first-out method.

PROBLEM 10-5A
LOWER-OF-COST-OR-
MARKET INVENTORY
Objective 7

If the working papers correlating with the textbook are not used, omit Problem 10-5A.

Data on the physical inventory of Lyons Co. as of December 31, the end of the current fiscal year, are presented in the working papers. The quantity of each commodity on hand has been determined and recorded on the inventory sheet. Unit market prices have also been determined as of December 31 and recorded on the sheet. The inventory is to be determined at cost and also at the lower of cost or market, using the first-in, first-out method. Quantity and cost data from the last purchases invoice of the year and the next-to-the-last purchases invoice are summarized below.

Description	Last Purchases Invoice		Next-to-the-Last Purchases Invoice	
	Quantity Purchased	Unit Cost	Quantity Purchased	Unit Cost
A71	20	$ 60	40	$ 59
C22	25	190	15	190
D82	15	145	15	142
E34	150	25	100	27
F17	6	550	15	540
J19	75	16	100	17
K41	8	400	5	410
P21	500	6	500	7
R72	70	17	50	16
T15	5	250	4	260
V55	1,000	10	500	10
AC2	100	45	100	46
BB7	5	410	5	400
BD1	100	20	100	19
CC1	50	15	40	16
EB2	40	29	50	28
FF7	55	28	50	28
GE4	6	690	5	700

**SPREADSHEET
PROBLEM**

Instructions

Record the appropriate unit costs on the inventory sheet and complete the pricing of the inventory. When there are two different unit costs applicable to an item, proceed as follows:

1. Draw a line through the quantity and insert the quantity and unit cost of the last purchase.
2. On the following line, insert the quantity and unit cost of the next-to-the-last purchase. The first item on the inventory sheet has been completed as an example.

PROBLEM 10-6A
ADJUSTING ENTRIES;
FINANCIAL STATEMENTS
Objectives 7, 8

Worden Sales is a distributor of imported motorcycles. Its unadjusted trial balance as of the end of the current fiscal year is as follows:

Cash	17,900	
Accounts Receivable	29,500	
Allowance for Doubtful Accounts		275
Merchandise Inventory	90,200	
Equipment	30,000	
Accumulated Depreciation—Equipment		12,250
Accounts Payable		24,500
Notes Payable		10,000
Robert Worden, Capital		71,750
Robert Worden, Drawing	36,000	
Sales		535,700
Purchases	395,800	
Operating Expenses (controlling account)	55,175	
Rent Income		1,200
Interest Expense	1,100	
	655,675	655,675

Data needed for adjustments at December 31:

    a. Merchandise inventory at December 31, $84,600, at lower of fifo cost or market.
    b. Uncollectible accounts expense for current year, estimated at $1,725.
    c. Depreciation of equipment for current year, $5,500.

Instructions

1. Journalize the necessary adjusting entries. All selling and administrative expenses are included in the operating expenses controlling account.
2. Prepare the following without the use of a conventional work sheet: (a) an income statement, (b) a statement of owner's equity, and (c) a balance sheet in report form.

Instructions for Solving Problem 10-6A Using Solutions Software

SOLUTIONS
SOFTWARE

1. Load opening balances.
2. Save the opening balances file to your drive and directory.
3. Set the run date to December 31 of the current year and enter your name.
4. Key the adjusting entries. Key ADJ.ENT. in the reference field.
5. Display the adjusting entries. Key ADJ.ENT. in the Reference Restriction area of the Selection Options screen.
6. Display the financial statements.
7. Save a backup copy of your data file.
8. Perform period-end closing.
9. Display a post-closing trial balance.
10. Save your data file to disk.
11. End the session.

PROBLEM 10-7A
RETAIL METHOD; GROSS PROFIT METHOD
Objective 9

Selected data on merchandise inventory, purchases, and sales for Wright Co. and C. F. Jones Co. are as follows:

	Cost	Retail
Wright Co.		
Merchandise inventory, January 1	$377,100	$579,100
Transactions during January:		
Purchases	186,600	298,400
Purchases discounts	2,100	
Sales		340,500
Sales returns and allowances		5,500
C. F. Jones Co.		
Merchandise inventory, July 1	$517,900	
Transactions during July and August:		
Purchases	425,500	
Purchases discounts	3,600	
Sales	570,250	
Sales returns and allowances	5,250	
Estimated gross profit rate	35%	

Instructions

SPREADSHEET PROBLEM

1. Determine the estimated cost of the merchandise inventory of Wright Co. on January 31 by the retail method, presenting details of the computations.
2. a. Estimate the cost of the merchandise inventory of C. F. Jones Co. on August 31 by the gross profit method, presenting details of the computations.
    b. Assume that C. F. Jones Co. took a physical inventory on August 31 and discovered that $565,000 of merchandise was on hand. What was the estimated loss of inventory due to theft or damage during July and August?

Series B

Condensed versions of the income statements for Gross Company for the past two fiscal years ended December 31 are as follows:

Gross Company
Income Statements
For Years Ended December 31, 1994 and 1993

	1994		1993	
Net sales		$950,000		$900,000
Cost of merchandise sold:				
Inventory, January 1	$ 85,000		$ 80,000	
Cost of merchandise purchased	670,000		640,000	
Merchandise available for sale	$755,000		$720,000	
Less Inventory, December 31	75,000		85,000	
Cost of merchandise sold		680,000		635,000
Gross profit		$270,000		$265,000
Operating expenses		190,000		185,000
Net income		$ 80,000		$ 80,000

In late 1995, it was discovered that the merchandise inventory had been overstated by $10,000 at December 31, 1993, and understated by $10,000 at December 31, 1994.

**SPREADSHEET
PROBLEM**

Instructions

1. Prepare corrected income statements for each of the two years ended December 31, 1993 and 1994.
2. If the accounts are not corrected, (a) will the net income for the year ended December 31, 1995, be overstated or understated, and in what amount; (b) what items on the balance sheet at December 31, 1995, will be overstated or understated, and in what amount(s)?

The following preliminary income statement of E. Banks Enterprises was prepared *before the accounts were adjusted or closed* at the end of the fiscal year. The company uses the periodic inventory system.

E. Banks Enterprises
Income Statement
For Year Ended December 31, 19—

Sales (net)		$985,750
Cost of merchandise sold:		
Merchandise inventory, January 1, 19—	$230,000	
Purchases (net)	695,000	
Merchandise available for sale	$925,000	
Less merchandise inventory, December 31, 19—	245,000	
Cost of merchandise sold		680,000
Gross profit		$305,750
Operating expenses		202,250
Net income		$103,500

The following errors in the ledger and on the inventory sheets were discovered by the independent CPA retained to conduct the annual audit:

a. A number of errors were discovered in pricing inventory items, in extending amounts, and in footing inventory sheets. The net effect of the errors, exclusive of those described below, was to overstate by $5,000 the amount of the ending inventory on the income statement.

b. A purchases invoice for merchandise of $1,500, dated December 30, had been received and correctly recorded, but the merchandise was not received until January 3 and had not been included in the December 31 inventory. Title had passed to E. Banks Enterprises on December 30.

c. A purchases invoice for merchandise of $3,000, dated December 31, was not received until January 4 and had not been recorded by December 31. However, the merchandise, to which title had passed, had arrived and had been included in the December 31 inventory.

d. A sales order for $10,000, dated December 31, had been recorded as a sale on that date, but title did not pass to the buyer until shipment was made on January 3. The merchandise, which had cost $6,500, was excluded from the December 31 inventory.

e. A sales invoice for $1,250, dated December 30, had not been recorded. The merchandise was shipped on December 30, FOB shipping point, and its cost, $775, was excluded from the December 31 inventory.

f. An item of office equipment, received on December 27, was erroneously included in the December 31 merchandise inventory at its cost of $8,500. The invoice had been recorded correctly.

Instructions

1. Journalize the entries to correct the general ledger accounts as of December 31, inserting the identifying letters in the date column. All purchases and sales were made on account.

2. Determine the correct inventory for December 31, beginning your analysis with the $245,000 inventory shown on the preliminary income statement. Assemble the corrections in two groupings, "Additions" and "Deductions," allowing six lines for each group. Identify each correction by the appropriate letter.

3. Prepare a revised income statement.

PROBLEM 10-3B
PERIODIC INVENTORY BY
THREE METHODS
Objective 5

A-1 Television uses the periodic inventory system. Details regarding the inventory of television sets at July 1, 1993, purchases invoices during the year, and the inventory count at June 30, 1994, are summarized as follows:

Model	Inventory, July 1	Purchases Invoices 1st	Purchases Invoices 2d	Purchases Invoices 3d	Inventory Count, June 30
A37	6 at $238	4 at $250	8 at $260	10 at $266	12
E15	6 at 77	5 at 82	8 at 89	8 at 99	10
L10	2 at 108	2 at 110	3 at 128	3 at 130	3
O18	8 at 88	4 at 79	3 at 85	6 at 92	8
K72	2 at 250	2 at 260	4 at 271	4 at 275	4
S91	5 at 160	4 at 170	4 at 175	7 at 180	8
V17	—	4 at 150	4 at 200	2 at 205	5

SPREADSHEET
PROBLEM

Instructions

1. Determine the cost of the inventory on June 30, 1994, by the first-in, first-out method. Present data in columnar form, using the following headings:

Model	Quantity	Unit Cost	Total Cost

If the inventory of a particular model is composed of one entire purchase plus a portion of another purchase acquired at a different unit cost, use a separate line for each purchase.

2. Determine the cost of the inventory on June 30, 1994, by the last-in, first-out method, following the procedures indicated in (1).

3. Determine the cost of the inventory on June 30, 1994, by the average cost method, using the columnar headings indicated in (1).

4. Discuss which method (fifo or lifo) would be preferred for income tax purposes in periods of (a) rising prices and (b) declining prices.

PROBLEM 10-4B
FIFO AND LIFO PERPETUAL
INVENTORY
Objective 6

The beginning inventory of soybeans at SW Co-Op and data on purchases and sales for a three-month period are as follows:

Date		Transaction	Number of Bushels	Per Unit	Total
July	1	Inventory	25,000	$6.10	$152,500
	10	Purchase	75,000	6.15	461,250
	15	Sale	35,000	7.00	245,000
	25	Sale	30,000	7.00	210,000
Aug.	8	Sale	10,000	7.10	71,000
	12	Purchase	50,000	6.20	310,000
	17	Sale	35,000	7.20	252,000
	28	Sale	20,000	7.15	143,000
Sep.	5	Purchase	60,000	6.10	366,000
	17	Sale	40,000	7.00	280,000
	20	Purchase	30,000	6.00	180,000
	30	Sale	45,000	7.00	315,000

Instructions

1. Record the inventory, purchases, and cost of merchandise sold data in a perpetual inventory record similar to the one illustrated in Exhibit 4, using the first-in, first-out method.
2. Determine the total sales and the total cost of soybeans sold for the period. Journalize the entries in the sales and cost of merchandise sold accounts. Assume that all sales were on account.
3. Determine the gross profit from sales of soybeans for the period.
4. Record the inventory, purchases, and cost of merchandise sold data in a perpetual inventory record similar to the one illustrated in Exhibit 5, using the last-in, first-out method.

If the working papers correlating with the textbook are not used, omit Problem 10-5B.

PROBLEM 10-5B
LOWER-OF-COST-OR-
MARKET INVENTORY
Objective 7

Data on the physical inventory of Klein Company as of December 31, the end of the current fiscal year, are presented in the working papers. The quantity of each commodity on hand has been determined and recorded on the inventory sheet. Unit market prices have also been determined as of December 31 and recorded on the sheet. The inventory is to be determined at cost and also at the lower of cost or market, using the first-in, first-out method. Quantity and cost data from the last purchases invoice of the year and the next-to-the-last purchases invoice are summarized below.

Description	Last Purchases Invoice Quantity Purchased	Unit Cost	Next-to-the-Last Purchases Invoice Quantity Purchased	Unit Cost
A71	20	$ 60	30	$ 59
C22	25	210	20	205
D82	10	145	25	142
E34	150	25	100	24
F17	10	560	10	570
J19	100	15	100	14
K41	10	380	5	385
P21	500	6	500	6
R72	80	17	50	18
T15	5	250	4	260
V55	700	9	500	9
AC2	100	45	50	46
BB7	5	420	5	425
BD1	100	20	75	19
CC1	60	16	40	17
EB2	50	29	25	28
FF7	75	26	60	25
GE4	5	710	5	715

**SPREADSHEET
PROBLEM**

Instructions

Record the appropriate unit costs on the inventory sheet and complete the pricing of the inventory. When there are two different unit costs applicable to an item, proceed as follows:

1. Draw a line through the quantity and insert the quantity and unit cost of the last purchase.
2. On the following line, insert the quantity and unit cost of the next-to-the-last purchase. The first item on the inventory sheet has been completed as an example.

PROBLEM 10-6B
ADJUSTING ENTRIES;
FINANCIAL STATEMENTS
Objectives 7, 8

Boyd Imports is a distributor of imported motorcycles. Its unadjusted trial balance as of the end of the current fiscal year is as follows:

Cash	22,550	
Accounts Receivable	37,500	
Allowance for Doubtful Accounts		275
Merchandise Inventory	85,200	
Equipment	37,500	
Accumulated Depreciation—Equipment		20,000
Accounts Payable		24,500
Notes Payable		10,000
P. L. Boyd, Capital		86,675
P. L. Boyd, Drawing	40,000	
Sales		850,200
Purchases	705,800	
Operating Expenses (controlling account)	63,200	
Rent Income		1,200
Interest Expense	1,100	
	992,850	992,850

Data needed for adjustments at December 31:

    a. Merchandise inventory at December 31, $89,600, at lower of fifo cost or market.
    b. Uncollectible accounts expense for current year, estimated at $1,900.
    c. Depreciation of equipment for current year, $6,800.

Instructions

1. Journalize the necessary adjusting entries. All selling and administrative expenses are included in the operating expenses controlling account.
2. Prepare the following without the use of a conventional work sheet: (a) an income statement, (b) a statement of owner's equity, and (c) a balance sheet in report form.

**SOLUTIONS
SOFTWARE**

Instructions for Solving Problem 10-6B Using Solutions Software

    1. Load opening balances.
    2. Save the opening balances file to your drive and directory.
    3. Set the run date to December 31 of the current year and enter your name.
    4. Key the adjusting entries. Key ADJ.ENT. in the reference field.
    5. Display the adjusting entries. Key ADJ.ENT. in the Reference Restriction area of the Selection Options screen.
    6. Display the financial statements.
    7. Save a backup copy of your data file.
    8. Perform period-end closing.
    9. Display a post-closing trial balance.
  10. Save your data file to disk.
  11. End the session.

PROBLEM 10-7B
RETAIL METHOD; GROSS
PROFIT METHOD
Objective 9

Selected data on merchandise inventory, purchases, and sales for Heims Co. and G. N. Palmer Co. are as follows:

	Cost	Retail
Heims Co.		
Merchandise inventory, July 1	$259,800	$370,000
Transactions during July:		
Purchases	366,840 ⎱	521,000
Purchases discounts	2,940 ⎰	
Sales		600,000
Sales returns and allowances		5,000
G. N. Palmer Co.		
Merchandise inventory, April 1	$317,500	
Transactions during April and May:		
Purchases	410,250	
Purchases discounts	5,250	
Sales	625,000	
Sales returns and allowances	5,000	
Estimated gross profit rate	40%	

SPREADSHEET
PROBLEM

Instructions

1. Determine the estimated cost of the merchandise inventory of Heims Co. on July 31 by the retail method, presenting details of the computations.
2. a. Estimate the cost of the merchandise inventory of G. N. Palmer Co. on May 31 by the gross profit method, presenting details of the computations.
   b. Assume that G. N. Palmer Co. took a physical inventory on May 31 and discovered that $338,750 of merchandise was on hand. What was the estimated loss of inventory due to theft or damage during April and May?

MINI-CASE 10 GARVEY COMPANY

Garvey Company began operations in 1993 by selling a single product. Data on purchases and sales for the year were as follows:

Purchases

Date	Units Purchased	Unit Cost	Total Cost
April 5	5,000	$13.20	$ 66,000
May 2	5,000	14.00	70,000
June 4	5,000	14.20	71,000
July 10	5,000	15.00	75,000
August 7	3,000	15.25	45,750
October 5	2,000	15.50	31,000
November 1	1,000	15.75	15,750
December 10	1,000	17.00	17,000
	27,000		$391,500

Sales

April	2,000 units	September	3,500 units
May	2,000	October	2,250
June	3,500	November	2,250
July	4,000	December	1,000
August	3,500		

Total sales $454,000

On January 3, 1994, the president of the company,

Laura Garvey, asked for your advice on costing the 3,000-unit physical inventory that was taken on December 31, 1993. Also, since the firm plans to expand its product line, she asked for your advice on the use of a perpetual inventory system in the future.

Instructions:

1. Determine the cost of the December 31, 1993 inventory under the periodic system, using the (a) first-in, first-out method, (b) last-in, first-out method, and (c) average cost method.
2. Determine the gross profit for the year under each of the three methods in (1).
3. a. ▪▪▪▪ ▸ In your opinion, which of the three inventory costing methods best reflects the results of operations for 1993? Why?
   b. ▪▪▪▪ ▸ In your opinion, which of the three inventory costing methods best reflects the replacement cost of the inventory on the balance sheet as of December 31, 1993? Why?
   c. ▪▪▪▪ ▸ Which inventory costing method would you choose to use for income tax purposes? Why?
   d. ▪▪▪▪ ▸ Discuss the advantages and disadvantages of using a perpetual inventory system. From the data presented in this case, is there any indication of the adequacy of inventory levels during the year?

ANSWERS TO SELF-EXAMINATION QUESTIONS

1. **C** The overstatement of inventory by $7,500 at the end of the year will cause the cost of merchandise sold for the year to be understated by $7,500, the gross profit for the year to be overstated by $7,500, and the net income for the year to be overstated by $7,500 (answer C).

2. **A** The fifo method (answer A) is based on the assumption that costs are charged against revenue in the order in which they were incurred. The lifo method (answer B) charges the most recent costs incurred against revenue, and the average cost method (answer C) charges a weighted average of unit costs of items sold against revenue. The perpetual inventory system (answer D) is a system that continuously discloses the amount of inventory.

3. **D** The fifo method of costing is based on the assumption that costs should be charged against revenue in the order in which they were incurred (first-in, first-out). Thus the most recent costs are assigned to inventory. The 35 units would be assigned a unit cost of $23 (answer D).

4. **A** The lifo method of costing is based on the assumption that costs should be charged against revenue in the reverse order in which costs were incurred. Thus the oldest costs are assigned to inventory. Thirty of the 35 units would be assigned a unit cost of $20 (since 10 of the beginning inventory units were sold on the first sale), and the remaining 5 units would be assigned a cost of $23 (answer A).

5. **B** When the price level is steadily rising, the earlier unit costs are lower than recent unit costs. Under the fifo method (answer B), these earlier costs are matched against revenue to yield the highest possible net income. The periodic inventory system (answer D) is a system and not a method of costing.

You and Accounting

Assume that your parents have offered to buy you a car for your 20th birthday, provided that you agree to pay all operating costs. You have found a 1980 Porsche 911 at a local car dealership. The sales manager has offered to sell you the car "as is" for $12,000. One of your friends who is a mechanic has inspected the car and has indicated that it needs a tune-up and new tires, shocks, and brakes. Should you ask your parents to pay for this mechanical work?

Normally, the cost of the car and the cost of getting it ready for use are costs of purchasing the car. Thus, you may be able to convince your parents to pay for the additional mechanical work. Once that work is completed, however, other mechanical work such as periodic tune-ups would normally be considered an operating cost.

This chapter discusses issues similar to the preceding example. For example, business enterprises must determine and record the total cost of assets acquired. The chapter also discusses other issues related to plant assets, such as accounting for costs that may significantly enhance or improve an asset after it is purchased.

Chapter 11
Plant Assets and Intangible Assets

Prior chapters have discussed assets that are classified as current assets. Such assets include cash or assets that are expected to be realized in cash or sold or used up normally within one year. This chapter describes and illustrates accounting principles and concepts for long-term assets of a relatively permanent nature. Such assets include land, buildings, equipment, patents, and copyrights. This chapter discusses the costs of acquiring such assets, accounting for their depreciation, depletion, or amortization, and accounting for their disposal.

LEARNING OBJECTIVES
After studying this chapter, you should be able to:

Objective 1
Define and give examples of plant assets and intangible assets.

Objective 2
Identify and list the costs of acquiring a plant asset.

Objective 3
Describe the nature of depreciation of plant assets.

Objective 4
Compute depreciation, using the following methods: straight-line, units-of-production, declining-balance, and sum-of-the-years-digits.

Objective 5
Compute depreciation, using the composite-rate method.

Objective 6
Classify plant asset costs as either capital expenditures or revenue expenditures.

Objective 7
Journalize entries for the disposal of plant assets.

Objective 8
Define a lease and summarize the accounting rules related to the leasing of plant assets.

Objective 9
Describe internal controls over plant assets and provide examples of such controls.

Objective 10
Compute depletion and journalize the entry for depletion.

Objective 11
Journalize the entries for acquiring and amortizing intangible assets, such as patents, copyrights, and goodwill.

Objective 12
Describe how depreciation expense is reported in an income statement and prepare a balance sheet that includes plant assets and intangible assets.

NATURE OF PLANT ASSETS AND INTANGIBLE ASSETS

Objective 1
Define and give examples of plant assets and intangible assets.

Plant assets are long-term or relatively permanent tangible assets that are used in the normal business operations. They are owned by the enterprise and are not held for sale in the ordinary course of business. Other descriptive titles for such assets are **fixed assets** or **property, plant, and equipment**. These assets may also be described in more specific terms, such as equipment, furniture, tools, machinery, buildings, and land.

Long-term assets that are without physical attributes and not held for sale but are useful in the operations of an enterprise are classified as **intangible assets**. Intangible assets include such items as patents, copyrights, and goodwill.

There is no standard rule as to the minimum length of life necessary for an asset to be classified as a plant asset or an intangible asset. Such assets must be capable of repeated use or benefit and are normally expected to last more than a year. However, an asset need not actually be used on an ongoing basis or even often. For example, items of standby equipment held for use in the event of a breakdown of regular equipment or for use only during peak periods of activity are included in plant assets.

Assets acquired for resale in the normal course of business are not classified as plant assets, regardless of their permanent nature or the length of time they are held. For example, undeveloped land or other real estate acquired as an investment for resale should be listed on the balance sheet in the asset section entitled *Investments*.

COSTS OF ACQUIRING PLANT ASSETS

Objective 2
Identify and list the costs of acquiring a plant asset.

The cost of acquiring a plant asset includes all expenditures necessary to get it in place and ready for use. For example sales tax, transportation charges, insurance while in transit, special foundations, and installation costs should be added to the asset's purchase price in determining the cost of a plant asset. Similarly, when a secondhand asset is purchased, the initial costs of getting it ready for use, such as expenditures for new parts, repairs, and painting, should be included as part of the asset cost. These expenditures should be debited to the asset account. On the other hand, costs related to acquiring a plant asset should be excluded from the asset account if they are not necessary for getting the asset ready for use and thus do not increase the asset's usefulness. For example, costs resulting from errors in installing an asset, from vandalism, or from other unusual occurrences do not increase the usefulness of the asset and should be treated as an expense.

The cost of constructing a building includes the fees paid to architects and engineers for plans and supervision. In addition, insurance incurred during construction and all other necessary expenditures related to the project are included in the cost of the building. Generally, interest incurred during the construction period on money borrowed to finance construction should also be treated as part of the cost of the building.[1]

The cost of land includes not only the negotiated price but also broker's commissions, title fees, surveying fees, and other expenditures of obtaining title. If delinquent real estate taxes are paid by the buyer, they also are charged to the land account. If unwanted buildings are located on land acquired for a plant site, the cost of their razing or removal, less any salvage recovered, is a cost of the land. The cost of leveling or otherwise changing the contour of the land is also a cost of the land.

Other expenditures related to land may be charged to Land, Buildings, or Land Improvements, depending upon the nature of the expenditure. If a property owner pays for the initial cost of paving a public street bordering the land, either by direct payment or by special tax assessment, the paving may be considered

[1] *Statement of Financial Accounting Standards, No. 34,* "Capitalization of Interest Cost" (Stamford: Financial Accounting Standards Board, 1979), par. 6.

part of the cost of the land. On the other hand, the cost of constructing walkways to and around a building may be added to the cost of the building if the walkways are expected to last only as long as the building. Expenditures for improvements that are neither as permanent as the land nor directly related to a building may be set apart in a land improvements account. Some of the more usual items of this nature are trees and shrubs, fences, outdoor lighting, and paved parking areas.

NATURE OF DEPRECIATION

Objective 3
Describe the nature of depreciation of plant assets.

As time passes, all plant assets except land lose their ability to provide services.[2] As a result, the cost of a plant asset should be transferred to an expense account, in a systematic manner, during the asset's expected useful life. This periodic cost expiration is called **depreciation**.

Factors that cause a decline in the ability of a plant asset to provide services may be divided into two categories. First, physical depreciation caused by wear and tear from use and from the action of the elements decreases usefulness. Second, functional depreciation caused by inadequacy and obsolescence decreases usefulness. A plant asset becomes inadequate if its capacity is not able to meet the demands of increased production. A plant asset is obsolete if the item that it produces is no longer in demand or if a newer machine can produce an item of better quality at the same or a lower cost. Advances in technology during this century have made obsolescence an increasingly important cause of depreciation.

The meaning of the term *depreciation* as used in accounting is often misunderstood because the same term is also used in business to mean a decline in the market value of an asset. However, the amount of a plant asset's unexpired cost reported in the balance sheet usually does not agree with the amount that could be realized from its sale. Plant assets are held for use in an enterprise rather than for sale. It is assumed that the enterprise will continue as a **going concern**. Thus, a decision to dispose of a plant asset is based mainly on the usefulness of the asset to the enterprise and not on its market value.

Another common misunderstanding is that depreciation accounting provides cash needed to replace plant assets as they wear out. The cash account is neither increased nor decreased by the periodic entries that transfer the cost of plant assets to depreciation expense accounts. The misunderstanding probably occurs because depreciation, unlike most expenses, does not require an outlay of cash in the period in which it is recorded.

ACCOUNTING FOR DEPRECIATION

Objective 4
Compute depreciation, using the following methods:

Straight-line method
Units-of-production method
Declining-balance method
Sum-of-the-years-digits method

Three factors are considered in determining the amount of depreciation expense to be recognized each period. These three factors are the (1) plant asset's initial cost, (2) its expected useful life, and (3) its estimated value at the end of its useful life. This third factor is called the **residual value, scrap value, salvage value,** or **trade-in value.** The relationship among the three factors and the periodic depreciation expense is shown in Exhibit 1.

If a plant asset is expected to have no residual value at the time that it is taken out of service, then its initial cost should be spread over its expected useful life as depreciation expense. Also, if a plant asset's estimated residual value at the time it is taken out of service is expected to be very small compared to the cost of the asset, this value may be ignored and the entire cost spread over the asset's expected useful life. If a plant asset is expected to have a significant residual value, the difference between its initial cost and this value is the cost (called **depreciable cost**) that should be spread over the asset's useful life as depreciation expense.

Neither *the period of usefulness* of a plant asset nor its *residual value* at the end of that period can be accurately determined until the asset is taken out of service.

---

[2] As discussed in this section, land is assumed to be used only as a location or site. Land acquired for its mineral deposits or other natural resources will be considered later in the chapter.

Exhibit 1
Factors that Determine
Depreciation Expense

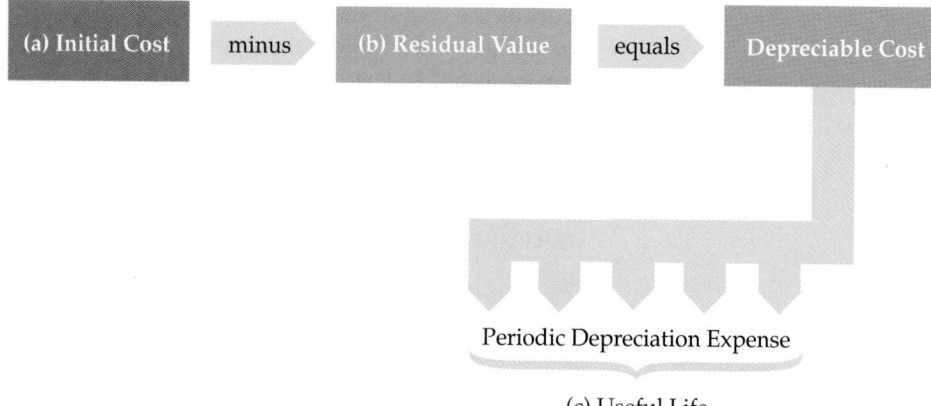

However, in determining the amount of the periodic depreciation, these two related factors must be estimated at the time the asset is placed in service. There are no set rules for estimating either factor, and both factors may be affected by management policies. For example, a company that provides its salespersons with a new automobile every year will have different estimates than a company that keeps its cars for five years. Such variables as climate, use, and maintenance will also affect the estimates.

Estimates of the useful life of assets are available from various trade association and other publications. For federal income tax purposes, the Internal Revenue Service has also established guidelines for useful lives. These guidelines may also be helpful in determining depreciation for financial reporting purposes.

In addition to the many factors that may affect the useful life of an asset, various degrees of accuracy may be used in the computations. A month is normally the smallest unit of time used. When this period of time is used, all assets placed in or taken out of service during the first half of a month are treated as if the event occurred on the first day of that month. Likewise, all plant asset additions and deductions during the second half of a month are treated as if the event occurred on the first day of the next month. In the absence of any statement to the contrary, this practice is assumed throughout this chapter.

It is not necessary that an enterprise use a single method of computing depreciation for all its depreciable assets. The methods used in the accounts and financial statements may also differ from the methods used in determining income taxes and property taxes. The four methods used most often are: (1) straight-line, (2) units-of-production, (3) declining-balance, and (4) sum-of-the-years-digits. The extent of the use of these methods in financial statements is shown in Exhibit 2.

Exhibit 2
Use of Depreciation Methods

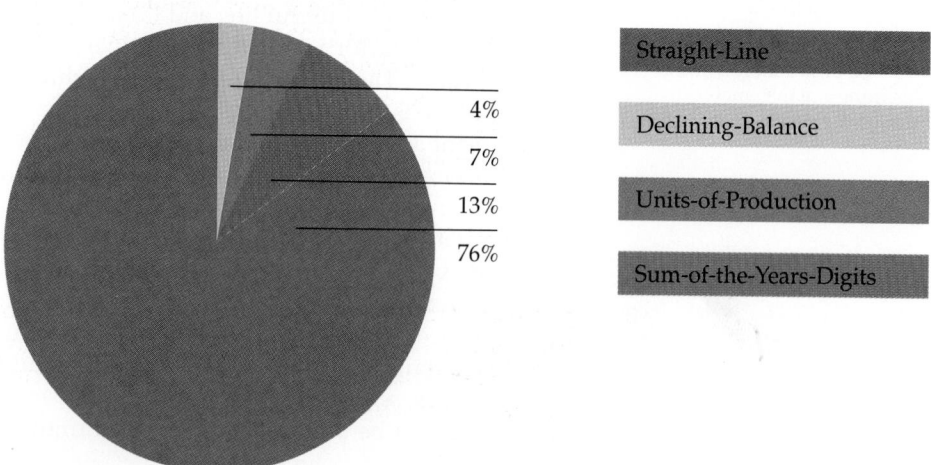

Source: *Accounting Trends & Techniques*, 45th ed. (New York: American Institute of Certified Public Accountants, 1991).

Straight-Line Method

The **straight-line depreciation method** provides for equal amounts of periodic expense over the estimated useful life of the asset. For example, assume that the cost of a depreciable asset is $16,000, its estimated residual value is $1,000, and its estimated life is 5 years. The annual depreciation is computed as follows:

$$\frac{\$16{,}000 \text{ cost} - \$1{,}000 \text{ estimated residual value}}{5 \text{ years estimated life}} = \$3{,}000 \text{ annual depreciation}$$

When an asset is used for only part of a year, the annual depreciation is prorated. For example, assume that the fiscal year ends on December 31 and that the asset in the above example is first used on October 15. The depreciation for the first fiscal year of use would be $750 ($3,000 × 3/12), computed on the basis of 3 months. If usage had begun on October 16, the depreciation for the year would have been $500 ($3,000 × 2/12).

For ease in applying the straight-line method, the annual depreciation may be converted to a percentage of depreciable cost. This percentage is determined by dividing 100 by the number of years of useful life. For example, a useful life of 20 years converts to a 5% (100 ÷ 20) rate, 8 years converts to a 12.5% (100 ÷ 8) rate, and so on.[3] To further illustrate, the straight-line rate in the above example is 20% (100 ÷ 5). The annual depreciation of $3,000 can be computed by multiplying the depreciable cost of $15,000 by this rate.

The straight-line method is simple and is widely used. It provides a reasonable allocation of costs to periodic expense when the usage of the asset and the related revenues from its use are about the same from period to period.

Units-of-Production Method

The **units-of-production depreciation method** yields depreciation expense that varies with the amount of the asset's usage. In applying this method, the useful life of the asset is expressed in terms of units of productive capacity, such as hours or miles. Depreciation is first computed for each unit of production. The total depreciation expense for each accounting period is then determined by multiplying the unit depreciation by the number of productive units used during the period. For example, assume that a machine with a cost of $16,000 and an estimated residual value of $1,000 is expected to have an estimated life of 10,000 operating hours. The depreciation for a unit of one hour is computed as follows:

$$\frac{\$16{,}000 \text{ cost} - \$1{,}000 \text{ estimated residual value}}{10{,}000 \text{ estimated hours}} = \$1.50 \text{ hourly depreciation}$$

Assuming that the machine was in operation for 2,200 hours during a year, the depreciation for that year would be $3,300 ($1.50 × 2,200 hours).

When the amount of use of a plant asset varies from year to year, the units-of-production method is more appropriate than the straight-line method. In such cases, the units-of-production method better matches the allocation of cost (depreciation expense) with the related revenue.

Declining-Balance Method

The **declining-balance depreciation method** provides for a declining periodic expense over the estimated useful life of the asset. To apply this method, the annual straight-line depreciation rate described previously is doubled. For example, the declining-balance rate for an asset with an estimated life of 5 years is 40%—double the straight-line rate of 20% (100 ÷ 5).

---

[3] The depreciation rate may also be expressed as a fraction. For example, the annual straight-line rate for an asset with a 3-year useful life is ⅓.

This rate is then multiplied by the cost of the asset for the first year of use. After the first year, the rate is multiplied by the declining **book value** (cost minus accumulated depreciation) of the asset. To illustrate, the annual declining-balance depreciation for an asset with an estimated 5-year life and a cost of $16,000 is shown below.

Year	Cost	Accum. Depr. at Beginning of Year	Book Value at Beginning of Year	Rate	Depreciation for Year	Book Value at End of Year
1	$16,000	—	$16,000.00	40%	$6,400.00	$9,600.00
2	16,000	$ 6,400.00	9,600.00	40%	3,840.00	5,760.00
3	16,000	10,240.00	5,760.00	40%	2,304.00	3,456.00
4	16,000	12,544.00	3,456.00	40%	1,382.40	2,073.60
5	16,000	13,926.40	2,073.60	40%	829.44	1,244.16

When the declining-balance method is used, the estimated residual value is not considered in determining the depreciation rate. It is also ignored in computing the periodic depreciation, except that the asset should not be depreciated below its estimated residual value. In the above example, it was assumed that the estimated residual value at the end of the fifth year approximates the book value of $1,244.16. If the estimated residual value were $1,500, the depreciation for the fifth year would have been $573.60 ($2,073.60 – $1,500.00) instead of $829.44.

In the example above, the first use of the asset is assumed to have occurred at the beginning of the fiscal year. This is normally not the case in practice, however, and depreciation for the first partial year of use must be computed. For example, assume that the asset above had been placed in service at the end of the third month of the fiscal year. In this case, only a portion (9/12) of the first full year's depreciation of $6,400 is allocated to the first fiscal year. Thus, depreciation of $4,800 (9/12 × $6,400) is allocated to the first partial year of use. The method of computing the depreciation for the following years would not be affected. Thus, the depreciation for the second fiscal year would be $4,480 [40% × ($16,000 – $4,800)].

Sum-of-the-Years-Digits Method

Under the **sum-of-the-years-digits depreciation method**, depreciation expense is determined by multiplying the original cost of the asset less its estimated residual value by a smaller fraction each year. Thus, the sum-of-the-years-digits method is similar to the declining-balance method, in that the depreciation expense declines each year.

The denominator of the fraction used in determining the depreciation expense is the sum of the digits of the years of the asset's useful life. For example, an asset with a useful life of 5 years would have a denominator of 15 (5 + 4 + 3 + 2 + 1).[4] The numerator of the fraction is the number of years of useful life remaining at the beginning of each year for which depreciation is being computed. Thus, the numerator decreases each year by 1. For a useful life of 5 years, the numerator is 5 the first year, 4 the second year, 3 the third year, and so on.

The following depreciation schedule illustrates the sum-of-the-years-digits method for an asset with a cost of $16,000, an estimated residual value of $1,000, and an estimated useful life of 5 years:

Year	Cost Less Residual Value	Rate	Depreciation for Year	Accum. Depr. at End of Year	Book Value at End of Year
1	$15,000	5/15	$5,000	$ 5,000	$11,000
2	15,000	4/15	4,000	9,000	7,000
3	15,000	3/15	3,000	12,000	4,000
4	15,000	2/15	2,000	14,000	2,000
5	15,000	1/15	1,000	15,000	1,000

[4] The denominator can also be determined from the following formula: $S = N[(N + 1)/2]$, where S = sum of the digits and N = number of years of estimated life.

When the date an asset is first put into service is not the beginning of a fiscal year, each full year's depreciation must be allocated between the two fiscal years benefited. To illustrate, assume that the asset in the above example was put into service at the beginning of the fourth month of the first fiscal year. The depreciation for that year would be \$3,750 ($9/12 \times 5/15 \times \$15{,}000$). The depreciation for the second year would be \$4,250, computed as follows:

$3/12 \times 5/15 \times \$15{,}000$	\$1,250
$9/12 \times 4/15 \times \$15{,}000$	3,000
Total depreciation for second fiscal year	\$4,250

Comparison of Depreciation Methods

The straight-line method provides for uniform periodic charges to depreciation expense over the life of the asset. The units-of-production method provides for periodic charges to depreciation expense that vary, depending upon the amount of usage of the asset.

Both the declining-balance and the sum-of-the-years-digits methods provide for a higher depreciation charge in the first year of use of the asset followed by a gradually declining periodic charge. For this reason, these methods are frequently called **accelerated depreciation methods.** They are most appropriate for situations in which the decline in an asset's productivity or earning power is greater in the early years of its use than in later years. Further, the use of these methods is often justified on the basis that repairs tend to increase with the age of an asset. The reduced amounts of depreciation in later years are thus offset to some extent by increased repairs expenses.

The periodic depreciation charges for the straight-line method and the accelerated methods are compared in Exhibit 3. This comparison is based on an asset cost of \$16,000, an estimated life of 5 years, and an estimated residual value of \$1,000.

Exhibit 3
Comparison of Depreciation Methods

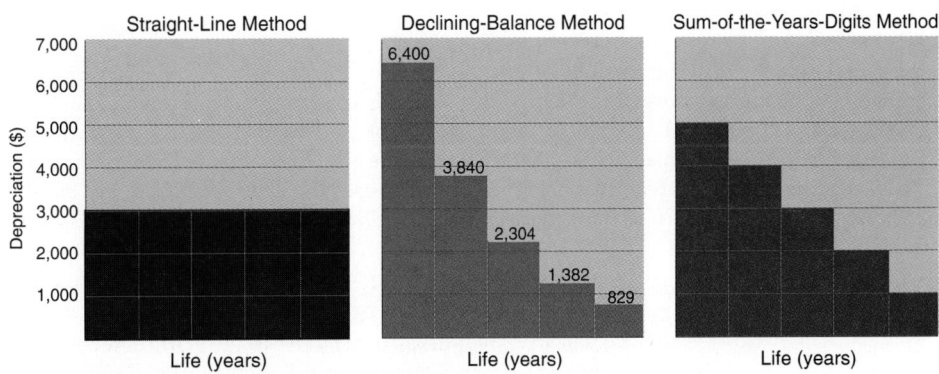

Depreciation for Federal Income Tax

Each of the four depreciation methods described in the preceding paragraphs can be used to determine depreciation expense for federal income tax purposes for plant assets acquired prior to 1981. The two accelerated depreciation methods (declining-balance and sum-of-the-years-digits) are widely used for tax purposes. Acceleration of the *write-off* of the asset reduces the income tax liability in the earlier years. Thus, the amount of cash available to pay for the asset or for other purposes is increased in those years.

For plant assets acquired after 1980 and before 1987, either the straight-line method or the Accelerated Cost Recovery System (ACRS) could be used for federal income tax purposes. ACRS provided for depreciation deductions that were similar to those that would be computed using the 150-percent declining-balance method.[5] For most business property, ACRS provided for three classes of useful life. Each class of useful life was often much shorter than the actual useful life of the asset in that class.

Under the Tax Reform Act of 1986, Modified ACRS (MACRS) provides for eight classes of useful life for plant assets acquired after 1986. The two most common classes, other than real estate, are the 5-year class and the 7-year class.[6] The 5-year class includes automobiles and light-duty trucks, and the 7-year class includes most machinery and equipment. The depreciation deduction for these two classes approximates the use of the declining-balance method using twice the straight-line rate.

The Internal Revenue Service has prescribed methods that use annual percentages (rates) in determining depreciation for each class of asset. In using these rates, residual value is ignored, and all plant assets are assumed to be put in service in the middle of the year and taken out of service in the middle of the year. Thus, for the 5-year-class assets, for example, depreciation is spread over six years, as shown in the following MACRS schedule of depreciation rates:

Year	5-Year-Class Depreciation Rates
1	20.0%
2	32.0
3	19.2
4	11.5
5	11.5
6	5.8
	100.0%

Two (Legal) Sets of Books

Many companies use one method of depreciation for financial reporting purposes (frequently the straight-line method) and a different method of depreciation for income tax purposes (often an accelerated method). The advantages of maintaining two sets of accounts is addressed in the following excerpt from an article in *The Wall Street Journal:*

. . . When you're dealing with the tax folks, quick depreciation . . . of equipment outlays makes a lot of sense. It cuts . . . profits and [therefore cuts] taxes . . . . [Such a policy also] leaves more cash for other uses. But good tax strategy can be bad business strategy.

David A. Tonneson, a Wakefield, Mass., accountant who specializes in advising small businesses, says the biggest mistake his clients make is to immediately deduct too much from profits [for depreciation of] equipment and installation costs. This results in undervalued [bases for] assets and makes borrowing more funds or selling the company more difficult. Small start-up

companies would be wiser to [spread depreciation over future years more evenly]. Though this boosts reported income [in the early years], it boosts their asset base, permitting them to borrow more and sell their concern for more.

Mr. Tonneson says one of his clients lost a chance for a $1 million contract because it had used accelerated depreciation for its equipment. Using straight-line depreciation, the equipment would have been valued on the books at $525,000, or enough to collateralize a $420,000 loan from a bank. But after accelerated depreciation, the books only showed the equipment at $300,000, so the bank would supply only a $240,000 loan. The company needed $400,000 to gear up for the new order. It lost the sale.

Many new small-business owners aren't aware that they can use accelerated depreciation [MACRS] to report income to the tax authorities but can keep their asset [book] values up by using straight-line depreciation to report to shareholders. . . . While this does entail keeping two sets of books, "it's well worth it."

Source: Lee Berton, "Dos and Don'ts," *The Wall Street Journal* (June 10, 1988), p. 34R.

---

[5] The 150-percent declining-balance method uses 150% of the straight-line rate, in contrast to double the straight-line rate (or 200%) as illustrated earlier in this chapter for the declining-balance method.
[6] Real estate is classified into 27½-year classes and 31½-year classes and is depreciated by the straight-line method.

Revision of Periodic Depreciation

Earlier in this chapter, it was noted that two of the factors that must be considered in computing the periodic depreciation of a plant asset are (1) its estimated residual value and (2) its estimated useful life. These factors must be estimated at the time the asset is placed in service. Revisions of these estimates are normal and tend to be recurring. When such revisions occur, the revised estimates are used to determine the depreciation expense to be charged to future periods.

To illustrate, assume that a plant asset was purchased for $130,000, was originally estimated to have a useful life of 30 years, and was estimated to have a residual value of $10,000. The asset has been depreciated for 10 years by the straight-line method. At the end of ten years, the asset's book value (undepreciated cost) is $90,000, determined as follows:

Asset cost	$130,000
Less accumulated depreciation ($4,000 per year × 10 years)	40,000
Book value (undepreciated cost), end of tenth year	$ 90,000

During the eleventh year, it is estimated that the remaining useful life is 25 years (instead of 20) and that the residual value is $5,000 (instead of $10,000). The depreciation expense for each of the remaining 25 years is $3,400, computed as follows:

Book value (undepreciated cost), end of tenth year	$90,000
Less revised estimated residual value	5,000
Revised remaining depreciable cost	$85,000
Revised annual depreciation expense ($85,000 ÷ 25)	$ 3,400

The revisions of the estimates used in determining depreciation does not affect the amounts of depreciation expense recorded in earlier years. The use of estimates and the resulting revisions of such estimates are inherent in the accounting process. Therefore, when such revisions are made, the amounts recorded for depreciation expense in the past are not corrected. Only future depreciation expense amounts are affected.[7]

Recording Depreciation

Depreciation may be recorded by an entry at the end of each month or an adjustment at the end of the year. As discussed in an earlier chapter, the entry to record depreciation is a debit to Depreciation Expense and a credit to a contra asset account entitled Accumulated Depreciation or Allowance for Depreciation. The use of a contra asset account allows the original cost to remain unchanged in the plant asset account. This amount is useful for computing periodic depreciation, preparing the balance sheet presentation of both cost and accumulated depreciation, and reporting for property tax and income tax purposes.

An exception to recording depreciation only monthly or annually is made when a plant asset is sold, traded in, or scrapped. As will be illustrated, a disposal is recorded by removing from the accounts both the cost of the asset and its related accumulated depreciation as of the date of the disposal. Depreciation for the current period should be recorded before the disposal of the asset is recorded.

Subsidiary Ledgers for Plant Assets

When depreciation is computed on a large number of individual assets, a subsidiary ledger is usually maintained. For example, assume that an enterprise owns 200 items of office equipment with a total cost of $100,000. Unless the business is new, the equipment would have been acquired over a number of years. The individual cost, estimated residual value, and estimated useful life would be

---

[7] The correction of material or large errors made in computing depreciation in prior periods is discussed in a later chapter.

different in each case. In addition, the makeup of the assets will continually change because of acquisitions and disposals.

The subsidiary records for depreciable assets may be maintained by a manual system or a computerized system. In either case, a separate ledger account may be maintained for each asset. The subsidiary ledger account shown in Exhibit 4 provides spaces for recording the acquisition and the disposal of the asset, the depreciation charged each period, the accumulated depreciation to date, and the book value. Other relevant data useful to management may also be included.

Exhibit 4
An Account in the Office Equipment Ledger

PLANT ASSET RECORD

Account No.: 123-215   General Ledger Account: Office Equipment
Item: SF 490 Copier
Serial No.: AT 47-3926
From Whom Purchased: Hamilton Office Machines Co.
Estimated Useful Life: 10 Years   Estimated Residual Value: $500   Depr. per Year: $240

Date	Asset Debit	Asset Credit	Asset Balance	Accumulated Depreciation Debit	Accumulated Depreciation Credit	Accumulated Depreciation Balance	Book Value
04/08/93	2,900		2,900				2,900
12/31/93					180	180	2,720
12/31/94					240	420	2,480

The number assigned to the account in Exhibit 4 is made up of the number of the office equipment account in the general ledger (123) followed by the number assigned to the specific item of office equipment purchased (215). A tag or plaque with the account number is attached to the asset for control purposes. Depreciation for the year in which the asset was acquired, computed for nine months on a straight-line basis, is $180. Depreciation for the following year is $240. The subsidiary ledger can therefore provide the data for the adjusting entries for depreciation at the end of each year.

When an asset is disposed of, the asset section of the subsidiary account is credited and the accumulated depreciation section is debited. Thus the balances of both sections are reduced to zero. The account is then removed from the ledger and filed for future reference.

Subsidiary ledgers for plant assets are useful to accountants in (1) determining periodic depreciation expense, (2) recording the disposal of individual items, (3) preparing tax returns, and (4) preparing insurance claims in the event of insured losses. The subsidiary account forms may also be expanded for accumulating data on the operating efficiency of the asset. Such information as number of breakdowns, length of time out of service, and cost of repairs may be useful to management. For example, when new equipment is to be purchased, these data may be useful in deciding upon size, model, and the best vendor.

Depreciation of Plant Assets of Low Unit Cost

Subsidiary ledgers are not usually maintained for classes of plant assets that are made up of individual items of low unit cost. Examples of such items are hand tools and other small portable equipment, dies, molds, patterns, and spare parts. Because of hard usage, breakage, and pilferage, such assets may be relatively short-lived and may require frequent replacement.

For plant assets with a low unit cost, the usual depreciation methods are generally not practical. One method of accounting for such assets is to treat them as expenses when they are acquired. Another method of accounting for assets with a low unit cost is to treat them as assets when they are acquired. Then, at the end of the year, an inventory of the items on hand is taken and their current value is estimated. The difference between this value and the assets' original cost or last year's value is debited to an expense account and credited to the plant asset account.

COMPOSITE-RATE DEPRECIATION METHOD

In the preceding examples, depreciation was computed for each individual plant asset. This procedure is normally used in the exercises and problems at the end of this chapter. Another method, called the **composite-rate depreciation method**, determines depreciation for groups of assets, using a single rate. The basis for grouping may be estimates of useful lives or other common traits. The groupings may be expanded to include all assets within a class, such as office equipment or factory equipment.

When depreciation is computed on the basis of a group of assets with differing useful lives, a rate based on an average must be developed. This rate is computed by (1) determining the annual depreciation for each asset, (2) determining the total annual depreciation, and (3) dividing the total annual depreciation by the total cost of the assets. An example of the composite-rate method is shown below.

Asset No.	Cost	Estimated Residual Value	Estimated Life	Annual Depreciation
101	$ 20,000	$4,000	10 years	$ 1,600
102	15,600	1,500	15 years	940
147	41,000	1,000	8 years	5,000
Total	$473,400			$49,707

$$\frac{\$49,707 \text{ annual depreciation}}{\$473,400 \text{ cost}} = 10.5\% \text{ composite rate}$$

Although new assets of differing useful lives and residual values will be added to the group and old assets will be taken out of service, the *mix* is assumed to remain relatively unchanged. Thus, the depreciation rate based on averages (10.5% in the example) also remains unchanged for an indefinite time in the future.

A composite rate can be applied to the total asset cost on a monthly basis, or some reasonable assumption regarding the timing of increases and decreases in the group may be made. A common practice is to assume that all additions and disposals occur uniformly throughout the year. The average of the beginning and the ending balances of the asset account is then multiplied by the composite rate. Another approach is to assume that all additions and disposals during the first half of the year occur as of the first day of the year. All additions and disposals during the second half of the year are then assumed to have occurred on the first day of the following year.

When assets within the composite group are taken out of service, no gain or loss is recognized. Instead, the asset account is credited for the cost of the asset, and the accumulated depreciation account is debited for the excess of the cost over the amount realized from the disposal. Any deficiency in the amount of depreciation recorded on the shorter-lived assets is presumed to be balanced by excessive depreciation on the longer-lived assets.

CAPITAL AND REVENUE EXPENDITURES

The costs of acquiring plant assets, adding to plant assets, and adding utility to plant assets for more than one accounting period are called **capital expenditures.** Such expenditures are either debited to the asset account or debited to the related accumulated depreciation account. Costs that benefit only the current period or costs incurred in order to maintain normal operating efficiency are called **revenue expenditures.** Such expenditures are debited to expense accounts.

It is important to distinguish between capital and revenue expenditures so that revenues and expenses are properly matched. Capital expenditures will affect the depreciation expense of more than one period, while revenue expenditures will affect the expenses of only the current period.

Capital Expenditures

Accounting for the initial costs of acquiring plant assets was discussed earlier in the chapter. Accounting for capital expenditures after a plant asset has been acquired—(a) additions, (b) betterments, and (c) extraordinary repairs—are discussed in the following paragraphs.

ADDITIONS TO PLANT ASSETS. An expenditure for an addition to a plant asset should be debited to the related plant asset account. The cost of an addition should be depreciated over the estimated useful life of the addition. For example, the cost of adding an air conditioning system to a building or of adding a wing to a building should be accounted for as a capital expenditure.

BETTERMENTS. An expenditure that increases the operating efficiency or capacity for the remaining useful life of a plant asset is called a **betterment**. Such an expenditure should be debited to the related plant asset account. For example, if the power unit attached to a machine is replaced by one of greater capacity, the cost should be debited to the machine account. Also, the cost and the accumulated depreciation related to the old power unit should be removed from the accounts. The cost of the new power unit is depreciated over its estimated useful life or the remaining useful life of the machine, whichever is shorter.

EXTRAORDINARY REPAIRS. An expenditure that increases the useful life of an asset beyond its original estimate is called an **extraordinary repair**. Such an expenditure should be debited to the related accumulated depreciation account. In such cases, the repairs are said to restore or *make good* a portion of the depreciation accumulated in prior years. The depreciation for future periods should be computed on the basis of the revised book value of the asset and the revised estimate of the remaining useful life.

To illustrate, assume that a machine costing $50,000 has no estimated residual value and an estimated useful life of 10 years. Assume also that the machine has been depreciated for 6 years by the straight-line method ($5,000 annual depreciation). At the beginning of the seventh year, an $11,500 extraordinary repair increases the remaining useful life of the machine to 7 years (instead of 4). The repair of $11,500 should be debited to Accumulated Depreciation. The annual depreciation for the remaining 7 years of use would be $4,500, computed as follows:

Cost of machine		$50,000
Less Accumulated Depreciation balance:		
Depreciation for first 6 years ($5,000 × 6)	$30,000	
Deduct debit for extraordinary repairs	11,500	
Balance of Accumulated Depreciation		18,500
Revised book value of machine after extraordinary repair		$31,500
Annual depreciation ($31,500 ÷ by 7 years remaining useful life)		$ 4,500

Revenue Expenditures

Expenditures for normal maintenance and repairs are classified as revenue expenditures. For example, the cost of replacing spark plugs in an automobile or the cost of repainting a building should be debited to expense accounts.

Small expenditures that are insignificant in amount are also normally debited to repair expense accounts, even though they may have the qualities of capital expenditures. The saving in time and record-keeping effort justifies the small loss of accuracy. Some businesses establish a minimum dollar amount required to classify an item as a capital expenditure.

Summary of Capital and Revenue Expenditures

The accounting for capital and revenue expenditures related to plant assets is summarized in Exhibit 5.

Exhibit 5
Capital and Revenue Expenditures

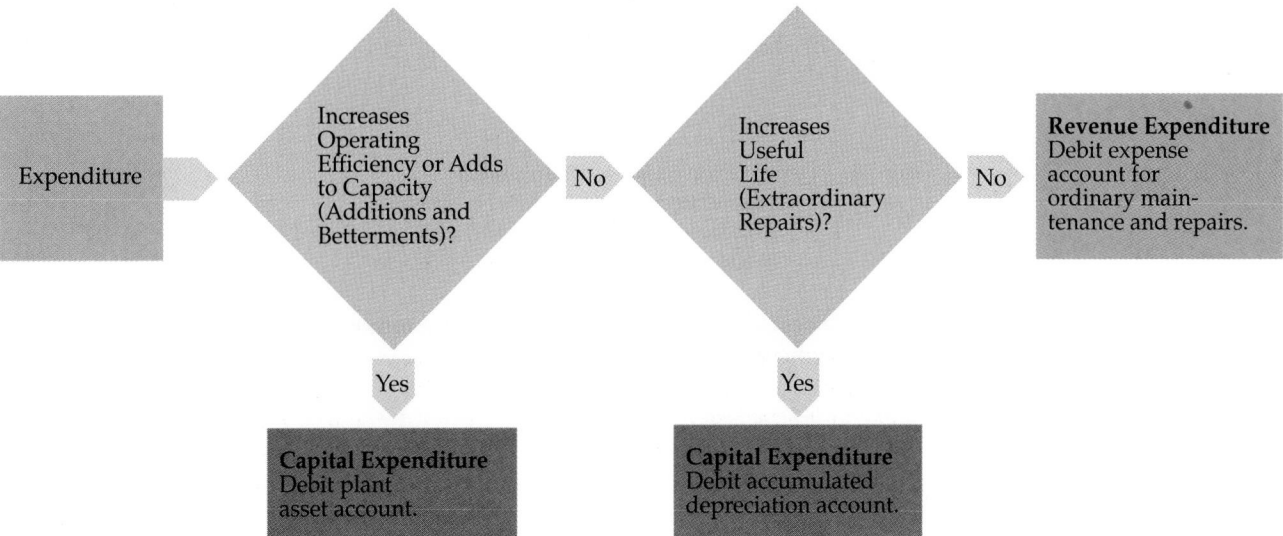

DISPOSAL OF PLANT ASSETS

Objective 7
Journalize entries for the disposal of plant assets.

Plant assets that are no longer useful may be discarded, sold, or traded for other plant assets. The details of the entry to record a disposal will vary. In all cases, however, the book value of the asset must be removed from the accounts. The entry for this purpose is a debit to the asset's accumulated depreciation account for its balance on the date of disposal and a credit to the asset account for the cost of the asset.

A plant asset should not be removed from the accounts only because it has been fully depreciated. If the asset is still used by the enterprise, the cost and accumulated depreciation should remain in the ledger. This maintains accountability for the asset in the ledger. If the book value of the asset were removed from the ledger, the accounts would contain no evidence of the continued existence of the asset. In addition, the cost and the accumulated depreciation data on such assets are often needed for property tax and income tax reports.

Discarding Plant Assets

When plant assets are no longer useful to the business and have no residual or market value, they are discarded. If the asset has been fully depreciated, no loss is realized. For example, assume that an item of equipment acquired at a cost of $25,000 is fully depreciated at December 31, the end of the preceding fiscal year. On February 14, the equipment is discarded as worthless. The entry to record the discarding of the asset is as follows:

Feb. 14	Accumulated Depreciation—Equipment	25,000	
	Equipment		25,000
	To write off equipment discarded.		

The depreciation for a plant asset must be brought up to date prior to removing it from service. In the preceding example, the equipment was fully depreciated at the end of the preceding fiscal year. If, however, the asset had not been fully depreciated, depreciation should be recorded prior to removing the asset from service and from the accounting records.

To illustrate, assume that equipment costing $6,000 is depreciated at an annual straight-line rate of 10%. In addition, assume that on December 31 of the preceding fiscal year, the accumulated depreciation balance, after adjusting entries, is $4,750. Finally, assume that the asset is removed from service on the following March 24. The entry to record the depreciation for the three months of the current period prior to the asset's removal from service is as follows:

Mar. 24	Depreciation Expense—Equipment	150	
	Accumulated Depreciation—Equipment		150
	To record current depreciation on equipment discarded		
	($600 × 3/12).		

The discarding of the equipment and its removal from service is recorded by the following entry:

Mar. 24	Accumulated Depreciation—Equipment	4,900	
	Loss on Disposal of Plant Assets	1,100	
	Equipment		6,000
	To write off equipment discarded.		

In the preceding example, a loss of $1,100 is recorded. A loss on the discarding of a plant asset will occur whenever the balance of the accumulated depreciation account ($4,900 in this example) is less than the balance in the equipment account ($6,000 in this example). Losses on the discarding of plant assets are nonoperating items and are normally reported in the Other Expense section of the income statement.

Sale of Plant Assets

The entry to record the sale of a plant asset is similar to the entries illustrated above, except that the cash or other asset received must also be recorded. If the selling price is more than the book value of the asset, the transaction results in a gain. If the selling price is less than the book value, there is a loss.

To illustrate, assume that equipment is acquired at a cost of $10,000 and is depreciated at an annual straight-line rate of 10%. The equipment is sold for cash on October 12 of the eighth year of its use. The balance of the accumulated depreciation account as of the preceding December 31 is $7,000. The entry to update the depreciation for the nine months of the current year is as follows:

Oct. 12	Depreciation Expense—Equipment	750	
	Accumulated Depreciation—Equipment		750
	To record current depreciation on equipment sold		
	($10,000 × 3/4 × 10%).		

After the current depreciation is recorded, the book value of the asset is $2,250 ($10,000 − $7,750). The entries to record the sale, assuming three different selling prices, are as follows:

Sold at book value, for $2,250. **No gain or loss.**	Oct. 12	Cash	2,250	
		Accumulated Depreciation—Equipment	7,750	
		Equipment		10,000

Sold below book value, for $1,000. Loss of $1,250.	Oct. 12	Cash	1,000	
		Accumulated Depreciation—Equipment	7,750	
		Loss on Disposal of Plant Assets	1,250	
		Equipment		10,000

Sold above book value, for $3,000. Gain of $750.	Oct. 12	Cash	3,000	
		Accumulated Depreciation—Equipment	7,750	
		Equipment		10,000
		Gain on Disposal of Plant Assets		750

Exchanges of Similar Plant Assets

Old equipment is often traded in for new equipment having a similar use. The trade-in allowance is deducted from the price of the new equipment, and the balance owed is paid according to the credit terms. This balance is often called **boot**. The trade-in allowance granted by the seller may be greater or less than the book value of the old equipment traded in.

GAINS ON EXCHANGES. At one time, it was acceptable to recognize gains on exchanges of plant assets. For example, a trade-in allowance of $1,500 on equipment with a book value of $1,000 would have resulted in a gain of $500. However, such gains are no longer recognized for financial reporting purposes. This is based on the theory that revenue occurs from the production and sale of goods produced by plant assets and not from the exchange of similar plant assets.

When the trade-in allowance exceeds the book value of an asset traded in and no gain is recognized, the cost of the new asset is the amount of boot given plus the book value of the old asset. For example, assume the following exchange:

Similar equipment acquired (new):

Price of new equipment	$5,000	
Trade-in allowance on old equipment	1,100	
Boot given (cash)		$3,900

Equipment traded in (old):

Cost of old equipment	$4,000	
Accumulated depreciation at date of exchange	3,200	
Book value at June 19, date of exchange		**800**
Cost of new equipment		**$4,700**

The entry to record this exchange and the assumed payment of cash is as follows:

June 19	Accumulated Depreciation—Equipment	3,200	
	Equipment	4,700	
	Equipment		4,000
	Cash		3,900

The nonrecognition of the $300 gain ($1,100 trade-in allowance minus $800 book value) at the time of the exchange reduces future depreciation expense. That is, the depreciation expense for the new asset is based on a cost of $4,700 rather than on the quoted price of $5,000. In effect, the unrecognized gain of $300 reduces the total amount of depreciation taken during the life of the equipment by $300.

In exchanges as described above, gains are also not recognized for federal income tax purposes. Specifically, the Internal Revenue Code (IRC) does not recognize gains when (1) the asset acquired by the taxpayer is similar in use to the asset given in exchange and (2) any boot involved is given (rather than received) by the taxpayer. Thus, in the above example, the cost of the new equipment for federal income tax purposes is $4,700.

LOSSES ON EXCHANGES. If the trade-in allowance is less than the book value of the old equipment, losses are recognized. To illustrate, assume the following exchange:

Similar equipment acquired (new):

Price of new equipment	$10,000
Trade-in allowance on old equipment	2,000
Boot given (cash)	$ 8,000

Equipment traded in (old):

Cost of old equipment	$ 7,000
Accumulated depreciation at date of exchange	4,600
Book value at September 7, date of exchange	$ 2,400

The amount of the loss recognized on the exchange is the excess of the book value of the equipment traded in ($2,400) over the trade-in allowance ($2,000), or $400. The entry to record the exchange is as follows:

Sep. 7	Accumulated Depreciation—Equipment	4,600	
	Equipment	10,000	
	Loss on Disposal of Plant Assets	400	
	Equipment		7,000
	Cash		8,000

For federal income tax purposes, losses are not recognized when (1) the asset acquired by the taxpayer is similar in use to the asset given in exchange and (2) any boot involved is given (rather than received) by the taxpayer. The cost of the new equipment is determined by adding the boot given to the book value of the equipment traded in. In the above example, the cost of the new equipment for federal income tax purposes is determined as follows:

Book value of equipment traded in	$ 2,400
Boot given (cash)	8,000
Cost of new equipment	$10,400

The unrecognized loss of $400 at the time of the exchange increases the cost of the new equipment. Thus, the total amount of depreciation expense increases by $400 during the useful life of the equipment.

SUMMARY OF ACCOUNTING FOR EXCHANGES. A summary of accounting for the exchanges of similar plant assets for financial and income tax reporting is shown in Exhibit 6, which is based on the following data:

Exhibit 6
Summary Illustration—
Accounting for Exchanges of
Similar Plant Assets

Quoted price of new equipment acquired	$15,000
Cost of old equipment traded in	$12,500
Accumulated depreciation at date of exchange	10,100
Book value at date of exchange	$ 2,400

CASE ONE (GAIN): Trade-in allowance is more than book value of asset traded in.
Trade-in allowance, $3,000; boot given, $12,000 ($15,000 – $3,000)

	Financial Reporting			Income Tax Reporting		
Cost of new asset	Boot plus book value of asset traded in, $14,400 ($12,000 + $2,400)			Boot plus book value of asset traded in, $14,400 ($12,000 + $2,400)		
Gain recognized	None			None		
Entry	Equipment	14,400		Equipment	14,400	
	Accumulated Depreciation	10,100		Accumulated Depreciation	10,100	
	Equipment		12,500	Equipment		12,500
	Cash		12,000	Cash		12,000

Exhibit 6 (concluded)

CASE TWO (LOSS): Trade-in allowance is less than book value of asset traded in.

Trade-in allowance, $2,000; boot given, $13,000 ($15,000 – $2,000)

	Financial Reporting	Income Tax Reporting
Cost of new asset	Quoted price of new asset acquired, $15,000	Boot plus book value of asset traded in, $15,400 ($13,000 + $2,400)
Loss recognized	$400	None

Entry	Equipment 15,000
	Accumulated Depreciation 10,100
	Loss on disposal 400
	     Equipment 12,500
	     Cash 13,000
		Equipment 15,400
		Accumulated Depreciation 10,100
		     Equipment 12,500
		     Cash 13,000

LEASING PLANT ASSETS

Objective 8
Define a lease and summarize the accounting rules related to the leasing of plant assets.

Instead of owning a plant asset, a business may acquire the use of a plant asset through a lease. For example, automobiles, computers, and airplanes are often leased. A **lease** is a contract for the use of an asset for a stated period of time. The two parties to a lease contract are the lessor and the lessee. The **lessor** is the party who owns the asset. The **lessee** is the party to whom the rights to use the asset are granted by the lessor. The lessee is obligated to make periodic rent payments for the lease term.

All leases are classified by the lessee as either capital leases or operating leases. **Capital leases** include one or more of the following elements:

1. The lease transfers ownership of the asset to the lessee at the end of the lease term.
2. The lease contains an option for a bargain purchase of the asset by the lessee.
3. The lease term extends over most of the economic life of the asset.
4. The lease requires rental payments that approximate the fair market value of the asset.[8]

A capital lease is accounted for as if the lessee has, in fact, purchased the asset. Thus, under a capital lease, the lessee debits an asset account for the fair market value of the asset. The offsetting credit is to a long-term lease liability account. The accounting for capital leases is discussed in detail in more advanced accounting texts.

Leases that do not meet the preceding criteria for a capital lease are classified as **operating leases**. The lease payments under an operating lease are accounted for as rent expense by the lessee. The rentals of assets described in the earlier chapters of this text were accounted for as operating leases. Neither future lease obligations nor the future rights to use the asset are recognized in the accounts. However, the lessee must disclose future lease commitments in footnotes to the financial statements.[9]

INTERNAL CONTROL OF PLANT ASSETS

Objective 9
Describe internal controls over plant assets and provide examples of such controls.

Because of the dollar value and the long-term nature of plant assets, it is important to design and implement effective internal controls over plant assets. Such controls should begin with authorization and approval procedures for the purchase of plant assets. Procedures should also exist to ensure that plant assets are acquired at the lowest possible costs. One procedure to achieve this objective is to require competitive bids from preapproved vendors.

---

[8] *Statement of Financial Accounting Standards, No. 13*, "Accounting for Leases" (Stamford: Financial Accounting Standards Board, 1976), par. 7.
[9] *Ibid.*, par. 16.

Like the assets discussed in earlier chapters, plant assets should be safeguarded from possible theft, misuse, or other damage. For example, plant assets that are highly marketable and susceptible to theft, such as computers, should be locked or otherwise safeguarded when not in use. Likewise, procedures should exist for training employees to properly operate plant assets such as equipment and machinery. Plant assets should also be insured against theft, fire, flooding, or other disasters.

As soon as a plant asset is received, it should be inspected and tagged for control purposes and an entry made in the plant asset subsidiary ledger. A company that maintains a computerized subsidiary ledger may use bar-coded tags, similar to the one on the back of this textbook, so that plant asset data can be directly scanned into computer records.

A physical inventory of plant assets should be taken periodically in order to verify the accuracy of the accounting records. Such an inventory would detect missing, obsolete, or idle plant assets. In addition, plant assets should be inspected periodically in order to determine their state of repair.

Careful control should also be exercised over the disposal of plant assets. All disposals should be properly authorized and approved. Fully depreciated assets should be retained in the accounting records until disposal has been authorized and they are removed from service. In this way, accountability for the asset is maintained throughout the period of ownership.

DEPLETION

Objective 10
Compute depletion and journalize the entry for depletion.

The periodic allocation of the cost of metal ores and other minerals removed from the earth is called **depletion.** This allocation to expense is based upon a depletion rate that is computed by dividing the cost of the mineral deposit by its estimated size. The amount of periodic depletion is determined by multiplying the quantity extracted during the period by the depletion rate.

To illustrate, assume that an enterprise paid $400,000 for the mining rights to a mineral deposit estimated at 1,000,000 tons of ore. The depletion rate is $.40 per ton ($400,000 ÷ 1,000,000 tons). If 90,000 tons are mined during the year, the periodic depletion is $36,000 (90,000 tons × $.40). The entry to record the depletion is shown below.

	Adjusting Entry		
Dec. 31	Depletion Expense	36,000	
	Accumulated Depletion		36,000

Like the accumulated depreciation account, the accumulated depletion account is a contra asset account. It is reported on the balance sheet as a deduction from the cost of the mineral deposit.

In determining income subject to the federal income tax, complex IRC rules regarding depletion deductions must be applied. In some cases, it is possible for the total depletion deductions to be more than the cost of the property. A detailed discussion of the tax law and the regulations regarding depletion is presented in tax textbooks.

INTANGIBLE ASSETS

Objective 11
Journalize the entries for acquiring and amortizing intangible assets, such as patents, copyrights, and goodwill.

The basic principles of accounting for intangible assets are like those described earlier for plant assets. The major concerns are (1) determining the initial cost and (2) recognizing the periodic cost expiration, called **amortization.** Amortization results from the passage of time or a decline in the usefulness of the intangible asset. These concerns as they affect patents, copyrights, and goodwill are discussed in the following paragraphs.

Patents

Manufacturers may acquire exclusive rights to produce and sell goods with one or more unique features. Such rights are granted by **patents**, which the federal government issues to inventors. These rights continue in effect for 17 years. An enterprise may purchase patent rights from others, or it may obtain patents developed by its own research and development efforts.

The initial cost of a purchased patent should be debited to an asset account. This cost should be written off, or amortized, over the years of the patent's expected usefulness. This period of time may be less than the remaining legal life of the patent. The estimated useful life of the patent may also change as technology or consumer tastes change. The straight-line method of amortization is used unless it can be shown that another method is better.[10]

A separate contra asset account is normally not credited for the write-off or amortization of patents. The credit is normally recorded directly in the patents account. This practice is common for all intangible assets.

To illustrate, assume that at the beginning of its fiscal year an enterprise acquires patent rights for $100,000. The patent had been granted 6 years earlier by the Federal Patent Office. Although the patent will not expire for 11 years, its remaining useful life is estimated as 5 years. The entry to amortize the patent at the end of the fiscal year is as follows:

	Adjusting Entry		
Dec. 31	Amortization Expense—Patents	20,000	
	Patents		20,000

Assume that after two years of use it appears that this patent will have only two years of remaining usefulness. The cost to be amortized in the third year is $30,000, which is the balance of the asset account, $60,000 ($100,000 – $40,000), divided by two years.

Rather than purchase patent rights, an enterprise may incur significant costs in developing patents through its own research and development efforts. Such costs, called **research and development costs**, are accounted for as current operating expenses in the period in which they are incurred.[11]

The expensing of research and development costs in the period they are incurred is justified for two reasons. First, there is a high degree of uncertainty about the future benefits from research and development efforts. In fact, most research and development efforts do not result in patents. Second, even if a patent is granted, it may be difficult to objectively estimate its cost. If many research projects are in process at the same time, for example, it is difficult to separate the costs of one project from another.

Whether patent rights are purchased or developed internally, an enterprise often incurs significant legal fees related to patents. For example, legal fees may be incurred in filing for patents or in defending the legal rights to patents. Such fees should be debited to an asset account and then amortized over the years of usefulness of the patents.

Copyrights

The exclusive right to publish and sell a literary, artistic, or musical composition is granted by a **copyright**. Copyrights are issued by the federal government and extend for 50 years beyond the author's death. The costs of a copyright include all costs of creating the work plus any administrative or legal costs of obtaining the

[10]*Opinions of the Accounting Principles Board, No. 17,* "Intangible Assets" (New York: American Institute of Certified Public Accountants, 1970), par. 30.

[11]*Statement of Financial Accounting Standards, No. 2,* "Accounting for Research and Development Costs" (Stamford: Financial Accounting Standards Board, 1974), par. 12.

copyright. A copyright that is purchased from another should be recorded at the price paid for it. Because of the uncertainty regarding the useful life of a copyright, it is normally amortized over a short period of time.

Goodwill

In business, **goodwill** refers to an intangible asset of an enterprise that is created from such favorable factors as location, product quality, reputation, and managerial skill. Goodwill allows an enterprise to earn a rate of return on its investment that is often in excess of the normal rate for other firms in the same business.

Generally accepted accounting principles permit the recording of goodwill in the accounts only if it is objectively determined by a transaction. An example of such a transaction is the purchase or sale of a business. In addition, goodwill should be amortized over its estimated useful life. The estimated useful life of goodwill, however, cannot exceed 40 years.[12]

FINANCIAL REPORTING FOR PLANT ASSETS AND INTANGIBLE ASSETS

Objective 12
Describe how depreciation expense is reported in an income statement and prepare a balance sheet that includes plant assets and intangible assets.

The amount of depreciation and amortization expense of a period should be reported separately in the income statement or disclosed in a footnote. A general description of the method or methods used in computing depreciation should also be reported.[13]

The balance of each major class of plant assets should be disclosed in the balance sheet or in footnotes. The related accumulated depreciation should also be disclosed, either by major class or in total.[14] If there are too many classes of plant assets, a single amount may be presented in the balance sheet, supported by a separate detailed listing.

Intangible assets are usually reported in the balance sheet in a separate section immediately following plant assets. The balance of each major class of intangible assets should be disclosed at an amount net of amortization taken to date.

An example of the reporting of plant assets and intangible assets is shown in the partial balance sheet in Exhibit 7.

Exhibit 7
Plant Assets and Intangible Assets in the Balance Sheet

Clinton Door Co.
Balance Sheet
December 31, 19—

Assets

	Cost	Accumulated Depreciation	Book Value	
Total current assets				$462,500
Plant assets:				
Land	$ 30,000	—	$ 30,000	
Buildings	110,000	$ 26,000	84,000	
Factory equipment	650,000	192,000	458,000	
Office equipment	120,000	13,000	107,000	
Total plant assets	$910,000	$231,000		679,000
Intangible assets:				
Patents			$ 75,000	
Goodwill			50,000	
Total intangible assets				125,000

[12]*Opinions of the Accounting Principles Board, No. 17*, "Intangible Assets," *op. cit.*, par. 29.
[13]*Opinions of the Accounting Principles Board, No. 22*, "Disclosure of Accounting Policies" (New York: American Institute of Certified Public Accountants, 1972), par. 13.
[14]*Opinions of the Accounting Principles Board, No. 12*, "Omnibus Opinion—1967" (New York: American Institute of Certified Public Accountants, 1967), par. 5.

CHAPTER REVIEW

Key Points

Objective 1. Define and give examples of plant assets and intangible assets.

Plant assets are long-term tangible assets that are owned by the enterprise and are used in the normal operations of the business. Examples of plant assets are equipment, buildings, and land. Long-term assets that are without physical attributes but are used in the business are classified as intangible assets. Examples of intangible assets are patents, copyrights, and goodwill.

Objective 2. Identify and list the costs of acquiring a plant asset.

The initial cost of a plant asset includes all expenditures necessary to get it in place and ready for use. For example, sales tax, transportation charges, insurance in transit, special foundations, and installation costs are all included in the cost of a plant asset.

Objective 3. Describe the nature of depreciation of plant assets.

Depreciation recognizes that, as time passes, all plant assets except land lose their ability to provide services. As a result, the cost of a plant asset should be transferred to an expense account, in a systematic manner, during the asset's expected useful life. This periodic cost expiration is called depreciation.

Objective 4. Compute depreciation, using the following methods: straight-line method, units-of-production method, declining-balance method, and sum-of-the-years-digits method.

In computing depreciation, three factors need to be considered: (1) the plant asset's initial cost, (2) the useful life of the asset, and (3) the residual value of the asset.

The straight-line method spreads the initial cost less the residual value equally over the useful life. The units-of-production method spreads the initial cost less the residual value equally over the units expected to be produced by the asset during its useful life.

The declining-balance method is applied by multiplying the declining book value of the asset by twice the straight-line rate. The sum-of-the-years-digits method is applied by multiplying the cost less the residual value by a smaller fraction each year.

Objective 5. Compute depreciation, using the composite-rate method.

Depreciation is computed under the composite-rate method by using a single rate for a group of assets.

Objective 6. Classify plant asset costs as either capital expenditures or revenue expenditures.

Costs for additions to plant assets and other costs related to improving efficiency or capacity are classified as capital expenditures. Costs for additions to an asset and costs that add to the utility of the asset for more than one period (called betterments) are also classified as capital expenditures. Also, costs that increase the useful life of an asset beyond the original estimate are a type of capital expenditure and are called extraordinary repairs. Expenditures that benefit only the current period or that maintain normal operating efficiency are debited to expense accounts and are classified as revenue expenditures.

Objective 7. Journalize entries for the disposal of plant assets.

The journal entries to record disposals of plant assets will vary. In all cases, however, any depreciation for the current period should be recorded, and the book value of the asset is then removed from the accounts. The entry to remove the book value from the accounts is a debit to the asset's accumulated depreciation account and a credit to the asset account for the cost of the asset. For assets retired from service, a loss may be recorded for any remaining book value of the asset.

When a plant asset is sold, the book value is removed and the cash or other asset received is also recorded. If the selling price is more than the book value of the asset, the transaction results in a gain. If the selling price is less than the book value, there is a loss.

When a plant asset is exchanged for another of similar nature, no gain is recognized on the exchange. The acquired asset's cost is adjusted for any gains. A loss on an exchange of similar assets is recorded.

Objective 8. Define a lease and summarize the accounting rules related to the leasing of plant assets.

A lease is a contract for the use of an asset for a period of time. A capital lease is accounted for as if the lessee has purchased the asset. The lease payments under an operating lease are accounted for as rent expense for the lessee.

Objective 9. Describe internal controls over plant assets and provide examples of such controls.

Internal controls over plant assets should include procedures for authorizing the purchase of assets. Once acquired, plant assets should be safeguarded from theft, misuse, or damage. A physical inventory of plant assets should be taken periodically.

Objective 10. Compute depletion and journalize the entry for depletion.

The amount of periodic depletion is computed by multiplying the quantity of minerals extracted during the period by a depletion rate. The depletion rate is computed by dividing the cost of the mineral deposit by its estimated size. The entry to record depletion debits a depletion expense account and credits an accumulated depletion account.

Objective 11. Journalize the entries for acquiring and amortizing intangible assets, such as patents, copyrights, and goodwill.

The initial cost of an intangible asset should be debited to an asset account. This cost should be written off, or amortized, over the years of the asset's expected usefulness by debiting an expense account and crediting the intangible asset account.

Objective 12. Describe how depreciation expense is reported in an income statement and prepare a balance sheet that includes plant assets and intangible assets.
The amount of depreciation expense and the method or methods used in computing depreciation should be disclosed

in the financial statements. In addition, each major class of plant assets should be disclosed, along with the related accumulated depreciation. Intangible assets are usually presented in the balance sheet in a separate section immediately following plant assets. Each major class of intangible assets should be disclosed at an amount net of the amortization recorded to date.

Glossary of Key Terms

Accelerated depreciation methods. Depreciation methods that provide for a high depreciation expense in the first year of use of an asset and a gradually declining expense thereafter. **Objective 4**

Amortization. The periodic expense attributed to the decline in usefulness of an intangible asset. **Objective 11**

Betterment. An expenditure that increases operating efficiency or capacity for the remaining useful life of a plant asset. **Objective 6**

Boot. The balance owed the supplier when an old asset is traded for a new asset. **Objective 7**

Capital expenditures. Costs that add to the utility of assets for more than one accounting period. **Objective 6**

Capital leases. Leases that include one or more of four provisions that result in treating the leased assets as purchased assets in the accounts. **Objective 8**

Composite-rate depreciation method. A method of depreciation based on the use of a single rate that applies to entire groups of assets. **Objective 5**

Declining-balance depreciation method. A method of depreciation that provides declining periodic depreciation expense over the estimated life of an asset. **Objective 4**

Depletion. The cost of metal ores and other minerals removed from the earth. **Objective 10**

Depreciation. The periodic cost expiration for the use of all plant assets except land. **Objective 3**

Extraordinary repair. An expenditure that increases the useful life of an asset beyond the original estimate. **Objective 6**

Goodwill. An intangible asset that attaches to a business as a result of such favorable factors as location, product superiority, reputation, and managerial skill. **Objective 11**

Intangible assets. Long-lived assets that are useful in the operations of an enterprise, are not held for sale, and are without physical qualities. **Objective 1**

Operating leases. Leases that do not meet the criteria for capital leases and thus are accounted for as operating expenses. **Objective 8**

Plant assets. Relatively permanent tangible assets used in the operations of a business enterprise. **Objective 1**

Residual value. The estimated recoverable cost of a depreciable asset as of the time of its removal from service. **Objective 4**

Revenue expenditures. Expenditures that benefit only the current period. **Objective 6**

Straight-line depreciation method. A method of depreciation that provides for equal periodic depreciation expense over the estimated life of an asset. **Objective 4**

Sum-of-the-years-digits depreciation method. A method of depreciation that provides for declining periodic depreciation expense over the estimated life of an asset. **Objective 4**

Units-of-production depreciation method. A method of depreciation that provides for depreciation expense based on the expected productive capacity of an asset. **Objective 4**

Self-Examination Questions
Answers at end of chapter.

1. Which of the following expenditures incurred in connection with the acquisition of machinery is a proper charge to the asset account?
   A. Transportation charges   C. Both A and B
   B. Installation costs   D. Neither A nor B

2. What is the amount of depreciation, using the sum-of-the-years-digits method, for the first year of use for equipment costing $9,500, with an estimated residual value of $500 and an estimated life of 3 years?
   A. $4,500   C. $3,000
   B. $3,166.67   D. $2,500

3. An example of an accelerated depreciation method is:
   A. straight-line   C. units-of-production
   B. sum-of-the-years-digits D. composite-rate

4. A plant asset priced at $100,000 is acquired by trading in a similar asset that has a book value of $25,000. Assuming that the trade-in allowance is $30,000 and that $70,000 cash is paid for the new asset, what is the cost of the new asset for financial reporting purposes?
   A. $100,000   C. $70,000
   B. $95,000   D. $30,000

5. Which of the following is an example of an intangible asset?
   A. Patents   C. Copyrights
   B. Goodwill   D. All of the above

ILLUSTRATIVE PROBLEM

Florence Company acquired new equipment at a cost of $75,000 at the beginning of the fiscal year. The equipment has an estimated life of 5 years and an estimated residual value of $6,000. Patrick Florence, the president, has requested information regarding alternative depreciation methods.

Instructions

1. Determine the annual depreciation for each of the five years of estimated useful life of the equipment, the accumulated depreciation at the end of each year, and the book value of the equipment at the end of each year by (a) the straight-line method, (b) the declining-balance method (at twice the straight-line rate), and (c) the sum-of-the-years-digits method.
2. Assume that the equipment was depreciated under the declining-balance method. In the first week of the fifth year, the equipment was traded in for similar equipment priced at $90,000. The trade-in allowance on the old equipment was $8,000, and cash was paid for the balance.
   a. Journalize the entry to record the exchange.
   b. What is the cost basis of the new equipment for computing the amount of depreciation allowable for income tax purposes?

Solution

1.

	Year	Depreciation Expense	Accumulated Depreciation, End of Year	Book Value, End of Year
a.	1	$13,800	$13,800	$61,200
	2	13,800	27,600	47,400
	3	13,800	41,400	33,600
	4	13,800	55,200	19,800
	5	13,800	69,000	6,000
b.	1	$30,000	$30,000	$45,000
	2	18,000	48,000	27,000
	3	10,800	58,800	16,200
	4	6,480	65,280	9,720
	5	3,720*	69,000	6,000
c.	1	$23,000	$23,000	$52,000
	2	18,400	41,400	33,600
	3	13,800	55,200	19,800
	4	9,200	64,400	10,600
	5	4,600	69,000	6,000

*The asset is not depreciated below the estimated residual value of $6,000.

2.

a.

Accumulated Depreciation—Equipment	65,280	
Equipment	90,000	
Loss on Disposal of Plant Assets	1,720	
Equipment		75,000
Cash		82,000

b.

Book value of old equipment	$ 9,720
Boot given (cash)	82,000
Cost basis of new equipment for income tax purposes	$91,720

REAL W🌐RLD FOCUS

35. A revision of depreciable plant asset lives resulted in an increase in the remaining lives of certain plant assets. The company would like to include, as income of the current period, the cumulative effect of the changes, which reduce the depreciation expense of past periods. Is this in accordance with generally accepted accounting principles? Discuss.

Source: "Q's and A's Technical Hotline," *Journal of Accountancy* (December 1991), p. 89.

REAL W🌐RLD FOCUS

36. The financial statements of La-Z-Boy Chair Company contain the following footnote:

The Company has several long-term leases covering manufacturing facilities. The lease agreements require the Company to insure and maintain the facilities and provide for annual payments, which include interest. These leases give the Company the option to purchase the facilities for nominal amounts, or in some instances to renew the leases for extended periods at nominal annual rentals.

Would these leases be classified as operating or capital leases? Discuss.

ETHICS DISCUSSION CASE

SHARPEN YOUR COMMUNICATION SKILLS

Alice Parker, CPA, is an assistant to the controller of Wilson Co. In her spare time, Alice also prepares tax returns and performs general accounting services for clients. Frequently, Alice performs these services after her normal working hours, using Wilson Co.'s microcomputers and laser printers. Occasionally, Alice's clients will call her at the office during regular working hours.

Discuss whether Alice Parker is performing in an ethical manner.

EXERCISES

EXERCISE 11-1
DETERMINING COST OF LAND
Objective 2

Lancaster Company acquired an adjacent lot to construct a new warehouse, paying $10,000 and giving a non-interest-bearing short-term note for $50,000. Legal fees paid were $2,500, delinquent taxes assumed were $4,000, and fees paid to remove an old building from the land were $5,500. Materials salvaged from the demolition of the building were sold for $1,000. A contractor was paid $112,500 to construct a new warehouse. Determine the cost of the land to be reported on the balance sheet.

EXERCISE 11-2
NATURE OF DEPRECIATION
Objective 3

SHARPEN YOUR COMMUNICATION SKILLS

Flowers Co. reported $725,000 for equipment and $510,000 for accumulated depreciation—equipment on its balance sheet.

Does this mean (a) that the replacement cost of the equipment is $725,000 and (b) that $510,000 is set aside in a special fund for the replacement of the equipment? Explain.

EXERCISE 11-3
DEPRECIATION BY UNITS-OF-PRODUCTION METHOD
Objective 4

A diesel-powered generator with a cost of $170,000 and estimated salvage value of $20,000 is expected to have a useful operating life of 50,000 hours. During November, the generator was operated 360 hours.

Determine the depreciation for the month.

EXERCISE 11-4
DEPRECIATION BY UNITS-OF-PRODUCTION METHOD
Objective 4

Prior to adjustment at the end of the year, the balance in Trucks is $109,600, and the balance in Accumulated Depreciation—Trucks is $53,500. Details of the subsidiary ledger are as follows:

Truck No.	Cost	Estimated Residual Value	Estimated Useful Life	Accumulated Depreciation at Beginning of Year	Miles Operated During Year
1	$45,000	$5,000	200,000 miles	$22,500	25,000 miles
2	17,600	2,600	100,000	7,700	20,000
3	28,000	4,000	150,000	23,300	4,500
4	19,000	1,000	200,000	—	12,000

ILLUSTRATIVE PROBLEM

Florence Company acquired new equipment at a cost of $75,000 at the beginning of the fiscal year. The equipment has an estimated life of 5 years and an estimated residual value of $6,000. Patrick Florence, the president, has requested information regarding alternative depreciation methods.

Instructions

1. Determine the annual depreciation for each of the five years of estimated useful life of the equipment, the accumulated depreciation at the end of each year, and the book value of the equipment at the end of each year by (a) the straight-line method, (b) the declining-balance method (at twice the straight-line rate), and (c) the sum-of-the-years-digits method.
2. Assume that the equipment was depreciated under the declining-balance method. In the first week of the fifth year, the equipment was traded in for similar equipment priced at $90,000. The trade-in allowance on the old equipment was $8,000, and cash was paid for the balance.
   a. Journalize the entry to record the exchange.
   b. What is the cost basis of the new equipment for computing the amount of depreciation allowable for income tax purposes?

Solution

1.

	Year	Depreciation Expense	Accumulated Depreciation, End of Year	Book Value, End of Year
a.	1	$13,800	$13,800	$61,200
	2	13,800	27,600	47,400
	3	13,800	41,400	33,600
	4	13,800	55,200	19,800
	5	13,800	69,000	6,000
b.	1	$30,000	$30,000	$45,000
	2	18,000	48,000	27,000
	3	10,800	58,800	16,200
	4	6,480	65,280	9,720
	5	3,720*	69,000	6,000
c.	1	$23,000	$23,000	$52,000
	2	18,400	41,400	33,600
	3	13,800	55,200	19,800
	4	9,200	64,400	10,600
	5	4,600	69,000	6,000

*The asset is not depreciated below the estimated residual value of $6,000.

2.

a.

Accumulated Depreciation—Equipment	65,280	
Equipment	90,000	
Loss on Disposal of Plant Assets	1,720	
Equipment		75,000
Cash		82,000

b.

Book value of old equipment	$ 9,720
Boot given (cash)	82,000
Cost basis of new equipment for income tax purposes	$91,720

DISCUSSION QUESTIONS

1. Which of the following qualities are characteristic of plant assets? (a) tangible, (b) intangible, (c) capable of repeated use in the operations of the business, (d) held for sale in the normal course of business, (e) used continuously in the operations of the business, (f) long-lived.

2. Tols Office Equipment Co. has a fleet of automobiles and trucks for use by salespersons and for delivery of office supplies and equipment. Holmes Auto Sales Co. has automobiles and trucks for sale. Under what caption would the automobiles and trucks be reported on the balance sheet of (a) Tols Office Equipment Co., (b) Holmes Auto Sales Co.?

3. W. C. Simons Co. acquired an adjacent vacant lot with the hope of selling it in the future at a gain. The lot is not intended to be used in Simons' business operations. Where should such real estate be listed in the balance sheet?

4. Tomlin Company solicited bids from several contractors to construct an addition to its office building. The lowest bid received was for $120,000. Tomlin Company decided to construct the addition itself at a cost of $105,000. What amount should be recorded in the building account?

5. Which of the following expenditures incurred in acquiring factory equipment should be debited to the asset account? (a) sales tax on purchase price, (b) transportation charges, (c) insurance while in transit, (d) cost of special foundation, (e) new parts to replace those damaged in unloading, (f) fee paid to factory representative for installation.

6. Which of the following expenditures incurred in purchasing a secondhand printing press should be debited to the asset account? (a) transportation charges, (b) installation costs, (c) repair of vandalism damage that occurred during installation, (d) replacement of worn-out parts.

7. To increase its parking area, Pineridge Shopping Center acquired adjoining land for $95,000 and a building located on the land for $50,000. The net cost of razing the building and leveling the land was $10,000, after amounts received from the sale of salvaged building materials were deducted. What accounts should be debited for (a) the cost of the land ($95,000), (b) the cost of the building ($50,000), (c) the net cost of preparing the land ($10,000)?

8. Are the amounts at which plant assets are reported in the balance sheet their approximate market values as of the balance sheet date? Discuss.

9. a. Does the recognition of depreciation in the accounts provide a special cash fund for the replacement of plant assets? Explain.
   b. Describe the nature of depreciation as the term is used in accounting.

10. Name the three factors that need to be considered in determining the amount of periodic depreciation.

11. West Company purchased a machine that has a manufacturer's suggested life of 12 years. The company plans to use the machine on a special project that will last 4 years. At the completion of the project, the machine will be sold. Over how many years should the machine be depreciated?

12. Is it necessary for an enterprise to use the same method of computing depreciation (a) for all classes of its depreciable assets, (b) in the financial statements and in the determination of income taxes?

13. Of the four common depreciation methods, which is most widely used?

14. A plant asset with a cost of $87,500 has an estimated residual value of $7,500 and an estimated useful life of 4 years. What is the amount of the annual depreciation computed by the straight-line method?

15. A plant asset with a cost of $95,000 has an estimated residual value of $5,000 and an estimated productive capacity of 600,000 units. What is the amount of depreciation computed by the units-of-production method for a year in which production is (a) 60,000 units, (b) 40,000 units?

16. Convert each of the following estimates of useful life to a straight-line depreciation rate, stated as a percentage, assuming that the residual value of the plant asset is to be ignored: (a) 4 years, (b) 5 years, (c) 10 years, (d) 20 years, (e) 25 years, (f) 40 years, (g) 50 years.

17. The declining-balance method, at double the straight-line rate, is to be used for an asset with a cost of $100,000, estimated residual value of $10,000, and estimated useful life of

10 years. What is the depreciation for the first fiscal year, assuming that the asset was placed in service at the beginning of the year?

18. An asset with a cost of $26,000, an estimated residual value of $1,000, and an estimated useful life of 4 years is to be depreciated by the sum-of-the-years-digits method. (a) What is the denominator of the depreciation fraction? (b) What is the amount of depreciation for the first full year of use? (c) What is the amount of depreciation for the second full year of use?

19. a. Under what conditions is the use of an accelerated depreciation method most appropriate?
    b. Why are the accelerated depreciation methods used frequently for income tax purposes?
    c. What is the Modified Accelerated Cost Recovery System (MACRS), and under what conditions is it used?

20. A plant asset with a cost of $205,000 has an estimated residual value of $5,000, an estimated useful life of 40 years, and is depreciated by the straight-line method. (a) What is the amount of the annual depreciation? (b) What is the book value at the end of the twentieth year of use? (c) If at the start of the twenty-first year it is estimated that the remaining life is 25 years and that the residual value is $5,000, what is the depreciation expense for each of the remaining 25 years?

21. The cost of the equipment in a composite group is $600,000 and the annual depreciation, computed on the individual items, totals $60,000. (a) What is the composite straight-line depreciation rate? (b) What would the rate be if the total depreciation amounted to $66,000 instead of $60,000?

22. a. Differentiate between capital expenditures and revenue expenditures.
    b. Why are some items that have the characteristics of capital expenditures treated as revenue expenditures?

23. Immediately after a used truck is acquired, a new motor is installed and the tires are replaced at a total cost of $3,950. Is this a capital expenditure or a revenue expenditure?

24. For some of the plant assets of an enterprise, the balance in Accumulated Depreciation is exactly equal to the cost of the asset. (a) Is it permissible to record additional depreciation on the assets if they are still useful to the enterprise? Explain. (b) When should an entry be made to remove the cost and the accumulated depreciation from the accounts?

25. In what sections of the income statement are gains and losses from the disposal of plant assets presented?

26. A plant asset priced at $120,000 is acquired by trading in a similar asset and paying cash for the difference between trade-in allowance and the price of the new asset. (a) Assuming that the trade-in allowance is $50,000, what is the amount of boot given? (b) Assuming that the book value of the asset traded in is $40,000, what is the cost of the new asset for financial reporting purposes? (c) What is the cost of the new asset for the computation of depreciation for federal income tax purposes?

27. Assume the same facts as in Question 26, except that the book value of the asset traded in is $60,000. (a) What is the cost of the new asset for financial reporting purposes? (b) What is the cost of the new asset for the computation of depreciation for federal income tax purposes?

28. Differentiate between a capital lease and an operating lease.

29. Describe the internal controls for acquiring plant assets.

30. Why is an inventory of plant assets necessary?

31. What is the term applied to the periodic charge for (a) ore removed from a mine, (b) the write-off of the cost of an intangible asset?

32. a. Over what period of time should the cost of a patent acquired by purchase be amortized?
    b. In general, what is the required treatment for research and development costs?

33. How should (a) plant assets and (b) intangible assets be reported in the balance sheet?

 34. A company has developed a tract of land into a ski resort. The company has cut the trees, cleared and graded the land and hills, and constructed ski lifts. (a) Should the tree cutting, land clearing, and grading costs of constructing the ski slopes be debited to the land account? (b) If such costs are debited to Land, should they be depreciated?

Source: "Technical Issues Feature," *Journal of Accountancy* (December 1987), p. 82.

REAL WORLD FOCUS

35. A revision of depreciable plant asset lives resulted in an increase in the remaining lives of certain plant assets. The company would like to include, as income of the current period, the cumulative effect of the changes, which reduce the depreciation expense of past periods. Is this in accordance with generally accepted accounting principles? Discuss.

Source: "Q's and A's Technical Hotline," *Journal of Accountancy* (December 1991), p. 89.

REAL WORLD FOCUS

36. The financial statements of La-Z-Boy Chair Company contain the following footnote:

The Company has several long-term leases covering manufacturing facilities. The lease agreements require the Company to insure and maintain the facilities and provide for annual payments, which include interest. These leases give the Company the option to purchase the facilities for nominal amounts, or in some instances to renew the leases for extended periods at nominal annual rentals.

Would these leases be classified as operating or capital leases? Discuss.

ETHICS DISCUSSION CASE

Alice Parker, CPA, is an assistant to the controller of Wilson Co. In her spare time, Alice also prepares tax returns and performs general accounting services for clients. Frequently, Alice performs these services after her normal working hours, using Wilson Co.'s microcomputers and laser printers. Occasionally, Alice's clients will call her at the office during regular working hours.

Discuss whether Alice Parker is performing in an ethical manner.

SHARPEN YOUR COMMUNICATION SKILLS

EXERCISES

EXERCISE 11-1
DETERMINING COST OF LAND
Objective 2

Lancaster Company acquired an adjacent lot to construct a new warehouse, paying $10,000 and giving a non-interest-bearing short-term note for $50,000. Legal fees paid were $2,500, delinquent taxes assumed were $4,000, and fees paid to remove an old building from the land were $5,500. Materials salvaged from the demolition of the building were sold for $1,000. A contractor was paid $112,500 to construct a new warehouse. Determine the cost of the land to be reported on the balance sheet.

EXERCISE 11-2
NATURE OF DEPRECIATION
Objective 3

Flowers Co. reported $725,000 for equipment and $510,000 for accumulated depreciation—equipment on its balance sheet.

Does this mean (a) that the replacement cost of the equipment is $725,000 and (b) that $510,000 is set aside in a special fund for the replacement of the equipment? Explain.

SHARPEN YOUR COMMUNICATION SKILLS

EXERCISE 11-3
DEPRECIATION BY UNITS-OF-PRODUCTION METHOD
Objective 4

A diesel-powered generator with a cost of $170,000 and estimated salvage value of $20,000 is expected to have a useful operating life of 50,000 hours. During November, the generator was operated 360 hours.
Determine the depreciation for the month.

EXERCISE 11-4
DEPRECIATION BY UNITS-OF-PRODUCTION METHOD
Objective 4

Prior to adjustment at the end of the year, the balance in Trucks is $109,600, and the balance in Accumulated Depreciation—Trucks is $53,500. Details of the subsidiary ledger are as follows:

Truck No.	Cost	Estimated Residual Value	Estimated Useful Life	Accumulated Depreciation at Beginning of Year	Miles Operated During Year
1	$45,000	$5,000	200,000 miles	$22,500	25,000 miles
2	17,600	2,600	100,000	7,700	20,000
3	28,000	4,000	150,000	23,300	4,500
4	19,000	1,000	200,000	—	12,000

a. Determine the depreciation rates per mile and the amount to be credited to the accumulated depreciation section of each of the subsidiary accounts for the miles operated during the current year.
b. Journalize the entry to record depreciation for the year.

EXERCISE 11-5
DEPRECIATION BY THREE
METHODS
Objective 4

A plant asset acquired on January 2 at a cost of $220,000 has an estimated useful life of 10 years. Assuming that it will have no residual value, determine the depreciation for each of the first two years (a) by the straight-line method, (b) by the declining-balance method, using twice the straight-line rate, and (c) by the sum-of-the-years-digits method.

EXERCISE 11-6
DEPRECIATION BY THREE
METHODS
Objective 4

A piece of machinery acquired at the beginning of the fiscal year at a cost of $45,200 has an estimated residual value of $2,000 and an estimated useful life of 8 years. Determine the following: (a) the amount of annual depreciation by the straight-line method, (b) the amount of depreciation for the **second year** computed by the declining-balance method (at twice the straight-line rate), (c) the amount of depreciation for the **second year** computed by the sum-of-the-years-digits method.

EXERCISE 11-7
DEPRECIATION BY
ACCELERATED
DEPRECIATION METHODS
Objective 4

An item of equipment acquired at a cost of $33,000 has an estimated residual value of $3,000 and an estimated useful life of 5 years. It was placed in service on April 1 of the current fiscal year, which ends on December 31. Determine the depreciation for the current fiscal year and for the following fiscal year by (a) the declining-balance method, at twice the straight-line rate, and (b) the sum-of-the-years-digits method.

EXERCISE 11-8
REVISION OF
DEPRECIATION
Objective 4

An item of equipment acquired on January 5, 1990, at a cost of $32,500, has an estimated residual value of $2,500 and an estimated useful life of 10 years. Depreciation has been recorded for the first four years ended December 31, 1993, by the straight-line method. Determine the amount of depreciation for the current year ended December 31, 1994, if the revised estimated residual value is $2,100 and the revised estimated remaining useful life (including the current year) is 8 years.

EXERCISE 11-9
COMPOSITE DEPRECIATION
RATE
Objective 5

A composite depreciation rate of 15% is applied annually to a plant asset account. Details of the account for the fiscal year ended December 31 are as follows:

Machinery			
Jan. 1 Balance	297,750	May 1	16,500
Mar. 2	27,250	Sep. 7	11,750
Apr. 29	14,000	Dec. 15	15,500
Aug. 22	20,500		
Nov. 14	17,500		

Determine the depreciation for the year according to each of the following assumptions: (a) that all additions and retirements have occurred uniformly throughout the year, (b) that additions and retirements during the first half of the year occurred on the first day of that year and those during the second half occurred on the first day of the succeeding year.

EXERCISE 11-10
MAJOR REPAIR TO PLANT
ASSET
Objective 6

A number of major structural repairs on a building were completed at the beginning of the current fiscal year at a cost of $90,000. The repairs are expected to extend the life of the building 10 years beyond the original estimate. The original cost of the building was $800,000, and it has been depreciated by the straight-line method for 25 years. The residual value is expected to be negligible and has been ignored. The balance of the related accumulated depreciation account after the depreciation adjustment at the end of the preceding year is $400,000.

a. What has the amount of annual depreciation been in past years?
b. To what account should the cost of repairs ($90,000) be debited?
c. What is the book value of the building after the repairs have been recorded?
d. What is the amount of depreciation for the current year using the straight-line method (assuming that the repairs were completed at the very beginning of the year)?

EXERCISE 11-11
ENTRIES FOR SALE OF
PLANT ASSET
Objective 7

A piece of equipment acquired on January 3, 1991, at a cost of $57,500, has an estimated useful life of 5 years, an estimated residual value of $7,500, and is depreciated by the straight-line method.

a. What was the book value of the equipment at December 31, 1994, the end of the fiscal year?
b. Assuming that the equipment was sold on July 1, 1995, for $9,000, journalize the entries to record (1) depreciation for the six months of the current year ending December 31, 1995, and (2) the sale of the equipment.

EXERCISE 11-12
DISPOSAL OF PLANT ASSET
Objective 7

A piece of equipment acquired on January 3, 1991, at a cost of $25,000, has an estimated useful life of 4 years and an estimated residual value of $5,000.

a. What was the annual amount of depreciation for the years 1991, 1992, and 1993, using the straight-line method of depreciation?
b. What was the book value of the equipment on January 1, 1994?
c. Assuming that the equipment was sold on January 2, 1994, for $8,500, journalize the entry to record the sale.
d. Assuming that the equipment had been sold for $11,500 on January 2, 1994, instead of $8,500, journalize the entry to record the sale.

EXERCISE 11-13
ENTRIES FOR LOSS ON
TRADE OF PLANT ASSET
Objective 7

On July 1, Lewis Co. acquired a new computer with a list price of $125,000. Lewis received a trade-in allowance of $15,000 on an old computer of a similar type, paid cash of $30,000, and gave a series of five notes payable for the remainder. The following information about the old computer is obtained from the account in the office equipment ledger: cost, $82,500; accumulated depreciation on December 31, the end of the preceding fiscal year, $50,000; annual depreciation, $15,000. Journalize the entries to record: (a) the current depreciation of the old computer to the date of trade-in, (b) the transaction on July 1 for financial reporting purposes.

EXERCISE 11-14
ENTRIES FOR GAIN ON
TRADE OF PLANT ASSET
Objective 7

On July 1, Klaus Co. acquired a new computer with a list price of $130,000. Klaus received a trade-in allowance of $20,000 on an old computer of a similar type, paid cash of $20,000, and gave a series of five notes payable for the remainder. The following information about the old computer is obtained from the account in the office equipment ledger: cost, $82,500; accumulated depreciation on December 31, the end of the preceding fiscal year, $62,500; annual depreciation, $15,000. Journalize the entries to record: (a) the current depreciation of the old computer to the date of trade-in, (b) the transaction on July 1 for financial reporting purposes.

EXERCISE 11-15
DEPRECIATION ON ASSET
ACQUIRED BY EXCHANGE
Objective 7

On the first day of the fiscal year, a delivery truck with a list price of $30,000 was acquired in exchange for an old delivery truck and $26,000 cash. The old truck had a book value of $2,500 at the date of the exchange. The new truck is to be depreciated over 5 years by the straight-line method. The estimated residual value is $2,000.

a. Determine the following:
   1. Annual depreciation for financial reporting purposes.
   2. Annual depreciation for income tax purposes.
b. Assuming that the book value of the old delivery truck was $5,000, determine the following:
   1. Annual depreciation for financial reporting purposes.
   2. Annual depreciation for income tax purposes.

EXERCISE 11-16
INTERNAL CONTROL OF
PLANT ASSETS
Objective 9

Programs Co. is a computer software company marketing software products in the United States and Canada. While Programs Co. has over 30 sales offices, all accounting is handled at the company's headquarters in Dayton, Ohio.

Programs Co. keeps all its plant asset records on a computerized system. The computer maintains a subsidiary ledger of all plant assets owned by the company and calculates depreciation automatically. Whenever a manager at one of the thirty sales offices wants to purchase a plant asset, a purchase request is submitted to headquarters for approval. Upon approval, the plant asset is purchased and the invoice is sent back to headquarters so that the asset can be entered into the plant asset system.

A manager who wants to dispose of a plant asset simply sells or disposes of the asset and notifies headquarters to remove the asset from the system. Company cars and personal computers are frequently purchased by employees when they are disposed of. Most pieces of office equipment are traded in when new assets are acquired.

■SHARPEN YOUR ▶
COMMUNICATION SKILLS

What internal control weakness exists in the procedures used to acquire and dispose of plant assets at Programs Co.?

EXERCISE 11-17
DEPLETION ENTRIES
Objective 10

Grace Co. acquired mineral rights for $3,000,000. The mineral deposit is estimated at 15,000,000 tons. During the current year, 600,000 tons were mined and sold for $750,000.

a. Determine the amount of depletion expense for the current year.
b. Journalize the adjusting entry to recognize the expense.

EXERCISE 11-18
AMORTIZATION ENTRIES
Objective 11

Mercedes Company acquired patent rights on January 3, 1991, for $59,500. The patent has a useful life equal to its legal life of 17 years. On January 5, 1994, Mercedes successfully defended the patent in a lawsuit at a cost of $19,600.

a. Determine the patent amortization expense for the current year ended Dec. 31, 1994.
b. Journalize the adjusting entry to recognize the amortization.

WhAT'S WRONG WITH THI2?

How many errors can you find in the following partial balance sheet?

Prague Company
Balance Sheet
December 31, 19—

Assets

	Replacement Cost	Accumulated Depreciation	Book Value	
Total current assets:				$397,500
Plant assets:				
Land	$ 50,000	$ 20,000	$ 30,000	
Buildings	160,000	76,000	84,000	
Factory equipment	450,000	192,000	258,000	
Office equipment	120,000	73,000	47,000	
Patents	60,000	—	60,000	
Goodwill	45,000	—	45,000	
Total plant assets	$885,000	$361,000		524,000

PROBLEMS
Series A

PROBLEM 11-1A
ALLOCATION OF PAYMENTS AND RECEIPTS TO PLANT ASSET ACCOUNTS
Objective 2

The following payments and receipts are related to land, land improvements, and buildings acquired for use in a business enterprise. The receipts are identified by an asterisk.

a. Cost of real estate acquired as a plant site: Land	$ 175,000
Building	50,000
b. Finder's fee paid to real estate agency	15,000
c. Fee paid to attorney for title search	900
d. Delinquent real estate taxes on property, assumed by purchaser	18,500
e. Cost of razing and removing building	11,250
f. Proceeds from sale of salvage materials from old building	1,500*
g. Cost of filling and grading land	13,500
h. Architect's and engineer's fees for plans and supervision	105,000
i. Premium on 1-year insurance policy during construction	9,000
j. Cost of paving parking lot to be used by customers	17,500
k. Cost of trees and shrubbery planted	10,000
l. Special assessment paid to city for extension of water main to the property	4,500
m. Cost of repairing windstorm damage during construction	3,500
n. Cost of repairing vandalism damage during construction	800
o. Proceeds from insurance company for windstorm and vandalism damage	3,300*
p. Interest incurred on building loan during construction	85,000
q. Money borrowed to pay building contractor	1,000,000*
r. Payment to building contractor for new building	1,250,000
s. Refund of premium on insurance policy (i) canceled after 10 months	750*

408   Part Three   Accounting Systems

SPREADSHEET PROBLEM

SHARPEN YOUR COMMUNICATION SKILLS

PROBLEM 11-2A
COMPARISON OF FOUR
DEPRECIATION METHODS
Objective 4

Instructions

1. Assign each payment and receipt to Land (permanently capitalized), Land Improvements (limited life), Building, or Other Accounts. Indicate receipts by an asterisk. Identify each item by letter and list the amounts in columnar form, as follows:

Item	Land	Land Improvements	Building	Other Accounts
	$	$	$	$

2. The costs assigned to the land, which is used as a plant site, will not be depreciated, while the costs assigned to land improvements will be depreciated. Explain this seemingly contradictory application of the concept of depreciation.

King Company purchased equipment on January 2, 1993, for $90,000. The equipment was expected to have a useful life of 3 years, or 7,000 operating hours, and a residual value of $6,000. The equipment was used for 2,000 hours during 1993, 2,800 hours in 1994, and 2,200 hours in 1995.

Instructions

Determine the amount of depreciation expense for the years ended December 31, 1993, 1994, and 1995 by (a) the straight-line method, (b) the units-of-production method, (c) the declining-balance method, using twice the straight-line rate, and (d) the sum-of-the-years-digits method. Also determine the total depreciation expense for the three years by each method. The following columnar headings are suggested for recording the depreciation expense amounts:

	Depreciation Expense			
Year	Straight-line method	Units-of-production method	Declining-balance method	Sum-of-the-years-digits method
1993				
1994				
1995				
Total				

PROBLEM 11-3A
DEPRECIATION BY FOUR
METHODS; PARTIAL YEARS
Objective 4

Robb Company purchased equipment on July 1, 1993, for $72,000. The equipment was expected to have a useful life of 3 years, or 6,900 operating hours, and a residual value of $3,000. The equipment was used for 700 hours during 1993, 2,800 hours in 1994, 2,400 hours in 1995, and 1,000 hours in 1996. The equipment was sold for $3,000 on July 1, 1996.

Instructions

Determine the amount of depreciation expense for the years ended December 31, 1993, 1994, 1995, and 1996 by (a) the straight-line method, (b) the units-of-production method, (c) the declining-balance method, using twice the straight-line rate, and (d) the sum-of-the-years-digits method.

PROBLEM 11-4A
DEPRECIATION BY THREE
METHODS; TRADE OF
PLANT ASSET
Objectives 4, 7

An item of new equipment, acquired at a cost of $80,000 at the beginning of a fiscal year, has an estimated useful life of 4 years and an estimated residual value of $5,000. The manager requested information regarding the effect of alternative methods on the amount of depreciation expense each year. Upon the basis of the data presented to the manager, the declining-balance method was selected.

In the first week of the fourth year, the equipment was traded in for similar equipment priced at $200,000. The trade-in allowance on the old equipment was $15,000, cash of $15,000 was paid, and a note payable was issued for the balance.

SPREADSHEET PROBLEM

Instructions

1. Determine the annual depreciation expense for each of the estimated 4 years of use, the accumulated depreciation at the end of each year, and the book value of the equipment at the end of each year by (a) the straight-line method, (b) the declining-balance method (at twice the straight-line rate), and (c) the sum-of-the-years-digits method. The following columnar headings are suggested for each schedule:

Year	Depreciation Expense	Accumulated Depreciation, End of Year	Book Value, End of Year

2. For financial reporting purposes, determine the cost of the new equipment acquired in the exchange.
3. Journalize the entry to record the exchange.
4. What is the cost of the new equipment for purposes of computing the amount of depreciation allowable for income tax purposes?
5. Journalize the entry to record the exchange, assuming that the trade-in allowance was $5,000 instead of $15,000.
6. What is the cost of the new equipment for purposes of computing the amount of depreciation allowable for income tax purposes, assuming the data presented in Instruction (5)?

PROBLEM 11-5A
CORRECTING ENTRIES
Objectives 2, 6, 7

The following recording errors occurred and were discovered during the current year:

a. The $750 cost of repairing factory equipment damaged in the process of installation was charged to Factory Equipment.
b. The sale of a computer for $475 was recorded by a $475 credit to Office Equipment. The original cost of the computer was $1,450, and the related balance in Accumulated Depreciation at the beginning of the current year was $925. Depreciation of $100 accrued during the current year, prior to the sale, had not been recorded.
c. Property taxes of $5,000 were paid on real estate acquired during the year and were debited to Property Tax Expense. Of this amount, $4,000 was for taxes that were delinquent at the time the property was acquired.
d. Office equipment with a book value of $11,200 was traded in for similar equipment with a list price of $60,000. The trade-in allowance on the old equipment was $15,000, and a note payable was given for the balance. A gain on the disposal of plant assets of $3,800 was recorded.
e. The $1,100 cost of a major motor overhaul expected to prolong the life of a truck two years beyond the original estimate was debited to Delivery Expense. The truck was acquired new four years earlier.
f. A $450 charge for incoming transportation on an item of factory equipment was debited to Transportation In.
g. The cost of a razed building, $30,000, was debited to Loss on Disposal of Plant Assets and credited to Building. The building and the land on which it was located had been acquired at a total cost of $110,000 ($80,000 debited to Land, $30,000 debited to Building) as a parking area for the adjacent plant.
h. The fee of $7,500 paid to the wrecking contractor to raze the building in (g) was debited to Miscellaneous Expense.
i. The $7,750 cost of repainting several interior rooms of a building was debited to Building. The building had been owned and occupied for 20 years.

Instructions
Journalize the entries to correct the errors during the current year. Identify each entry by letter.

PROBLEM 11-6A
TRANSACTIONS FOR PLANT ASSETS, INCLUDING TRADE
Objectives 2, 6, 7

The following transactions, adjusting entries, and closing entries were completed by Stucky Furniture Co. during 3 fiscal years ending on June 30. All are related to the use of delivery equipment. The declining-balance method (at twice the straight-line rate) of depreciation is used.

1993-1994 Fiscal Year
July   3. Purchased a used delivery truck for $15,000, paying cash.
      6. Paid $1,000 to replace the automatic transmission and install new brakes on the truck. (Debit Delivery Equipment.)
Dec. 7. Paid garage $215 for changing the oil, replacing the oil filter, and tuning the engine on the delivery truck.
June 30. Recorded depreciation on the truck for the fiscal year. The estimated useful life of the truck is 8 years, with a residual value of $3,000.
     30. Closed the appropriate accounts to the income summary account.

1994-1995 Fiscal Year
Aug.29. Paid garage $240 to tune the engine and make other minor repairs on the truck.
Oct. 31. Traded in the used truck for a new truck priced at $28,000, receiving a trade-in allowance of $12,000 and paying the balance in cash. (Record depreciation to date in 1994.)
June 30. Recorded depreciation on the truck. It has an estimated trade-in value of $2,750 and an estimated life of 10 years.
     30. Closed the appropriate accounts to the income summary account.

1995-1996 Fiscal Year

Apr. 1. Purchased a new truck for $30,000, paying cash.
     2. Sold the truck purchased October 31, 1994, for $20,500. (Record depreciation for the year.)

June 30. Recorded depreciation on the remaining truck. It has an estimated residual value of $4,500 and an estimated useful life of 8 years.
    30. Closed the appropriate accounts to the income summary account.

Instructions

Journalize the transactions and the adjusting and closing entries. Post to the following accounts in the ledger and extend the balances after each posting:

122   Delivery Equipment
123   Accumulated Depreciation—Delivery Equipment
616   Depreciation Expense—Delivery Equipment
617   Truck Repair Expense
812   Gain on Disposal of Plant Assets

PROBLEM 11-7A
PLANT ASSET
TRANSACTIONS AND
SUBSIDIARY PLANT LEDGER
Objectives 4, 7

If the working papers correlating with the textbook are not used, omit Problem 11-7A.

Langford Press Co. maintains a subsidiary equipment ledger for the printing equipment and accumulated depreciation accounts in the general ledger. A small portion of the subsidiary ledger, the two controlling accounts, and a journal are presented in the working papers. The company computes depreciation on each individual item of equipment. Transactions and adjusting entries affecting the printing equipment are described as follows:

1993

June 30. Purchased a binder (Model G, Serial No. C3721) from Kunz Manufacturing Co. on account for $108,000. The estimated useful life of the asset is 12 years, it is expected to have no residual value, and the straight-line method of depreciation is to be used. (This is the only transaction of the year that directly affected the printing equipment account.)

Dec. 31. Recorded depreciation for the year in subsidiary accounts 125-30 to 125-32 and inserted the new balances. (An assistant recorded the depreciation and the new balances in accounts 125-1 to 125-29.)

   31. Journalized and posted the annual adjusting entry for depreciation on printing equipment. The depreciation for the year, recorded in subsidiary accounts 125-1 to 125-29, totaled $61,200, to which was added the depreciation entered in accounts 125-30 to 125-32.

1994

Sep. 30. Purchased a Model 722 rotary press from Gross Press Co., priced at $60,000, giving the Model G3 flatbed press (Account No. 125-31) in exchange, plus $20,000 cash and a series of ten $2,500 notes payable, maturing at 6-month intervals. The estimated useful life of the new press is 10 years, and it is expected to have a residual value of $6,250. (Recorded depreciation to date in 1994 on item traded in.)

Instructions

1. Journalize the transaction of June 30. Post to Printing Equipment in the general ledger and to Account No. 125-32 in the subsidiary ledger.
2. Journalize the adjusting entry on December 31 and post to Accumulated Depreciation—Printing Equipment in the general ledger.
3. Journalize the entries required by the purchase of printing equipment on September 30. Post to Printing Equipment and to Accumulated Depreciation—Printing Equipment in the general ledger and to Account Nos. 125-31 and 125-33 in the subsidiary ledger.
4. If the rotary press purchased on September 30 had been depreciated by the declining-balance method at twice the straight-line rate, determine the depreciation on this press for the fiscal years ending (a) December 31, 1994, and (b) December 31, 1995.

PROBLEM 11-8A
INCOME STATEMENT AND
BALANCE SHEET
Objectives 5, 11, 12

The trial balance of Martin Company at the end of the current calendar year, before adjustments, is as follows:

Cash	30,100	
Accounts Receivable	60,200	
Allowance for Doubtful Accounts		500
Merchandise Inventory	178,700	
Prepaid Expense	11,250	
Land	50,000	
Buildings	225,000	
Accumulated Depreciation—Buildings		86,000
Office Equipment	31,100	
Accumulated Depreciation—Office Equipment		11,600
Store Equipment	51,500	
Accumulated Depreciation—Store Equipment		21,400
Delivery Equipment	57,850	
Accumulated Depreciation—Delivery Equipment		21,750
Patents	18,000	
Accounts Payable		40,200
Notes Payable (short-term)		20,000
R. C. Martin, Capital		429,750
R. C. Martin, Drawing	70,000	
Sales (net)		996,950
Purchases (net)	702,350	
Operating Expenses (controlling account)	140,500	
Interest Expense	1,600	
	1,628,150	1,628,150

Data needed for year-end adjustments:

a. Estimated uncollectible accounts at December 31, $6,100.
b. Insurance and other prepaid operating expenses expired during the year, $7,250.
c. Merchandise inventory at December 31, $171,000.
d. Depreciation is computed at composite rates on the average of the beginning and the ending balances of the plant asset accounts. The beginning balances and rates are as follows:

    Office Equipment, $27,900; 10%   Delivery Equipment, $57,150; 20%
    Store Equipment, $48,500; 8%   Buildings, $225,000; 2%

e. Amortization of patents, computed for the year, $3,000.
f. Accrued liabilities at the end of the year, $3,000, of which $300 is for interest on the notes and $2,700 is for wages and other operating expenses.

Instructions

1. Prepare a multiple-step income statement for the current year.
2. Prepare a balance sheet in report form, presenting the plant assets in the manner illustrated in this chapter.

Instructions for Solving Problem 11-8A Using Solutions Software

1. Load opening balances.
2. Save the opening balances file to your drive and directory.
3. Set the run date to December 31 of the current year and enter your name.
4. Key the adjusting entries. Key ADJ.ENT. in the reference field.
5. Display the adjusting entries.
6. Display the financial statements.
7. Save a back-up copy of your data file.
8. Perform period-end closing.
9. Display a post-closing trial balance.
10. Save your data file to disk.
11. End the session.

SOLUTIONS
SOFTWARE

PROBLEM 11-9A
AMORTIZATION AND
DEPLETION ENTRIES
Objectives 10, 11

Data related to the acquisition of timber rights and intangible assets during the current year ended December 31 are as follows:

  a. Timber rights on a tract of land were purchased for $50,000 on February 5. The stand of timber is estimated at 500,000 board feet. During the current year, 75,000 board feet of timber were cut.

  b. Goodwill in the amount of $160,000 was purchased on January 4. It is decided to amortize over the maximum period allowable.

  c. Governmental and legal costs of $24,800 were incurred on July 10 in obtaining a patent with an estimated economic life of 8 years. Amortization is to be for one-half year.

Instructions

1. Determine the amount of the amortization or depletion expense for the current year for each of the foregoing items.
2. Journalize the adjusting entries to record the amortization or depletion expense for each item.

Series B

PROBLEM 11-1B
ALLOCATION OF PAYMENTS
AND RECEIPTS TO PLANT
ASSET ACCOUNTS
Objective 2

The following payments and receipts are related to land, land improvements, and buildings acquired for use in a business enterprise. The receipts are identified by an asterisk.

a. Cost of real estate acquired as a plant site: Land	$ 150,000
Building	40,000
b. Delinquent real estate taxes on property, assumed by purchaser	8,750
c. Cost of razing and removing building	5,800
d. Fee paid to attorney for title search	900
e. Cost of filling and grading land	9,700
f. Architect's and engineer's fees for plans and supervision	60,000
g. Premium on 1-year insurance policy during construction	5,500
h. Payment to building contractor for new building	750,000
i. Cost of repairing windstorm damage during construction	1,500
j. Cost of paving parking lot to be used by customers	12,500
k. Cost of trees and shrubbery planted	15,000
l. Special assessment paid to city for extension of water main to the property	2,500
m. Cost of repairing vandalism damage during construction	500
n. Interest incurred on building loan during construction	39,000
o. Cost of floodlights installed on parking lot	13,500
p. Proceeds from sale of salvage materials from old building	1,100*
q. Money borrowed to pay building contractor	600,000*
r. Proceeds from insurance company for windstorm damage	1,000*
s. Refund of premium on insurance policy (g) canceled after 11 months	350*

Instructions

SPREADSHEET
PROBLEM

1. Assign each payment and receipt to Land (permanently capitalized), Land Improvements (limited life), Building, or Other Accounts. Indicate receipts by an asterisk. Identify each item by letter and list the amounts in columnar form, as follows:

Item	Land	Land Improvements	Building	Other Accounts
	$	$	$	$

**SHARPEN YOUR
COMMUNICATION SKILLS**

2. The costs assigned to the land, which is used as a plant site, will not be depreciated, while the costs assigned to land improvements will be depreciated. Explain this seemingly contradictory application of the concept of depreciation.

PROBLEM 11-2B
COMPARISON OF FOUR
DEPRECIATION METHODS
Objective 4

Taylor Company purchased equipment on January 3, 1993, for $99,000. The equipment was expected to have a useful life of 3 years, or 9,000 operating hours, and a residual value of $9,000. The equipment was used for 3,000 hours during 1993, 3,800 hours in 1994, and 2,200 hours in 1995.

Instructions

Determine the amount of depreciation expense for the years ended December 31, 1993, 1994, and 1995 by (a) the straight-line method, (b) the units-of-production method, (c) the declining-balance method, using twice the straight-line rate, and (d) the sum-of-the-years-digits method. Also determine the total depreciation expense for the three years by each method. The following columnar headings are suggested for recording the depreciation expense amounts:

	Depreciation Expense			
Year	*Straight-line method*	*Units-of-production method*	*Declining-balance method*	*Sum-of-the-years-digits method*
1993				
1994				
1995				
Total				

PROBLEM 11-3B
DEPRECIATION BY FOUR
METHODS; PARTIAL YEARS
Objective 4

XL Company purchased machinery on July 1, 1993, for $90,000. The equipment was expected to have a useful life of 3 years, or 14,000 operating hours, and a residual value of $6,000. The equipment was used for 1,400 hours during 1993, 5,600 hours in 1994, 4,800 hours in 1995, and 2,200 hours in 1996.

Instructions

Determine the amount of depreciation expense for the years ended December 31, 1993, 1994, 1995, and 1996 by (a) the straight-line method, (b) the units-of-production method, (c) the declining-balance method, using twice the straight-line rate, and (d) the sum-of-the-years-digits method.

PROBLEM 11-4B
DEPRECIATION BY THREE
METHODS; TRADE OF
PLANT ASSET
Objectives 4, 7

An item of new equipment, acquired at a cost of $125,000 at the beginning of a fiscal year, has an estimated useful life of 5 years and an estimated residual value of $5,000. The manager requested information regarding the effect of alternative methods on the amount of depreciation expense each year. Upon the basis of the data presented to the manager, the declining-balance method was selected.

In the first week of the fifth year, the equipment was traded in for similar equipment priced at $170,000. The trade-in allowance on the old equipment was $20,000, cash of $25,000 was paid, and a note payable was issued for the balance.

**SPREADSHEET
PROBLEM**

Instructions

1. Determine the annual depreciation expense for each of the estimated 5 years of use, the accumulated depreciation at the end of each year, and the book value of the equipment at the end of each year by (a) the straight-line method, (b) the declining-balance method (at twice the straight-line rate), and (c) the sum-of-the-years-digits method. The following columnar headings are suggested for each schedule:

Year	*Depreciation Expense*	*Accumulated Depreciation, End of Year*	*Book Value, End of Year*

2. For financial reporting purposes, determine the cost of the new equipment acquired in the exchange.

3. Journalize the entry to record the exchange.
4. What is the cost of the new equipment for purposes of computing the amount of depreciation allowable for income tax purposes?
5. Journalize the entry to record the exchange, assuming that the trade-in allowance was $10,000 instead of $20,000.
6. What is the cost of the new equipment for purposes of computing the amount of depreciation allowable for income tax purposes, assuming the data presented in Instruction (5)?

PROBLEM 11-5B
CORRECTING ENTRIES
Objectives 2, 6, 7

The following recording errors occurred and were discovered during the current year:

a. The $900 cost of repairing equipment damaged in the process of installation was charged to Equipment.
b. Store equipment with a book value of $6,700 was traded in for similar equipment with a list price of $50,000. The trade-in allowance on the old equipment was $10,500, and a note payable was given for the balance. A gain on the disposal of plant assets of $3,800 was recorded.
c. Property taxes of $5,000 were paid on real estate acquired during the year and were debited to Property Tax Expense. Of this amount, $3,000 was for taxes that were delinquent at the time the property was acquired.
d. The sale of a computer for $1,750 was recorded by a $1,750 credit to Office Equipment. The original cost of the computer was $7,800, and the related balance in Accumulated Depreciation at the beginning of the current year was $6,000. Depreciation of $800 accrued during the current year, prior to the sale, had not been recorded.
e. The $2,250 cost of a major motor overhaul expected to prolong the life of a truck two years beyond the original estimate was debited to Delivery Expense. The truck was acquired new four years earlier.
f. The $12,500 cost of repainting several interior rooms of a building was debited to Building. The building had been owned and occupied for 20 years.
g. The cost of a razed building, $25,000, was debited to Loss on Disposal of Plant Assets and credited to Building. The building and the land on which it was located had been acquired at a total cost of $100,000 ($75,000 debited to Land, $25,000 debited to Building) as a parking area for the adjacent plant.
h. The fee of $4,000 paid to the wrecking contractor to raze the building in (g) was debited to Miscellaneous Expense.
i. A $250 charge for incoming transportation on an item of store equipment was debited to Transportation In.

Instructions

Journalize the entries to correct the errors during the current year. Identify each entry by letter.

PROBLEM 11-6B
TRANSACTIONS FOR PLANT ASSETS, INCLUDING TRADE
Objectives 2, 6, 7

The following transactions, adjusting entries, and closing entries were completed by Keck Furniture Co. during a 3-year period. All are related to the use of delivery equipment. The declining-balance method (at twice the straight-line rate) of depreciation is used.

1993
Jan.   2. Purchased a used delivery truck for $10,800, paying cash.
         5. Paid $1,200 for major repairs to the truck.
Sep. 17. Paid garage $225 for miscellaneous repairs to the truck.
Dec. 31. Recorded depreciation on the truck for the fiscal year. The estimated useful life of the truck is 4 years, with a residual value of $1,800.
       31. Closed the appropriate accounts to the income summary account.

1994
June 30. Traded in the used truck for a new truck priced at $25,000, receiving a trade-in allowance of $5,000 and paying the balance in cash. (Record depreciation to date in 1994.)
Nov. 4. Paid garage $195 for miscellaneous repairs to the truck.
Dec. 31. Recorded depreciation on the truck. It has an estimated trade-in value of $4,500 and an estimated life of 5 years.
       31. Closed the appropriate accounts to the income summary account.

1995

Oct. 1. Purchased a new truck for $24,400, paying cash.

2. Sold the truck purchased June 30, 1994, for $15,000. (Record depreciation for the year.)

Dec. 31. Recorded depreciation on the remaining truck. It has an estimated residual value of $1,500 and an estimated useful life of 8 years.

31. Closed the appropriate accounts to the income summary account.

Instructions

Journalize the transactions and the adjusting and closing entries. Post to the following accounts in the ledger and extend the balances after each posting:

122   Delivery Equipment
123   Accumulated Depreciation—Delivery Equipment
616   Depreciation Expense—Delivery Equipment
617   Truck Repair Expense
812   Gain on Disposal of Plant Assets

PROBLEM 11-7B
PLANT ASSET
TRANSACTIONS AND
SUBSIDIARY PLANT LEDGER
Objectives 4, 7

If the working papers correlating with the textbook are not used, omit Problem 11-7B.

Dunn Press Co. maintains a subsidiary equipment ledger for the printing equipment and accumulated depreciation accounts in the general ledger. A small portion of the subsidiary ledger, the two controlling accounts, and a journal are presented in the working papers. The company computes depreciation on each individual item of equipment. Transactions and adjusting entries affecting the printing equipment are described as follows:

1993

Sep. 1. Purchased a power binder (Model 14B, Serial No. 6725) from King Manufacturing Co. on account for $60,000. The estimated useful life of the asset is 10 years, it is expected to have no residual value, and the straight-line method of depreciation is to be used. (This is the only transaction of the year that directly affected the printing equipment account.)

Dec. 31. Recorded depreciation for the year in subsidiary accounts 125-30 to 125-32 and inserted the new balances. (An assistant recorded the depreciation and the new balances in accounts 125-1 to 125-29.)

31. Journalized and posted the annual adjusting entry for depreciation on printing equipment. The depreciation for the year, recorded in subsidiary accounts 125-1 to 125-29, totaled $68,200, to which was added the depreciation entered in accounts 125-30 to 125-32.

1994

Mar. 31. Purchased a Model 4B rotary press from Carson Press, priced at $50,000, giving the Model G3 flatbed press (Account No. 125-31) in exchange, plus $7,500 cash and a series of four $5,000 notes payable, maturing at 6-month intervals. The estimated useful life of the new press is 10 years, and it is expected to have a residual value of $2,000. (Recorded depreciation to date in 1994 on item traded in.)

Instructions

1. Journalize the transaction of September 1. Post to Printing Equipment in the general ledger and to Account No. 125-32 in the subsidiary ledger.
2. Journalize the adjusting entry on December 31 and post to Accumulated Depreciation—Printing Equipment in the general ledger.
3. Journalize the entries required by the purchase of printing equipment on March 31. Post to Printing Equipment and to Accumulated Depreciation—Printing Equipment in the general ledger and to Account Nos. 125-31 and 125-33 in the subsidiary ledger.
4. If the rotary press purchased on March 31 had been depreciated by the declining-balance method at twice the straight-line rate, determine the depreciation on this press for the fiscal years ending (a) December 31, 1994, and (b) December 31, 1995.

PROBLEM 11-8B
INCOME STATEMENT AND
BALANCE SHEET
Objectives 5, 11, 12

The trial balance of Treadway Company at the end of the current calendar year, before adjustments, is as follows:

Cash	30,700	
Accounts Receivable	62,600	
Allowance for Doubtful Accounts		500
Merchandise Inventory	179,200	
Prepaid Expense	10,750	
Land	55,000	
Buildings	225,000	
Accumulated Depreciation—Buildings		90,000
Office Equipment	41,100	
Accumulated Depreciation—Office Equipment		17,600
Store Equipment	52,200	
Accumulated Depreciation—Store Equipment		22,100
Delivery Equipment	57,850	
Accumulated Depreciation—Delivery Equipment		21,750
Patents	18,000	
Accounts Payable		43,200
Notes Payable (short-term)		30,000
D. D. Treadway, Capital		430,250
D. D. Treadway, Drawing	70,000	
Sales (net)		999,750
Purchases (net)	706,550	
Operating Expenses (controlling account)	144,600	
Interest Expense	1,600	
	1,655,150	1,655,150

Data needed for year-end adjustments:

a. Estimated uncollectible accounts at December 31, $7,200.
b. Merchandise inventory at December 31, $171,000.
c. Insurance and other prepaid operating expenses expired during the year, $6,750.
d. Depreciation is computed at composite rates on the average of the beginning and the ending balances of the plant asset accounts. The beginning balances and rates are as follows:

Office Equipment, $37,900; 10%   Delivery Equipment, $57,150; 20%
Store Equipment, $49,200; 8%   Buildings, $225,000; 2%

e. Amortization of patents computed for the year, $3,000.
f. Accrued liabilities at the end of the year, $2,000, of which $250 is for interest on the notes and $1,750 is for wages and other operating expenses.

Instructions
1. Prepare a multiple-step income statement for the current year.
2. Prepare a balance sheet in report form, presenting the plant assets in the manner illustrated in this chapter.

SOLUTIONS
SOFTWARE

Instructions for Solving Problem 11-8B Using Solutions Software
1. Load opening balances.
2. Save the opening balances file to your drive and directory.
3. Set the run date to December 31 of the current year and enter your name.
4. Key the adjusting entries. Key ADJ.ENT. in the reference field.
5. Display the adjusting entries.
6. Display the financial statements.
7. Save a back-up copy of your data file.
8. Perform period-end closing.
9. Display a post-closing trial balance.
10. Save your data file to disk.
11. End the session.

PROBLEM 11-9B
AMORTIZATION AND
DEPLETION ENTRIES
Objectives 10, 11

Data related to the acquisition of timber rights and intangible assets during the current year ended December 31 are as follows:

a. Timber rights on a tract of land were purchased for $60,000 on March 5. The stand of timber is estimated at 500,000 board feet. During the current year, 50,000 board feet of timber were cut.

b. Goodwill in the amount of $150,000 was purchased on January 3. It is decided to amortize over the maximum period allowable.

c. Governmental and legal costs of $20,000 were incurred on July 1 in obtaining a patent with an estimated economic life of 8 years. Amortization is to be for one-half year.

Instructions

1. Determine the amount of the amortization or depletion expense for the current year for each of the foregoing items.
2. Journalize the adjusting entries required to record the amortization or depletion for each item.

MINI-CASE 1 WILDE AND COMPANY

Ann Wilde, president of Wilde and Company, is considering the purchase of plant assets on July 1, 1994, for $120,000. The plant assets have a useful life of 5 years and no residual value. In the past, all plant assets have been leased. For tax purposes, Wilde is considering depreciating the plant assets by the straight-line method. She discussed the matter with her CPA and learned that, although the straight-line method could be elected, it was to her advantage to use the modified accelerated cost recovery system (MACRS) for tax purposes. She asked for your advice as to which method to use for tax purposes.

Instructions:

1. Compute depreciation for each of the years (1994, 1995, 1996, 1997, 1998, and 1999) of useful life by (a) the straight-line method and (b) MACRS. In using the straight-line method, one-half year's depreciation should be computed for 1994 and 1999. Use the MACRS rates presented in the chapter.

2. Assuming that income before depreciation and income tax is estimated to be $200,000 uniformly per year and that the income tax rate is 30%, compute the net income for each of the years 1994, 1995, 1996, 1997, 1998, and 1999 if (a) the straight-line method is used and (b) MACRS is used.

3. ▮▮▮➤ What factors would you present for Wilde's consideration in the selection of a depreciation method?

ANSWERS TO SELF-EXAMINATION QUESTIONS

1. **C** All expenditures necessary to get a plant asset (such as machinery) in place and ready for use are proper charges to the asset account. In the case of machinery acquired, the transportation charges (answer A) and the installation costs (answer B) are both (answer C) proper charges to the machinery account.

2. **A** The periodic charge for depreciation under the sum-of-the-years-digits method is determined by multiplying a fraction by the original cost of the asset after the estimated residual value has been subtracted. The denominator of the fraction, which remains constant, is the sum of the digits representing the years of life, or 6 (3+2+1) in this question. The numerator of the fraction, which changes each year, is the number of years of life remaining at the beginning of the year for which depreciation is being computed, or 3 for the first year, 2 for the second year, and 1 for the third year in this question. The $4,500 (answer A) of depreciation for the first year is determined as follows:

3. **B** Depreciation methods that provide for a higher depreciation charge in the first year of the use of an asset and a gradually declining periodic charge thereafter are called accelerated depreciation methods. Examples of such methods are the sum-of-the-years-digits (answer B) and the declining-balance methods.

4. **B** The acceptable method of accounting for an exchange of similar assets in which the trade-in allowance ($30,000) exceeds the book value of the old asset ($25,000) requires that the cost of the new asset be determined by adding the amount of boot given ($70,000) to the book value of the old asset ($25,000), which totals $95,000.

5. **D** Long-lived assets that are useful in operations, not held for sale, and without physical qualities are called intangible assets. Patents, goodwill, and copyrights are examples of intangible assets (answer D).

$$\frac{\text{Years of Life Remaining at Beginning of Year}}{\text{Sum of Digits for Years of Life}} \times \left[\begin{array}{c} \text{Estimated} \\ \text{Cost} - \text{Residual Value} \end{array} \right]$$

$$\frac{3}{3+2+1} \times (\$9,500 - \$500) = \frac{1}{2} \times \$9,000 = \$4,500$$

You and Accounting

Have you ever checked the accuracy of your payroll check? For each pay period, your paycheck is less than the total amount you earned during the period. Various deductions from your total earnings are made for such items as federal income tax and FICA tax. For example, if you worked 20 hours last week at $10 per hour, you are paid weekly, you are single with no dependents, and your employer withholds federal income tax and FICA tax, your payroll check could appear as follows:

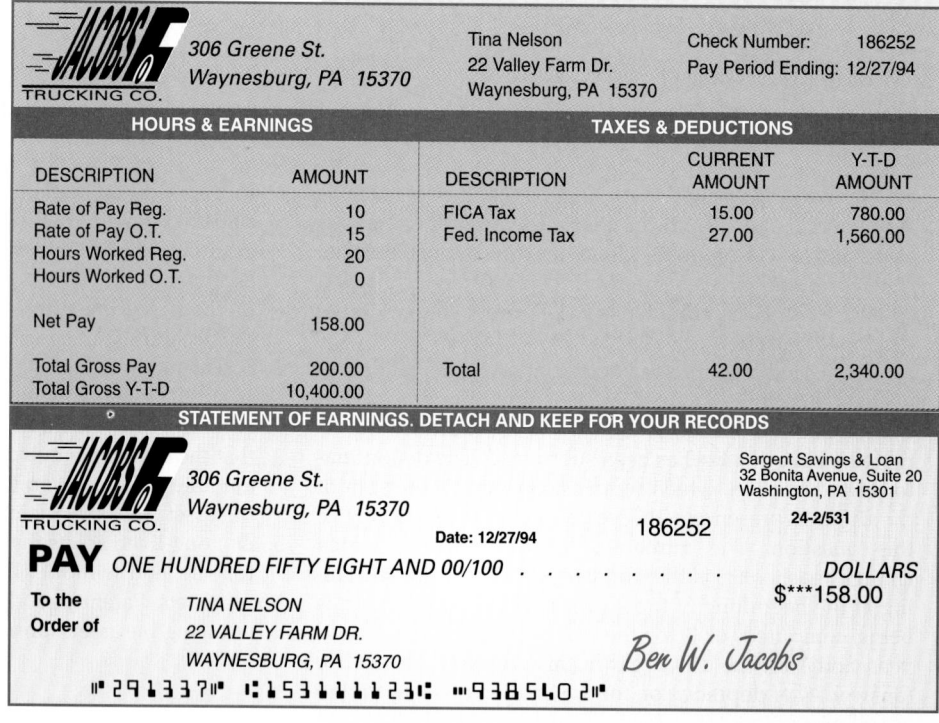

This chapter discusses computations affecting employee pay, so that you can verify whether you are being paid the correct amount each pay period.

Chapter 12
Payroll, Notes Payable, and Other Current Liabilities

LEARNING OBJECTIVES
After studying this chapter, you should be able to:

Objective 1
Determine employer's liabilities for payroll, including liabilities arising from employee earnings and deductions from earnings.

Objective 2
Record payroll and payroll taxes, using a payroll register, employees' earnings records, and a general journal.

Objective 3
Journalize entries for employee fringe benefits, including vacation pay and pensions.

Objective 4
Journalize entries for short-term notes payable.

Objective 5
Journalize entries for product warranties.

Payables are the opposite of receivables. They are debts owed by an enterprise to its creditors. Money claims against a firm may be created in many ways. For example, payables are created by purchases of merchandise or services on account, loans from banks, and purchases of equipment and marketable securities on a credit basis. At a point in time, a business may also owe its employees for wages or salaries accrued, banks or other creditors for interest accrued on notes, and governmental agencies for taxes.

Some types of current liabilities, such as accounts payable, have been discussed in earlier chapters. Additional types of current liabilities, including liabilities arising from payrolls, vacation pay, pensions, notes payable, and product warranties, are discussed in this chapter.

Objective 1
Determine employer's liabilities
for payroll, including liabilities
arising from employee earnings
and deductions from earnings.

PAYROLL AND PAYROLL TAXES

The term **payroll** refers to the amount paid to employees for services provided during a period. An enterprise's payroll is usually significant for several reasons. First, employees are sensitive to payroll errors and irregularities. Maintaining good employee morale requires that the payroll be paid on a timely, accurate basis. Second, payroll expenditures are subject to various federal and state regulations. Finally, payroll expenditures and related payroll taxes have a significant effect on the net income of most business enterprises. Although the amount of such expenses varies widely, it is not unusual for a business to expend nearly a third of its revenue for payroll and payroll-related expenses.

Liability for Employee Earnings

The term **salary** usually refers to payment for managerial, administrative, or similar services. The rate of salary is normally expressed in terms of a month or a year. The term **wages** usually refers to payment for manual labor, both skilled and unskilled. The rate of wages is normally stated on an hourly or weekly basis. In practice, the terms salary and wages are often used interchangeably.

The basic salary or wage of an employee may be increased by commissions, bonuses, profit sharing, or cost-of-living adjustments. Although payment is usually made in cash, it may take such forms as securities, notes, lodging, or other property or services. Generally, the form of payment has no effect on how salaries and wages are treated by either the employer or the employee.

Salary and wage rates are determined by agreement between the employer and the employees. Enterprises engaged in interstate commerce must follow the requirements of the Fair Labor Standards Act. Employers covered by this legislation, which is commonly called the Federal Wage and Hour Law, are required to pay a minimum rate of $1\frac{1}{2}$ times the regular rate for all hours worked in excess of 40 hours per week. Exemptions are provided for executive, administrative, and certain supervisory positions. Premium rates for overtime or for working at night, holidays, or other less desirable times are fairly common, even when not required by law. In some cases, the premium rates may be as much as twice the base rate.

DETERMINING EMPLOYEE EARNINGS. To illustrate the computation of the earnings of an employee, assume that John T. McGrath is employed at the rate of $20 per hour. Any hours in excess of 40 hours per week are paid at a rate of $1\frac{1}{2}$ times the normal rate, or $30 ($20 + $10) per hour. For the week ended December 27, McGrath's time card indicates that he worked 50 hours. His earnings for that week are computed as follows:

Earnings at base rate (40 × $20)	$ 800
Earnings at overtime rate (10 × $30)	300
Total earnings	$1,100

DETERMINING INCOME-SHARING BONUSES. Many enterprises pay their employees an annual bonus in addition to a regular salary or wage. The amount of the bonus is often based on some measure of productivity of the employees. One productivity measure commonly used for managers is income or profit of the enterprise. Such income-sharing bonuses are treated in the same manner as salaries and wages.

The method used in determining the amount of an income-sharing bonus should be stated in the contract between the employer and the employees. When the bonus is expressed as a percentage of income, the percentage may be applied to one of the following four income measures:

1. Income before deducting the bonus and income taxes.
2. Income after deducting the bonus but before deducting income taxes.

3. Income before deducting the bonus but after deducting income taxes.
4. Net income after deducting both the bonus and income taxes.

Determining a 10% bonus using each of the four income measures is shown below. In these illustrations, the employer's income before deducting the bonus and income taxes is $150,000, and the income tax rate is 40%. Bonus and income taxes are abbreviated as B (bonus) and T (taxes).

1. Bonus based on income before deducting bonus and taxes.

$$B = .10 (\$150,000)$$
$$\text{Bonus} = \$15,000$$

2. Bonus based on income after deducting bonus but before deducting taxes.

$$B = .10(\$150,000 - B)$$

Simplifying: $B = \$15,000 - .10B$

Transposing: $1.10B = \$15,000$

$$\text{Bonus} = \$13,636.36$$

3. Bonus based on income before deducting bonus but after deducting taxes.

B equation: $B = .10(\$150,000 - T)$

T equation: $T = .40(\$150,000 - B)$

Substituting for T in the B equation and solving for B:

$$B = .10[\$150,000 - .40(\$150,000 - B)]$$

Simplifying: $B = .10(\$150,000 - \$60,000 + .40B)$

Simplifying: $B = \$15,000 - \$6,000 + .04B$

Transposing: $.96B = \$9,000$

$$\text{Bonus} = \$9,375$$

4. Bonus based on net income after deducting bonus and taxes.

B equation: $B = .10(\$150,000 - B - T)$

T equation: $T = .40(\$150,000 - B)$

Substituting for T in the B equation and solving for B:

$$B = .10[\$150,000 - B - .40(\$150,000 - B)]$$

Simplifying: $B = .10(\$150,000 - B - \$60,000 + .40B)$

Simplifying: $B = \$15,000 - .10B - \$6,000 + .04B$

Transposing: $1.06B = \$9,000$

$$\text{Bonus} = \$8,490.57$$

In the preceding examples, the amount of the bonus ranges from a high of $15,000 to a low of $8,490.57. It is obvious that strictly following the bonus agreement is important. If the bonus is to be shared by all of the employees, the agreement must also indicate how the bonus is divided among the employees. A common method is to express the bonus as a percentage of total earnings for the year. For example, if the bonus was $15,000 and total employee earnings before the bonus were $100,000, the bonus for each of the employees could be stated as 15% of their earnings.

Deductions from Employee Earnings

The total earnings of an employee for a payroll period, including bonuses and overtime pay, are called **gross pay**. From this amount is subtracted one or more **deductions** to arrive at the net pay. **Net pay** is the amount the employer must pay the employee. The deductions for federal taxes are usually the largest deduction. Deductions may also be required for state or local income taxes. Other deductions may be made for medical insurance, contributions to pensions, and for items authorized by individual employees.

FICA TAX. Most employers are required by the Federal Insurance Contributions Act (FICA) to withhold a portion of the earnings of each of their employees. The amount of **FICA tax** withheld is the employees' contribution to two federal programs. The first program, referred to as social security, is for old age, survivors, and disability insurance. The second program, referred to as Medicare, is for health insurance.

With very few exceptions, employers are required to withhold from each employee a tax based on the amount of earnings paid in the calendar year. Although both the schedule of future tax rates and the maximum amount subject to tax are revised often by Congress, such changes have little effect on the basic payroll system.[1] In this text, a combined rate of 7.5% on the first $60,000 of annual earnings and a rate of 1.5% on annual earnings from $60,000 to $140,000 will be used.

To illustrate, assume that John T. McGrath's annual earnings prior to the current payroll period total $59,200. Assume also that the current period earnings are $1,100. The FICA tax of $64.50 is determined as follows:[2]

Earnings subject to 7.5% FICA tax		
($60,000 − $59,200)	$800.00	
FICA tax rate	7.5%	
FICA tax		$60.00
Earnings subject to 1.5% FICA tax		
($59,200 + $1,100 − $60,000)	$300.00	
FICA tax rate	1.5%	
FICA tax		4.50
Total FICA tax		$64.50

Your Social Security Taxes

In its 1936 publication, *Security in Your Old Age*, the Social Security Board set forth the following explanation of how the social security tax would affect a worker's paycheck:

The taxes called for in this law will be paid both by your employer and by you. For the next 3 years you will pay maybe 15 cents a week, maybe 25 cents a week, maybe 30 cents or more, according to what you earn. That is to say, during the next 3 years, beginning January 1, 1937, you will pay 1 cent for every dollar you earn, and at the same time your employer will pay 1 cent for every dollar you earn, up to $3,000 a year. Twenty-six million other workers and their employers will be paying at the same time.

After the first 3 years—that is to say, beginning in 1940— you will pay, and your employer will pay, 1½ cents for each dollar you earn, up to $3,000 a year. This will be the tax for 3 years, and then beginning in 1943, you will pay 2 cents, and so will your employer, for every dollar you earn for the next three years. After that, you and your employer will each pay half a cent more for 3 years, and finally, beginning in 1949, twelve years from now, you and your employer will each pay 3 cents on each dollar you earn, up to $3,000 a year. That is the most you will ever pay.

The rate on January 1, 1992, is 7.65 cents per dollar earned (7.65%). The social security portion is 6.2% on the first $55,500 of earnings. The Medicare portion is 1.45% on the first $130,200 of earnings.

Source: Adapted from Arthur Lodge, "That Is the Most You Will Ever Pay," *Journal of Accountancy* (October 1985), p. 44.

FEDERAL INCOME TAX. Except for certain types of employment, all employers must withhold a portion of employee earnings for payment of the employees' federal income tax. As a basis for determining the amount to be withheld, each employee completes and submits to the employer an "Employee's Withholding Allowance Certificate," often called a W-4. An example of a completed W-4 form is shown in Exhibit 1.

On the W-4, each employee indicates marital status, the number of withholding allowances, and whether any additional withholdings are authorized. A

[1] The FICA rates for 1992 are 6.2% for the first $55,500 of earnings and 1.45% for earnings between $55,500 and $130,200.
[2] Tables are available from the Internal Revenue Service for determining FICA withholding.

Exhibit 1
Form W-4

Form **W-4**	Employee's Withholding Allowance Certificate	OMB No. 1545-0010

Department of the Treasury
Internal Revenue Service

► For Privacy Act and Paperwork Reduction Act Notice, see reverse.

19**92**

1 Type or print your first name and middle initial	Last name	2 Your social security number
John T.	McGrath	381-48-9120

Home address (number and street or rural route)	3 ☒ Single ☐ Married ☐ Married, but withhold at higher Single rate.
1830 4th Street	**Note:** *If married, but legally separated, or spouse is a nonresident alien, check the Single box.*

City or town, state, and ZIP code	4 If your last name differs from that on your social security card,
Clinton, Iowa 52732-6142	check here and call 1-800-772-1213 for more information ► ☐

5	Total number of allowances you are claiming (from line G above or from the Worksheets on back if they apply)	5	1
6	Additional amount, if any, you want deducted from each paycheck	6	$

7 I claim exemption from withholding and I certify that I meet **ALL** of the following conditions for exemption:
- Last year I had a right to a refund of **ALL** Federal income tax withheld because I had **NO** tax liability; **AND**
- This year I expect a refund of **ALL** Federal income tax withheld because I expect to have **NO** tax liability; **AND**
- This year if my income exceeds $600 and includes nonwage income, another person cannot claim me as a dependent.

If you meet all of the above conditions, enter the year effective and "EXEMPT" here . . . ► | 7 | 19

8 Are you a full-time student? (**Note:** *Full-time students are not automatically exempt.*) . . . . | 8 ☐ Yes ☒ No

Under penalties of perjury, I certify that I am entitled to the number of withholding allowances claimed on this certificate or entitled to claim exempt status.

Employee's signature ► *John T. McGrath*   Date ►   June 2   , 19 91

9 Employer's name and address (Employer: Complete 9 and 11 only if sending to the IRS)	10 Office code (optional)	11 Employer identification number

single employee may claim one withholding allowance. A married employee may claim an additional allowance for a spouse. An employee may also claim an allowance for each dependent other than a spouse. Each allowance claimed reduces the amount of federal income tax withheld from the employee's check.

The amount that must be withheld for income tax differs, depending upon each employee's gross pay and completed W-4. Most employers use wage bracket withholding tables furnished by the Internal Revenue Service to determine the amount to be withheld.[3]

An example of a wage bracket withholding table is shown in Exhibit 2. This table is for a single employee who is paid weekly. Other tables are used for employees who are married or who are paid biweekly, semimonthly, monthly, or at other time periods. Unlike FICA tax, there is no ceiling on the amount of employee earnings subject to federal income tax withholding.

In using the withholding table, the employee's wage bracket is first located in the left-hand column. The number of withholding allowances is then located across the horizontal columns. The intersection of the employee's wage bracket with the appropriate withholding allowance column indicates the federal withholding. For example, assume that John T. McGrath, who is single and has declared one withholding allowance, made $1,100 for the week ended December 27. Using the withholding table in Exhibit 2, the amount of federal income tax withheld is $238.

OTHER DEDUCTIONS. Deductions from gross earnings for payment of taxes are required. Neither the employer nor the employee has any choice in the matter. In addition, however, there may be other deductions authorized by individual employees. For example, an employee may authorize deductions for the purchase of U.S. Savings Bonds, for contributions to charitable organizations, for premiums on employee insurance, or for retirement annuities. A union contract may also require the deduction of union dues.

Computing Employee Net Pay

Gross earnings less payroll deductions equals the amount to be paid to an employee for the payroll period. This amount is the **net pay**, which is often called the **take-home pay**. The amount to be paid John T. McGrath for the week ended December 27 is $772.50, as shown below.

---

[3] Current federal income tax withholding tables are available from the Internal Revenue Service as part of *Circular E*, "Employer's Tax Guide."

Gross earnings for the week		$1,100.00
Deductions:		
FICA tax	$ 64.50	
Federal income tax	238.00	
U.S. savings bonds	20.00	
United Fund	5.00	
Total deductions		327.50
Net pay		$ 772.50

The determination of the gross earnings and the FICA tax and federal income tax withheld for McGrath was illustrated earlier. It is assumed that the deductions for the purchase of bonds and for the United Fund contribution were authorized by McGrath.

Exhibit 2
Wage Bracket
Withholding Table

WEEKLY PAYROLL PERIOD—continued SINGLE PERSONS

Wages: $550–$1,200 and over

And the wages are—		And the number of withholding allowances claimed is—										
At least	But less than	0	1	2	3	4	5	6	7	8	9	10
		The amount of income tax to be withheld shall be—										
$550	$560	$95	$82	$70	$60	$53	$46	$40	$33	$26	$20	$13
560	570	98	85	73	61	54	48	41	35	28	21	15
570	580	100	88	76	63	56	49	43	36	29	23	16
580	590	103	91	78	66	57	51	44	38	31	24	18
590	600	106	94	81	69	59	52	46	39	32	26	19
600	610	109	96	84	72	60	54	47	41	34	27	21
610	620	112	99	87	74	62	55	49	42	35	29	22
620	630	114	102	90	77	65	57	50	44	37	30	24
630	640	117	105	92	80	68	58	52	45	38	32	25
640	650	120	108	95	83	70	60	53	47	40	33	27
650	660	123	110	98	86	73	61	55	48	41	35	28
660	670	126	113	101	88	76	64	56	50	43	36	30
670	680	128	116	104	91	79	66	58	51	44	38	31
680	690	131	119	106	94	82	69	59	53	46	39	33
690	700	134	122	109	97	84	72	61	54	47	41	34
700	710	137	124	112	100	87	75	62	56	49	42	36
710	720	140	127	115	102	90	78	65	57	50	44	37
720	730	142	130	118	105	93	80	68	59	52	45	39
730	740	145	133	120	108	96	83	71	60	53	47	40
740	750	148	136	123	111	98	86	74	62	55	48	42
750	760	151	138	126	114	101	89	76	64	56	50	43
760	770	154	141	129	116	104	92	79	67	58	51	45
770	780	156	144	132	119	107	94	82	70	59	53	46
780	790	159	147	134	122	110	97	85	72	61	54	48
790	800	162	150	137	125	112	100	88	75	63	56	49
800	810	165	152	140	128	115	103	90	78	66	57	51
810	820	168	155	143	130	118	106	93	81	68	59	52
820	830	170	158	146	133	121	108	96	84	71	60	54
830	840	173	161	148	136	124	111	99	86	74	62	55
840	850	176	164	151	139	126	114	102	89	77	65	57
850	860	179	166	154	142	129	117	104	92	80	67	58
860	870	182	169	157	144	132	120	107	95	82	70	60
870	880	184	172	160	147	135	122	110	98	85	73	61
880	890	187	175	162	150	138	125	113	100	88	76	63
890	900	190	178	165	153	140	128	116	103	91	79	66
900	910	193	180	168	156	143	131	118	106	94	81	69
910	920	196	183	171	158	146	134	121	109	96	84	72
920	930	198	186	174	161	149	136	124	112	99	87	75
930	940	201	189	176	164	152	139	127	114	102	90	77
940	950	204	192	179	167	154	142	130	117	105	93	80
950	960	207	194	182	170	157	145	132	120	108	95	83
960	970	210	197	185	172	160	148	135	123	110	98	86
970	980	212	200	188	175	163	150	138	126	113	101	89
980	990	215	203	190	178	166	153	141	128	116	104	91
990	1,000	218	206	193	181	168	156	144	131	119	107	94
1,000	1,010	221	208	196	184	171	159	146	134	122	109	97
1,010	1,020	224	211	199	186	174	162	149	137	124	112	100
1,020	1,030	226	214	202	189	177	164	152	140	127	115	103
1,030	1,040	230	217	204	192	180	167	155	142	130	118	105
1,040	1,050	233	220	207	195	182	170	158	145	133	121	108
1,050	1,060	236	222	210	198	185	173	160	148	136	123	111
1,060	1,070	239	225	213	200	188	176	163	151	138	126	114
1,070	1,080	242	228	216	203	191	178	166	154	141	129	117
1,080	1,090	245	231	218	206	194	181	169	156	144	132	119
1,090	1,100	248	234	221	209	196	184	172	159	147	135	122
1,100	1,110	251	238	224	212	199	187	174	162	150	137	125
1,110	1,120	254	241	227	214	202	190	177	165	152	140	128
1,120	1,130	257	244	230	217	205	192	180	168	155	143	131
1,130	1,140	261	247	233	220	208	195	183	170	158	146	133
1,140	1,150	264	250	236	223	210	198	186	173	161	149	136
1,150	1,160	267	253	239	226	213	201	188	176	164	151	139
1,160	1,170	270	256	242	229	216	204	191	179	166	154	142
1,170	1,180	273	259	246	232	219	206	194	182	169	157	145
1,180	1,190	276	262	249	235	222	209	197	184	172	160	147
1,190	1,200	279	265	252	238	224	212	200	187	175	163	150

$1,200 and over   Use Table 1(a) for a **SINGLE** person on page 29.

Liability for Employer's Payroll Taxes

So far, payroll taxes have been discussed from the employees' point of view. These taxes are assessed against employees and are withheld by employers. Most employers are also subject to federal and state payroll taxes based on the amount paid their employees. Such taxes are an operating expense of the business.

FICA TAX. Employers are required to contribute to the Federal Insurance Contributions Act (FICA) program for each employee. The tax rates are the same as those discussed and illustrated earlier for employees.

FEDERAL UNEMPLOYMENT COMPENSATION TAX. Unemployment insurance provides temporary payments to those who become unemployed as a result of layoffs due to economic causes beyond their control. Types of employment subject to the unemployment insurance program are similar to those covered by the FICA tax. The tax of .8% is levied on employers only, rather than on both employers and employees.[4] It is applied to only the first $7,000 of the earnings of each covered employee during a calendar year. The rate and the maximum earnings subject to federal unemployment compensation tax are often revised by Congress. The funds collected by the federal government are not paid directly to the unemployed, but are allocated among the states for use in state programs.

STATE UNEMPLOYMENT COMPENSATION TAX. The amounts paid as benefits to unemployed persons are obtained, for the most part, by taxes levied upon employers only. A very few states also require employee contributions. The rates of tax and the tax bases vary. In most states, employers who provide stable employment for their employees are granted reduced rates. The employment experience and the status of each employer's tax account are reviewed annually, and the tax rates are adjusted accordingly.[5]

ACCOUNTING SYSTEMS FOR PAYROLL AND PAYROLL TAXES

Objective 2
Record payroll and payroll taxes, using a payroll register, employees' earnings records, and a general journal.

The employees of an enterprise expect and are entitled to payment at regular intervals at the end of each payroll period. Regardless of the number of employees, the payroll system must be designed to process payroll data quickly and accurately.

In designing payroll systems, the requirements of various federal, state, and local agencies for payroll data must be considered. Payroll data must not only be maintained for each payroll period, but also for each employee. Periodic reports using payroll data must be submitted to governmental agencies. The payroll data itself must be retained for possible inspection by the various agencies.

Payroll systems should also be designed to provide useful data for management decision-making needs. Such needs might include settling employee grievances and negotiating retirement or other benefits with employees.

Although payroll systems differ among enterprises, the major components common to most payroll systems are the payroll register, employee's earnings record, and payroll checks. Each of these major components is discussed and illustrated below. The illustrations have been kept relatively simple and may be modified in practice to meet the needs of each individual enterprise.

Payroll Register

The **payroll register** is a multicolumn form used in assembling and summarizing the data needed each payroll period. Its design varies according to the number and classes of employees and the extent to which computers are used. A form suitable for a small number of employees is illustrated in Exhibit 3.

---

[4] The rate on January 1, 1992, was 6.2%, which may be reduced to 0.8% for credits for state unemployment compensation tax.
[5] As of January 1, 1992, the maximum state rate recognized by the federal unemployment system was 5.4% of the first $7,000 of each employee's earnings during a calendar year.

Exhibit 3
Payroll Register

| | | | PAYROLL FOR WEEK ENDING |
| | | EARNINGS | |
Employee Name	Total Hours	Regular	Overtime	Total
Abrams, Julie S.	40	500.00		500.00
Elrod, Fred G.	44	392.00	58.80	450.80
Gomez, Jose C.		840.00		840.00
McGrath, John T.	50	800.00	300.00	1,100.00
Wilkes, Glenn K.	40	480.00		480.00
Zumpano, Michael W.		600.00		600.00
Total		13,328.00	574.00	13,902.00

The nature of the data appearing in the payroll register is evident from the columnar headings. The number of hours worked and the earnings and deduction data are inserted in their proper columns. The sum of the deductions for each employee is then deducted from the total earnings to yield the amount to be paid. The check numbers are recorded in the payroll register as evidence of payment.

The last two columns of the payroll register are used to accumulate the total wages or salaries to be charged to the various expense accounts. This process is usually called **payroll distribution**. If a large number of accounts are to be debited, the data may be accumulated on a separate payroll distribution sheet.

The format of the payroll register in Exhibit 3 aids in determining the mathematical accuracy of the payroll before checks are issued to employees. All columnar totals should be cross-verified, as shown below.

Earnings:
  Regular $13,328.00
  Overtime   574.00
    Total $13,902.00

Deductions:
  FICA tax $ 851.60
  Federal income tax   3,332.00
  U.S. savings bonds   680.00
  United Fund   470.00
  Accounts receivable   50.00
    Total   5,383.60
Paid—net amount $ 8,518.40

Accounts debited:
  Sales Salaries Expense $11,122.00
  Office Salaries Expense   2,780.00
    Total (as above) $13,902.00

RECORDING EMPLOYEES' EARNINGS. Amounts in the payroll register may be posted directly to the accounts. An alternative is to use the payroll register as a supporting record for a compound journal entry. The entry based on the payroll register in Exhibit 3 follows.

DECEMBER 27, 19--									
	DEDUCTIONS					PAID		ACCOUNTS DEBITED	
FICA Tax	Federal Income Tax	U.S. Savings Bonds	Miscel-laneous		Total	Net Amount	Check No.	Sales Salaries Expense	Office Salaries Expense
37.50	74.00	20.00	UF 10.00		141.50	358.50	6857	500.00	
33.81	62.00		UF 50.00		145.81	304.99	6858		450.80
12.60	173.00	25.00	UF 10.00		220.60	619.40	6859	840.00	
64.50	238.00	20.00	UF 5.00		327.50	772.50	6860	1,100.00	
36.00	69.00	10.00			115.00	365.00	6880	480.00	
45.00	71.00	5.00	UF 2.00		123.00	477.00	6881		600.00
851.60	3,332.00	680.00	UF 470.00		5,383.60	8,518.40		11,122.00	2,780.00
			AR 50.00						
Miscellanous Deductions UF–United Fund; AR–Accounts Receivable									

Dec. 27	Sales Salaries Expense	11,122.00	
	Office Salaries Expense	2,780.00	
	FICA Tax Payable		851.60
	Employees Federal Income Tax Payable		3,332.00
	Bond Deductions Payable		680.00
	United Fund Deductions Payable		470.00
	Accounts Receivable—Fred G. Elrod		50.00
	Salaries Payable		8,518.40
	Payroll for week ended December 27.		

The total expense incurred for the services of employees is recorded by the debits to the salary expense accounts. Amounts withheld from employees' earnings have no effect on the debits to these accounts. Five of the credits in the preceding entry increase liability accounts and one credit decreases the accounts receivable account.

RECORDING AND PAYING PAYROLL TAXES. All employer's payroll taxes become liabilities when the related payroll is *paid* to employees. In addition, employers are required to compute and report payroll taxes on a *calendar-year* basis. The calendar year must be used for payroll taxes, even if a different fiscal year is used for financial reporting and income tax purposes.

To illustrate the accounting implications of the preceding requirement, assume that Everson Company's fiscal year ends on April 30. Also, assume that Everson Company owes its employees $26,000 of wages on December 31. The following portions of the $26,000 of wages are subject to payroll taxes on December 31:

	Earnings Subject to Payroll Taxes
FICA—Social Security and Medicare (7.5%)	$18,000
FICA—Medicare only (1.5%)	8,000
State and Federal Unemployment Compensation	1,000

If the payroll is paid on December 31, the payroll taxes will be based on the preceding amounts. If the payroll is paid on January 2, however, the *entire* $26,000 will be subject to payroll taxes.

Each time the payroll is prepared, the amounts of employer payroll taxes should be determined. The payroll tax expense accounts are then debited and related liability accounts credited.

To illustrate, the payroll register in Exhibit 3 indicates that the amount of FICA tax withheld is $851.60. Since the employer must match the employees' FICA contributions, the employer's FICA payroll tax will also be $851.60. Further, assume that the earnings subject to state and federal unemployment compensation taxes are $2,710. Multiplying this amount by the state (5.4%) and federal (.8%) unemployment tax rates yields the unemployment compensation taxes shown below.

FICA tax	$ 851.60
State unemployment compensation tax (5.4% × $2,710)	146.34
Federal unemployment compensation tax (.8% × $2,710)	21.68
Total payroll tax expense	$1,019.62

The entry to journalize the payroll tax expense for the week and the liability for the taxes accrued is shown below. Payment of the liabilities for payroll taxes is recorded in the same manner as the payment of other liabilities.

Dec. 27	Payroll Tax Expense	1,019.62	
	FICA Tax Payable		851.60
	State Unemployment Tax Payable		146.34
	Federal Unemployment Tax Payable		21.68
	Payroll taxes for week ended December 27.		

FICA contributions (both the employees' and employer's amounts) and federal income taxes must be deposited periodically in a federal depository bank. An "Employer's Quarterly Federal Tax Return" (Form 941) must be filed by the end of the first month following each calendar quarter. A portion of a completed Form 941 is shown in Exhibit 4.

Form **941**
(Rev. January 1992)
Department of the Treasury
Internal Revenue Service

4141

Employer's Quarterly Federal Tax Return
▶ See Circular E for more information concerning employment tax returns.
Please type or print.

#	Description		Amount
2	Total wages and tips subject to withholding, plus other compensation . . . . ▶ **2**		40,180 5
3	Total income tax withheld from wages, tips, pensions, annuities, sick pay, gambling, etc. . ▶ **3**		6,520 00
4	Adjustment of withheld income tax for preceding quarters of calendar year (see instructions) . ▶ **4**		
5	Adjusted total of income tax withheld (line 3 as adjusted by line 4—see instructions) . . . **5**		6,520 00
6a	Taxable social security wages (**Complete** $ 40,180 50 × 12.4% (.124) = **6a**		4,982 38
b	Taxable social security tips (**line 7**) $ × 12.4% (.124) = **6b**		
7	Taxable Medicare wages and tips . . . $ × 2.9% (.029) = **7**		
8	Total social security and Medicare taxes (add lines 6a, 6b, and 7) **8**		4,982 38
9	Adjustment of social security and Medicare taxes (see instructions for required explanation) . **9**		
10	Adjusted total of social security and Medicare taxes (line 8 as adjusted by line 9—see instructions) . ▶ **10**		4,982 38
11	Backup withholding (see instructions) **11**		
12	Adjustment of backup withholding tax for preceding quarters of calendar year **12**		
13	Adjusted total of backup withholding (line 11 as adjusted by line 12) **13**		
14	**Total taxes** (add lines 5, 10, and 13) **14**		11,502 38
15	Advance earned income credit (EIC) payments made to employees, if any . . . . . . ▶ **15**		
16	Net taxes (subtract line 15 from line 14). **This should equal line IV below** (plus line IV of Schedule A (Form 941) if you have treated backup withholding as a separate liability) . . . **16**		11,502 38
17	**Total deposits for quarter,** including overpayment applied from a prior quarter, from your records . ▶ **17**		11,502 38
18	**Balance due** (subtract line 17 from line 16). This should be less than $500. Pay to Internal Revenue Service . . ▶ **18**		0

Unemployment compensation tax returns and payments are required by the federal government on an annual basis. Earlier payments are required when the tax exceeds a certain minimum. Unemployment compensation tax returns and payments are required by most states on a basis similar to that required by the federal government.

Employee's Earnings Record

The amount of each employee's earnings to date must be readily available at the end of each payroll period. This cumulative amount is required in order to compute each employee's earnings subject to FICA tax and federal and state unemployment taxes. Without this cumulative amount, there would be no means of determining the employee's FICA tax withholding and employer's payroll taxes. It is essential, therefore, that a detailed payroll record be maintained for each employee. This record is called an **employee's earnings record.**

A portion of the employee's earnings record for John T. McGrath is shown in Exhibit 5. The relationship between this record and the payroll register can be seen by tracing the amounts entered on McGrath's earnings record for December 27 back to its source—the fourth line of the payroll register in Exhibit 3.

In addition to spaces for recording data for each payroll period and the cumulative total of earnings, the employee's earnings record has spaces for quarterly totals and the yearly total. These totals are used in various reports for tax, insurance, and other purposes. One such report is the Wage and Tax Statement, commonly called a Form W-2. This form must be provided annually to each employee as well as to the Social Security Administration. The amounts reported in the example of a Form W-2 shown below were taken from John T. McGrath's employee's earnings record.

1 Control number	**22222**	For Official Use Only ► OMB No. 1545-0008			
2 Employer's name, address, and ZIP code		6 Statutory employee ☐ Deceased ☐ Pension plan ☐ Legal rep. ☐ 942 emp. ☐ Subtotal ☐ Deferred compensation ☐ Void ☐			
McDermott Supply Co. 415 5th Ave. So. Dubuque, Iowa 52736-0142		7 Allocated tips		8 Advance EIC payment	
		9 Federal income tax withheld 12,500.00		10 Wages, tips, other compensation 60,300.00	
3 Employer's identification number 61-843652	4 Employer's state I.D. number	11 Social security tax withheld 4,500.00		12 Social security wages 60,000.00	
5 Employee's social security number 381-48-9120		13 Social security tips		14 Medicare wages and tips	
19a Employee's name (first, middle initial, last) John T. McGrath		15 Medicare tax withheld		16 Nonqualified plans	
1830 4th St. Clinton, Iowa 52732-6142		17 See Instrs. for Form W-2		18 Other	
19b Employee's address and ZIP code					
20	21	22 Dependent care benefits		23 Benefits included in Box 10	
24 State income tax	25 State wages, tips, etc.	26 Name of state	27 Local income tax	28 Local wages, tips, etc.	29 Name of locality

Copy A For Social Security Administration   Cat. No. 10134D   Department of the Treasury—Internal Revenue Service

Form **W-2 Wage and Tax Statement 1992**

Payroll Checks

At the end of each pay period, one of the major outputs of the payroll system is a series of **payroll checks.** These checks are prepared from the payroll register, in which each line applies to an employee. Normally, the payroll check includes a detachable statement showing the details of how the net pay was computed. An example of the payroll check for John T. McGrath is shown in Exhibit 6.

When the voucher system is used, it is necessary to prepare a voucher for the net amount to be paid the employees. The voucher is then recorded in the voucher register as a debit to Salaries Payable and a credit to Accounts Payable. The payment of the voucher is recorded in the check register in the usual manner. If the voucher system is not used, the payment is recorded by a debit to Salaries Payable and a credit to Cash.

The compound journal entry to record the payroll should precede the entries just described. The information for this entry is taken from the payroll register.

Exhibit 5
Employee's Earnings Record

John T. McGrath
1830 4th Street
Clinton, IA 52732-6142

PHONE: 555-3148

MARRIED   NUMBER OF
              WITHHOLDING   PAY
              ALLOWANCES: 1   RATE: $800.00 Per Week
OCCUPATION: Salesperson   EQUIVALENT HOURLY RATE: $20

EARNINGS

Period Ended	Total Hours	Regular Earnings	Overtime	Total Earnings	Cumulative Total
SEP. 27	51	800.00	330.00	1,130.00	45,700.00
THIRD QUARTER		10,400.00	4,770.00	15,170.00	
OCT. 4	50	800.00	300.00	1,100.00	46,800.00
NOV. 15	48	800.00	240.00	1,040.00	54,000.00
NOV. 22	50	800.00	300.00	1,100.00	55,100.00
NOV. 29	46	800.00	180.00	980.00	56,080.00
DEC. 6	50	800.00	300.00	1,100.00	57,180.00
DEC. 13	46	800.00	180.00	980.00	58,160.00
DEC. 20	48	800.00	240.00	1,040.00	59,200.00
DEC. 27	50	800.00	300.00	1,100.00	60,300.00
FOURTH QUARTER		10,400.00	4,200.00	14,600.00	
YEARLY TOTAL		41,600.00	18,700.00	60,300.00	

Also, the entire amount paid is normally recorded as a single amount, regardless of the number of employees. There is no need to record each payroll check separately in the journal, since all of the details are available in the payroll register.

Exhibit 6
Payroll Check

McDermott Supply Co.
415 5th Ave. So.
Dubuque, IA 52736-0142

John T. McGrath
1830 4th St.
Clinton, IA 52732-6142

Check Number: 291337
Pay Period Ending: 12/27/94

HOURS & EARNINGS

DESCRIPTION	AMOUNT
Rate of Pay Reg.	20
Rate of Pay O.T.	30
Hours Worked Reg.	40
Hours Worked O.T.	10
Net Pay	772.50
Total Gross Pay	1,100.00
Total Gross Y-T-D	60,300.00

TAXES & DEDUCTIONS

DESCRIPTION	CURRENT AMOUNT	Y-T-D AMOUNT
FICA Tax	64.50	4,504.50
Fed. Income Tax	238.00	14,181.00
U.S. Savings Bonds	20.00	1,040.00
United Fund	5.00	100.00
Total	327.50	19,825.50

STATEMENT OF EARNINGS. DETACH AND KEEP FOR YOUR RECORDS

McDermott Supply Co.
415 5th Ave. So.
Dubuque, IA 52736-0142

LaGesse Savings & Loan
33 Katie Avenue, Suite 33
Clinton, IA 52736-3581

Date: 12/27/94   291337   24-2/531

PAY SEVEN HUNDRED SEVENTY-TWO AND 50/100 . . . .   **DOLLARS**

$***772.50

To the
Order of   JOHN T. MCGRATH
            1830 4TH ST.
            CLINTON, IA 52732-6142

Franklin D. McDermott

⑈291337⑈ ⑆153111123⑈ ⑈938540 2⑈

SOC. SEC. NO.: 381-48-9120

EMPLOYEE NO.: 814

DATE OF BIRTH: February 15, 1974

DATE EMPLOYMENT TERMINATED:

		DEDUCTIONS				PAID	
FICA Tax	Federal Income Tax	U.S. Bonds	Other		Total	Net Amount	Check No.
84.75	247.00	20.00			351.75	778.25	6175
1,137.75	3,185.00	260.00	UF	40.00	4,622.75	10,547.25	
82.50	238.00	20.00	UF	5.00	345.50	754.50	6225
78.00	220.00	20.00			318.00	722.00	6530
82.50	238.00	20.00			340.50	759.50	6582
73.50	203.00	20.00			296.50	683.50	6640
82.50	238.00	20.00	UF	5.00	345.50	754.50	6688
73.50	203.00	20.00			296.50	683.50	6743
78.00	220.00	20.00			318.00	722.00	6801
64.50	238.00	20.00	UF	5.00	327.50	772.50	6860
1,072.50	3,090.00	260.00	UF	15.00	4,437.50	10,162.50	
4,504.50	14,181.00	1,040.00	UF	100.00	19,825.50	40,474.50	

For paying their payroll, most employers use payroll checks drawn on a special bank account. After the data for the payroll period have been recorded and summarized in the payroll register, a single check for the total amount to be paid is written on the firm's regular bank account. This check is then deposited in the special payroll bank account. Individual payroll checks are written from the payroll account, and the numbers of the payroll checks are inserted in the payroll register.

The use of payroll checks relieves the treasurer or other executives of the task of signing a large number of regular checks each payday. The task of signing payroll checks may be given to a paymaster, or a check-signing machine may be used to imprint the checks with the treasurer's signature.

Another advantage of using a separate payroll bank account is that the task of reconciling the bank statements is simplified. The paid payroll checks are returned by the bank with a bank statement for the payroll account. If all the payroll checks have been cashed by employees, the balance of the payroll account should be zero or the amount initially required by the bank to open the account. This is because the amount of each deposit is equal to the total amount of payroll checks written. Any payroll checks not cashed by employees will appear as outstanding checks on the bank reconciliation. After a period of time, funds for payroll checks that have not been cashed are transferred to the regular bank account. This establishes control over these items and prevents the theft or misuse of uncashed payroll checks.

Currency may be used to pay payroll. For example, currency is often used for payment of part-time workers or for employees who are paid at remote locations where cashing checks is difficult. In such cases, a single check, payable to Payroll, is written for the entire amount to be paid. The check is then cashed at the bank and the money is inserted in individual pay envelopes. The employees should be asked for identification and should be required to sign a receipt when picking up their pay envelopes. Journalizing the payroll is the same as if payroll checks were used.

Payroll System Diagram

The flow of data within the payroll segment of an accounting system is shown in the diagram in Exhibit 7. The diagram indicates the relationships among the primary components of the payroll system described in this chapter. The need to update the employee's earnings record is indicated by the dotted line.

Exhibit 7
Flow of Data in a Payroll System

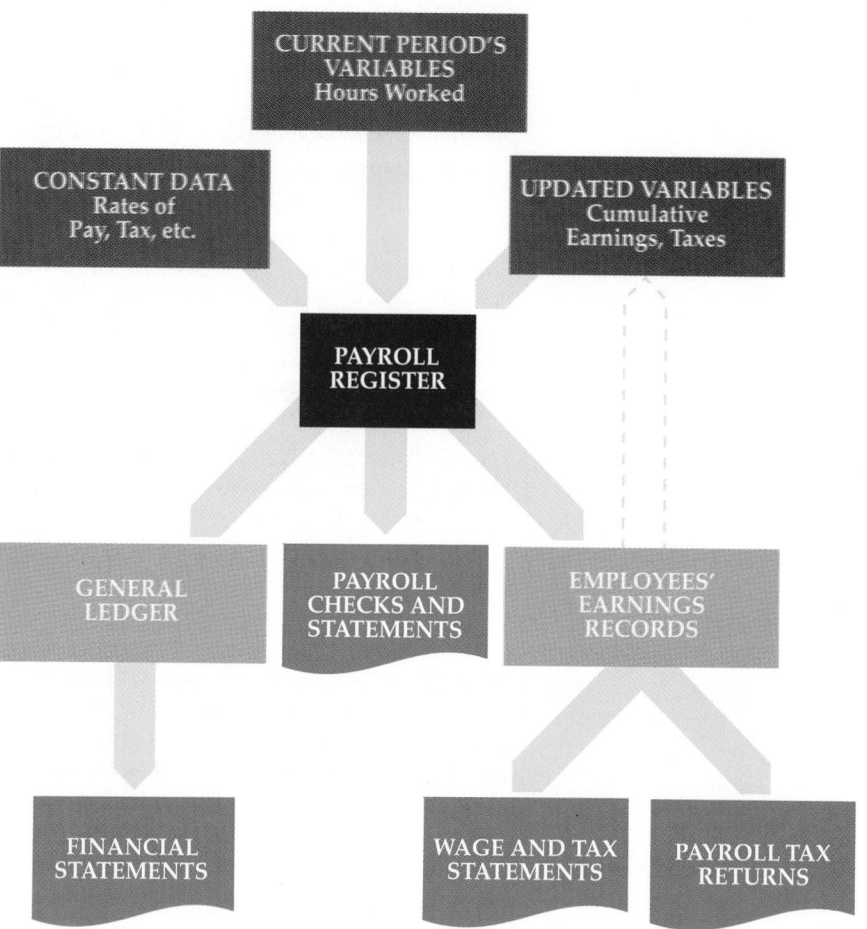

The focus in the preceding discussion has been on the outputs of a payroll system: the payroll register, payroll checks, the employee's earnings record, and tax and other reports. As shown in the diagram in Exhibit 7, the inputs into a payroll system may be classified as either constants or variables. Constants are data that remain unchanged from payroll to payroll and thus do not need to be inputted into the system each pay period. Variables are data that change from payroll to payroll and thus must be inputted into the system each pay period.

Examples of constants include such data as each employee's name and social security number, marital status, number of income tax withholding allowances, rate of pay, payroll category (office, sales, etc.), and department where employed. The FICA tax rates and various tax tables are also constants that apply to all employees. Examples of variables include such data as the number of hours or days worked for each employee during the payroll period, days of sick leave with pay, vacation credits, and cumulative earnings and taxes withheld. If salespersons are paid commissions, the amount of their sales would also vary from period to period.

Internal Controls for Payroll Systems

The processing of payroll, as discussed above, requires the input of a large amount of data, along with numerous, sometimes complex, computations. These factors, combined with the large dollar amounts involved, require controls to ensure that payroll payments are timely and accurate. In addition, the system must also provide adequate safeguards against theft or other misuse of funds.

One scheme to misuse payroll funds was portrayed in the movie *Superman III*. In this movie, actor Richard Pryor played a computer programmer, Gus Gorman, who embezzled payroll funds. Gus programmed the computer to round down each employee's payroll amount to the nearest penny. The amount "rounded out" was then added to Gus's payroll check. For example, if an employee's total payroll was $458.533, the payroll program would pay the employee $458.53 and add the $.003 to a special account. The total in this special account would be transferred to Gus's paycheck at the end of the processing of the payroll. In this way, Gus's check increased from $143.80 to $85,000 in one pay period.

The cash payment controls discussed in the cash chapter also apply to payrolls. Thus, it is normally desirable to use a voucher system that includes procedures for proper authorization and approval of payroll. When a check-signing machine is used, it is important that blank payroll checks and access to the machine be carefully controlled to prevent the theft or misuse of payroll funds.

It is especially important to authorize and approve in writing the additions and deletions of employees and changes in pay rates. For example, numerous payroll frauds have occurred where fictitious employees have been added to the payroll by a supervisor. The supervisor then cashes the fictitious employees' checks. Similar frauds have occurred where employees have been fired, but the Payroll Department is not notified. As a result, payroll checks to the fired employees are prepared and cashed by a supervisor.

To prevent or detect frauds such as those described above, employees' attendance records should be controlled. For example, many companies use "In and Out" cards on which employees record their time of arrival to and departure from work. These cards are inserted in a time clock, which automatically records the time. A Payroll Department employee may be stationed near the time clock during normal arrival and departure times in order to verify that employees only "clock in" once and only for themselves. Employee identification cards or badges may also be used to verify that only authorized employees are clocking in and are permitted entrance to work areas. When payroll checks are distributed, employee identification cards may be used to deter one employee from picking up another's check.

Other controls include verification and approval of all payroll rate changes. In addition, in a computerized system, all program changes should be properly approved and tested by employees who are independent of the payroll system. This would prevent or detect any changes such as those portrayed in the movie mentioned above. The use of a special payroll bank account, as discussed earlier in the chapter, also enhances control over payroll.

EMPLOYEES' FRINGE BENEFITS

Objective 3
Journalize entries for employee fringe benefits, including vacation pay and pensions.

Many companies provide their employees a variety of benefits in addition to salary and wages earned. These benefits are often called **fringe benefits**. Such benefits may take many forms, including vacations, pension plans, and health, life, and disability insurance. When the employer pays part or all of the cost of the fringe benefits, these costs must be recognized as expenses. To properly match revenues and expenses, the estimated cost of these benefits should be recorded as an expense during the period in which the employee earns the benefit. The following paragraphs discuss applying this matching concept to vacation pay and pension costs.

Vacation Pay

Most employers grant vacation rights, sometimes called compensated absences, to their employees. To properly match revenues and expense, employees' vacation pay should be accrued as a liability as the vacation rights are earned.[6] The entry to accrue vacation pay may be recorded in total at the end of each fiscal year, or it may be recorded at the end of each pay period. To illustrate this latter case, assume that employees earn one day of vacation for each month worked during the year. Assume also that the estimated vacation pay for the payroll period ending May 5 is $2,000. The entry to record the accrued vacation pay for this pay period is shown below.

May 5	Vacation Pay Expense	2,000	
	Vacation Pay Payable		2,000
	Vacation pay for week ended May 5.		

If employees are required to take all their vacation time within one year, the vacation payable is reported on the balance sheet as a current liability. If employees are allowed to accumulate their vacation time from year to year, the estimated portion of vacation payable that is applicable to time that will not be taken within one year is reported as a long-term liability on the balance sheet.

When payroll is prepared for the period in which the employees have taken vacations, the vacation payable is reduced. The entry debits Vacation Pay Payable and credits Salaries Payable and the other related accounts for recording taxes and withholdings.

Pensions

In the past twenty years, retirement pension plans have increased rapidly in number, variety, and complexity. Although such plans vary from employer to employer, pension benefits are normally based on employee age, years of service, and salary level. In 1974, Congress enacted the Employee Retirement Income Security Act (ERISA), which set forth guidelines for safeguarding employee benefits.

Pension plans may be classified as contributory or noncontributory, funded or unfunded, and qualified or unqualified. A **contributory plan** requires the employer to withhold a portion of each employee's earnings as a contribution to the plan. The employer then makes a contribution according to the provisions of the plan. A **noncontributory plan** requires the employer to bear the entire cost.

A **funded plan** requires the employer to set aside funds to meet future pension benefits by making payments to an independent funding agency. The funding agency is responsible for managing the assets of the pension fund and for disbursing the pension benefits to employees. For many pension plans, insurance companies serve as the funding agency. An **unfunded plan** is managed entirely by the employer instead of by an independent agency.

A **qualified plan** is designed to comply with federal income tax requirements. Plans meeting these requirements allow the employer to deduct pension contributions for tax purposes and exempt the pension fund income from tax. Most pension plans are qualified.

The accounting for pension plans is usually very complex due to the uncertainties of projecting future pension obligations. Such obligations depend upon such factors as employee life expectancies, expected employee compensation levels, and investment income on pension contributions. Pension funding obligations are estimated by using sophisticated mathematical and statistical models.

The employer's cost of an employee's pension plan in a given period is called the **net periodic pension cost**. This cost is debited to an operating expense ac-

---

[6] *Statement of Financial Accounting Standards, No. 43,* "Accounting for Compensated Absences" (Stamford: Financial Accounting Standards Board, 1980), par. 6.

count, Pension Expense.[7] Cash is credited if the pension cost is fully funded. If the pension cost is partially funded, any unfunded amount is credited to Unfunded Pension Liability. For example, assume that the pension plan of Flossmoor Industries requires an annual pension cost of $25,000, and Flossmoor Industries pays $15,000 to the fund trustee, Equity Insurance Company. The entry to record the transaction is as follows:

Pension Expense		25,000	
Cash			15,000
Unfunded Pension Liability			10,000

If the unfunded pension liability is to be paid within one year, it will be classified on the balance sheet as a current liability. That portion of the liability to be paid beyond one year is classified as a long-term liability.

An entity's financial statements should fully disclose the nature of its pension plans and pension obligations. These disclosures are usually included as footnotes to the financial statements. They should include the net periodic pension cost and a description of the plan, which includes such items as the employees covered and the accounting and funding policies used. In addition, any changes that affect the ability to compare pension costs and obligations among years should be disclosed.

When a pension plan is first adopted or later changed, the employer must decide whether to grant employees credit for prior years' service. If a company does grant credit to employees for prior service, a prior service cost obligation is recognized. A prior service cost is normally funded over a number of years, thus creating a long-term prior service pension liability. The complex nature of accounting for prior service costs is left for more advanced accounting study.

SHORT-TERM NOTES PAYABLE

Objective 4
Journalize entries for short-term notes payable.

Notes may be issued to creditors to temporarily satisfy an account payable created earlier. They may also be issued at the time merchandise or other assets are purchased. For example, assume that an enterprise issues a 90-day, 12% note for $1,000, dated August 1, 1994, to Murray Co. for a $1,000 overdue account. The entry to record the issuance of the note is as follows:

Aug. 1	Accounts Payable—Murray Co.	1,000	
	Notes Payable		1,000
	Issued a 90-day, 12% note on account.		

At the time the note matures, the entry to record the payment of $1,030 ($1,000 principal plus $30 interest) is as follows:

Oct. 30	Notes Payable	1,000	
	Interest Expense	30	
	Cash		1,030

The interest expense account is closed at December 31, and the amount is reported in the Other Expense section of the income statement for the year ended December 31, 1994.

---

[7] *Statement of Financial Accounting Standards*, No. 87, "Employers' Accounting for Pensions" (Stamford: Financial Accounting Standards Board, 1985), par. 6.

The preceding entries for notes payable are similar to those discussed in an earlier chapter for notes receivable. Notes payable entries are presented from the viewpoint of the borrower, while notes receivable entries are presented from the viewpoint of the creditor or lender. To illustrate, the following entries are journalized for a borrower (Bowden Co.), who issues a note payable to a creditor (Coker Co.):

	Bowden Co. (Borrower)			Coker Co. (Creditor)		

May 1. Bowden Co. purchased merchandise on account from Coker Co., $10,000, 2/10, n/30.	Purchases
	   Accounts Payable
		10,000	10,000	Accounts Receivable
				   Sales
					10,000	10,000

May 31. Bowden Co. issued a 60-day, 12% note for $10,000 to Coker Co. on account.	Accounts Payable
	   Notes Payable
		10,000	10,000	Notes Receivable
				   Accounts Receivable
					10,000	10,000

July 30. Bowden Co. paid Coker Co. the amount due on the note of May 31. Interest: $10,000 × 12% × 60/360	Notes Payable
	Interest Expense
	   Cash
		10,000
		200
			10,200	Cash
				   Interest Income
				   Notes Receivable
					10,200	200
						10,000

Notes may also be issued when money is borrowed from banks. Although the terms may vary, many banks would accept from the borrower an interest-bearing note for the amount of the loan. For example, assume that on September 19 a firm borrows $4,000 from the First National Bank by giving the bank a 90-day, 15% note. The entry to record the receipt of cash and the issuance of the note is as follows:

Sep. 19	Cash	4,000	
	Notes Payable		4,000

On the due date of the note (December 18), the borrower owes $4,000, the principal of the note, plus interest of $150. The entry to record the payment of the note is as follows:

Dec. 18	Notes Payable	4,000	
	Interest Expense	150	
	Cash		4,150

Sometimes a borrower will issue a non-interest-bearing note to the bank rather than an interest-bearing note. The face amount of the note is the amount that is to be paid at maturity. Although such a note does not specify an interest rate, the bank sets a rate of interest and deducts the interest from the maturity value of the note. The borrower is given the remainder. This deduction of interest from the maturity value is called **discounting**. The rate used in computing the amount deducted is called the **discount rate,** and the deduction is called the **discount**. The net amount received by the borrower is called the **proceeds**.

To illustrate, assume that on August 10 an enterprise issues to a bank a $4,000, 90-day, non-interest-bearing note, which the bank discounts at a rate of 15%. The amount of the discount is $150, and the proceeds are $3,850. The entry to record the issuance of the note is as follows:

Aug. 10	Cash	3,850	
	Interest Expense	150	
	Notes Payable		4,000

Cash is debited for the proceeds received from the bank from issuance of the note. Since most discounted notes mature within a short period of time, the amount of the discount is normally debited to Interest Expense at the time of issuance. If the accounting period ends before the maturity date of the note, an adjusting entry should be prepared, allocating the interest expense between accounting periods. Notes Payable is credited for the face amount of the note, which is also its maturity value.

When the note in the preceding illustration is paid, the following entry is recorded:

| Nov. 8 | Notes Payable | 4,000 | |
| | Cash | | 4,000 |

Short-term notes payable are presented in the Current Liabilities section of the balance sheet. If the market (fair) value of short-term notes payable differs from the carrying (book) value, the market value of the notes should be disclosed in notes to the financial statements.[8] In most cases, however, the carrying value of short-term notes payable approximates the market value, and such disclosures are unnecessary.

PRODUCT WARRANTY LIABILITY

Objective 5
Journalize entries for product warranties.

At the time of sale, a company may grant a warranty on a product. To match revenues and expenses properly, warranty costs should be recognized as expenses in the same period in which the revenues to which they relate are recorded. In other words, estimated warranty costs should be recognized as expenses in the period in which the sale is recorded.[9] Later, when the product is repaired or replaced, the liability will be reduced.

To illustrate, assume that during June a company sells $60,000 of a product, on which there is a 36-month warranty for repairing defects in the product. Past experience indicates that the average cost to repair defects is 5% of the sales price. The entry to record the estimated warranty expense for June is as follows:

June 30	Product Warranty Expense	3,000	
	Product Warranty Payable		3,000
	Product warranty for June, 5% × $60,000.		

When the defective product is repaired, the repair costs are recorded by debiting Product Warranty Payable and crediting Cash, Supplies, or other appropriate accounts.

---

[8] *Statement of Financial Accounting Standards, No. 107*, "Disclosures about Fair Value of Financial Instruments" (Norwalk: Financial Accounting Standards Board, 1991), pars. 10 and 13.
[9] *Statement of Financial Accounting Standards, No. 5*, "Accounting for Contingencies" (Stamford: Financial Accounting Standards Board, 1975), pars. 8 and 24.

CHAPTER REVIEW

Key Points

Objective 1. Determine employer's liabilities for payroll, including liabilities arising from employee earnings and deductions from earnings.

An employer's liability for payroll is calculated by determining employees' total earnings for a payroll period, including bonuses and overtime pay. From this amount is subtracted employee deductions to arrive at the net pay to be paid each employee. Employer's liabilities for employee deductions are recognized at the time the payroll is recorded. Most employers also incur liabilities for payroll taxes, such as FICA tax, federal unemployment compensation tax, and state unemployment compensation tax.

Objective 2. Record payroll and payroll taxes, using a payroll register, employees' earnings records, and a general journal.

The payroll register is a multicolumn form used in assembling and summarizing the data needed each payroll period. The data recorded in the payroll register include the number of hours worked and the earnings and deduction data for each employee. The sum of the deductions for each employee is subtracted from the total earnings to yield the amount to be paid. Check numbers are recorded in the payroll register as evidence of payment to each employee. The payroll register also includes columns for accumulating total wages or salaries to be debited to the various expense accounts.

Amounts in the payroll register may be posted directly to the accounts. Alternatively, the payroll register may be used as a supporting record for recording the payroll for the period in the general journal. The payroll register is supported by a detailed payroll record for each employee, called an employee's earnings record.

Objective 3. Journalize entries for employee fringe benefits, including vacation pay and pensions.

Fringe benefits should be recognized as expenses of the period in which the employees earn the benefits. Fringe benefits are recorded by debiting an expense account and crediting a liability account. For example, the entry to record accrued vacation pay debits Vacation Pay Expense and credits Vacation Pay Payable.

Objective 4. Journalize entries for short-term notes payable.

A note issued to a creditor to temporarily satisfy an account payable is recorded as a debit to Accounts Payable and a credit to Notes Payable. At the time the note is paid, Notes Payable and Interest Expense are debited and Cash is credited. Notes may also be issued to purchase merchandise or other assets or to borrow money from a bank. When a non-interest-bearing note is issued to a bank, Interest (discount) Expense is debited for the interest deduction at the time of issuance, Cash is debited for the proceeds, and Notes Payable is credited for the face value of the note.

Objective 5. Journalize entries for product warranties.

If a company grants a warranty on a product, an estimated warranty expense and liability should be recorded in the period of the sale. The expense and the liability are recorded by debiting Product Warranty Expense and crediting Product Warranty Payable.

Glossary of Key Terms

Discount. The interest deducted from the maturity value of a note. **Objective 4**

Discount rate. The rate used in computing the interest to be deducted from the maturity value of a note. **Objective 4**

Employee's earnings record. A detailed record of each employee's earnings. **Objective 2**

FICA tax. Federal Insurance Contributions Act tax used to finance federal programs for old-age and disability benefits (social security) and health insurance for the aged (Medicare). **Objective 1**

Gross pay. The total earnings of an employee for a payroll period. **Objective 1**

Net pay. Gross pay less payroll deductions; the amount the employer is obligated to pay the employee. **Objective 1**

Payroll. The total amount paid to employees for a certain period. **Objective 1**

Payroll register. A multicolumn form used to assemble and summarize payroll data at the end of each payroll period. **Objective 2**

Proceeds. The net amount available from discounting a note. **Objective 4**

Self-Examination Questions

Answers at end of chapter.

1. An employee's rate of pay is $20 per hour, with time and a half for all hours worked in excess of 40 during a week. The FICA rate is 7.5% on the first $60,000 of annual earnings and 1.5% on earnings between $60,000 and $140,000. The following additional data are available:

Hours worked during current week 45
Year's cumulative earnings prior to current week $59,400
Federal income tax withheld 212

Based on these data, the amount of the employee's net pay for the current week is:

A. $620.50
B. $641.50
C. $666.75
D. $687.75

2. Which of the following taxes are employers usually not required to withhold from employees?
   A. Federal income tax
   B. Federal unemployment compensation tax
   C. FICA tax
   D. State and local income taxes

3. With limitations on the maximum earnings subject to the tax, employers do not incur operating costs for which of the following payroll taxes?
   A. FICA tax
   B. Federal unemployment compensation tax
   C. State unemployment compensation tax
   D. Employees' federal income tax

4. An enterprise issued a $5,000, 60-day, 12% note to the bank. The amount due at maturity is:
   A. $4,900
   B. $5,000
   C. $5,100
   D. $5,600

5. An enterprise issued a $5,000, 60-day, non-interest-bearing note to the bank, and the bank discounts the note at 12%. The proceeds are:
   A. $4,400
   B. $4,900
   C. $5,000
   D. $5,100

ILLUSTRATIVE PROBLEM

Selected transactions of Grainger Company, completed during the fiscal year ended December 31, are as follows:

Mar. 1. Purchased merchandise on account from Perry Co., $15,000.
Apr. 10. Issued a 60-day, 12% note for $15,000 to Perry Co. on account.
June 9. Paid Perry Co. the amount owed on the note of April 10.
Aug. 1. Issued a 90-day, non-interest-bearing note for $30,000 to Atlantic Coast National Bank. The bank discounted the note at 15%.
Oct. 30. Paid Atlantic Coast National Bank the amount due on the note of August 1.
Dec. 27. Journalized the entry to record the biweekly payroll. A summary of the payroll record follows:

Salary distribution:		
Sales	$50,800	
Officers	25,800	
Office	6,400	$83,000
Deductions:		
FICA tax	$ 4,820	
Federal income tax withheld	13,280	
State income tax withheld	3,840	
Savings bond deductions	630	
Medical insurance deductions	960	23,530
Net amount		$59,470

30. Issued a check in payment of employees' federal income tax of $13,280 and FICA tax of $9,640 due.
31. Issued a check for $8,600 to the pension fund trustee to fully fund the pension cost for December.
31. Journalized an entry to record the employees' accrued vacation pay, $32,200.
31. Journalized an entry to record the estimated accrued product warranty liability, $41,360.

Instructions
Journalize the preceding transactions, using a general journal.

Solution

Mar. 1	Purchases	15,000	
	Accounts Payable—Perry Co.		15,000
Apr. 10	Accounts Payable—Perry Co.	15,000	
	Notes Payable		15,000
June 9	Notes Payable	15,000	
	Interest Expense	300	
	Cash		15,300

Aug.	1	Cash	28,875	
		Interest Expense	1,125	
		Notes Payable		30,000
Oct.	30	Notes Payable	30,000	
		Cash		30,000
Dec.	27	Sales Salaries Expense	50,800	
		Officers Salaries Expense	25,800	
		Office Salaries Expense	6,400	
		FICA Tax Payable		4,820
		Employees Federal Income Tax Payable		13,280
		Employees State Income Tax Payable		3,840
		Bond Deductions Payable		630
		Medical Insurance Payable		960
		Salaries Payable		59,470
	30	Employees Federal Income Tax Payable	13,280	
		FICA Tax Payable	9,640	
		Cash		22,920
	31	Pension Expense	8,600	
		Cash		8,600
	31	Vacation Pay Expense	32,200	
		Vacation Pay Payable		32,200
	31	Product Warranty Expense	41,360	
		Product Warranty Payable		41,360

DISCUSSION QUESTIONS

1. What term is frequently used to refer to the total amount paid to employees for a certain period?
2. If an employee is granted an income-sharing bonus, is the amount of the bonus (a) part of the employee's earnings and (b) deductible as an expense of the enterprise in determining the federal income tax?
3. The general manager of a business enterprise is entitled to an annual income-sharing bonus of 6%. For the current year, income before bonus and income taxes is $250,000, and income taxes are estimated at 35% of income before income taxes. Calculate the amount of the bonus, assuming that the bonus is based on net income after deducting both bonus and income taxes.
4. What is (a) gross pay? (b) net, or take-home, pay?
5. What programs are funded by the FICA (Federal Insurance Contributions Act) tax?
6. a. Identify the federal taxes that most employers are required to withhold from employees.
   b. Give the titles of the accounts to which the amounts withheld are credited.
7. For each of the following payroll-related taxes, indicate whether there is a ceiling on the annual earnings subject to the tax: (a) FICA tax, (b) federal income tax, (c) federal unemployment compensation tax.
8. An employee earns $18 per hour and 1½ times that rate for all hours in excess of 40 per week. If the employee worked 50 hours during the current week, what was the gross pay for the week?
9. Based on the data presented in Question 8, calculate the net pay for the current week assuming that gross pay prior to the current week totaled $49,760, the FICA tax rate was 7.5% (with earnings up to $60,000 subject to the 7.5% rate), and federal income tax to be withheld was $195.
10. Identify the payroll taxes levied against employers.
11. Why are deductions from employees' earnings classified as liabilities for the employer?
12. Do payroll taxes levied against employers become liabilities at the time the liabilities for wages are incurred or at the time the wages are paid?
13. Taylor Company, with 20 employees, is expanding operations. It is trying to decide whether to hire one employee full-time for $25,000 or two employees part-time for a total of $25,000. Would any of the employer's payroll taxes discussed in this chapter have a bearing on this decision? Explain.

14. For each of the following payroll-related taxes, indicate whether they generally apply to (a) employees only, (b) employers only, (c) both employees and employers:
    1. FICA tax
    2. Federal income tax
    3. Federal unemployment compensation tax
    4. State unemployment compensation tax

15. What type of information is recorded in the employee's earnings record and for what purpose is this information used?

16. An employer pays the employees in currency, and the pay envelopes are prepared by an employee rather than by the bank. (a) Why would it be advisable to obtain from the bank the exact amount of money needed for a payroll? (b) How could the exact number of each bill and coin denomination needed be determined efficiently in advance?

17. What are the principal reasons for using a special payroll checking account?

18. A company uses a weekly payroll period and a special bank account for payroll. (a) When should deposits be made in the account? (b) How is the amount of the deposit calculated? (c) Is it necessary to have in the general ledger an account entitled "Cash—Special Payroll Account"? Explain. (d) The bank statement for the payroll bank account for the month ended June 30 indicates a bank balance of $7,127.50. Assuming that the bank has made no errors, what does this amount represent?

19. In a payroll system, what type of input data are referred to as (a) constants, (b) variables?

20. To strengthen internal controls, what department should provide written authorizations for the addition of names to the payroll?

21. Explain how a payroll system that is properly designed and operated tends to ensure (a) that wages paid are based upon hours actually worked, and (b) that payroll checks are not issued to fictitious employees.

22. What are employee fringe benefits? Give three examples of such fringe benefits.

23. To match revenues and expenses properly, should the expense for employee vacation pay be recorded in the period during which the vacation privilege is earned or during the period in which the vacation is taken? Discuss.

24. Differentiate between a contributory and a noncontributory pension plan.

25. Identify several factors that influence the future pension obligation of an enterprise.

26. How does prior service cost arise in a new or revised pension plan?

27. Where should the unfunded pension liability be reported on the balance sheet?

28. A bank has two alternatives in making a $30,000 loan: (1) accepting a $30,000, 60-day, 10% note or (2) discounting a $30,000 non-interest-bearing note at 10%. Which alternative is more favorable to the bank? Explain.

29. A business enterprise issued a 90-day, 10% note for $15,000 to a creditor on account. Give the entries to record (a) the issuance of the note and (b) the payment of the note at maturity, including interest of $375.

30. In borrowing money from a bank, an enterprise issued a $50,000, 60-day, non-interest-bearing note, which the bank discounted at 12%. Are the proceeds $50,000? Explain.

31. When should the liability associated with a product warranty be recorded? Discuss.

REAL WORLD FOCUS

32. The 1991 annual report for Maytag Corporation reported the following data with respect to product warranties in the liability section of its December 31, 1991 balance sheet:

    Accrued Liabilities:
        Warranties $48,614,000

    a. What entry would have been made to record the accrued product warranty costs at December 31, 1991, assuming that no entry had been made in prior years?
    b. How would costs of repairing a defective product be recorded?

REAL WORLD FOCUS

33. The "Questions and Answers Technical Hotline" in the *Journal of Accountancy* included the following question:

    Several years ago, Company B instituted legal action against Company A. Under a memorandum of settlement and agreement, Company A agreed to pay Company B a total of $17,500 in three installments—$5,000 on March 1, $7,500 on July 1 and the remaining $5,000 on December 31. Company A paid the first two installments during its fiscal year ended September 30. Should the unpaid amount of $5,000 be presented as a current liability at September 30?

    How would you answer this question?

ETHICS DISCUSSION CASE

Ellen Burks, a CPA and staff assistant for a local CPA firm, noticed on her payroll stub covering the two-week period of April 5-18 that her overtime pay had been computed on the basis of 2 times her regular pay rate, rather than 1½ times her regular rate. Ellen has decided to cash the payroll check. If her employer later catches the error, Ellen plans to deny having originally noticed the mistake.

Discuss whether Ellen Burks is behaving in an ethical manner.

SHARPEN YOUR ►
COMMUNICATION SKILLS

EXERCISES

EXERCISE 12-1
INCOME-SHARING BONUS
Objective 1

The general manager of a business enterprise is entitled to an annual income-sharing bonus of 5%. For the current year, income before bonus and income taxes is $400,000, and income taxes are estimated at 35% of income before income taxes.

Calculate the amount of the bonus, assuming that (a) the bonus is based on income before deductions for bonus and income taxes, and (b) the bonus is based on income after deductions for bonus and income taxes.

EXERCISE 12-2
SUMMARY PAYROLL DATA
Objectives 1, 2

In the following summary of data for a payroll period, some amounts have been intentionally omitted:

Earnings:
1. At regular rate   ? *88,900*
2. At overtime rate $6,100
3. Total earnings   ? *95,000*

Deductions:
4. FICA tax $ 6,500
5. Income tax withheld   10,750
6. Medical insurance   1,050
7. Union dues   ? *1,150*
8. Total deductions   19,450
9. Net amount paid   75,550

Accounts debited:
10. Factory Wages $71,500
11. Sales Salaries   ? *16,000*
12. Office Salaries   7,500

a. Calculate the amounts omitted in lines (1), (3), (7), and (11).
b. Journalize the entry to record the payroll.
c. In general journal form, journalize the entry to record the voucher for the payroll.
d. In general journal form, journalize the entry to record the payment of the voucher.
e. From the data given in this exercise and your answer to (a), would you conclude that this payroll was paid sometime during the first few weeks of the calendar year? Explain.

SHARPEN YOUR ►
COMMUNICATION SKILLS

EXERCISE 12-3
INTERNAL CONTROL
PROCEDURES
Objective 2

Gem City Sounds is a retail store specializing in the sale of jazz compact disks and cassettes. The store employs 3 full-time and 10 part-time workers. The store's weekly payroll averages $1,800 for all 13 workers.

Gem City Sounds uses a personal computer to assist with the preparation of paychecks. Each week, the store's accountant collects employee time cards and enters the hours worked into the payroll program. The payroll program calculates each employee's pay and prints a paycheck. The accountant uses a check-signing machine to sign the paychecks. Next, a voucher is prepared to transfer funds from the store's regular bank account to the payroll account. This voucher is authorized by the store's owner.

For the week of May 10, the accountant accidentally recorded 400 hours worked instead of 40 hours for one of the full-time employees. Does Gem City have internal controls in place to catch this error? If so, how will this error be detected?

EXERCISE 12-4
INTERNAL CONTROL
PROCEDURES
Objective 2

Smart Shop Inc. is a small manufacturer of home workshop power tools. The company employs 30 production workers and 10 administrative persons. The following procedures are used to process the company's weekly payroll:

a. Smart Shop maintains a separate checking account for payroll checks. Each week, the total net pay for all employees is transferred from the company's regular bank account to the payroll account.
b. Paychecks are signed by using a check-signing machine. This machine is located in the main office, so that it can be easily accessed by anyone needing a check signed.

c. All employees are required to record their hours worked by clocking in and out on a time clock. Employees must clock out for lunch break. Due to congestion around the time clock area at lunch time, management has not objected to having one employee clock in and out for an entire department.

d. Whenever an employee receives a pay raise, the supervisor must fill out a wage adjustment form, which is signed by the company president. This form is used to change the employee's wage rate in the payroll system.

e. Whenever a salaried employee is terminated, Personnel authorizes Payroll to remove the employee from the payroll system. However, this procedure is not required when an hourly worker is terminated. Hourly employees only receive a paycheck if their time card shows hours worked. The computer automatically drops an employee from the payroll system when that employee has six consecutive weeks with no hours worked.

SHARPEN YOUR COMMUNICATION SKILLS ►

State whether each of the procedures is appropriate or inappropriate after considering the principles of internal control. If a procedure is inappropriate, state what action must be taken to correct it.

EXERCISE 12-5
PAYROLL TAX ENTRIES
Objective 2

According to a summary of the payroll of O'Hare Publishing Co., the amount of earnings for the payroll paid on November 30 of the current year was $540,000. Of this amount, $510,000 was subject to the 7.5% FICA tax rate and $30,000 was subject to the 1.5% FICA tax rate. Also, $15,000 was subject to state and federal unemployment taxes.

a. Calculate the employer's payroll taxes expense on the payroll, using the following rates: state unemployment, 4.3%; federal unemployment, 0.8%.

b. Journalize the entry to record the accrual of payroll taxes.

EXERCISE 12-6
ACCRUED VACATION PAY
Objective 3

A business enterprise provides its employees with varying amounts of vacation per year, depending on the length of employment. The estimated amount of the current year's vacation pay is $186,000. Journalize the adjusting entry required on January 31, the end of the first month of the current year, to record the accrued vacation pay.

EXERCISE 12-7
PENSION PLAN ENTRIES
Objective 3

Tice Company maintains a funded pension plan for its employees. The plan requires quarterly installments to be paid to the funding agent, Interstate Insurance Company, by the fifteenth of the month following the end of each quarter. If the pension cost is $75,000 for the quarter ended December 31, journalize entries to record (a) the accrued pension liability on December 31 and (b) the payment to the funding agent on January 15.

EXERCISE 12-8
ENTRIES FOR DISCOUNTING NOTES
Objective 4

Clark Co. issues a 60-day, non-interest-bearing note for $100,000 to First National Bank and Trust Co., and the bank discounts the note at 12%.

a. Journalize the maker's entries to record:
   1. the issuance of the note.
   2. the payment of the note at maturity.

b. Journalize the payee's entries to record:
   1. the receipt of the note.
   2. the receipt of payment of the note at maturity.

EXERCISE 12-9
CALCULATION OF INTEREST ON NOTES ISSUED
Objective 4

In negotiating a 90-day loan, an enterprise has the option of either (1) issuing a $250,000, non-interest-bearing note that will be discounted at the rate of 10%, or (2) issuing a $250,000 note that bears interest at the rate of 10% and that will be accepted at face value.

a. Calculate the amount of the interest expense for each option.

b. Calculate the amount of the proceeds for each option.

SHARPEN YOUR COMMUNICATION SKILLS ►

c. Which option is more favorable to the borrower? Explain.

EXERCISE 12-10
PLANT ASSET PURCHASES WITH NOTE
Objective 4

On June 30, Candice Company purchased land for $200,000 and a building for $670,000, paying $150,000 cash and issuing a 10% note for the balance, secured by a mortgage on the property. The terms of the note provide for 18 semiannual payments of $40,000 on the principal plus the interest accrued from the date of the preceding payment. Journalize the entry to record (a) the transaction on June 30, (b) the payment of the first installment on December 31, and (c) the payment of the second installment the following June 30.

EXERCISE 12-11
ACCRUED PRODUCT WARRANTY
Objective 5

Blair Company warrants its products for one year. The estimated product warranty is 2% of sales. If sales were $750,000 for January, journalize the adjusting entry required at January 31, the end of the first month of the current year, to record the accrued product warranty.

WhAT'S WROnG
WITH THi2?

The fiscal year for K. L. Clark Co. ends on June 30. However, the company computes and reports payroll taxes on the calendar-year basis. What is wrong with these procedures for accounting for payroll taxes?

PROBLEMS

Series A

PROBLEM 12-1A
INCOME-SHARING
BONUSES
Objective 1

The Chief Operating Officer (COO) of TX Co. is entitled to an annual income-sharing bonus of 5%. For the current year, income before bonus and income taxes is $309,000, and income taxes are estimated at 40% of income before income taxes.

Instructions

1. Calculate the amount of the bonus, assuming that:
   a. The bonus is based on income before deductions for bonus and income taxes.
   b. The bonus is based on income after deduction for bonus but before deduction for income taxes.
   c. The bonus is based on income after deduction for income taxes but before deduction for bonus.
   d. The bonus is based on income after deductions for bonus and income taxes.

SHARPEN YOUR ►
COMMUNICATION SKILLS

2. a. Which bonus plan would the COO prefer? Discuss.
   b. Would this plan always be the COO's choice, regardless of TX Co.'s income level? Discuss.

PROBLEM 12-2A
ENTRIES FOR PAYROLL AND
PAYROLL TAXES
Objectives 1, 2

The following information relative to the payroll for the week ended December 30 was obtained from the records of D. N. Bonnar Co.:

Salaries:		Deductions:	
Sales salaries	$ 86,500	Income tax withheld	$18,050
Warehouse salaries	18,980	FICA tax withheld	8,175
Office salaries	9,520	Group insurance	1,350
	$115,000	U.S. savings bonds	1,200

Tax rates assumed:
  FICA, 7.5% on first $60,000 and 1.5% on $60,000 to $140,000 of annual earnings
  State unemployment (employer only), 4.2%
  Federal unemployment, 0.8%

Instructions

1. Assuming that the payroll for the last week of the year is to be paid on December 31, journalize the following entries:
   a. December 30, to record the payroll.
   b. December 30, to record the employer's payroll taxes on the payroll to be paid on December 31. Of the total payroll for the last week of the year, $9,000 is subject to unemployment compensation taxes.
2. Assuming that the payroll for the last week of the year is to be paid on January 5 of the following year, journalize the following entries:
   a. December 31, to record the payroll.
   b. January 5, to record the employer's payroll taxes on the payroll to be paid on January 5.

If the working papers correlating with the textbook are not used, omit Problem 12-3A.

PROBLEM 12-3A
PAYROLL REGISTER
Objectives 1, 2

The payroll register for C. L. Pugh Co. for the week ended December 12 of the current fiscal year is presented in the working papers.

Instructions

1. Journalize the entry to record the payroll for the week.
2. Assuming the use of a voucher system and payment by regular check, journalize the entries, in general journal form, to record the payroll voucher and the issuance of the checks to employees.

3. Journalize the entry to record the employer's payroll taxes for the week. Assume the following tax rates: state unemployment, 3.1%; federal unemployment, 0.8%. Of the earnings, $1,020 is subject to unemployment taxes.

4. Journalize the entries, in general journal form, to record the following selected transactions:

Dec. 16. Prepared a voucher, payable to Burbank National Bank, for employees' income taxes, $937.00, and FICA taxes, $766.06.

16. Issued a check to Burbank National Bank in payment of the voucher.

PROBLEM 12-4A
WAGE AND TAX
STATEMENT DATA AND
EMPLOYER FICA TAX
Objectives 1, 2

Graham Company began business on January 2 of last year. Salaries were paid to employees on the last day of each month, and both FICA tax and federal income tax were withheld in the required amounts. An employee who is hired in the middle of the month receives half the monthly salary for that month. All required payroll tax reports were filed and the correct amount of payroll taxes was remitted by the company for the calendar year. Before the Wage and Tax Statements (Form W-2) could be prepared for distributing to employees and filing with the Social Security Administration, the employees' earnings records were inadvertently destroyed.

None of the employees resigned or were discharged during the year, and there were no changes in salary rates. The FICA tax was withheld at the rate of 7.5% on the first $60,000 of salary and at the rate of 1.5% on salary from $60,000 to $140,000. Data on dates of employment, salary rates, and employees' income taxes withheld, which are summarized as follows, were obtained from personnel records and payroll records.

Employee	Date First Employed	Monthly Salary	Monthly Income Tax Withheld
Alvarez	Jan. 16	$2,800	$ 471
Cruz	Nov. 1	2,500	394
Funk	Jan. 2	4,200	895
Little	July 16	3,400	636
Powell	Jan. 2	5,400	1,374
Soong	May 1	3,600	652
Wilson	Feb. 16	4,000	864

Instructions

SPREADSHEET
PROBLEM

1. Calculate the amounts to be reported on each employee's Wage and Tax Statement (Form W-2) for the year, arranging the data in the following form:

Employee	Gross Earnings	Federal Income Tax Withheld	FICA Tax Withheld

2. Calculate the following employer payroll taxes for the year: (a) FICA; (b) state unemployment compensation at 4.2% on the first $7,000 of each employee's earnings; (c) federal unemployment compensation at 0.8% on the first $7,000 of each employee's earnings; (d) total.

PROBLEM 12-5A
PAYROLL REGISTER
Objectives 1, 2

The following data for Butler Co. relate to the payroll for the week ended December 7, 1993:

Employee	Hours Worked	Hourly Rate	Weekly Salary	Federal Income Tax	U.S. Savings Bonds	Accumulated Earnings, Nov. 30
A	40	$20.00		$166	$25.00	$38,880
B	42	20.00		265	37.50	40,500
C			$1,200	300	50.00	60,000
D	40	11.00		68		22,000
E	40	15.00		115	25.00	30,000
F	48	12.75		125		15,300
G	40	14.00		93	25.00	28,000
H			350	35		2,100
I	20	11.00		15		2,700
J	40	15.00		81		30,000

Employees C and H are office staff, and all of the other employees are sales personnel. All sales personnel are paid 1½ times the regular rate for all hours in excess of 40 hours per week. The FICA tax rate is 7.5% on the first $60,000 of annual earnings and 1.5% of annual earnings from $60,000 to $140,000 for each employee. The next payroll check to be used is No. 818.

Instructions

1. Prepare a payroll register for Butler Co., similar to the one in Exhibit 3, for the week ended December 7, 1993.
2. Journalize the entry to record the payroll for the week.

SPREADSHEET PROBLEM

PROBLEM 12-6A
PAYROLL ACCOUNTS, ENTRIES WITH VOUCHER AND CHECK REGISTERS, AND YEAR-END ENTRIES
Objectives 1, 2

The following accounts, with the balances indicated, appear in the ledger of Becker Company on December 1 of the current year:

212	Salaries Payable	—
213	FICA Tax Payable	$ 6,000
214	Employees Federal Income Tax Payable	7,500
215	Employees State Income Tax Payable	13,260
216	State Unemployment Tax Payable	1,710
217	Federal Unemployment Tax Payable	360
218	Bond Deductions Payable	715
219	Medical Insurance Payable	3,875
611	Sales Salaries Expense	631,300
711	Officers Salaries Expense	311,800
712	Office Salaries Expense	85,500
719	Payroll Taxes Expense	92,430

The following transactions relating to payroll, payroll deductions, and payroll taxes occurred during December:

Dec. 2. Prepared Voucher No. 637 for $715, payable to Marine National Bank, to purchase U.S. savings bonds for employees.
     2. Issued Check No. 620 in payment of Voucher No. 637.
     3. Prepared Voucher No. 638 for $13,500, payable to Marine National Bank for $6,000 of FICA tax and $7,500 of employees' federal income tax due.
     3. Issued Check No. 621 in payment of Voucher No. 638.
    14. Journalized the entry to record the biweekly payroll. A summary of the payroll record follows:

Salary distribution:		
Sales	$30,600	
Officers	15,200	
Office	3,800	$49,600
Deductions:		
FICA tax	$ 3,250	
Federal income tax withheld	7,790	
State income tax withheld	1,920	
Savings bond deductions	315	
Medical insurance deductions	480	13,755
Net amount		$35,845

    14. Prepared Voucher No. 646, payable to Payroll Bank Account, for the net amount of the biweekly payroll.
    14. Issued Check No. 627 in payment of Voucher No. 646.
    14. Journalized the entry to record payroll taxes on employees' earnings of December 14: FICA, $3,250; state unemployment tax, $163; federal unemployment tax, $35.
    17. Prepared Voucher No. 647 for $14,290, payable to Marine National Bank for $6,500 of FICA tax and $7,790 of employees' federal income tax due.
    17. Issued Check No. 633 in payment of Voucher No. 647.
    18. Prepared Voucher No. 650 for $3,875, payable to Wilson Insurance Company, for the semiannual premium on the group medical insurance policy.
    19. Issued Check No. 639 in payment of Voucher No. 650.
    28. Journalized the entry to record the biweekly payroll. A summary of the payroll record follows:

Salary distribution:

Sales	$28,500	
Officers	15,200	
Office	3,800	$47,500

Deductions:

FICA tax	$ 3,010	
Federal income tax withheld	7,565	
State income tax withheld	1,845	
Savings bond deductions	315	12,735
Net amount		$34,765

28. Prepared Voucher No. 684, payable to Payroll Bank Account, for the net amount of the biweekly payroll.

28. Issued check No. 671 in payment of Voucher No. 684.

28. Journalized the entry to record payroll taxes on employees' earnings of December 28: FICA, $3,010; state unemployment tax, $160; federal unemployment tax, $33.

30. Prepared Voucher No. 690 for $630, payable to Marine National Bank, to purchase U.S. savings bonds for employees.

30. Issued Check No. 680 in payment of Voucher No. 690.

30. Prepared Voucher No. 691 for $13,260, payable to Marine National Bank, for employees' state income tax due on December 31.

30. Issued Check No. 681 in payment of Voucher No. 691.

Instructions

1. Enter the balances in the accounts as of December 1.

2. Journalize the transactions, using a voucher register, a check register, and a general journal. The only amount columns needed in the voucher register are Accounts Payable Cr. and Other Accounts Dr. (subdivided into Account, Post. Ref., and Amount). The only amount columns needed in the check register are Accounts Payable Dr. and Cash in Bank Cr. Post to the accounts.

3. Journalize the adjusting entry on December 31 to record salaries for the incomplete payroll period. Salaries accrued are as follows: sales salaries, $2,950; officers salaries, $1,640; office salaries, $410. The payroll taxes are immaterial and are not accrued. Post to the accounts.

4. Journalize the entry to close the salary expense and payroll taxes expense accounts to Income Summary, and post to the accounts.

SOLUTIONS SOFTWARE

Instructions for Solving Problem 12-6A Using Solutions Software

1. Load opening balances.

2. Save the opening balances file to your drive and directory.

3. Set the run date to December 31 of the current year and enter your name.

4. Key the transactions, using the General Journal, the New Vouchers Journal, and the Cash Payments Journal.

5. Display a report for the entries in the General Journal, the New Vouchers Journal, and the Cash Payments Journal.

6. Display a trial balance.

7. Key the adjusting entries for payroll only. All other adjustments have been made. Key ADJ.ENT. in the reference field.

8. Display the financial statements.

9. Save a backup copy of your data file.

10. Perform period-end closing.

11. Display a post-closing trial balance.

12. Save your data file to disk.

13. End the session.

PROBLEM 12-7A
PURCHASES AND NOTES
PAYABLE TRANSACTIONS
Objectives 3, 4, 5

The following items were selected from among the transactions completed by Landon Co. during the current year:

Jan. 15. Purchased merchandise on account from Wyatt Co., $7,800.

Mar. 1. Purchased merchandise on account from Evans Co., $9,600.

6. Issued a 30-day, 12% note for $7,800 to Wyatt Co., on account.

10. Paid Evans Co. for the invoice of March 1, less 1% discount.

Apr. 5. Paid Wyatt Co. the amount owed on the note on March 6.

July 15. Borrowed $8,000 from Royal National Bank, issuing a 90-day, 13% note.

25. Issued a 120-day, non-interest-bearing note for $20,000 to Barnett State Bank. The bank discounted the note at the rate of 15%.

Oct. 13. Paid Royal National Bank the interest due on the note of July 15 and renewed the loan by issuing a new 30-day, 15% note for $8,000. (Journalize both the debit and credit to the notes payable account.)

Nov. 12. Paid Royal National Bank the amount due on the note of October 13.

    22. Paid Barnett State Bank the amount due on the note of July 25.

Dec. 1. Purchased office equipment from Bunn Equipment Co. for $57,500, paying $7,500 and issuing a series of ten 12% notes for $5,000 each, coming due at 30-day intervals.

    31. Paid the amount due Bunn Equipment Co. on the first note in the series issued on December 1.

    31. Paid $27,500 of the annual pension cost of $40,000. (Record both the payment and unfunded pension liability.)

Instructions

1. Journalize the transactions.
2. Journalize the adjusting entries for each of the following accrued expenses for the current year:
   a. Vacation pay $15,000
   b. Product warranty cost   12,750
3. Journalize the adjusting entry for the accrued interest at December 31 on the nine notes owed to Bunn Equipment Co.
4. Assume that a single note for $50,000 had been issued on December 1 instead of the series of ten notes and that its terms required principal payments of $5,000 each 30 days, with interest at 12% on the principal balance before applying the $5,000 payment. Calculate the amount that would have been due and payable on December 31.

Instructions for Solving Problem 12-7A Using Solutions Software

1. Load opening balances.
2. Save the opening balances file to your drive and directory.
3. Set the run date to December 31 of the current year and enter your name.
4. Select the General Journal Entries option and key the journal entries. Leave the reference field blank. Note: To review the chart of accounts, select F-1.
5. Display a journal entries report.
6. Display a trial balance.
7. Key the adjusting entries. Key ADJ.ENT. in the reference field.
8. Display the financial statements.
9. Save a backup copy of your data file.
10. Perform period-end closing.
11. Display a post-closing trial balance.
12. Save your data file to disk.
13. End the session.

SOLUTIONS SOFTWARE

Series B

PROBLEM 12-1B
INCOME-SHARING
BONUSES
Objective 1

The Chief Operating Officer (COO) of General Products Co. is entitled to an annual income-sharing bonus of 4%. For the current year, income before bonus and income taxes is $720,000, and income taxes are estimated at 40% of income before income taxes.

Instructions

1. Calculate the amount of the bonus, assuming that:
   a. The bonus is based on income before deductions for bonus and income taxes.
   b. The bonus is based on income after deduction for bonus but before deduction for income taxes.
   c. The bonus is based on income after deduction for income taxes but before deduction for bonus.
   d. The bonus is based on income after deductions for bonus and income taxes.

SHARPEN YOUR COMMUNICATION SKILLS

2. a. Which bonus plan would the COO prefer? Discuss.
   b. Would this plan always be the COO's choice, regardless of General Products Co.'s income level? Discuss.

PROBLEM 12-2B
ENTRIES FOR PAYROLL AND
PAYROLL TAXES
Objectives 1, 2

The following information relative to the payroll for the week ended December 30 was obtained from the records of E. Thurmond Co.:

Salaries:		Deductions:	
Sales salaries	$148,700	Income tax withheld	$33,850
Warehouse salaries	21,280	FICA tax withheld	8,460
Office salaries	12,020	U.S. savings bonds	4,400
	$182,000	Group insurance	2,800

Tax rates assumed:

FICA, 7.5% on first $60,000 and 1.5% on $60,000 to $140,000 of annual earnings

State unemployment (employer only), 3.8%

Federal unemployment, 0.8%

Instructions

1. Assuming that the payroll for the last week of the year is to be paid on December 31, journalize the following entries:
   a. December 30, to record the payroll.
   b. December 30, to record the employer's payroll taxes on the payroll to be paid on December 31. Of the total payroll for the last week of the year, $15,000 is subject to unemployment compensation taxes.
2. Assuming that the payroll for the last week of the year is to be paid on January 4 of the following fiscal year, journalize the following entries:
   a. December 30, to record the payroll.
   b. January 4, to record the employer's payroll taxes on the payroll to be paid on January 4.

If the working papers correlating with the textbook are not used, omit Problem 12-3B.

PROBLEM 12-3B
PAYROLL REGISTER
Objectives 1, 2

The payroll register for L. C. Herbert Co. for the week ended December 12 of the current fiscal year is presented in the working papers.

Instructions

1. Journalize the entry to record the payroll for the week.
2. Assuming the use of a voucher system and payment by regular check, journalize the entries, in general journal form, to record the payroll voucher and the issuance of the checks to employees.
3. Journalize the entry to record the employer's payroll taxes for the week. Assume the following tax rates: state unemployment, 3.8%; federal unemployment, 0.8%. Of the earnings, $1,020 is subject to unemployment taxes.
4. Journalize the entries, in general journal form, to record the following selected transactions:

   Dec. 15. Prepared a voucher, payable to Second National Bank, for employees' income taxes, $937.00, and FICA taxes, $766.06.
         15. Issued a check to Second National Bank in payment of the voucher.

PROBLEM 12-4B
WAGE AND TAX
STATEMENT DATA AND
EMPLOYER FICA TAX
Objectives 1, 2

Griffin Company began business on January 2 of last year. Salaries were paid to employees on the last day of each month, and both FICA tax and federal income tax were withheld in the required amounts. An employee who is hired in the middle of the month receives half the monthly salary for that month. All required payroll tax reports were filed and the correct amount of payroll taxes was remitted by the company for the calendar year. Before the Wage and Tax Statements (Form W-2) could be prepared for distributing to employees and filing with the Social Security Administration, the employees' earnings records were inadvertently destroyed.

None of the employees resigned or were discharged during the year, and there were no changes in salary rates. The FICA tax was withheld at the rate of 7.5% on the first $60,000 of salary and at the rate of 1.5% on salary from $60,000 to $140,000. Data on dates of employment, salary rates, and employees' income taxes withheld, which are summarized as follows, were obtained from personnel records and payroll records.

Employee	Date First Employed	Monthly Salary	Monthly Income Tax Withheld
Allen	June 2	$2,500	$ 417
Cox	Jan. 2	4,200	854
Gower	Mar. 1	3,800	748
Nunn	Jan. 2	4,000	810
Quinn	Nov. 15	3,600	652
Ruiz	Apr. 15	2,800	461
Wu	Jan. 16	5,300	1,261

**SPREADSHEET
PROBLEM**

Instructions

1. Calculate the amounts to be reported on each employee's Wage and Tax Statement (Form W-2) for the year, arranging the data in the following form:

Employee	Gross Earnings	Federal Income Tax Withheld	FICA Tax Withheld

2. Calculate the following employer payroll taxes for the year: (a) FICA; (b) state unemployment compensation at 3.8% on the first $7,000 of each employee's earnings; (c) federal unemployment compensation at 0.8% on the first $7,000 of each employee's earnings; (d) total.

PROBLEM 12-5B
PAYROLL REGISTER
Objectives 1, 2

The following data for Butler Co. relate to the payroll for the week ended December 7, 1993:

Employee	Hours Worked	Hourly Rate	Weekly Salary	Federal Income Tax	U.S. Savings Bonds	Accumulated Earnings, Nov. 30
A	44	$20.00		$280	$37.50	$44,700
B	40	20.00		166	25.00	38,880
C			$1,120	270	50.00	60,000
D	40	15.00		81		30,000
E	40	15.00		115	25.00	30,000
F	48	12.75		125		15,300
G	40	14.00		93	25.00	28,000
H			400	40		3,200
I	20	11.00		15		2,700
J	40	11.00		68		22,000

Employees C and H are office staff, and all of the other employees are sales personnel. All sales personnel are paid 1½ times the regular rate for all hours in excess of 40 hours per week. The FICA tax rate is 7.5% on the first $60,000 of annual earnings and 1.5% of annual earnings from $60,000 to $140,000 for each employee. The next payroll check to be used is No. 981.

Instructions

1. Prepare a payroll register for Butler Co. for the week ended December 7, 1993.
2. Journalize the entry to record the payroll for the week.

PROBLEM 12-6B
PAYROLL ACCOUNTS,
ENTRIES WITH VOUCHER
AND CHECK REGISTERS,
AND YEAR-END ENTRIES
Objectives 1, 2

The following accounts, with the balances indicated, appear in the ledger of Sims and Coen Co. on December 1 of the current year:

212	Salaries Payable	—
213	FICA Tax Payable	$ 7,550
214	Employees Federal Income Tax Payable	9,070
215	Employees State Income Tax Payable	14,586
216	State Unemployment Tax Payable	1,881
217	Federal Unemployment Tax Payable	396
218	Bond Deductions Payable	800
219	Medical Insurance Payable	3,200
611	Sales Salaries Expense	694,430
711	Officers Salaries Expense	342,980
712	Office Salaries Expense	94,050
719	Payroll Taxes Expense	101,673

The following transactions relating to payroll, payroll deductions, and payroll taxes occurred during December:

Dec. 2. Prepared Voucher No. 745 for $800, payable to First National Bank, to purchase U.S. savings bonds for employees.
　　2. Issued Check No. 728 in payment of Voucher No. 745.
　　3. Prepared Voucher No. 746 for $16,620, payable to First National Bank for $7,550 of FICA tax and $9,070 of employees' federal income tax due.
　　3. Issued Check No. 729 in payment of Voucher No. 746.
　14. Journalized the entry to record the biweekly payroll. A summary of the payroll record follows:

Salary distribution:

Sales	$33,660	
Officers	16,720	
Office	4,180	$54,560

Deductions:

FICA tax	$ 3,575	
Federal income tax withheld	8,569	
State income tax withheld	2,112	
Savings bond deductions	375	
Medical insurance deductions	528	15,159
Net amount		$39,401

Dec. 14. Prepared Voucher No. 757, payable to Payroll Bank Account, for the net amount of the biweekly payroll.

14. Issued Check No. 738 in payment of Voucher No. 757.

14. Journalized the entry to record payroll taxes on employees' earnings of December 14: FICA, $3,575; state unemployment tax, $162; federal unemployment tax, $35.

17. Prepared Voucher No. 758 for $15,719, payable to First National Bank for $7,150 of FICA tax and $8,569 of employees' federal income tax due.

17. Issued Check No. 744 in payment of Voucher No. 758.

18. Prepared Voucher No. 760 for $3,200, payable to Pico Insurance Company, for the semiannual premium on the group medical insurance policy.

19. Issued Check No. 750 in payment of Voucher No. 760.

28. Journalized the entry to record the biweekly payroll. A summary of the payroll record follows:

Salary distribution:

Sales	$31,350	
Officers	16,720	
Office	4,180	$52,250

Deductions:

FICA tax	$ 3,311	
Federal income tax withheld	8,322	
State income tax withheld	2,029	
Savings bond deductions	375	14,037
Net amount		$38,213

28. Prepared Voucher No. 795, payable to Payroll Bank Account, for the net amount of the biweekly payroll.

28. Issued Check No. 782 in payment of Voucher No. 795.

28. Journalized the entry to record payroll taxes on employees' earnings of December 28: FICA, $3,311; state unemployment tax, $161; federal unemployment tax, $33.

30. Prepared Voucher No. 801 for $750, payable to First National Bank, to purchase U.S. savings bonds for employees.

30. Issued Check No. 791 in payment of Voucher No. 801.

30. Prepared Voucher No. 802 for $14,586, payable to First National Bank, for employees' state income tax due on December 31.

30. Issued Check No. 792 in payment of Voucher No. 802.

Instructions

1. Enter the balances in the accounts as of December 1.

2. Journalize the transactions, using a voucher register, a check register, and a general journal. The only amount columns needed in the voucher register are Accounts Payable Cr. and Other Accounts Dr. (subdivided into Account, Post. Ref., and Amount). The only amount columns needed in the check register are Accounts Payable Dr. and Cash in Bank Cr. Post to the accounts.

3. Journalize the adjusting entry on December 31 to record salaries for the incomplete payroll period. Salaries accrued are as follows: sales salaries, $3,245; officers salaries, $1,800; office salaries, $450. The payroll taxes are immaterial and are not accrued. Post to the accounts.

4. Journalize the entry to close the salary expense and payroll taxes expense accounts to Income Summary, and post to the accounts.

Instructions for Solving Problem 12-6B Using Solutions Software

1. Load opening balances.
2. Save the opening balances file to your drive and directory.
3. Set the run date to December 31 of the current year and enter your name.
4. Key the transactions, using the General Journal, the New Vouchers Journal, and the Cash Payments Journal.
5. Display a report for the entries in the General Journal, the New Vouchers Journal, and the Cash Payments Journal.
6. Display a trial balance.
7. Key the adjusting entries for payroll only. All other adjustments have been made. Key ADJ.ENT. in the reference field.
8. Display the financial statements.
9. Save a backup copy of your data file.
10. Perform period-end closing.
11. Display a post-closing trial balance.
12. Save your data file to disk.
13. End the session.

PROBLEM 12-7B
PURCHASES AND NOTES
PAYABLE TRANSACTIONS
Objectives 3, 4, 5

The following items were selected from among the transactions completed by Otis Co. during the current year:

Mar. 2. Purchased merchandise on account from Clark Co., $5,000.
        8. Purchased merchandise on account from Malone Co., $10,000.
       12. Paid Clark Co. for the invoice of March 2, less 2% discount.
Apr. 1. Issued a 60-day, 12% note for $10,000 to Malone Co., on account.
May 10. Issued a 120-day, non-interest-bearing note for $45,000 to Garden City Bank. The bank discounted the note at the rate of 14%.
       31. Paid Malone Co. the amount owed on the note of April 1.
Aug. 5. Borrowed $7,500 from First Financial Corporation, issuing a 60-day, 14% note for that amount.
Sep. 7. Paid Garden City Bank the amount due on the note of May 10.
Oct. 4. Paid First Financial Corporation the interest due on the note of August 5 and renewed the loan by issuing a new 30-day, 16% note for $7,500. (Record both the debit and credit to the notes payable account.)
Nov. 3. Paid First Financial Corporation the amount due on the note of October 4.
       15. Purchased store equipment from Sims Equipment Co. for $50,000, paying $8,000 and issuing a series of seven 12% notes for $6,000 each, coming due at 30-day intervals.
Dec. 15. Paid the amount due Sims Equipment Co. on the first note in the series issued on November 15.
       31. Paid $32,400 of the annual pension cost of $45,000. (Record both the payment and the unfunded pension liability.)

Instructions

1. Journalize the transactions.
2. Journalize the adjusting entries for each of the following accrued expenses for the current year:
   a. Vacation pay $17,900
   b. Product warranty cost   15,000
3. Journalize the adjusting entry for the accrued interest at December 31 on the six notes owed to Sims Equipment Co.
4. Assume that a single note for $42,000 had been issued on November 15 instead of the series of seven notes and that its terms required principal payments of $6,000 each 30 days, with interest at 12% on the principal balance before applying the $6,000 payment. Calculate the amount that would have been due and payable on December 15.

Instructions for Solving Problem 12-7B Using Solutions Software

1. Load opening balances.
2. Save the opening balances file to your drive and directory.
3. Set the run date to December 31 of the current year and enter your name.
4. Select the General Journal Entries option and key the journal entries. Leave the reference field blank. Note: To review the chart of accounts, select F-1.

5. Display a journal entries report.
6. Display a trial balance.
7. Key the adjusting entries. Key ADJ.ENT. in the reference field.
8. Display the financial statements.
9. Save a backup copy of your data file.
10. Perform period-end closing.
11. Display a post-closing trial balance.
12. Save your data file to disk.
13. End the session.

MINI-CASE 12 E. ROBB AND CO.

In 1992, your mother retired as president of the family-owned business, E. Robb and Co., and a new president was recruited by an executive search firm. The new president's contract called for an annual base salary of $80,000 plus a bonus of 12% of income after deducting the bonus but before deducting income taxes.

In 1993, the first full year under the new president, E. Robb and Co. reported income of $910,000 before deducting the bonus and income taxes. After being fired on January 3, 1994, the new president demanded immediate payment of a $109,200 bonus for 1993.

Your mother was concerned about the accounting practices used during 1993, and she has asked you to help her in reviewing the accounting records before the bonus is paid. Upon investigation, you have discovered the following facts:

a. The payroll for December 27-31, 1993, was not accrued at the end of the year. The salaries for the five-day period and the applicable payroll taxes are as follows:

Sales salaries	$9,000
Office salaries	3,000
FICA tax	7.5%
State unemployment tax (employer only)	3.2%
Federal unemployment tax	.8%

The payroll was paid on January 9, 1994, for the period December 27, 1993, through January 7, 1994.

b. The semiannual pension cost of $22,500 was not accrued for the last half of 1993. The pension cost was paid to Reliance Insurance Company on January 12, 1994, and was journalized by a debit to Pension Expense and a credit to Cash for $22,500.
c. The estimated product warranty liability of $12,000 for products sold during the year ended December 31, 1993, was not journalized.
d. On July 1, 1993, a one-year insurance policy was purchased for $10,640, debiting the cost to Prepaid Insurance. No adjusting entry was made for insurance expired at December 31, 1993.
e. The vacation pay liability of $12,000 for the year ended December 1993, was not journalized.

Instructions

1. Based on reported 1993 income of $910,000 before deducting the bonus and income taxes, was the president's calculation of the $109,200 bonus correct? Explain.
2. What accounting errors were made in 1993 that would affect the amount of the president's bonus?
3. Based on the employment contract and your answer to (2), what is the correct amount of the president's bonus for 1993?
4. How much did the president's demand for a $109,200 bonus exceed the correct amount of the bonus under the employment contract?
5. ▪▪▪ ▸ Describe the major advantage and disadvantage of using income-sharing bonuses in employment contracts.

COMPREHENSIVE PROBLEM 4

Selected transactions completed by Key Company during its first fiscal year ending December 31 were as follows:

a. Prepared a voucher to establish a petty cash fund of $300 and issued a check in payment of the voucher. (Journalize two entries.)
b. Prepared a voucher to replenish the petty cash fund, based on the following summary of petty cash receipts: office supplies, $95; miscellaneous selling expense, $97; miscellaneous administrative expense, $90.
c. Prepared a voucher for the purchase of $5,000 of merchandise, 1/10, n/30. Purchase invoices are recorded at the net amount.
d. Paid the invoice in (c) after the discount period had passed.
e. Received cash from daily cash sales for $9,050. The amount indicated by the cash register was $9,060.
f. Received a 60-day, 10% note for $30,000 on account.

g. Discounted note received in (f) at the bank, 30 days prior to maturity, at 12%.
h. Received notice from the bank that the note discounted in (g) had been dishonored. Paid the bank the maturity value of the note.
i. Received amount owed on dishonored note in (h) plus interest for 36 days at 10% computed on the maturity value of the note.
j. Received $800 on account and wrote off the remainder owed on a $1,500 accounts receivable balance. (The allowance method is used in accounting for uncollectible receivables.)
k. Reinstated the account written off in (j) and received $700 cash in full payment.
l. Traded office equipment on May 31 for new equipment with a list price of $125,000. A trade-in allowance of $30,000 was received on the old equipment that had cost $90,000 and had accumulated depreciation of $65,000 as of May 31. A voucher was prepared for the amount owed of $95,000.
m. Journalized the monthly payroll for November, based on the following data:

Salaries:		Deductions:	
Sales salaries	$ 9,500	Income tax withheld	$2,950
Office salaries	4,500	FICA tax withheld	900
	$14,000		

Unemployment tax rates assumed:
State unemployment, 3.8%
Federal unemployment, .8%
Amount subject to unemployment taxes:
State unemployment $2,000
Federal unemployment 2,000

n. Journalized the employer's payroll taxes on the payroll in (m).
o. Issued a 90-day, non-interest-bearing note for $25,000 to the bank, which discounted it at 12%.
p. Journalized voucher for payment of the note in (o) at maturity.
q. The pension cost for the year was $34,000, and a voucher was prepared for $25,000, payable to the trustee for the funded portion.

Instructions

1. Journalize the selected transactions in general journal form.
2. Based on the following data, prepare a bank reconciliation for November of the current year:
   a. Balance according to the bank statement at November 30, $89,030.
   b. Balance according to the ledger at November 30, $60,130.
   c. Checks outstanding at November 30, $56,630.
   d. Deposit in transit, not recorded by bank, $27,600.
   e. Bank debit memorandum for service charges, $40.
   f. A check for $100 in payment of a voucher was erroneously recorded in the accounts as $10.
3. Based on the bank reconciliation prepared in (2), journalize in general journal form the entry or entries to be made by Key Company.
4. Based on the following selected data, journalize the adjusting entries as of December 31 of the current year:
   a. Estimated uncollectible accounts at December 31, $5,950. The balance of Allowance for Doubtful Accounts at December 31 was $900 (debit).
   b. Merchandise inventory data are indicated in the following schedule:

Purchases Invoices

Item	1st	2d	3d	Inventory Count at December 31
C10	50 at $1,940	30 at $1,950	60 at $2,000	45
D35	25 at 1,100	20 at 1,185	25 at 1,200	30
L11	75 at 550	100 at 575	100 at 575	80
K72	10 at 2,600	10 at 2,600	10 at 2,675	15
V17	5 at 4,100	7 at 4,200	—	4

The inventory is determined by the periodic method and is costed by the last-in, first-out method.

c. Prepaid insurance expired during the year, $18,400.

d. Office supplies used during the year, $5,100.

e. Depreciation is computed as follows:

Asset	Cost	Residual Value	Acquisition Date	Useful Life in Years	Depreciation Method Used
Buildings	$225,000	0	January 2	50	Straight-line
Office Equip.	120,000	$12,000	July 1	5	Sum-of-the-years-digits
Store Equip.	60,000	10,000	January 3	8	Declining-balance (at twice the straight-line rate)

f. A patent costing $18,000 when acquired on January 2 has a remaining legal life of 9 years, and was expected to have value for 6 years.

g. The cost of mineral rights was $50,000. Of the estimated deposit of 25,000 tons of ore, 6,000 tons were mined during the year.

h. Total vacation pay expense for the year, $7,000.

i. A product warranty was granted beginning December 1 and covering a one-year period. The estimated cost is 3% of sales, which totaled $150,000 in December.

5. Based on the following post-closing trial balance and other data, prepare a balance sheet in report form at December 31 of the current year:

Key Company
Post-Closing Trial Balance
December 31, 19—

Petty Cash	300	
Cash	59,250	
Marketable Equity Securities	40,000	
Allowance for Decline to Market		4,510
Notes Receivable	50,000	
Accounts Receivable	152,300	
Allowance for Doubtful Accounts		5,950
Merchandise Inventory	220,250	
Prepaid Insurance	12,950	
Office Supplies	2,300	
Land	50,000	
Buildings	225,000	
Accumulated Depreciation—Buildings		4,500
Office Equipment	120,000	
Accumulated Depreciation—Office Equipment		18,000
Store Equipment	60,000	
Accumulated Depreciation—Store Equipment		15,000
Mineral Rights	50,000	
Accumulated Depletion		12,000
Patents	15,000	
FICA Tax Payable		2,100
Employees Federal Income Tax Payable		2,950
State Unemployment Tax Payable		1,520
Federal Unemployment Tax Payable		320
Salaries Payable		14,000
Accounts Payable		88,000
Product Warranty Payable		4,500
Vacation Pay Payable		7,000
Unfunded Pension Liability		2,000
Notes Payable		450,000
Jim Key, Capital		425,000
	1,057,350	1,057,350

The following information relating to the balance sheet accounts at December 31 is obtained from supplementary records:

Notes receivable is a current asset.
The merchandise inventory is stated at cost by the lifo method.
The product warranty payable is a current liability.
Vacation pay payable:

Current liability	$5,000
Long-term liability	2,000

The unfunded pension liability is a long-term liability.
Notes payable:

Current liability	$50,000
Long-term liability	400,000

6. Assuming that the general manager had been granted a 4% income-sharing bonus (based on income after deduction for the bonus) and income before the bonus was $208,000, what would have been the amount of the bonus?

7. On February 7 of the following year, the merchandise inventory was destroyed by fire. Based on the following data obtained from the accounting records, estimate the cost of the merchandise destroyed:

Jan. 1 Merchandise inventory	$220,250
Jan. 1–Feb. 7 Purchases (net)	189,750
Sales (net)	350,000
Estimated gross profit rate	35%

Instructions for Solving Comprehensive Problem 4 Using Solutions Software

SOLUTIONS
SOFTWARE

1. Load opening balances.
2. Save the opening balances file to your drive and directory.
3. Set the run date to December 31 of the current year and enter your name.
4. Select the General Journal Entries option and key the journal entries. Use December 31 of the current year as the date for each entry. Key (a), (b), etc., in the reference field to identify each transaction.
5. Display a journal entries report.
6. Display a trial balance.
7. Key the adjusting entries. Key ADJ.ENT. in the reference field.
8. Display the financial statements.
9. Save a backup copy of your data file.
10. Perform period-end closing.
11. Display a post-closing trial balance.
12. Save your data file to disk.
13. End the session.

ANSWERS TO SELF-EXAMINATION QUESTIONS

1. **D** The amount of net pay of $687.75 (answer D) is determined as follows:

Gross pay:

40 hours at $20	$800.00	
5 hours at $30	150.00	$950.00
Deductions:		
Federal income tax withheld	$212.00	
FICA:		
$600 × .075	$45.00	
$350 × .015	5.25	50.25	262.25
Net pay		$687.75

2. **B** Employers are usually required to withhold a portion of the earnings of their employees for payment of federal income taxes (answer A), FICA tax (answer C), and state and local income taxes (answer D). Generally, federal unemployment compensation taxes (answer B) are levied against the employer only and thus are not deducted from employee earnings.

3. **D** The employer incurs operating costs for FICA tax (answer A), federal unemployment compensation tax (answer B), and state unemployment compensation tax (answer C). The employees' federal income tax (answer D) is not an operating cost of the employer. It is withheld from the employees' earnings.

4. **C** The maturity value is $5,100, determined as follows:

Face amount of note	$5,000
Plus interest ($5,000 × 12/100 × 60/360)	100
Maturity value	$5,100

5. **B** The net amount available to a borrower from discounting a note payable is called the proceeds. The proceeds of $4,900 (answer B) is determined as follows:

Face amount of note	$5,000
Less discount ($5,000 × 12/100 × 60/360)	100
Proceeds	$4,900

Part 4

Accounting Principles

CHAPTER 13
Concepts and
Principles

You and Accounting

How many triangles are there in the figure below?[1]

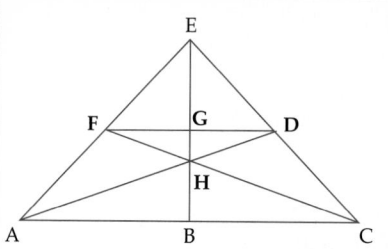

The answer to this puzzle is at the end of this chapter, following the answers to the self-examination questions. Given the physical principles and concepts of geometry, there is only one correct answer to this puzzle. Unlike geometry, however, concepts and principles of accounting are developed through consensus and general acceptance. In many cases, there are equally acceptable methods of recording transactions. This chapter discusses the development of accounting concepts and principles. Ten of the most important concepts and principles are discussed and illustrated.

[1] Pat Battaglia, *So You Think You're Smart*, "150 Fun and Challenging Brain Teasers" (Tab Books: Blue Ridge Summit, Pa., 1988), p. 34.

Chapter 13
Concepts and Principles

The evolution of accounting has been closely related to the economic development of the United States. In the early stages of the American economy, a business enterprise was very often managed by its owner. The accounting records and reports were used mainly by the owner-manager in conducting business operations. Bankers and other lenders often relied on their personal relationship with the owner, rather than on financial statements, as the basis for making loans to a business. If a large amount was owed to a bank or supplier, the creditor might participate in management decisions.

As business enterprises grew in size and complexity, *outsiders* became less familiar with management and day-to-day operations of the business enterprise. As a result, the outsiders group, which includes owners, creditors, government, labor unions, customers, and the general public, demanded accurate financial information for use in evaluating the performance of management. In addition, as the size of business enterprises and the complexity of transactions increased, the accounting issues involved in preparing financial statements became more and more complex. With these developments came a need for a framework of concepts and principles to serve as guidelines for preparing financial statements. In this chapter, the basic accounting concepts and principles are discussed and illustrated.

DEVELOPMENT OF CONCEPTS AND PRINCIPLES

Objective 1
Describe the role of the FASB and other groups in the development of accounting concepts and principles.

Accounting *principles* represent guides based on reason and observation. They do not have the same universal authority as principles relating to the natural sciences, such as astronomy, physics, or chemistry. The primary criterion of use of an accounting concept or principle is its general acceptance among users of financial statements and members of the accounting profession. In most cases, accounting concepts and principles have been selected from among many alternatives. In some areas, a clear consensus and acceptance is still lacking. In addition, accounting concepts and principles are continually reexamined and revised in keeping pace with the increasing complexity of business operations.

The responsibility for developing accounting concepts and principles has rested primarily on practicing accountants and accounting educators. These individuals, working independently or under the sponsorship of various organizations, strive to develop sound accounting practices to meet user needs. Accounting concepts and principles have also been influenced by business practices and customs, ideas and beliefs of the users of the financial statements, governmental agencies, stock exchanges, and other business groups.

Financial Accounting Standards Board

The **Financial Accounting Standards Board (FASB)** is currently the primary body developing accounting principles. In 1973, the FASB replaced the **Accounting Principles Board (APB)**, which was the primary body developing accounting principles from 1959 to 1973. The APB was composed of eighteen accountants who were members of the American Institute of Certified Public Accountants (AICPA). These individuals served without pay and continued their employment with their firms or institutions.

The FASB is appointed by the Financial Accounting Foundation (FAF). The FAF is an independent, nonprofit organization that was created in 1972 to oversee the accounting standard-setting process. Its duties include appointing members of standard-setting boards (the FASB and the Governmental Accounting Standards Board) and advisory councils. It also raises funds for the operation of the standard-setting process.

The FASB is composed of seven members, four of whom must be CPAs drawn from public practice. These seven members serve full-time, receive a salary, and must resign from the firm or institution with which they have been employed.

The FASB employs a full-time research and administrative staff and often uses task forces to study specific issues in financial reporting. As these issues in financial reporting arise, the FASB conducts extensive research to identify the primary concerns involved and the possible solutions. Generally, after issuing discussion memoranda and preliminary proposals and evaluating comments from interested parties, the Board issues *Statements of Financial Accounting Standards*. These *Standards* become part of generally accepted accounting principles. To explain, clarify, or elaborate on existing standards, the Board also issues *Interpretations*, which have the same authority as the *Standards*.

As an ongoing project, the board has committed to developing a broad conceptual framework for financial accounting. This project is an attempt to develop a "constitution" that can be used to evaluate current and future standards. Although this project is expected to take many years to complete, six *Statements of Financial Accounting Concepts* have been published. These *Concepts* are briefly described below.

■ **Objectives of Financial Reporting by Business Enterprises (No. 1)**
Sets forth three broad objectives of financial reporting:

1. To provide financial information that is useful in making rational investment, credit, and similar decisions;

2. To provide financial information to enable users to predict cash flows to the business and subsequently to themselves;

3. To provide financial information about business resources (assets), claims to these resources (liabilities and owner's equity), and changes in these resources and claims.

■ **Qualitative Characteristics of Accounting Information (No. 2)**
Identifies the essential qualities of the accounting information included in financial reports as follows: usefulness, understandability, relevance, reliability, verifiability, timeliness, neutrality, completeness, and comparability.

■ **Elements of Financial Statements of Business Enterprises (No. 3)**
Replaced by Statement No. 6.

■ **Objectives of Financial Reporting by Nonbusiness Organizations (No. 4)**
Sets forth the objectives that guide the preparation of the financial statements for nonbusiness organizations.

■ **Recognition and Measurement in Financial Statements of Business Enterprises (No. 5)**
Identifies the financial statements that should be prepared to meet the objectives of financial reporting for business enterprises.

■ **Elements of Financial Statements (No. 6)**
Replaces Statement No. 3 and defines the interrelated elements of financial statements that are directly related to measuring the performance and status of businesses and nonprofit organizations.

The Importance of Accounting Standards

No amount of policing by the public accounting profession or regulatory agencies to prevent abuses in financial reporting can satisfy the public need for comparable information from all companies. Only financial accounting and reporting standards can satisfy that need. The challenge to the FASB is to strike a reasonable balance between the prevention of abuses and the portrayal of economic reality. As standard setters, we must try to avoid the concern about potential abuses leading to standards that make significantly different situations look the same—in other words, forcing square pegs into round holes.

Source: Donald J. Kirk, FASB chairman (From a speech before the National Association of Accountants Second Annual International-European Conference, Paris, April 19, 1985).

Governmental Accounting Standards Board

The **Governmental Accounting Standards Board (GASB)** was formed in 1984 as an extension of the Financial Accounting Foundation. The GASB has a full-time chairperson and four part-time members who are responsible for establishing accounting principles to be followed by state and municipal governments. The GASB employs a full-time research staff and administrative staff.

Accounting Organizations

Among the oldest and most influential organizations of accountants are the **American Institute of Certified Public Accountants (AICPA)** and the **American Accounting Association (AAA)**. Each organization publishes monthly or quarterly periodicals and often publishes research studies, technical opinions, and monographs. There are also other national accounting organizations as well as many state societies and local chapters of the national and state organizations. These groups provide forums for the interchange of ideas and discussion of accounting concepts and principles.

Government Organizations

Of the various governmental agencies, the **Securities and Exchange Commission (SEC)** is one of the most influential. Established by an act of Congress in 1934, the SEC regulates securities traded on the public stock exchanges and over the counter. The SEC's rules and regulations must be used in preparing financial statements and other reports filed with the Commission.

The **Internal Revenue Service (IRS)** oversees the laws and regulations for preparing federal tax returns. These laws and regulations determine how income is reported for federal income tax purposes. These rules sometimes conflict with generally accepted accounting principles for preparing financial statements. As a result, many enterprises maintain two sets of records to satisfy both reporting requirements. To avoid the costs of this increased record keeping, firms may adopt tax accounting methods for preparing financial statements. This is usually done when the results of using tax methods do not materially affect the financial statements.[2]

Other regulatory agencies exercise a major influence over the accounting principles of the industries under their jurisdiction. For example, the Controller of the Currency and the Federal Deposit Insurance Corporation greatly influence generally accepted accounting principles used by banks. In rare situations, Congress may also enact special laws that require firms to use specific accounting methods. These laws usually involve accounting methods for which no clear consensus has been reached within the profession.

Other Influential Organizations

The **Financial Executives Institute (FEI)**, whose membership consists of top financial executives, sponsors accounting research projects on major issues. The FEI also comments on proposed standards of the FASB, the SEC, and other organizations.

The **Institute of Management Accountants** (formerly the **National Association of Accountants**) is primarily concerned with management's use of accounting information. However, since management accountants prepare financial statements, the Institute is also interested in accounting principles that affect financial reporting. As a result, the Institute often comments on proposed principles.

In addition to the preceding organizations, other organizations representing users of accounting reports have had an influence on accounting principles. These organizations include the **Financial Analysts Federation** (investors and investment advisors) and the **Securities Industry Associates** (investment bankers).

Many accounting principles have been introduced and discussed in earlier chapters. The remainder of this chapter discusses the concepts and principles of greatest importance and use. Application of these principles to specific situations will also be illustrated.

BUSINESS ENTITY CONCEPT

Objective 2a
Describe and apply the business entity concept.

Under the **business entity concept,** it is assumed that a business enterprise is separate from the persons who supply its assets. This separation exists regardless of the legal form of the business organization. The business entity concept is implied by the accounting equation, Assets = Equities, or Assets = Liabilities + Owner's Equity. That is, the business owns the assets and must account for the use of the assets to the various equity holders (owners and creditors). Thus, accounting is mainly concerned with the enterprise as an economic (business) entity and reporting changes in its assets and related obligations.

The business entity concept used in accounting for a sole proprietorship is different from the legal concept of a sole proprietorship. In accounting for a sole

---

[2] A discussion of the nature of the income tax is presented in Appendix E.

proprietorship, the nonbusiness assets, liabilities, revenues, and expenses are excluded from the business accounts. If a sole proprietor owns two or more enterprises, each one is treated as a separate business entity for accounting purposes. Legally, however, a sole proprietor is personally liable for all business debts and may be required to use nonbusiness assets to satisfy the business creditors. Likewise, business assets may be required under law to be used to satisfy the claims of the sole proprietor's personal creditors.

Differences between the business entity concept and the legal nature of other forms of business organization will be considered in later chapters. Under generally accepted accounting principles, however, the revenue and expenses of an enterprise are viewed as affecting the business assets and liabilities, not the individual investor's assets and liabilities.

GOING CONCERN CONCEPT

Objective 2b

Only in rare cases is a business organized with the expectation of operating for only a certain period of time. In most cases, the amount of time an enterprise will operate is not known, so an assumption must be made. The assumption will affect the recording of the business transactions, which, in turn, will affect the financial statements.

It is normal to assume that a business entity expects to continue in business at a profit for an indefinite period of time. This **going concern concept** justifies recording plant assets at cost and depreciating them without reference to their current realizable (market) values. Under the going concern concept, it is assumed that plant assets will be used in the normal operations of the entity to generate revenues. If the plant assets are not expected to be sold, there is little reason to report them on the balance sheet at their market values. This is true regardless of whether the market values are less or more than the book values. Changes in market values do not affect the usefulness of the assets.

The going concern assumption also supports the recording of prepaid expenses as assets, even though in many cases they cannot be sold. For example, assume that on the last day of its fiscal year, a retail firm receives from a printer a $20,000 order of special sales catalogs. Without assuming a going concern, the catalogs would be worthless scrap paper with little value. In contrast, the going concern concept allows for the recording of the catalogs as a prepaid expense at a cost of $20,000. As the catalogs are distributed and generate revenues, the cost will be charged to expense.

When doubt exists as to the ability of an enterprise to continue as a going concern, this fact should be disclosed in a note to the financial statements. An example of such a note taken from the financial statements of The Wurlitzer Company is shown below.

The Company's . . . financial statements have been presented on the basis that it is a going concern, which contemplates the realization of assets and the satisfaction of liabilities in the normal course of business. . . .

The Company's continued existence is dependent upon its ability to resolve its liquidity problems, principally by obtaining additional debt financing and equity capital. While pursuing additional debt and equity funding, the Company must continue to operate on limited cash flow generated internally. The Company has experienced a net loss from continuing operations for the quarter ended June 30 . . . of $926,000 (unaudited) compared to a net loss from continuing operations for the [comparable quarter last year]. . . of $1,580,000 (unaudited).

When there is pervasive evidence that a business entity has a limited life, the accounting methods used should reflect the expected terminal date of the entity. For example, changes in normal accounting methods may be needed for business organizations in receivership or bankruptcy. In such cases, the financial statements should disclose the limited life of the enterprise. In addition, the statements should be prepared from the *quitting concern* or liquidation point of view, rather than from a *going concern* point of view.

OBJECTIVITY PRINCIPLE

Objective 2c
Describe and apply the objectivity principle.

The objectivity principle requires that entries in the accounting records and data reported on financial statements be based on objective evidence. If this principle is not followed, the confidence of the many users of the financial statements could not be maintained. For example, such evidence as invoices and vouchers for purchases, bank statements for the amount of cash in bank, and physical counts of merchandise on hand supports the accounting entries and records. Such evidence is objective and can be verified.

In some cases, judgments, estimates, and other subjective factors must be used in preparing financial statements. In such situations, the most objective evidence available should be used. For example, the provision for doubtful accounts is an estimate of the losses expected from failure to collect credit sales. This estimate should be based as much as possible on objective factors, such as the enterprise's past experience with bad debts and economic forecasts of future business conditions.

UNIT OF MEASUREMENT CONCEPT

Objective 2d
Describe and apply the unit of measurement concept.

All business transactions are recorded in dollars. Other relevant, nonfinancial data may also be recorded, such as terms of contracts and the purpose, amount, and term of insurance policies. However, it is only through the use of dollar amounts that diverse transactions and activities of a business may be measured, summarized, reported, and compared. Money is common to all business transactions and thus is a unit of measurement that allows for the reporting of uniform financial data.

The use of the monetary unit for recording and reporting the activities of an enterprise has two major limitations. First, it limits the scope of accounting reports; secondly, it assumes a stable unit of measure.

Scope of Accounting Reports

Many factors affecting the activities and the future prospects of an enterprise cannot be expressed in monetary terms. In general, accounting does not attempt to report such factors. For example, information regarding the abilities of management, the fairness of an employee health program, and the strengths and weaknesses of competitors cannot be expressed in monetary terms. Although such matters may be important to investors or other interested parties, accounting does not report such data in the financial statements.

Changes in the Value of the Dollar

As a unit of measure, the dollar differs from such measures as the kilogram, liter, or meter, which have not changed for centuries. It is a well-known fact that the value of the dollar, sometimes called its purchasing power, continually changes. Accountants are also aware of the potential impact of the changing value of the dollar on the financial condition of a business enterprise. In the past, however, this impact has not been recognized in the accounts or in the financial statements.

To indicate the potential impact of the changing value of the dollar, assume that the plant assets acquired by an enterprise for $100,000 twenty years ago are now to be replaced with similar assets. The cost of similar plant assets at current price levels is $200,000. Assume also that during the twenty-year period the plant assets were fully depreciated and the net income of the enterprise was $300,000. The plant assets generated revenue through their use, which in turn contributed towards the total enterprise net income of $300,000. During this same time, depreciation expense of $100,000 was recognized. However, the depreciation expense of $100,000 amounts to only half of the cost of replacing the plant assets. Because of the increase in the cost of replacing the plant assets, the enterprise has suffered a loss of purchasing power. Taking into consideration the cost of replacing the plant assets, the enterprise has, in effect, earned only $200,000 of net income ($300,000 less the $100,000 increase in the price of the plant assets) during the twenty-year period.

Assuming that the dollar is stable allows for greater objectivity in preparing financial statements. This is because changes in price levels can be difficult to measure across a wide variety of assets. Thus, historical-dollar financial statements are still considered more useful than statements based on changing price levels. There are, however, two widely discussed methods for supplementing historical-dollar statements with disclosures on the impact of changing price levels. The first method discloses supplemental financial data based on current costs. The second method discloses supplemental financial data based on constant dollars. Each of these methods of disclosure is briefly discussed below.

CURRENT COST DATA. **Current cost** is the amount that would have to be paid currently to acquire assets of the same age and in the same condition as existing assets. When current costs are used as the basis for financial reporting, assets, liabilities, and owner's equity are stated at current values. Likewise, expenses are stated at the current cost of doing business. The use of current costs identifies gains and losses resulting from holding assets during periods of changes in price levels. For example, assume that a firm acquired land at the beginning of the fiscal year for $50,000, and that at the end of the year its current cost (value) is $60,000. The land could be reported at its current cost of $60,000, and the $10,000 increase in value could be reported as an unrealized gain from holding the land.

The major disadvantage in the use of current costs is the lack of standards for determining such costs. However, many accountants believe that adequate standards will evolve over time through experimenting with actual applications.

CONSTANT DOLLAR DATA. **Constant dollar** data, also known as general price-level data, are historical costs that have been restated to constant dollars through the use of a price-level index. In this manner, financial statement elements are reported in dollars, which have the same (that is, constant) purchasing power.

A **price-level index** is the ratio of the total cost of a group of goods at a specific time to the total cost of the same group of goods at an earlier base time. The total cost of the goods at the base time is assigned a value of 100. The price-level indexes for all later times are expressed as a ratio to 100. For example, assume that the cost of a group of goods is $12,000 at the base time and $13,200 today. The price index for the earlier, or base, time becomes 100 and the current price index is 110 [(13,200 ÷ 12,000) × 100].

A general price-level index may be used to restate financial statement items to **constant dollar equivalents**. For example, assume a price index of 120 at the time of purchasing land for $10,000. The current price index is 150. The constant dollar equivalent of the original cost of $10,000 is computed as follows:

$$\frac{\text{Current Price Index}}{\text{Price Index at Date of Purchase}} \times \text{Original Cost} = \text{Constant Dollar Equivalent}$$

$$\frac{150}{120} \times \$10,000 \qquad = \$12,500$$
$$\text{Constant Dollar Equivalent}$$

REPORTING PRICE-LEVEL CHANGES. In 1979, the Financial Accounting Standards Board began a program to experiment with reporting the effects of changing prices. The FASB required about 1,300 large, publicly held enterprises to disclose specific current cost and constant dollar data annually as supplemental data. In 1984, after reviewing the experiences with these disclosures, the FASB concluded that the current cost data were more useful than the constant dollar data. In 1986, the FASB eliminated all requirement disclosures on the effects of changing prices. However, the FASB still encourages companies to disclose such data voluntarily.[3] An example of such a disclosure is shown in the following footnote from an annual report of The Pillsbury Company:

Financial statements, prepared using historical costs as required by generally accepted accounting principles, may not reflect the full impact of current costs and general inflation.

The following supplementary disclosures attempt to remeasure certain historical financial information to recognize the effects of changes in current costs using specific price indices. The current cost information is then expressed in average . . . dollars to reflect the effects of general inflation based on the U.S. Consumer Price Index. . . .

ACCOUNTING PERIOD CONCEPT

Objective 2e
Describe and apply the accounting period concept.

A complete and accurate reporting of an enterprise's success or failure cannot be obtained until it discontinues operations, converts its assets into cash, and pays off its debts. Then, and only then, is it possible to determine its net income. But many decisions regarding the business must be made by management and interested outsiders during its existence. It is therefore necessary to prepare periodic reports on operations, financial position, and cash flows.

Reports may be prepared when a certain job or project is completed, but more often they are prepared at specified time intervals. For a number of reasons, including custom and various legal requirements, the longest interval between reports is normally one year.

The accounting period concept creates many areas of concern and difficulty in accountancy. The basic difficulty is determining periodic net income. For example, adjusting entries, as discussed in earlier chapters, are needed because of the reporting of net income for a period of time. The difficulties of inventory costing, estimating uncollectible receivables, and selecting depreciation methods are also directly related to the periodic income measurement process. In addition, the amounts of the assets and the equities reported on the balance sheet are also affected by the methods used in determining net income. For example, the cost flow assumption used in determining the cost of merchandise sold during the accounting period affects the amount of cost assigned to the remaining inventory.

MATCHING CONCEPT

Objective 2f
Describe and apply the matching concept.

During the early stages of the evolution of accounting, the balance sheet was viewed as the primary financial statement. Over the years, the emphasis has shifted to the income statement, as users of financial statements have become more concerned with the results of business operations than with financial position.

Determining periodic net income is a two-fold process of **matching** (1) revenue for the period with (2) expenses incurred in generating revenues. The difference between the revenues and expenses is the net income (loss) for the period.

Revenue Realization

Revenue is the amount of assets received by rendering services to customers or selling merchandise to them. The preparation of periodic financial statements creates an issue of timing; that is, at what point is the revenue recorded? When revenue is recorded, it is said to be realized. For a given accounting period, the question is whether revenue items should be realized and reported in the current period or whether they should be realized and reported in a future period.

---

[3] *Statement of Financial Accounting Standards, No. 89,* "Financial Reporting and Changing Prices" (Stamford: Financial Accounting Standards Board, 1986).

Various criteria are acceptable for determining when revenue is realized. Generally, the criteria used should agree with any contractual terms with the customer and should be based on objective evidence. The criteria most often used are described below.

POINT OF SALE. Revenue from the sale of merchandise is usually determined using the **point-of-sale method.** Under this method, revenue is realized at the time title passes to the buyer. At the point of sale, the sale price has been agreed upon, the buyer acquires the right of ownership of the merchandise, and the seller has a legal claim against the buyer. The revenue from the sale of services is normally realized in the same manner. That is, revenue is realized when the services have been performed. For example, assume that a contract for repair services has been signed. The price agreed to in the contract does not become revenue until the work has been performed.

In theory, revenue from producing and selling goods and rendering services is earned as the effort is expended. As a practical matter, however, it is usually not possible to objectively determine the amount of revenue earned until (1) a contract has been signed and (2) the seller's portion of the contract has been completed.

RECEIPT OF PAYMENT. In some cases, the realization of revenue may be delayed until payment is received. That is, revenue is realized at the time the cash is collected, regardless of when the sale was made. This method of realizing revenue is referred to as the cash basis. The cash basis is widely used by physicians, attorneys, and other enterprises in which professional services are rendered. In theory, this method has little justification. However, it is simple, and losses from bad debts do not have to be estimated. Its wide use in practice is influenced by the fact that it may be used in determining federal income tax. It is not, however, a proper method of realizing revenue from the sale of merchandise.

INSTALLMENT METHOD. In some businesses, especially in the retail field, it is common to make sales on the installment plan. In a typical installment sale, the buyer makes a down payment and agrees to pay the remainder in periodic payments over a period of time. The seller may retain title to the goods or may use other contractual means to make repossession of the goods easier if the buyer defaults on the payments. Despite such provisions, installment sales should normally be recorded in the same manner as any other sale on account. That is, the revenue is considered to be realized at the point of sale.

In rare cases, the collection of receivables from installment sales may not be reasonably assured. In these cases, the **installment method** of realizing revenue may be used.[4] Under this method, revenue is realized upon the receipt of cash. Each cash receipt is considered to be (1) part cost of merchandise sold and (2) part gross profit on the sale.

To illustrate, assume that in the first year of operations, a dealer in household appliances had total installment sales of $300,000, with a related cost of $180,000 of merchandise sold. Assume also that collections of the installment accounts receivable are spread over three years as follows: first year, $140,000; second year, $100,000; third year, $60,000. Under the point-of-sale method, all of the revenue would be recognized in the first year, and the gross profit realized in that year would be as follows:

Point-of-sale method:	
Installment sales	$300,000
Cost of merchandise sold	180,000
Gross profit	$120,000

[4] *Opinions of the Accounting Principles Board, No. 10,* "Omnibus Opinion—1966" (New York: American Institute of Certified Public Accountants, 1966), par. 12.

Under the installment method, gross profit is allocated according to the amount of receivables collected in each year. This allocation is based on the percent of gross profit to sales. The rate of gross profit to sales is determined as follows:

$$\frac{\text{Gross Profit}}{\text{Installment Sales}} = \frac{\$120,000}{\$300,000} = 40\%$$

The amounts reported as gross profit for each of the three years in the illustration, based on collections of installment accounts receivable, are as follows:

Installment method:

1st year collections: $140,000 × 40%		$ 56,000
2d year collections: 100,000 × 40%		40,000
3d year collections: 60,000 × 40%		24,000
Total	$300,000	$120,000

PERCENTAGE OF COMPLETION. Enterprises engaged in large construction projects may take years to complete a contract. For example, assume that a contractor begins a project that will require three years to complete at a total contract price of $50,000,000. Also assume that the total estimated cost to be incurred over the three-year period is $44,000,000. Using the point-of-sale method, no revenue or expense would be recognized until the project is completed. Thus, the entire net income from the contract would be reported in the third year. This method of realizing revenue from long-term contracts is called the **completed-contract method.**

Whenever the total cost of a long-term contract and the project's progress can be reasonably estimated, revenue is often realized over the entire life of the contract by the **percentage-of-completion method.**[5] The amount of revenue realized in a period is determined on the basis of the estimated percentage of the contract that has been completed during the period. The percentage of completion can be estimated by comparing the amount of incurred costs with the estimated total costs. Other methods of estimating the percentage of completion include using estimates developed by engineers, architects, or other qualified personnel.

Continuing with the preceding example, assume that by the end of the first fiscal year the contract is estimated to be one-fourth completed. The costs incurred during the first year were $11,200,000. Using the percentage-of-completion method, the revenue realized and the income for the year are as follows:

Revenue realized ($50,000,000 × 25%)	$12,500,000
Costs incurred	11,200,000
Income (Year 1)	$ 1,300,000

The 1991 edition of *Accounting Trends & Techniques* indicated that 66% of the surveyed companies with long-term contracts used the percentage-of-completion method. This method involves estimates and hence possible inaccuracies in determining and reporting revenue. However, the financial statements are often considered more informative and more useful than if the completed-contract method is used.

Whichever method is used to recognize revenue on a long-term contract, it should be disclosed in the financial statements. The following excerpt taken from a note to the financial statements of Martin Marietta Corporation is an example of such a disclosure:

Revenue Recognition

Sales under long-term contracts generally are recognized under the percentage-of-completion method, and include a proportion of the earnings expected to be realized on the contract. . . . Other sales are recorded upon shipment of products or performance of services.

---

[5] *Accounting Research and Terminology Bulletins—Final Edition*, "No. 45, Long-term Construction-type Contracts" (New York: American Institute of Certified Public Accountants, 1961), par. 15.

Expense Recognition

An expense is the using up of an asset to generate revenues. The amount of an asset's cost that is used up is a measure of the expense. Each expense must be matched against its related revenue in order to properly determine the amount of net income or net loss for the period.

The concepts and methods used to record expenses have been discussed and illustrated in previous chapters. For example, the recording of salaries in the period in which they helped generate revenue was discussed. This often involved the use of adjusting entries at the end of the period to properly match revenues and expenses. Also, the allocation of the cost of plant assets to expense was discussed. This required the use of adjusting entries for depreciation expense at the end of the period to properly match expenses with related revenues.

ADEQUATE DISCLOSURE CONCEPT

Objective 2g
Describe and apply the adequate disclosure concept.

Financial statements, including all their related footnotes and other disclosures, should contain all of the relevant data essential to a user's understanding of the entity's financial status. The decision as to whether **adequate disclosure,** or **full disclosure**, has been achieved is often more subjective than objective.

Although all essential data should be disclosed within the financial statements or in notes attached to those statements, nonessential data should be excluded to avoid clutter. For example, the balance of each cash account is usually not reported separately. Instead, the balances are normally grouped together and reported as one total. In some cases, the investments in temporary marketable securities are also included with cash and reported as *cash and cash equivalents.*

In most cases, all relevant data needed by users cannot be presented in the financial statements. Therefore, the statements normally include explanatory data in accompanying notes. For example, a note used to present supplemental information related to the effects of inflation on the financial statements of The Pillsbury Company was previously illustrated. Other matters that are normally disclosed in notes are briefly discussed and illustrated in the following paragraphs. Many of the illustrations were taken from annual reports where they appeared in a section entitled "Notes to Financial Statements."

Accounting Methods Used

Many times there are several acceptable accounting methods that can be used in preparing the financial statements. The method used should be disclosed if its use has a significant effect on the statements. For example, the inventory cost flow method used (lifo, fifo, or average) usually has a significant impact on reported net income. Other examples include depreciation methods and revenue recognition methods.

There is wide variation in the format for disclosing accounting methods in the financial statements. One form of disclosure is to present "Significant Accounting Policies" as the first note. Some examples of such notes are shown below.

Digital Equipment Corporation

Note A—Significant Accounting Policies

Inventories—Inventories are stated at the lower of cost (first-in, first-out) or market. Property, Plant and Equipment—Depreciation expense is computed principally on the following bases:

Classification	Depreciation Lives and Methods
Buildings	*33 years (straight-line)*
Machinery and equipment	*8 and 10 years (sum-of-years)*
	4 and 5 years (double-declining-balance)

Atico Financial Corporation

Sales of home sites are recorded under the installment method of accounting. All depreciable assets are recorded at cost; depreciation is calculated using the straight-line method.

Changes in Accounting Estimates

There are many cases in accounting in which the use of estimates is necessary. These estimates should be revised when additional data or later developments allow for better, more accurate estimates. If the effect of such a change on net income is significant, it should be disclosed in the financial statements for the year in which the change is made.[6] An example of such a disclosure appeared in an annual report of Time Incorporated:

Change in Estimate

. . . The Company changed the rate of amortization of its pay-TV programming costs to more closely reflect audience viewing patterns. The effect of this change was to reduce programming costs by $58 million . . . , resulting in increased net income of $35 million . . . , or $.58 per share. . . .

Contingent Liabilities

As discussed earlier, contingent liabilities are potential obligations that will become liabilities only if certain events occur in the future. If the liability is probable and the amount of the liability can be reasonably estimated, it should be recorded in the accounts. Examples of such liabilities include vacation pay payable and product warranty payable. Although the vacation pay liability depends upon employees taking vacations, the liability is probable and is reasonably estimated. Likewise, although the product warranty liability depends upon customers presenting products for repair, the liability is probable and is reasonably estimated.

If the amount of the potential obligation cannot be reasonably estimated, the facts of the contingency should be disclosed.[7] For example, the following footnote taken from the 1991 annual report of Harley-Davidson, Inc., describes a potential liability for environmental contamination:

6. Commitments and Contingencies

The Company is involved in various environmental matters, including soil contamination at its York, Pennsylvania facility (the Facility), with various governmental and environmental agencies. During the third quarter of 1991, the Company discovered additional soil contamination at the Facility in an area formerly owned and used by the U.S. Navy and AMF, (the predecessor corporation of Minstar) from whom the Company was purchased in 1981. Based on the preliminary information available to the Company, the Company is unable to determine what remediation will be necessary, what the costs of such remediation will be and what the Company's share of such costs might be, relative to either the Navy's share or other former owner's share. The Company is therefore unable to determine at this time whether the potential liability relating to this matter will have a material effect on the Company's financial condition. Based on preliminary information available to the Company and admission by the Navy in the pending . . . action, the Company believes that the Navy should be liable for a substantial portion of the on-going investigation and future cleanup of the Facility.

Common examples of contingent liabilities disclosed in notes to the financial statements are litigation, guarantees, and discounting receivables. The 1991 edition of *Accounting Trends & Techniques* indicated that 65% of the surveyed companies disclosed contingencies for litigations, 35.5% for guarantees, and 13% for discounting receivables. These contingent liabilities are briefly discussed below.

LITIGATION. Most companies have lawsuits filed against them at one time or another. In many cases, litigation takes many months or years to complete. Although it is often difficult to estimate the amount of the liability, if any, the litigation should

---

[6] *Opinions of the Accounting Principles Board*, No. 20, "Accounting Changes" (New York: American Institute of Certified Public Accountants, 1971), pars. 31-33.
[7] *Statement of Financial Accounting Standards*, No. 5, "Accounting for Contingencies" (Stamford: Financial Accounting Standards Board, 1975), pars. 8, 10, 12.

be disclosed. An example of a note in the 1991 financial statements of Pier 1 Imports, Inc., disclosing a contingent liability arising from litigation, is shown below.

Note 9 — Litigation

In August 1988, a suit was filed in the 113th District Court of Harris County, Texas against Wolfe Nursery, Inc. (a wholly owned subsidiary of the Company), an apartment complex owner, a chemical distributor, a chemical manufacturer, and others, alleging that the improper use of chemicals and a failure to warn resulted in personal injury, and in certain cases, wrongful death. The plaintiffs seek $90 million. One defendant, a chemical manufacturer, has settled with the plaintiffs and has been dismissed from the lawsuit. The Company continues to deny liability in this action and intends to vigorously pursue all available defenses. The Company believes that its ultimate liability, if any, will not have a material adverse effect on the Company.

GUARANTEES. Companies sometimes guarantee a loan for another company, often an affiliate, supplier, or major customer. In such cases, the company is obligated to pay the loan if the borrower fails to make payment. Such a contingency may be disclosed in a note to the financial statements, such as that shown below for PepsiCo, Inc.:

At year-end 1991 and 1990, PepsiCo was contingently liable under direct and indirect guarantees aggregating $86 million and $97 million, respectively. The guarantees are primarily issued to support financial arrangements of certain restaurant and bottling franchisees and PepsiCo joint ventures. PepsiCo manages the risk associated with these guarantees by performing appropriate credit reviews in addition to retaining certain rights as a franchisor or joint venture partner.

DISCOUNTED RECEIVABLES. The contingent liability arising from discounting a note receivable was discussed in a previous chapter. A similar obligation may also arise from the sale of receivables. The contingent liability exists until the due date for discounted receivables. An example of a note disclosing such an obligation is shown below for The Wurlitzer Company.

7 (in part): Commitments and Contingent Liabilities

During the year ended March 31, . . . the Company negotiated an agreement to sell at face value approximately $6,100,000 of accounts receivable to an outside finance company. Cash proceeds of the sale were approximately $6,000,000: the remaining $100,000 is held by the outside finance company as security for the uncollected recourse receivables. At March 31, . . . the Company remained contingently liable on approximately $1,900,000 of the sold receivables; however, management believes that the allowance for doubtful accounts will be adequate for any such uncollectible receivables.

Financial Instruments

In the past decade there has been a widespread growth in the variety and types of financial instruments issued by enterprises. A **financial instrument** is cash, a security that evidences ownership interest in an entity, or a contract that imposes certain obligations and rights upon another entity.[8] Examples of financial instruments include such items as cash, accounts receivable, notes receivable, accounts payable, notes payable, bonds payable, and other securities traded in the marketplace.

Generally accepted accounting principles require specific disclosures related to financial instruments. These disclosures include the market (fair) value of the financial instruments.[9] In addition, any unusual risks related to the financial instruments in excess of the amounts reported in the financial statements must also

[8] *Statement of Financial Accounting Standards, No. 107,* "Disclosures about Fair Value of Financial Instruments," (Norwalk: Financial Accounting Standards Board, 1991), par. 3.
[9] *Ibid.,* par. 10.

be disclosed. Finally, any unusual credit risks must also be reported.[10] For example, a retailer whose receivables are concentrated in one geographical area should disclose this fact in the notes to the financial statements.

Segment of a Business

Many companies are involved in more than one type of business activity or market. For example, a company may operate both radio and television stations in both domestic and foreign markets. The individual segments of such companies normally experience differing rates of profit, degrees of risk, and growth. To help financial statement users assess operating results, the financial statements should disclose segment information. The information reported for each major segment includes revenue, income from operations, and identifiable assets related to the segment.[11] An example of financial reporting for segments is shown in Exhibit 1 in the note adapted from the 1991 financial statements of The Gillette Company.

Exhibit 1
Disclosure of Segment Information

Financial Information by Business Segment

(Millions of Dollars)

1991	Blades & Razors	Toiletries & Cosmetics	Stationery Products	Braun Products	Oral-B Products	Other	Corporate	Total
Net sales	$1,750.1	$946.9	$460.3	$1,215.8	$308.1	$2.7	$ —	$4,683.9
Profit from operations	555.6	114.1	48.8	145.3	38.8	(.1)	(40.9)	861.6
Identifiable assets	1,477.9	486.9	423.2	883.2	248.4	2.3	364.8	3,886.7
Capital expenditures	126.5	37.6	27.8	78.0	11.1	—	5.0	286.0
Depreciation	71.6	19.1	11.9	56.3	7.8	.3	5.4	172.4

Events Subsequent to Date of Statements

Events that have a significant effect on the financial statements may occur or become known after the close of the fiscal period. Such events should be disclosed in the financial statements.[12] For example, an enterprise might suffer a loss from a fire, flood, or other natural disaster between the end of its fiscal year and the issuance of statements for that year. In such a case, the facts of the event should be disclosed, even though the event occurred after the end of the fiscal year. Likewise, the issuance of long-term debt or the purchase of another business enterprise after the close of the period should be disclosed. Delta Air Lines Inc. reported a subsequent event in a note to its financial statements for the year ended June 30, 1991, as follows:

Subsequent Event

On July 27, 1991, Delta entered into an asset purchase agreement, as amended, with Pan Am Corporation and certain of its subsidiaries (Pan Am) providing for Delta's purchase of a package of Pan Am assets, including Pan Am's New York to Europe routes, its Frankfurt hub operation, its Miami-London and Detroit-London routes, its Boston-New York-Washington, D.C. Shuttle, Pan Am's leasehold or other interests in up to 45 aircraft, and various related assets and facilities. Delta's purchase price for the asset acquisition is $416 million. In addition, Delta has agreed to assume certain liabilities, including approximately $70 million in mortgages on assets to be acquired by Delta and up to $100 million of Pan Am passenger tickets under certain circumstances. As part of the asset purchases, Delta has also agreed to offer employment to 6,600 Pan Am personnel.

[10]*Statement of Financial Accounting Standards, No. 105*, "Disclosure of Information about Financial Instruments with Off-Balance Sheet Risk and Financial Instruments with Concentrations of Credit Risk," (Norwalk: Financial Accounting Standards Board, 1990), pars. 18 and 20.
[11]*Statement of Financial Accounting Standards, No. 14*, "Financial Reporting for Segments of a Business Enterprise" (Stamford: Financial Accounting Standards Board, 1976). Nonpublic corporations are exempted from this requirement by *Statement of Financial Accounting Standards, No. 21*, "Suspension of the Reporting of Earnings per Share and Segment Information by Nonpublic Enterprises" (Stamford: Financial Accounting Standards Board, 1978).
[12]*Statement on Auditing Standards, No. 1*, "Codification of Auditing Standards and Procedures" (New York: American Institute of Certified Public Accountants, 1988), section 560.

CONSISTENCY CONCEPT

Objective 2h
Describe and apply the
consistency concept.

The amount and direction of change in net income and financial position from period to period may influence readers' judgments and decisions. Readers of financial statements should be able to assume that the financial statements of an enterprise are based on the same principles from period to period. Otherwise, the changes and trends reported in the statements could be the result of changes in principles rather than changes in operations.

A number of alternative generally accepted accounting principles have been discussed in this text. These principles may significantly affect the financial statements. Because of these potential effects, a consistency standard is needed to ensure that financial statements can be compared across fiscal periods.

The **consistency** concept does not prohibit changes in the accounting principles used. Changes are allowed if the change will more fairly report net income and financial position. Examples of changes in accounting principles include changes in inventory cost flow assumptions, changes in depreciation methods, and changes in realizing revenue from long-term construction contracts. Changes in accounting principles must meet the following general rule for disclosure of such changes:

The nature of and justification for a change in accounting principle and its effect on income should be disclosed in the financial statements of the period in which the change is made. The justification for the change should explain clearly why the newly adopted accounting principle is preferable.[13]

An example of a disclosure of a change in accounting method, taken from the 1991 annual report of General Motors Corporation, is shown below.

Accounting Change

Effective January 1, 1991, accounting procedures were changed to include in inventory general purpose spare parts previously charged directly to expense. The Corporation believes this change is preferable because it provides a better matching of costs with related revenues. The effect of this change on 1991 earnings was a favorable adjustment of $306.5 million . . .

There are various ways of reporting the effect of a change in an accounting principle on net income. The cumulative effect of the change on net income may be reported on the income statement of the period in which the change is made. In some cases, the effect of the change could be applied to past periods by reporting revised income statements for the earlier years. Methods of disclosure of such effects are discussed in more detail in a later chapter.

The consistency concept does not require that an accounting method be used throughout an enterprise. For example, it is not unusual for enterprises to use different costing and pricing methods for different segments of their inventories.

This is illustrated by the following note from the 1991 financial statements of Hartmarx Corporation:

Objective i
Describe and apply the
materiality concept.

. . . Approximately 23% and 26% of the Company's inventories at November 30, 1991 and 1990, primarily work in process and finished goods, are valued using the last-in, first-out (LIFO) method. The first-in, first-out (FIFO) method is used for substantially all raw materials and the remaining manufacturing and retail inventories.

MATERIALITY CONCEPT

Generally accepted accounting principles should be applied to all significant items in preparing the financial statements. Insignificant items may be treated in the easiest manner. Determining what is and what is not significant or material requires judgment. Precise criteria cannot be developed.

The Financial Accounting Standards Board's *Statement of Financial Accounting Concepts, No. 2* defines **materiality** as follows:

---

[13]*Opinions of the Accounting Principles Board, No. 20,* "Accounting Changes" (New York: American Institute of Certified Public Accountants, 1971), par. 17.

The omission or misstatement of an item in a financial report is material if, in light of the surrounding circumstances, the magnitude of the item is such that it is probable that the judgment of a reasonable person relying upon the report would have been changed or influenced by the inclusion or correction of the item.[14]

Concerning the Gnat and the Camel

This is the story as it comes to us: An accountant . . . was [asked] to check the cash of a concern, which may be called the XYZ Corporation. This concern among its activities included a selling department where goods of small value were sold in fairly large quantities. When the cash of the selling department was counted it was found that the amount on hand was, let us say, $2.04—a fictitious amount greater than the actual sum—more than it should have been. Now this incident happened in the city of New York where, as all citizens know to their sorrow, there is a two percent tax on sales. Evidently, therefore, this excessive sum of $2.04 represented the sale of some article for $2, plus a tax of four cents. . . . Apparently a careless member of the staff had sold such an article, placed the proceeds in the till and forgotten to make the proper record of the whole stupendous transaction. The carelessness was unpardonable, of course. No member of any staff anywhere should forget anything. However, the error occurred and the perspicacious young [accountant] discovered it, as he could not very well avoid doing. He found the unaccountable excess and, like a well-trained man, conscious of his complete efficiency, he set to work to trace the mistake and to expose the guilty person. Here was a chance for him to demonstrate his incalculable value to his firm. . . . Such wrongdoing must not escape unchallenged. Relying upon his supposed authority he began a search, a veritable inquisition, and after two or three days of earnest effort,

during which he had interrupted the work of the entire . . . office and had . . . considerable . . . time expended, he was compelled to admit that he could not find a shortage in the inventory to account for the surplus cash, nor could he rightfully determine who had committed the crime. At last he regretfully reported the matter to his superior and confessed himself defeated. What the superior had to say about the matter is not recorded; but one can imagine the attitude of the [superior] and can form a reasonably accurate notion of the comments which were made. . . .

This little story bears a moral which every accountant may well take to heart. It might be unwise to say that errors should be overlooked or that carelessness should be condoned. But surely there is no sense whatever in a ridiculous adherence to meticulous detail when the sole purpose is to trace something which is not worth tracing. . . . What the [accountant] should have done in the present case is clear. He should have made a note of the excess, and, after spending a few minutes in trying to trace it to its source, he should have gone on to weightier things. It is a great pity that this sort of incident ever occurs; but we are told that the case before us is not unique. There are many little fellows who revel in the most microscopic minutiae. They can't help it. They probably were born that way, but they should never, never, be employed in the work of accountancy, which, after all, is a matter of principles, not of pin points.

Source: A. P. Richardson, *The Journal of Accountancy* (October, 1936), pp. 233–235.

In assessing the materiality of an item, the size of the item, its nature, and relationship to other items in the financial statements should be considered. For example, an error in classifying a $10,000 asset on a balance sheet with total assets of $10,000,000 would probably be immaterial. If the assets totaled only $100,000, however, the error would be material. If the $10,000 were a note receivable from an officer of the enterprise, it might well be material even in the first case. Assume further that the loan increased to $100,000 between the end of the fiscal period and the issuance of the financial statements. In this case, the nature of the item, its amount at the balance sheet date, and its subsequent increase in amount should be disclosed in the statements.

The materiality concept may also be applied to the recording of transactions. For example, as mentioned in a previous chapter, many companies record small expenditures for plant assets as an expense of the period rather than as an asset. In setting the dollar cutoff between revenue and capital expenditures, factors such as the following should be considered: (1) the amount of plant assets, (2) the amount of other assets, (3) the number of such expenditures, (4) the nature and expected life of the plant assets, and (5) the effect on reported net income.

A common use of the materiality concept is the practice of omitting cents in preparing financial statements. Many large companies round financial statement

[14]*Statement of Financial Accounting Concepts*, No. 2, "Qualitative Characteristics of Accounting Information" (Stamford: Financial Accounting Standards Board, 1980), par. 132.

items to thousands or even millions of dollars for reporting purposes. For example, the 1991 edition of *Accounting Trends & Techniques* indicated that 55 of 600 companies reported amounts to the nearest dollar, 394 to the nearest thousand dollars, and 151 to the nearest million dollars.

Some companies use "whole-dollar" accounting in which the cents amounts are eliminated from accounting records at the earliest possible point in the accounting process. Any differences introduced into the accounts by rounding tend to balance out, and any final difference is usually not material. There may be some accounts, however, such as those with customers and creditors, for which it may not be feasible to use "whole-dollar" accounting.

CONSERVATISM CONCEPT

Objective 2j
Describe and apply the conservatism concept.

The financial statements are significantly affected by the selection of accounting principles and other value judgments. In accounting, there has been a tendency for accountants to be conservative in selecting among principles and in making estimates. The method that yielded the lesser amount of net income or of asset value was often selected. This attitude of **conservatism** was often expressed in the statement to "anticipate no profits and provide for all losses."

Examples of the conservatism concept still exist today. Generally accepted accounting principles require that merchandise inventory be reported at the lower of cost or market. If market price is higher than cost, the higher amount is ignored in the accounts. Likewise, temporary marketable securities are valued at the lower of cost or market.

Current accounting thought has shifted away from the conservatism concept. Conservatism is no longer considered to be the dominant factor in selecting among alternatives. The objectivity and matching principles and the concepts of consistency, disclosure, and materiality are more important than the conservatism concept. The latter concept is only a factor when the others do not play a significant role.

CHAPTER REVIEW

Key Points

Objective 1. Describe the role of the FASB and other groups in the development of accounting concepts and principles.

The FASB, which issues *Statements of Financial Accounting Standards, Interpretations,* and *Statements of Financial Accounting Concepts,* is the dominant accounting standard-setting body. The Governmental Accounting Standards Board is responsible for establishing accounting principles to be followed by state and municipal governments.

Other influential organizations that impact the development of accounting concepts and principles include the American Institute of Certified Public Accountants, the American Accounting Association, the Securities and Exchange Commission, the Internal Revenue Service, the Financial Executives Institute, the Institute of Management Accountants, the Financial Analysts Federation, and the Securities Industry Associates.

Objective 2a. Describe and apply the business entity concept.

Under the business entity concept, it is assumed that a business enterprise is separate from the persons who supply its assets. This separation exists regardless of the legal form of the organization. The application of the business entity concept justifies the recording of transactions affecting an enterprise's assets separately from the owner's assets.

Objective 2b. Describe and apply the going concern concept.

Under the going concern concept, it is assumed that a business entity will continue in business at a profit for an indefinite period of time. The application of the going concern concept justifies recording plant assets at cost and depreciating them without reference to their current realizable (market) values.

Objective 2c. Describe and apply the objectivity principle.

The objectivity principle requires that entries in the accounting records and data reported on financial statements be based on objectively determined evidence. Examples of such evidence include invoices and vouchers for purchases, bank statements for the amount of cash in the bank, and physical counts for merchandise on hand.

Objective 2d. Describe and apply the unit of measurement concept.

The unit of measurement concept requires that all business transactions be recorded in terms of money. The monetary unit is also assumed to be stable. The financial statements may, however, be supplemented to disclose changes in price levels through using current costs or constant dollars.

**Objective 2e. Describe and apply
the accounting period concept.**
The accounting period concept requires that periodic reports on operations, financial position, and cash flows of a business enterprise be prepared so that management and others can make informed decisions regarding the business.

Objective 2f. Describe and apply the matching principle.
The matching concept requires that expenses be properly matched and reported with their related revenues in determining net income. Thus, periodic net income is determined by a two-fold process of (1) recognizing revenues during the period and (2) matching the related expenses with the revenues.

Revenues may be realized at the point of sale, upon receipt of payment, or under the installment method. Revenues for long-term projects may be recognized using the percentage-of-completion method.

An expense is the using up of an asset to generate revenues. The amount of an asset's cost that is used up is a measure of the expense. The proper matching of each expense with its related revenue often requires the use of adjusting entries at the end of the period for such items as depreciation and accrued salaries.

**Objective 2g. Describe and apply
the adequate disclosure concept.**
The adequate disclosure concept requires that financial statements and their accompanying footnotes or other explanatory materials contain all of the relevant data essential to the user's understanding of the enterprise's financial status. Applying this concept requires such disclosures as the account-

ing methods used, changes in accounting estimates, contingent liabilities, financial instruments, segment data, and subsequent events.

**Objective 2h. Describe and apply
the consistency concept.**
The consistency concept implies that the financial statements should be prepared by applying the same principles year after year. If changes in principles do occur, their effect on the financial statements should be disclosed.

**Objective 2i. Describe and apply
the materiality concept.**
The materiality concept requires accountants to consider the relative importance of any event, accounting procedure, or change in procedure that affects the financial statements. In applying the materiality concept, generally accepted accounting principles should be applied to all material items in preparing the financial statements. Immaterial items may be treated in the easiest manner.

**Objective 2j. Describe and apply
the conservatism concept.**
The conservatism concept implies that, in selecting among alternative accounting principles, the principle that yields the lesser amount of net income or asset value is chosen. An example of applying the conservatism concept is the reporting of merchandise inventory at the lower of cost or market. If market price is higher than cost, the higher amount is ignored in the accounts. The conservatism concept is no longer considered to be a dominant factor in selecting among alternatives.

Glossary of Key Terms

Adequate disclosure. The concept that financial statements and their accompanying footnotes should contain all of the pertinent data believed essential to the reader's understanding of an enterprise's financial status. **Objective 2g**

Business entity concept. The concept that assumes that accounting applies to individual economic units and that each unit is separate and distinct from the persons who supply its assets. **Objective 2a**

Completed-contract method. The method that recognizes revenue from long-term construction contracts when the project is completed. **Objective 2f**

Conservatism. The concept that dictates that in selecting among alternatives, the method or procedure that yields the lesser amount of net income or asset value should be selected. **Objective 2j**

Consistency. The concept that assumes that the same generally accepted accounting principles have been applied in the preparation of successive financial statements. **Objective 2h**

Constant dollar. Historical costs that have been converted into dollars of constant value through the use of a price-level index. **Objective 2d**

Current cost. The amount of cash that would have to be paid currently to acquire assets of the same age and in the same condition as existing assets. **Objective 2d**

Financial Accounting Standards Board (FASB). The current authoritative body for the development of accounting

principles for all entities except state and municipal governments. **Objective 1**

Going concern concept. The concept that assumes that a business entity has a reasonable expectation of continuing in business at a profit for an indefinite period of time. **Objective 2b**

Installment method. The method of recognizing revenue, whereby each receipt of cash from installment sales is considered to be part cost of merchandise sold and part gross profit. **Objective 2f**

Matching. The principle of accounting that all revenues should be matched with the expenses incurred in earning those revenues during a period of time. **Objective 2f**

Materiality. The concept that recognizes the practicality of ignoring small or insignificant deviations from generally accepted accounting principles. **Objective 2i**

Percentage-of-completion method. The method of recognizing revenue from long-term contracts over the entire life of the contract. **Objective 2f**

Point-of-sale method. The method of recognizing revenue, whereby the revenue is determined to be realized at the time that title passes to the buyer. **Objective 2f**

Price-level index. The ratio of the total cost of a group of commodities prevailing at a particular time to the total cost of the same group of commodities at an earlier base time. **Objective 2d**

Self-Examination Questions
Answers at end of chapter.

1. Equipment that was acquired for $250,000 has a current book value of $100,000 and an estimated market value of $120,000. If the replacement cost of the equipment is $350,000, at what amount should the equipment be reported in the balance sheet?
   A. $100,000
   B. $120,000
   C. $150,000
   D. $350,000

2. Merchandise costing $140,000 was sold on the installment plan for $200,000 during the current year. Down payments of $40,000 and installment payments of $35,000 were received during the current year. If the installment method of accounting is used, what is the amount of gross profit to be realized in the current year?
   A. $22,500
   B. $60,000
   C. $75,000
   D. $140,000

3. The total contract price for the construction of an ocean liner was $20,000,000, and the estimated construction costs were $17,000,000. During the current year, the project was estimated to be 40% completed and the costs incurred totaled $7,050,000. Under the percentage-of-completion method of accounting, what amount of income would be recognized for the current year?
   A. $950,000
   B. $1,200,000
   C. $2,820,000
   D. $3,000,000

4. The consistency concept requires that the nature of and justification for a change in an accounting principle and its effect on income be disclosed in the financial statements of the period in which the change is made. An example of a change that is not a change in an accounting principle is a:
   A. change in method of inventory pricing
   B. change in depreciation method for previously recorded plant assets
   C. change in method of accounting for installment sales
   D. change in method of reporting cents in the financial statements

5. A corporation's financial statements do not report cents amounts. This is an example of the application of which of the following concepts?
   A. Business entity
   B. Going concern
   C. Consistency
   D. Materiality

ILLUSTRATIVE PROBLEM

Town and Country Furniture Company makes all sales on the installment basis and recognizes revenue at the point of sale. Condensed income statements and the amounts collected from customers for each of the first three years of operations are as follows:

	1994	1995	1996
Sales	$190,000	$240,000	$170,000
Cost of merchandise sold	133,000	163,200	122,400
Gross profit	$ 57,000	$ 76,800	$ 47,600
Operating expenses	33,900	41,500	30,000
Net income	$ 23,100	$ 35,300	$ 17,600
Collected from sales of first year	$ 50,000	$110,000	$ 30,000
Collected from sales of second year		80,000	120,000
Collected from sales of third year			60,000

Instructions

1. Determine the gross profit percentages for each year.
2. Using the installment method, determine the amount of net income or loss that would have been reported in each year.

Solution

1. Gross profit percentages:

   1994: $57,000 ÷ $190,000 = 30%
   1995: $76,800 ÷ $240,000 = 32%
   1996: $47,600 ÷ $170,000 = 28%

2.

	1994	1995	1996
Gross profit realized on collections from sales of:			
1994: 30% × $ 50,000	$ 15,000		
30% × $110,000		$33,000	
30% × $ 30,000			$ 9,000
1995: 32% × $ 80,000		25,600	
32% × $120,000			38,400
1996: 28% × $ 60,000			16,800
Total gross profit realized	$ 15,000	$58,600	$64,200
Operating expenses	33,900	41,500	30,000
Net income (loss)	$(18,900)	$17,100	$34,200

DISCUSSION QUESTIONS

1. Accounting principles are broad guides to accounting practice. (a) How do these principles differ from the principles relating to the physical sciences? (b) Of what significance is acceptability in the development of accounting principles? (c) Why must accounting principles be continually reexamined and revised?

2. What role does the Financial Accounting Foundation play in the development of accounting principles?

3. What body is currently dominant in the development of (a) generally accepted accounting principles for business enterprises and (b) principles for state and municipal governments?

4. Briefly discuss the process by which the Financial Accounting Standards Board (FASB) develops *Statements of Financial Accounting Standards.*

5. Organizations that have an interest in the development of generally accepted accounting principles are represented by the following abbreviations. What is the name of each organization?

    a. FASB   e. AAA
    b. FAF   f. SEC
    c. GASB   g. IRS
    d. AICPA

6. What accounting concept assumes that a business enterprise is separate and distinct from the persons who supply its assets?

7. For accounting purposes, what is the nature of the assumption as to the length of life of an enterprise?

8. A business enterprise is in receivership and the receiver expects to dissolve it. Should the going concern concept be used as the basis for preparing the current financial statements? Discuss.

9. Why should the most objective evidence available be used as the basis for data reported on financial statements?

10. Plant assets are reported on the balance sheet at a total cost of $500,000 less accumulated depreciation of $300,000. (a) Is it possible that the assets might realize considerably more or considerably less than $200,000 if the business was discontinued and the assets were sold separately? (b) Why aren't plant assets reported on the balance sheet at their estimated market values?

11. During the current year, a mortgage note payable for $1,000,000, issued by Pendleton Company 8 years ago, became due and was paid. Assuming that the general price level had increased by 50% during the 8-year period, did the loan result in an increase or a decrease in Pendleton Company's purchasing power? Explain.

12. A machine with a cost of $75,000 and accumulated depreciation of $65,000 will soon need to be replaced by a similar machine that will cost $120,000. (a) At what amount should the machine presently owned be reported on the balance sheet? (b) What amount should management use in planning for the cash required to replace the machine?

13. During May, merchandise costing $125,000 was sold for $175,000 in cash. Because the purchasing power of the dollar has declined, it will cost $130,000 to replace the mer-

chandise. (a) What is the amount of gross profit in May? (b) Assuming that all operating expenses for the month are paid in cash and that the owner withdraws cash in the amount of the net income, would there be enough cash remaining from the $175,000 of sales to replace the merchandise sold? Discuss.

14. Conventional financial statements do not give recognition to the instability of the purchasing power of the dollar. How can the effect of the fluctuating dollar on business operations be presented to the users of the financial statements?

15. What is the current cost of an asset?

16. If land was purchased for $50,000 when the general price-level index was 175, and the general price-level index has risen to 210, what is the constant dollar equivalent of the original cost of the land?

17. If a complete and accurate picture of an enterprise's success or failure is desired, what accounting period must be used to report on operations?

18. Is revenue from sales of merchandise on account more commonly recognized at the time of sale or at the time of cash receipt?

19. During the current year, merchandise costing $480,000 was sold on the installment plan for $800,000. The down payments and the installment payments received during the current year totaled $300,000. What is the amount of gross profit realized in the current year, applying (a) the point-of-sale method and (b) the installment method of revenue recognition?

20. During the current year, Cross Construction Company obtained a contract to build an apartment building. The total contract price was $9,000,000, and the estimated construction costs were $7,950,000. During the current year, the project was estimated to be 40% completed, and the costs incurred totaled $3,110,000. Under the percentage-of-completion method of revenue recognition, what amount of (a) revenue, (b) cost, and (c) income should be recognized from the contract for the current year?

21. On January 3 of the current year, Cogdal Realty Company acquired a 10-acre tract of land for $300,000. Before the end of the year, $125,000 was spent on subdividing the tract and paving streets. The market value of the land at the end of the year was estimated at $500,000. Although no lots were sold during the year, the income statement for the year reported revenue of $200,000, expenses of $125,000, and net income of $75,000 from the project. Were generally accepted accounting principles followed? Discuss.

22. Mini-Storage Company constructed a warehouse at a cost of $175,000 after a local contractor had submitted a bid of $200,000. The building was recorded at $200,000, and income of $25,000 was recognized. Were generally accepted accounting principles followed? Discuss.

23. Gaston Company purchased equipment for $120,000 at the beginning of a fiscal year. The equipment could be sold for $130,000 at the end of the fiscal year. It was proposed that since the equipment was worth more at the end of the year than at the beginning of the year, (a) no depreciation should be recorded for the current year, and (b) the gain of $10,000 should be recorded. Discuss the propriety of the proposals.

24. When there are several acceptable alternative accounting methods that could be used, the method used by an enterprise should be disclosed in the financial statements. Give examples of accounting methods that fall in this category.

25. If significant changes are made in the accounting principles applied from one period to the next, why should the effect of these changes be disclosed in the financial statements?

26. You have just been employed by a relatively small merchandising business that records its revenues only when cash is received and its expenses only when cash is paid. You are aware of the fact that the enterprise should record its revenues and expenses on the accrual basis. Would changing to the accrual basis violate the principle of consistency? Discuss.

27. For many years, Whitson Company has used the sum-of-the-years-digits method of computing depreciation. For the current year, the straight-line method was used, depreciation expense amounted to $125,000, and net income amounted to $90,000. Depreciation computed by the sum-of-the-years-digits method would have been $155,000. (a) What is the quantitative effect of the change in method on the net income for the current year? (b) Is the effect of the change material? (c) Should the effect of the change in method be disclosed in the financial statements?

28. The accountant for a large department store charged the acquisition of a pencil sharpener to an expense account, even though the asset had an estimated useful life of 10 years. Which accounting concept supports this treatment of the expenditure?

29. In 1975, Olson Co. acquired a building, with a useful life of 50 years, and depreciated it by the declining-balance method. Is this practice conservative (a) for the year 1975 and (b) for the year 2024? Explain.

REAL W🌐RLD FOCUS   30. A real estate development company would like to reflect appraised values of land held for development in its financial statements. This would increase its asset valuation and enhance its borrowing capability. Is appraisal value a proper basis for presenting the land in the financial statements?

Source: "Technical Issues Feature," *Journal of Accountancy* (April 1990), p. 97.

REAL W🌐RLD FOCUS   31. The following footnote was taken from the 1991 annual report of Maytag Corporation:

INVENTORIES

In thousands	1991	1990
Finished products	$314,493	$335,417
Work in process, raw materials and supplies	174,589	200,370
	$489,082	$535,787

If . . . [current costs had] been used for all inventories, they would have been $72.3 million and $76.8 million higher than reported at December 31, 1991 and 1990.

Maytag Corporation reported operating income before income taxes of $191,507,000 for the year ended December 31, 1991. Based upon the preceding data, determine the income before income taxes that would have been reported in 1991 if inventories had been valued using current costs.

REAL W🌐RLD FOCUS   32. In the annual reports of the 600 companies surveyed for the forty-fifth edition of *Accounting Trends & Techniques*, there were 284 subsequent event disclosures in notes to the statements. (a) What is a subsequent event? (b) Give two examples of subsequent events.

ETHICS DISCUSSION CASE

Janet Smoltz is negotiating the sale of her law practice to Richard Statham. As part of the negotiations, Janet has prepared a list of her clients, with an estimate of fees expected to be earned from each. In some cases, the estimated fees differ from the amounts earned from clients and included in the preceding year's financial statements. In other cases, an amount has been listed as an expected fee from a client for whom no services have been rendered in the past.

SHARPEN YOUR COMMUNICATION SKILLS

Discuss whether Janet Smoltz is behaving in an ethical manner.

EXERCISES

EXERCISE 13-1
EFFECT OF PRICE-LEVEL CHANGE ON INVESTMENT IN LAND
Objective 2d

Several years ago, Valen Company purchased land as a future building site for $100,000. The price-level index at that time was 150. On February 25 of the current year, when the price-level index was 240, the land was sold for $170,000.

a. Determine the amount of the gain that would be realized according to conventional accounting.
b. Indicate the amount of the gain that may be (1) attributed to the change in purchasing power and (2) considered a true gain in terms of current dollars.

EXERCISE 13-2
RECOGNITION OF REVENUE
Objective 2f

Each of the following items involves revenue for a different company:

a. Season tickets for a series of five concerts were sold for $90,000. Two concerts were played during the current year.
b. Merchandise on hand at the end of the current fiscal year, costing $317,500, is expected to be sold in the following year for $420,000.
c. Sixty days before the end of the current fiscal year, $100,000 was loaned at 9% for 90 days.

Chapter Thirteen   Concepts and Principles

481

d. Sales of merchandise on terms of n/30 and delivered during the current year totaled $955,000. No cash was received on these credit sales during the current year.
e. The contract price for building a bridge is $11,000,000. During the current year, the first year of construction, the bridge is estimated to be 20% completed and the costs incurred totaled $1,950,000. Revenue is recognized by the percentage-of-completion method.
f. A tract of land was leased on the first day of the ninth month of the current year, and one year's rent of $60,000 was received.
g. Salespersons submitted orders in the current year for merchandise to be delivered in the following year. The merchandise had a cost of $35,000 and a selling price of $49,250.
h. Cash of $10,000 was received in the current year on the sale of gift certificates to be redeemed in merchandise in the following year.
i. Thirty days before the end of the current fiscal year, a $60,000, 90-day, non-interest-bearing note was accepted at a discount of 9%. Proceeds in the amount of $58,650 were given to the maker of the note.

SHARPEN YOUR COMMUNICATION SKILLS

Indicate for each of the following items the amount of revenue that should be reported for the current year and the amount of revenue that should be postponed to a future period. Give a reason for your answer.

EXERCISE 13-3
GROSS PROFIT BY POINT-OF-SALE AND INSTALLMENT METHODS
Objective 2f

SPREADSHEET PROBLEM

Diana Company makes all sales on the installment plan. Data related to merchandise sold during the current fiscal year are as follows:

Sales	$950,000
Cash received on the $950,000 of installment contracts	350,000
Merchandise inventory, beginning of year	175,000
Merchandise inventory, end of year	167,500
Purchases	657,500

Determine the amount of gross profit that would be recognized for the current fiscal year according to (a) the point-of-sale method and (b) the installment method.

EXERCISE 13-4
DETERMINATION OF COST OF PRODUCTS AND SERVICES ACQUIRED
Objective 2f

Properties and services acquired by an enterprise are generally recorded at cost. For each of the following, determine the cost.

a. Materials and supplies costing $7,500 were purchased for the construction of a display case. An additional $4,500 was paid to hire a carpenter to build the display case. A similar case would cost $15,000 if purchased from a manufacturer.
b. An adjacent tract of land was acquired for $60,000 to provide additional parking for customers. The structures on the land were removed at a cost of $7,500. The salvaged material from the structures was sold for $500. The cost of grading the land was $1,750.
c. Equipment was purchased for $50,000 under terms of n/30, FOB shipping point. The freight charge amounted to $725, and installation costs totaled $1,500.

EXERCISE 13-5
EFFECTS ON FINANCIAL STATEMENTS OF FAILURE TO ACCRUE COMMISSIONS
Objective 2f

Salespersons for Wood Realty receive a commission of 3% of sales, the amount of commissions due on sales of one month being paid in the middle of the following month. At the end of each of the first three years of operations, the accountant failed to record accrued sales commissions expense as follows: first year, $20,000; second year, $27,500; third year, $23,500. In each case, the commissions were paid during the first month of the succeeding year and were charged as an expense of that year. Accrued sales commissions expense was properly recorded at the end of the fourth year.

a. Determine the amount by which net income was overstated or understated for each of the four years.
b. Determine the items on the balance sheet that would have been overstated or understated at the end of each of the four years and the amount of overstatement or understatement.

EXERCISE 13-6
EFFECT ON FINANCIAL STATEMENTS OF FAILURE TO RECORD SALES
Objective 2f

Speelberg Company sells most of its products on a cash basis, but extends short-term credit to a few of its customers. Invoices for sales on account are placed in a file and are not recorded until cash is received, at which time the sale is recorded in the same manner as a cash sale. The net income reported for the first three years of operations was $191,500, $180,000, and $202,000, respectively. The total amount of the uncollected sales invoices in the file at the end of each of the three years was $6,500, $5,000, and $7,500, respectively. In each case, the entire amount was collected during the first month of the succeeding year.

a. Determine the amount by which net income was overstated or understated for each of the three years.

b. Determine the items on the balance sheet that were overstated or understated, and the amount of overstatement or understatement, as of the end of each year.

EXERCISE 13-7
DETERMINATION OF
MATERIALITY
Objectives 2g, 2i

Of the following matters, considered individually, indicate those that are material and that should be disclosed in the financial statements or in accompanying explanatory notes.

a. A merchandising company employs the first-in, first-out cost flow assumption and prices its inventory at the lower of cost or market.

b. A change in the estimate of the remaining usefulness of computer equipment decreased the amount of net income that would otherwise have been reported from $1,100,000 to $800,000.

c. A company is facing litigation involving restraint of trade. Damages might amount to $5,000,000. Annual net income reported in the past few years has ranged from $10,000,000 to $13,500,000.

d. A change in accounting for depreciation of plant assets was adopted in the current year. The amount of net income that would otherwise have been reported decreased from $990,000 to $975,000.

e. Between the end of the fiscal year and the date of publication of the annual report, a fire completely destroyed one of three principal plants. The loss was estimated at $5,000,000 and was fully covered by insurance. The net income for the fiscal year was $1,125,000.

EXERCISE 13-8
EFFECT OF DIFFERENT
INVENTORY COST
METHODS ON NET INCOME
Objectives 2g, 2i

The cost of merchandise inventory at the end of the first fiscal year of operations, according to three different methods, is as follows: fifo, $90,000; average, $86,500; lifo, $80,000. If the average cost method is used, the net income reported will be $65,000.

a. What will be the amount of net income reported if the lifo method is adopted?

b. What will be the amount of net income reported if the fifo method is adopted?

c. Which of the three methods is the most conservative in terms of net income?

d. Is the particular method adopted of sufficient materiality to require disclosure in the financial statements?

EXERCISE 13-9
IDENTIFICATION OF
GENERALLY ACCEPTED
ACCOUNTING PRINCIPLES
Objective 2

Each of the following statements represents a decision made by an accountant:

a. In preparing the balance sheet, detailed information as to the amount due to dozens of creditors was omitted. The total amount was presented under the caption *Accounts Payable*.

b. Land, used as a parking lot, was purchased 20 years ago for $50,000. Since its market value is now $250,000, the land account is debited for $200,000 and a gain account is credited for a like amount. The gain is presented as an *Other income* item in the income statement.

c. All minor expenditures for office equipment are charged to an expense account.

d. Merchandise transferred to other parties on a consignment basis and not sold was included in merchandise inventory.

e. Used computer equipment, with an estimated useful life of 5 years and no salvage value, was purchased early in the current fiscal year for $250,000. Since the company planned to purchase new equipment, costing $400,000, to replace this equipment at the end of five years, depreciation expense of $80,000 was recorded for the current year. The depreciation expense thus provided for one-fifth of the cost of the replacement.

f. Merchandise inventory at the end of the current year was estimated by the general manager, who "eye-balled" the inventory on hand and then determined its cost, based on an estimate of current costs. The accountant used the general manager's estimate for recording the cost of the inventory in the accounts.

g. Thirty days before the end of the current year, sales catalogs were acquired for $75,000. Although the catalogs are not salable, the unused portion is included as an asset in the balance sheet at the end of the year.

h. Net income for the current year is expected to be larger than normal. Therefore, the accountant used the declining-balance method for determining depreciation for the current year to reduce the net income to a more normal amount. The accountant plans to use the straight-line method in future years. The straight-line method has been used in all past years for determining income.

i. Financial statements adjusted to eliminate the effects of inflation (using the current cost method) were presented as supplementary financial data.

SHARPEN YOUR ►
COMMUNICATION SKILLS

State whether or not you agree with the decision. Support your answer with reference to generally accepted accounting principles that are applicable in the circumstances.

WhAT'S WRONG WITH THIS?

Drabek Department Stores has been reporting merchandise inventory by the lower-of-cost-or-market method. However, the replacement cost of its inventory has risen significantly during the current year. Therefore, Drabek Department Stores elected to report the merchandise inventory at the end of the current year at current market prices. The change in method was disclosed in a note to the financial statements that fully reported the effect of the use of market prices on the balance sheet and income statement. Is there anything wrong with the reporting?

PROBLEMS

Series A

PROBLEM 13-1A
INSTALLMENT SALES
Objective 2f

Puckett Co. makes all sales on the installment basis and recognizes revenue at the point of sale. Condensed income statements and the amounts collected from customers for each of the first three years of operations are as follows:

	First Year	Second Year	Third Year
Sales	$398,750	$340,000	$382,000
Cost of merchandise sold	271,150	227,800	248,300
Gross profit	$127,600	$112,200	$133,700
Operating expenses	60,000	51,500	62,250
Net income	$ 67,600	$ 60,700	$ 71,450
Collected from sales of first year	$121,250	$157,500	$120,000
Collected from sales of second year		95,000	145,000
Collected from sales of third year			99,000

Instructions

1. Determine the gross profit percentage for each year.
2. Determine the amount of net income or loss that would have been reported in each year if the installment method of recognizing revenue had been used, ignoring the possible effects of uncollectible accounts on the computation.

PROBLEM 13-2A
INSTALLMENT SALE AND
REPOSSESSION
Objective 2f

Martino Video uses the installment method of recognizing gross profit for sales made on the installment plan. Details of a particular installment sale, amounts collected from the buyer, and the repossession of the item sold are as follows:

First year:
   Sold for $800 a television set having a cost of $640; received a down payment of $150.
Second year:
   Received 12 monthly payments of $25 each.
Third year:
   The buyer defaulted on the monthly payments, the set was repossessed, and the remaining 14 installments were canceled. The set was sold for $250.

Instructions

1. Determine the gross profit to be recognized in the first year.
2. Determine the gross profit to be recognized in the second year.
3. Determine the gain or loss to be recognized from the repossession and sale of the set in the third year. (*Suggestion*: First determine the amount of the unrecovered cost in the canceled installments. The gain or loss will then be the difference between this unrecovered cost and the sales price of the repossessed set.)

PROBLEM 13-3A
PERCENTAGE-OF-
COMPLETION METHOD
Objective 2f

Munoz Company began construction on three contracts during 1993. The contract prices and construction activities for 1993, 1994, and 1995 were as follows:

Contract	Contract Price	1993 Costs Incurred	1993 Percent Completed	1994 Costs Incurred	1994 Percent Completed	1995 Costs Incurred	1995 Percent Completed
1	$ 5,000,000	$1,810,000	40%	$1,575,000	35%	$1,090,000	25%
2	10,000,000	2,550,000	30	2,625,000	30	2,695,000	30
3	8,000,000	3,710,000	50	3,815,000	50	—	—

SPREADSHEET PROBLEM

Instructions

Determine the amount of revenue and the income to be recognized for each of the years, 1993, 1994, and 1995. Revenue is to be recognized by the percentage-of-completion method.

PROBLEM 13-4A
EFFECT ON NET INCOME FROM CHANGES IN THREE ACCOUNTING PRINCIPLES
Objective 2f

Gagne Co. was organized on January 3, 1993. During its first three years of operations, the company calculated uncollectible accounts expense by the direct write-off method, the cost of the merchandise inventory at the end of the period by the first-in, first-out method, and depreciation expense by the straight-line method. The amount of net income reported and the amounts of the foregoing items for each of the three years were as follows:

	First Year	Second Year	Third Year
Net income reported	$105,000	$142,000	$175,000
Uncollectible accounts expense	1,125	2,800	5,950
Ending merchandise inventory	60,750	82,000	112,000
Depreciation expense	20,000	26,800	35,000

The firm is considering the possibility of changing to the following methods in determining net income for the fourth and subsequent years: provision for doubtful accounts through the use of an allowance account, last-in, first-out inventory, and declining-balance depreciation at twice the straight-line rate. To consider the probable future effect of these changes on the determination of net income, the management requests that net income of the past three years be recomputed on the basis of the proposed methods. The uncollectible accounts expense, inventory, and depreciation expense for the past three years, computed in accordance with the proposed methods, are as follows:

	First Year	Second Year	Third Year
Uncollectible accounts expense	$ 2,625	$ 3,500	$ 4,250
Ending merchandise inventory	59,000	70,100	92,750
Depreciation expense	40,000	38,840	34,100

Instructions

Recompute the net income for each of the three years, presenting the figures in the following format:

	First Year	Second Year	Third Year
Net income reported			
Increase (decrease) in net income attributable to change in method of determining:			
Uncollectible accounts expense			
Ending merchandise inventory			
Depreciation expense			
Total			
Net income as recomputed			

PROBLEM 13-5A
ADJUSTING AND CORRECTING ENTRIES
Objective 2

You are engaged to review the accounting records of Maldonado Company prior to the closing of the revenue and expense accounts as of December 31, the end of the current fiscal year. The following information comes to your attention during the review:

   a. Accounts receivable include $8,000 owed by J. J. Jeffries Co., a bankrupt company. There is no prospect of collecting any of the receivable. The allowance method of accounting for receivables is used.

b. Land recorded in the accounts at a cost of $75,000 was appraised at $112,500 by two expert appraisers.

c. The company is being sued for $2,000,000 by a customer who claims damages for personal injury allegedly caused by a defective product. Company attorneys and outside legal counsel feel extremely confident that the company will have no liability for damages resulting from this case.

d. The prepaid insurance account has a balance of $7,175. At December 31, the unexpired premiums were $2,200.

e. Since net income for the current year is expected to be considerably less than it was for the preceding year, depreciation on buildings has not been recorded. Depreciation for the year, determined in a manner consistent with the preceding year, amounts to $52,100.

f. No interest has been accrued on a $100,000, 12%, 90-day note receivable, dated November 1 of the current year.

g. Merchandise inventory at December 31 of the current year has been recorded in the accounts at cost, $277,150. Current market price of the inventory is $286,500.

Instructions

SHARPEN YOUR COMMUNICATION SKILLS ►
Journalize any entries required to adjust or correct the accounts, identifying each entry by letter. For those items for which no entry is necessary, explain why an entry should not be made.

PROBLEM 13-6A
ADJUSTMENTS AND CORRECTIONS ON WORK SHEET; FINANCIAL STATEMENTS
Objective 2

Chris Bosio owns and manages The Gallery on a full-time basis. He also maintains the accounting records. At the end of the first year of operations, he prepared the following balance sheet and income statement:

The Gallery
Balance Sheet
December 31, 19—

Cash	$ 7,750
Equipment	17,250
Chris Bosio	$25,000

The Gallery
Income Statement
For Year Ended December 31, 19—

Sales		$98,700
Purchases		73,500
Gross profit		$25,200
Operating expenses:		
Salary expense	$17,850	
Rent expense	13,000	
Utilities expense	5,100	
Miscellaneous expense	1,750	
Total operating expenses		37,700
Net loss		$12,500

Because of the large net loss reported on the income statement, Bosio is considering discontinuing operations. Before making a decision, he asks you to review the accounting methods used and, if material errors are found, to prepare revised statements. The following information is obtained during the course of the review:

a. The only transactions recorded have been those in which cash was received or paid.

b. The accounts have not been closed for the year.

c. The business was established on January 3 by an investment of $30,000 in cash by the owner. An additional investment of $7,500 was made in cash on June 10.

d. The equipment listed on the balance sheet at $17,250 was purchased for cash on January 5. Equipment purchased July 1 for $5,000 in cash was debited to Purchases. Equipment purchased on December 31 for $4,000, for which a 60-day, 12% note was issued, was not recorded.

e. Depreciation on equipment has not been recorded. The equipment is estimated to have a useful life of 10 years and no salvage value. (Use the straight-line method.)

f. Accounts receivable from customers at December 31 total $6,700.

g. Uncollectible accounts are estimated at $475.
h. The merchandise inventory at December 31, as nearly as can be determined, has a cost of $12,750.
i. Insurance premiums of $850 were debited to Miscellaneous Expense during the year. The unexpired portion at December 31 is $350.
j. Supplies of $1,000 purchased during the year were debited to Purchases. An estimated $250 of supplies were on hand at December 31.
k. A total of $5,000 is owed to merchandise creditors on account at December 31.
l. Rent Expense includes an advance payment of $1,000 for the month of January in the subsequent year.
m. Salaries owed but not paid on December 31 total $350.
n. The classification of operating expenses as *selling* and *administrative* is not considered to be sufficiently important to justify the cost of the analysis.
o. The proprietor made no withdrawals during the year.

Instructions

1. On the basis of the financial statements presented, prepare an unadjusted trial balance, as of December 31, on an eight-column work sheet. Leave an extra line blank after *Equipment* and *Purchases*.
2. Enter the adjustments and the corrections in the Adjustments columns. Complete the work sheet by extending the adjusted trial balance amounts directly to the appropriate Income Statement or Balance Sheet columns.
3. Prepare a multiple-step income statement, a statement of owner's equity, and a report form balance sheet.

Instructions for Solving Problem 13-6A Using Solutions Software

SOLUTIONS
SOFTWARE

1. Load opening balances.
2. Save the opening balances file to your drive and directory.
3. Set the run date to December 31 of the current year and enter your name.
4. Key the adjusting entries. Key ADJ.ENT. in the reference field.
5. Display the adjusting entries. Key ADJ.ENT. in the Reference Restriction area of the Selection Options screen.
6. Display the financial statements.
7. Save a backup copy of your data file.
8. Perform period-end closing.
9. Display a post-closing trial balance.
10. Save your data file to disk.
11. End the session.

Series B

PROBLEM 13-1B
INSTALLMENT SALES
Objective 2f

D. J. Aguilera Co. makes all sales on the installment basis and recognizes revenue at the point of sale. Condensed income statements and the amounts collected from customers for each of the first three years of operations are as follows:

	First Year	Second Year	Third Year
Sales	$300,000	$340,000	$440,000
Cost of merchandise sold	195,000	224,400	281,600
Gross profit	$105,000	$115,600	$158,400
Operating expenses	62,500	68,500	98,400
Net income	$ 42,500	$ 47,100	$ 60,000
Collected from sales of first year	$ 75,000	$125,000	$100,000
Collected from sales of second year		110,000	180,000
Collected from sales of third year			115,000

Instructions

1. Determine the gross profit percentage for each year.
2. Determine the amount of net income or loss that would have been reported in each year if the installment method of recognizing revenue had been used, ignoring the possible effects of uncollectible accounts on the computation.

PROBLEM 13-2B
INSTALLMENT SALE AND
REPOSSESSION
Objective 2f

Higuera Video uses the installment method of recognizing gross profit for sales made on the installment plan. Details of a particular installment sale, amounts collected from the buyer, and the repossession of the item sold are as follows:

First year:
  Sold for $900 a television set having a cost of $720; received a down payment of $150.
Second year:
  Received 12 monthly payments of $30 each.
Third year:
  The buyer defaulted on the monthly payments, the set was repossessed, and the remaining 13 installments were canceled. The set was sold for $350.

Instructions

1. Determine the gross profit to be recognized in the first year.
2. Determine the gross profit to be recognized in the second year.
3. Determine the gain or loss to be recognized from the repossession and sale of the set in the third year. (*Suggestion*: First determine the amount of the unrecovered cost in the canceled installments. The gain or loss will then be the difference between this unrecovered cost and the sales price of the repossessed set.)

PROBLEM 13-3B
PERCENTAGE-OF-
COMPLETION METHOD
Objective 2f

T. Rodriguez Company began construction on three contracts during 1993. The contract prices and construction activities for 1993, 1994, and 1995 were as follows:

SPREADSHEET
PROBLEM

		1993		1994		1995	
Contract	Contract Price	Costs Incurred	Percent Completed	Costs Incurred	Percent Completed	Costs Incurred	Percent Completed
1	$6,000,000	$2,175,000	40%	$3,250,000	60%	—	—
2	4,000,000	600,000	20	1,375,000	40	$1,500,000	40%
3	3,500,000	455,000	15	985,000	30	1,575,000	50

Instructions
Determine the amount of revenue and the income to be recognized for each of the years, 1993, 1994, and 1995. Revenue is to be recognized by the percentage-of-completion method.

PROBLEM 13-4B
EFFECT ON NET INCOME
FROM CHANGES IN THREE
ACCOUNTING PRINCIPLES
Objective 2f

Tabler Co. was organized on January 3, 1993. During its first three years of operations, the company calculated uncollectible accounts expense by the direct write-off method, the cost of the merchandise inventory at the end of the period by the first-in, first-out method, and depreciation expense by the straight-line method. The amount of net income reported and the amounts of the foregoing items for each of the three years were as follows:

	First Year	Second Year	Third Year
Net income reported	$40,200	$60,750	$69,900
Uncollectible accounts expense	1,050	2,350	4,250
Ending merchandise inventory	49,750	54,000	58,150
Depreciation expense	19,000	19,900	20,900

The firm is considering the possibility of changing to the following methods in determining net income for the fourth and subsequent years: provision for doubtful accounts through the use of an allowance account, last-in, first-out inventory, and declining-balance depreciation at twice the straight-line rate. To consider the probable future effect of these changes on the determination of net income, the management requests that net income of the past three years be recomputed on the basis of the proposed methods. The uncollectible accounts expense, inventory, and depreciation expense for the past three years, computed in accordance with the proposed methods, are as follows:

	First Year	Second Year	Third Year
Uncollectible accounts expense	$ 1,625	$ 2,900	$ 4,000
Ending merchandise inventory	53,000	52,900	59,650
Depreciation expense	38,000	32,000	27,520

Instructions

Recompute the net income for each of the three years, presenting the figures in the following format:

	First Year	Second Year	Third Year
Net income reported			
Increase (decrease) in net income attributable to change in method of determining:			
Uncollectible accounts expense			
Ending merchandise inventory			
Depreciation expense			
Total			
Net income as recomputed			

PROBLEM 13-5B
ADJUSTING AND
CORRECTING ENTRIES
Objective 2

You are engaged to review the accounting records of Leo Gomez Company prior to the closing of the revenue and expense accounts as of June 30, the end of the current fiscal year. The following information comes to your attention during the review:

a. Since net income for the current year is expected to be considerably less than it was for the preceding year, depreciation on equipment has not been recorded. Depreciation for the year, determined in a manner consistent with the preceding year, amounts to $29,600.

b. Land recorded in the accounts at a cost of $75,000 was appraised at $120,000 by two expert appraisers.

c. No interest has been accrued on a $50,000, 12%, 90-day note payable, dated May 31 of the current year.

d. The office supplies account has a balance of $7,250. The cost of the office supplies at June 30, as determined by a physical count, was $1,250.

e. Merchandise inventory at June 30 of the current year has been recorded in the accounts at cost, $215,200. Current market price of the inventory is $218,750.

f. Accounts receivable includes $14,625 owed by Baker and Wilson Co., a bankrupt company. Leo Gomez Company expects to receive twenty cents on each dollar owed. The allowance method of accounting for receivables is used.

g. The company is being sued for $1,500,000 by a customer who claims damages for personal injury allegedly caused by a defective product. Company attorneys and outside legal counsel feel extremely confident that the company will have no liability for damages resulting from this case.

h. The company received a debit memorandum with the bank statement from Palmer National Bank, indicating that a customer note discounted at the bank has been dishonored. The 12%, 90-day note is from Cowens Co. and has a $40,000 face value. Leo Gomez Company has not recorded the memorandum, which included a protest fee of $15.

SHARPEN YOUR COMMUNICATION SKILLS

Instructions

Journalize any entries required to adjust or correct the accounts, identifying each entry by letter. For those items for which no entry is necessary, explain why an entry should not be made.

PROBLEM 13-6B
ADJUSTMENTS AND
CORRECTIONS ON WORK
SHEET; FINANCIAL
STATEMENTS
Objective 2

Alice Marx owns and manages The Art Mart on a full-time basis. She also maintains the accounting records. At the end of the first year of operations, she prepared the following balance sheet and income statement:

The Art Mart
Balance Sheet
December 31, 19—

Cash		$ 8,000
Equipment		12,000
Alice Marx		$20,000

The Art Mart
Income Statement
For Year Ended December 31, 19—

Sales		$146,750
Purchases		90,500
Gross profit		$ 56,250
Operating expenses:		
Salary expense	$38,410	
Rent expense	16,800	
Utilities expense	4,225	
Miscellaneous expense	2,315	
Total operating expenses		61,750
Net loss		$ 5,500

Because of the large net loss reported on the income statement, Marx is considering discontinuing operations. Before making a decision, she asks you to review the accounting methods used and, if material errors are found, to prepare revised statements. The following information is discovered during the course of the review:

a. The only transactions recorded have been those in which cash was received or paid.
b. The accounts have not been closed for the year.
c. The classification of operating expenses as *selling* and *administrative* is not considered to be sufficiently important to justify the cost of the analysis.
d. The proprietor made no withdrawals during the year.
e. The business was established on January 26 by an investment of $17,500 in cash by the owner. An additional investment of $8,000 was made in cash on June 1.
f. Accounts receivable from customers at December 31 total $10,250.
g. The merchandise inventory at December 31, as nearly as can be determined, has a cost of $23,425.
h. Rent Expense includes an advance payment of $1,400 for the month of January in the subsequent year.
i. Salaries owed but not paid on December 31 total $925.
j. The equipment listed on the balance sheet at $12,000 was purchased for cash on February 1. Equipment purchased April 1 for $6,000 in cash was debited to Purchases. Equipment purchased on December 31 for $7,000, for which a 90-day, 12% note was issued, was not recorded.
k. Uncollectible accounts are estimated at $950.
l. A total of $17,500 is owed to merchandise creditors on account at December 31.
m. Depreciation on equipment has not been recorded. The equipment is estimated to have a useful life of 10 years and no salvage value. (Use the straight-line method.)
n. Insurance premiums of $1,250 were debited to Miscellaneous Expense during the year. The unexpired portion at December 31 is $400.
o. Supplies of $2,400 purchased during the year were debited to Purchases. An estimated $800 of supplies were on hand at December 31.

Instructions

1. On the basis of the financial statements presented, prepare an unadjusted trial balance, as of December 31, on an eight-column work sheet. Leave an extra line blank after *Equipment* and *Purchases*.
2. Enter the adjustments and the corrections in the Adjustments columns. Complete the work sheet by extending the adjusted trial balance amounts directly to the appropriate Income Statement or Balance Sheet columns.
3. Prepare a multiple-step income statement, a statement of owner's equity, and a report form balance sheet.

**SOLUTIONS
SOFTWARE**

Instructions for Solving Problem 13-6B Using Solutions Software

1. Load opening balances.
2. Save the opening balances file to your drive and directory.
3. Set the run date to December 31 of the current year and enter your name.
4. Key the adjusting entries. Key ADJ.ENT. in the reference field.

5. Display the adjusting entries. Key ADJ.ENT. in the Reference Restriction area of the Selection Options screen.
6. Display the financial statements.
7. Save a backup copy of your data file.
8. Perform period-end closing.
9. Display a post-closing trial balance.
10. Save your data file to disk.
11. End the session.

MINI-CASE 13 J. B. PARTS CO.

J. B. Parts Co. operates ten cash-and-carry auto parts stores in the Southeast. In an effort to expand sales, the company has decided to offer two additional sales plans:

a. Credit sales to commercial enterprises, such as body and repair shops, with free 24-hour delivery.
b. Installment sales of major dollar items, with payments spread over 36 months.

The company president has asked you when the revenue from each of the two new plans would be recognized in the accounting records and statements.

Instructions:

1. Indicate to the president when the revenue from each type of sale should be journalized in the accounting records.
2. While discussing the concepts in (1), the president raised the following questions related to various accounting concepts. How would you respond to each?

a. ▥▥ ▸ "Many businesses cease operating each year; so why do accountants assume a going concern concept when preparing the financial statements?"
b. ▥▥ ▸ "To assume that the value of the dollar does not change and that we don't have inflation is wrong! An automatic transmission that cost $400 five years ago costs $500 today. Why wouldn't it be better to use current dollars, at least for the inventory?"
c. ▥▥ ▸ "With so many different accounting methods that can be used, why can't I switch methods to improve net income this year?"
d. ▥▥ ▸ "Our annual bonuses to store managers are based on store profits. It is not fair to 'anticipate no profits and provide for all losses.'"

ANSWERS TO SELF-EXAMINATION QUESTIONS

1. **A** In the balance sheet, the equipment should be reported at its cost less accumulated depreciation, $100,000 (answer A). The effect of the declining value of the dollar on plant assets, the market value of plant assets, and the replacement cost of plant assets are not recognized in the basic historical cost statements.

2. **A** Under the installment method of accounting, gross profit is realized in accordance with the amount of cash collected in each year, based on the percent of gross profit to sales. For this question, the amount of gross profit to be realized for the current year is $22,500 (answer A), determined as follows:

Percent of gross profit to sales:
$60,000 ÷ $200,000 = 30%

Gross profit realized:
$75,000 × 30% = $22,500

3. **A** Under the percentage-of-completion method of accounting, the amount of revenue to be recognized during a period is determined on the basis of the estimated percentage of the contract that has been completed during the period. The costs incurred during the period are deducted from this revenue to yield the income from the contract. The $950,000 of income (answer A) is determined as follows:

Revenue realized (40% × $20,000,000)	$8,000,000
Costs incurred	7,050,000
Income	$ 950,000

4. **D** In some situations, there are a number of accepted alternative principles that can be used. To ensure a high degree of comparability of the financial statements between periods, a change from one accepted principle to another should be disclosed. A change in method of inventory pricing (answer A), a change in depreciation method for previously recorded plant assets (answer B), and a change in method of accounting for installment sales (answer C) are examples of changes in accepted alternative principles that should be appropriately disclosed. A change in the method of reporting cents in the financial statements (answer D) is not a change in a principle.

5. **D** The concept of materiality (answer D) relates to the acceptance of a procedure that deviates from absolute accuracy for insignificant or immaterial items, such as reporting cents in financial statements .

Answer to Triangle Puzzle

Twenty-four triangles are in the figure, as follows: ABE, ABH, ACD, ACE, ACF, ACH, ADE, ADF, AEH, AFH, BCE, BCH, CDF, CDH, CEF, CEH, DEF, DEG, DEH, DFH, DGH, EFG, EFH, FGH

Part 5

Partnerships

CHAPTER 14
Partnership
Formation, Income
Division, and
Liquidation

You and Accounting

Assume that you and your roommate have an idea for starting a part-time business to earn some extra spending money.

What does it take to start a business operated by two or more individuals? How much money should each individual (you and your roommate) contribute to start the business? How will the profits be divided? Can you withdraw money from the business whenever you want, or do you have to have your roommate's (partner's) approval? Can your roommate bring someone else into the business as a partner without your approval? Could you or your roommate quit the business at any time? Will you be liable for commitments made by your roommate, even if they were made without your knowledge? Is the amount you can lose in the business, if it's not successful, limited to the amount you initially invested?

This chapter discusses the partnership form of organization, which is the form you and your friend would be using in operating your business. The answers to the questions above and the accounting for partnerships will be addressed throughout this discussion.

Chapter 14
Partnership Formation, Income Division, and Liquidation

LEARNING OBJECTIVES
After studying this chapter, you should be able to:

Objective 1
Identify and list the basic characteristics of the partnership form of organization.

Objective 2
List the major advantages and disadvantages of the partnership form of organization.

Objective 3
Summarize the basic accounting system for partnerships.

Objective 4
Journalize the entries for the formation of partnerships.

Objective 5
Journalize the entries for dividing partnership net income and net loss.

Objective 6
Prepare financial statements for partnerships.

Objective 7
Journalize the entries for partnership dissolution, including admission of new partners and the withdrawal or death of partners.

Objective 8
Journalize the entries for liquidating partnerships.

The partnership form of business organization allows two or more persons to combine capital, managerial talent, and experience with a minimum of effort. This form is widely used by small businesses. In many cases, the only alternative to the partnership form of organization is the corporate form. Some states, however, do not permit the corporate form for certain types of businesses. For example, physicians, attorneys, and certified public accountants often organize as partnerships. Medical and legal partnerships made up of 20 or more partners are not unusual, and the number of partners in some national CPA firms exceeds 1,000.

The preceding chapters focused on the accounting for sole proprietorships. This chapter describes and illustrates the accounting for the partnership form of organization.

CHARACTERISTICS OF PARTNERSHIPS

Objective 1
Identify and list the basic
characteristics of the partnership
form of organization.

A **partnership** is "an association of two or more persons to carry on as co-owners a business for profit."[1] Partnerships have several characteristics with accounting implications. These characteristics are described in the following paragraphs.

A partnership has a **limited life**. Dissolution of a partnership occurs whenever a partner ceases to be a member of the firm. For example, a partnership is dissolved if a withdrawal of a partner occurs due to bankruptcy, incapacity, or death. Likewise, the admission of a new partner dissolves the old partnership. When a partnership is dissolved, a new partnership must be formed if operations of the business are to continue. This situation often occurs in professional partnerships. Their membership changes as new partners join the firm and others retire.

Most partnerships are *general partnerships*, in which the partners have **unlimited liability**. Each partner is individually liable to creditors for debts incurred by the partnership. Thus, if a partnership becomes insolvent, the partners must contribute sufficient personal assets to settle the debts of the partnership. In some states, a *limited partnership* may be formed. In a limited partnership, the liability of some partners may be limited to the amount of their capital investment. However, a limited partnership must have at least one general partner who has unlimited liability. In this chapter, the discussion focuses on the general partnership.

Partners have **co-ownership of partnership property**. The property invested in a partnership by a partner becomes the property of all the partners jointly. When a partnership is dissolved, the partners' claims against the assets are measured by the amount of the balances in their capital accounts.

Another characteristic of a partnership is **mutual agency**. This means that each partner is an agent of the partnership. Thus, each partner has the authority to enter into contracts for the partnership. The acts of each partner bind the entire partnership and become the obligations of all partners.

An important right of partners is **participation in income** of the partnership. Net income and net loss are distributed among the partners according to their agreement. In the absence of any agreement, all partners share equally. If the agreement indicates a profit distribution but is silent as to losses, the losses are shared in the same manner as profits.

A partnership, like a sole proprietorship, is a **nontaxable entity** and thus does not pay federal income taxes. However, revenue and expense and other results of partnership operations must be reported annually to the Internal Revenue Service. This reporting is done on information returns. The partners must, in turn, report their share of partnership income on their personal tax returns.

A partnership is created by a contract. It is not necessary that the contract be in writing, nor even that its terms be specifically expressed. However, good business practice requires that the contract be in writing and that it clearly expresses the intentions of the partners. The contract is known as the partnership agreement or **articles of partnership**. It should include statements regarding such matters as amounts to be invested, limits on withdrawals, distributions of income and losses, and admission and withdrawal of partners.

ADVANTAGES AND DISADVANTAGES OF PARTNERSHIPS

Objective 2
List the major advantages and
disadvantages of the partnership
form of organization.

The partnership form of business organization is less widely used than are the sole proprietorship and corporate forms. For many business purposes, however, the advantages of the partnership form are greater than its disadvantages.

A partnership is relatively easy and inexpensive to organize, requiring only an agreement between two or more persons. A partnership has the advantage of bringing together more capital, managerial skills, and experience than does a sole proprietorship. Since a partnership is a nontaxable entity, the combined income

---

[1] This definition of a partnership is included in the Uniform Partnership Act, which has been adopted by over ninety percent of the states.

taxes paid by the individual partners may be lower than the income taxes that would be paid by a corporation, which is a taxable entity.

The disadvantages of a partnership are that its life is limited, each partner has unlimited liability, and one partner can bind the partnership to contracts. Also, raising large amounts of capital is more difficult for a partnership than for a corporation.

ACCOUNTING FOR PARTNERSHIPS

Objective 3
Summarize the basic accounting system for partnerships.

Most of the day-to-day accounting for a partnership is the same as the accounting for any other form of business organization. The accounting system described in previous chapters may, with little change, be used by a partnership. For example, the journals described may be used unchanged. The chart of accounts, with the exception of drawing and capital accounts for each partner, does not differ from the chart of accounts of a similar business conducted by a single owner. It is in the areas of the formation, income distribution, dissolution, and liquidation of partnerships that transactions unique to partnerships arise. The remainder of this chapter discusses accounting principles related to these areas.

FORMATION OF A PARTNERSHIP

Objective 4
Journalize the entries for the formation of partnerships.

A separate entry is made for the investment of each partner in a partnership. The assets contributed by a partner are debited to the partnership asset accounts. If liabilities are assumed by the partnership, the partnership liability accounts are credited. The partner's capital account is credited for the net amount.

To illustrate, assume that Joseph A. Stevens and Earl S. Foster, sole owners of competing hardware stores, agree to combine their businesses in a partnership. Each is to contribute certain amounts of cash and other business assets. It is also agreed that the partnership is to assume the liabilities of the separate businesses. The entry to record the assets contributed and the liabilities transferred by Stevens is as follows:

Apr. 1	Cash	7,200	
	Accounts Receivable	16,300	
	Merchandise Inventory	28,700	
	Store Equipment	5,400	
	Office Equipment	1,500	
	Allowance for Doubtful Accounts		1,500
	Accounts Payable		2,600
	Joseph A. Stevens, Capital		55,000

A similar entry would record the assets contributed and the liabilities transferred by Foster. In each entry, the noncash assets are recorded at values agreed upon by the partners. These values represent the acquisition cost to the new partnership. The agreed-upon values normally represent current market values and therefore usually differ from the book values of the assets in the records of the separate businesses. For example, the store equipment recorded at $5,400 in the preceding entry may have had a book value of $3,500 in Stevens's ledger (cost of $10,000 less accumulated depreciation of $6,500).

Receivables contributed to the partnership are recorded at their face amount. Future bad debts are provided for by crediting a contra account. Only accounts that are likely to be collected are normally transferred to the partnership. For example, assume that in the prior example the accounts receivable ledger of Stevens totaled $17,600. Of this total, accounts of $1,300 are considered worthless. The remaining receivables of $16,300 were transferred to the partnership accounts by a debit to the accounts receivable account in the general ledger. A subsidiary ledger is set up by debiting each customer's individual account. Finally, an allowance for possible uncollectible accounts is recorded by crediting Allowance for Doubtful Accounts for $1,500.

DIVIDING NET INCOME OR NET LOSS

Objective 5
Journalize the entries for dividing partnership net income and net loss.

The net income of a partnership should be divided among partners in a fair and equitable manner. Partners are not legally employees of the partnership, nor are their capital contributions a loan. If each partner contributes equal services and amounts of capital, an equal division of partnership net income would be equitable. However, if one partner contributes a larger portion of capital than the others, then the division of net income should provide for the unequal capital contributions. Likewise, if the services rendered by one partner are more important than those of the others, the unequal service contributions should be recognized in dividing net income. Such differences among partners should be agreed upon by the partners in their partnership agreement.

Executive Compensation—A Partnership vs. a Corporation

In a report prepared for a Congressional subcommittee, Deloitte, Haskins & Sells (now Deloitte & Touche, a public accounting partnership) described its view of partner compensation and the division of the firm's income. Excerpts from that report are as follows:

. . . As a general rule, compensation in major mid-sized corporations (to which we might be compared based on revenue size, number of personnel, etc.) consists of current cash, deferred payments, payments made on behalf of an individual for retirement benefits, and perquisites. In addition, options to purchase stock at potentially favorable prices may also be an attractive compensation component. Unlike a corporation, partners . . . must provide from their own earnings for their own retirement benefits, as well as paying for self-employment taxes, group insurance, and other benefit programs. As a partnership, of course, our partners . . . do not have stock options available. . . .

Each year the majority of the firm's earnings are distributed to the partners. Some small percentage is usually retained for working capital needs. No amounts are guaranteed, like a "preset" annual salary. If earnings decline, partners'. . . individual earnings also decline. Partners . . . are also required to invest capital in the firm. As such, part of their earnings represent a return on their investment. . . . With regard to their firm activities, partners have a much broader exposure to personal liability than do most corporate officers.

The factors mentioned above must be considered in making meaningful comparisons of partners' compensation with other business executives. To simply compare amounts would be misleading.

The average earnings of all of our partners for fiscal year 1985 was approximately $143,000. As to our five most highly compensated partners, their individual earnings ranged from $385,000 to $725,000, and their average was $500,000. . . .

Source : Deloitte, Haskins & Sells, *A Report for Congress and the Public* (September 1985).

It should be noted that dividing the net income or the net loss among the partners in exact accordance with their partnership agreement is essential. In the absence of a partnership agreement or if the agreement is silent on dividing net income or net losses, all partners share equally. This is true regardless of differences among the partners in the amounts of capital contributed, skills possessed, or time devoted to the business. In preparing a partnership agreement, accountants are often called upon to advise partners on fair and equitable methods of dividing income and losses. Examples of partnership agreements that recognize differences in capital contributions and services among partners are presented next.

Income Division—Services of Partners

Differences in ability and in amount of time devoted to the business may be recognized in dividing net income. One method of doing so is to provide for salary allowances to partners. Such allowances are treated as divisions of partnership net income and are credited to the partners' capital accounts. Accountants should be careful to distinguish between salary allowances and partner withdrawals. Partner withdrawals are debited to the partners' drawing accounts.

To illustrate, assume that the partnership agreement of Jennifer L. Stone and Crystal R. Mills provides for monthly salary allowances. Jennifer Stone is to receive a monthly allowance of $2,500, and Crystal Mills is to receive $2,000 a month. Any remaining net income after the salary allowances is to be divided equally. Assume also that the net income for the year is $75,000.

A report of the division of net income may be presented as a separate statement to accompany the balance sheet and the income statement. Another format is to add the division to the bottom of the income statement. If the latter format is used, the lower part of the income statement would appear as follows:

Net income $75,000

Division of net income:

	J. L. Stone	C. R. Mills	Total
Salary allowance	$30,000	$24,000	$54,000
Remaining income	10,500	10,500	21,000
Net income	$40,500	$34,500	$75,000

The division of net income is recorded as a closing entry, even if the partners do not actually withdraw the amounts of their salary allowances. The entry for the division of net income is as follows:

Dec. 31	Income Summary	75,000	
	Jennifer L. Stone, Capital		40,500
	Crystal R. Mills, Capital		34,500

If Stone and Mills had withdrawn their salary allowances monthly, the withdrawals would have been debited to their drawing accounts during the year. At the end of the year, the debit balances of $30,000 and $24,000 in their drawing accounts would be transferred to their capital accounts.

It is important to distinguish between the division of net income and partner withdrawals. The division of net income is determined by the partnership agreement, or in the absence of an agreement, the net income is shared equally. In most cases, the amount of net income distributed to each partner's capital account at the end of the year will differ from the amount the partner withdraws during the year.

Income Division—Services of Partners and Investment

Partners may agree that the most equitable plan of income division is to provide for (1) salary allowances and (2) interest on capital investments. Any remaining net income is then divided as agreed. For example, assume that the partnership agreement for Stone and Mills allows for the following division of income:

1. Monthly salary allowances of $2,500 for Stone and $2,000 for Mills.
2. Interest of 12% on each partner's capital balance on January 1.
3. Any remaining net income to be divided equally between the partners.

Stone had a credit balance of $80,000 in her capital account on January 1 of the current fiscal year, and Mills had a credit balance of $60,000 in her capital account. The division of the $75,000 net income for the year is shown below.

Net income			$75,000

Division of net income:

	J. L. Stone	C. R. Mills	Total
Salary allowance	$30,000	$24,000	$54,000
Interest allowance	9,600	7,200	16,800
Remaining income	2,100	2,100	4,200
Net income	$41,700	$33,300	$75,000

For the above example, the entry to close the income summary account is shown below.

Dec. 31	Income Summary	75,000	
	Jennifer L. Stone, Capital		41,700
	Crystal R. Mills, Capital		33,300

Income Division—Allowances Exceed Net Income

In the examples so far, the net income has exceeded the total of the salary and interest allowances. If the net income is less than the total of the allowances, the *remaining balance* will be a negative amount. This amount must be divided among the partners as though it were a net loss.

To illustrate, assume the same salary and interest allowances as in the above example, but assume that the net income is $50,000. The salary and interest allowances total $39,600 for Stone and $31,200 for Mills. The sum of these amounts, $70,800, exceeds the net income of $50,000 by $20,800. It is necessary to divide the $20,800 excess between Stone and Mills. Under the partnership agreement, any net income or net loss remaining after deducting the allowances is divided equally between Stone and Mills. Thus, each partner is allocated one-half of the $20,800, and $10,400 is deducted from each partner's share of the allowances. The final division of net income between Stone and Mills is shown below.

Net income			$50,000

Division of net income:

	J. L. Stone	C. R. Mills	Total
Salary allowance	$30,000	$24,000	$54,000
Interest allowance	9,600	7,200	16,800
Total	$39,600	$31,200	$70,800
Excess of allowances over income	10,400	10,400	20,800
Net income	$29,200	$20,800	$50,000

In closing Income Summary at the end of the year, $29,200 would be credited to Jennifer L. Stone, Capital, and $20,800 would be credited to Crystal R. Mills, Capital.

FINANCIAL STATEMENTS FOR PARTNERSHIPS

Objective 6
Prepare financial statements for partnerships.

The division of net income among partners should be disclosed in the financial statements prepared at the end of the fiscal period. This disclosure may be reported by adding a section to the income statement, as illustrated earlier. The disclosure may also be reported in a separate statement.

The balance of the capital account of each partner is usually reported on the partnership balance sheet. In addition, the changes in the owner's equity of a partnership during the period should be reported. These changes are normally reported in a statement of owner's equity. The purpose of this statement is similar to that of the statement of owner's equity for a sole proprietorship.

There are a number of different forms of the partnership statement of owner's equity. One such format is shown below for the Stone and Mills partnership.

	Stone and Mills Statement of Owner's Equity For Year Ended December 31, 19—		
	Jennifer L. Stone	Crystal R. Mills	Total
Capital, January 1, 19—	$ 80,000	$60,000	$140,000
Additional investment during the year		5,000	5,000
	$ 80,000	$65,000	$145,000
Net income for the year	41,700	33,300	75,000
	$121,700	$98,300	$220,000
Withdrawals during the year	30,000	24,000	54,000
Capital, December 31, 19—	$ 91,700	$74,300	$166,000

PARTNERSHIP DISSOLUTION

Objective 7
Journalize the entries for partnership dissolution, including admission of new partners and the withdrawal or death of partners.

One of the basic characteristics of the partnership form of organization is its limited life. Any change in the ownership dissolves the partnership. Thus, admission of a new partner dissolves the old firm. Likewise, death, bankruptcy, or withdrawal of a partner dissolves the partnership.

When a partnership dissolves, its affairs are not necessarily wound up. For example, a partnership of two partners may admit a third partner. Or if one of the partners in a business withdraws, the remaining partners may continue to operate the business. In such cases, a new partnership is formed and a new partnership agreement should be prepared.

Admission of a Partner

A person may be admitted to a partnership only with the consent of all the current partners, through either of two methods:[2]

1. Purchasing an interest from one or more of the current partners.
2. Contributing assets to the partnership.

When the first method is used, the capital interest of the incoming partner is obtained from current partners, and *neither the total assets nor the total owner's equity of the business is affected.* When the second method is used, *both the total assets and the total owner's equity of the business are increased.* Each of these methods is further discussed in the following paragraphs.

PURCHASING AN INTEREST IN A PARTNERSHIP. A person may be admitted to a partnership by purchasing an interest from one or more of the existing partners. The purchase and sale of the partnership interest occurs between the new partner and the existing partners acting as individuals. Thus, the purchase price is paid directly to the selling partners. Neither the total assets nor the total owner's equity of the business are affected. The only entry needed in the records of the partnership is to transfer owner's equity amounts from the capital accounts of the selling partners to the capital account established for the incoming partner.

As an example, assume that partners Tom Andrews and Nathan Bell have capital balances of $50,000 each. On June 1, each sells one-fifth of his equity to Joe Canter for $10,000 in cash. The exchange of cash is not a partnership transaction and thus is not recorded by the partnership. The only entry required in the partnership accounts is as follows:

---

[2] Although an individual cannot become a partner without the consent of the other partners, the rights of a partner, such as the right to share in the income of a partnership, may be assigned to others without the consent of the other partners. Such issues are discussed in business law textbooks.

June 1	Tom Andrews, Capital	10,000	
	Nathan Bell, Capital	10,000	
	Joe Canter, Capital		20,000

The effect of the transaction on the partnership accounts is presented in the following diagram:

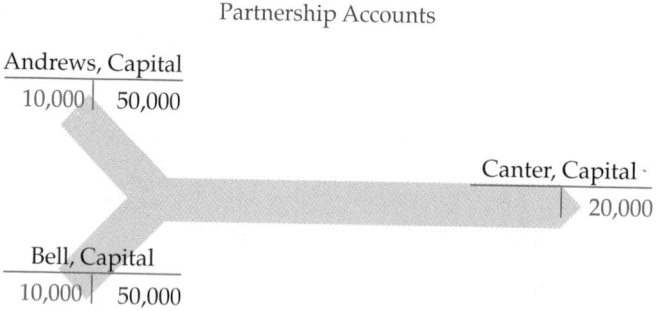

Partnership Accounts

The preceding entry is not affected by the amount paid by Canter for the one-fifth interest. If the firm had been earning a high rate of return on the investment, Canter might have paid more than $20,000. If the existing partners had been eager to sell, he might have acquired the one-fifth interest for less than $20,000. In either case, the entry to transfer the capital interests is the same as shown above.

After Canter is admitted to the partnership, the total owner's equity of the firm is still $100,000. Canter now has a one-fifth interest, or a $20,000 capital balance. However, Canter may not be entitled to a one-fifth share of the partnership net income. Division of net income or net loss will be made according to the new partnership agreement.

CONTRIBUTING ASSETS TO A PARTNERSHIP. Instead of purchasing an interest from the current partners, the incoming partner may contribute assets to the partnership. In this case, both the assets and the owner's equity of the firm increase. For example, assume that Donald Lewis and Gerald Morton are partners with capital accounts of $35,000 and $25,000. On June 1, Sharon Nelson invests $20,000 cash in the business for an ownership equity of $20,000. The entry to record this transaction is as follows:

| June 1 | Cash | 20,000 | |
| | Sharon Nelson, Capital | | 20,000 |

The major difference between the admission of Nelson and the admission of Canter in the preceding examples may be observed by comparing the following diagram with the preceding diagram.

Partnership Accounts

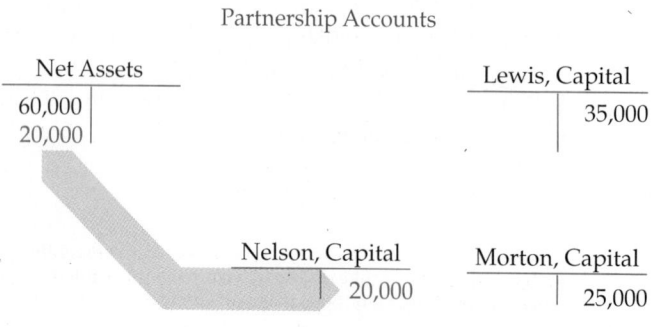

With the admission of Nelson, the total owners' equity of the new partnership becomes $80,000, of which Nelson has a one-fourth interest, or $20,000. The extent of Nelson's share in partnership net income will be determined by the partnership agreement.

REVALUATION OF ASSETS. A partnership's asset account balances should be stated at current values at the time of the admission of a new partner. If the accounts do not approximate current market values, the accounts should be adjusted. The net adjustment (increase or decrease) in asset values is divided among the capital accounts of the existing partners according to their income-sharing ratio. Failure to adjust the accounts for current values may result in the new partner sharing in asset gains or losses that arose in prior periods.

To illustrate, assume that in the preceding example for the Lewis and Morton partnership, the balance of the merchandise inventory account is $14,000 and the current replacement value is $17,000. Assuming that Lewis and Morton share net income equally, the revaluation is recorded as follows:

June 1	Merchandise Inventory	3,000	
	Donald Lewis, Capital		1,500
	Gerald Morton, Capital		1,500

If a number of assets are revalued, the adjustments may be debited or credited to a temporary account entitled Asset Revaluations. After all adjustments are made, this account is closed to the partner capital accounts.

PARTNER BONUSES. When a new partner is admitted to a partnership, the incoming partner may pay a bonus to the existing partners for the privilege of joining the partnership. Such a bonus is usually paid in expectation of high partnership profits in the future due to the contributions of the existing partners. Alternatively, the existing partners may pay the incoming partner a bonus to join the partnership. In this case, the bonus is usually paid in recognition of special qualities or skills that the incoming partner is bringing to the partnership. These qualities or skills are expected to increase partnership profits in the future. The amount of any bonus paid to the partnership is distributed among the partner capital accounts.[3]

To illustrate, assume that on March 1 the partnership of Marsha Jenkins and Helen Kramer is considering admitting a new partner, William Larson. After the assets of the partnership have been adjusted to current market values, the capital balance of Jenkins is $20,000, and the capital balance of Kramer is $24,000. Jenkins and Kramer agree to admit Larson to the partnership for $31,000. In return, Larson will receive a one-third equity in the partnership and will share equally with Jenkins and Kramer in partnership income or losses.

In this case, Larson is paying Jenkins and Kramer a $6,000 bonus to join the partnership. This bonus is computed as follows:

Equity of Jenkins	$ 20,000
Equity of Kramer	24,000
Contribution of Larson	31,000
Total equity after admission of Larson	$ 75,000
Larson's equity interest after admission	× 1/3
Larson's equity after admission	$ 25,000
Contribution of Larson	$ 31,000
Larson's equity after admission	25,000
Bonus paid to Jenkins and Kramer	$ 6,000

[3] Another method is sometimes used to record the admission of partners in situations such as that described in this paragraph. This method attributes goodwill rather than a bonus to the partners. This method is discussed in advanced accounting textbooks.

The bonus is distributed to Jenkins and Kramer according to their income-sharing ratio. Assuming that Jenkins and Kramer share profits and losses equally, the entry to record the admission of Larson to the partnership is as follows:

Mar. 1	Cash	31,000	
	William Larson, Capital		25,000
	Marsha Jenkins, Capital		3,000
	Helen Kramer, Capital		3,000

If a new partner possesses unique qualities or skills, the existing partners may agree to pay the new partner a bonus to join the partnership. To illustrate, assume that after adjustment to market values the capital balance of Janice Cowen is $80,000 and the capital balance of Steve Dodd is $40,000. Cowen and Dodd agree to admit Sandra Ellis to the partnership on June 1 for an investment of $30,000. In return, Ellis will receive a one-fourth equity interest in the partnership and will share in one-fourth of the profits and losses.

In this case, Cowen and Dodd are paying Ellis a $7,500 bonus to join the partnership. This bonus is computed as follows:

Equity of Cowen	$ 80,000
Equity of Dodd	40,000
Contribution of Ellis	30,000
Total equity after admission of Ellis	$150,000
Ellis's equity interest after admission	× 25%
Ellis's equity after admission	$ 37,500
Contribution of Ellis	30,000
Bonus paid to Ellis	$ 7,500

Assuming that the income-sharing ratio of Cowen and Dodd was 2:1 before the admission of Ellis, the entry to record the bonus and admission of Ellis to the partnership is as follows:

June 1	Cash	30,000	
	Janice Cowen, Capital	5,000	
	Steve Dodd, Capital	2,500	
	Sandra Ellis, Capital		37,500

Withdrawal of a Partner

When a partner retires or withdraws from a partnership, one or more of the remaining partners may purchase the withdrawing partner's interest. The firm may then continue its operations uninterrupted. In such cases, the purchase and sale of the partnership interest is between the partners as individuals. The only entry on the partnership's records is to debit the capital account of the partner withdrawing and to credit the capital account of the partner or partners purchasing the additional interest.

If the withdrawing partner sells the interest directly to the partnership, both the assets and the owner's equity of the partnership are reduced. Before the sale, the asset accounts should be adjusted to current values, so that the withdrawing partner's equity may be accurately determined. The net amount of the adjustment should be divided among the capital accounts of the partners according to their income-sharing ratio. If not enough partnership cash or other assets are available to pay the withdrawing partner, a liability may be created (credited) for the amount owed the withdrawing partner.

Death of a Partner

The death of a partner dissolves the partnership. In the absence of an agreement, the accounts should be closed as of the date of death. The net income for this part of the current year should be determined and divided among the partners' capital accounts. It is not unusual, however, for the partnership agreement to indicate that the accounts should remain open until the end of the current fiscal year. At that time, the net income of the entire period is divided, as provided by the agreement, between the periods before and after the partner's death.

The balance in the capital account of the deceased partner is then transferred to a liability account with the deceased's estate. The remaining partner or partners may continue the business, or the affairs may be terminated. If the partnership continues in business, the procedures for settling with the estate are the same as those discussed for the withdrawal of a partner.

LIQUIDATING PARTNERSHIPS

Objective 8
Journalize the entries for liquidating partnerships.

When a partnership goes out of business, it usually sells the assets, pays the creditors, and distributes the remaining cash or other assets to the partners. This winding-up process is called the **liquidation** of the partnership. Although liquidating refers to the payment of liabilities, it is often used to include the entire winding-up process.

When the partnership goes out of business and the normal operations are discontinued, the accounts should be adjusted and closed. The only accounts remaining open will be the asset, contra asset, liability, and owner's equity accounts.

The sale of the assets is called **realization**. As cash is realized, it is used to pay the claims of creditors. After all liabilities have been paid, the remaining cash is distributed to the partners based on the balances in their capital accounts.

The liquidating process may extend over a long period of time as individual assets are sold. This delays the distribution of cash to partners, but does not affect the amount each partner will receive.

As a basis for illustration, assume that Farley, Greene, and Hall share income and losses in a ratio of 5:3:2 (5/10, 3/10, 2/10). On April 9, after discontinuing business operations of the partnership and closing the accounts, the following trial balance in summary form was prepared:

Cash	11,000	
Noncash Assets	64,000	
Liabilities		9,000
Jean Farley, Capital		22,000
Brad Greene, Capital		22,000
Alice Hall, Capital		22,000
Total	75,000	75,000

Based on these facts, accounting for liquidating the partnership will be shown using three different selling prices for the noncash assets. To simplify, it is assumed that all noncash assets are sold in a single transaction, and that all liabilities are paid at one time. In addition, *Noncash Assets* and *Liabilities* will be used as account titles in place of the various asset, contra asset, and liability accounts.

Gain on Realization

Between April 10 and April 30 of the current year, Farley, Greene, and Hall sell all noncash assets for $72,000. Thus, a gain of $8,000 ($72,000 − $64,000) is realized. The gain is divided among the capital accounts in the income-sharing ratio of 5:3:2. The liabilities are paid, and the remaining cash is distributed to the partners. *The cash is distributed to the partners based on the balances in their capital accounts.* A statement of partnership liquidation, which summarizes the liquidation process, is shown in Exhibit 1.

Exhibit 1
Gain on Realization

	Farley, Greene, and Hall Statement of Partnership Liquidation For Period April 10–30, 19—					
					Capital	
	Cash +	Noncash = Assets	Liabilities +	Farley + (50%)	Greene + (30%)	Hall (20%)
Balances before realization	$11,000	$64,000	$9,000	$22,000	$22,000	$22,000
Sale of assets and division of gain	+72,000	−64,000	—	+ 4,000	+ 2,400	+ 1,600
Balances after realization	$83,000	0	$9,000	$26,000	$24,400	$23,600
Payment of liabilities	− 9,000	—	−9,000	—	—	—
Balances after payment of liabilities	$74,000	0	0	$26,000	$24,400	$23,600
Distribution of cash to partners	−74,000	—	—	−26,000	−24,400	−23,600
Final balances	0	0	0	0	0	0

The entries to record the steps in the liquidating process are as follows:

Sale of assets	Cash	72,000	
	Noncash Assets		64,000
	Loss and Gain on Realization		8,000

Division of gain	Loss and Gain on Realization	8,000	
	Jean Farley, Capital		4,000
	Brad Greene, Capital		2,400
	Alice Hall, Capital		1,600

Payment of liabilities	Liabilities	9,000	
	Cash		9,000

Distribution of cash to partners	Jean Farley, Capital	26,000	
	Brad Greene, Capital	24,400	
	Alice Hall, Capital	23,600	
	Cash		74,000

As shown in Exhibit 1, the cash is distributed to the partners based on the balances of their capital accounts. These balances are determined after the gain on realization has been divided among the partners. *The income-sharing ratio should not be used as a basis for distributing the cash to partners.*

Loss on Realization

Assume that in the preceding example, Farley, Greene, and Hall dispose of all noncash assets for $44,000. A loss of $20,000 ($64,000 − $44,000) is realized. The steps in liquidating the partnership are summarized in Exhibit 2.

Exhibit 2
Loss on Realization

	Cash +	Noncash = Assets	Liabilities +	Capital		
				Farley (50%) +	Greene (30%) +	Hall (20%)
Balances before realization	$11,000	$64,000	$9,000	$22,000	$22,000	$22,000
Sale of assets and division of loss	+44,000	−64,000	—	−10,000	− 6,000	− 4,000
Balances after realization	$55,000	0	$9,000	$12,000	$16,000	$18,000
Payment of liabilities	− 9,000	—	−9,000	—	—	—
Balances after payment of liabilities	$46,000	0	0	$12,000	$16,000	$18,000
Distribution of cash to partners	−46,000	—	—	−12,000	−16,000	−18,000
Final balances	0	0	0	0	0	0

Farley, Greene, and Hall
Statement of Partnership Liquidation
For Period April 10–30, 19—

The entries to liquidate the partnership are as follows:

Sale of assets	Cash	44,000	
	Loss and Gain on Realization	20,000	
	Noncash Assets		64,000
Division of loss	Jean Farley, Capital	10,000	
	Brad Greene, Capital	6,000	
	Alice Hall, Capital	4,000	
	Loss and Gain on Realization		20,000
Payment of liabilities	Liabilities	9,000	
	Cash		9,000
Distribution of cash to partners	Jean Farley, Capital	12,000	
	Brad Greene, Capital	16,000	
	Alice Hall, Capital	18,000	
	Cash		46,000

Loss on Realization—Capital Deficiency

In the preceding example, the capital account of each partner was large enough to absorb the partner's share of the loss from realization. The partners received cash to the extent of the remaining balances in their capital accounts. The share of loss on realization may, however, exceed the balance in the partner's capital account. The resulting debit balance in the capital account is called a **deficiency**. It represents a claim of the partnership against the partner.

To illustrate, assume that Farley, Greene, and Hall sell all of the noncash assets for $10,000. A loss of $54,000 ($64,000 − $10,000) is realized. The share of the loss allocated to Farley, $27,000 (50% of $54,000), exceeds the $22,000 balance in her capital account. This $5,000 deficiency represents an amount that Farley owes the partnership. Assuming that Farley pays the entire deficiency to the partnership, sufficient cash is available to distribute to the remaining partners according to their capital balances. The steps in liquidating the partnership in this case are summarized in Exhibit 3.

Exhibit 3
Loss on Realization—Capital Deficiency

					Capital		
	Cash +	Noncash = Assets	Liabilities +	Farley + (50%)	Greene + (30%)	Hall (20%)
Balances before realization	$11,000	$64,000	$9,000	$22,000	$22,000	$22,000
Sale of assets and division of loss	+10,000	−64,000	—	−27,000	−16,200	−10,800
Balances after realization	$21,000	0	$9,000	$ 5,000(Dr.)	$ 5,800	$11,200
Payment of liabilities	− 9,000	—	−9,000	—	—	—
Balances after payment of liabilities	$12,000	0	0	$ 5,000(Dr.)	$ 5,800	$11,200
Receipt of deficiency	+ 5,000	—	—	+ 5,000	—	—
Balances	$17,000	0	0	0	$ 5,800	$11,200
Distribution of cash to partners	−17,000	—	—	—	− 5,800	−11,200
Final balances	0	0	0	0	0	0

The table is titled:

Farley, Greene, and Hall
Statement of Partnership Liquidation
For Period April 10–30, 19—

The entries to record the liquidation are as follows:

		Debit	Credit
Sale of assets	Cash	10,000	
	Loss and Gain on Realization	54,000	
	Noncash Assets		64,000
Division of loss	Jean Farley, Capital	27,000	
	Brad Greene, Capital	16,200	
	Alice Hall, Capital	10,800	
	Loss and Gain on Realization		54,000
Payment of liabilities	Liabilities	9,000	
	Cash		9,000
Receipt of deficiency	Cash	5,000	
	Jean Farley, Capital		5,000
Distribution of cash to partners	Brad Greene, Capital	5,800	
	Alice Hall, Capital	11,200	
	Cash		17,000

If cash is not collected from a deficient partner, the partnership cash will not be large enough to pay the other partners in full. Any uncollected deficiency becomes a loss to the partnership and is divided among the remaining partners' capital balances, based on their income-sharing ratio. The cash balance will then equal the sum of the capital account balances. Cash is then distributed to the remaining partners, based on the balances of their capital accounts.[4]

---

[4] The accounting for uncollectible deficiencies of partners is discussed and illustrated in advanced accounting texts.

Errors in Liquidation

The type of error that occurs most often in liquidating a partnership is an improper distribution of cash to the partners. Such errors usually occur because the distribution of cash to partners in liquidation is confused with the division of gains and losses on realization.

Gains and losses on realization result from the disposal of assets to outsiders. *Realization gains and losses should be divided among the partner capital accounts in the same manner as net income or net loss from normal business operations—using the income-sharing ratio.* On the other hand, the distribution of cash (or other assets) to the partners in liquidation is not directly related to the income-sharing ratio. The distribution of assets to the partners in liquidation is the exact reverse of the contribution of assets by the partners at the time the partnership was established. *The distribution of assets to partners in liquidation is equal to the credit balances in their capital accounts after all gains and losses on realization have been divided and allowances have been made for any partner deficiencies.*

CHAPTER REVIEW

Key Points

Objective 1. Identify and list the basic characteristics of the partnership form of organization.
A partnership is "an association of two or more persons to carry on as co-owners a business for profit." Partnership characteristics that have accounting implications are limited life, unlimited liability, co-ownership of property, mutual agency, and participation in income.

Objective 2. List the major advantages and disadvantages of the partnership form of organization.
The principal advantages of a partnership include the ease with which it can be organized, bringing together capital of one or more individuals, and the fact that it is a nontaxable entity. The major disadvantages of a partnership are its limited life, its unlimited liability, and its limitations for raising large amounts of capital.

Objective 3. Summarize the basic accounting system for partnerships.
The basic accounting system for partnerships is the same as for most other forms of business organization for the recording of day-to-day transactions. It is in the areas of partnership formation, income distribution, dissolution, and liquidation that transactions unique to partnerships arise.

Objective 4. Journalize the entries for the formation of partnerships.
When a partnership is formed, accounts are debited for the assets contributed, accounts are credited for the liabilities assumed, and the partners' capital accounts are credited for their respective net amounts. Noncash assets are recorded at amounts agreed upon by the partners.

Objective 5. Journalize the entries for dividing partnership net income and net loss.
The net income (net loss) of a partnership is divided among the partners by debiting (crediting) Income Summary and crediting (debiting) the partners' capital accounts. The net income or net loss may be divided on the basis of services rendered by individual partners and/or on the basis of the investments of the individual partners. In the absence of any agreement, net income is divided equally among the partners.

Objective 6. Prepare financial statements for partnerships.
The financial statements for partnerships are similar to other forms of business organization, except that the division of partnership net income should be disclosed in the partnership financial statements. In addition, changes in the owner's equity during the period should be reported in the statement of owner's equity.

Objective 7. Journalize the entries for partnership dissolution, including admission of new partners and the withdrawal or death of partners.
Any change in the personnel or ownership dissolves the partnership. A partnership may be dissolved by admission of a new partner, withdrawal of a partner, or death of a partner. A partnership's asset account balances should be stated at current values at the time of dissolution of the partnership.

A new partner may be admitted to a partnership by purchasing an interest from one or more of the existing partners. The admission of the new partner is recorded by debiting the capital accounts of the selling partners and crediting the capital account of the new partner.

A new partner may be admitted to a partnership by contributing assets to the partnership. The admission of the new partner is recorded by debiting asset accounts for the fair market value of the assets contributed and crediting the capital account of the new partner.

When a new partner is admitted to a partnership, the incoming partner may pay a bonus to the existing partners. Alternatively, the existing partners may pay a bonus to the new partner to join the partnership.

When a partner retires, dies, or withdraws from a partnership, one or more of the remaining partners may purchase the withdrawing partner's interest. The only entry for the partnership is to debit the capital account of the withdrawing partner and to credit the capital account of the partner or partners purchasing the additional interest.

Objective 8. Journalize the entries for liquidating partnerships.

When a partnership liquidates, it sells its noncash assets, pays the creditors, and distributes the remaining cash or other assets to the partners. The journal entries for the sale of noncash assets and the payment of liabilities are similar to those illustrated in earlier chapters. Any gain or loss on the sale of the noncash assets should be divided among the partners according to their income-sharing ratio. The final asset distribution to partners is based on the balances of the partners' capital accounts after all noncash assets have been sold and liabilities paid. The journal entry for the final distribution of assets debits the partners' capital accounts and credits the asset accounts.

Glossary of Key Terms

Deficiency. The debit balance in the owner's equity account of a partner. **Objective 8**

Liquidation. The winding-up process when a partnership goes out of business. **Objective 8**

Partnership. An unincorporated business of two or more persons to carry on as co-owners a business for profit. **Objective 1**

Partnership agreement. The formal written contract creating a partnership. **Objective 1**

Realization. The sale of assets when a partnership is being liquidated. **Objective 8**

Self-Examination Questions

Answers at end of chapter.

1. As part of the initial investment, a partner contributes office equipment that had cost $20,000 and on which accumulated depreciation of $12,500 had been recorded. If the partners agree on a valuation of $9,000 for the equipment, what amount should be debited to the office equipment account?
   A. $7,500   C. $12,500
   B. $9,000   D. $20,000

2. X and Y agree to form a partnership. X is to contribute $50,000 in assets and to devote one-half time to the partnership. Y is to contribute $20,000 and to devote full time to the partnership. How will X and Y share in the division of net income or net loss?
   A. 5:2   C. 1:1
   B. 1:2   D. 2.5:1

3. X and Y invest $100,000 and $50,000 respectively in a partnership and agree to a division of net income that provides for an allowance of interest at 10% on original investments, salary allowances of $12,000 and $24,000 respectively, with the remainder divided equally. What would be X's share of a periodic net income of $45,000?
   A. $22,500   C. $19,000
   B. $22,000   D. $10,000

4. X and Y are partners who share income in the ratio of 2:1 and who have capital balances of $65,000 and $35,000 respectively. If P, with the consent of Y, acquired one-half of X's interest for $40,000, for what amount would P's capital account be credited?
   A. $32,500   C. $50,000
   B. $40,000   D. $72,500

5. X and Y share gains and losses in the ratio of 2:1. After selling all assets for cash, dividing the losses on realization, and paying liabilities, the balances in the capital accounts were as follows: X, $10,000 Cr.; Y, $2,000 Cr. How much of the cash of $12,000 would be distributed to X?
   A. $2,000   C. $10,000
   B. $8,000   D. $12,000

ILLUSTRATIVE PROBLEM

Ryan, Shaw, and Todd, who share in income and losses in the ratio of 4:2:4, decided to discontinue operations as of April 30 and liquidate their partnership. After the accounts were closed on April 30, the following trial balance was prepared:

Cash	8,100	
Noncash Assets	70,600	
Liabilities		27,500
Ryan, Capital		23,300
Shaw, Capital		12,100
Todd, Capital		15,800
Total	78,700	78,700

ILLUSTRATIVE PROBLEM

Between May 1 and May 18, the noncash assets were sold for $20,600, and the liabilities were paid.

Instructions

1. Assuming that the partner with the capital deficiency pays the entire amount owed to the partnership, prepare a statement of partnership liquidation.
2. Journalize the entries to record (a) the sale of the assets, (b) the division of loss on the sale of the assets, (c) the payment of the liabilities, (d) the receipt of the deficiency, and (e) the distribution of cash to the partners.

Solution

1.

Ryan, Shaw, and Todd
Statement of Partnership Liquidation
For Period May 1–18, 19—

	Cash +	Noncash = Assets	Liabilities +	Ryan (40%) +	Shaw (20%) +	Todd (40%)
				Capital		
Balances before realization	$ 8,100	$70,600	$27,500	$23,300	$12,100	$15,800
Sale of assets and division of loss	+20,600	−70,600	—	−20,000	−10,000	−20,000
Balances after realization	$28,700	0	$27,500	$ 3,300	$ 2,100	$ 4,200 (Dr.)
Payment of liabilities	−27,500	—	−27,500	—	—	—
Balances after payment of liabilities	$ 1,200	0	0	$ 3,300	$ 2,100	$ 4,200 (Dr.)
Receipt of deficiency	+ 4,200	—	—	—	—	+ 4,200
Balances	$ 5,400	0	0	$ 3,300	$ 2,100	0
Distribution of cash to partners	− 5,400	—	—	− 3,300	− 2,100	—
Final balances	0	0	0	0	0	0

2. a. Cash   20,600
       Loss and Gain on Realization   50,000
         Noncash Assets   70,600

   b. Ryan, Capital   20,000
       Shaw, Capital   10,000
       Todd, Capital   20,000
         Loss and Gain on Realization   50,000

   c. Liabilities   27,500
         Cash   27,500

   d. Cash   4,200
         Todd, Capital   4,200

   e. Ryan, Capital   3,300
       Shaw, Capital   2,100
         Cash   5,400

DISCUSSION QUESTIONS

1. In a *general* partnership, what is the liability of the partners?
2. In a *limited* partnership, what is the liability of the partners?
3. Alan Biles and Joan Crandall joined together to form a partnership. Is it possible for them to lose a greater amount than the amount of their investment in the partnership enterprise? Explain.
4. Must a partnership (a) file a federal income tax return or (b) pay federal income taxes? Explain.
5. The partnership agreement between Roberta Baker and Jose Cruz provides for the sharing of partnership net income in the ratio of 3:2. Since the agreement is silent concerning the sharing of net losses, in what ratio will they be shared?
6. In the absence of an agreement, how will the net income be distributed between Michael Evans and Janice Farr, partners in the firm of E and F Environmental Consultants?

7. Paul Boyer, Fran Carrick, and Ed DiPano are contemplating the formation of a partnership. According to the partnership agreement, Boyer is to invest $60,000 and devote one-half time, Carrick is to invest $40,000 and devote three-fourths time, and DiPano is to make no investment and devote full time. Would DiPano be correct in assuming that, since he is not contributing any assets to the firm, he is risking nothing? Explain.

8. What are the disadvantages of the partnership over the corporation as a form of organization for a profit-making business enterprise?

9. As a part of the initial investment, a partner contributes delivery equipment that had originally cost $50,000 and on which accumulated depreciation of $37,500 had been recorded. The partners agree on a valuation of $15,000. How should the delivery equipment be recorded in the accounts of the partnership?

10. All partners agree that $200,000 of accounts receivable invested by a partner will be collectible to the extent of 90%. How should the accounts receivable be recorded in the general ledger of the partnership?

11. Ramon Flores and Joel Garcia are contemplating the formation of a partnership in which Flores is to devote full time and Garcia is to devote one-half time. In the absence of any agreement, will the partners share in net income or net loss in the ratio of 2:1? Explain.

12. During the current year, Helen Bray withdrew $3,000 monthly from the partnership of Bray and Cox Water Management Consultants. Is it possible that her share of partnership net income for the current year might be more or less than $36,000? Explain.

13. a. What accounts are debited and credited to record a partner's cash withdrawal in lieu of salary?

    b. At the end of the fiscal year, what accounts are debited and credited to record the division of net income among partners?

    c. The articles of partnership provide for a salary allowance of $5,000 per month to partner C. If C withdrew only $4,000 per month, would this affect the division of the partnership net income?

14. How can the division of net income be disclosed in the financial statements of a partnership?

15. Harry Imes, a partner in the firm of Greene, Herbert, and Imes, sells his investment (capital balance of $75,000) to Agnes Smith. (a) Does the withdrawal of Imes dissolve the partnership? (b) Are Greene and Herbert required to admit Smith as a partner?

16. Explain the difference between the admission of a new partner to a partnership (a) by purchase of an interest from another partner and (b) by contribution of assets to the partnership.

17. Terry Kirk and Arthur Loebel are partners who share in net income equally and have capital balances of $90,000 and $62,500 respectively. Kirk, with the consent of Loebel, sells one-third of his interest to Nancy Taylor. What entry is required by the partnership if the sale price is (a) $20,000? (b) $40,000?

18. Why is it important to state all partnership assets in terms of current prices at the time of the admission of a new partner?

19. When a new partner is admitted to a partnership and agrees to pay a bonus to the original partners, how should the amount of the bonus be allocated to the capital accounts of the original partners?

20. Why might a partnership pay a bonus to a newly admitted partner?

21. a. Differentiate between *dissolution* and *liquidation* of a partnership.

    b. What does *realization* mean when used in connection with liquidation of a partnership?

22. In the liquidation process, (a) how are losses and gains on realization divided among the partners, and (b) how is cash distributed among the partners?

23. Logan and Mayes are partners, sharing gains and losses equally. At the time they decide to terminate their partnership, their capital balances are $5,000 and $20,000 respectively. After all noncash assets are sold and all liabilities are paid, there is a cash balance of $20,000. (a) What is the amount of gain or loss on realization? (b) How should the gain or loss be divided between Logan and Mayes? (c) How should the cash be divided between Logan and Mayes?

24. Pecci, Quinlan, and Reed share equally in net income and net loss. After the partnership sells all the assets for cash, divides the losses on realization, and pays the liabilities, the balances in the capital accounts are as follows: Pecci, $20,000 Cr.; Quinlan, $57,500 Cr.; Reed, $17,500 Dr. (a) What term is applied to the debit balance in Reed's capital account? (b) What is the amount of cash on hand? (c) What transaction must take place for Pecci and Quinlan to receive cash in the liquidation process equal to their capital account balances?

25. Short, Tull, and Wade are partners sharing income 3:2:1. After the firm's loss from liquidation is distributed, Short's capital account has a debit balance of $15,000. If Short is personally bankrupt and unable to pay any of the $15,000, how will the loss be divided between Tull and Wade?

26. In November 1990, the CPA firm of Laventhol & Horwath filed for bankruptcy. At the time of filing for bankruptcy, the firm had at least 100 lawsuits pending against it for claims totaling perhaps as much as $2 billion. If Laventhol & Horwath should have to pay all these damages and if the firm itself had no assets after paying existing liabilities, approximately how much would each of the 350 partners have to pay out of their personal assets?

Source: Peter Pae, "Laventhol Bankruptcy Filing Indicates Liabilities May Be as Much as $2 Billion," *The Wall Street Journal*, November 23, 1990.

REAL WRLD FOCUS

ETHICS DISCUSSION CASE

Donald Newton and Eileen Logan are partners in Newton & Logan, CPAs. Without notifying Eileen Logan, Donald Newton recently signed a contract for the firm to utilize a national computerized tax preparation service. The contract, for $200,000 of use over a five-year period, provides that Newton & Logan, CPAs, will have exclusive use of the service in the immediate geographic area.

Discuss whether Donald Newton behaved in an ethical manner.

SHARPEN YOUR COMMUNICATION SKILLS

EXERCISES

EXERCISE 14-1
ENTRY FOR PARTNER'S
ORIGINAL INVESTMENT
Objective 4

Albert Sommers and C. T. Tibbs decide to form a partnership by combining the assets of their separate businesses. Sommers contributes the following assets to the partnership: cash, $4,500; accounts receivable with a face amount of $97,500 and an allowance for doubtful accounts of $6,600; merchandise inventory with a cost of $85,000; and equipment with a cost of $140,000 and accumulated depreciation of $90,000.

The partners agree that $5,000 of the accounts receivable are completely worthless and are not to be accepted by the partnership, that $7,500 is a reasonable allowance for the uncollectibility of the remaining accounts, that the merchandise inventory is to be recorded at the current market price of $81,500, and that the equipment is to be valued at $75,000.

Journalize the partnership's entry to record Sommer's investment.

EXERCISE 14-2
DIVISION OF PARTNERSHIP
INCOME
Objective 5

SPREADSHEET PROBLEM

Lewis Kahn and Marcy Lell formed a partnership, investing $120,000 and $60,000 respectively. Determine their participation in the year's net income of $60,000 under each of the following independent assumptions: (a) no agreement concerning division of net income; (b) divided in the ratio of original capital investment; (c) interest at the rate of 10% allowed on original investments and the remainder divided in the ratio of 2:3; (d) salary allowances of $20,000 and $25,000 respectively, and the balance divided equally; (e) allowance of interest at the rate of 10% on original investments, salary allowances of $20,000 and $25,000 respectively, and the remainder divided equally.

EXERCISE 14-3
DIVISION OF PARTNERSHIP
INCOME
Objective 5

Determine the participation of Kahn and Lell in the year's net income of $90,000, according to each of the five assumptions as to income division listed in Exercise 14-2.

EXERCISE 14-4
DIVISION OF PARTNERSHIP
NET LOSS
Objective 5

Ruth Neff and Don Raub formed a partnership in which the partnership agreement provided for salary allowances of $20,000 and $30,000 respectively. Determine the division of a $10,000 net loss for the current year.

EXERCISE 14-5
PARTNERSHIP ENTRIES
AND STATEMENT OF
OWNER'S EQUITY
Objective 6

The capital accounts of J. C. Reed and Victor Scott have balances of $80,000 and $95,000 respectively on January 1, the beginning of the current fiscal year. On April 10, Reed invested an additional $10,000. During the year, Reed and Scott withdrew $36,000 and $42,000 respectively, and net income for the year was $80,000. The articles of partnership make no reference to the division of net income.

a. Journalize the entries to close (1) the income summary account and (2) the drawing accounts.
b. Prepare a statement of owner's equity for the current year for the partnership of Reed and Scott.

EXERCISE 14-6
REAL WORLD FOCUS
Objective 7

REAL W⬤RLD FOCUS

▌SHARPEN YOUR ▶
COMMUNICATION SKILLS

The international public accounting partnership of Arthur Andersen & Co. disclosed revenues of $4,947,800,000 for 1991. The revenues were attributable to 2,393 active partners.

a. What was the average revenue per active partner for 1991? Round to nearest $1,000.
b. Assuming that the total partners' capital is $500,000,000 and that it approximates the fair market value of the firm's net assets, what would be considered a minimum contribution for the admission of a new partner to the firm? Round to nearest $10,000.
c. Why might the amount to be contributed by a new partner for admission to the firm exceed the amount determined in (b)?

EXERCISE 14-7
ADMISSION OF NEW
PARTNERS BY PURCHASE
OF AN INTEREST AND BY
CONTRIBUTION OF ASSETS
Objective 7

The capital accounts of Alan Evans and Mary Farr have balances of $80,000 and $70,000 respectively. Don Reese and Gloria Swain are to be admitted to the partnership. Reese purchases one-fourth of Evan's interest for $22,500 and one-fifth of Farr's interest for $15,000. Swain contributes $30,000 cash to the partnership, for which she is to receive an ownership equity of $30,000.

a. Journalize the entries to record the admission of (1) Reese and (2) Swain.
b. What are the capital balances of each partner after the admission of the new partners?

EXERCISE 14-8
ADMISSION OF NEW
PARTNER BY
CONTRIBUTION OF ASSETS
Objective 7

After the tangible assets have been adjusted to current market prices, the capital accounts of Mike Cash and Ed Doerr have balances of $56,000 and $54,000 respectively. Paula Goles is to be admitted to the partnership, contributing $40,000 cash to the partnership, for which she is to receive an ownership equity of $50,000. All partners share equally in income.

a. Journalize the entry to record the admission of Goles, who is to receive a bonus of $10,000.
b. What are the capital balances of each partner after the admission of the new partner?

EXERCISE 14-9
WITHDRAWAL OF PARTNER
Objective 7

Paul Blasi is to retire from the partnership of Blasi and Associates as of March 31, the end of the current fiscal year. After closing the accounts, the capital balances of the partners are as follows: Paul Blasi, $200,000; Sandra Young, $125,000; and Ralph Zimmer, $140,000. They have shared net income and net losses in the ratio of 3:2:2. The partners agree that the merchandise inventory should be increased by $7,500, and the allowance for doubtful accounts should be increased by $1,550. Blasi agrees to accept an interest-bearing note for $150,000 in partial settlement of his ownership equity. The remainder of his claim is to be paid in cash. Young and Zimmer are to share equally in the net income or net loss of the new partnership.

Journalize the entries to record (a) the adjustment of the assets to bring them into agreement with current market prices, and (b) the withdrawal of Blasi from the partnership.

EXERCISE 14-10
DISTRIBUTION OF CASH ON
LIQUIDATION
Objective 8

John Bond and Angelo Fico, with capital balances of $51,000 and $36,000 respectively, decided to liquidate their partnership. After selling the noncash assets and paying the liabilities, there is $67,000 of cash remaining. If the partners share income and losses equally, how should the cash be distributed?

EXERCISE 14-11
DISTRIBUTION OF CASH ON
LIQUIDATION
Objective 8

Delores Gray, Ted Hall, and James Ide arranged to import and sell orchid corsages for a university dance. They agreed to share equally the net income or net loss of the venture. Gray and Hall advanced $175 and $125 of their own respective funds to pay for advertising and other expenses. After collecting for all sales and paying creditors, the partnership has $525 in cash.

a. How should the money be distributed?
b. Assuming that the partnership has only $150 instead of $525, do any of the three partners have a capital deficiency? If so, how much?

EXERCISE 14-12
STATEMENT OF
PARTNERSHIP
LIQUIDATION
Objective 8

After closing the accounts on July 1, prior to liquidating the partnership, the capital account balances of Gertz, Hart, and Imes are $24,000, $28,000, and $14,000 respectively. Cash, non-cash assets, and liabilities total $11,000, $85,000, and $30,000 respectively. Between July 1 and July 29, the noncash assets are sold for $49,000, the liabilities are paid, and the remaining cash is distributed to the partners. The partners share net income and loss in the ratio of 3:2:1. Prepare a statement of partnership liquidation for the period July 1–29.

WhAT'S WRONG
WITH THIS?

Sixty-year-old Jim Ebers retired from his computer consulting business in Boston and moved to Florida. There he met 27-year-old Ann Bowers, who had just graduated from Eldon Community College with an associate degree in computer science. Jim and Ann formed a partnership called E&B Computer Consultants. Jim contributed $15,000 for startup costs and devoted one-half time to the business. Ann devoted full time to the business. The monthly drawings were $1,500 for Jim and $3,000 for Ann.

At the end of the first year of operations, the two partners disagreed on the division of net income. Jim reasoned that the division should be equal. Although he devoted only one-half time to the business, he contributed all of the startup funds. Ann reasoned that the income-sharing ratio should be 2:1 in her favor because she devoted full-time to the business and her monthly drawings were twice those of Jim. Can you identify any flaws in the partners' reasoning regarding the income-sharing ratio?

PROBLEMS

Series A

PROBLEM 14-1A
ENTRIES AND BALANCE
SHEET FOR PARTNERSHIP
Objectives 4, 6

On May 1 of the current year, Anna Austin and Dave Walls form a partnership. Austin agrees to invest $10,500 in cash and merchandise inventory valued at $39,500. Walls invests certain business assets at valuations agreed upon, transfers business liabilities, and contributes sufficient cash to bring his total capital to $40,000. Details regarding the book values of the business assets and liabilities, and the agreed valuations, follow:

	Walls' Ledger Balance	Agreed Valuation
Accounts Receivable	$20,750	$19,500
Allowance for Doubtful Accounts	950	800
Equipment	79,100 }	45,000
Accumulated Depreciation	35,200 }	
Accounts Payable	14,000	14,000
Notes Payable	15,000	15,000

The partnership agreement includes the following provisions regarding the division of net income: interest on original investments at 10%, salary allowances of $18,000 and $21,000 respectively, and the remainder equally.

Instructions

1. Journalize the entries to record the investments of Austin and Walls in the partnership accounts.
2. Prepare a balance sheet as of May 1, the date of formation of the partnership of Austin and Walls.
3. After adjustments and the closing of revenue and expense accounts at April 30, the end of the first full year of operations, the income summary account has a credit balance of $68,000, and the drawing accounts have debit balances of $20,000 (Austin) and $26,000 (Walls). Journalize the entries to close the income summary account and the drawing accounts at April 30.

PROBLEM 14-2A
DIVISION OF PARTNERSHIP
INCOME
Objective 5

Bode and Dyke have decided to form a partnership. They have agreed that Bode is to invest $100,000 and that Dyke is to invest $50,000. Bode is to devote one-half time to the business and Dyke is to devote full time. The following plans for the division of income are being considered:

a. Equal division.
b. In the ratio of original investments.

c. In the ratio of time devoted to the business.
d. Interest of 12% on original investments and the remainder equally.
e. Interest of 12% on original investments, salary allowances of $15,000 to Bode and $30,000 to Dyke, and the remainder equally.
f. Plan (e), except that Dyke is also to be allowed a bonus equal to 20% of the amount by which net income exceeds the salary allowances.

Instructions

For each plan, determine the division of the net income under each of the following assumptions: (1) net income of $45,000 and (2) net income of $120,000. Present the data in tabular form, using the following columnar headings:

Plan	$45,000		$120,000	
	Bode	Dyke	Bode	Dyke

PROBLEM 14-3A
FINANCIAL STATEMENTS
FOR PARTNERSHIP
Objectives 5, 6

The ledger of Acosta and Morris, attorneys-at-law, contains the following accounts and balances after adjustments have been recorded on December 31, the end of the current fiscal year:

Cash	$ 17,000
Accounts Receivable	28,900
Supplies	1,900
Land	25,000
Building	130,000
Accumulated Depreciation—Building	69,200
Office Equipment	39,000
Accumulated Depreciation—Office Equipment	21,500
Accounts Payable	2,100
Salaries Payable	2,000
Juan Acosta, Capital	75,000
Juan Acosta, Drawing	60,000
Marsha Morris, Capital	55,000
Marsha Morris, Drawing	75,000
Professional Fees	265,650
Salary Expense	75,500
Depreciation Expense—Building	10,500
Property Tax Expense	8,000
Heating and Lighting Expense	7,900
Supplies Expense	2,850
Depreciation Expense—Office Equipment	2,800
Miscellaneous Expense	6,100

The balance in Morris's capital account includes an additional investment of $5,000 made on August 10 of the current year.

Instructions

1. Prepare an income statement for the current fiscal year, indicating the division of net income. The articles of partnership provide for salary allowances of $30,000 to Acosta and $40,000 to Morris; allowances of 12% on each partner's capital balance at the beginning of the fiscal year; and equal division of the remaining net income or net loss.
2. Prepare a statement of owner's equity for the current fiscal year.
3. Prepare a balance sheet in report form as of the end of the current fiscal year.

PROBLEM 14-4A
ADMISSION OF NEW
PARTNER
Objectives 6, 7

Dave Eagan and Agnes Mobley have operated a successful firm for many years, sharing net income and net losses equally. Ann Wild is to be admitted to the partnership on May 1 of the current year, in accordance with the following agreement:

a. Assets and liabilities of the old partnership are to be valued at their book values as of April 30, except for the following:
  • Accounts receivable amounting to $2,500 are to be written off, and the allowance for doubtful accounts is to be increased to 5% of the remaining accounts.
  • Merchandise inventory is to be valued at $52,900.
  • Equipment is to be valued at $95,000.

b. Wild is to purchase $20,000 of the ownership interest of Mobley for $25,000 cash and to contribute $20,000 cash to the partnership for a total ownership equity of $40,000.

c. The income-sharing ratio of Eagan, Mobley, and Wild is to be 2:1:1.

The post-closing trial balance of Eagan and Mobley as of April 30 is as follows:

Eagan and Mobley
Post-Closing Trial Balance
April 30, 19—

Cash	7,900	
Accounts Receivable	22,500	
Allowance for Doubtful Accounts		550
Merchandise Inventory	50,600	
Prepaid Insurance	1,650	
Equipment	145,000	
Accumulated Depreciation—Equipment		65,000
Accounts Payable		12,100
Notes Payable		10,000
Dave Eagan, Capital		80,000
Agnes Mobley, Capital		60,000
	227,650	227,650

Instructions

1. Journalize the entries as of April 30 to record the revaluations, using a temporary account entitled Asset Revaluations. The balance in the accumulated depreciation account is to be eliminated.

2. Journalize the additional entries to record the remaining transactions relating to the formation of the new partnership. Assume that all transactions occur on May 1.

3. Present a balance sheet for the new partnership as of May 1.

Instructions for Solving Problem 14-4A Using Solutions Software

SOLUTIONS SOFTWARE

1. Load opening balances.
2. Save the opening balances file to your drive and directory.
3. Set the run date to April 30 of the current year and enter your name.
4. Select the General Journal Entries option and key the journal entries to record the revaluations. Leave the reference field blank. Note: To review the chart of accounts, select F-1.
5. Display a journal entries report.
6. Display a trial balance.
7. Save a backup copy of your data file.
8. Set the run date to May 1 of the current year and change company name to "Eagan, Mobley, and Wild."
9. Select the General Journal Entries option and key the journal entries to record the formation of the new partnership. Leave the reference field blank.
10. Display a journal entries report.
11. Display a balance sheet.
12. Save your data file to disk.
13. End the session.

PROBLEM 14-5A
STATEMENT OF PARTNER-
SHIP LIQUIDATION
Objective 8

After the accounts are closed on May 3, prior to liquidating the partnership, the capital accounts of Donna Ark, Jane Birk, and Sue Case are $20,000, $3,900, and $10,000 respectively. Cash and noncash assets total $1,900 and $62,000 respectively. Amounts owed to creditors total $30,000. The partners share income and losses in the ratio of 2:1:1. Between May 3 and May 29, the noncash assets are sold for $22,000, the partner with the capital deficiency pays her deficiency to the partnership, and the liabilities are paid.

SPREADSHEET PROBLEM

Instructions

1. Prepare a statement of partnership liquidation, indicating (a) the sale of assets and division of loss, (b) the receipt of the deficiency (from the appropriate partner), and (c) the payment of liabilities.

SHARPEN YOUR COMMUNICATION SKILLS ►

2. If the partner with the capital deficiency declares bankruptcy and is unable to pay the deficiency, explain how the deficiency would be divided between the partners.

If the working papers correlating with the textbook are not used, omit Problem 14-6A.

PROBLEM 14-6A
PARTNERSHIP
LIQUIDATION
Objective 8

Tom Gray, Clyde Hale, and Curtis Ives decided to discontinue business operations and liquidate their partnership. A summary of the various transactions that have occurred thus far is presented in the working papers in a partial statement of liquidation.

Instructions

1. Assuming that the partner with the capital deficiency pays the entire amount owed to the partnership, prepare a statement of partnership liquidation.
2. Journalize the entries to record (a) the sale of assets, (b) the division of loss on the sale of assets, (c) the payment of liabilities, (d) the receipt of the deficiency, and (e) the distribution of cash to partners.

PROBLEM 14-7A
STATEMENT OF
PARTNERSHIP
LIQUIDATION
Objective 8

On October 1, the date the firm of Just, Kane, and Lowe decided to liquidate their partnership, the partners have capital balances of $100,000, $90,000, and $30,000 respectively. The cash balance is $20,000, the book values of noncash assets total $250,000, and liabilities total $50,000. The partners share income and losses in the ratio of 2:2:1.

Instructions

Prepare a statement of partnership liquidation, covering the period October 1 through October 30 for each of the following independent assumptions:

1. All of the noncash assets are sold for $300,000 in cash, the creditors are paid, and the remaining cash is distributed to the partners.
2. All of the noncash assets are sold for $150,000 in cash, the creditors are paid, and the remaining cash is distributed to the partners.
3. All of the noncash assets are sold for $80,000 in cash, the creditors are paid, the partner with the debit capital balance pays the amount owed to the firm, and the remaining cash is distributed to the partners.

Instructions for Solving Problem 14-7A Using Solutions Software
(Note: Solve the three assumptions and save your data files using three different file names.)

SOLUTIONS
SOFTWARE

1. Load opening balances.
2. Save the opening balances file to your drive and directory.
3. Set the run date to October 31 of the current year and enter your name.
4. Display the trial balance.
5. Select the General Journal Entries option and key the journal entries to record the liquidation, assuming that the noncash assets are sold for $300,000 in cash. Leave the reference field blank. Note: To review the chart of accounts, select F-1.
6. Display a journal entries report.
7. Display a trial balance. Note: All accounts should have a zero balance; therefore, the trial balance will be blank.
8. Save a backup copy of your data file.
9. Load opening balances.
10. Save the opening balances file to your drive and directory.
11. Set the run date to October 31 of the current year and enter your name.
12. Display the trial balance.
13. Select the General Journal Entries option and key the journal entries to record the liquidation, assuming that the noncash assets are sold for $150,000 in cash. Leave the reference field blank. Note: To review the chart of accounts, select F-1.
14. Display a journal entries report.
15. Display a trial balance. Note: All accounts should have a zero balance; therefore, the trial balance will be blank.
16. Save a backup copy of your data file.
17. Load opening balances.
18. Save the opening balances file to your drive and directory.
19. Set the run date to October 31 of the current year and enter your name.
20. Display the trial balance.
21. Select the General Journal Entries option and key the journal entries to record the liquidation, assuming that the noncash assets are sold for $80,000 in cash. Leave the reference field blank. Note: To review the chart of accounts, select F-1.
22. Display a journal entries report.
23. Display a trial balance. Note: All accounts should have a zero balance; therefore, the trial balance will be blank.
24. Save your data file to disk.
25. End the session.

Series B

PROBLEM 14-1B
ENTRIES AND BALANCE
SHEET FOR PARTNERSHIP
Objectives 4, 6

On November 1 of the current year, Dan Neja and Paul Ott form a partnership. Neja agrees to invest $10,000 cash and merchandise inventory valued at $55,000. Ott invests certain business assets at valuations agreed upon, transfers business liabilities, and contributes sufficient cash to bring his total capital to $85,000. Details regarding the book values of the business assets and liabilities, and the agreed valuations, follow:

	Ott's Ledger Balance	Agreed Valuation
Accounts Receivable	$33,250	$30,500
Allowance for Doubtful Accounts	500	1,000
Merchandise Inventory	42,500	40,900
Equipment	50,000	27,750
Accumulated Depreciation	29,700	
Accounts Payable	9,700	9,700
Notes Payable	10,000	10,000

The partnership agreement includes the following provisions regarding the division of net income: interest of 10% on original investments, salary allowances of $24,000 and $18,000 respectively, and the remainder equally.

Instructions

1. Journalize the entries to record the investments of Neja and Ott in the partnership accounts.
2. Prepare a balance sheet as of November 1, the date of formation of the partnership of Neja and Ott.
3. After adjustments and the closing of revenue and expense accounts at October 31, the end of the first full year of operations, the income summary account has a credit balance of $65,000, and the drawing accounts have debit balances of $26,000 (Neja) and $17,500 (Ott). Journalize the entries to close the income summary account and the drawing accounts at October 31.

PROBLEM 14-2B
DIVISION OF PARTNERSHIP
INCOME
Objective 5

Mary Logan and Robert Mair have decided to form a partnership. They have agreed that Logan is to invest $60,000 and that Mair is to invest $90,000. Logan is to devote full time to the business and Mair is to devote one-half time. The following plans for the division of income are being considered:

a. Equal division.
b. In the ratio of original investments.
c. In the ratio of time devoted to the business.
d. Interest of 10% on original investments and the remainder in the ratio of 3:2.
e. Interest of 10% on original investments, salary allowances of $30,000 to Logan and $15,000 to Mair, and the remainder equally.
f. Plan (e), except that Logan is also to be allowed a bonus equal to 20% of the amount by which net income exceeds the salary allowances.

Instructions

For each plan, determine the division of the net income under each of the following assumptions: (1) net income of $75,000 and (2) net income of $45,000. Present the data in tabular form, using the following columnar headings:

	$75,000		$45,000	
Plan	Logan	Mair	Logan	Mair

PROBLEM 14-3B
FINANCIAL STATEMENTS
FOR PARTNERSHIP
Objectives 5, 6

The ledger of Ed Muzi and Ellen Nall, attorneys-at-law, contains the following accounts and balances after adjustments have been recorded on December 31, the end of the current fiscal year:

Cash	$ 19,500
Accounts Receivable	30,500
Supplies	2,400
Land	50,000
Building	150,000
Accumulated Depreciation—Building	77,500

Office Equipment	$ 40,000
Accumulated Depreciation—Office Equipment	22,400
Accounts Payable	1,000
Salaries Payable	1,500
Ed Muzi, Capital	75,000
Ed Muzi, Drawing	50,000
Ellen Nall, Capital	55,000
Ellen Nall, Drawing	60,000
Professional Fees	296,750
Salary Expense	79,500
Depreciation Expense—Building	10,500
Property Tax Expense	10,000
Heating and Lighting Expense	9,900
Supplies Expense	5,750
Depreciation Expense—Office Equipment	5,000
Miscellaneous Expense	6,100

The balance in Nall's capital account includes an additional investment of $5,000 made on April 5 of the current year.

Instructions

1. Prepare an income statement for the current fiscal year, indicating the division of net income. The articles of partnership provide for salary allowances of $25,000 to Muzi and $35,000 to Nall; allowances of 12% on each partner's capital balance at the beginning of the fiscal year; and equal division of the remaining net income or net loss.
2. Prepare a statement of owner's equity for the current fiscal year.
3. Prepare a balance sheet in report form as of the end of the current fiscal year.

PROBLEM 14-4B
ADMISSION OF NEW
PARTNER
Objectives 6, 7

Alan Lair and Don Mara have operated a successful firm for many years, sharing net income and net losses equally. Fran Voss is to be admitted to the partnership on June 1 of the current year, in accordance with the following agreement:

a. Assets and liabilities of the old partnership are to be valued at their book values as of May 31, except for the following:
   • Accounts receivable amounting to $4,250 are to be written off, and the allowance for doubtful accounts is to be increased to 5% of the remaining accounts.
   • Merchandise inventory is to be valued at $61,200.
   • Equipment is to be valued at $110,000.
b. Voss is to purchase $25,000 of the ownership interest of Lair for $37,500 cash and to contribute $25,000 cash to the partnership for a total ownership equity of $50,000.
c. The income-sharing ratio of Lair, Mara, and Voss is to be 2:1:1.

The post-closing trial balance of Lair and Mara as of May 31 is as follows:

Lair and Mara
Post-Closing Trial Balance
May 31, 19—

Cash	9,500	
Accounts Receivable	29,250	
Allowance for Doubtful Accounts		500
Merchandise Inventory	60,100	
Prepaid Insurance	2,000	
Equipment	162,000	
Accumulated Depreciation—Equipment		72,500
Accounts Payable		9,850
Notes Payable		20,000
Alan Lair, Capital		120,000
Don Mara, Capital		40,000
	262,850	262,850

Instructions

1. Journalize the entries as of May 31 to record the revaluations, using a temporary account entitled Asset Revaluations. The balance in the accumulated depreciation account is to be eliminated.
2. Journalize the additional entries to record the remaining transactions relating to the formation of the new partnership. Assume that all transactions occur on June 1.
3. Present a balance sheet for the new partnership as of June 1.

SOLUTIONS SOFTWARE

Instructions for Solving Problem 14-4B Using Solutions Software

1. Load opening balances.
2. Save the opening balances file to your drive and directory.
3. Set the run date to May 31 of the current year and enter your name.
4. Select the General Journal Entries option and key the journal entries to record the revaluations. Leave the reference field blank. Note: To review the chart of accounts, select F-1.
5. Display a journal entries report.
6. Display a trial balance.
7. Save a backup copy of your data file.
8. Set the run date to June 1 of the current year and change company name to "Lair, Mara, and Voss."
9. Select the General Journal Entries option and key the journal entries to record the formation of the new partnership. Leave the reference field blank.
10. Display a journal entries report.
11. Display a balance sheet.
12. Save your data file to disk.
13. End the session.

PROBLEM 14-5B
STATEMENT OF PARTNERSHIP LIQUIDATION
Objective 8

After the accounts are closed on May 10, prior to liquidating the partnership, the capital accounts of Mathew Fox, Conrad Gove, and Jennifer Howe are $27,800, $8,300, and $13,900 respectively. Cash and noncash assets total $6,500 and $89,100 respectively. Amounts owed to creditors total $45,600. The partners share income and losses in the ratio of 2:1:1. Between May 10 and 30, the noncash assets are sold for $33,500, the partner with the capital deficiency pays his or her deficiency to the partnership, and the liabilities are paid.

Instructions

1. Prepare a statement of partnership liquidation, indicating (a) the sale of assets and division of loss, (b) the receipt of the deficiency (from the appropriate partner), and (c) the payment of liabilities.

2. If the partner with the capital deficiency delcares bankruptcy and is unable to pay the deficiency, explain how the deficiency would be divided between the partners.

If the working papers correlating with the textbook are not used, omit Problem 14-6B.

PROBLEM 14-6B
PARTNERSHIP LIQUIDATION
Objective 8

Tom Gray, Clyde Hale, and Curtis Ives decided to discontinue business operations and liquidate their partnership. A summary of the various transactions that have occurred thus far is presented in the working papers in a partial statement of liquidation.

Instructions

1. Prepare a statement of partnership liquidation. Assume that the partner with the capital deficiency is bankrupt and the deficiency is divided between the remaining partners. Allocate $5,000 of the deficiency to Gray and $2,000 to Ives.
2. Journalize the entries to record (a) the sale of assets, (b) the division of loss on the sale of assets, (c) the payment of liabilities, (d) the division of the partner's deficiency, and (e) the distribution of cash to partners.

PROBLEM 14-7B
STATEMENT OF
PARTNERSHIP
LIQUIDATION
Objective 8

On May 3, the date the firm of Anku, Bass, and Cox decided to liquidate their partnership, the partners have capital balances of $30,000, $90,000, and $120,000 respectively. The cash balance is $10,000, the book values of noncash assets total $285,000, and liabilities total $55,000. The partners share income and losses in the ratio of 1:2:2.

Instructions

Prepare a statement of partnership liquidation, covering the period May 3 through May 29 for each of the following independent assumptions:

1. All of the noncash assets are sold for $335,000 in cash, the creditors are paid, and the remaining cash is distributed to the partners.
2. All of the noncash assets are sold for $185,000 in cash, the creditors are paid, and the remaining cash is distributed to the partners.
3. All of the noncash assets are sold for $115,000 in cash, the creditors are paid, the partner with the debit capital balance pays the amount owed to the firm, and the remaining cash is distributed to the partners.

Instructions for Solving Problem 14-7B Using Solutions Software

(Note: Solve the three assumptions and save your data files using three different file names.)

1. Load opening balances.
2. Save the opening balances file to your drive and directory.
3. Set the run date to May 31 of the current year and enter your name.
4. Display the trial balance.
5. Select the General Journal Entries option and key the journal entries to record the liquidation, assuming that the noncash assets are sold for $335,000 in cash. Leave the reference field blank. Note: To review the chart of accounts, select F-1.
6. Display a journal entries report.
7. Display a trial balance. Note: All accounts should have a zero balance; therefore, the trial balance will be blank.
8. Save a backup copy of your data file.
9. Load opening balances.
10. Save the opening balances file to your drive and directory.
11. Set the run date to May 31 of the current year and enter your name.
12. Display the trial balance.
13. Select the General Journal Entries option and key the journal entries to record the liquidation, assuming that the noncash assets are sold for $185,000 in cash. Leave the reference field blank. Note: To review the chart of accounts, select F-1.
14. Display a journal entries report.
15. Display a trial balance. Note: All accounts should have a zero balance; therefore, the trial balance will be blank.
16. Save a backup copy of your data file.
17. Load opening balances.
18. Save the opening balances file to your drive and directory.
19. Set the run date to May 31 of the current year and enter your name.
20. Display the trial balance.
21. Select the General Journal Entries option and key the journal entries to record the liquidation, assuming that the noncash assets are sold for $115,000 in cash. Leave the reference field blank. Note: To review the chart of accounts, select F-1.
22. Display a journal entries report.
23. Display a trial balance. Note: All accounts should have a zero balance; therefore, the trial balance will be blank.
24. Save your data file to disk.
25. End the session.

MINI-CASE 14 L AND M COMPANY

Twelve years ago, Robert Lewis and Lynn Meyer formed L and M Company as a partnership by each contributing $100,000 in capital. The partnership agreement indicated the following division of net income: salary allowances of $20,000 and $30,000 to Lewis and Meyer respectively, and all remaining net income divided equally.

Meyer recently expressed concern with the manner in which profits are being divided. Specifically, the income-sharing agreement did not consider changes in the amounts invested by each partner as reflected in the balances of their capital accounts. Over the years, Lewis has consistently withdrawn more from the partnership than Meyer, with the result that the capital balances as of January 1, 1994, indicated an investment of $200,000 by Lewis and $362,500 by Meyer.

Lewis agreed with Meyer that a change in the income-sharing agreement was warranted and accordingly proposed the following two alternatives:

Proposal I:

a. The salary allowances of Lewis and Meyer would be increased to $30,000 and $45,000 respectively.
b. Interest of 8% would be allowed on the January 1 balances of the capital accounts.
c. All remaining income would be divided equally.

Proposal II:

a. The salary allowances of Lewis and Meyer would not be changed.
b. No interest would be allowed on the capital balances.
c. Meyer would be allowed a bonus of 20% of the amount by which net income exceeds salary allowances, and the remainder would be divided equally.

Meyer has asked for your advice on which of the two proposals she should accept.

Instructions:

1. For each proposal, prepare an analysis of the distribution of net income between Lewis and Meyer for 1994 for net income levels of $100,000, $140,000, and $200,000.
2. ■■■ ▸ Which proposal would you recommend that Meyer accept?
3. Elizabeth Brill has offered to purchase for $250,000 a one-fourth interest in the partnership capital and net income. Assuming that the net tangible assets of the partnership approximate their fair market values at January 1, 1994, how much bonus is Brill paying to the partnership?

ANSWERS TO SELF-EXAMINATION QUESTIONS

1. **B** Noncash assets contributed to a partnership should be recorded at the amounts agreed upon by the partners. The preferred practice is to record the office equipment at $9,000 (answer B).
2. **C** Net income and net loss are divided among the partners in accordance with their agreement. In the absence of any agreement, all partners share equally (answer C).
3. **C** X's share of the $45,000 of net income is $19,000 (answer C), determined as follows:

	X	Y	Total
Interest allowance	$10,000	$ 5,000	$15,000
Salary allowance	12,000	24,000	36,000
Total	$22,000	$29,000	$51,000
Excess of allowances over income	3,000	3,000	6,000
Net income distribution	$19,000	$26,000	$45,000

4. **A** When an additional person is admitted to a partnership by purchasing an interest from one or more of the partners, the purchase price is paid directly to the selling partner(s). The amount of capital transferred from the capital account(s) of the selling partner(s) to the capital account of the incoming partner is the capital interest acquired from the selling partner(s). In the question, the amount is $32,500 (answer A), which is one-half of X's capital balance of $65,000.
5. **C** Partnership cash would be distributed in accordance with the credit balances in the partners' capital accounts. Therefore, $10,000 (answer C) would be distributed to X (X's $10,000 capital balance).

Part 6

Corporations

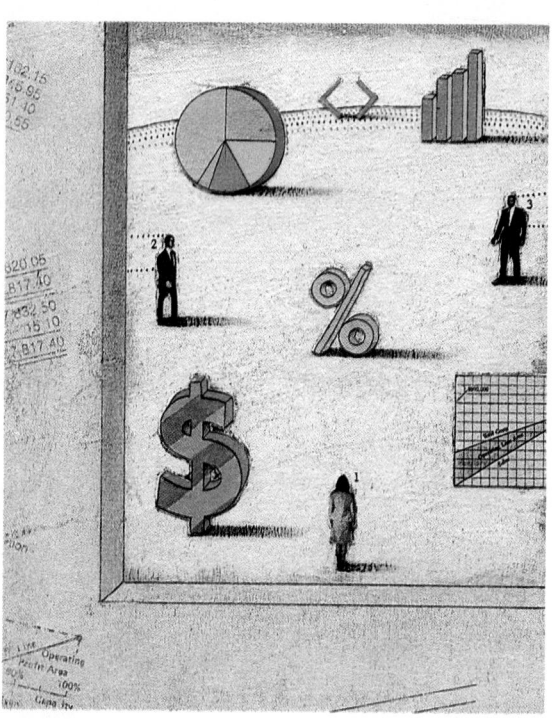

The following stock quotations for Grumman Corporation were taken from the June 5, 1992 issue of *The Wall Street Journal*. The first stock is a common stock, and the second stock is a preferred stock.

NEW YORK STOCK EXCHANGE COMPOSITE TRANSACTIONS											
52 Weeks					**Yld**		**Vol**				**Net**
Hi	**Lo**	**Stock**	**Sym**	**Div**	**%**	**PE**	**100s**	**Hi**	**Lo**	**Close**	**Chg**
21¹/₂	15⁵/₈	Grumman	GQ	1.00	4.8	7	375	21¹/₈	20⁵/₈	21	+¹/₄
27⁵/₈	25³/₈	Grumman pf		2.80	10.6	···	19	26¹/₂	26³/₈	26¹/₂	···

The preceding quotations are interpreted as follows:

Hi	Highest price during the past 52 weeks
Lo	Lowest price during the past 52 weeks
Stock	Name of the company
Sym	Stock exchange symbol (GQ for Grumman)
Div	Dividends paid per share during the past year
Yld %	Annual dividend yield per share based on the closing price (Grumman's 4.8% yield on common stock is computed as $1 ÷ $21)
PE	Price-earnings ratio on common stock (discussed in a later chapter)
Vol	The volume of stock traded in 100s
Hi	Highest price the previous day
Lo	Lowest price the previous day
Close	Closing price the previous day
Net Chg	The net change in price from the previous day

This chapter discusses the corporate form of organization and accounting for stocks, such as those listed above. This will enable you to better understand corporations and corporate stocks as a potential investment.

Chapter 15
Corporations: Organization and Equity Rights

In the Dartmouth College case in 1819, Chief Justice Marshall of the United States Supreme Court stated:

"A corporation is an artificial being, invisible, intangible, and existing only in contemplation of the law."

The concept underlying the preceding definition has become the basis for the legal doctrine that a corporation is an artificial person, created by law and having a distinct existence separate and apart from the natural persons who are responsible for its creation and operation. Almost all large business enterprises in the United States are organized as corporations.

This chapter discusses the nature of corporations, including the main sources of stockholders' equity. In addition, the accounting for capital stock and related transactions is described and illustrated.

CHARACTERISTICS OF A CORPORATION

As a separate legal entity, a corporation has certain characteristics that make it different from other forms of business organizations. The most important characteristics with accounting implications are briefly described below.

A corporation has a **separate legal existence**. It may acquire, own, and dispose of property in its corporate name. It may also incur liabilities and enter into other types of contracts according to the rights granted by its charter or articles of incorporation.

The ownership of a corporation, of which there may be several classes, is divided into units called **shares of stock.** Each share of stock has the same rights as every other share of stock in its class. The owners of the shares of stock own the corporation and are called stockholders or **shareholders**.

Shares of stock may be bought and sold without affecting the operations or continued existence of the corporation. This is in contrast to the partnership form of organization, in which changes in the ownership dissolve the partnership. Corporations whose shares of stock are traded in public markets are called **public corporations**. Corporations whose shares are not traded publicly are usually owned by a small group of investors and are called **nonpublic** or **private corporations**.

The stockholders of a corporation have **limited liability**. A corporation is responsible for its own acts and obligations under law. Therefore, a corporation's creditors usually may not go beyond the assets of the corporation to satisfy their claims. Thus, the financial loss that a stockholder may suffer is limited to the amount invested. This limited liability feature contributed to the rapid growth of the corporate form of organization.

Stockholders exercise control over the management of a corporation's operations and activities by electing a **board of directors**. Under the authority of the corporate charter, the board of directors meets periodically to establish corporate policies. The Board also selects the chief executive officer (CEO) and other major officers to manage the day-to-day affairs of the corporation. The **organizational structure** of a corporation is shown below.

Exhibit 1
Organizational Structure of a Corporate Enterprise

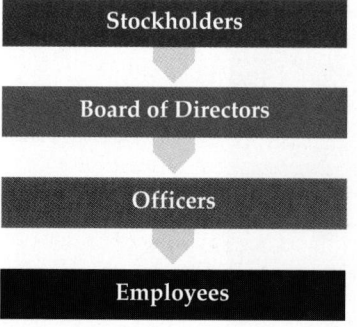

As a separate legal entity, a corporation is subject to additional **taxes**. Thus, unlike the sole proprietorship and partnership forms of organization, corporations must pay federal income taxes. Some states also require corporations to pay income taxes. In addition, when an enterprise is initially organized (incorporated), it usually pays a fee to the state. State incorporation laws may differ significantly, and large corporations usually organize in those states with the more favorable laws.

A corporation distributes its earnings (income) to stockholders in the form of **dividends**. Although corporations must pay federal and, in some cases, state income taxes, income distributed in the form of dividends is taxed again as income to those receiving the dividends. This *double taxation* of corporate earnings is viewed as a major disadvantage of the corporate form of organization. This double taxation does not occur for sole proprietorships and partnerships, which are not taxed as separate entities.[1]

---

[1] Under the *Internal Revenue Code*, a corporation with a few stockholders may elect to be treated like a partnership for income tax purposes. Such corporations are known as Subchapter S Corporations.

Corporations generally have less freedom of action in their operations than do sole proprietorships or partnerships. For example, government regulations often restrict corporations in such matters as ownership of real estate, retention of earnings, and purchase of their own stock.

Corporations may be organized for nonprofit reasons, such as recreational, educational, charitable, or humanitarian purposes. However, most corporations are organized to earn a profit and a fair rate of return for their stockholders. The remainder of this chapter discusses corporations organized for profit.

STOCKHOLDERS' EQUITY

Objective 2
List the two main sources of stockholders' equity.

The owners' equity in a corporation is commonly called **stockholders' equity, shareholders' equity, shareholders' investment**, or **capital**. In a corporation balance sheet, the owners' equity section is called the Stockholders' Equity section. This section reports the amount of each of the two main sources of stockholders' equity. The first source is capital contributed directly by the stockholders, called **paid-in capital** or **contributed capital**. The second source is net income retained in the business, called **retained earnings.** An example of a Stockholders' Equity section of a corporation balance sheet is shown below.

Stockholders' Equity		
Paid-in capital:		
Common stock	$330,000	
Retained earnings	80,000	
Total stockholders' equity		$410,000

The paid-in capital contributed by the stockholders is recorded in separate accounts for each class of stock. If there is only one class of stock, the account is entitled Common Stock or Capital Stock.

Retained earnings results from transferring the balance in the income summary account (the net income) to a retained earnings account at the end of a fiscal year. The dividends account, which is similar to the drawings account for a sole proprietorship or partnership, is also closed to Retained Earnings.

The changes in retained earnings during a fiscal period are summarized in a retained earnings statement. This statement is similar to the statement of owner's equity for a sole proprietorship. An example of a retained earnings statement is shown in Exhibit 2.

Exhibit 2
Retained Earnings Statement

C. L. Eller Inc. Retained Earnings Statement For Year Ended December 31, 1994		
Retained earnings, January 1, 1994		$56,000
Net income for the year	$40,000	
Less dividends	16,000	
Increase in retained earnings		24,000
Retained earnings, December 31, 1994		$80,000

As a result of net losses, a debit balance in Retained Earnings may occur. Such a balance is called a **deficit.** In the Stockholders' Equity section of the balance sheet, a deficit is deducted from paid-in capital in determining total stockholders' equity.

There are a number of alternative terms used for retained earnings, including *earnings retained for use in the business* and *earnings reinvested in the business.* These terms refer to the *use* of retained earnings and not to an amount of *surplus cash* or *cash left over for dividends.* Earnings retained in the business normally are used by management to improve or expand operations. Over time, as the amount of retained earnings from profitable operations increases, it will have less and less of a relationship to the amount of cash on hand.

CHARACTERISTICS OF CAPITAL STOCK

Objective 3
Identify the common characteristics of capital stock and their effects on distributions of earnings.

The general term applied to the shares of ownership of a corporation is **capital stock**. The number of shares that a corporation is authorized to issue is set forth in its charter. The term *issued* is applied to the shares issued to the stockholders. A corporation may, under circumstances discussed later in the chapter, reacquire some of the stock that it has issued. The stock remaining in the hands of stockholders is then called **outstanding stock**.

The shares of capital stock are often assigned a monetary figure, known as **par**. As a written representation of ownership, corporations may issue certificates, called **stock certificates**, to stockholders.[2] On a stock certificate is printed the par value of the stock, the name of the stockholder, and the number of shares owned. Stock may also be issued without par, in which case it is called **no-par** stock. Some states require the board of directors to assign a **stated value** to no-par stock.

Because of the limited liability feature of corporations, creditors have no claim against the personal assets of stockholders. However, some state laws require that corporations maintain a minimum contribution by the stockholders as protection for creditors. This minimum amount is called **legal capital**. The amount of required legal capital varies among the states, but it usually includes the amount of par or stated value of the shares of capital stock issued.

The major rights that accompany ownership of a share of stock are as follows:

1. The right to vote in matters concerning the corporation.
2. The right to share in distributions of earnings.
3. The **preemptive right**, which is the right to maintain the same fractional interest in the corporation by purchasing shares of any additional issuances of stock.[3]
4. The right to share in assets upon liquidation.

If a corporation issues only **common stock**, each share generally has equal rights. In order to appeal to a broader investment market, a corporation may issue one or more classes of stock with various preference rights. A common preference right is the right to share in distributions of earnings. Such stock is generally called **preferred stock**.

The board of directors has the sole authority to distribute earnings to the stockholders in the form of **dividends**. When such action is taken, the directors are said to *declare* a dividend. Since dividends are normally based upon earnings, a corporation cannot guarantee dividends to its stockholders. Rather than distribute dividends, the board of directors may decide to retain earnings in the corporation to provide for expansion, to offset possible future losses, or to provide for other contingencies.

A corporation with both preferred stock and common stock may declare dividends on the common only after it meets the dividend preference of the preferred stock. The dividend preference of the preferred stock may be stated in monetary terms or as a percent of par. For example, $4 preferred stock has a prior claim to an annual $4 per share dividend. If the par value of the preferred stock were $50, the same claim on dividends could be stated as 8% preferred stock.

Nonparticipating and Participating Preferred Stock

The preferred stockholders' dividend preference is usually limited to a certain amount. Such stock is said to be **nonparticipating preferred stock**. To continue

---

[2] Some corporations have stopped issuing stock certificates except upon special request. In these cases, records of ownership are maintained by the corporation, using electronic media.
[3] In recent years, stockholders of a number of corporations have, by formal action, given up their preemptive rights.

the above example, assume that a corporation has 1,000 shares of $4 nonparticipating preferred stock and 4,000 shares of common stock outstanding. Also assume that the net income, amount of earnings retained, and the amount of earnings distributed by the board of directors for the first three years of operations are as follows:

	First Year	Second Year	Third Year
Net income	$20,000	$55,000	$100,000
Amount retained	10,000	20,000	40,000
Amount distributed	$10,000	$35,000	$ 60,000

The distribution of the earnings between the preferred stock and the common stock for each year is shown in Exhibit 3.

Exhibit 3
Dividends to Nonparticipating Preferred Stock

	First Year	Second Year	Third Year
Amount distributed	$10,000	$35,000	$60,000
Preferred dividend (1,000 shares)	4,000	4,000	4,000
Common dividend (4,000 shares)	$ 6,000	$31,000	$56,000
Dividends per share:			
Preferred	$4.00	$4.00	$ 4.00
Common	$1.50	$7.75	$14.00

In the above example, the preferred stockholders received an annual dividend of $4 per share, compared to the common stockholders' dividends of $1.50, $7.75, and $14.00 per share. The preferred stockholders have a greater chance of receiving regular dividends than do the common stockholders. On the other hand, common stockholders have a greater chance of receiving larger dividends than do the preferred stockholders.

Preferred stock may provide for the possibility of receiving additional dividends if certain conditions are met. These conditions often include reaching a certain level of earnings and distributing a certain amount of dividends to common stockholders. Such stock is called **participating preferred stock**.[4] Preferred shares may participate with common shares to varying degrees, and the agreement with the shareholders must be examined to determine the extent of the participation.

To illustrate, assume that the preferred stock contract in the preceding example provides the following order of dividend distribution:

1. Regular preferred stock dividends.
2. Common stock dividends per share equal to the regular preferred dividends per share.
3. Excess dividends in proportion to the number of shares outstanding of both preferred and common.

Under the above terms, the $60,000 dividend distribution in the third year would be allocated as shown in Exhibit 4.

Exhibit 4
Dividends to Participating Preferred Stock

	Preferred Dividend	Common Dividend	Total Dividends
Regular dividend to preferred (1,000 × $4)	$ 4,000	—	$ 4,000
Comparable dividend to common (4,000 × $4)	—	$16,000	16,000
Remainder to 5,000 shares ratably ($8 per share)	8,000	32,000	40,000
Total	$12,000	$48,000	$60,000
Dividends per share	$12	$12	

---

[4] Although participating preferred stock was common at one time, it is used infrequently in today's financial markets.

Cumulative and Noncumulative Preferred Stock

As has been discussed, most preferred stock is nonparticipating. The preferred stock contract, however, may contain special provisions if regular preferred dividends are passed (not declared) by the board of directors. These provisions normally prohibit the payment of any common stock dividends if any preferred dividends have been passed in prior years. Such preferred stock is said to be **cumulative preferred stock**, and any preferred dividends that have been passed are said to be *in arrears*. Preferred stock not having this cumulative right is called **noncumulative preferred stock**.

To illustrate, assume that a corporation has outstanding 5,000 shares of cumulative preferred 9% stock, $100 par. In addition, assume that preferred dividends have been passed for the preceding two years. In the current year, no dividend may be declared on the common stock unless preferred dividends of $90,000 for the past two years and $45,000 for the current year are declared.

Other Preferential Rights

The preceding discussion of the preference rights of preferred stock concerned dividend distributions. Preferred stock may also be given preference rights on assets in liquidation of the corporation. However, claims of creditors must be satisfied first before any assets are distributed to stockholders. Any assets remaining after the creditors have been paid are first distributed to preferred stockholders. Any remaining assets are then distributed to common stockholders.

A corporation may have more than one class of preferred stock, with differences as to the amount of dividends, preferences in liquidation, and voting rights. The rights of a class of stock may be determined by reference to the corporate charter, stock certificate, or stock contract.

Preferred Stock—Risks vs. Rewards

Preferred stocks shield shareholders somewhat from the lows of corporate fortunes. If dividend payments must be reduced, preferred stockholders receive dividends before common shareholders. However, preferred stockholders often miss out on the highs of corporate fortunes. If dividend payments are large, because most preferred stock is nonparticipating, preferred shareholders receive a fixed dividend and the bulk of the large dividends goes to common shareholders. These "safe-but-stodgy" equities can offer dramatic profits, however, as described in the following excerpt from an article in *Business Week*:

. . . In times of grave financial trouble, dividends on preferreds are often suspended and placed in arrears. . . . If and when the company reinstates dividends, current shareholders are entitled to all the back payments, whether or not they owned stock during the arrearage period—if the preferred is cumulative. . . .

The gains [from purchasing preferred stock with dividends in arrears] can be impressive. Bethlehem Steel announced in April that it would pay $22.5 million in arrears and resume the regular quarterly dividend on its two classes of preferred stock. Because Bethlehem had missed four payments, investors receive an extra year's worth of dividends: One class that usually pays $1.25 quarterly will return $6.25—not bad on a stock that traded in the low 30s just a few months ago.

Playing preferreds in arrears requires patience. Long Island Lighting, for instance, recently announced that it would try to resume paying dividends next year after a four-year hiatus. But the larger concern lies in the fact that you're betting on a turnaround. And all bets are off if the company goes bankrupt: You not only lose arrearages but you're also sure to see the share price plummet. On the repayment totem pole, preferreds occupy the second-lowest notch—before the common shareholders but after the creditors and bondholders. . . .

Source: Troy Segal, "Preferred Stock: The Risky Hunt for Hidden Rewards," *Business Week* (June 13, 1988), p. 114.

ISSUANCE OF CAPITAL STOCK

Objective 4
Journalize the entries for the issuance of capital stock.

The entries to record investments of stockholders in a corporation are similar to those for owners of sole proprietorships or partnerships. The cash and other assets received by the corporation are debited and any liabilities assumed are credited. The credit to owner's equity accounts, however, differs in that a stock account is credited rather than an owner's capital account. A separate account is used for each class of stock.

For example, assume that a corporation is authorized to issue 10,000 shares of preferred stock, $100 par, and 100,000 shares of common stock, $20 par. One-half of each class of authorized shares is issued at par for cash. The entry to record the stockholders' investment and the receipt of the cash is as follows:

Cash	1,500,000	
Preferred Stock		500,000
Common Stock		1,000,000

The capital stock accounts (Preferred Stock, Common Stock) are controlling accounts. A record of each stockholder's name, address, and number of shares held is normally kept in a subsidiary ledger. This subsidiary ledger is called the **stockholders ledger**. It provides the source for issuing dividend checks, annual meeting notices, and financial reports to individual stockholders.

Par stock is often issued by a corporation at a price other than par. This is because the par value of a stock is simply a way of dividing owners' equity into units of ownership. The price at which stock can be sold by a corporation generally depends upon such factors as the following:

1. The financial condition, earnings record, and dividend record of the corporation.
2. Investor expectations of the corporation's potential earning power.
3. General business and economic conditions and prospects.

When par stock is issued for a price that is more than its par, the stock has sold at a **premium**. When par stock is issued for a price that is less than its par, the stock has sold at a **discount**. Thus, if stock with a par of $50 is issued for a price of $60, the stock has sold at a premium of $10. If the same stock is issued for a price of $45, the stock has sold at a discount of $5.

Many states do not permit the issuance of stock at a discount. In others, it may be done only under unusual conditions. Since capital stock is not often issued at a discount, transactions involving discounts are not discussed and illustrated in this text.

Premium on Capital Stock

When capital stock is issued at a premium, Cash or other asset accounts are debited for the amount received. The stock account is then credited for the par amount. The excess of the amount paid over par is a part of the total investment of the stockholders in the corporation. Therefore, such an amount in excess of par should be classified as a part of the paid-in capital. An account entitled Paid-In Capital in Excess of Par is usually credited for this amount.

To illustrate, if Caldwell Company issues 2,000 shares of $50 par preferred stock for cash at $55, the entry to record the transaction is as follows:

Cash	110,000	
Preferred Stock		100,000
Paid-In Capital in Excess of Par—Preferred Stock		10,000

Although the $10,000 in excess of par is a part of the paid-in capital, it is recorded in an account separate from the stock account to which it relates. This is because, in some states, the amount received in excess of par may not be considered a part of legal capital. If so, this amount may be used for dividends to stockholders. However, if this amount is used for dividends, stockholders should be clearly notified that the dividend is a return of paid-in capital rather than a distribution of earnings.

The balance of the paid-in capital in excess of par account should be presented in the Stockholders' Equity section of the balance sheet. An example of such a presentation is shown in Exhibit 5.

Exhibit 5
Stockholders' Equity Section of Balance Sheet

Stockholders' Equity			
Paid-in capital:			
Preferred 10% stock, cumulative, $50 par			
(2,000 shares authorized and issued)	$100,000		
Excess of issue price over par	10,000	$110,000	
Common stock, $25 par (50,000 shares			
authorized, 20,000 shares issued)	$500,000		
Excess of issue price over par	40,000	540,000	
Total paid-in capital		$650,000	
Retained earnings		175,000	
Total stockholders' equity			$825,000

The Stockholders' Equity section in Exhibit 6 reports a deficit and illustrates the use of terms that are different from the preceding example.

Exhibit 6
Stockholders' Equity Section with Deficit

Shareholders' Equity			
Paid-in capital:			
Preferred $3 stock, cumulative,			
$25 par (10,000 shares			
authorized and issued)	$ 250,000		
Excess over par	20,000	$ 270,000	
Common stock, $10 par			
(200,000 shares authorized,			
100,000 shares issued)	$1,000,000		
Excess over par	100,000	1,100,000	
Total paid in by shareholders		$1,370,000	
Less deficit		75,000	
Total shareholders' equity			$1,295,000

No-Par Stock

In most states, both preferred and common stock may be issued without a par value. Preferred stock, however, is normally assigned a par value. When no-par stock is issued, the entire proceeds are credited to the capital stock account. This is true even though the issuance price varies from time to time. For example, assume that at the time of organization a corporation issues 10,000 shares of no-par common stock at $40 a share and at a later date issues 1,000 additional shares at $36. The entries to record the issuances of the no-par stock would be as follows:

Original issuance of 10,000 shares of no-par common at $40.

Cash	400,000	
Common Stock		400,000

Subsequent issuance of 1,000 shares of no-par common at $36.

Cash	36,000	
Common Stock		36,000

The laws of some states require that the entire proceeds from the issuance of no-par stock be regarded as legal capital. The preceding entries follow this principle. In other states, no-par stock may be assigned a *stated value* per share. The stated value is treated similarly to par value, and the excess of the proceeds over the stated value is credited to Paid-In Capital in Excess of Stated Value. Assuming that in the above example the stated value is $25, the issuance of the no-par stock would be recorded as follows.

Original issuance of 10,000 shares of no-par common at $40, stated value $25.	Cash	400,000	
	Common Stock		250,000
	Paid-In Capital in Excess of Stated Value		150,000

Subsequent issuance of 1,000 shares of no-par common at $36, stated value $25.	Cash	36,000	
	Common Stock		25,000
	Paid-In Capital in Excess of Stated Value		11,000

Issuing Stock for Assets Other Than Cash

When capital stock is issued in exchange for assets other than cash, such as land, buildings, and equipment, the assets acquired should be recorded at their fair market value. If the fair market value of the assets cannot be objectively determined, the fair market price of the stock issued may be used.

To illustrate, assume that a corporation acquired land for which the fair market value cannot be determined. In exchange, the corporation issued 10,000 shares of its $10 par common. Assuming the stock has a current market price of $12 per share, the transaction is recorded as follows:

Land	120,000	
Common Stock		100,000
Paid-In Capital in Excess of Par—Common Stock		20,000

Subscriptions and Stock Issuance

When a corporation is initially issuing capital stock or when stockholders have waived their preemptive rights in a subsequent issuance, a corporation may sell its stock to an **underwriter**. The underwriter then resells the shares to investors at a price high enough to earn a profit from the sale. In these cases, the corporation is relieved of the task of marketing the stock to investors. It receives the entire amount of cash without delay and can proceed immediately with its plans for the use of the funds.

A corporation may also sell its stock directly to investors or others, such as employees, under stock purchase plans. In such cases, the buyer may enter into an agreement with the corporation to *subscribe* to shares at a stated price per share. Payment for the stock may be received in full, or installment payments may be arranged over a period of time.

When stock is subscribed for at par, the subscription price is debited to Stock Subscriptions Receivable and credited to Stock Subscribed. When stock is subscribed for at a price above par, the Stock Subscriptions Receivable is debited for the subscription price, Stock Subscribed is credited at par, and the difference between the subscription price and par is credited to Paid-In Capital in Excess of Par.

After a subscriber has fully paid for the stock, the corporation issues the stock certificate. The stock subscribed account is then debited for the total par of the shares issued, and the capital stock account is credited for the same amount. For example, assume that the newly organized Ledway Corporation receives subscriptions, collects cash, and issues stock certificates as follows:

Received subscriptions to 10,000 shares of $20 par common stock at $21 per share, with a down payment of 40% of the subscription price.	Mar. 1	Common Stock Subscriptions Receivable	210,000	
		Common Stock Subscribed		200,000
		Paid-In Capital in Excess of Par—Common Stock		10,000
	1	Cash	84,000	
		Common Stock Subscriptions Receivable		84,000

| Received 30% of subscription price from subscribers. | May 1 | Cash | 63,000 | |
| | | Common Stock Subscriptions Receivable | | 63,000 |

Received final 30% of subscription price from subscribers and issued the stock certificates.	July 1	Cash	63,000	
		Common Stock Subscriptions Receivable		63,000
	1	Common Stock Subscribed	200,000	
		Common Stock		200,000

The stock subscriptions receivable account is a current asset account, and the stock subscribed account is a paid-in capital account. Thus, a balance sheet prepared after the transactions of March 1 would list Subscriptions Receivable as a current asset and Stock Subscribed and Paid-In Capital in Excess of Par as paid-in capital. The balance sheet of Ledway Corporation as of March 1 is shown in Exhibit 7.

Exhibit 7
Balance Sheet with
Stock Subscriptions

Ledway Corporation
Balance Sheet
March 1, 19—

Assets		Stockholders' Equity	
Current assets:		Paid-in capital:	
Cash	$ 84,000	Common stock subscribed	$200,000
Common stock subscriptions receivable	126,000	Excess of issue price over par	10,000
Total assets	$210,000	Total stockholders' equity	$210,000

The stock subscriptions receivable account is a controlling account. Individual subscriber accounts are kept in a subsidiary **subscribers ledger**. It is used in much the same manner as the accounts receivable ledger.

After all the subscriptions have been collected, the common stock subscriptions receivable account will have a zero balance. The stock certificates will then be issued and the common stock subscribed account will have a zero balance. The ultimate effect of the series of transactions is a debit to Cash of $210,000, a credit to Common Stock of $200,000, and a credit to Paid-In Capital in Excess of Par of $10,000.

TREASURY STOCK

Objective 5
Journalize the entries for treasury stock.

Although some state laws restrict the practice, a corporation may purchase shares of its own outstanding stock from stockholders. A corporation may buy its own stock in order to provide shares for resale to employees, for reissuance as a bonus to employees, or to support the market price of the stock. For example, General Motors bought back its common stock and stated that two primary uses of the treasury stock would be for incentive compensation plans and employee savings plans.

The term **treasury stock** is used for a corporation's stock that:

1. has been issued as fully paid,
2. has been reacquired by the corporation, and
3. has not been canceled or reissued.

A commonly used method of accounting for the purchase and the resale of treasury stock is the **cost method**.[5] When the stock is purchased by the corporation, the

---

[5] Another method, called the *par value method*, is infrequently used and is discussed in advanced accounting texts.

account Treasury Stock is debited for its cost (the price paid for it). The par value and the price at which the stock was originally issued are ignored. When the stock is resold, Treasury Stock is credited for its cost and any difference between the cost and the selling price is normally debited or credited to a paid-in capital account. This latter account is entitled *Paid-In Capital from Sale of Treasury Stock*.

To illustrate the cost method, assume that the paid-in capital of a corporation is as follows:

Common stock, $25 par (20,000 shares authorized and issued)	$500,000
Excess of issue price over par	150,000

The transactions involving treasury stock and the related entries are shown below.

Purchased 1,000 shares of treasury stock at $45.	Treasury Stock	45,000	
	Cash		45,000
Sold 200 shares of treasury stock at $60.	Cash	12,000	
	Treasury Stock		9,000
	Paid-In Capital from Sale of Treasury Stock		3,000
Sold 200 shares of treasury stock at $40.	Cash	8,000	
	Paid-In Capital from Sale of Treasury Stock	1,000	
	Treasury Stock		9,000

Paid-In Capital from Sale of Treasury Stock is reported in the Paid-In Capital section of the balance sheet. Treasury Stock is deducted from the total of the paid-in capital and retained earnings. After the above transactions have been recorded, the Stockholders' Equity section of the balance sheet would appear as shown in Exhibit 8.

Exhibit 8
Stockholders' Equity Section with Treasury Stock

Stockholders' Equity		
Paid-in capital:		
Common stock, $25 par (20,000 shares authorized and issued)	$500,000	
Excess of issue price over par—common stock	150,000	$650,000
From sale of treasury stock		2,000
Total paid-in capital		$652,000
Retained earnings		130,000
Total		$782,000
Deduct treasury stock (600 shares at cost)		27,000
Total stockholders' equity		$755,000

The Stockholders' Equity section of the balance sheet indicates that 20,000 shares of stock were issued, of which 600 are held as treasury stock. The number of shares outstanding is therefore 19,400. If cash dividends are declared at this time, the declaration would apply to only 19,400 shares of stock. Similarly, owners of 19,400 shares would have the right to vote at a stockholders' meeting.

As shown in the preceding illustration, a sale of treasury stock may result in a decrease in paid-in capital. To the extent that Paid-in Capital from Sale of Treasury Stock has a credit balance, it should be debited for any decrease. Any remaining decrease should then be debited to the retained earnings account.

EQUITY PER SHARE

The stockholders' equity is often reported in the financial press in terms of **equity per share** or **book value per share**. If there is only one class of stock, equity per share is determined by dividing the total stockholders' equity by the number of shares outstanding.

For a corporation with both preferred and common stock, total stockholders' equity must be allocated between the two classes of stock. This allocation must consider any liquidation rights and any participating and cumulative dividend features of the preferred stock. After the total equity is allocated, the equity per share for preferred stock and common stock is determined.

To illustrate, assume that as of the end of the current fiscal year, a corporation has preferred and common shares outstanding, no preferred dividends are in arrears, and preferred stock is entitled to $105 per share upon liquidation. The stockholders' equity and the computation of the equity per share is shown below.

Stockholders' Equity

Preferred $9 stock, cumulative, $100 par (1,000 shares outstanding)	$100,000
Excess of issue price over par—preferred stock	2,000
Common stock, $10 par (50,000 shares outstanding)	500,000
Excess of issue price over par—common stock	50,000
Retained earnings	253,000
Total stockholders' equity	$905,000

Allocation of Total Equity to Preferred and Common Stock

Total stockholders' equity	$905,000
Allocated to preferred stock:	
Liquidation price	105,000
Allocated to common stock	$800,000

Equity per Share

$$\text{Equity per share of preferred stock} = \frac{\text{Total dollar equity of preferred stock}}{\text{Number of shares of preferred stock outstanding}}$$

$$\text{Equity per share of preferred stock} = \frac{\$105,000}{1,000 \text{ shares}} = \$105 \text{ per share}$$

$$\text{Equity per share of common stock} = \frac{\text{Total dollar equity of common stock}}{\text{Number of shares of common stock outstanding}}$$

$$\text{Equity per share of common stock} = \frac{\$800,000}{50,000 \text{ shares}} = \$16 \text{ per share}$$

Assume that the preferred stock is entitled to dividends in arrears upon liquidation and dividends are in arrears for two years. The equity per share in the preceding example would then be determined as follows:

Total stockholders' equity		$905,000
Allocated to preferred stock:		
Liquidation price	$105,000	
Dividends in arrears	18,000	123,000
Allocated to common stock		$782,000

$$\text{Equity per share of preferred stock} = \frac{\$123,000}{1,000 \text{ shares}} = \$123 \text{ per share}$$

$$\text{Equity per share of common stock} = \frac{\$782,000}{50,000 \text{ shares}} = \$15.64 \text{ per share}$$

Equity per share is one of the many factors affecting the market price of stock. Earnings potential, dividend rates, and future expectations also affect the market price of stocks. For example, so-called "hot" stocks may sell at multiples of more than ten times their equity per share. On the other hand, stock of corporations that have reported losses or unfavorable earnings trends may sell at less than the equity per share.

ORGANIZATION COSTS

Objective 7
Give examples of organization costs and journalize the entries for such costs.

Significant costs are often incurred in organizing a corporation. These costs include legal fees, taxes, state incorporation fees, and promotional costs. Such costs are debited to an intangible asset account entitled *Organization Costs*. Although such costs have no value upon liquidation, they are accounted for as an asset, since the corporation could not have been created without them.

To illustrate, assume that on January 5 Schafer Inc. paid an attorney $8,500 for services rendered in organizing the corporation. The entry to record the organization costs is as follows:

Jan.	5	Organization Costs	8,500	
		Cash		8,500

At the time of organization, it is normally assumed that the corporation will continue in existence indefinitely. Thus, it could be argued that organization costs should be carried in the accounts as an asset until such time that the corporation ceases its operations and liquidates. As a practical matter, however, organization costs are amortized.

The *Internal Revenue Code* allows the amortization of organization costs equally over a period of not less than sixty months (5 years), beginning with the month the corporation begins business. Since the effect of organization costs on the financial statements is generally small, such costs are normally amortized over five years.

The entry on December 31 to amortize the preceding organization costs is as follows:

Dec. 31	Amortization Expense—Organization Costs	1,700	
	Organization Costs		1,700
	($8,500 ÷ 5 years = $1,700)		

CHAPTER REVIEW

Key Points

Objective 1. Describe the characteristics of the corporate form of organization that have accounting implications.
Corporation characteristics with accounting implications are separate legal existence, transferable units of stock, and limited liability. Corporations are also subject to federal income taxes.

Objective 2. List the two main sources of stockholders' equity.
The two main sources of stockholders' equity are (1) capital contributed directly by the stockholders, called paid-in capital, and (2) net income retained in the business, called retained earnings. Stockholders' equity is reported in a corporation balance sheet according to these two sources.

Objective 3. Identify the common characteristics of capital stock and their effects on distributions of earnings.
The stock of a corporation may be classified according to its par, right to vote, preference as to dividends, and preference as to liquidation rights. Types of stock include par common stock, no-par common stock, nonparticipating preferred stock, participating preferred stock, cumulative preferred stock, and noncumulative preferred stock.

If the preferred stockholders' dividend preference is limited to a certain amount, the stock is nonparticipating preferred stock. If the preferred stockholders are entitled to receive additional dividends when certain conditions are met, the stock is participating preferred stock. If common dividends cannot be declared until previously passed preferred dividends have been paid, the preferred stock is cumulative preferred stock. If the preferred stock does not have this right, it is noncumulative stock.

Objective 4. Journalize the entries for the issuance of capital stock.

When a corporation issues stock at par for cash, the cash account is debited and the class of stock issued is credited for its par amount. When a corporation issues stock at more than par, Paid-In Capital in Excess of Par is credited for the difference between the cash received and the par value of the stock. When capital stock is issued and exchanged for assets other than cash, the assets acquired should be recorded at their fair market price.

When no-par stock is issued, the entire proceeds are credited to the capital stock account. No-par stock may be assigned a stated value per share, and the excess of the proceeds over the stated value may be credited to Paid-In Capital in Excess of Stated Value.

Investors may subscribe to shares of stock directly from a corporation. When stock is subscribed, the subscription price is debited to an asset account, Stock Subscriptions Receivable, and credited to a capital stock account, Stock Subscribed. If the subscription price exceeds the par or stated value of the stock, Paid-In Capital in Excess of Par is credited. When the stock subscription is fully paid, the corporation issues the stock certificate. The stock subscribed account is debited and the capital stock account is credited.

Objective 5. Journalize the entries for treasury stock.

When a corporation purchases its own stock, the cost method of accounting is normally used. Treasury stock is debited for its cost and Cash is credited. If the stock is resold, Treasury Stock is credited for its cost and any difference between the cost and the selling price is normally debited or credited to Paid-In Capital from Sale of Treasury Stock.

Objective 6. Compute equity per share of stock.

If there is only one class of stock, equity per share is determined by dividing the total stockholders' equity by the number of shares outstanding. For a corporation with both preferred and common stock, the total stockholders' equity must be allocated between the two classes of stock. This allocation must consider any liquidation rights and any participating and cumulative dividend features of the preferred stock. After the total equity is allocated, the equity per share for preferred stock and common stock is determined as follows:

$$\text{Equity per share of preferred stock} = \frac{\text{Total dollar equity of preferred stock}}{\text{Number of shares of preferred stock outstanding}}$$

$$\text{Equity per share of common stock} = \frac{\text{Total dollar equity of common stock}}{\text{Number of shares of common stock outstanding}}$$

Objective 7. Give examples of organization costs and journalize the entries for such costs.

Costs often incurred in organizing a corporation include legal fees, taxes, state incorporation fees, and promotional costs. Such costs are debited to an intangible asset account entitled Organization Costs. This account is normally amortized to expense over a period of five years by debiting Amortization Expense—Organization Costs and crediting Organization Costs.

Glossary of Key Terms

Capital stock. Shares of ownership of a corporation. **Objective 3**

Common stock. The basic ownership class of corporate capital stock. **Objective 3**

Cumulative preferred stock. Preferred stock that is entitled to current and past dividends before dividends may be paid on common stock. **Objective 3**

Deficit. A debit balance in the retained earnings account. **Objective 2**

Discount. The excess of par value of stock over its sales price. **Objective 4**

Equity per share. The ratio of stockholders' equity to the related number of shares of stock outstanding. **Objective 6**

Nonparticipating preferred stock. Preferred stock where dividend preference is limited to a certain amount. **Objective 3**

Outstanding stock. The stock that has been issued to stockholders. **Objective 3**

Paid-in capital. The capital acquired from stockholders. **Objective 2**

Par. The monetary amount printed on a stock certificate. **Objective 3**

Preemptive right. The right of each shareholder to maintain the same fractional interest in the corporation by purchasing shares of any additional issuances of stock. **Objective 3**

Preferred stock. A class of stock with preferential rights over common stock. **Objective 3**

Premium. The excess of the sales price of stock over its par amount. **Objective 4**

Retained earnings. Net income retained in a corporation. **Objective 2**

Stated value. A value approved by the board of directors of a corporation for no-par stock. Similar to par value. **Objective 3**

Stockholders. The owners of a corporation. **Objective 1**

Stockholders' equity. The equity of the shareholders in a corporation. **Objective 2**

Treasury stock. A corporation's own outstanding stock that has been reacquired. **Objective 5**

Self-Examination Questions

Answers at end of chapter.

1. The owners' equity in a corporation is commonly called:
   A. stockholders' equity
   B. shareholders' investment
   C. capital
   D. all of the above

2. If a corporation has outstanding 1,000 shares of $9 cumulative preferred stock of $100 par and dividends have been passed for the preceding three years, what is the amount of preferred dividends that must be declared in the current year before a dividend can be declared on common stock?
   A. $9,000
   B. $27,000
   C. $36,000
   D. $45,000

3. The Stockholders' Equity section of the balance sheet may include:
   A. Common Stock
   B. Common Stock Subscribed
   C. Preferred Stock
   D. all of the above

4. If a corporation reacquires its own stock, the stock is listed on the balance sheet in the:
   A. Current Assets section
   B. Long-Term Liabilities section
   C. Stockholders' Equity section
   D. Investments section

5. A corporation's balance sheet includes 10,000 outstanding shares of $8 cumulative preferred stock of $100 par; 100,000 outstanding shares of $20 par common stock; paid-in capital in excess of par—common stock of $100,000; and retained earnings of $540,000. If preferred dividends are three years in arrears and the preferred stock is entitled to dividends in arrears plus $110 per share in the event of liquidation, what is the equity per common share?
   A. $20.00
   B. $22.20
   C. $23.00
   D. $25.40

ILLUSTRATIVE PROBLEM

The stockholders' equity and related accounts of Rockton Manufacturing Corporation as of November 1, 1993, the beginning of the fiscal year, are as follows:

Preferred Stock Subscriptions Receivable	$ 120,000
Preferred 8% Stock, $50 par (100,000 shares authorized, 20,000 shares issued)	1,000,000
Preferred Stock Subscribed (3,000 shares)	150,000
Paid-In Capital in Excess of Par—Preferred Stock	80,000
Common Stock, $25 par (500,000 shares authorized, 100,000 shares issued)	2,500,000
Paid-In Capital in Excess of Par—Common Stock	600,000
Retained Earnings	3,150,000

During the fiscal year ended October 31, 1994, Rockton Manufacturing Corporation completed the following transactions affecting stockholders' equity:

a. Purchased 5,000 shares of treasury common for $130,000.
b. Received balance due on preferred stock subscribed and issued the certificates.
c. Sold 3,000 shares of treasury common for $81,000.
d. Received subscriptions to 4,000 shares of preferred 8% stock at $51, collecting one-third of the subscription price.
e. Issued 40,000 shares of common stock at $27, receiving cash.
f. Sold 1,000 shares of treasury common for $24,000.

Instructions

1. Journalize the entries to record the transactions listed, identifying each transaction by the appropriate letter.
2. Prepare the Stockholders' Equity section of the October 31, 1994 balance sheet. The beginning retained earnings balance must be increased by the net income for the year, $710,000, and reduced by the dividends declared and paid, $280,000.

Solution

1.

a.	Treasury Stock	130,000	
	Cash		130,000
b.	Cash	120,000	
	Preferred Stock Subscriptions Receivable		120,000
	Preferred Stock Subscribed	150,000	
	Preferred Stock		150,000

c. Cash   81,000
        Treasury Stock   78,000
        Paid-In Capital from Sale of Treasury Stock   3,000

d. Preferred Stock Subscriptions Receivable   204,000
        Preferred Stock Subscribed   200,000
        Paid-In Capital in Excess of Par—Preferred Stock   4,000

    Cash   68,000
        Preferred Stock Subscriptions Receivable   68,000

e. Cash   1,080,000
        Common Stock   1,000,000
        Paid-In Capital in Excess of Par—Common Stock   80,000

f. Cash   24,000
    Paid-In Capital from Sale of Treasury Stock   2,000
        Treasury Stock   26,000

2.

Stockholders' Equity

Paid-in capital:
    Preferred 8% stock, $50 par (100,000 shares
        authorized, 23,000 shares issued) $1,150,000
    Preferred stock subscribed, $50 par (4,000 shares)   200,000
    Excess of issue price over par—preferred stock   84,000 $1,434,000
    Common stock, $25 par (500,000 shares
        authorized, 140,000 shares issued) $3,500,000
    Excess of issue price over par—common stock   680,000   4,180,000
    From sale of treasury stock   1,000
        Total paid-in capital $5,615,000
Retained earnings   3,580,000
Total $9,195,000
Deduct treasury common stock (1,000 shares at cost)   26,000
Total stockholders' equity $9,169,000

DISCUSSION QUESTIONS

1. Contrast the owners' liability to creditors of (a) a partnership (partners) and (b) a corporation (stockholders).
2. Why is it said that the earnings of a corporation are subject to *double taxation*? Discuss.
3. Why are most large business enterprises organized as corporations?
4. What are the two principal sources of stockholders' equity?
5. Distinguish between paid-in capital and retained earnings of a corporation.
6. The retained earnings account of a corporation at the beginning of the year had a credit balance of $125,000. The only other entry in the account during the year was a debit of $170,000 transferred from the income summary account at the end of the year. (a) What is the term applied to the $170,000 debit? (b) What is the balance in Retained Earnings at the end of the year? (c) What is the term applied to the balance determined in (b)?
7. The charter of a corporation provides for the issuance of a maximum of 50,000 shares of $100 par common stock. The corporation issued 30,000 shares of common stock, and two years later it reacquired 5,000 shares. After the reacquisition, what is the number of shares of stock (a) authorized, (b) issued, and (c) outstanding?
8. Of two corporations organized at approximately the same time and engaged in competing businesses, one issued $25 par common stock and the other issued $10 par common stock. Do the par designations provide any indication as to which stock is preferable as an investment? Explain.
9. What are the four basic rights that accompany ownership of a share of common stock?
10. a. Differentiate between common stock and preferred stock.
    b. Describe briefly (1) nonparticipating preferred stock and (2) cumulative preferred stock.

11. Assume that a corporation has had outstanding 50,000 shares of $7 cumulative preferred stock of $100 par and dividends were passed for the preceding three years. What amount of total dividends must be paid to the preferred stockholders before the common stockholders are entitled to any dividends in the current year?

12. If common stock of $20 par is sold for $30, what is the $10 difference between the issue price and par called?

13. What are some of the factors that influence the market price of a corporation's stock?

14. When a corporation issues stock at a premium, is the premium income? Explain.

15. In which section of the corporation balance sheet would Paid-In Capital in Excess of Par—Preferred Stock appear?

16. The Stockholders' Equity section of a corporation balance sheet is composed of the following items:

Preferred $4 stock, $50 par	$300,000		
Excess of issue price over par—preferred stock	30,000	$330,000	
Common stock, $10 par	$500,000		
Excess of issue price over par—common stock	70,000	570,000	$900,000
Retained earnings			275,000 $1,175,000

What is the amount of each of the following: (a) paid-in capital attributable to preferred stock, (b) paid-in capital attributable to common stock, (c) earnings retained for use in the business, and (d) total stockholders' equity?

17. Land is acquired by a corporation for 5,000 shares of its $25 par common stock, which is currently selling for $35 per share on a national stock exchange. (a) At what value should the land be recorded? (b) What accounts and amounts should be credited to record the transaction?

18. A newly organized corporation receives subscriptions to 5,000 shares of $20 par common stock from various subscribers at $24 per share, with a down payment of 25% of the subscription price. Subsequently, another payment of 25% of the subscription price is received. Assuming that financial statements are prepared at this point, determine the following account balances: (a) Subscriptions Receivable, (b) Common Stock Subscribed, (c) Paid-In Capital in Excess of Par—Common Stock, and (d) Common Stock.

19. a. In what respect does treasury stock differ from unissued stock?
    b. How should treasury stock be presented on the balance sheet?

20. A corporation reacquires 2,000 shares of its own $40 par common stock for $95,000, recording it at cost. (a) What effect does this transaction have on revenue or expense of the period? (b) What effect does it have on stockholders' equity?

21. The treasury stock in Question 20 is resold for $125,000. (a) What is the effect on the corporation's revenue of the period? (b) What is the effect on stockholders' equity?

22. A corporation that had issued 25,000 shares of $10 par common stock subsequently reacquired 1,000 shares, which it now holds as treasury stock. If the board of directors declares a cash dividend of $1 per share, what will be the total amount of the dividend?

23. The Stockholders' Equity section of a corporation balance sheet is composed of total paid-in capital of $560,000, retained earnings of $240,000, and treasury stock of $50,000. What is the total stockholders' equity?

24. At the end of the current period, a corporation has 5,000 shares of preferred stock and 50,000 shares of common stock outstanding. Assuming that there are no preferred dividends in arrears, that the preferred stock is entitled to receive $56 per share upon liquidation, and that total stockholders' equity is $1,750,000, determine the following amounts: (a) equity per share of preferred stock and (b) equity per share of common stock.

25. Differentiate between equity per share and market price per share of stock.

26. Common stock has a par of $10 per share, the current equity per share is $22.50, and the market price per share is $55. Suggest reasons for the comparatively high market price in relation to par and to equity per share.

27. a. What type of expenditure is charged to the organization costs account?
    b. Give examples of such expenditures.
    c. In what section of the balance sheet is the balance of Organization Costs listed?

28. Identify each of the following accounts as asset, liability, stockholders' equity, revenue, or expense, and indicate the normal balance of each:
    a. Common Stock
    b. Paid-In Capital from Sale of Treasury Stock
    c. Common Stock Subscribed

Continued

d. Common Stock Subscriptions Receivable
e. Retained Earnings
f. Organization Costs
g. Paid-In Capital in Excess of Par—Common Stock
h. Preferred Stock
i. Paid-In Capital in Excess of Par—Preferred Stock
j. Treasury Stock

REAL W●RLD FOCUS   29. A stockbroker advises a client to "buy cumulative preferred stock. . . . With that type of stock, . . .[you] will never have to worry about losing the dividends." Is the broker right?

Source: "Investors Guide," *Naples Daily News* (July 21, 1991), p. 13E.

REAL W●RLD FOCUS   30. The total stockholders' equity of The Woolworth Corporation was $2,031,000,000 as of January 25, 1992. In addition to 130,342,000 shares of common stock outstanding on January 25, 1992, The Woolworth Corporation also had 131,365 shares of $8 cumulative, convertible, Series A preferred stock outstanding. The following excerpt was taken from the footnotes to The Woolworth Corporation's 1992 annual report:

PREFERRED STOCK

At January 25, 1992, the 131,365 outstanding shares of $2.20 Series A Preferred Stock had a liquidation value of $45.00 per share.

(a) If no dividends were in arrears on January 25, 1992, what was the total liquidation value of the Series A preferred stock? (b) What was the equity per share of the outstanding common stock as of January 25, 1992?

ETHICS DISCUSSION CASE

Ignacio Maglie and Don Tomlin are organizing Mines Unlimited Inc. to undertake a high-risk gold mining venture in Mexico. Maglie and Tomlin tentatively plan to request authorization for 100,000,000 shares of common stock to be sold to the general public. Maglie and Tomlin have decided to establish par of $.10 per share in order to appeal to a wide variety of potential investors. Maglie and Tomlin feel that investors would be more willing to invest in the company if they received a large quantity of shares for what might appear to be a "bargain" price.

SHARPEN YOUR COMMUNICATION SKILLS

Discuss whether Maglie and Tomlin are behaving in an ethical manner.

EXERCISES

EXERCISE 15-1
RETAINED EARNINGS
STATEMENT
Objective 2

The following data were extracted from the records of CFA Corporation for the current year ended December 31:

Retained earnings balance, January 1	$96,765
Dividends declared during the year	65,000
Net income for the year	83,450

Prepare a retained earnings statement for the current year ended December 31.

EXERCISE 15-2
DIVIDENDS PER SHARE
Objective 3

Lance Company has stock outstanding as follows: 10,000 shares of $8 (8%) cumulative, nonparticipating preferred stock of $100 par, and 100,000 shares of $20 par common. During its first five years of operations, the following amounts were distributed as dividends: first year, none; second year, $120,000; third year, $180,000; fourth year, $230,000; fifth year, $200,000. Calculate the dividends per share on each class of stock for each of the five years.

EXERCISE 15-3
DIVIDENDS PER SHARE
Objective 3

TDD Inc. has outstanding stock composed of 1,000 shares of 10% ($10) participating preferred stock of $100 par and 10,000 shares of no-par common stock. The preferred stock is entitled to participate equally with the common, on a share-for-share basis, in any dividend distributions that exceed the regular preferred dividend and a $2 per share common dividend. The directors declare dividends of $41,000 for the current year. Calculate the amount of the dividend per share on (a) the preferred stock and (b) the common stock.

EXERCISE 15-4
ENTRIES FOR ISSUANCE OF
PAR STOCK
Objective 4

On April 25, Bonn Company issued for cash 5,000 shares of $10 par common stock at $14, and on August 7 it issued for cash 1,000 shares of $50 par preferred stock at $54.

a. Journalize the entries for April 25 and August 7.
b. What is the total amount invested (total paid-in capital) by all stockholders as of August 7?

EXERCISE 15-5
ENTRIES FOR ISSUANCE OF
NO-PAR STOCK
Objective 4

On January 25, Campbell Company issued for cash 5,000 shares of no-par common stock (with a stated value of $20) at $22, and on August 15 it issued for cash 2,000 shares of $50 par preferred stock at $52.

a. Journalize the entries for January 25 and August 15, assuming that the common stock is to be credited with the stated value.
b. What is the total amount invested (total paid-in capital) by all stockholders as of August 15?

EXERCISE 15-6
ISSUANCE OF STOCK FOR
ASSETS OTHER THAN CASH
Objective 4

On February 9, Morris Corporation acquired land in exchange for 5,000 shares of $25 par common stock with a current market price of $40. Journalize the entry to record the transaction.

EXERCISE 15-7
STOCK SUBSCRIPTIONS
Objective 4

On February 1, Oliver Company received its charter authorizing 10,000 shares of $50 par common stock. On March 5, the corporation received subscriptions to 5,000 shares of stock at $60. Cash for one-half of the subscription price accompanied the subscriptions. On June 5, the remaining half was received from all subscribers and the stock was issued.

a. Journalize entries to record the transactions of March 5.
b. Journalize entries to record the transactions of June 5.
c. By what amount did the corporation's stockholders' equity increase on February 1, March 5, and June 5?
d. Name two controlling accounts used in the transactions and identify the related subsidiary ledgers.

EXERCISE 15-8
STOCKHOLDERS' EQUITY
SECTION OF BALANCE
SHEET
Objectives 4, 5

The following accounts and their balances appear in the ledger of ITC Inc. on June 30 of the current year:

Common Stock, $20 par	$300,000
Paid-In Capital in Excess of Par	90,000
Paid-In Capital from Sale of Treasury Stock	5,000
Retained Earnings	115,000
Treasury Stock	15,000

Prepare the Stockholders' Equity section of the balance sheet as of June 30. Twenty-five thousand shares of common stock are authorized and 1,000 shares have been reacquired.

EXERCISE 15-9
ISSUANCE OF STOCK;
STOCKHOLDERS' EQUITY
SECTION OF BALANCE
SHEET
Objective 4

Slezak Company, with an authorization of 5,000 shares of preferred stock and 50,000 shares of common stock, completed several transactions involving its capital stock on April 1, the first day of operations. The trial balance at the close of the day follows:

Cash	390,000	
Common Stock Subscriptions Receivable	260,000	
Land	90,000	
Buildings	410,000	
Preferred $12 Stock, $100 par		450,000
Paid-In Capital in Excess of Par—Preferred Stock		50,000
Common Stock, $20 par		300,000
Paid-In Capital in Excess of Par—Common Stock		150,000
Common Stock Subscribed		200,000
	1,150,000	1,150,000

All shares within each class of stock were sold or subscribed at the same price, the preferred stock was issued in exchange for the land and buildings, and no cash was received on the unissued common stock subscribed.

a. Journalize the three compound entries to record the transactions summarized in the trial balance.
b. Prepare the Stockholders' Equity section of the balance sheet as of April 1.

EXERCISE 15-10
TREASURY STOCK
TRANSACTIONS
Objective 5

On March 1 of the current year, Curtis Company reacquired 1,000 shares of its common stock at $22 per share. On August 10, 500 of the reacquired shares were sold at $25 per share. The remaining 500 shares were sold at $20 per share on December 19.

a. Journalize the transactions of March 1, August 10, and December 19.
b. What is the balance in Paid-In Capital from Sale of Treasury Stock on December 31 of the current year?
c. Where will the balance in Paid-In Capital from Sale of Treasury Stock be reported on the balance sheet?

■ SHARPEN YOUR ▶
COMMUNICATION SKILLS

d. For what reasons might Curtis Company have purchased the treasury stock?

EXERCISE 15-11
EQUITY PER SHARE
Objective 6

The stockholders' equity accounts of DeViro Company at the end of the current fiscal year are as follows: Preferred $5 Stock, $50 par, $1,000,000; Common Stock, $25 par, $5,000,000; Paid-In Capital in Excess of Par—Common Stock, $200,000; Paid-In Capital in Excess of Par—Preferred Stock, $40,000; Retained Earnings, $860,000.

SPREADSHEET
PROBLEM

a. Calculate the equity per share of each class of stock, assuming that the preferred stock is entitled to receive $60 upon liquidation.
b. Calculate the equity per share of each class of stock, assuming that the preferred stock is to receive $60 per share plus the dividends in arrears in the event of liquidation, and that only the dividends for the current year are in arrears.

EXERCISE 15-12
TREASURY STOCK AND
EQUITY PER SHARE
Objectives 5, 6

The following items were listed in the Stockholders' Equity section of the balance sheet of April 30: Common stock, $10 par (50,000 shares outstanding), $500,000; Paid-in capital in excess of par—common stock, $150,000; Retained earnings, $190,000. On May 1, the corporation purchased 2,000 shares of its stock for $24,000.

a. Calculate the equity per share of stock on April 30.
b. Journalize the entry to record the purchase of the stock on May 1.
c. Calculate the equity per share on May 1.

EXERCISE 15-13
EQUITY PER SHARE;
LIQUIDATION AMOUNTS
Objective 6

The following items were listed in the Stockholders' Equity section of the balance sheet on June 30: Preferred stock, $50 par, $500,000; Common stock, $20 par, $1,500,000; Paid-in capital in excess of par—common stock, $150,000; Deficit, $250,000. On July 1, the board of directors voted to dissolve the corporation immediately. A short time later, after all noncash assets were sold and liabilities were paid, cash of $1,525,000 remained for distribution to stockholders.

a. Assuming that preferred stock is entitled to preference in liquidation of $55 per share, calculate the equity per share on June 30 of (1) preferred stock and (2) common stock.
b. Calculate the amount of the $1,525,000 that will be distributed for each share of (1) preferred stock and (2) common stock.

■ SHARPEN YOUR ▶
COMMUNICATION SKILLS

c. Explain the reason for the difference between the common stock equity per share on June 30 and the amount of the cash distribution per common share.

EXERCISE 15-14
CORPORATE
ORGANIZATION;
STOCKHOLDERS' EQUITY
SECTION OF BALANCE
SHEET
Objectives 4, 7

Shaw Products Inc. was organized on January 17 of the current year, with an authorization of 10,000 shares of $9 noncumulative preferred stock, $100 par, and 100,000 shares of $10 par common stock.

The following selected transactions were completed during the first year of operations:

Jan. 17. Issued 20,000 shares of common stock at par for cash.
    17. Issued 950 shares of common stock to an attorney in payment of legal fees for organizing the corporation.
Feb. 4. Issued 20,000 shares of common stock in exchange for land, buildings, and equipment with fair market prices of $40,000, $120,000, and $45,000 respectively.
Oct. 15. Issued 2,000 shares of preferred stock at $104 for cash.

a. Journalize the transactions.
b. Prepare the Stockholders' Equity section of the balance sheet as of December 31, the end of the current year. The net income for the year amounted to $37,500.

WhAT'S WROnG
WITH THi?

How many errors can you find in the following Stockholders' Equity section of the balance sheet prepared as of the end of the current year?

Stockholders' Equity

Paid-in capital:

Preferred $4 stock, cumulative, $50 par			
(5,000 shares authorized and issued)	$250,000		
Excess of issue price over par	60,000	$310,000	
Retained earnings		140,000	
Total paid-in capital		$450,000	
Common stock, $20 par (50,000 shares			
authorized, 30,000 shares issued)	$600,000		
Excess of issue price over par	210,000	810,000	
Total stockholders' equity			$1,260,000

PROBLEMS

Series A

PROBLEM 15-1A
DIVIDENDS ON PREFERRED
AND COMMON STOCK
Objective 3

Sanford Company has declared the following annual dividends over a six-year period: 1990, $6,000; 1991, $9,000; 1992, $30,000; 1993, $84,000; 1994, $72,000; and 1995, $21,000. During the entire period, the outstanding stock of the company was composed of 1,000 shares of cumulative, participating, $10 preferred stock, $100 par, and 10,000 shares of common stock, $50 par. The preferred stock contract provides that the preferred stock shall participate in distributions of additional dividends after allowance of a $5 dividend per share on the common stock, the additional dividends to be prorated among common and preferred shares on the basis of the total par of the stock outstanding.

Instructions

SPREADSHEET
PROBLEM

1. Calculate the total dividends and the per share dividends declared on each class of stock for each of the six years. There were no dividends in arrears on January 1, 1990. Summarize the data in tabular form, using the following column headings:

		Preferred Dividends		Common Dividends	
Year	Total Dividends	Total	Per Share	Total	Per Share
1990	$ 6,000				
1991	9,000				
1992	30,000				
1993	84,000				
1994	72,000				
1995	21,000				

2. Calculate the average annual dividend per share for each class of stock for the six-year period.
3. Assuming that the preferred stock was sold at par and common stock was sold at $40 at the beginning of the six-year period, calculate the percentage return on initial shareholders' investment, based on the average annual dividend per share (a) for preferred stock and (b) for common stock.

PROBLEM 15-2A
STOCKHOLDERS' EQUITY
SECTION OF BALANCE
SHEET
Objectives 4, 5

The following accounts and their balances appear in the ledger of A and K Inc. on December 31, the end of the current year:

Common Stock, $20 par	$550,000
Paid-In Capital in Excess of Par—Common Stock	127,500
Paid-In Capital in Excess of Par—Preferred Stock	37,500
Paid-In Capital from Sale of Treasury Stock—Common	875
Preferred $4 Stock, $50 par	500,000
Retained Earnings	417,000
Treasury Stock—Common	7,500

Instructions

Prepare the Stockholders' Equity section of the balance sheet as of December 31, the end of the current year. Ten thousand shares of preferred and 50,000 shares of common stock are authorized. Two hundred fifty shares of common stock are held as treasury stock.

PROBLEM 15-3A
CORPORATE EXPANSION;
STOCKHOLDERS' EQUITY
SECTION OF BALANCE
SHEET
Objective 4

The following accounts and their balances appear in the ledger of Janet Combs Corp. on March 31 of the current year:

Preferred $9 Stock, $100 par (10,000 shares authorized, 5,000 shares issued)	$ 500,000
Paid-In Capital in Excess of Par—Preferred Stock	20,000
Common Stock, $20 par (100,000 shares authorized, 75,000 shares issued)	1,500,000
Paid-In Capital in Excess of Par—Common Stock	225,000
Retained Earnings	305,000

At the annual stockholders' meeting on April 11, the board of directors presented a plan for modernizing and expanding plant operations at a cost of approximately $500,000. The plan provided (a) that the corporation borrow $175,000, (b) that 1,000 shares of the unissued preferred stock be issued through an underwriter, and (c) that a building, valued at $180,000, and the land on which it is located, valued at $40,000, be acquired in accordance with preliminary negotiations by the issuance of 10,000 shares of common stock. The plan was approved by the stockholders and accomplished by the following transactions:

May   7. Issued 10,000 shares of common stock in exchange for land and building in accordance with the plan.
       20. Issued 1,000 shares of preferred stock, receiving $105 per share in cash from the underwriter.
       31. Borrowed $175,000 from Highland National Bank, giving a 12% mortgage note.

No other transactions occurred during May.

Instructions

1. Journalize the entries to record the foregoing transactions.
2. Prepare the Stockholders' Equity section of the balance sheet as of May 31.

PROBLEM 15-4A
STOCK TRANSACTIONS;
STOCKHOLDERS' EQUITY
SECTION OF BALANCE
SHEET
Objectives 4, 5

The following selected accounts appear in the ledger of Helms Corporation on July 1, the beginning of the current fiscal year:

Preferred Stock Subscriptions Receivable	$ 26,750
Preferred 10% Stock, $50 par (10,000 shares authorized, 5,000 shares issued)	250,000
Preferred Stock Subscribed (2,000 shares)	100,000
Paid-In Capital in Excess of Par—Preferred Stock	28,000
Common Stock, $20 par (50,000 shares authorized, 25,000 shares issued)	500,000
Paid-In Capital in Excess of Par—Common Stock	90,000
Retained Earnings	337,000

During the year, the corporation completed a number of transactions affecting the stockholders' equity. They are summarized as follows:

    a. Purchased 1,000 shares of treasury common for $27,500.
    b. Received balance due on preferred stock subscribed and issued the certificates.
    c. Sold 500 shares of treasury common for $15,000.
    d. Issued 2,500 shares of common stock at $30, receiving cash.
    e. Received subscriptions to 1,000 shares of preferred 10% stock at $52.50, collecting 25% of the subscription price.
    f. Sold 250 shares of treasury common for $6,500.

Instructions

1. Journalize the entries to record the transactions. Identify each entry by letter. (The use of T accounts for stockholders' equity accounts will facilitate the determination of the amounts needed in recording some of the transactions and in completing Instruction (2).)
2. Prepare the Stockholders' Equity section of the balance sheet as of June 30, the end of the current fiscal year. The net income for the year was $185,000, and cash dividends declared and paid during the year were $105,000.

Instructions for Solving Problem 15-4A Using Solutions Software

1. Load opening balances.
2. Save the opening balances file to your drive and directory.
3. Set the run date to June 30 of the current year and enter your name.
4. Select the General Journal Entries option and key the journal entries. Leave the reference field blank. Note: To review the chart of accounts, select F-1.

SOLUTIONS
SOFTWARE

5. Display a journal entries report.
6. Display a balance sheet.
7. Save your data file to disk.
8. End the session.

PROBLEM 15-5A
CORPORATION
ORGANIZATION;
STOCKHOLDERS' EQUITY
SECTION OF BALANCE
SHEET
Objectives 4, 7

Payne Company was organized by Bows, Howe, and Radner. The charter authorized 10,000 shares of common stock with a par of $50. The following transactions affecting stockholders' equity were completed during the first year of operations:

a. Issued 1,000 shares of stock at par to Bows for cash.
b. Issued 100 shares of stock at par to Howe for promotional services rendered in connection with the organization of the corporation, and issued 900 shares of stock at par to Howe for cash.
c. Purchased land and a building from Radner. The building is mortgaged for $125,000 for 22 years at 12%, and there is accrued interest of $4,000 on the mortgage note at the time of the purchase. It is agreed that the land is to be priced at $49,000 and the building at $130,000, and that Radner's equity will be exchanged for stock at par. The corporation agreed to assume responsibility for paying the mortgage note and the accrued interest.
d. Issued 2,000 shares of stock at $60 to various investors for cash.
e. Purchased equipment for $75,000. The seller accepted a 6-month, 11% note for $25,000 and 1,000 shares of stock in exchange for the equipment.

Instructions

1. Journalize the entries to record the transactions.
2. Prepare the Stockholders' Equity section of the balance sheet as of the end of the first year of operations. The Retained Earnings balance is the net income for the year, $67,200, less dividends declared and paid during the year, $5 per share on each share of stock issued.

PROBLEM 15-6A
STOCK TRANSACTIONS
AND CORRECTIONS;
BALANCE SHEET
Objectives 4, 5, 7

Grady Company was organized on March 1 of the current year. The accounting clerk prepared the first balance sheet the following December 31, the date that had been adopted as the end of the fiscal year. This balance sheet is as follows:

Grady Company
Balance Sheet
March 1 to December 31, 19—

Assets		Liabilities	
Cash	$ 51,700	Accounts payable	$ 93,000
Accounts receivable	208,900	Preferred stock	200,000
Merchandise inventory	122,500	Common stock	300,000
Prepaid insurance	9,100	Paid-in capital in excess	
Treasury common stock	20,000	of par—common stock	30,000
Equipment	130,000		
Retained earnings (deficit)	80,800		
Total assets	$623,000	Total liabilities	$623,000

You are retained by the board of directors to audit the accounts and to prepare a revised balance sheet. The relevant facts developed during the course of your engagement are:

a. Stock authorized: 5,000 shares of $100 par, $8 preferred, and 50,000 shares of $20 par common.
b. Stock issued: 2,000 shares of fully paid preferred at $102.50 and 15,000 shares of common at $22. The premium on preferred stock was credited to Retained Earnings.
c. The company reacquired 1,000 shares of the issued common stock at $25. The difference between par and the price paid was debited to Retained Earnings. (It is decided that the treasury stock is to be recorded at cost.)
d. Included in merchandise inventory is $4,000 of office supplies.
e. Land to be used as a future building site cost $30,000 and was debited to Equipment.
f. No depreciation has been recognized. The equipment is to be depreciated for 9 months by the straight-line method, using an estimated life of 10 years and assuming no residual value.
g. Organization costs of $12,000 were debited to Advertising Expense. (The organization costs are to be amortized over 60 months, beginning with March 1 of the current year.)
h. No dividends have been declared or paid.

Instructions

1. Journalize the entries to record the corrections. Corrections of net income should be recorded as adjustments to Retained Earnings.
2. Prepare a six-column work sheet, with columns for (a) balances per balance sheet, (b) corrections, and (c) corrected balances. In listing the accounts, leave an extra line blank following the retained earnings account. Complete the work sheet.
3. Prepare a corrected balance sheet in report form as of the end of the fiscal year.
4. Explain why a premium on the sale of capital stock is not considered to be a part of retained earnings.

SHARPEN YOUR COMMUNICATION SKILLS

Instructions for Solving Problem 15-6A Using Solutions Software

SOLUTIONS SOFTWARE

1. Load opening balances.
2. Save the opening balances file to your drive and directory.
3. Set the run date to December 31 of the current year and enter your name.
4. Select the General Journal Entries option and key the journal entries. Leave the reference field blank. Note: To review the chart of accounts, select F-1.
5. Display a journal entries report.
6. Display a balance sheet.
7. Save your data file to disk.
8. End the session.

PROBLEM 15-7A
EQUITY PER SHARE
Objective 6

Selected data from the balance sheets of six corporations, identified by letter, are as follows:

A. Common stock, $10 par $ 500,000
   Paid-in capital in excess of par—common stock   100,000
   Deficit   75,000

B. Preferred $2 stock, $25 par $ 500,000
   Common stock, $20 par   1,500,000
   Paid-in capital in excess of par—common stock   130,000
   Retained earnings   410,000
   Preferred stock has prior claim to assets on liquidation to the extent
   of par.

C. Preferred $9 stock, $100 par $1,000,000
   Paid-in capital in excess of par—preferred stock   50,000
   Common stock, no par, 25,000 shares outstanding   1,250,000
   Deficit   200,000
   Preferred stock has prior claim to assets on liquidation to the extent
   of par.

D. Preferred 11% stock, $50 par $2,000,000
   Paid-in capital in excess of par—preferred stock   275,000
   Common stock, $25 par   3,750,000
   Retained earnings   450,000
   Preferred stock has prior claim to assets on liquidation to the extent
   of 110% of par.

E. Preferred 9% stock, $100 par $1,200,000
   Common stock, $50 par   4,000,000
   Paid-in capital in excess of par—common stock   340,000
   Retained earnings   108,000
   Dividends on preferred stock are in arrears for 2 years, including the
   dividend passed during the current year. Preferred stock is entitled
   to par plus unpaid cumulative dividends upon liquidation to the
   extent of retained earnings.

F. Preferred $2 stock, $25 par $ 500,000
   Common stock, $10 par   2,000,000
   Deficit   170,000
   Dividends on preferred stock are in arrears for 3 years, including the
   dividend passed during the current year. Preferred stock is entitled
   to par plus unpaid cumulative dividends upon liquidation,
   regardless of the availability of retained earnings.

Instructions

Calculate for each corporation the equity per share of each class of stock, presenting the total shareholders' equity allocated to each class and the number of shares outstanding.

Series B

PROBLEM 15-1B
DIVIDENDS ON PREFERRED
AND COMMON STOCK
Objective 3

Peabody Company has declared the following annual dividends over a six-year period: 1990, $62,000; 1991, $128,000; 1992, $12,000; 1993, $5,000; 1994, $6,000; and 1995, $45,000. During the entire period, the outstanding stock of the company was composed of 2,000 shares of cumulative, participating, $5 preferred stock, $50 par, and 20,000 shares of common stock, $10 par. The preferred stock contract provides that the preferred stock shall participate in distributions of additional dividends after allowance of a $2 dividend per share on the common stock, the additional dividends to be prorated among common and preferred shares on the basis of the total par of the stock outstanding.

SPREADSHEET
PROBLEM

Instructions

1. Calculate the total dividends and the per share dividends declared on each class of stock for each of the six years. There were no dividends in arrears on January 1, 1990. Summarize the data in tabular form, using the following column headings:

Year	Total Dividends	Preferred Dividends		Common Dividends	
		Total	Per Share	Total	Per Share
1990	$ 62,000				
1991	128,000				
1992	12,000				
1993	5,000				
1994	6,000				
1995	45,000				

2. Calculate the average annual dividend per share for each class of stock for the six-year period.
3. Assuming that the preferred stock was sold at par and common stock was sold at $28 at the beginning of the six-year period, calculate the percentage return on initial shareholders' investment, based on the average annual dividend per share (a) for preferred stock and (b) for common stock.

PROBLEM 15-2B
STOCKHOLDERS' EQUITY
SECTION OF BALANCE
SHEET
Objectives 4, 5

The following accounts and their balances appear in the ledger of C. C. Clausen Inc. on December 31, the end of the current year:

Common Stock, $10 par	$3,500,000
Paid-In Capital in Excess of Par—Common Stock	850,000
Paid-In Capital in Excess of Par—Preferred Stock	55,000
Paid-In Capital from Sale of Treasury Stock—Common	3,500
Preferred $9 Stock, $100 par	1,450,000
Retained Earnings	1,112,500
Treasury Stock—Common	60,000

Instructions

Prepare the Stockholders' Equity section of the balance sheet as of December 31, the end of the current year. Twenty thousand shares of preferred and 500,000 shares of common stock are authorized. Five thousand shares of common stock are held as treasury stock.

PROBLEM 15-3B
CORPORATE EXPANSION;
STOCKHOLDERS' EQUITY
SECTION OF BALANCE
SHEET
Objective 4

The following accounts and their balances appear in the ledger of Fred Putman Corp. on June 30 of the current year:

Preferred $9 Stock, $100 par (10,000 shares authorized, 8,000 shares issued)	$ 800,000
Paid-In Capital in Excess of Par—Preferred Stock	16,000
Common Stock, $20 par (100,000 shares authorized, 75,000 shares issued)	1,500,000
Paid-In Capital in Excess of Par—Common Stock	210,000
Retained Earnings	305,000

At the annual stockholders' meeting on July 9, the board of directors presented a plan for modernizing and expanding plant operations at a cost of approximately $500,000. The plan provided (a) that the corporation borrow $200,000, (b) that 1,000 shares of the unissued preferred stock be issued through an underwriter, and (c) that a building, valued at $155,000, and the land on which it is located, valued at $40,000, be acquired in accordance with preliminary negotiations by the issuance of 8,000 shares of common stock. The plan was approved by the stockholders and accomplished by the following transactions:

July 29. Issued 8,000 shares of common stock in exchange for land and building in accordance with the plan.
    30. Issued 1,000 shares of preferred stock, receiving $105 per share in cash from the underwriter.
    31. Borrowed $200,000 from Palmer National Bank, giving a 14% mortgage note.

No other transactions occurred during July.

Instructions

1. Journalize the entries to record the foregoing transactions.
2. Prepare the Stockholders' Equity section of the balance sheet as of July 31.

PROBLEM 15-4B
STOCK TRANSACTIONS;
STOCKHOLDERS' EQUITY
SECTION OF BALANCE
SHEET
Objectives 4, 5

The following selected accounts appear in the ledger of Hirchfield Corporation on July 1, the beginning of the current fiscal year:

Preferred Stock Subscriptions Receivable	$ 65,900
Preferred 12% Stock, $100 par (20,000 shares authorized,	
10,000 shares issued)	1,000,000
Preferred Stock Subscribed (2,500 shares)	250,000
Paid-In Capital in Excess of Par—Preferred Stock	62,500
Common Stock, $10 par (500,000 shares authorized,	
300,000 shares issued)	3,000,000
Paid-In Capital in Excess of Par—Common Stock	600,000
Retained Earnings	1,450,000

During the year, the corporation completed a number of transactions affecting the stockholders' equity. They are summarized as follows:

   a. Received balance due on preferred stock subscribed and issued the certificates.
   b. Purchased 10,000 shares of treasury common for $120,000.
   c. Sold 3,000 shares of treasury common for $45,000.
   d. Received subscriptions to 2,000 shares of preferred 12% stock at $105, collecting 25% of the subscription price.
   e. Issued 50,000 shares of common stock at $15, receiving cash.
   f. Sold 2,000 shares of treasury common for $22,000.

Instructions

1. Journalize the entries to record the transactions. Identify each entry by letter. (The use of T accounts for stockholders' equity accounts will facilitate the determination of the amounts needed in recording some of the transactions and in completing Instruction (2).)
2. Prepare the Stockholders' Equity section of the balance sheet as of June 30, the end of the current fiscal year. The net income for the year was $550,000, and cash dividends declared and paid during the year were $420,000.

Instructions for Solving Problem 15-4B Using Solutions Software

1. Load opening balances.
2. Save the opening balances file to your drive and directory.
3. Set the run date to June 30 of the current year and enter your name.
4. Select the General Journal Entries option and key the journal entries. Leave the reference field blank. Note: To review the chart of accounts, select F-1.
5. Display a journal entries report.
6. Display a balance sheet.
7. Save your data file to disk.
8. End the session.

PROBLEM 15-5B
CORPORATION
ORGANIZATION;
STOCKHOLDERS' EQUITY
SECTION OF BALANCE
SHEET
Objectives 4, 7

Bonita East Corp. was organized by Dunn, Edwards, and Gardner. The charter authorized 50,000 shares of common stock with a par of $10. The following transactions affecting stockholders' equity were completed during the first year of operations:

a. Issued 5,000 shares of stock at par to Dunn for cash.
b. Issued 500 shares of stock at par to Edwards for promotional services rendered in connection with the organization of the corporation, and issued 4,500 shares of stock at par to Edwards for cash.
c. Purchased land and a building from Gardner. The building is mortgaged for $95,500 for 16 years at 13%, and there is accrued interest of $4,000 on the mortgage note at the time of the purchase. It is agreed that the land is to be priced at $40,000 and the building at $125,000, and that Gardner's equity will be exchanged for stock at par. The corporation agreed to assume responsibility for paying the mortgage note and the accrued interest.
d. Issued 10,000 shares of stock at $12 to various investors for cash.
e. Purchased equipment for $75,000. The seller accepted a 6-month, 11% note for $25,000 and 5,000 shares of stock in exchange for the equipment.

Instructions

1. Journalize the entries to record the transactions.
2. Prepare the Stockholders' Equity section of the balance sheet as of the end of the first year of operations. The Retained Earnings balance is the net income for the year, $77,500, less dividends declared and paid during the year, $1 per share on each share of stock issued.

PROBLEM 15-6B
STOCK TRANSACTIONS
AND CORRECTIONS;
BALANCE SHEET
Objectives 4, 5, 7

Abrams Company was organized on April 1 of the current year. The accounting clerk prepared the first balance sheet the following December 31, the date that had been adopted as the end of the fiscal year. This balance sheet is as follows:

Abrams Company
Balance Sheet
April 1 to December 31, 19—

Assets		Liabilities	
Cash	$ 65,750	Accounts payable	$ 85,000
Accounts receivable	215,000	Preferred stock	200,000
Merchandise inventory	145,250	Common stock	300,000
Prepaid insurance	6,500	Paid-in capital in excess	
Treasury common stock	20,000	of par—common stock	30,000
Equipment	130,000		
Retained earnings (deficit)	32,500		
Total assets	$615,000	Total liabilities	$615,000

You are retained by the board of directors to audit the accounts and to prepare a revised balance sheet. The relevant facts developed during the course of your engagement are:

a. Stock authorized: 5,000 shares of $100 par, $11 preferred, and 50,000 shares of $20 par common.
b. Stock issued: 1,000 shares of fully paid preferred at $105 and 15,000 shares of common at $22. The premium on preferred stock was credited to Retained Earnings.
c. Stock subscribed but not issued: 1,000 shares of preferred at par, on which all subscribers have paid one-half of the subscription price. Unpaid subscriptions are included in accounts receivable and are collectible in 60 days.
d. The company reacquired 1,000 shares of the issued common stock at $30. The difference between par and the price paid was debited to Retained Earnings. (It is decided that the treasury stock is to be recorded at cost.)
e. Included in merchandise inventory is $1,500 of office supplies.
f. Land to be used as a future building site cost $30,000 and was debited to Equipment.
g. No depreciation has been recognized. The equipment is to be depreciated for 9 months by the straight-line method, using an estimated life of 10 years and assuming no residual value.
h. Organization costs of $6,000 were debited to Advertising Expense. (The organization costs are to be amortized over 60 months, beginning with April 1 of the current year.)
i. No dividends have been declared or paid.
j. In balancing the common stockholders ledger with the common stock controlling account, it was discovered that the account with James Wade contained a posting for an issuance of 100 shares, while the copy of the stock certificate indicated that 1,000 shares had been issued. The stock certificate was found to be correct.

Instructions

1. Journalize the entries to record the corrections. Corrections of net income should be recorded as adjustments to Retained Earnings.
2. Prepare a six-column work sheet, with columns for (a) balances per balance sheet, (b) corrections, and (c) corrected balances. In listing the accounts, leave an extra line blank following the retained earnings account. Complete the work sheet.
3. Prepare a corrected balance sheet in report form as of the end of the fiscal year.
4. Explain why a premium on the sale of capital stock is not considered to be a part of retained earnings.

 SHARPEN YOUR COMMUNICATION SKILLS

Instructions for Solving Problem 15-6B Using Solutions Software

 SOLUTIONS SOFTWARE

1. Load opening balances.
2. Save the opening balances file to your drive and directory.
3. Set the run date to December 31 of the current year and enter your name.
4. Select the General Journal Entries option and key the journal entries. Leave the reference field blank. Note: To review the chart of accounts, select F-1.
5. Display a journal entries report.
6. Display a balance sheet.
7. Save your data file to disk.
8. End the session.

PROBLEM 15-7B
EQUITY PER SHARE
Objective 6

Selected data from the balance sheets of six corporations, identified by letter, are as follows:

A. Common stock, no par, 50,000 shares outstanding $ 750,000
    Deficit   90,000

B. Preferred $2 stock, $25 par $ 750,000
    Common stock, $10 par   2,000,000
    Paid-in capital in excess of par—common stock   50,000
    Retained earnings   450,000
    Preferred stock has prior claim to assets on liquidation to the extent of par.

C. Preferred $12 stock, $100 par $ 500,000
    Paid-in capital in excess of par—preferred stock   30,000
    Common stock, $5 par   1,000,000
    Paid-in capital in excess of par—common stock   55,000
    Deficit   205,000
    Preferred stock has prior claim to assets on liquidation to the extent of par.

D. Preferred 10% stock, $100 par $ 750,000
    Paid-in capital in excess of par—preferred stock   100,000
    Common stock, $20 par   2,500,000
    Deficit   75,000
    Preferred stock has prior claim to assets on liquidation to the extent of 110% of par.

E. Preferred 11% stock, $100 par $ 800,000
    Common stock, $5 par   2,000,000
    Paid-in capital in excess of par—common stock   300,000
    Retained earnings   104,000
    Dividends on preferred stock are in arrears for 2 years, including the dividend passed during the current year. Preferred stock is entitled to par plus unpaid cumulative dividends upon liquidation to the extent of retained earnings.

F. Preferred $2 stock, $25 par $ 500,000
    Paid-in capital in excess of par—preferred stock   10,000
    Common stock, $10 par   1,500,000
    Deficit   55,000
    Dividends on preferred stock are in arrears for 3 years, including the dividend passed during the current year. Preferred stock is entitled to par plus unpaid cumulative dividends upon liquidation, regardless of the availability of retained earnings.

Instructions

Calculate for each corporation the equity per share of each class of stock, presenting the total shareholders' equity allocated to each class and the number of shares outstanding.

MINI-CASE 15 MARSHALL VALLEY COOPERATIVE ELECTRIC CORPORATION

Marshall Valley Cooperative Electric Corporation needs $2,000,000 to finance a plant expansion. To raise the $2,000,000, the board of directors suggested that the cooperative first offer common stock for sale at a price equal to the January 1, 1994 equity per share of common stock. By setting the price in this way, the value of the current common stockholders' interest in the cooperative would be preserved. Any additional funds that might be needed after this offer expired could be obtained from the issuance of preferred stock. Since no preferred stock is authorized, the board is considering characteristics of the stock, such as the dividend rate and the cumulative and participating features. So as not to jeopardize common stockholder dividends, the board of directors tentatively approved a dividend rate of 4% for the preferred stock. The board agreed to delay any final action on other aspects of the financing plan until the legal counsel can be contacted to determine the procedures necessary to seek authorization of the preferred sotck.

As of January 1, 1994, the stockholders' equity is as follows:

Paid-in capital:

Common stock, $50 par (100,000 shares authorized, 60,000 shares issued)	$3,000,000
Excess of issue price over par	450,000
Total paid-in capital	$3,450,000
Retained earnings	1,350,000
Total stockholders' equity	$4,800,000

Instructions

1. Calculate the equity per share of common stock on January 1, 1994.
2. a. ▓▓▓ ▸ During the board meeting, you were asked for your opinion of the suggestion for determining the selling price of the common stock. How would you respond?
   b. ▓▓▓ ▸ What characteristics might you suggest the board consider in designing the preferred stock? Comment on the low preferred stock dividend rate tentatively approved by the board.

ANSWERS TO SELF-EXAMINATION QUESTIONS

1. **D** The owners' equity in a corporation is commonly called stockholders' equity (answer A), shareholders' investment (answer B), capital (answer C), or shareholders' equity.
2. **C** If a corporation has cumulative preferred stock outstanding, dividends that have been passed for prior years plus the dividend for the current year must be paid before dividends may be declared on common stock. In this case, dividends of $27,000 ($9,000 × 3) have been passed for the preceding three years and the current year's dividends are $9,000, making a total of $36,000 (answer C) that must be paid to preferred stockholders before dividends can be declared on common stock.
3. **D** The Stockholders' Equity section of corporate balance sheets is divided into two principal subsections: (1) investments contributed by the stockholders and (2) net income retained in the business. Included as part of the investments by stockholders is the par of common stock (answer A); the par of stock subscribed (answer B); and the par of preferred stock (answer C).
4. **C** Reacquired stock, known as treasury stock, should be listed in the Stockholders' Equity section (answer C) of the balance sheet. The price paid for the treasury stock is de-

ducted from the total of all of the stockholders' equity accounts.

5. **C** The total stockholders' equity is determined as follows:

Preferred stock	$1,000,000
Common stock	2,000,000
Excess of issue price over par— common stock	100,000
Retained earnings	540,000
Total equity	$3,640,000

The amount allocated to common stock is determined as follows:

Total equity		$3,640,000
Allocated to preferred stock:		
Liquidation price	$1,100,000	
Dividends in arrears	240,000	1,340,000
Allocated to common stock		$2,300,000

The equity per common share is determined as follows:

$2,300,000 ÷ 100,000 shares = $23 per share

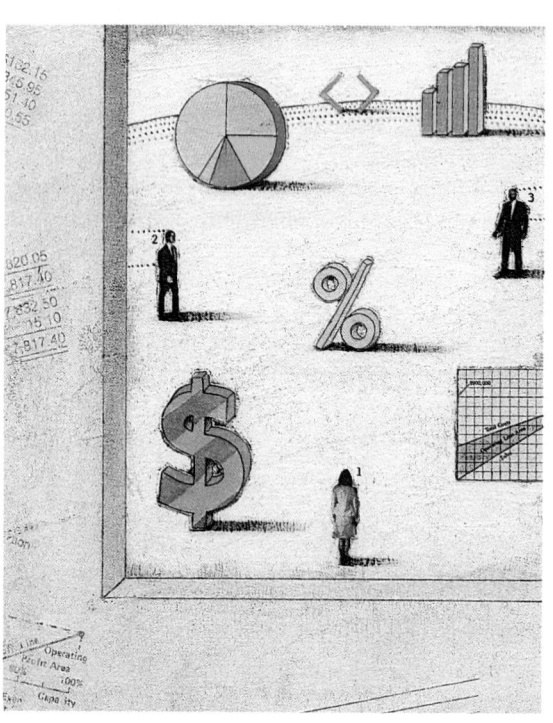

You and Accounting

As a potential investor, you should be able to interpret stock market quotations reported in the financial press. The following are some of the explanatory notes that accompany the stock quotations in *The Wall Street Journal*:

c—Liquidating dividend
k—Indicates dividend declared or paid this year on cumulative issues with dividends in arrears
s—Stock split or stock dividend amounting to 25% or more in the past 52 weeks
x—Ex-dividend

Among other matters related to corporate reporting and dividends, this chapter discusses liquidating dividends, dividends in arrears, stock dividends, stock splits, and ex-dividends. This discussion will help you make informed investment decisions.

Chapter 16
Stockholders' Equity, Earnings, and Dividends

LEARNING OBJECTIVES
After studying this chapter, you should be able to:

Objective 1
Prepare the Paid-In Capital section of a corporate balance sheet.

Objective 2
Journalize the entries for corporate income taxes and prepare an income statement that includes income taxes.

Objective 3
Journalize the entries to account for differences between income before taxes on the income statement and taxable income.

Objective 4
Prepare corporate financial statements reporting the following unusual items:

Discontinued operations
Extraordinary items
Changes in accounting principles
Prior-period adjustments

Objective 5
Prepare a corporate income statement reporting earnings per share data.

Objective 6
Journalize appropriations of retained earnings.

Objective 7
Prepare a retained earnings statement.

Objective 8
Journalize the entries for cash dividends and stock dividends.

Objective 9
State the effect of stock splits on corporate financial statements.

As the financial markets and users of financial statements have become more sophisticated and demanding, there has been an increasing emphasis on full disclosure and clarity in financial reporting. This has not always been the case. For example, at one time it was not unusual to present for stockholders' equity only the amount of the par of the preferred and common stock outstanding and an amount called *surplus*. Users of the financial statements could only assume that the amount reported for par was the amount paid in by stockholders. Likewise, users had to assume that surplus represented retained earnings. Such reporting practices are unacceptable for today's financial statements.

This chapter focuses on current corporate reporting practices for stockholders' equity and earnings. In addition, the accounting for dividends and stock splits will be described and illustrated.

PAID-IN CAPITAL

Objective 1
Prepare the Paid-In Capital section of a corporate balance sheet.

The Stockholders' Equity section of the balance sheet is divided into two major subdivisions, paid-in capital (or contributed capital) and retained earnings. In practice, there is a wide variety in the format, detail, and captions used in reporting stockholders' equity. Regardless of these differences, the primary objective is to report the major sources of stockholders' equity.

As indicated in the preceding chapter, the main source of paid-in capital is from the issuance of stock. Separate capital stock accounts are used for each class of stock. If par stock is issued at a price above or below par, the difference is recorded in a separate paid-in capital account. Also, two accounts are normally used in recording the issuance of no-par stock: one for the stated value and the other for any excess over stated value. Another account for paid-in capital discussed in the preceding chapter was *Paid-In Capital from Sale of Treasury Stock.*

Paid-in capital may arise from donations of real estate or other properties to a corporation. Civic groups and municipalities sometimes give land or buildings to a corporation as an incentive to locate or remain in a community. In such cases, the corporation debits the assets for their fair market value and credits *Donated Capital.*

Paid-in capital may also arise from the redemption of capital stock by a corporation. Preferred stock contracts sometimes provide that the issuing corporation may redeem (retire) the stock at a specific redemption price. When the stock is redeemed, the redemption price may be less than the original issuance price of the stock. In this case, the excess of the original issuance price over the redemption price is credited to *Paid-In Capital from Preferred Stock Redemption.* On the other hand, the redemption price may be greater than the original issuance price of the stock. In this case, the excess of the redemption price over the original issuance price is debited to Retained Earnings.

As with other sections of the balance sheet, alternative terms and formats may be used in reporting paid-in capital. Some examples of alternative terms and formats are presented below.

Stockholders' Equity

Paid-in capital:			
Common stock, $20 par (50,000 shares authorized, 45,000 shares issued)	$900,000		
Excess of issue price over par	132,000	$1,032,000	
From stock redemption		60,000	
From sale of treasury stock		25,000	
Total paid-in capital			$1,117,000

Shareholders' Equity

Paid-in capital:			
Common stock, $20 par (50,000 shares authorized, 45,000 shares issued)		$ 900,000	
Premium on common stock	$132,000		
From redemption of common stock	60,000		
From transactions in own stock	25,000	217,000	
Total paid-in capital			$1,117,000

Shareholders' Investment

Contributed capital:		
Common stock, $20 par (50,000 shares authorized, 45,000 shares issued)	$ 900,000	
Additional paid-in capital	217,000	
Total contributed capital		$1,117,000

In the preceding examples, the common stock is reported first, followed by the other paid-in capital accounts. Instead of reporting each paid-in capital account, the paid-in capital accounts may be combined. When this is done, the capital stock accounts are listed first, followed by a single item described as *Additional paid-in capital, Capital in excess of par (or stated value) of shares,* or other similar title.

Significant changes in paid-in capital during a period should also be disclosed. Such disclosures may be presented either in a *statement of stockholders' equity* or in notes to the financial statements.[1]

CORPORATE EARNINGS AND INCOME TAXES

Objective 2
Journalize the entries for corporate income taxes and prepare an income statement that includes income taxes.

The net income or net loss of a corporation is determined and reported in a manner similar to that of a sole proprietorship or partnership. However, unlike sole proprietorships and partnerships, corporations are taxable entities and must pay income taxes. Some corporations pay not only federal income taxes, but also state and local income taxes. Although the following discussion is limited to federal income taxes, the basic concepts also apply to state and local income taxes.

Most corporations are required to pay estimated federal income taxes in four installments throughout the year. For example, assume that a corporation with a calendar-year accounting period estimates its income tax expense for the year as $84,000. The entry to record each of the four estimated tax payments of $21,000 (1/4 of $84,000) is as follows:

Income Tax	21,000	
Cash		21,000

At year end, the actual taxable income and the actual tax are determined. If additional taxes are owed, this liability must be recorded. To illustrate, assume that in the preceding example the corporation's tax, based on actual taxable income, is $86,000 instead of $84,000. The entry to record the additional tax and liability is as follows:

Dec. 31	Income Tax	2,000	
	Income Tax Payable		2,000

The total estimated tax payments may be greater than the actual tax liability based on actual income. In this case, the overpayment should be debited to a receivable account and credited to Income Tax.

A corporation's income tax returns and supporting records are subject to audits by taxing authorities. Such audits can normally be conducted for a period of three years after the return is filed. A corporation may be assessed additional taxes based upon the results of audits. Because of this possibility, the liability for income taxes is sometimes described in the balance sheet as *Estimated income tax payable*.

Because income tax is often a significant amount, it is normally reported on the income statement as a special deduction, as shown below.

Palmer Corporation	
Income Statement	
For Year Ended December 31, 19—	
Sales	$980,000
Income before income tax	$200,000
Income tax	82,500
Net income	$117,500

---

[1] The statement of stockholders' equity is described and illustrated in a later chapter.

ALLOCATION OF INCOME TAX BETWEEN PERIODS

Objective 3
Journalize the entries to account for differences between income before taxes on the income statement and taxable income.

The **taxable income** of a corporation must be determined according to the tax laws. As a result, it is often different from the *income before income tax* determined and reported according to generally accepted accounting principles. Thus, the income tax based upon *taxable income* usually differs from the income tax based upon *income before taxes* in the income statement. This difference may need to be allocated between various financial statement periods, depending upon the nature of the items causing the differences.

Some differences between *taxable income* and *income before income tax* are created because items are recognized in one period for tax purposes and in another period for income statement purposes. Such differences, called **temporary differences,** reverse or turn around in later years. Some examples of items that create temporary differences are listed below.[2]

1. Revenues or gains are taxed after they are reported in the income statement. Example: The point-of-sale method of realizing revenue is used for financial statement reporting, and the installment method of realizing revenue is used for tax reporting.
2. Expenses or losses are deducted in determining taxable income after they are reported in the income statement. Example: Product warranty expense estimated and reported in the year of the sale for financial statement reporting is deducted for tax reporting when paid.
3. Revenues or gains are taxed before they are reported in the income statement. Example: Cash received in advance for magazine subscriptions is included in taxable income when received, but included in the income statement only when earned in a future period.
4. Expenses or losses are deducted in determining taxable income before they are reported in the income statement. Example: An accelerated depreciation method is used for tax purposes, and the straight-line method is used for financial reporting purposes.

Over the life of an enterprise, temporary differences do not change or reduce the total amount of tax paid. Temporary differences only affect the *timing* of when the taxes are paid. In most cases, temporary differences defer the payment of taxes to later years. As a result, at the end of each year the amount of the current tax liability and the postponed (deferred) liability must be recorded.

To illustrate, assume that a corporation that sells its product on the installment basis realizes the revenue using the point-of-sale method. At the end of the first year of operations, the income before income tax recorded in the ledger is $300,000. In order to reduce current income taxes, the corporation elects the installment method of realizing revenue for tax purposes. The installment method yields taxable income of $100,000. Assuming an income tax rate of 40%, the income tax on $300,000 of income is $120,000.[3] The income tax actually due for the year would only be $40,000 (40% of $100,000). The $80,000 difference between the two amounts is created by the timing difference in realizing revenue. It represents a deferment of $80,000 of income tax to future years. As the installment accounts receivable are collected in later years, the additional $200,000 of income will be included in the taxable income, and the $80,000 deferment (40% of $200,000) will become a tax liability of those years.[4] The example is summarized below.

[2] *Statement of Financial Accounting Standards, No. 109,* "Accounting for Income Taxes" (Norwalk: Financial Accounting Standards Board, 1992), par. 11.
[3] For purposes of illustration, the 40% tax rate is assumed to include all federal, state, and local income taxes.
[4] If the tax rates change, companies are required to recompute their tax liabilities and to recognize the effect of the change in net income. This topic is discussed in more detail in advanced texts.

Income tax based on $300,000 reported income at 40%	$120,000
Income tax based on $100,000 taxable income at 40%	40,000
Income tax deferred to future years	$ 80,000

The income tax reported on the income statement is the total tax ($120,000 in the above example) expected to result from the net income for the year. In this way, the expenses (including income tax) are matched against the revenue to which they relate on the income statement. This matching occurs even though the tax related to the revenue will be paid in a later period. This allocation of income tax between periods is illustrated in the following journal entry:

Income Tax	120,000	
Income Tax Payable		40,000
Deferred Income Tax Payable		80,000

Continuing with the example, the $80,000 in Deferred Income Tax Payable will be transferred to Income Tax Payable as the remaining $200,000 of income becomes taxable in later years. To illustrate, if $120,000 of untaxed income of the first year of the corporation's operations becomes taxable in the second year, the journal entry would be as follows:

| Deferred Income Tax Payable | 48,000 | |
| Income Tax Payable | | 48,000 |

The balance of Deferred Income Tax Payable at the end of a year will be reported as a liability. The amount due within one year is classified as a current liability. The remainder is classified as a long-term liability or reported in a Deferred Credits section following the Long-Term Liabilities section.[5]

During periods of growth, the amount of deferred income taxes for enterprises may increase rapidly and become large in amount. The amounts of deferred income taxes listed as long-term liabilities on the 1991 annual reports of nine major companies were as follows:

Walgreen Co.	$175,592,000
The Boeing Company	102,000,000
Circus Circus Enterprises, Inc.	58,830,000
Tandy Corporation	62,010,000
The Quaker Oats Company	366,700,000
Toys "R" Us, Inc.	136,626,000
H. J. Heinz Company	344,834,000
Super Valu Stores, Inc.	50,845,000
Delta Air Lines, Inc.	378,246,000

Differences between taxable income and income (before tax) reported on the income statement may also arise because certain revenues are exempt from tax and certain expenses are not deductible in determining taxable income.[6] For example, interest income on municipal bonds may be exempt from taxation. Such differences create no special financial reporting problems, since the amount of income tax determined in accordance with the tax laws is the same amount reported on the income statement.

---

[5] In some cases, a deferred tax asset may arise for tax benefits to be received in the future. Such deferred tax assets are reported as either a current or long-term asset, depending upon when the expected benefits are expected to be realized.
[6] Such differences, which will not reverse with the passage of time, are sometimes called *permanent differences.*

Are Deferred Taxes Really a Liability?

For those companies that show a significant amount of deferred taxes on their balance sheets, the question that may arise is whether such amounts really are liabilities. For example, the reporting of a liability for "deferred income taxes, $267.7 million," on an Anheuser-Busch balance sheet was discussed in Forbes. In this article, excerpts from which follow, it was noted that Anheuser-Busch's deferred tax liability was equal to 19% of the total liabilities and 26% of the stockholders' equity.

. . . Says Harvey D. Moskowitz, national director of accounting and auditing for Seidman & Seidman, "The deferred taxes on the balance sheet bear no relationship to what is actually going to be owed" . . . .

Here's the explanation for this curious state of affairs: Anheuser-Busch had pretax income of $271.5 million, so, using standard corporate tax rates (less credits), it owed $99.7 million to Uncle Sam. That's what it set aside as "provision for income taxes" on its income statement. But it's not what the company actually paid. Like most businesses Anheuser keeps two sets of books, one for tax purposes, one for stock owners. It uses accelerated depreciation for taxes but straight line for reporting to investors. . . . So, out-of-pocket, it really had to pay only $31.9 million in taxes . . . the line marked "current" on the income statement. The other $67.8 million, called "deferred," represents cash that's squirreled away in liabilities on the balance sheet, under the assumption that the company will pay those taxes eventually—when accelerated depreciation runs out, for example.

That assumption is probably wrong, though. As long as the company keeps growing—in real terms or because of inflation—it will keep adding new assets and new interest costs to replace the ones that are running out. That means those deferred taxes, instead of getting paid, will simply roll over. And over and over and over. It could almost make you dizzy.

Source: Jane Carmichael, "Rollover," Forbes (January 18, 1982), pp. 75, 78.

REPORTING UNUSUAL ITEMS IN THE FINANCIAL STATEMENTS

Objective 4
Prepare corporate financial statements reporting the following unusual items:

Discontinued operations
Extraordinary items
Changes in accounting principles
Prior-period adjustments

Significant time and effort have been spent by the accounting profession in developing guidelines for reporting unusual items in the financial statements. Generally, unusual items affect either the current or a prior year's net income. Thus, these items may be described as follows:

1. Items that affect the current year's net income and are reported on the current year's income statement.
2. Items that affect a prior year's net income and are reported on the current year's retained earnings statement.

Each of the preceding types of unusual items are discussed and illustrated in the following paragraphs. This discussion assumes that the items illustrated are material to the financial statements. Immaterial items would not affect the normal financial statement presentation.

Items that Affect the Current Year's Net Income

Three types of unusual items may affect the current year's net income and are reported separately in the income statement. These three types of items are listed below.

1. The results of discontinued operations.
2. Extraordinary items of gain or loss.
3. A change from one generally accepted accounting principle to another.

DISCONTINUED OPERATIONS. A gain or loss resulting from the disposal of a segment of a business is reported on the income statement as a gain or loss from **discontinued operations.** The term *discontinued* refers to "the operations of a segment of a business . . . that has been sold, abandoned, spun off, or otherwise disposed of or . . . is the subject of a formal plan for disposal."[7]

---

[7] *Opinions of the Accounting Principles Board, No. 30,* "Reporting the Results of Operations" (New York: American Institute of Certified Public Accountants, 1973), par. 8.

The term *segment of a business* refers to a part of an enterprise whose activities represent a major line of business, such as a division or department or a certain class of customer.[8] For example, assume that an enterprise owns newspapers, television stations, and radio stations. If the enterprise were to sell its radio stations, the results of the sale would be reported as a gain or loss on discontinued operations.

When an enterprise discontinues a segment of its operations, both the *gain or loss from discontinued operations* and the results from *continuing operations* should be reported. The results from continuing operations are presented first, followed by the gain or loss from discontinued operations. Additional data concerning the disposal should also be presented. Such data include the identity of the segment, the disposal date, a description of the segment's assets and liabilities, and the manner of disposal. These data are often disclosed in a note to the financial statements.[9]

EXTRAORDINARY ITEMS. Extraordinary gains and losses result from "events and transactions that are unusual in nature and infrequent in occurrence."[10] Such gains and losses, other than those from the disposal of a segment of a business, should be reported in the income statement as **extraordinary items.** To be classified as an extraordinary item, an event must meet both of the following requirements:[11]

1. Unusual nature—the event should be significantly different from the typical or the normal operating activities of the entity.
2. Infrequent occurrence—the event should not be expected to recur often.

Events that meet both of the preceding requirements are uncommon. For example, the 1991 edition of *Accounting Trends & Techniques* indicated that only 63 of the 600 industrial and merchandising companies surveyed reported extraordinary items on their income statements. Usually, extraordinary items result from natural disasters, such as floods, earthquakes, and fires that are not expected to recur. Gains or losses from condemning land or buildings for public use are also considered extraordinary.

Sometimes extraordinary events result in unusual financial results. For example, in its 1989 income statement, Delta Air Lines reported an extraordinary *gain* of over $5.5 million as the result of the crash of one of its 727 airplanes earlier in the fiscal year. The plane that crashed was insured for $6.5 million, but its book value in Delta's accounting records was $962,000.

Gains and losses on the disposal of plant assets are not extraordinary items. This is because (1) they are not unusual and (2) they recur from time to time in the normal operations of an enterprise. Likewise, gains and losses from the sale of investments are usual and recurring for most enterprises. However, if a company has owned only one type of investment during its entire existence, a gain or loss on its sale might qualify as an extraordinary item, provided there was no intention of acquiring other similar investments in the future.

CHANGES IN ACCOUNTING PRINCIPLES. A change in accounting principle "results from adoption of a generally accepted accounting principle different from the one used previously for reporting purposes."[12] A change in generally accepted accounting principles or methods should be disclosed in the financial statements (or in notes to the statements) of the period in which the change is made. This disclosure should include the nature of the change and its justification. In addition, the effects of the change should be disclosed as follows:

---

[8] *Ibid.*, par. 13.
[9] *Ibid.*, par. 18.
[10]*Ibid.*, par. 20.
[11]*Ibid.*
[12]*Opinions of the Accounting Principles Board, No. 20,* "Accounting Changes" (New York: American Institute of Certified Public Accountants, 1971), par. 7.

1. The effect on the current year's net income should be disclosed.
2. The cumulative effect of the change on the net income of prior periods should be reported in a special section of the income statement.

The special section in which the cumulative effect is reported should follow any extraordinary items and immediately precede the net income.[13] If financial statements of prior periods are presented on a comparative basis with the current period's statements, the following additional disclosures should be made:

1. The financial statements of the prior periods should be restated as if the change had been made in the prior periods.
2. The effect of the restatement of the prior periods' statements should be reported either on the face of the statements or in a note to the statements.

ALLOCATION OF INCOME TAX TO UNUSUAL ITEMS. The related tax effects of unusual items should be reported with the item to which they are associated. Thus, gains or losses from discontinued operations, extraordinary items, or cumulative effects of a change in accounting principle should be reported net of any related income tax. The amount of income tax related to each of these items may be disclosed on the face of the financial statements or in a note to the statements.

REPORTING UNUSUAL ITEMS IN THE INCOME STATEMENT. Many different terms and formats may be used in reporting unusual items in the income statement. An example of the reporting of unusual items in the income statement is illustrated in Exhibit 1 for Jones Corporation.

Exhibit 1
Unusual Items
in Income Statement

Jones Corporation Income Statement For Year Ended December 31, 1994	
Net Sales	$9,600,000
Income from continuing operations before income tax	$1,310,000
Income tax	620,000
Income from continuing operations	$ 690,000
Loss on discontinued operations (Note A)	100,000
Income before extraordinary items and cumulative effect of a change in accounting principle	$ 590,000
Extraordinary item:	
Gain on condemnation of land, net of applicable income tax of $65,000	150,000
Cumulative effect on prior years of changing to a different depreciation method (Note B)	92,000
Net income	$ 832,000

Note A.

On July 1 of the current year, the electrical products division of the corporation was sold at a loss of $100,000, net of applicable income tax of $50,000. The net sales of the division for the current year were $2,900,000. The assets sold were composed of inventories, equipment and plant totaling $2,100,000. The purchaser assumed liabilities of $600,000.

---

[13]Two exceptions to these disclosures are made for a change from the last-in, first-out inventory method or for a change in the method of accounting for long-term construction contracts. The disclosures for these changes are discussed in advanced accounting texts.

Note B.

Depreciation of all property, plant, and equipment has been computed by the straight-line method in 1994. Prior to 1994, depreciation of equipment for one of the divisions had been computed on the double-declining-balance method. In 1994, the straight-line method was adopted for this division in order to achieve uniformity and to better match depreciation charges with the estimated economic utility of such assets. Consistent with APB Opinion No. 20, this change in depreciation has been applied to prior years. The effect of the change was to increase income before extraordinary items for 1994 by $30,000. The adjustment of $92,000 (after reduction for income tax of $88,000) to apply the new method to prior years is also included in income for 1994.

Unusual Items that Affect the Retained Earnings Statement

Material errors in a prior period's net income may arise from mathematical mistakes and from mistakes in applying accounting principles. The effect of material errors that are not discovered within the same fiscal period in which they occurred should not be included in determining net income for the current period.[14] Corrections of such errors are called **prior-period adjustments.** Such errors are reported as an adjustment of the retained earnings balance at the beginning of the period in which the error is discovered and corrected.[15] For example, the correction of a material error in computing a prior period's depreciation expense is a prior-period adjustment. In addition, a change from an unacceptable accounting principle to an acceptable accounting principle is considered to be a correction of a material error and is reported as a prior-period adjustment. For example, a change from reporting plant assets at market values to historical costs would be a prior-period adjustment.

Differences arising from the use of estimates are not prior-period adjustments. Estimates must be used throughout the accounting process. For example, income taxes and uncollectible accounts receivable must be estimated in preparing the financial statements. As a result, differences between estimated and actual amounts will arise. These differences are not considered errors or prior-period adjustments, but they are included in determining the current period's net income.

The reporting of a prior-period adjustment in the retained earnings statement is illustrated in Exhibit 2.

Exhibit 2
Retained Earnings Statement with Prior-Period Adjustment

Casper Company Retained Earnings Statement For Year Ended December 31, 1994		
Retained earnings, January 1, 1994		$310,500
Less prior-period adjustment:		
Correction of error in depreciation expense in 1993, net of applicable income tax of $13,000		29,200
Corrected retained earnings, January 1, 1994		$281,300
Net income for year	$77,350	
Less dividends	40,000	
Increase in retained earnings		37,350
Retained earnings, December 31, 1994		$318,650

Like unusual items on the income statement, prior-period adjustments are reported net of any related income tax. If only the current period's financial statements

---

[14]Corrections of errors that are discovered in the same period in which they occur were discussed in a previous chapter.
[15]*Statement of Financial Accounting Standards, No. 16,* "Prior Period Adjustments" (Stamford: Financial Accounting Standards Board, 1977), par. 11.

are presented, the effect of the adjustment on the net income of the preceding period should also be disclosed. If financial statements for prior periods are presented on a comparative basis, the prior periods' statements should be restated and the amount of the adjustment disclosed.

Prior-period adjustments are rare in financial reporting. Annual audits by independent public accountants, combined with good internal control policies and procedures, reduce the chance of such errors.

EARNINGS PER COMMON SHARE

Objective 5
Prepare a corporate income statement reporting earnings per share data.

The amount of net income is often used by investors and creditors in evaluating a company's profitability. However, net income by itself is difficult to use in comparing companies of different sizes. For example, a net income of $750,000 may be acceptable for a small computer software company, but it would be unacceptable for Apple Computer Inc. Also, trends in net income may be difficult to evaluate, using only net income, when there have been significant changes in a company's stockholders' equity.

In addressing the above concerns, the profitability of companies is often expressed as earnings per share. **Earnings per share,** often called **EPS,** is the net income per share of common stock outstanding during a period. Corporations whose stock is traded on stock exchanges, referred to as public companies, must report earnings per share on the income statement.[16] Because of its importance, earnings per share is reported in the financial press and by various investor services, such as *Moodys* and *Standard & Poors*.

If a company has only common stock outstanding, the earnings per share of common stock is determined by dividing net income by the number of common shares outstanding. If preferred stock is outstanding, the net income must be reduced by the amount of any preferred dividend requirements before dividing by the number of common shares outstanding.

The effect of unusual items should be considered in computing earnings per share. Otherwise, a single earnings per share amount based on net income could be misleading. For example, assume that Jones Corporation, whose partial income statement for 1994 was presented in Exhibit 1, reported net income of $700,000 for 1993. Also assume that no extraordinary or other special items were reported in 1993. The corporation's capital stock was composed of 200,000 common shares outstanding during 1993 and 1994. The earnings per share is $3.50 ($700,000 ÷ 200,000) for 1993 and $4.16 ($832,000 ÷ 200,000) for 1994. Comparing the two earnings per share amounts for 1993 and 1994 would suggest that operations had significantly improved. However, the current year's per share amount that is comparable to $3.50 is $3.45, which is the income from continuing operations of $690,000 divided by 200,000 shares of common stock outstanding. This latter amount indicates a slight downward trend in normal operations.

When unusual items exist, earnings per share should be reported for the following items:

1. Income from continuing operations.
2. Income before extraordinary items and the cumulative effect of a change in accounting principle.
3. The cumulative effect of a change in accounting principle.
4. Net income.[17]

---

[16]Nonpublic corporations are exempt from reporting earnings per share under *Statement of Financial Accounting Standards, No. 21*, "Suspension of the Reporting of Earnings Per Share and Segment Information by Nonpublic Enterprises" (Stamford: Financial Accounting Standards Board, 1978).
[17]*Opinions of the Accounting Principles Board, No. 15*, "Earnings per Share" (New York: American Institute of Certified Public Accountants, 1969) as amended by *Opinions of the Accounting Principles Board, No. 20*, and *Opinions of the Accounting Principles Board, No. 30*.

The reporting of earnings per share for the gain or loss on discontinued operations and for extraordinary items is optional. Earnings per share data may be
shown in parentheses or added at the bottom of the statement, as shown in Exhibit 3 for Jones Corporation.

Exhibit 3
Income Statement
with Earnings per Share

Jones Corporation
Income Statement
For Year Ended December 31, 1994

Income from continuing operations	$690,000
Net income	$832,000
Earnings per common share:	
Income from continuing operations	$3.45
Loss on discontinued operations	.50
Income before extraordinary item and cumulative effect	
of a change in accounting principle	$2.95
Extraordinary item	.75
Cumulative effect on prior years of changing to a different	
depreciation method	.46
Net income	$4.16

In computing the earnings per share of common stock, all factors that could affect the number of common shares outstanding should be considered. For example, an issue of preferred stock or bonds (debt) with the right to convert to
common stock may be outstanding. Such securities that are convertible to common stock are often classified as **common stock equivalents.**[18]

When common stock equivalents exist, two amounts for earnings per share are
normally reported. One amount is computed without regard to the conversion
privilege. This amount is called *Earnings per common share—assuming no dilution* or
Primary earnings per share. The second amount is based on the assumption that the
preferred stock or bonds are converted to common stock. This amount is called
Earnings per common share—assuming full dilution or *Fully diluted earnings per
share.*[19]

A note accompanying the financial statements normally explains how the
earnings per share were computed. An example of such a note, taken from the
1991 statements of The Polaroid Corporation is shown below.

Earnings Per Common Share:

*Primary earnings per common share are computed by dividing net income available to
common stockholders (net income less preferred dividends) by the weighted average number of common shares and dilutive common stock equivalents outstanding for the period.*

    *Fully diluted earnings per common share reflect the maximum dilution that would
result from the exercise of . . . preferred stock, the warrants, stock options, and the
convertible debentures.*

APPROPRIATIONS OF RETAINED EARNINGS

Objective 6
Journalize appropriations of
retained earnings.

A corporation's retained earnings available for use as dividends may be limited
(restricted) by action of its board of directors. The amount restricted is called an
appropriation or a **reserve.** This amount remains a part of retained earnings and
is reported as such in the financial statements.

[18]In order to be classified as a common stock equivalent, a security must satisfy certain requirements set forth
in *Opinions of the Accounting Principles Board, No. 15,* "Earnings per Share" (New York: American Institute of
Certified Public Accountants, 1969).
[19]Additional issues related to computing earnings per share are discussed in advanced accounting texts.

An appropriation is usually reflected in the accounts by transferring the amount from the retained earnings account to a special account. This special account is identified as an appropriation, with a description of its purpose. An example of such an account would be *Appropriation for Plant Expansion.*

In some cases, appropriations may be required by law or contract. For example, some states require appropriations for the amounts paid for treasury stock. To illustrate, assume that a corporation with retained earnings of $200,000 purchases treasury stock for $50,000. An appropriation of $50,000 would be transferred to the account Appropriation for Treasury Stock. This appropriation would restrict the payment of dividends to not more than $150,000. In this way, the corporation's legal capital will not be used for dividends. The entry to record the appropriation is as follows:

| Apr. 24 | Retained Earnings | 50,000 | |
| | Appropriation for Treasury Stock | | 50,000 |

When a part or all of an appropriation is no longer needed, the appropriation is transferred back to the retained earnings account. In the above example, when the corporation sells the treasury stock, the following entry is made:

| Nov. 10 | Appropriation for Treasury Stock | 50,000 | |
| | Retained Earnings | | 50,000 |

When a corporation borrows a large amount of money, it may issue notes or bonds, which are a form of interest-bearing note. The lender or the bond agreement may require restrictions on dividends until the debt is paid. The amount to be restricted is usually equal to the amount of the debt outstanding. The appropriation of retained earnings may be made in total, or an annual buildup of appropriations may be required. For example, assume that a corporation borrows $700,000 on ten-year bonds. If equal annual appropriations are required over the life of the bonds, there would be a series of ten entries, each in the amount of $70,000. The annual entry for the appropriation is shown below.

| Apr. 24 | Retained Earnings | 70,000 | |
| | Appropriation for Bonded Indebtedness | | 70,000 |

Even if the bond agreement does not require the appropriation of retained earnings, the corporation's board of directors might make such an appropriation. In this case, the appropriation is said to be **discretionary** rather than **contractual.** The entries are the same in either case.

An appropriation of retained earnings is not related to any specific assets. Thus, an appropriation does not mean that there is an equivalent amount of cash or other assets set aside in a special fund. The only purpose of an appropriation is to restrict dividend distributions to stockholders. The cash that otherwise might be distributed as dividends could be invested in other assets, such as plant and equipment, or used to reduce liabilities.

The board of directors of a corporation may as a separate action set aside assets such as cash or marketable securities for a specific purpose. This setting aside of assets may also be accompanied by an appropriation of retained earnings. In this case, the appropriation is said to be **funded**. Accumulation of such funds is discussed in a later chapter.

The board of directors may establish appropriations for purposes other than those discussed in the preceding paragraphs. For example, a board of directors may appropriate retained earnings for contingencies, such as inventory price declines, a possible settlement of a pending lawsuit, or possible losses from self-insurance.

REPORTING RETAINED EARNINGS

Objective 7
Prepare a retained earnings statement.

As illustrated in previous chapters, retained earnings is reported in the balance sheet. Changes in retained earnings may be reported in a separate retained earnings statement. The reporting of retained earnings is discussed in the following paragraphs. In addition, the combining of the retained earnings statement and the income statement is described and illustrated.

Reporting Retained Earnings in the Balance Sheet

In the balance sheet, retained earnings should be reported so that readers of the statement can clearly distinguish between the *appropriated* and *unappropriated* portions. An example of such a presentation is shown below.

Retained earnings:
  Appropriated:
    For plant expansion $ 250,000
  Unappropriated   1,800,000
    Total retained earnings $2,050,000

Presentations, other than the above, could be used to report retained earnings in the balance sheet. For example, the preceding data could be presented in a note accompanying the balance sheet. Such a presentation, including the note, might appear as follows:

Retained earnings (see note) $2,050,000

Note:

Retained earnings in the amount of $250,000 are appropriated for expansion of plant facilities; the remaining $1,800,000 is unappropriated.

Retained Earnings Statement

When a separate retained earnings statement is prepared, it is normal to divide the statement into two major sections: (1) appropriated and (2) unappropriated. The first section presents for each appropriation account its beginning balance, any additions or deductions during the period, and its ending balance. The second section presents for the unappropriated retained earnings account its beginning balance, net income or net loss for the period, dividends, transfers to and from the appropriation accounts, and the ending balance. The final figure on the statement is the total retained earnings as of the end of the period. An example of this form of retained earnings statement is shown in Exhibit 4 for Lester Corporation.

Exhibit 4
Retained Earnings Statement
with Appropriations

Lester Corporation Retained Earnings Statement For Year Ended December 31, 1994			
Appropriated:			
Appropriation for plant expansion, January 1, 1994		$ 180,000	
Additional appropriation (see below)		100,000	
Retained earnings appropriated, December 31, 1994			$ 280,000
Unappropriated:			
Balance, January 1, 1994	$1,414,500		
Net income for the year	580,000	$1,994,500	
Cash dividends declared	$ 125,000		
Transfer to appropriation for plant expansion (see above)	100,000	225,000	
Retained earnings unappropriated, December 31, 1994			1,769,500
Total retained earnings, December 31, 1994			$2,049,500

Combined Income and Retained Earnings Statement

An alternative format for presenting the retained earnings statement is to combine it with the income statement. This combined form was used by 30 of the 600 industrial and merchandising companies surveyed in the 1991 edition of *Accounting Trends & Techniques*. An example of the combined income and retained earnings statement is shown in Exhibit 5 for the Wm. Wrigley Jr. Company.

Exhibit 5
Combined Income and Retained
Earnings Statement

Wm. Wrigley Jr. Company Combined Income and Retained Earnings Statement For Year Ended December 31, 1991	
YEAR ENDED DECEMBER 31	1991
	In thousands of dollars except for per share amounts
EARNINGS	
Revenues:	
Net sales	$1,148,875
Investment and other interest income	10,888
Total revenues	1,159,763
Costs and expenses:	
Cost of sales	507,795
Selling, distribution, and general administrative	442,575
Interest	1,379
Total costs and expenses	951,749
Earnings before income taxes	208,014
Income taxes	79,362
Net income	128,652
RETAINED EARNINGS	
Retained earnings at beginning of the year	515,615
Dividends declared	(64,602)
Retained earnings at end of the year	$ 579,665

An advantage of the combined format is that it emphasizes net income as the connecting link between the income statement and the retained earnings portion of stockholders' equity. A disadvantage of the combined form is that the net income figure is buried in the body of the statement.

DIVIDENDS

Objective 8
Journalize the entries for cash dividends and stock dividends.

A dividend usually represents a distribution of retained earnings. Dividends may be paid in cash, in stock of the company, or in other property. A dividend may also represent a distribution of paid-in capital. Cash dividends, stock dividends, and liquidating dividends are discussed in the following paragraphs.

Cash Dividends

A cash distribution of earnings by a corporation to its shareholders is called a **cash dividend.** Cash dividends are the most common form of dividend. There are usually three conditions that must be met to pay a cash dividend:

1. Sufficient unappropriated retained earnings
2. Sufficient cash
3. Formal action by the board of directors

A large amount of retained earnings does not always mean that a corporation is able to pay dividends. There must also be enough cash in excess of normal operating needs. The board of directors of a corporation is not required by law to declare dividends. This is true even if both retained earnings and cash are large enough to justify a dividend. When a dividend has been *declared*, however, it becomes a liability of the corporation.

Most corporations try to maintain a stable dividend record in order to make their stock attractive to investors. Dividends may be paid once a year or on a semiannual or quarterly basis. The general tendency is to pay quarterly dividends on both common and preferred stock. In periods of high profitability, the board of directors may declare an *extra* dividend on common stock. It may be paid at one of the usual dividend dates or at some other date. The use of the term *extra* dividend indicates that the board of directors does not anticipate an increase in the amount of the *regular* dividend.

Dividend declarations are usually announced and reported in financial newspapers and investor services. Three dates are important in a dividend announcement:

1. The date of declaration
2. The date of record
3. The date of payment

The date of declaration is the date the board of directors takes formal action to declare the dividend. The date of record is the date on which ownership of shares is to be determined. The date of payment is the date on which the dividend is to be paid. For example, a dividend announcement might read:

On June 26, the board of directors of Campbell Soup Co. declared a quarterly cash dividend of $.33 per common share to stockholders of record as of the close of business on July 8, payable on July 31.

The liability for a dividend is recorded on the declaration date. No entry is required on the date of record. This date merely sets the date for determining the identity of the stockholders who will receive the dividend. The period of time between the record date and the payment date allows for the preparation of the dividend checks. During this period, a stock's price is usually quoted as selling *ex-dividends*. This means that since the date of record has passed, a new investor will not receive the unpaid dividends. On the date of payment, the corporation's dividend liability is paid by mailing the dividend checks.

The entries required in the declaration and the payment of cash dividends are illustrated below for Hiber Corporation. As a basis for the illustration, assume that on December 1 the board of directors of Hiber Corporation declares both a preferred stock and common stock dividend. The preferred stock dividend is a regular quarterly dividend of $2.50 on the 5,000 shares of $100 par, 10% preferred stock outstanding (total dividend of $12,500). The common stock dividend is a quarterly dividend of $0.30 on the 100,000 shares of $10 par common stock outstanding (total dividend of $30,000). The record date is December 10, and checks are to be issued to stockholders on January 2. The entry to record the declaration of the dividends is as follows:

| Dec. 1 | Cash Dividends | 42,500 | |
| | Cash Dividends Payable | | 42,500 |

The balance in Cash Dividends will be transferred to Retained Earnings as a part of the closing process. Cash Dividends Payable will be listed on the December 31 balance sheet as a current liability. The entry to record the payment of the dividends on January 2 is as follows:

| Jan. 2 | Cash Dividends Payable | 42,500 | |
| | Cash | | 42,500 |

If a corporation that holds treasury stock declares a cash dividend, the dividends are not paid on the treasury shares. To do so would place the corporation in the position of earning income through dealing with itself. For example, if Hiber Corporation in the preceding illustration had held 5,000 shares of its own common stock, the cash dividends on the common stock would have been $28,500 [(100,000 − 5,000) × $.30] instead of $30,000.

Dividends on cumulative preferred stock do not become a liability of the corporation until formal action is taken by the board of directors. However, dividends in arrears at a balance sheet date should be disclosed. This disclosure may be made by a footnote, a parenthetical note, or a segregation of retained earnings, as shown below.

Retained earnings:
Required to meet dividends in arrears on preferred stock	$ 50,000	
Remainder, unrestricted	116,000	
Total retained earnings		$166,000

Stock Dividends

A pro rata distribution of shares of stock to stockholders through a transfer of retained earnings to paid-in capital is a **stock dividend.** Such distributions are usually in common stock and are issued to holders of common stock. It is possible to issue common stock to preferred stockholders or vice versa, but such stock dividends are rare.

Stock dividends are different from cash dividends, in that there is no distribution of cash or other assets to stockholders. Stock dividends are often issued by corporations that are experiencing rapid growth. Such corporations use most of the cash generated from operations to acquire new facilities or to expand their operations.

When a corporation holding treasury stock declares a stock dividend, the number of shares to be issued may be based on either (1) the number of shares outstanding or (2) the number of shares issued. In practice, the number of shares held as treasury stock usually is a small percent of the number of shares issued. Also, the rate of dividend is normally small, so that the difference between the methods is usually not significant.

The effect of a stock dividend on the stockholders' equity of the issuing corporation is to transfer retained earnings to paid-in capital. The amount of this transfer, however, has been subject to some debate in the accounting profession. The laws of most states require that a minimum amount equal to the par or stated value of a stock dividend be transferred from retained earnings to paid-in capital.

For nonpublic (private) corporations, the minimum is usually transferred from retained earnings to paid-in capital. This minimum transfer is often justified on the basis that stockholders of nonpublic corporations have direct knowledge of the affairs of the corporation. Because of this knowledge, the stockholders are able to assess the impact of the stock dividend on the corporation. In addition, since stock of nonpublic corporations is not actively traded, the fair value of the shares of stock issued in a stock dividend usually cannot be objectively determined.

For large public corporations, the *fair value* of the shares issued in a stock dividend is the amount transferred from retained earnings to paid-in capital. The justification for the transfer of *fair value* for public corporations is expressed as follows:

. . . Many recipients of stock dividends look upon them as distributions of corporate earnings and usually in an amount equivalent to the fair value of the additional shares received. . . . [Such] views . . . are . . . strengthened in those instances, which by far are the most numerous where the [stock dividends] are so small in comparison with the shares previously outstanding that they do not have any apparent effect upon the share market price and, consequently, the market value of the shares previously held remains substantially unchanged. . . . [where] these circumstances exist the corporation should in the public interest . . . [transfer] from [retained earnings] to . . . [paid-in capital] . . . an amount equal to the fair value of the additional shares issued. . . .[20]

Using the preceding method, Stock Dividends is debited for the fair value of the stock issued as a dividend. Stock Dividends Distributable is credited for the par or stated value of the common stock to be issued. The remaining difference between the fair value of the stock and its par or stated value is credited to Paid-In Capital in Excess of Par—Common Stock. When the stock is issued on the date of payment, Stock Dividends Distributable is debited and Common Stock is credited for the par or stated value of the stock issued. At the end of the period, the stock dividends account is closed to Retained Earnings.

To illustrate a stock dividend for a public corporation, assume that the stockholders' equity accounts of Hendrix Corporation as of December 15 are as follows:

Common Stock, $20 par (2,000,000 shares issued)	$40,000,000
Paid-In Capital in Excess of Par—Common Stock	9,000,000
Retained Earnings	26,600,000

On December 15, the board of directors declares a 5% stock dividend (100,000 shares, $20 par) to be issued on January 10. The market price of the stock on the declaration date is $31 a share. The entry to record the declaration is shown below.

Dec. 15	Stock Dividends	3,100,000	
	Stock Dividends Distributable		2,000,000
	Paid-In Capital in Excess of Par—Common Stock		1,100,000

[20]*Accounting Research and Terminology Bulletins—Final Edition*, "No. 43, Restatement and Revision of Accounting Research Bulletins" (New York: American Institute of Certified Public Accountants, 1961), Ch. 7, Sec. B, par. 10.

The $3,100,000 debit to Stock Dividends is transferred to Retained Earnings as a part of the closing process at the end of the period. The entry to record the issuance of the stock on January 10 is shown below.

| Jan. 10 | Stock Dividends Distributable | 2,000,000 | |
| | Common Stock | | 2,000,000 |

The effect of the stock dividend is to transfer $3,100,000 from retained earnings to paid-in capital and to increase by 100,000 the number of shares outstanding. There is no change in the assets, liabilities, or total stockholders' equity of the corporation. If financial statements are prepared between the date of declaration and the date of issuance, the stock dividends distributable account should be listed in the Paid-In Capital section of the balance sheet.

The issuance of the additional stock dividend shares does not affect the total amount of a stockholder's equity. A stock dividend also does not affect a stockholder's proportionate interest (equity) in the corporation. This is illustrated below for a stockholder who owns 1,000 shares of a corporation's stock.

The Corporation	Before Stock Dividend	After Stock Dividend
Common stock	$40,000,000	$42,000,000
Excess of issue price over par	9,000,000	10,100,000
Retained earnings	26,600,000	23,500,000
Total stockholders' equity	$75,600,000	$75,600,000
Number of shares outstanding	2,000,000	2,100,000
Equity per share	$37.80	$36.00
A Stockholder		
Number of shares owned	1,000	1,050
Total equity	$37,800	$37,800
Portion of corporation owned	5%	5%

Liquidating Dividends

The term **liquidating dividend** refers to a distribution to stockholders from paid-in capital. Such dividends are rare and are usually paid when a corporation is permanently reducing its operations or winding up its affairs completely. Since dividends are normally paid from retained earnings, dividends that reduce paid-in capital should be identified as liquidating dividends when paid.

STOCK SPLITS

Objective 9
State the effect of stock splits on corporate financial statements.

Corporations sometimes reduce the par or stated value of their common stock and issue a proportionate number of additional shares. When this is done, a corporation is said to have *split its stock*, and the process is a **stock split** or **stock split-up**.

When stock is split, the reduction in par or stated value applies to all shares, including the unissued, issued, and treasury shares. A major objective of a stock split is to reduce the market price per share of the corporation's stock. The lower stock price encourages more investors to enter the market for the stock. This, in turn, tends to increase or broaden the types and numbers of a corporation's stockholders. For example, when Nature's Sunshine Products Inc. declared a two-for-one stock split, the company president said:

We believe the split will place our stock price in a range attractive to both individual and institutional investors, broadening the market for the stock.

To illustrate a stock split, assume that the board of directors of Rojek Corporation, which has 10,000 shares of $100 par common stock outstanding, reduces the par to $20 and increases the number of shares to 50,000. The amount of common stock outstanding is $1,000,000 both before and after the stock split. Only the number of shares and the par per share are changed. Since there are no changes in the balances of any of the corporation's accounts, no entry to record a stock split is required.

Each shareholder in a corporation whose stock is split owns the same total par amount of stock before and after the stock split. For example, a Rojek Corporation stockholder who owned 100 shares of $100 par stock before the split (total par of $10,000) would own 500 shares of $20 par stock after the split (total par of $10,000).

CHAPTER REVIEW

Key Points

Objective 1. Prepare the Paid-In Capital section of a corporate balance sheet.
The format and the terms used in preparing the Paid-In Capital section of the balance sheet may vary. In all cases, however, significant changes in paid-in capital during a period should be disclosed. Such changes include the issuance of stock, the donation of assets, and redemptions of a corporation's own stock.

Objective 2. Journalize the entries for corporate income taxes and prepare an income statement that includes income taxes.
Corporations are subject to federal income tax and are required to make estimated payments throughout the year. To record the payment of estimated tax, Income Tax is debited and Cash is credited. If additional taxes are owed at the end of the year, Income Tax is debited and Income Tax Payable is credited for the amount owed. If the estimated tax payments are greater than the actual tax liability, a receivable account is debited and Income Tax is credited. Because income taxes are a significant amount, they are normally reported on the income statement as a special deduction.

Objective 3. Journalize the entries to account for differences between income before taxes on the income statement and taxable income.
The taxable income is often different from income before income tax reported in the income statement. This is because some items are recognized in one period for income statement purposes and in another period for tax purposes. The tax effects of such differences, called temporary differences, must be allocated between periods. The journal entry for such allocations normally debits Income Tax and credits Income Tax Payable and Deferred Income Tax Payable. A portion of Deferred Income Tax Payable is normally a current liability; the remainder is a long-term liability.

Objective 4. Prepare corporate financial statements reporting the following unusual items: discontinued operations, extraordinary items, changes in accounting principles, and prior-period adjustments.
Discontinued operations: A gain or loss resulting from the disposal of a segment of a business should be identified on the income statement, net of any related income tax, as a gain or loss from discontinued operations. The results of continuing operations should also be identified on the income statement.

Extraordinary items: Gains and losses may result from events and transactions that are unusual in nature and infrequent in occurrence. Such items, net of any related income tax, should be identified on the income statement as extraordinary items.
Changes in accounting principles: A change in an accounting principle results from the adoption of a generally accepted accounting principle different from the one used previously for reporting purposes. The effect of the change in principle on net income in the current period, as well as the cumulative effect on income of prior periods, should be disclosed in the financial statements. The effects of a change in an accounting principle should be reported net of the related income tax.
Prior-period adjustments: Material errors related to a prior period are called prior-period adjustments and are reported as an adjustment to the retained earnings balance at the beginning of the period in which the correction is made.

Objective 5. Prepare a corporate income statement reporting earnings per share data.
Earnings per share data are reported on the income statements of public corporations. If there are nonrecurring items on the income statement, the per share amount should be presented for (1) income from continuing operations, (2) income before extraordinary items and the cumulative effect of a change in accounting principle, (3) the cumulative effect of a change in accounting principle, and (4) net income.

Objective 6. Journalize appropriations of retained earnings.
The retained earnings available for distribution to stockholders may be limited by action of the board of directors or by law or contract. An appropriation is usually recorded in the accounts by debiting Retained Earnings and crediting a special appropriated retained earnings account. An example of such an account is Appropriation for Plant Expansion. When a part or all of an appropriation is no longer needed, the appropriation is transferred back to the retained earnings account. The entry for this transfer is to debit the appropriated retained earnings account and credit Retained Earnings.

Objective 7. Prepare a retained earnings statement.
The retained earnings statement is often divided into two major sections: (1) appropriated and (2) unappropriated.

Each of these sections should identify the beginning balance and any additions or deductions during the period. An alternative format for reporting retained earnings is to combine the retained earnings statement and the income statement.

Objective 8. Journalize the entries for cash dividends and stock dividends.

The entry for a dividend is recorded on the declaration date. The entry for a cash dividend debits Dividends and credits Dividends Payable for the amount of the dividend. No entry is required on the date of record. When the dividend is paid, Dividends Payable is debited and Cash is credited.

A stock dividend is a pro rata distribution of shares of stock to stockholders. The effect of a stock dividend on the capital structure of the issuing corporation is to transfer accumulated earnings to paid-in capital. Stock Dividends is debited for the fair value of the stock declared as a dividend. Stock Dividends Distributable is credited for the par or stated value of the common stock to be issued. The difference between the fair value of the stock and its par or stated value is credited to Paid-In Capital in Excess of Par—Common Stock. When the stock is issued, Stock Dividends Distributable is debited and Common Stock is credited for the par or stated value of the stock issued. At the end of the period, the stock dividends account is closed to Retained Earnings.

Objective 9. State the effect of stock splits on corporate financial statements.

When a corporation reduces the par or stated value of its common stock and issues a proportionate number of additional shares, a stock split or stock split-up has occurred. There are no changes in the balances of any corporation accounts, and no entry is required for a stock split.

Glossary of Key Terms

Appropriation. The amount of a corporation's retained earnings that has been restricted and therefore is not available for distribution to shareholders as dividends. **Objective 6**

Cash dividend. A cash distribution of earnings by a corporation to its shareholders. **Objective 8**

Discontinued operations. The operations of a business segment that have been disposed of. **Objective 4**

Earnings per share (EPS). The profitability ratio of net income available to common shareholders to the number of common shares outstanding. **Objective 5**

Extraordinary items. Events or transactions that are unusual and infrequent. **Objective 4**

Funded. An appropriation of retained earnings accompanied by a segregation of cash or marketable securities. **Objective 6**

Liquidating dividend. A distribution out of paid-in capital when a corporation permanently reduces its operations or winds up its affairs completely. **Objective 8**

Prior-period adjustments. Corrections of material errors related to a prior period or periods, excluded from the determination of net income. **Objective 4**

Stock dividend. Distribution of a company's own stock to its shareholders. **Objective 8**

Stock split. A reduction in the par or stated value of a share of common stock and the issuance of a proportionate number of additional shares. **Objective 9**

Taxable income. The base on which the amount of income tax is determined. **Objective 3**

Temporary differences. Differences between income before income tax and taxable income created by items that are recognized in one period for income statement purposes and in another period for tax purposes. Such differences reverse or turn around in later years. **Objective 3**

Self-Examination Questions
Answers at end of chapter.

1. Paid-in capital for a corporation may originate from which of the following sources?
   A. Real estate donated to the corporation
   B. Redemption of the corporation's own stock
   C. Sale of the corporation's treasury stock
   D. All of the above

2. During its first year of operations, a corporation elected to use the straight-line method of depreciation for financial reporting purposes and the sum-of-the-years-digits method in determining taxable income. If the income tax is 40% and the amount of depreciation expense is $60,000 under the straight-line method and $100,000 under the sum-of-the-years-digits method, what is the amount of income tax deferred to future years?
   A. $16,000   C. $40,000
   B. $24,000   D. $60,000

3. A material gain resulting from the condemnation of land for public use would be reported on the income statement as:
   A. an extraordinary item   C. revenue from sales
   B. an other income item   D. a change in estimate

4. An item treated as a prior-period adjustment should be reported in the financial statements as:
   A. an extraordinary item
   B. an other expense item
   C. an adjustment of the beginning balance of Retained Earnings
   D. a change in estimate

5. An appropriation for plant expansion would be reported on the balance sheet in the:
   A. Plant Assets section
   B. Long-Term Liabilities section
   C. Stockholders' Equity section
   D. Current Liabilities section

ILLUSTRATIVE PROBLEM

During its current fiscal year ended December 31, 1994, Block Inc. completed the following selected transactions:

Jan.   9. Purchased 1,500 shares of its own common stock at $16, recording the stock at cost. (Prior to the purchase, there were 70,000 shares of $10 par common stock outstanding.)

Mar. 16. Discovered that a receipt of $500 cash on account from I. Jonson had been posted in error to the account of I. Johnson. The transaction was journalized correctly.

May 18. Declared a semiannual dividend of $1 on the 10,000 shares of preferred stock and a 20¢ dividend on the common stock to stockholders of record on May 28, payable on June 10.

June 10. Paid the cash dividends.

Aug. 23. Sold 1,000 shares of treasury stock at $18, receiving cash.

Nov. 12. Declared semiannual dividends of $1 on the preferred stock and 20¢ on the common stock. In addition, a 5% common stock dividend was declared on the common stock outstanding, to be capitalized at the fair market value of the common stock, which is estimated at $16.

Dec.   4. Paid the cash dividends and issued the certificates for the common stock dividend.

     31. Recorded $75,000 additional federal income tax allocable to net income for the year. Of this amount, $65,600 is a current liability and $9,400 is deferred.

     31. The board of directors authorized the appropriation necessitated by the holding of treasury stock.

Instructions

Journalize the entries to record the transactions for Block Inc.

Solution

1994

Jan.	9	Treasury Stock	24,000	
		Cash		24,000
Mar.	16	No entry. Error can be corrected by revising the postings in the subsidiary accounts receivable ledger.		
May	18	Cash Dividends	23,700	
		Cash Dividends Payable		23,700*
		*(10,000 × $1) + [(70,000 − 1,500) × $.20]		
June	10	Cash Dividends Payable	23,700	
		Cash		23,700
Aug.	23	Cash	18,000	
		Treasury Stock		16,000
		Paid-In Capital from Sale of Treasury Stock		2,000
Nov.	12	Cash Dividends	23,900*	
		Cash Dividends Payable		23,900
		*(10,000 × $1) + [(70,000 − 500) × $.20]		
		Stock Dividends	55,600*	
		Stock Dividends Distributable		34,750
		Paid-In Capital in Excess of Par—Common Stock		20,850
		*(70,000 − 500) × 5% × $16		
Dec.	4	Cash Dividends Payable	23,900	
		Stock Dividends Distributable	34,750	
		Cash		23,900
		Common Stock		34,750
	31	Income Tax	75,000	
		Income Tax Payable		65,600
		Deferred Income Tax Payable		9,400
	31	Retained Earnings	8,000	
		Appropriation for Treasury Stock		8,000*
		*(500 × $16)		

DISCUSSION QUESTIONS

1. What are the titles of the two principal subdivisions of the Stockholders' Equity section of a corporate balance sheet?
2. Indicate which of the following accounts would be reported as part of paid-in capital on the balance sheet:
   a. Retained Earnings
   b. Common Stock
   c. Donated Capital
   d. Preferred Stock
3. If a corporation is given land as an inducement to locate in a particular community, (a) how should the amount of the debit to the land account be determined, and (b) what is the title of the account that should be credited for the same amount?
4. A corporation has paid $250,000 of federal income tax during the year on the basis of its estimated income. What entry should be recorded as of the end of the year if it determines that (a) it owes an additional $20,000; (b) it overpaid its tax by $10,000?
5. The income before income tax reported on the income statement for the year is $790,000. Because of temporary differences between accounting and tax methods, the taxable income for the same year is $650,000. Assuming an income tax rate of 40%, determine (a) the amount of income tax to be deducted from the $790,000 on the income statement, (b) the amount of the actual income tax that should be paid for the year, and (c) the amount of the deferred income tax liability.
6. How would the amount of deferred income tax payable be reported in the balance sheet if (a) it is payable within one year, and (b) it is payable beyond one year?
7. What two criteria must be met to classify an item as an *extraordinary item* on the income statement?
8. Indicate where the following should be reported in the financial statements, assuming that financial statements are presented only for the current year:
   a. Loss by a Florida citrus firm from crop damage caused by frost. Frost damage occurs one or two times on the average each decade.
   b. Loss on disposal of equipment considered to be obsolete.
   c. Uninsured loss on building due to hurricane damage. The firm was organized in 1920, and had not previously incurred hurricane damage.
9. Classify each of the following revenue and expense items as either (a) normally recurring or (b) extraordinary. Assume that the amount of each item is material.
   (1) Loss on sale of plant assets.
   (2) Interest income on notes receivable.
   (3) Uninsured flood loss. (Flood insurance is unavailable because of periodic flooding in the area.)
   (4) Salaries of corporate officers.
   (5) Gain on sale of land condemned for public use.
   (6) Uncollectible accounts expense.
10. During the current year, twenty acres of land that cost $100,000 were condemned for construction of an interstate highway. Assuming that an award of $140,000 in cash was received and that the applicable income tax on this transaction is 30%, how would this information be presented in the income statement?
11. If significant changes are made in the accounting principles applied from one period to the next, why should the effect of these changes be disclosed in the financial statements?
12. Indicate how prior-period adjustments would be reported on the financial statements presented only for the current period.
13. A corporation reports earnings per share of $9.50 for the most recent year and $7.00 for the preceding year. The $9.50 includes a $3.00 per share gain from a sale of the only investment owned since the business was organized in 1940. (a) Should the composition of the $9.50 be disclosed in the financial reports? (b) What is the earnings per share amount for the most recent year that is comparable to the $7.00 earnings per share of the preceding year? (c) On the basis of the limited information presented, would you conclude that operations had improved or declined?
14. Appropriations of retained earnings may be (a) required by law, (b) required by contract, or (c) made at the discretion of the board of directors. Give an illustration of each type of appropriation.
15. A credit balance in Retained Earnings does not represent cash. Explain.

16. The board of directors votes to appropriate $250,000 of retained earnings for bonded indebtedness. What is the effect of this action on (a) cash, (b) total retained earnings, and (c) retained earnings available for dividends?

17. a. What two financial statements are frequently combined and presented as a single statement?
    b. What is the major disadvantage of the combined statement?

18. What are the three conditions for the declaration and the payment of a cash dividend?

19. The dates in connection with the declaration of a cash dividend are April 1, May 15, and May 30. Identify each date.

20. A corporation with both cumulative preferred stock and common stock outstanding has a substantial credit balance in its retained earnings account at the beginning of the current fiscal year. Although net income for the current year is sufficient to pay the preferred dividend of $50,000 each quarter and a common dividend of $200,000 each quarter, the board of directors declares dividends only on the preferred stock. Suggest possible reasons for passing the dividends on the common stock.

21. The board of directors declared a 5% stock dividend on 1,000 shares of $50 par common stock. If the market price is $65 per share on the date of declaration, for what amount should the stock dividends account be debited to record the declaration?

22. State the effect of the following actions on a corporation's total assets, liabilities, and stockholders' equity: (a) declaration of a cash dividend; (b) payment of the cash dividend declared in (a); (c) declaration of a stock dividend; (d) issuance of stock certificates for the stock dividend declared in (c); (e) authorization and issuance of stock certificates in a stock split.

23. An owner of 200 shares of Dunston Company common stock receives a stock dividend of 4 shares. (a) What is the effect of the stock dividend on the equity per share of the stock? (b) How does the total equity of 204 shares compare with the total equity of 200 shares before the stock dividend?

24. What term is used to identify a distribution to stockholders from paid-in capital?

25. A corporation with 10,000 shares of no-par common stock issued, of which 1,000 shares are held as treasury stock, declares a cash dividend of $2 a share. What is the total amount of the dividend?

26. a. What is a stock split?
    b. What is the primary purpose of a stock split?

27. a. Where should a declared but unpaid cash dividend be reported on the balance sheet?
    b. Where should a declared but unissued stock dividend be reported on the balance sheet?

28. If a corporation with 5,000 shares of common stock outstanding has a 5-for-1 stock split (4 additional shares for each share issued), what will be the number of shares outstanding after the split?

29. If the common stock in Question 28 had a market price of $150 per share before the stock split, what would be an approximate market price per share after the split?

REAL WORLD FOCUS   30. The 1991 annual report of The Quaker Oats Company disclosed the discontinuance of its Fisher-Price operations. The estimated loss on disposal of the operations was $30 million, net of $20 million of tax benefits. Indicate how the loss from discontinued operations should be reported by The Quaker Oats Company on its income statement for the year ended June 30, 1991.

REAL WORLD FOCUS   31. Corporation A received an insurance refund of $45,000 in December 1994. After a limited investigation into why the money was received, Corporation A concluded that the refund was an adjustment of premiums previously paid. The $45,000 was reflected in the income statement for the year ended December 31, 1994, as a reduction of insurance expense.

Subsequently in 1995, Corporation A was notified that the amount had been refunded in error and paid the insurance company $45,000. How should it be reported in the income statement for the year ended December 31, 1995?

Source: "Technical Hotline," *Journal of Accountancy* (June 1989), p. 31

REAL WORLD FOCUS   32. Corporation X realized a material gain when its facilities at a designated floodway were acquired by the urban renewal agency. How should the gain be reported in the income statement?

Source: "Technical Hotline," *Journal of Accountancy* (June 1989), p. 32.

ETHICS DISCUSSION CASE

L. Lancaster Inc. discontinued its cellular telephone operations on July 1, 1994. In preparing the income statement for the year ended December 31, 1994, Ann Johnson, the controller, omitted the earnings per share amount for the discontinued operations. The per share loss on the discontinued operations was $1.25, while the net income per share was $4.00.

SHARPEN YOUR ►
COMMUNICATION SKILLS

Discuss whether Ann Johnson is behaving in an ethical manner.

EXERCISES

EXERCISE 16-1
PAID-IN CAPITAL SECTION
OF BALANCE SHEET
Objective 1

The following accounts and their balances were selected from the unadjusted trial balance of Spielman Company at December 31, the end of the current fiscal year:

Preferred $3 Stock, $25 par	$500,000
Paid-In Capital in Excess of Par—Preferred Stock	75,000
Common Stock, no par, $20 stated value	750,000
Paid-In Capital in Excess of Par—Common Stock	200,000
Paid-In Capital from Redemption of Common Stock	10,000
Paid-In Capital from Sale of Treasury Stock	7,500
Donated Capital	100,000
Retained Earnings	350,000

Prepare the Paid-In Capital portion of the Stockholders' Equity section of the balance sheet. There are 50,000 shares of common stock authorized and 20,000 shares of preferred stock authorized.

EXERCISE 16-2
INCOME TAX ENTRIES
Objectives 2, 3

Journalize the entries to record the following selected transactions of Anson Inc.:

Apr. 15. Paid the first installment of the estimated income tax for the current fiscal year ending December 31, $175,000. No entry had been made to record the liability.
June 15. Paid the second installment of $175,000.
Sep. 15. Paid the third installment of $175,000.
Dec. 31. Recorded the estimated income tax liability for the year just ended and the deferred income tax liability, based on the transactions above and the following data:

Income tax rate	40%
Income before income tax	$1,900,000
Taxable income according to tax return	1,775,000

Jan. 15. Paid the fourth installment of $175,000.

EXERCISE 16-3
RETAINED EARNINGS
STATEMENT WITH PRIOR-
PERIOD ADJUSTMENT
Objective 4

C. C. Littler and Company reported the following results of transactions affecting retained earnings for the current year ended December 31, 1994:

Net income	$102,500
Dividends	60,000
Prior-period adjustment for understatement of merchandise inventory on December 31, 1993, net of applicable income tax of $9,000	11,000

Assuming that the retained earnings balance reported on the retained earnings statement as of December 31, 1993, was $212,500, prepare a retained earnings statement for the year ended December 31, 1994.

EXERCISE 16-4
EXTRAORDINARY ITEM
Objective 4

A company received life insurance proceeds on the death of its president before the end of its fiscal year. It intends to report the amount in its income statement as an extraordinary item.

SHARPEN YOUR ►
COMMUNICATION SKILLS

Would this be in conformity with generally accepted accounting principles? Discuss.

Source: "Technical Hotline," *Journal of Accountancy*, (June 1989), p. 31.

EXERCISE 16-5
INCOME STATEMENT
Objectives 4, 5

On the basis of the following data for the current fiscal year ended September 30, prepare an income statement for Root Company, including an analysis of earnings per share in the form illustrated in this chapter. There were 50,000 shares of $20 par common stock outstanding throughout the year.

Administrative expenses	$ 46,250
Cost of merchandise sold	622,500
Cumulative effect on prior years of changing to a different depreciation method (increase in income)	70,000
Gain on condemnation of land (extraordinary item)	57,750
Income tax applicable to change in depreciation method	22,000
Income tax applicable to gain on condemnation of land	16,750
Income tax reduction applicable to loss from discontinued operations	22,500
Income tax applicable to ordinary income	108,000
Loss on discontinued operations	74,500
Sales	992,500
Selling expenses	74,750

EXERCISE 16-6
ENTRIES FOR TREASURY
STOCK AND
APPROPRIATION
Objective 6

A corporation purchased for cash 2,500 shares of its own $20 par common stock at $30 a share. In the following year, it sold 1,000 of the treasury shares at $36 a share for cash.

a. Journalize the entries (1) to record the purchase (treasury stock is recorded at cost) and (2) to provide for the appropriation of retained earnings.
b. Journalize the entries (1) to record the sale of the stock and (2) to reduce the appropriation.

EXERCISE 16-7
RETAINED EARNINGS
STATEMENT
Objective 7

Jenkins Corporation reports the following results of transactions affecting net income and retained earnings for its first fiscal year of operations ended on December 31:

Appropriation for plant expansion	$ 25,000
Cash dividends declared	60,000
Income before income tax	160,000
Income tax	52,000

Prepare a retained earnings statement for the fiscal year ended December 31.

EXERCISE 16-8
COMBINED INCOME AND
RETAINED EARNINGS
STATEMENT
Objective 7

Summary operating data for R. G. Kline Inc. during the current year ended August 31, 1994, are as follows: administrative expenses, $125,000; cost of merchandise sold, $850,000; income tax, $65,000; interest expense, $30,000; net sales, $1,400,000; and selling expenses, $200,000. Assuming that the balance of Retained Earnings was $415,000 on September 1, 1993, and that $90,000 of dividends were paid during the year, prepare a combined income and retained earnings statement for R. G. Kline Inc. (Use the multiple-step form for the income statement portion.)

EXERCISE 16-9
ENTRIES FOR CASH
DIVIDENDS
Objective 8

The dates of importance in connection with a cash dividend of $25,000 on a corporation's common stock are January 9, January 25, and February 7. Journalize the entries required on each date.

EXERCISE 16-10
STOCK DIVIDENDS; EQUITY
PER SHARE
Objective 8

The following account balances appear on the balance sheet of Long Company: Common stock (10,000 shares authorized), $50 par, $400,000; Paid-in capital in excess of par—common stock, $72,500; and Retained earnings, $199,500. The board of directors declared a 5% stock dividend when the market price of the stock was $65 a share.

a. Journalize the entries to record (1) the declaration of the dividend, capitalizing an amount equal to market value, and (2) the issuance of the stock certificates.
b. Determine the equity per share (1) before the stock dividend and (2) after the stock dividend.
c. Cathy Owens owned 100 shares of the common stock before the stock dividend was declared. Determine the total equity of her holdings (1) before the stock dividend and (2) after the stock dividend.

EXERCISE 16-11
STOCK SPLIT
Objective 9

The board of directors of Dugan Corporation authorized the reduction of par of its common shares from $100 to $25, increasing the number of outstanding shares to 400,000. The market price of the stock immediately before the stock split was $200 a share.

a. Determine the number of outstanding shares prior to the stock split.

■SHARPEN YOUR   ►
COMMUNICATION SKILLS

b. Is a journal entry required to record the stock split? If not, explain how the stock split would be reflected in the accounting records.
c. At approximately what price would a share of stock be expected to sell immediately after the stock split?

WhAT'S WRONG WITH THi2?

How many errors can you find in the following retained earnings statement prepared for the current year ended December 31?

Stoner Corporation
Retained Earnings Statement
December 31, 19—

Appropriated:			
Appropriation for plant expansion,			
January 1, 19—		$ 400,000	
Additional appropriation (see below)		100,000	
Net income for the year		625,000	
Retained earnings appropriated,			
December 31, 19—			$1,125,000
Unappropriated:			
Balance, January 1, 19—		$1,500,000	
Less: Cash dividends declared	$300,000		
Transfer to appropriation for			
plant expansion (see below)	100,000	400,000	
Retained earnings unappropriated,			
December 31, 19—			1,100,000
Total retained earnings, December 31, 19—			$2,225,000

PROBLEMS

Series A

PROBLEM 16-1A
INCOME TAX ALLOCATION
Objective 3

Differences between the accounting methods applied to accounts and financial reports and those used in determining taxable income yielded the following amounts for the first four years of a corporation's operations:

	First Year	Second Year	Third Year	Fourth Year
Income before income tax	$236,250	$337,500	$506,250	$549,000
Taxable income	168,750	292,500	483,750	582,750

The income tax rate for each of the four years was 40% of taxable income, and each year's taxes were promptly paid.

Instructions

1. Determine for each year the amounts described in the following columnar captions, presenting the information in the form indicated:

Year	Income Tax Deducted on Income Statement	Income Tax Payments for the Year	Deferred Income Tax Payable	
			Year's Addition (Deduction)	Year-End Balance

2. Total the first three amount columns.

PROBLEM 16-2A
INCOME STATEMENT
Objectives 4, 5

The following data were selected from the records of A. P. Ryan, Inc. for the current fiscal year ended December 31:

Advertising expense	$ 27,250
Delivery expense	19,750
Depreciation expense—office equipment	5,200
Depreciation expense—store equipment	9,000
Gain on condemnation of land	20,000
Income tax:	
Applicable to continuing operations	35,000
Applicable to loss from disposal of a segment of the business (reduction)	8,200
Applicable to gain on condemnation of land	4,000

Insurance expense	$ 9,000
Interest expense	25,200
Loss from disposal of a segment of the business	40,200
Merchandise inventory (January 1)	130,000
Merchandise inventory (December 31)	135,500
Miscellaneous administrative expense	4,550
Miscellaneous selling expense	8,600
Office salaries expense	42,750
Office supplies expense	1,700
Purchases	605,500
Rent expense	21,000
Sales	997,500
Sales commissions expense	53,500
Sales salaries expense	42,500
Store supplies expense	7,500

SPREADSHEET PROBLEM

Instructions

Prepare a multiple-step income statement, concluding with a section for earnings per share in the form illustrated in this chapter. There were 25,000 shares of common stock (no preferred) outstanding throughout the year. Assume that the gain on condemnation of land is an extraordinary item.

PROBLEM 16-3A
RETAINED EARNINGS
STATEMENT
Objectives 6, 7

The retained earnings accounts of Yoder Corporation for the current fiscal year ended December 31 are as follows:

ACCOUNT **APPROPRIATION FOR PLANT EXPANSION**   ACCOUNT NO. 3201

Date		Item	Debit	Credit	Balance Debit	Balance Credit
19—						
Jan.	1	Balance				150,000
Dec.	31	Retained earnings		50,000		200,000

ACCOUNT **APPROPRIATION FOR TREASURY STOCK**   ACCOUNT NO. 3202

Date		Item	Debit	Credit	Balance Debit	Balance Credit
19—						
Jan.	1	Balance				375,000
Dec.	31	Retained earnings	125,000			250,000

ACCOUNT **RETAINED EARNINGS**   ACCOUNT NO. 3301

Date		Item	Debit	Credit	Balance Debit	Balance Credit
19—						
Jan.	1	Balance				515,000
Dec.	31	Income summary		175,000		690,000
	31	Appropriation for plant expansion	50,000			640,000
	31	Appropriation for treasury stock		125,000		765,000
	31	Cash dividends	90,000			675,000
	31	Stock dividends	185,000			490,000

ACCOUNT **CASH DIVIDENDS**   ACCOUNT NO. 3302

Date		Item	Debit	Credit	Balance Debit	Balance Credit
19—						
July	27		90,000		90,000	
Dec.	31	Retained earnings		90,000	—	—

ACCOUNT STOCK DIVIDENDS   ACCOUNT NO. 3303

Date		Item	Debit	Credit	Balance Debit	Credit
19—						
July	27		185,000		185,000	
Dec.	31	Retained earnings		185,000	—	—

Instructions
Prepare a retained earnings statement for the fiscal year ended December 31.

PROBLEM 16-4A
ENTRIES FOR SELECTED
CORPORATE
TRANSACTIONS
Objectives 6, 8

The stockholders' equity accounts of Zellner Enterprises Inc., with balances on January 1 of the current fiscal year, are as follows:

Common Stock, $25 stated value (100,000 shares authorized,
   50,000 shares issued) $1,250,000
Paid-In Capital in Excess of Stated Value   300,000
Appropriation for Plant Expansion   150,000
Appropriation for Treasury Stock   120,000
Retained Earnings   425,000
Treasury Stock (4,000 shares, at cost)   120,000

The following selected transactions occurred during the year:

Jan. 15. Received land from the city as a donation. The land had an estimated fair market value of $65,000.

    30. Paid cash dividends of $1 per share on the common stock. The dividend had been properly recorded when declared on December 20 of the preceding fiscal year for $46,000.

Feb. 25. Sold all of the treasury stock for $150,000.

Apr. 1. Issued 5,000 shares of common stock for $190,000.

July 1. Declared a 4% stock dividend on common stock, to be capitalized at the market price of the stock, which is $40 a share.

Aug. 11. Issued the certificates for the dividend declared on July 1.

Nov. 20. Purchased 2,000 shares of treasury stock for $72,000.

Dec. 21. The board of directors authorized an increase of the appropriation for plant expansion by $50,000.

    21. Declared a $1.10 per share dividend on common stock.

    21. Decreased the appropriation for treasury stock to $72,000.

    31. Closed the credit balance of the income summary account, $196,700.

    31. Closed the two dividends accounts to Retained Earnings.

Instructions

1. Enter the January 1 balances in T accounts for the stockholders' equity accounts listed. Also prepare T accounts for the following: Paid-In Capital from Sale of Treasury Stock; Donated Capital; Stock Dividends Distributable; Stock Dividends; Cash Dividends .

2. Journalize the entries to record the transactions and post to the eleven selected accounts.

3. Prepare the Stockholders' Equity section of the balance sheet as of December 31 of the current fiscal year.

Instructions for Solving Problem 16-4A Using Solutions Software

SOLUTIONS
SOFTWARE

1. Load opening balances.
2. Save the opening balances file to your drive and directory.
3. Set the run date to December 31 of the current year and enter your name.
4. Select the General Journal Entries option and key the journal entries, including the two closing entries. Leave the reference field blank. Note: To review the chart of accounts, select F-1.
5. Display a journal entries report.
6. Display a balance sheet.
7. Save your data file to disk.
8. End the session.

PROBLEM 16-5A
STOCKHOLDERS' EQUITY
TRANSACTIONS AND
STATEMENTS
Objectives 6, 7, 8

The Stockholders' Equity section of the balance sheet of DCF Industries as of January 1 is as follows:

Stockholders' Equity

Paid-in capital:		
Common stock, $20 par (100,000 shares		
authorized, 40,000 shares issued)	$800,000	
Excess of issue price over par	150,000	
Total paid-in capital		$ 950,000
Retained earnings:		
Appropriated for bonded indebtedness	$275,000	
Unappropriated	530,000	
Total retained earnings		805,000
Total		$1,755,000
Deduct treasury stock (5,000 shares at cost)		125,000
Total stockholders' equity		$1,630,000

The following selected transactions occurred during the fiscal year:

Jan. 30. Issued 10,000 shares of stock in exchange for land and buildings with an estimated fair market value of $100,000 and $400,000 respectively. The property was encumbered by a mortgage of $250,000, and the company agreed to assume the responsibility for paying the mortgage note.

Mar. 5. Sold all of the treasury stock for $150,000.

June 25. Declared a cash dividend of $2 per share to stockholders of record on July 15, payable on July 30.

July 30. Paid the cash dividend declared on June 25.

Sep. 2. Received additional land valued at $50,000. The land was donated for a plant site by the Bonita Industrial Development Council.

Dec. 1. Issued 1,000 shares of stock to officers as a salary bonus. The market price of the stock is $30 a share. (Debit Officers Salaries Expense.)

10. Declared a 4% stock dividend on the stock outstanding to stockholders of record on December 30, to be issued on January 20. The market price of the stock is $30 a share.

31. Increased the appropriation for bonded indebtedness by $25,000.

31. Closed the income summary account, which has a credit balance of $195,000. (All revenue and expense accounts have been closed.)

31. Closed the two dividends accounts to Retained Earnings.

Instructions

1. Enter the January 1 balances in T accounts for the accounts appearing in the Stockholders' Equity section of the balance sheet. Also prepare T accounts for the following: Paid-In Capital from Sale of Treasury Stock; Donated Capital; Cash Dividends; Stock Dividends; Stock Dividends Distributable.
2. Journalize the entries to record the transactions and post to the ten selected accounts.
3. Prepare the Stockholders' Equity section of the balance sheet as of December 31, the end of the fiscal year.
4. Prepare a retained earnings statement for the fiscal year ended December 31.

PROBLEM 16-6A
ENTRIES FOR CASH AND
STOCK DIVIDENDS; STOCK
SPLIT
Objectives 8, 9

As of January 1, the beginning of the current fiscal year, Snyder Corporation had issued 40,000 common, $100 par shares of the 50,000 shares authorized. The retained earnings balance was $947,500. The only transactions affecting common stock during the fiscal year are as follows:

Mar. 1. The board of directors declared a $2 per share dividend on the common stock , payable on April 10 to stockholders of record on March 22.

Apr. 10. Paid the dividends declared on March 1.

May 5. Purchased 1,000 shares of treasury stock for $210,000.

June 1. The board of directors declared a $2 per share dividend on the common stock outstanding, payable on July 12 to stockholders of record on May 25.

July 12. Paid the dividends declared on June 1.

Aug. 21. Sold the treasury stock purchased on May 5 for $216,500.

MINI-CASE 16 KOLBY CO.

Kolby Co. has paid quarterly cash dividends since 1987. These dividends have steadily increased from $.20 per share to the latest dividend declaration of $.50 per share. The board of directors would like to continue this trend and are hesitant to suspend or decrease the amount of quarterly dividends. Unfortunately, sales dropped sharply in the fourth quarter of 1994 due to worsening economic conditions and increased competition. As a result, the board is uncertain as to whether it should declare a dividend for the last quarter of 1994.

On November 1, 1994, Kolby Co. borrowed $500,000 from Second National Bank to use in modernizing its retail stores and to expand its product line in reaction to its competition. The terms of the 10-year, 12% loan require Kolby Co. to:

a. Pay monthly the total interest due.
b. Pay $50,000 of the principal each November 1, beginning in 1995.
c. Maintain a current ratio (current assets ÷ current liabilities) of 2:1.
d. Appropriate $500,000 of retained earnings until the loan is fully paid.
e. Maintain a minimum balance of $25,000 (called a compensating balance) in its Second National Bank account.

On December 31, 1994, 25% of the $500,000 loan had been disbursed in modernization of the retail stores and in expansion of the product line, and the remainder is temporarily invested in U.S. Treasury Notes. Kolby Co.'s balance sheet as of December 31, 1994, is as follows:

Kolby Co.
Balance Sheet
December 31, 1994

Assets

Current assets:			
Cash			$ 40,000
Marketable securities, at cost (market price, $379,500)			375,000
Accounts receivable	$ 91,500		
Less allowance for doubtful accounts	6,500	85,000	
Merchandise inventory		120,500	
Prepaid expenses		4,500	
Total current assets			$ 625,000
Plant assets:			
Land		$150,000	
Buildings	$950,000		
Less accumulated depreciation	215,000	735,000	
Equipment	$460,000		
Less accumulated depreciation	110,000	350,000	
Total plant assets			1,235,000
Total assets			$1,860,000

Liabilities

Current liabilities:		
Accounts payable	$ 71,800	
Notes payable (Second National Bank)	50,000	
Salaries payable	3,200	
Total current liabilities		$125,000
Long-term liabilities:		
Notes payable (Second National Bank)	450,000	
Total liabilities		$ 575,000

Stockholders' Equity

Paid-in capital:		
Common stock, $20 par (50,000 shares authorized, 25,000 shares issued)	$500,000	
Excess of issue price over par	40,000	
Total paid-in capital		$540,000
Retained earnings:		
Appropriated for provision of Second National Bank loan	$500,000	
Unappropriated	245,000	
Total retained earnings		745,000
Total stockholders' equity		1,285,000
Total liabilities and stockholders' equity		$1,860,000

PROBLEM 16-5A
STOCKHOLDERS' EQUITY
TRANSACTIONS AND
STATEMENTS
Objectives 6, 7, 8

The Stockholders' Equity section of the balance sheet of DCF Industries as of January 1 is as follows:

Stockholders' Equity

Paid-in capital:		
Common stock, $20 par (100,000 shares		
authorized, 40,000 shares issued)	$800,000	
Excess of issue price over par	150,000	
Total paid-in capital		$ 950,000
Retained earnings:		
Appropriated for bonded indebtedness	$275,000	
Unappropriated	530,000	
Total retained earnings		805,000
Total		$1,755,000
Deduct treasury stock (5,000 shares at cost)		125,000
Total stockholders' equity		$1,630,000

The following selected transactions occurred during the fiscal year:

Jan. 30. Issued 10,000 shares of stock in exchange for land and buildings with an estimated fair market value of $100,000 and $400,000 respectively. The property was encumbered by a mortgage of $250,000, and the company agreed to assume the responsibility for paying the mortgage note.

Mar. 5. Sold all of the treasury stock for $150,000.

June 25. Declared a cash dividend of $2 per share to stockholders of record on July 15, payable on July 30.

July 30. Paid the cash dividend declared on June 25.

Sep.   2. Received additional land valued at $50,000. The land was donated for a plant site by the Bonita Industrial Development Council.

Dec.   1. Issued 1,000 shares of stock to officers as a salary bonus. The market price of the stock is $30 a share. (Debit Officers Salaries Expense.)

      10. Declared a 4% stock dividend on the stock outstanding to stockholders of record on December 30, to be issued on January 20. The market price of the stock is $30 a share.

      31. Increased the appropriation for bonded indebtedness by $25,000.

      31. Closed the income summary account, which has a credit balance of $195,000. (All revenue and expense accounts have been closed.)

      31. Closed the two dividends accounts to Retained Earnings.

Instructions

1. Enter the January 1 balances in T accounts for the accounts appearing in the Stockholders' Equity section of the balance sheet. Also prepare T accounts for the following: Paid-In Capital from Sale of Treasury Stock; Donated Capital; Cash Dividends; Stock Dividends; Stock Dividends Distributable.

2. Journalize the entries to record the transactions and post to the ten selected accounts.

3. Prepare the Stockholders' Equity section of the balance sheet as of December 31, the end of the fiscal year.

4. Prepare a retained earnings statement for the fiscal year ended December 31.

PROBLEM 16-6A
ENTRIES FOR CASH AND
STOCK DIVIDENDS; STOCK
SPLIT
Objectives 8, 9

As of January 1, the beginning of the current fiscal year, Snyder Corporation had issued 40,000 common, $100 par shares of the 50,000 shares authorized. The retained earnings balance was $947,500. The only transactions affecting common stock during the fiscal year are as follows:

Mar. 1. The board of directors declared a $2 per share dividend on the common stock , payable on April 10 to stockholders of record on March 22.

Apr. 10. Paid the dividends declared on March 1.

May   5. Purchased 1,000 shares of treasury stock for $210,000.

June 1. The board of directors declared a $2 per share dividend on the common stock outstanding, payable on July 12 to stockholders of record on May 25.

July 12. Paid the dividends declared on June 1.

Aug. 21. Sold the treasury stock purchased on May 5 for $216,500.

Sep.   1. The board of directors declared a 5% common stock dividend to be distributed on October 16 to stockholders of record on September 20. The market price of the stock is $220 per share.

Oct.   16. Distributed the stock dividend declared on September 1.

Dec.   1. The board of directors authorized the reduction of par of its common shares from $100 to $25, increasing the number of outstanding shares to 168,000. The number of authorized shares was increased to 200,000.

Instructions

1. Journalize the entries to record the transactions.
2. Explain how the transactions for which no entry is required are reflected in the accounting records.

SHARPEN YOUR COMMUNICATION SKILLS

PROBLEM 16-7A
CORRECTING ENTRIES AND
FINANCIAL STATEMENTS
Objectives 2, 4, 5, 6, 7, 8

B. G. Cox Company is in need of additional cash to expand operations. To raise the needed funds, the company is applying to Barnett County Bank for a loan. For this purpose, the bank requests that the financial statements be audited. To assist the auditor, B. G. Cox Company's accountant prepared the following financial statements related to the current year:

B. G. Cox Company
Balance Sheet
December 31, 19—

Current assets:		
Cash	$ 55,650	
Accounts receivable	65,900	
Merchandise inventory	86,250	
Supplies	6,750	$214,550
Plant assets:		
Land	$100,000	
Buildings	315,000	
Equipment	132,500	
Patents	45,000	592,500
Total assets		$807,050
Current liabilities:		
Accounts payable	$ 46,400	
Salaries payable	3,600	$ 50,000
Deferred charges:		
Accumulated depreciation—buildings	$ 72,500	
Accumulated depreciation—equipment	37,500	
Allowance for doubtful accounts	4,500	114,500
Stockholders' equity:		
Common stock (100,000 shares authorized, $20 par)	$350,000	
Excess of issue price over par	45,000	
Retained earnings	165,000	
Net income	82,550	642,550
Total liabilities and stockholders' equity		$807,050

B. G. Cox Company
Income Statement
For Year Ended December 31, 19—

Revenues:		
Net sales	$802,500	
Gain on expropriation of land	42,000	
Total revenues		$844,500
Expenses:		
Cost of merchandise sold	$500,500	
Salary expense	72,000	
Depreciation expense—buildings	36,900	
Loss on discontinued operations	35,550	
Utilities expense	19,000	
Insurance expense	15,400	
Depreciation expense—equipment	8,500	
Amortization expense—patents	5,000	
Uncollectible accounts expense	3,750	
Miscellaneous administrative expense	8,350	
Income tax	32,000	
Dividends expense	25,000	
Total expenses		761,950
Net income		$ 82,550

In the course of the audit, the auditor examined the common stock and retained earnings accounts, which appeared as follows:

ACCOUNT COMMON STOCK ($20 PAR)   ACCOUNT NO. 3200

Date		Item	Debit	Credit	Balance Debit	Balance Credit
19—						
Jan.	1	Balance—15,000 shares				300,000
July	2	Issued 1,500 shares for patents		50,000		350,000

ACCOUNT RETAINED EARNINGS   ACCOUNT NO. 3300

Date		Item	Debit	Credit	Balance Debit	Balance Credit
19—						
Jan.	1	Balance				97,500
Feb.	1	Donation of land		50,000		147,500
	10	Error correction	7,500			140,000
Dec.	28	Appropriation for land acquisition		25,000		165,000

A closer examination of the transactions in these and other accounts revealed the following details:

a. A computational error was made in the calculation of a prior year's dividend. The corrected amount of the dividend was paid on February 10 and debited to the retained earnings account.

b. On February 1, the company received a donation of land. The land account was debited for $50,000, the fair market value of the land at that date.

c. The patent acquired on July 2 by an issuance of 1,500 shares of common stock had a fair market value of $50,000 and an estimated useful life of 5 years.

d. A $2 cash dividend declared on December 10 and payable on January 20 of the next fiscal year was not recorded. The $25,000 of dividends expense represents the mid-year cash dividend paid on July 30 of the current year.

e. After three years of using the straight-line method of depreciation for the buildings, the company changed to the sum-of-the-years-digits method. The following entry recorded this change:

Depreciation Expense—Buildings	26,900	
Accumulated Depreciation—Buildings		26,900

f. In anticipation of further land acquisition, the board of directors on December 28 authorized a $25,000 appropriation of retained earnings that resulted in a debit to Land and a credit to Retained Earnings.

g. The income tax of $32,000 is the estimated tax paid during the year. The tax based on the corrected net income was determined to be $33,950, allocated as follows:

Income from continuing operations	$44,500
Loss from discontinued operations	14,100
Gain on expropriation of land	12,300
Cumulative effect of change in depreciation method	8,750

The tax owed of $1,950 at December 31 had not been recorded.

Instructions

1. Journalize the necessary correcting entries for the items discovered by the independent auditor. Assume that the accounts have not been closed for the current fiscal year.
2. Prepare a multiple-step income statement for the current fiscal year, including the appropriate earnings per share disclosure. Operating expenses need not be divided into selling and administrative expense categories.
3. Prepare the retained earnings statement for the current fiscal year.
4. Prepare a balance sheet as of the end of the current fiscal year.

PROBLEM 16-8A
ENTRIES FOR SELECTED
CORPORATE
TRANSACTIONS
Objectives 3, 6, 8, 9

Selected transactions completed by Neuman Corporation during the current fiscal year are as follows:

Feb.   1. Split the common stock 4 for 1 and reduced the par from $100 to $25 per share. After the split, there were 40,000 common shares outstanding.

Mar. 10. Purchased 1,000 shares of the corporation's own common stock at $62, recording the stock at cost.

Apr. 11. Discovered that a receipt of $450 cash on account from A. Allen had been posted in error to the account of N. Alden. The transaction was recorded correctly in the journal.

May   1. Declared semiannual dividends of $5 on 5,000 shares of preferred stock and $1 on the common stock to stockholders of record on May 20, payable on July 15.

July 15. Paid the cash dividends.

Aug. 22. Sold 500 shares of treasury stock at $70, receiving cash.

Nov. 30. Declared semiannual dividends of $5 on the preferred stock and $1.25 on the common stock. In addition, a 5% common stock dividend was declared on the common stock outstanding. The fair market value of the common stock is estimated at $72.

Dec. 30. Paid the cash dividends and issued the certificates for the common stock dividend.

       30. Recorded $76,500 additional federal income tax allocable to net income for the year. Of this amount, $51,500 is a current liability and $25,000 is deferred.

       30. The board of directors authorized the appropriation necessitated by the holding of treasury stock.

Instructions
Journalize the transactions.

SOLUTIONS
SOFTWARE

Instructions for Solving Problem 16-8A Using Solutions Software

1. Load opening balances.
2. Save the opening balances file to your drive and directory.
3. Set the run date to December 31 of the current year and enter your name.
4. Select the General Journal Entries option and key the journal entries. Leave the reference field blank. Note: To review the chart of accounts, select F-1.
5. Display a journal entries report.
6. Save a backup copy of your data file.
7. Perform period-end closing.
8. Display a balance sheet.
9. Save your data file to disk.
10. End the session.

Series B

PROBLEM 16-1B
INCOME TAX ALLOCATION
Objective 3

Differences between the accounting methods applied to accounts and financial reports and those used in determining taxable income yielded the following amounts for the first four years of a corporation's operations:

	First Year	Second Year	Third Year	Fourth Year
Income before income tax	$326,250	$416,250	$517,500	$495,000
Taxable income	270,000	382,500	528,750	540,000

The income tax rate for each of the four years was 40% of taxable income, and each year's taxes were promptly paid.

Instructions

1. Determine for each year the amounts described in the following columnar captions, presenting the information in the form indicated:

SPREADSHEET
PROBLEM

Year	Income Tax Deducted on Income Statement	Income Tax Payments for the Year	Deferred Income Tax Payable	
			Year's Addition (Deduction)	Year-End Balance

2. Total the first three amount columns.

PROBLEM 16-2B
INCOME STATEMENT
Objectives 4, 5

The following data were selected from the records of Cullen Inc. for the current fiscal year ended December 31:

Advertising expense	$ 22,500
Delivery expense	10,400
Depreciation expense—office equipment	4,250
Depreciation expense—store equipment	11,500
Gain on condemnation of land	50,000
Income tax:	
Applicable to continuing operations	55,000
Applicable to loss from disposal of a segment of the business (reduction)	5,000
Applicable to gain on condemnation of land	15,000
Insurance expense	9,100
Interest income	13,700
Loss from disposal of a segment of the business	25,000
Merchandise inventory (January 1)	97,750
Merchandise inventory (December 31)	105,000
Miscellaneous administrative expense	2,800
Miscellaneous selling expense	3,500
Office salaries expense	46,000
Office supplies expense	1,750

Purchases	$602,250
Rent expense	30,000
Sales	987,500
Sales commissions expense	44,900
Sales salaries expense	56,900
Store supplies expense	2,600

**SPREADSHEET
PROBLEM**

Instructions

Prepare a multiple-step income statement, concluding with a section for earnings per share in the form illustrated in this chapter. There were 50,000 shares of common stock (no preferred) outstanding throughout the year. Assume that the gain on condemnation of land is an extraordinary item.

PROBLEM 16-3B
RETAINED EARNINGS
STATEMENT
Objectives 6, 7

The retained earnings accounts of Elder Corporation for the current fiscal year ended December 31 are as follows:

ACCOUNT APPROPRIATION FOR PLANT EXPANSION   ACCOUNT NO. 3201

Date		Item	Debit	Credit	Balance Debit	Balance Credit
19—						
Jan.	1	Balance				300,000
Dec.	31	Retained earnings		50,000		350,000

ACCOUNT APPROPRIATION FOR TREASURY STOCK   ACCOUNT NO. 3202

Date		Item	Debit	Credit	Balance Debit	Balance Credit
19—						
Jan.	1	Balance				250,000
Dec.	31	Retained earnings	30,000			220,000

ACCOUNT RETAINED EARNINGS   ACCOUNT NO. 3301

Date		Item	Debit	Credit	Balance Debit	Balance Credit
19—						
Jan.	1	Balance				515,000
Dec.	31	Income summary		190,000		705,000
	31	Appropriation for plant expansion	50,000			655,000
	31	Appropriation for treasury stock		30,000		685,000
	31	Cash dividends	50,000			635,000
	31	Stock dividends	100,000			535,000

ACCOUNT CASH DIVIDENDS   ACCOUNT NO. 3302

Date		Item	Debit	Credit	Balance Debit	Balance Credit
19—						
Apr.	10		25,000		25,000	
Oct.	13		25,000		50,000	
Dec.	31	Retained earnings		50,000	—	—

ACCOUNT STOCK DIVIDENDS   ACCOUNT NO. 3303

Date		Item	Debit	Credit	Balance Debit	Balance Credit
19—						
Oct.	13		100,000		100,000	
Dec.	31	Retained earnings		100,000	—	—

Instructions

Prepare a retained earnings statement for the fiscal year ended December 31.

PROBLEM 16-4B
ENTRIES FOR SELECTED
CORPORATE
TRANSACTIONS
Objectives 6, 8

The stockholders' equity accounts of Collins Enterprises Inc., with balances on January 1 of the current fiscal year, are as follows:

Common Stock, $10 stated value (100,000 shares authorized, 80,000 shares issued)	$800,000
Paid-In Capital in Excess of Stated Value	120,000
Appropriation for Plant Expansion	75,000
Appropriation for Treasury Stock	37,500
Retained Earnings	397,750
Treasury Stock (3,000 shares, at cost)	37,500

The following selected transactions occurred during the year:

Feb. 1. Paid cash dividends of $1 per share on the common stock. The dividend had been properly recorded when declared on December 28 of the preceding fiscal year.

Apr. 7. Sold all of the treasury stock for $45,000.

May 5. Issued 10,000 shares of common stock for $130,000.

June 11. Received land from the Naples City Council as a donation. The land had an estimated fair market value of $50,000.

July 30. Declared a 5% stock dividend on common stock, to be capitalized at the market price of the stock, which is $15 a share.

Aug. 27. Issued the certificates for the dividend declared on July 30.

Oct. 8. Purchased 2,500 shares of treasury stock for $25,000.

Dec. 20. Declared a $1 per share dividend on common stock.

      20. The board of directors authorized an increase of the appropriation for plant expansion by $25,000.

      20. Decreased the appropriation for treasury stock to $25,000.

      31. Closed the credit balance of the income summary account, $132,500.

      31. Closed the two dividends accounts to Retained Earnings.

Instructions

1. Enter the January 1 balances in T accounts for the stockholders' equity accounts listed. Also prepare T accounts for the following: Paid-In Capital from Sale of Treasury Stock; Donated Capital; Stock Dividends Distributable; Stock Dividends; Cash Dividends.
2. Journalize the entries to record the transactions and post to the eleven selected accounts.
3. Prepare the Stockholders' Equity section of the balance sheet as of December 31 of the current fiscal year.

Instructions for Solving Problem 16-4B Using Solutions Software

1. Load opening balances.
2. Save the opening balances file to your drive and directory.
3. Set the run date to December 31 of the current year and enter your name.
4. Select the General Journal Entries option and key the journal entries, including the two closing entries. Leave the reference field blank. Note: To review the chart of accounts, select F-1.
5. Display a journal entries report.
6. Display a balance sheet.
7. Save your data file to disk.
8. End the session.

SOLUTIONS
SOFTWARE

PROBLEM 16-5B
STOCKHOLDERS' EQUITY
TRANSACTIONS AND
STATEMENTS
Objectives 6, 7, 8

The Stockholders' Equity section of the balance sheet of Foley Industries as of January 1 is as follows:

Stockholders' Equity

Paid-in capital:		
Common stock, $10 par (100,000 shares authorized, 60,000 shares issued)	$600,000	
Excess of issue price over par	150,000	
Total paid-in capital		$ 750,000
Retained earnings:		
Appropriated for bonded indebtedness	$250,000	
Unappropriated	790,000	
Total retained earnings		1,040,000
Total		$1,790,000
Deduct treasury stock (5,000 shares at cost)		220,000
Total stockholders' equity		$1,570,000

The following selected transactions occurred during the fiscal year:

Feb.   5. Sold all of the treasury stock for $275,000.
Mar. 20. Issued 20,000 shares of stock in exchange for land and buildings with an estimated fair market value of $75,000 and $225,000 respectively. The property was encumbered by a mortgage of $60,000, and the company agreed to assume the responsibility for paying the mortgage note.
June 10. Declared a cash dividend of $1 per share to stockholders of record on July 10, payable on July 31.
July 31. Paid the cash dividend declared on June 10.
Sep. 12. Received additional land valued at $100,000. The land was donated for a plant site by the Mayberry Industrial Development Council.
Oct. 11. Issued 1,000 shares of stock to officers as a salary bonus. The market price of the stock is $13 a share. (Debit Officers Salaries Expense.)
Dec. 5. Declared a 2% stock dividend on the stock outstanding to stockholders of record on December 28, to be issued on January 28. The market price of the stock is $13 a share.
      31. Increased the appropriation for bonded indebtedness by $50,000.
      31. Closed the income summary account, which has a credit balance of $315,000 (all revenue and expense accounts have been closed.)
      31. Closed the two dividends accounts to Retained Earnings.

Instructions

1. Enter the January 1 balances in T accounts for the accounts appearing in the Stockholders' Equity section of the balance sheet. Also prepare T accounts for the following: Paid-In Capital from Sale of Treasury Stock; Donated Capital; Cash Dividends; Stock Dividends; Stock Dividends Distributable.
2. Journalize the entries to record the transactions and post to the ten selected accounts.
3. Prepare the Stockholders' Equity section of the balance sheet as of December 31, the end of the fiscal year.
4. Prepare a retained earnings statement for the fiscal year ended December 31.

PROBLEM 16-6B
ENTRIES FOR CASH AND
STOCK DIVIDENDS; STOCK
SPLIT
Objectives 8, 9

As of January 1, the beginning of the current fiscal year, Doyle Company had issued 70,000 common, $50 par shares of the 100,000 shares authorized. The retained earnings balance was $995,000. The only transactions affecting common stock during the fiscal year are as follows:

Mar.   8. The board of directors declared a $2 per share dividend on the common stock, payable on April 10 to stockholders of record on March 22.

Apr.   10. Paid the dividends declared on March 8.

May   5. Purchased 1,000 shares of treasury stock for $107,000.

June   7. The board of directors declared a $2 per share dividend on the common stock outstanding, payable on July 12 to stockholders of record on May 25.

July   12. Paid the dividends declared on June 7.

Aug.   21. Sold the treasury stock purchased on May 5 for $116,500.

Sep.   6. The board of directors declared a 5% common stock dividend to be distributed on October 16 to stockholders of record on September 20. The market price of the stock is $110 per share.

Oct.   16. Distributed the stock dividend declared on September 6.

Dec.   8. The board of directors authorized the reduction of par of its common shares from $50 to $10, increasing the number of outstanding shares to 367,500. The number of authorized shares was increased to 500,000.

Instructions

1. Journalize the entries to record the transactions.
2. Explain how the transactions for which no entry is required are reflected in the accounting records.

SHARPEN YOUR COMMUNICATION SKILLS

PROBLEM 16-7B
CORRECTING ENTRIES AND FINANCIAL STATEMENTS
Objectives 2, 4, 5, 6, 7, 8

Decker Company is in need of additional cash to expand operations. To raise the needed funds, the company is applying to First National Bank for a loan. For this purpose, the bank requests that the financial statements be audited. To assist the auditor, Decker's accountant prepared the following financial statements related to the current year:

Decker Company
Balance Sheet
December 31, 19—

Current assets:		
Cash	$ 52,950	
Accounts receivable	65,700	
Merchandise inventory	79,850	
Supplies	8,250	$206,750
Plant assets:		
Land	$100,000	
Buildings	325,000	
Equipment	132,500	
Patents	35,000	592,500
Total assets		$799,250
Current liabilities:		
Accounts payable	$ 39,500	
Salaries payable	3,500	$ 43,000
Deferred charges:		
Accumulated depreciation—buildings	$ 72,500	
Accumulated depreciation—equipment	37,500	
Allowance for doubtful accounts	3,700	113,700
Stockholders' equity:		
Common stock (100,000 shares authorized, $10 par)	$350,000	
Excess of issue price over par	45,000	
Retained earnings	165,000	
Net income	82,550	642,550
Total liabilities and stockholders' equity		$799,250

Decker Company
Income Statement
For Year Ended December 31, 19—

Revenues:
Net sales	$842,500	
Gain on expropriation of land	42,000	
Total revenues		$884,500

Expenses:
Cost of merchandise sold	$560,500	
Salary expense	60,250	
Depreciation expense—buildings	36,900	
Loss on discontinued operations	35,550	
Utilities expense	20,750	
Insurance expense	10,400	
Depreciation expense—equipment	8,500	
Amortization expense—patents	5,000	
Uncollectible accounts expense	3,750	
Miscellaneous administrative expense	3,350	
Income tax	32,000	
Dividends expense	25,000	
Total expenses		801,950
Net income		$ 82,550

In the course of the audit, the auditor examined the common stock and retained earnings accounts, which appeared as follows:

ACCOUNT COMMON STOCK ($10 PAR)   ACCOUNT NO. 3200

Date		Item	Debit	Credit	Balance Debit	Balance Credit
19—						
Jan.	1	Balance—30,000 shares				300,000
	2	Issued 3,000 shares for patents		50,000		350,000

ACCOUNT RETAINED EARNINGS   ACCOUNT NO. 3300

Date		Item	Debit	Credit	Balance Debit	Balance Credit
19—						
Jan.	1	Balance				97,500
Feb.	1	Donation of land		50,000		147,500
	10	Error correction	7,500			140,000
Dec.	28	Appropriation for land acquisition		25,000		165,000

A closer examination of the transactions in these and other accounts revealed the following details:

a. The patent acquired on January 2 by an issuance of 3,000 shares of common stock had a fair market value of $50,000 and an estimated useful life of 10 years.
b. On February 1, the company received a donation of land. The land account was debited for $50,000, the fair market value of the land at that date.
c. A computational error was made in the calculation of a prior year's dividend. The corrected amount of the dividend was paid on February 10 and debited to the retained earnings account.
d. In anticipation of further land acquisition, the board of directors on December 28 authorized a $25,000 appropriation of retained earnings that resulted in a debit to Land and a credit to Retained Earnings.
e. After three years of using the straight-line method of depreciation for the buildings, the company changed to the sum-of-the-years-digits method. The following entry recorded this change:

Depreciation Expense—Buildings	26,900	
Accumulated Depreciation—Buildings		26,900

f. A $1 cash dividend declared on December 28 and payable on February 9 of the next fiscal year was not recorded. The $25,000 of dividends expense represents the mid-year cash dividend paid on July 30 of the current year.

g. The income tax of $32,000 is the estimated tax paid during the year. The tax based on the corrected net income was determined to be $33,950, allocated as follows:

Income from continuing operations	$44,500
Loss from discontinued operations	14,100
Gain on expropriation of land	12,300
Cumulative effect of change in depreciation method	8,750

The tax owed of $1,950 at December 31 had not been recorded.

Instructions

1. Journalize the necessary correcting entries for the items discovered by the independent auditor. Assume that the accounts have not been closed for the current fiscal year.
2. Prepare a multiple-step income statement for the current fiscal year, including the appropriate earnings per share disclosure. Operating expenses need not be divided into selling and administrative expense categories.
3. Prepare the retained earnings statement for the current fiscal year.
4. Prepare a balance sheet as of the end of the current fiscal year.

PROBLEM 16-8B
ENTRIES FOR SELECTED
CORPORATE
TRANSACTIONS
Objectives 3, 6, 8, 9

Selected transactions completed by Penrod Corporation during the current fiscal year are as follows:

Jan. 7. Split the common stock 5 for 1 and reduced the par from $50 to $10 per share. After the split, there were 80,000 common shares outstanding.

Feb. 3. Declared semiannual dividends of $5 on 10,000 shares of preferred stock and $0.50 on the 80,000 shares of $10 par common stock to stockholders of record on February 28, payable on March 15.

Mar. 15. Paid the cash dividends.
    30. Purchased 5,000 shares of the corporation's own common stock at $16, recording the stock at cost.

Apr. 29. Discovered that a receipt of $750 cash on account from A. C. Green Co. had been posted in error to the account of Greenberg Co. The transaction was recorded correctly in the journal.

July 10. Sold 1,000 shares of treasury stock at $22, receiving cash.
    23. Declared semiannual dividends of $5 on the preferred stock and $0.50 on the common stock. In addition, a 2% common stock dividend was declared on the common stock outstanding, to be capitalized at the fair market value of the common stock, which is estimated at $20.

Aug. 25. Paid the cash dividends and issued the certificates for the common stock dividend.

Nov. 8. Discovered that an invoice of $825 for utilities expense for the month of October was debited to Office Supplies.

Dec. 31. Recorded $112,500 additional federal income tax allocable to net income for the year. Of this amount, $83,000 is a current liability and $29,500 is deferred.
    31. The board of directors authorized the appropriation necessitated by the holding of treasury stock.

Instructions
Journalize the transactions.

SOLUTIONS
SOFTWARE

Instructions for Solving Problem 16-8B Using Solutions Software

1. Load opening balances.
2. Save the opening balances file to your drive and directory.
3. Set the run date to December 31 of the current year and enter your name.
4. Select the General Journal Entries option and key the journal entries. Leave the reference field blank. Note: To review the chart of accounts, select F-1.
5. Display a journal entries report.
6. Save a backup copy of your datafile.
7. Perform period-end closing.
8. Display a balance sheet.
9. Save your data file to disk.
10. End the session.

MINI-CASE 16 KOLBY CO.

Kolby Co. has paid quarterly cash dividends since 1987. These dividends have steadily increased from $.20 per share to the latest dividend declaration of $.50 per share. The board of directors would like to continue this trend and are hesitant to suspend or decrease the amount of quarterly dividends. Unfortunately, sales dropped sharply in the fourth quarter of 1994 due to worsening economic conditions and increased competition. As a result, the board is uncertain as to whether it should declare a dividend for the last quarter of 1994.

On November 1, 1994, Kolby Co. borrowed $500,000 from Second National Bank to use in modernizing its retail stores and to expand its product line in reaction to its competition. The terms of the 10-year, 12% loan require Kolby Co. to:

a. Pay monthly the total interest due.
b. Pay $50,000 of the principal each November 1, beginning in 1995.
c. Maintain a current ratio (current assets ÷ current liabilities) of 2:1.
d. Appropriate $500,000 of retained earnings until the loan is fully paid.
e. Maintain a minimum balance of $25,000 (called a compensating balance) in its Second National Bank account.

On December 31, 1994, 25% of the $500,000 loan had been disbursed in modernization of the retail stores and in expansion of the product line, and the remainder is temporarily invested in U.S. Treasury Notes. Kolby Co.'s balance sheet as of December 31, 1994, is as follows:

Kolby Co.
Balance Sheet
December 31, 1994

Assets

Current assets:
Cash		$ 40,000
Marketable securities, at cost (market price, $379,500)		375,000
Accounts receivable	$ 91,500	
Less allowance for doubtful accounts	6,500	85,000
Merchandise inventory		120,500
Prepaid expenses		4,500
Total current assets		$ 625,000

Plant assets:
Land		$150,000	
Buildings	$950,000		
Less accumulated depreciation	215,000	735,000	
Equipment	$460,000		
Less accumulated depreciation	110,000	350,000	
Total plant assets			1,235,000
Total assets			$1,860,000

Liabilities

Current liabilities:
Accounts payable	$ 71,800	
Notes payable (Second National Bank)	50,000	
Salaries payable	3,200	
Total current liabilities		$125,000

Long-term liabilities:
Notes payable (Second National Bank)		450,000
Total liabilities		$ 575,000

Stockholders' Equity

Paid-in capital:
Common stock, $20 par (50,000 shares authorized, 25,000 shares issued)	$500,000	
Excess of issue price over par	40,000	
Total paid-in capital		$540,000

Retained earnings:
Appropriated for provision of Second National Bank loan	$500,000	
Unappropriated	245,000	
Total retained earnings		745,000
Total stockholders' equity		1,285,000
Total liabilities and stockholders' equity		$1,860,000

The board of directors is scheduled to meet January 10, 1995, to discuss the results of operations for 1994 and to consider the declaration of dividends for the fourth quarter of 1994. The chairman of the board has asked for your advice on the declaration of dividends.

Instructions:

1. What factors should the board consider in deciding whether to declare a cash dividend?

2. ▪▪▪▪ ▸ The board is considering the declaration of a stock dividend instead of a cash dividend. Discuss the issuance of a stock dividend from the point of view of (a) a stockholder and (b) the board of directors.

ANSWERS TO SELF-EXAMINATION QUESTIONS

1. **D** Paid-in capital is one of the two major subdivisions of the stockholders' equity of a corporation. It may result from many sources, including the receipt of donated real estate (answer A), the redemption of a corporation's own stock (answer B), and the sale of a corporation's treasury stock (answer C).

2. **A** The amount of income tax deferred to future years is $16,000 (answer A), determined as follows:

Depreciation expense, sum-of-the-years-digits method	$100,000
Depreciation expense, straight-line method	60,000
Excess expense in determination of taxable income	$ 40,000
Income tax rate	× 40%
Income tax deferred to future years	$ 16,000

3. **A** Events and transactions that are distinguished by their unusual nature and by the infrequency of their occurrence, such as a gain on condemnation of land for public use, are reported in the income statement as extraordinary items (answer A).

4. **C** The correction of a material error related to a prior period should be excluded from the determination of net income of the current period and reported as an adjustment of the balance of retained earnings at the beginning of the current period (answer C).

5. **C** An appropriation for plant expansion is a portion of total retained earnings and would be reported in the Stockholders' Equity section of the balance sheet (answer C).

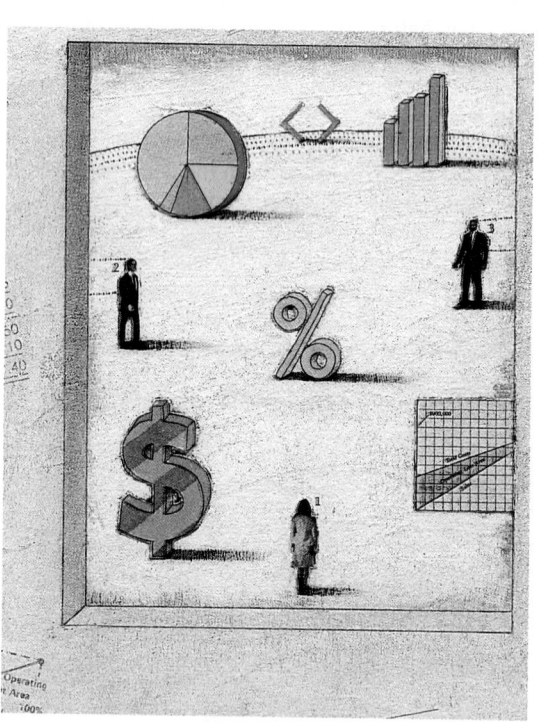

You and Accounting

On June 25, 1992, *The Wall Street Journal* reported that American Telephone & Telegraph Inc. (AT&T) bonds due in 2003, paying 7⅛% interest, were selling for 97⅜. Does this mean that you could buy these bonds on this date for $97.375 each?

The Wall Street Journal also reported that Walt Disney Co.'s zero-coupon bonds due in 2005 were selling for 47. Why are these bonds selling at such a low price?

The answers to these and other questions related to bonds are discussed in this chapter.

Chapter 17
Long-Term Liabilities and Investments in Bonds

Cash and other assets may be obtained by a corporation through issuing its stock. A corporation may also finance operations through retained earnings, which in some cases is accompanied by the issuance of stock dividends. These methods of financing a corporation's operations were discussed in preceding chapters.

A corporation may finance its operations by borrowing money on a long-term basis. This chapter discusses accounting principles and concepts related to the issuance of long-term debt. The accounting by investors who acquire such debt is also discussed.

FINANCING CORPORATIONS

Objective 1
Compute the potential impact of long-term borrowing on the earnings per share of a corporation.

A corporation may finance the expansion of its operations by borrowing money on a long-term basis. In doing so, the corporation normally issues either notes or bonds. A **bond** is a form of interest-bearing note. Long-term notes may be issued to a few lending agencies or to a single investor, such as an insurance company. Bonds are usually sold to underwriters who are dealers and brokers in securities. Underwriters, in turn, sell them to investors. This chapter focuses on the accounting principles and concepts for bonds. However, much of the discussion also applies to long-term notes.

When funds are borrowed through the issuance of bonds, there is a definite commitment to pay interest and to repay the principal at a stated future date. Bondholders are creditors of the issuing corporation, and their claims for interest and for repayment of principal rank ahead of the claims of stockholders.

Many factors influence the board of directors of a corporation in deciding whether to issue debt or equity to obtain funds for financing long-term operations. To illustrate, assume that three alternative plans for financing a $4,000,000 corporation are being considered by its organizers (board of directors). In each case, the securities are issued at their par or face amount. It is estimated that the corporation will earn $800,000 annually, before deducting interest on the bonds and income tax estimated at 40% of income. Exhibit 1 shows the effect of the three plans on the income of a corporation and its common stockholders.

Exhibit 1
Effect of Alternative Financing Plans—$800,000 Earnings

	Plan 1	Plan 2	Plan 3
12% bonds	—	—	$2,000,000
Preferred 9% stock, $50 par	—	$2,000,000	1,000,000
Common stock, $10 par	$4,000,000	2,000,000	1,000,000
Total	$4,000,000	$4,000,000	$4,000,000
Earnings before interest and income tax	$ 800,000	$ 800,000	$ 800,000
Deduct interest on bonds	—	—	240,000
Income before income tax	$ 800,000	$ 800,000	$ 560,000
Deduct income tax	320,000	320,000	224,000
Net income	$ 480,000	$ 480,000	$ 336,000
Dividends on preferred stock	—	180,000	90,000
Available for dividends on common stock	$ 480,000	$ 300,000	$ 246,000
Shares of common stock outstanding	400,000	200,000	100,000
Earnings per share on common stock	$1.20	$1.50	$2.46

Under Plan 1, all the financing is from issuing common stock. In this case, the earnings per share on the common stock is $1.20 per share. Under Plan 2, one-half of the financing is from issuing 9% preferred stock, and one-half is from issuing common stock. In this case, earnings per common share is $1.50. Under Plan 3, one-half of the financing is from issuing 12% bonds, and the remaining one-half is equally split between issuing 9% preferred and common stock. In this case, earnings per common share is $2.46.

In Exhibit 1, Plan 3 is the most attractive for common stockholders. If the estimated earnings are increased beyond $800,000, the difference between the earnings per share to common stockholders under Plan 1 and Plan 3 is even greater. However, if smaller earnings occur, Plans 2 and 3 become less attractive. The effect of earnings of $440,000 rather than $800,000 is shown in Exhibit 2.

In addition to effect on earnings per share, other factors should be considered when alternative methods of financing are evaluated. For example, issuing bonds requires a fixed interest charge that, in contrast to dividends, is not subject to corporate control. Also, the eventual repayment of the principal amount of the bonds is required, in contrast to the absence of any such requirement to stockholders. On the other hand, financing a corporation entirely through issuing common stock often requires a significant investment by one or a small group of stockholders who desire to control the corporation. Another factor to be considered is the current climate of the financial markets. If interest rates are low, corporations usually

Exhibit 2
Effect of Alternative Financing Plans—$440,000 Earnings

	Plan 1	Plan 2	Plan 3
12% bonds	—	—	$2,000,000
Preferred 9% stock, $50 par	—	$2,000,000	1,000,000
Common stock, $10 par	$4,000,000	2,000,000	1,000,000
Total	$4,000,000	$4,000,000	$4,000,000
Earnings before interest and income tax	$ 440,000	$ 440,000	$ 440,000
Deduct interest on bonds	—	—	240,000
Income before income tax	$ 440,000	$ 440,000	$ 200,000
Deduct income tax	176,000	176,000	80,000
Net income	$ 264,000	$ 264,000	$ 120,000
Dividends on preferred stock	—	180,000	90,000
Available for dividends on common stock	$ 264,000	$ 84,000	$ 30,000
Shares of common stock outstanding	400,000	200,000	100,000
Earnings per share on common stock	$.66	$.42	$.30

finance their operations with the issuance of debt by either issuing notes or bonds. For example, as interest rates fell in early 1992, corporations rushed to issue new debt. In one day alone, more than $4.5 billion dollars of debt was issued.[1]

How Refinancing Works

Some of the same factors that influence a corporation's decision on financing are also considered when a company refinances, or changes the structure of its debt and stockholders' equity. These concerns are described in the following excerpt from an article in *USA TODAY*.

When a major company like Allegis Corp. announces that it is "recapitalizing" [refinancing], many shareholders may be baffled. . . . Recapitalization plans aren't as complicated as they seem, however. Here are some basic questions and answers:

What is capital?

Simply put, it's a company's money. It can come from two sources: stockholders and lenders.

The stockholders' share is called equity. It represents cash the company has raised by selling stock, and profits the company has built up.

The other part of capital is money borrowed from banks or raised by selling bonds.

How companies balance equity and debt is up to them. At IBM Corp., only 11% of total capital is debt. Sears, Roebuck and Co. has 46% debt. The level of debt a company keeps depends on the risk its managers are willing to assume.

What does risk have to do with it?

It's no different for a company than for an individual. The more debt you have, the greater the risk. Reason: Any profit you earn first must go to meet interest payments. If earnings aren't sufficient to cover the interest owed, you'll have to deplete your savings—or sell something—to raise the needed cash.

What happens in a recapitalization?

A company decides to borrow heavily to raise cash for a large, one-time cash . . . payment to shareholders. . . . [In addition,] . . . shareholders also receive new shares to replace their old shares in the company. . . . [In] the process, the company generally [reduces its equity]. It's replaced with debt.

How can the company afford the debt load?

The company is forced to operate more efficiently than ever. It will have to slash expenses to keep earnings up in the face of higher interest expenses. Owens-Corning Fiberglas Corp., for example, pared its research costs significantly after its recapitalization last year. . . .

Is there any advantage in being so heavily in debt?

Debt does have a good side. By borrowing, you gain "leverage"—the ability to control more assets by using someone else's money. That can magnify the return to shareholders, if business is good and the firm operates efficiently. . . .

Source: Neil Budde, "How Company Recapitalization Plans Work," *USA TODAY* (June 8, 1987).

CHARACTERISTICS OF BONDS

Objective 2
List the characteristics of bonds.

When a corporation issues bonds, it enters into a contract, called a **bond indenture** or **trust indenture** with the bondholders. A bond issue is normally divided into a number of individual bonds, which may be of varying denominations. Usually the principal of each bond, called the **face value**, is $1,000 or a multiple of $1,000. The interest on bonds may be payable annually, semiannually, or quarterly. Most bonds pay interest semiannually.

[1] Kenneth N. Gilpin, "More Corporate Issues Are Offered," *The Wall Street Journal* (January 9, 1992), p. C16.

The prices of bonds are quoted on bond exchanges as a percentage of the bonds' face value. Thus, AT&T bonds quoted at 97⅜ could be purchased for $973.75. Likewise, bonds quoted at 109 could be purchased for $1,090.

Registered bonds may be transferred from one owner to another by endorsement on the bond certificate. The issuing corporation records or registers the name and the address of each bondholder. Interest payments are then made to each registered bondholder. Title to **coupon bonds**, also called **bearer bonds**, is transferred merely by delivery. Thus, the issuing corporation does not know the identity of the bondholders. Interest coupons, in the form of checks or drafts payable to bearer, are attached to the bond certificate. At each interest date, the holder detaches the appropriate coupon and presents it to a bank for payment. Although coupon bonds were issued often in the past, they are rarely issued today.

When all bonds of an issue mature at the same time, they are called **term bonds**. If the maturities are spread over several dates, they are called **serial bonds**. For example, one-tenth of an issue of $1,000,000 bonds, or $100,000, may mature sixteen years from the issuance date, another $100,000 in the seventeenth year, and so on until the final $100,000 matures in the twenty-fifth year.

Bonds that may be exchanged for other securities under certain conditions are called **convertible bonds**. Bonds issued by a corporation that reserves the right to redeem bonds before maturity are called **callable bonds**.

A **secured bond** is one that gives the bondholder a claim on specific assets in case the issuing corporation fails to meet its liabilities on the bonds. The properties mortgaged or pledged may be specific buildings and equipment, the entire plant, or stocks and bonds of other companies owned by the corporation. Unsecured bonds issued on the basis of the general credit of the corporation are called **debenture bonds**.

THE PRESENT-VALUE CONCEPT AND BONDS PAYABLE

Objective 3
Explain the present-value concept and the present value of bonds payable.

The concept of present value plays an important role in many accounting analyses and business decisions. For example, accounting analyses based on the present-value concept are useful for evaluating proposals for long-term investments in plant and equipment. Such analyses will be discussed in a later chapter. In this chapter, the concept of present value will be discussed as it relates to bonds.

The concept of **present value** is based on the time value of money. That is, an amount of cash to be received at some date in the future is not the equivalent of the same amount of cash held at an earlier date. In other words, a sum of cash to be received in the future is not as valuable as the same sum on hand today. This is because cash on hand today can be invested to earn income. For example, $100 on hand today would be more valuable than $100 received a year from today. In this case, if the $100 cash on hand today can be invested to earn 10% per year, the $100 will accumulate to $110 ($100 plus $10 earnings) in one year. The $100 on hand today is the present-value amount that is equivalent to $110 to be received a year from today.

When a corporation issues bonds, it usually incurs a liability to pay two separate amounts. The price that a buyer is willing to pay for the right to receive these amounts is the sum of their present values. These amounts are:

1. The face amount of the bonds at a maturity date.
2. Periodic interest at a specified percentage of the face amount.

Present Value of the Face Amount of Bonds

The present value of the face amount of bonds is the value today of the amount to be received at the maturity date. For example, assume that $1,000 is to be paid in one year and that the rate of interest is 12%. The present-value amount is $892.86 ($1,000 ÷ 1.12). If the $1,000 is to be paid one year later (two years in all), with the interest compounded at the end of the first year, the present value is $797.20 ($892.86 ÷ 1.12).

The present value of a cash sum to be received in the future can be determined by a series of divisions as illustrated above. In practice, however, it is normal to use a table of present values for this purpose. The **present value of $1 table** can be used to find the present-value factor for $1 to be received for the appropriate number of periods in the future. The amount of the future cash sum is then multiplied by this factor to determine its present value. A partial table of the present value of $1 is shown in Exhibit 3.[2]

Exhibit 3
Present Value of $1 at Compound Interest

Periods	5%	5½%	6%	6½%	7%	10%	11%	12%	13%	14%
1	0.9524	0.9479	0.9434	0.9390	0.9346	0.9091	0.9009	0.8929	0.8850	0.8772
2	0.9070	0.8985	0.8900	0.8817	0.8734	0.8264	0.8116	0.7972	0.7832	0.7695
3	0.8638	0.8516	0.8396	0.8278	0.8163	0.7513	0.7312	0.7118	0.6931	0.6750
4	0.8227	0.8072	0.7921	0.7773	0.7629	0.6830	0.6587	0.6355	0.6133	0.5921
5	0.7835	0.7651	0.7473	0.7299	0.7130	0.6209	0.5935	0.5674	0.5428	0.5194
6	0.7462	0.7252	0.7050	0.6853	0.6663	0.5645	0.5346	0.5066	0.4803	0.4556
7	0.7107	0.6874	0.6651	0.6435	0.6228	0.5132	0.4817	0.4523	0.4251	0.3996
8	0.6768	0.6516	0.6274	0.6042	0.5820	0.4665	0.4339	0.4039	0.3762	0.3506
9	0.6446	0.6176	0.5919	0.5674	0.5439	0.4241	0.3909	0.3606	0.3329	0.3075
10	0.6139	0.5854	0.5584	0.5327	0.5083	0.3855	0.3522	0.3220	0.2946	0.2697
11	0.5847	0.5549	0.5268	0.5002	0.4751	0.3505	0.3173	0.2875	0.2607	0.2366
12	0.5568	0.5260	0.4970	0.4697	0.4440	0.3186	0.2858	0.2567	0.2307	0.2076
13	0.5303	0.4986	0.4688	0.4410	0.4150	0.2897	0.2575	0.2292	0.2042	0.1821
14	0.5051	0.4726	0.4423	0.4141	0.3878	0.2633	0.2320	0.2046	0.1807	0.1597
15	0.4810	0.4479	0.4173	0.3888	0.3624	0.2394	0.2090	0.1827	0.1599	0.1401
16	0.4581	0.4246	0.3936	0.3651	0.3387	0.2176	0.1883	0.1631	0.1415	0.1229
17	0.4363	0.4024	0.3714	0.3428	0.3166	0.1978	0.1696	0.1456	0.1252	0.1078
18	0.4155	0.3815	0.3503	0.3219	0.2959	0.1799	0.1528	0.1300	0.1108	0.0946
19	0.3957	0.3616	0.3305	0.3022	0.2765	0.1635	0.1377	0.1161	0.0981	0.0829
20	0.3769	0.3427	0.3118	0.2838	0.2584	0.1486	0.1240	0.1037	0.0868	0.0728

For the preceding example, Exhibit 3 indicates that the present value of $1 to be received in two years with interest of 12% a year is 0.7972. Multiplying $1,000 by 0.7972 yields $797.20. This is the same amount that was determined previously by two consecutive divisions. In Exhibit 3, the Periods column represents the number of compounding periods and the Percentage columns represent the compound interest rate per period. For example, 12% for two years compounded annually, as in the preceding example, is 12% for two periods. Likewise, 12% for two years compounded semiannually would be 6% (12% per year ÷ 2 semiannual periods) for four periods (2 years × 2 semiannual periods). Similarly, 12% for three years compounded semiannually would be 6% (12% ÷ 2) for six periods (3 years × 2 semiannual periods).

Present Value of the Periodic Bond Interest Payments

The present value of the periodic bond interest payments is the value today of the amount of interest to be received at the end of each interest period. Such a series of fixed payments at fixed intervals is called an **annuity.**

A partial table of the **present value of an annuity** of $1 at compound interest is presented in Exhibit 4. Exhibit 4 indicates the present value of $1 to be received at the end of each period for various compound rates of interest. For example, the present value of $1,000 to be received at the end of each of the next 5 periods at 10% compound interest per period is $3,790.80 ($1,000 × 3.7908).

[2] The tables presented in this chapter are limited to 20 periods for a small number of interest rates, and the amounts are carried to only four decimal places. Books of tables are available with as many as 360 periods, 45 interest rates (including many fractional rates), and amounts carried to eight decimal places. More complete interest tables are provided in Appendix A.

Exhibit 4
Present Value of Annuity of $1 at Compound Interest

Periods	5%	5½%	6%	6½%	7%	10%	11%	12%	13%	14%
1	0.9524	0.9479	0.9434	0.9390	0.9346	0.9091	0.9009	0.8929	0.8850	0.8772
2	1.8594	1.8463	1.8334	1.8206	1.8080	1.7355	1.7125	1.6901	1.6681	1.6467
3	2.7232	2.6979	2.6730	2.6485	2.6243	2.4869	2.4437	2.4018	2.3612	2.3216
4	3.5460	3.5052	3.4651	3.4258	3.3872	3.1699	3.1024	3.0373	2.9745	2.9137
5	4.3295	4.2703	4.2124	4.1557	4.1002	3.7908	3.6959	3.6048	3.5172	3.4331
6	5.0757	4.9955	4.9173	4.8410	4.7665	4.3553	4.2305	4.1114	3.9976	3.8887
7	5.7864	5.6830	5.5824	5.4845	5.3893	4.8684	4.7122	4.5638	4.4226	4.2883
8	6.4632	6.3346	6.2098	6.0888	5.9713	5.3349	5.1461	4.9676	4.7988	4.6389
9	7.1078	6.9522	6.8017	6.6561	6.5152	5.7590	5.5370	5.3283	5.1317	4.9464
10	7.7217	7.5376	7.3601	7.1888	7.0236	6.1446	5.8892	5.6502	5.4262	5.2161
11	8.3064	8.0925	7.8869	7.6890	7.4987	6.4951	6.2065	5.9377	5.6869	5.4527
12	8.8632	8.6185	8.3838	8.1587	7.9427	6.8137	6.4924	6.1944	5.9176	5.6603
13	9.3936	9.1171	8.8527	8.5997	8.3577	7.1034	6.7499	6.4235	6.1218	5.8424
14	9.8986	9.5896	9.2950	9.0138	8.7455	7.3667	6.9819	6.6282	6.3025	6.0021
15	10.3797	10.0376	9.7123	9.4027	9.1079	7.6061	7.1909	6.8109	6.4624	6.1422
16	10.8378	10.4622	10.1059	9.7678	9.4467	7.8237	7.3792	6.9740	6.6039	6.2651
17	11.2741	10.8646	10.4773	10.1106	9.7632	8.0216	7.5488	7.1196	6.7291	6.3729
18	11.6896	11.2461	10.8276	10.4325	10.0591	8.2014	7.7016	7.2497	6.8399	6.4674
19	12.0853	11.6077	11.1581	10.7347	10.3356	8.3649	7.8393	7.3658	6.9380	6.5504
20	12.4622	11.9504	11.4699	11.0185	10.5940	8.5136	7.9633	7.4694	7.0248	6.6231

ACCOUNTING FOR BONDS PAYABLE

Objective 4
Journalize entries for bonds payable.

The interest rate specified in the bond indenture is called the **contract** or **coupon rate**. This rate may differ from the market rate of interest at the time the bonds are issued. If the **market** or **effective rate** is higher than the contract rate, the bonds will sell at a **discount**, or less than their face amount. This is because buyers are unwilling to pay the face amount for bonds whose contract rate is lower than the market rate. The discount, in effect, represents the amount necessary to make up for the difference in the market and the contract interest rates. In contrast, if the market rate is lower than the contract rate, the bonds will sell at a **premium**, or more than their face amount. In this case, buyers are willing to pay more than the face amount for bonds whose contract rate is higher than the market rate.

Bonds Issued at Face Amount

To illustrate the journal entries for issuing bonds, assume that on January 1 a corporation issues for cash $100,000 of 12%, five-year bonds, with interest of $6,000 payable semiannually. The market rate of interest at the time the bonds are issued is 12%. Since the contract rate and the market rate of interest are the same, the bonds will sell at their face amount. This amount is the sum of (1) the present value of the face amount of $100,000 to be repaid in 5 years and (2) the present value of 10 semiannual interest payments of $6,000 each. This computation is shown below.[3]

Present value of face amount of $100,000 due in 5 years, at 12%
  compounded semiannually: $100,000 × 0.5584 (present value of $1
  for 10 periods at 6%).. $ 55,840
Present value of 10 semiannual interest payments of $6,000, at 12%
  compounded semiannually: $6,000 × 7.3601 (present value of
  annuity of $1 for 10 periods at 6%).. 44,160
Total present value of bonds.. $100,000

---

[3] Because the present-value tables are rounded to four decimal places, minor rounding differences may appear in the illustrations.

The basic data for computing the above amounts were obtained from the pre-sent-value tables in Exhibits 3 and 4. The first of the two amounts, **$55,840**, is the present value of the $100,000 that is to be repaid in 5 years. The $55,840 is deter-mined as follows:

1. The present value of $1 for 10 periods (5 years of semiannual payments) at 6% semiannually (12% annual rate) is located in Exhibit 3.
2. The present-value factor in (1) is multiplied by $100,000.

If the bond indenture provided that no interest would be paid during the en-tire 5-year period, the bonds would be worth only $55,840 at the time of their is-suance. To express the concept of present value from a different viewpoint, if $55,840 were invested today, with interest at 12% compounded semiannually, the sum accumulated at the end of 10 semiannual periods would be $100,000.

The second of the two amounts, **$44,160**, is the present value of the series of ten $6,000 interest payments. The $44,160 is determined as follows:

1. The present value of an annuity of $1 for 10 periods (5 years of semiannual payments) at 6% semiannually (12% annual rate) is located in Exhibit 4.
2. The present-value factor in (1) is multiplied by $6,000.

The present value of $44,160 can also be viewed as the amount that must be deposited today at an interest rate of 12% compounded semiannually to provide ten semiannual withdrawals of $6,000 each. At the end of the tenth withdrawal, the original deposit will be reduced to zero.

The entry to record the issuance of the $100,000 bonds at their face amount is shown below.

| Jan. 1 | Cash | 100,000 | |
| | Bonds Payable | | 100,000 |

At six-month intervals following the issuance of the 12% bonds, interest pay-ments of $6,000 are made. The interest payment is recorded in the usual manner by a debit to Interest Expense and a credit to Cash. At the maturity date, the pay-ment of the principal sum of $100,000 is recorded by a debit to Bonds Payable and a credit to Cash.

Bonds Issued at a Discount

If the market rate of interest is 13% and the contract rate is 12%, the bonds will sell at a discount. The present value of the five-year, $100,000 bonds is computed as follows:

Present value of face amount of $100,000 due in 5 years, at 13% compounded semiannually: $100,000 × 0.5327 (present value of $1 for 10 periods at 6½%)..	$53,270
Present value of 10 semiannual interest payments of $6,000, at 13% compounded semiannually: $6,000 × 7.1888 (present value of an annuity of $1 for 10 periods at 6½%)...	43,133
Total present value of bonds..	$96,403

The two present values that make up the total are both less than the compara-ble amounts in the preceding example. This is because the market rate of interest was 12% in the first example, while the market rate of interest was 13% in the above example. The present value of a future amount becomes less and less as the interest rate used to compute the present value increases. Stated in another way, the amount that has to be invested today to equal a future amount becomes less and less as the interest rate that is assumed to be earned on the investment increases.

The entry to record the issuance of the preceding 12% bonds is shown below.

Jan. 1	Cash	96,403	
	Discount on Bonds Payable	3,597	
	Bonds Payable		100,000

When bonds payable are issued at a discount, the amount of the discount is recorded in a separate contra account. The $3,597 discount may be viewed as the amount that is needed to entice investors to accept a contract rate of interest that is below the market rate. In other words, the discount is the market's way of adjusting a bond's contract rate of interest to the higher market rate of interest. In this sense, the discount represents an additional interest expense beyond the amounts paid as periodic interest based on the contract rate of interest. The discount is paid to the bondholders at the maturity date. That is, in the above example the issuer must pay the bondholders $100,000 at maturity, even though only $96,403 was initially received when the bonds were issued.

As noted above, a discount represents additional interest expense above the amounts paid as periodic interest. Because of this, generally accepted accounting principles require the amortization of discounts to increase the interest expense over the life of a bond issue.

There are two methods of amortizing discount to interest expense over the life of a bond issue: (1) the **straight-line method** and (2) the **effective interest rate method.** Both methods amortize the same total amount of discount over the life of the bonds. However, the effective interest rate method, often called simply the **interest method,** more accurately reports the interest expense on a year-to-year basis. Because of this, the interest method is required by generally accepted accounting principles.[4] The straight-line method is acceptable if the results obtained do not materially differ from the results that would be obtained by the use of the interest method.[5] Because it illustrates the basic concept of amortizing discounts and is simpler, the straight-line method is discussed first. The interest method is illustrated later in the chapter.

The straight-line method of amortizing bond discount provides for amortization in equal periodic amounts. Applying this method to the preceding example yields amortization of $\frac{1}{10}$ of $3,597, or $359.70, each half year. The amount of the interest expense on the bonds remains constant for each half year at $6,000 plus $359.70, or $6,359.70. The entry to record the first interest payment and the amortization of the related amount of discount is shown below.

June 30	Interest Expense	6,359.70	
	Discount on Bonds Payable		359.70
	Cash		6,000.00

Instead of recording the amortization each time the interest is paid, it may be recorded only at the end of the year. When this procedure is used, each interest payment is recorded on the periodic payment date as shown below.

| Interest Expense | 6,000.00 | |
| Cash | | 6,000.00 |

---

[4] *Opinions of the Accounting Principles Board, No. 21,* "Interest on Receivables and Payables" (New York: American Institute of Certified Public Accountants, 1971), par. 14.
[5] *Ibid.*

The entry to amortize the discount at the end of the first year is shown below. The amount of the discount amortized, $719.40, is made up of the two semiannual amortization amounts of $359.70.

| Dec. 31 | Interest Expense | 719.40 | |
| | Discount on Bonds Payable | | 719.40 |

Bonds Issued at a Premium

If the market rate of interest is 11% and the contract rate is 12%, the bonds will sell at a premium. The present value of the five-year, $100,000 bonds is computed as follows:

Present value of face amount of $100,000 due in 5 years, at 11% compounded semiannually: $100,000 × 0.5854 (present value of $1 for 10 periods at 5½%)...	$ 58,540
Present value of 10 semiannual interest payments of $6,000, at 11% compounded semiannually: $6,000 × 7.5376 (present value of an annuity of $1 for 10 periods at 5½%)...	45,226
Total present value of bonds...	$103,766

The entry to record the issuance of the bonds is as follows:

Jan. 1	Cash	103,766	
	Bonds Payable		100,000
	Premium on Bonds Payable		3,766

The amortization of bond premiums is basically the same as that for bond discounts, except that interest expense is decreased. In the above example, the straight-line method yields amortization of 1/10 of $3,766, or $376.60, each half year. The entry to record the first interest payment and the amortization of the related premium is as follows:

June 30	Interest Expense	5,623.40	
	Premium on Bonds Payable	376.60	
	Cash		6,000.00

If the amortization of the premium is recorded only at the end of the year, each interest payment is recorded by debiting Interest Expense and crediting Cash. The amortization of the premium at the end of the first year is then recorded as shown below. The amount of the premium amortized, $753.20, is the sum of the two semiannual amounts of $376.60.

| Dec. 31 | Premium on Bonds Payable | 753.20 | |
| | Interest Expense | | 753.20 |

Effective Interest Rate Method of Amortization

The effective interest rate method of amortization of discounts and premiums provides for a constant *rate of interest* on the **carrying amount** (also called **book value**) of the bonds at the beginning of each period. This is in contrast to the straight-line method, which provides for a constant *amount* of interest expense.

The interest rate used in the interest method of amortization is the market rate on the date the bonds are issued. The carrying amount of the bonds to which the interest rate is applied is the face amount of the bonds minus any unamortized discount or plus any unamortized premium. Under the interest method, the interest expense to be reported on the income statement is computed by multiplying the effective interest rate by the carrying amount of the bonds. The difference between the interest expense computed in this way and the periodic interest payment is the amount of discount or premium to be amortized for the period.

AMORTIZATION OF DISCOUNT BY THE INTEREST METHOD. To illustrate the interest method for amortizing bond discounts, assume the following data from the earlier illustration of the issuance of $100,000 bonds at a discount:

Face value of 12%, five-year bonds, interest compounded semiannually.............. $100,000
Present value of bonds at effective (market) rate of interest of 13%......................   96,403
Discount on bonds payable.. $ 3,597

Applying the interest method to these data yields the amortization table in Exhibit 5. The following items should be noted in this table:

1. The interest paid (Column A) remains constant at 6% of $100,000, the face amount of the bonds.
2. The interest expense (Column B) is computed at 6½% of the bond carrying amount at the beginning of each period. This results in an increasing interest expense each period.
3. The excess of the interest expense over the interest payment of $6,000 is the amount of discount to be amortized (Column C).
4. The unamortized discount (Column D) decreases from the initial balance, $3,597, to a zero balance at the maturity date of the bonds.
5. The carrying amount (Column E) increases from $96,403, the amount received for the bonds, to $100,000 at maturity.

Exhibit 5
Amortization of Discount on Bonds Payable—Interest Method

Interest Payment	A Interest Paid (6% of Face Amount)	B Interest Expense (6½% of Bond Carrying Amount)	C Discount Amortization (B − A)	D Unamortized Discount (D − C)	E Bond Carrying Amount ($100,000 − D)
				$3,597	$ 96,403
1	$6,000	$6,266 (6½% of $96,403)	$266	3,331	96,669
2	6,000	6,284 (6½% of $96,669)	284	3,047	96,953
3	6,000	6,302 (6½% of $96,953)	302	2,745	97,255
4	6,000	6,322 (6½% of $97,255)	322	2,423	97,577
5	6,000	6,343 (6½% of $97,577)	343	2,080	97,920
6	6,000	6,365 (6½% of $97,920)	365	1,715	98,285
7	6,000	6,389 (6½% of $98,285)	389	1,326	98,674
8	6,000	6,415 (6½% of $98,674)	415	911	99,089
9	6,000	6,441 (6½% of $99,089)	441	470	99,530
10	6,000	6,470 (6½% of $99,530)	470	—	100,000

The entry to record the first interest payment on June 30 and the related discount amortization is as follows:

June 30	Interest Expense	6,266	
	Discount on Bonds Payable		266
	Cash		6,000

If the amortization is recorded only at the end of the year, the amount of the discount amortized on December 31 would be $550. This is the sum of the first two semiannual amortization amounts ($266 and $284) from Exhibit 5.

AMORTIZATION OF PREMIUM BY THE INTEREST METHOD. To illustrate the interest method for amortizing bond premiums, assume the following data from the earlier illustration of the issuance of $100,000 bonds at a premium:

Present value of bonds at effective (market) rate of interest of 11%.......................... $103,766
Face value of 12%, five-year bonds, interest compounded semiannually............... 100,000
Premium on bonds payable .... $ 3,766

Using the interest method to amortize the above premium yields the amortization table in Exhibit 6. The following items should be noted in this table:

1. The interest paid (Column A) remains constant at 6% of $100,000, the face amount of the bonds.
2. The interest expense (Column B) is computed at 5½% of the bond carrying amount at the beginning of each period. This results in a decreasing interest expense each period.
3. The excess of the periodic interest payment of $6,000 over the interest expense is the amount of premium to be amortized (Column C).
4. The unamortized premium (Column D) decreases from the initial balance, $3,766, to a zero balance at the maturity date of the bonds.
5. The carrying amount (Column E) decreases from $103,766, the amount received for the bonds, to $100,000 at maturity.

Exhibit 6
Amortization of Premium on Bonds Payable—Interest Method

Interest Payment	A Interest Paid (6% of Face Amount)	B Interest Expense (5½% of Bond Carrying Amount)	C Premium Amortization (A − B)	D Unamortized Premium (D − C)	E Bond Carrying Amount ($100,000 + D)
				$3,766	$103,766
1	$6,000	$5,707 (5½% of $103,766)	$293	3,473	103,473
2	6,000	5,691 (5½% of $103,473)	309	3,164	103,164
3	6,000	5,674 (5½% of $103,164)	326	2,838	102,838
4	6,000	5,657 (5½% of $102,838)	343	2,495	102,495
5	6,000	5,638 (5½% of $102,495)	362	2,133	102,133
6	6,000	5,618 (5½% of $102,133)	382	1,751	101,751
7	6,000	5,597 (5½% of $101,751)	403	1,348	101,348
8	6,000	5,575 (5½% of $101,348)	425	923	100,923
9	6,000	5,551 (5½% of $100,923)	449	474	100,474
10	6,000	5,526 (5½% of $100,474)	474	—	100,000

The entry to record the first interest payment on June 30 and the related premium amortization is as follows:

June 30	Interest Expense	5,707	
	Premium on Bonds Payable	293	
	Cash		6,000

If the amortization is recorded only at the end of the year, the amount of the premium amortized on December 31 would be $602. This is the sum of the first two semiannual amortization amounts ($293 and $309) from Exhibit 6.

Zero-Coupon Bonds

Some enterprises issue bonds that do not provide for interest payments. Such bonds are called **zero-coupon bonds**. For example, Walt Disney Co. has issued zero-coupon bonds maturing in 2005.

Zero-coupon bonds provide for only the payment of the face amount of the bonds at the maturity date. Because the bonds do not provide for interest payments, they sell at a large discount. For example, Walt Disney Co.'s zero-coupon bonds maturing in 2005 were selling for 47 on June 25, 1992.

To further illustrate, if the market rate of interest for five-year bonds that pay interest semiannually is 13%, the present value of $100,000 zero-coupon, five-year bonds is as follows:

Present value of $100,000 due in 5 years, at 13% compounded
    semiannually: $100,000 × 0.5327 (present value of $1 for
    10 periods at 6½%) $53,270

The accounting for zero-coupon bonds is similar to that for interest-bearing bonds that have been sold at a discount. The entry to record the issuance of the bonds is as follows:

Cash	53,270	
Discount on Bonds Payable	46,730	
Bonds Payable		100,000

The discount of $46,730 is amortized as interest expense over the life of the bonds. The discount may be amortized using either the straight-line method or the interest method.

BOND SINKING FUNDS

Objective 5
Journalize entries for bond sinking funds, using future-value concepts.

As discussed in a previous chapter, the bond indenture may restrict dividends by an appropriation of retained earnings as a means of increasing the assurance that the bonds will be paid at maturity. Assuming that a corporation is required by a bond indenture to appropriate $10,000 of retained earnings each year for the 10 years, the following entry would be made annually:

Retained Earnings	10,000	
Appropriation for Bonded Indebtedness		10,000

In addition to or instead of an appropriation, the bond indenture may require that funds for the payment of the face value of the bonds at maturity be set aside over the life of the bond issue. The amounts set aside are kept separate from other assets in a special fund called a **sinking fund**.

An appropriation for bonded indebtedness has no direct effect on the existence of a sinking fund. Each is independent of the other. When there is both a fund and an appropriation for the same purpose, the appropriation is referred to as **funded**.

Cash deposited in a sinking fund is usually invested in income-producing securities. The periodic deposits plus the earnings on the investments should accumulate to the face value of the bonds at maturity. To compute the amount of these periodic deposits, the concept of future value can be used.

Future-Value Concepts

Future value is the amount that will accumulate at some future date as a result of an investment or a series of investments. For example, if $1,000 is invested to earn 10% per year, the future value at the end of one year will be $1,100 ($1,000 plus $100 earnings). If the $1,100 is left to accumulate additional earnings for three years, the future value at the end of the second year will be $1,210 ($1,100 plus $110 earnings), and at the end of the third year, $1,331 ($1,210 plus $121 earnings).

The future value of an investment can also be determined by using a table of future values. A partial table of the future value of $1 is shown in Exhibit 7.

Exhibit 7
Future Value of $1 at Compound Interest

Periods	5%	5½%	6%	6½%	7%	10%	11%	12%	13%	14%
1	1.0500	1.0550	1.0600	1.0650	1.0700	1.1000	1.1100	1.1200	1.1300	1.1400
2	1.1025	1.1130	1.1236	1.1342	1.1449	1.2100	1.2321	1.2544	1.2769	1.2996
3	1.1576	1.1742	1.1910	1.2080	1.2250	1.3310	1.3676	1.4049	1.4429	1.4815
4	1.2155	1.2388	1.2625	1.2865	1.3108	1.4641	1.5181	1.5735	1.6305	1.6890
5	1.2763	1.3070	1.3382	1.3701	1.4026	1.6105	1.6851	1.7623	1.8424	1.9254
6	1.3401	1.3788	1.4185	1.4591	1.5007	1.7716	1.8704	1.9738	2.0820	2.1950
7	1.4071	1.4547	1.5036	1.5540	1.6058	1.9487	2.0762	2.2107	2.3526	2.5023
8	1.4775	1.5347	1.5939	1.6550	1.7182	2.1436	2.3045	2.4760	2.6584	2.8526
9	1.5513	1.6191	1.6895	1.7626	1.8385	2.3580	2.5580	2.7731	3.0040	3.2520
10	1.6289	1.7081	1.7909	1.8771	1.9672	2.5937	2.8394	3.1059	3.3946	3.7072
11	1.7103	1.8021	1.8983	1.9992	2.1049	2.8531	3.1518	3.4786	3.8359	4.2262
12	1.7959	1.9012	2.0122	2.1291	2.2522	3.1384	3.4985	3.8960	4.3345	4.8179
13	1.8857	2.0058	2.1329	2.2675	2.4099	3.4523	3.8833	4.3635	4.8980	5.4924
14	1.9799	2.1161	2.2609	2.4149	2.5785	3.7975	4.3104	4.8871	5.5348	6.2614
15	2.0789	2.2325	2.3966	2.5718	2.7590	4.1773	4.7846	5.4736	6.2543	7.1379
16	2.1829	2.3553	2.5404	2.7390	2.9522	4.5950	5.3109	6.1304	7.0673	8.1373
17	2.2920	2.4848	2.6928	2.9171	3.1588	5.0545	5.8951	6.8660	7.9861	9.2765
18	2.4066	2.6215	2.8543	3.1067	3.3799	5.5599	6.5436	7.6900	9.0243	10.5752
19	2.5270	2.7657	3.0256	3.3086	3.6165	6.1159	7.2633	8.6128	10.1974	12.0557
20	2.6533	2.9178	3.2071	3.5237	3.8697	6.7275	8.0623	9.6463	11.5231	13.7435

For the above example, the table indicates that the future value of $1 in three years (periods), with earnings at the rate of 10% a year, is 1.331. The future value of the investment of $1,000 is computed by multiplying $1,000 by 1.331, which yields $1,331. This is the same amount as determined above.

Future value may also arise from an annuity—a series of equal investments made at fixed intervals. For example, assume that $1,000 is invested at the end of each year to earn 10% per year compounded annually. The future value of the annuity at the end of the third year is $3,310, as shown below.

Year	Beginning Balance	Earnings During Year (10% × Beginning Balance)	Annual Deposit (End of Year)	Accumulation at End of Year
1	—	—	$1,000	$1,000
2	$1,000	$100	1,000	2,100
3	2,100	210	1,000	3,310

The future value of a series of investments can also be determined by using a table of future values. A partial table of the future value of an annuity of $1 is shown in Exhibit 8.

Exhibit 8
Future Value of Annuity of $1 at Compound Interest (Investments at End of Period)

Periods	5%	5½%	6%	6½%	7%	10%	11%	12%	13%	14%
1	1.0000	1.0000	1.0000	1.0000	1.0000	1.0000	1.0000	1.0000	1.0000	1.0000
2	2.0500	2.0550	2.0600	2.0650	2.0700	2.1000	2.1100	2.1200	2.1300	2.1400
3	3.1525	3.1680	3.1836	3.1992	3.2149	3.3100	3.3421	3.3744	3.4069	3.4396
4	4.3101	4.3423	4.3746	4.4072	4.4399	4.6410	4.7097	4.7793	4.8498	4.9211
5	5.5256	5.5811	5.6371	5.6936	5.7507	6.1051	6.2278	6.3529	6.4803	6.6101
6	6.8019	6.8881	6.9753	7.0637	7.1533	7.7156	7.9129	8.1152	8.3227	8.5355
7	8.1420	8.2669	8.3938	8.5229	8.6540	9.4872	9.7833	10.0890	10.4047	10.7305
8	9.5491	9.7216	9.8975	10.0769	10.2598	11.4359	11.8594	12.2997	12.7573	13.2328
9	11.0266	11.2563	11.4913	11.7319	11.9780	13.5795	14.1640	14.7757	15.4157	16.0854
10	12.5779	12.8754	13.1808	13.4944	13.8165	15.9374	16.7220	17.5487	18.4198	19.3373
11	14.2068	14.5835	14.9716	15.3716	15.7836	18.5312	19.5614	20.6546	21.8143	23.0445
12	15.9171	16.3856	16.8699	17.3707	17.8885	21.3843	22.7132	24.1331	25.6502	27.2708
13	17.7130	18.2868	18.8821	19.4998	20.1406	24.5227	26.2116	28.0291	29.9847	32.0887
14	19.5986	20.2926	21.0151	21.7673	22.5505	27.9750	30.0949	32.3926	34.8827	37.5811
15	21.5786	22.4087	23.2760	24.1822	25.1290	31.7725	34.4054	37.2797	40.4175	43.8424
16	23.6575	24.6411	25.6725	26.7540	27.8881	35.9497	39.1900	42.7533	46.6717	50.9804
17	25.8404	26.9964	28.2129	29.4930	30.8402	40.5447	44.5008	48.8837	53.7391	59.1176
18	28.1324	29.4812	30.9057	32.4101	33.9990	45.5992	50.3959	55.7497	61.7251	68.3941
19	30.5390	32.1027	33.7600	35.5167	37.3790	51.1591	56.9395	63.4397	70.7494	78.9692
20	33.0660	34.8683	36.7856	38.8253	40.9955	57.2750	64.2028	72.0524	80.9468	91.0249

For the previous example, the table indicates that the future value of an annuity of $1 in three years (periods), with earnings at the rate of 10% a year, is 3.310. The future value of the series of investments of $1,000 is computed by multiplying $1,000 by 3.310, which yields $3,310. This is the same amount as determined above.

To illustrate the use of the future-value concept to determine the periodic deposits in a bond sinking fund, assume that a corporation issues $100,000 of 10-year bonds, dated January 1. A bond sinking fund for the payment of the bonds at maturity is to be established, with deposits to be made at the end of each year. If the deposits are expected to earn 14% per year, the annual deposit would be $5,171, determined as follows:

$$\text{Annual Deposit} = \frac{\text{Maturity Value of Bonds}}{\text{Future Value of Annuity of \$1 for 10 Periods at 14\%}}$$

$$\text{Annual Deposit} = \frac{\$100,000}{19.3373}$$

Annual Deposit = $5,171 (rounded)

Accounting for Bond Sinking Funds

When cash is transferred to the sinking fund, an account called Sinking Fund Cash is debited and Cash is credited. The purchase of investments is recorded by a debit to Sinking Fund Investments and a credit to Sinking Fund Cash. As income (interest or dividends) is received, the cash is debited to Sinking Fund Cash and Sinking Fund Income is credited.

To illustrate the accounting for a bond sinking fund to retire $100,000 of 10-year bonds, assume that annual sinking fund deposits are $5,171. When invested in securities yielding 14% per year, these deposits will accumulate to $100,000 at the end of 10 years. Some selected transactions and related entries for this sinking fund during the 10-year period are illustrated below.

| Deposit of cash in the fund | Sinking Fund Cash | 5,171 | |
| | Cash | | 5,171 |

The first deposit in the sinking fund is recorded. A similar entry would be recorded as deposits are made at the end of each of the 9 remaining years.

| Purchase of investments | Sinking Fund Investments | 5,000 | |
| | Sinking Fund Cash | | 5,000 |

The purchases of securities after the first deposit was made are recorded in a summary entry. The time of purchase and the amount invested at any one time may vary, depending upon market conditions and the unit price of securities purchased.

| Receipt of income from invest-
ments | Sinking Fund Cash | 700 | |
| | Sinking Fund Income | | 700 |

The receipt of income for the year on the securities purchased is recorded in a summary entry. Interest and dividends are received at different times during the year, and the amount earned per year normally increases as the fund increases.

Sale of investments	Sinking Fund Cash	85,100	
	Sinking Fund Investments		82,480
	Gain on Sale of Investments		2,620

The sale of all securities at the end of the tenth year is recorded. Investments may be sold from time to time and the proceeds reinvested. Prior to maturity, all investments are converted into cash.

Payment of bonds	Bonds Payable	100,000	
	Cash	1,791	
	Sinking Fund Cash		101,791

The payment of the bonds and the transfer of the remaining sinking fund cash to the cash account are recorded. The cash available in the fund at the end of the tenth year is assumed to be composed of the following:

Proceeds from sale of investments	$ 85,100
Income earned during tenth year	11,520
Last annual deposit	5,171
Total	$101,791

In the above example, the amount of the fund exceeded the amount of the liability by $1,791. This excess is transferred to the regular cash account. The amount of the fund, however, might have been less than the amount of the liability. For example, assume that the fund totaled only $99,500 at the end of the tenth year. In this case, the $500 deficiency would have been made up by writing a check on the regular cash account.

Sinking fund income represents earnings of the corporation and is reported in the income statement as *Other income*. The cash and the securities making up the sinking fund are reported in the balance sheet as *Investments*, immediately below the Current Assets section.

BOND REDEMPTION

Objective 6
Journalize entries for bond redemptions.

Callable bonds can be redeemed by the issuing corporation within the period of time and at the price stated in the bond indenture. The call price is normally above the face value. If the market rate of interest declines after the issuance of the bonds, the corporation may sell new bonds at a lower interest rate and use the funds to redeem the original bond issue. In this way, the corporation can save on future interest expenses. A corporation may also redeem its bonds by purchasing them on the open market.

A corporation may redeem its bonds at a price below their carrying amount or book value. In this case, the difference between the carrying amount and the price paid for the redemption is recorded as a gain. If the price paid for the redemption is above the carrying amount, a loss is recorded.[6]

To illustrate, assume that on June 30 a corporation has a bond issue of $100,000 outstanding, on which there is an unamortized premium of $4,000. The corporation has the option of calling the bonds for $105,000, which it exercises on this date. The entry to record the redemption is as follows:

June 30	Bonds Payable	100,000	
	Premium on Bonds Payable	4,000	
	Loss on Redemption of Bonds	1,000	
	Cash		105,000

Even when a bond issue is not callable, the corporation may still purchase its bonds on the open market. Assuming that the preceding corporation purchases one-fourth ($25,000) of the bonds for $24,000 on June 30, the entry to record the redemption is as follows:

June 30	Bonds Payable	25,000	
	Premium on Bonds Payable	1,000	
	Cash		24,000
	Gain on Redemption of Bonds		2,000

In the preceding entry, only a portion of the premium relating to the redeemed bonds is written off. The difference between the carrying amount of the bonds purchased, $26,000 ($25,000 + $1,000), and the price paid for the redemption, $24,000, is recorded as a gain.

BALANCE SHEET PRESENTATION OF BONDS PAYABLE

Objective 7
Describe the balance sheet presentation of bonds payable.

Bonds payable are usually reported on the balance sheet as long-term liabilities. If there are two or more bond issues, the details of each should be reported on the balance sheet or in a supporting schedule or note. Separate accounts are normally maintained for each bond issue.

When the balance sheet date is within one year of the maturity date of the bonds, the bonds may require classification as a current liability. This would be the case if the bonds are to be paid out of current assets. If the bonds are to be paid from a sinking fund or if they are to be refinanced with another bond issue, they should remain in the noncurrent category. In this case, the details of the retirement of the bonds are normally disclosed in a note to the financial statements.

The balance in a discount on bonds payable account is reported in the balance sheet as a deduction from the related bonds payable. Conversely, the balance in a bond premium account is reported as an addition to the related bonds payable. Ei-

---

[6] Gains and losses on the redemption of bonds are reported in the income statement as extraordinary items. See *Statement of Financial Accounting Standards, No. 4*, "Reporting Gains and Losses from Extinguishment of Debt" (Stamford: Financial Accounting Standards Board, 1975), par. 8.

ther on the face of the financial statements or in accompanying notes, a description of the bonds (terms, security, due date, and coupon and effective interest rates) should also be disclosed. In addition, the maturities and sinking fund requirements should be disclosed for each of the next five years.[7] Finally, the market (fair) value of the bonds payable should also be disclosed.[8]

INVESTMENTS IN BONDS

Objective 8
Journalize entries for the purchase, interest, discount and premium amortization, and sale of bond investments.

Up until now, bonds and related transactions have been discussed from the standpoint of the issuing corporation (the debtor). However, these transactions also affect investors. The remainder of this chapter discusses the accounting for bonds from the point of view of investors.

Investments in bonds or other debt securities that are not intended as a ready source of cash for normal operations are classified as **long-term investments**. A business may make long-term investments because it has cash that is not needed in its normal operations. A corporation may also purchase bonds in order to establish or maintain business relations with the issuing company. Cash and securities in bond sinking funds are considered long-term investments, because they will be used for paying a bond liability.

Investments in bonds may be purchased directly from the issuing corporation or from other investors. The services of a broker are usually employed in buying and selling bonds listed on the organized bond exchanges. The record of transactions on bond exchanges is reported daily in the financial pages of newspapers. This record usually includes data on the bond interest rate, maturity date, volume of sales, and the high, low, and closing prices for each corporation's bonds traded during the day. Prices for bonds are quoted as a percentage of the face amount. Thus, the price of a $1,000 bond quoted at 104½ would be $1,045.

Accounting for Bond Investments—Purchase, Interest, and Amortization

A long-term investment in debt securities is usually carried at cost. The cost of bonds purchased includes the amount paid to the seller plus other costs related to the purchase. For example, such costs would include a broker's commission.

When bonds are purchased between interest dates, the buyer normally pays the seller the interest accrued from the last interest payment date to the date of purchase. The amount of the interest paid is normally debited to Interest Income, since it is an offset against the amount that will be received at the next interest date.

To illustrate, assume that a $1,000 bond is purchased at 102 plus a brokerage fee of $5.30 and accrued interest of $10.20. The transaction is recorded by the following entry:

Apr. 2	Investment in Lewis Co. Bonds	1,025.30	
	Interest Income	10.20	
	Cash		1,035.50

The cost of the bond is recorded in a single investment account. The face amount of the bond and the premium (or discount) are normally not recorded in separate accounts. This is different from the accounting for bonds payable. Separate premium and discount accounts are usually not maintained by investors, since bond investments are often not held by business enterprises until their maturity dates.

---

[7] *Statement of Financial Accounting Standards, No. 47*, "Disclosure of Long-Term Obligations" (Stamford: Financial Accounting Standards Board, 1981), par. 10.
[8] *Statement of Financial Accounting Standards, No. 107*, "Disclosures about Fair Value of Financial Instruments" (Norwalk: Financial Accounting Standards Board, 1991), par. 10.

When bonds held as long-term investments are purchased at a price other than the face amount, such as above, the premium or discount should be amortized over the remaining life of the bonds. The amortization of premium decreases the amount of the investment in bonds account and interest income. The amortization of discount increases the amount of the investment in bonds account and interest income. The amortization of the premium or discount can be determined using either the straight-line or interest methods. Unlike bonds payable, the amortization of premiums and discounts on bond investments are usually recorded at the end of the period, rather than when interest is received.

Interest received on bond investments is recorded by a debit to Cash and a credit to Interest Income. At the end of a period, the interest accrued should be recorded by a debit to Interest Receivable and a credit to Interest Income.

To illustrate, assume that $50,000 of 8% bonds of Deitz Corporation, due in 8¾ years, are purchased by Crenshaw Inc. on July 1. Crenshaw Inc. purchases the bonds directly from Deitz Corporation to yield an effective interest rate of 11%. The purchase price is $41,706 plus interest of $1,000 ($50,000 × 8% × 3/12) accrued from April 1, the date of the last semiannual interest payment. Entries in the accounts of Crenshaw Inc. at the time of purchase and for the remainder of the fiscal period ending December 31 are as follows:

Payment for investment in bonds and accrued interest	July 1	Investment in Deitz Corp. Bonds Interest Income Cash	41,706 1,000	 42,706

Cost of $50,000 of Deitz Corp. bonds $41,706
Interest accrued ($50,000 × 8% × 3/12)   1,000
Total $42,706

Receipt of semiannual interest for April 1–October 1 ($50,000 × 8% × 6/12)	Oct. 1	Cash Interest Income	2,000	 2,000

Adjusting entry for accrued interest from October 1–December 31 ($50,000 × 8% × 3/12)	Dec. 31	Interest Receivable Interest Income	1,000	 1,000

Adjusting entry for amortization of discount by straight-line method for July 1–December 31	Dec. 31	Investment in Deitz Corp. Bonds Interest Income	474	 474

Face value of bonds $50,000
Cost of bond investment   41,706
Discount on bond investment $ 8,294

Number of months to maturity (8¾ years × 12)   105 months
Monthly amortization (rounded to nearest dollar)
    ($8,294 ÷ 105 months) $79 per month

Amortization for 6 months ($79 × 6) $474

The entries in the interest income account in the above illustration are summarized below.

July	1	Paid accrued interest—3 months	$(1,000)
Oct.	1	Received interest payment—6 months	2,000
Dec.	31	Recorded accrued interest—3 months	1,000
	31	Recorded amortization of discount—6 months	474
		Interest earned—6 months	$ 2,474

Accounting for Bond Investments—Sale

Many long-term investments in bonds are sold before their maturity date. When this occurs, the seller receives the sales price (less commissions and other selling costs) plus any accrued interest since the last interest payment date. Before recording the cash proceeds, the seller should amortize any discount or premium for the current period up to the date of sale. Any gain or loss on the sale can then be recorded when the cash proceeds are recorded.

To illustrate, assume that the Deitz Corporation bonds in the above example are sold for $47,350 plus accrued interest on June 30, seven years after their purchase. The carrying amount of the bonds (cost plus amortized discount) as of *January 1* of the year of sale (78 months after their purchase) is $47,868 [$41,706 + ($79 per mo. × 78 months)]. The entries to amortize the discount for the current year and to record the sale of the bonds are as follows:

Amortization of $474 of discount for current year ($79 × 6 months)	June 30	Investment in Deitz Corp. Bonds	474	
		Interest Income		474

Receipt of interest and proceeds from sale of bonds and recognition of loss on sale of bonds	June 30	Cash	48,350	
		Loss on Sale of Investments	992	
		Interest Income		1,000
		Investment in Deitz Corp. Bonds		48,342

Interest for April 1–June 30 ($50,000 × 8% × 3/12)	$ 1,000
Carrying amount of bonds on January 1	$47,868
Discount amortized, Jan. 1–June 30	474
Carrying amount of bonds on June 30	$48,342
Proceeds of sale	47,350
Loss on sale	$ 992

Financial Statement Presentation of Investments in Bonds

The carrying value of a bond investment is normally reported in the balance sheet under the caption *Investments*, following current assets. In addition, the market (fair) value of the bond investment should be disclosed, either on the face of the balance sheet or in an accompanying note.[9] Any gain or loss on the sale of bond investments is normally reported in the Other Income section of the income statement.

[9] *Ibid.*, par. 10.

CHAPTER REVIEW

Key Points

Objective 1. Compute the potential impact of long-term borrowing on the earnings per share of a corporation.
Three alternative plans for financing a corporation by issuing common stock, preferred stock, or bonds are illustrated in Exhibits 1 and 2. The effects of alternative financing on the earnings per share vary significantly, depending upon the level of earnings.

Objective 2. List the characteristics of bonds.
The characteristics of bonds depend upon the type of bonds issued by a corporation. Bonds that may be issued include registered bonds, bearer bonds, coupon bonds, term bonds, serial bonds, convertible bonds, callable bonds, secured bonds, and debenture bonds.

Objective 3. Explain the present-value concept and the present value of bonds payable.
The concept of present value is based on the time value of money. That is, an amount of cash to be received at some date in the future is not the equivalent of the same amount of cash held at an earlier date. For example, if $100 cash today can be invested to earn 10% per year, the $100 today is referred to as the present value amount that is equivalent to $110 to be received a year from today.

A price that a buyer is willing to pay for a bond is the sum of (1) the present value of the face amount of the bonds at the maturity date and (2) the present value of the periodic interest payments.

Objective 4. Journalize entries for bonds payable.
The journal entry for issuing bonds payable debits Cash for the proceeds received and credits Bonds Payable for the face value of the bonds. Any difference between the face value of the bonds and the proceeds is debited to Discount on Bonds Payable or credited to Premium on Bonds Payable.

A discount or premium on bonds payable is amortized to interest expense over the life of the bonds by using either the straight-line method or the effective interest rate method. The entry to amortize a discount debits Interest Expense and credits Discount on Bonds Payable. The entry to amortize a premium debits Premium on Bonds Payable and credits Interest Expense.

Objective 5. Journalize entries for bond sinking funds, using future-value concepts.
The amounts set aside to pay a bond at its maturity date are accumulated in a sinking fund. The concept of future value may be used to determine the amount of the periodic deposits in a sinking fund. The journal entry to record deposits

in a sinking fund debits Sinking Fund Cash and credits Cash. Investments are recorded by debiting Sinking Fund Investments and crediting Sinking Fund Cash. Income from sinking fund investments is recorded in a sinking fund income account.

At maturity, Bonds Payable is debited for the face value of the bonds and Sinking Fund Cash is credited. Any surplus of sinking fund cash is returned to the regular cash account. Any shortage of sinking fund cash is transferred to the sinking fund from the regular cash account.

Objective 6. Journalize entries for bond redemptions.
When a corporation redeems bonds, Bonds Payable is debited for the face value of the bonds, the premium (discount) on bonds account is debited (credited) for its balance, Cash is credited, and any gain or loss on the redemption is recorded.

Objective 7. Describe the balance sheet presentation of bonds payable.
Bonds payable are usually reported on the balance sheet as long-term liabilities. When the balance sheet date is within one year of the bond maturity date, the bonds should be classified as a current liability if they are to be paid out of current assets. If the bonds are to be paid from a sinking fund or refinanced, they should remain in the noncurrent category. A discount on bonds should be reported in the balance sheet as a deduction from the related bonds payable. A premium on bonds should be reported as an addition to the related bonds payable.

Objective 8. Journalize entries for the purchase, interest, discount and premium amortization, and sale of bond investments.
A long-term investment in bonds is carried at cost and is recorded by debiting Investment in Bonds. When bonds are purchased between interest dates, the amount of the interest paid should be debited to Interest Income. Any discount or premium on bond investments should be amortized, using the straight-line or effective interest rate methods. The amortization of a discount is recorded by debiting Investment in Bonds and crediting Interest Income. The amortization of a premium is recorded by debiting Interest Income and crediting Investment in Bonds.

When bonds held as long-term investments are sold, any discount or premium for the current period should first be amortized. Cash is then debited for the proceeds of the sale, Investment in Bonds is credited for its balance, and any gain or loss is recorded.

Glossary of Key Terms

Annuity. A series of equal cash flows at fixed intervals. **Objective 3**

Bond. A form of interest-bearing note employed by corporations to borrow on a long-term basis. **Objective 1**

Bond indenture. The contract between a corporation issuing bonds and the bondholders. **Objective 2**

Carrying amount. The amount at which a temporary or a long-term investment or a long-term liability is reported on the balance sheet; also called basis or book value. **Objective 4**

Contract rate. The interest rate specified on a bond; sometimes called the coupon rate of interest. **Objective 4**

Discount. The excess of the face amount of bonds over their issue price. **Objective 4**

Effective rate. The market rate of interest at the time bonds are issued. **Objective 4**

Future value. The amount that will accumulate at some future date as a result of an investment or a series of investments. **Objective 5**

Long-term investments. Investments that are not intended to be a ready source of cash in the normal operations of a business and that are listed in the Investments section of the balance sheet. **Objective 8**

Premium. The excess of the issue price of bonds over the face amount. **Objective 4**

Present value. The estimated present worth of an amount of cash to be received (or paid) in the future. **Objective 3**

Present value of an annuity. The sum of the present values of a series of equal cash flows to be received at fixed intervals. **Objective 3**

Sinking fund. Assets set aside in a special fund to be used for a specific purpose. **Objective 5**

Self-Examination Questions
Answers at end of chapter.

1. If a corporation plans to issue $1,000,000 of 12% bonds at a time when the market rate for similar bonds is 10%, the bonds can be expected to sell at:
   - A. their face amount
   - B. a premium
   - C. a discount
   - D. a price below their face amount

2. If the bonds payable account has a balance of $500,000 and the discount on bonds payable account has a balance of $40,000, what is the carrying amount of the bonds?
   - A. $460,000
   - B. $500,000
   - C. $540,000
   - D. $580,000

3. The cash and the securities that make up the sinking fund established for the payment of bonds at maturity are classified on the balance sheet as:
   - A. current assets
   - B. investments
   - C. long-term liabilities
   - D. current liabilities

4. If a firm purchases $100,000 of bonds of X Company at 101 plus accrued interest of $2,000 and pays broker's commissions of $50, the amount debited to Investment in X Company Bonds would be:
   - A. $100,000
   - B. $101,050
   - C. $103,000
   - D. $103,050

5. The balance in the discount on bonds payable account would usually be reported in the balance sheet in the:
   - A. Current Assets section
   - B. Current Liabilities section
   - C. Long-Term Liabilities section
   - D. Investments section

ILLUSTRATIVE PROBLEM

Dent Inc.'s fiscal year ends December 31. Selected transactions for the period 1993 through 2000, involving bonds payable issued by Dent Inc., are as follows:

1993

June 30.   Issued $4,000,000 of 25-year, 9% callable bonds dated June 30, 1993, for cash of $3,840,000. Interest is payable semiannually on June 30 and December 31.

Dec. 31.   Paid the semiannual interest on the bonds.

   31.   Recorded straight-line amortization of $3,200 discount on the bonds.

   31.   Closed the interest expense account.

1994

June 30.   Paid the semiannual interest on the bonds.

Dec. 31.   Paid the semiannual interest on the bonds.

   31.   Recorded straight-line amortization of $6,400 discount on the bonds.

   31.   Closed the interest expense account.

2000

June 30.   Recorded the redemption of the bonds, which were called at 102. The balance in the bond discount account is $115,200 after the payment of interest and amortization of discount have been recorded. (Record the redemption only.)

ILLUSTRATIVE PROBLEM ILLUSTRATIVE PROBLEM ILLUSTRATIVE PROBLEM ILLUSTRATIVE PROBLEM

Instructions

1. Journalize entries to record the preceding transactions.
2. Determine the amount of interest expense for 1993 and 1994.
3. Estimate the effective annual interest rate by dividing the interest expense for 1993 by the bond carrying amount at the time of issuance and multiplying by 2.
4. Determine the carrying amount of the bonds as of December 31, 1994.

Solution

1.

1993

June 30	Cash	3,840,000	
	Discount on Bonds Payable	160,000	
	Bonds Payable		4,000,000
Dec. 31	Interest Expense	180,000	
	Cash		180,000
31	Interest Expense	3,200	
	Discount on Bonds Payable		3,200
31	Income Summary	183,200	
	Interest Expense		183,200

1994

June 30	Interest Expense	180,000	
	Cash		180,000
Dec. 31	Interest Expense	180,000	
	Cash		180,000
31	Interest Expense	6,400	
	Discount on Bonds Payable		6,400
31	Income Summary	366,400	
	Interest Expense		366,400

2000

June 30	Bonds Payable	4,000,000	
	Loss on Redemption of Bonds Payable	195,200	
	Discount on Bonds Payable		115,200
	Cash		4,080,000

2. a. 1993 — $183,200
   b. 1994 — $366,400
3. $183,200 ÷ $3,840,000 = 4.77% rate for six months of a year
   4.77% × 2 = 9.54% annual rate
4.

Initial carrying amount of bonds	$3,840,000
Discount amortized on December 31, 1993	3,200
Discount amortized on December 31, 1994	6,400
Carrying amount of bonds, December 31, 1994	$3,849,600

DISCUSSION QUESTIONS

1. When underwriters are used by corporations issuing bonds, what function do the underwriters perform?
2. Explain the meaning of each of the following terms as they relate to a bond issue: (a) secured, (b) convertible, (c) callable, and (d) debenture.
3. Describe the two distinct obligations incurred by a corporation when issuing bonds.
4. If you asked your broker to purchase for you a 9% bond when the market interest rate for such bonds was 10%, would you expect to pay more or less than the face value for the bond? Explain.
5. A corporation issues $5,000,000 of 10% coupon bonds to yield interest at the rate of 9%. (a) Was the amount of cash received from the sale of the bonds greater or less than $5,000,000? (b) Identify the following terms related to the bond issue: (1) face amount, (2) market or effective rate of interest, (3) contract or coupon rate of interest, and (4) maturity amount.

6. If bonds issued by a corporation are sold at a premium, is the market rate of interest greater or less than the coupon rate?
7. What is the present value of $1,000 due in 2 years, if the market rate of interest is 11%?
8. What is the present value of $1,000 to be received in each of the next 2 years, if the market rate of interest is 11%?
9. If the bonds payable account has a balance of $2,000,000 and the premium on bonds payable account has a balance of $25,500, what is the carrying amount of the bonds?
10. The following data are related to a $750,000, 12% bond issue for a selected semiannual interest period:

Bond carrying amount at beginning of period	$796,500
Interest paid at end of period	45,000
Interest expense allocable to the period	42,675

(a) Were the bonds issued at a discount or at a premium? (b) What is the balance of the discount or premium account at the beginning of the period? (c) How much amortization of discount or premium is allocable to the period?

11. A corporation issues 10%, 20-year debenture bonds, with a face amount of $5,000,000, for 102½ at the beginning of the current year. Assuming that the premium is to be amortized on a straight-line basis, what is the total amount of interest expense for the current year?
12. In the entry made at year end, indicate the title of (a) the account to be debited and (b) the account to be credited for amortization of (1) discount on bonds payable and (2) premium on bonds payable.
13. When the premium on bonds payable is amortized by the interest method, does the interest expense increase or decrease over the amortization period?
14. What is the purpose of a bond sinking fund?
15. If the earnings rate is 9% compounded annually, what would be the value at the end of the second year for a $1,000 investment?
16. If the earnings rate is 12% compounded annually, what would be the value at the end of the sixth year for a $5,000 investment? Use the table of the future value of $1 presented in this chapter to determine the value.
17. What would be the value at the end of the second year from a series of investments of $5,000 each to be made at the end of each of the first two years, with earnings of 12% compounded annually?
18. If Power Company invests $5,000 at the end of each of the next 5 years in a sinking fund and the fund investments yield 10% per year compounded annually, what is the value of the fund at the end of 5 years? Use the table of the future value of an annuity of $1 presented in this chapter to determine the value.
19. What amount must be invested at the end of each of the next 5 years, in a sinking fund that earns 12% compounded annually, to accumulate to $25,000 at the end of the fifth year? Use the table of the future value of an annuity of $1 presented in this chapter to determine the amount.
20. If the amount accumulated in a sinking fund account exceeds the amount of liability at the redemption date, to what account is the excess transferred?
21. How are cash and securities comprising a sinking fund classified on the balance sheet?
22. Bonds Payable has a balance of $500,000 and Discount on Bonds Payable has a balance of $7,500. If the issuing corporation redeems the bonds at 98, what is the amount of gain or loss on redemption?
23. Indicate how the following accounts should be reported in the balance sheet: (a) Premium on Bonds Payable, and (b) Discount on Bonds Payable.
24. Under what caption are *long-term investments in bonds* listed on the balance sheet?
25. The quoted price of Steale Inc. bonds on April 1 is 103. On the same day, the interest accrued is 4% of the face amount. (a) Does the quoted price include accrued interest? (b) If $10,000 face amount of Steale Inc. bonds is purchased on April 1 at the quoted price, what is the cost of the bonds, exclusive of commission?
26. An investor sells $10,000 of bonds of Juniper Corp., carried at $10,200, for $10,600 plus accrued interest of $500. The broker remits the balance due after deducting a commission of $250. Journalize the entry to record this transaction.

REAL W RLD FOCUS

27. A company purchased a $1,000, 20-year zero-coupon bond for $189 to yield 8.5% to maturity. How is the interest income computed?

Source: "Technical Hotline," *Journal of Accountancy* (January 1989), p. 100.

ETHICS DISCUSSION CASE

Restono Inc. has outstanding a $50,000,000, 25-year, 11% debenture bond issue dated July 1, 1978. The bond issue is due June 30, 2003. The bond indenture requires a sinking fund, which has a balance of $30,000,000 as of July 1, 1993. Restono Inc. is currently experiencing a shortage of funds due to a recent plant expansion. Grace Barker, treasurer of Restono, has suggested using the sinking fund cash to temporarily relieve the shortage of funds. Barker's brother-in-law, who is trustee of the sinking fund, is willing to loan Restono Inc. the necessary funds from the sinking fund.

▌SHARPEN YOUR ▶
COMMUNICATION SKILLS

Discuss whether Grace Barker is behaving in an ethical manner.

EXERCISES

EXERCISE 17-1
EFFECT OF FINANCING ON
EARNINGS PER SHARE
Objective 1

Two companies are financed as follows:

	Feld Co.	Barr Inc.
Bonds payable, 10% (issued at face value)	$2,000,000	$1,000,000
Preferred $9 stock (nonparticipating), $100 par	2,000,000	1,000,000
Common stock, $20 par	2,000,000	4,000,000

Income tax is estimated at 40% of income.

SPREADSHEET
PROBLEM

a. Determine for each company the earnings per share of common stock, assuming that the income before bond interest and income tax for each company is (1) $600,000, (2) $1,000,000, and (3) $1,600,000.

▌SHARPEN YOUR ▶
COMMUNICATION SKILLS

b. Discuss factors other than earnings per share that should be considered in evaluating such financing plans.

EXERCISE 17-2
REAL WORLD FOCUS
Objective 3

K Mart Corporation 8⅜% bonds due in 2017 were reported in *The Wall Street Journal* as selling for 98½ on June 4, 1992.

▌SHARPEN YOUR ▶
COMMUNICATION SKILLS

Were the bonds selling at a premium or at a discount on June 4, 1992? Explain.

EXERCISE 17-3
ENTRIES FOR ISSUANCE OF
BONDS
Objective 4

C. C. Cox Co. issued $10,000,000 of 20-year, 11% bonds on April 1 of the current year, with interest payable on April 1 and October 1. The fiscal year of the company is the calendar year. Journalize the entries to record the following selected transactions for the current year:

Apr.   1. Issued the bonds for cash at their face amount.
Oct.   1. Paid the interest on the bonds.
Dec. 31. Recorded accrued interest for three months.

EXERCISE 17-4
ENTRIES FOR BOND
ISSUANCE; AMORTIZATION
OF DISCOUNT BY
STRAIGHT-LINE METHOD
Objective 4

On the first day of its fiscal year, Mitchell Company issued $10,000,000 of 10-year, 10% bonds, interest payable semiannually, at an effective interest rate of 12%, receiving cash of $8,852,950.

a. Journalize the entries to record the following:
  1. Sale of the bonds.
  2. First semiannual interest payment. (Amortization of discount is to be recorded annually.)
  3. Second semiannual interest payment.
  4. Amortization of discount at the end of the first year, using the straight-line method.
b. Determine the amount of the bond interest expense for the first year.

EXERCISE 17-5
AMORTIZATION OF
DISCOUNT BY INTEREST
METHOD
Objective 4

Using the data presented in Exercise 17-4, compute the following:

a. Amortization of discount at the end of the first year, using the interest method. (Round to the nearest dollar.)
b. The amount of the bond interest expense for the first year.

EXERCISE 17-6
COMPUTATION OF BOND
PROCEEDS, ENTRIES FOR
BOND ISSUANCE, AND
AMORTIZATION BY
STRAIGHT-LINE METHOD
Objectives 3, 4

On March 1, 1994, Brown Corporation issued $1,000,000 of 10-year, 12% bonds at an effective interest rate of 11%. Interest is payable semiannually on March 1 and September 1. Journalize the entries to record the following:

a. Sale of bonds on March 1, 1994. (Use the tables of present values in the chapter to determine the bond proceeds.)
b. First interest payment on September 1, 1994, and amortization of bond premium for 6 months, using the straight-line method. (Round to the nearest dollar.)

EXERCISE 17-7
COMPUTATION OF BOND
PROCEEDS, AMORTIZATION
BY INTEREST METHOD,
AND INTEREST EXPENSE
Objectives 3, 4

On the first day of its fiscal year, Kane Inc. issued $10,000,000 of 10-year, 12% bonds at an effective interest rate of 10%, with interest payable semiannually. Compute the following, presenting figures used in your computations and rounding to the nearest dollar:

SPREADSHEET
PROBLEM

a. The amount of cash proceeds from the sale of the bonds. (Use the tables of present values in the chapter.)
b. The amount of premium to be amortized for the first semiannual interest payment period, using the interest method.
c. The amount of premium to be amortized for the second semiannual interest payment period, using the interest method.
d. The amount of the bond interest expense for the first year.

EXERCISE 17-8
COMPUTATION OF
AMORTIZATION BY BOTH
STRAIGHT-LINE AND
INTEREST METHODS
Objectives 3, 4, 8

On July 1 of the current fiscal year, Farrow Company purchased $100,000 of 10-year, 10% bonds as a long-term investment, directly from the issuing company, for $88,530. The effective rate of interest is 12%, and the interest is payable semiannually. Compute the amount of discount to be amortized for the first semiannual interest payment period, using (a) the straight-line method and (b) the interest method.

EXERCISE 17-9
DETERMINATION OF
SINKING FUND DEPOSIT
AND ENTRY
Objective 5

L. D. Riley Inc. issued $5,000,000 of 20-year bonds on January 1 of the current year. The bond indenture requires that equal deposits be made in a bond sinking fund at the end of each of the 20 years. The fund is expected to be invested in securities that will yield 12% per year, compounded annually.

a. Determine the amount of each of the 20 deposits to be made in the bond sinking fund.
b. Journalize the entry to record the first deposit made in the sinking fund.

EXERCISE 17-10
ENTRIES FOR BOND
SINKING FUND
Objective 5

Hood Corporation issued $20,000,000 of 10-year bonds on the first day of the fiscal year. The bond indenture provides that a sinking fund be accumulated, assuming 10% interest, by 10 annual deposits of $1,254,910, beginning at the end of the first year.
 Journalize the entries to record the following selected transactions related to the bond issue:

a. The required amount is deposited in the sinking fund.
b. Investments in securities made from the first sinking fund deposit total $1,250,000.
c. The sinking fund earned $123,600 during the year following the first deposit (summarizing entry).
d. The bonds are paid at maturity, and excess cash of $55,800 in the fund is transferred to the cash account.

EXERCISE 17-11
ENTRIES FOR BOND
SINKING FUND AND
APPROPRIATION OF
RETAINED EARNINGS
Objectives 5, 6

Higgins Corporation issued $10,000,000 of 20-year bonds on the first day of the fiscal year. The bond indenture provides that a sinking fund be accumulated by 20 annual deposits of $275,000, beginning at the end of the first year.
 Journalize the entries to record the following selected transactions related to the bond issue:

a. The required amount is deposited in the sinking fund.
b. Investments in securities from the first sinking fund deposit total $270,500.
c. Retained earnings of $500,000 are appropriated for bonded indebtedness.
d. The sinking fund earns $18,500 during the year following the first deposit (summarizing entry).
e. The bonds are paid at maturity, and excess cash of $47,750 in the fund is transferred to the cash account.
f. The appropriation for bonded indebtedness balance of $10,000,000 is transferred back to retained earnings.

EXERCISE 17-12
ENTRIES FOR ISSUANCE
AND CALLING OF BONDS
Objectives 4, 6

Kline Corp. issued $5,000,000 of 20-year, 12% callable bonds on March 1, 1994, with interest payable on March 1 and September 1. The fiscal year of the company is the calendar year. Journalize the entries to record the following selected transactions:

1994
Mar. 1. Issued the bonds for cash at their face amount.
Sep. 1. Paid the interest on the bonds.

1999
Sep. 1. Called the bond issue at 102, the rate provided in the bond indenture. (Omit entry for payment of interest.)

EXERCISE 17-13
ENTRIES FOR PURCHASE
AND SALE OF INVESTMENT
IN BONDS
Objective 8

Journalize the entries to record the following selected transactions of Fitch Company:

a. Purchased for cash $200,000 of Gray Co. 11% bonds at 102 plus accrued interest of $5,500.
b. Received first semiannual interest.
c. Amortized $360 on the bond investment at the end of the first year.
d. Sold the bonds at 100 plus accrued interest of $2,775. The bonds were carried at $201,750 at the time of the sale.

WhAT'S WROnG
WITH THiS?

At the beginning of the current year, two bond issues (A and B) were outstanding. During the year, bond issue A was redeemed and a significant loss on the redemption of bonds was reported as Other Expense on the income statement. At the end of the year, bond issue B was reported as a current liability because its maturity date was early in the following year. A sinking fund of cash and securities sufficient to pay the series B bonds was reported in the balance sheet as *Investments*. Can you find any flaws in the reporting practices related to the two bond issues?

PROBLEMS

Series A

PROBLEM 17-1A
EFFECT OF FINANCING ON
EARNINGS PER SHARE
Objective 1

Three different plans for financing a $10,000,000 corporation are under consideration by its organizers. Under each of the following plans, the securities will be issued at their par or face amount and the income tax rate is estimated at 40% of income.

	Plan 1	Plan 2	Plan 3
12% bonds			$ 5,000,000
Preferred 8% stock, $100 par		$ 5,000,000	2,500,000
Common stock, $20 par	$10,000,000	5,000,000	2,500,000
Total	$10,000,000	$10,000,000	$10,000,000

SPREADSHEET
P R O B L E M

Instructions

1. Determine for each plan the earnings per share of common stock, assuming that the income before bond interest and income tax is $1,500,000.
2. Determine for each plan the earnings per share of common stock, assuming that the income before bond interest and income tax is $1,100,000.

SHARPEN YOUR ►
COMMUNICATION SKILLS

3. Discuss the advantages and disadvantages of each plan.

PROBLEM 17-2A
ENTRIES FOR BONDS
PAYABLE TRANSACTIONS
Objective 4

On July 1, 1994, Curry Corporation issued $10,000,000 of 10-year, 12% bonds at an effective interest rate of 11%. Interest on the bonds is payable semiannually on December 31 and June 30. The fiscal year of the company is the calendar year.

Instructions

1. Journalize the entry to record the amount of the cash proceeds from the sale of the bonds. Use the tables of present values in this chapter to compute the cash proceeds, rounding to the nearest dollar.

2. Journalize the entries to record the following:
   a. The first semiannual interest payment on December 31, 1994, and the amortization of the bond premium, using the straight-line method.
   b. The interest payment on June 30, 1995, and the amortization of the bond premium, using the straight-line method.
3. Journalize the entries for Instruction (2), using the interest method of amortization. (Round to nearest dollar.)
4. Determine the total interest expense for 1994 under (a) the straight-line method of premium amortization and (b) the interest method of premium amortization.
5. Will the annual interest expense using the interest method of premium amortization always be greater than the annual interest expense using the straight-line method of premium amortization? Explain.

SHARPEN YOUR ►
COMMUNICATION SKILLS

PROBLEM 17-3A
ENTRIES FOR BOND AND
SINKING FUND
TRANSACTIONS
Objectives 4, 5

The following transactions relate to the issuance of $1,000,000 of 10-year, 10% bonds dated January 1, 1985, and the accumulations in a sinking fund to redeem the bonds at maturity. Interest on the bonds is payable on June 30 and December 31.

1985
Jan.   2. Sold the bond issue at 100.
June 30. Paid semiannual interest on bonds.
Dec. 31. Paid semiannual interest on bonds and deposited $58,000 in a bond sinking fund.

1986
Jan.   13. Purchased $56,100 of investments with bond sinking fund cash.
June 30. Paid semiannual interest on bonds.
Oct. 22. Received $4,125 income on investments.
Dec. 31. Paid semiannual interest on bonds.

(Assume that all intervening transactions have been properly recorded.)

1995
Jan.   2. Sold all investments in the bond sinking fund for $980,500. The sinking fund investments had a carrying value of $999,200.
       11. Paid the bonds at maturity from the sinking fund cash and the regular cash account. The cash available in the sinking fund at this date was $991,900.

Instructions
Journalize the entries to record the foregoing transactions.

PROBLEM 17-4A
ENTRIES FOR BOND AND
SINKING FUND
TRANSACTIONS,
INCLUDING
APPROPRIATION OF
RETAINED EARNINGS
Objectives 4, 5

During 1994 and 1995, Norris Company completed the following transactions relating to its $5,000,000 issue of 20-year, 12% bonds dated July 1, 1994. Interest is payable on June 30 and December 31. The corporation's fiscal year is the calendar year.

1994
July   1. Sold the bond issue for $5,402,000 cash.
Dec. 31. Paid the semiannual interest on the bonds.
       31. Recorded bond premium amortization of $10,050, which was determined by using the straight-line method.
       31. Deposited $144,000 cash in a bond sinking fund.
       31. Appropriated $125,000 of retained earnings for bonded indebtedness.
       31. Closed the interest expense account.

1995
Jan.   9. Purchased various securities with sinking fund cash, cost $136,500.
June 30. Paid the semiannual interest on the bonds.
Dec. 20. Recorded the receipt of $10,150 of income on sinking fund securities, depositing the cash in the sinking fund.
       31. Paid the semiannual interest on the bonds.
       31. Recorded bond premium amortization of $20,100, which was determined by using the straight-line method.
       31. Deposited $288,000 cash in the sinking fund.
       31. Appropriated $250,000 of retained earnings for bonded indebtedness.
       31. Closed the interest expense account.

Instructions

1. Journalize the entries to record the foregoing transactions.
2. Prepare a columnar table, using the following headings, and list the information for each of the two years.

Account Balances at End of Year

Year	Bond Interest Expense for Year	Sinking Fund Income for Year	Bonds Payable	Premium on Bonds	Sinking Fund		Appropriation for Bonded Indebtedness
					Cash	Investments	

SOLUTIONS SOFTWARE

Instructions for Solving Problem 17-4A Using Solutions Software

1. Load opening balances.
2. Save the opening balances file to your drive and directory.
3. Set the run date to December 31, 1994, and enter your name.
4. Select the General Journal Entries option and key the journal entries for 1994. Leave the reference field blank. Note: To review the chart of accounts, select F-1.
5. Display a journal entries report.
6. Display a trial balance.
7. Set the run date to December 31, 1995.
8. Select the General Journal Entries option and key the journal entries for 1995. Leave the reference field blank. Note: Be certain to change the year to 1995 when entering the General Journal entries.
9. Display a journal entries report for 1995.
10. Display a trial balance.
11. Save your data file to disk.
12. End the session.

PROBLEM 17-5A
ENTRIES FOR BONDS
PAYABLE TRANSACTIONS
Objectives 4, 6

The following transactions were completed by L. L. Lang Inc., whose fiscal year is the calendar year:

1994

July 1. Issued $5,000,000 of 10-year, 8% callable bonds dated July 1, 1994, at an effective rate of 10%, receiving cash of $4,376,940. Interest is payable semiannually on December 31 and June 30.

Dec. 31. Paid the semiannual interest on the bonds.
   31. Recorded bond discount amortization of $18,847, which was determined by using the interest method.
   31. Closed the interest expense account.

1995

June 30. Paid the semiannual interest on the bonds.
Dec. 31. Paid the semiannual interest on the bonds.
   31. Recorded bond discount amortization of $40,568, which was determined by using the interest method.
   31. Closed the interest expense account.

2002

June 30. Recorded the redemption of the bonds, which were called at 101. The balance in the bond discount account is $177,184 after the payment of interest and amortization of discount have been recorded. (Record the redemption only.)

Instructions

1. Journalize the entries to record the foregoing transactions.
2. Indicate the amount of the interest expense in (a) 1994 and (b) 1995.
3. Determine the effective interest rate by dividing the interest expense for 1994 by the bond carrying amount at the time of issuance and converting the result to an annual rate.
4. Determine the carrying amount of the bonds as of December 31, 1995.

PROBLEM 17-6A
ENTRIES FOR BOND
INVESTMENTS
Objective 8

The following selected transactions relate to certain securities acquired as a long-term investment by J. Matson Inc., whose fiscal year ends on December 31:

1994

Sep. 1. Purchased $300,000 of Payne Company 10-year, 14% bonds dated July 1, 1994, directly from the issuing company, for $305,900 plus accrued interest of $7,000.

Dec. 31. Received the semiannual interest on the Payne Company bonds.

     31. Recorded bond premium amortization of $200 on the Payne Company bonds. The amortization amount was determined by using the straight-line method.

(Assume that all intervening transactions and adjustments have been properly recorded, and that the number of bonds owned has not changed from December 31, 1994, to December 31, 1999.)

2000

June 30. Received the semiannual interest on the Payne Company bonds.

July 31. Sold one-half of the Payne Company bonds at 102 plus accrued interest. The broker deducted $700 for commission, etc., remitting the balance. Prior to the sale, $175 of premium on one-half of the bonds is to be amortized, reducing the carrying amount of those bonds to $151,175.

Dec. 31. Received the semiannual interest on the Payne Company bonds.

     31. Recorded bond premium amortization of $300 on the Payne Company bonds.

Instructions
Journalize the entries to record the foregoing transactions.

Series B

PROBLEM 17-1B
EFFECT OF FINANCING ON
EARNINGS PER SHARE
Objective 1

Three different plans for financing a $10,000,000 corporation are under consideration by its organizers. Under each of the following plans, the securities will be issued at their par or face amount and the income tax rate is estimated at 40% of income.

SPREADSHEET
PROBLEM

	Plan 1	Plan 2	Plan 3
14% bonds			$ 5,000,000
Preferred $4 stock, $50 par		$ 5,000,000	2,500,000
Common stock, $20 par	$10,000,000	5,000,000	2,500,000
Total	$10,000,000	$10,000,000	$10,000,000

Instructions

1. Determine for each plan the earnings per share of common stock, assuming that the income before bond interest and income tax is $1,500,000.
2. Determine for each plan the earnings per share of common stock, assuming that the income before bond interest and income tax is $1,100,000.

■ SHARPEN YOUR ►
COMMUNICATION SKILLS

3. Discuss the advantages and disadvantages of each plan.

PROBLEM 17-2B
ENTRIES FOR BONDS
PAYABLE TRANSACTIONS
Objective 4

On July 1, 1994, Allen Corporation issued $12,000,000 of 10-year, 10% bonds at an effective interest rate of 11%. Interest on the bonds is payable semiannually on December 31 and June 30. The fiscal year of the company is the calendar year.

Instructions

1. Journalize the entry to record the amount of the cash proceeds from the sale of the bonds. Use the tables of present values in this chapter to compute the cash proceeds, rounding to the nearest dollar.
2. Journalize the entries to record the following:
   a. The first semiannual interest payment on December 31, 1994, and the amortization of the bond discount, using the straight-line method.
   b. The interest payment on June 30, 1995, and the amortization of the bond discount, using the straight-line method.
3. Journalize the entries for Instruction (2), using the interest method of amortization. (Round to nearest dollar.)
4. Determine the total interest expense for 1994 under (a) the straight-line method of discount amortization and (b) the interest method of discount amortization.

■ SHARPEN YOUR ►
COMMUNICATION SKILLS

5. Will the annual interest expense using the straight-line method of discount amortization always be greater than the annual interest expense using the interest method of discount amortization? Explain.

PROBLEM 17-3B
ENTRIES FOR BOND AND
SINKING FUND
TRANSACTIONS
Objectives 4, 5

The following transactions relate to the issuance of $900,000 of 10-year, 8% bonds dated January 1, 1985, and the accumulations in a sinking fund to redeem the bonds at maturity. Interest on the bonds is payable on June 30 and December 31.

1985

Jan.   2. Sold the bond issue at 100.

June 30. Paid semiannual interest on bonds.

Dec. 31. Paid semiannual interest on bonds and deposited $50,000 in a bond sinking fund.

1986

Jan.   6. Purchased $49,200 of investments with bond sinking fund cash.

June 30. Paid semiannual interest on bonds.

Nov. 11. Received $4,050 income on investments.

Dec. 31. Paid semiannual interest on bonds.

(Assume that all intervening transactions have been properly recorded.)

1995

Jan.   2. Sold all investments in the bond sinking fund for $885,750. The sinking fund investments had a carrying value of $899,200.

         3. Paid the bonds at maturity from the sinking fund cash and the regular cash account. The cash available in the sinking fund at this date was $893,500.

Instructions

Journalize the entries to record the foregoing transactions.

PROBLEM 17-4B
ENTRIES FOR BOND AND
SINKING FUND
TRANSACTIONS,
INCLUDING
APPROPRIATION OF
RETAINED EARNINGS
Objectives 4, 5

During 1994 and 1995, Pryor Company completed the following transactions relating to its $4,500,000 issue of 30-year, 11% bonds dated July 1, 1994. Interest is payable on June 30 and December 31. The corporation's fiscal year is the calendar year.

1994

July   1. Sold the bond issue for $4,197,600 cash.

Dec. 31. Paid semiannual interest on the bonds.

        31. Recorded bond discount amortization of $5,040, which was determined by using the straight-line method.

        31. Deposited $30,000 cash in a bond sinking fund.

        31. Appropriated $75,000 of retained earnings for bonded indebtedness.

        31. Closed the interest expense account.

1995

Jan. 15. Purchased various securities with sinking fund cash, cost $27,400.

June 30. Paid the semiannual interest on the bonds.

Dec. 15. Recorded the receipt of $2,900 of income on sinking fund securities, depositing the cash in the sinking fund.

        31. Paid the semiannual interest on the bonds.

        31. Recorded bond discount amortization of $10,080, which was determined by using the straight-line method.

        31. Deposited $60,000 cash in the sinking fund.

        31. Appropriated $150,000 of retained earnings for bonded indebtedness.

        31. Closed the interest expense account.

Instructions

1. Journalize the entries to record the foregoing transactions.
2. Prepare a columnar table, using the following headings, and list the information for each of the two years.

Account Balances at End of Year

Year	Bond Interest Expense for Year	Sinking Fund Income for Year	Bonds Payable	Discount on Bonds	Sinking Fund Cash	Investments	Appropriation for Bonded Indebtedness

SOLUTIONS
SOFTWARE

Instructions for Solving Problem 17-4B Using Solutions Software

1. Load opening balances.
2. Save the opening balances file to your drive and directory.
3. Set the run date to December 31, 1994, and enter your name.
4. Select the General Journal Entries option and key the journal entries. Leave the reference field blank. Note: To review the chart of accounts, select F-1.

   5. Display a journal entries report.
   6. Display a trial balance.
   7. Set the run date to December 31, 1995.
   8. Select the General Journal Entries option and key the journal entries for 1995. Leave the reference field blank. Note: Be certain to change the year to 1995 when entering the General Journal entries.
   9. Display a journal entries report for 1995.
  10. Display a trial balance.
  11. Save your data file to disk.
  12. End the session.

PROBLEM 17-5B
ENTRIES FOR BONDS
PAYABLE TRANSACTIONS
Objectives 4, 6

The following transactions were completed by Logan Co., whose fiscal year is the calendar year:

1994
July   1. Issued $20,000,000 of 10-year, 14% callable bonds dated July 1, 1994, at an effective rate of 12%, receiving cash of $22,293,860. Interest is payable semiannually on December 31 and June 30.
Dec. 31. Paid the semiannual interest on the bonds.
     31. Recorded bond premium amortization of $62,368, which was determined by using the interest method.
     31. Closed the interest expense account.

1995
June 30. Paid the semiannual interest on the bonds.
Dec. 31. Paid the semiannual interest on the bonds.
     31. Recorded bond premium amortization of $136,187, which was determined by using the interest method.
     31. Closed the interest expense account.

2000
July   1. Recorded the redemption of the bonds, which were called at 106. The balance in the bond premium account is $1,360,103 after the payment of interest and amortization of premium have been recorded. (Record the redemption only.)

Instructions

1. Journalize the entries to record the foregoing transactions.
2. Indicate the amount of the interest expense in (a) 1994 and (b) 1995.
3. Determine the effective interest rate by dividing the interest expense for 1994 by the bond carrying amount at the time of issuance and converting the result to an annual rate.
4. Determine the carrying amount of the bonds as of December 31, 1995.

PROBLEM 17-6B
ENTRIES FOR BOND
INVESTMENTS
Objective 8

The following selected transactions relate to certain securities acquired by Marsh Company, whose fiscal year ends on December 31:

1994
Sep.   1. Purchased $500,000 of Ellis Company 20-year, 9% bonds dated July 1, 1994, directly from the issuing company, for $476,200 plus accrued interest of $7,500.
Dec. 31. Received the semiannual interest on the Ellis Company bonds.
     31. Recorded bond discount amortization of $400 on the Ellis Company bonds. The amortization amount was determined by using the straight-line method.

(Assume that all intervening transactions and adjustments have been properly recorded, and that the number of bonds owned has not changed from December 31, 1994, to December 31, 1998.)

1999
June 30. Received the semiannual interest on the Ellis Company bonds.
July 31. Sold one-half of the Ellis Company bonds at 95 plus accrued interest. The broker deducted $750 for commission, etc., remitting the balance. Prior to the sale, $350 of discount on one-half of the bonds was amortized, reducing the carrying amount of those bonds to $241,050.
Dec. 31. Received the semiannual interest on the Ellis Company bonds.
     31. Recorded bond discount amortization of $600 on the Ellis Company bonds.

Instructions
Journalize the entries to record the foregoing transactions.

628

MINI-CASE 17 ST BOTTLING CO.

You hold a 25% common stock interest in the family-owned business, a soft drink bottling distributorship. Your sister, who is the manager, has proposed an expansion of plant facilities at an expected cost of $1,500,000. Two alternative plans have been suggested as methods of financing the expansion. Each plan is briefly described as follows:

Plan 1. Issue $1,500,000 of 20-year, 12% bonds at face amount.

Plan 2. Issue an additional 20,000 shares of $20 par common stock at $25 per share, and $1,000,000 of 20-year, 12% bonds at face amount.

The balance sheet as of the end of the previous fiscal year is as follows:

Net income has remained relatively constant over the past several years. The expansion program is expected to increase yearly income before bond interest and income tax from $300,000 to $500,000.

Your sister has asked you, as the company treasurer, to prepare an analysis of each financing plan.

Instructions:

1. Prepare a tabulation indicating the expected earnings per share on the common stock under each plan. Assume an income tax rate of 40%.

2. a. ▇▇ ▸ Discuss the factors that should be considered in evaluating the two plans.

   b. ▇▇ ▸ Which plan offers the greater benefit to the present stockholders? Give reasons for your opinion.

ST Bottling Co.
Balance Sheet
December 31, 19—

Assets	
Current assets	$2,350,000
Plant assets	5,150,000
Total assets	$7,500,000

Liabilities and Stockholders' Equity	
Current liabilities	$2,000,000
Common stock, $20	600,000
Paid-in capital in excess of par	150,000
Retained earnings	4,750,000
Total liabilities and stockholders' equity	$7,500,000

COMPREHENSIVE PROBLEM 5

Selected transactions completed by Walton Inc. during the fiscal year ending March 31, 1994, were as follows:

a. Issued 5,000 shares of $25 par common stock at $35, receiving cash.

b. Received subscriptions to 5,000 shares of $100 par preferred 8% stock at $110, collecting one-half of the subscription price.

c. Collected the remaining one-half of the subscriptions for the preferred stock and issued the 5,000 shares of preferred stock.

d. Declared a dividend of $0.25 per share on common stock and $2 per share on preferred stock. On the date of record, 100,000 shares of common stock were outstanding, no treasury shares were held, and 15,000 shares of preferred stock were outstanding.

e. Paid the cash dividends declared in (d).

f. Redeemed $500,000 of 8-year, 13% bonds at 98. The balance in the bond discount account is $3,900 after the payment of interest and amortization of discount have been recorded. (Record only the redemption of the bonds payable.)

g. Transferred $500,000 of the appropriation for bonded indebtedness back to retained earnings for the bonds redeemed in (f).

h. Purchased 2,000 shares of treasury common stock at $40 per share.

i. Issued $1,000,000 of 10-year, 12% bonds at an effective interest rate of 10%, with interest payable semiannually.

j.   Declared a 5% stock dividend on common stock and a $2 cash dividend per share on preferred stock. On the date of declaration, the market value of the common stock was $41 per share. On the date of record, 100,000 shares of common stock were outstanding, 2,000 shares of treasury common stock were held, and 15,000 shares of preferred stock were outstanding.

k.   Issued the stock certificates for the stock dividends declared in (j) and paid the cash dividends to the preferred stockholders.

l.   Sold, at $45 per share, 1,000 shares of treasury common stock purchased in (h).

m.   Purchased $50,000 of Hanson Inc. 10-year, 15% bonds, directly from the issuing company, for $48,500 plus accrued interest of $1,875.

n.   Recorded the payment of semiannual interest on the bonds issued in (i) and the amortization of the premium for six months. The amortization was determined using the straight-line method. (Round the amortization to the nearest dollar.)

o.   Deposited $20,000 in a bond sinking fund.

p.   Appropriated $50,000 of retained earnings for bonded indebtedness.

q.   Accrued interest for four months on the Hanson Inc. bonds purchased in (m). Also recorded amortization of $50.

Instructions

1.   Journalize the selected transactions.
2.   After all of the transactions for the year ended March 31, 1994, had been posted (including the transactions recorded in (1) and all adjusting entries), the following data were selected from the records of Walton Inc.:

Income statement data:

Advertising expense	$ 85,000
Delivery expense	17,000
Depreciation expense—office equipment	13,100
Depreciation expense—store equipment	45,000
Gain on redemption of bonds	6,100
Income tax:	
Applicable to continuing operations	308,975
Applicable to loss from disposal of a	
segment of the business	21,100
Applicable to gain from redemption of bonds	1,150
Interest expense	68,500
Interest income	675
Loss from disposal of a segment of the business	80,500
Merchandise inventory (April 1, 1993)	375,000
Merchandise inventory (March 31, 1994)	425,000
Miscellaneous administrative expenses	1,600
Miscellaneous selling expenses	6,300
Office rent expense	25,000
Office salaries expense	85,000
Office supplies expense	5,300
Purchases	4,050,000
Sales	5,500,000
Sales commissions	95,000
Sales salaries expense	280,000
Store supplies expense	9,500

Retained earnings and balance sheet data:

Accounts payable	$ 149,500
Accounts receivable	280,500
Accumulated depreciation—office equipment	835,250
Accumulated depreciation—store equipment	2,214,750
Allowance for doubtful accounts	11,500
Bond sinking fund cash	20,000
Bonds payable, 12%, due 2003	1,000,000
Cash	125,500
Common stock, $25 par (400,000 shares authorized; 104,900	
shares outstanding)	2,622,500
Deferred income tax payable (current portion, $4,700)	25,700

Dividends:	
Cash dividends for common stock	$ 100,000
Cash dividends for preferred stock	110,000
Stock dividends for common stock	200,900
Dividends payable	25,000
Income tax payable	55,900
Interest receivable	2,500
Investment in Hanson Inc. bonds (long-term)	48,550
Marketable securities at cost, held as a short-term investment (market value, $80,500)	77,500
Merchandise inventory (March 31, 1994), at lower of cost (fifo) or market	425,000
Office equipment	2,410,100
Organization costs	55,000
Paid-in capital from sale of treasury stock	5,000
Paid-in capital in excess of par—common stock	325,000
Paid-in capital in excess of par—preferred stock	240,000
Preferred 8% stock, $100 par (30,000 shares authorized; 15,000 shares issued)	1,500,000
Premium on bonds payable	118,400
Prepaid expenses	15,900
Retained earnings:	
Appropriated for bonded indebtedness (April 1, 1993)	500,000
Appropriated for bonded indebtedness (March 31, 1994)	50,000
Appropriated for treasury stock (April 1, 1993)	—
Appropriated for treasury stock (March 31, 1994)	40,000
Unappropriated, April 1, 1993	2,485,950
Store equipment	8,603,950
Treasury stock (1,000 shares of common stock at cost of $40 per share)	40,000

a. Prepare a multiple-step income statement for the year ended March 31, 1994, concluding with earnings per share. In computing earnings per share, assume that the average number of common shares outstanding was 100,000 and preferred dividends were $110,000. Round to nearest cent.

b. Prepare a retained earnings statement for the year ended March 31, 1994.

c. Prepare a balance sheet in report form as of March 31, 1994.

SOLUTIONS SOFTWARE

Instructions for Solving Comprehensive Problem 5 Using Solutions Software

1. Load opening balances.
2. Save the opening balances file to your drive and directory.
3. Set the run date to March 31, 1994, and enter your name.
4. Select the General Journal Entries option and key the journal entries, including the adjusting entries for the amortization of premium on the bonds payable, accrued interest income, and the amortization of discount on the bond investment.
5. Display a journal entries report.
6. Display a trial balance.
7. Display the financial statements.
8. Save a backup copy of your data file.
9. Perform period-end closing.
10. Display a post-closing trial balance.
11. Save your data file to disk.
12. End the session.

ANSWERS TO SELF-EXAMINATION QUESTIONS

1. **B** Since the contract rate on the bonds is higher than the prevailing market rate, a rational investor would be willing to pay more than the face amount, or a premium (answer B), for the bonds. If the contract rate and the market rate were equal, the bonds could be expected to sell at their face amount (answer A). Likewise, if the market rate is higher than the contract rate, the bonds would sell at a price below their face amount (answer D) or at a discount (answer C).

2. **A** The bond carrying amount, sometimes called the book value, is the face amount plus unamortized premium or less unamortized discount. For this question, the carrying amount is $500,000 less $40,000, or $460,000 (answer A).

3. **B** Although the sinking fund may consist of cash as well as securities, the fund is listed on the balance sheet as an investment (answer B) because it is to be used to pay the long-term liability at maturity.

4. **B** The amount debited to the investment account is the cost of the bonds, which includes the amount paid to the seller for the bonds (101% × $100,000) plus broker's commissions ($50), or $101,050 (answer B). The $2,000 of accrued interest that is paid to the seller should be debited to Interest Income, since it is an offset against the amount that will be received as interest at the next interest date.

5. **C** The balance of Discount on Bonds Payable is usually reported as a deduction from Bonds Payable in the Long-Term Liabilities section (answer C) of the balance sheet. Likewise, a balance in a premium on bonds payable account would usually be reported as an addition to Bonds Payable in the Long-Term Liabilities section of the balance sheet.

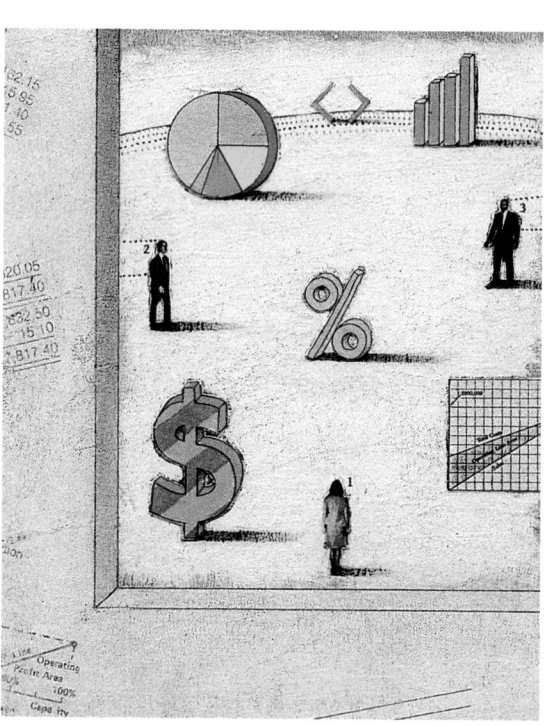

You and Accounting

If you converted 100 U.S. dollars to German deutsche marks, how much foreign currency would you receive? The answer to this question is essential for anyone traveling to Germany. The amount you would receive for $100 of U.S. currency is 165.79 marks.

The amount of German marks received for 100 U.S. dollars was determined by multiplying $100 by the proper exchange rate (1.6579) from a foreign exchange table such as the following:

	Dollar
Canada	1.1854
France	5.6360
Germany	1.6579
Italy	1244.0
Japan	129.80
Switzerland	1.5055
United Kingdom	.57488

Source: *The Wall Street Journal*, February 26, 1992.

If you ordered merchandise priced in a foreign currency, you would also need to be able to determine the equivalent price in U.S. dollars. For example, assume that you ordered a place setting of china from a British firm for an advertised price of 89 pounds. How much is this in U.S. dollars? The answer is $154.81, which is calculated by dividing the amount of foreign currency (89 pounds) by the exchange rate (.57488).

Many business enterprises enter into transactions with foreign companies. Computations such as those shown on the previous page are required to determine the amounts to be received and paid. Among other topics, this chapter discusses the accounting for international transactions.

Chapter 18
Investments in Stocks; Consolidated Statements; International Operations

The principles of accounting for long-term investments in bonds were discussed in an earlier chapter. This chapter focuses on long-term investments in stocks, including the accounting for business combinations.

LEARNING OBJECTIVES
After studying this chapter, you should be able to:

Objective 1
Explain why and how business enterprises make long-term investments in stocks.

Objective 2
Journalize entries for long-term investments in stocks, using the cost method and the equity method.

Objective 3
List and describe three alternative methods of combining businesses.

Objective 4
Describe consolidated financial statements.

Objective 5
Prepare consolidated financial statements, using the purchase method and the pooling-of-interests method.

Objective 6
Prepare a consolidated balance sheet and a statement of stockholders' equity.

Objective 7
Journalize entries for international transactions.

INVESTMENTS IN STOCKS

Objective 1
Explain why and how business
enterprises make long-term
investments in stocks.

A business may purchase long-term investments in **equity securities** (preferred
stock and common stock) for a variety of reasons. One reason may be that the enterprise has excess cash that it does not need for normal operations. A corporation
may also purchase stocks as a means of developing or maintaining business relationships with the issuing company. In other cases, a corporation may purchase
voting stock of another corporation in order to gain control of its activities. Likewise, a corporation may organize a new corporation for other business purposes,
such as developing a new product line.

Investments in stocks are purchased either directly from the issuing corporation or from other investors. Preferred and common stocks may be listed on an organized stock exchange or they may be unlisted. Stocks that are unlisted are said
to be bought or sold *over the counter*. The services of a stockbroker are usually used
in buying and selling both listed and unlisted securities.

A record of the purchases and sales of a corporation's stock on a stock exchange is reported daily in the financial press. This record usually includes each
stock's high and low price for the past year, the current annual dividend, the volume of sales for the day, and the high, low, and closing price for the day. Prices for
stocks are quoted in fractional dollars, such as ½, ⅛, or 1/16 of a dollar. Thus, a price
of 40½ per share equals $40.50; a price of 40⅜ equals $40.375.

The following paragraphs discuss the principles underlying the accounting for
investments in stocks that are not intended as a ready source of cash in the normal
operations of a business. Such investments are identified as long-term investments and are reported in the balance sheet under the caption *Investments*.

ACCOUNTING FOR LONG-TERM INVESTMENTS IN STOCK

Objective 2
Journalize entries for long-term
investments in stocks, using the
cost method and the equity
method.

There are two methods of accounting for long-term investments in stock: (1) the
cost method and (2) the **equity method**. The method used depends upon whether
the investor has a significant influence over the operating and financing activities
of the company (the investee) whose stock is owned. If the investor does not have
a significant influence, the cost method is used. If the investor has a significant influence, the equity method is used. Evidence of such influence includes the percentage of ownership, the existence of intercompany transactions, and the
interchange of managerial personnel. A general guideline used to determine
whether significant influence exists is as follows:

*". . . [An] investment (direct or indirect) of 20% or more of the voting stock of an investee
should lead to a presumption that . . . an investor has the ability to exercise significant influence over an investee. Conversely, an investment of less than 20% of the voting stock of
an investee should lead to a presumption that an investor does not have the ability to exercise significant influence. . . ."*[1]

Cost Method

As with the purchase of other assets, the cost of stocks purchased includes all expenditures necessary to acquire the stocks. For example, the cost of stocks
includes not only the amount paid to the seller, but also such costs as a broker's
commission. The total cost of a stock purchased is debited to an investment
account.

A stock may be purchased between the dividend dates, that is, the date of declaration, the date of record, or the date of payment. For example, when a stock is
purchased between the date of declaration and the date of record, the *buyer* owns
the stock on the date of record. Therefore, the buyer receives the dividend. In the
financial press, a stock that is selling between the dividend's declaration date and
the date of record is reported as selling *with dividends*.

[1] *Opinions of the Accounting Principles Board, No. 18*, "The Equity Method of Accounting for Investments in
Common Stock" (New York: American Institute of Certified Public Accountants, 1971), par. 17.

When a stock is purchased between the date of record and the date of payment, the *seller* owns the stock on the date of record. Therefore, the seller receives the dividend. A stock that is selling between the date of record and the date of payment is reported as selling *ex-dividends* in the financial press.

When a stock is purchased between the declaration date and the date of record (with dividends), the buyer debits a dividends receivable account for the amount of the dividend and an investment in stock account for the remainder of the purchase price. When the dividend is received, the cash account is debited and the dividends receivable account is credited.

To illustrate, assume that Lee Inc. purchases 1,000 common shares of Murphy Corporation stock on June 5 for $46,850. Further, assume that a dividend of $1.20 per share has been declared on June 1, payable on July 31 to stockholders of record on June 30. The entries to record the purchase of the stock and the receipt of the dividend ($1.20 × 1,000 shares) are as follows:

Purchase of Murphy Corp. common stock	June 5	Investment in Murphy Corp. Stock	45,650	
		Dividends Receivable	1,200	
		Cash		46,850

| Receipt of cash dividends on Murphy Corp. common stock | July 31 | Cash | 1,200 | |
| | | Dividends Receivable | | 1,200 |

After the date of purchase, cash dividends may be declared and received on capital stock held as an investment. When the cost method is used, such dividends are recorded as an increase (debit) to an asset account and an increase (credit) to a dividend income account.

To illustrate, assume that on March 1 Makowski Corporation purchases 100 shares of Compton Corporation common stock at 59 plus a brokerage fee of $40. On April 30, Compton Corporation declares a $2 per share cash dividend payable on June 15 to stockholders of record on May 15. The entries in the accounts of Makowski Corporation to record the purchase of the stock and the receipt of the dividends are as follows:

| Purchase of Compton Corp. common stock | Mar. 1 | Investment in Compton Corp. Stock | 5,940 | |
| | | Cash | | 5,940 |

| Receipt of cash dividends on Compton Corp. common stock | June 15 | Cash | 200 | |
| | | Dividend Income | | 200 |

A dividend in the form of additional shares of stock (a stock dividend) is not considered income to the investor. Thus, no entry is needed beyond a notation as to the additional number of shares received. The receipt of a stock dividend does, however, affect the carrying value (book value) of each share of stock. For example, assume that a 5-share common stock dividend is received on 100 shares of common stock acquired at $42 per share, or $4,200. The book value of the stock before the stock dividend is $42 per share. After the receipt of the stock dividend, the book value is $40 per share ($4,200 ÷ 105 shares).

Under the cost method, investments in stocks are reported in the financial statements using a lower-of-cost-or-market rule. This rule is applied on the balance sheet date to all stock investments taken as a whole. If the total cost of the investments is lower than the total market value, no special reporting is necessary. If the total market value is lower, the investments are reported at the market value. The decrease in value is not, however, reported on the income statement as a loss.

Instead, the decrease in value is reported as a separate item in the Stockholders' Equity section of the balance sheet.[2]

An exception to the preceding lower-of-cost-or-market rule is made if the decrease in the market value for an individual stock is considered a permanent decrease. This might be the case, for example, if a corporation has filed for bankruptcy. In this case, the carrying amount (cost) of the individual stock is written down (decreased), and the amount of the write-down is reported as a loss on the income statement. After the write-down, the revised carrying value of the individual stock is treated as its cost and is not increased for later recoveries in market value.[3]

Equity Method

Under the equity method, a stock purchase is recorded at its cost in the same manner as if the cost method were used. The equity method, however, is different from the cost method in the way in which net income and cash dividends of the investee are recorded. The equity method of recording these items is summarized below.

1. The investor's share of the periodic net income of the investee is recorded as an increase in the investment account on the balance sheet. This increase is also recorded on the income statement as revenue for the period. Likewise, the investor's share of an investee's net loss is recorded as a decrease in the investment and as a loss for the period.
2. The investor's share of cash dividends is recorded as an increase in the cash account and a decrease in the investment account.

To illustrate, assume that on January 2, Hally Inc. pays cash of $350,000 for 40% of the common (voting) stock of Brock Corporation. Assume also that, for the year ending December 31, Brock Corporation reports net income of $105,000 and declares and pays $45,000 in dividends. Using the equity method, Hally Inc. (the investor) records these transactions as follows:

Purchase of 40% of Brock Corp. common stock	Jan. 2	Investment in Brock Corp. Stock Cash	350,000	350,000
Share (40%) of Brock Corp. net income of $105,000	Dec. 31	Investment in Brock Corp. Stock Income of Brock Corp.	42,000	42,000
Share (40%) of cash dividends of $45,000 paid by Brock Corp.	Dec. 31	Cash Investment in Brock Corp. Stock	18,000	18,000

The combined effect of recording 40% of Brock Corporation's net income and dividends is to increase Cash by $18,000, Investment in Brock Corp. Stock by $24,000, and Income of Brock Corp. by $42,000.

Sale of Long-Term Investments in Stocks

When shares of stock are sold, the investment account is credited for the carrying value of the shares sold. The cash or receivable account is debited for the proceeds (sales price less commission and other selling costs). Any difference between the proceeds and the carrying value is recorded as a gain or loss on the sale.

---

[2] *Statement of Financial Accounting Standards, No. 12*, "Accounting for Certain Marketable Securities" (Stamford: Financial Accounting Standards Board, 1975), par. 11.
[3] *Ibid.*, par. 21.

To illustrate, assume that an investment in Drey Inc. stock has a carrying value of $15,700. If the proceeds from the sale of the stock are $17,500, the entry to record the transaction is as follows:

Cash	17,500	
Investment in Drey Inc. Stock		15,700
Gain on Sale of Investments		1,800

BUSINESS COMBINATIONS

Objective 3
List and describe three alternative methods of combining businesses.

Each year many business enterprises combine to achieve such objectives as efficiencies of large-scale production, broadening of markets, increased sales volume, diversification of product lines, and savings in income taxes. For example, in one year in the United States, more than 3,500 combinations took place involving the exchange of cash, debt obligations, or capital stock of roughly $170 billion.[4]

The combining of businesses is often announced to the public in the financial press. For example, the announcement shown in Exhibit 1 appeared in *The Wall Street Journal* on February 26, 1992, when Great Northern Paper, Inc., was acquired by Bowater Incorporated.

Exhibit 1
Announcement of a Business Combination

Bowater Incorporated

has acquired

Great Northern Paper, Inc.

from

Georgia-Pacific Corporation

———————

*The undersigned assisted in the negotiations
and acted as financial advisor
to Bowater Incorporated.*

LIPPER & COMPANY

February 26, 1992

A business combination may occur through a merger or consolidation, in which two or more corporations are combined to form a single unit. Two or more corporations may also combine by means of stock ownership, in which a parent-

---

[4] "Takeovers + Divestitures: Full Speed Ahead," Edward T. O'Toole, *Barron's*, May 23, 1988.

subsidiary relationship is created. Each of these types of combinations is discussed in the following paragraphs.

Mergers and Consolidations

A **merger** is the joining of two enterprises in which one corporation acquires the properties of another corporation that is then dissolved. Usually, all of the assets and liabilities of the acquired company are taken over by the acquiring company. The acquiring enterprise may use cash, debt obligations, or its own capital stock as the form of payment. Whatever the form of payment, the amount received by the dissolving corporation is distributed to its stockholders in final liquidation.

A **consolidation** is the creation of a new corporation, to which is transferred the assets and liabilities of two or more existing corporations. The new corporation usually issues its own stock in exchange for the net assets acquired. The original corporations are then dissolved.

The Language of Hostile Takeovers

In some ways, business can be viewed as a game in which winners or losers are determined by profits and losses. Businesses combine to form stronger, more diverse organizations as part of this game. In the past two decades, however, many mergers have been viewed as *takeovers* because they are considered *unfriendly* or *hostile* to the current management. Individuals attempting the takeover are called *raiders*. The following excerpts from an article in *Management Accounting* describe some of the unique language that characterizes these types of takeovers.

Bear hug. Slang term for a takeover.

Crown jewels. Vital assets of a target company; jewels can be high-technology equipment, certain securities or investments, or even key personnel.

Golden parachutes. An amount of money paid to an executive of a merged company for services previously rendered; this amount is paid only after a merger in the event that the executive decides to leave the merged entity.

Tin parachute. Similar to, though smaller than, a golden parachute; it is a sum of money paid to any employee whose job is adversely affected by a takeover.

Pac-Man defense. A technique in which the targeted company attempts to purchase controlling interest in the raiding company before the raiding company can purchase a controlling interest in the target.

Shark repellents. Provisions introduced into corporate bylaws that make it more difficult for a prospective shareholder to obtain a majority of the outstanding stock.

Poison pills. An overall term used to encompass all types of shark repellents.

White knight. A company that comes to the aid of another company that is attempting to fend off a hostile tender offer; the targeted company allows itself to be acquired in a friendly takeover by the white knight.

Source: Cecily Raiborn, Dinah Payne, and Chandra Schorg, "It Helps to Know How to Play the Game," *Management Accounting* (March 1991), p. 31.

Parent and Subsidiary Corporations

Business combinations may also occur when one corporation buys a controlling share of the outstanding voting stock of one or more other corporations. In this case, none of the participating corporations dissolve. All continue as separate legal entities. The corporation owning all or a majority of the voting stock of the other corporation is called the **parent company**. The corporation that is controlled is called the **subsidiary company**. Two or more corporations closely related through stock ownership are sometimes called **affiliated** or **associated** companies.

In accounting terms, parent and subsidiary relationships are created by either a *purchase* or a *pooling of interests*. A corporation may acquire the controlling share of the voting common stock of another corporation by paying cash, exchanging other assets, issuing debt, or some combination of these methods. The stockholders of the acquired company, in turn, transfer their stock to the parent corporation. In such cases, the transaction is recorded like a normal purchase of assets and the combination is accounted for by the **purchase method**.

A parent-subsidiary relationship may be created by exchanging the voting common stock of the acquiring corporation (the parent) for the common stock of the acquired corporation (the subsidiary). If at least 90% of the stock of the subsidiary is acquired in this way, the transaction is called a **pooling of interests** and the combination is accounted for by the **pooling-of-interests method.** In a pooling of interests, the stockholders of the acquired company (the subsidiary) become stockholders of the acquiring company (the parent).

The accounting for a purchase and a pooling of interests are significantly different. A purchase is accounted for as a *sale-purchase* transaction, while a pooling of interests is accounted for as a *joining of ownership interests*.

Generally accepted accounting principles set forth very strict criteria that must be met before the pooling-of-interests method can be used.[5] As a result, only a few business combinations are accounted for by the pooling-of-interests method. The 1991 edition of *Accounting Trends & Techniques* reported that 95% of the business combinations surveyed were accounted for by the purchase method.

NATURE OF CONSOLIDATED FINANCIAL STATEMENTS

Objective 4
Describe consolidated financial statements.

Although the corporations that make up a parent-subsidiary affiliation may operate as a single economic unit, they continue to maintain separate accounting records and prepare their own periodic financial statements. The parent corporation uses the equity method of accounting for its investment in the stock of a subsidiary.

After the parent-subsidiary relationship has been established, the investment account of the parent is increased by its share of the subsidiary's net income and decreased by its share of dividends received from the subsidiary. At the end of each fiscal year, the parent reports the investment account balance on its own balance sheet as a long-term investment. The parent reports its share of the subsidiary's net income on its own income statement as a separate item.

In addition to the interrelationship through stock ownership, there are usually other intercompany transactions that have an effect on the financial statements of both the parent and the subsidiary. For example, either may own bonds or other debt issued by the other, and either may purchase or sell goods or services to the other.

The results of operations and the financial position of a parent company and its subsidiaries should usually be presented as if the group were a single company. Such statements are more meaningful to stockholders of the parent company than separate statements for each corporation. This is because the parent company, *in substance*, controls the subsidiaries, even though the parent and its subsidiaries are separate entities.

The financial statements resulting from the combining of parent and subsidiary statements are called **consolidated statements.** Such statements are usually identified by the addition of "and subsidiary(ies)" to the name of the parent corporation, or by addition of "consolidated" to the statement title.[6]

PREPARATION OF CONSOLIDATED FINANCIAL STATEMENTS

Objective 5
Prepare consolidated financial statements, using the purchase method and the pooling-of-interests method.

When the data on the financial statements of the parent corporation and its subsidiaries are combined to form the consolidated statements, special attention should be given to intercompany transactions. Intercompany transactions by their very nature affect accounts on the ledgers of both the parent and its subsidiary. For example, assume that the parent company issued a $200,000 note to its subsidiary for cash. In this case, the parent's ledger would include Notes Payable with a $200,000 balance. Likewise, the subsidiary's ledger would include Notes Receivable with a balance of $200,000. The corresponding accounts in the parent's and subsidiary's ledgers are sometimes called **reciprocal accounts.**[7] Examples of other accounts often affected by intercompany transactions include accounts re-

---

[5] *Opinions of the Accounting Principles Board, No. 16*, "Business Combinations" (New York: American Institute of Certified Public Accountants, 1970).
[6] Examples of actual consolidated statements are presented in Appendix G.
[7] In some cases, the intercompany accounts on the ledgers of the parent and its subsidiaries may not be entirely reciprocal or equal in amount. Such differences are discussed in advanced accounting textbooks.

ceivable and accounts payable, interest receivable and interest payable, sales and purchases (or cost of merchandise sold), and interest expense and interest income.

The effects of intercompany transactions must be eliminated when the financial statements of the parent and subsidiary are consolidated. For example, the preceding reciprocal accounts—the $200,000 note receivable and note payable—must be eliminated when consolidated financial statements are prepared. This is because consolidated financial statements are prepared as if the parent and subsidiary are one operating unit. Thus, in the preceding example, an entity cannot owe itself $200,000 on a note.

The eliminations referred to above are not actually recorded in the ledgers of the parent and the subsidiary. Rather, the effects of intercompany transactions are eliminated only in preparing the consolidated financial statements. A work sheet, as discussed later, is often used as an aid in preparing consolidated financial statements and in eliminating the effects of intercompany transactions.

After the intercompany transactions have been eliminated, the remaining items on the financial statements of the parent and subsidiary are combined (consolidated) for purposes of the consolidated financial statements. In order to simplify the following examples, the term *net assets* will be used in place of the specific assets and liabilities of the parent and subsidiary. The illustrative companies will be identified as Parent and Subsidiary.

Purchase Method—Date of Acquisition

Under the purchase method, the basic principles of accounting for a sale-purchase transaction are used in accounting for a business combination. At the date of acquisition, the parent debits its investment in subsidiary account for the fair market value of the assets used to acquire the subsidiary's stock. In preparing the consolidated balance sheet, the subsidiary's net assets are reported using this fair market value. Any difference between the fair market value and the book value of the subsidiary's net assets is recognized in preparing the consolidated balance sheet.

WHOLLY OWNED (100%) SUBSIDIARY. Assume that Parent creates Subsidiary by transferring to it $120,000 of assets and $20,000 of liabilities. Parent receives in exchange 10,000 shares of $10 par common stock of Subsidiary. Parent debits Investment in Subsidiary for the net assets transferred, $100,000 ($120,000 − $20,000). The effect of this transaction on Parent's ledger is to show Subsidiary's various assets and liabilities (net assets of $100,000) in a single account: Investment in Subsidiary, $100,000. Parent's investment in subsidiary account and the balance sheet data of Subsidiary immediately after the transaction are shown below.

	Assets	Stockholders' Equity
Parent:		
Investment in Subsidiary, 10,000 shares	$100,000	
Subsidiary:		
Net assets	$100,000	
Common stock, 10,000 shares, $10 par		$100,000

When the balance sheets of the two corporations are consolidated, the reciprocal accounts are eliminated. In this illustration, the two reciprocal accounts are Parent's Investment in Subsidiary and Subsidiary's Common Stock. Subsidiary's net assets (Cash, Equipment, etc.) are then added to Parent's net assets (Cash, Equipment, etc.). The consolidated balance sheet is completed by listing Parent's paid-in capital accounts and retained earnings.

Instead of creating a new subsidiary, a corporation may acquire an existing corporation by purchasing all its stock. In such cases, the stock's total cost to the parent usually differs from the book value of the subsidiary's net assets.

To illustrate, assume that Parent acquires for $180,000 all of the outstanding stock of Subsidiary. Assume also that the book value of Subsidiary's net assets is $150,000 and that the stockholders' equity of Subsidiary consists of common stock, $100,000 (10,000 shares, $10 par) and retained earnings, $50,000. Under the purchase method, Parent debits Investment in Subsidiary for the total cost of acquiring subsidiary's stock, $180,000, even though the book value of Subsidiary's net assets is only $150,000. The effect of the transaction on Parent and Subsidiary is shown below.

	Assets	Stockholders' Equity
Parent:		
Investment in Subsidiary, 10,000 shares	$180,000	
Subsidiary:		
Net assets	$150,000	
Common stock, 10,000 shares, $10 par		$100,000
Retained earnings		50,000

The purchase transaction does not affect Subsidiary's ledger and its accounts. However, the balance of Parent's investment in subsidiary account differs from Parent's share of the book value of Subsidiary's stockholders' equity. This difference in reciprocal accounts is $30,000 ($180,000 – $150,000). Thus, if the reciprocal accounts are eliminated against each other in preparing the consolidated balance sheet, the consolidated balance sheet would be out of balance by $30,000.

The accounting for the $30,000 difference depends upon the reason that Parent paid more than book value for its interest in Subsidiary. Parent may have paid more than book value because the fair value of Subsidiary's assets exceeds the book value of its assets. In this case, the book value of the assets should be revised upward by $30,000.

To illustrate, assume that Subsidiary acquired land several years ago at a cost of $50,000 (book value). The land now has a current market value of $80,000. In this case, the land's book value should be increased from $50,000 to $80,000 in preparing the consolidated balance sheet.

Parent may have paid more than book value because Subsidiary has prospects for high future earnings. In this case, the $30,000 difference is reported on the consolidated balance sheet as an intangible asset. This asset is identified as *Goodwill* or *Excess of cost of business acquired over related net assets.*

Parent may have paid more than book value because of both an excess of market value over book value of assets and prospects for high future earnings. In this case, the difference of cost over book value is allocated among the assets and goodwill.[8]

To illustrate, assume that the $30,000 difference is due to a $20,000 excess of market value over book value of Subsidiary's land. The remaining difference is due to Subsidiary prospects for high future earnings. In this case, the book value of the land is increased from $50,000 to $70,000. In addition, goodwill of $10,000 is reported on the consolidated balance sheet.

All of the stock of a corporation may be acquired from its stockholders at a cost that is less than its book value. In this case, the parent has acquired the subsidiary at an apparent *bargain purchase*. The accounting and the reasons for the difference are generally the opposite of those explained above. Since this type of purchase rarely occurs in practice, it is not illustrated.

PARTIALLY OWNED SUBSIDIARY. One corporation may gain control over another corporation by purchase of its stock. However, it may not be necessary or even possible to acquire all of the stock. To illustrate, assume that Parent acquires 80% of the stock of Subsidiary for $190,000. Subsidiary's stockholders' equity consists of

[8] *Opinions of the Accounting Principles Board, No. 16, op. cit.,* par. 87.

common stock of $100,000 (10,000 shares, $10 par) and retained earnings of $80,000. The balance sheet data immediately after the stock is acquired is as follows:

	Assets	Stockholders' Equity
Parent:		
Investment in Subsidiary, 8,000 shares	$190,000	
Subsidiary:		
Net assets	$180,000	
Common stock, 10,000 shares, $10 par		$100,000
Retained earnings		80,000

The analysis of the $10,000 difference between the investment in subsidiary account and the book value of Subsidiary's stockholders' equity is more complex than in the preceding example. There are two reasons for this:

1. The amount paid for the stock is greater than 80% of the book value of Subsidiary's stockholders' equity.
2. Only 80% of Subsidiary's stock was purchased.

Since Parent acquired 8,000 shares or 80% of Subsidiary's outstanding stock, only 80% of the stockholders' equity of Subsidiary is eliminated. The remaining 20% of Subsidiary's stockholders' equity is owned by outsiders. These outsiders are called the **minority interest.** The amounts eliminated and reported on the consolidated balance sheet are shown below.

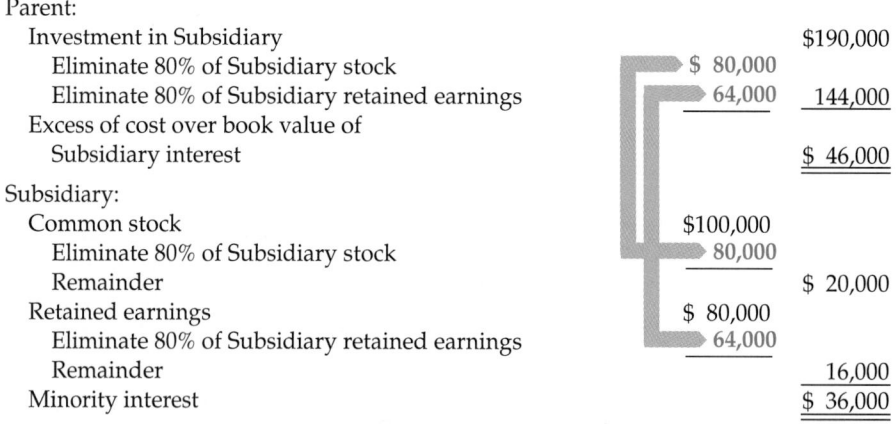

Parent:			
Investment in Subsidiary			$190,000
Eliminate 80% of Subsidiary stock		$ 80,000	
Eliminate 80% of Subsidiary retained earnings		64,000	144,000
Excess of cost over book value of Subsidiary interest			$ 46,000
Subsidiary:			
Common stock		$100,000	
Eliminate 80% of Subsidiary stock		80,000	
Remainder			$ 20,000
Retained earnings		$ 80,000	
Eliminate 80% of Subsidiary retained earnings		64,000	
Remainder			16,000
Minority interest			$ 36,000

The excess of cost over Parent's interest in the book value of Subsidiary is $46,000. This is the amount by which the book values of Subsidiary's net assets are increased to their market values or goodwill is recognized in preparing the consolidated balance sheet.

The minority interest of $36,000 is the amount of Subsidiary's book value owned by outsiders. Minority interest is reported on the consolidated balance sheet, usually preceding stockholders' equity. The 1991 edition of *Accounting Trends & Techniques* indicates that most of the companies surveyed reported minority interest in the Long-Term Liabilities section.

Purchase Method—Subsequent to Acquisition

After a subsidiary is acquired, the parent company uses the equity method to account for its investment in the subsidiary. Thus, the parent company's investment account increases each year for its share of the subsidiary's earnings. Likewise, the parent's investment account decreases for any dividends received. Through its normal operations, the subsidiary's retained earnings account also increases for yearly net income and decreases for dividends. Thus, the eliminations required in preparing the consolidated balance sheet will change each year.

To illustrate, assume the same data as in the preceding illustration, where Parent acquired 80% of Subsidiary's common stock. Also assume that in the year after the acquisition, Subsidiary earned net income of $50,000 and paid dividends of $20,000. The net effect of the subsequent year's transactions on Subsidiary is shown below.

	Net Assets	Common Stock	Retained Earnings
Subsidiary:			
Date of acquisition	$180,000	$100,000	$ 80,000
Add net income	50,000		50,000
Deduct dividends	(20,000)		(20,000)
Date subsequent to acquisition	$210,000	$100,000	$110,000

Parent's entries to record its 80% share of Subsidiary's net income and dividends are as follows:

Investment in Subsidiary	40,000	
Income of Subsidiary		40,000
Cash	16,000	
Investment in Subsidiary		16,000

The net effect of the above entries on Parent's investment in subsidiary account is to increase its balance by $24,000. This effect is shown below.

Parent:
  Investment in subsidiary, 8,000 shares:

Date of acquisition		$190,000
Add 80% of Subsidiary's net income	$40,000	
Deduct 80% of Subsidiary's dividends	(16,000)	24,000
One year subsequent to acquisition		$214,000

The amounts eliminated in preparing the consolidated balance sheet are shown below. The amounts reported on the consolidated balance sheet are also shown.

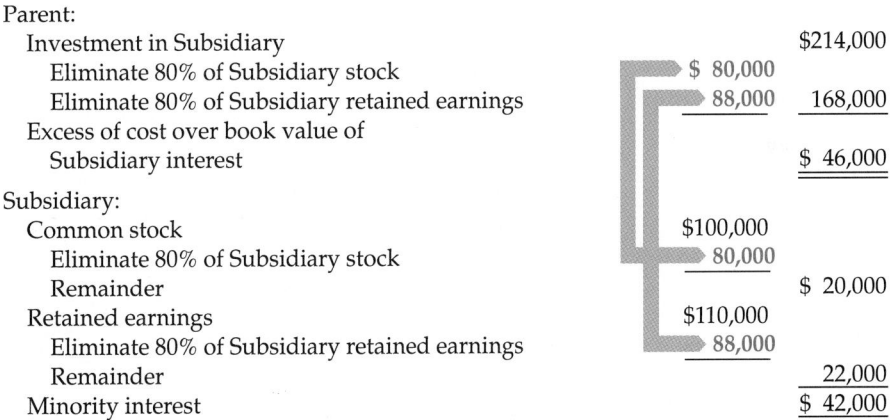

Parent:		
Investment in Subsidiary		$214,000
Eliminate 80% of Subsidiary stock	$ 80,000	
Eliminate 80% of Subsidiary retained earnings	88,000	168,000
Excess of cost over book value of		
Subsidiary interest		$ 46,000
Subsidiary:		
Common stock	$100,000	
Eliminate 80% of Subsidiary stock	80,000	
Remainder		$ 20,000
Retained earnings	$110,000	
Eliminate 80% of Subsidiary retained earnings	88,000	
Remainder		22,000
Minority interest		$ 42,000

A comparison of the consolidated balance sheets on the date of acquisition with one year after acquisition reveals the following:

1. The minority interest increased $6,000 (from $36,000 to $42,000). This is equal to 20% of the $30,000 net increase ($50,000 of net income less $20,000 of dividends) in Subsidiary's retained earnings.
2. The excess of cost over book value of the subsidiary interest remained unchanged at $46,000.

To simplify, it was assumed that the $46,000 excess of cost over book value at the date of acquisition is related to a nondepreciable asset, such as land. Otherwise, this $46,000 excess would be depreciated or amortized as goodwill.

Purchase Method—Consolidated Work Sheet

The preceding discussion focused on the basic concepts of preparing consolidated balance sheets. Consolidation work sheets are often used when the consolidation process becomes complex or when a large amount of data are involved. Such a work sheet is illustrated in Exhibit 2. Whether or not a work sheet is used, the basic concepts and the consolidated balance sheet are not affected.

Exhibit 2
Work Sheet for Consolidated
Balance Sheet—Purchase Method

Parent and Subsidiary
Work Sheet for Consolidated Balance Sheet
December 31, 19—

	Parent	Subsidiary	Eliminations Debit	Eliminations Credit	Consolidated Balance Sheet
Investment in Subsidiary	214,000			(a) 168,000	
				(b) 46,000	
Land	100,000	60,000	(b) 46,000		206,000
Other Assets	400,000	200,000			600,000
	714,000	260,000			806,000
Liabilities	164,000	50,000			214,000
Common Stock:					
Parent	300,000				300,000
Subsidiary		100,000	(a) 80,000		20,000 minority interest
Retained Earnings:					
Parent	250,000				250,000
Subsidiary		110,000	(a) 88,000		22,000 minority interest
	714,000	260,000	214,000	214,000	806,000

To illustrate, assume that Parent had purchased 80% of Subsidiary stock for $190,000. Also, assume that the excess of the cost of the investment over book value is due to the excess of market value over book value of Subsidiary's land. For the year after acquisition, Parent debited the investment account for its share of Subsidiary earnings. Parent also credited the investment account for its share of dividends declared by Subsidiary.

The balance sheet data for Parent and Subsidiary as of December 31 of the year after the acquisition are as follows:

	Parent	Subsidiary
Investment in Subsidiary	$214,000	
Land	100,000	$ 60,000
Other assets	400,000	200,000
	$714,000	$260,000
Liabilities	$164,000	$ 50,000
Common stock:		
Parent	300,000	
Subsidiary		100,000
Retained earnings:		
Parent	250,000	
Subsidiary		110,000
	$714,000	$260,000

The account balances at December 31 are entered on the consolidation work sheet in Exhibit 2. The entries eliminating reciprocal amounts in the Parent and Subsidiary accounts are also entered on the work sheet. The amounts are then extended to the Consolidated Balance Sheet column, as shown in Exhibit 2.

Each of the entries in the Eliminations columns of the work sheet is explained below.

a. This entry eliminates the reciprocal amounts related to Parent's share of Subsidiary's common stock and retained earnings from the investment in subsidiary account. Parent's share of Subsidiary's common stock is $80,000, and Parent's share of the retained earnings is $88,000. The total amount eliminated is $168,000.

   After Parent's share of $80,000 is eliminated, the remaining balance in Subsidiary's common stock account, $20,000, represents minority interest. Likewise, the remaining balance in Subsidiary's retained earnings account, $22,000, represents minority interest. The minority interests are identified in the consolidation work sheet as an aid in preparing the consolidated balance sheet.

b. This entry eliminates the remaining balance of the investment in subsidiary account. This remaining balance represents the excess of cost over Parent's interest in the book value of Subsidiary's net assets. It is allocated to the subsidiary's assets and goodwill, as explained earlier. In this illustration, the $46,000 excess of cost over book value is related to Subsidiary's land. Thus, the land account is debited for $46,000.

Any other intercompany items to be eliminated would also be entered in the Eliminations columns of the work sheet. For example, the face value of a note payable from a subsidiary to its parent would be eliminated from both notes receivable and notes payable in the work sheet.

The consolidated balance sheet for Parent and Subsidiary is shown in Exhibit 3. In this balance sheet, the amount reported for land is $206,000, and the amount reported for minority interest is $42,000. Both of these amounts were identified on the work sheet in Exhibit 2.

Exhibit 3
Consolidated Balance Sheet—
Purchase Method

Parent and Subsidiary Consolidated Balance Sheet December 31, 19—	
Assets	
Land	$206,000
Other assets	600,000
Total assets	$806,000
Liabilities and Stockholders' Equity	
Liabilities	$214,000
Minority interest in subsidiary	42,000
Common stock	300,000
Retained earnings	250,000
Total liabilities and stockholders' equity	$806,000

Pooling-of-Interests Method—Date of Affiliation

When two companies are joined together by the exchange of ownership interests (stock), the business combination is accounted for as a pooling of interests. Thus, a pooling of interests is characterized by an exchange of stock rather than assets.

In a pooling of interests, the parent debits Investment in Subsidiary for the book value of the subsidiary's net assets. Any difference between the book value of the subsidiary's net assets and their fair value is not recorded. This is because, in contrast to the purchase method, the pooling-of-interests method treats the combination as a *joining of ownership interests* rather than as a *sale-purchase transaction*. Since the parent's investment in the subsidiary account equals the parent's share of the book value of the subsidiary's net assets, no *excess of cost over book value* or *excess of book value over cost* exists.

At the date of affiliation, the parent debits its investment in subsidiary account for an amount equal to its share of the book value of the subsidiary's net assets. The parent credits its stockholders' equity accounts for the stock issued.

In addition to the parent's common stock account, its paid-in capital and retained earnings account may be affected. Under the pooling-of-interests concept of the joining of ownership interests, subsidiary earnings accumulated prior to the affiliation should be combined with those of the parent. For purposes of preparing the consolidated balance sheet, it is as though the companies had been operating as a single economic unit from the time the enterprises were initially organized.

To illustrate the pooling-of-interests method, the financial positions of Parent and Subsidiary immediately prior to the exchange of stock are as follows:

	Assets	Stockholders' Equity
Parent:		
Net assets	$230,000	
Common stock, 4,000 shares, $25 par		$100,000
Retained earnings		130,000
Subsidiary:		
Net assets	$150,000	
Common stock, 10,000 shares, $10 par		$100,000
Retained earnings		50,000

To use the pooling-of-interests method, almost all (90% or more) of the stock of the subsidiary must be exchanged. In this illustration, assume that 100% of the stock was exchanged. Also, assume that the market value of the net assets of both companies is greater than their book values shown above and that goodwill exists. Based on negotiations, the managements of both companies agree that Parent's common stock will be valued at $45 a share and Subsidiary's at $18 a share.[9]

According to the agreement, the exchange of stock will be completed as follows:

Parent issues 4,000 shares valued at $45 per share	$180,000
in exchange for	
Subsidiary's 10,000 shares valued at $18 per share	$180,000

Unlike the purchase method, the excess of the $180,000 value of Parent's stock issued over its share (100%) of the book value of Subsidiary's net assets ($150,000) is ignored. Parent records the investment as follows:

Investment in Subsidiary	150,000	
Common Stock		100,000
Retained Earnings		50,000

After the above entry has been recorded, the balance sheet data for the two companies are as follows:

	Assets	Stockholders' Equity
Parent:		
Investment in Subsidiary, 10,000 shares	$150,000	
Other net assets	230,000	
Common stock, 8,000 shares, $25 par		$200,000
Retained earnings		180,000
Subsidiary:		
Net assets	$150,000	
Common stock, 10,000 shares, $10 par		$100,000
Retained earnings		50,000

[9] In practice, it may be necessary to pay cash for fractional shares or for subsidiary shares held by dissenting stockholders.

In preparing the consolidated balance sheet, Parent's investment account and Subsidiary's common stock and retained earnings accounts are eliminated. Under the pooling-of-interests method, the book values of the net assets of the two companies are combined without any change in valuation. Thus, the net assets of the two companies, $230,000 and $150,000, are combined for total consolidated net assets of $380,000. Total consolidated stockholders' equity of $380,000 consists of Parent's common stock of $200,000 and retained earnings of $180,000.

Pooling-of-Interests Method—Subsequent to Affiliation

The equity method is used by the parent corporation in recording changes in its investment account after the acquisition. Thus, the investment in subsidiary account is debited for the parent's share of the subsidiary's earnings and credited for its share of subsidiary dividends.

To illustrate, assume that in the preceding illustration Subsidiary's net income is $20,000 for the first year after the acquisition. Also, assume that dividends of $5,000 are paid during the year. Thus, Parent's investment in subsidiary account increased by $15,000 for Subsidiary's operations during the year. Likewise, Subsidiary's net assets and retained earnings increased by $15,000. At the end of the first year, the account balances are as follows:

	Assets	Stockholders' Equity
Parent:		
Investment in Subsidiary, 10,000 shares	$165,000	
Subsidiary:		
Net assets	$165,000	
Common stock, 10,000 shares, $10 par		$100,000
Retained earnings		65,000

When the balance sheets of Parent and Subsidiary are consolidated, the reciprocal accounts are eliminated. The reciprocal accounts are highlighted in color in the above data. The $165,000 of net assets of Subsidiary are then combined with those of Parent.

Pooling-of-Interests Method—Consolidated Work Sheet

A work sheet may be useful in assembling data for preparing a consolidated balance sheet when the pooling-of-interests method is used. To illustrate, the data from the preceding illustration are used, except that amounts for land, other assets, and liabilities have been added. The total net assets and stockholders' equity amounts, however, are the same as in the preceding illustration. The balance sheet data for Parent and Subsidiary as of December 31 of the year after acquisition are as follows:

	Parent	Subsidiary
Investment in Subsidiary	$165,000	
Land	80,000	$ 40,000
Other assets	325,000	175,000
	$570,000	$215,000
Liabilities	$140,000	$ 50,000
Common stock:		
Parent	200,000	
Subsidiary		100,000
Retained earnings:		
Parent	230,000	
Subsidiary		65,000
	$570,000	$215,000

The account balances at December 31 and the eliminations for the reciprocal accounts have been entered on the work sheet in Exhibit 4.

Exhibit 4
Work Sheet for Consolidated
Balance Sheet—Pooling-of-Interests Method

<table>
<tr><td colspan="6" align="center">Parent and Subsidiary
Work Sheet for Consolidated Balance Sheet
December 31, 19—</td></tr>
<tr><td></td><td></td><td></td><td colspan="2" align="center">*Eliminations*</td><td>*Consolidated*</td></tr>
<tr><td></td><td>*Parent*</td><td>*Subsidiary*</td><td>*Debit*</td><td>*Credit*</td><td>*Balance Sheet*</td></tr>
<tr><td>Investment in Subsidiary</td><td>165,000</td><td></td><td></td><td>165,000</td><td></td></tr>
<tr><td>Land</td><td>80,000</td><td>40,000</td><td></td><td></td><td>120,000</td></tr>
<tr><td>Other Assets</td><td>325,000</td><td>175,000</td><td></td><td></td><td>500,000</td></tr>
<tr><td></td><td>570,000</td><td>215,000</td><td></td><td></td><td>620,000</td></tr>
<tr><td>Liabilities</td><td>140,000</td><td>50,000</td><td></td><td></td><td>190,000</td></tr>
<tr><td>Common Stock:</td><td></td><td></td><td></td><td></td><td></td></tr>
<tr><td> Parent</td><td>200,000</td><td></td><td></td><td></td><td>200,000</td></tr>
<tr><td> Subsidiary</td><td></td><td>100,000</td><td>100,000</td><td></td><td></td></tr>
<tr><td>Retained Earnings:</td><td></td><td></td><td></td><td></td><td></td></tr>
<tr><td> Parent</td><td>230,000</td><td></td><td></td><td></td><td>230,000</td></tr>
<tr><td> Subsidiary</td><td></td><td>65,000</td><td>65,000</td><td></td><td></td></tr>
<tr><td></td><td>570,000</td><td>215,000</td><td>165,000</td><td>165,000</td><td>620,000</td></tr>
</table>

The reciprocal accounts—Subsidiary's Common Stock and Retained Earnings and Parent's Investment in Subsidiary—are eliminated as shown in the Eliminations columns of the work sheet. The accounts for the two companies are then combined and are reported on the consolidated balance sheet.

Consolidated Income Statement and Other Statements

Consolidations of income statements and other statements of affiliated companies are usually simpler to prepare than the consolidated balance sheet. This is largely because of the nature of the statements. The balance sheet reports cumulative effects of all transactions from the very beginning of an enterprise to a current date. In contrast, the income statement, the retained earnings statement, and the statement of cash flows report transactions for a period of time, usually one year.

The consolidation of income statements of a parent and its subsidiaries are the same, regardless of whether the purchase or pooling-of-interests method is used. The effects of all intercompany transactions, such as sales of merchandise, management fees, or interest on loans charged by one company to another, are eliminated. For intercompany sales of merchandise, any profits included in inventories at the end of the year are also eliminated. The remaining amounts for Sales, Cost of Merchandise Sold, Operating Expenses, and Other Revenues and Expenses are then combined. The eliminations required in consolidating the retained earnings statement and other statements are based on data assembled in consolidating the balance sheet and income statement.

CORPORATION FINANCIAL STATEMENTS

Objective 6
Prepare a consolidated balance sheet and a statement of stockholders' equity.

The financial statements for corporate enterprises were described and illustrated in preceding chapters. The consolidated balance sheet in Exhibit 6 illustrates for a corporation the presentation of many of the items discussed in this and preceding chapters. These items include bond sinking funds, investments in bonds, goodwill, deferred income taxes, bonds payable and unamortized discount, minority interest in subsidiaries, and appropriation of retained earnings.

The income statement, the retained earnings statement, and the combined income and retained earnings statement were also illustrated in preceding chapters. In addition to these basic statements, significant changes in stockholders' equity should be reported for the period in which they occur. These changes are often reported in a **statement of stockholders' equity.**

The statement of stockholders' equity may be prepared in a columnar format, where each column represents a major stockholders' equity classification. Changes in each classification are then described in the left-hand column. An illustration of a statement of stockholders' equity for Telex Inc. is shown in Exhibit 5.

Exhibit 5
Statement of Stockholders' Equity

Telex Inc.
Statement of Stockholders' Equity
For Year Ended December 31, 1994

	Preferred Stock	Common Stock	Paid-In Capital in Excess of Par— Common Stock	Unappropriated Retained Earnings	Retained Earnings Appropriated for Treasury Stock	Treasury (Common) Stock	Total
Balance, Jan. 1, 1994	$5,000,000	$10,000,000	$3,000,000	$1,500,000	$500,000	$(500,000)	$19,500,000
Net income				850,000			850,000
Dividends on preferred stock				(250,000)			(250,000)
Dividends on common stock				(400,000)			(400,000)
Issuance of additional common stock		500,000	50,000				550,000
Purchase of treasury stock						(30,000)	(30,000)
Increase in appropriation for treasury stock				(30,000)	30,000		
Balance, Dec. 31, 1994	$5,000,000	$10,500,000	$3,050,000	$1,670,000	$530,000	$(530,000)	$20,220,000

ACCOUNTING FOR INTERNATIONAL OPERATIONS

Objective 7
Journalize entries for international transactions.

Many U.S. companies enter into transactions with foreign business enterprises, either as sellers or buyers of products or services. These transactions may require the payment or receipt of currencies other than the U.S. dollar. The basic principles used in accounting for such transactions are discussed in the following paragraphs.

Many U.S. companies also own foreign subsidiaries. The preparation of consolidated statements for domestic and foreign companies that are affiliated is also briefly discussed.

Accounting for International Transactions

If transactions with foreign companies require payment or receipt in U.S. dollars, no special accounting problems arise.[10] Such transactions are recorded as described and illustrated earlier in this text. For example, the sale of merchandise to a Japanese company that is billed in and paid for in dollars would be recorded by

---

[10]This discussion is from the point of view of a U.S. company. Unless otherwise indicated, the reference to the dollar refers to the U.S. dollar rather than a dollar of another country, such as Canada.

Exhibit 6
Balance Sheet of a Corporation

Escoe Corporation
Consolidated
December

Assets

Current assets:

Cash		$ 255,000
Marketable securities, at cost (market price, $160,000)		152,500
Accounts and notes receivable	$ 722,000	
Less allowance for doubtful receivables	37,000	685,000
Inventories, at lower of cost (first-in, first-out) or market		917,500
Prepaid expenses		70,000
Total current assets		$2,080,000

Investments:

Bond sinking fund		$ 422,500
Investment in bonds of Dalton Company		240,000
Total investments		662,500

	Cost	Accumulated Depreciation	Book Value
Plant assets (depreciated by the straight-line method):			
Land	$ 250,000	—	$ 250,000
Buildings	920,000	$ 379,955	540,045
Machinery and equipment	2,764,400	766,200	1,998,200
Total plant assets	$3,934,400	$1,146,155	2,788,245

Intangible assets:

Goodwill		$ 300,000
Organization costs		50,000
Total intangible assets		350,000
Total assets		$5,880,745

the U.S. company in the normal manner. However, if the transaction is billed and payment is to be received in Japanese yen, the U.S. company may incur an exchange gain or loss.

Where Was Your Car Made?

American manufacturers depend heavily upon foreign suppliers for many of the parts that are used in "Made in the USA" products. For example, 27% of the parts for Ford Motor Co.'s *Crown Victoria* are imported from foreign suppliers. Some of these parts and foreign suppliers are listed as follows:

Windshield	Mexico
Instrument panel	Mexico
Electronic engine control	Spain
Electronic control for antilock brake system	Germany
Fuel tank	Mexico
Shock absorbers	Japan
Seats	Mexico
Front wheel spindle	England

Source: Alex Taylor III, "Do You Know Where Your Car Was Made?" *Fortune* (June 17, 1991).

and Subsidiaries
Balance Sheet
31, 19—

Liabilities

Current liabilities:		
Accounts payable	$ 508,810	
Income tax payable	120,500	
Dividends payable	94,000	
Accrued liabilities	81,400	
Deferred income tax payable	10,000	
Total current liabilities		$ 814,710
Long-term liabilities:		
Debenture 8% bonds payable, due		
December 31, 19—	$1,000,000	
Less unamortized discount	60,000	$ 940,000
Minority interest in subsidiaries		115,000
Total long-term liabilities		1,055,000
Deferred credits:		
Deferred income tax payable		85,500
Total liabilities		$1,955,210

Stockholders' Equity

Paid-in capital:		
Common stock, $20 par		
(250,000 shares authorized,		
100,000 shares issued)	$2,000,000	
Excess of issue price over par	320,000	
Total paid-in capital		$2,320,000
Retained earnings:		
Appropriated for bonded		
indebtedness	$ 250,000	
Unappropriated	1,355,535	
Total retained earnings		1,605,535
Total stockholders' equity		3,925,535
Total liabilities and stockholders'		
equity		$5,880,745

REALIZED CURRENCY EXCHANGE GAINS AND LOSSES. A U.S. company may enter into a transaction with a foreign company requiring either the receipt of a foreign currency or payment in a foreign currency. When funds are received in a foreign currency, the amount of foreign currency received must be converted to its equivalent in U.S. dollars for recording in the accounts. When payment is to be made in a foreign currency, U.S. dollars must be exchanged for the foreign currency for payment.

To illustrate, assume that a U.S. company purchases merchandise from a British company that requires payment in British pounds. In this case, U.S. dollars ($) must be exchanged for British pounds (£) to pay for the merchandise. This exchange of one currency into another involves the use of an exchange rate. The **exchange rate** is the rate at which one unit of currency (the dollar, for example) can be converted into another currency (the British pound, for example).

To continue the example, assume that the U.S. company had purchased merchandise for £1,000 from a British company on June 1, when the exchange rate was $1.40 per British pound. Thus, $1,400 must be exchanged for £1,000 to make the purchase.[11] Since the U.S. company maintains its accounts in dollars, the transaction is recorded as follows:

---

[11] Foreign exchange rates are quoted in major financial reporting services. Because the exchange rates are quite volatile, those used in this chapter are assumed rates.

June 1	Purchases	1,400	
	Cash		1,400
	Payment of Invoice No. 1725 from W. A.		
	Sterling Co., £1,000; exchange rate, $1.40		
	per British pound.		

Instead of a cash purchase, the purchase may be made on account. In this case, the exchange rate may change between the date of purchase and the payment of the account payable in the foreign currency. In practice, exchange rates vary on a day-to-day basis.

To illustrate, assume that the preceding purchase was made on account. The entry to record it is as follows:

June 1	Purchases	1,400	
	Accounts Payable—W. A. Sterling Co.		1,400
	Purchase on account; Invoice No. 1725 from		
	W. A. Sterling Co., £1,000; exchange rate,		
	$1.40 per British pound.		

Assume that on the date of payment, June 15, the exchange rate was $1.45 per pound. The £1,000 account payable must be settled by exchanging $1,450 (£1,000 × $1.45) for £1,000. In this case, the U.S. company incurs an exchange loss of $50, because $1,450 was needed to settle a $1,400 account payable. The cash payment is recorded as follows:

June 15	Accounts Payable—W. A. Sterling Co.	1,400	
	Exchange Loss	50	
	Cash		1,450
	Cash paid on Invoice No. 1725, for £1,000, or		
	$1,400, when exchange rate was $1.45 per pound.		

All transactions with foreign companies can be analyzed in the manner described above. For example, assume that a sale on account for $1,000 to a Swiss company on May 1 was billed in Swiss francs. If the exchange rate was $.25 per Swiss franc (F) on May 1, the transaction is recorded as follows:

May 1	Accounts Receivable—D. W. Robinson Co.	1,000	
	Sales		1,000
	Invoice No. 9772, F4,000; exchange rate, $.25 per		
	Swiss franc.		

Assume that the exchange rate increases to $.30 per Swiss franc on May 31 when cash is received. In this case, the U.S. company realizes an exchange gain of $200. This gain is realized because the F4,000, which had a value of $1,000 on the date of sale, has increased in value to $1,200 (F4,000 × $.30) on May 31 when the payment is received. The receipt of the cash is recorded as follows:

May 31	Cash	1,200	
	Accounts Receivable—D. W. Robinson Co.		1,000
	Exchange Gain		200
	Cash received on Invoice No. 9772, for F4,000,		
	or $1,000, when exchange rate was $.30 per		
	Swiss franc.		

UNREALIZED CURRENCY EXCHANGE GAINS AND LOSSES. In the previous examples, the transactions were completed by either the receipt or the payment of cash. On the date the cash was received or paid, any related exchange gain or loss was realized and was recorded in the accounts. However, financial statements may be prepared between the date of the sale or purchase on account and the date the cash is received or paid. In this case, any exchange gain or loss created by a change in exchange rates between the date of the original transaction and the balance sheet date must be recorded. Such an exchange gain or loss is reported in the financial statements as an unrealized exchange gain or loss.

To illustrate, assume that a sale on account for $1,000 had been made to a German company on December 20 and had been billed in deutsche marks (DM). On this date, the exchange rate was $.50 per deutsche mark. The transaction is recorded as follows:

Dec. 20	Accounts Receivable—T. A. Mueller Inc.	1,000	
	Sales		1,000
	Invoice No. 1793, DM2,000; exchange rate, $.50 per deutsche mark.		

Assume that the exchange rate decreases to $.45 per deutsche mark on December 31, the date of the balance sheet. Thus, the $1,000 account receivable on December 31 only has a value of $900 (DM2,000 × $.45). This *unrealized* loss of $100 ($1,000 − $900) is recorded as follows:

Dec. 31	Exchange Loss	100	
	Accounts Receivable—T. A. Mueller Inc.		100
	Invoice No. 1793, DM2,000 × $.05 decrease in exchange rate.		

Any additional change in the exchange rate during the following period is recorded when the cash is received. To continue the illustration, assume that the exchange rate declines from $.45 to $.42 per deutsche mark by January 19, when the DM2,000 is received. The receipt of the cash on January 19 is recorded as follows:

Jan. 19	Cash (DM2,000 × $.42)	840	
	Exchange Loss ($.03DM × 2,000)	60	
	Accounts Receivable—T. A. Mueller Inc.		900
	Cash received on Invoice No. 1793, for DM2,000, or $900, when exchange rate was $.42 per deutsche mark.		

In contrast, assume that in the preceding example the exchange rate increases between December 31 and January 19. In this case, an exchange gain would be recorded on January 19. For example, if the exchange rate increases from $.45 to $.47 per deutsche mark during this period, Exchange Gain would be credited for $40 ($.02 × DM2,000).

A balance in the exchange loss account at the end of the fiscal period is reported in the Other Expense section of the income statement. A balance in the exchange gain account is reported in the Other Income section.

Consolidated Financial Statements with Foreign Subsidiaries

Before the financial statements of domestic and foreign companies are consolidated, the amounts shown on the statements for the foreign companies must be converted to U.S. dollars. Asset and liability amounts are normally converted to U.S. dollars by using the exchange rates as of the balance sheet date. Revenues and expenses are normally converted by using the exchange rates that were in effect when those transactions were executed. However, for practical purposes, a weighted average rate for the period is generally used. The adjustments (gains or losses) resulting from the conversion are reported as a separate item in the Stockholders' Equity section of the balance sheets of the foreign companies.[12]

After the foreign company statements have been converted to U.S. dollars, the financial statements of U.S. and foreign subsidiaries are consolidated in the manner described earlier in this chapter.

CHAPTER REVIEW

Key Points

Objective 1. Explain why and how business enterprises make long-term investments in stocks.

A business may make long-term investments in equity securities (preferred and common shares) to earn income with excess cash not needed for normal operations, to establish business relations with another company, or to gain control of another corporation. Investments in stocks are purchased either directly from the issuing corporation or from other investors.

Objective 2. Journalize entries for long-term investments in stocks, using the cost method and the equity method.

The cost of purchasing a long-term investment in a stock includes all expenditures necessary to acquire the stock. The total cost of a stock purchased is debited to an investment account. If a stock is purchased between the dividend declaration date and the date of record (with dividends), the buyer debits a dividends receivable account for the amount of the dividend. When the dividend is received, the cash account is debited and the dividends receivable account is credited.

When the cost method is used, cash dividends are recorded as an increase in the cash account (debit) and an increase in the dividend income account (credit). The lower-of-cost-or-market rule is applied to the total cost or total market price of the stock as of the date of the balance sheet. If total market is lower, the difference is reported as a separate item in the Stockholders' Equity section of the balance sheet. If the decline in market value for an individual security is permanent, the individual security is written down and the write-down is reported as a realized loss on the income statement.

Under the equity method, the investor records its share of periodic net income of the investee as an increase in the investment account (debit) and as an increase in an income account (credit). The investor's share of the investee's periodic net loss is recorded in a loss account (debit) and as a decrease in the investment account (credit). The investor records its share of cash dividends as an increase in the cash account (debit) and as a decrease in the investment account (credit).

When shares of stock held as a long-term investment are sold, cash or a receivable account is debited for the proceeds and the investment account is credited for the carrying amount of the shares sold. Any difference between the proceeds and the carrying amount is recorded as a gain or loss on the sale.

Objective 3. List and describe three alternative methods of combining businesses.

Businesses may combine in a merger or a consolidation. A merger is the joining of two enterprises. One corporation acquires the properties of another corporation, which is then dissolved. A consolidation is the creation of a new corporation by the transfer of the assets and liabilities from two or more existing corporations. Business combinations may also occur when one corporation acquires a controlling share of the outstanding voting stock of another corporation. In this case, a parent-subsidiary relationship exists and the companies are called affiliated or associated companies.

Objective 4. Describe consolidated financial statements.

Although the corporations that make up a parent-subsidiary affiliation may operate as a single economic unit, they usually continue to maintain separate accounting records and prepare their own periodic financial statements. The financial statements prepared by combining the parent and subsidiary statements are called consolidated statements.

Objective 5. Prepare consolidated financial statements, using the purchase method and the pooling-of-interests method.

Under the purchase method, the parent corporation purchases all or a major part of the subsidiary's stock. The parent's investment account at the date of acquisition is reciprocal to the parent's share of the subsidiary's stockholders' equity accounts. If the parent pays more than the book value for the subsidiary's stock, the excess is allocated to the subsidiary's net assets or identified as goodwill on the consolidated balance sheet. When a parent corporation purchases less than 100% of the subsidiary's stock, the remaining stockholders' equity is identified as minority interest. The minority interest is reported on the consolidated balance sheet, usually preceding stockholders' equity.

Under the pooling-of-interests method, the parent corporation acquires the stock of a subsidiary in exchange for its

---

[12]*Statement of Financial Accounting Standards, No. 52,* "Foreign Currency Translation" (Stamford: Financial Accounting Standards Board, 1981).

own stock. The parent investment in the subsidiary account equals the carrying amount of the subsidiary's net assets. The net assets of both companies are combined in preparing the consolidated financial statements.

The principles used in preparing consolidated income statements of a parent and its subsidiary are the same under both the purchase and the pooling-of-interests methods. All amounts from intercompany transactions, such as management fees or interest on loans charged by one affiliate to another, are eliminated. Any intercompany sales of merchandise and any profit included in inventories are also eliminated.

Objective 6. Prepare a consolidated balance sheet and a statement of stockholders' equity.

A consolidated balance sheet of a corporation, containing many of the items discussed in this and preceding chapters, is presented in Exhibit 5. A statement of stockholders' equity is prepared when significant changes occur in stockholders' eq-

uity other than retained earnings. An example of a statement of stockholders' equity is presented in Exhibit 6.

Objective 7. Journalize entries for international transactions.

When a U.S. company enters into a transaction with a company in a foreign country using a currency other than the dollar, an exchange rate is used to convert the foreign currency into dollars. The transaction is then recorded in dollars, similar to other transactions.

When foreign currency is received in payment of a receivable or when foreign currency is paid in payment of a payable, a foreign exchange gain or loss may be realized. Such a gain or loss will be realized if the foreign exchange rate changes between the initial recording of the transaction and the receipt or payment of the foreign currency. If a foreign transaction has not been completed by the end of the year, an adjusting entry to record any unrealized currency exchange gains or losses may need to be recorded.

Glossary of Key Terms

Consolidated statements. Financial statements resulting from combining parent and subsidiary company statements. **Objective 4**

Consolidation. The creation of a new corporation by the transfer of assets and liabilities from two or more existing corporations. **Objective 3**

Cost method. A method of accounting for an investment in common stock, by which the investor recognizes as income its share of cash dividends of the investee. **Objective 2**

Equity method. A method of accounting for investments in common stock, by which the investment account is adjusted for the investor's share of periodic net income and property dividends of the investee. **Objective 2**

Equity securities. Preferred or common stock. **Objective 1**

Exchange rate. The rate at which one currency can be converted into another currency. **Objective 7**

Merger. The combining of two corporations by the acquisition of the properties of one corporation by another, with the dissolution of one of the corporations. **Objective 3**

Minority interest. The portion of a subsidiary corporation's capital stock that is not owned by the parent corporation. **Objective 5**

Parent company. The company owning a majority of the voting stock of another corporation. **Objective 3**

Pooling-of-interests method. A method of accounting for an affiliation of two corporations resulting from an exchange of voting stock of one corporation for substantially all of the voting stock of the other corporation. **Objective 3**

Purchase method. The accounting method employed when a parent company acquires a controlling share of the voting stock of a subsidiary other than by the exchange of voting common stock. **Objective 3**

Statement of stockholders' equity. A summary of the changes in the stockholders' equity of a corporation that have occurred during a specific period of time. **Objective 6**

Subsidiary company. The corporation that is controlled by a parent company. **Objective 3**

Self-Examination Questions
Answers at end of chapter.

1. Which of the following are characteristic of a parent-subsidiary relationship known as a pooling of interests?
   A. Parent acquires substantially all of the voting stock of subsidiary in exchange for cash.
   B. Parent acquires substantially all of the voting stock of subsidiary in exchange for its bonds payable.
   C. Parent acquires substantially all of the voting stock of subsidiary in exchange for its voting common stock.
   D. All of the above

2. P Co. purchased the entire outstanding stock of S Co. for $1,000,000 in cash. If at the date of acquisition S Co.'s

stockholders' equity consisted of $750,000 of common stock and $150,000 of retained earnings, what is the amount of the difference between cost and book value of the subsidiary interest?
   A. Excess of cost over book value of subsidiary interest, $250,000
   B. Excess of cost over book value of subsidiary interest, $100,000
   C. Excess of book value over cost of subsidiary interest, $250,000
   D. Excess of book value over cost of subsidiary interest, $100,000

3. If, in Question 2, P Co. had purchased 90% of the outstanding stock of S Co. for $1,000,000, what is the amount of the difference between cost and book value of subsidiary interest?
   A. Excess of cost over book value of subsidiary interest, $100,000
   B. Excess of cost over book value of subsidiary interest, $190,000
   C. Excess of cost over book value of subsidiary interest, $250,000
   D. Excess of cost over book value of subsidiary interest, $300,000

4. Based on the data in Question 3, what is the amount of the minority interest at the date of acquisition?
   A. $15,000   C. $90,000
   B. $75,000   D. $100,000

5. On July 9, 1994, a sale on account for $10,000 to a Mexican company was billed for 25,000,000 pesos. The exchange rate was $.0004 per peso on July 9 and $.0005 per peso on August 8, 1994, when the cash was received on account. Which of the following statements identifies the exchange gain or loss for the fiscal year ended December 31, 1994?
   A. Realized exchange loss, $2,500
   B. Realized exchange gain, $2,500
   C. Unrealized exchange loss, $2,500
   D. Unrealized exchange gain, $2,500

ILLUSTRATIVE PROBLEM

All of Stereophonic Inc.'s outstanding shares of stock were acquired on October 1, 1994, by Piedmont Inc. After lengthy negotiations with Stereophonic Inc.'s major shareholder, it was agreed that (1) the current management of Stereophonic Inc. would be retained for a minimum of five years, (2) Stereophonic Inc. would be operated as an independent subsidiary, and (3) Piedmont Inc. would issue 1,200 shares of its own $100 par common stock in exchange for all of Stereophonic Inc.'s stock.

The balance sheets of the two corporations on September 30, 1994, were as follows:

	Piedmont Inc.	Stereophonic Inc.
Assets		
Cash	$ 124,200	$ 18,120
Accounts receivable	238,150	36,810
Inventory	405,750	61,300
Land	120,000	50,000
Plant and equipment (net)	612,300	120,450
	$1,500,400	$286,680
Liabilities and Stockholders' Equity		
Accounts payable	$ 136,400	$ 41,500
Common stock	900,000	120,000
Retained earnings	464,000	125,180
	$1,500,400	$286,680

Instructions

1. Journalize the entry that should be made by Piedmont Inc. to record the combination as a pooling of interests.
2. Assuming the business combination is to be recorded as a pooling of interests, prepare a consolidated balance sheet for Piedmont Inc. and Stereophonic Inc. as of October 1, 1994.
3. Assume that Piedmont Inc. paid $106,000 in cash and issued 1,500 shares of Piedmont Inc. common stock with a fair market value of $212,000 for all the common stock of Stereophonic Inc. Journalize the entry for Piedmont Inc. to record the combination as a purchase.
4. Assuming that the business combination is to be recorded as a purchase and that the book values of the net assets of Stereophonic Inc. are approximately equal to their fair market values, prepare a consolidated balance sheet for Piedmont Inc. and Stereophonic Inc. as of October 1, 1994.

Solution

1.

Investment in Stereophonic Inc.	245,180	
Common Stock		120,000
Retained Earnings		125,180

2.

Piedmont Inc. and Subsidiary Stereophonic Inc.
Consolidated Balance Sheet
October 1, 1994

Assets

Current assets:		
Cash	$ 142,320	
Accounts receivable	274,960	
Inventory	467,050	
Total current assets		$ 884,330
Plant assets:		
Land	$ 170,000	
Plant and equipment (net)	732,750	
Total plant assets		902,750
Total assets		$1,787,080

Liabilities

Accounts payable		$ 177,900

Stockholders' Equity

Common stock	$1,020,000	
Retained earnings	589,180	
Total stockholders' equity		1,609,180
Total liabilities and stockholders' equity		$1,787,080

3.

Investment in Stereophonic Inc.	318,000	
Cash		106,000
Common Stock		150,000
Paid-In Capital in Excess of Par—Common Stock		62,000

4.

Piedmont Inc. and Subsidiary Stereophonic Inc.
Consolidated Balance Sheet
October 1, 1994

Assets

Current assets:		
Cash ($124,200 + $18,120 – $106,000)	$ 36,320	
Accounts receivable	274,960	
Inventory	467,050	
Total current assets		$ 778,330
Plant assets:		
Land	$ 170,000	
Plant and equipment (net)	732,750	
Total plant assets		902,750
Intangible assets:		
Goodwill ($318,000 – $245,180)		72,820
Total assets		$1,753,900

Liabilities

Accounts payable		$ 177,900

Stockholders' Equity

Common stock	$1,050,000	
Excess of issue price over par—common stock	62,000	
Retained earnings	464,000	
Total stockholders' equity		1,576,000
Total liabilities and stockholders' equity		$1,753,900

DISCUSSION QUESTIONS

1. a. What are two methods of accounting for long-term investments in stock?
   b. Under what caption are long-term investments in stock reported on the balance sheet?

2. Carson Company purchased 500 shares of XD Corporation stock on February 2 of the current year. XD Corporation had declared a $2 per share dividend on January 10 of the current year, payable on February 15, to stockholders of record on January 30. Will Carson Company receive the dividend? Explain.

3. Fox Co., which owns 1,000 shares of Pryor Inc. common stock, received 20 shares as a stock dividend. If the current market price of Pryor Inc. common stock is $32 per share, how much income should Fox Co. report on its income statement?

4. TC Corporation holds 1,000 shares of Boritz Co. common stock, acquired at a total cost of $41,000, as a long-term investment. It receives a common stock dividend of 25 shares. What is the carrying amount per share after the stock dividend?

5. What terms are applied to the following: (a) a corporation that is controlled by another corporation through ownership of a controlling interest in its stock; (b) a corporation that owns a controlling interest in the voting stock of another corporation; (c) a group of corporations related through stock ownership?

6. Which method of accounting for long-term investments in stock (cost or equity) should be used by the parent company in accounting for its investments in stock of subsidiaries?

7. What are the two methods by which the relationship of parent-subsidiary may be established?

8. The relationships of parent and subsidiary were established by the following transactions. Identify each affiliation as a purchase or a pooling of interests.
   a. Company P receives 100% of the voting common stock of Company S in exchange for cash and long-term bonds payable.
   b. Company P receives 95% of the voting common stock of Company S in exchange for voting common stock of Company P.
   c. Company P receives 95% of the voting common stock of Company S in exchange for cash.
   d. Company P receives 70% of the voting common stock of Company S in exchange for voting common stock of Company P.

9. What are consolidated (financial) statements?

10. At the end of the fiscal year, the amount of notes receivable and notes payable reported on the respective balance sheets of a parent and its wholly owned subsidiary are as follows:

	Parent	Subsidiary
Notes receivable	$500,000	$75,000
Notes payable	175,000	70,000

If $50,000 of Subsidiary's notes receivable are owed by Parent, determine the amount of notes receivable and notes payable to be reported on the consolidated balance sheet.

11. Sales and purchases of merchandise by a parent corporation and its wholly owned subsidiary during the year were as follows:

	Parent	Subsidiary
Sales	$5,000,000	$975,000
Purchases	3,200,000	605,000

If $500,000 of the sales of Parent were made to Subsidiary, determine the amount of sales and purchases to be reported on the consolidated income statement.

12. P Company purchases for $10,000,000 the entire common stock of S Corporation. What accounts on S's balance sheet are reciprocal to the investment account on P's balance sheet?

13. Are the eliminations of the reciprocal accounts in consolidating the balance sheets of P and S in Question 12 recorded in the respective ledgers of the two companies? Explain.

14. Price Company purchased from stockholders the entire outstanding stock of Simpson Inc. for a total of $2,500,000 in cash. At the date of acquisition, Simpson Inc. had $3,500,000 of liabilities and total stockholders' equity of $2,000,000. (a) As of the acquisition date, what was the total amount of the assets of Simpson Inc.? (b) As of the acquisition date, what was the amount of the net assets of Simpson Inc.? (c) What is the amount of difference between the investment account and the book equity of the subsidiary interest acquired by Price Company?

15. What is the possible explanation of the difference determined in Question 14(c), and how will it affect the reporting of the difference on the consolidated balance sheet?

16. If, in Question 14, Price Company had paid only $1,700,000 for the stock of Simpson Inc., what would the solution to part (c) have been?

17. Parent Corporation owns 90% of the outstanding common stock of Subsidiary Corporation, which has no preferred stock. (a) What is the term applied to the remaining 10% interest? (b) If the total stockholders' equity of Subsidiary Corporation is $750,000, what is the amount of Subsidiary's book equity allocable to outsiders? (c) Where is the amount determined in (b) reported on the consolidated balance sheet?

18. P Corporation owns 85% of the outstanding common stock of S Co., which has no preferred stock. Net income of S Co. was $500,000 for the year, and cash dividends declared and paid during the year amounted to $200,000. What entries should be made by P Corporation to record its share of S Co.'s (a) net income and (b) dividends? (c) What is the amount of the net increase in the equity of the minority interest?

19. a. What purpose is served by the work sheet for a consolidated balance sheet?
    b. Is the work sheet a substitute for the consolidated balance sheet?

20. Which of the following procedures for consolidating the balance sheet of a parent and wholly owned subsidiary are characteristic of acquisition of control by purchase and which are characteristic of a pooling of interests? (a) Retained earnings of the subsidiary at date of acquisition are eliminated. (b) Retained earnings of the subsidiary at date of acquisition are combined with retained earnings of the parent. (c) Assets are not revalued. (d) Goodwill may not be recognized.

21. Can a U.S. company incur an exchange gain or loss because of fluctuations in the exchange rate if its transactions with foreign countries, involving receivables or payables, are executed in (a) dollars, (b) the foreign currency?

22. A U.S. company purchased merchandise for 20,000 francs on account from a French company. If the exchange rate was $.19 per franc on the date of purchase and $.18 per franc on the date of payment of the account, what was the amount of exchange gain or loss realized by the U.S. company?

23. What two conditions give rise to unrealized currency exchange gains and losses from sales and purchases on account that are to be settled in the foreign currency?

24. The 1991 annual report of The Campbell Soup Company reported on its income statement $2.4 million as "equity in earnings of affiliates." Journalize the entry that Campbell would have made to record this equity in earnings of affiliates.

25. A note to the consolidated financial statements of Johnson & Johnson for the year ended December 31, 1991, stated: "The consolidated financial statements include the accounts of Johnson & Johnson and subsidiaries. Intercompany accounts and transactions are eliminated." Why are these eliminations necessary in preparing consolidated statements?

ETHICS DISCUSSION CASE

Marchant Company has recently begun selling merchandise to foreign customers. Roberta Douglas, the controller, has implemented a policy that requires all foreign transactions to be executed in U.S. dollars. In this way, Douglas transfers to the customers all risks of foreign transactions on sales to foreign markets.

Discuss whether Roberta Douglas's policy is ethical.

SHARPEN YOUR ►
COMMUNICATION SKILLS

EXERCISES

EXERCISE 18-1
REAL WORLD FOCUS
Objective 2

The following note to the consolidated financial statements for The Goodyear Tire and Rubber Co. related to the principles of consolidation used in preparing the financial statements:

The Company's investments in 20% to 50% owned companies in which it has the ability to exercise significant influence over operating and financial policies are accounted for by the equity method. Accordingly, the Company's share of the earnings of these companies is included in consolidated net income.

■ SHARPEN YOUR ►
COMMUNICATION SKILLS

Is it a requirement that Goodyear use the equity method in this situation? Explain.

EXERCISE 18-2
STOCK DIVIDEND ON
INVESTMENT IN STOCK
Objective 2

Etley Company purchased 500 shares of Gross Inc. common stock at 40 plus commission and postage charges of $150 on February 28. On December 15 of the current year, a 4% stock dividend was received when the current market price was $44 per share.

■ SHARPEN YOUR ►
COMMUNICATION SKILLS

a. Explain how the stock dividend will be recorded in the accounting records of Etley Company.
b. What is the carrying amount of each share of stock immediately after the stock dividend is received?

EXERCISE 18-3
ENTRIES FOR INVESTMENT
IN STOCK, RECEIPT OF
DIVIDENDS, AND SALE OF
SHARES
Objective 2

On February 10, Gregory Corporation acquired 500 shares of the 50,000 outstanding shares of Dawson Co. common stock at 52¾ plus commission and postage charges of $400. On August 3, a cash dividend of $3 per share and a 5% stock dividend were received. On October 15, 100 shares were sold at 55½ less commission and postage charges of $175. Journalize the entries to record (a) the purchase of the stock, (b) the receipt of the dividends, and (c) the sale of the 100 shares.

EXERCISE 18-4
ENTRIES USING EQUITY
METHOD FOR STOCK
INVESTMENT
Objective 2

At a total cost of $1,500,000, Tower Corporation acquired 100,000 shares of Enviro-Systems Co. common stock as a long-term investment. Tower Corporation uses the equity method of accounting for this investment. Enviro-Systems Co. has 250,000 shares of common stock outstanding, including the shares acquired by Tower Corporation. Journalize the entries by Tower Corporation to record the following information:

a. Enviro-Systems Co. reports net income of $500,000 for the current period.
b. A cash dividend of $1 per common share is paid by Enviro-Systems Co. during the current period.

EXERCISE 18-5
DETERMINATION AND
REPORTING OF ITEMS
RELATED TO
CONSOLIDATED
STATEMENTS
Objective 5

On the last day of the fiscal year, Perry Inc. purchased 85% of the common stock of Scott Company for $600,000, at which time Scott Company reported the following on its balance sheet: assets, $930,000; liabilities, $250,000; common stock, $5 par, $500,000; retained earnings, $180,000. In negotiating the stock sale, it was determined that the book carrying amounts of Scott's recorded assets and equities approximated their current market values.

a. Indicate for each of the following the section, the title of the item, and the amount to be reported on the consolidated balance sheet as of the date of acquisition:
1. Difference between cost and book value of subsidiary interest.
2. Minority interest.
b. During the following year, Perry Inc. realized net income of $310,000, exclusive of the income of the subsidiary, and Scott Company realized net income of $150,000. In preparing a consolidated income statement, indicate in what amounts the following would be reported:
1. Minority interest's share of net income.
2. Consolidated net income.

EXERCISE 18-6
CONSOLIDATED BALANCE
SHEET FROM AFFILIATION
EFFECTED AS A PURCHASE
Objective 5

On December 31 of the current year, P Corporation purchased 90% of the stock of S Company. The data reported on their separate balance sheets immediately after the acquisition are as follows:

	P Corporation	S Company
Assets		
Cash	$ 40,100	$ 21,250
Accounts receivable (net)	52,700	35,000
Inventories	141,000	61,750
Investment in S Company	450,000	—
Equipment (net)	500,000	391,500
	$1,183,800	$509,500
Liabilities and Stockholders' Equity		
Accounts payable	$ 129,000	$ 49,500
Common stock, $10 par	750,000	300,000
Retained earnings	304,800	160,000
	$1,183,800	$509,500

The fair value of S Company's assets corresponds to the book carrying amounts, except for equipment, which is valued at $425,000 for consolidation purposes. Prepare a consolidated balance sheet as of December 31, in report form, omitting captions for current assets, plant assets, etc. (A work sheet need not be used.)

EXERCISE 18-7
CONSOLIDATED BALANCE SHEET FROM AFFILIATION EFFECTED AS A POOLING OF INTERESTS
Objective 5

As of July 31 of the current year, Phelps Corporation exchanged 5,000 shares of its $10 par common stock for the 10,000 shares of Stern Company $5 par common stock held by Stern stockholders. The separate balance sheets of the two enterprises, immediately after the exchange of shares, are as follows:

	Phelps Corporation	Stern Company
Assets		
Cash	$ 30,500	$ 20,500
Accounts receivable (net)	29,100	22,500
Inventories	75,750	35,250
Investment in Stern Company	92,500	—
Equipment (net)	300,000	44,250
	$527,850	$122,500
Liabilities and Stockholders' Equity		
Accounts payable	$ 75,000	$ 30,000
Common stock	300,000	50,000
Retained earnings	152,850	42,500
	$527,850	$122,500

Prepare a consolidated balance sheet as of July 31, in report form, omitting captions for current assets, plant assets, etc. (A work sheet need not be used.)

EXERCISE 18-8
DETERMINATION OF AMOUNTS FROM CONSOLIDATED STATEMENTS
Objective 5

On April 30, Pryor Corp. issued 10,000 shares of its $25 par common stock, with a total market value of $380,000, to the stockholders of Stark Inc. in exchange for all of Stark's common stock. Pryor Corp. records its investment at $350,000. The net assets and stockholders' equities of the two companies just prior to the affiliation are summarized as follows:

	Pryor Corp.	Stark Inc.
Net assets	$950,000	$350,000
Common stock	$700,000	$250,000
Retained earnings	250,000	100,000
	$950,000	$350,000

a. At what amounts would the following be reported on the consolidated balance sheet as of July 31, applying the pooling-of-interests method?
   1. Net assets
   2. Retained earnings
b. Assume that, instead of issuing shares of stock, Pryor Corp. had given $380,000 in cash and long-term notes. At what amounts would the following be reported on the consolidated balance sheet as of July 31?
   1. Net assets
   2. Retained earnings

EXERCISE 18-9
ELIMINATIONS ON WORK
SHEET
Objective 5

On December 31 of the current year, Peterson Co., which held 80% of the common stock of Schafer Co., had a balance of $225,000 in Investment in Schafer Co. The common stock and retained earnings of Schafer Co. at December 31 were $150,000 and $100,000 respectively. The fair value of Schafer Co.'s assets corresponds to the book carrying amounts.

a. Prepare the elimination entry that would be made on the work sheet for the consolidated balance sheet at December 31.
b. How much minority interest would be reported on the consolidated balance sheet at December 31?
c. How much goodwill would be reported on the consolidated balance sheet at December 31?

EXERCISE 18-10
CONSOLIDATED INCOME
STATEMENT
Objective 5

For the current year ended June 30, the results of operations of Paley Corporation and its wholly owned subsidiary, Sims Enterprises, are as follows:

	Paley Corporation		Sims Enterprises	
Sales		$950,000		$400,000
Cost of merchandise sold	$625,000		$240,000	
Selling expenses	155,000		55,000	
Administrative expenses	85,000		35,000	
Interest expense (income)	(12,000)	853,000	12,000	342,000
Net income		$ 97,000		$ 58,000

During the year, Paley sold merchandise to Sims for $75,000. The merchandise was sold by Sims to nonaffiliated companies for $100,000. Paley's interest income was realized from a long-term loan to Sims.

a. Prepare a consolidated income statement for the current year for Paley Corporation and its subsidiary. Use the single-step form and disregard income taxes. (A work sheet need not be used.)
b. Assuming that none of the merchandise sold by Paley to Sims had been sold during the year to nonaffiliated companies and that Paley's cost of the merchandise had been $60,000, determine the amounts that would have been reported for the following items on the consolidated income statement: (1) sales, (2) cost of merchandise sold, (3) net income.

EXERCISE 18-11
DETERMINATION OF
CONSOLIDATED BALANCE
SHEET AMOUNTS FOR
AFFILIATION EFFECTED AS
A POOLING OF INTERESTS
AND AS A PURCHASE
Objective 5

Summarized data from the balance sheets of P Company and S Inc., as of June 30 of the current year, are as follows:

	P Company	S Inc.
Net assets	$850,000	$80,000
Common stock:		
25,000 shares, $20 par	500,000	
5,000 shares, $10 par		50,000
Retained earnings	350,000	30,000

a. On July 1 of the current year, the two companies combine. P Company issues 2,500 shares of its $20 par common stock, valued at $90,000, to S Inc.'s stockholders in exchange for the 5,000 shares of S Inc.'s $10 par common stock, also valued at $90,000. Assuming that the affiliation is effected as a pooling of interests, what are the amounts that would be reported for net assets, common stock, and retained earnings as of July 1 of the current year?
b. Assume that P Company had paid cash of $90,000 for all of S Inc.'s common stock on July 1 of the current year and that the book value of the net assets of S Inc. is deemed to reflect fair value. (1) What are the amounts that would be reported for net assets, common stock, and retained earnings as of July 1 of the current year, using the purchase method? (2) How much goodwill will be reported on the combined balance sheet?

EXERCISE 18-12
STATEMENT OF
STOCKHOLDERS' EQUITY
Objective 6

The stockholders' equity accounts of Reese Corporation for the current fiscal year ended December 31 are as follows:

ACCOUNT COMMON STOCK, $10 PAR   ACCOUNT NO.

Date		Item	Debit	Credit	Balance Debit	Balance Credit
19— Jan.	1	Balance				800,000
	20	Issued 10,000 shares		100,000		900,000

ACCOUNT PAID-IN CAPITAL IN EXCESS OF PAR   ACCOUNT NO.

Date		Item	Debit	Credit	Balance Debit	Balance Credit
19— Jan.	1	Balance				180,000
	20	Issued 10,000 shares		25,000		205,000

ACCOUNT TREASURY STOCK   ACCOUNT NO.

Date		Item	Debit	Credit	Balance Debit	Balance Credit
19— Nov.	30	Purchased 1,000 shares	11,000		11,000	

ACCOUNT APPROPRIATION FOR TREASURY STOCK   ACCOUNT NO.

Date		Item	Debit	Credit	Balance Debit	Balance Credit
19— Dec.	31	Retained Earnings		11,000		11,000

ACCOUNT RETAINED EARNINGS   ACCOUNT NO.

Date		Item	Debit	Credit	Balance Debit	Balance Credit
19— Jan.	1	Balance				575,000
Dec.	31	Income summary		215,000		790,000
	31	Appropriation for treasury stock	11,000			779,000
	31	Cash dividends	100,000			679,000

ACCOUNT CASH DIVIDENDS   ACCOUNT NO.

Date		Item	Debit	Credit	Balance Debit	Balance Credit
19— Apr.	12		50,000		50,000	
Oct.	17		50,000		100,000	
Dec.	31	Closing		100,000	—	—

Prepare a statement of stockholders' equity for the fiscal year ended December 31.

EXERCISE 18-13
ENTRIES FOR SALES MADE
IN FOREIGN CURRENCY
Objective 7

Robb Company makes sales on account to several Swedish companies that it bills in kronas. Journalize the entries for the following selected transactions completed during the current year:

Feb. 2. Sold merchandise on account, 10,000 kronas; exchange rate, $.16 per krona.
Mar. 4. Received cash from sale of February 2, 10,000 kronas; exchange rate, $.17 per krona.
May 30. Sold merchandise on account, 12,000 kronas; exchange rate, $.17 per krona.
June 30. Received cash from sale of May 30, 12,000 kronas; exchange rate, $.16 per krona.

EXERCISE 18-14
ENTRIES FOR PURCHASES
MADE IN FOREIGN
CURRENCY
Objective 7

Holzer Company purchases merchandise from a German company that requires payment in deutsche marks. Journalize the entries for the following selected transactions completed during the current year:

June 10. Purchased merchandise on account, net 30, 5,000 deutsche marks; exchange rate, $.58 per deutsche mark.

July 10. Paid invoice of June 10; exchange rate, $.59 per deutsche mark.

Sep. 1. Purchased merchandise on account, net 30, 4,000 deutsche marks; exchange rate, $.59 per deutsche mark.

Oct. 1. Paid invoice of September 1; exchange rate, $.57 per deutsche mark.

WhAT'S WRONG
WITH THIS?

How many errors can you find in the following balance sheet?

Simpson Inc. and Subsidiaries
Consolidated Balance Sheet
January 31, 19—

Assets

	Cost	Accumulated Depreciation	Book Value		
Current assets:					
Cash				$ 127,500	
Investment in bonds of Fox Company				100,000	
Accounts and notes receivable			$ 360,000		
Less allowance for doubtful receivables			18,500	341,500	
Inventories, at lower of cost (first-in, first-out) or market				460,750	
Prepaid expenses				20,000	
Unamortized discount on bonds payable				15,000	
Total current assets					$1,064,750
Investments:					
Bond sinking fund				$ 210,500	
Marketable securities, at lower of cost or market (cost, $80,000)				76,250	
Total investments					286,750
Plant assets:	Cost	Accumulated Depreciation	Book Value		
Goodwill	$ 400,000		$ 400,000		
Buildings	500,000	$ 190,600	309,400		
Machinery and equipment	1,382,200	583,100	799,100		
Total plant assets	$2,282,200	$ 773,700			1,508,500
Intangible assets:					
Land				$ 150,000	
Organization costs				100,000	
Total intangible assets					250,000
Total assets					$3,110,000

Liabilities

Current liabilities:

Accounts payable		$ 250,000	
Income tax payable		60,250	
Accrued liabilities		40,750	
Deferred income tax payable		5,000	
Total current liabilities			$ 356,000

Long-term liabilities:

Debenture 10% bonds payable, due January 31, 2001		$ 500,000	
Minority interest in subsidiaries		57,500	
Total long-term liabilities			557,500

Deferred credits:

Deferred income tax payable			40,000
Total liabilities			$ 953,500

Stockholders' Equity

Paid-in capital:

Common stock, $10 par (500,000 shares authorized, 100,000 shares issued)		$1,000,000	
Excess of issue price over par—common stock		160,000	
Total paid-in capital			$1,160,000

Retained earnings:

Appropriated:				
For bonded indebtedness	$500,000			
For plant expansion	250,000	$ 750,000		
Unappropriated		234,000		
Total retained earnings			984,000	
Cash dividends payable			12,500	
Total stockholders' equity				2,156,500
Total liabilities and stockholders' equity				$3,110,000

PROBLEMS

Series A

PROBLEM 18-1A
ENTRIES FOR INVESTMENTS IN STOCK
Objective 2

The following transactions relate to certain securities acquired by Hidy Company, whose fiscal year ends on December 31:

1993

Feb. 11. Purchased 1,000 shares of the 25,000 outstanding common shares of Huston Corporation at 35 plus commission and other costs of $175.

June 5. Received the regular cash dividend of $1 a share on Huston Corporation stock.

Dec. 5. Received the regular cash dividend of $1 a share plus an extra dividend of $.25 a share on Huston Corporation stock.

(Assume that all intervening transactions have been recorded properly and that the number of shares of stock owned have not changed from December 31, 1993, to December 31, 1997.)

1998

June 7. Received the regular cash dividend of $1 a share and a 5% stock dividend on the Huston Corporation stock.

July 20. Sold 500 shares of Huston Corporation stock at 40. The broker deducted commission and other costs of $125, remitting the balance.

Dec. 9. Received a cash dividend at the new rate of $1.10 a share on the Huston Corporation stock.

Instructions

Journalize the entries for the foregoing transactions.

PROBLEM 18-2A
WORK SHEET AND
CONSOLIDATED BALANCE
SHEET FROM AFFILIATION
EFFECTED AS A PURCHASE
Objective 5

On June 30 of the current year, Powell Company purchased 85% of the stock of Sawyer Company. On the same date, Powell Company loaned Sawyer Company $25,000 on a 60-day note. The data reported on their separate balance sheets immediately after the acquisition and loan are as follows:

	Powell Company	Sawyer Company
Assets		
Cash	$ 49,500	$ 45,000
Accounts receivable (net)	102,250	55,000
Notes receivable	75,000	—
Inventories	178,250	98,000
Investment in Sawyer Company	520,000	—
Equipment (net)	425,000	430,000
	$1,350,000	$628,000
Liabilities and Stockholders' Equity		
Accounts payable	$ 210,000	$ 45,000
Notes payable	—	25,000
Common stock, $20 par	800,000	—
Common stock, $10 par	—	400,000
Retained earnings	340,000	158,000
	$1,350,000	$628,000

SPREADSHEET PROBLEM

The fair value of Sawyer Company's assets corresponds to the book carrying amounts, except for equipment, which is valued at $450,000 for consolidation purposes.

Instructions

1. Prepare a work sheet for a consolidated balance sheet as of June 30 of the current year.
2. Prepare in report form a consolidated balance sheet as of June 30, omitting captions for current assets, plant assets, etc.
3. Do the eliminations included on the work sheet in (1) affect the accounts of Powell Company and Sawyer Company? Explain.

SHARPEN YOUR COMMUNICATION SKILLS

PROBLEM 18-3A
CONSOLIDATED BALANCE
SHEET FROM BOTH
POOLING-OF-INTERESTS
AND PURCHASE METHODS
Objective 5

On April 30 of the current year, after several months of negotiations, Power Company issued 7,500 shares of its own $20 par common stock for all of Sabo Inc.'s outstanding shares of stock. The fair market value of the Power Company shares issued is $45 per share, or a total of $337,500. Sabo Inc. is to be operated as a separate subsidiary. The balance sheets of the two firms on April 30 of the current year are as follows:

	Power Company	Sabo Inc.
Assets		
Cash	$ 192,500	$ 19,500
Accounts receivable (net)	255,000	45,900
Inventory	428,250	61,450
Land	120,000	50,000
Plant and equipment (net)	504,250	123,150
	$1,500,000	$300,000
Liabilities and Stockholders' Equity		
Accounts payable	$ 145,000	$ 52,500
Common stock, $20 par	1,000,000	150,000
Retained earnings	355,000	97,500
	$1,500,000	$300,000

Instructions

1. a. What entry would be made by Power Company to record the combination as a pooling of interests?
   b. Prepare a consolidated balance sheet for Power Company and Sabo Inc. as of April 30 of the current year, assuming that the business combination has been recorded as a pooling of interests. (A work sheet is not required.)

Liabilities

Current liabilities:		
Accounts payable	$ 250,000	
Income tax payable	60,250	
Accrued liabilities	40,750	
Deferred income tax payable	5,000	
Total current liabilities		$ 356,000
Long-term liabilities:		
Debenture 10% bonds payable,		
due January 31, 2001	$ 500,000	
Minority interest in sub-		
sidiaries	57,500	
Total long-term liabilities		557,500
Deferred credits:		
Deferred income tax payable		40,000
Total liabilities		$ 953,500

Stockholders' Equity

Paid-in capital:			
Common stock, $10 par			
(500,000 shares authorized,			
100,000 shares issued)		$1,000,000	
Excess of issue price over			
par—common stock		160,000	
Total paid-in capital			$1,160,000
Retained earnings:			
Appropriated:			
For bonded indebtedness	$500,000		
For plant expansion	250,000	$ 750,000	
Unappropriated		234,000	
Total retained earnings			984,000
Cash dividends payable			12,500
Total stockholders' equity			2,156,500
Total liabilities and stock-			
holders' equity			$3,110,000

PROBLEMS

Series A

PROBLEM 18-1A
ENTRIES FOR INVESTMENTS IN STOCK
Objective 2

The following transactions relate to certain securities acquired by Hidy Company, whose fiscal year ends on December 31:

1993
Feb. 11. Purchased 1,000 shares of the 25,000 outstanding common shares of Huston Corporation at 35 plus commission and other costs of $175.
June 5. Received the regular cash dividend of $1 a share on Huston Corporation stock.
Dec. 5. Received the regular cash dividend of $1 a share plus an extra dividend of $.25 a share on Huston Corporation stock.

(Assume that all intervening transactions have been recorded properly and that the number of shares of stock owned have not changed from December 31, 1993, to December 31, 1997.)

1998
June 7. Received the regular cash dividend of $1 a share and a 5% stock dividend on the Huston Corporation stock.
July 20. Sold 500 shares of Huston Corporation stock at 40. The broker deducted commission and other costs of $125, remitting the balance.
Dec. 9. Received a cash dividend at the new rate of $1.10 a share on the Huston Corporation stock.

Instructions
Journalize the entries for the foregoing transactions.

PROBLEM 18-2A
WORK SHEET AND
CONSOLIDATED BALANCE
SHEET FROM AFFILIATION
EFFECTED AS A PURCHASE
Objective 5

On June 30 of the current year, Powell Company purchased 85% of the stock of Sawyer Company. On the same date, Powell Company loaned Sawyer Company $25,000 on a 60-day note. The data reported on their separate balance sheets immediately after the acquisition and loan are as follows:

	Powell Company	Sawyer Company
Assets		
Cash	$ 49,500	$ 45,000
Accounts receivable (net)	102,250	55,000
Notes receivable	75,000	—
Inventories	178,250	98,000
Investment in Sawyer Company	520,000	—
Equipment (net)	425,000	430,000
	$1,350,000	$628,000
Liabilities and Stockholders' Equity		
Accounts payable	$ 210,000	$ 45,000
Notes payable	—	25,000
Common stock, $20 par	800,000	—
Common stock, $10 par	—	400,000
Retained earnings	340,000	158,000
	$1,350,000	$628,000

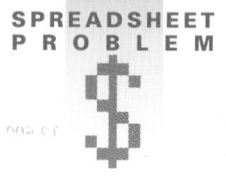

SPREADSHEET PROBLEM

The fair value of Sawyer Company's assets corresponds to the book carrying amounts, except for equipment, which is valued at $450,000 for consolidation purposes.

Instructions

1. Prepare a work sheet for a consolidated balance sheet as of June 30 of the current year.
2. Prepare in report form a consolidated balance sheet as of June 30, omitting captions for current assets, plant assets, etc.

▶ **SHARPEN YOUR COMMUNICATION SKILLS**

3. Do the eliminations included on the work sheet in (1) affect the accounts of Powell Company and Sawyer Company? Explain.

PROBLEM 18-3A
CONSOLIDATED BALANCE
SHEET FROM BOTH
POOLING-OF-INTERESTS
AND PURCHASE METHODS
Objective 5

On April 30 of the current year, after several months of negotiations, Power Company issued 7,500 shares of its own $20 par common stock for all of Sabo Inc.'s outstanding shares of stock. The fair market value of the Power Company shares issued is $45 per share, or a total of $337,500. Sabo Inc. is to be operated as a separate subsidiary. The balance sheets of the two firms on April 30 of the current year are as follows:

	Power Company	Sabo Inc.
Assets		
Cash	$ 192,500	$ 19,500
Accounts receivable (net)	255,000	45,900
Inventory	428,250	61,450
Land	120,000	50,000
Plant and equipment (net)	504,250	123,150
	$1,500,000	$300,000
Liabilities and Stockholders' Equity		
Accounts payable	$ 145,000	$ 52,500
Common stock, $20 par	1,000,000	150,000
Retained earnings	355,000	97,500
	$1,500,000	$300,000

Instructions

1. a. What entry would be made by Power Company to record the combination as a pooling of interests?
   b. Prepare a consolidated balance sheet for Power Company and Sabo Inc. as of April 30 of the current year, assuming that the business combination has been recorded as a pooling of interests. (A work sheet is not required.)

2. a. Assume that Power Company paid $150,000 in cash and issued 6,250 shares of Power common stock with a fair market value of $187,500 for all the common stock of Sabo Inc. What entry would Power Company make to record the combination as a purchase?

b. Prepare a consolidated balance sheet as of April 30 of the current year, assuming that the business combination has been recorded as a purchase, and that the book values of the net assets of Sabo Inc. are deemed to represent fair value. (A work sheet is not required.)

3. Assume the same situation as in (2), except that the fair value of the land of Sabo Inc. was $60,000 for consolidation purposes. Prepare a consolidated balance sheet as of April 30 of the current year. (A work sheet is not required.)

PROBLEM 18-4A
ELIMINATIONS FOR AND
PREPARATION OF
CONSOLIDATED BALANCE
SHEET AND INCOME
STATEMENT
Objective 5

On January 4 of the current year, Porter Corporation exchanged 30,000 shares of its $10 par common stock for 12,000 shares (the entire issue) of Strong Company's $25 par common stock. Strong purchased from Porter Corporation $125,000 of its $250,000 issue of bonds payable, at face amount. All of the items for interest appearing on the balance sheets and income statements of both corporations are related to the bonds.

During the year, Porter Corporation sold merchandise with a cost of $138,000 to Strong Company for $230,000, all of which was sold by Strong Company before the end of the year.

Porter Corporation has correctly recorded the income and dividends reported for the year by Strong Company. Data for the income statements for both companies for the current year are as follows:

	Porter Corporation	Strong Company
Revenues:		
Sales	$1,600,000	$500,000
Income of subsidiary	110,000	—
Interest income	—	12,500
	$1,710,000	$512,500
Expenses:		
Cost of merchandise sold	$ 950,000	$280,000
Selling expenses	165,000	52,000
Administrative expenses	125,000	37,000
Interest expense	25,000	—
Income tax	195,000	33,500
	$1,460,000	$402,500
Net income	$ 250,000	$110,000

Data for the balance sheets of both companies as of the end of the current year are as follows:

	Porter Corporation	Strong Company
Assets		
Cash	$ 62,500	$ 27,050
Accounts receivable (net)	165,000	51,800
Dividends receivable	50,000	—
Interest receivable	—	6,250
Inventories	275,000	126,300
Investment in Strong Company (12,000 shares)	641,550	—
Investment in Porter Corp. bonds (at face amount)	—	125,000
Plant and equipment	1,150,000	496,950
Accumulated depreciation	(650,000)	(108,350)
	$1,694,050	$725,000
Liabilities and Stockholders' Equity		
Accounts payable	$ 75,200	$ 27,750
Income tax payable	20,510	5,700
Dividends payable	30,000	50,000
Interest payable	12,500	—
Bonds payable, 10% (due in 2006)	250,000	—
Common stock, $10 par	1,000,000	—
Common stock, $25 par	—	300,000
Paid-in capital in excess of par	100,000	50,000
Retained earnings	205,840	291,550
	$1,694,050	$725,000

**SPREADSHEET
PROBLEM**

Instructions

1. Determine the amounts to be eliminated from the following items in preparing the consolidated balance sheet as of December 31 of the current year: (a) dividends receivable and dividends payable; (b) interest receivable and interest payable; (c) investment in Strong Company and stockholders' equity; (d) investment in Porter Corporation bonds and bonds payable.
2. Prepare a detailed consolidated balance sheet as of December 31 in report form.
3. Determine the amounts to be eliminated from the following items in preparing the consolidated income statement for the current year ended December 31: (a) sales and cost of merchandise sold; (b) interest income and interest expense; (c) income of subsidiary and net income.
4. Prepare a single-step consolidated income statement, inserting the earnings per share in parentheses on the same line with net income.
5. Determine the amount of the reduction in consolidated inventories, net income, and retained earnings if Strong Company's inventory had included $50,000 of the merchandise purchased from Porter Corporation.

PROBLEM 18-5A
WORK SHEET AND
CONSOLIDATED BALANCE
SHEET; YEAR-END
MINORITY INTEREST;
INCREASE IN INVESTMENT
ACCOUNT DURING YEAR
Objectives 5, 6

On July 31, Palmer Company purchased 80% of the outstanding stock of Stewart Company for $600,000. Balance sheet data for the two corporations immediately after the transaction are as follows:

	Palmer Company	Stewart Company
Assets		
Cash and marketable securities	$ 288,200	$ 40,400
Accounts receivable	344,225	61,225
Allowance for doubtful accounts	(30,150)	(12,075)
Inventories	735,375	183,150
Investment in Stewart Company	600,000	—
Land	300,000	132,500
Building and equipment	1,093,950	741,900
Accumulated depreciation	(348,600)	(392,850)
	$2,983,000	$754,250
Liabilities and Stockholders' Equity		
Accounts payable	$ 398,575	$126,725
Income tax payable	63,000	9,075
Bonds payable (due in 2010)	600,000	—
Common stock, $20 par	1,125,000	—
Common stock, $5 par	—	450,000
Retained earnings	796,425	168,450
	$2,983,000	$754,250

Instructions

1. Prepare a work sheet for a consolidated balance sheet as of the date of acquisition. The fair value of Stewart Company's assets is deemed to correspond to the book carrying amounts, except for land, which is to be increased by $70,000 for consolidation purposes.
2. Prepare in report form a detailed consolidated balance sheet as of the date of acquisition.
3. Assuming that Stewart Company earns net income of $150,000 and pays cash dividends of $90,000 during the following fiscal year and that Palmer Company records its share of the earnings and dividends, determine the following as of the end of the year:
   a. The net amount added to Palmer Company's investment account as a result of Stewart Company's earnings and dividends.
   b. The amount of the minority interest.

PROBLEM 18-6A
CONSOLIDATED BALANCE
SHEET FROM AFFILIATION
EFFECTED AS A PURCHASE
Objectives 5, 6

Several years ago, Pond Corporation purchased 18,000 shares of the 20,000 outstanding shares of stock of Sax Company. Since the date of acquisition, Pond Corporation has debited the investment account for its share of the subsidiary's earnings and has credited the account for its share of dividends declared. Balance sheet data for the two corporations as of December 31 of the current year are as follows:

	Pond Corporation	Sax Company
Assets		
Cash	$ 62,750	$ 16,050
Notes receivable	35,000	15,000
Accounts receivable (net)	140,750	49,650
Interest receivable	3,000	600
Dividends receivable	4,500	—
Inventories	199,500	70,000
Prepaid expenses	5,100	1,700
Investment in Sax Company	180,180	—
Land	75,000	45,000
Buildings and equipment	411,000	240,000
Accumulated depreciation	(200,000)	(95,400)
	$916,780	$342,600
Liabilities and Stockholders' Equity		
Notes payable	$ 45,000	$ 35,000
Accounts payable	99,500	80,500
Income tax payable	35,000	13,900
Dividends payable	15,000	5,000
Interest payable	2,450	3,000
Common stock, $20 par	600,000	—
Common stock, $5 par	—	100,000
Paid-in capital in excess of par	—	25,000
Retained earnings	119,830	80,200
	$916,780	$342,600

Pond Corporation holds $35,000 of short-term notes of Sax Company, on which there is accrued interest of $3,000. Sax Company owes Pond Corporation $15,000 for a management advisory fee for the year. It has been recorded by both corporations in their respective accounts payable and accounts receivable accounts.

Instructions

Prepare in report form a detailed consolidated balance sheet as of December 31 of the current year. (A work sheet is not required.) The excess of book value in Sax Company over the balance of Pond Corporation's investment account is attributable to overvaluation of Sax Company's land.

PROBLEM 18-7A
CONSOLIDATED BALANCE
SHEET
Objective 6

The following data were extracted from the records of Furstner Inc. after adjustment at December 31, 1994, the end of the current fiscal year:

Accounts and notes receivable	$ 400,000
Accounts payable	290,000
Accrued liabilities	40,750
Accumulated depreciation—buildings	240,600
Accumulated depreciation—machinery and equipment	583,100
Allowance for doubtful receivables	18,500
Appropriation for bonded indebtedness	300,000
Appropriation for plant expansion	250,000
Bonds payable, 12% debenture bonds due March 1, 2002	500,000
Bond sinking fund	260,500
Buildings	550,000
Cash	132,500
Common stock, $10 par, 500,000 shares authorized,	
125,000 shares issued	1,250,000
Deferred income tax payable ($10,000 due within one year)	50,000
Discount on bonds payable	15,000
Dividends payable	12,500
Goodwill	400,000
Income tax payable	60,250
Inventories, at lower of cost (first-in, first-out) or market	460,750
Investment in bonds of Maxwell Company	100,000
Land	150,000
Machinery and equipment	1,382,200
Marketable securities, at lower of cost or market	
(original cost, $80,000)	76,250
Minority interest in subsidiaries	57,500
Organization costs	100,000
Paid-in capital in excess of par	160,000
Prepaid expenses	20,000
Retained earnings (unappropriated)	234,000

Instructions

Prepare a report form consolidated balance sheet for Furstner Inc.

PROBLEM 18-8A
FOREIGN CURRENCY
TRANSACTIONS
Objective 7

Benton Company sells merchandise to and purchases merchandise from various companies in Canada and the Philippines. These transactions are settled in the foreign currency. The following selected transactions were completed during the current fiscal year:

May 10. Sold merchandise on account to Salas Company, net 30, 300,000 pesos; exchange rate, $.048 per Philippines peso.

June 9. Received cash from Salas Company; exchange rate, $.047 per Philippines peso.

July 5. Purchased merchandise on account from Mason Company, net 30, $5,000 Canadian; exchange rate, $.82 per Canadian dollar.

Aug. 4. Issued check for amount owed to Mason Company; exchange rate, $.81 per Canadian dollar.

    31. Sold merchandise on account to Marcos Company, net 30, 300,000 pesos; exchange rate, $.044 per Philippines peso.

Sep. 30. Received cash from Marcos Company; exchange rate, $.046 per Philippines peso.

Oct. 10. Purchased merchandise on account from Chevalier Company, net 30, $20,000 Canadian; exchange rate, $.83 per Canadian dollar.

Nov. 9. Issued check for amount owed to Chevalier Company; exchange rate, $.84 per Canadian dollar.

Dec. 15. Sold merchandise on account to Adams Company, net 30, $50,000 Canadian; exchange rate, $.85 per Canadian dollar.

16. Purchased merchandise on account from Santos Company, net 30, 250,000 pesos; exchange rate, $.047 per Philippines peso.

31. Recorded unrealized currency exchange gain and/or loss on transactions of December 15 and 16. Exchange rates on December 31: $.86 per Canadian dollar; $.048 per Philippines peso.

Instructions

1. Journalize the entries to record the transactions and adjusting entries for the year.
2. Journalize the entries to record the payment of the December 16 purchase, on January 15, when the exchange rate was $.046 per Philippines peso, and the receipt of cash from the December 15 sale, on January 17, when the exchange rate was $.87 per Canadian dollar.

SOLUTIONS
SOFTWARE

Instructions for Solving Problem 18-8A Using Solutions Software

1. Load opening balances.
2. Save the opening balances file to your drive and directory.
3. Set the run date to December 31 of the current year and enter your name.
4. Select the General Journal Entries option and key the journal entries, including the entries to record the exchange gains and losses. Leave the reference field blank. Note: To review the chart of accounts, select F-1.
5. Display a journal entries report.
6. Display a trial balance.
7. Display an income statement and a balance sheet.
8. Save a backup copy of your data file.
9. Perform period-end closing.
10. Display a post-closing trial balance.
11. Set the run date to January 31 of the following year.
12. Key the journal entries of January 15 and January 17.
13. Display a journal entries report.
14. Display a trial balance.
15. Save your data file to disk.
16. End the session.

Series B

PROBLEM 18-1B
ENTRIES FOR INVESTMENTS
IN STOCK
Objective 2

The following transactions relate to certain securities acquired by Barnett Company, whose fiscal year ends on December 31:

1993
Feb. 20. Purchased 1,000 shares of the 20,000 outstanding common shares of Stevens Corporation at 35 plus commission and other costs of $175.
May 15. Received the regular cash dividend of $1 a share on Stevens Corporation stock.
Nov. 15. Received the regular cash dividend of $1 a share plus an extra dividend of $.20 a share on Stevens Corporation stock.

(Assume that all intervening transactions have been recorded properly and that the number of shares of stock owned have not changed from December 31, 1993, to December 31, 1997.)

1998
May 20. Received the regular cash dividend of $1 a share and a 5% stock dividend on the Stevens Corporation stock.
July 20. Sold 500 shares of Stevens Corporation stock at 30. The broker deducted commission and other costs of $125, remitting the balance.
Nov. 18. Received a cash dividend at the new rate of $1.20 a share on the Stevens Corporation stock.

Instructions
Journalize the entries for the foregoing transactions.

PROBLEM 18-2B
WORK SHEET AND
CONSOLIDATED BALANCE
SHEET FROM AFFILIATION
EFFECTED AS A PURCHASE
Objective 5

On April 1 of the current year, P Company purchased 90% of the stock of S Company. On the same date, P Company loaned S Company $30,000 on a 60-day note. The data reported on their separate balance sheets immediately after the acquisition and loan are as follows:

	P Company	S Company
Assets		
Cash	$ 49,250	$ 25,750
Accounts receivable (net)	50,000	32,000
Notes receivable	30,000	—
Inventories	164,750	32,250
Investment in S Company	290,000	—
Equipment (net)	340,000	215,000
	$924,000	$305,000
Liabilities and Stockholders' Equity		
Accounts payable	$155,000	$ 29,500
Notes payable	—	30,000
Common stock, $20 par	500,000	—
Common stock, $10 par	—	200,000
Retained earnings	269,000	45,500
	$924,000	$305,000

The fair value of S Company's assets correspond to the book carrying amounts, except for equipment, which is valued at $250,000 for consolidation purposes.

Instructions

1. Prepare a work sheet for a consolidated balance sheet as of April 1 of the current year.
2. Prepare in report form a consolidated balance sheet as of April 1, omitting captions for current assets, plant assets, etc.

SPREADSHEET
PROBLEM

SHARPEN YOUR
COMMUNICATION SKILLS

3. Do the eliminations included on the work sheet in (1) affect the accounts of P Company and S Company? Explain.

PROBLEM 18-3B
CONSOLIDATED BALANCE
SHEET FROM BOTH
POOLING-OF-INTERESTS
AND PURCHASE METHODS
Objective 5

On May 1 of the current year, after several months of negotiations, Parr Company issued 7,500 shares of its own $20 par common stock for all of Sharp Inc.'s outstanding shares of stock. The fair market value of the Parr Company shares issued is $45 per share, or a total of $337,500. Sharp Inc. is to be operated as a separate subsidiary. The balance sheets of the two firms on April 30 of the current year are as follows:

	Parr Company	Sharp Inc.
Assets		
Cash	$ 252,500	$ 23,500
Accounts receivable (net)	295,000	31,900
Inventory	428,250	61,450
Land	120,000	50,000
Plant and equipment (net)	504,250	123,150
	$1,600,000	$290,000
Liabilities and Stockholders' Equity		
Accounts payable	$ 245,000	$ 42,500
Common stock, $20 par	1,000,000	150,000
Retained earnings	355,000	97,500
	$1,600,000	$290,000

Instructions

1. a. What entry would be made by Parr Company to record the combination as a pooling of interests?
   b. Prepare a consolidated balance sheet for Parr Company and Sharp Inc. as of May 1 of the current year, assuming that the business combination has been recorded as a pooling of interests. (A work sheet is not required.)
2. a. Assume that Parr Company paid $150,000 in cash and issued 6,250 shares of Parr common stock with a fair market value of $187,500 for all the common stock of

Sharp Inc. What entry would Parr Company make to record the combination as a purchase?

b. Prepare a consolidated balance sheet as of May 1 of the current year, assuming that the business combination has been recorded as a purchase, and that the book values of the net assets of Sharp Inc. are deemed to represent fair value. (A work sheet is not required.)

3. Assume the same situation as in (2), except that the fair value of the land of Sharp Inc. was $60,000 for consolidation purposes. Prepare a consolidated balance sheet as of May 1 of the current year. (A work sheet is not required.)

PROBLEM 18-4B
ELIMINATIONS FOR AND
PREPARATION OF
CONSOLIDATED BALANCE
SHEET AND INCOME
STATEMENT
Objective 5

On January 1 of the current year, Parks Corporation exchanged 25,000 shares of its $10 par common stock for 50,000 shares (the entire issue) of Sota Company's $5 par common stock. Later in the year, Sota purchased from Parks Corporation $100,000 of its $200,000 issue of bonds payable, at face amount. All of the items for interest appearing on the balance sheets and income statements of both corporations are related to the bonds.

During the year, Parks Corporation sold merchandise with a cost of $175,000 to Sota Company for $250,000, all of which was sold by Sota Company before the end of the year.

Parks Corporation has correctly recorded the income and dividends reported for the year by Sota Company. Data for the income statements for both companies for the current year are as follows:

	Parks Corporation	Sota Company
Revenues:		
Sales	$1,950,000	$575,000
Income of subsidiary	125,000	—
Interest income	—	3,125
	$2,075,000	$578,125
Expenses:		
Cost of merchandise sold	$1,219,600	$315,750
Selling expenses	185,000	62,275
Administrative expenses	135,000	37,000
Interest expense	12,500	—
Income tax	155,100	38,100
	$1,707,200	$453,125
Net income	$ 367,800	$125,000

Data for the balance sheets of both companies as of the end of the current year are as follows:

	Parks Corporation	Sota Company
Assets		
Cash	$ 66,200	$ 29,150
Accounts receivable (net)	108,400	70,800
Dividends receivable	12,500	—
Interest receivable	—	3,125
Inventories	549,550	199,000
Investment in Sota Company (50,000 shares)	505,800	—
Investment in Parks Corp. bonds (at face amount)	—	100,000
Plant and equipment	837,850	312,000
Accumulated depreciation	(230,300)	(164,075)
	$1,850,000	$550,000
Liabilities and Stockholders' Equity		
Accounts payable	$ 104,400	$ 26,100
Income tax payable	20,000	5,600
Dividends payable	20,000	12,500
Interest payable	6,250	—
Bonds payable, $12\frac{1}{2}$% (due in 2009)	200,000	—
Common stock, $10 par	1,000,000	—
Common stock, $5 par	—	250,000
Paid-in capital in excess of par	40,000	80,000
Retained earnings	459,350	175,800
	$1,850,000	$550,000

Instructions

1. Determine the amounts to be eliminated from the following items in preparing the consolidated balance sheet as of December 31 of the current year: (a) dividends receivable and dividends payable; (b) interest receivable and interest payable; (c) investment in Sota Company and stockholders' equity; (d) investment in Parks Corporation bonds and bonds payable.
2. Prepare a detailed consolidated balance sheet as of December 31 in report form.
3. Determine the amounts to be eliminated from the following items in preparing the consolidated income statement for the current year ended December 31: (a) sales and cost of merchandise sold; (b) interest income and interest expense; (c) income of subsidiary and net income.
4. Prepare a single-step consolidated income statement, inserting the earnings per share in parentheses on the same line with net income.
5. Determine the amount of the reduction in consolidated inventories, net income, and retained earnings if Sota Company's inventory had included $100,000 of the merchandise purchased from Parks Corporation.

PROBLEM 18-5B
WORK SHEET AND
CONSOLIDATED BALANCE
SHEET; YEAR-END
MINORITY INTEREST;
INCREASE IN INVESTMENT
ACCOUNT DURING YEAR
Objectives 5, 6

On March 31, Poke Company purchased 80% of the outstanding stock of Stark Company for $375,000. Balance sheet data for the two corporations immediately after the transaction are as follows:

	Poke Company	Stark Company
Assets		
Cash and marketable securities	$ 64,000	$ 24,720
Accounts receivable	105,500	59,160
Allowance for doubtful accounts	(9,500)	(1,320)
Inventories	475,000	115,440
Investment in Stark Company	375,000	—
Land	100,000	21,000
Building and equipment	990,000	297,000
Accumulated depreciation	(200,000)	(66,000)
	$1,900,000	$450,000
Liabilities and Stockholders' Equity		
Accounts payable	$ 129,800	$ 36,660
Income tax payable	41,500	5,940
Bonds payable (due in 2010)	500,000	—
Common stock, $20 par	900,000	—
Common stock, $10 par	—	300,000
Retained earnings	328,700	107,400
	$1,900,000	$450,000

Instructions

1. Prepare a work sheet for a consolidated balance sheet as of the date of acquisition. The fair value of Stark Company's assets is deemed to correspond to the book carrying amounts, except for land, which is to be increased by $30,000 for consolidation purposes.
2. Prepare in report form a detailed consolidated balance sheet as of the date of acquisition.
3. Assuming that Stark Company earns net income of $80,000 and pays cash dividends of $50,000 during the following fiscal year and that Poke Company records its share of the earnings and dividends, determine the following as of the end of the year:
   a. The net amount added to Poke Company's investment account as a result of Stark Company's earnings and dividends.
   b. The amount of the minority interest.

PROBLEM 18-6B
CONSOLIDATED BALANCE
SHEET FROM AFFILIATION
EFFECTED AS A PURCHASE
Objectives 5, 6

Several years ago, Pratt Corporation purchased 9,000 shares of the 10,000 outstanding shares of stock of Saks Company. Since the date of acquisition, Pratt Corporation has debited the investment account for its share of the subsidiary's earnings and has credited the account for its share of dividends declared. Balance sheet data for the two corporations as of June 30 of the current year are as follows:

	Pratt Corporation	Saks Company
Assets		
Cash	$ 40,970	$ 28,450
Notes receivable	40,000	15,000
Accounts receivable (net)	140,750	49,650
Interest receivable	3,000	600
Dividends receivable	4,500	—
Inventories	199,500	65,000
Prepaid expenses	5,100	1,700
Investment in Saks Company	180,180	—
Land	75,000	45,000
Buildings and equipment	411,000	240,000
Accumulated depreciation	(200,000)	(95,400)
	$900,000	$350,000
Liabilities and Stockholders' Equity		
Notes payable	$ 45,000	$ 50,000
Accounts payable	82,720	72,900
Income tax payable	35,000	13,900
Dividends payable	15,000	5,000
Interest payable	2,450	3,000
Common stock, $20 par	600,000	—
Common stock, $10 par	—	100,000
Paid-in capital in excess of par	—	25,000
Retained earnings	119,830	80,200
	$900,000	$350,000

Pratt Corporation holds $35,000 of short-term notes of Saks Company, on which there is accrued interest of $3,000. Saks Company owes Pratt Corporation $15,000 for a management advisory fee for the year. It has been recorded by both corporations in their respective accounts payable and accounts receivable accounts.

Instructions

Prepare in report form a detailed consolidated balance sheet as of December 31 of the current year. (A work sheet is not required.) The excess of book value in Saks Company over the balance of the Pratt Corporation's investment account is attributable to overvaluation of Saks Company's land.

PROBLEM 18-7B
CONSOLIDATED BALANCE SHEET
Objective 6

The following data were extracted from the records of Bromley Inc. after adjustment at December 31, 1994, the end of the current fiscal year:

Accounts and notes receivable	$ 357,500
Accounts payable	255,000
Accrued liabilities	35,750
Accumulated depreciation—buildings	190,600
Accumulated depreciation—machinery and equipment	583,100
Allowance for doubtful receivables	18,500
Appropriation for bonded indebtedness	300,000
Appropriation for plant expansion	250,000
Bonds payable, 11% mortgage bonds due December 31, 2002	500,000
Bond sinking fund	210,500
Buildings	500,000
Cash	130,000
Common stock, $20 par, 100,000 shares authorized, 50,000 shares issued	1,000,000
Deferred income tax payable ($10,000 due within one year)	50,000
Discount on bonds payable	15,000
Dividends payable	12,500
Goodwill	425,000
Income tax payable	55,250
Inventories, at lower of cost (first-in, first-out) or market	457,750
Investment in bonds of Spears Company	100,000
Land	150,000

Machinery and equipment	$1,382,200
Marketable securities, at lower of cost or market (original cost, $80,000)	76,250
Minority interest in subsidiaries	57,500
Organization costs	75,000
Paid-in capital in excess of par	160,000
Prepaid expenses	23,000
Retained earnings (unappropriated)	434,000

Instructions

Prepare a report form consolidated balance sheet for Bromley Inc.

PROBLEM 18-8B
FOREIGN CURRENCY
TRANSACTIONS
Objective 7

Lynn Company sells merchandise to and purchases merchandise from various Canadian and Japanese companies. These transactions are settled in the foreign currency. The following selected transactions were completed during the current fiscal year:

Jan. 20. Purchased merchandise on account from Ridge Company, net 30, $50,000 Canadian; exchange rate, $.84 per Canadian dollar.

Feb. 16. Issued check for amount owed to Ridge Company; exchange rate, $.86 per Canadian dollar.

Mar. 3. Sold merchandise on account to Niko Company, net 30, 500,000 yen; exchange rate, $.008 per Japanese yen.

Apr. 2. Received cash from Niko Company; exchange rate, $.009 per Japanese yen.

May 30. Purchased merchandise on account from Andrews Company, net 30, $30,000 Canadian; exchange rate, $.87 per Canadian dollar.

June 29. Issued check for amount owed to Andrews Company; exchange rate, $.86 per Canadian dollar.

July 3. Sold merchandise on account to Oh Company, net 30, 1,000,000 yen; exchange rate, $.0085 per Japanese yen.

Aug. 2. Received cash from Oh Company; exchange rate, $.007 per Japanese yen.

Dec. 6. Sold merchandise on account to Claude Company, net 45, $8,000 Canadian; exchange rate, $.85 per Canadian dollar.

     20. Purchased merchandise on account from Toko Company, net 30, 3,000,000 yen; exchange rate, $.006 per Japanese yen.

     31. Recorded unrealized currency exchange gain and/or loss on transactions of December 6 and 20. Exchange rates on December 31: $.83 per Canadian dollar; $.005 per Japanese yen.

Instructions

1. Journalize the entries to record the transactions and adjusting entries for the year.
2. Journalize the entries to record the payment of the December 20 purchase, on January 19, when the exchange rate was $.0055 per Japanese yen, and the receipt of cash from the December 6 sale, on January 20, when the exchange rate was $.82 per Canadian dollar.

Instructions for Solving Problem 18-8B Using Solutions Software

1. Load opening balances.
2. Save the opening balances file to your drive and directory.
3. Set the run date to December 31 of the current year and enter your name.
4. Select the General Journal Entries option and key the journal entries, including the entries to record the exchange gains and losses. Leave the reference field blank. Note: To review the chart of accounts, select F-1.
5. Display a journal entries report.
6. Display a trial balance.
7. Display an income statement and a balance sheet.
8. Save a backup copy of your data file.
9. Perform period-end closing.

SOLUTIONS
SOFTWARE

10. Display a post-closing trial balance.
11. Set the run date to January 31 of the following year.
12. Key the journal entries of January 19 and January 20.
13. Display a journal entries report.
14. Display a trial balance.
15. Save your data file to disk.
16. End the session.

MINI-CASE 18 MAXINE MCNEAL

Your grandmother recently retired, sold her home in Chicago, and moved to a retirement community in Sarasota. With some of the proceeds from the sale of her home, she is considering investing $250,000 in the stock market.

In the process of selecting among alternative stock investments, your grandmother collected annual reports from twenty different companies. In reviewing these reports, however, she has become confused and has questions concerning several items which appear in the financial reports. She has asked for your help and has written down the following questions for you to answer:

a. *"In reviewing the annual reports, I noticed many references to 'consolidated financial statements.' What are consolidated financial statements?"*

b. *" 'Excess of cost of business acquired over related net assets' appears on the consolidated balance sheets in several annual reports. What does this mean? Is it an asset (it appears with other assets)?"*

c. *"What is minority interest?"*

d. *"A footnote to one of the consolidated statements indicated interest and the amount of a loan from one company to another had been eliminated. Is this good accounting? A loan is a loan. How can a company just eliminate a loan that hasn't been paid off?"*

e. *"How can financial statements for an American company (in dollars) be combined with a British subsidiary (in pounds)?"*

Instructions:

1. ▩▩▩▩ ► Briefly respond to each of your grandmother's questions.

2. While discussing the items in (1) with your grandmother, she asked for your advice on whether she should limit her investment to one stock. What would you advise?

ANSWERS TO SELF-EXAMINATION QUESTIONS

1. **C** When parent acquires substantially all of the voting stock of subsidiary in exchange for its voting common stock (answer C), the affiliation is termed a pooling of interests. When parent acquires substantially all of the voting stock of subsidiary in exchange for cash (answer A), other assets, issuances of debt obligations (answer B), or a combination of the foregoing, it is termed a purchase.

2. **B** The excess of cost over book value of interest in S Co. is $100,000 (answer B), determined as follows:

Investment in S Co. (cost)	$1,000,000
Eliminate 100% of S Co. stock	(750,000)
Eliminate 100% of S Co. retained earnings	(150,000)
Excess of cost over book value of subsidiary interest	$ 100,000

3. **B** The excess of cost over book value of interest in S Co. is $190,000 (answer B), determined as follows:

Investment in S Co. (cost)	$1,000,000
Eliminate 90% of S Co. stock	(675,000)
Eliminate 90% of S Co. retained earnings	(135,000)
Excess of cost over book value of subsidiary interest	$ 190,000

4. **C** The 10% of the stock owned by outsiders is called the minority interest. It amounts to $90,000 (answer C), determined as follows:

10% of common stock	$75,000
10% of retained earnings	15,000
Total minority interest	$90,000

5. **B** The 25,000,000 pesos billed, which had a value of $10,000 (25,000,000 pesos × $.0004) on July 9, 1994, had increased in value to $12,500 (25,000,000 pesos × $.0005) on August 8, 1994, when payment was received. The gain, which was realized because the transaction was completed by the receipt of cash, was $2,500 (answer B).

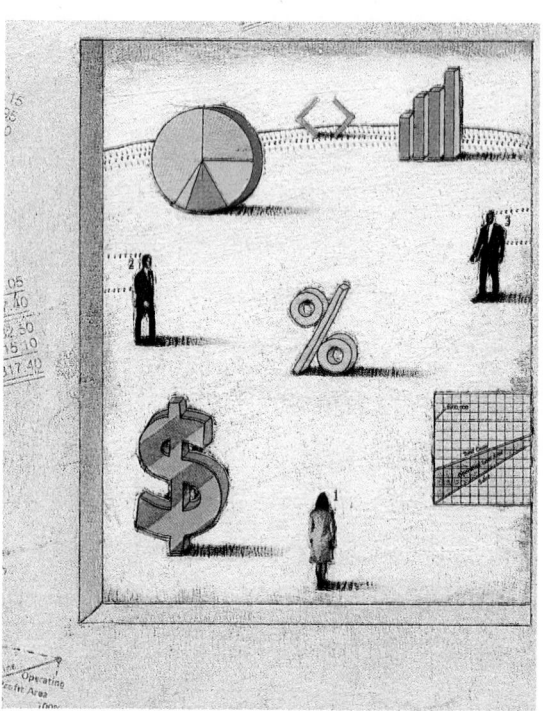

You and Accounting

How much cash do you now have in the bank or in your wallet or purse? How much cash did you have at the beginning of this month? The difference between these two amounts is the net change in your cash during the month. Knowing the reasons for the change in cash may be useful in evaluating whether your financial position has improved and whether you will be able to pay your bills in the future.

For example, assume that you had $200 at the beginning of the month and $550 at the end of the month. The net change in cash is $350. Based on this net change, it appears that your financial position has improved. However, this conclusion may or may not be valid, depending upon how the change of $350 was created. If you *borrowed* $1,000 during the month from your parents and spent $650 on living expenses, your cash would have increased by $350. On the other hand, if you *earned* $1,000 and spent $650 on living expenses, your cash would have also increased by $350 but your financial position is not the same.

To assess whether your financial position during a period has improved, it is useful to analyze individual cash transactions. These transactions can then be classified according to basic cash activities. This chapter discusses and illustrates the statement of cash flows, which reports the results of such analyses for a business.

Chapter 19
Statement of Cash Flows

The basic financial statements are the (1) income statement, (2) retained earnings statement (or statement of owner's equity), (3) balance sheet, and (4) statement of cash flows. The preparation and use of the first three statements were thoroughly described and illustrated in previous chapters. In addition, the statement of cash flows was briefly described and illustrated for a small service enterprise.

In this chapter, the basic concept of the statement of cash flows is presented. The purpose of this chapter is to provide an understanding of the preparation, interpretation, and use of the statement of cash flows.

PURPOSE OF THE STATEMENT OF CASH FLOWS

Objective 1
Explain why the statement of cash flows is one of the basic financial statements.

The **statement of cash flows** reports a firm's major cash inflows and outflows for a period.[1] It provides useful information about a firm's ability to generate cash from operations, maintain and expand its operating capacity, meet its financial obligations, and pay dividends.

The statement of cash flows is one of the basic financial statements.[2] It is useful to managers in evaluating past operations and in planning future investing and financing activities. It is useful to investors, creditors, and others in assessing the firm's profit potential. In addition, it provides a basis for assessing the ability of the firm to pay its maturing debt.

Focus on Cash Flow

In the past, investors have relied heavily on a company's earnings information in judging the company's performance. But this information may be misleading. As a result, more and more investors are focusing on cash flows, as described below.

Follow the money.

That's a guiding principle for . . . stock analysts and investors who study corporate cash flows. While none of them advocate using cash-flow analysis by itself, they say it can be an important tool in piercing the camouflage that sometimes makes reported earnings misleading.

As the term suggests, cash flow is basically a measure of the money flowing into—or out of—a business. If large companies were run, like lemonade stands, on a cash basis, earnings and cash flow would be identical.

Every major corporation, however, keeps its books on an accrual basis. . . . [This] can give a truer picture of corporate profitability, but sometimes it obscures important developments.

Take a company that spent $140 million on new machinery last year. If it depreciates the equipment over a seven-year period, it will be subtracting $20 million from reported profits each year.

But if the machines will stay up to date and useful for 25 years, the company's reported earnings may understate its true strength. . . .

Sometimes the reverse is true. If a company has been neglecting capital spending, its earnings may look good. But on a cash-flow basis, it will look no better, perhaps worse, than its competitors.

In another article, analysts raised questions about the ability of McDonald's Corp. to continue its growth, given the rate at which McDonald's is consuming cash. Some of these concerns, which illustrate the importance of cash-flow analysis, are presented in the following excerpts.

[To raise cash] McDonald's started selling off more company-owned restaurants as domestic sales went softer. . . .

McDonald's received $131 million cash from sales of [300] restaurants. . . . That works out to an average of $436,000 per store—30% of the previous year's revenues of an average store. A longtime rule of thumb in the fast-food industry is that stores are sold for between 50% and 90% of revenues. . . .

One real surprise . . . is "the magnitude of cash McDonald's needs to consume every year to continue its earnings."

Through last year, the company plowed all of its operating cash flow into capital spending—meaning the business was consuming cash at least as fast as it was generating it. Faster, in fact. . . .

Last year, . . . cash flow from operations was $1.3 billion, while $1.1 billion was spent to build 641 new stores and another $500 million went for other capital expenditures. Add to that figure $133 million in dividends and $160 million to repurchase stock. . . .

[McDonald's] plans include a cut in capital spending to the level of increased operating cash flow this year. . . .

Sources: John R. Dorfman, "Stock Analysts Increase Focus on Cash Flow," *The Wall Street Journal* (February 17, 1987), Section 2, page 1; Dana Wechsler Linden, "R. McDonald, CPA," *Forbes* (September 16, 1991), p. 44.

REPORTING CASH FLOWS

Objective 2
Summarize the types of cash flow activities reported in the statement of cash flows.

The statement of cash flows reports cash flows by three types of activities:[3]

1. **Cash flows from operating activities** are cash flows from transactions that affect net income. Examples of such transactions include the purchase and sale of merchandise by a retailer.

---

[1] As used in this chapter, *cash* refers to *cash and cash equivalents.* Examples of cash equivalents include marketable securities, certificates of deposit, U.S. Treasury bills, and money market funds.
[2] *Statement of Financial Accounting Standards, No. 95*, "Statement of Cash Flows" (Stamford: Financial Accounting Standards Board, 1987).
[3] *Ibid.*

2. **Cash flows from investing activities** are cash flows from transactions that affect the investments in noncurrent assets. Examples of such transactions include the sale and purchase of plant assets, such as equipment and buildings.

3. **Cash flows from financing activities** are cash flows from transactions that affect the equity and debt of the entity. Examples of such transactions include the issuance or retirement of equity and debt securities.

The cash flows from operating activities is normally presented first, followed by the cash flows from investing activities and financing activities. The total of the net cash flow from these activities is the net increase or decrease in cash for the period. The cash balance at the beginning of the period is added to the net increase or decrease in cash, and the cash balance at the end of the period is reported. The ending cash balance on the statement of cash flows equals the cash reported on the balance sheet.

Common cash flow transactions reported in each of the three sections of the statement of cash flows are shown in Exhibit 1. By reporting cash flows by operating, investing, and financing activities, significant relationships within and among the activities can be evaluated. For example, cash receipts from issuing bonds can be related to repayments of borrowings when both are reported as financing activities. Also, the impact of each of the three activities (operating, investing, and financing) on cash flows can be evaluated. This allows investors and creditors to evaluate the effects of cash flows on a firm's profits and ability to pay debt.

Exhibit 1
Cash Flows

OPERATING ACTIVITIES (receipts from revenues and payments for expenses)

INVESTING ACTIVITIES (receipts from sale of noncurrent assets and payments for acquisition of noncurrent assets)

CASH

FINANCING ACTIVITIES (receipts from issuance of equity and debt securities; payments for treasury stock and dividends and for redemption of debt securities)

Cash Flows from Operating Activities

The most frequent and often the most important cash flows of an enterprise relate to operating activities. There are two alternative methods for reporting cash flows from operating activities in the statement of cash flows. These methods are (1) the direct method and (2) the indirect method.

The **direct method** reports the sources of operating cash and the uses of operating cash. The major source of operating cash is cash received from customers. The major uses of operating cash include cash paid to suppliers for merchandise and services and cash paid to employees for wages. The difference between these operating cash receipts and cash payments is the **net cash flow from operating activities**.

The primary advantage of the direct method is that it reports the sources and uses of cash in the statement of cash flows. Its primary disadvantage is that the necessary data may not be readily available and may be costly to gather.

The **indirect method** reports the operating cash flows by beginning with net income and adjusting it for revenues and expenses that do not involve the receipt or payment of cash. In other words, net income is adjusted to determine the net amount of cash flows from operating activities.

A major advantage of the indirect method is that it focuses on the differences between net income and cash flows from operations. In this sense, it shows the relationship between the income statement and the statement of cash flows. Because the data are readily available, the indirect method is normally less costly to use than the direct method.

Cash Flows from Investing Activities

Cash inflows from investing activities normally arise from the sale of plant assets, investments, and intangible assets. Cash outflows normally include payments to acquire plant assets, investments, and intangible assets.

Cash flows from investing activities are reported on the statement of cash flows by first listing the cash inflows. The cash outflows are then presented. If the inflows are greater than the outflows, **net cash flow provided by investing activities** is reported. If the cash inflows are less than the cash outflows, **net cash flow used for investing activities** is reported.

Cash Flows from Financing Activities

Cash inflows from financing activities normally arise from issuing debt or equity securities. Examples of such inflows include the issuance of bonds, notes payable, and preferred and common stocks. Cash outflows from financing activities include the payment of cash dividends, the repayment of debt, and the acquisition of treasury stock.

Cash flows from financing activities are reported on the statement of cash flows by first listing the cash inflows. The cash outflows are then presented. If the inflows are greater than the outflows, **net cash flow provided by financing activities** is reported. If the cash inflows are less than the cash outflows, **net cash flow used for financing activities** is reported.

Illustrations of the Statement of Cash Flows

Two illustrations of the statement of cash flows are presented in Exhibit 2. Both statements are for the same accounting period for Computer King, which was used in illustrations in the first chapter of this text. The first statement reports cash flows from operating activities by the direct method. The second statement reports cash flows from operating activities by the indirect method. The same amount of net cash flow from operating activities is reported, regardless of the method. Both methods are illustrated in detail later in this chapter.

Exhibit 2
Statements of Cash Flows

Computer King Statement of Cash Flows—Direct Method For Month Ended November 30, 1993		
Cash flows from operating activities:		
Cash received from customers	$ 7,500	
Deduct cash payments for expenses and payment		
to creditors	4,600	
Net cash flow from operating activities		$ 2,900
Cash flows from investing activities:		
Cash payments for acquisition of land		(10,000)
Cash flows from financing activities:		
Cash received from owner's investment	$15,000	
Deduct cash withdrawal by owner	2,000	
Net cash flow from financing activities		13,000
Net cash flow and November 30, 1993 cash balance		$ 5,900

Exhibit 2 (concluded)

Computer King
Statement of Cash Flows—Indirect Method
For Month Ended November 30, 1993

Cash flows from operating activities:		
Net income, per income statement	$ 3,050	
Add increase in accounts payable	400	
	$ 3,450	
Deduct increase in supplies	550	
Net cash flow from operating activities		$ 2,900
Cash flows from investing activities:		
Cash payments for acquisition of land		(10,000)
Cash flows from financing activities:		
Cash received from owner's investment	$15,000	
Deduct cash withdrawal by owner	2,000	
Net cash flow from financing activities		13,000
Net cash flow and November 30, 1993 cash balance		$ 5,900

Noncash Investing and Financing Activities

An enterprise may enter into investing and financing activities that do not directly involve cash. For example, an enterprise may issue common stock to retire long-term debt. Such a transaction does not have a direct effect on cash. However, the transaction does eliminate the need for a future cash payment to retire the bonds. In addition, future cash payments for interest are eliminated. Thus, such transactions should be reported to readers of the financial statements because of their future effect on cash flows.

When noncash investing and financing transactions occur during a period, their effect is reported in a separate schedule. This schedule accompanies the statement of cash flows. Other examples of noncash investing and financing transactions include acquiring plant assets by issuing bonds or capital stock and issuing common stock in exchange for convertible preferred stock.

Cash Flow per Share

The term *cash flow per share* is sometimes reported in the financial press. Often, the term is used to mean "cash flow **from operations** per share." Such reporting may be misleading to users of the financial statements. For example, users might interpret cash flow per share as the amount available for dividends. This would not be the case if most of the cash generated by operations is required for repaying loans or for reinvesting in the business. Users might also think that cash flow per share is equivalent or perhaps superior to earnings per share. For these reasons, the financial statements, including the statement of cash flows, should not report cash flow per share.

STATEMENT OF CASH FLOWS—THE INDIRECT METHOD

Objective 3
Prepare a statement of cash flows, using the indirect method.

The indirect method of reporting cash flows from operating activities is normally less costly and more efficient than the direct method. In addition, when the direct method is used, the indirect method must also be used in preparing a supplemental reconciliation of net income with cash flows from operations. The 45th Edition (1991) of *Accounting Trends & Techniques* reported that 97% of the companies surveyed used the indirect method. For these reasons, the indirect method of preparing the statement of cash flows is discussed first.

To collect the data for the statement of cash flows, all the cash receipts and cash payments for a period could be analyzed and then reported by activity (operating, investing, or financing). However, this procedure is expensive and time-consuming. A more efficient approach is to analyze the changes in the noncash balance sheet accounts. The logic of this approach is that a change in any balance sheet account (including cash) can be analyzed in terms of changes in the other balance sheet accounts. To illustrate, the accounting equation is rewritten below to focus on the cash account.

$$\text{Assets} = \text{Liabilities} + \text{Stockholders' Equity}$$
$$\text{Cash} + \text{Noncash Assets} = \text{Liabilities} + \text{Stockholders' Equity}$$
$$\text{Cash} = \text{Liabilities} + \text{Stockholders' Equity} - \text{Noncash Assets}$$

Any change in the cash account results in a change in one or more noncash balance sheet accounts. That is, if the cash account changes, then a liability, stockholders' equity, or noncash asset account must also change.

Additional explanatory data are also obtained by analyzing the income statement accounts and supporting records. For example, since the net income or net loss for the period is closed to Retained Earnings, a change in the retained earnings account can be partially explained by the net income or net loss reported on the income statement.

There is no order in which the noncash balance sheet accounts must be analyzed. However, it is usually more efficient to analyze the accounts in the reverse order in which they appear on the balance sheet. Thus, the analysis of retained earnings provides the starting point for determining the cash flows from operating activities, which is the first section of the statement of cash flows.

The comparative balance sheet for Rundell Inc. on December 31, 1994 and 1993, is used to illustrate the indirect method. This balance sheet is shown in Exhibit 3. Selected ledger accounts and other data are presented as needed.[4]

Retained Earnings

The comparative balance sheet for Rundell Inc. shows that retained earnings increased $60,500 during the year. An analysis of the entries posted to the retained earnings account indicates how this change occurred. The retained earnings account for Rundell Inc. is shown below.

ACCOUNT RETAINED EARNINGS   ACCOUNT NO.

Date		Item	Debit	Credit	Balance Debit	Balance Credit
1994						
Jan.	1	Balance				112,000
Dec.	31	Net income		90,500		
	31	Cash dividends	30,000			172,500

The retained earnings account must be carefully analyzed because some of the entries to retained earnings may not affect cash. For example, a decrease in retained earnings resulting from an issuance of a stock dividend does not affect cash. Likewise, an appropriation of retained earnings does not affect cash. Such transactions are not reported on the statement of cash flows.

For Rundell Inc., the retained earnings account indicates that the $60,500 change resulted from net income of $90,500 and cash dividends declared of $30,000. The effect of each of these items on cash flows is discussed below.

CASH FLOWS FROM OPERATING ACTIVITIES. The net income of $90,500 reported by Rundell Inc. normally is not equal to the amount of cash generated from operations during the period. This is because net income is determined using the accrual method of accounting.

Under the accrual method of accounting, there is often a difference between when revenues and expenses are recorded and when cash is received or paid. For example, merchandise may be sold on account and the cash received at a later

[4] An appendix that discusses the use of a work sheet as an aid in assembling data for the statement of cash flows is presented at the end of this chapter. This appendix illustrates a work sheet that can be used with the indirect method and a work sheet that can be used with the direct method of reporting cash flows from operating activities.

Exhibit 3
Comparative Balance Sheet

			Rundell Inc.		
			Comparative Balance Sheet		
			December 31, 1994 and 1993		
		1994	1993	Increase Decrease*
Assets				
Cash		$ 49,000	$ 26,000	$ 23,000
Trade receivables (net)		74,000	65,000	9,000
Inventories		172,000	180,000	8,000*
Prepaid expenses		4,000	3,000	1,000
Investments (long-term)		—	45,000	45,000*
Land		90,000	40,000	50,000
Building		200,000	200,000	—
Accumulated depreciation—building		(36,000)	(30,000)	(6,000)
Equipment		290,000	142,000	148,000
Accumulated depreciation—equipment		(43,000)	(40,000)	(3,000)
Total assets		$800,000	$631,000	$169,000
Liabilities				
Accounts payable (merchandise creditors)		$ 45,000	$ 28,200	$ 16,800
Accrued expenses (operating expenses)		5,000	3,800	1,200
Income tax payable		2,500	4,000	1,500*
Dividends payable		15,000	8,000	7,000
Bonds payable		120,000	245,000	125,000*
Total liabilities		$187,500	$289,000	$101,500*
Stockholders' Equity				
Preferred stock		$150,000	—	$150,000
Paid-in capital in excess of par—preferred stock		10,000	—	10,000
Common stock		280,000	$230,000	50,000
Retained earnings		172,500	112,000	60,500
Total stockholders' equity		$612,500	$342,000	$270,500
Total liabilities and stockholders' equity		$800,000	$631,000	$169,000

date. Likewise, insurance expense represents the amount of insurance expired during the period. The premiums for the insurance may have been paid in a prior period. Thus, the net income reported on the income statement must be adjusted in determining cash flows from operating activities. The typical adjustments to net income are summarized in Exhibit 4.

Exhibit 4
Adjustments to Net Income—
Indirect Method

Net income, per income statement			$XX
Add:	Depreciation of plant assets	$XX	
	Amortization of bond payable discount and intangible assets	XX	
	Decreases in current assets (receivables, inventories, prepaid expenses)	XX	
	Increases in current liabilities (accounts and notes payable, accrued liabilities)	XX	
	Losses on disposal of assets and retirement of debt	XX	XX
Deduct:	Amortization of bond payable premium	$XX	
	Increases in current assets (receivables, inventories, prepaid expenses)	XX	
	Decreases in current liabilities (accounts and notes payable, accrued liabilities)	XX	
	Gains on disposal of assets and retirement of debt	XX	XX
Net cash flow from operating activities			$XX

Some of the adjustment items in Exhibit 4 are for expenses that affect noncurrent accounts but not cash. For example, depreciation of plant assets and amortization of intangible assets are deducted from revenue but do not affect cash.

Likewise, the amortization of premium on bonds payable decreases interest expense but does not affect cash.

Some of the adjustment items in Exhibit 4 are for revenues and expenses that affect current assets and current liabilities but not cash flows. For example, a sale of $10,000 on account increases accounts receivable by $10,000. However, cash is not affected. Thus, the increase in accounts receivable of $10,000 is deducted from net income in arriving at cash flows from operating activities.

Cash flows from operating activities should not include investing or financing transactions. For example, assume that land costing $50,000 was sold for $90,000 (a gain of $40,000). The sale should be reported as an investing activity: "Cash receipts from the sale of land, $90,000." However, the $40,000 gain on the sale of the land is included in net income on the income statement. Thus, the $40,000 gain is *deducted from* net income in determining cash flows from operations. Losses from the sale of plant assets are *added to* net income in determining cash flows from operations. Likewise, losses on the retirement of debt are added to net income and gains are deducted from net income in determining cash flows from operating activities.

The effect of dividends payable on cash flows from operating activities is omitted from Exhibit 4. Dividends payable is omitted because dividends do not affect net income. The reporting of dividends in the statement of cash flows will be discussed later in the chapter.

In the following paragraphs, the adjustment of Rundell Inc.'s net income to "Cash flows from operating activities" is discussed and illustrated.

DEPRECIATION. The comparative balance sheet in Exhibit 3 indicates that Accumulated Depreciation—Equipment increased by $3,000 and Accumulated Depreciation—Building by $6,000. As shown below, these two accounts indicate that depreciation for the year was $12,000 for the equipment and $6,000 for the building, or a total of $18,000.

ACCOUNT ACCUMULATED DEPRECIATION—EQUIPMENT   ACCOUNT NO.

Date		Item	Debit	Credit	Balance Debit	Balance Credit
1994						
Jan.	1	Balance				40,000
May	9	Discarded, no salvage	9,000			
Dec.	31	Depreciation for year		12,000		43,000

ACCOUNT ACCUMULATED DEPRECIATION—BUILDING   ACCOUNT NO.

Date		Item	Debit	Credit	Balance Debit	Balance Credit
1994						
Jan.	1	Balance				30,000
Dec.	31	Depreciation for year		6,000		36,000

The $18,000 of depreciation expense reduced net income but did not require an outflow of cash. Thus, the $18,000 is added to net income in determining cash flows from operating activities, as follows:

Cash flows from operating activities:
    Net income $90,500
    Add: Depreciation   18,000 $108,500

CURRENT ASSETS AND CURRENT LIABILITIES. As shown in Exhibit 4, decreases in noncash current assets and increases in current liabilities are *added to* net income. In contrast, increases in noncash current assets and decreases in current liabilities are *deducted from* net income. The current asset and current liability accounts of Rundell Inc. are as follows:

Accounts	December 31		Increase Decrease*
	1994	1993	
Trade receivables (net)	$ 74,000	$ 65,000	$ 9,000
Inventories	172,000	180,000	8,000*
Prepaid expenses	4,000	3,000	1,000
Accounts payable (merchandise creditors)	45,000	28,200	16,800
Accrued expenses (operating expenses)	5,000	3,800	1,200
Income taxes payable	2,500	4,000	1,500*

The $9,000 increase in **trade receivables** indicates that the sales on account during the year are $9,000 more than collections from customers on account. The amount reported as sales on the income statement therefore includes $9,000 that did not result in a cash inflow during the year. Thus, $9,000 is deducted from net income.

The $8,000 decrease in **inventories** indicates that the merchandise sold exceeds the cost of the merchandise purchased by $8,000. The amount deducted as cost of merchandise sold on the income statement therefore includes $8,000 that did not require a cash outflow during the year. Thus, $8,000 is added to net income.

The $1,000 increase in **prepaid expenses** indicates that the cash payments for prepaid expenses exceed the amount deducted as an expense during the year by $1,000. Thus, $1,000 is deducted from net income.

The $16,800 increase in **accounts payable** indicates that the amount incurred during the year for merchandise purchased on account exceeds the cash payments made on account by $16,800. The amount reported on the income statement for cost of merchandise sold therefore includes $16,800 that did not require a cash outflow during the year. Thus, $16,800 is added to net income.

The $1,200 increase in **accrued expenses** indicates that the amount incurred during the year for operating expenses exceeds the cash payments by $1,200. The amount reported on the income statement for operating expenses therefore includes $1,200 that did not require a cash outflow during the year. Thus, $1,200 is added to net income.

The $1,500 decrease in **income taxes payable** indicates that the amount paid for taxes exceeds the amount owed during the year by $1,500. The amount reported on the income statement for income tax therefore is less than the amount paid by $1,500. Thus, $1,500 is deducted from net income.

The preceding adjustments to net income are summarized below.

Cash flows from operating activities:				
Net income			$ 90,500	
Add: Depreciation		$18,000		
Decrease in inventories		8,000		
Increase in accounts payable		16,800		
Increase in accrued expenses		1,200	44,000	
			$134,500	
Deduct: Increase in trade receivables		$ 9,000		
Increase in prepaid expenses		1,000		
Decrease in income taxes payable		1,500	11,500	$123,000

GAIN ON SALE OF INVESTMENTS. The ledger or income statement of Rundell Inc. indicates that the sale of investments resulted in a gain of $30,000. As discussed previously, the sale proceeds, which include the gain and the carrying value of the investments, are included in cash flows from investing activities.[5] The gain is also included in net income. Thus, to avoid double reporting, the gain of

---

[5]The reporting of the proceeds (cash flows) from the sale of investments as part of the investing activities is discussed in a later paragraph.

$30,000 is deducted from net income in determining cash flows from operating activities, as shown below.

Cash flows from operating activities:
Net income	$90,500
Deduct: Gain on sale of investments	30,000

REPORTING CASH FLOWS FROM OPERATING ACTIVITIES. All the necessary adjustments to convert the net income to cash flows from operating activities for Rundell Inc. have now been presented. These adjustments are summarized in Exhibit 5 in a format suitable for the statement of cash flows.

Exhibit 5
Cash Flows from Operating
Activities—Indirect Method

Cash flows from operating activities:			
Net income, per income statement			$ 90,500
Add: Depreciation	$ 18,000		
Decrease in inventories	8,000		
Increase in accounts payable	16,800		
Increase in accrued expenses	1,200	44,000	
		$134,500	
Deduct: Increase in trade receivables	$ 9,000		
Increase in prepaid expenses	1,000		
Decrease in income taxes payable	1,500		
Gain on sale of investments	30,000	41,500	
Net cash flow from operating activities			$93,000

CASH FLOWS USED FOR PAYMENT OF DIVIDENDS. According to the retained earnings account of Rundell Inc., shown earlier in the chapter, cash dividends of $30,000 were declared during the year. However, the dividends payable account, shown below, indicates that dividends of only $23,000 were paid during the year.

ACCOUNT DIVIDENDS PAYABLE   ACCOUNT NO.

Date		Item	Debit	Credit	Balance Debit	Balance Credit
1994						
Jan.	1	Balance				8,000
	10	Cash paid	8,000		—	—
June	20	Dividend declared		15,000		15,000
July	10	Cash paid	15,000		—	—
Dec.	20	Dividend declared		15,000		15,000

The $23,000 of dividend payments represents a cash outflow that is reported in the financing activities section as follows:

Cash flows from financing activities:
Cash paid for dividends	$23,000

Common Stock

The common stock account increased by $50,000 as shown below. This increase results from the issuance of stock in exchange for land valued at $50,000.

ACCOUNT COMMON STOCK   ACCOUNT NO.

Date		Item	Debit	Credit	Balance Debit	Balance Credit
1994						
Jan.	1	Balance				230,000
Dec.	28	Issued at par in exchange for land		50,000		280,000

Although no inflow or outflow of cash occurred, the transaction represents a significant investing and financing activity. Such transactions, as discussed previously, are reported in a separate schedule accompanying the statement of cash flows. In this schedule, the transaction is reported as follows:

Noncash investing and financing activities:
    Acquisition of land by issuance of common stock $50,000

Preferred Stock

The preferred stock account increased by $150,000 and the paid-in capital in excess of par—preferred stock account increased by $10,000, as shown below. These increases result from the issuance of preferred stock for $160,000.

ACCOUNT PREFERRED STOCK, $50 PAR   ACCOUNT NO.

Date		Item	Debit	Credit	Balance Debit	Balance Credit
1994 Nov.	1	3,000 shares issued for cash		150,000		150,000

                        PAID-IN CAPITAL IN EXCESS OF PAR—
ACCOUNT PREFERRED STOCK   ACCOUNT NO.

Date		Item	Debit	Credit	Balance Debit	Balance Credit
1994 Nov.	1	3,000 shares issued for cash		10,000		10,000

This cash inflow is reported in the financing activities section as follows:

Cash flows from financing activities:
    Cash received from sale of preferred stock $160,000

Bonds Payable

The bonds payable account decreased by $125,000, as shown below. This decrease results from retiring the bonds by a cash payment for their face value.

ACCOUNT BONDS PAYABLE   ACCOUNT NO.

Date		Item	Debit	Credit	Balance Debit	Balance Credit
1994 Jan.	1	Balance				245,000
June	30	Retired by payment of cash at face amount	125,000			120,000

This cash outflow is reported in the financing activities section as follows:

Cash flows from financing activities:
    Cash paid to retire bonds payable $125,000

Equipment

The equipment account increased by $148,000, and the accumulated depreciation—equipment account increased by $3,000, as shown below.

ACCOUNT EQUIPMENT   ACCOUNT NO.

Date		Item	Debit	Credit	Balance Debit	Balance Credit
1994						
Jan.	1	Balance			142,000	
May	9	Discarded, no salvage		9,000		
Dec.	7	Purchased for cash	157,000		290,000	

ACCOUNT ACCUMULATED DEPRECIATION—EQUIPMENT   ACCOUNT NO.

Date		Item	Debit	Credit	Balance Debit	Balance Credit
1994						
Jan.	1	Balance				40,000
May	9	Discarded, no salvage	9,000			
Dec.	31	Purchased for cash		12,000		43,000

The $148,000 increase in the equipment account resulted from two separate transactions. The first transaction is the discarding of equipment with a cost of $9,000. The credit of $9,000 in the equipment account and the debit of $9,000 in the accumulated depreciation—equipment account indicate that the discarded equipment was fully depreciated. In addition, the memorandum entry in the accounts indicates that no salvage was realized from the disposal of the equipment. Thus, the first transaction of discarding the equipment did not affect cash and is not reported on the statement of cash flows.

The second transaction is the purchase of equipment for cash of $157,000. This transaction is reported as an outflow of cash in the investing activities section, as follows:

Cash flows from investing activities:
    Cash paid for purchase of equipment $157,000

The credit of $12,000 in the accumulated depreciation account represents depreciation expense for the year. This depreciation expense of $12,000 on the equipment has already been considered as an addition to net income in determining cash flows from operating activities, as reported in Exhibit 5.

Building

The comparative balance sheet in Exhibit 3 indicates no change in buildings during the year. Also, the ledger indicates that no entries were made to the building account during the year. For this reason, the account is not shown.

The credit in the accumulated depreciation—building account, shown earlier, represents depreciation expense for the year. This depreciation expense of $6,000 on the building has already been considered as an addition to net income in determining cash flows from operating activities, as reported in Exhibit 5.

Land

The land account increased by $50,000 as shown below. This increase results from acquiring the land by issuing common stock at par.

ACCOUNT LAND   ACCOUNT NO.

Date		Item	Debit	Credit	Balance Debit	Balance Credit
1994 Jan.	1	Balance			40,000	
Dec.	28	Aquired by issuance of common stock at par	50,000		90,000	

Although no inflow or outflow of cash occurred, the transaction represents a significant investing and financing activity. Such transactions, as discussed previously, are reported in a separate schedule accompanying the statement of cash flows. In this schedule, the transaction is reported as follows:

Noncash investing and financing activities:
   Acquisition of land by issuance of common stock $50,000

Investments

The investments account decreased by $45,000 as shown below. This decrease results from selling the investments for $75,000 in cash.

ACCOUNT INVESTMENTS   ACCOUNT NO.

Date		Item	Debit	Credit	Balance Debit	Balance Credit
1994 Jan.	1	Balance			45,000	
June	8	Sold for $75,000 cash		45,000	—	—

The $75,000 proceeds received from the sale of the investments is reported as a cash flow from investing activities, as follows:

Cash flows from investing activities:
   Cash received from sale of investments (includes $30,000 gain
   reported in net income) $75,000

The proceeds of $75,000 include the $30,000 gain on the sale of investments and the $45,000 carrying value of the investments. As shown in Exhibit 5, the $30,000 gain is also deducted from net income in the cash flows from operating activities section. This is necessary so that the $30,000 cash inflow related to the gain is not included twice as a cash inflow.

Preparing the Statement of Cash Flows

The statement of cash flows for Rundell Inc. is prepared from the data assembled and analyzed above. Using the indirect method, the statement of cash flows for Rundell Inc. is shown in Exhibit 6. The statement indicates that the cash position increased by $23,000 during the year. The most significant increase in net cash flows, $93,000, was from operating activities. The most significant use of cash, $82,000, was for investing activities.

Exhibit 6
Statement of Cash Flows—
Indirect Method

Rundell Inc.
Statement of Cash Flows
For Year Ended December 31, 1994

Cash flows from operating activities:			
Net income, per income statement			$ 90,500
Add: Depreciation	$ 18,000		
Decrease in inventories	8,000		
Increase in accounts payable	16,800		
Increase in accrued expenses	1,200	44,000	
		$134,500	
Deduct: Increase in trade receivables	$ 9,000		
Increase in prepaid expenses	1,000		
Decrease in income taxes payable	1,500		
Gain on sale of investments	30,000	41,500	
Net cash flow from operating activities			$93,000
Cash flows from investing activities:			
Cash received from sale of investments		$ 75,000	
Less: Cash paid for purchase of equipment		157,000	
Net cash flow used for investing activities			(82,000)
Cash flows from financing activities:			
Cash received from sale of preferred stock		$160,000	
Less: Cash paid for dividends	$ 23,000		
Cash paid to retire bonds payable	125,000	148,000	
Net cash flow provided by financing activities			12,000
Increase in cash			$23,000
Cash at the beginning of the year			26,000
Cash at the end of the year			$49,000
Schedule of Noncash Investing and Financing Activities:			
Acquisition of land by issuance of common stock			$50,000

STATEMENT OF CASH FLOWS—THE DIRECT METHOD

Objective 4
Prepare a statement of cash flows, using the direct method.

As discussed previously, the direct method and the indirect method will report the same amount of cash flows from operating activities. In addition, the manner of reporting cash flows from investing and financing activities is the same under both methods. The methods differ in how the cash flow from operating activities data are obtained, analyzed, and reported.

To illustrate how the data for cash flows from operating activities are obtained and analyzed under the direct method, the comparative balance sheet and the income statement for Rundell Inc. will be used. In this way, the statement of cash flows under the direct method and the indirect method can be compared.

The changes in the current asset and liability account balances for Rundell Inc. are shown in Exhibit 7. Additional data for Rundell Inc. are shown in the income statement in Exhibit 7.

Exhibit 7
Balance Sheet and Income
Statement Data for Direct Method

| Accounts | December 31 | | Increase Decrease* |
	1994	1993	
Cash	$ 49,000	$ 26,000	$23,000
Trade receivables (net)	74,000	65,000	9,000
Inventories	172,000	180,000	8,000*
Prepaid expenses	4,000	3,000	1,000
Accounts payable (merchandise creditors)	45,000	28,200	16,800
Accrued expenses (operating expenses)	5,000	3,800	1,200
Income taxes payable	2,500	4,000	1,500*

Rundell Inc.
Income Statement
For Year Ended December 31, 1994

Sales		$960,000
Cost of merchandise sold		580,000
Gross profit		$380,000
Operating expenses:		
Depreciation expense	$ 18,000	
Other operating expenses	260,000	
Total operating expenses		278,000
Income from operations		$102,000
Other income:		
Gain on sale of investments	$ 30,000	
Other expense:		
Interest expense	14,000	16,000
Income before income tax		$118,000
Income tax		27,500
Net income		$ 90,500

The direct method reports cash flows from operating activities by major classes of operating cash receipts and operating cash payments. These classes are described and illustrated in the following paragraphs. The difference between the major classes of total operating cash receipts and total operating cash payments is the net cash flow from operating activities.

Cash Received from Customers

The $960,000 of sales for Rundell Inc. is reported using the accrual method. To determine the cash received from sales made to customers, the $960,000 must be adjusted. The adjustments necessary to convert the sales reported on the income statement to the cash received from customers is summarized below.

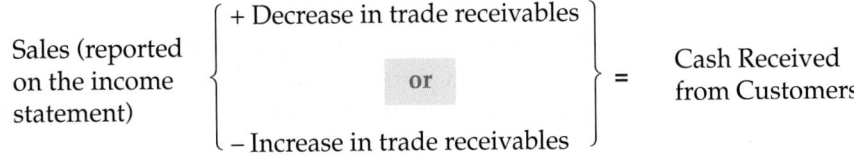

For Rundell Inc., the cash received from customers is $951,000, as shown below.

Sales	$960,000
Less increase in trade receivables	9,000
Cash received from customers	$951,000

The additions to **trade receivables** for sales on account during the year were $9,000 more than the amounts collected from customers on account. Sales reported on the income statement therefore included $9,000 that did not result in a cash inflow during the year. In other words, the increase of $9,000 in trade receivables during 1994 indicates that sales on account exceeded cash received from customers by $9,000. Thus, $9,000 is deducted from sales to determine the cash received from customers. The $951,000 of cash received from customers is reported in the cash flows from operating activities section of the cash flow statement.

Cash Payments for Merchandise

The $580,000 of cost of merchandise sold is reported on the income statement for Rundell Inc., using the accrual method. The adjustments necessary to convert the cost of merchandise sold to cash payments for merchandise made during 1994 are summarized below.

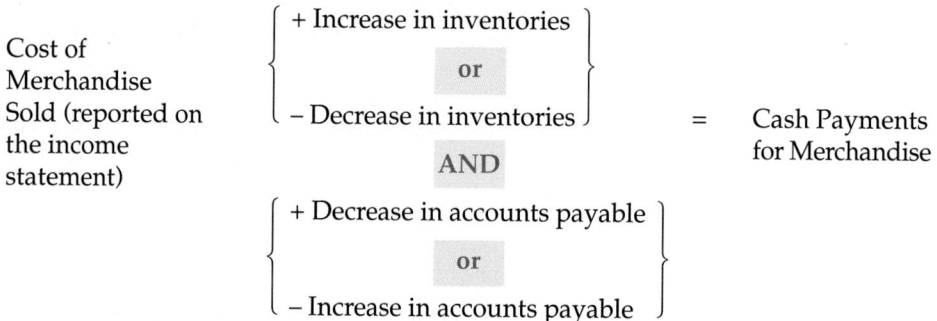

For Rundell Inc., the amount of cash payments for merchandise is $555,200, as determined below.

Cost of merchandise sold		$580,000
Deduct: Decrease in inventories	$ 8,000	
Increase in accounts payable	16,800	24,800
Cash payments for merchandise		$555,200

The $8,000 decrease in **inventories** indicates that the merchandise sold exceeded the cost of the merchandise purchased by $8,000. The amount reported on the income statement for cost of merchandise sold therefore includes $8,000 that did not require a cash outflow during the year. Thus, $8,000 is deducted from the cost of merchandise sold in determining the cash payments for merchandise.

The $16,800 increase in **accounts payable** (merchandise creditors) indicates that merchandise purchases include $16,800 for which there was no cash outflow (payment) during the year. In other words, the increase in accounts payable indicates that cash payments for merchandise were $16,800 less than the purchases on account during 1994. Thus, $16,800 is deducted from the cost of merchandise sold in determining the cash payments for merchandise.

Cash Payments for Operating Expenses

The $18,000 of depreciation expense reported on the income statement did not require a cash outflow. Thus, under the direct method, it is not reported on the statement of cash flows. The adjustment of the $260,000 reported for other operating expenses to cash payments for operating expenses is summarized below.

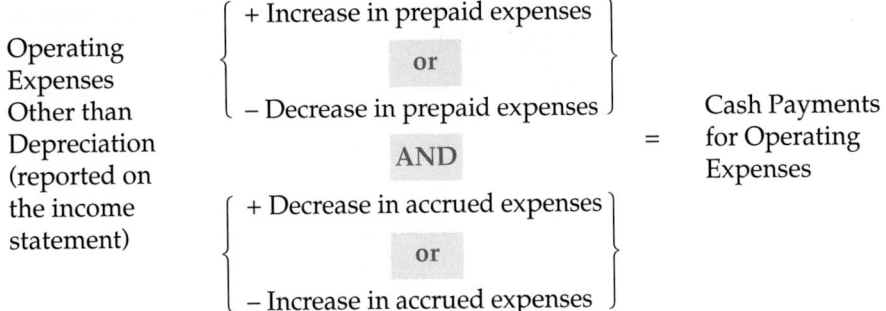

For Rundell Inc., the amount of cash payments for operating expenses is $259,800, determined as follows:

Operating expenses other than depreciation	$260,000
Add increase in prepaid expenses	1,000
	$261,000
Deduct increase in accrued expenses	1,200
Cash payments for operating expenses	$259,800

The outflow of cash for **prepaid expenses** exceeded by $1,000 the amount deducted as an expense during the year. Hence, $1,000 is added to the amount of operating expenses (other than depreciation) reported on the income statement in determining the cash payments for operating expenses.

The increase in **accrued expenses** (operating expenses) indicates that operating expenses include $1,200 for which there was no cash outflow (payment) during the year. In other words, the increase in accrued expenses indicates that the cash payments for operating expenses were $1,200 less than the amount reported as an expense during the year. Thus, $1,200 is deducted from the operating expenses on the income statement in determining the cash payments for operating expenses.

Gain on Sale of Investments

A gain of $30,000 on the sale of investments is reported on the income statement for Rundell Inc. in Exhibit 7. As discussed previously, the gain is included in the proceeds from the sale of investments, which is reported as part of the cash flows from investing activities.

Interest Expense

Interest expense of $14,000 is reported on the income statement for Rundell Inc. in Exhibit 7. The interest expense is related to the bonds payable that were outstanding during the year. It is assumed that interest on the bonds is paid on June 30 and December 31. Thus, the interest expense of $14,000 is reported as a cash outflow from operating activities on the statement of cash flows.

If interest payable had existed at the end of the year, the interest expense would be adjusted for any increase or decrease in interest payable from the beginning to the end of the year. That is, a decrease in interest payable would be added to and an increase in interest payable would be subtracted from interest expense. This is similar to the adjustment for changes in income taxes payable, which is illustrated in the following paragraph.

Cash Payments for Income Taxes

The adjustment to convert the income tax reported on the income statement to the cash basis is summarized below.

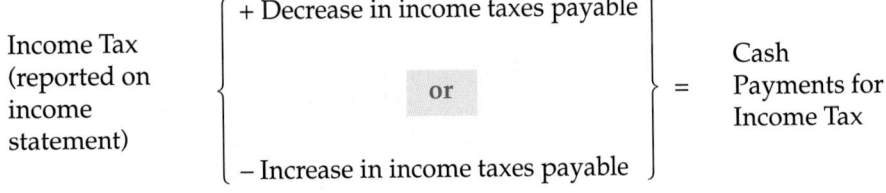

For Rundell Inc., the amount of cash payments for income tax is $29,000, determined as follows:

Income tax	$27,500
Add decrease in income taxes payable	1,500
Cash payments for income tax	$29,000

The outflow of cash for **income taxes** exceeded by $1,500 the income tax deducted as an expense during the period. Thus, $1,500 is added to the amount of income tax reported on the income statement to determine the cash payments for income tax.

Reporting Cash Flows from Operating Activities—Direct Method

A complete statement of cash flows for Rundell Inc. using the direct method for reporting cash flow from operating activities is presented in Exhibit 8. The portions of this statement that differ from the indirect method are highlighted in color. Also included in Exhibit 8 is the separate schedule reconciling net income and net cash flow from operating activities. As mentioned earlier, this schedule must accompany the statement of cash flows when the direct method is used. This schedule is similar to the cash flows from operating activities section of the statement of cash flows prepared by using the indirect method.

Exhibit 8
Statement of Cash Flows—
Direct Method

Rundell Inc.
Statement of Cash Flows
For Year Ended December 31, 1994

Cash flows from operating activities:			
Cash received from customers		$951,000	
Deduct: Cash payments for merchandise	$555,200		
Cash payments for operating expenses	259,800		
Cash payments for interest	14,000		
Cash payments for income tax	29,000	858,000	
Net cash flow from operating activities			$93,000
Cash flows from investing activities:			
Cash received from sale of investments		$ 75,000	
Less: Cash paid for purchase of equipment		157,000	
Net cash flow used for investing activities			(82,000)
Cash flows from financing activities:			
Cash received from sale of preferred stock		$160,000	
Less: Cash paid for dividends	$ 23,000		
Cash paid to retire bonds payable	125,000	148,000	
Net cash flow provided by financing activities			12,000
Increase in cash			$23,000
Cash at the beginning of the year			26,000
Cash at the end of the year			$49,000
Schedule of Noncash Investing and Financing Activities:			
Acquisition of land by issuance of common stock			$50,000
Schedule Reconciling Net Income with Cash Flows from Operating Activities:			
Net income, per income statement		$ 90,500	
Add: Depreciation	$ 18,000		
Decrease in inventories	8,000		
Increase in accounts payable	16,800		
Increase in accrued expenses	1,200	44,000	
		$134,500	
Deduct: Increase in trade receivables	$ 9,000		
Increase in prepaid expenses	1,000		
Decrease in income taxes payable	1,500		
Gain on sale of investments	30,000	41,500	
Net cash flow from operating activities			$93,000

APPENDIX

WORK SHEET FOR STATEMENT OF CASH FLOWS

Some accountants prefer to use a work sheet to assist them in assembling data for the statement of cash flows. Although a work sheet is not essential, it may be useful when a large number of transactions are to be analyzed. Whether or not a work sheet is used, the concepts of cash flow and the statements of cash flows presented in this chapter are not affected.

This appendix describes and illustrates the use of work sheets in preparing the statement of cash flows. Work sheets for both the indirect method and the direct method are discussed.

WORK SHEET—INDIRECT METHOD

The data for Rundell Inc., presented in Exhibit 3, are used as a basis for illustrating the work sheet for the indirect method. The procedures used in preparing this work sheet, shown in Exhibit 9, are outlined as follows:

1. List the title of each balance sheet account in the Accounts column. For each account, enter its balance as of December 31, 1993, in the first column, and its balance as of December 31, 1994, in the last column. Place the credit balances in parentheses. The column totals should equal zero, since the total of the debits in a column should equal the total of the credits in a column.
2. Analyze the change during the year in each account to determine the net increase (decrease) in cash and the cash flows from operating activities, investing activities, financing activities, and the noncash investing and financing activities. Show the effect of the change on cash flows by making entries in the Transactions columns.

Analysis of Accounts

As discussed in this chapter, an efficient method of analyzing cash flows is to determine the type of cash flow activity that led to changes in balance sheet accounts during the period. As each noncash account is analyzed, entries for specific types of cash flow activities related to the noncash accounts are made on the work sheet. After all the noncash accounts have been analyzed, an entry is made for the increase (decrease) in cash during the period. *These entries, however, are not posted to the ledger.* They only aid in assembling the data on the work sheet for use in preparing the statement of cash flows.

The order in which the accounts are analyzed is unimportant. However, it is more efficient to begin with the retained earnings account and proceed upward in the accounts listing.

RETAINED EARNINGS. The work sheet shows a Retained Earnings balance of $112,000 at December 31, 1993, and $172,500 at December 31, 1994. Thus, retained earnings increased $60,500 during the year. This increase resulted from two factors: (1) net income of $90,500 and (2) declaration of cash dividends of $30,000. To identify the cash flows by activity, two entries are made on the work sheet. These entries also serve to account for or explain, in terms of cash flows, the increase of $60,500.

In closing the accounts at the end of the year, the retained earnings account was credited for the net income of $90,500. The $90,500 is reported on the statement of cash flows as "cash flows from operating activities." The following entry is made in the Transactions columns on the work sheet. This entry (1) accounts for the credit portion of the closing entry (to Retained Earnings) and (2) identifies the cash flow in the bottom portion of the work sheet.

(a) Operating Activities—Net Income   90,500
        Retained Earnings   90,500

Exhibit 9
Work Sheet for Statement of Cash
Flows—Indirect Method

Rundell Inc.
Work Sheet for Statement of Cash Flows
For Year Ended December 31, 1994

Accounts	Balance, Dec. 31, 1993	Transactions Debit	Transactions Credit	Balance, Dec. 31, 1994
Cash	26,000	(s) 23,000		49,000
Trade Receivables	65,000	(r) 9,000		74,000
Inventories	180,000		(q) 8,000	172,000
Prepaid Expenses	3,000	(p) 1,000		4,000
Investments	45,000		(o) 45,000	—
Land	40,000	(n) 50,000		90,000
Building	200,000			200,000
Accumulated Depreciation—Building	(30,000)		(m) 6,000	(36,000)
Equipment	142,000	(l) 157,000	(k) 9,000	290,000
Accumulated Depreciation—Equipment	(40,000)	(k) 9,000	(j) 12,000	(43,000)
Accounts Payable	(28,200)		(h) 16,800	(45,000)
Accrued Expenses	(3,800)		(i) 1,200	(5,000)
Income Taxes Payable	(4,000)	(g) 1,500		(2,500)
Dividends Payable	(8,000)		(f) 7,000	(15,000)
Bonds Payable	(245,000)	(e) 125,000		(120,000)
Preferred Stock	—		(d) 150,000	(150,000)
Paid-In Capital in Excess of Par—Preferred Stock	—		(d) 10,000	(10,000)
Common Stock	(230,000)		(c) 50,000	(280,000)
Retained Earnings	(112,000)	(b) 30,000	(a) 90,500	(172,500)
Totals	0	405,500	405,500	0
Operating activities:				
Net Income		(a) 90,500		
Decrease in income taxes payable			(g) 1,500	
Increase in accounts payable		(h) 16,800		
Increase in accrued expenses		(i) 1,200		
Depreciation of equipment		(j) 12,000		
Depreciation of building		(m) 6,000		
Gain on sale of investments			(o) 30,000	
Increase in prepaid expenses			(p) 1,000	
Decrease in inventories		(q) 8,000		
Increase in trade receivables			(r) 9,000	
Investing activities:				
Purchase of equipment			(l) 157,000	
Sale of investments		(o) 75,000		
Financing activities:				
Declaration of cash dividends			(b) 30,000	
Issuance of preferred stock		(d) 160,000		
Retirement of bonds payable			(e) 125,000	
Increase in dividends payable		(f) 7,000		
Schedule of noncash investing and financing activities:				
Acquisition of land by issuance of common stock		(c) 50,000	(n) 50,000	
Net increase in cash			(s) 23,000	
Totals		426,500	426,500	

In closing the accounts at the end of the year, the retained earnings account was debited for dividends declared of $30,000. The $30,000 is reported as a financing activity on the statement of cash flows. The following entry on the work sheet (1) accounts for the debit portion of the closing entry (to Retained Earnings) and (2) identifies the cash flow in the bottom portion of the work sheet.

(b) Retained Earnings	30,000	
Financing Activities—Declaration of Cash Dividends		30,000

The $30,000 of declared dividends will be adjusted later for the actual amount of cash dividends paid during the year.

OTHER ACCOUNTS. The analysis of the changes in the other accounts and their effect on cash flows are discussed in the chapter and therefore are not repeated in this appendix. The related entries are made in the work sheet in a manner similar to entries (a) and (b). A summary of these entries is as follows:

(c) Schedule of Noncash Investing and Financing Activities—		
Acquisition of Land by Issuance of Common Stock	50,000	
Common Stock		50,000
(d) Financing Activities—Issuance of Preferred Stock	160,000	
Preferred Stock		150,000
Paid-In Capital in Excess of Par—Preferred Stock		10,000
(e) Bonds Payable	125,000	
Financing Activities—Retirement of Bonds Payable		125,000
(f) Financing Activities—Increase in Dividends Payable	7,000	
Dividends Payable		7,000
(g) Income Taxes Payable	1,500	
Operating Activities—Decrease in Income Taxes Payable		1,500
(h) Operating Activities—Increase in Accounts Payable	16,800	
Accounts Payable		16,800
(i) Operating Activities—Increase in Accrued Expenses	1,200	
Accrued Expenses		1,200
(j) Operating Activities—Depreciation of Equipment	12,000	
Accumulated Depreciation—Equipment		12,000
(k) Accumulated Depreciation—Equipment	9,000	
Equipment		9,000
(l) Equipment	157,000	
Investing Activities—Purchase of Equipment		157,000
(m) Operating Activities—Depreciation of Building	6,000	
Accumulated Depreciation—Building		6,000
(n) Land	50,000	
Schedule of Noncash Investing and Financing		
Activities—Acquisition of Land by Issuance of		
Common Stock		50,000
(o) Investing Activities—Sale of Investments	75,000	
Operating Activities—Gain on Sale of Investments		30,000
Investments		45,000
(p) Prepaid Expenses	1,000	
Operating Activities—Increase in Prepaid Expenses		1,000
(q) Operating Activities—Decrease in Inventories	8,000	
Inventories		8,000
(r) Trade Receivables	9,000	
Operating Activities—Increase in Trade Receivables		9,000
(s) Cash	23,000	
Net Increase in Cash		23,000

Completing the Work Sheet

After all the balance sheet accounts have been analyzed and the entries made on the work sheet, all the operating, investing, and financing activities are identified in the bottom portion of the work sheet. The accuracy of the work sheet entries is verified by the equality of the totals of the debit and credit Transactions columns.

Preparation of the Statement of Cash Flows

The statement of cash flows prepared from the work sheet is identical to the statement in Exhibit 6. The data for the three sections of the statement are obtained from the bottom portion of the work sheet. Some of these data may not be reported exactly as they appear in the work sheet. For example, in reporting the cash flows from operating activities, the total depreciation expense ($18,000) is reported instead of the two separate amounts ($12,000 and $6,000).

In the cash flows from operating activities section, the effect of depreciation is normally presented first. The effects of increases and decreases in current assets and current liabilities are then presented. The effects of any gains and losses on operating activities are normally reported last. The cash paid for dividends is reported as $23,000 instead of the amount of dividends declared ($30,000) less the increase in dividends payable ($7,000). The issuance of the common stock for land ($50,000) is reported in a separate schedule.

WORK SHEET—DIRECT METHOD

A work sheet can also be used as an aid in assembling data for preparing a statement of cash flows under the direct method. As a basis for illustration, the balance sheet data for Rundell Inc. in Exhibit 3 and the income statement data in Exhibit 7 are used. The procedures used in preparing the work sheet shown in Exhibit 10 are outlined as follows:

1. List the title of each asset account in the Accounts column. For each account, enter its balance as of December 31, 1993, in the first column, and its balance as of December 31, 1994, in the last column. Place the contra asset account balances (credit balances) in parentheses. Enter the amount of the total assets for December 31, 1993 and 1994, on the work sheet.
2. List the title of each liability and stockholders' equity account in the Accounts column. For each account, enter its balance as of December 31, 1993, in the first column, and its balance as of December 31, 1994, in the last column. Enter the total liabilities and stockholders' equity for December 31, 1993 and 1994, on the work sheet. The total assets and the total liabilities and stockholders' equity should be equal for each year.
3. List the title of each income statement account and "Net Income" on the work sheet.
4. Analyze the effect of each income statement item on cash flows from operating activities. Beginning with sales, enter the balance of each item in the proper Transactions column. Complete the entry in the Transactions columns to show the effect on cash flows.
5. Analyze the change during the year in each balance sheet account to determine the net increase (decrease) in cash and the cash flows from operating activities, investing activities, financing activities, and the noncash investing and financing activities. Show the effect of the change on cash flows by making entries in the Transactions columns.

Analysis of Accounts

Under the direct method of reporting cash flows from operating activities, the analysis of accounts begins with the income statement. As each income statement account is analyzed, entries that show its effect on cash flows from operating activities are made on the work sheet. After the income statement accounts have been analyzed, changes in the balance sheet accounts are analyzed.

The order in which the balance sheet accounts are analyzed is unimportant. However, it is more efficient to begin with the retained earnings account and proceed upward in the account listing. As each noncash balance sheet account is analyzed, entries for the related cash flow activities are made on the work sheet. After all the noncash accounts have been analyzed, an entry is made for the increase (decrease) in cash during the period.

Exhibit 10   *Work Sheet for Statement of Cash Flows—Direct Method*

Rundell Inc.
Work Sheet for Statement of Cash Flows
For Year Ended December 31, 1994

Accounts	Balance, Dec. 31, 1993	Transactions Debit	Transactions Credit	Balance, Dec. 31, 1994
Balance Sheet				
Cash	26,000	(w) 23,000		49,000
Trade Receivables	65,000	(v) 9,000		74,000
Inventories	180,000		(u) 8,000	172,000
Prepaid Expenses	3,000	(t) 1,000		4,000
Investments	45,000		(e) 45,000	—
Land	40,000	(s) 50,000		90,000
Building	200,000			200,000
Accumulated Depreciation—Building	(30,000)		(c) 6,000	(36,000)
Equipment	142,000	(r) 157,000	(q) 9,000	290,000
Accumulated Depreciation—Equipment	(40,000)	(q) 9,000	(c) 12,000	(43,000)
Total Assets	631,000			800,000
Accounts Payable	28,200		(p) 16,800	45,000
Accrued Expenses	3,800		(o) 1,200	5,000
Income Taxes Payable	4,000	(n) 1,500		2,500
Dividends Payable	8,000		(m) 7,000	15,000
Bonds Payable	245,000	(l) 125,000		120,000
Preferred Stock	—		(k) 150,000	150,000
Paid-In Capital in Excess of Par—Preferred Stock	—		(k) 10,000	10,000
Common Stock	230,000		(j) 50,000	280,000
Retained Earnings	112,000	(i) 30,000	(h) 90,500	172,500
Total Liabilities and Stockholders' Equity	631,000			800,000
Income Statement				
Sales			(a) 960,000	
Cost of Merchandise Sold		(b) 580,000		
Depreciation Expense		(c) 18,000		
Other Operating Expenses		(d) 260,000		
Gain on Sales of Investments			(e) 30,000	
Interest Expense		(f) 14,000		
Income Taxes		(g) 27,500		
Net Income		(h) 90,500		
Cash Flows				
Operating activities:				
Cash received from customers		(a) 960,000	(v) 9,000	
Cash payments:				
Merchandise		(p) 16,800	(b) 580,000	
		(u) 8,000		
Operating expenses		(o) 1,200	(d) 260,000	
			(t) 1,000	
Interest expense			(f) 14,000	
Income taxes			(g) 27,500	
			(n) 1,500	
Investing activities:				
Sale of investments		(e) 75,000		
Purchase of equipment			(r) 157,000	
Financing activities:				
Declaration of cash dividends			(i) 30,000	
Issuance of preferred stock		(k) 160,000		
Retirement of bonds payable			(l) 125,000	
Increase in dividends payable		(m) 7,000		
Schedule of noncash investing & financing activities:				
Acquisition of land by issuance of common stock		(j) 50,000	(s) 50,000	
Net increase in cash			(w) 23,000	
Totals		2,673,500	2,673,500	

SALES. The income statement for Rundell Inc. shows sales of $960,000 for the year. Sales for cash provide cash when the sale is made. Sales on account provide cash when customers pay their bills. The entry on the work sheet is as follows:

(a)   Operating Activities—Receipts from Customers   960,000
        Sales   960,000

COST OF MERCHANDISE SOLD. The income statement for Rundell Inc. shows cost of merchandise sold of $580,000 for the year. The cost of merchandise sold requires cash payments for cash purchases of merchandise. For purchases on account, cash payments are made when the invoices are due. The entry on the work sheet is as follows:

(b)   Cost of Merchandise Sold   580,000
        Operating Activities—Payments for Merchandise   580,000

DEPRECIATION EXPENSE. The income statement for Rundell Inc. shows depreciation expense of $18,000. Depreciation expense does not require a cash outflow and thus is not reported on the statement of cash flows. The entry on the work sheet to fully account for the depreciation expense is as follows:

(c)   Depreciation Expense   18,000
        Accumulated Depreciation—Building   6,000
        Accumulated Depreciation—Equipment   12,000

OTHER ACCOUNTS. The analysis of the changes in the other accounts and their effect on cash flows are discussed in the chapter and therefore are not repeated in this appendix. The related entries are made on the work sheet in a manner similar to entries (a), (b), and (c). A summary of these entries is as follows:

(d)   Other Operating Expenses   260,000
        Operating Activities—Payments for
            Operating Expenses   260,000
(e)   Investing Activities—Sales of Investments   75,000
        Investments   45,000
        Gain on Sales of Investments   30,000
(f)   Interest Expense   14,000
        Operating Activities—Payments for Interest   14,000
(g)   Income Taxes   27,500
        Operating Activities—Payments for Income Taxes   27,500
(h)   Net Income   90,500
        Retained Earnings   90,500
(i)   Retained Earnings   30,000
        Financing Activities—Declaration of
            Cash Dividends   30,000
(j)   Schedule of Noncash Investing and Financing Activities—
      Acquisition of Land by Issuance of Common Stock   50,000
        Common Stock   50,000

(k)	Financing Activities—Issuance of Preferred Stock	160,000	
	Preferred Stock		150,000
	Paid-In Capital in Excess of Par—Preferred Stock		10,000
(l)	Bonds Payable	125,000	
	Financing Activities—Retirement of Bonds Payable		125,000
(m)	Financing Activities—Increase in Dividends Payable	7,000	
	Dividends Payable		7,000
(n)	Income Taxes Payable	1,500	
	Operating Activities—Decrease in Income Taxes Payable		1,500
(o)	Operating Activities—Cash Payments for		
	Operating Expenses	1,200	
	Accrued Expenses		1,200
(p)	Operating Activities—Cash Payments for Merchandise	16,800	
	Accounts Payable		16,800
(q)	Accumulated Depreciation—Equipment	9,000	
	Equipment		9,000
(r)	Equipment	157,000	
	Investing Activities—Purchase of Equipment		157,000
(s)	Land	50,000	
	Schedule of Noncash Investing and Financing Activities—		
	Acquisition of Land by Issuance of Common Stock		50,000
(t)	Prepaid Expenses	1,000	
	Operating Activities—Cash Payments for		
	Operating Expenses		1,000
(u)	Operating Activities—Cash Payments for Merchandise	8,000	
	Inventories		8,000
(v)	Trade Receivables	9,000	
	Operating Activities—Cash Received from Customers		9,000
(w)	Cash	23,000	
	Net Increase in Cash		23,000

Completing the Work Sheet

After all the income statements and balance sheet accounts have been analyzed and the entries made on the work sheet, all the operating, investing, and financing activities are identified in the bottom portion of the work sheet. The mathematical accuracy of the work sheet entries is verified by the equality of the totals of the debit and credit Transactions columns.

Preparation of the Statement of Cash Flows

The statement of cash flows prepared from the work sheet is identical to the statement in Exhibit 8. The data for the three sections of the statement are obtained from the bottom portion of the work sheet. Some of these data may not be reported exactly as they appear on the work sheet.

CHAPTER REVIEW

Key Points

Objective 1. Explain why the statement of cash flows is one of the basic financial statements.

The statement of cash flows is one of the basic financial statements because it reports useful information about a firm's ability to generate cash from operations, maintain and expand its operating capacity, meet its financial obligations, and pay dividends. This information assists investors, creditors, and others in assessing the firm's profit potential and its ability to pay its maturing debt. The statement of cash flows is also useful to managers in evaluating past operations and in planning future operating, investing, and financing activities.

Objective 2. Summarize the type of cash flow activities reported in the statement of cash flows.

The statement of cash flows reports cash receipts and cash payments by three types of activities: operating activities, investing activities, and financing activities.

Cash flows from operating activities are cash flows from transactions that affect net income. There are two methods of reporting cash flows from operating activities: (1) the direct method and (2) the indirect method.

Cash inflows from investing activities are cash flows from the sale of investments, plant assets, and intangible assets. Cash outflows generally include payments to acquire investments, plant assets, and intangible assets.

Cash inflows from financing activities include proceeds from the issuance of equity securities, such as preferred and common stock. Cash inflows also arise from the issuance of bonds, mortgage notes payable, and other long-term debt. Cash outflows from financing activities include the payment of cash dividends, the purchase of treasury stock, and the repayment of amounts borrowed.

Investing and financing for an enterprise may be affected by transactions that do not involve cash. The effect of such transactions should be reported in a separate schedule accompanying the statement of cash flows.

Because it may be misleading, cash flow per share is not reported in the statement of cash flows.

Objective 3. Prepare a statement of cash flows, using the indirect method.

To prepare the statement of cash flows, changes in the noncash balance sheet accounts are analyzed. This logic relies on the fact that a change in any balance sheet account can by analyzed in terms of changes in the other balance sheet accounts. Thus, by analyzing the noncash balance sheet accounts, those activities that resulted in cash flows can be identified. Although the noncash balance sheet accounts may be analyzed in any order, it is usually more efficient to begin with retained earnings. Additional data are obtained by analyzing the income statement accounts and supporting records.

The preparation of the statement of cash flows using the indirect method of reporting cash flows from operating activities is illustrated in this chapter.

Objective 4. Prepare a statement of cash flows, using the direct method.

The direct method and the indirect method will report the same amount of cash flows from operating activities. Also, the manner of reporting cash flows from investing and financing activities is the same under both methods. The methods differ in how the cash flow from operating activities data are obtained, analyzed, and reported.

The direct method reports cash flows from operating activities by major classes of operating cash receipts and cash payments. The difference between the major classes of total operating cash receipts and total operating cash payments is the net cash flow from operating activities.

The data for reporting cash flows from operating activities by the direct method can be obtained by analyzing the cash flows related to the revenues and expenses reported on the income statement. The revenues and expenses are adjusted from the accrual basis of accounting to the cash basis for purposes of preparing the statement of cash flows.

When the direct method is used, a reconciliation of net income and net cash flow from operating activities is reported in a separate schedule. This schedule is similar to the cash flows from operating activities section of the statement of cash flows prepared using the indirect method.

The preparation of the statement of cash flows using the direct method is illustrated in this chapter.

Glossary of Key Terms

Cash flows from financing activities. The section of the statement of cash flows which reports cash flows from transactions that affect the equity and debt of the entity. **Objective 2**

Cash flows from investing activities. The section of the statement of cash flows which reports cash flows from transactions that affect investments in noncurrent assets. **Objective 2**

Cash flows from operating activities. The section of the statement of cash flows which reports the cash transactions that affect the determination of net income. **Objective 2**

Direct method. A method of reporting the cash flows from operating activities as the difference between the operating cash receipts and the operating cash payments. **Objective 2**

Indirect method. A method of reporting the cash flows from operating activities as the net income from operations adjusted for all deferrals of past cash receipts and payments and all accruals of expected future cash receipts and payments. **Objective 2**

Statement of cash flows. A summary of the major cash receipts and cash payments for a period. **Objective 1**

Self-Examination Questions
Answers at end of chapter.

1. An example of a cash flow from an operating activity is:
   A. receipt of cash from the sale of capital stock
   B. receipt of cash from the sale of bonds
   C. payment of cash for dividends
   D. receipt of cash from customers on account

2. An example of a cash flow from an investing activity is:
   A. receipt of cash from the sale of equipment
   B. receipt of cash from the sale of capital stock
   C. payment of cash for dividends
   D. payment of cash to acquire treasury stock

3. An example of a cash flow from a financing activity is:
   A. receipt of cash from customers on account
   B. receipt of cash from the sale of equipment
   C. payment of cash for dividends
   D. payment of cash to acquire marketable securities

4. Which of the following methods of reporting cash flows from operating activities adjusts net income for revenues and expenses not involving the receipt or payment of cash?
   A. Direct method   C. Reciprocal method
   B. Purchase method   D. Indirect method

5. The net income reported on the income statement for the year was $55,000, and depreciation of plant assets for the year was $22,000. The balances of the current asset and current liability accounts at the beginning and end of the year are as follows:

	End	Beginning
Cash	$ 65,000	$ 70,000
Trade receivables	100,000	90,000
Inventories	145,000	150,000
Prepaid expenses	7,500	8,000
Accounts payable (merchandise creditors)	51,000	58,000

The total amount reported for cash flows from operating activities in the statement of cash flows, using the indirect method, is:
A. $33,000   C. $65,500
B. $55,000   D. $77,000

ILLUSTRATIVE PROBLEM

The comparative balance sheet of Nesbitt Inc. for December 31, 1994 and 1993, is as follows:

Nesbitt Inc.
Comparative Balance Sheet
December 31, 1994 and 1993

	1994	1993
Assets		
Cash	$ 65,100	$ 42,500
Trade receivables (net)	91,350	61,150
Inventories	104,500	109,500
Prepaid expenses	3,600	2,700
Investments (long-term)	—	35,000
Land	30,000	50,000
Buildings	345,000	210,000
Accumulated depreciation—buildings	(120,600)	(110,400)
Machinery and equipment	255,000	255,000
Accumulated depreciation—machinery and equipment	(92,000)	(65,000)
Patents	35,000	40,000
	$716,950	$630,450
Liabilities and Stockholders' Equity		
Accounts payable (merchandise creditors)	$ 42,800	$ 65,950
Accrued expenses (operating expenses)	18,000	12,600
Income taxes payable	7,000	4,000
Dividends payable	15,000	10,000
Mortgage note payable, due 2001	60,000	—
Bonds payable	—	75,000
Common stock, $20 par	300,000	250,000
Excess of issue price over par—common stock	100,000	75,000
Retained earnings	174,150	137,900
	$716,950	$630,450

ILLUSTRATIVE PROBLEM ILLUSTRATIVE PROBLEM ILLUSTRATIVE PROBLEM

The income statement for Nesbitt Inc. is shown below.

Nesbitt Inc.
Income Statement
For Year Ended December 31, 1994

Sales		$800,000
Cost of merchandise sold		480,000
Gross profit		$320,000
Operating expenses:		
Depreciation expense	$ 37,200	
Patent amortization	5,000	
Other operating expenses	140,500	
Total operating expenses		182,700
Income from operations		$137,300
Other income:		
Gain on sale of investments	$ 15,000	
Other expense:		
Interest expense	6,500	8,500
Income before income tax		$145,800
Income tax		49,550
Net income		$ 96,250

An examination of the accounting records revealed the following additional information applicable to 1994:

  a. Land costing $20,000 was sold for $20,000.
  b. A mortgage note was issued for $60,000.
  c. A building costing $135,000 was constructed.
  d. 2,500 shares of common stock were issued at 30 in exchange for the bonds payable.
  e. Cash dividends declared were $60,000.

Instructions

1. Prepare a statement of cash flows using the indirect method of reporting cash flows from operating activities.
2. Prepare a statement of cash flows using the direct method of reporting cash flows from operating activities.

Solution

1.

Nesbitt Inc.
Statement of Cash Flows—Indirect Method
For Year Ended December 31, 1994

Cash flows from operating activities:			
Net income, per income statement		$ 96,250	
Add: Depreciation	$37,200		
Amortization of patents	5,000		
Decrease in inventories	5,000		
Increase in accrued expenses	5,400		
Increase in income taxes payable	3,000	55,600	
		$151,850	
Deduct: Increase in trade receivables (net)	$30,200		
Increase in prepaid expenses	900		
Decrease in accounts payable	23,150		
Gain on sales of investments	15,000	69,250	
Net cash flow from operating activities			$82,600
Cash flows from investing activities:			
Cash received from sale of:			
Investments	$50,000		
Land	20,000	$ 70,000	
Less: Cash paid for construction of building		135,000	
Net cash flow used for investing activities			(65,000)

Cash flows from financing activities:
   Cash received from issuance of mortgage
     note payable $ 60,000
   Less: Cash paid for dividends   55,000
   Net cash flow provided by financing activities   5,000
Increase in cash $22,600
Cash at the beginning of the year   42,500
Cash at the end of the year $65,100

Schedule of Noncash Investing and Financing Activities:
   Issuance of common stock to retire bonds payable $75,000

2.

Nesbitt Inc.
Statement of Cash Flows—Direct Method
For Year Ended December 31, 1994

Cash flows from operating activities:
   Cash received from customers[1] $769,800
   Deduct: Cash payments for merchandise[2] $498,150
         Cash payments for operating
          expenses[3]   136,000
         Cash payments for interest expense   6,500
         Cash payments for income tax[4]   46,550   687,200
   Net cash flow from operating activities $82,600
Cash flows from investing activities:
   Cash received from sale of:
     Investments $ 50,000
     Land   20,000 $ 70,000
   Less: Cash paid for construction of building   135,000
   Net cash flow used for investing activities   (65,000)
Cash flows from financing activities:
   Cash received from issuance of mortgage
     note payable $ 60,000
   Less: Cash paid for dividends[5]   55,000
   Net cash flow provided by financing activities   5,000
Increase in cash $22,600
Cash at the beginning of the year   42,500
Cash at the end of the year $65,100

Schedule of Noncash Investing and Financing Activities:
   Issuance of common stock to retire bonds payable $75,000

Computations: [1]$800,000 - $30,200 = $769,800
              [2]$480,000 - $5,000 + $23,150 = $498,150
              [3]$140,500 + $900 - $5,400 = $136,000
              [4]$49,550 - $3,000 = $46,550
              [5]$60,000 + $10,000 – $15,000 = $55,000

DISCUSSION QUESTIONS

1.   Which financial statement is most useful in evaluating past operations and in planning future investing and financing activities?
2.   What are the three types of activities reported on the statement of cash flows?
3.   State the effect (cash receipt or payment, and amount) of each of the following transactions, considered individually, on cash flows:
   a.   Sold a new issue of $100,000 of bonds at 101.
   b.   Sold equipment with a book value of $37,500 for $40,000.
   c.   Sold 5,000 shares of $20 par common stock at $35 per share.
   d.   Retired $500,000 of bonds on which there was $2,500 of unamortized bond discount for $501,000.

4. Identify each of the following as to type of cash flow activity (operating, investing, or financing):
   a. purchase of buildings
   b. issuance of common stock
   c. sale of investments
   d. net income
   e. issuance of bonds
   f. redemption of bonds
   g. purchase of treasury stock
   h. payment of cash dividends
   i. purchase of patents
   j. issuance of preferred stock
   k. sale of equipment

5. Name the two alternative methods of reporting cash flows from operating activities in the statement of cash flows.

6. What is the principal disadvantage of the direct method of reporting cash flows from operating activities?

7. What are the major advantages of the indirect method of reporting cash flows from operating activities?

8. On the statement of cash flows, if the cash inflows from investing activities exceed the cash outflows, how is the difference described?

9. On the statement of cash flows, if the cash outflows from investing activities exceed the cash inflows, how is the difference described?

10. On the statement of cash flows, if the cash inflows from financing activities exceed the cash outflows, how is the difference described?

11. On the statement of cash flows, if the cash outflows from financing activities exceed the cash inflows, how is the difference described?

12. A corporation issued $200,000 of common stock in exchange for $200,000 of plant assets. Where would this transaction be reported on the statement of cash flows?

13. A corporation acquired as a long-term investment all of the capital stock of XL Co., valued at $5,000,000, by issuance of $5,000,000 of its own common stock. Where should the transaction be reported on the statement of cash flows?

14. a. What is the effect on cash flows of the declaration and issuance of a stock dividend?
    b. Is the stock dividend reported on the statement of cash flows?

15. What is the effect on cash flows of an appropriation of retained earnings for bonded indebtedness?

16. Indicate whether each of the following would be added to or deducted from net income in determining net cash flow from operating activities by the indirect method:
    a. increase in notes payable due in 90 days
    b. decrease in accounts payable
    c. gain on retirement of long-term debt
    d. depreciation of plant assets
    e. increase in merchandise inventory
    f. amortization of discount on bonds payable
    g. increase in notes receivable due in 90 days
    h. decrease in accounts receivable
    i. loss on disposal of plant assets
    j. amortization of premium on bonds payable
    k. decrease in accrued salaries payable
    l. amortization of patents
    m. decrease in prepaid expenses

17. A retail enterprise, using the accrual method of accounting, owed merchandise creditors (accounts payable) $290,000 at the beginning of the year and $315,000 at the end of the year. What adjustment for the $25,000 increase must be made to net income in determining the amount of cash flows from operating activities by the indirect method? Explain.

18. If revenue from sales amounted to $900,000 for the year and trade receivables totaled $120,000 at the beginning of the year and $95,000 at the end of the year, what was the amount of cash received from customers during the year?

19. If salaries payable was $75,000 at the beginning of the year and $65,000 at the end of the year, should $10,000 be added to or deducted from income to determine the amount of cash flows from operating activities by the indirect method? Explain.

20. The board of directors declared cash dividends totaling $120,000 during the current year. The comparative balance sheet indicates dividends payable of $25,000 at the be-

ginning of the year and $30,000 at the end of the year. What was the amount of cash payments to stockholders during the year?

21. A long-term investment in bonds with a cost of $75,000 was sold for $80,000 cash. (a) What was the gain or loss on the sale? (b) What was the effect of the transaction on cash flows? (c) How should the transaction be reported in the statement of cash flows if cash flows from operating activities are reported by the indirect method?

22. A corporation issued $5,000,000 of 20-year bonds for cash at 105. How would the transaction be reported on the statement of cash flows?

23. Fully depreciated equipment costing $55,000 was discarded. What was the effect of the transaction on cash flows if (a) $5,000 cash is received, (b) there is no salvage value?

24. For the current year, Accord Company decided to switch from the indirect method to the direct method for reporting cash flows from operating activities on the statement of cash flows. Will the change cause the amount of net cash flow from operating activities to be (a) larger, (b) smaller, or (c) the same as if the indirect method had been used? Explain.

25. Name five common major classes of operating cash receipts or operating cash payments presented on the statement of cash flows when the cash flows from operating activities are reported by the direct method.

26. The cash flows from operating activities are reported by the direct method on the statement of cash flows. If sales for the current year were $750,000 and trade receivables decreased by $25,000 during the year, what was the amount of cash received from customers?

27. The cash flows from operating activities are reported by the direct method on the statement of cash flows. If income tax for the current year was $100,000 and income tax payable decreased by $25,000 during the year, what was the amount of cash payments for income tax?

REAL W⬤RLD FOCUS   28. In its 1991 annual report, PepsiCo, Inc. reported that during 1991 it issued treasury stock and debt of $162.7 million for acquisitions. How would this be reported on the statement of cash flows?

ETHICS DISCUSSION CASE

Alice Bowers, controller of Ortiz Inc., has decided to add *cash flow per share* to the financial statements. She feels that such reporting, although different from past reporting, would be useful to the readers. The *cash flow per share* would be reported on the statement of cash flows. On a comparative basis with the preceding year, the *cash flow per share* figure for the current year increased by 20% (as contrasted with a slight decline in net income and earnings per share).

■SHARPEN YOUR ▶   Discuss whether Alice Bowers is behaving in an ethical manner.
COMMUNICATION SKILLS

EXERCISES

EXERCISE 19-1
CASH FLOWS FROM
OPERATING ACTIVITIES—
NET LOSS
Objective 2

On its income statement for the current year, Carson company reported a net loss of $60,000 from operations. On its statement of cash flows, it reported $15,000 of cash flows from operating activities.

■SHARPEN YOUR ▶
COMMUNICATION SKILLS
EXERCISE 19-2
CASH FLOWS FROM
OPERATING ACTIVITIES—
INDIRECT METHOD
Objectives 2, 3

Explain what seems to be a contradiction between the loss and the cash flows.

The net income reported on the income statement for the current year was $87,100. Depreciation recorded on equipment and a building amounted to $31,750 for the year. Balances of the current asset and current liability accounts at the beginning and end of the year are as follows:

	End of Year	Beginning of Year
Cash	$ 64,250	$ 60,500
Trade receivables (net)	98,750	91,250
Inventories	110,000	95,000
Prepaid expenses	6,400	7,650
Accounts payable (merchandise creditors)	77,200	72,700
Salaries payable	3,250	5,750

a. Prepare the cash flows from operating activities section of the statement of cash flows, using the indirect method.
b. If the direct method had been used, would the net cash flow from operating activities have been the same? Explain.

EXERCISE 19-3
CASH FLOWS FROM
OPERATING ACTIVITIES—
INDIRECT METHOD
Objectives 2, 3

The net income reported on an income statement for the current year was $92,125. Depreciation recorded on store equipment for the year amounted to $43,500. Balances of the current asset and current liability accounts at the beginning and end of the year are as follows:

	End of Year	Beginning of Year
Cash	$ 70,150	$66,500
Trade receivables (net)	79,250	83,750
Merchandise inventory	110,000	97,000
Prepaid expenses	8,000	7,500
Accounts payable (merchandise creditors)	70,200	73,200
Wages payable	6,900	5,650

**SPREADSHEET
PROBLEM**

Prepare the cash flows from operating activities section of a statement of cash flows, using the indirect method.

EXERCISE 19-4
REPORTING CHANGES IN
EQUIPMENT ON STATEMENT
OF CASH FLOWS
Objectives 2, 3

An analysis of the general ledger accounts indicates that office equipment, which had cost $75,000 and on which accumulated depreciation totaled $67,500 on the date of sale, was sold for $7,000 during the year. Using this information, indicate the items to be reported on the statement of cash flows.

EXERCISE 19-5
REPORTING CHANGES IN
EQUIPMENT ON STATEMENT
OF CASH FLOWS
Objectives 2, 3

An analysis of the general ledger accounts indicates that delivery equipment, which had cost $45,000 and on which accumulated depreciation totaled $39,000 on the date of sale, was sold for $7,750 during the year. Using this information, indicate the items to be reported on the statement of cash flows.

EXERCISE 19-6
REPORTING LAND
TRANSACTIONS ON
STATEMENT OF CASH
FLOWS
Objectives 2, 3

On the basis of the details of the following plant asset account, indicate the items to be reported on the statement of cash flows:

ACCOUNT LAND   ACCOUNT NO.

Date		Item	Debit	Credit	Balance Debit	Balance Credit
19—						
Jan.	1	Balance			500,000	
Feb.	5	Purchased for cash	150,000			
Oct.	30	Sold for $75,000		40,000	610,000	

EXERCISE 19-7
REPORTING
STOCKHOLDERS' EQUITY
ITEMS ON STATEMENT OF
CASH FLOWS
Objectives 2, 3

On the basis of the following stockholders' equity accounts, indicate the items, exclusive of net income, to be reported on the statement of cash flows. There were no unpaid dividends at either the beginning or the end of the year.

ACCOUNT COMMON STOCK, $10 PAR   ACCOUNT NO.

Date		Item	Debit	Credit	Balance Debit	Balance Credit
19—						
Jan.	1	Balance, 50,000 shares				500,000
Feb.	11	5,000 shares issued for cash		50,000		
June	30	2,750-share stock dividend		27,500		577,500

PAID-IN CAPITAL IN EXCESS OF PAR—
ACCOUNT COMMON STOCK   ACCOUNT NO.

Date		Item	Debit	Credit	Balance Debit	Balance Credit
19—						
Jan.	1	Balance				90,000
Feb.	11	5,000 shares issued for cash		20,000		
June	30	Stock dividend		10,000		120,000

ACCOUNT RETAINED EARNINGS   ACCOUNT NO.

Date		Item	Debit	Credit	Balance Debit	Balance Credit
19—						
Jan.	1	Balance				275,000
June	30	Stock dividend	37,500			
Dec.	30	Cash dividend	55,000			
	31	Net income		97,500		280,000

EXERCISE 19-8
REPORTING LAND
ACQUISITION FOR CASH
AND MORTGAGE NOTE ON
STATEMENT OF CASH
FLOWS
Objectives 2, 3

On the basis of the details of the following asset account, indicate the items to be reported on the statement of cash flows:

ACCOUNT LAND   ACCOUNT NO.

Date		Item	Debit	Credit	Balance Debit	Balance Credit
19—						
Jan.	1	Balance			450,000	
Feb.	10	Purchased for cash	50,000			
Nov.	20	Purchased with long-term mortgage note	150,000		650,000	

EXERCISE 19-9
DETERMINATION OF NET
INCOME FROM NET CASH
FLOW FROM OPERATING
ACTIVITIES
Objectives 2, 3

Austin Inc. reported a net cash flow from operating activities of $46,500 on its statement of cash flows for the year ended December 31, 1994. The following information was reported in the cash flows from operating activities section of the statement of cash flows, using the indirect method:

Decrease in income tax payable	$ 1,250
Decrease in inventories	5,500
Depreciation	9,400
Gain on sale of investments	14,250
Increase in accounts payable	7,300
Increase in prepaid expenses	500
Increase in trade receivables	4,700

Determine the net income reported by Austin Inc. for the year ended December 31, 1994.

EXERCISE 19-10
DETERMINATION OF
SELECTED AMOUNTS FOR
CASH FLOWS FROM
OPERATING ACTIVITIES—
DIRECT METHOD
Objectives 2, 4

Selected data taken from the accounting records of Brown Company for the current year ended December 31 are as follows:

	Balance January 1	Balance December 31
Accrued expenses (operating expenses)	$12,000	$ 5,500
Accounts payable (merchandise creditors)	85,000	70,000
Inventories	62,500	53,500
Prepaid expenses	17,500	12,500

During the current year, the cost of merchandise sold was $790,000 and the operating expenses other than depreciation were $275,000. The direct method is used for presenting the cash flows from operating activities on the statement of cash flows.

Determine the amount reported on the statement of cash flows for (a) cash payments for merchandise and (b) cash payments for operating expenses.

EXERCISE 19-11
CASH FLOWS FROM
OPERATING ACTIVITIES—
DIRECT METHOD
Objectives 2, 4

The income statement of Jackson Company for the current year ended June 30 is as follows:

Sales		$995,000
Cost of merchandise sold		600,000
Gross profit		$395,000
Operating expenses:		
Depreciation expense	$ 31,500	
Other operating expenses	248,500	
Total operating expenses		280,000
Income before income tax		$115,000
Income tax		35,000
Net income		$ 80,000

712

Changes in the balances of selected accounts from the beginning to the end of the current year are as follows:

	Increase (Decrease)
Trade receivables (net)	$(26,000)
Inventories	11,200
Prepaid expenses	(1,250)
Accounts payable (merchandise creditors)	(17,500)
Accrued expenses (operating expenses)	6,800
Income tax payable	(7,100)

Prepare the cash flows from operating activities section of the statement of cash flows, using the direct method.

EXERCISE 19-12
CASH FLOWS FROM
OPERATING ACTIVITIES—
DIRECT METHOD
Objectives 2, 4

The income statement for Regal Company for the current year ended June 30 and balances of selected accounts at the beginning and the end of the year are as follows:

Sales		$872,500
Cost of merchandise sold		500,000
Gross profit		$372,500
Operating expenses:		
Depreciation expense	$ 32,250	
Other operating expenses	213,750	
Total operating expenses		246,000
Income before income tax		$126,500
Income tax		30,900
Net income		$ 95,600

	End of Year	Beginning of Year
Trade receivables (net)	$ 90,000	$80,000
Inventories	102,500	87,500
Prepaid expenses	6,900	7,650
Accounts payable (merchandise creditors)	74,200	69,700
Accrued expenses (operating expenses)	3,750	6,250
Income tax payable	2,225	2,225

Prepare the cash flows from operating activities section of the statement of cash flows, using the direct method.

EXERCISE 19-13
CASH FLOWS FROM
OPERATING ACTIVITIES—
DIRECT METHOD
Objectives 2, 4

The income statement for the current year and balances of selected accounts at the beginning and end of the current year are as follows:

Sales		$1,250,000
Cost of merchandise sold		750,000
Gross profit		$ 500,000
Operating expenses:		
Depreciation expense	$ 43,500	
Other operating expenses	327,875	
Total operating expenses		371,375
Operating income		$ 128,625
Other expense:		
Interest expense		9,000
Income before income tax		$ 119,625
Income tax		27,500
Net income		$ 92,125

	End of Year	Beginning of Year
Trade receivables	$79,750	$84,250
Inventories	99,500	86,500
Prepaid expenses	8,100	7,600
Accounts payable (merchandise creditors)	69,700	72,700
Accrued expenses (operating expenses)	6,900	5,650
Interest payable	1,750	1,750
Income tax payable	3,000	4,500

Prepare the cash flows from operating activities section of the statement of cash flows, using the direct method.

EXERCISE 19-14
CASH FLOWS FROM
OPERATING ACTIVITIES
Objectives 2, 4

Selected data from the income statement and statement of cash flows of Toys "R" Us, Inc., for the year ending February 1, 1992, are as follows:

Income Statement Data (dollars in thousands)

REAL WORLD FOCUS

Net earnings	$339,529
Depreciation and amortization	100,701
Deferred taxes (expense)	23,604

Statement of Cash Flows Data (dollars in thousands)

Decrease in accounts receivable	$ 9,092
Increase in merchandise inventories	115,436
Increase in prepaid expenses and other operating assets	16,176
Increase in accounts payable, accrued expenses, and taxes	461,436

Prepare the cash flows from operating activities section of the statement of cash flows (using the indirect method) for Toys "R" Us, Inc., for the year ending February 1, 1992.

WhAT'S WRONG
WITH THi2?

How many errors can you find in the following statement of cash flows? The cash balance at the beginning of the year was $70,700. All other figures are correct.

Environmental Products Inc.
Statement of Cash Flows
For Year Ended December 31, 19—

Cash flows from operating activities:			
Net income, per income statement			$ 90,300
Add: Depreciation		$ 49,000	
Increase in trade receivables		11,200	60,200
			$150,500
Deduct: Increase in accounts payable		$ 4,400	
Increase in inventories		22,200	
Gain on sale of investments		5,000	
Decrease in accrued expenses		1,600	33,200
Net cash flow from operating activities			$117,300
Cash flows from investing activities:			
Cash received from sale of investments			$ 85,000
Less: Cash paid for purchase of land		$ 70,000	
Cash paid for purchase of equipment		150,100	220,100
Net cash flow used for investing activities			(135,100)
Cash flows from financing activities:			
Cash received from sale of common stock			$107,000
Plus cash paid for dividends			45,500
Net cash flow provided by financing activities			152,500
Increase in cash			$134,700
Cash at the end of the year			100,800
Cash at the beginning of the year			$235,500

PROBLEMS

Series A

PROBLEM 19-1A
STATEMENT OF CASH
FLOWS—INDIRECT
METHOD
Objective 3

The comparative balance sheet of C. T. Green Inc. for June 30, 1994 and 1993, is as follows:

	June 30, 1994	June 30, 1993
Assets		
Cash	$ 82,000	$ 64,800
Trade receivables (net)	104,800	91,000
Inventories	127,400	108,900
Investments	—	90,000
Land	102,000	—
Equipment	425,700	329,700
Accumulated depreciation	(171,800)	(135,800)
	$670,100	$548,600
Liabilities and Stockholders' Equity		
Accounts payable (merchandise creditors)	$ 70,900	$ 63,000
Accrued expenses (operating expenses)	6,100	5,000
Dividends payable	14,400	12,000
Common stock, $10 par	360,000	300,000
Paid-in capital in excess of par—common stock	31,400	19,400
Retained earnings	187,300	149,200
	$670,100	$548,600

The following additional information was taken from the records of C. T. Green Inc.:

    a. Equipment and land were acquired for cash.
    b. There were no disposals of equipment during the year.
    c. The investments were sold for $98,000 cash.
    d. The common stock was issued for cash.
    e. There was a $88,500 credit to Retained Earnings for net income.
    f. There was a $50,400 debit to Retained Earnings for cash dividends declared.

Instructions
Prepare a statement of cash flows, using the indirect method of presenting cash flows from operating activities.

PROBLEM 19-2A
STATEMENT OF CASH
FLOWS—INDIRECT
METHOD
Objective 3

The comparative balance sheet of Kane Inc. at June 30, 1994 and 1993, is as follows:

	June 30, 1994	June 30, 1993
Assets		
Cash	$ 45,100	$ 64,600
Trade receivables (net)	116,300	129,300
Merchandise inventory	354,700	346,400
Prepaid expenses	5,200	3,600
Plant assets	440,000	396,800
Accumulated depreciation—plant assets	(232,300)	(266,600)
	$729,000	$674,100
Liabilities and Stockholders' Equity		
Accounts payable (merchandise creditors)	$ 71,300	$ 65,400
Mortgage note payable	—	101,300
Common stock, $30 par	300,000	270,000
Paid-in capital in excess of par—common stock	39,800	34,800
Retained earnings	317,900	202,600
	$729,000	$674,100

Additional data obtained from the income statement and from an examination of the accounts in the ledger are as follows:

a. Net income, $155,300.
b. Depreciation reported on the income statement, $38,600.
c. An addition to the building was constructed at a cost of $116,100, and fully depreciated equipment costing $72,900 was discarded, with no salvage realized.
d. The mortgage note payable was not due until 2000, but the terms permitted earlier payment without penalty.
e. 1,000 shares of common stock were issued at 35 for cash.
f. Cash dividends declared and paid, $40,000.

Instructions

Prepare a statement of cash flows, using the indirect method of presenting cash flows from operating activities.

PROBLEM 19-3A
STATEMENT OF CASH
FLOWS—INDIRECT
METHOD
Objective 3

The comparative balance sheet of Paton Corporation at December 31, 1994 and 1993, is as follows:

	Dec. 31, 1994	Dec. 31, 1993
Assets		
Cash	$ 72,400	$ 66,800
Trade receivables (net)	87,900	100,500
Inventories	192,100	178,600
Prepaid expenses	6,400	2,900
Land	75,000	75,000
Buildings	480,600	316,800
Accumulated depreciation—buildings	(157,500)	(144,000)
Machinery and equipment	206,300	206,300
Accumulated depreciation—machinery and equipment	(93,000)	(81,300)
Patents	30,000	37,500
	$900,200	$759,100
Liabilities and Stockholders' Equity		
Accounts payable (merchandise creditors)	$ 27,200	$ 38,900
Dividends payable	18,800	15,000
Salaries payable	7,900	14,600
Mortgage note payable, due 1999	120,000	—
Bonds payable	—	70,000
Common stock, $10 par	410,000	360,000
Paid-in capital in excess of par—common stock	65,000	45,000
Retained earnings	251,300	215,600
	$900,200	$759,100

An examination of the income statement and the accounting records revealed the following additional information applicable to 1994:

a. Net income, $63,200.
b. Depreciation expense reported on the income statement: buildings, $13,500; machinery and equipment, $11,700.
c. Patent amortization reported on the income statement, $7,500.
d. A building was constructed for $163,800.
e. A mortgage note for $120,000 was issued for cash.
f. 5,000 shares of common stock were issued at 14 in exchange for the bonds payable.
g. Cash dividends declared, $27,500.

SPREADSHEET
PROBLEM

Instructions

Prepare a statement of cash flows, using the indirect method of presenting cash flows from operating activities.

PROBLEM 19-7A
STATEMENT OF CASH
FLOWS—DIRECT AND
INDIRECT METHODS
Objectives 3, 4

An income statement and a comparative balance sheet for DABCO Company are as follows:

DABCO Company
Income Statement
For Year Ended December 31, 1994

Sales		$1,520,700
Cost of merchandise sold		1,110,200
Gross profit		$ 410,500
Operating expenses		
Depreciation expense	$ 39,990	
Other operating expenses	227,110	
Total operating expenses		267,100
		$ 143,400
Other income:		
Gain on sale of land	$ 20,500	
Gain on sale of investments	11,000	
	$ 31,500	
Other expense:		
Interest expense	25,000	6,500
Income before income tax		$ 149,900
Income tax		38,500
Net income		$ 111,400

DABCO Company
Comparative Balance Sheet
December 31, 1994 and 1993

	1994	1993
Assets		
Cash	$ 57,870	$ 66,200
Trade receivables (net)	137,180	117,800
Inventories	211,500	190,150
Prepaid expenses	5,160	6,120
Investments	44,500	93,500
Land	77,250	75,000
Buildings	412,500	225,000
Accumulated depreciation—buildings	(91,260)	(81,220)
Equipment	493,700	437,500
Accumulated depreciation—equipment	(179,700)	(149,750)
Total assets	$1,168,700	$980,300
Liabilities and Stockholders' Equity		
Accounts payable (merchandise creditors)	$ 58,715	$ 51,875
Accrued expenses (operating expenses)	11,000	10,500
Interest payable	1,875	1,875
Income tax payable	5,000	8,500
Dividends payable	15,660	12,500
Mortgage note payable	175,000	—
Bonds payable	100,000	250,000
Common stock, $25 par	450,000	375,000
Paid-in capital in excess of par—common stock	47,250	41,250
Retained earnings	304,200	228,800
Total liabilities and stockholders' equity	$1,168,700	$980,300

The following additional information on cash flows during the year was obtained from an examination of the ledger:

a. Investments (long-term) were purchased for $40,500.
b. Investments (long-term) costing $89,500 were sold for $100,500.
c. Equipment was purchased for $56,200. There were no disposals.
d. A building valued at $187,500 and land valued at $62,500 were acquired by a cash payment of $250,000.
e. Land which cost $60,250 was sold for $80,750 cash.

Additional data obtained from the income statement and from an examination of the accounts in the ledger are as follows:

    a. Net income, $155,300.
    b. Depreciation reported on the income statement, $38,600.
    c. An addition to the building was constructed at a cost of $116,100, and fully depreciated equipment costing $72,900 was discarded, with no salvage realized.
    d. The mortgage note payable was not due until 2000, but the terms permitted earlier payment without penalty.
    e. 1,000 shares of common stock were issued at 35 for cash.
    f. Cash dividends declared and paid, $40,000.

Instructions

Prepare a statement of cash flows, using the indirect method of presenting cash flows from operating activities.

PROBLEM 19-3A
STATEMENT OF CASH FLOWS—INDIRECT METHOD
Objective 3

The comparative balance sheet of Paton Corporation at December 31, 1994 and 1993, is as follows:

	Dec. 31, 1994	Dec. 31, 1993
Assets		
Cash	$ 72,400	$ 66,800
Trade receivables (net)	87,900	100,500
Inventories	192,100	178,600
Prepaid expenses	6,400	2,900
Land	75,000	75,000
Buildings	480,600	316,800
Accumulated depreciation—buildings	(157,500)	(144,000)
Machinery and equipment	206,300	206,300
Accumulated depreciation—machinery and equipment	(93,000)	(81,300)
Patents	30,000	37,500
	$900,200	$759,100
Liabilities and Stockholders' Equity		
Accounts payable (merchandise creditors)	$ 27,200	$ 38,900
Dividends payable	18,800	15,000
Salaries payable	7,900	14,600
Mortgage note payable, due 1999	120,000	—
Bonds payable	—	70,000
Common stock, $10 par	410,000	360,000
Paid-in capital in excess of par—common stock	65,000	45,000
Retained earnings	251,300	215,600
	$900,200	$759,100

An examination of the income statement and the accounting records revealed the following additional information applicable to 1994:

    a. Net income, $63,200.
    b. Depreciation expense reported on the income statement: buildings, $13,500; machinery and equipment, $11,700.
    c. Patent amortization reported on the income statement, $7,500.
    d. A building was constructed for $163,800.
    e. A mortgage note for $120,000 was issued for cash.
    f. 5,000 shares of common stock were issued at 14 in exchange for the bonds payable.
    g. Cash dividends declared, $27,500.

SPREADSHEET PROBLEM

Instructions

Prepare a statement of cash flows, using the indirect method of presenting cash flows from operating activities.

PROBLEM 19-4A
STATEMENT OF CASH
FLOWS—INDIRECT
METHOD
Objective 3

The comparative balance sheet of B. L. Nelson Inc. at December 31, 1994 and 1993, is as follows:

	Dec. 31, 1994	Dec. 31, 1993
Assets		
Cash	$ 97,100	$ 81,400
Trade receivables (net)	170,000	151,700
Income tax refund receivable	9,000	—
Inventories	255,600	269,400
Prepaid expenses	9,300	11,100
Investments	50,000	250,000
Land	180,000	230,000
Buildings	820,000	450,000
Accumulated depreciation—buildings	(207,700)	(193,800)
Equipment	608,400	470,400
Accumulated depreciation—equipment	(218,000)	(205,700)
	$1,773,700	$1,514,500
Liabilities and Stockholders' Equity		
Accounts payable (merchandise creditors)	$ 96,000	$ 108,720
Income tax payable	—	10,880
Bonds payable	350,000	—
Discount on bonds payable	(29,000)	—
Common stock, $10 par	630,000	600,000
Paid-in capital in excess of par—common stock	81,000	72,000
Appropriation for plant expansion	280,000	230,000
Retained earnings	365,700	492,900
	$1,773,700	$1,514,500

The noncurrent asset, the noncurrent liability, and the stockholders' equity accounts for 1994 are as follows:

ACCOUNT INVESTMENTS   ACCOUNT NO.

Date		Item	Debit	Credit	Balance Debit	Balance Credit
1994						
Jan.	1	Balance			250,000	
Mar.	22	Realized $220,000 cash from sale		200,000	50,000	—

ACCOUNT LAND   ACCOUNT NO.

Date		Item	Debit	Credit	Balance Debit	Balance Credit
1994						
Jan.	1	Balance			230,000	
Apr.	20	Realized $62,500 cash from sale		50,000	180,000	

ACCOUNT BUILDINGS   ACCOUNT NO.

Date		Item	Debit	Credit	Balance Debit	Balance Credit
1994						
Jan.	1	Balance			450,000	
Nov.	15	Acquired for cash	370,000		820,000	

ACCOUNT ACCUMULATED DEPRECIATION—BUILDINGS   ACCOUNT NO.

Date		Item	Debit	Credit	Balance Debit	Balance Credit
1994						
Jan.	1	Balance				193,800
Dec.	31	Depreciation for year		13,900		207,700

ACCOUNT EQUIPMENT   ACCOUNT NO.

Date		Item	Debit	Credit	Balance Debit	Balance Credit
1994						
Jan.	1	Balance			470,400	
	26	Discarded, no salvage		48,000		
May	27	Purchased for cash	96,000			
Aug.	11	Purchased for cash	90,000		608,400	

ACCOUNT ACCUMULATED DEPRECIATION—EQUIPMENT   ACCOUNT NO.

Date		Item	Debit	Credit	Balance Debit	Balance Credit
1994						
Jan.	1	Balance				205,700
	26	Equipment discarded	48,000			
Dec.	31	Depreciation for year		60,300		218,000

ACCOUNT BONDS PAYABLE   ACCOUNT NO.

Date		Item	Debit	Credit	Balance Debit	Balance Credit
1994						
May	1	Issued 20-year bonds		350,000		350,000

ACCOUNT DISCOUNT ON BONDS PAYABLE   ACCOUNT NO.

Date		Item	Debit	Credit	Balance Debit	Balance Credit
1994						
May	1	Bonds issued	30,000		30,000	
Dec.	31	Amortization		1,000	29,000	

ACCOUNT COMMON STOCK, $10 PAR   ACCOUNT NO.

Date		Item	Debit	Credit	Balance Debit	Balance Credit
1994						
Jan.	1	Balance				600,000
Dec.	7	Stock dividend		30,000		630,000

ACCOUNT PAID-IN CAPITAL IN EXCESS OF PAR—COMMON STOCK   ACCOUNT NO.

Date		Item	Debit	Credit	Balance Debit	Balance Credit
1994						
Jan.	1	Balance				72,000
Dec.	7	Stock dividend		9,000		81,000

ACCOUNT APPROPRIATION FOR PLANT EXPANSION   ACCOUNT NO.

Date		Item	Debit	Credit	Balance Debit	Balance Credit
1994						
Jan.	1	Balance				230,000
Dec.	31	Appropriation		50,000		280,000

ACCOUNT RETAINED EARNINGS   ACCOUNT NO.

Date		Item	Debit	Credit	Balance Debit	Balance Credit
1994						
Jan.	1	Balance				492,900
Dec.	7	Stock dividend	39,000			
	31	Net loss	6,700			
	31	Cash dividends	31,500			
	31	Appropriated	50,000			365,700

Instructions

Prepare a statement of cash flows, using the indirect method of presenting cash flows from operating activities.

PROBLEM 19-5A
STATEMENT OF CASH
FLOWS—DIRECT METHOD
Objective 4

The comparative balance sheet of C. C. Conley Inc. for December 31, 1994 and 1993, is as follows:

	Dec. 31, 1994	Dec. 31, 1993
Assets		
Cash	$ 72,000	$ 50,500
Trade receivables (net)	88,000	80,000
Inventories	105,900	91,400
Investments	—	50,000
Land	50,000	—
Equipment	375,000	275,000
Accumulated depreciation	(149,000)	(114,000)
	$541,900	$432,900
Liabilities and Stockholders' Equity		
Accounts payable (merchandise creditors)	$ 59,000	$ 57,000
Accrued expenses (operating expenses)	5,000	7,000
Dividends payable	15,000	10,000
Common stock, $40 par	320,000	250,000
Paid-in capital in excess of par—common stock	17,000	12,000
Retained earnings	125,900	96,900
	$541,900	$432,900

The income statement for the year ended December 31, 1994, is as follows:

Sales		$919,500
Cost of merchandise sold		550,000
Gross profit		$369,500
Operating expenses:		
Depreciation expense	$ 35,000	
Other operating expenses	260,000	
Total operating expenses		295,000
Operating income		$ 74,500
Other income:		
Gain on sale of investments		10,000
Income before income tax		$ 84,500
Income tax		20,000
Net income		$ 64,500

The following additional information was taken from Conley's records:

a. The investments were sold for $60,000 cash at the beginning of the year.
b. Equipment and land were acquired for cash.
c. There were no disposals of equipment during the year.
d. The common stock was issued for cash.
e. There was a $35,500 debit to Retained Earnings for cash dividends declared.

SPREADSHEET
P R O B L E M

SOLUTIONS
S O F T W A R E

Instructions
Prepare a statement of cash flows, using the direct method of presenting cash flows from operating activities.

Instructions for Solving Problem 19-5A Using Solutions Software

1. Load opening balances.
2. Save the opening balances file to your drive and directory.
3. Set the run date to December 31, 1994, and enter your name.
4. Display a statement of cash flows.
5. Save your data file to disk.
6. End the session.

PROBLEM 19-6A
STATEMENT OF CASH
FLOWS—DIRECT METHOD
APPLIED TO PROBLEM 19-1A
Objective 4

The comparative balance sheet of C. T. Green Inc. for June 30, 1994 and 1993, is as follows:

	June 30, 1994	June 30, 1993
Assets		
Cash	$ 82,000	$ 64,800
Trade receivables (net)	104,800	91,000
Inventories	127,400	108,900
Investments	—	90,000
Land	102,000	—
Equipment	425,700	329,700
Accumulated depreciation	(171,800)	(135,800)
	$670,100	$548,600
Liabilities and Stockholders' Equity		
Accounts payable (merchandise creditors)	$ 70,900	$ 63,000
Accrued expenses (operating expenses)	6,100	5,000
Dividends payable	14,400	12,000
Common stock, $10 par	360,000	300,000
Paid-in capital in excess of par—common stock	31,400	19,400
Retained earnings	187,300	149,200
	$670,100	$548,600

The income statement for the year ended June 30, 1994, is as follows:

Sales		$1,194,000
Cost of merchandise sold		708,900
Gross profit		$ 485,100
Operating expenses:		
Depreciation expense	$ 36,000	
Other operating expenses	336,000	
Total operating expenses		372,000
Operating income		$ 113,100
Other income:		
Gain on sale of investments		8,000
Income before income tax		$ 121,100
Income tax		32,600
Net income		$ 88,500

The following additional information was taken from the records of C. T. Green Inc.:

a. Equipment and land were acquired for cash.
b. There were no disposals of equipment during the year.
c. The investments were sold for $98,000.
d. The common stock was issued for cash.
e. There was a $50,400 debit to Retained Earnings for cash dividends declared.

Instructions
Prepare a statement of cash flows, using the direct method of presenting cash flows from operating activities.

PROBLEM 19-7A
STATEMENT OF CASH
FLOWS—DIRECT AND
INDIRECT METHODS
Objectives 3, 4

An income statement and a comparative balance sheet for DABCO Company are as follows:

DABCO Company
Income Statement
For Year Ended December 31, 1994

Sales		$1,520,700
Cost of merchandise sold		1,110,200
Gross profit		$ 410,500
Operating expenses		
Depreciation expense	$ 39,990	
Other operating expenses	227,110	
Total operating expenses		267,100
		$ 143,400
Other income:		
Gain on sale of land	$ 20,500	
Gain on sale of investments	11,000	
	$ 31,500	
Other expense:		
Interest expense	25,000	6,500
Income before income tax		$ 149,900
Income tax		38,500
Net income		$ 111,400

DABCO Company
Comparative Balance Sheet
December 31, 1994 and 1993

	1994	1993
Assets		
Cash	$ 57,870	$ 66,200
Trade receivables (net)	137,180	117,800
Inventories	211,500	190,150
Prepaid expenses	5,160	6,120
Investments	44,500	93,500
Land	77,250	75,000
Buildings	412,500	225,000
Accumulated depreciation—buildings	(91,260)	(81,220)
Equipment	493,700	437,500
Accumulated depreciation—equipment	(179,700)	(149,750)
Total assets	$1,168,700	$980,300
Liabilities and Stockholders' Equity		
Accounts payable (merchandise creditors)	$ 58,715	$ 51,875
Accrued expenses (operating expenses)	11,000	10,500
Interest payable	1,875	1,875
Income tax payable	5,000	8,500
Dividends payable	15,660	12,500
Mortgage note payable	175,000	—
Bonds payable	100,000	250,000
Common stock, $25 par	450,000	375,000
Paid-in capital in excess of par—common stock	47,250	41,250
Retained earnings	304,200	228,800
Total liabilities and stockholders' equity	$1,168,700	$980,300

The following additional information on cash flows during the year was obtained from an examination of the ledger:

a. Investments (long-term) were purchased for $40,500.
b. Investments (long-term) costing $89,500 were sold for $100,500.
c. Equipment was purchased for $56,200. There were no disposals.
d. A building valued at $187,500 and land valued at $62,500 were acquired by a cash payment of $250,000.
e. Land which cost $60,250 was sold for $80,750 cash.

f. A mortgage note payable for $175,000 was issued for cash.
g. Bonds payable of $150,000 were retired by the payment of their face amount.
h. 3,000 shares of common stock were issued for cash at 27.
i. Cash dividends of $36,000 were declared.

SPREADSHEET
P R O B L E M

■SHARPEN YOUR ▶
COMMUNICATION SKILLS

Instructions

1. Prepare a statement of cash flows, using the direct method of presenting cash flows from operating activities.
2. Prepare a statement of cash flows, using the indirect method of presenting cash flows from operating activities.
3. Which method of reporting cash flows from operating activities is more widely used? Explain.

Series B

PROBLEM 19-1B
STATEMENT OF CASH
FLOWS—INDIRECT
METHOD
Objective 3

The comparative balance sheet of T. A. Kolby Inc. for December 31, 1994 and 1993, is as follows:

	Dec. 31, 1994	Dec. 31, 1993
Assets		
Cash	$ 90,500	$ 60,400
Trade receivables (net)	123,200	112,000
Inventories	150,300	128,100
Investments	—	80,000
Land	70,000	—
Equipment	874,600	724,500
Accumulated depreciation	(208,600)	(159,600)
	$1,100,000	$945,400
Liabilities and Stockholders' Equity		
Accounts payable (merchandise creditors)	$ 75,000	$ 70,600
Accrued expenses (operating expenses)	4,800	6,400
Dividends payable	21,000	14,000
Common stock, $10 par	450,000	350,000
Paid-in capital in excess of par—common stock	23,800	16,800
Retained earnings	525,400	487,600
	$1,100,000	$945,400

The following additional information was taken from the records:

a. The investments were sold for $85,000 cash.
b. Equipment and land were acquired for cash.
c. There were no disposals of equipment during the year.
d. The common stock was issued for cash.
e. There was an $87,800 credit to Retained Earnings for net income.
f. There was a $50,000 debit to Retained Earnings for cash dividends declared.

Instructions
Prepare a statement of cash flows, using the indirect method of presenting cash flows from operating activities.

PROBLEM 19-2B
STATEMENT OF CASH
FLOWS—INDIRECT
METHOD
Objective 3

The comparative balance sheet of Roth Corporation at December 31, 1994 and 1993, is as follows:

	Dec. 31, 1994	Dec. 31, 1993
Assets		
Cash	$ 78,300	$ 64,000
Trade receivables (net)	69,300	73,700
Merchandise inventory	121,900	97,400
Prepaid expenses	7,660	5,860
Plant assets	472,440	425,240
Accumulated depreciation—plant assets	(138,500)	(157,500)
	$611,100	$508,700

Liabilities and Stockholders' Equity

Accounts payable (merchandise creditors)	$ 69,100	$ 53,500
Mortgage note payable	—	60,000
Common stock, $25 par	300,000	250,000
Paid-in capital in excess of par—common stock	34,500	31,500
Retained earnings	207,500	113,700
	$611,100	$508,700

Additional data obtained from the income statement and from an examination of the accounts in the ledger are as follows:

a. Net income, $108,800.
b. Depreciation reported on the income statement, $34,600.
c. An addition to the building was constructed at a cost of $100,800, and fully depreciated equipment costing $53,600 was discarded, with no salvage realized.
d. The mortgage note payable was not due until 2003, but the terms permitted earlier payment without penalty.
e. 2,000 shares of common stock were issued at $26.50 for cash.
f. Cash dividends declared and paid, $15,000.

Instructions

Prepare a statement of cash flows, using the indirect method of presenting cash flows from operating activities.

PROBLEM 19-3B
STATEMENT OF CASH
FLOWS—INDIRECT
METHOD
Objective 3

The comparative balance sheet of Courier Corporation at December 31, 1994 and 1993, is as follows:

	Dec. 31, 1994	Dec. 31, 1993
Assets		
Cash	$ 60,900	$ 52,800
Trade receivables (net)	86,100	70,000
Inventories	126,600	136,700
Prepaid expenses	4,400	3,100
Land	65,000	65,000
Buildings	381,500	291,500
Accumulated depreciation—buildings	(154,600)	(143,400)
Machinery and equipment	300,500	300,500
Accumulated depreciation—machinery and equipment	(101,200)	(71,500)
Patents	30,800	38,500
	$800,000	$743,200
Liabilities and Stockholders' Equity		
Accounts payable (merchandise creditors)	$ 58,800	$ 88,800
Dividends payable	9,400	8,250
Salaries payable	5,000	5,450
Mortgage note payable, due 2003	55,000	—
Bonds payable	—	110,000
Common stock, $10 par	450,000	350,000
Paid-in capital in excess of par—common stock	80,000	70,000
Retained earnings	141,800	110,700
	$800,000	$743,200

An examination of the income statement and the accounting records revealed the following additional information applicable to 1994:

a. Net income, $66,100.
b. Depreciation expense reported on the income statement: buildings, $11,200; machinery and equipment, $29,700.
c. A building was constructed for $90,000.
d. Patent amortization reported on the income statement, $7,700.
e. A mortgage note for $55,000 was issued for cash.
f. 10,000 shares of common stock were issued at 11 in exchange for the bonds payable.
g. Cash dividends declared, $35,000.

SPREADSHEET PROBLEM

$

PROBLEM 19-4B
STATEMENT OF CASH FLOWS—INDIRECT METHOD
Objective 3

Instructions

Prepare a statement of cash flows, using the indirect method of presenting cash flows from operating activities.

The comparative balance sheet of Brodell Inc. at December 31, 1994 and 1993, is as follows:

	Dec. 31, 1994	Dec. 31, 1993
Assets		
Cash	$ 36,200	$ 38,800
Trade receivables (net)	60,800	54,100
Inventories	136,750	121,000
Prepaid expenses	3,850	4,100
Investments	—	45,000
Land	28,500	28,500
Buildings	190,000	126,000
Accumulated depreciation—buildings	(46,200)	(41,400)
Equipment	286,200	239,500
Accumulated depreciation—equipment	(86,100)	(77,400)
	$610,000	$538,200
Liabilities and Stockholders' Equity		
Accounts payable (merchandise creditors)	$ 38,700	$ 48,300
Income tax payable	3,600	2,800
Bonds payable	50,000	—
Discount on bonds payable	(2,900)	—
Common stock, $20 par	315,000	300,000
Paid-in capital in excess of par—common stock	40,200	33,000
Appropriation for plant expansion	50,000	30,000
Retained earnings	115,400	124,100
	$610,000	$538,200

The noncurrent asset, the noncurrent liability, and the stockholders' equity accounts for 1994 are as follows:

ACCOUNT **INVESTMENTS**   ACCOUNT NO.

Date		Item	Debit	Credit	Balance Debit	Balance Credit
1994						
Jan.	1	Balance			45,000	
Mar.	5	Realized $40,500 cash from sale		45,000	—	—

ACCOUNT **LAND**   ACCOUNT NO.

Date		Item	Debit	Credit	Balance Debit	Balance Credit
1994						
Jan.	1	Balance			28,500	

ACCOUNT **BUILDINGS**   ACCOUNT NO.

Date		Item	Debit	Credit	Balance Debit	Balance Credit
1994						
Jan.	1	Balance			126,000	
July	1	Acquired for cash	64,000		190,000	

ACCOUNT **ACCUMULATED DEPRECIATION—BUILDINGS**   ACCOUNT NO.

Date		Item	Debit	Credit	Balance Debit	Balance Credit
1994						
Jan.	1	Balance				41,400
Dec.	31	Depreciation for year		4,800		46,200

ACCOUNT EQUIPMENT   ACCOUNT NO.

Date		Item	Debit	Credit	Balance Debit	Balance Credit
1994						
Jan.	1	Balance			239,500	
Mar.	1	Discarded, no salvage		21,000		
	5	Purchased for cash	40,000			
Dec.	1	Purchased for cash	27,700		286,200	

ACCOUNT ACCUMULATED DEPRECIATION—EQUIPMENT   ACCOUNT NO.

Date		Item	Debit	Credit	Balance Debit	Balance Credit
1994						
Jan.	1	Balance				77,400
Mar.	1	Equipment discarded	21,000			
Dec.	31	Depreciation for year		29,700		86,100

ACCOUNT BONDS PAYABLE   ACCOUNT NO.

Date		Item	Debit	Credit	Balance Debit	Balance Credit
1994						
May	1	Issued 20-year bonds		50,000		50,000

ACCOUNT DISCOUNT ON BONDS PAYABLE   ACCOUNT NO.

Date		Item	Debit	Credit	Balance Debit	Balance Credit
1994						
May	1	Bonds issued	3,000		3,000	
Dec.	31	Amortization		100	2,900	

ACCOUNT COMMON STOCK, $20 PAR   ACCOUNT NO.

Date		Item	Debit	Credit	Balance Debit	Balance Credit
1994						
Jan.	1	Balance				300,000
June	29	Stock dividend		15,000		315,000

ACCOUNT PAID-IN CAPITAL IN EXCESS OF PAR— COMMON STOCK   ACCOUNT NO.

Date		Item	Debit	Credit	Balance Debit	Balance Credit
1994						
Jan.	1	Balance				33,000
June	29	Stock dividend		7,200		40,200

ACCOUNT APPROPRIATION FOR PLANT EXPANSION   ACCOUNT NO.

Date		Item	Debit	Credit	Balance Debit	Balance Credit
1994						
Jan.	1	Balance				30,000
Dec.	31	Appropriation		20,000		50,000

ACCOUNT RETAINED EARNINGS   ACCOUNT NO.

Date		Item	Debit	Credit	Balance Debit	Balance Credit
1994						
Jan.	1	Balance				124,100
June	29	Stock dividend	22,200			
Dec.	31	Net income		53,500		
	31	Cash dividends	20,000			
	31	Appropriated	20,000			115,400

Instructions

Prepare a statement of cash flows, using the indirect method of presenting cash flows from operating activities.

PROBLEM 19-5B
STATEMENT OF CASH
FLOWS—DIRECT METHOD
Objective 4

The comparative balance sheet of A. C. North Co. for December 31, 1994 and 1993, is as follows:

	Dec. 31, 1994	Dec. 31, 1993
Assets		
Cash	$ 59,200	$ 44,900
Trade receivables (net)	91,500	80,000
Inventories	105,900	90,500
Investments	—	75,000
Land	85,000	—
Equipment	362,400	282,400
Accumulated depreciation	(149,000)	(119,000)
	$555,000	$453,800
Liabilities and Stockholders' Equity		
Accounts payable (merchandise creditors)	$ 62,450	$ 55,000
Accrued expenses (operating expenses)	6,000	4,000
Dividends payable	12,000	10,000
Common stock, $20 par	300,000	250,000
Paid-in capital in excess of par—common stock	22,000	12,000
Retained earnings	152,550	122,800
	$555,000	$453,800

The income statement for the year ended December 31, 1994, is as follows:

Sales		$995,000
Cost of merchandise sold		590,750
Gross profit		$404,250
Operating expenses:		
Depreciation expense	$ 30,000	
Other operating expenses	280,000	
Total operating expenses		310,000
Operating income		$ 94,250
Other income:		
Gain on sale of investments		5,000
Income before income tax		$ 99,250
Income tax		22,500
Net income		$ 76,750

The following additional information was taken from the records:

a. Equipment and land were acquired for cash.
b. There were no disposals of equipment during the year.
c. The investments were sold for $80,000 cash.
d. The common stock was issued for cash.
e. There was a $47,000 debit to Retained Earnings for cash dividends declared.

Instructions

Prepare a statement of cash flows, using the direct method of presenting cash flows from operating activities.

Instructions for Solving Problem 19-5B Using Solutions Software

1. Load opening balances.
2. Save the opening balances file to your drive and directory.
3. Set the run date to December 31, 1994, and enter your name.
4. Display a statement of cash flows.
5. Save your data file to disk.
6. End the session.

PROBLEM 19-6B
STATEMENT OF CASH
FLOWS—DIRECT METHOD
APPLIED TO PROBLEM 19-1B
Objective 4

The comparative balance sheet of T. A. Kolby Inc. for December 31, 1994 and 1993, is as follows:

	Dec. 31, 1994	Dec. 31, 1993
Assets		
Cash	$ 90,500	$ 60,400
Trade receivables (net)	123,200	112,000
Inventories	150,300	128,100
Investments	—	80,000
Land	70,000	—
Equipment	874,600	724,500
Accumulated depreciation	(208,600)	(159,600)
	$1,100,000	$945,400
Liabilities and Stockholders' Equity		
Accounts payable (merchandise creditors)	$ 75,000	$ 70,600
Accrued expenses (operating expenses)	4,800	6,400
Dividends payable	21,000	14,000
Common stock, $10 par	450,000	350,000
Paid-in capital in excess of par—common stock	23,800	16,800
Retained earnings	525,400	487,600
	$1,100,000	$945,400

The income statement for the year ended December 31, 1994, is as follows:

Sales		$1,287,300
Cost of merchandise sold		770,000
Gross profit		$ 517,300
Operating expenses:		
Depreciation expense	$ 49,000	
Other operating expenses	364,000	
Total operating expenses		413,000
Operating income		$ 104,300
Other income:		
Gain on sale of investments		5,000
Income before income tax		$ 109,300
Income tax		21,500
Net income		$ 87,800

The following additional information was taken from the records:

a. The investments were sold for $85,000 cash at the beginning of the year.
b. Equipment and land were acquired for cash.
c. There were no disposals of equipment during the year.
d. The common stock was issued for cash.
e. There was a $50,000 debit to Retained Earnings for cash dividends declared.

Instructions

Prepare a statement of cash flows, using the direct method of presenting cash flows from operating activities.

PROBLEM 19-7B
STATEMENT OF CASH
FLOWS—DIRECT AND
INDIRECT METHODS
Objectives 3, 4

An income statement and a comparative balance sheet for Yoder Company are as follows:

Yoder Company
Income Statement
For Year Ended December 31, 1994

Sales		$1,255,000
Cost of merchandise sold		830,000
Gross profit		$ 425,000
Operating expenses		
Depreciation expense	$ 39,990	
Other operating expenses	220,010	
Total operating expenses		260,000
		$ 165,000
Other income:		
Gain on sale of land	$ 18,750	
Gain on sale of investments	14,250	
	$ 33,000	
Other expense:		
Interest expense	27,500	5,500
Income before income tax		$ 170,500
Income tax		59,100
Net income		$ 111,400

Yoder Company
Comparative Balance Sheet
December 31, 1994 and 1993

	1994	1993
Assets		
Cash	$ 52,370	$ 60,700
Trade receivables (net)	130,080	116,700
Inventories	215,400	188,050
Prepaid expenses	5,160	6,120
Investments	34,250	93,500
Land	65,000	75,000
Buildings	435,000	225,000
Accumulated depreciation—buildings	(91,260)	(81,220)
Equipment	493,700	437,500
Accumulated depreciation—equipment	(179,700)	(149,750)
Total assets	$1,160,000	$971,600
Liabilities and Stockholders' Equity		
Accounts payable (merchandise creditors)	$ 54,640	$ 48,300
Accrued expenses (operating expenses)	12,000	11,000
Interest payable	3,000	3,000
Income tax payable	6,250	9,750
Dividends payable	15,660	12,500
Mortgage note payable	175,000	—
Bonds payable	100,000	250,000
Common stock, $25 par	450,000	375,000
Paid-in capital in excess of par—common stock	47,250	41,250
Retained earnings	296,200	220,800
Total liabilities and stockholders' equity	$1,160,000	$971,600

The following additional information on cash flows during the year was obtained from an examination of the ledger:

    a. Investments (long-term) were purchased for $34,500.
    b. Investments (long-term) costing $93,750 were sold for $108,000.
    c. Equipment was purchased for $56,200. There were no disposals.

d. A building valued at $210,000 and land valued at $40,000 were acquired by a cash payment of $250,000.
e. Land which cost $50,000 was sold for $68,750 cash.
f. A mortgage note payable for $175,000 was issued for cash.
g. Bonds payable of $150,000 were retired by the payment of their face amount.
h. 3,000 shares of common stock were issued for cash at 27.
i. Cash dividends of $36,000 were declared.

SPREADSHEET PROBLEM

$

SHARPEN YOUR COMMUNICATION SKILLS ▶

Instructions

1. Prepare a statement of cash flows using the direct method of presenting cash flows from operating activities.
2. Prepare a statement of cash flows using the indirect method of presenting cash flows from operating activities.
3. Which method of reporting cash flows from operating activities is more widely used? Explain.

MINI-CASE 19 A. J. JOHNS INC.

Alan Johns is the president and majority shareholder of A. J. Johns Inc., a small retail store chain. Recently, Johns submitted a loan application for A. J. Johns Inc. to Bonita National Bank. It called for a $200,000, 11%, 10-year loan to help finance the construction of a building and the purchase of store equipment, costing a total of $250,000 to enable A. J. Johns Inc. to open a store in Bonita. Land for this purpose was acquired last year. The bank's loan officer re-

quested a statement of cash flows in addition to the most recent income statement, balance sheet, and retained earnings statement that Johns had submitted with the loan application.

As a close family friend, Johns asked you to prepare a statement of cash flows. From the records provided, you prepared the following statement:

A. J. Johns Inc.
Statement of Cash Flows
For Year Ended December 31, 19—

Cash flows from operating activities:			
Net income, per income statement			$ 82,500
Add: Depreciation	$28,000		
Decrease in trade receivables	11,500	39,500	
		$122,000	
Deduct: Increase in inventory	$10,000		
Increase in prepaid expenses	1,500		
Decrease in accounts payable	3,000		
Gain on sale of investments	7,500	22,000	
Net cash flow from operating activities			$100,000
Cash flows from investing activities:			
Cash received from investments sold		$ 42,500	
Less: Cash paid for purchase of store equipment		35,000	
Net cash flow from investing activities			7,500
Cash flows from financing activities:			
Cash paid for dividends		$ 50,000	
Net cash flow used for financing activities			(50,000)
Increase in cash			$ 57,500
Cash at the beginning of the year			27,500
Cash at the end of the year			$ 85,000
Schedule of Noncash Financing and Investing Activities:			
Issuance of common stock at par for land			$ 40,000

After reviewing the statement, Johns telephoned you and commented, "Are you sure this statement is right?" Johns then raised the following questions:

a. "How can depreciation be a cash flow?"
b. "The issuance of common stock for the land is listed in a separate schedule. This transaction has nothing to do with cash! Shouldn't this transaction be eliminated from the statement?"
c. "How can the gain on sale of investments be a deduction from net income in determining the cash flow from operating activities?"

d. "Why does the bank need this statement anyway? They can compute the increase in cash from the balance sheets for the last two years."

After jotting down Johns' questions, you assured him that this statement was "right." However, to alleviate Johns' concern, you arranged a meeting for the following day.

Instructions:

1. How would you respond to each of Johns' questions?
2. ▮▮▮ ▸ Do you think that the statement of cash flows enhances the chances of A. J. Johns Inc. receiving the loan? Discuss.

ANSWERS TO SELF-EXAMINATION QUESTIONS

1. **D** Cash flows from operating activities affect transactions that enter into the determination of net income such as the receipt of cash from customers on account (answer D). Receipts of cash from the sale of capital stock (answer A) and the sale of bonds (answer B) and payments of cash for dividends (answer C) are cash flows from financing activities.

2. **A** Cash flows from investing activities include receipts from the sale of noncurrent assets, such as equipment (answer A), and payments for the acquisition of noncurrent assets. Receipts of cash from the sale of capital stock (answer B) and payments of cash for dividends (answer C) and to acquire treasury stock (answer D) are cash flows from financing activities.

3. **C** Payment of cash dividends (answer C) is an example of a financing activity. The receipt of cash from customers on account (answer A) is an operating activity. The receipt of cash from the sale of equipment (answer B) is an investing activity. The payment of cash to acquire marketable securities (answer D) is an example of an investing activity.

4. **D** The indirect method (answer D) reports cash flows from operating activities by beginning with net income and adjusting it for revenues and expenses not involving the receipt or payment of cash.

5. **C** The cash flows from operating activities section of the statement of cash flows would report net cash flow from operating activities of $65,500, determined as follows:

Net income			$55,000
Add: Depreciation		$22,000	
Decrease in inventories		5,000	
Decrease in prepaid			
expenses		500	27,500
			$82,500
Deduct: Increase in trade			
receivables		$10,000	
Decrease in accounts			
payable		7,000	17,000
Net cash flow from			
operating activities			$65,500

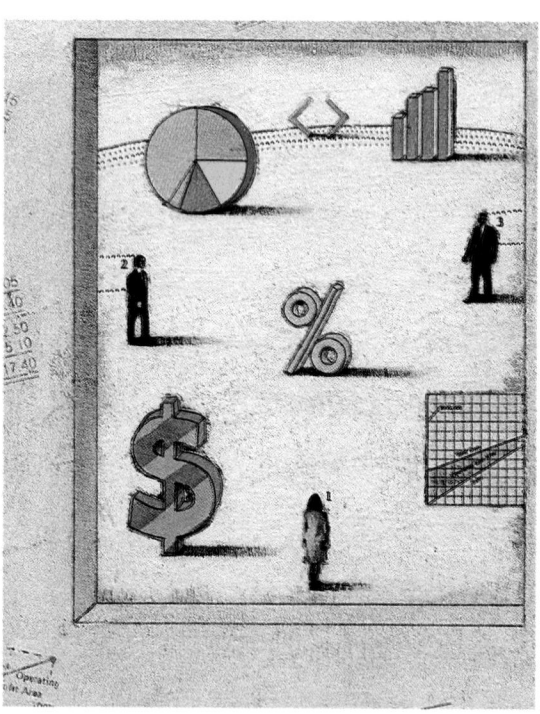

You and Accounting

The Wall Street Journal (July 2, 1992) reported that the common stock of International Business Machines (IBM) was selling for $98¼. If you had funds to invest, would you invest in IBM common stock?

IBM is a well-known, international company. However, Eastern Airlines, Pan Am, W. T. Grant Company, and Orion Pictures were also well-known companies. They share the common characteristic of having declared bankruptcy!

Obviously, being well-known is not necessarily a good basis for investing. Knowledge that a company has a good product, by itself, may also be an inadequate basis for investing in the company. Even with a good product, a company may go bankrupt for a variety of reasons, such as inadequate financing. For example, Orion Pictures went bankrupt, even though it produced the award-winning motion pictures *Dances With Wolves* and *Silence of the Lambs*.

How, then, does one decide on the companies in which to invest? This chapter describes and illustrates common financial data that can be analyzed to assist you in making investment decisions. In addition, the contents of corporate annual reports are also discussed.

Chapter 20
Financial Statement Analysis and Annual Reports

LEARNING OBJECTIVES
After studying this chapter, you should be able to:

Objective 1
List basic financial statement analytical procedures.

Objective 2
Explain the two aspects of financial statement analysis.

Objective 3
Apply financial statement analysis to assess the solvency of an enterprise.

Objective 4
Apply financial statement analysis to assess the profitability of an enterprise.

Objective 5
Summarize the uses and limitations of analytical measures.

Objective 6
Describe the contents of corporate annual reports.

The financial condition and the results of operations of business enterprises are of interest to many users. These user groups include owners, managers, creditors, governmental agencies, employees, and prospective owners and creditors. The basic financial statements provide much of the information users need to make economic decisions about business enterprises. Various ways in which financial statement data are analyzed are discussed in this chapter.

The contents of corporate annual reports are also discussed in this chapter. These reports normally contain, in addition to the basic financial statements, a summary of activities for the past year and management's plans for the future. Annual reports may also contain financial analyses and other useful data about the enterprise.

BASIC ANALYTICAL PROCEDURES

Objective 1
List basic financial statement analytical procedures.

The analytical measures obtained from financial statements are usually expressed as ratios or percentages. For example, the relationship of $150,000 to $100,000 ($150,000 ÷ $100,000, or $150,000 : $100,000) may be expressed as 1.5, 1.5 : 1, or 150%. This ease by which financial relationships can be summarized by ratios and percentages is a major reason for their widespread use.

Analytical procedures may be used to compare items on a current statement with related items on earlier statements. For example, cash of $150,000 on the current balance sheet may be compared with cash of $100,000 on the balance sheet of a year earlier. The current year's cash may be expressed as 1.5 or 150% of the earlier amount. The relationship may also be expressed in terms of change. That is, the increase of $50,000 may be stated as a 50% increase.

Analytical procedures are also widely used to examine relationships within a financial statement. To illustrate, assume that cash of $50,000 and inventories of $250,000 are included in the total assets of $1,000,000 on a balance sheet. In relative terms, the cash balance is 5% of the total assets, and the inventories are 25% of the total assets. Individual current asset amounts could also be related to total current assets. Assuming that the total of the current assets is $500,000 in the preceding example, cash represents 10% of the total and inventories represent 50% of the total.

Increases or decreases in items may be expressed in percentage terms only when the initial or base amount is positive. If the base amount is zero or a negative value, the amount of change cannot be expressed as a percentage. For example, assume that comparative balance sheets indicate no liability for notes payable on the initial, or base, date and a liability of $10,000 on the later date. The increase of $10,000 cannot be expressed as a percent of zero. Likewise, if a net loss of $10,000 is followed by a net income of $5,000, the increase of $15,000 cannot be stated as a percent of the loss of the base year.

In the following discussion, the importance of each of the various analytical measures illustrated is emphasized. The measures are not ends in themselves; they are only guides in evaluating financial and operating data. Many other factors, such as trends in the industry and general economic conditions, should also be considered.

Horizontal Analysis

The percentage analysis of increases and decreases in related items in comparative financial statements is called **horizontal analysis**. The amount of each item on the most recent statement is compared with the related item on one or more earlier statements. The amount of increase or decrease in the item is listed, along with the percent of increase or decrease.

An analysis may include a comparison between two statements. In this case, the earlier statement is used as the base. In other situations, an analysis may include three or more comparative statements. In this case, the earliest date or period may be used as the base for comparing all later dates or periods. Another approach is to compare each statement to the immediately preceding statement. These two approaches are illustrated in Exhibit 1.

Exhibit 1
Horizontal Analysis

BASE: EARLIEST YEAR

| | | | | Increase (Decrease*) | | | |
| | | | | *1993–94* | | *1993–95* | |
Item	*1993*	*1994*	*1995*	*Amount*	*Percent*	*Amount*	*Percent*
A	$100,000	$150,000	$200,000	$ 50,000	50%	$100,000	100%
B	100,000	200,000	150,000	100,000	100%	50,000	50%

BASE: PRECEDING YEAR

| | | | | Increase (Decrease*) | | | |
| | | | | *1993–94* | | *1994–95* | |
Item	*1993*	*1994*	*1995*	*Amount*	*Percent*	*Amount*	*Percent*
A	$100,000	$150,000	$200,000	$ 50,000	50%	50,000	33%
B	100,000	200,000	150,000	100,000	100%	50,000*	25%*

A condensed comparative balance sheet for two years, with horizontal analysis, is illustrated in Exhibit 2.

Exhibit 2
Comparative Balance Sheet—
Horizontal Analysis

	1994	1993	Amount	Percent
Marlea Company **Comparative Balance Sheet** **December 31, 1994 and 1993**				
			Increase (Decrease*)	
Assets				
Current assets	$ 550,000	$ 533,000	$ 17,000	3.2%
Long-term investments	95,000	177,500	82,500*	46.5%*
Plant assets (net)	444,500	470,000	25,500*	5.4%*
Intangible assets	50,000	50,000	—	
Total assets	$1,139,500	$1,230,500	$ 91,000*	7.4%*
Liabilities				
Current liabilities	$ 210,000	$ 243,000	$ 33,000*	13.6%*
Long-term liabilities	100,000	200,000	100,000*	50.0%*
Total liabilities	$ 310,000	$ 443,000	$133,000*	30.0%*
Stockholders' Equity				
Preferred 6% stock, $100 par	$ 150,000	$ 150,000	—	—
Common stock, $10 par	500,000	500,000	—	—
Retained earnings	179,500	137,500	$ 42,000	30.5%
Total stockholders' equity	$ 829,500	$ 787,500	$ 42,000	5.3%
Total liabilities and stockholders' equity	$1,139,500	$1,230,500	$ 91,000*	7.4%*

The significance of the various increases and decreases in the items shown in Exhibit 2 cannot be fully evaluated without additional information. Although total assets at the end of 1994 were $91,000 (7.4%) less than at the beginning of the year, liabilities were reduced by $133,000 (30%) and stockholders' equity increased $42,000 (5.3%). It appears that the reduction of $100,000 in long-term liabilities was achieved mostly through the sale of long-term investments.

The balance sheet in Exhibit 2 may be expanded to include the details of the various categories of assets and liabilities. An alternative is to present the details in separate schedules. A supporting schedule with horizontal analysis is illustrated in Exhibit 3.

Exhibit 3
Comparative Schedule of Current
Assets—Horizontal Analysis

	1994	1993	Amount	Percent
Marlea Company **Comparative Schedule of Current Assets** **December 31, 1994 and 1993**				
			Increase (Decrease*)	
Cash	$ 90,500	$ 64,700	$25,800	39.9%
Marketable securities	75,000	60,000	15,000	25.0%
Accounts receivable (net)	115,000	120,000	5,000*	4.2%*
Inventories	264,000	283,000	19,000*	6.7%*
Prepaid expenses	5,500	5,300	200	3.8%
Total current assets	$550,000	$533,000	$17,000	3.2%

The decrease in accounts receivable may be due to changes in credit terms or improved collection policies. Likewise, a decrease in inventories during a period of increased sales may indicate an improvement in the management of inventories.

The changes in the current assets in Exhibit 3 appear favorable. This assessment is supported by the 24.8% increase in net sales shown in Exhibit 4.

Exhibit 4
Comparative Income Statement—
Horizontal Analysis

			Increase (Decrease*)	
Marlea Company Comparative Income Statement December 31, 1994 and 1993				
	1994	1993	Amount	Percent
Sales	$1,530,500	$1,234,000	$296,500	24.0%
Sales returns and allowances	32,500	34,000	1,500*	4.4%*
Net sales	$1,498,000	$1,200,000	$298,000	24.8%
Cost of goods sold	1,043,000	820,000	223,000	27.2%
Gross profit	$ 455,000	$ 380,000	$ 75,000	19.7%
Selling expenses	$ 191,000	$ 147,000	$ 44,000	29.9%
Administrative expenses	104,000	97,400	6,600	6.8%
Total operating expenses	$ 295,000	$ 244,400	$ 50,600	20.7%
Operating income	$ 160,000	$ 135,600	$ 24,400	18.0%
Other income	8,500	11,000	2,500*	22.7%*
	$ 168,500	$ 146,600	$ 21,900	14.9%
Other expense	6,000	12,000	6,000*	50.0%*
Income before income tax	$ 162,500	$ 134,600	$ 27,900	20.7%
Income tax	71,500	58,100	13,400	23.1%
Net income	$ 91,000	$ 76,500	$ 14,500	19.0%

An increase in net sales may not have a favorable effect on operating performance. The percentage increase in Marlea Company's net sales is accompanied by a greater percentage increase in the cost of goods (merchandise) sold.[1] This has the effect of reducing gross profit. Selling expenses increased significantly, and administrative expenses increased slightly. Overall operating expenses increased by 20.7%, while gross profit increased by only 19.7%.

The increase in operating income and in net income is favorable. However, the company's operations may or may not be at maximum efficiency. A study of the expenses and additional analyses and comparisons should be made before reaching a conclusion.

The income statement illustrated in Exhibit 4 is in condensed form. Such a condensed statement usually provides enough information for all interested groups except management. If necessary, the statement may be expanded or supplemental schedules may be prepared to present details of the cost of goods sold, selling expenses, administrative expenses, other income, and other expense.

A comparative retained earnings statement with horizontal analysis is illustrated in Exhibit 5. Exhibit 5 reveals an increase of 30.5% in retained earnings for the year. The increase is due to net income of $91,000 for the year less dividends of $49,000.

Vertical Analysis

A percentage analysis may also be used to show the relationship of each component to the total within a single statement. This type of analysis is called **vertical**

[1] The term *cost of goods sold* is often used in practice in place of *cost of merchandise sold*. Such usage is followed in this chapter.

Exhibit 5
Comparative Retained Earnings
Statement—Horizontal Analysis

Marlea Company
Comparative Retained Earnings Statement
December 31, 1994 and 1993

	1994	1993	*Increase (Decrease*)* Amount	Percent
Retained earnings, January 1	$137,500	$100,000	$37,500	37.5%
Net income for the year	91,000	76,500	14,500	19.0%
Total	$228,500	$176,500	$52,000	29.5%
Dividends:				
On preferred stock	$ 9,000	$ 9,000	—	—
On common stock	40,000	30,000	$10,000	33.3%
Total	$ 49,000	$ 39,000	$10,000	25.6%
Retained earnings, December 31	$179,500	$137,500	$42,000	30.5%

analysis. Like horizontal analysis, the statements may be prepared in either detailed or condensed form. In the latter case, additional details of the changes in individual items may be presented in supporting schedules. In such schedules, the percentage analysis may be based on either the total of the schedule or the statement total. Although vertical analysis is limited to an individual statement, its significance may be improved by preparing comparative statements.

In vertical analysis of the balance sheet, each asset item is stated as a percent of the total assets. Each liability and stockholders' equity item is stated as a percent of the total liabilities and stockholders' equity. A condensed comparative balance sheet with vertical analysis is illustrated in Exhibit 6.

Exhibit 6
Comparative Balance Sheet—
Vertical Analysis

Marlea Company
Comparative Balance Sheet
December 31, 1994 and 1993

	1994 Amount	Percent	1993 Amount	Percent
Assets				
Current assets	$ 550,000	48.3%	$ 533,000	43.3%
Long-term investments	95,000	8.3	177,500	14.4
Plant assets (net)	444,500	39.0	470,000	38.2
Intangible assets	50,000	4.4	50,000	4.1
Total assets	$1,139,500	100.0%	$1,230,500	100.0%
Liabilities				
Current liabilities	$ 210,000	18.4%	$ 243,000	19.7%
Long-term liabilities	100,000	8.8	200,000	16.3
Total liabilities	$ 310,000	27.2%	$ 443,000	36.0%
Stockholders' Equity				
Preferred 6% stock, $100 par	$ 150,000	13.2%	$ 150,000	12.2%
Common stock, $10 par	500,000	43.9	500,000	40.6
Retained earnings	179,500	15.7	137,500	11.2
Total stockholders' equity	$ 829,500	72.8%	$ 787,500	64.0%
Total liabilities and stockholders' equity	$1,139,500	100.0%	$1,230,500	100.0%

The major percentage changes in Marlea Company's assets are in the current asset and long-term investment categories. In the Liabilities and Stockholders' Equity sections of the balance sheet, the greatest percentage changes are in long-term liabilities and retained earnings. Stockholders' equity increased from 64% to 72.8% of total liabilities and stockholders' equity in 1994. There is a comparable decrease in liabilities.

In a vertical analysis of the income statement, each item is stated as a percent of net sales. A condensed comparative income statement with vertical analysis is illustrated in Exhibit 7.

Exhibit 7
Comparative Income Statement—
Vertical Analysis

Marlea Company
Comparative Income Statement
For Years Ended December 31, 1994 and 1993

	1994		1993	
	Amount	*Percent*	*Amount*	*Percent*
Sales	$1,530,500	102.2%	$1,234,000	102.8%
Sales returns and allowances	32,500	2.2	34,000	2.8
Net sales	$1,498,000	100.0%	$1,200,000	100.0%
Cost of goods sold	1,043,000	69.6	820,000	68.3
Gross profit	$ 455,000	30.4%	$ 380,000	31.7%
Selling expenses	$ 191,000	12.8%	$ 147,000	12.3%
Administrative expenses	104,000	6.9	97,400	8.1
Total operating expenses	$ 295,000	19.7%	$ 244,400	20.4%
Operating income	$ 160,000	10.7%	$ 135,600	11.3%
Other income	8,500	.6	11,000	.9
	$ 168,500	11.3%	$ 146,600	12.2%
Other expense	6,000	.4	12,000	1.0
Income before income tax	$ 162,500	10.9%	$ 134,600	11.2%
Income tax	71,500	4.8%	58,100	4.8
Net income	$ 91,000	6.1%	$ 76,500	6.4%

Care must be used in judging the significance of differences between percentages for the two years. For example, the decline of the gross profit rate from 31.7% in 1993 to 30.4% in 1994 is only 1.3 percentage points. In terms of dollars of potential gross profit, however, it represents a decline of approximately $19,500 (1.3% × $1,498,000).

Common-Size Statements

Horizontal and vertical analyses with both dollar and percentage amounts are useful in assessing relationships and trends in financial condition and operations of an enterprise. Vertical analysis with both dollar and percentage amounts is also useful in comparing one company with another or with industry averages. Such comparisons are easier to make with the use of *common-size statements*. In a **common-size statement** all items are expressed in percentages.

Common-size statements are useful in comparing the current period with prior periods, individual businesses, or one business with industry percentages. Industry data are often available from trade associations and financial information services. A comparative common-size income statement for two enterprises is illustrated in Exhibit 8.

Exhibit 8 indicates that Marlea Company has a slightly higher rate of gross profit than Gram Corporation. However, this advantage is more than offset by Marlea Company's higher percentage of selling and administrative expenses. As a

Exhibit 8
Common-Size Income Statement

**Marlea Company and Gram Corporation
Condensed Common-Size Income Statement
For Year Ended December 31, 1994**

	Marlea Company	Gram Corporation
Sales	102.2%	102.3%
Sales returns and allowances	2.2	2.3
Net sales	100.0%	100.0%
Cost of goods sold	69.6	70.0
Gross profit	30.4%	30.0%
Selling expenses	12.8%	11.5%
Administrative expenses	6.9	4.1
Total operating expenses	19.7%	15.6%
Operating income	10.7%	14.4%
Other income	.6	.6
	11.3%	15.0%
Other expense	.4	.5
Income before income tax	10.9%	14.5%
Income tax	4.8	5.5
Net income	6.1%	9.0%

result, the operating income of Marlea Company is 10.7% of net sales, compared with 14.4% for Gram Corporation—an unfavorable difference of 3.7 percentage points.

Other Analytical Measures

In addition to the preceding analyses, there are other relationships that may be expressed in ratios and percentages. Often, these items are taken from the financial statements and thus are a type of vertical analysis. Comparison of these items with items from earlier periods is a type of horizontal analysis.

FOCUS OF FINANCIAL STATEMENT ANALYSES

Objective 2
Explain the two aspects of financial statement analysis.

Some aspects of an enterprise's financial condition and operations are of greater importance to some users than others. However, all users are interested in the ability of an enterprise to pay its debts as they are due and to earn income. These two aspects of an enterprise are called factors of **solvency** and **profitability**.

An enterprise that cannot pay its debts on a timely basis may experience difficulty in obtaining credit. A lack of available credit may, in turn, lead to a decline in the enterprise's profitability. Eventually, the enterprise may be forced into bankruptcy. Likewise, an enterprise that is less profitable than its competitors is likely to be at a disadvantage in obtaining credit or new capital from stockholders. Thus, the factors of solvency and profitability are interrelated.

Analyses of historical data are useful in assessing the past performance of an enterprise and in forecasting its future performance. The results of financial analyses may be even more useful when they are compared with those of competing enterprises and with industry averages.

Various types of financial analyses useful in evaluating the solvency and profitability of an enterprise are discussed in the following paragraphs. The examples are based on Marlea Company's financial statements presented earlier. In some cases, data from Marlea Company's financial statements of the preceding year and from other sources are also used.

SOLVENCY ANALYSIS

Solvency is the ability of a business to meet its financial obligations (debts) as they are due. Solvency analysis, therefore, focuses on the ability of an enterprise to pay or otherwise satisfy its current and noncurrent liabilities. This ability is normally assessed by examining balance sheet relationships. Major analyses used in assessing solvency include the following:

1. Current position analysis.
2. Accounts receivable analysis.
3. Inventory analysis.
4. The ratio of plant assets to long-term liabilities.
5. The ratio of stockholders' equity to liabilities.
6. The number of times interest charges are earned.

Current Position Analysis

To be useful in assessing solvency, a ratio or other financial measure must relate to an enterprise's ability to pay or otherwise satisfy its liabilities. The use of such measures to assess the ability of an enterprise to pay its current liabilities is called **current position analysis**. Such analysis is of special interest to short-term creditors.

WORKING CAPITAL. The excess of the current assets of an enterprise over its current liabilities is called **working capital**. *The working capital is often used in evaluating a company's ability to meet currently maturing debts.* It is especially useful in making monthly or other period-to-period comparisons for a company. However, amounts of working capital are difficult to assess when comparing companies of different sizes or in comparing such amounts with industry figures. For example, working capital of $250,000 may be adequate for a small residential contractor, but it may be inadequate for a large commercial contractor.

CURRENT RATIO. Another means of expressing the relationship between current assets and current liabilities is the **current ratio**. This ratio is sometimes called the **working capital ratio** or **bankers' ratio**. The ratio is computed by dividing the total current assets by the total current liabilities. For Marlea Company, working capital and the current ratio for 1994 and 1993 are as follows:

	1994	1993
Current assets	$550,000	$533,000
Current liabilities	210,000	243,000
Working capital	$340,000	$290,000
Current ratio	2.6:1	2.2:1

The current ratio is a more reliable indicator of solvency than is working capital. To illustrate, assume that as of December 31, 1994, the working capital of a competitor is much greater than $340,000, but its current ratio is only 1.3:1. Considering these facts alone, Marlea Company, with its current ratio of 2.6:1, is in a more favorable position to obtain short-term credit than the competitor, which has the greater amount of working capital.

ACID-TEST RATIO. The working capital and the current ratio are two solvency measures that indicate a company's ability to pay its current debts. However, these measures do not consider the makeup of the current assets. To illustrate the importance of this consideration, the current position data for Marlea Company and Wilson Corporation as of December 31, 1994, are as follows:

	Marlea Company	Wilson Corporation
Current assets:		
Cash	$ 90,500	$ 45,500
Marketable securities	75,000	25,000
Accounts receivable (net)	115,000	90,000
Inventories	264,000	380,000
Prepaid expenses	5,500	9,500
Total current assets	$550,000	$550,000
Current liabilities	210,000	210,000
Working capital	$340,000	$340,000
Current ratio	2.6:1	2.6:1

Both companies have working capital of $340,000 and a current ratio of 2.6:1. But the ability of each company to pay its current debts is significantly different. Wilson Corporation has more of its current assets in inventories. Some of these inventories must be sold and the receivables collected before the current liabilities can be paid in full. Thus, a large amount of time may be necessary to convert these inventories into cash. Declines in market prices and a reduction in demand could also impair the ability to pay current liabilities. In contrast, Marlea Company has cash and current assets (marketable securities and accounts receivable) that can generally be converted to cash rather quickly to meet its current liabilities.

A ratio that measures the "instant" debt-paying ability of a company is called the **acid-test ratio** or **quick ratio**. It is the ratio of the total quick assets to the total current liabilities. **Quick assets** are cash and other current assets that can be quickly converted to cash. Quick assets normally include cash, marketable securities, and receivables. The acid-test ratio data for Marlea Company are as follows:

	1994	1993
Quick assets:		
Cash	$ 90,500	$ 64,700
Marketable securities	75,000	60,000
Accounts receivable (net)	115,000	120,000
Total	$280,500	$244,700
Current liabilities	$210,000	$243,000
Acid-test ratio	1.3:1	1.0:1

An analysis of a firm's current position normally includes determining the working capital, the current ratio, and the acid-test ratio. The current and acid-test ratios are most useful when analyzed together and compared to previous periods and other firms in the industry.

Accounts Receivable Analysis

The size and makeup of accounts receivable change constantly during business operations. Sales on account increase accounts receivable, while collections from customers decrease accounts receivable. Firms that grant long credit terms usually have larger accounts receivable balances than those granting short credit terms. Increases or decreases in the volume of sales also affect the balance of accounts receivable.

It is desirable to collect receivables as promptly as possible. The cash collected from receivables improves solvency. In addition, the cash generated by prompt collections from customers may be used in operations for such purposes as purchasing merchandise in large quantities at lower prices. The cash may also be used for payment of dividends to stockholders or for other investing or financing purposes. Prompt collection also lessens the risk of loss from uncollectible accounts.

ACCOUNTS RECEIVABLE TURNOVER. The relationship between credit sales and accounts receivable may be stated as the **accounts receivable turnover.** This ratio is computed by dividing net sales on account by the average net accounts receivable. It is desirable to base the average on monthly balances, which allows for seasonal changes in sales. When such data are not available, it may be necessary to use the average of the accounts receivable balance at the beginning and the end of the year. If there are trade notes receivable as well as accounts, the two may be combined. The accounts receivable turnover data for Marlea Company are as follows. All sales were made on account.

	1994	1993
Net sales on account	$1,498,000	$1,200,000
Accounts receivable (net):		
Beginning of year	$ 120,000	$ 140,000
End of year	115,000	120,000
Total	$ 235,000	$ 260,000
Average	$ 117,500	$ 130,000
Accounts receivable turnover	12.7	9.2

The increase in the accounts receivable turnover for 1994 indicates that there has been an improvement in the collection of receivables. This may be due to a change in the granting of credit or the collection practices, or both.

NUMBER OF DAYS' SALES IN RECEIVABLES. Another measure of the relationship between credit sales and accounts receivable is the **number of days' sales in receivables.** This ratio is computed by dividing the net accounts receivable at the end of the year by the average daily sales on account. Average daily sales on account is determined by dividing net sales on account by 365 days. The number of days' sales in receivables is computed for Marlea Company below.

	1994	1993
Accounts receivable (net), end of year	$ 115,000	$ 120,000
Net sales on account	$1,498,000	$1,200,000
Average daily sales on account	$ 4,104	$ 3,288
Number of days' sales in receivables	28.0	36.5

The number of days' sales in receivables is an estimate of the length of time the accounts receivable have been outstanding. Comparing this measure with the credit terms provides information on the efficiency in collecting receivables. For example, assume that the number of days' sales in receivables for Empire Inc. is 40. If Empire Inc.'s credit terms are n/45, then an efficient collection process is indicated. On the other hand, if Empire Inc.'s credit terms are n/30, an inefficient collection process is indicated. A comparison with other firms in the same industry and with prior years also provides useful information. Such comparisons may indicate efficiency of collection procedures and trends in credit management.

Inventory Analysis

An enterprise should keep enough inventory on hand to meet the needs of its customers and its operations. At the same time, however, an excessive amount of inventory reduces solvency by tying up funds. Excess inventories also increase insurance expense, property taxes, storage costs, and other related expenses. These expenses further reduce funds that could be used elsewhere to improve operations. Finally, excess inventory also increases the risk of losses because of price declines or obsolescence of the inventory.

As with many types of financial analyses, it is possible to determine more than one measure to express the relationship between the cost of goods sold and inventory. As discussed in the following paragraphs, both the inventory turnover and the number of days' sales in inventory are useful for evaluating the management of inventory. Whether both measures are used or whether one measure is preferred over the other is a matter for the individual analyst to decide.

INVENTORY TURNOVER. The relationship between the volume of goods (merchandise) sold and inventory may be stated as the inventory turnover. It is computed by dividing the cost of goods sold by the average inventory. If monthly data are not available, the average of the inventories at the beginning and the end of the year may be used. The inventory turnover for Marlea Company is computed as follows:

	1994	1993
Cost of goods sold	$1,043,000	$820,000
Inventories:		
Beginning of year	$ 283,000	$311,000
End of year	264,000	283,000
Total	$ 547,000	$594,000
Average	$ 273,500	$297,000
Inventory turnover	3.8	2.8

The inventory turnover improved for Marlea Company because of an increase in the cost of goods sold and a decrease in the average inventories. Differences across inventories, companies, and industries are too great to allow a general statement as to what is a good inventory turnover. For example, a firm selling food should have a higher turnover than a firm selling furniture or jewelry. Likewise, the perishable foods department of a supermarket should have a higher turnover than the soaps and cleansers department. However, for each business or each department within a business, there is a reasonable turnover rate. A turnover lower than this rate could mean that inventory is not being managed properly. In such cases, an investigation should be undertaken to determine the causes of the lower turnover rate.

NUMBER OF DAYS' SALES IN INVENTORY. Another measure of the relationship between the cost of goods sold and inventory is the number of days' sales in inventory. This measure is computed by dividing the inventory at the end of the year by the average daily cost of goods sold (cost of goods sold divided by 365). The number of days' sales in inventory for Marlea Company is computed as follows:

	1994	1993
Inventories, end of year	$ 264,000	$283,000
Cost of goods sold	$1,043,000	$820,000
Average daily cost of goods sold	$ 2,858	$ 2,247
Number of days' sales in inventory	92.4	125.9

The number of days' sales in inventory is a rough measure of the length of time it takes to acquire, sell, and replace the inventory. For Marlea Company there is a major improvement in the number of days' sales in inventory during 1994. However, a comparison with earlier years and similar firms would be useful in assessing Marlea Company's overall inventory management.

Ratio of Plant Assets to Long-Term Liabilities

Long-term notes and bonds are often secured by mortgages on plant assets. The **ratio of total plant assets to long-term liabilities** *is a solvency measure that indicates the margin of safety of the noteholders or bondholders. It also indicates the ability of the enterprise to borrow additional funds on a long-term basis.* The ratio of plant assets to long-term liabilities for Marlea Company is as follows:

	1994	1993
Plant assets (net)	$444,500	$470,000
Long-term liabilities	$100,000	$200,000
Ratio of plant assets to long-term liabilities	4.4:1	2.4:1

The major increase in the above ratio at the end of 1994 is mainly due to the liquidation of one-half of Marlea Company's long-term liabilities. If the company needs to borrow additional funds on a long-term basis in the future, it is in a strong position to do so.

Ratio of Stockholders' Equity to Liabilities

Claims against the total assets of an enterprise are divided into two groups: (1) claims of creditors and (2) claims of owners. *The relationship between the total claims of the creditors and owners is a solvency measure that indicates the margin of safety for creditors. It also indicates the ability of the enterprise to withstand adverse business conditions.* When the claims of creditors are large in relation to the equity of the stockholders, there are usually significant interest payments. If earnings decline to the point where the company is unable to meet its interest payments, the business may be taken over by the creditors.

The relationship between stockholder and creditor equity is shown in the vertical analysis of the balance sheet. For example, the balance sheet of Marlea Company in Exhibit 6 indicates that on December 31, 1994, stockholders' equity represented 72.8% and liabilities represented 27.2% of the total liabilities and stockholders' equity (100.0%). Instead of expressing each item as a percent of the total, this relationship may be expressed as a ratio of one to the other, as follows:

	1994	1993
Total stockholders' equity	$829,500	$787,500
Total liabilities	$310,000	$443,000
Ratio of stockholders' equity to liabilities	2.7:1	1.8:1

The balance sheet of Marlea Company shows that the major factor affecting the change in the ratio was the $100,000 decrease in long-term liabilities during 1994. The ratio at the end of both years shows a large margin of safety for the creditors.

Number of Times Interest Charges Earned

Corporations in some industries, such as public utilities, normally have high ratios of debt to stockholders' equity. For such corporations, *the relative risk of the debtholders is normally measured as the* **number of times the interest charges are earned** during the year. The higher the ratio, the lower the risk that interest payments will not be made if earnings decrease. In other words, the higher the ratio, the greater the assurance that interest payments will be made on a continuing basis. *This measure also indicates the general financial strength of the enterprise, which is of interest to stockholders and employees as well as creditors.*

The amount available to meet interest charges is not affected by taxes on income. This is because interest is deductible in determining taxable income. Thus, the number of times interest charges are earned is computed as shown below.

	1994	1993
Income before income tax	$ 900,000	$ 800,000
Add interest expense	300,000	250,000
Amount available to meet interest charges	$1,200,000	$1,050,000
Number of times interest charges earned	4	4.2

Analysis like that above can also be applied to dividends on preferred stock. In such a case, net income is divided by the amount of preferred dividends to yield the number of times preferred dividends are earned. This measure indicates the risk that dividends to preferred stockholders may not be paid.

PROFITABILITY ANALYSIS

Objective 4
Apply financial statement analysis to assess the profitability of an enterprise.

Profitability is the ability of an entity to earn profits. This ability to earn profits depends upon the effectiveness and efficiency of operations as well as resources available to the enterprise. Profitability analysis, therefore, focuses primarily upon the relationship between operating results as reported in the income statement and resources available to the enterprise as reported in the balance sheet. Major analyses used in assessing profitability include the following:

1. Ratio of net sales to assets
2. Rate earned on total assets
3. Rate earned on stockholders' equity
4. Rate earned on common stockholders' equity
5. Earnings per share on common stock
6. Price-earnings ratio
7. Dividend yield

Ratio of Net Sales to Assets

The **ratio of net sales to assets** *is a profitability measure that shows how effectively a firm utilizes its assets.* For example, two competing enterprises have equal amounts of assets. If the sales of one are double the sales of the other, the enterprise with the higher sales is making better use of its assets.

In computing the ratio of net sales to assets, any long-term investments are excluded from total assets. This is because such investments are unrelated to normal operations involving the sale of goods or services. Assets may be measured as the total at the end of the year, the average at the beginning and the end of the year, or the average of monthly totals. The basic data and the computation of this ratio for Marlea Company are as follows:

	1994	1993
Net sales	$1,498,000	$1,200,000
Total assets (excluding long-term investments):		
Beginning of year	$1,053,000	$1,010,000
End of year	1,044,500	1,053,000
Total	$2,097,500	$2,063,000
Average	$1,048,750	$1,031,500
Ratio of net sales to assets	1.4:1	1.2:1

There was an improvement in this ratio during 1994. This was primarily due to an increase in sales volume. A comparison with similar companies or industry averages would be helpful in assessing the effectiveness of Marlea Company's use of its assets.

Rate Earned on Total Assets

The **rate earned on total assets** *measures the profitability of total assets, without considering how the assets are financed.* This rate is therefore not affected by whether the assets are financed primarily by creditors or stockholders.

The rate earned on total assets is computed by adding interest expense to net income and dividing this sum by the average total assets. The addition of interest expense to net income eliminates the effect of whether the assets are financed by debt or equity. The rate earned by Marlea Company on total assets is computed as follows:

	1994	1993
Net income	$ 91,000	$ 76,500
Plus interest expense	6,000	12,000
Total	$ 97,000	$ 88,500
Total assets:		
Beginning of year	$1,230,500	$1,187,500
End of year	1,139,500	1,230,500
Total	$2,370,000	$2,418,000
Average	$1,185,000	$1,209,000
Rate earned on total assets	8.2%	7.3%

The rate earned on total assets of Marlea Company during 1994 improved over that of 1993. A comparison with similar companies and industry averages would be useful in evaluating Marlea Company's profitability on total assets.

Sometimes it may be desirable to compute the rate of operating income to total assets. This is especially true if significant amounts of nonoperating income and expense are reported on the income statement. In this case, any assets related to the nonoperating income and expense items should be excluded from total assets in computing the rate. In addition, the use of operating income (which is before tax) has the advantage of eliminating the effects of any changes in the tax structure on the rate of earnings. When evaluating published data on rates earned on assets, the reader should be careful to determine the exact nature of the measure that is reported.

Rate Earned on Stockholders' Equity

Another measure of profitability is the **rate earned on stockholders' equity.** It is computed by dividing net income by average total stockholders' equity. In contrast to the rate earned on total assets, *this measure emphasizes the rate of income earned on the amount invested by the stockholders.*

The total stockholders' equity may vary throughout a period. For example, an enterprise may issue or retire stock, pay dividends, and earn net income. If monthly amounts are not available, the average of the stockholders' equity at the beginning and the end of the year is normally used to compute this rate. For Marlea Company, the rate earned on stockholders' equity is computed as follows:

	1994	1993
Net income	$ 91,000	$ 76,500
Stockholders' equity:		
Beginning of year	$ 787,500	$ 750,000
End of year	829,500	787,500
Total	$1,617,000	$1,537,500
Average	$ 808,500	$ 768,750
Rate earned on stockholders' equity	11.3%	10.0%

The rate earned by an enterprise on the equity of its stockholders is usually higher than the rate earned on total assets. This occurs when the amount earned on assets acquired with creditors' funds is more than the interest paid to creditors. This difference in the rate on stockholders' equity and the rate on total assets is called **leverage.**

Marlea Company's rate on stockholders' equity for 1994, 11.3%, is greater than the rate of 8.2% earned on total assets. The leverage of 3.1% (11.3% − 8.2%) for 1994 compares favorably with the 2.7% (10.0% − 7.3%) leverage for 1993. The 1994 and 1993 leverage for Marlea Company is shown in Exhibit 9.

Rate Earned on Common Stockholders' Equity

A corporation may have both preferred and common stock outstanding. In this case, the common stockholders have the residual claim on earnings. The **rate earned on common stockholders' equity** focuses only on the rate of profits

Exhibit 9
Leverage

earned on the amount invested by the common stockholders. It is computed by subtracting preferred dividend requirements from the net income and dividing by the average common stockholders' equity.

Marlea Company has $150,000 of 6% nonparticipating preferred stock outstanding on December 31, 1994 and 1993. Thus, the annual preferred dividend requirement is $9,000 ($150,000 × 6%). The common stockholders' equity equals the total stockholders' equity, including retained earnings, less the par of the preferred stock ($150,000). The basic data and the rate earned on common stockholders' equity for Marlea Company are as follows:

	1994	1993
Net income	$ 91,000	$ 76,500
Preferred dividends	9,000	9,000
Remainder—identified with common stock	$ 82,000	$ 67,500
Common stockholders' equity:		
Beginning of year	$ 637,500	$ 600,000
End of year	679,500	637,500
Total	$1,317,000	$1,237,500
Average	$ 658,500	$ 618,750
Rate earned on common stockholders' equity	12.5%	10.9%

The rate earned on common stockholders' equity differs from the rates earned by Marlea Company on total assets and total stockholders' equity. This occurs if there are borrowed funds and also preferred stock outstanding, which rank ahead of the common shares in their claim on earnings. Thus, the concept of leverage, as discussed in the preceding section, can also be applied to the use of funds from the sale of preferred stock as well as borrowing. Funds from both sources can be used in an attempt to increase the return on common stockholders' equity.

Earnings per Share on Common Stock

One of the profitability measures most commonly quoted by the financial press is **earnings per share (EPS) on common stock**. It is also normally reported in the income statement in corporate annual reports. If a company has issued only one class of stock, the earnings per share is computed by dividing net income by the number of shares of stock outstanding. If preferred and common stock are outstanding, the net income is first reduced by the amount of preferred dividend requirements.

Any changes in the number of shares outstanding during the year, such as from stock dividends or stock splits, should be disclosed in reporting earnings per share on common stock. Also, if there are any nonrecurring items in the income statement, such as an extraordinary item, the income per share before such items should be reported. The net income per share is then reported. If there are convertible bonds or convertible preferred stock outstanding, the amount reported as net income per share is reported with and without considering the conversion privilege.

The data on the earnings per share of common stock for Marlea Company are as follows:

	1994	1993
Net income	$91,000	$76,500
Preferred dividends	9,000	9,000
Remainder—identified with common stock	$82,000	$67,500
Shares of common stock outstanding	50,000	50,000
Earnings per share on common stock	$1.64	$1.35

Since earnings are the primary basis for dividends, earnings per share and dividends per share on common stock are commonly used by investors in assessing alternative stock investments. Earnings per share can be reported with dividends per share to indicate the relationship between earnings and dividends. A comparison of these two per share amounts indicates the extent to which the corporation is retaining its earnings for use in operations. Exhibit 10 shows these relationships for Marlea Company:

Exhibit 10
Earnings and Dividends per Share of Common Stock

Price-Earnings Ratio

Another profitability measure commonly quoted by the financial press is the **price-earnings (P/E) ratio** on common stock. *The price-earnings ratio is an indicator of a firm's future earnings prospects.* It is computed by dividing the market price per share of common stock at a specific date by the annual earnings per share. To illustrate, assume that the market prices per common share are 20½ at the end of 1994 and 13½ at the end of 1993. The price-earnings ratio on common stock of Marlea Company is computed as follows:

	1994	1993
Market price per share of common stock	$20.50	$13.50
Earnings per share on common stock	$ 1.64	$ 1.35
Price-earnings ratio on common stock	12.5	10.0

The price-earnings ratio indicates that a share of common stock of Marlea Company was selling for 10 times the amount of earnings per share at the end of 1993. At the end of 1994, the common stock was selling for 12.5 times the amount of earnings per share.

Dividend Yield

The **dividend yield** on common stock is a profitability measure that shows the rate of return to common stockholders in terms of cash dividends. It is of special interest to investors whose main investment objective is to receive current returns (dividends) on an investment rather than an increase in the market price of the investment. The dividend yield is computed by dividing the annual dividends paid per share of common stock by the market price per share on a specific date. To illustrate, assume that dividends were $0.80 per common share and the market price was 20½ at the end of 1994. Dividends were $0.60 per share, and the market price was 13½ at the end of 1993. The dividend yield on common stock of Marlea Company is as follows:

	1994	1993
Dividends per share of common stock	$ .80	$ .60
Market price per share of common stock	$20.50	$13.50
Dividend yield on common stock	3.9%	4.4%

SUMMARY OF ANALYTICAL MEASURES

Objective 5
Summarize the uses and limitations of analytical measures.

Exhibit 11 presents a summary of the analytical measures discussed in this chapter. These measures can be computed for most medium-size enterprises. Depending upon the specific enterprise being analyzed, some measures might be omitted or additional measures could be developed. The type of industry, the capital structure, and the diversity of the enterprise's operations usually affect the measures used. For example, analysis for an airline might include revenue per passenger mile and cost per available seat as measures. Likewise, analysis for a hotel might focus on occupancy rates.

Percentage analyses, ratios, turnovers, and other measures of financial position and operating results are useful analytical measures. They are helpful in assessing an enterprise's past performance and predicting its future. They are not, however, a substitute for sound judgment. In selecting and interpreting analytical measures, conditions peculiar to an enterprise or its industry should be considered. In addition, the influence of the general economic and business environment should be considered.

In determining trends, the interrelationship of the measures used in assessing an enterprise should be carefully studied. Comparable indexes of earlier periods should also be studied. Data from competing enterprises may be useful in assessing the efficiency of operations for the firm under analysis. In making such comparisons, however, the effects of differences in the accounting methods used by the enterprises should be considered.

Exhibit 11
Summary of Analytical Measures

	Method of Computation	*Use*
Solvency measures:		
Working capital	Current assets – Current liabilities	To indicate the ability to meet currently maturing obligations
Current ratio	$\dfrac{\text{Current assets}}{\text{Current liabilities}}$	
Acid-test ratio	$\dfrac{\text{Quick assets}}{\text{Current liabilities}}$	To indicate instant debt-paying ability
Accounts receivable turnover	$\dfrac{\text{Net sales on account}}{\text{Average accounts receivable}}$	To assess the efficiency in collecting receivables and in the management of credit
Number of days' sales in receivables	$\dfrac{\text{Accounts receivable, end of year}}{\text{Average daily sales on account}}$	
Inventory turnover	$\dfrac{\text{Cost of goods sold}}{\text{Average inventory}}$	To assess the efficiency in the management of inventory
Number of days' sales in inventory	$\dfrac{\text{Inventory, end of year}}{\text{Average daily cost of goods sold}}$	

Exhibit 11 (concluded)

Solvency measures:	*Method of Computation*	*Use*
Ratio of plant assets to long-term liabilities	$\dfrac{\text{Plant assets (net)}}{\text{Long-term liabilities}}$	To indicate the margin of safety to long-term creditors
Ratio of stockholders' equity to liabilities	$\dfrac{\text{Total stockholders' equity}}{\text{Total liabilities}}$	To indicate the margin of safety to creditors
Number of times interest charges earned	$\dfrac{\text{Income before income tax + Interest expense}}{\text{Interest expense}}$	To assess the risk to debtholders in terms of number of times interest charges were earned

Profitability measures:		
Ratio of net sales to assets	$\dfrac{\text{Net sales}}{\text{Average total assets (excluding long-term investments)}}$	To assess the effectiveness in the use of assets
Rate earned on total assets	$\dfrac{\text{Net income + Interest expense}}{\text{Average total assets}}$	To assess the profitability of the assets
Rate earned on stockholders' equity	$\dfrac{\text{Net income}}{\text{Average total stockholders' equity}}$	To assess the profitability of the investment by stockholders
Rate earned on common stockholders' equity	$\dfrac{\text{Net income – Preferred dividends}}{\text{Average common stockholders' equity}}$	To assess the profitability of the investment by common stockholders
Earnings per share on common stock	$\dfrac{\text{Net income – Preferred dividends}}{\text{Shares of common stock outstanding}}$	
Dividends per share of common stock	$\dfrac{\text{Dividends}}{\text{Shares of common stock outstanding}}$	To indicate the extent to which earnings are being distributed to common stockholders
Price-earnings ratio	$\dfrac{\text{Market price per share of common stock}}{\text{Earnings per share of common stock}}$	To indicate future earnings prospects, based on the relationship between market value of common stock and earnings
Dividend yield	$\dfrac{\text{Dividends per share of common stock}}{\text{Market price per share of common stock}}$	To indicate the rate of return to common stockholders in terms of dividends

Perceptions of Financial Ratios

Financial statements serve as the primary financial reporting focus of an entity, both internally and externally. An analysis of the financial information reported by these statements includes the computation and interpretation of financial ratios.

A survey of financial executives indicated that financial ratios are an important tool in analyzing the financial results of a company and in managing a company. In addition, 93 of the 100 respondents to the survey indicated that their firms use financial ratios as part of their corporate objectives. The ratios most significant to the respondents are those that measure the ability of the firm to earn a profit.

Financial ratios are often more useful when they are compared with similar ratios of other companies or groups of companies. For this purpose, average ratios for many industries are compiled by various financial services and trade associations. In this process, however, it should be remembered that averages are just that—averages—and care should be taken in their use. The danger in interpreting averages was noted by Eldon Grimm, a Wall Street analyst who said: "A statistician is an individual who has his head in the refrigerator, his feet in the oven and on the average feels comfortable."

Sources: Charles H. Gibson, "How Industry Perceives Financial Ratios," *Management Accounting* (April 1982), pp. 13–19; "Twenty-Five Years Ago in Forbes" *Forbes* (August 16, 1982), p. 107.

CORPORATE ANNUAL REPORTS

Objective 6
Describe the contents of corporate annual reports.

Corporations normally issue annual reports to their stockholders and other interested parties. Such reports summarize the corporation's operating activities for the past year and plans for the future. There are many variations in the form and order of presentation of the major sections of annual reports. However, one section of the annual report is devoted to the financial statements, including the accompanying notes. In addition, annual reports usually include the following sections and information:

1. Selected data called the Financial Highlights
2. The President's Letter
3. The Independent Auditors' Report
4. The Management Report
5. A five- or ten-year Historical Summary of financial data

As a way to enhance relationships with stockholders, many corporations also include pictures of their products and officers in the annual report. The following paragraphs describe the portions of annual reports commonly related to financial matters, with the exception of the financial statements, examples of which appear in Appendix G.

Financial Highlights

The Financial Highlights section summarizes the operating results for the last year or two. It is sometimes called *Results in Brief*. It is usually presented on the first one or two pages of the annual report. Such items as sales, income before income tax, net income, net income per common share, cash dividends, cash dividends per common share, and the amount of capital expenditures are typically presented. An example of a Financial Highlights section is shown in Exhibit 12.

Exhibit 12
Financial Highlights Section

FINANCIAL HIGHLIGHTS

(Dollars in thousands except per share amounts)

For the Year	Current Year	Preceding Year
Sales	$1,336,750	$ 876,400
Income before income tax	149,550	90,770
Net income	105,120	66,190
Per common share	4.03	2.62
Dividends declared on common stock	34,990	33,150
Per common share	1.48	1.40
Capital expenditures and investments	265,120	157,050

At Year End		
Working capital	$ 415,410	$ 423,780
Total assets	1,712,170	1,457,240
Long-term debt	440,680	457,350
Stockholders' equity	840,350	692,950

There are many variations in format and content of the Financial Highlights section. In addition to the selected income statement data, information about the financial position at year end may be presented. As shown in Exhibit 12, such information may include the amount of working capital, total assets, long-term debt, and stockholders' equity. Other year-end data often reported are the number of common and preferred shares outstanding, number of common and preferred stockholders, and number of employees.

President's Letter

A letter from the company president to the stockholders is also presented in most annual reports. Such letters usually discuss such items as reasons for an increase or decrease in net income, changes in existing plants or purchase or construction of new plants, significant new financing commitments, social responsibility issues, and future plans. A condensed version of a President's Letter adapted from a corporation's annual report is presented in Exhibit 13.

Exhibit 13
President's Letter Section

PRESIDENT'S LETTER

To the Stockholders:

FISCAL YEAR REVIEWED
The record net income in this fiscal year resulted from very strong product demand experienced for about two-thirds of the fiscal year, more complete utilization of plants, and a continued improvement in sales mix. Income was strong both domestically and internationally during this period.

PLANT EXPANSION CONTINUES
Capital expenditures during the year were $14.5 million. Expansions were in progress or completed at all locations. Portions of the Company's major new expansion at one of its West Coast plants came on stream in March of this year and will provide much needed capacity in existing and new product areas. Capital expenditures will be somewhat less during next year.

ENVIRONMENTAL CONCERN
The Company recognizes its responsibility to provide a safe and healthy environment at each of its plants. The Company expects to spend approximately $1 million in the forthcoming year to help continue its position as a constructive corporate citizen.

OUTLOOK
During the past 10 years the Company's net income and sales have more than tripled. Net income increased from $3.1 million to $10.7 million, and sales from $45 million to $181 million.

The Company's employees are proud of this record and are determined to carry the momentum into the future. The current economic slowdown makes results for the new fiscal year difficult to predict. However, we are confident and enthusiastic about the Company's prospects for continued growth over the longer term.

Respectfully submitted,

Frances B. Davis

Frances B. Davis
President

March 24, 1995

During recent years, many corporate enterprises have become active in accepting environmental and other social goals. In addition to the brief discussion that may be included in the President's Letter, a more detailed analysis of the company's social goals and programs may be included elsewhere in the annual report. Managers recognize that a failure to accept social responsibilities can have an unfavorable, long-run impact on a corporation. In the future, a function of accounting may be to assist managers in developing a social responsibilities statement listing goals, programs, and results.

Independent Auditors' Report

Before issuing annual statements, all publicly held corporations are required to have an independent audit of their financial statements. Certified public accountants (CPAs) are engaged to conduct an audit (examination) of the financial statements. The purpose of an independent audit is to add credibility to the financial statements that have been prepared by management.

Upon completion of the audit, which for large corporations may take several weeks or longer, an *Independent Auditors' Report* is issued. This report accompanies the financial statements. The normal audit report includes the following three paragraphs:

1. An introductory paragraph identifying the financial statements audited.
2. A *scope* paragraph describing the nature of the audit.
3. An *opinion* paragraph presenting the auditor's opinion as to the fairness of the statements.[2]

The audit report for Winn-Dixie Stores, Inc., shown in Exhibit 14, uses standard report language. For the financial statements of most companies, the auditors render an opinion such as the one in Exhibit 14. Such an opinion is called an *unqualified* or *clean* opinion. However, it is possible that accounting methods used by the corporation do not conform with generally accepted accounting principles. In such cases, a *qualified* opinion is rendered and the exception is briefly described. If the departure from accepted principles is severe, an *adverse* or *negative* opinion is issued and the exception described. In rare cases, the auditors may be unable to reach an opinion on the financial statements. The auditor then issues a *disclaimer* and briefly describes why an opinion could not be reached.

Exhibit 14
Independent Auditors' Report
Section

Independent Auditor's Report

The Shareholders and the Board of Directors
Winn-Dixie Stores, Inc.:

We have audited the accompanying consolidated balance sheets of Winn-Dixie Stores, Inc. and subsidiaries as of June 29, 1991 and June 24, 1990, and the related consolidated statements of earnings, shareholders' equity, and cash flows for each of the years in the three-year period ended June 29, 1991. These consolidated financial statements are the responsibility of the Company's management. Our responsibility is to express an opinion on these consolidated financial statements based on our audits.

We conducted our audits in accordance with generally accepted auditing standards. Those standards require that we plan and perform the audit to obtain reasonable assurance about whether the financial statements are free of material misstatement. An audit includes examining, on a test basis, evidence supporting the amounts and disclosures in the financial statements. An audit also includes assessing the accounting principles used and significant estimates made by management, as well as evaluating the overall financial statement presentation. We believe that our audits provide a reasonable basis for our opinion.

In our opinion, the consolidated financial statements referred to above present fairly, in all material respects, the financial position of Winn-Dixie Store, Inc. and subsidiaries at June 29, 1991 and June 24, 1990, and the results of their operations and their cash flows for the years then ended in conformity with generally accepted accounting principles.

Peat Marwick Main & Co.

Certified Public Accountants

Jacksonville, Florida
August 22, 1991

---

[2] *Statements on Auditing Standards, No. 58*, "Reports on Audited Financial Statements" (New York: American Institute of Certified Public Accountants, 1988), par. 8.

Management Report

The management of the corporation is responsible for the corporation's accounting system and financial statements. In the *Management Report*, the chief financial officer or other corporate officer normally includes the following:

1. A statement that the financial statements are management's responsibility and that they have been prepared according to generally accepted accounting principles.
2. Management's assessment of the company's internal accounting control system.
3. Comments on any other relevant matters related to the accounting system, the financial statements, and the examination by the independent auditor.

Many corporations include a Management Report in the corporation's annual report. The 1991 edition of *Accounting Trends & Techniques* reported that 56% of the companies surveyed included a Management Report in their annual report. An example of such a report taken from the 1991 annual report for Toys "R" Us is shown in Exhibit 15.

Exhibit 15
Management Report Section

Report of Management

Responsibility for the integrity and objectivity of the financial information presented in this Annual Report rests with Toys "R" Us management. The accompanying financial statements have been prepared from accounting records which management believes fairly and accurately reflect the operations and financial position of the Company. Management has established a system of internal controls to provide reasonable assurance that assets are maintained and accounted for in accordance with its policies and that transactions are recorded accurately on the Company's books and records.

The Company's comprehensive internal audit program provides for constant evaluation of the adequacy of and adherence to management's established policies and procedures. The Company has distributed to key employees its policies for conducting business affairs in a lawful and ethical manner.

The financial statements of the Company have been examined by Touche Ross & Co., independent certified public accountants. Their accompanying report is based on an examination conducted in accordance with generally accepted auditing standards, including a review of internal accounting controls and financial reporting matters.

Charles Lazarus

Charles Lazarus
Chairman of the Board

Michael Goldstein

Michael Goldstein
Executive Vice President—
Finance and Administration

Historical Summary

The Historical Summary section reports selected financial and operating data of past periods, usually for five or ten years. It is usually presented in close proximity to the financial statements for the current year. There are wide variations in the types of data reported and the title of this section. An example of a portion of such a report is shown in Exhibit 16.

Other Information

The preceding paragraphs described the most commonly presented sections of annual reports related to the financial statements. Some annual reports may include other financial information, such as forecasts that indicate financial plans and expectations for the year ahead and other supplemental data.

Exhibit 16
Historical Summary Section

Five-Year Consolidated Financial and Statistical Summary
for Years Ended December 31
(Dollar amounts in millions except for per share data)

For the Year	1995	1994	1993
Net sales	$1,759.7	$1,550.1	$ 997.4
Gross profit	453.5	402.8	270.8
Percent to net sales	25.8%	26.0%	27.2%
Interest expense	33.9	21.3	15.0
Income before income tax	172.7	163.4	87.5
Income tax	82.8	77.8	40.2
Net income	89.9	85.6	47.3
Percent to net sales	5.1%	5.5%	4.7%
Per common share:			
Net income	5.19	4.84	2.54
Dividends	1.80	1.65	1.40
Return on stockholders' equity	15.9%	16.4%	11.2%
Common share market price:			
High	31	41½	40⅞
Low	18	22⅜	22¼
Depreciation and amortization	43.3	41.0	23.6
Capital expenditures	98.5	72.1	55.5
At Year End			
Working capital	$ 443.9	$ 434.8	$ 254.6
Plant assets—gross	704.7	620.3	453.7
Plant assets—net	420.0	362.7	263.4
Stockholders' equity	594.3	536.9	447.6
Stockholders' equity per common share	33.07	29.69	23.02
Number of holders of common shares	39,503	39,275	43,852
Number of employees	50,225	50,134	42,826

CHAPTER REVIEW

Key Points

Objective 1. List basic financial statement analytical procedures.

The analysis of percentage increases and decreases in related items in comparative financial statements is called horizontal analysis. The analysis of percentages of component parts to the total in a single statement is called vertical analysis. Financial statements in which all amounts are expressed in percentages for purposes of analysis are called common-size statements.

Objective 2. Explain the two aspects of financial statement analysis.

The primary focus of financial statement analysis is the assessment of solvency and profitability. All users are interested in the ability of an enterprise to pay its debts as they come due (solvency) and to earn income (profitability). Financial statement analysis is useful in assessing the past performance of an enterprise and in predicting its future.

Objective 3. Apply financial statement analysis to assess the solvency of an enterprise.

Solvency analysis focuses mainly on balance sheet relationships that indicate the ability to pay liabilities. Major analy-

ses used in assessing solvency include (1) current position analysis, (2) accounts receivable analysis, (3) inventory analysis, (4) the ratio of plant assets to long-term liabilities, (5) the ratio of stockholders' equity to liabilities, and (6) the number of times interest charges are earned. The computation of the financial ratios related to each of these analyses are summarized in Exhibit 11.

Objective 4. Apply financial statement analysis to assess the profitability of an enterprise.

Profitability analysis focuses mainly on the relationship between operating results (income statement) and resources available (balance sheet). Major analyses used in assessing profitability include (1) the ratio of net sales to assets, (2) the rate earned on total assets, (3) the rate earned on stockholders' equity, (4) the rate earned on common stockholders' equity, (5) earnings per share on common stock, (6) the price-earnings ratio, and (7) dividend yield. The computation of each of these profitability measures is summarized in Exhibit 11.

Objective 5. Summarize the uses and limitations of analytical measures.

In selecting and interpreting analytical measures, conditions peculiar to an enterprise or its industry should be considered. For example, the type of industry, capital structure, and diversity of the enterprise's operations affect the measures used. In addition, the influence of the general economic and business environment should be considered.

Objective 6. Describe the contents of corporate annual reports.

Corporate annual reports normally include a Financial Highlights section, the President's Letter, the Independent Auditors' Report, financial statements and related notes, the Management Report, and a Historical Summary of operations.

Glossary of Key Terms

Accounts receivable turnover. The relationship between credit sales and accounts receivable, computed by dividing net sales on account by the average net accounts receivable. **Objective 3**

Acid-test ratio. The ratio of the sum of cash, receivables, and marketable securities to current liabilities. **Objective 3**

Common-size statement. A financial statement in which all items are expressed only in relative terms. **Objective 1**

Current ratio. The ratio of current assets to current liabilities. **Objective 3**

Earnings per share (EPS) on common stock. The profitability ratio of net income available to common shareholders to the number of common shares outstanding. **Objective 4**

Horizontal analysis. The percentage of increases and decreases in corresponding items in comparative financial statements. **Objective 1**

Inventory turnover. The relationship between the volume of goods sold and inventory, computed by dividing the cost of goods sold by the average inventory. **Objective 3**

Leverage. The tendency of the rate earned on stockholders' equity to vary from the rate earned on total assets because the amount earned on assets acquired through the use of funds provided by creditors varies from the interest paid to these creditors. **Objective 4**

Number of days' sales in inventory. The relationship between the volume of sales and inventory, computed by dividing the inventory at the end of the year by the average daily cost of goods sold. **Objective 3**

Number of days' sales in receivables. The relationship between credit sales and accounts receivable, computed by dividing the net accounts receivable at the end of the year by the average daily sales on account. **Objective 3**

Price-earnings (P/E) ratio. The ratio of the market price per share of common stock, at a specific date, to the annual earnings per share. **Objective 4**

Profitability. The ability of a firm to earn income. **Objective 4**

Quick assets. The sum of cash, receivables, and marketable securities. **Objective 3**

Rate earned on common stockholders' equity. A measure of profitability computed by dividing net income, reduced by preferred dividend requirements, by common stockholders' equity. **Objective 4**

Rate earned on stockholders' equity. A measure of profitability computed by dividing net income by total stockholders' equity. **Objective 4**

Rate earned on total assets. A measure of the profitability of assets, without regard to the equity of creditors and stockholders in the assets. **Objective 4**

Solvency. The ability of a firm to pay its debts as they come due. **Objective 3**

Vertical analysis. The percentage analysis of component parts in relation to the total of the parts in a single financial statement. **Objective 1**

Working capital. The excess of total current assets over total current liabilities at some point in time. **Objective 3**

Self-Examination Questions
Answers at end of chapter.

1. What type of analysis is indicated by the following?

	Amount	Percent
Current assets	$100,000	20%
Plant assets	400,000	80
Total assets	$500,000	100%

   A. Vertical analysis
   B. Horizontal analysis
   C. Differential analysis
   D. Contribution margin analysis

2. Which of the following measures is useful as an indication of the ability of a firm to liquidate current liabilities?
   A. Working capital
   B. Current ratio
   C. Acid-test ratio
   D. All of the above

3. The ratio determined by dividing total current assets by total current liabilities is:
   A. current ratio
   B. working capital ratio
   C. bankers' ratio
   D. all of the above

4. The ratio of the quick assets to current liabilities, which indicates the "instant" debt-paying ability of a firm, is:
   A. current ratio
   B. working capital ratio
   C. acid-test ratio
   D. bankers' ratio

5. A measure useful in evaluating the efficiency in the management of inventories is:
   A. working capital ratio
   B. acid-test ratio
   C. number of days' sales in inventory
   D. ratio of plant assets to long-term liabilities

ILLUSTRATIVE PROBLEM

Fleming Inc.'s comparative financial statements for the years ending December 31, 1994 and 1993, are as follows. The market price of Fleming Inc.'s common stock was $30 on December 31, 1993, and $25 on December 31, 1994.

Fleming Inc.
Comparative Income Statement
For Years Ended December 31, 1994 and 1993

	1994	1993
Sales (all on account)	$5,125,000	$3,257,600
Sales returns and allowances	125,000	57,600
Net sales	$5,000,000	$3,200,000
Cost of goods sold	3,400,000	2,080,000
Gross profit	$1,600,000	$1,120,000
Selling expenses	$ 650,000	$ 464,000
Administrative expenses	325,000	224,000
Total operating expenses	$ 975,000	$ 688,000
Operating income	$ 625,000	$ 432,000
Other income	25,000	19,200
	$ 650,000	$ 451,200
Other expense (interest)	105,000	64,000
Income before income tax	$ 545,000	$ 387,200
Income tax	300,000	176,000
Net income	$ 245,000	$ 211,200

Fleming Inc.
Comparative Retained Earnings Statement
For Years Ended December 31, 1994 and 1993

	1994	1993
Retained earnings, January 1	$ 723,000	$ 581,800
Add net income for year	245,000	211,200
Total	$ 968,000	$ 793,000
Deduct dividends:		
On preferred stock	$ 40,000	$ 40,000
On common stock	45,000	30,000
Total	$ 85,000	$ 70,000
Retained earnings, December 31	$ 883,000	$ 723,000

Fleming Inc.
Comparative Balance Sheet
December 31, 1994 and 1993

	1994	1993
Assets		
Current assets:		
Cash	$ 175,000	$ 125,000
Marketable securities	150,000	50,000
Accounts receivable (net)	425,000	325,000
Inventories	720,000	480,000
Prepaid expenses	30,000	20,000
Total current assets	$1,500,000	$1,000,000
Long-term investments	250,000	225,000
Plant assets	2,093,000	1,948,000
Total assets	$3,843,000	$3,173,000

	1994	1993

Liabilities

Current liabilities	$ 750,000	$ 650,000
Long-term liabilities:		
Mortgage note payable, 10%, due 2003	$ 410,000	—
Bonds payable, 8%, due 2006	800,000	$ 800,000
Total long-term liabilities	$1,210,000	$ 800,000
Total liabilities	$1,960,000	$1,450,000

Stockholders' Equity

Preferred 8% stock, $100 par	$ 500,000	$ 500,000
Common stock, $10 par	500,000	500,000
Retained earnings	883,000	723,000
Total stockholders' equity	$1,883,000	$1,723,000
Total liabilities and stockholders' equity	$3,843,000	$3,173,000

Instructions

Determine the following measures for 1994:

1. Working capital
2. Current ratio
3. Acid-test ratio
4. Accounts receivable turnover
5. Number of days' sales in receivables
6. Inventory turnover
7. Number of days' sales in inventory
8. Ratio of plant assets to long-term liabilities
9. Ratio of stockholders' equity to liabilities
10. Number of times interest charges earned
11. Number of times preferred dividends earned
12. Ratio of net sales to assets
13. Rate earned on total assets
14. Rate earned on stockholders' equity
15. Rate earned on common stockholders' equity
16. Earnings per share on common stock
17. Price-earnings ratio
18. Dividend yield

Solution

1. Working capital: $750,000
   $1,500,000 − $750,000
2. Current ratio: 2.0:1
   $1,500,000 ÷ $750,000
3. Acid-test ratio: 1.0:1
   $750,000 ÷ $750,000
4. Accounts receivable turnover: 13.3
   $$5,000,000 \div \frac{\$425,000 + \$325,000}{2}$$
5. Number of days' sales in receivables: 31 days
   $5,000,000 ÷ 365 = $13,699
   $425,000 ÷ $13,699
6. Inventory turnover: 5.7
   $$3,400,000 \div \frac{\$720,000 + \$480,000}{2}$$
7. Number of days' sales in inventory: 77.3 days
   $3,400,000 ÷ 365 = $9,315
   $720,000 ÷ $9,315
8. Ratio of plant assets to long-term liabilities: 1.7:1
   $2,093,000 ÷ $1,210,000
9. Ratio of stockholders' equity to liabilities: 1.0:1
   $1,883,000 ÷ $1,960,000
10. Number of times interest charges earned: 6.2
    ($545,000 + $105,000) ÷ $105,000

11. Number of times preferred dividends earned: 6.1
    $245,000 ÷ $40,000

12. Ratio of net sales to assets: 1.5:1

$$\$5,000,000 \div \frac{\$3,593,000 + \$2,948,000}{2}$$

13. Rate earned on total assets: 10.0%

$$(\$245,000 + \$105,000) \div \frac{\$3,843,000 + \$3,173,000}{2}$$

14. Rate earned on stockholders' equity: 13.6%

$$\$245,000 \div \frac{\$1,883,000 + \$1,723,000}{2}$$

15. Rate earned on common stockholders' equity: 15.7%

$$(\$245,000 - \$40,000) \div \frac{\$1,383,000 + \$1,223,000}{2}$$

16. Earnings per share on common stock: $4.10
    ($245,000 − $40,000) ÷ 50,000

17. Price-earnings ratio: 6.1
    $25 ÷ $4.10

18. Dividend yield: 3.6%

$$\frac{(\$45,000 \div 50,000 \text{ shares})}{\$25}$$

DISCUSSION QUESTIONS

1. What is the difference between horizontal and vertical analysis of financial statements?
2. Using the following data taken from a comparative balance sheet, illustrate (a) horizontal analysis and (b) vertical analysis.

	Current Year	Preceding Year
Accounts payable	$ 600,000	$ 500,000
Total current liabilities	1,250,000	1,000,000

3. What is the advantage of using comparative statements for financial analysis rather than statements for a single date or period?
4. The current year's amount of net income (after income tax) is 15% larger than that of the preceding year. Does this indicate an improved operating performance? Discuss.
5. What are common-size financial statements?
6. In the analysis of the financial status of an enterprise, what is meant by *solvency* and *profitability*?
7. a. Name the major ratios useful in assessing solvency and profitability.
   b. Why is it important not to rely on only one ratio or measure in assessing the solvency or profitability of an enterprise?
8. Identify the measure of current position analysis described by each of the following: (a) the excess of the current assets over current liabilities, (b) the ratio of current assets to current liabilities, (c) the ratio of quick assets to current liabilities.
9. Selected condensed data taken from the balance sheet of Farrow Company at December 31, the end of the current fiscal year, are as follows:

Cash, marketable securities, and receivables	$300,000
Other current assets	450,000
Total current assets	$750,000
Current liabilities	$250,000

At December 31, what are (a) the working capital, (b) the current ratio, and (c) the acid-test ratio?

10. For Lindsay Corporation, the working capital at the end of the current year is $50,000 greater than the working capital at the end of the preceding year, reported as follows. Does this mean that the current position has improved? Explain.

	Current Year	Preceding Year
Current assets:		
Cash, marketable securities, and receivables	$340,000	$300,000
Inventories	510,000	325,000
Total current assets	$850,000	$625,000
Current liabilities	425,000	250,000
Working capital	$425,000	$375,000

11. A company that grants terms of n/30 on all sales has a yearly accounts receivable turnover, based on monthly averages, of 6. Is this a satisfactory turnover? Discuss.

12. What does an increase in the number of days' sales in receivables ordinarily indicate about the credit and collection policy of the firm?

13. a. Why is it advantageous to have a high inventory turnover?
    b. Is it possible for the inventory turnover to be too high? Discuss.
    c. Is it possible to have a high inventory turnover and a high number of days' sales in inventory? Discuss.

14. What do the following data taken from a comparative balance sheet indicate about the company's ability to borrow additional funds on a long-term basis in the current year as compared to the preceding year?

	Current Year	Preceding Year
Plant assets (net)	$1,750,000	$1,700,000
Total long-term liabilities	700,000	850,000

15. What does an increase in the ratio of stockholders' equity to liabilities indicate about the margin of safety for a firm's creditors and the ability of the firm to withstand adverse business conditions?

16. In computing the ratio of net sales to assets, why are long-term investments excluded in determining the amount of the total assets?

17. In determining the number of times interest charges are earned, why are interest charges added to income before income tax?

18. In determining the rate earned on total assets, why is interest expense added to net income before dividing by total assets?

19. a. Why is the rate earned on stockholders' equity by a thriving enterprise ordinarily higher than the rate earned on total assets?
    b. Should the rate earned on common stockholders' equity normally be higher or lower than the rate earned on total stockholders' equity? Explain.

20. The net income (after income tax) of A. L. Gibson Inc. was $25 per common share in the latest year and $40 per common share for the preceding year. At the beginning of the latest year, the number of shares outstanding was doubled by a stock split. There were no other changes in the amount of stock outstanding. What were the earnings per share in the preceding year, adjusted for comparison with the latest year?

21. The price-earnings ratio for the common stock of Essian Company was 10 at December 31, the end of the current fiscal year. What does the ratio indicate about the selling price of the common stock in relation to current earnings?

22. Why would the dividend yield differ significantly from the rate earned on common stockholders' equity?

23. Favorable business conditions may bring about certain seemingly unfavorable ratios, and unfavorable business operations may result in apparently favorable ratios. For example, Sanchez Company increased its sales and net income substantially for the current year, yet the current ratio at the end of the year is lower than at the beginning of the year. Discuss some possible causes of the apparent weakening of the current position while sales and net income have increased substantially.

24. a. What are the major components of an annual report?
    b. Indicate the purpose of the Financial Highlights section and the President's Letter.

25. a. The typical independent auditors' report expressing an unqualified opinion consists of three paragraphs. What is reported in each paragraph?
    b. Under what condition does an auditor give a qualified opinion?

REAL WORLD FOCUS 26. The rate of return on total assets based upon The Home Depot, Inc.'s 1991 annual report is 12.6%. The rate of return on stockholders' equity for the same period is 18.5%. What is the explanation for the difference in the two rates?

REAL W●RLD FOCUS   27. Apple Computer, Inc., paid an annual cash dividend of $.48 per share on its common stock when the market price of the stock was $45⅜. What was (a) the dividend yield and (b) the price-earnings ratio if the annual earnings per share were $2.58?

ETHICS DISCUSSION CASE

Barbara Becker, president of Becker Equipment Co., prepared a draft of the *President's Letter* to be included with Becker Equipment Co.'s 1994 annual report. The letter mentions a 10% increase in sales and a recent expansion of plant facilities, but fails to mention the net loss of $175,000 for the year. You have been asked to review the letter for inclusion in the annual report.

SHARPEN YOUR ▶
COMMUNICATION SKILLS

How would you respond to the omission of the net loss of $175,000? Specifically, is such an action ethical?

EXERCISES

EXERCISE 20-1
VERTICAL ANALYSIS OF
INCOME STATEMENT
Objective 1

Revenue and expense data for N. L. Munoz Inc. are as follows:

	1994	1993
Sales	$900,000	$800,000
Cost of goods sold	540,000	472,000
Selling expenses	135,000	144,000
Administrative expenses	63,000	64,000
Income tax	54,000	40,000

a. Prepare an income statement in comparative form, stating each item for both 1994 and 1993 as a percent of sales.

SHARPEN YOUR ▶
COMMUNICATION SKILLS

b. Comment on the significant changes disclosed by the comparative income statement.

EXERCISE 20-2
VERTICAL ANALYSIS OF
INCOME STATEMENT
Objective 1

REAL W●RLD FOCUS

The following comparative income statement (in thousands of dollars) for the years ending December 31, 1991 and 1990, was adapted from the 1991 annual report of William Wrigley Jr. Company:

	1991	1990
Revenues	$1,159,763	$1,123,508
Costs and expenses:		
Cost of sales	$ 507,795	$ 508,957
Selling, distribution, and administrative expenses	442,575	425,175
Interest expense	1,379	1,117
Total costs and expenses	$ 951,749	$ 935,249
Earnings before income taxes	$ 208,014	$ 188,259
Income taxes	79,362	70,897
Net earnings	$ 128,652	$ 117,362

a. Prepare a comparative income statement for 1991 and 1990 in vertical form, stating each item as a percent of revenues.

SHARPEN YOUR ▶
COMMUNICATION SKILLS

b. Based upon the 1991 income statement, comment on the significant changes.

EXERCISE 20-3
HORIZONTAL ANALYSIS OF
BALANCE SHEET
Objective 1

Balance sheet data for Weaver Company on December 31, the end of the fiscal year, are as follows:

	1994	1993
Current assets	$356,000	$322,000
Plant assets	544,000	501,800
Intangible assets	50,000	56,200
Current liabilities	100,000	90,000
Long-term liabilities	250,000	275,000
Common stock	300,000	250,000
Retained earnings	300,000	265,000

SPREADSHEET
PROBLEM

Prepare a comparative balance sheet with horizontal analysis, indicating the increase (decrease) for 1994 when compared with 1993.

EXERCISE 20-4
CURRENT POSITION
ANALYSIS
Objective 3

SPREADSHEET
PROBLEM

The following data were abstracted from the balance sheet of Thompson Company:

	Current Year	Preceding Year
Cash	$ 89,500	$102,000
Marketable securities	50,000	50,000
Accounts and notes receivable (net)	190,500	198,000
Inventories	280,500	189,000
Prepaid expenses	19,500	11,000
Accounts and notes payable (short-term)	245,000	202,500
Accrued liabilities	55,000	47,500

a. Determine for each year (1) the working capital, (2) the current ratio, and (3) the acid-test ratio.

SHARPEN YOUR COMMUNICATION SKILLS ▶

b. What conclusions can be drawn from these data as to the company's ability to meet its currently maturing debts?

EXERCISE 20-5
ACCOUNTS RECEIVABLE
ANALYSIS
Objective 3

The following data are taken from the financial statements of West Company. Terms of all sales are 1/10, n/60.

	Current Year	Preceding Year
Accounts receivable, end of year	$ 676,100	$ 611,900
Monthly average accounts receivable (net)	627,000	550,100
Net sales on account	5,016,000	3,850,700

a. Determine for each year (1) the accounts receivable turnover and (2) the number of days' sales in receivables.

SHARPEN YOUR COMMUNICATION SKILLS ▶

b. What conclusions can be drawn from these data concerning the composition of the accounts receivable?

EXERCISE 20-6
INVENTORY ANALYSIS
Objective 3

The following data were abstracted from the income statement of Ryan Corporation:

	Current Year	Preceding Year
Sales	$4,425,000	$4,300,000
Beginning inventories	642,500	607,500
Purchases	2,675,000	2,785,000
Ending inventories	677,500	642,500

a. Determine for each year (1) the inventory turnover and (2) the number of days' sales in inventory.

SHARPEN YOUR COMMUNICATION SKILLS ▶

b. What conclusions can be drawn from these data concerning the composition of the inventories?

EXERCISE 20-7
SIX MEASURES OF
SOLVENCY OR
PROFITABILITY
Objectives 3, 4

The following data were taken from the financial statements of C. C. Wagner and Co. for the current fiscal year:

Plant assets (net)		$1,300,000
Liabilities:		
Current liabilities		$ 400,000
Mortgage note payable, 10%, issued 1986, due 1996		500,000
Total liabilities		$ 900,000
Stockholders' equity		
Preferred $4 stock, $50 par, cumulative, nonparticipating (no change during year)		$ 200,000
Common stock, $10 par (no change during year)		1,000,000
Retained earnings:		
Balance, beginning of year	$687,500	
Net income	193,500	$881,000
Preferred dividends	$ 16,000	
Common dividends	65,000	81,000
Balance, end of year		800,000
Total stockholders' equity		$2,000,000
Net sales		$4,240,000
Interest expense		50,000

SPREADSHEET PROBLEM

Assuming that long-term investments totaled $175,000 throughout the year and that total assets were $2,750,000 at the beginning of the year, determine the following: (a) ratio of plant assets to long-term liabilities, (b) ratio of stockholders' equity to liabilities, (c) ratio of net sales to assets, (d) rate earned on total assets, (e) rate earned on stockholders' equity, (f) rate earned on common stockholders' equity.

EXERCISE 20-8
FIVE MEASURES OF SOLVENCY OR PROFITABILITY
Objectives 3, 4

The balance sheet for Vincent Corporation at the end of the current fiscal year indicated the following:

Bonds payable, 10% (issued in 1980, due in 2000)	$2,400,000
Preferred $8 stock, $100 par	1,000,000
Common stock, $25 par	5,000,000

Income before income tax was $720,000, and income taxes were $320,000 for the current year. Cash dividends paid on common stock during the current year totaled $250,000. The common stock was selling for $16 per share at the end of the year. Determine each of the following: (a) number of times bond interest charges were earned, (b) number of times preferred dividends were earned, (c) earnings per share on common stock, (d) price-earnings ratio, and (e) dividend yield.

EXERCISE 20-9
EARNINGS PER SHARE
Objective 4

The net income reported on the income statement of T. L. Sweeney Co. was $2,800,000. There were 250,000 shares of $20 par common stock and 100,000 shares of $8 cumulative preferred stock outstanding throughout the current year. The income statement included two extraordinary items: a $750,000 gain from condemnation of land and a $250,000 loss arising from flood damage, both after applicable income tax. Determine the per share figures for common stock for (a) income before extraordinary items and (b) net income.

WhAT'S WRONG WITH THi2?

The bond indenture for the 10-year, 7½% debenture bonds dated January 2, 1994, required working capital of $300,000, a current ratio of 1.5:1, and an acid-test ratio of 1:1 at the end of each calendar year until the bonds mature. At December 31, 1994, the three measures were computed as follows:

a. Current assets:

Cash	$205,000	
Marketable securities	125,000	
Accounts and notes receivable (net)	185,000	
Inventories	350,000	
Prepaid expenses	35,000	
Goodwill	90,000	
Total current assets		$990,000
Current liabilities:		
Accounts and notes payable	$500,000	
Accrued liabilities	160,000	
Total current liabilities		660,000
Working capital		$330,000

b. Current ratio = 1.5:1 ($990,000 ÷ $660,000)
c. Acid-test ratio = 1.03:1 ($515,000 ÷ $500,000)

Can you find any errors in the determination of the three measures of current position analysis?

PROBLEMS

Series A

PROBLEM 20-1A
HORIZONTAL ANALYSIS FOR INCOME STATEMENT
Objective 1

For 1994, Getz Company reported its most significant increase in net income in years. At the end of the year, Jane Getz, the president, is presented with the following condensed comparative income statement:

Getz Company
Comparative Income Statement
For Years Ended December 31, 1994 and 1993

	1994	1993
Sales	$907,200	$803,200
Sales returns and allowances	7,200	3,200
Net sales	$900,000	$800,000
Cost of goods sold	557,000	488,000
Gross profit	$343,000	$312,000
Selling expenses	$108,000	$136,000
Administrative expenses	81,000	65,000
Total operating expenses	$189,000	$201,000
Operating income	$154,000	$111,000
Other income	2,000	1,000
Income before income tax	$156,000	$112,000
Income tax	48,000	32,000
Net income	$108,000	$ 80,000

Instructions

1. Prepare a comparative income statement with horizontal analysis for the two-year period, using 1993 as the base year.
2. To the extent the data permit, comment on the significant relationships revealed by the horizontal analysis prepared in (1).

SHARPEN YOUR ►
COMMUNICATION SKILLS

PROBLEM 20-2A
VERTICAL ANALYSIS FOR
INCOME STATEMENT
Objective 1

For 1994, Hartley Company initiated an extensive sales promotion campaign that included the expenditure of an additional $50,000 for advertising. At the end of the year, Ann Hartley, the president, is presented with the following condensed comparative income statement:

Hartley Company
Comparative Income Statement
For Years Ended December 31, 1994 and 1993

	1994	1993
Sales	$612,000	$363,600
Sales returns and allowances	12,000	3,600
Net sales	$600,000	$360,000
Cost of goods sold	372,000	216,000
Gross profit	$228,000	$144,000
Selling expenses	$108,000	$ 57,600
Administrative expenses	24,000	16,200
Total operating expenses	$132,000	$ 73,800
Operating income	$ 96,000	$ 70,200
Other income	1,800	1,440
Income before income tax	$ 97,800	$ 71,640
Income tax	22,800	16,200
Net income	$ 75,000	$ 55,440

SPREADSHEET
PROBLEM

Instructions

1. Prepare a comparative income statement for the two-year period, presenting an analysis of each item in relationship to net sales for each of the years.
2. To the extent the data permit, comment on the significant relationships revealed by the vertical analysis prepared in (1).

SHARPEN YOUR ►
COMMUNICATION SKILLS

PROBLEM 20-3A
COMMON-SIZE INCOME
STATEMENT
Objective 1

Revenue and expense data for the current calendar year for Harpo Publishing Company and for the publishing industry are as follows. The Harpo Publishing Company data are expressed in dollars; the publishing industry averages are expressed in percentages.

	Harpo Publishing Company	Publishing Industry Average
Sales	$8,072,000	100.5%
Sales returns and allowances	72,000	.5
Cost of goods sold	5,760,000	69.0
Selling expenses	656,000	9.0
Administrative expenses	496,000	8.2
Other income	48,000	.6
Other expense	104,000	1.4
Income tax	384,000	5.0

Instructions

1. Prepare a common-size income statement comparing the results of operations for Harpo Publishing Company with the industry average.

SHARPEN YOUR COMMUNICATION SKILLS

2. As far as the data permit, comment on significant relationships revealed by the comparisons.

PROBLEM 20-4A
EFFECT OF TRANSACTIONS ON CURRENT POSITION ANALYSIS
Objective 3

Data pertaining to the current position of Osborn Inc. are as follows:

Cash	$137,000
Marketable securities	40,000
Accounts and notes receivable (net)	303,000
Inventories	490,500
Prepaid expenses	29,500
Accounts payable	297,500
Notes payable (short-term)	75,000
Accrued expenses	27,500

Instructions

1. Compute (a) the working capital, (b) the current ratio, and (c) the acid-test ratio.
2. List the following captions on a sheet of paper:

Transaction	Working Capital	Current Ratio	Acid-Test Ratio

Compute the working capital, the current ratio, and the acid-test ratio after each of the following transactions, and record the results in the appropriate columns. Consider each transaction separately and assume that only that transaction affects the data given above.
a. Sold marketable securities, $40,000.
b. Paid accounts payable, $100,000.
c. Purchased goods on account, $80,000.
d. Paid notes payable, $75,000.
e. Declared a cash dividend, $50,000.
f. Declared a common stock dividend on common stock, $72,500.
g. Borrowed cash from bank on a long-term note, $200,000.
h. Received cash on account, $150,000.
i. Issued additional shares of stock for cash, $150,000.
j. Paid cash for prepaid expenses, $40,000.

PROBLEM 20-5A
EFFECT OF ERRORS ON CURRENT POSITION ANALYSIS
Objective 3

Prior to approving an application for a short-term loan, Citizens National Bank required that Fite Company provide evidence of working capital of at least $300,000, a current ratio of at least 1.5 : 1, and an acid-test ratio of at least 1.0 : 1. The chief accountant of Fite Company compiled the following data pertaining to the current position:

Fite Company
Schedule of Current Assets and Current Liabilities
December 31, 1994

Current assets:		Current liabilities:	
Cash	$115,250	Accounts payable	$325,000
Marketable securities	101,250	Notes payable	75,000
Accounts receivable	330,500	Total current liabilities	$400,000
Notes receivable	50,000		
Interest receivable	3,000		
Inventories	179,250		
Supplies	20,750		
Total current assets	$800,000		

Instructions

1. Compute (a) the working capital, (b) the current ratio, and (c) the acid-test ratio.
2. At the request of the bank, a firm of independent auditors was retained to examine data submitted with the loan application. This examination disclosed several errors. Prepare correcting entries for each of the following errors:
   a. A canceled check indicates that a bill for $25,000 for repairs on factory equipment had not been recorded in the accounts.
   b. Accounts receivable of $30,500 are uncollectible and should be immediately written off. In addition, it was estimated that of the remaining receivables, 5% would eventually become uncollectible. An allowance should be made for these future uncollectible accounts.
   c. Six months' interest had been accrued on the $50,000, 12%, six-month note receivable dated October 1, 1994.
   d. Supplies on hand at December 31, 1994, total $9,750.
   e. The marketable securities portfolio includes $50,000 of Porter Company stock that is held as a long-term investment.
   f. The notes payable account consists of a 12%, 90-day note dated November 1, 1994. No interest had been accrued on the note.
   g. Accrued wages as of December 31, 1994, totaled $30,000.
   h. Rental Income had been credited upon receipt of $72,000, which was the full amount of a year's rent for warehouse space leased to C. Pena and Son, effective July 1, 1994.
3. Giving effect to each of the preceding errors separately and assuming that only that error affects the current position of Fite Company, compute (a) the working capital, (b) the current ratio, and (c) the acid-test ratio. Use the following column headings for recording your answers:

   Error   *Working Capital*   *Current Ratio*   *Acid-Test Ratio*

4. Prepare a revised schedule of working capital as of December 31, 1994, and recompute the current ratio and the acid-test ratio, giving effect to the corrections of all of the preceding errors.

SHARPEN YOUR COMMUNICATION SKILLS ▶ 5. Discuss the action you would recommend that the bank take regarding the pending loan application.

PROBLEM 20-6A
EIGHTEEN MEASURES OF SOLVENCY AND PROFITABILITY
Objectives 3, 4

The comparative financial statements of C. C. Shelton and Co. are as follows. The market price of C. C. Shelton and Co. common stock was $30.25 on December 31, 1993, and $27 on December 31, 1994.

C. C. Shelton and Co.
Comparative Income Statement
For Years Ended December 31, 1994 and 1993

	1994	1993
Sales (all on account)	$7,779,200	$6,528,000
Sales returns and allowances	299,200	128,000
Net sales	$7,480,000	$6,400,000
Cost of goods sold	4,874,800	3,840,000
Gross profit	$2,605,200	$2,560,000
Selling expenses	$1,205,200	$ 985,600
Administrative expenses	540,000	526,400
Total operating expenses	$1,745,200	$1,512,000
Operating income	$ 860,000	$1,048,000
Other income	140,000	112,000
	$1,000,000	$1,160,000
Other expense (interest)	200,000	180,000
Income before income tax	$ 800,000	$ 980,000
Income tax	320,000	400,000
Net income	$ 480,000	$ 580,000

C. C. Shelton and Co.
Comparative Retained Earnings Statement
For Years Ended December 31, 1994 and 1993

	1994	1993
Retained earnings, January 1	$2,416,000	$1,936,000
Add net income for year	480,000	580,000
Total	$2,896,000	$2,516,000
Deduct dividends:		
On preferred stock	$ 30,000	$ 30,000
On common stock	50,000	70,000
Total	$ 80,000	$ 100,000
Retained earnings, December 31	$2,816,000	$2,416,000

C. C. Shelton and Co.
Comparative Balance Sheet
December 31, 1994 and 1993

	1994	1993
Assets		
Current assets:		
Cash	$ 105,000	$ 95,000
Marketable securities	225,000	175,000
Accounts receivable (net)	440,000	400,000
Inventories	769,600	674,800
Prepaid expenses	70,400	35,200
Total current assets	$1,610,000	$1,380,000
Long-term investments	300,000	250,000
Plant assets	4,506,000	4,086,000
Total assets	$6,416,000	$5,716,000
Liabilities		
Current liabilities	$ 700,000	$ 600,000
Long-term liabilities:		
Mortgage note payable, 10%, due 2001	$ 200,000	—
Bonds payable, 15%, due 2009	1,200,000	$1,200,000
Total long-term liabilities	$1,400,000	$1,200,000
Total liabilities	$2,100,000	$1,800,000
Stockholders' Equity		
Preferred $6 stock, $100 par	$ 500,000	$ 500,000
Common stock, $10 par	1,000,000	1,000,000
Retained earnings	2,816,000	2,416,000
Total stockholders' equity	$4,316,000	$3,916,000
Total liabilities and stockholders' equity	$6,416,000	$5,716,000

SPREADSHEET PROBLEM

Instructions

Determine the following measures for 1994:

1. Working capital.
2. Current ratio.
3. Acid-test ratio.
4. Accounts receivable turnover.
5. Number of days' sales in receivables.
6. Inventory turnover.
7. Number of days' sales in inventory.
8. Ratio of plant assets to long-term liabilities.
9. Ratio of stockholders' equity to liabilities.
10. Number of times interest charges earned.
11. Number of times preferred dividends earned.
12. Ratio of net sales to assets.

13. Rate earned on total assets.
14. Rate earned on stockholders' equity.
15. Rate earned on common stockholders' equity.
16. Earnings per share on common stock.
17. Price-earnings ratio.
18. Dividend yield.

PROBLEM 20-7A
REPORT ON DETAILED
FINANCIAL ANALYSIS
Objectives 3, 4, 5

Ann Raines is considering making a substantial investment in C. C. Shelton and Co. The company's comparative financial statements for 1994 and 1993 are given in Problem 20-6A. To assist in the evaluation of the company, Raines secured the following additional data taken from the balance sheet at December 31, 1992:

Accounts receivable (net)	$ 350,000
Inventories	654,800
Long-term investments	250,000
Total assets	5,284,000
Total stockholders' equity (preferred and common stock outstanding same as in 1993)	3,684,000

SHARPEN YOUR COMMUNICATION SKILLS

Instructions

Prepare a report for Raines, based on an analysis of the financial data presented. In preparing your report, include all ratios and other data that will be useful in arriving at a decision regarding the investment. (Note: If you are using the Solutions Software, you may want to complete the instructions below before you prepare this report.)

SOLUTIONS SOFTWARE

Instructions for Solving Problem 20-7A Using Solutions Software

1. Load opening balances.
2. Save the opening balances file to your drive and directory.
3. Set the run date to December 31, 1994, and enter your name.
4. Display a horizontal analysis of the income statement.
5. Display a vertical analysis of the income statement.
6. Display a horizontal analysis of the balance sheet.
7. Display a vertical analysis of the balance sheet.
8. Save your data file to disk.
9. End the session.

Series B

PROBLEM 20-1B
HORIZONTAL ANALYSIS
FOR INCOME STATEMENT
Objective 1

For 1995, Meyer Company reported its most significant increase in net income in years. At the end of the year, John Meyer, the president, is presented with the following condensed comparative income statement:

Meyer Company
Comparative Income Statement
For Years Ended December 31, 1995 and 1994

	1995	1994
Sales	$906,000	$804,000
Sales returns and allowances	6,000	4,000
Net sales	$900,000	$800,000
Cost of goods sold	548,000	480,000
Gross profit	$352,000	$320,000
Selling expenses	$117,000	$144,000
Administrative expenses	81,000	65,000
Total operating expenses	$198,000	$209,000
Operating income	$154,000	$111,000
Other income	900	1,000
Income before income tax	$154,900	$112,000
Income tax	57,900	42,000
Net income	$ 97,000	$ 70,000

Instructions

1. Prepare a comparative income statement with horizontal analysis for the two-year period, using 1994 as the base year.

■ SHARPEN YOUR ▶

COMMUNICATION SKILLS

2. To the extent the data permit, comment on the significant relationships revealed by the horizontal analysis prepared in (1).

PROBLEM 20-2B
VERTICAL ANALYSIS FOR
INCOME STATEMENT
Objective 1

For 1995, Dunlap Company initiated an extensive sales promotion campaign that included the expenditure of an additional $75,000 for advertising. At the end of the year, Jane Dunlap, the president, is presented with the following condensed comparative income statement:

Dunlap Company
Comparative Income Statement
For Years Ended December 31, 1995 and 1994

	1995	1994
Sales	$833,250	$683,400
Sales returns and allowances	8,250	3,400
Net sales	$825,000	$680,000
Cost of goods sold	519,750	435,200
Gross profit	$305,250	$244,800
Selling expenses	$198,000	$102,000
Administrative expenses	36,300	40,800
Total operating expenses	$234,300	$142,800
Operating income	$ 70,950	$102,000
Other income	2,475	2,720
Income before income tax	$ 68,475	$ 99,280
Income tax	14,475	19,280
Net income	$ 54,000	$ 80,000

SPREADSHEET
PROBLEM

Instructions

1. Prepare a comparative income statement for the two-year period, presenting an analysis of each item in relationship to net sales for each of the years.

■ SHARPEN YOUR ▶

COMMUNICATION SKILLS

2. To the extent the data permit, comment on the significant relationships revealed by the vertical analysis prepared in (1).

PROBLEM 20-3B
COMMON-SIZE INCOME
STATEMENT
Objective 1

Revenue and expense data for the current calendar year for Sands Publishing Company and for the publishing industry are as follows. The Sands Publishing Company data are expressed in dollars; the publishing industry averages are expressed in percentages.

	Sands Publishing Company	Publishing Industry Average
Sales	$9,595,000	100.6%
Sales returns and allowances	95,000	.6
Cost of goods sold	6,840,000	69.0
Selling expenses	779,000	9.0
Administrative expenses	589,000	8.2
Other income	47,500	.6
Other expense	114,000	1.4
Income tax	551,000	6.0

Instructions

1. Prepare a common-size income statement comparing the results of operations for Sands Publishing Company with the industry average.

■ SHARPEN YOUR ▶

COMMUNICATION SKILLS

2. As far as the data permit, comment on significant relationships revealed by the comparisons.

PROBLEM 20-4B
EFFECT OF TRANSACTIONS
ON CURRENT POSITION
ANALYSIS
Objective 3

Data pertaining to the current position of Jefferson Inc. are as follows:

Cash	$ 75,000
Marketable securities	50,000
Accounts and notes receivable (net)	125,000
Inventories	225,000
Prepaid expenses	25,000
Accounts payable	150,000
Notes payable (short-term)	75,000
Accrued expenses	25,000

Instructions

1. Compute (a) the working capital, (b) the current ratio, and (c) the acid-test ratio.
2. List the following captions on a sheet of paper:

Transaction	Working Capital	Current Ratio	Acid-Test Ratio

Compute the working capital, the current ratio, and the acid-test ratio after each of the following transactions, and record the results in the appropriate columns. Consider each transaction separately and assume that only that transaction affects the data given above.

a. Declared a cash dividend, $50,000.
b. Issued additional shares of stock for cash, $100,000.
c. Paid accounts payable, $60,000.
d. Purchased goods on account, $50,000.
e. Borrowed cash from bank on a long-term note, $50,000.
f. Paid cash for prepaid expenses, $20,000.
g. Paid notes payable, $75,000.
h. Received cash on account, $75,000.
i. Declared a stock dividend on common stock, $100,000.
j. Sold marketable securities, $50,000.

PROBLEM 20-5B
EFFECT OF ERRORS ON
CURRENT POSITION
ANALYSIS
Objective 3

Prior to approving an application for a short-term loan, Palmer National Bank required that Kinney Company provide evidence of working capital of at least $300,000, a current ratio of at least 1.5 : 1, and an acid-test ratio of at least 1.0 : 1. The chief accountant of Kinney Company compiled the following data pertaining to the current position:

Kinney Company
Schedule of Current Assets and Current Liabilities
December 31, 1994

Current assets:	
Cash	$ 60,750
Marketable securities	81,750
Accounts receivable	351,250
Notes receivable	100,000
Interest receivable	6,250
Inventories	188,250
Supplies	11,750
Total current assets	$800,000
Current liabilities:	
Accounts payable	$300,000
Notes payable	100,000
Total current liabilities	$400,000

Instructions

1. Compute (a) the working capital, (b) the current ratio, and (c) the acid-test ratio.
2. At the request of the bank, a firm of independent auditors was retained to examine data submitted with the loan application. This examination disclosed several errors. Prepare correcting entries for each of the following errors:
   a. A canceled check indicates that $27,500 of computers purchased for cash had not been recorded in the accounts.
   b. Accounts receivable of $41,500 are uncollectible and should be immediately written off. In addition, it was estimated that of the remaining receivables, $15,000 would

eventually become uncollectible. An allowance should be made for these future uncollectible accounts.

c. Six months' interest had been accrued on the $125,000, 10%, six-month note receivable dated October 1, 1994.

d. Supplies on hand at December 31, 1994, total $4,750.

e. The marketable securities portfolio includes $50,000 of TC Inc. stock that is held as a long-term investment.

f. The notes payable account consists of a 12%, 90-day note dated November 1, 1994. No interest had been accrued on the note.

g. Accrued wages as of December 31, 1994, totaled $30,000.

h. Rental Income had been credited upon receipt of $72,000, which was the full amount of a year's rent for warehouse space leased effective July 1, 1994.

3. Giving effect to each of the preceding errors separately and assuming that only that error affects the current position of Kinney Company, compute (a) the working capital, (b) the current ratio, and (c) the acid-test ratio. Use the following column headings for recording your answers:

| Error | Working Capital | Current Ratio | Acid-Test Ratio |

4. Prepare a revised schedule of working capital as of December 31, 1994, and recompute the current ratio and the acid-test ratio, giving effect to the corrections of all of the preceding errors.

5. Discuss the action you would recommend that the bank take regarding the pending loan application.

SHARPEN YOUR COMMUNICATION SKILLS

PROBLEM 20-6B
EIGHTEEN MEASURES OF
SOLVENCY AND
PROFITABILITY
Objectives 3, 4

The comparative financial statements of Farrell Company are as follows. The market price of Farrell Company's common stock was $176 on December 31, 1994, and $153 on December 31, 1995.

Farrell Company
Comparative Income Statement
For Years Ended December 31, 1995 and 1994

	1995	1994
Sales (all on account)	$9,387,400	$8,016,000
Sales returns and allowances	37,400	16,000
Net sales	$9,350,000	$8,000,000
Cost of goods sold	5,890,500	4,800,000
Gross profit	$3,459,500	$3,200,000
Selling expenses	$1,589,500	$1,232,000
Administrative expenses	673,200	658,000
Total operating expenses	$2,262,700	$1,890,000
Operating income	$1,196,800	$1,310,000
Other income	149,600	136,000
	$1,346,400	$1,446,000
Other expense (interest)	240,000	210,000
Income before income tax	$1,106,400	$1,236,000
Income tax	506,400	596,000
Net income	$ 600,000	$ 640,000

Farrell Company
Comparative Retained Earnings Statement
For Years Ended December 31, 1995 and 1994

	1995	1994
Retained earnings, January 1	$2,770,000	$2,420,000
Add net income for year	600,000	640,000
Total	$3,370,000	$3,060,000
Deduct dividends:		
On preferred stock	$ 90,000	$ 90,000
On common stock	210,000	200,000
Total	$ 300,000	$ 290,000
Retained earnings, December 31	$3,070,000	$2,770,000

Farrell Company
Comparative Balance Sheet
December 31, 1995 and 1994

	1995	1994
Assets		
Current assets:		
Cash	$ 400,000	$ 370,000
Marketable securities	150,000	125,000
Accounts receivable (net)	550,000	495,000
Inventories	792,000	726,000
Prepaid expenses	88,000	44,000
Total current assets	$1,980,000	$1,760,000
Long-term investments	275,000	220,000
Plant assets	5,665,000	5,280,000
Total assets	$7,920,000	$7,260,000
Liabilities		
Current liabilities	$1,100,000	$ 990,000
Long-term liabilities:		
Mortgage note payable, 12%, due 1997	$ 250,000	—
Bonds payable, 14%, due 2014	1,500,000	$1,500,000
Total long-term liabilities	$1,750,000	$1,500,000
Total liabilities	$2,850,000	$2,490,000
Stockholders' Equity		
Preferred $9 stock, $100 par	$1,000,000	$1,000,000
Common stock, $20 par	1,000,000	1,000,000
Retained earnings	3,070,000	2,770,000
Total stockholders' equity	$5,070,000	$4,770,000
Total liabilities and stockholders' equity	$7,920,000	$7,260,000

SPREADSHEET PROBLEM

Instructions
Determine the following measures for 1995:

1. Working capital.
2. Current ratio.
3. Acid-test ratio.
4. Accounts receivable turnover.
5. Number of days' sales in receivables.
6. Inventory turnover.
7. Number of days' sales in inventory.
8. Ratio of plant assets to long-term liabilities.
9. Ratio of stockholders' equity to liabilities.
10. Number of times interest charges earned.
11. Number of times preferred dividends earned.
12. Ratio of net sales to assets.
13. Rate earned on total assets.
14. Rate earned on stockholders' equity.
15. Rate earned on common stockholders' equity.
16. Earnings per share on common stock.
17. Price-earnings ratio.
18. Dividend yield.

PROBLEM 20-7B
REPORT ON DETAILED FINANCIAL ANALYSIS
Objectives 3, 4, 5

Don Strait is considering making a substantial investment in Farrell Company. The company's comparative financial statements for 1995 and 1994 are given in Problem 20-6B. To assist in the evaluation of the company, Strait secured the following additional data taken from the balance sheet at December 31, 1993:

Accounts receivable (net)	$ 440,000
Inventories	674,000
Long-term investments	100,000
Total assets	6,700,000
Total stockholders' equity (preferred and common stock outstanding same as in 1994)	4,200,000

SHARPEN YOUR COMMUNICATION SKILLS ▶ **Instructions**

Prepare a report for Strait, based on an analysis of the financial data presented. In preparing your report, include all ratios and other data that will be useful in arriving at a decision regarding the investment. (Note: If you are using the Solutions Software, you may want to complete the instructions below before you prepare this report.)

SOLUTIONS SOFTWARE

Instructions for Solving Problem 20-7B Using Solutions Software

1. Load opening balances.
2. Save the opening balances file to your drive and directory.
3. Set the run date to December 31, 1995, and enter your name.
4. Display a horizontal analysis of the income statement.
5. Display a vertical analysis of the income statement.
6. Display a horizontal analysis of the balance sheet.
7. Display a vertical analysis of the balance sheet.
8. Save your data file to disk.
9. End the session.

MINI-CASE 20 DC INC. AND ST INC.

You and your sister are both presidents of companies in the same industry, DC Inc. and ST Inc., respectively. Both companies were originally operated as a single-family business. But shortly after your father's death in 1982, the business was divided into two companies. Your sister took over DC Inc., located in San Diego, while you took over ST Inc., located in San Francisco.

During a recent family reunion, your sister referred to the much larger rate of return to her stockholders than was the case in your company and suggested that you consider rearranging the method of financing your corporation. The difference is highlighted by the following chart, which compares the rates earned on the stockholders' equity and the assets of the two companies:

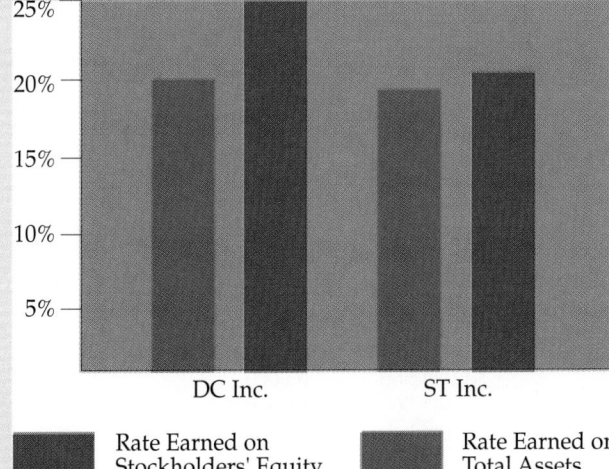

Rate Earned on Stockholders' Equity

Rate Earned on Total Assets

Since 1982, the growth in your sister's company has been financed largely through borrowing and yours largely through the issuance of additional common stock. Both companies have about the same volume of sales, gross profit, operating income, and total assets.

The income statements for the year ended December 31, 1995, and the balance sheets at December 31, 1995, for both companies are as follows:

Income Statements	DC Inc.	ST Inc.
Sales	$2,040,000	$1,965,000
Sales returns and allowances	40,000	35,000
Net sales	$2,000,000	$1,930,000
Cost of goods sold	1,350,000	1,279,000
Gross profit	$ 650,000	$ 651,000
Selling expenses	$ 235,000	$ 235,750
Administrative expenses	171,000	145,250
Total operating expenses	$ 406,000	$ 381,000
Operating income	$ 244,000	$ 270,000
Interest expense	30,000	10,500
Income before income tax	$ 214,000	$ 259,500
Income tax	86,000	103,500
Net income	$ 128,000	$ 156,000

Balance Sheets	DC Inc.	ST Inc.
Assets		
Current assets	$ 90,000	$ 75,000
Plant assets (net)	750,000	800,000
Intangible assets	10,000	25,000
Total assets	$ 850,000	$ 900,000
Liabilities		
Current liabilities	$ 35,000	$ 40,000
Long-term liabilities	300,000	100,000
Total liabilities	$ 335,000	$ 140,000
Stockholders' Equity		
Common stock, $10 par	$ 100,000	$ 400,000
Retained earnings	415,000	360,000
Total stockholders' equity	$ 515,000	$ 760,000
Total liabilities and stockholders' equity	$ 850,000	$ 900,000

In addition to the 1995 financial statements, the following data were taken from the balance sheet at December 31, 1994:

	DC Inc.	ST Inc.
Total assets	$800,000	$860,000
Total stockholders' equity	495,000	740,000

Instructions:

1. Determine for 1995 the following ratios and other measures for both companies.
   a. Ratio of plant assets to long-term liabilities.
   b. Ratio of stockholders' equity to liabilities.
   c. Ratio of net sales to assets.
   d. Rate earned on total assets.
   e. Rate earned on stockholders' equity.

2. a. ▌▊▶ For both DC Inc. and ST Inc., the rate earned on stockholders' equity is greater than the rate earned on total assets. Explain.
   b. ▌▊▶ Why is the rate of return on stockholders' equity for DC Inc. approximately 20% greater than for ST Inc.?
   c. ▌▊▶ Comment on your sister's suggestion for rearranging the financing of ST Inc.

COMPREHENSIVE PROBLEM 6

The comparative financial statements of Malone Company are as follows. The market price of Malone Company's common stock was $64 on December 31, 1993, and $82 on December 31, 1994.

Malone Company
Comparative Income Statement
For Years Ended December 31, 1994 and 1993

	1994	1993
Sales (all on account)	$6,860,000	$4,880,000
Sales returns and allowances	110,000	80,000
Net sales	$6,750,000	$4,800,000
Cost of goods sold	4,590,000	3,120,000
Gross profit	$2,160,000	$1,680,000
Selling expenses	$ 877,500	$ 741,000
Administrative expenses	438,750	336,000
Total operating expenses	$1,316,250	$1,077,000
Operating income	$ 843,750	$ 603,000
Other income	33,750	30,000
	$ 877,500	$ 633,000
Other expense (interest)	193,800	120,000
Income before income tax	$ 683,700	$ 513,000
Income tax	316,200	226,500
Net income	$ 367,500	$ 286,500

Malone Company
Comparative Retained Earnings Statement
For Years Ended December 31, 1994 and 1993

	1994	1993
Retained earnings, January 1	$1,084,500	$ 903,000
Add net income for year	367,500	286,500
Total	$1,452,000	$1,189,500
Deduct dividends:		
On preferred stock	$ 60,000	$ 60,000
On common stock	67,500	45,000
Total	$ 127,500	$ 105,000
Retained earnings, December 31	$1,324,500	$1,084,500

Malone Company
Comparative Balance Sheet
December 31, 1994 and 1993

	1994	1993
Assets		
Current assets:		
Cash	$ 337,500	$ 262,500
Trade receivable (net)	787,500	487,500
Inventories	1,080,000	720,000
Prepaid expenses	45,000	30,000
Total current assets	$2,250,000	$1,500,000
Long-term investments	375,000	337,500
Plant assets (net)	3,139,500	2,922,000
Total assets	$5,764,500	$4,759,500
Liabilities		
Current liabilities:		
Accounts payable	$1,000,000	$ 840,000
Accrued expenses	100,000	105,000
Income tax payable	25,000	30,000
Total current liabilities	$1,125,000	$ 975,000
Long-term liabilities:		
Note payable, 13%, due 2001	$ 400,000	—
Mortgage note payable, 12%, due 2002	215,000	—
Bonds payable, 10%, due 2000	1,200,000	$1,200,000
Total long-term liabilities	$1,815,000	$1,200,000
Total liabilities	$2,940,000	$2,175,000
Stockholders' Equity		
Preferred $8 stock, $100 par	$ 750,000	$ 750,000
Common stock, $25 par	750,000	750,000
Retained earnings	1,324,500	1,084,500
Total stockholders' equity	$2,824,500	$2,584,500
Total liabilities and stockholders' equity	$5,764,500	$4,759,500

Additional information extracted from the accounting records for 1994 revealed the following:
   a. Depreciation expense on plant assets, $182,500.
   b. Plant assets were acquired in exchange for a $400,000, 13%, note due 1999.
   c. Long-term investments were acquired for $37,500 cash.
   d. Mortgage note payable due 2000 was issued for cash, $215,000.
   e. Cash dividends paid, $127,500.

SPREADSHEET PROBLEM

Instructions

1. Prepare a statement of cash flows for the year ended December 31, 1994, using the indirect method of reporting cash flows from operating activities.
2. Prepare a statement of cash flows for the year ended December 31, 1994, using the direct method for reporting cash flows from operating activities. In using the direct method, cash received from other income should be reported at $33,750.
3. Determine the following measures for 1994:
   a. Working capital.
   b. Current ratio.
   c. Acid-test ratio.
   d. Accounts receivable turnover.
   e. Number of days' sales in receivables.
   f. Inventory turnover.

g. Number of days' sales in inventory.
h. Ratio of plant assets to long-term liabilities.
i. Ratio of stockholders' equity to liabilities.
j. Number of times interest charges earned.
k. Number of times preferred dividends earned.
l. Ratio of net sales to assets.
m. Rate earned on total assets.
n. Rate earned on stockholders' equity.
o. Rate earned on common stockholders' equity.
p. Earnings per share on common stock.
q. Price-earnings ratio.
r. Dividend yield

SOLUTIONS
SOFTWARE

Instructions for Solving Comprehensive Problem 6 Using Solutions Software

1. Load opening balances.
2. Save the opening balances file to your drive and directory.
3. Set the run date to December 31, 1994, and enter your name.
4. Display a statement of cash flows.
5. Display a horizontal analysis of the income statement.
6. Display a vertical analysis of the income statement.
7. Display a horizontal analysis of the balance sheet.
8. Display a vertical analysis of the balance sheet.
9. Save your data file to disk.
10. End the session.

ANSWERS TO SELF-EXAMINATION QUESTIONS

1. **A** Percentage analysis indicating the relationship of the component parts to the total in a financial statement, such as the relationship of current assets to total assets (20% to 100%) in the question, is called vertical analysis (answer A). Percentage analysis of increases and decreases in corresponding items in comparative financial statements is called horizontal analysis (answer B). An example of horizontal analysis would be the presentation of the amount of current assets in the preceding balance sheet, along with the amount of current assets at the end of the current year, with the increase or decrease in current assets between the periods expressed as a percentage. Differential analysis (answer C) and contribution margin analysis (answer D) are discussed in later managerial accounting chapters.

2. **D** Various solvency measures, categorized as current position analysis, indicate a firm's ability to meet currently maturing obligations. Each measure contributes in the analysis of a firm's current position and is most useful when viewed with other measures and when compared with similar measures for other periods and for other firms. Working capital (answer A) is the excess of current assets over current liabilities; the current ratio (answer B) is the ratio of current assets to current liabilities; and the

acid-test ratio (answer C) is the ratio of the sum of cash, receivables, and marketable securities to current liabilities.

3. **D** The ratio of current assets to current liabilities is usually called the current ratio (answer A). It is sometimes called the working capital ratio (answer B) or bankers' ratio (answer C).

4. **C** The ratio of the sum of cash, receivables, and marketable securities (sometimes called quick assets) to current liabilities is called the acid-test ratio (answer C) or quick ratio. The current ratio (answer A), working capital ratio (answer B), and bankers' ratio (answer D) are terms that describe the ratio of current assets to current liabilities.

5. **C** The number of days' sales in inventory (answer C), which is determined by dividing the inventories at the end of the year by the average daily cost of goods sold, expresses the relationship between the cost of goods sold and inventory. It indicates the efficiency in the management of inventory. The working capital ratio (answer A) indicates the ability of the enterprise to meet currently maturing obligations (debt). The acid-test ratio (answer B) indicates the "instant" debt-paying ability of the enterprise. The ratio of plant assets to long-term liabilities (answer D) indicates the margin of safety for long-term creditors.

Part 7

Managerial Accounting Principles and Systems

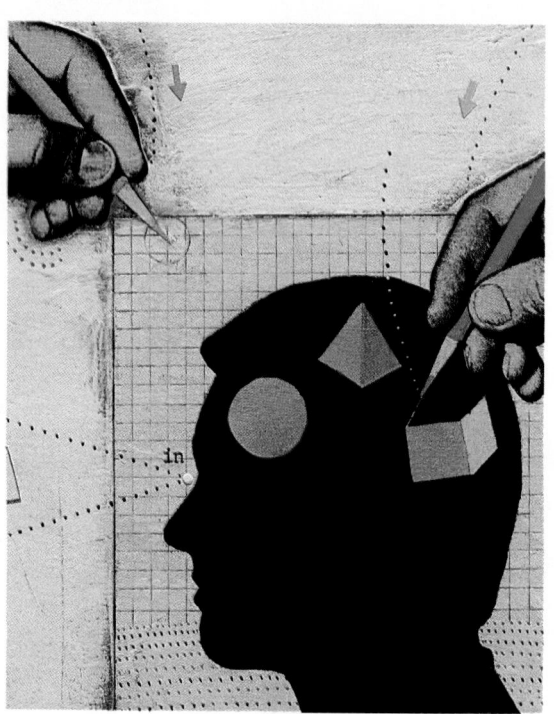

You and Accounting

How much will it cost you to attend college this term? How you answer this question depends upon why the information is needed. For example, you may need to know this cost in order to be reimbursed from a scholarship fund for all costs directly related to attending college. These costs would include books, tuition, room and board, and student fees. On the other hand, you may need to know these costs in order to determine whether you need to borrow money to finish the term. In this case, costs that have been paid by the scholarship fund are not relevant. Only costs that you will incur in finishing the term, such as travel to and from college, laundry, toiletries, etc., are important for your decision.

In gathering and reporting information for use by managers, accountants also recognize that different costs are important for different purposes. One primary focus of the discussion in this chapter is cost concepts used in managerial accounting. These concepts may also be useful to you in making day-to-day decisions.

Chapter 21
Managerial Accounting Concepts and Principles

LEARNING OBJECTIVES
After studying this chapter, you should be able to:

Objective 1
Compare and contrast managerial accounting and financial accounting.

Objective 2
Diagram the management process and describe each of the functions.

Objective 3
State and give examples of the role of managerial accounting in the management process.

Objective 4
List the characteristics of accounting reports prepared for use by management.

Objective 5
Define and give an example of the following cost concepts:

Direct costs and indirect costs
Differential costs
Sunk costs
Controllable costs and noncontrollable costs
Discretionary costs
Variable costs and fixed costs
Opportunity costs

Objective 6
Contrast merchandising and manufacturing operations, and define each of the following costs:

Direct materials
Direct labor
Factory overhead

Objective 7
Prepare financial statements for a manufacturing enterprise, including the statement of cost of goods manufactured.

Objective 8
Describe the major trends in manufacturing and service enterprises.

Accounting has been described as an information system that provides reports about the economic activities of an entity to various users. Such information aids users in making informed judgments and decisions. One important user of accounting information is management, who has the responsibility of directing the operations of an enterprise. The types of information needed and the use of this information by management in directing operations are the focus of the remainder of this text.

This chapter begins by describing managerial accounting, often called management accounting, and its relationship to financial accounting. The chapter then describes the management process and the role of managerial accounting in this process. The characteristics of managerial accounting reports and various accounting terms that often appear in such reports are also discussed. The chapter concludes with a discussion of the basic financial statements of a manufacturing enterprise and trends in manufacturing and service enterprises.

MANAGERIAL ACCOUNTING AND FINANCIAL ACCOUNTING

Although economic information can be classified in many ways, accountants often divide accounting information into two types: financial and managerial. A brief discussion of each of these is useful in understanding the nature of the information needed by management.

Financial accounting information is reported in statements that are prepared according to **generally accepted accounting principles (GAAP).** These statements report the results of past financial activities. They are prepared primarily for the use of persons who are "outside" or external to the enterprise. Examples of such users include shareholders, creditors, government agencies, and the general public. These statements are also useful to management in directing the operations of the enterprise. For example, in planning future operations, management often begins by evaluating the results of past activities as reported in the financial statements.

Managerial accounting information includes both historical and estimated data that management uses in conducting daily operations, planning future operations, and developing overall business strategies. For example, in controlling inflows and outflows of cash, management relies upon accounting to provide information. Such information includes the amount owed to each creditor, the amount owed by each customer, and the date each amount is due. The treasurer uses these data and other data in the management of cash. Production managers use managerial accounting information in making decisions to improve future operations.

The diagram in Exhibit 1 illustrates the relationship between managerial accounting and financial accounting. To the extent that management uses the financial statements in directing current operations and planning future operations, the two areas of accounting overlap. However, managerial accounting extends beyond financial accounting in providing additional information and reports for management's use. In providing this information, the accountant is not restricted by generally accepted accounting principles. Since these data are used only by management, the accountant can provide the data in any format that is useful to management. This principle of *usefulness* guides the preparation of management accounting reports.

Exhibit 1
Financial Accounting and
Managerial Accounting

THE MANAGEMENT PROCESS

The management process involves the following four basic functions:

1. Planning
2. Organizing and directing
3. Controlling
4. Decision making

Although decision making has the central role in the management process, all four functions interact. As shown in Exhibit 2, these functions drive an enterprise's operations.

Exhibit 2
Diagram of Management Process

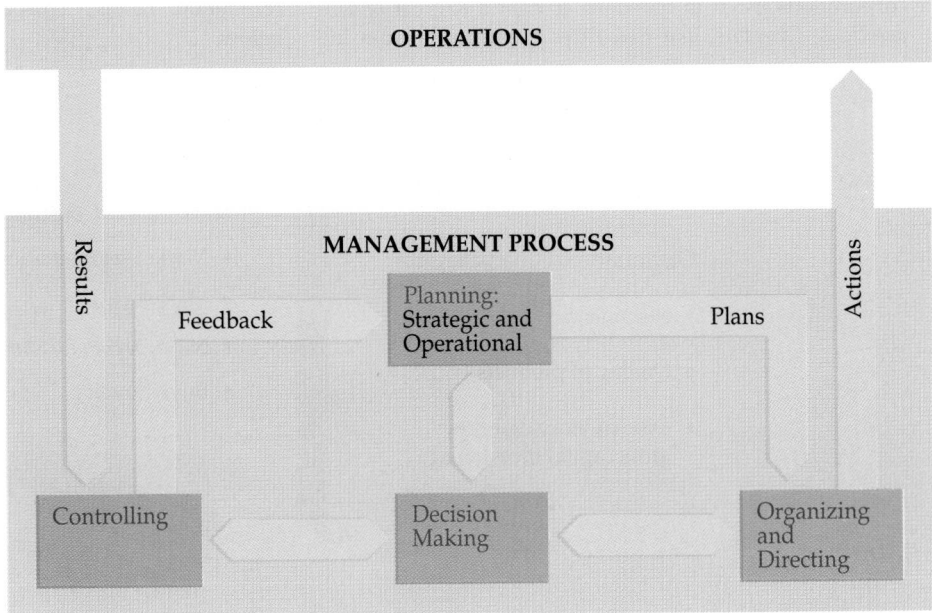

Planning

Planning is the process by which management develops a course of action to achieve enterprise goals. Planning involves such activities as setting selling prices, arranging financing for operations, and developing new products. Planning can be classified as either strategic planning or operational planning.

Strategic planning is the development of a long-range course of action to achieve goals. A strategic plan often involves periods ranging from five to ten years. Such a plan sets policy and priorities for activities such as research and development, marketing, financing, and plant expansion. A strategic plan serves as the basis for the commitment of enterprise resources.

A strategic plan is normally approved by the highest levels of management. It should integrate all aspects of the enterprise operations necessary to achieve long-range goals. Because of its long-range nature, a strategic plan may be significantly influenced by the changing environment within which the enterprise operates. Thus, strategic plans should be continually reviewed and revised. For example, rising stock prices might accelerate a decision to expand operations by issuing additional common stock. Likewise, falling interest rates might lead management to refinance existing debt by issuing new bonds.

Operational planning, sometimes called tactical planning, is the development of short-term plans to achieve goals identified in the strategic plan. Thus, operational plans complement the strategic plan. They are usually developed for time periods ranging from a week or a month to several years. An example of operational planning is the setting of the current month's production levels by a manufacturer. Operational planning for a merchandise enterprise might include the hiring of part-time employees for a holiday shopping period.

Effective communication among all levels of management within an enterprise is essential for effective strategic and operational planning. Only in this way can the necessary coordination be obtained to meet the operational and strategic plans. Accounting reports play an important part in this communication process.

Strategic Planning

A survey of 180 executives selected from manufacturing corporations listed in Standard & Poor's *Register of Corporations, Directors, and Executives* identified factors important for developing strategic plans. Some of the environmental factors considered important are shown below.

Environmental Factors To Include in Strategic Plans

Organizational Characteristics

- Market share
- Quality of products
- Discretionary cashflow/ gross capital investment

Marketing & Consumer Behavior

- Market segmentation
- Market size
- New market development
- Buyer loyalty

Supplier

- Major changes in availability of raw materials

Industry Structure

- Rate of technological change in products or processes
- Degree of product differentiation
- Industry price/cost structure
- Economies of scale

Social, Economic & Political

- GNP trend
- Interest rates
- Energy availability
- Government established & legally enforceable regulations

Source: James F. Brown, Jr., "How U.S. Firms Conduct Strategic Planning," *Management Accounting* (February 1986), pp. 38-44, 55.

Organizing and Directing

Organizing is the process by which management assigns responsibility to individuals for achieving enterprise goals. Each enterprise has its own unique organizational structure that management has established to implement strategic and operational plans. Some managers favor a highly centralized and autocratic organizational structure. Other managers favor decentralized structures with significant lower-management independence. No one organizational structure is best in all situations.

Directing is the process by which managers run day-to-day operations. A production supervisor's efforts at keeping the production line moving smoothly throughout a work shift is an example of directing.

Controlling

Controlling is the process by which managers attempt to achieve the goals identified in the strategic and operational plans. This process normally involves overseeing operations and comparing the expected results with actual results. This feedback allows management to isolate significant variations for further investigation and possible action. It may also lead to a revision of future plans. This philosophy of controlling is sometimes called **management by exception**. For example, if the actual materials costs to manufacture a product significantly exceed the expected costs, an investigation may determine the cause of the variation so that corrective action can be taken.

Decision Making

Decision making is the process by which managers select one course of action over another. Decision making is inherent in each of the three management functions described in the preceding paragraphs. For example, in developing a strategic plan, managers must decide between competing courses of action to achieve long-range goals and objectives. Likewise, in organizing and directing operations, managers must decide on an organizational structure and on specific actions to take in day-to-day operations. In controlling operations, managers must decide whether variances are worth investigating.

ROLE OF MANAGERIAL ACCOUNTING IN THE MANAGEMENT PROCESS

Objective 3
State and give examples of the role of managerial accounting in the management process.

For the management process to succeed, relevant information must be provided to managers on a timely basis. The role of managerial accounting in the management process is to provide this information. The following paragraphs describe how managerial accounting provides information for use by managers in planning, organizing and directing, controlling, and decision making.

Managerial accounting aids managers in **planning** by providing reports that estimate the effects of alternative actions on an enterprise's ability to achieve its goals. For example, an enterprise might establish a 25% market share as a long-term strategic goal. To achieve this goal, the enterprise might consider increasing its advertising and/or lowering its unit selling prices. Managerial accounting could report the estimated effects of the increased advertising, based on past experience, industry advertising statistics, market surveys, and other data. Likewise, managerial accounting could provide reports estimating effects of lowering the selling prices.

Managerial accounting aids managers in **organizing** and **directing** by providing reports that allow managers to adjust operations for changing conditions. For example, reports organized by product line may provide useful information on the effects of combining or eliminating product lines. Likewise, daily or weekly sales reports may be used by a retail store manager in deciding which items should be reordered.

Managerial accounting aids managers in **controlling** operations by providing reports of variances between expected and actual operating results. Such reports serve as a basis for taking necessary corrective actions to control operations. For example, a production supervisor might receive weekly or daily reports comparing actual materials costs with estimated costs. Significant variances could be isolated and corrective action taken. An excess of actual materials costs over estimated costs might be caused by high levels of scrap due to the use of poor quality materials. To correct this problem, a change in suppliers might be warranted. Another example would be a partner in a law firm receiving weekly reports on the amount of staff time spent on each case. An excessive amount of staff time spent on any particular case should be investigated.

Managerial accounting aids managers in **decision making** by providing the basic information used in selecting among alternative courses of action. For example, a report might indicate the contribution of an automotive service department to the profits of a retail store. This information could aid the store manager in deciding whether to discontinue the department.

Managerial accounting provides information to management to carry out all the basic functions of the management process. Without this information, it would be difficult for managers to be effective. To illustrate the types of decisions made on the basis of information provided by managerial accounting, the following excerpt is taken from the article "Huge GM Write-Off Positions Auto Maker to Show New Growth," which appeared in the December 1, 1990 *Wall Street Journal.*

"[Write-offs to cover plant closings are], a major element in GM's long-term strategic plan to improve the competitiveness and profitability of its North American operations," said Chairman Robert C. Stempel. "That means GM intends to run fewer factories faster and make more money . . . ."

". . . [GM intends to close] at least 7 of its 38 assembly plants in the U.S. and Canada and . . . related parts factories as well, affecting more than 20,000 workers. . . . By the time the shutdowns end, GM estimates, it will have cut roughly $1 billion from its yearly operating costs."

Organization of the Managerial Accounting Function

In most large business enterprises, departments or similar units are assigned responsibilities for specific functions or activities. This operating structure of an enterprise can be diagrammed in an organization chart. An organization chart for Baker Inc., a small manufacturing enterprise, is shown in Exhibit 3.

Exhibit 3
Organization Chart for Baker Inc.

The individual reporting units in an enterprise can be viewed as having either (1) line or (2) staff responsibilities. A **line** department or unit is directly involved in the basic objectives of the organization. For Baker Inc., the vice-president of production and the managers of the manufacturing plants occupy line positions. These are line positions because the managers are responsible for the manufacture of Baker's product. Likewise, the vice-president of sales occupies a line position because the vice-president of sales is responsible for generating revenues.

A **staff** department or unit provides services, assistance, and advice to other departments. A staff department has no direct authority over a line department. The organization chart for Baker Inc. indicates that two staff vice-president positions report to the chief executive officer. The vice-president of personnel occupies a staff position because the Personnel Department assists line managers and others in staffing their departments. Likewise, the vice-president of finance occupies a staff position, to which two other staff positions—the controller and the treasurer—report. In large organizations, staff positions may also exist for such functions as engineering, research and development, and marketing.

The chief accountant of a division or other segment of a business enterprise occupies a staff position and is often called a **controller**. Controllers provide advice and assistance to management but assume no direct responsibility for the operations of the business. However, in providing information for management's use, a controller must be thoroughly familiar with the operations of the business. Because of this critical role, controllers are often considered members of management.

The controller's staff often includes several accountants. Each accountant is responsible for a specialized accounting function. Examples of such functions include systems and procedures, general accounting, budgets and budget analyses, special reports and analyses, and cost accounting. The organization chart in Exhibit 4 is typical for an Accounting Department that reports to the controller.

Exhibit 4
Organization Chart—Controller's Department

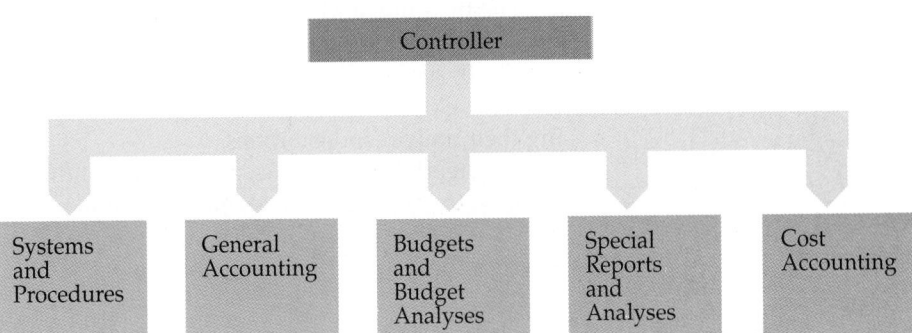

The Magic of 3M

3M was listed along with 61 other corporate high achievers in the best seller, *In Search of Excellence*, by Thomas J. Peters and Robert H. Waterman, Jr. In *A Passion for Excellence*, by Peters and Nancy Austin, 3M was again listed as a model for product innovation and entrepreneurship.

Some of the reasons for 3M's success, based on interviews with 3M executives, are as follows:

". . . [accounting] expertise, long recognized as one of 3M's greatest assets, is a major contributor to the corporation's success. 3M uses its [accounting] system to encourage . . . creativity . . ."

". . . we (controllers) get intimately involved with day-to-day activities . . . with forecasting and planning activities of business units. . . . Our controllers' view their roles as not to always challenge management, but as being a cooperative effort to develop a better business."

"3M's (division) controllers have been able to support 3M's strategic objectives while keeping management focused on [operations] . . . we do a fair, if not a good, job of balancing strategic and operational considerations."

"Our organization is not a negatively focused accounting organization. . . . We are supportive and positive in dealing with line management. We have tried to understand the business while doing our jobs."

"I (division controller) view the controller's function as [a] consultant . . . the person who brings to a division the financial information."

"I (vice president of finance) tell our people, 'Your job is to help the operating people achieve what they're trying to achieve.'. . . The first principle is working with the operating people."

Source: Kathy Williams, "The Magic of 3M: Management Accounting Excellence," *Management Accounting* (February 1986), pp. 20-27.

Managerial Accounting as a Profession

Managerial accounting is gaining recognition as a profession because of its unique nature and its importance to the effective management of business enterprises. Two important characteristics of this profession—certification and ethics—have received increasing emphasis in recent years.

The Institute of Certified Management Accountants offers the **Certificate in Management Accounting (CMA)** program. The primary purpose of the CMA program is to provide evidence of competence in managerial accounting through the awarding of the CMA certificate.

The requirements for the CMA designation include education, experience, and the passing of a 2-day examination. The examination reflects the interdisciplinary nature of managerial accounting and consists of the following four parts:

1. Economics, finance, and management
2. Financial accounting and reporting
3. Management reporting, analysis, and behavioral issues
4. Decision analysis and information systems

Certified Management Accountants are required to participate in a program of continuing professional education. In addition, they must adhere to a professional code of ethics.

The Institute of Management Accountants has developed the *Standards of Ethical Conduct for Management Accountants*. These *Standards*, which appear in Appendix B, serve as a guide to professional conduct. In addition, many companies have developed their own codes of conduct to guide their employees in performing their daily responsibilities.

Managerial accountants, as members of the management team, are in a unique position to influence management decision making. By providing relevant ethical considerations concerning alternative courses of action, management accountants can promote proper business behavior.

CHARACTERISTICS OF MANAGERIAL ACCOUNTING REPORTS

Objective 4
List the characteristics of accounting reports prepared for use by management.

Accounting reports provide essential information for management in planning, organizing and directing, controlling, and decision making. The principle of *usefulness to management* is the primary criterion for preparing managerial accounting reports. To be useful, these reports should possess the characteristics of (1) relevance, (2) timeliness, (3) accuracy, (4) clarity, and (5) conciseness. Each of these characteristics is described in the following paragraphs.

Relevance

Relevance requires that the economic information reported be applicable to the action being considered by management. In applying this concept, the accountant must be thoroughly familiar with the operations of the firm and the information needs of management. With this knowledge, the accountant selects the relevant information from the available data for reporting to management. To illustrate, assume that management is considering the replacement of fully depreciated equipment, which cost $100,000, with new equipment costing $150,000. It is the $150,000 that is relevant for an analysis of financing the replacement. The original cost, $100,000, is irrelevant for this decision.

In applying the concept of relevance, some accounting information may have little or no relevance for one use but may be relevant for another use. For example, in the previous illustration, the $100,000 was irrelevant for evaluating the financing of the replacement equipment. For tax purposes, however, the $100,000 (and its accumulated depreciation) may be relevant for determining the amount of the gain from sale if the old equipment can be sold.

In today's environment, large amounts of data can be processed and stored using computerized information systems. As a result, the process of selecting and reporting only relevant information from the large amount of data available is becoming more and more important.

Timeliness

Timeliness requires that accounting reports include up-to-date information. Reports received late or reports that include outdated information can lead to unwise decisions. For example, if outdated costs are relied upon in setting the selling price of a product, the selling price may not cover current costs and provide a profit.

In some cases, the timeliness concept requires the preparation of accounting reports on a regular schedule. For example, daily reports of cash receipts and payments are useful in managing the use of cash on a day-to-day basis. Weekly departmental expense reports may be adequate for administrative expenses.

In other cases, reports are prepared on an irregular basis or only as they are needed. For example, management of a retail enterprise may be evaluating the possibility of a Thanksgiving Day sales promotion. A report of estimated costs and sales would be needed in time for management to fully consider the proposal and make a decision.

Accuracy

Accuracy requires that accounting reports be correct within the constraints of the use of the report and the inherent inaccuracies in the measurement process. If the report is not accurate, management's decision may be unwise. For example, if an inaccurate report on a customer's past payment practices is presented to management, an unwise decision in granting credit may be made.

The concept of accuracy is applied within the constraints of management's use of the report. In some cases, accuracy may be sacrificed for less precise data that are more useful to management. For example, in planning production, estimates (forecasts) of future sales are normally more useful than only data from past sales.

Clarity

Clarity requires that accounting reports be clear and understandable in format and content. Such reports better enable management to focus on the important factors for planning and controlling operations. For example, for management's use in controlling costs of manufacturing a product, a report that compares actual costs with expected costs and clearly indicates the differences enables management to focus its attention on significant differences. Management can then take any necessary corrective actions.

Conciseness

Conciseness requires that accounting reports be brief and to the point. As indicated previously, an accounting report should include only relevant information. The inclusion of unnecessary information wastes management's time and makes it more difficult for management to focus on the important factors affecting a decision. The concept of conciseness also recognizes that information may be relevant for some levels of management and not for others. For example, reports prepared for the top level of management are usually broad in scope and present summaries of data rather than small details.

Costs vs. Benefits of Managerial Accounting Reports

The characteristics of managerial accounting reports provide general guidelines for preparing reports to meet management's needs. In applying these guidelines, the specific needs of each manager must be considered. In addition, the costs of preparing the report should also be considered. These costs should not exceed the value of the reports to management. No matter how much information a report may contain, the report should not be prepared if its expected cost exceeds its expected benefits. The relationship between the characteristics of accounting reports and the cost-benefit consideration is shown in Exhibit 5.

Exhibit 5
Managerial Accounting Reports

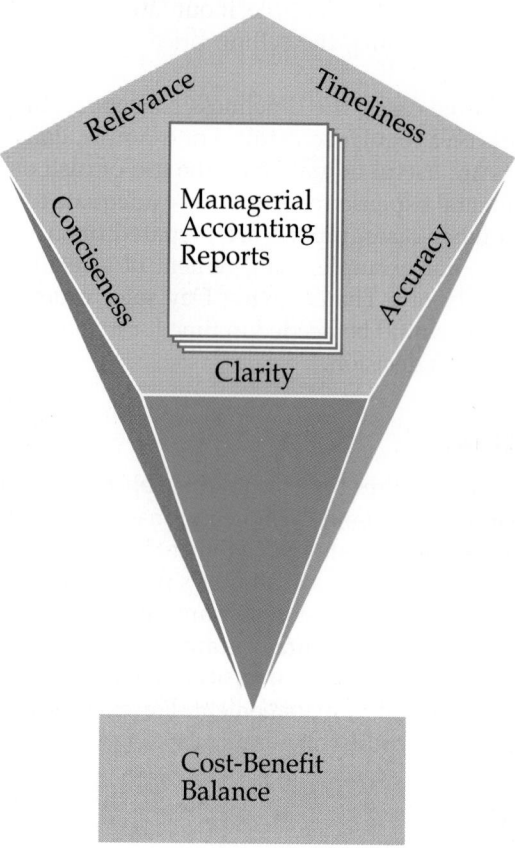

COST CONCEPTS AND TERMINOLOGY

Objective 5
Define and give an example of the following cost concepts:

Direct costs and indirect costs
Differential costs
Sunk costs
Controllable costs and
  noncontrollable costs
Discretionary costs
Variable costs and fixed costs
Opportunity costs

The information reported to management for use in decision making is often related to the costs of operations. A *cost* is a payment of cash or its equivalent or the commitment to pay cash in the future for the purpose of generating revenues. For example, cash (or credit) used to purchase equipment is the cost of the equipment. Likewise, if equipment is purchased by exchanging assets other than cash, the current market value of the assets is the cost of the equipment purchased. The following paragraphs describe and illustrate common cost concepts used in managerial accounting. Such an understanding provides a foundation for later discussions and illustrations of more complex, real-world decision-making situations.

Direct and Indirect Costs

For management's use in making decisions, costs are often classified in terms of how they relate to some object or segment of operations, often called a *cost object*. A cost object may be a product, a sales territory, a department, or some activity, such as research and development. Costs that can be traced directly to the cost object are called *direct costs*. Costs that cannot be traced accurately to a cost object are *indirect costs* for that cost object.

Cost objects are determined by management according to their decision-making needs. Classifying a cost as a direct or an indirect cost first requires that the cost object be identified by management. Next, whether the cost can be traced accurately to the cost object must be determined. For example, assume that the

management of Midway Taxi is evaluating the cost effectiveness of its various taxis. In this case, the cost object is each taxi. The cost of gasoline consumed and repair parts used in operating each taxi are direct costs. On the other hand, the salary of the Maintenance Shop supervisor whose department repairs and services the taxis is an indirect cost of each taxi. This is because the supervisor's salary normally cannot be traced to individual taxis. If the cost object was the Maintenance Shop, however, the salary of the Maintenance shop supervisor is a direct cost. Thus, a cost can be either direct or indirect, depending upon the cost object identified by management.

Differential Costs

Differential cost, sometimes called **incremental cost,** is the increase or decrease in cost that is expected from one course of action as compared to another course of action. For example, the management of a microcomputer manufacturer must decide whether to purchase carrying cases for its computers from an outside supplier or to produce the carrying cases itself. If the cost of purchasing the carrying cases is $20 per case and the cost of producing the carrying cases is $18 per case, the difference between the two alternatives ($2) is the differential cost per unit. To further illustrate, if a proposed increase in advertising costs from $100,000 to $150,000 is being considered, the differential cost of the proposal is $50,000.

Sunk Costs

Sunk costs are costs that have been incurred and that cannot be reversed by subsequent decisions. Sunk costs are irrelevant for future decision making and therefore are often excluded from managerial accounting reports. To illustrate, assume that a major airline is operating a fleet of Boeing 727 passenger jets, which originally cost $300 million and on which depreciation of $250 million has been taken. In considering whether to spend $500 million to upgrade its fleet of aircraft to newer, more fuel-efficient 767 passenger jets, the original $300 million cost is irrelevant. The $300 million has been spent, and regardless of whether the original decision was wise or unwise, this expenditure cannot be reversed. For this reason, the $300 million original cost of the 727 jets is a sunk cost. Likewise, the $50 million book value (the original cost less the accumulated depreciation) and the $250 million accumulated depreciation are irrelevant. The cost savings resulting from the use of the more fuel-efficient 767, when compared to the proposed expenditure of $500 million, are the relevant costs that should be considered by management in making the decision.

Controllable and Noncontrollable Costs

All costs are controllable by someone within a business enterprise, but not all costs are controllable at the same level of management. **Controllable costs** are therefore costs that can be influenced or controlled by a specific manager. For example, plant managers are usually responsible for the use of materials in their departments. Since the plant managers can significantly influence or control materials costs, these costs are controllable costs to the plant managers. On the other hand, advertising costs are **noncontrollable costs** to plant managers because they have no significant influence or control over these costs. Advertising costs are, however, controllable costs to the vice-president of sales. The classification of costs as controllable and noncontrollable is useful in fixing the responsibility for the incurrence of costs. It is also useful in investigating differences between actual and expected costs.

In some cases, time is important in classifying costs as controllable or noncontrollable. Some costs cannot be controlled in the short run but can be controlled in the long run. For example, a plant manager may not be able, in the short run, to control the wages of factory employees who have union contracts. In the long run, however, the wages become controllable as the union contracts expire and are subject to renegotiation.

Discretionary Costs

A **discretionary cost** is a cost that is not essential to short-term operations. Thus, discretionary costs can be reduced or eliminated in the short run without harming operations. For example, costs incurred in management training courses are often classified as discretionary costs. Other examples of discretionary costs include advertising expenses, management consulting fees, and charitable contributions.

Management normally reviews discretionary costs periodically to determine whether the costs should continue to be incurred. Discretionary costs are usually the first to be reduced or eliminated during periods of worsening economic conditions. This is because their reduction or elimination will result in an immediate increase in profit. Although discretionary costs do not have a significant effect on short-term operations, they can have a long-term impact on an enterprise. For example, research and development costs are often viewed as discretionary, but their elimination could be disastrous in the long run. This is especially true in high-tech industries, such as the computer industry. Likewise, the elimination of management training courses could harm the quality of managerial decision making in the long run.

Variable Costs and Fixed Costs

Costs are often classified by their behavior, that is, how they change with changes in some measure of business activity. As business activity increases or decreases, some costs change significantly, while other costs do not change. Knowledge of such cost behavior is useful for management in directing current operations and planning future operations.

VARIABLE COSTS. A **variable cost** varies proportionately in total dollar amount as the level of activity changes. The level of activity is normally expressed in terms of an **activity base** or **activity driver**. For example, materials cost is a variable cost for the number of units produced because the total materials cost varies proportionately with the number of units produced (the activity base). To illustrate, assume that Micro-Systems Inc. produces a standard microcomputer containing a 640K memory board. If each memory board costs $50, the total materials cost of the memory boards for the production of 1,000 computers is $50,000 ($50 × 1,000); for 2,000 computers, the total cost is $100,000. Thus, materials cost is a variable cost for the number of units (computers) produced.

FIXED COSTS. A **fixed cost** remains constant in total dollar amount as the level of activity changes. As with variable costs, the level of activity is normally expressed in terms of an activity base. Straight-line depreciation on factory equipment is a fixed cost for the number of units produced. This is because the total depreciation does not vary with the number of units produced (the activity base). For example, straight-line depreciation of $15,000 per year on Micro-Systems Inc.'s assembly and testing equipment would not vary with the number of computers produced. The total straight-line depreciation would be $15,000, regardless of whether 1,000, 2,000, or 6,000 microcomputers are produced.

MIXED COSTS. Some costs have both variable and fixed characteristics. These costs are often called **mixed costs** or **semivariable** or **semifixed costs**. These mixed costs can often be separated into variable and fixed components. For example, the rental charge for a copier might be $100 per month plus $.01 per copy. The

$100-per-month portion of the rental charge is a fixed cost, and the $.01-per-copy portion is a variable cost for the activity base of number of copies.

Opportunity Costs

An opportunity cost is unlike the cost concepts discussed in the preceding paragraphs because a cash payment or equivalent has not occurred. Instead, an **opportunity cost** is the amount of income that is forgone by selecting one alternative over another. To illustrate, assume that $100,000 is invested in a money market account yielding 5% interest. If U.S. Treasury Bills are yielding 6%, the opportunity cost of not investing in the Treasury Bills is $6,000 ($100,000 × 6%) per year. Thus, consideration might be given to changing investments to earn a higher rate of return.

Although opportunity costs differ from the other costs that have been discussed, they should be considered in all management decisions involving the commitment of resources. For example, assume that management is considering acquiring an international subsidiary in order to expand into European markets. In making this decision, management should consider the opportunity costs of forgoing competing investments, such as the expansion into other product lines or domestic markets.

Classification of Costs

Many of the costs described in the preceding paragraphs can be classified in more than one way, depending upon the decision-making needs of management. For example, in estimating the cost of products manufactured, materials costs would be classified as a variable cost for the number of units produced (the activity base). In determining responsibility for cost control, the materials costs would also be classified as a controllable cost of the production supervisor. This concept is often expressed as "different costs for different purposes."

MANUFACTURING OPERATIONS: COSTS AND TERMINOLOGY

The operations of business enterprises can be classified as service, merchandising, or manufacturing. A **service enterprise** renders services to its customers. A **merchandising enterprise** purchases goods in a form ready for sale and then retails the merchandise to consumers. A **manufacturing enterprise** converts materials into a finished product through the use of machinery and labor.

The cost concepts discussed in the preceding paragraphs are used in managerial accounting for all three types of business enterprises. In addition, most of the managerial accounting concepts described in the remaining chapters of this text are applicable to all three types of businesses. In the remainder of this chapter, cost concepts and terms that are unique to manufacturing enterprises are described and illustrated.

Objective 6
Contrast merchandising and manufacturing operations, and define each of the following costs:

Direct materials
Direct labor
Factory overhead

Manufacturing Costs

The cost of a manufactured product includes the cost of materials used in producing the product as well as the costs incurred in converting the materials into a finished product. The cost of a manufactured product normally consists of direct materials cost, direct labor cost, and factory overhead cost.

DIRECT MATERIALS COST. The cost of materials that are an integral part of the manufactured product is classified as **direct materials cost**. This cost is sometimes called **raw materials cost**. For example, the direct materials cost for Seawind Company, a manufacturer of fishing boats, would include fiberglass and paint. The *cost object*, in this case, is the product (a fishing boat).

As a practical matter, a direct materials cost must not only be an integral part of the finished product, but it must also be a significant portion of the total cost of the product. For Seawind Company, the costs of fiberglass and paint are a significant portion of the total cost of each boat. Other examples of direct materials costs are the cost of paper and ink for a printer, lumber for a furniture manufacturer, silicon wafers for a producer of microcomputer chips, and tires for an automobile manufacturer.

DIRECT LABOR COST. The cost of wages of employees who are directly involved in converting materials into the manufactured product is classified as **direct labor cost**. As with direct materials, the *cost object* for direct labor cost is the product. For example, the direct labor cost of Seawind Company includes the wages of the employees who paint the boat hulls. Other examples of direct labor costs are the wages of carpenters for a construction contractor, mechanics' wages in an automotive repair shop, machine operators' wages in a tool manufacturing plant, and assemblers' wages in a microcomputer assembly plant.

As a practical matter, a direct labor cost must not only be an integral part of the finished product, but it must also be a significant portion of the total cost of the product. For Seawind Company, the painters' wages are a significant portion of the total cost of each boat.

FACTORY OVERHEAD COST. Costs other than direct materials cost and direct labor cost incurred in the manufacturing process are classified as **factory overhead cost**. Factory overhead is sometimes called **manufacturing overhead** or **factory burden**. For example, factory overhead cost includes the cost of heating and lighting the factory, repair and maintenance of factory equipment, and property taxes, insurance, and depreciation on factory plant and equipment. Factory overhead cost also includes materials and labor costs that do not enter directly into the finished product. For example, the cost of oil used to lubricate machinery is a materials cost that does not enter directly into finished products. Other examples of such costs are the wages of janitorial, supervisory, and quality control personnel.

As a practical matter, if the costs of direct materials or direct labor are not a significant portion of the total product cost, these costs may be classified as factory overhead. In Seawind Company, for example, the cost of the metal tag identifying each boat's serial number enters directly into the manufacture of each boat. However, because its cost is insignificant, it is classified as factory overhead. For many industries, the increased use of automated machinery and robotics has decreased labor costs to a level where they are a small amount of the total product cost. In this situation, direct labor costs of manufactured products are often included as part of factory overhead cost.

PRIME COSTS AND CONVERSION COSTS. As discussed above, the total cost of a manufactured product normally consists of three elements: direct materials, direct labor, and factory overhead costs. These costs may be grouped together for analysis and reporting purposes. Two common groupings of manufacturing costs are prime costs and conversion costs.

Prime costs consist of direct materials and direct labor costs. **Conversion costs** consist of direct labor and factory overhead costs. Conversion costs represent the costs of converting the materials into a finished, manufactured product. Exhibit 6 summarizes the classification of manufacturing costs into prime costs and conversion costs.

Product Costs and Period Costs

For financial reporting purposes, costs are often classified as either product costs or period costs. **Product costs** consist of the three elements of manufacturing cost: direct materials, direct labor, and factory overhead. From the time product costs are incurred until the products are manufactured and sold, product costs are ac-

Exhibit 6
Prime Costs and Conversion Costs

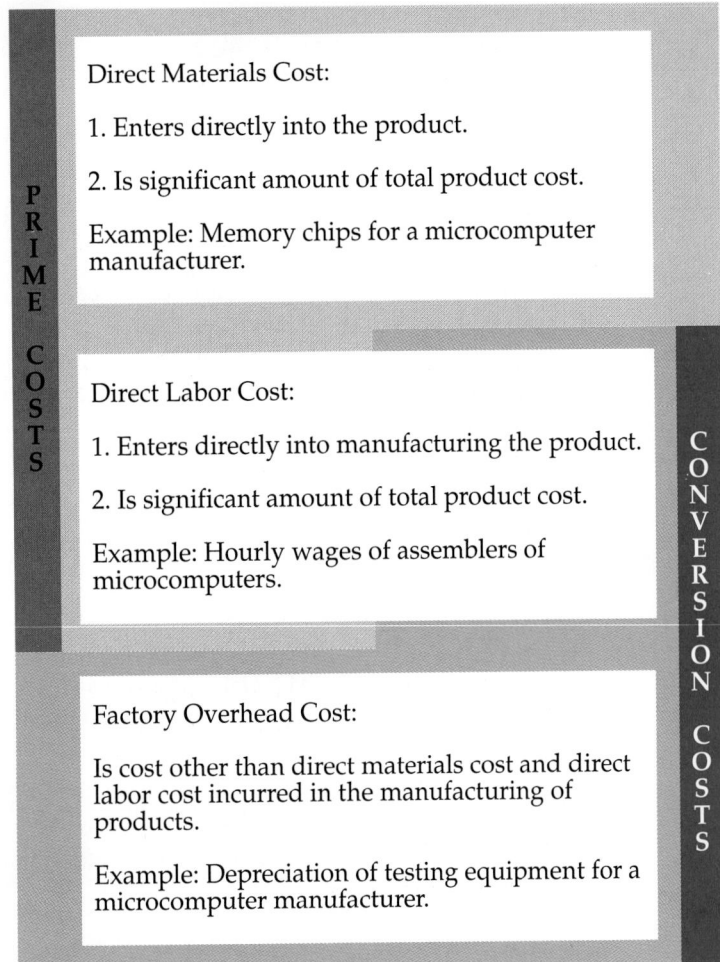

Direct Materials Cost:

1. Enters directly into the product.

2. Is significant amount of total product cost.

Example: Memory chips for a microcomputer manufacturer.

PRIME COSTS

Direct Labor Cost:

1. Enters directly into manufacturing the product.

2. Is significant amount of total product cost.

Example: Hourly wages of assemblers of microcomputers.

CONVERSION COSTS

Factory Overhead Cost:

Is cost other than direct materials cost and direct labor cost incurred in the manufacturing of products.

Example: Depreciation of testing equipment for a microcomputer manufacturer.

counted for as assets. As such, they are reported on the balance sheet as inventory and are sometimes called inventoriable costs. Thus, direct materials, direct labor, and factory overhead costs will not appear on the income statement as expenses until the products with which they are associated are sold. Financial statements for manufacturing enterprises are described and illustrated later in this chapter.

Period costs are recognized as expenses in the period in which they arise. Period costs are generally classified into two categories: selling and administrative. Selling expenses are incurred in marketing the product and delivering the sold product to customers. Examples of selling expenses are salaries of marketing personnel, advertising expenditures, sales commissions, salespersons' salaries, and depreciation of store equipment. Administrative expenses are incurred in the administration of the business and are not related to the manufacturing or selling functions. Examples of administrative expenses are office salaries, office supplies, and depreciation on office buildings and equipment.

The classification of costs between product costs and period costs is summarized in Exhibit 7.

Classifying period costs as selling or administrative assists management in controlling the costs of these two major functional activities. Different levels of responsibility for these activities may be shown in managerial reports. For example, selling expenses may be reported by product, salespersons, departments, divisions, or geographic territories. Likewise, administrative expenses may be reported by functional area, such as personnel, computer services, accounting, finance, or office support. The concepts and principles of planning and controlling manufacturing costs also apply to selling and administrative expenses.

Exhibit 7
Product Costs and Period Costs

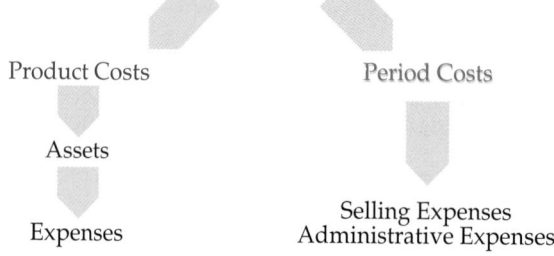

Examples of product costs and period costs for a furniture manufacturer are presented in Exhibit 8.

Exhibit 8
Examples of Product Costs and Period Costs—Furniture Manufacturer

Examples
(Furniture Manufacturer)

Product (Manufacturing) Costs	Direct Materials Costs	Lumber costs Paint costs Varnish costs
	Direct Labor Costs	Wages of saw operator Wages of sander Wages of painter
	Factory Overhead Costs	Utility costs of factory Depreciation of factory equipment Maintenance and repair costs
Period (Nonmanufacturing) Costs	Selling Expenses	Advertising expenses Sales salaries expense Commission expense
	Administrative Expenses	Office salaries expense Office supplies expense Depreciation expense–office equipment

FINANCIAL STATEMENTS FOR MANUFACTURING ENTERPRISES

Objective 7
Prepare financial statements for a manufacturing enterprise, including the statement of cost of goods manufactured.

The financial statements for manufacturing enterprises are more complex than those for service and merchandising enterprises. This is because a manufacturing enterprise makes the products that it sells. As a result, manufacturing costs must be properly accounted for and reported in the financial statements. These manufacturing costs primarily affect the preparation of the balance sheet and the income statement. The retained earnings and cash flow statements for merchandising and manufacturing enterprises are similar and therefore are not discussed here.

Balance Sheet for a Manufacturing Enterprise

A manufacturing enterprise reports the following three types of inventory on its balance sheet:

1. Direct materials inventory
2. Work in process inventory
3. Finished goods inventory

The **direct materials inventory** for a manufacturing enterprise consists of the cost of the direct materials that have not yet entered the manufacturing process.[1] The **work in process inventory** consists of the direct materials costs, the direct labor costs, and the factory overhead costs that have entered the manufacturing process but are associated with products that have not been completed. The **finished goods inventory** consists of the completed (or finished) products on hand that have not been sold. For example, The Polaroid Corporation reported the following inventories in its 1991 annual report:

Inventories (in millions of dollars):
Raw materials $107.3
Work in process   220.2
Finished goods   196.8

The flow of manufacturing costs into the manufacturing process and the related inventories of a manufacturing enterprise are illustrated in Exhibit 9.

Exhibit 9
Flow of Manufacturing Costs to Balance Sheet

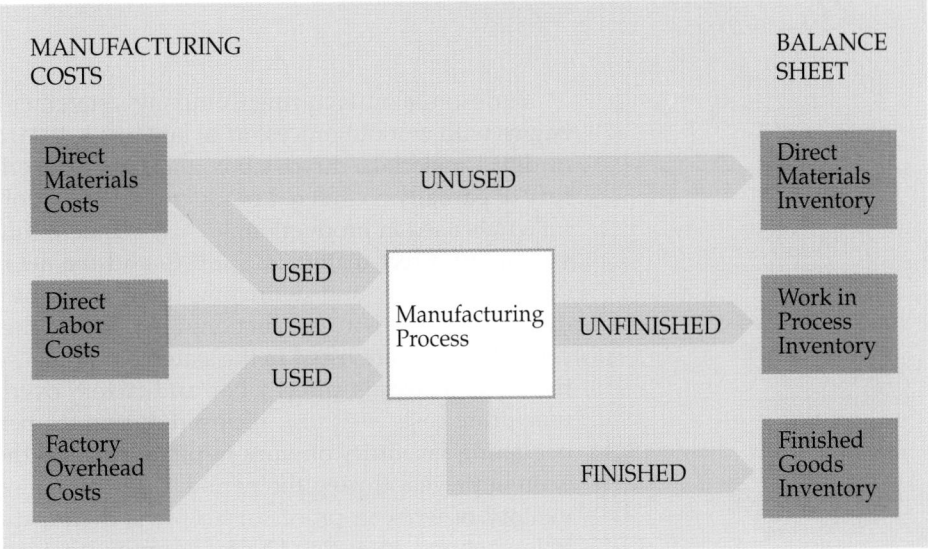

Income Statement for a Manufacturing Enterprise

The major difference in the income statements for merchandising and manufacturing enterprises is in the reporting of cost of products sold during the period. A merchandising enterprise purchases merchandise (products) in a finished state for resale to customers. The merchandise that is sold is generally called the **cost of merchandise sold**.

A manufacturing enterprise makes the products it sells, using direct materials, direct labor, and factory overhead. The cost of the product sold is generally called the **cost of goods sold**. For a manufacturing enterprise, the total cost of making the product is comparable to purchases reported by a merchandising enterprise.

The difference between the income statements for a merchandising enterprise and a manufacturing enterprise are illustrated in Exhibits 10 and 11. In Exhibit 10, the income statement for Loose Inc., a merchandiser, reports **cost of merchandise sold**. In Exhibit 11, the income statement for Burleson Manufacturing Company reports **cost of goods manufactured** and **cost of goods sold**. The Burleson Manu-

[1] Direct materials inventory, sometimes called materials inventory, includes only direct materials to be used in the manufacturing process. Indirect materials are classified as factory supplies.

facturing Company income statement is supported by a **statement of cost of goods manufactured**, which provides the details of the cost of goods manufactured.

Exhibit 10
Merchandising Enterprise—
Income Statement

Loose Inc. Income Statement For the Year Ended December 31, 1994		
Sales		$1,100,000
Cost of merchandise sold:		
Merchandise inventory, Jan. 1, 1994	$ 90,000	
Purchases	900,000	
Merchandise available for sale	$990,000	
Less merchandise inventory, Dec. 31, 1994	120,000	
Cost of merchandise sold		870,000
Gross profit		$ 230,000
Operating expenses:		
Selling expenses	$ 85,000	
Administrative expenses	75,000	
Total operating expenses		160,000
Net income		$ 70,000

Burleson Manufacturing Company's statement of cost of goods manufactured begins with work in process as of January 1, 1994, of $55,000. This amount consists of direct materials, direct labor, and factory overhead costs related to the inventory of partially completed products on hand as of January 1. The cost of the direct materials used in production, $224,075, is determined by adding the beginning inventory of direct materials, $62,000, and the net cost of the direct materials purchased, $220,800, and deducting the ending inventory, $58,725. The amount of direct labor used in production, $218,750, is then listed. The factory overhead costs, $118,850, are listed in the statement or in a supporting schedule. The sum of the direct materials, direct labor, and factory overhead costs equals the total manufacturing costs, $561,675, incurred during the period. Adding to this amount the beginning inventory of work in process equals the total cost of the work that has been in process during the period, $616,675. The estimated cost of the ending inventory of work in process, $65,800, is then deducted to yield the cost of goods manufactured, $550,875. This is the amount reported on the income statement.

TRENDS IN MANUFACTURING AND SERVICE ENTERPRISES

Objective 8
Describe the major trends in manufacturing and service enterprises.

Managerial accounting continues to evolve with changes in the business environment and management philosophies. In recent years, this evolution has been especially rapid for manufacturing enterprises. Competitive world-wide pressures have forced many manufacturers to rethink their techniques and philosophies. This has lead to the adoption of innovative approaches to managing and manufacturing. At the same time, the U. S. economy is becoming more and more service-oriented. This service orientation has resulted in a renewed emphasis on applying managerial accounting concepts to service enterprises.

The following paragraphs provide an overview of the major trends and innovations occurring in the manufacturing and service industries. The impact of each of these trends on managerial accounting is also briefly discussed.

Just-in-Time Manufacturing

To achieve greater productivity and efficiency, many manufacturing enterprises have implemented **just-in-time (JIT) manufacturing** systems. These systems are sometimes called **flexible flow manufacturing systems**. In such systems the em-

Exhibit 11
Manufacturing Enterprise—
Income Statement with Statement
of Cost of Goods Manufactured

Burleson Manufacturing Company
Income Statement
For Year Ended December 31, 1994

Sales		$915,800
Cost of goods sold:		
Finished goods inventory, January 1, 1994	$ 78,500	
Cost of goods manufactured	550,875	
Cost of finished goods available for sale	$629,375	
Less finished goods inventory, December 31, 1994	91,000	
Cost of goods sold		538,375
Gross profit		$377,425
Operating expenses:		
Selling expenses	$165,000	
Administrative expenses	84,425	
Total operating expenses		249,425
Net income		$128,000

Burleson Manufacturing Company
Statement of Cost of Goods Manufactured
For Year Ended December 31, 1994

Work in process inventory, January 1, 1994			$ 55,000
Direct materials:			
Inventory, January 1, 1994	$ 62,000		
Purchases	220,800		
Cost of materials available for use	$282,800		
Less inventory, December 31, 1994	58,725		
Cost of materials placed in production		$224,075	
Direct labor		218,750	
Factory overhead:			
Indirect labor	$ 49,300		
Depreciation of factory equipment	22,300		
Heat, light, and power	21,800		
Property taxes	9,750		
Depreciation of buildings	6,000		
Insurance expense	4,750		
Factory supplies expense	2,900		
Miscellaneous factory costs	2,050		
Total factory overhead		118,850	
Total manufacturing costs			561,675
Total work in process during period			$616,675
Less work in process inventory, December 31, 1994			65,800
Cost of goods manufactured			$550,875

phasis is on manufacturing products or product components only as they are needed (demanded) by the next stage of production or by the marketplace. Because the demand initiates the manufacturing process, just-in-time systems are often called *demand-pull* systems. In contrast, traditional manufacturing systems tend to *push* materials through the production process in order to avoid idle time for employees. The emphasis on keeping the production line moving often results in the buildup of manufacturing inventories.

Because just-in-time systems produce only what is needed by the next stage of production, inventories are reduced to low or insignificant levels. Suppliers are required to deliver raw materials just in time to enter the production process. Since one of a manufacturer's goals is to respond quickly to customer orders, just-in-time systems also focus on reducing the time required to manufacture a product from when an order is received until it is shipped to the customer. This time is called the **cycle time** or **throughput time**. As a result, the cost of products in the process of manufacture (work in process) is reduced to a low enough level that it is often not accounted for as a separate inventory. This allows managerial accountants to focus more on providing information for managerial decision making, rather than measuring inventory for use in preparing financial statements.

Just-in-time manufacturing also places a greater emphasis on quality control. This is because a defective part will have the effect of stopping the production line until the part can be reworked or a new part manufactured. As mentioned above, just-in-time systems require the timely delivery of raw materials by suppliers. This requires a greater emphasis on purchasing high-quality raw materials from reliable suppliers who can meet strict production deadlines. Thus, in just-in-time systems, managerial accountants devote significant time and effort in measuring the costs and benefits of quality control systems, cycle time, and the reliability and performance of suppliers.[2]

Total Quality Control

During the 1950s and 1960s, price was a primary vehicle for competition among manufacturers. During that period, for example, Japanese products were primarily known for their low prices. During the last decade, however, foreign competitors, such as Japan, have implemented new manufacturing techniques. These techniques have been accompanied by stringent quality control standards. As a result, in many cases, Japan has supplied world markets with higher quality products at lower prices than U.S. manufacturers. Thus, many U.S. manufacturers realize that they cannot compete in the world markets on lower prices alone. Superior product quality must be a major manufacturing goal.

Although quality control programs are an integral part of just-in-time manufacturing systems, other manufacturers have also implemented such programs in order to improve product quality. **Total quality control (TQC)** programs begin with product design and continue throughout the production process. Such programs involve an ongoing commitment to improving product quality. Managerial accountants play a vital role in total quality control programs by providing information on the costs of poor quality and the benefits of high quality. The costs of poor quality include the costs of reworks, scrap, defect prevention, customer dissatisfaction, and warranty obligations. The benefits of improved quality include greater customer satisfaction and increased sales.

Computer-Integrated Manufacturing

Computer-integrated manufacturing (CIM) involves the use of automated equipment to perform routine, repetitive tasks with a minimum of human involvement. The automated equipment may be in the form of computer-aided machinery, such as robots. Since some automated machines perform a variety of repetitive tasks, computer-integrated manufacturing adds flexibility to the manufacturing process. This, in turn, allows manufacturers to respond quickly to changing market conditions. Computer-integrated manufacturing is often used with just-in-time manufacturing systems.

The use of automated equipment increases factory overhead costs through increases in depreciation, maintenance, repairs, and insurance, for example. At the same time, automation normally reduces the amount of direct labor used in the

---

[2] JIT manufacturing systems are further discussed in an appendix at the end of this chapter.

manufacturing process. In some cases, direct labor is reduced to such a low level that it is treated as factory overhead. As a result, there has been an increased emphasis in managerial accounting on controlling and properly accounting for overhead. For example, increased emphasis has been placed on identifying activities that cause the incurrence of overhead. Once identified, overhead costs for these activities are then closely monitored.

International Competition

After World War II the United States experienced a period of rapid growth and prosperity. Most of the industrial capacity in Europe and Japan was destroyed by the War, leaving the United States the major supplier of world markets. Whatever was produced could generally be sold either domestically or internationally.

In the decades following the 1950s, the remainder of the world slowly rebuilt its manufacturing plants. As a result, since the late 1970s and early 1980s the United States has faced increasing competition from foreign suppliers. The affects of this competition can be readily seen in retail stores throughout the United States. For example, twenty-five years ago electronics stores carried mostly U.S. brand-name products, such as GE, RCA, and Zenith. The same stores today carry mostly foreign products made by such companies as Sony and Toshiba.

The pressures of increased international competition have forced U.S. manufacturers to re-examine their manufacturing processes. This has resulted in the implementation of new manufacturing processes, such as just-in-time and computer-integrated manufacturing. As mentioned, many companies have also implemented total quality control programs. By providing relevant information to managers, managerial accounting plays an essential role in designing and implementing these new manufacturing processes.

Factory Automation

In the mid-1980s, several U.S. companies were competing with Japanese companies for what was expected to be a $2 billion business in the manufacture of factory automated equipment. By 1990, most of the U.S. companies had "quit the business, whipped by the Japanese . . . " and " . . . robots installed in the U.S. . . . had an estimated value of just $437 million."

"Saddled with high labor costs, the auto industry, particularly, saw robotics as a way to match Japan's lower car production costs. . . ." To meet this demand for factory au-

tomated equipment, U.S. companies focused on the development of hydraulic robots, while the Japanese companies stressed electric robots. The electric robot won out, partly because hydraulics "cost $48,000 on average, while electric robots sold for more than $70,000 . . . however, . . . it cost $12,000 a year to run a hydraulic robot, but only $6,000 for electric." Also important factors were that electric robots have 30% fewer parts and a higher reliability rate than hydraulic robots.

Source: "How U.S. Robots Lost the Market to Japan in Factory Automation," *The Wall Street Journal*, November 6, 1990.

Service Industry Awareness

Many service industries within the United States, such as the airline and trucking industries, are struggling for survival. As a result, service enterprises are increasingly looking to managerial accounting for analyses that will enable them to compete more effectively. Many of the managerial accounting techniques and concepts discussed in the remainder of this text are applicable to service enterprises. For example, hospital administrators need accurate cost information in order to properly bill patients for such health-care services as X-rays, nursing care, and laboratory tests. Likewise, airlines need accurate cost and revenue estimates in setting fares.

APPENDIX

TRADITIONAL VS. JUST-IN-TIME MANUFACTURING SYSTEMS

Just-in-time (JIT) manufacturing systems typically utilize computers and automated machinery such as robots. A JIT system attempts to achieve productive efficiencies and flexibility by reorganizing the traditional production process.

In a traditional production process, a product moves from process to process as each function or step is completed. Each worker is assigned a specific job, which is performed repeatedly as unfinished products are received from the preceding department. For example, a furniture manufacturer might use seven production departments to perform the operating functions necessary to manufacture furniture, as shown in the diagram in Exhibit 12.

Exhibit 12
Traditional Production Line—
Furniture Manufacturer

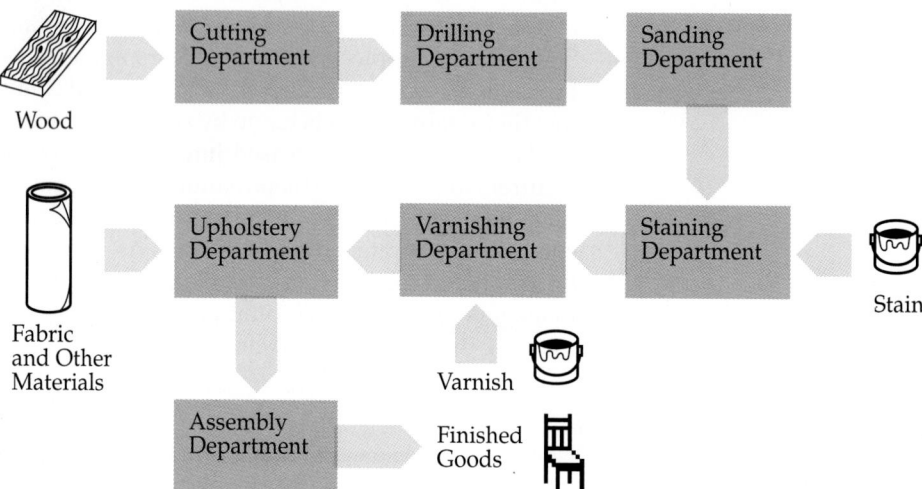

For the furniture maker in the illustration, manufacturing would begin in the Cutting Department, where the wood would be cut to design specifications. Next, the Drilling Department would perform the drilling function, after which the Sanding Department would sand the wood, the Staining Department would stain the furniture, and the Varnishing Department would apply varnish and other protective coatings. Then, the Upholstery Department would add fabric and other materials. Finally, the Assembly Department would assemble the furniture to complete the manufacturing process.

In the traditional production process, production supervisors attempt to enter enough materials into the manufacturing process to keep all the manufacturing departments operating. Some departments, however, may process materials more rapidly than others. In addition, if one department stops production because of machine breakdowns, for example, the preceding departments usually continue production in order to avoid idle time. This unevenness may result in a build-up of work in some departments. Furthermore, if bottlenecks occur, the entire production line slows or stops because the unfinished product is not passed on to the next department.

In a just-in-time manufacturing system, processing functions are combined into work centers, sometimes called manufacturing cells. For example, the seven departments illustrated above for the furniture manufacturer might be reorganized into three work centers. As shown in the diagram in Exhibit 13, Work Center One would perform the cutting, drilling, and sanding functions, Work Center Two would perform the staining and varnishing functions, and Work Center Three would perform the upholstery and assembly functions.

Exhibit 13
Just-In-Time
Production Line—Furniture
Manufacturer

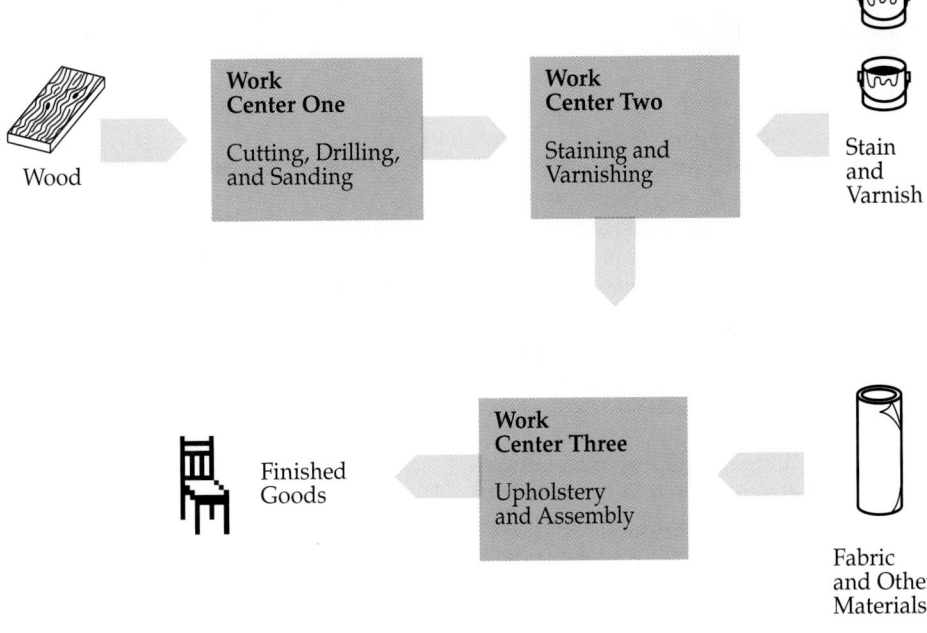

In the traditional production line, as described previously, a worker typically performs only one function on a continuous basis. However, in a work center in which several manufacturing functions take place, the workers are often cross-trained to perform more than one function. Research has indicated that workers who perform several manufacturing functions identify better with the end product. This identification creates pride in the product and improves quality and productivity.

The just-in-time reorganization of the manufacturing departments may also result in a reorganization of activities involving services to these departments. Specifically, the service activities may be assigned to individual work centers, rather than to traditional centralized service departments. For example, each work center may be assigned the responsibility for the repair and maintenance of its machinery and equipment. The acceptance of this responsibility creates an environment in which workers gain a better understanding of the production process and machinery limitations. In turn, workers tend to take better care of the machinery, which decreases repairs and maintenance costs, reduces machine downtime, and improves product quality.

In a just-in-time manufacturing system, the non-value-added activity of moving the product and materials is reduced. The product is often placed on a movable carrier that is centrally located in the work center. After the workers in a work center have completed their activities with the product, the entire carrier and any additional materials are moved to the next work center just in time to be completed and to satisfy the demand or need of that work center. In this sense, the product is said to be "pulled through." Each work center is relatively independent of other work centers, and a work center that has idle time may often contract for special jobs outside the company.

In summary, the primary benefit of just-in-time manufacturing systems is the increased efficiency of operations, which is achieved by eliminating waste and reducing or eliminating non-value-adding activities. At the same time, just-in-time manufacturing systems emphasize continuous improvement in the manufacturing process and the improvement of product quality.

CHAPTER REVIEW

Key Points

Objective 1. Compare and contrast managerial accounting and financial accounting.

Managerial accounting information includes both historical and estimated data for management's use in conducting daily operations and in planning future operations. The principle of usefulness is dominant in guiding the accountant in preparing management reports. In contrast, financial accounting information is presented in statements that are prepared, primarily for external users, according to generally accepted accounting principles.

Objective 2. Diagram the management process and describe each of the functions.

The management process is diagrammed in Exhibit 2. It consists of the basic functions of planning, organizing and directing, controlling, and decision making. Planning is the process by which management develops a course of action to achieve enterprise goals. Organizing is the process by which management assigns responsibility to individuals for achieving enterprise goals. Directing is the process by which managers, given their assigned level of responsibilities, run day-to-day operations. Controlling is the process by which managers attempt to achieve the goals identified in the strategic and operational plans. Decision making is the process by which managers select one course of action over another.

Objective 3. State and give examples of the role of managerial accounting in the management process.

Managerial accounting provides information to management. For example, managerial accounting provides reports that estimate costs for planning, summarize costs of combining operations for organizing and directing, compare actual and expected costs for controlling, and identify effects of alternative actions for decision making.

Objective 4. List the characteristics of accounting reports prepared for use by management.

Managerial accounting reports should possess the characteristics of (1) relevance, (2) timeliness, (3) accuracy, (4) clarity, and (5) conciseness. The principle of usefulness to management is the primary criterion for the preparation of managerial accounting reports.

Objective 5. Define and give an example of the following cost concepts: direct costs and indirect costs, differential costs, sunk costs, controllable costs and noncontrollable costs, discretionary costs, variable costs and fixed costs, and opportunity costs.

A direct cost can be traced directly to a cost object, while an indirect cost cannot. An example of a direct cost of a taxi is the cost of gasoline used in operating it. An indirect cost of the taxi is the salary of the maintenance shop supervisor.

A differential cost is the increase or decrease in cost that is expected from one action compared to another action. An example of a differential cost is the cost of going to a movie tomorrow night.

A sunk cost is one that has been incurred and cannot be reversed by subsequent decisions. The cost of having gone to the movie last night is a sunk cost.

A controllable cost is one that can be influenced or controlled by a specific manager, while a noncontrollable cost cannot. A discretionary cost is one that is not essential to short-term operations. The cost of renting a VCR tape to watch a movie tonight is a controllable cost as well as a discretionary cost.

A variable cost varies proportionately in total dollar amount as the level of activity changes. A fixed cost remains constant in total dollar amount as the level of activity changes. A mixed cost has both fixed and variable characteristics. Insurance premiums on an automobile are a fixed cost, while the cost of gasoline is a variable cost if the activity base is miles driven.

An opportunity cost is the amount of income forgone by selecting one alternative over another. The interest you could earn if you deposit $1,000 in a savings account rather than spend it on a stereo system is an opportunity cost.

Objective 6. Contrast merchandising and manufacturing operations, and define each of the following costs: direct materials, direct labor, and factory overhead.

A merchandising enterprise purchases goods in a form ready for sale and then retails the merchandise to consumers. In contrast, a manufacturing enterprise converts materials into a finished product through the use of machinery and labor. The cost of materials that are an integral part of the manufactured product is direct materials cost. The cost of wages of employees who are directly involved in converting materials into the manufactured product is direct labor cost. Costs other than direct materials cost and direct labor cost incurred in the manufacturing process are factory overhead costs.

Objective 7. Prepare financial statements for a manufacturing enterprise, including the statement of cost of goods manufactured.

The retained earnings statement and the statement of cash flows are similar for merchandising and manufacturing enterprises. The balance sheet is also similar, except that a manufacturing enterprise reports direct materials, work in process, and finished goods inventories. The income statement and the supporting statement of cost of goods manufactured for Burleson Manufacturing Company are presented in Exhibit 11.

Objective 8. Describe the major trends in manufacturing and service enterprises.

In just-in-time manufacturing systems, products or components are manufactured only as they are needed. Total quality control programs begin with product design and continue throughout the production process. Computer-integrated manufacturing systems involve the use of automated equipment to perform routine, repetitive tasks. International competition and an increased service industry orientation have increased the demand for managerial accounting information.

Glossary of Key Terms

Computer-integrated manufacturing (CIM). The use of automated equipment to perform routine, repetitive tasks with a minimum of human involvement. **Objective 8**

Controllable costs. Costs that can be directly controlled by a specific level of management. **Objective 5**

Controller. The chief managerial accountant of a division or other segment of a business enterprise. **Objective 3**

Controlling. The process by which managers attempt to achieve the goals identified in an enterprise's strategic and operational plans. **Objective 2**

Conversion costs. The combination of direct labor and factory overhead costs. **Objective 6**

Cost. A disbursement of cash (or a commitment to pay cash in the future) for the purpose of generating revenues. **Objective 5**

Cost object. The object or segment of operations to which costs are related for management's use, such as a product or department. **Objective 5**

Cost of goods sold. The cost of the manufactured product sold. **Objective 7**

Cost of merchandise sold. The cost of merchandise purchased by a merchandise enterprise and sold. **Objective 7**

Cycle time. The time required to manufacture a product from receipt of an order until it is shipped to the customer. Sometimes referred to as throughput time. **Objective 8**

Decision making. The process by which managers select one course of action over another. **Objective 2**

Differential cost. The amount of increase or decrease in cost that is expected from a particular course of action compared with an alternative. **Objective 5**

Direct costs. Costs that can be traced directly to a cost object. **Objective 5**

Directing. The process by which managers, given their assigned level of responsibilities, run day-to-day operations. **Objective 2**

Direct labor cost. Wages of factory workers who are directly involved in converting materials into a finished product. **Objective 6**

Direct materials cost. The cost of materials that are an integral part of the finished product. **Objective 6**

Direct materials inventory. The cost of direct materials which have not yet entered into the manufacturing process. **Objective 7**

Discretionary cost. A cost that is not essential to short-term operations. **Objective 5**

Factory overhead cost. All of the costs of operating the factory except for direct materials and direct labor. **Objective 6**

Financial accounting. The branch of accounting that is concerned with the recording of transactions using generally accepted accounting principles (GAAP) for a business enterprise or other economic unit and with a periodic preparation of various statements from such records. **Objective 1**

Finished goods inventory. The cost of finished products on hand that have not been sold. **Objective 7**

Fixed cost. A cost (expense) that tends to remain constant in amount regardless of variations in an activity base. **Objective 5**

Indirect costs. Costs that cannot be traced directly to a cost object. **Objective 5**

Just-in-time (JIT) manufacturing systems. Systems of manufacturing in which a primary emphasis is on the manufacture of products only as they are needed by the next stage of production or by the marketplace. **Objective 8**

Management by exception. The philosophy of managing which involves monitoring the operating results of implemented plans and comparing the expected results with the actual results. This feedback allows management to isolate significant variations for further investigation and possible remedial action. **Objective 2**

Managerial accounting. The branch of accounting that uses both historical and estimated data in providing information which management uses in conducting daily operations and in planning future operations and developing overall business strategies. **Objective 1**

Mixed costs. Costs with both variable and fixed characteristics, sometimes referred to as semivariable or semifixed costs. **Objective 5**

Noncontrollable costs. Costs that cannot be directly controlled by specific level of management. **Objective 5**

Operational planning. The development of short-term plans to achieve goals identified in an enterprise's strategic plan. Sometimes referred to as tactical planning. **Objective 2**

Opportunity cost. The amount of income that would result from the best available alternative to a proposed use of cash or its equivalent. **Objective 5**

Organizing. The process by which management assigns responsibility to individuals for achieving enterprise goals. **Objective 2**

Period costs. Those costs that are used up in generating revenue during the current period and that are not involved in the manufacturing process. These costs are recognized as expenses on the current period's income statement. **Objective 6**

Planning. The process of setting goals for the use of an organization's resources and developing ways to achieve these goals. **Objective 2**

Prime costs. The combination of direct materials and direct labor costs. **Objective 6**

Product costs. The three components of manufacturing cost: direct materials, direct labor, and factory overhead costs. **Objective 6**

Statement of cost of goods manufactured. A separate statement for a manufacturer that reports the cost of goods manufactured during a period. **Objective 7**

Strategic planning. The development of a long-range course of action to achieve enterprise goals. **Objective 2**

Sunk costs. Costs that are not affected by subsequent decisions. **Objective 5**

Total quality control (TQC). A quality control program that begins with product design and continues through production; it involves an ongoing commitment to improving product quality. **Objective 8**

Variable cost. A cost that varies in total dollar amount as the level of activity changes. **Objective 5**

Work in process inventory. The direct materials costs, the direct labor costs, and the factory overhead costs which have entered into the manufacturing process, but are associated with products that have not been finished. **Objective 7**

Self-Examination Questions
Answers at end of chapter.

1. Which of the following designations serves as evidence of professional competence in managerial accounting?
   A. Certified Public Accountant
   B. Certified Management Accountant
   C. Certified Internal Auditor
   D. Certified Financial Planner

2. Which of the following is *not* a characteristic of managerial accounting reports?
   A. Timeliness
   B. Relevance
   C. Conciseness
   D. Cost-benefit balance

3. Which of the following is *not* considered a cost of manufacturing a product?
   A. Direct materials cost
   B. Factory overhead cost
   C. Sales salaries
   D. Direct labor cost

4. Which of the following costs would be included as part of the factory overhead costs of a microcomputer manufacturer?
   A. The cost of memory chips
   B. Depreciation of testing equipment
   C. Wages of computer assemblers
   D. The cost of disk drives

5. Which of the following costs would normally be considered a variable cost?
   A. Direct materials cost
   B. Direct labor cost
   C. Electricity to operate factory equipment
   D. All of the above

ILLUSTRATIVE PROBLEM

The following pre-closing trial balance of Mahaney Inc. was prepared as of December 31, 1994, the end of the current fiscal year:

Cash	50,000	
Accounts Receivable	160,000	
Allowance for Doubtful Accounts		20,000
Finished Goods Inventory	180,000	
Work in Process Inventory	75,000	
Direct Materials Inventory	40,000	
Prepaid Insurance	12,000	
Factory Supplies	7,000	
Land	100,000	
Factory Buildings	400,000	
Accumulated Depreciation—Factory Buildings		220,000
Factory Equipment	250,000	
Accumulated Depreciation—Factory Equipment		125,000
Accounts Payable		30,000
Wages Payable		14,000
Income Tax Payable		10,000
Common Stock		100,000
Retained Earnings		711,000
Dividends	20,000	
Sales		1,500,000
Direct Materials Purchases	750,000	
Direct Labor	300,000	
Indirect Factory Labor	150,000	
Depreciation—Factory Equipment	25,000	
Factory Heat, Light, and Power	20,000	
Depreciation—Factory Buildings	20,000	
Factory Property Taxes	18,000	
Insurance Expense—Factory	12,000	
Factory Supplies Expense	6,000	
Miscellaneous Factory Costs	4,000	
Selling Expenses	60,000	
Administrative Expenses	50,000	
Income Tax	21,000	
	2,730,000	2,730,000

Inventories at December 31, 1994, were as follows:

Finished goods	$200,000
Work in process	70,000
Direct materials	42,000

Instructions

1. Prepare a statement of cost of goods manufactured.
2. Prepare an income statement.
3. Prepare a retained earnings statement.
4. Prepare a balance sheet.

Solution

1.

Mahaney Inc.
Statement of Cost of Goods Manufactured
For Year Ended December 31, 1994

Work in process inventory, January 1, 1994		$ 75,000
Direct materials:		
Inventory, January 1, 1994	$ 40,000	
Purchases	750,000	
Cost of materials available for use	$790,000	
Less inventory, December 31, 1994	42,000	
Cost of materials placed in production	$748,000	
Direct labor	300,000	
Factory overhead:		
Indirect labor	$150,000	
Depreciation—factory equipment	25,000	
Factory heat, light, and power	20,000	
Depreciation—factory buildings	20,000	
Factory property taxes	18,000	
Insurance expense—factory	12,000	
Factory supplies expense	6,000	
Miscellaneous factory costs	4,000	
Total factory overhead	255,000	
Total manufacturing costs		1,303,000
Total work in process during period		$1,378,000
Less work in process inventory, December 31, 1994		70,000
Cost of goods manufactured		$1,308,000

2.

Mahaney Inc.
Income Statement
For Year Ended December 31, 1994

Sales		$1,500,000
Costs of goods sold:		
Finished goods inventory, January 1, 1994	$ 180,000	
Cost of goods manufactured	1,308,000	
Cost of finished goods available for sale	$1,488,000	
Less finished goods inventory, December 31, 1994	200,000	
Cost of goods sold		1,288,000
Gross profit		$ 212,000
Operating expenses:		
Selling expenses	$ 60,000	
Administrative expenses	50,000	
Total operating expenses		110,000
Income before income tax		$ 102,000
Income tax		21,000
Net income		$ 81,000

3.

Mahaney Inc.
Retained Earnings Statement
For Year Ended December 31, 1994

Retained earnings, January 1, 1994		$711,000
Net income for year	$81,000	
Less dividends	20,000	
Increase in retained earnings		61,000
Retained earnings, December 31, 1994		$772,000

4.

Mahaney Inc.
Balance Sheet
December 31, 1994

Assets

Current assets:			
Cash		$ 50,000	
Accounts receivable	$160,000		
Less allowance for doubtful accounts	20,000	140,000	
Inventories:			
Finished goods	$200,000		
Work in process	70,000		
Direct materials	42,000	312,000	
Prepaid insurance		12,000	
Factory supplies		7,000	
Total current assets			$521,000
Plant assets:			
Land		$100,000	
Factory buildings	$400,000		
Less accumulated depreciation	220,000	180,000	
Factory equipment	$250,000		
Less accumulated depreciation	125,000	125,000	
Total plant assets			405,000
Total assets			$926,000

Liabilities

Current liabilities:		
Accounts payable	$ 30,000	
Wages payable	14,000	
Income tax payable	10,000	
Total current liabilities		$ 54,000

Stockholders' Equity

Common stock	$100,000	
Retained earnings	772,000	
Total stockholders' equity		872,000
Total liabilities and stockholders' equity		$926,000

DISCUSSION QUESTIONS

1. What term refers to the individuals who are responsible for directing an enterprise?
2. Describe the field of managerial accounting.
3. What are the four basic functions of the management process?
4. What is the term for a plan that encompasses a period ranging from five to ten years and that serves as a basis for commitment of enterprise resources?

5. What is the process by which management assigns responsibility to individuals for achieving enterprise goals?
6. Describe what is meant by *management by exception*.
7. a. Differentiate between a department with line responsibility and a department with staff responsibility.
   b. In an organization that has a Sales Department and a Personnel Department, among others, which of the two departments has (1) line responsibility and (2) staff responsibility?
8. a. What is the role of the controller in a business organization?
   b. Does the controller have a line or a staff responsibility?
9. a. What do the initials CMA signify?
   b. Briefly describe the requirements for the CMA designation.
10. Describe what *proper ethical conduct* implies.
11. What is the dominant principle that guides the managerial accountant in preparing management reports?
12. A bank loan officer is evaluating a request for a loan that is to be secured by a mortgage on the borrower's property. The property cost $100,000 thirty years ago and has a current market value of $900,000. Which amount, $100,000 or $900,000, is relevant for the loan officer's use in evaluating the request for the loan? Discuss.
13. What is meant by cost-benefit balance as it relates to the preparation of management reports?
14. What term describes a payment in cash (or its equivalent or the commitment to pay cash in the future) for the purpose of generating revenues?
15. For a company that produces microcomputers, would memory chips be considered a direct or an indirect cost of each microcomputer produced?
16. In deciding between the purchase of truck E or truck F, what would be the differential cost?
17. a. What is meant by sunk costs?
   b. A company is contemplating replacing an old piece of machinery that cost $500,000 and has $465,000 accumulated depreciation to date. A new machine costs $825,000. What is the sunk cost in this situation?
18. In considering the purchase of a new automobile, would the book value (the original cost less accumulated depreciation) of the automobile traded in be considered a sunk cost?
19. For a production line supervisor, would depreciation on the factory plant be considered a controllable or a noncontrollable cost?
20. How might the discontinuance or reduction of discretionary costs affect long-term operations? Use research and development costs as the basis for an example.
21. A variable cost remains constant in total dollar amount as the level of activity changes. Do you agree? Explain.
22. If the activity base is the number of units produced, classify each of the following costs as either (a) variable cost or (b) fixed cost:
   (1) Direct labor cost
   (2) Straight-line depreciation of factory equipment
   (3) $3,000 per month rent on factory building used for warehouse
   (4) Property taxes of factory plant and equipment
   (5) Property insurance on factory building
   (6) Direct materials cost
   (7) Electricity (power) usage by robotic machinery
   (8) Monthly salary of factory supervisor
23. a. What is meant by opportunity cost?
   b. Burkett Company is currently earning 8% on $150,000 invested in marketable securities. It proposes to use the $150,000 to acquire plant facilities to manufacture a new product line that is expected to add $14,000 annually to net income. What is the opportunity cost involved in the decision to manufacture the new product?
24. What three costs make up the cost of manufacturing a product?
25. What manufacturing cost term is used to describe the cost of materials that are an integral part of the manufactured end product?
26. If the cost of wages paid to employees who are directly involved in converting raw materials into a manufactured end product is not a significant portion of the total product cost, how would the wages cost be classified as to type of manufacturing cost?

27. Indicate whether each of the following costs of an airplane manufacturer would be classified as (a) direct materials cost, (b) direct labor cost, or (c) factory overhead cost:
    (1) Steel used in landing gear
    (2) Controls for flight deck
    (3) Welding machinery lubricants
    (4) Salary of test pilot
    (5) Wages of assembly-line worker
    (6) Tires
    (7) Aircraft engines
    (8) Depreciation of welding equipment
28. Distinguish between prime costs and conversion costs.
29. What is the difference between a product cost and a period cost?
30. Name the three inventory accounts for a manufacturing business, and describe what each balance represents at the end of an accounting period.
31. What are the three categories of manufacturing costs included in the cost of finished goods and the cost of work in process?
32. For a manufacturing enterprise, what is the description of the amount that is comparable to a merchandising concern's cost of merchandise purchased?
33. What statement is used to summarize the manufacturing costs incurred during a period?
34. What term is sometimes used to refer to just-in-time manufacturing systems?
35. Why are just-in-time manufacturing systems said to be *demand-pull* systems?
36. Does the amount of inventory normally increase or decrease with the implementation of a just-in-time manufacturing system?
37. Why does the implementation of a just-in-time manufacturing system increase the emphasis placed on quality control?
38. What are some of the implications of just-in-time manufacturing systems for management accounting?
39. What is meant by a total quality control system?
40. a. Why does the increased use of automated manufacturing equipment increase factory overhead costs?
    b. What is the implication of increased factory overhead costs for managerial accountants?
41. Why are managers of service enterprises increasingly looking to managerial accountants for analyses and information that will enable them to compete more effectively?

REAL W●RLD FOCUS   42. The management of Trico Products Inc., a manufacturer of windshield wipers in Buffalo, New York, was faced with a decision on whether to locate several new plants in New York or on the Mexican border. The management decided to locate the plants on the Mexican border. Why would the employee hourly wage rate be a major differential operating cost of the two locations for purposes of this decision?

ETHICS DISCUSSION CASE

Helen West, assistant controller for Zimmerman Inc., is preparing a report for a proposed expansion of plant facilities at one of two possible locations—Palm City and Townsend. In preparing the report, West intentionally omitted the fact that Townsend's property tax rates are significantly higher than Palm City's. West has several relatives who own property in Townsend. If the plant is built in Townsend, property values should significantly increase.

SHARPEN YOUR
COMMUNICATION SKILLS   Discuss whether Helen West is behaving in an ethical manner.

EXERCISES

EXERCISE 21-1
MANAGERIAL
ACCOUNTING
TERMINOLOGY
Objectives 1, 2, 3, 4

Choose the appropriate term from the choices presented in parentheses for completing each of the following sentences:

a. Long-range plans of action to achieve goals are called (strategic, operational) plans.
b. The function of the management process that involves the development of a course of action to attain enterprise goals is called (planning, controlling).

c. The function of the management process that involves the assignment of responsibility to individuals for achieving enterprise goals is (directing, organizing).

d. The vice-president of production would occupy a (line, staff) position within a manufacturing company.

e. (Accuracy, Conciseness) refers to the need for a managerial accounting report to be correct within the constraints of the use of the report.

f. (Clarity, Relevance) refers to the need for a managerial accounting report to be clear and understandable in both format and content.

g. The primary criterion for the preparation of managerial accounting reports is the principle of (timeliness, usefulness).

EXERCISE 21-2
RELEVANCE CONCEPT
Objective 4

Chandler Inc. is contemplating the expansion of its operations through the purchase of the assets of Quality Tile Inc. Included among the assets of Quality Tile Inc. is inventory purchased for $75,000 and having a current replacement cost of $120,000.

▌SHARPEN YOUR ►
COMMUNICATION SKILLS

Which cost, $75,000 or $120,000, is relevant for the decision to be made by Chandler Inc.? Briefly explain the reason for your answer.

EXERCISE 21-3
ANALYSIS OF
DIFFERENTIAL COSTS
Objective 5

Wilbanks Inc. has been manufacturing carrying cases for its laptop computers at a price of $8 per case. If Wilbanks Inc. purchases the carrying cases, the cases are expected to cost $10 per case.

a. What is the differential cost of purchasing the carrying cases, compared to the alternative of manufacturing the cases?

▌SHARPEN YOUR ►
COMMUNICATION SKILLS

b. Should Wilbanks Inc. purchase or manufacture the cases? Explain.

EXERCISE 21-4
CLASSIFICATION OF COSTS
Objective 5

The following is a list of costs that were incurred in producing this textbook. With respect to the manufacture and sale of this text, classify each cost as either variable or fixed, and as either indirect or direct. For purposes of classifying each cost as variable or fixed, use the number of books produced and sold as the activity base. For purposes of classifying each cost as direct or indirect, use the textbook as the cost object.

a. Insurance on the factory building and equipment
b. Wages of the vice-president of finance
c. Hourly wages of printing press operators during production
d. Straight-line depreciation of the printing presses used to manufacture the text
e. Electricity used to run the presses during the printing of the text
f. Sales commissions paid to textbook representatives for each text sold
g. Paper on which the text is printed
h. Ink used to print the text
i. Royalty paid to the authors for each text sold
j. Salary of staff used to develop artwork for the text

EXERCISE 21-5
CLASSIFICATION AS
PRODUCT COST OR PERIOD
COST
Objective 6

For a manufacturing enterprise, classify each of the following costs as either a product (inventoriable) cost or a period cost:

a. Depreciation of factory equipment
b. Factory janitorial supplies
c. Direct materials used during production
d. Sales commissions
e. Depreciation of office equipment
f. Property taxes on factory building and equipment
g. Advertising expenses
h. Factory supervisors' salaries
i. Repairs and maintenance costs for factory equipment
j. Salary of production quality control supervisor
k. Oil used to lubricate factory equipment
l. Travel costs of salespersons
m. Utility costs for office building
n. Controller's salary
o. Wages of assembly workers

You and Accounting

You have probably taken a car into an automotive dealership or garage for maintenance or repair work. When you left the car, you signed a repair order authorizing the services to be rendered. When you paid the bill and picked up the car, you received a copy of the completed repair order, similar to the one shown below.

CITY WIDE Truck & Auto Repair & Wrecker Service

184 Elbert St. • Athens, GA 30601
404-**353-1536** • 24 Hours a Day
Complete Towing and Repair Service
24 Hour Wrecker and Road Service

Name	Alan Statler		Date of Order	9-9-94
Address	355 Versailles Rd.			
City Athens		Phone 353-2771		**0810**
Cust.'s Order No.		Order Written by	Time Promised	4:00
Yr, Make & Model	Serial No.		License No.	XNU-602
1991 Ford Escort	Motor No.		Odometer	21,004

Qty.	Part No. & Description	Amount		Description of Work			Amount	
1	Oil filter	5	50	Lubrication ☒ Change Oil ☒ Oil Filter ☒ Tune Up ☐			15	00
1	A.C. belt	15	80	Transmission ☐ Differential ☐ Wash ☐ Polish ☐				
				Replace air conditioner belt			12	50
(MAY BE CONTINUED ON OTHER SIDE) Total Parts		21	30	Liters/Gals. of Gas @		Total Labor	27	50
				Liters/Qts. of Oil @ $1.75	8.75	Total Parts	21	30
Accessories				kg/Lbs. of Grease @		Accessories		
				I hereby authorize the above repair work to be done along with the necessary materials. You and your employees may operate above vehicle for purposes of testing, inspection, or delivery at my risk. An express mechanics lien is acknowledged on above vehicle to secure the amount of repairs thereto. It is also understood that you will not be held responsible for loss or damage to cars or articles left in cars in case of fire, theft or any other cause beyond your control.		Gas, Oil & Grease	8	75
						Outside Repairs		
Total Accessories						Tax	1	71
				Signature Alan Statler		Total	59	26

The completed repair order includes spaces to record the amount of labor and parts used in repairing the car. This is an example of a type of job order cost system, where the repair shop treats each car worked on as a separate job. You may recognize other examples of the use of such systems in your day-to-day activities.

c. The function of the management process that involves the assignment of responsibility to individuals for achieving enterprise goals is (directing, organizing).

d. The vice-president of production would occupy a (line, staff) position within a manufacturing company.

e. (Accuracy, Conciseness) refers to the need for a managerial accounting report to be correct within the constraints of the use of the report.

f. (Clarity, Relevance) refers to the need for a managerial accounting report to be clear and understandable in both format and content.

g. The primary criterion for the preparation of managerial accounting reports is the principle of (timeliness, usefulness).

EXERCISE 21-2
RELEVANCE CONCEPT
Objective 4

Chandler Inc. is contemplating the expansion of its operations through the purchase of the assets of Quality Tile Inc. Included among the assets of Quality Tile Inc. is inventory purchased for $75,000 and having a current replacement cost of $120,000.

SHARPEN YOUR ►
COMMUNICATION SKILLS

Which cost, $75,000 or $120,000, is relevant for the decision to be made by Chandler Inc.? Briefly explain the reason for your answer.

EXERCISE 21-3
ANALYSIS OF
DIFFERENTIAL COSTS
Objective 5

Wilbanks Inc. has been manufacturing carrying cases for its laptop computers at a price of $8 per case. If Wilbanks Inc. purchases the carrying cases, the cases are expected to cost $10 per case.

a. What is the differential cost of purchasing the carrying cases, compared to the alternative of manufacturing the cases?

SHARPEN YOUR ►
COMMUNICATION SKILLS

b. Should Wilbanks Inc. purchase or manufacture the cases? Explain.

EXERCISE 21-4
CLASSIFICATION OF COSTS
Objective 5

The following is a list of costs that were incurred in producing this textbook. With respect to the manufacture and sale of this text, classify each cost as either variable or fixed, and as either indirect or direct. For purposes of classifying each cost as variable or fixed, use the number of books produced and sold as the activity base. For purposes of classifying each cost as direct or indirect, use the textbook as the cost object.

a. Insurance on the factory building and equipment
b. Wages of the vice-president of finance
c. Hourly wages of printing press operators during production
d. Straight-line depreciation of the printing presses used to manufacture the text
e. Electricity used to run the presses during the printing of the text
f. Sales commissions paid to textbook representatives for each text sold
g. Paper on which the text is printed
h. Ink used to print the text
i. Royalty paid to the authors for each text sold
j. Salary of staff used to develop artwork for the text

EXERCISE 21-5
CLASSIFICATION AS
PRODUCT COST OR PERIOD
COST
Objective 6

For a manufacturing enterprise, classify each of the following costs as either a product (inventoriable) cost or a period cost:

a. Depreciation of factory equipment
b. Factory janitorial supplies
c. Direct materials used during production
d. Sales commissions
e. Depreciation of office equipment
f. Property taxes on factory building and equipment
g. Advertising expenses
h. Factory supervisors' salaries
i. Repairs and maintenance costs for factory equipment
j. Salary of production quality control supervisor
k. Oil used to lubricate factory equipment
l. Travel costs of salespersons
m. Utility costs for office building
n. Controller's salary
o. Wages of assembly workers

EXERCISE 21-6
COST CONCEPTS AND
TERMINOLOGY
Objectives 5, 6, 7

Choose the appropriate term from the choices presented in parentheses for completing each of the following sentences:

a. A product, sales territory, department, or activity to which costs are traced is a (cost driver, cost object).
b. The increase or decrease in cost that is expected from a particular course of action as compared with an alternative is a (differential cost, sunk cost).
c. Insurance premiums on factory equipment would be a (controllable, noncontrollable) cost for an assembly-line supervisor.
d. Research and development costs are usually viewed as (discretionary, opportunity) costs.
e. Factory overhead costs combined with direct labor costs are called (prime, conversion) costs.
f. The implementation of automated, robotic factory equipment normally (increases, decreases) the direct labor component of product costs.

EXERCISE 21-7
COST CONCEPTS AND
TERMINOLOGY
Objectives 5, 6, 8

Choose the appropriate term from the choices presented in parentheses for completing each of the following sentences:

a. A cost that has been incurred and cannot be reversed by subsequent decisions is an example of a (fixed, sunk) cost.
b. Since the amount of overtime worked by assembly workers can be determined by the production supervisor through proper scheduling, overtime pay is considered a (controllable, noncontrollable) cost for the production supervisor.
c. If the activity base is the number of units produced, the wages of assembly workers are considered a (fixed, variable) cost.
d. The (opportunity, prime) cost of not investing in U.S. Treasury securities that are yielding 10% is the interest forgone on the possible investment.
e. Direct materials costs combined with direct labor costs are called (prime, conversion) costs.
f. The wages of an assembly worker are normally considered an inventoriable or (period, product) cost.
g. The time required to manufacture a product from when an order is received until it is shipped is called the (process time, cycle time).

EXERCISE 21-8
STATEMENT OF COST OF
GOODS MANUFACTURED
Objective 7

The following accounts were selected from the trial balance of Sanford Co. at August 31, 1994, the end of the current fiscal year:

Administrative Expense	$ 59,750
Direct Labor	230,400
Direct Materials Inventory	62,000
Direct Materials Purchases	257,200
Factory Overhead	92,000
Finished Goods Inventory	91,800
Interest Expense	8,750
Sales	797,500
Selling Expense	86,000
Work in Process Inventory	76,000

Inventories at August 31 were as follows:

Finished Goods	$ 89,950
Work in Process	71,500
Direct Materials	54,800

**SPREADSHEET
PROBLEM**

Prepare the statement of cost of goods manufactured.

EXERCISE 21-9
COST OF GOODS SOLD
Objective 7

On the basis of the data presented in Exercise 21-8, prepare the cost of goods sold section of the income statement.

How many errors can you find in the following statement of cost of goods manufactured?

R. R. Barney Inc.
Statement of Cost of Goods Manufactured
For Year Ended March 31, 1994

Work in process inventory, March 31, 1994		$ 180,800
Direct materials:		
Inventory, April 1, 1993	$170,000	
Purchases	800,000	
Cost of materials available for use	$970,000	
Less inventory, March 31, 1994	200,000	
Cost of materials placed in production	$770,000	
Direct labor	590,000	
Factory overhead:		
Indirect labor	$132,000	
Sales salaries	90,000	
Depreciation of factory equipment	81,200	
Heat, light and power	80,500	
Depreciation of factory buildings	56,000	
Property taxes	35,000	
Insurance expense	25,400	
Factory supplies expense	17,200	
Miscellaneous factory costs	13,500	
Total factory overhead	530,800	
Total manufacturing costs		1,890,800
Total work in process during period		$2,071,600
Less work in process inventory, April 1, 1993		160,000
Cost of goods manufactured		$1,911,600

PROBLEMS

Series A

PROBLEM 21-1A
MANAGERIAL
ACCOUNTING
TERMINOLOGY
Objectives 1, 2, 3, 4, 5, 6, 8

The following statements define, describe, or apply terms used in this chapter:

a. The field of accounting that specializes in providing accounting information for use by managers in making decisions is (financial accounting, managerial accounting).

b. The development of short-term plans is called (operational, strategic) planning.

c. The function of the management process that involves the attempt to achieve the goals identified in the strategic and operational plans is called (controlling, directing).

d. The function of the management process that involves selecting one course of action from alternatives is called (directing, decision making).

e. In a merchandising enterprise, the vice-president of sales occupies a (line, staff) position within the organization.

f. In a division or other segment of a business organization, the chief accountant is called the (controller, treasurer).

g. The characteristic of managerial accounting reports that refers to the economic information reported being pertinent to the specific action being considered by management is (relevance, timeliness).

h. The principle of (relevance, usefulness) is the primary criterion for the preparation of managerial accounting reports.

i. Costs that cannot be traced to a specific cost object are said to be (direct, indirect) costs with respect to that cost object.

j. Costs that are irrelevant for future decision making because they have already been incurred and cannot be reversed are called (indirect, sunk) costs.

k. The cost of external consultants is normally considered an example of a (discretionary, sunk) cost.

l. If the activity base is the number of units produced, the salary of a quality control inspector is normally considered a (variable, fixed) cost.

m. The charge of $30 per day plus $.30 per mile for a rental car is an example of a (discretionary, mixed) cost.

n. If the activity base is the number of units produced, straight-line depreciation of factory equipment is considered a (fixed, variable) cost.

o. The (opportunity, prime) cost of not investing in U.S. Treasury securities that are yielding 10% is the interest forgone on the possible investment.

p. The cost of materials that are an integral part of the manufactured end product is classified as part of the (direct materials, factory overhead) cost.

q. The cost of wages of employees who are directly involved in converting raw materials into the manufactured end product is classified as (direct labor, factory overhead) cost.

r. Costs such as property taxes and insurance on factory buildings are normally classified as (direct materials, factory overhead) cost.

s. Prime costs include direct materials cost and (direct labor, factory overhead) cost.

t. Product costs would normally not include (depreciation of factory equipment, the salary of the controller).

u. In a just-in-time manufacturing system, inventories usually (increase, decrease) in amount.

v. In just-in-time manufacturing systems, managerial accountants devote considerable time to measuring (cycle time, inventory values).

Instructions

Choose the appropriate term from the choices presented in parentheses for completing each of the above sentences.

PROBLEM 21-2A
CLASSIFICATION OF COSTS
Objective 5

Case One: The Quality Control Department of a manufacturing enterprise is a cost object. Each of the following costs is either a direct cost or an indirect cost:

a. Salary of the Quality Control Department supervisor
b. Executive bonuses paid to the president and all vice-presidents of the company
c. Depreciation of office equipment used in the Quality Control Department
d. Payroll taxes paid on the wages of Quality Control Department employees
e. Costs of maintaining the factory cafeteria used by all factory employees, including quality control employees

Case Two: Management is considering replacing a 1985 Ford pickup used for deliveries to customers with a 1994 Chrysler mini-van. Each of the following costs is either a differential cost or a sunk cost:

a. Remaining book value of the 1985 truck
b. $25 fee for transfer of the mini-van's title to the company
c. Sales taxes on the purchase of the mini-van
d. Cost of painting the truck last year
e. Increase in insurance premiums on purchase of the mini-van

Case Three: For an emergency room supervisor at a local hospital, each of the following costs is either a controllable cost or a noncontrollable cost on a day-to-day basis:

a. Salaries of emergency room doctors negotiated on a yearly basis by hospital administrators
b. Cost of medical supplies used in treating patients
c. Straight-line depreciation of X-ray equipment
d. Cost of office supplies used in processing patients
e. Health insurance premiums on emergency room staff

Case Four: Each of the following costs would normally be classified as a discretionary cost or a nondiscretionary cost for most business enterprises:

a. Advertising costs
b. Direct materials costs
c. Research and development costs
d. Depreciation of factory equipment
e. Charitable contributions to the local United Fund

Case Five: If the activity base is the number of employees, each of the following costs is either a variable cost or a fixed cost:

a. Wages of assembly workers
b. $5,000 paid to an outside consulting firm to provide employees' safety training
c. Salary of vice-president of human resources
d. Health insurance premiums paid on behalf of each employee
e. Salary of production supervisors

Instructions

For each of the preceding cases, properly classify the costs as indicated.

PROBLEM 21-3A
COST IDENTIFICATION AND CLASSIFICATION
Objective 5

The management of Wadley Inc., a motorcycle retailer and distributor, is considering expanding operations by adding a Repair and Maintenance Department. Wadley Inc. constructed its building to accommodate future expansion. For the past several years, it has rented a 1,500-square-foot section of the building to Jim's Video-for-View for $750 per month. At the end of Jim's lease, this section of the building will be converted for use by the Repair and Maintenance Department.

Repair and maintenance equipment costing $6,000 will be purchased. It will be depreciated using the straight-line method. Existing store fixtures used by Jim's Video-for-View have a book value of $800 and will be converted for use by the Repair and Maintenance Department. An experienced mechanic will be hired for $1,350 per month, and an assistant mechanic will be hired for $5 per hour. A $7,500 inventory of spare parts will be ordered. Wadley Inc.'s insurance premiums are expected to increase by $100 per month, once the Repair and Maintenance Department opens for business.

To obtain as much visibility as possible, a one-time special advertising promotion is planned at a cost of $400.

Instructions

1. Classify the costs of the proposed Repair and Maintenance Department into the following categories:

   Variable costs when the activity base is the number of repair and maintenance orders
   Fixed costs when the activity base is the number of repair and maintenance orders
   Differential costs of expansion
   Sunk costs of expansion

SHARPEN YOUR ▶
COMMUNICATION SKILLS

2. What is the opportunity cost of expanding operations for Wadley Inc.? Explain.

PROBLEM 21-4A
CLASSIFICATION OF COSTS
Objective 5

The following is a list of costs that were incurred in the production and sale of lawnmowers:

a. Property taxes on the factory building and equipment
b. Wages of vice-president of marketing
c. Hourly wages of operators of robotic machinery used in production
d. Factory cafeteria cashier's salary
e. Electricity used to run the robotic machinery
f. Commissions paid to sales representatives, based upon the number of lawnmowers sold
g. Steel used in producing the lawnmowers
h. Paint used to paint the lawnmowers
i. Telephone charges for controller's office
j. License fees for use of patent for lawnmower blade, based upon the number of lawnmowers produced
k. Straight-line depreciation on the robotic machinery used to manufacture the lawnmowers
l. Maintenance costs for new robotic factory equipment, based upon hours of usage
m. Attorney fees for drafting a new lease for headquarters offices
n. Engine oil used in mower engines prior to shipment
o. Cost paid to outside firm for janitorial services for factory
p. Rivets, bolts, and other fasteners used in lawnmowers
q. Salary of quality control supervisor, who inspects each lawnmower before it is shipped
r. Plastic for outside housing of lawnmowers
s. Cost of advertising lawnmowers in a national magazine
t. Tires for lawnmowers
u. Salary of factory supervisor
v. Gasoline engines used for lawnmowers
w. Premiums on insurance policy for factory buildings
x. Cost of boxes used in storing and shipping lawnmowers
y. Filter for spray gun used to paint the lawnmowers
z. Payroll taxes on hourly assembly line employees

Instructions

Classify each cost as either variable or fixed, and as either indirect or direct. For purposes of classifying each cost as variable or fixed, use the number of lawnmowers produced and sold as the activity base. For purposes of classifying each cost as direct or indirect, use the lawnmower as the cost object. Assume that the factory also produces other lawn maintenance equipment besides lawnmowers. Use the following headings for your answer, placing an "X" in the appropriate column.

	Variable Cost		Fixed Cost	
Cost	Direct Cost	Indirect Cost	Direct Cost	Indirect Cost

PROBLEM 21-5A
CLASSIFICATION OF COSTS
Objective 6

A list of costs incurred in the production and sale of lawnmowers is presented in Problem 21-4A.

Instructions

Classify each cost as either a product cost or a period cost. Indicate whether each product cost is a direct materials cost, a direct labor cost, or a factory overhead cost. Indicate whether each period cost is a selling expense or an administrative expense. Use the following headings for your answer, placing an "X" in the appropriate column.

	Product Cost			Period Cost	
Cost	Direct Materials Cost	Direct Labor Cost	Factory Overhead Cost	Selling Expense	Administrative Expense

PROBLEM 21-6A
CLASSIFICATION AS
PRODUCT COSTS AND
PERIOD COSTS
Objective 6

The following is a list of costs incurred by several business enterprises:

a. Tires for an automobile manufacturer
b. Shipping supplies for products sold
c. Costs for television advertisement
d. Disk drives for a microcomputer manufacturer
e. Seed for grain farmer
f. Executive bonus for vice-president of marketing
g. Wages of a machine operator on the production line
h. Hourly wages of controller's secretary
i. Factory operating supplies
j. First-aid supplies for factory workers
k. Sum-of-the-years-digits depreciation of factory equipment
l. Salary of quality control supervisor
m. Maintenance and repair costs for factory equipment
n. Sales commissions
o. Cost of hogs for meat processor
p. Health insurance premiums paid for factory workers
q. Lumber used by furniture manufacturer
r. Ink used by commercial printer
s. Paper used by Computer Department in processing various managerial reports
t. Hourly wages of warehouse laborers
u. Costs of operating a research laboratory
v. Entertainment expenses for sales representatives
w. Protective glasses for factory machine operators
x. Cost of telephone operators for a toll-free hotline to help customers operate products

Instructions

Classify each of the preceding costs as product costs or period costs. Indicate whether each product cost is a direct materials cost, a direct labor cost, or a factory overhead cost. Indicate whether each period cost is a selling expense or an administrative expense. Use the following headings for preparing your answer, placing an "X" in the appropriate column.

	Product Cost			Period Cost	
Cost	Direct Materials Cost	Direct Labor Cost	Factory Overhead Cost	Selling Expense	Administrative Expense

PROBLEM 21-7A
STATEMENT OF COST OF
GOODS MANUFACTURED;
COST OF GOODS SOLD
Objective 7

The following accounts related to the manufacturing operations of Wofford Inc. were selected from the trial balance at October 31, 1994, the end of the current fiscal year:

Depreciation of Factory Buildings	$ 60,000
Depreciation of Factory Equipment	75,200
Direct Labor	590,000
Direct Materials Inventory	155,000
Direct Materials Purchases	800,000
Factory Supplies Expense	17,200
Finished Goods Inventory	245,000
Heat, Light, and Power	80,500
Indirect Labor	132,000
Insurance Expense	25,400
Miscellaneous Factory Costs	13,500
Property Taxes	35,000
Work in Process Inventory	150,000

Inventories at October 31 were as follows:

Finished Goods	$260,000
Work in Process	175,000
Direct Materials	190,000

Instructions

1. Prepare a statement of cost of goods manufactured.
2. Prepare the cost of goods sold section of the income statement.

PROBLEM 21-8A
FINANCIAL STATEMENTS
FOR A MANUFACTURING
ENTERPRISE
Objective 7

The following trial balance of Howe Inc. was prepared as of July 31, 1994, the end of the current fiscal year:

Cash	35,000	
Accounts Receivable	120,000	
Allowance for Doubtful Accounts		12,000
Finished Goods Inventory	160,000	
Work in Process Inventory	55,000	
Direct Materials Inventory	42,000	
Prepaid Insurance	12,000	
Factory Supplies	7,000	
Land	100,000	
Factory Buildings	350,000	
Accumulated Depreciation—Factory Buildings		220,000
Factory Equipment	175,000	
Accumulated Depreciation—Factory Equipment		75,000
Accounts Payable		45,000
Wages Payable		18,000
Income Tax Payable		10,000
Common Stock		200,000
Retained Earnings		445,000
Dividends	30,000	
Sales		1,250,000
Direct Materials Purchases	520,000	
Direct Labor	250,000	
Indirect Labor	110,000	
Factory Heat, Light, and Power	28,000	
Depreciation—Factory Equipment	20,000	
Factory Property Taxes	15,000	
Depreciation—Factory Buildings	14,000	
Insurance Expense—Factory	9,000	
Factory Supplies Expense	8,000	
Miscellaneous Factory Costs	5,000	
Selling Expenses	120,000	
Administrative Expenses	60,000	
Income Tax	30,000	
	2,275,000	2,275,000

Inventories at July 31, 1994, were as follows:

Finished Goods	$140,000
Work in Process	50,000
Direct Materials	48,000

Instructions

1. Prepare a statement of cost of goods manufactured.
2. Prepare an income statement.
3. Prepare a retained earnings statement.
4. Prepare a balance sheet in report form.

Series B

PROBLEM 21-1B
MANAGERIAL
ACCOUNTING
TERMINOLOGY
Objectives 1, 2, 3, 4, 5, 6, 8

The following statements define, describe, or apply terms used in this chapter:

   a. The management process involves (three, four) basic functions.
   b. The function of the management process by which managers with assigned responsibilities run day-to-day operations is (directing, organizing).
   c. The comparisons of actual results with expected results is (controlling, feedback).
   d. Long-range plans of action to achieve goals are (strategic, operational) plans.
   e. The operating structure of an enterprise can be diagrammed in (organization charts, charts of accounts).
   f. The controller occupies a (line, staff) position within an organization.
   g. To provide more recognition of managerial accounting as a profession, the Institute of Certified Management Accountants grants the (Certificate in Management Accounting, Certificate in Public Accounting).
   h. The characteristic of managerial accounting reports that refers to the need for the report to be correct within the constraints of the use of the report is (accuracy, clarity).
   i. Increases in costs that are expected from a particular course of action as compared to an alternative course of action are (differential, opportunity) costs.
   j. Costs over which a manager has no significant influence are (controllable, noncontrollable) costs for that manager.
   k. If the activity base is the number of units produced, the hourly wages of assembly workers are normally considered a (variable, fixed) cost.
   l. If the activity base is the number of patients, the yearly premium for malpractice insurance for a doctor is normally considered a (variable, fixed) cost.
   m. The amount of income forgone by selecting one alternative over another is an (indirect, opportunity) cost.
   n. Costs that can be traced to a cost object are (direct, indirect) costs with respect to that cost object.
   o. For a television manufacturer, the cost of picture tubes is a (direct materials, factory overhead) cost.
   p. An assembly-line worker's hourly wages for an automobile manufacturer is an example of (direct labor, factory overhead) costs.
   q. The cost that is common to both prime costs and conversion costs is (direct materials, direct labor) cost.
   r. Conversion costs include direct labor costs and (direct materials, factory overhead) costs.
   s. Period costs would normally include (advertising costs, power costs used by factory equipment).
   t. Just-in-time manufacturing systems are often referred to as (demand-pull, demand-push) systems.
   u. The implementation of automated equipment normally (increases, decreases) factory overhead costs.
   v. Recent trends in the service sector of the economy have (increased, decreased) the demand for managerial accounting analyses and reports.
   w. Manufacturing systems that emphasize the manufacture of products only as they are needed by the next stage of production or by the marketplace are called (job order cost, just-in-time) systems.

Instructions

Choose the appropriate term from the choices presented in parentheses for completing each of the above sentences.

PROBLEM 21-2B
CLASSIFICATION OF COSTS
Objective 5

Case One: The hamburger at a fast food restaurant is a cost object. Each of the following costs is either a direct cost or an indirect cost:

  a. Salary of restaurant manager
  b. Hamburger patty
  c. Pickles put on each hamburger
  d. Hourly wages of cook
  e. Hamburger bun

Case Two: Management is considering whether to continue to lease office space in a downtown location or move to a suburban location. Each of the following costs is either a differential cost or a sunk cost:

  a. Cost of attorney's fees for negotiating the new lease
  b. Initial deposit of $4,000 for prepayment of one month's rent at the new suburban location
  c. Book value of lease improvements already made at the current location
  d. Costs to move to new location
  e. Nonrefundable deposit of $3,000 made under the original downtown lease agreement

Case Three: For the general manager of a professional baseball team, each of the following costs is either a controllable cost or a noncontrollable cost on a day-to-day basis:

  a. Salaries of the managers and players
  b. Annual stadium rental fee
  c. Hotel, meals, and transportation costs for away games
  d. Field maintenance and facility repair costs
  e. Executive entertainment expenses

Case Four: Each of the following costs would normally be classified as a discretionary cost or a nondiscretionary cost for most business enterprises:

  a. Sales salaries
  b. Salary of media consultant
  c. Executive bonuses
  d. Attorney fees for regulatory filings with the state
  e. Costs of sponsoring local golf tournament to benefit a community center for troubled children

Case Five: Each of the following costs would be classified as an opportunity cost or as some other type of cost:

  a. President's salary
  b. Interest that could be earned on investing in 8%, 10-year bonds instead of acquiring equipment with a 10-year life
  c. Revenues that could have been earned from renting a building rather than selling it
  d. Cost of insurance on sales representatives' automobiles
  e. Income a student could earn from working a full-time job rather than attending college

Instructions
For each of the preceding cases, properly classify the costs as indicated.

PROBLEM 21-3B
COST IDENTIFICATION AND
CLASSIFICATION
Objective 5

The management of Owens Grocery Inc., a local grocer, is considering expanding operations by adding a small Pharmacy Department. The space for the pharmacy is currently being rented by a flower shop for $5,000 per month.

New store fixtures costing $200,000 will be purchased. The new store fixtures will be depreciated using straight-line depreciation. Existing store fixtures having a book value of $350,000 will be used in the pharmacy.

An experienced pharmacist will be hired for $2,500 per month and an assistant will be hired. The assistant will be paid a sales commission of 5%. An inventory of $18,000 of medicines and drugs will be ordered. Owens Grocery Inc.'s insurance premiums are expected to increase by $200 per month, once the Pharmacy Department opens for business.

To obtain as much visibility as possible for the new pharmacy, a one-time special advertising promotion is planned at a cost of $1,000.

Instructions

1. Classify the costs of the proposed Pharmacy Department into the following categories:

   Direct costs
   Fixed costs when the activity base is sales dollars
   Variable costs when the activity base is sales dollars
   Differential costs
   Sunk costs

SHARPEN YOUR COMMUNICATION SKILLS ►

2. What is the opportunity cost of operating a Pharmacy Department for Owens Grocery Inc.? Explain.

PROBLEM 21-4B
CLASSIFICATION OF COSTS
Objective 5

The following is a list of costs that were incurred in the production and sale of boats:

a. Legal Department costs for the year
b. Fiberglass for producing the boat hull
c. Salary of president of company
d. Paint for boats
e. Annual fee to pro-fisherman Jim Bo Wilks to promote the boats
f. Decals for boat hull
g. Salary of shop supervisor
h. Executive end-of-the-year bonuses
i. Glue for boats
j. Oil to lubricate factory equipment
k. Yearly cost of maintenance contract for robotic equipment
l. Power used by sanding equipment
m. Masks for use by sanders in smoothing boat hulls
n. Special boating advertising campaign in *Bass World*
o. Steering wheels
p. Wood paneling for use in interior boat trim
q. Straight-line depreciation on factory equipment
r. Premiums on business interruption insurance in case of a natural disaster
s. Hourly wages of assembly-line workers
t. Cost of paving the employee parking lot
u. Cost of metal hardware for boats, such as ornaments and tie-down grasps
v. Cost of normal scrap from defective hulls
w. Cost of electrical wiring for boats
x. Memberships for key executives in the Bass World Association
y. Cost of boat for "grand prize" promotion in local bass tournament
z. Commissions to sales representatives, based upon the number of boats sold

Instructions

Classify each cost as either variable or fixed, and as either indirect or direct. For purposes of classifying each cost as variable or fixed, use the number of boats produced and sold as the activity base. For purposes of classifying each cost as direct or indirect, use the boat as the cost object. Assume that the factory also produces other sporting goods besides boats. Use the following headings for your answer, placing an "X" in the appropriate column.

	Variable Cost		Fixed Cost	
Cost	Direct Cost	Indirect Cost	Direct Cost	Indirect Cost

PROBLEM 21-5B
CLASSIFICATION OF COSTS
Objective 6

A list of costs incurred in the production and sale of boats is presented in Problem 21-4B.

Instructions

Classify each cost as either a product cost or a period cost. Indicate whether each product cost is a direct materials cost, a direct labor cost, or a factory overhead cost. Indicate whether each period cost is a selling expense or an administrative expense. Use the following headings for your answer, placing an "X" in the appropriate column.

	Product Cost			Period Cost	
Cost	Direct Materials Cost	Direct Labor Cost	Factory Overhead Cost	Selling Expense	Administrative Expense

PROBLEM 21-6B
CLASSIFICATION AS
PRODUCT COSTS AND
PERIOD COSTS
Objective 6

The following is a list of costs incurred by several business enterprises:

   a. Cost of dyes used by a clothing manufacturer
   b. Salary of the vice-president of manufacturing logistics
   c. Wages of a machine operator on the production line
   d. Travel costs of marketing executives to annual sales meeting
   e. Cost of sewing machine needles used by a shirt manufacturer
   f. Depreciation of microcomputers used in the factory to coordinate and monitor the production schedules
   g. Pens, paper, and other supplies used by Accounting Department in preparing various managerial reports
   h. Electricity used to operate factory machinery
   i. Factory janitorial supplies
   j. Fees paid to lawn service for office grounds upkeep
   k. Wages of computer programmer for production of microcomputer software
   l. Depreciation of copying machines used by the Marketing Department
   m. Telephone charges by president's office
   n. Cost of plastic for a telephone being manufactured
   o. Oil lubricants for factory plant and equipment
   p. Cost of a 30-second television commercial
   q. Depreciation of robot used to assemble a product
   r. Wages of production quality control personnel
   s. Maintenance and repair costs for factory equipment
   t. Depreciation of tools used in production
   u. Rent for a warehouse used to store finished products
   v. Maintenance costs for factory equipment
   w. Fees charged by collection agency on past-due customer accounts
   x. Charitable contribution to United Fund

Instructions
Classify each of the preceding costs as product costs or period costs. Indicate whether each product cost is a direct materials cost, a direct labor cost, or a factory overhead cost. Indicate whether each period cost is a selling expense or an administrative expense. Use the following headings for preparing your answer, placing an "X" in the appropriate column.

	Product Cost			Period Cost	
Cost	Direct Materials Cost	Direct Labor Cost	Factory Overhead Cost	Selling Expense	Administrative Expense

PROBLEM 21-7B
STATEMENT OF COST OF
GOODS MANUFACTURED;
COST OF GOODS SOLD
Objective 7

The following accounts related to manufacturing operations of Searcy Inc. were selected from the trial balance at November 30, 1994, the end of the current fiscal year:

Depreciation of Factory Buildings	$ 12,000
Depreciation of Factory Equipment	14,500
Direct Labor	120,000
Direct Materials Inventory	30,000
Direct Materials Purchases	150,600
Factory Supplies Expense	3,200
Finished Goods Inventory	55,000
Heat, Light, and Power	14,300
Indirect Labor	24,500
Insurance Expense	5,000
Miscellaneous Factory Costs	2,400
Property Taxes	6,100
Work in Process Inventory	38,400

Inventories at November 30 were as follows:

Finished Goods	$60,000
Work in Process	43,200
Direct Materials	32,500

Instructions

1. Prepare a statement of cost of goods manufactured.
2. Prepare the cost of goods sold section of the income statement.

PROBLEM 21-8B
FINANCIAL STATEMENTS
FOR A MANUFACTURING
ENTERPRISE
Objective 7

The following trial balance of Hirch Inc. was prepared as of January 31, 1994, the end of the current fiscal year:

Cash	25,000	
Accounts Receivable	80,000	
Allowance for Doubtful Accounts		4,000
Finished Goods Inventory	80,000	
Work in Process Inventory	65,000	
Direct Materials Inventory	50,000	
Prepaid Insurance	9,000	
Factory Supplies	8,000	
Land	75,000	
Factory Buildings	370,000	
Accumulated Depreciation—Factory Buildings		180,000
Factory Equipment	420,000	
Accumulated Depreciation—Factory Equipment		200,000
Accounts Payable		60,000
Wages Payable		8,000
Income Tax Payable		5,000
Common Stock		100,000
Retained Earnings		543,000
Dividends	20,000	
Sales		900,000
Direct Materials Purchases	250,000	
Direct Labor	175,000	
Indirect Labor	45,000	
Depreciation—Factory Equipment	32,000	
Factory Heat, Light, and Power	22,000	
Factory Property Taxes	15,000	
Depreciation—Factory Buildings	20,000	
Insurance Expense—Factory	6,000	
Factory Supplies Expense	5,000	
Miscellaneous Factory Costs	3,000	
Selling Expenses	90,000	
Administrative Expenses	75,000	
Income Tax	60,000	
	2,000,000	2,000,000

Inventories at January 31, 1994 were as follows:

Finished Goods	$85,000
Work in Process	70,000
Direct Materials	55,000

Instructions

1. Prepare a statement of cost of goods manufactured.
2. Prepare an income statement.
3. Prepare a retained earnings statement.
4. Prepare a balance sheet in report form.

MINI-CASE 1 PRESCOTT COMPUTERS INC.

Prescott Computers Inc. began operations on September 5, 1994, in the garage of Scott Pressley. During the weekends, Scott assembled microcomputers from commercially available parts and components. The microcomputers were assembled according to customer needs and specifications. Because of customer demand, Scott is considering moving to a vacant office building and devoting full time to the business. Scott is currently employed as the assistant manager of Boland Food Stores, where he makes $18,000 a year.

Scott has estimated the following costs of opening the new business:

Purchase of new testing equipment	$ 6,000
Purchase of used delivery van	12,000
Purchase of tables and other furnishings	8,000
Monthly rent	1,500
Wages of assistant	8 per hour
Insurance	120 per month
Local advertising	125 per month
Business licenses	500 per year

Scott plans to move the existing equipment from his garage to the new business. The existing equipment has an original cost of $9,000 and accumulated depreciation of $5,000. Straight-line depreciation is used to depreciate all assets.

Instructions:

1. Classify each of the preceding costs of opening the new business, using the following categories:

   Variable costs when the activity base is the number of orders
   Fixed costs when the activity base is the number of orders
   Differential costs
   Discretionary costs
   Opportunity costs
   Sunk costs
   Note: Some costs may be classified into more than one category.

2. Assuming that Scott opens the new business, list (a) costs that are controllable on a day-to-day basis, and (b) costs that are noncontrollable on a day-to-day basis.

3. List direct costs and indirect costs of assembling a specific microcomputer.

4. ■■■■ ▸ Explain for Scott how a cost may be classified in more than one category. Include in your explanation an example of such a cost.

ANSWERS TO SELF-EXAMINATION QUESTIONS

1. **B** The Certified Management Accountant designation (answer B) serves as evidence of professional competence in managerial accounting. A Certified Public Accountant (answer A) has professional competence in financial accounting and auditing. A Certified Internal Auditor (answer C) has professional competence in internal auditing. A Certified Financial Planner (answer D) has professional competence in financial planning.

2. **D** Cost-benefit balance (answer D) is not a characteristic of managerial accounting reports, but is a general guideline for the preparation of managerial accounting reports. Timeliness (answer A), relevance (answer B), and conciseness (answer C) are all characteristics of useful managerial accounting reports.

3. **C** Sales salaries (answer C) is a selling expense and is not considered a cost of manufacturing a product. Direct ma-

terials cost (answer A), factory overhead cost (answer B), and direct labor cost (answer D) are costs of manufacturing a product.

4. **B** Depreciation of testing equipment (answer B) is included as part of the factory overhead costs of the microcomputer manufacturer. The cost of memory chips (answer A) and the cost of disk drives (answer D) are both considered a part of direct materials cost. The wages of microcomputer assemblers (answer C) are part of direct labor costs.

5. **D** Direct materials cost (answer A), direct labor cost (answer B), and electricity to operate factory equipment (answer C) all vary with changes in the level of activity and are therefore variable costs.

You and Accounting

You have probably taken a car into an automotive dealership or garage for maintenance or repair work. When you left the car, you signed a repair order authorizing the services to be rendered. When you paid the bill and picked up the car, you received a copy of the completed repair order, similar to the one shown below.

CITY WIDE

Truck & Auto Repair & Wrecker Service

184 Elbert St. • Athens, GA 30601
404-353-1536 • 24 Hours a Day
Complete Towing and Repair Service
24 Hour Wrecker and Road Service

Name	Alan Statler		Date of Order	9-9-94
Address	355 Versailles Rd.			
City	Athens	Phone 353-2771		**0810**
Cust.'s Order No.	Order Written by	Time Promised		4:00
Yr, Make & Model	Serial No.	License No.		XNU-602
1991 Ford Escort	Motor No.	Odometer		21,004

Qty.	Part No. & Description	Amount		Description of Work		Amount	
1	Oil filter	5	50	Lubrication ☒ Change Oil ☒ Oil Filter ☒ Tune Up ☐		15	00
1	A.C. belt	15	80	Transmission ☐ Differential ☐ Wash ☐ Polish ☐			
				Reploace air conditioner belt		12	50
(MAY BE CONTINUED ON OTHER SIDE) Total Parts		21	30	Liters/Gals. of Gas @		Total Labor	27	50
				Liters/Qts. of Oil @ $1.75 8.75		Total Parts	21	30
Accessories				kg/Lbs. of Grease @		Accessories		
				I hereby authorize the above repair work to be done along with the necessary materials. You and your employees may operate above vehicle for purposes of testing, inspection, or delivery at my risk. An express mechanics lien is acknowledged on above vehicle to secure the amount of repairs thereto. It is also understood that you will not be		Gas, Oil & Grease	8	75
				held responsible for loss or damage to cars or		Outside Repairs		
Total Accessories				articles left in cars in case of fire, theft or any other cause beyond your control.		Tax	1	71
				Signature Alan Statler		Total	59	26

The completed repair order includes spaces to record the amount of labor and parts used in repairing the car. This is an example of a type of job order cost system, where the repair shop treats each car worked on as a separate job. You may recognize other examples of the use of such systems in your day-to-day activities.

Chapter 22
Job Order
Cost Systems

For manufacturing enterprises, it is important to properly account for product costs. As discussed in Chapter 21, product costs consist of direct materials, direct labor, and factory overhead costs. To properly account for product costs, a manufacturing enterprise must identify and allocate product costs to the units of production. This chapter briefly describes the basic types of accounting systems used by manufacturing enterprises to account for product costs. The job order cost system and traditional methods of allocating factory overhead costs to products are described and illustrated. The use of activity-based costing to allocate factory overhead costs is also discussed. The chapter concludes with a brief discussion of how a job order cost accounting system can be adapted for use by service enterprises.

LEARNING OBJECTIVES
After studying this chapter, you should be able to:

Objective 1
Give examples of the usefulness of product costs.

Objective 2
Compare general accounting systems and cost accounting systems used by manufacturing enterprises.

Objective 3
List and describe the basic characteristics of a job order cost accounting system.

Objective 4
Illustrate the use of a job order cost accounting system, including journal entries.

Objective 5
Explain how factory overhead costs are allocated in activity-based costing.

Objective 6
Diagram the flow of costs for a service enterprise that uses a job order cost accounting system.

USEFULNESS OF PRODUCT COSTS

The primary function of managerial accounting is to provide useful information to managers for planning and controlling operations. Much of this information is developed in the process of accounting for product costs.

Product costs are used by managers for a wide variety of purposes. For example, the unit cost of a finished product is useful for establishing product prices. Product costs are also useful in deciding whether to make a component of a product or to purchase the component from an outside source. Accurate product costs also enable managers to effectively and efficiently manage operations. A variety of other managerial decisions requiring the use of product costs is discussed throughout the remainder of this text.

Product costs are also used in preparing the financial statements of the enterprise. Product costs are necessary for valuing work in process and finished goods inventories on the balance sheet. Product costs are also necessary in determining the cost of goods sold on the income statement.

TYPES OF ACCOUNTING SYSTEMS

Two basic accounting systems used by manufacturers are general accounting systems and cost accounting systems. A **general accounting system** uses a periodic inventory system to account for manufacturing operations. A **cost accounting system** uses a perpetual inventory system to account for manufacturing operations.

In the following paragraphs, a general accounting system is briefly discussed. This is followed by a discussion and illustration of one of two types of cost accounting systems. The second type of cost accounting system is discussed in the following chapter.

General Accounting Systems

A general accounting system may be used when the manufacturing operations are relatively simple. This might be the case when a single product or several similar products are manufactured. Because such simple manufacturing situations are rare, the basic principles of a general accounting system for manufacturing operations are only briefly discussed.

A general accounting system is essentially an extension of the periodic system of inventory accounting used in merchandising enterprises. The periodic inventory system is applied to the three manufacturing inventories: direct materials, work in process, and finished goods. In addition, the manufacturing accounts are summarized periodically in an account titled Manufacturing Summary. At the end of the period, the manufacturing costs are reported in the statement of cost of goods manufactured, which is illustrated for Burleson Manufacturing Company in Exhibit 1.

In a general accounting system, the process of adjusting the inventory and manufacturing accounts is similar to that for a merchandising enterprise. Adjustments to the merchandise inventory account are replaced by adjusting entries to the three manufacturing inventories. Direct Materials Inventory and Work in Process Inventory are adjusted through Manufacturing Summary, and Finished Goods Inventory is adjusted through Income Summary.[1]

At the end of the period, the accounts used in preparing the statement of cost of goods manufactured are closed to Manufacturing Summary. This account's balance, which equals the cost of goods manufactured during the period, is then closed to Income Summary. The remaining temporary accounts (sales, expenses, etc.) are closed to Income Summary in the normal manner.

---

[1] A work sheet may be used in preparing the adjusting entries, the closing entries, and the financial statements for a manufacturing enterprise that uses a periodic inventory system. A description and illustration of such a work sheet is presented in Appendix F.

Exhibit 1
Statement of Cost of Goods Manufactured

Burleson Manufacturing Company
Statement of Cost of Goods Manufactured
For Year Ended December 31, 1994

Work in process inventory, January 1, 1994			$ 55,000
Direct materials:			
Inventory, January 1, 1994	$ 62,000		
Purchases	220,800		
Cost of materials available for use	$282,800		
Less inventory, December 31, 1994	58,725		
Cost of materials placed in production		$224,075	
Direct labor		218,750	
Factory overhead:			
Indirect labor	$ 49,300		
Depreciation of factory equipment	22,300		
Heat, light, and power	21,800		
Property taxes	9,750		
Depreciation of buildings	6,000		
Insurance expense	4,750		
Factory supplies expense	2,900		
Miscellaneous factory costs	2,050		
Total factory overhead		118,850	
Total manufacturing costs			561,675
Total work in process during period			$616,675
Less work in process inventory, December 31, 1994			65,800
Cost of goods manufactured			$550,875

The manufacturing summary account and a portion of the income summary account for Burleson Manufacturing Company are shown in Exhibit 2. To simplify this illustration, the factory overhead is posted in total to the manufacturing summary account. In practice, each factory overhead account would be posted individually.

Exhibit 2
Manufacturing Summary and Income Summary Accounts

Manufacturing Summary

Dec. 31	Work in process inventory, Jan. 1	55,000	Dec. 31	Work in process inventory, Dec. 31		65,800
31	Direct materials inventory, Jan. 1	62,000	31	Direct materials inventory, Dec. 31		58,725
31	Direct materials purchases	220,800	31	To Income Summary		550,875
31	Direct labor	218,750				
31	Factory overhead	118,850				
		675,400				675,400

Income Summary

Dec. 31	Finished goods inventory, Jan. 1	78,500	Dec. 31	Finished goods inventory, Dec. 31		91,000
31	From Manufacturing Summary	550,875				

Cost Accounting Systems

Through the use of perpetual inventory systems, cost accounting systems normally provide more accurate product costs than general accounting systems provide. Cost accounting systems improve control by supplying data on the costs incurred by each manufacturing department or process. Such systems not only provide useful data for minimizing costs, but also may provide management with other valuable data. For example, cost accounting systems may provide data on the efficiency of production methods.

There are two main types of cost accounting systems for manufacturing operations—job order cost and process cost. Each of the two systems is widely used. A manufacturer may use a job order cost system for some of its products and a process cost system for others.

A **job order cost system** provides a separate record of the cost of each quantity of product that passes through the factory. It is best suited to industries that manufacture goods to fill special orders from customers or that produce different lines of products for stock. It may also be used when standard products are manufactured in batches rather than on a continuous basis. In a job order cost system, a summary of the costs incurred in completing a job is prepared. An example of such a summary is shown below.

Job 565
1,000 Units of Product X200

Direct materials used	$2,380
Direct labor used	4,400
Factory overhead applied	3,080
Total cost	$9,860
Unit cost ($9,860 ÷ 1,000)	$ 9.86

Under a **process cost system**, the costs are accumulated for each of the departments or processes within the factory. A process system is best used by manufacturers of like units of product that are not distinct from each other during a continuous production process.

Perpetual Inventory Procedures

In a cost accounting system, perpetual inventory controlling accounts and subsidiary ledgers are maintained for direct materials, work in process, and finished goods inventories. Each inventory account is debited for all additions and is credited for all deductions. The balance of each account thus represents the inventory on hand.

All product costs move through the work in process account, the finished goods account, and finally the cost of goods sold account. The flow of costs through the perpetual inventory accounts is shown in Exhibit 3.

Exhibit 3
Flow of Costs Through Perpetual Inventory Accounts

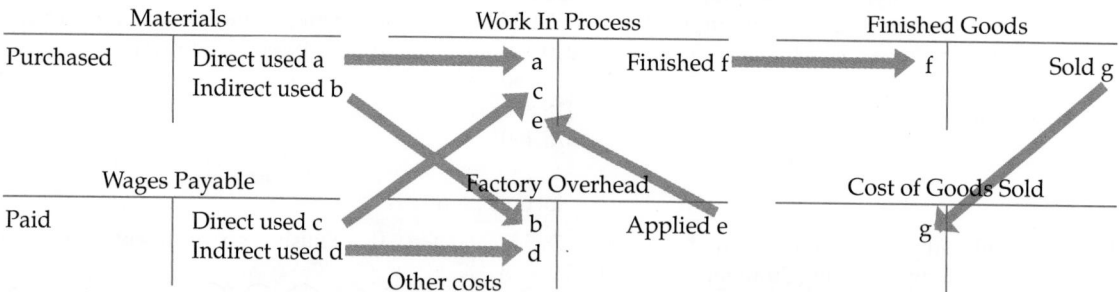

Materials and labor used in production are classified as either direct or indirect. Materials and labor that can be traced to the product are classified as direct and are debited to Work in Process (a and c in the diagram). Materials and labor that do not enter directly into the finished product are debited to Factory Overhead (b and d in the diagram). Examples of indirect materials are oils and greases, abrasives and polishes, cleaning supplies, gloves, and brushes. Examples of indirect labor are salaries of supervisors, inspectors, material handlers, security guards, and janitors.

Factory overhead cost is allocated (applied) to the product manufactured by using a rate determined at the beginning of the period. The applied factory overhead cost is debited to Work in Process (e in the diagram). The costs of the goods finished are transferred from Work in Process to Finished Goods (f in the diagram). When the goods are sold, their costs are transferred from Finished Goods to Cost of Goods Sold (g in the diagram).

The number of accounts presented in the flow chart was limited to simplify the illustration. In practice, manufacturing operations may require many processing departments. In such cases, a separate work in process and a factory overhead account would be used for each department.

JOB ORDER COST SYSTEMS FOR MANUFACTURING ENTERPRISES

Objective 3
List and describe the basic characteristics of a job order cost accounting system.

The basic concepts of job order cost systems are discussed in this chapter. Process cost systems are discussed in the next chapter. The following discussion focuses on the uses of cost accounting data in planning and controlling operations. Also discussed are source documents that are the basis for the entries in the job order cost system.

Materials

The procedures used to purchase, store, and issue materials to production often differ among manufacturers. The following discussion focuses on basic principles rather than minor variations and details.

Prior to the production of a given item, a **bill of materials** is prepared, listing all materials necessary for the item's manufacture. The department responsible for scheduling production then informs the Purchasing Department, by means of a **purchase requisition,** of the materials that will need to be purchased. The Purchasing Department issues the necessary **purchase orders** to suppliers. When the goods are received and inspected, a **receiving report** is prepared by Receiving Department personnel. The receiving report lists the quantity of materials received and their condition. When the supplier's **invoice** is received, the quantities, unit costs, and total costs of the goods billed are compared with the purchase order and the receiving report. This comparison verifies that the amounts billed agree with the materials ordered and received. After the invoice has been approved, it is recorded as a debit to Materials and a credit to Accounts Payable.

The materials account in the general ledger is a controlling account. A separate account for each type of material is maintained in a subsidiary **materials ledger.** Details as to quantity and cost of materials received are recorded in the materials ledger on the basis of the purchase invoices or receiving reports. A typical form of materials ledger account is shown in Exhibit 4.

Exhibit 4
Materials Ledger Account

MATERIAL NO. 23							ORDER POINT 1,000		
RECEIVED			ISSUED				BALANCE		
Rec. Report No.	Quantity	Amount	Mat. Req. No.	Quantity	Amount	Date	Quantity	Amount	Unit Price
						Jan. 1	1,200	600.00	.50
			672	500	250.00	4	700	350.00	.50
196	3,000	1,620.00				8	700	350.00	.50
							3,000	1,620.00	.54
			704	800	404.00	18	2,900	1,566.00	.54

The materials ledger may also be used as an aid in maintaining proper inventory quantities on hand. Comparisons of quantities on hand with predetermined order points enable management to avoid idle time caused by lack of materials. The subsidiary ledger may also include columns for recording quantities ordered and dates of the purchase orders.

Materials are released from the storeroom to the factory in response to **materials requisitions.** Materials requisitions may be issued by the manufacturing department responsible for production or by a central scheduling department. Storeroom personnel record the issuances on the materials requisition by inserting the physical quantity data. Transfer of responsibility for the materials is evidenced by the signature or initials of the storeroom personnel releasing the materials and the factory personnel receiving the materials. A copy of the materials requisition is then routed to the materials ledger clerk, who inserts unit prices and amounts. A typical materials requisition is shown in Exhibit 5.

Exhibit 5
Materials Requisition

MATERIALS REQUISITION

Job No. 62   Requisition No. 704

Authorized by R.A. Sanders   Date January 18, 19--

Description	Quantity Authorized	Quantity Issued	Unit Price	Amount
Material No. 23	800	700	$.50	$350
		100	.54	54
Total issued				$404

Issued by M.K.   Received by J.B.

The completed materials requisition serves as the basis for posting quantities and dollar data to the materials ledger accounts. The amounts can be determined by using either the first-in, first-out, the last-in, first-out, or the average cost methods. In the illustration, the first-in, first-out method is used.

A summary of the materials requisitions completed during the month is the basis for the entry debiting Work in Process and Factory Overhead and crediting Materials in the general ledger.[2] This flow of materials into production is illustrated as follows:

Work in Process	13,000	
Factory Overhead	840	
Materials		13,840

The use of the perpetual inventory system for materials has three important advantages. First, it provides for prompt and accurate charging of materials to jobs and factory overhead. Second, it permits the work of inventory-taking to be spread out over the year rather than scheduled only at the end of the year. Third, it aids in the timely detection of inventory shortages. When the physical quantities of the various materials are counted, they are compared with the balances in the

---

[2] Materials may be accounted for electronically in an advanced computer system by using scanning devices that read the bar codes attached to the materials.

subsidiary ledger. Any major differences between the two inventory amounts should be promptly investigated so that any necessary actions can be taken.

Factory Labor

Unlike materials, factory labor is not tangible, nor is it acquired and stored in advance of its use. Hence, there is no perpetual inventory account for labor. There are two primary objectives in accounting for factory labor. One objective is to determine the correct amount to be paid each employee for each payroll period. A second objective is to properly allocate factory labor costs to factory overhead and individual job orders.

The amount of time spent by an employee in the factory is usually recorded on **clock cards**. These cards are sometimes called **in-and-out cards**. The amount of time spent by each employee and the labor cost incurred for each individual job, or for factory overhead, are recorded on **time tickets**. A typical time ticket form is shown in Exhibit 6.

Exhibit 6
Time Ticket

TIME TICKET

Employee Name Gail Berry   No. 4521

Employee No. 240   Date January 18, 19--

Description of Work Finishing   Job No. 62

Time Started	Time Stopped	Hours Worked	Hourly Rate	Cost
10:00	12:00	2	$6.50	$13.00
1:00	2:00	1	6.50	6.50
Total cost				$19.50

Approved by *T.D.*

The times reported on an employee's time tickets are compared with the related clock cards as an internal check on the accuracy of the payroll. A summary of the time tickets at the end of each month is the basis for recording the direct and indirect labor costs. The flow of labor costs into production is illustrated by the following entry:

Work in Process	10,000	
Factory Overhead	2,200	
Wages Payable		12,200

Factory Overhead

Factory overhead includes all manufacturing costs except direct materials and direct labor. Examples of factory overhead costs, in addition to indirect materials and indirect labor, are depreciation, electricity, fuel, insurance, and property taxes. It is normal to have a factory overhead controlling account in the general ledger. Details of the individual overhead costs are then accumulated in a subsidiary ledger.

Debits to Factory Overhead come from various sources. For example, the cost of indirect materials is obtained from the summary of the materials requisitions. The cost of indirect labor is obtained from the summary of the time tickets. The cost of electricity and water are obtained from invoices. The cost of depreciation and expired insurance may be recorded as adjustments at the end of the accounting period.

Although factory overhead normally cannot be identified with individual jobs, it is an essential component of manufacturing costs. As factories have become more highly automated, factory overhead has become a larger part of the total product costs. Many items of factory overhead cost are related to the entire factory and cannot be traced to individual jobs. This problem is further complicated because some items of factory overhead cost are fixed, while others vary with production.

The total factory overhead for a period cannot be determined with certainty until the end of the accounting period. However, to wait until the end of an accounting period to allocate factory overhead to individual jobs is not acceptable. To be useful, a cost accounting system must provide accurate cost data throughout the period as each job is completed. This timely reporting of cost data is needed for management decision making, such as setting the selling price of a product. Thus, in order to provide timely cost data, factory overhead costs are assigned or applied to production by using a predetermined rate.

PREDETERMINED FACTORY OVERHEAD RATE. The **predetermined factory overhead rate** is calculated by relating the estimated amount of factory overhead for the period to an activity base. The activity base chosen should have a cause-and-effect relationship to the incurrence of the overhead. That is, the activity base should represent an activity that causes overhead to be incurred. Common activity bases used include machine hours, direct labor costs, and direct labor hours.

The term **activity driver** is often used to describe an activity base that is used to assign overhead costs to jobs. For example, if a machine is used in manufacturing a product, machine hours would likely be identified as the activity driver for assigning to jobs the factory overhead costs of operating the machine. Once the proper activity driver has been identified and the factory overhead cost has been estimated, the predetermined factory overhead rate can be calculated.

To illustrate, assume that machine hours, estimated to be 20,000, has been identified as the relevant activity driver. Also, assume that the total factory overhead cost for the year is estimated as $100,000. The predetermined factory overhead rate is computed as $5 per machine hour, as follows:

$$\text{Predetermined Factory Overhead Rate} = \frac{\text{Estimated Total Factory Overhead Costs}}{\text{Activity Driver}}$$

$$\text{Predetermined Factory Overhead Rate} = \frac{\$100,000}{20,000 \text{ machine hours}} = \textbf{\$5 per machine hour}$$

As factory overhead costs are incurred, they are debited to Factory Overhead. Factory overhead costs are periodically applied to production by crediting Factory Overhead and debiting Work in Process. To illustrate, assume a predetermined factory overhead rate of $5 per machine hour and the use of 1,600 machine hours during the period. The entry to apply the $8,000 ($5 × 1,600 machine hours) of factory overhead is as follows:

Work in Process	8,000	
Factory Overhead		8,000

The factory overhead costs applied and the actual factory overhead costs incurred during a period will usually differ. If the amount applied exceeds the actual costs, the factory overhead account will have a credit balance. This credit is described as **overapplied** or **overabsorbed factory overhead**. If the amount applied is less than the actual costs, the account will have a debit balance. This debit is described as **underapplied** or **underabsorbed factory overhead**. Both cases are illustrated in the following account:

ACCOUNT FACTORY OVERHEAD   ACCOUNT NO.

Date		Item	Debit	Credit	Balance Debit	Balance Credit
May	1	Balance				200
	31	Cost incurred	8,320			
	31	Cost applied		8,000	120	

Underapplied Balance
Overapplied Balance

The Implications of Automation for Allocating Factory Overhead—A Case Study

For some departments at Amerock Corporation, the allocation of overhead on the basis of direct labor became less accurate and less useful as manufacturing processes became more automated. The solution was to change from direct labor hours to machine hours for these departments.

Amerock Corporation, a manufacturer of cabinet and decorative hardware, found that the only disadvantages to using machine hours as a basis for allocating factory overhead were the time it would take to develop the system and the need for additional reporting by the machine operators. The potential benefits clearly outweighed any disadvantages. In the accounting area, a major advantage would be the ability to allocate overhead when one worker tended several machines. Better cost estimating would also be possible because overhead allocation would be more accurate. Forecasting and the calculation of actual costs would be easier. In the manufacturing area, machine utilization information would be more useful in understanding and controlling production and reporting.

Amerock Corporation's change in its overhead allocation basis has made it possible for accounting to capture costs accurately and for manufacturing to measure performance efficiently. The results have been so successful that Amerock plans to convert most of its departments to a machine-hour basis as more of its plants become automated.

Source: Gregory Hakala, "Measuring Costs with Machine Hours," *Management Accounting* (October 1985), pp. 57-61.

DISPOSAL OF FACTORY OVERHEAD BALANCE. The balance in the factory overhead account is carried forward from month to month until the end of the year. The balance is reported on interim balance sheets as a deferred item.

The balance in the factory overhead account (underapplied or overapplied), as well as the amount, may change during the year. If the balance increases in only one direction and the balance becomes large, the balance and the overhead rate should be investigated. For example, if a large balance is caused by changes in manufacturing methods or in production goals, the factory overhead rate should be revised. On the other hand, a large underapplied balance may indicate a serious control problem caused by inefficiencies in production methods, excessive costs, or a combination of factors.

Regardless of how carefully the predetermined overhead rate is estimated, Factory Overhead will usually have a balance at the end of the fiscal year. Since this balance applies to the operations of the year just ended, it should not be carried over to the next year and reported as a deferred item on the balance sheet.

There are two possibilities for disposing of the balance of factory overhead at the end of the year. First, the balance may be allocated among the work in process, finished goods, and cost of goods sold accounts. Such an allocation is usually based on the total amount of applied factory overhead included in each of these account balances at the end of the year. The alternative method transfers the entire overapplied or underapplied balance to the cost of goods sold account.

In theory, the first method of allocating over- or underapplied overhead is best because it corrects the estimated overhead rate and brings the accounts into agreement with the costs actually incurred. However, this method is more time-consuming than the second method. In addition, in most manufacturing enterprises, most of the total manufacturing costs for the year pass through the work in process and finished goods accounts into the cost of goods sold account before the end of the year. Thus, unless the balance is large, the total amount of overapplied or underapplied overhead is transferred to Cost of Goods Sold.

Work in Process

Product costs incurred for individual jobs are debited to Work in Process. The job costs described in the preceding sections are summarized below.

- **Direct materials, $13,000**—Work in Process debited and Materials credited; data obtained from summary of materials requisitions.
- **Direct labor, $10,000**—Work in Process debited and Wages Payable credited; data obtained from summary of time tickets.
- **Factory overhead, $8,000**—Work in Process debited and Factory Overhead credited; data obtained from summary of machine usage reports.

The work in process account to which these costs were debited is shown in Exhibit 7.

Exhibit 7
Work in Process Account

ACCOUNT WORK IN PROCESS   ACCOUNT NO.

Date		Item	Debit	Credit	Balance Debit	Balance Credit
May	1	Balance			3,000	
	31	Direct materials	13,000		16,000	
	31	Direct labor	10,000		26,000	
	31	Factory overhead	8,000		34,000	
	31	Jobs completed		31,920	2,080	

Work in Process is a controlling account that contains summary entries only. The supporting cost data for each job order are maintained in a subsidiary ledger called the **cost ledger**. Each cost ledger account is represented by a **job cost sheet**. This sheet has spaces for recording direct materials, direct labor, and factory overhead applied at the predetermined rate. Postings to the job cost sheets for direct materials and direct labor are made from materials requisitions and time tickets or summaries of these documents. The postings for factory overhead are based upon summary reports of the activity driver used in applying the overhead. For example, if the predetermined overhead rate is based upon machine hours, machine usage reports would be the source of the postings for factory overhead.

The four cost sheets in the subsidiary ledger for the work in process account shown in Exhibit 7 are summarized below.

Job 71 (Summary)	
Balance	3,000
Direct materials	2,000
Direct labor	2,400
Factory overhead	1,920
	9,320

Job 73 (Summary)	
Direct materials	6,000
Direct labor	4,000
Factory overhead	3,200
	13,200

Job 72 (Summary)	
Direct materials	4,000
Direct labor	3,000
Factory overhead	2,400
	9,400

Job 74 (Summary)	
Direct materials	1,000
Direct labor	600
Factory overhead	480
	2,080

The relationship between the work in process controlling account in Exhibit 7 and the subsidiary cost ledger is illustrated in Exhibit 8.

Exhibit 8
Subsidiary Cost Ledger

Work in Process (Controlling)		Cost Ledger (Subsidiary)	
Beginning balance	$ 3,000	{ Beginning Balance	
		Job 71	$ 3,000
		Direct materials	
		Job 71	$ 2,000
Direct materials	$13,000	Job 72	4,000
		Job 73	6,000
		Job 74	1,000
			$13,000
		Direct labor	
		Job 71	$ 2,400
		Job 72	3,000
Direct labor	$10,000	Job 73	4,000
		Job 74	600
			$10,000
		Factory overhead	
		Job 71	$ 1,920
		Job 72	2,400
Factory overhead	$ 8,000	Job 73	3,200
		Job 74	480
			$ 8,000
		Jobs completed	
		Job 71	$ 9,320
Jobs completed	$31,920	Job 72	9,400
		Job 73	13,200
			$31,920
Ending balance	$ 2,080	{ Ending balance	
		Job 74	$ 2,080

The data in the cost ledger are presented in summary form for illustrative purposes. A job cost sheet for Job 72 is shown in Exhibit 9. In this job cost sheet, the direct materials, direct labor, and factory overhead costs were totaled and entered in the Summary column when Job 72 was completed. The total cost of the job, **$9,400**, is then determined. This amount is divided by the number of units produced, **5,000**, to yield the unit cost of **$1.88** for the Type C Containers produced.

When Job 72 was completed, its job cost sheet was removed from the cost ledger and filed for future reference. At the end of the accounting period, the sum of the total costs on all cost sheets completed during the period is determined. This amount is the basis for the following entry to record jobs completed during the period:

Finished Goods	31,920	
Work in Process		31,920

The remaining balance in the work in process account represents the total product costs of the uncompleted jobs.

Exhibit 9
Job Cost Sheet

Job No.	72					Date	May 7, 19--	
Item	5,000 Type C Containers					Date wanted	May 23, 19--	
For	Stock					Date completed	May 21, 19--	

Direct Materials		Direct Labor				Summary	
Mat. Req. No.	Amount	Time Summary No.	Amount	Time Summary No.	Amount	Item	Amount
834	800.00	2202	83.60	2248	122.50	Direct	
838	1,000.00	2204	208.40	2250	187.30	materials	4,000.00
841	1,400.00	2205	167.00	2253	155.40	Direct Labor	3,000.00
864	800.00	2210	229.00		3,000.00	Factory	
	4,000.00	2211	198.30			overhead	
		2213	107.20			(80% of	
		2216	110.00			direct	
		2222	277.60			labor cost)	2,400.00
		2224	217.40			Total cost	9,400.00
		2225	106.30				
		2231	153.20			No. of unite	
		2234	245.20			finished	5,000
		2237	170.00			Cost per unit	1.88
		2242	261.60				

Finished Goods and Cost of Goods Sold

The finished goods account is a controlling account. Its related subsidiary ledger, which has an account for each product, is called the **finished goods ledger** or **stock ledger**. Each account in the finished goods ledger contains cost data for the units manufactured, units sold, and units on hand. An account in the finished goods ledger is as follows:

ITEM: TYPE C CONTAINER

MANUFACTURED			SHIPPED				BALANCE		
JOB ORDER NO.	QUAN- TITY	AMOUNT	SHIP ORDER NO.	QUAN- TITY	AMOUNT	DATE	QUAN- TITY	AMOUNT	UNIT COST
						May 1	2,000	3,920.00	1.96
			643	2,000	3,920.00	8	—	—	—
72	5,000	9,400.00				21	5,000	9,400.00	1.88
			646	2,000	3,760.00	23	3,000	5,640.00	1.88

Just as there are various methods of costing materials entering into production, there are various methods of determining the cost of the finished goods sold. In the illustration, the first-in, first-out method is used. The quantities shipped are posted to the finished goods ledger from a copy of the shipping order or other memorandum. The finished goods ledger clerk then records on the copy of the shipping order the unit cost and the total amount of the commodity sold. A summary of the cost data on these shipping orders becomes the basis for the following entry:

Cost of Goods Sold	30,168	
Finished Goods		30,168

If goods are returned by a buyer and are put back in stock, Finished Goods is debited and Cost of Goods Sold is credited for the cost of the returned goods.

Sales

For each sale of finished goods, a record of both the cost and the selling price of the goods sold must be maintained. As previously stated, the cost data may be recorded on the shipping orders. As each sale occurs, the cost of the goods billed is recorded by debiting Cost of Goods Sold and crediting Finished Goods. The selling price of the goods sold is recorded by debiting Accounts Receivable (or Cash) and crediting Sales.

ILLUSTRATION OF JOB ORDER COST ACCOUNTING

Objective 4
Illustrate the use of a job order cost accounting system, including journal entries.

The use of a job order cost accounting system is illustrated in the following comprehensive example for Petrocelli Co. The general ledger trial balance on January 1, 1994, the first day of the fiscal year, is as follows:

Petrocelli Co. Trial Balance January 1, 1994		
Cash	85,000	
Accounts Receivable	73,000	
Finished Goods	40,000	
Work in Process	20,000	
Materials	30,000	
Prepaid Expenses	2,000	
Plant Assets	850,000	
Accumulated Depreciation—Plant Assets		473,000
Accounts Payable		70,000
Wages Payable		15,000
Common Stock		500,000
Retained Earnings		42,000
	1,100,000	1,100,000

In practice, the transactions for Petrocelli Co. would be recorded daily. To simplify, however, the January transactions and adjustments are presented in summary form.

(a) Materials purchased and prepaid expenses incurred

Materials	66,000	
Prepaid Expenses	1,000	
Accounts Payable		67,000

Summary of invoices and receiving reports:

Material A	$29,000
Material B	17,000
Material C	16,000
Material D	4,000
Total	$66,000

(b) Materials requisitioned for
    use

Work in Process	60,000	
Factory Overhead	3,000	
Materials		63,000

Summary of requisitions:

By Use:
Job 1001	$12,000	
Job 1002	26,000	
Job 1003	22,000	$60,000
Factory Overhead		3,000
Total		63,000

By Types:
Material A	$27,000
Material B	18,000
Material C	15,000
Material D	3,000
Total	$63,000

(c) Factory labor used

Work in Process	100,000	
Factory Overhead	20,000	
Wages Payable		120,000

Summary of time tickets:

Job 1001	$60,000	
Job 1002	30,000	
Job 1003	10,000	$100,000
Factory Overhead		20,000
Total		$120,000

(d) Other costs incurred

Factory Overhead	56,000	
Selling Expenses	25,000	
Administrative Expenses	10,000	
Accounts Payable		91,000

(e) Expiration of prepaid
    expenses

Factory Overhead	1,000	
Selling Expenses	100	
Administrative Expenses	100	
Prepaid Expenses		1,200

(f) Depreciation

Factory Overhead	7,000	
Selling Expenses	200	
Administrative Expenses	100	
Accumulated Depreciation—Plant Assets		7,300

(g) Application of factory over-
    head costs to jobs

Work in Process	90,000	
Factory Overhead		90,000

    The predetermined rate was $2 per machine hour. Summary of factory overhead applied:

Job 1001 ($2 × 27,000 machine hours)	$54,000
Job 1002 ($2 × 13,500 machine hours)	27,000
Job 1003 ($2 × 4,500 machine hours)	9,000
Total	$90,000

(h) Jobs completed

Finished Goods	229,000	
Work in Process		229,000

Summary of completed job cost sheets:

Job 1001	$146,000
Job 1002	83,000
Total	$229,000

(i) Sales and cost of goods sold

Accounts Receivable	290,000	
Sales		290,000
Cost of Goods Sold	220,000	
Finished Goods		220,000

Summary of sales invoices and shipping orders:

	Sales Price	Cost Price
Product X	$ 19,600	$ 15,000
Product Y	165,100	125,000
Product Z	105,300	80,000
Total	$290,000	$220,000

(j) Cash received

Cash	300,000	
Accounts Receivable		300,000

(k) Cash paid

Accounts Payable	190,000	
Wages Payable	125,000	
Cash		315,000

The flow of costs through the manufacturing accounts, including the summary details of the subsidiary ledgers, is shown in Exhibit 10. Entries in the accounts are identified by letters as an aid to tracing the flow to the preceding journal entries.

The trial balance of Petrocelli Co. on January 31 is as follows:

Petrocelli Co.
Trial Balance
January 31, 1994

Cash	70,000	
Accounts Receivable	63,000	
Finished Goods	49,000	
Work in Process	41,000	
Materials	33,000	
Prepaid Expenses	1,800	
Plant Assets	850,000	
Accumulated Depreciation—Plant Assets		480,300
Accounts Payable		38,000
Wages Payable		10,000
Common Stock		500,000
Retained Earnings		42,000
Sales		290,000
Cost of Goods Sold	220,000	
Factory Overhead		3,000
Selling Expenses	25,300	
Administrative Expenses	10,200	
	1,363,300	1,363,300

Exhibit 10
Flow of Costs Through Job Order Cost Accounts

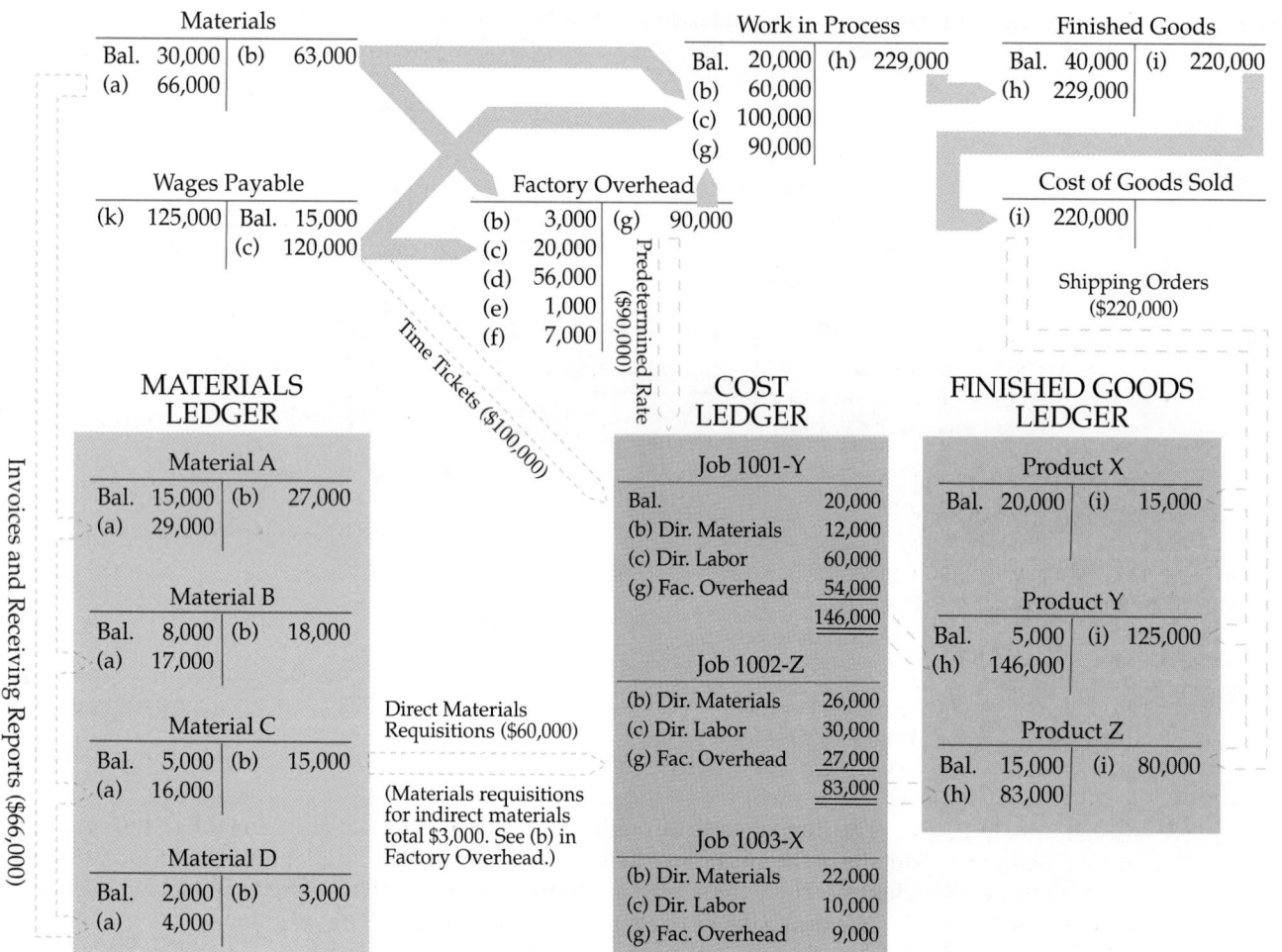

The balances of the three inventory accounts—Finished Goods, Work in Process, and Materials—represent the ending inventories on January 31. The balances of the general ledger controlling accounts should equal the totals of their subsidiary ledgers, as shown below.

Controlling Accounts		Subsidiary Ledgers		
Account	*Balance*	*Account*		*Balance*
Finished Goods	$49,000	Product X	$ 5,000	
		Product Y	26,000	
		Product Z	18,000	$49,000
Work in Process	$41,000	Job 1003		$41,000
Materials	$33,000	Material A	$17,000	
		Material B	7,000	
		Material C	6,000	
		Material D	3,000	$33,000

The financial statements in Exhibit 11 are based on the data for Petrocelli Co. Since the financial statements are prepared for only one month (January), the overapplied factory overhead on January 31 is reported on the balance sheet as a deferred item.

Exhibit 11
Financial Statements for a
Manufacturer Using a Job Order
Cost System

Petrocelli Co.
Income Statement
For Month Ended January 31, 1994

Sales		$290,000
Cost of goods sold		220,000
Gross profit		$ 70,000
Operating expenses:		
Selling expenses	$25,300	
Administrative expenses	10,200	
Total operating expenses		35,500
Income from operations		$ 34,500

Petrocelli Co.
Retained Earnings Statement
For Month Ended January 31, 1994

Retained earnings, January 1, 1994	$42,000
Income for the month	34,500
Retained earnings, January 31, 1994	$76,500

Petrocelli Co.
Balance Sheet
January 31, 1994

Assets

Current assets:			
Cash		$ 70,000	
Accounts receivable		63,000	
Inventories:			
Finished goods	$49,000		
Work in process	41,000		
Materials	33,000	123,000	
Prepaid expenses		1,800	
Total current assets			$257,800
Plant assets		$850,000	
Less accumulated depreciation		480,300	369,700
Total assets			$627,500

Liabilities

Current liabilities:			
Accounts payable		$38,000	
Wages payable		10,000	
Total current liabilities		$ 48,000	
Deferred credits:			
Factory overhead		3,000	
Total liabilities			$ 51,000

Stockholders' Equity

Common stock		$500,000	
Retained earnings		76,500	
Total stockholders' equity			576,500
Total liabilities and stockholders' equity			$627,500

ACTIVITY-BASED COSTING

In the preceding illustration, one work in process account, one factory overhead account, and a single factory overhead rate of $2 per machine hour were used. In more complex manufacturing processes, separate work in process and factory overhead accounts may be maintained for each production department or operation. In addition, if the processing operations differ significantly among departments, a single overhead rate may not be adequate. In such cases, a different factory overhead rate may be used for each department. For example, in a factory with three manufacturing departments, one department might use an overhead rate of $3.50 per machine hour, another a rate of 110% of direct labor cost, and another a rate of $4 per direct labor hour.

In some cases, even departmental overhead rates may not adequately allow for differences in how overhead is incurred by the departments or operations. Therefore, to more accurately allocate overhead, some manufacturers are using a new cost allocation approach called activity-based costing.[3] **Activity-based costing (ABC)** is a method of accumulating and allocating factory overhead costs by activities rather than by departments.

In applying activity-based costing, the activities causing the overhead are first identified. These activities are later used as a basis for allocating overhead costs to products. For example, the activities causing overhead might include the storage of raw materials, the quality control inspection of products, the movement of materials between work stations, and the number of machine setups necessary to produce a product. Thus, instead of allocating quality control costs by using a plant-wide or a departmental overhead rate such as machine hours, the number of inspections might be used.[4]

JOB ORDER COST SYSTEMS FOR SERVICE ENTERPRISES

A job order cost accounting system may be useful to the management of a service enterprise in planning and controlling operations. For example, an advertising agency, an attorney, and a physician all share the common characteristic of rendering services to individual customers, clients, or patients. In such cases, the customer, client, or patient can be viewed as an individual job for which costs are accumulated.

Since the "product" of a service enterprise is service, management's focus is on direct labor and overhead costs. The cost of any materials or supplies used in rendering services for a client is usually small and is normally included as part of the overhead.

The direct labor and overhead costs of rendering services to clients are accumulated in a work in process account. This account is supported by a cost ledger. A job cost sheet is used to accumulate the costs for each client's job. When a job is completed and the client is billed, the costs are transferred to a cost of services account. This account is similar to the cost of merchandise sold account for a merchandising enterprise or the cost of goods sold account for a manufacturing enterprise. A finished goods account and related finished goods ledger are not necessary, since the revenues associated with the services are recorded after the services have been rendered. The flow of costs through a service enterprise using a job order cost accounting system is shown in Exhibit 12.

In practice, additional accounting considerations unique to service enterprises may need to be considered. For example, a service enterprise may bill clients on a weekly or monthly basis rather than waiting until a job is completed. In these situations, a portion of the costs related to each billing should be transferred from the work in process account to the cost of services account. This treatment is similar to the percentage-of-completion method used by construction contractors. A service enterprise may also have advance billings that would be accounted for as deferred revenue until the services have been completed.

---

[3]A recent survey conducted by the Cost Management Group of the Institute of Management Accountants found that 11% of U.S. companies are using ABC and 19% are considering it.
[4]Activity-based costing is further discussed and illustrated in an appendix at the end of the process cost system chapter.

Exhibit 12
Flow of Costs Through a Service
Enterprise

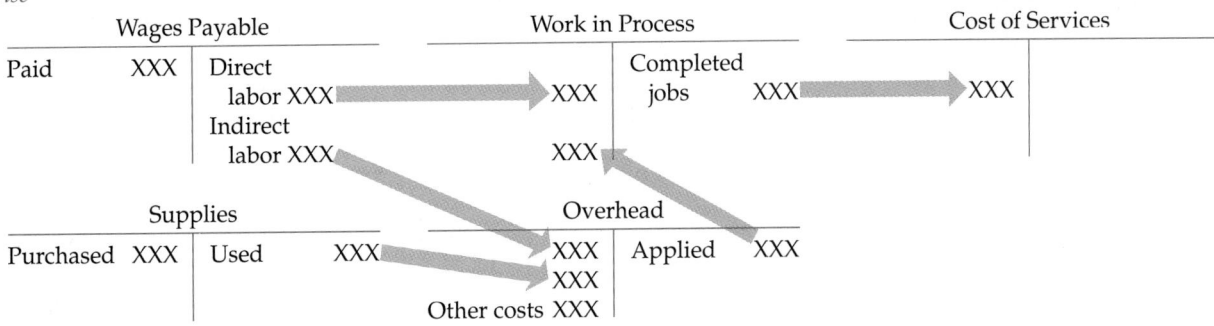

CHAPTER REVIEW

Key Points

Objective 1. Give examples of the usefulness of product costs.
Product costs are used by management for a wide variety of decisions, such as setting product prices and deciding whether to make a component of a product or to purchase the component from an outside source. Product costs are also used in preparing the financial statements.

Objective 2. Compare general accounting systems and cost accounting systems used by manufacturing enterprises.
A general accounting system uses periodic inventory procedures for materials, work in process, and finished goods inventories. A cost accounting system uses perpetual inventory procedures for manufacturing inventories, which include controlling accounts and subsidiary ledgers for materials, work in process, and finished goods. The two primary cost accounting systems are the job order cost and process cost systems.

Objective 3. List and describe the basic characteristics of a job order cost accounting system.
A job order cost system provides for a separate record of the cost of each particular quantity of product that passes through the factory. The product costs are accumulated in a subsidiary cost ledger, in which each account is represented by a job cost sheet. Work in Process is the controlling account

for the cost ledger. As a job is finished, it is transferred to the finished goods ledger, for which Finished Goods is the controlling account.

Objective 4. Illustrate the use of a job order cost accounting system, including journal entries.
An illustration of a job order cost accounting system for Petrocelli Co., including journal entries, is presented in this chapter.

Objective 5. Explain how factory overhead costs are allocated in activity-based costing.
In activity-based costing, overhead costs are accumulated and allocated by activities rather than by departments. The activities that cause the overhead are identified. These activities are then used as the basis for allocating overhead to products.

Objective 6. Diagram the flow of costs for a service enterprise that uses a job order cost accounting system.
A diagram of the flow of costs for a service enterprise using a job order cost accounting system is shown in Exhibit 12. For a service enterprise, the cost of materials or supplies used is normally included as part of the overhead. The direct labor and overhead costs of rendering services are accumulated in a work in process account. When a job is completed and the client is billed, the costs are transferred to a cost of services account.

Glossary of Key Terms

Activity-based costing (ABC). A method of accumulating and allocating overhead costs by the activities that cause the overhead. **Objective 5**

Activity driver. An activity base used to assign overhead costs to jobs. **Objective 3**

Bill of materials. A list of all materials required to manufacture a product. **Objective 3**

Cost accounting system. An accounting system that uses the perpetual system of inventory accounting for the three manufacturing inventories: direct materials, work in process, and finished goods. **Objective 2**

Cost ledger. A subsidiary ledger used in a job order cost system. It contains an account for each job order. **Objective 3**

Finished goods ledger. The subsidiary ledger that contains the individual accounts for each kind of product. **Objective 3**

General accounting system. An accounting system that extends the periodic system of inventory accounting used by merchandising enterprises to the three manufacturing inventories: direct materials, work in process, and finished goods. **Objective 2**

Job cost sheet. An account in the cost ledger in which the costs charged to a particular job order are recorded. **Objective 3**

Job order cost system. A type of cost system that provides a separate record of the cost of each particular quantity of product that passes through the factory. **Objective 2**

Materials ledger. The subsidiary ledger containing the individual accounts for each type of material. **Objective 3**

Materials requisitions. Forms used by the appropriate manufacturing department to authorize the issuance of materials from the storeroom. **Objective 3**

Overapplied factory overhead. The amount of factory overhead applied in excess of the actual factory overhead costs incurred for production during a period. **Objective 3**

Predetermined factory overhead rate. The rate used to apply factory overhead costs to the goods manufactured. **Objective 3**

Process cost system. A type of cost system that accumulates costs for each of the various departments or processes within a factory. **Objective 2**

Purchase orders. Forms issued by the Purchasing Department to suppliers, requesting the delivery of materials. **Objective 3**

Purchase requisition. The form used to inform the Purchasing Department that items are needed by a business. **Objective 3**

Receiving report. The form used by the Receiving Department to indicate that materials have been received and inspected. **Objective 3**

Time tickets. The form on which the amount of time spent by each employee and the labor cost incurred for each individual job, or for factory overhead, are recorded. **Objective 3**

Underapplied factory overhead. The amount of actual factory overhead in excess of the factory overhead applied to production during a period. **Objective 3**

Self-Examination Questions
Answers at end of chapter.

1. The account maintained by a manufacturing business for inventory of goods in the process of manufacture is:
   A. Finished Goods
   B. Materials
   C. Work in Process
   D. Merchandise Inventory

2. For a manufacturing business, finished goods inventory includes:
   A. direct materials costs
   B. direct labor costs
   C. factory overhead costs
   D. all of the above

3. An example of a factory overhead cost is:
   A. wages of factory assembly-line workers
   B. salaries of factory plant supervisors
   C. bearings for electric motors being manufactured
   D. all of the above

4. For which of the following would the job order cost system be appropriate?
   A. Antique furniture repair shop
   B. Rubber manufacturer
   C. Coal manufacturer
   D. All of the above

5. If the factory overhead account has a credit balance, factory overhead is said to be:
   A. underapplied
   B. overapplied
   C. underabsorbed
   D. in error

ILLUSTRATIVE PROBLEM

Shelton Signs Inc. specializes in the production of neon signs and uses a job order cost system. The following data summarize the operations related to production for November, the first month of operations:

a. Materials purchased on account, $21,750.
b. Materials requisitioned and factory labor used:

	Materials	Factory Labor
Job No. 1	$2,750	$1,700
Job No. 2	3,800	2,000
Job No. 3	2,990	1,450
Job No. 4	5,950	3,800
Job No. 5	3,250	1,900
Job No. 6	900	600
For general factory use	595	500

c. Factory overhead costs incurred on account, $4,300.
d. Depreciation of machinery, $1,450.
e. The factory overhead rate is 60% of direct labor cost.
f. Jobs completed: Nos. 1, 2, 4, and 5.
g. Jobs 1, 2, and 4 were shipped and customers were billed for $7,900, $10,500, and $18,100, respectively.

Instructions

1. Journalize the entries to record the foregoing summarized operations.
2. Determine the account balances for Work in Process and Finished Goods.
3. Prepare a schedule of unfinished jobs to support the balance in the work in process account.
4. Prepare a schedule of completed jobs on hand to support the balance in the finished goods account.

Solution

1. a. Materials   21,750
      Accounts Payable   21,750

   b. Work in Process   31,090
      Factory Overhead   1,095
         Materials   20,235
         Wages Payable   11,950

   c. Factory Overhead   4,300
      Accounts Payable   4,300

   d. Factory Overhead   1,450
      Accumulated Depreciation—Machinery   1,450

   e. Work in Process   6,870
      Factory Overhead (60% of $11,450)   6,870

   f. Finished Goods   30,790
      Work in Process   30,790

   Computation of the cost of jobs finished:

Job No.	Direct Materials	Direct Labor	Factory Overhead	Total
1	$2,750	$1,700	$1,020	$ 5,470
2	3,800	2,000	1,200	7,000
4	5,950	3,800	2,280	12,030
5	3,250	1,900	1,140	6,290
				$30,790

   g. Accounts Receivable   36,500
      Sales   36,500

      Cost of Goods Sold   24,500
      Finished Goods   24,500

   Computation of the cost of jobs sold:

Job No. 1	$ 5,470
Job No. 2	7,000
Job No. 4	12,030
	$24,500

2. Work in Process: $7,170 ($31,090 + $6,870 − $30,790)
   Finished Goods: $6,290 ($30,790 − $24,500)

3.
Schedule of Unfinished Jobs

Job No.	Direct Materials	Direct Labor	Factory Overhead	Total
3	$2,990	$1,450	$870	$5,310
6	900	600	360	1,860
Balance of Work in Process, November 30				$7,170

4.
Schedule of Completed Jobs

Job No. 5:	Direct materials	$3,250
	Direct labor	1,900
	Factory overhead	1,140
	Balance of Finished Goods, November 30	$6,290

DISCUSSION QUESTIONS

1. What are two important uses of product cost information by managers?
2. What are the two basic accounting systems commonly used by manufacturers?
3. What two manufacturing-related inventories are reported in the statement of cost of goods manufactured?
4. In a general accounting system, which of the following amounts is not closed to Manufacturing Summary?
   a. Direct materials inventory as of the beginning of the year
   b. Direct materials inventory as of the end of the year
   c. Finished goods inventory as of the beginning of the year
   d. Factory overhead
5. What are the principal advantages of cost accounting systems over general accounting systems?
6. a. Name the two principal types of cost accounting systems.
   b. Which system provides for a separate record of each particular quantity of product that passes through the factory?
   c. Which system accumulates the costs for each department or process within the factory?
7. Which type of cost accounting system, job order cost or process cost, would be best suited for (a) a cereal manufacturer and (b) a custom yacht manufacturer?
8. In a cost accounting system, what are the titles of the three perpetual inventory controlling accounts?
9. Distinguish between the purchase requisition and the purchase order used in acquiring materials.
10. Briefly discuss how the purchase order, purchase invoice, and receiving report can be used to assist in controlling cash payments for materials acquired.
11. What document is the source for (a) debiting the accounts in the materials ledger and (b) crediting the accounts in the materials ledger?
12. Briefly discuss how the accounts in the materials ledger can be used as an aid in maintaining appropriate inventory quantities of stock items.
13. How does the materials requisition help control the issuance of materials from the storeroom?
14. Discuss the major advantages of a perpetual inventory system over a periodic system for materials.
15. a. Differentiate between the clock card and the time ticket.
    b. Why should the total time reported on an employee's time tickets for a payroll period be compared with the time reported on the employee's clock cards for the same period?
16. Which of the following items are properly classified as part of factory overhead?
    a. Interest expense
    b. Factory supplies used
    c. Amortization of factory patents
    d. Property taxes on factory buildings
    e. Direct materials
    f. Sales commissions
17. Discuss how the predetermined factory overhead rate can be used in job order cost accounting to assist management in pricing jobs.
18. a. How is a predetermined factory overhead rate calculated?
    b. Name three common bases used in calculating the rate.
19. a. What is (1) overapplied factory overhead and (2) underapplied factory overhead?
    b. If the factory overhead account has a debit balance, was factory overhead underapplied or overapplied?
    c. If the factory overhead account has a credit balance at the end of the first month of the fiscal year, where will the amount of this balance be reported on the interim balance sheet?
20. At the end of a fiscal year, there was a relatively minor balance in the factory overhead account. What is the simplest satisfactory procedure for the disposition of the balance in the account?
21. What name is given to the individual accounts in the cost ledger?
22. What document serves as the basis for posting to (a) the direct materials section of the job cost sheet, and (b) the direct labor section of the job cost sheet?
23. Describe the source of the data for debiting Work in Process for (a) direct materials, (b) direct labor, and (c) factory overhead.
24. What account is the controlling account for (a) the materials ledger, (b) the cost ledger, and (c) the finished goods ledger or stock ledger?

25. Describe activity-based costing.
26. Would a job order cost or a process cost system be best suited for use by a law firm? Explain.
27. In a cost accounting system for a service enterprise, the cost of any materials or supplies used in rendering services for a client is normally debited to what account?
28. When a job is completed and the client is billed, the costs are transferred to what account in a cost accounting system for a service enterprise?

REAL W  **RLD FOCUS** 29. Hewlett-Packard Company manufactures printed circuit boards in which a high volume of standardized units are fabricated, machined, assembled, and tested. Is the job order cost system appropriate in this situation?

ETHICS DISCUSSION CASE

Sexton Manufacturing Enterprises allows employees to purchase for personal use, at cost, manufacturing materials, such as lumber. To purchase materials for personal use, an employee must complete a materials requisition form, which must then be approved by the employee's immediate supervisor. John Green, an assistant cost accountant, charges the employee an amount based upon Sexton's net purchase cost.

John Green is in the process of replacing a deck on his home and has requisitioned lumber for personal use, which has been approved in accordance with company policy. In computing the cost of the lumber, Green reviewed all the purchase invoices for the past year. He then used the lowest price to compute the amount due the company for the lumber.

SHARPEN YOUR ►
COMMUNICATION SKILLS

Discuss whether John Green behaved in an ethical manner.

EXERCISES

EXERCISE 22-1
COST OF MATERIALS
ISSUED, USING FIFO AND
LIFO METHODS
Objectives 2, 3

The balance of Material X3 on April 1 and the receipts and issuances during April are as follows:

Balance:	April 1	240 units at $40.00
Received:	April 6	600 units at $42.00
	14	480 units at $42.60
	26	360 units at $43.20
Issued:	April 7	360 units for Job 99
	17	300 units for Job 102
	28	420 units for Job 110

a. Determine the cost of each of the three issuances under a perpetual system, using (1) the first-in, first-out method and (2) the last-in, first-out method.

SHARPEN YOUR ►
COMMUNICATION SKILLS

b. Explain how the materials ledger might be used as an aid in maintaining inventory quantities on hand.

EXERCISE 22-2
ENTRY FOR ISSUANCE OF
MATERIALS
Objectives 3, 4

Materials were issued for the current month as follows:

Requisition No.	Material	Job. No.	Amount
711	P-51	1020	$4,820
712	E-16	1060	1,690
713	W-3	1035	3,860
714	A-16	General factory use	750
715	J-48	1018	4,640

Journalize the entry to record the issuances of materials.

EXERCISE 22-3
ENTRY FOR FACTORY
LABOR COSTS
Objectives 3, 4

A summary of the time tickets for the current month follows:

Job. No.	Amount	Job. No.	Amount
673	$2,100	677	$ 800
674	7,250	Indirect labor	1,180
675	3,170	678	6,250
676	4,000	679	5,200

Journalize the entry to record the factory labor costs.

EXERCISE 22-4
FACTORY OVERHEAD
RATES, ENTRIES, AND
ACCOUNT BALANCE
Objectives 3, 4

Andrews Company, which maintains departmental accounts for work in process and factory overhead, applies factory overhead to jobs on the basis of machine hours in Department 3 and on the basis of direct labor costs in Department 4. Estimated factory overhead costs, direct labor costs, and machine hours for January are as follows:

	Department 3	Department 4
Estimated factory overhead cost for year	$65,000	$243,600
Estimated direct labor costs for year		$580,000
Estimated machine hours for year	20,000	
Actual factory overhead costs for January	$ 6,050	$ 20,100
Actual direct labor costs for January		$ 48,500
Actual machine hours for January	1,800	

a. Determine the factory overhead rate for Department 3.
b. Determine the factory overhead rate for Department 4.
c. Journalize the entries to apply factory overhead to production for January.
d. Determine the balances of the departmental factory accounts as of January 31, and indicate whether the amounts represent overapplied or underapplied factory overhead.

▶ SHARPEN YOUR
COMMUNICATION SKILLS

e. Explain how balances in the factory overhead accounts are disposed of at the end of the year. In your explanation, discuss the treatment of both material and immaterial balances.

EXERCISE 22-5
ENTRY FOR JOBS
COMPLETED; COST OF
UNFINISHED JOBS
Objectives 3, 4

The following account appears in the ledger after only part of the postings have been completed for November:

Work in Process		
Balance, November 1	18,500	
Direct Materials	41,750	
Direct Labor	67,500	
Factory Overhead	37,000	

Jobs finished during November are summarized as follows:

Job 320 $25,400   Job 327 $40,300
Job 326   46,100   Job 330   26,100

a. Journalize the entry to record the jobs completed.
b. Determine the cost of the unfinished jobs at November 30.

EXERCISE 22-6
ENTRIES FOR FACTORY
COSTS AND JOBS
COMPLETED
Objectives 3, 4

Atlantic Inc. began manufacturing operations on April 1. Jobs 1 and 2 were completed during the month, and all costs applicable to them were recorded on the related cost sheets. Jobs 3 and 4 are still in process at the end of the month, and all applicable costs except factory overhead have been recorded on the related cost sheets. In addition to the materials and labor charged directly to the jobs, $9,100 of indirect materials and $24,900 of indirect labor were used during the month. The cost sheets for the four jobs entering production during the month are as follows, in summary form:

Job 1		Job 2	
Direct materials	15,750	Direct materials	28,200
Direct labor	12,600	Direct labor	20,160
Factory overhead	7,560	Factory overhead	12,096
Total	35,910	Total	60,456

Job 3		Job 4	
Direct materials	21,400	Direct materials	5,500
Direct labor	17,640	Direct labor	7,800
Factory overhead		Factory overhead	

Prepare an entry to record each of the following operations for the month (one entry for each operation):

a. Direct and indirect materials used.
b. Direct and indirect labor used.
c. Factory overhead applied (a single overhead rate is used, based on direct labor cost).
d. Completion of Jobs 1 and 2.

EXERCISE 22-7
TRANSACTION IN A JOB
ORDER COST SYSTEM
Objective 4

Five selected transactions for the current month are indicated by letters in the following T accounts in a job order cost accounting system:

Materials		Work in Process	
	(a)	(a)	(d)
		(b)	
		(c)	

Wages Payable		Finished Goods	
	(b)	(d)	(e)

Factory Overhead		Cost of Goods Sold	
(a)	(c)	(e)	
(b)			

Describe each of the 5 transactions.

EXERCISE 22-8
JOB ORDER COST
ACCOUNTING ENTRIES FOR
SERVICE ENTERPRISE
Objective 6

Selected transactions for May for Arthur Kline & Co., CPAs, are as follows:

1. Labor incurred as reported by time reports for May:

Direct labor:
Heath Inc. (Job 1)	$ 4,000
Riley Co. (Job 2)	2,800
Shuster Co. (Job 3)	3,500
Foster Inc. (Job 4)	12,250
Ashby Co. (Job 5)	1,250
	$23,800
Indirect labor	4,100
Total	$27,900

2. The following other costs were incurred on account: overhead cost, $10,500; rent expense, $6,000; and office supplies expense, $2,100.
3. Overhead is applied to individual jobs at a rate of $5 per computer hour. Computer hours used, as reported by usage summaries for May:

Job 1	480
Job 2	336
Job 3	420
Job 4	1,470
Job 5	150
Total	2,856

4. Jobs completed and amount billed to clients:

Heath Inc. (Job 1)	$ 8,800
Riley Co. (Job 2)	6,525
Shuster Co. (Job 3)	7,175
Total billings	$22,500

a. Journalize the entries to record the transactions.
b. Prepare a summary of jobs in work in process as of May 31.

How many errors can you find in the following balance sheet that was prepared at the end of the first month of the current fiscal year?

Lorek Inc.
Balance Sheet
February 28, 19—

Assets

Current assets:			
Cash		$ 78,370	
Accounts receivable		103,590	
Finished goods		111,750	
Inventories:			
Work in process	$39,636		
Materials	50,340	89,976	
Prepaid expenses		11,505	
Total current assets			$395,191
Plant assets		$873,600	
Less accumulated depreciation		502,800	
Total plant assets			370,800
Deferred charges:			
Overapplied factory overhead			1,551
Total assets			$767,542

Liabilities

Current liabilities:		
Accounts payable	$ 30,150	
Wages payable	2,250	
Total current liabilities		$ 32,400

Stockholders' Equity

Common stock	$150,000	
Retained earnings	582,040	
Total stockholders' equity		732,040
Total liabilities and stockholders' equity		$764,440

PROBLEMS

Series A

PROBLEM 22-1A
ENTRIES FOR COSTS IN A
JOB ORDER COST SYSTEM
Objectives 3, 4

O'Shea Company uses a job order cost system. The following data summarize the operations related to production for June:

a. Materials purchased on account, $96,500.
b. Materials requisitioned, $97,200, of which $2,900 was for general factory use.
c. Factory labor used, $80,000, of which $11,500 was factory overhead.
d. Other costs incurred on account were for factory overhead, $27,150, selling expenses, $10,500, and administrative expenses, $9,000.
e. Prepaid expenses expired for factory overhead were $950, for selling expenses, $250, and for administrative expenses, $150.
f. Depreciation of factory equipment was $9,100, of store equipment, $400, and of office equipment, $300.
g. Application of factory overhead costs to jobs, $52,500.
h. Jobs completed, $210,500.
i. Cost of goods sold, $199,750.

Instructions
Journalize the entries to record the summarized operations.

PROBLEM 22-2A
ENTRIES AND SCHEDULES
FOR UNFINISHED AND
COMPLETED JOBS
Objectives 3, 4

Simons Printing Company uses a job order cost system. The following data summarize the operations related to production for July, the first month of operations:

a. Materials purchased on account, $57,420.
b. Materials requisitioned and factory labor used:

	Materials	Factory Labor
Job 101	$11,600	$9,150
Job 102	3,400	1,960
Job 103	8,520	4,690
Job 104	4,280	1,900
Job 105	6,830	2,800
Job 106	6,180	4,610
For general factory use	1,310	3,000

c. Factory overhead costs incurred on account, $11,300.

d. Depreciation of machinery and equipment, $5,400.

e. The factory overhead rate is $14 per machine hour. Machine hours used:

Job 101	457.5
Job 102	98.0
Job 103	234.5
Job 104	95.0
Job 105	140.0
Job 106	230.5
Total	1,255.5

f. Jobs completed: 101, 102, 104, and 105.

g. Jobs were shipped and customers were billed as follows: Job 101, $36,200; Job 102, $8,400; Job 104, $10,350.

Instructions

1. Journalize the entries to record the summarized operations.
2. Post the appropriate entries to T accounts for Work in Process and Finished Goods, using the identifying letters as dates. Insert memorandum account balances as of the end of the month.
3. Prepare a schedule of unfinished jobs to support the balance in the work in process account.
4. Prepare a schedule of completed jobs on hand to support the balance in the finished goods account.

If the working papers correlating with the textbook are not used, omit Problem 22-3A.

PROBLEM 22-3A
JOB ORDER COST SHEET
Objectives 3, 4

Manford Furniture Company refinishes and reupholsters furniture. Manford uses a job order cost system.

When a prospective customer asks for a price quote on a job, the estimated cost data are inserted on an unnumbered job cost sheet. If the offer is accepted, a number is assigned to the job and the costs incurred are recorded in the usual manner on the job cost sheet. After the job is completed, reasons for the variances between the estimated and actual costs are noted on the sheet. The data are then available to management in evaluating the efficiency of operations and in preparing quotes on future jobs.

On March 5, an estimate of $360 for reupholstering a chair and couch was given to Alice Bowers. The estimate was based on the following data:

Estimated direct materials:	
10 meters at $12 per meter	$120
Estimated direct labor:	
8 hours at $15 per hour	120
Estimated factory overhead (40% of direct labor cost)	48
Total estimated costs	$288
Markup (25% of production costs)	72
Total estimate	$360

On March 9, the chair and couch were picked up from the residence of Alice Bowers, 979 Park Shore Dr., Ft. Myers, with a commitment to return it on March 26. The job was completed on March 23.

The related materials requisitions and time tickets are summarized as follows:

Materials Requisition No.	Description	Amount
U642	10 meters at $12	$120
U651	2 meters at $12	24

Time Ticket No.	Description	Amount
1519	6 hours at $15	$ 90
1520	3 hours at $15	45

SPREADSHEET PROBLEM

SHARPEN YOUR COMMUNICATION SKILLS

Instructions

1. Complete that portion of the job order cost sheet that would be prepared when the estimate is given to the customer.

2. Assign number 94-3-1 to the job, record the costs incurred, and complete the job order cost sheet. Comment on the reasons for the variances between actual costs and estimated costs. For this purpose, assume that 2 meters of materials were spoiled, the factory overhead rate has been proved to be satisfactory, and an inexperienced employee performed the work.

PROBLEM 22-4A
JOB ORDER COST
TRANSACTIONS AND
FINANCIAL STATEMENTS
Objectives 3, 4

The trial balance of Bluebill Inc. at the beginning of the current fiscal year is as follows:

Bluebill Inc.
Trial Balance
July 1, 19—

Cash	30,020	
Accounts Receivable	164,890	
Finished Goods	104,750	
Work in Process	41,540	
Materials	50,300	
Prepaid Expenses	15,400	
Plant Assets	879,100	
Accumulated Depreciation—Plant Assets		501,280
Accounts Payable		51,050
Wages Payable		—
Common Stock		300,000
Retained Earnings		433,670
Sales		—
Cost of Goods Sold	—	
Factory Overhead	—	
Selling Expenses	—	
Administrative Expenses	—	
	1,286,000	1,286,000

Transactions completed during July and adjustments required on July 31 are summarized as follows:

a.	Materials purchased on account		$ 39,200
b.	Materials requisitioned for factory use:		
	Direct	$40,350	
	Indirect	480	40,830
c.	Factory labor costs incurred:		
	Direct	$20,200	
	Indirect	2,690	22,890
d.	Other costs and expenses incurred on account:		
	Factory overhead	$10,125	
	Selling expenses	9,855	
	Administrative expenses	7,200	27,180
e.	Cash paid:		
	Accounts payable	$65,700	
	Wages payable	18,400	84,100

f. Prepaid expenses expired:
    Chargeable to factory $ 960
    Chargeable to selling expenses   225
    Chargeable to administrative expenses   430   1,615
g. Depreciation charged:
    Factory equipment $ 6,480
    Office equipment   540   7,020
h. Applied factory overhead at a predetermined rate
    based on machine hours   22,220
i. Total cost of jobs completed   80,250
j. Sales, all on account:
    Selling price   120,900
    Cost   78,800
k. Cash received on account   140,600

Instructions

1. Record the July 1 balances in T accounts, identifying each as "Bal."
2. Record the transactions directly in the T accounts, using the identifying letters in place
    of dates.
3. Prepare an income statement for the month ended July 31, 19—.
4. Prepare a retained earnings statement for the month ended July 31, 19—.
5. Prepare a balance sheet as of July 31, 19—.

**SOLUTIONS
SOFTWARE**

?

Instructions for Solving Problem 22-4A Using Solutions Software

1. Load opening balances.
2. Save the opening balances file to your drive and directory.
3. Set the run date to July 31 of the current year and enter your name.
4. Select the General Journal Entries option and key the journal entries. Leave the refer-
    ence field blank. Note: To review the chart of accounts, select F-1.
5. Display a journal entries report.
6. Display a trial balance.
7. Display an income statement, a retained earnings statement, and a balance sheet.
8. Save your data file to disk.
9. End the session.

PROBLEM 22-5A
ENTRIES, TRIAL BALANCE,
AND FINANCIAL
STATEMENTS
Objectives 3, 4

The trial balance of the general ledger of Payne Corporation as of January 31, the end of the
first month of the current fiscal year, is shown below.

Payne Corporation
Trial Balance
January 31, 19—

Cash	54,840	
Accounts Receivable	111,180	
Finished Goods	106,800	
Work in Process	36,840	
Materials	44,340	
Plant Assets	474,600	
Accumulated Depreciation—Plant Assets		211,740
Accounts Payable		79,780
Wages Payable		9,000
Capital Stock		200,000
Retained Earnings		311,700
Sales		160,980
Cost of Goods Sold	120,000	
Factory Overhead	1,200	
Selling and Administrative Expenses	23,400	
	973,200	973,200

As of the same date, balances in the accounts of selected subsidiary ledgers are as follows:

Finished goods ledger:
  Commodity E, 3,500 units, $42,000
  Commodity F, 1,800 units, $27,000
  Commodity G, 1,400 units, $37,800
Cost ledger:
  Job 580, $36,840.
Materials ledger:
  Material M, $17,700
  Material N, $22,140
  Material O, $4,500

The transactions completed during February are summarized as follows:

a. Materials were purchased on account as follows:

Material M	$33,000
Material N	23,100
Material O	900

b. Materials were requisitioned from inventory as follows:

Job 580, Material M, $16,200; Material N, $14,178	$30,378
Job 581, Material M, $8,280; Material N, $3,324	11,604
Job 582, Material M, $12,720; Material N, $10,118	22,838
For general factory use, Material O	960

c. Time tickets for the month were chargeable as follows:

Job 580	$11,760	Job 582	$9,840
Job 581	10,080	Indirect labor	3,600

d. Factory payroll checks for $38,640 were issued.
e. Various factory overhead charges of $13,425 were incurred on account.
f. Depreciation of $5,400 of factory plant and equipment was recorded.
g. Factory overhead was applied to jobs at 70% of direct labor cost.
h. Jobs completed during the month were as follows: Job 580 produced 5,700 units of Commodity F; Job 582 produced 1,460 units of Commodity G.
i. Selling and administrative expenses of $22,920 were incurred on account.
j. Payments on account were $85,800.
k. Total sales on account were $167,800. The goods sold were as follows (use first-in, first-out method): 1,500 units of Commodity E; 3,200 units of Commodity F; 1,600 units of Commodity G.
l. Cash of $150,600 was received on accounts receivable.

Instructions

1. Record the January 31 balances in T accounts, identifying them as "Bal." Use a general ledger, a finished goods ledger, a cost ledger, and a materials ledger. Record the quantities as well as the dollar amounts in the finished goods ledger.
2. Journalize the entries to record the February transactions. After recording each transaction, post to the T accounts, using the identifying letters as dates. When posting to the finished goods ledger, record quantities as well as dollar amounts.
3. Prepare a trial balance.
4. Prepare schedules of the account balances in the finished goods ledger, the cost ledger, and the materials ledger.
5. Prepare an income statement for the two months ended February 28.

Instructions for Solving Problem 22-5A Using Solutions Software

1. Load opening balances.
2. Save the opening balances file to your drive and directory.
3. Set the run date to February 28 of the current year and enter your name.

SOLUTIONS
SOFTWARE

4. Enter the transactions in the General Journal. Key the letter of each transaction in the reference field. Note that in transactions (a), (b), and (c), accounts for specific materials (M,N, and O) and jobs (580, 581, and 582) are not available on the computer. Use the materials, work in process, and factory overhead accounts for these transactions.
5. Display a journal entries report.
6. Display a trial balance.
7. Display an income statement.
8. Save your data file to disk.
9. End the session.

PROBLEM 22-6A
DETERMINATION OF
AMOUNTS MISSING FROM
SELECTED ACCOUNTS IN
JOB COST SYSTEM
Objectives 3, 4

Following are selected accounts for Jenkins Products. For the purposes of this problem, some of the debits and credits have been omitted.

Accounts Receivable

Mar. 1	Balance	79,500	Mar. 31	Collections	118,400
31	Sales	(A)			

Materials

Mar. 1	Balance	17,500	Mar. 31	Requisitions	(B)
31	Purchases	45,000			

Work in Process

Mar. 1	Balance	24,000	Mar. 31	Goods finished	(E)
31	Direct materials	(C)			
31	Direct labor	48,200			
31	Factory overhead	(D)			

Finished Goods

Mar. 1	Balance	12,800	Mar. 31	Cost of goods sold	(G)
31	Goods finished	(F)			

Factory Overhead

Mar. 1	Balance	300	Mar. 31	Applied	28,920
1-31	Costs incurred	28,800			

Cost of Goods Sold

Mar. 31	(H)	

Sales

	Mar. 31	(I)

Selected balances at March 31:

Accounts receivable	$78,750
Finished goods	22,000
Work in process	27,300
Materials	15,000

Materials requisitions for March included $1,300 of materials issued for general factory use. All sales are made on account, terms n/30.

Instructions

1. Determine the amounts represented by the letters (A) through (I), presenting your computations.
2. Determine the amount of factory overhead overapplied or underapplied as of March 31.

Series B

PROBLEM 22-1B
ENTRIES FOR FLOW OF
COSTS THROUGH JOB
ORDER COST SYSTEM
Objectives 3, 4

L. Morrow Inc. uses a job order cost system. The following data summarize the operations related to production for June:

a. Materials purchased on account, $81,500.
b. Materials requisitioned, $79,200, of which $2,900 was for general factory use.
c. Factory labor used, $73,000, of which $7,500 was factory overhead.
d. Other costs incurred on account were for factory overhead, $25,150, selling expenses, $9,500, and administrative expenses, $7,500.
e. Prepaid expenses expired for factory overhead were $750, for selling expenses, $250, and for administrative expenses, $150.
f. Depreciation of factory equipment was $8,100, of store equipment, $500, and of office equipment, $300.
g. Application of factory overhead costs to jobs, $45,000.
h. Jobs completed, $190,500.
i. Cost of goods sold, $199,750.

Instructions
Journalize the entries to record the summarized operations.

PROBLEM 22-2B
ENTRIES AND SCHEDULES
FOR UNFINISHED AND
COMPLETED JOBS
Objectives 3, 4

Weaver Printing Inc. uses a job order cost system. The following data summarize the operations related to production for April, the first month of operations:

a. Materials purchased on account, $110,160.
b. Materials requisitioned and factory labor used:

	Materials	Factory Labor
Job 601	$15,840	$ 9,500
Job 602	10,380	7,040
Job 603	13,900	5,100
Job 604	20,950	13,380
Job 605	11,440	6,680
Job 606	7,100	2,900
For general factory use	2,300	1,760

c. Factory overhead costs incurred on account, $21,200.
d. Depreciation of machinery and equipment, $7,760.
e. The factory overhead rate is $15 per machine hour. Machine hours used:

Job 601	475
Job 602	352
Job 603	255
Job 604	669
Job 605	334
Job 606	145
Total	2,230

f. Jobs completed: 601, 602, 603, and 605.
g. Jobs were shipped and customers were billed as follows: Job 601: $49,250; Job 602: $31,100; and Job 605: $31,280.

Instructions

1. Journalize the entries to record the summarized operations.
2. Post the appropriate entries to T accounts for Work in Process and Finished Goods, using the identifying letters as dates. Insert memorandum account balances as of the end of the month.
3. Prepare a schedule of unfinished jobs to support the balance in the work in process account.
4. Prepare a schedule of completed jobs on hand to support the balance in the finished goods account.

If the working papers correlating with the textbook are not used, omit Problem 22-3B.

PROBLEM 22-3B
JOB ORDER COST SHEET
Objectives 3, 4

Ann Logan and Daughter Furniture repairs, refinishes, and reupholsters furniture. Logan uses a job order cost system.

When a prospective customer asks for a price quote on a job, the estimated cost data are inserted on an unnumbered job cost sheet. If the offer is accepted, a number is assigned to the job and the costs incurred are recorded in the usual manner on the job cost sheet. After the job is completed, reasons for the variances between the estimated and actual costs are noted on the sheet. The data are then available to management in evaluating the efficiency of operations and in preparing quotes on future jobs.

On April 9, an estimate of $665 for reupholstering a chair and couch was given to Alan Dodds. The estimate was based on the following data:

Estimated direct materials:	
8½ meters at $10 per meter	$ 85
Estimated direct labor:	
20 hours at $13 per hour	260
Estimated factory overhead (50% of direct labor cost)	130
Total estimated costs	$475
Markup (40% of production costs)	190
Total estimate	$665

On April 12, the chair and couch were picked up from the residence of Alan Dodds, 1927 Oak Tree Way, Columbus, with a commitment to return it on April 28. The job was completed on April 24.

The related materials requisitions and time tickets are summarized as follows:

Materials Requisition No.	Description	Amount
3480	8½ meters at $10	$ 85
3492	2 meters at $10	20

Time Ticket No.	Description	Amount
H143	15 hours at $13	$195
H151	7 hours at $13	91

SPREADSHEET PROBLEM

Instructions

1. Complete that portion of the job order cost sheet that would be prepared when the estimate is given to the customer.

SHARPEN YOUR COMMUNICATION SKILLS ►

2. Assign number R6-18 to the job, record the costs incurred, and complete the job order cost sheet. Comment on the reasons for the variances between actual costs and estimated costs. For this purpose, assume that 2 meters of materials were spoiled, the factory overhead rate has been proved to be satisfactory, and an inexperienced employee performed the work.

PROBLEM 22-4B
JOB ORDER COST
TRANSACTIONS AND
FINANCIAL STATEMENTS
Objectives 3, 4

The trial balance of Sloan Company at the beginning of the current fiscal year is as follows:

Sloan Company
Trial Balance
July 1, 19—

Cash	46,300	
Accounts Receivable	70,260	
Finished Goods	66,500	
Work in Process	24,360	
Materials	32,200	
Prepaid Expenses	8,600	
Plant Assets	582,400	
Accumulated Depreciation—Plant Assets		330,500
Accounts Payable		23,700
Wages Payable		—
Common Stock		100,000
Retained Earnings		376,420
Sales		—
Cost of Goods Sold	—	
Factory Overhead	—	
Selling Expenses	—	
Administrative Expenses	—	
	830,620	830,620

Transactions completed during July and adjustments required on July 31 are summarized as follows:

a. Materials purchased on account $27,480
b. Materials requisitioned for factory use:
    Direct $25,800
    Indirect   320   26,120
c. Factory labor costs incurred:
    Direct $12,960
    Indirect   1,840   14,800
d. Other costs and expenses incurred on account:
    Factory overhead $ 6,750
    Selling expenses   6,570
    Administrative expenses   4,800   18,120
e. Cash paid:
    Accounts payable $49,200
    Wages payable   13,300   62,500
f. Depreciation charged:
    Factory equipment $ 4,320
    Office equipment   360   4,680
g. Prepaid expenses expired:
    Chargeable to factory $ 640
    Chargeable to selling expenses   150
    Chargeable to administrative expenses   140   930
h. Applied factory overhead at a predetermined rate
    based on machine hours   14,256
i. Total cost of jobs completed   51,600
j. Sales, all on account:
    Selling price   67,200
    Cost   43,600
k. Cash received on account   68,400

Instructions

1. Record the July 1 balances in T accounts, identifying each as "Bal."
2. Record the transactions directly in the T accounts, using the identifying letters in place of dates.
3. Prepare an income statement for the month ended July 31, 19—.
4. Prepare a retained earnings statement for the month ended July 31, 19—.
5. Prepare a balance sheet as of July 31, 19—.

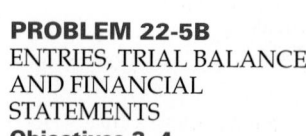
SOLUTIONS
SOFTWARE

Instructions for Solving Problem 22-4B Using Solutions Software

1. Load opening balances.
2. Save the opening balances file to your drive and directory.
3. Set the run date to July 31 of the current year and enter your name.
4. Select the General Journal Entries option and key the journal entries. Leave the reference field blank. Note: To review the chart of accounts, select F-1.
5. Display a journal entries report.
6. Display a trial balance.
7. Display an income statement, a retained earnings statement, and a balance sheet.
8. Save your data file to disk.
9. End the session.

PROBLEM 22-5B
ENTRIES, TRIAL BALANCE,
AND FINANCIAL
STATEMENTS
Objectives 3, 4

The trial balance of the general ledger of William Stark Co. as of July 31, the end of the first month of the current fiscal year, is shown below.

William Stark Co.
Trial Balance
July 31, 19—

Cash	92,000	
Accounts Receivable	185,300	
Finished Goods	187,600	
Work in Process	62,000	
Materials	72,900	
Plant Assets	810,000	
Accumulated Depreciation—Plant Assets		360,000
Accounts Payable		125,000
Wages Payable		15,000
Capital Stock		100,000
Retained Earnings		738,700
Sales		280,000
Cost of Goods Sold	168,000	
Factory Overhead	900	
Selling and Administrative Expenses	40,000	
	1,618,700	1,618,700

As of the same date, balances in the accounts of selected subsidiary ledgers are as follows:

Finished goods ledger:
   Commodity X, 2,000 units, $40,000
   Commodity Y, 6,000 units, $90,000
   Commodity Z, 3,200 units, $57,600
Cost ledger:
   Job 700, $62,000
Materials ledger:
   Material R15, $38,600
   Material Z10, $31,600
   Material W01, $2,700

The transactions completed during August are summarized as follows:

a. Materials were purchased on account as follows:

Material R15	$55,000
Material Z10	38,500
Material W01	1,500

b. Materials were requisitioned from inventory as follows:

Job 700, Material R15, $21,040; Material Z10, $16,800	$37,840
Job 701, Material R15, $27,000; Material Z10, $23,120	50,120
Job 702, Material R15, $13,800; Material Z10, $6,130	19,930
For general factory use, Material WO1	1,600

c. Time tickets for the month were chargeable as follows:

Job 700	$19,600	Job 702	$16,400
Job 701	16,800	Indirect labor	5,000

d. Factory payroll checks for $59,400 were issued.
e. Various factory overhead charges of $11,200 were incurred on account.
f. Selling and administrative expenses of $38,200 were incurred on account.
g. Payments on account were $140,000.
h. Depreciation of $10,300 of factory plant and equipment was recorded.
i. Factory overhead was applied to jobs at 60% of direct labor cost.
j. Jobs completed during the month were as follows: Job 700 produced 6,400 units of Commodity X; Job 701 produced 5,000 units of Commodity Y.
k. Total sales on account were $383,200. The goods sold were as follows (use first-in, first-out method): 4,600 units of Commodity X; 7,500 units of Commodity Y; 2,000 units of Commodity Z.
l. Cash of $250,000 was received on accounts receivable.

Instructions

1. Record the July 31 balances in T accounts, identifying them as "Bal." Use a general ledger, a finished goods ledger, a cost ledger, and a materials ledger. Record the quantities as well as the dollar amounts in the finished goods ledger.
2. Journalize the entries to record the August transactions. After recording each transaction, post to the T accounts, using the identifying letters as dates. When posting to the finished goods ledger, record quantities as well as dollar amounts.
3. Prepare a trial balance.
4. Prepare schedules of the account balances in the finished goods ledger, the cost ledger, and the materials ledger.
5. Prepare an income statement for the two months ended August 31.

Instructions for Solving Problem 22-5B Using Solutions Software

SOLUTIONS SOFTWARE

1. Load opening balances.
2. Save the opening balances file to your drive and directory.
3. Set the run date to August 31 of the current year and enter your name.
4. Enter the transactions in the General Journal. Key the letter of each transaction in the reference field. Note that in transactions (a), (b), and (c), accounts for specific materials (R15, Z10, and W01) and jobs (700, 701, and 702) are not available on the computer. Use the materials, work in process, and factory overhead accounts for these transactions.
5. Display a journal entries report.
6. Display a trial balance.
7. Display an income statement.
8. Save your data file to disk.
9. End the session.

PROBLEM 22-6B
DETERMINATION OF AMOUNTS MISSING FROM SELECTED ACCOUNTS IN JOB COST SYSTEM
Objectives 3, 4

Following are selected accounts for Marshall Products. For the purposes of this problem, some of the debits and credits have been omitted.

Accounts Receivable

Oct. 1	Balance	51,100	Oct. 31 Collections	105,500
31	Sales	(A)		

Materials

Oct. 1	Balance	12,100	Oct. 31 Requisitions	(B)
31	Purchases	16,300		

Work in Process

Oct. 1	Balance	21,000	Oct. 31 Goods finished	(E)
31	Direct materials	(C)		
31	Direct labor	22,400		
31	Factory overhead	(D)		

Finished Goods

Oct. 1	Balance	38,900	Oct. 31 Cost of goods sold	(G)
31	Goods finished	(F)		

Factory Overhead

Oct. 1	Balance	120	Oct. 31 Applied	17,920
1-31	Costs incurred	17,500		

Cost of Goods Sold

Oct. 31	(H)		

Sales

		Oct. 31	(I)

Selected balances at October 31:

Accounts receivable	$52,000
Finished goods	24,000
Work in process	17,800
Materials	9,500

Materials requisitions for October included $500 of materials issued for general factory use. All sales are made on account, terms n/30.

Instructions

1. Determine the amounts represented by the letters (A) through (I), presenting your computations.
2. Determine the amount of factory overhead overapplied or underapplied as of October 31.

MINI-CASE 22 ADLER INDUSTRIES

As an assistant cost accountant for Adler Industries, you have been assigned to review the activity driver for the predetermined factory overhead rate. The president, Calvin Adler, has expressed concern that the over- or underapplied overhead has fluctuated excessively over the years.

An analysis of the company's operations and use of the current overhead base (direct materials usage) has narrowed the possible alternative overhead bases to direct labor cost and machine hours. For the past five years, the following data have been gathered:

Instructions:

1. Calculate a predetermined factory overhead rate for each alternative base, assuming that the rates would have been determined by relating the amount of factory overhead for the past five years to the base.
2. For each of the past five years, determine the over- or underapplied overhead, based on the two predetermined overhead rates developed in (1).
3. ▓▓▓▓ ▸ Which predetermined overhead rate would you recommend? Discuss the basis for your recommendation.

	1994	1993	1992	1991	1990
Actual overhead	$ 840,000	$ 820,000	$ 900,000	$ 735,000	$ 705,000
Applied overhead	812,000	847,500	921,000	750,000	656,000
(Over) under-applied over-head	$ 28,000	$ (27,500)	$ (21,000)	$ (15,000)	$ 49,000
Direct labor cost	$3,350,000	$3,300,000	$3,625,000	$2,925,000	$2,800,000
Machine hours	663,000	645,000	726,000	597,000	569,000

ANSWERS TO SELF-EXAMINATION QUESTIONS

1. **C** Inventory accounts are maintained by manufacturing businesses for (1) goods in the process of manufacture (Work in Process—answer C), (2) goods in the state in which they are to be sold (Finished Goods—answer A), and (3) goods in the state in which they were acquired (Materials—answer B). Merchandise Inventory (answer D) is not a type of manufacturing inventory, but is inventory for a merchandising enterprise.

2. **D** The finished goods inventory is composed of three categories of manufacturing costs: direct materials (answer A), direct labor (answer B), and factory overhead (answer C).

3. **B** Factory overhead includes all manufacturing costs, except direct materials and direct labor. Salaries of plant supervisors (answer B) is an example of a factory overhead item. Wages of factory assembly-line workers (answer A) is a direct labor item, and bearings for electric motors (answer C) are direct materials.

4. **A** Job order cost systems are best suited to businesses manufacturing for special orders from customers, such as would be the case for a repair shop for antique furniture (answer A). A process cost system is best suited for manufacturers of homogeneous units of product, such as rubber (answer B) and coal (answer C).

5. **B** If the amount of factory overhead applied during a particular period exceeds the actual overhead costs, the factory overhead account will have a credit balance and is said to be overapplied (answer B) or overabsorbed. If the amount applied is less than the actual costs, the account will have a debit balance and is said to be underapplied (answer A) or underabsorbed (answer C). Since an "estimated" predetermined overhead rate is used to apply overhead, a credit balance does not necessarily represent an error (answer D).

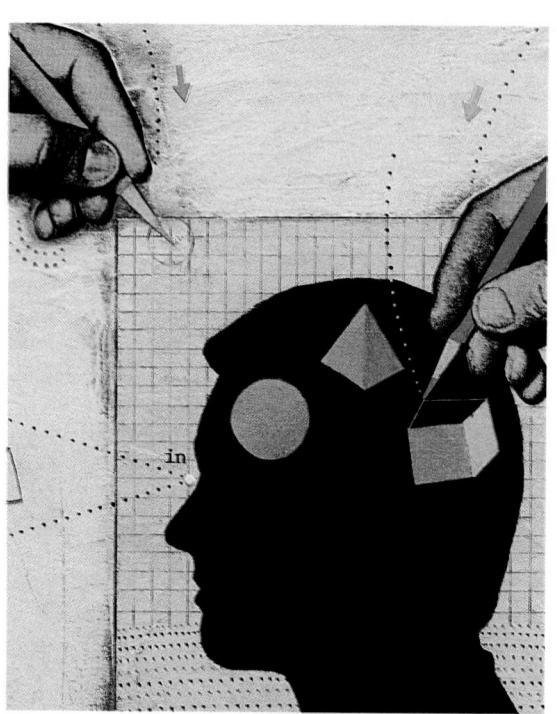

You and Accounting

Assume that you are planning on baking a birthday cake for your roommate. You would probably buy a cake mix and other necessary ingredients at the local grocery store. You would then follow the instructions on the cake box, mixing water, sugar, etc., with the dry mix and baking the cake at the proper temperature, and finally, add icing and the candles.

You probably wouldn't be too concerned with the total cost of the cake in this case. However, businesses are concerned with determining the cost of producing their products. For example, the cost of a product is a major concern in setting a product's selling price.

To illustrate the complexity of computing product costs, consider the problem of estimating the cost of the birthday cake. The cost of the cake mix and other ingredients can be easily determined. However, if you purchased a 5-lb. bag of sugar, you would need to allocate part of the total cost of the sugar to the cake. And what about the time you spent baking the cake? In business, the cost of labor must also be allocated to finished products. In addition, the cost of water used, electricity or gas used to operate the oven, and depreciation of the oven should be allocated to the cake.

Determining the cost of products in process at the end of the period is even more difficult. This chapter discusses how costs are accumulated and allocated to products in a manufacturing process that mass-produces large quantities of identical products, such as cakes.

Chapter 23
Process Cost Systems

After studying this chapter, you should be able to:

Objective 1
Compare and contrast a job order cost system and a process cost system.

Objective 2
Explain the flow of costs in a process cost system.

Objective 3
Explain the accounting for inventories of partially processed units, including the computation of equivalent units.

Objective 4
Prepare a cost of production report.

Objective 5
Allocate service department costs to producing departments.

Objective 6
Allocate product costs to joint products and by-products.

Objective 7
Illustrate the flow of costs, including journal entries, through a process cost accounting system.

Objective 8
Compute equivalent units of production, using the average cost method of inventory costing.

Objective 9
Explain the nature of hybrid cost accounting systems.

There are two primary types of cost accounting systems—job order cost and process cost. The job order cost system has been discussed. The use of a process cost system is discussed in this chapter. The chapter concludes with a brief discussion of hybrid cost systems, which are a combination of job order costing and process costing.

JOB ORDER COSTING AND PROCESS COSTING DISTINGUISHED

Objective 1
Compare and contrast a job order cost system and a process cost system.

The job order cost system is best suited to industries that fill special orders from customers or manufacture standard products in batches. Industries that normally use job order cost systems include special-order printing, custom-made tailoring, furniture manufacturing, shipbuilding, and construction. The process cost system is best suited for industries that mass-produce identical units of a product. Industries that commonly use process cost systems include chemicals, oil, cement, and food processing.

Process cost and job order cost systems are similar in many ways. Both systems accumulate product costs—direct materials, direct labor, and factory overhead—and allocate these costs to the units produced. For example, both systems maintain perpetual inventory accounts with subsidiary ledgers for materials, work in process, and finished goods. Both systems also provide product cost data to management for planning, organizing and directing, controlling, and decision making. The main difference between the two systems is the format in which the product costs are accumulated and reported.

In a job order cost system, product costs are accumulated by individual jobs and are summarized on job order cost sheets. The job order cost sheets provide unit cost information and can be used by management for such purposes as product pricing and cost control. In the process cost system, there is no need to accumulate costs by job orders, since the units of product that pass through several stages of production are identical. Thus, in the process cost system, costs are accumulated by department or process and are summarized in a cost of production report. The cost of production report provides unit cost information that is often used by management for such purposes as cost control.

FLOW OF COSTS IN A PROCESS COST SYSTEM

Objective 2
Explain the flow of costs in a process cost system.

In process cost accounting, product costs are accumulated in each department. In the processing departments, the costs incurred are accumulated in factory overhead and work in process accounts. If there is only one processing department, the cost accounting procedures are simple. In this case, product costs are debited to a single work in process account. The unit cost of the finished product is determined by dividing the total product cost by the number of units produced.

The manufacture of most products requires a sequence of different manufacturing processes. The output of Process 1 becomes the direct materials of Process 2, the output of Process 2 becomes the direct materials of Process 3, and so on until the product is finished. The product costs transferred from preceding departments and the costs of direct materials and direct labor incurred in each processing department are debited to the department's work in process account. Each departmental work in process account is also debited for the factory overhead applied.[1] All product costs are summarized periodically, usually at the end of the month. The costs related to the output of each department during the month are then transferred to the next processing department or to Finished Goods, as the case may be. This flow of costs through a work in process account for Bergen Manufacturing Inc. is illustrated in Exhibit 1.

Exhibit 1
Flow of Costs Through a Work in Process Account

Work in Process—Sanding Department

10,000 units at $9.60 from Assembly Dept.		96,000	To Polishing Dept., 10,000 units	160,000
Direct labor	36,800		(Cost per unit:	
Factory overhead	27,200	64,000	$160,000 ÷ 10,000 = $16)	
		160,000		160,000

The three debits in the work in process account in Exhibit 1 are normally grouped into two separate categories. The first category includes direct materials or

---

[1] The use of activity-based costing for accumulating and allocating overhead costs is discussed and illustrated in an appendix at the end of this chapter.

partially processed materials received from another department. In Exhibit 1, this is composed of 10,000 units received from the Assembly Department, with a total cost of $96,000. The second category includes direct labor and factory overhead applied in the Sanding Department, which in Exhibit 1 totals $64,000. This second category of costs is often called the **conversion cost** or **processing cost** for the department.

In Exhibit 1, all of the 10,000 units were completely processed in the Sanding Department and were transferred to the Polishing Department. The unit cost of the product transferred to the Polishing Department is $16. It is made up of Assembly Department cost of $9.60 ($96,000 ÷ 10,000 units) and conversion cost of $6.40 ($64,000 ÷ 10,000 units) incurred in the Sanding Department.

A New Way to Build Cars

One of the major industries that uses process cost accounting is the automobile manufacturing industry. Typically, cars are built as they move along an assembly line that provides little flexibility for the installation of the many options common to today's vehicles. Therefore, automakers are turning to modern technology in modifying the traditional assembly line. For example, in two assembly plants, hundreds of motorized, unmanned carriers move cars through the assembly process. The effect of using these carriers, called automated guided vehicles, in the production of cars is described in the following excerpts from an article in *The New York Times*:

When Henry Ford perfected the assembly line, he was making only one type of car, the Model T, which came in just one color, black. Since then, options have proliferated and today there can be as much as a 30 percent difference in the content of a stripped-down model and one fully loaded.

Because current lines move at a constant speed, regardless of the model mix, plant managers have had to hire enough workers to build the most complex car in the assigned amount of time. This means that some people are idle when base models come down the line. And because stopping the line to fix something

would idle thousands, most workers only tag an incorrectly fitting part and hope it will be repaired at the end of the line.

With the carriers, the notion of a "line" begins to fade, although the vehicles generally follow a prescribed path, receiving their instructions from wires buried in the plant floor. If a particular car has a heavy load of options, though, the vehicle may be directed to move out of the main [path] to have those parts installed, while less heavily equipped models continue along the route. G.M. engineers call this "decoupling the line." With this flexibility, plant managers will be able to balance the work force more closely with the workload....

The carriers also fit into the modular assembly concept that G.M. officials have called one of the keys to cutting manufacturing costs in its Saturn program. Instead of installing thousands of parts, one by one, on a car, a whole module, such as an instrument panel, will be built off the line, tested and only installed if it passes the tests. Since a carrier can be programmed to stop and go as needed, it could roll to the completed instrument panels and then stop to ease the installation....

"We couldn't have done this a few years ago," said ... the director of operations for G.M.'s Chevrolet-Pontiac-Canada group. "We need computers that can keep track of hundreds of carriers and decide on a minute-by-minute basis what station to assign them to, based on variations in the model mix."

Source: John Holusha, "A New Way to Build Cars," *The New York Times*, March 13, 1986.

INVENTORIES OF PARTIALLY PROCESSED UNITS

Objective 3
Explain the accounting for inventories of partially processed units, including the computation of equivalent units.

In Exhibit 1, all materials entering the Sanding Department were completely processed at the end of the accounting period. In such cases, determining unit costs is simple. The total product costs transferred from other departments plus the direct materials, the direct labor, and the factory overhead incurred within the department are divided by the number of units completed. Often, however, some partially processed materials remain in various stages of production in a department at the end of a period. In these cases, the product costs in work in process must be allocated between the completed and the partially completed units. The completed units will have been transferred to the next manufacturing department or to finished goods. Thus, the only costs that remain in the work in process account relate to the partially completed products.

Flow of Materials

To allocate product costs between the completed and partially completed units, it is necessary to determine how materials are added during the manufacturing process. For some products, materials are added uniformly throughout the manufacturing process. In these cases, the materials are added at approximately the same rate as conversion costs (direct labor and factory overhead) are incurred. In other situations, materials may enter the manufacturing process at relatively few points, which may or may not be evenly spaced throughout the process.

For many manufacturing processes, materials are added at the beginning of production, and the units are moved through the production processes in a first-in, first-out (fifo) flow. That is, the first units entering the production process are the first to be completed. The following discussion and illustrations will assume such a production process, where all materials are placed into production at the beginning of a process in a fifo order. The related manufacturing costs will also be allocated by the fifo cost method. Later in the chapter, an alternate method—the average cost method—will be discussed.

Equivalent Units of Production

When all materials are assumed to enter production at the beginning of a process, materials costs are allocated by multiplying the material unit costs by the number of units completed and the number of units partially completed. However, conversion costs (direct labor and factory overhead) are normally incurred uniformly during the production process. Thus, in order to allocate conversion costs, it is necessary to determine the number of equivalent units of production during the period. The **equivalent units of production** are the number of units that could have been manufactured from start to finish during the period.

During a period, a manufacturing department will normally have worked on the following three categories of units:

1. Partially completed units at the beginning of a period, which are completed during the period. At the end of the period, these units will have been transferred to the next department or to finished goods.
2. Units started and completed during the period. At the end of the period, these units will have been transferred to the next department or to finished goods.
3. Units started during the period but only partially completed at the end of the period. These units make up the department's ending work in process.

The computation of equivalent units for each of these three categories of units is illustrated below. For this illustration, the following data are assumed for the Polishing Department of Bergen Manufacturing Inc.:

Work in process inventory within Polishing Department on March 1	600 units; 1/3 completed
Units started during March (received from Sanding Department)	10,000 units
Completed in Polishing Department and transferred to finished goods during March	9,800 units, completed
Work in process inventory within Polishing Department on March 31	800 units, 2/5 completed

The equivalent units of production are determined as follows:

To process units in inventory on March 1 (600 units × 2/3)	400
To process units started and completed in March (9,800 units completed – 600 units in March 1 inventory)	9,200
To process units in inventory on March 31 (800 units × 2/5)	320
Equivalent units of production in March	9,920

The equivalent units of production necessary to complete the March 1 work in process inventory is determined by multiplying the number of units, 600, by the portion that needed to be completed during March. In this example, since the 600 units were 1/3 complete on March 1, the equivalent portion that was necessary to complete production during March is 2/3. Thus, the equivalent units related to the March 1 inventory is 400 (600 units × 2/3).

The units started and completed during March, 9,200, is computed by subtracting the 600 units in the March 1 work in process inventory from the total number of units completed, 9,800. The units started and completed during March could also be computed by subtracting the 800 units in work in process on March 31 from the total number of units started during March, 10,000.

The equivalent units for the March 31 inventory is determined by multiplying the number of units, 800, by the portion that was completed during March, 2/5. The 9,920 total equivalent units of production in March represents the number of units that would have been produced if there had been no inventories in process either at the beginning or at the end of the period.

Continuing the above illustration, the next step is to allocate the product costs incurred in the Polishing Department between the units completed during March and those remaining in process at the end of March. As noted earlier, it is assumed that all materials enter production at the beginning of the process. Thus, the full materials cost per unit is assigned to the uncompleted units. The conversion costs (direct labor and factory overhead) are allocated to the finished and the uncompleted units on the basis of equivalent units of production. These allocations and their effect on the Polishing Department's work in process account are shown in Exhibit 2.

Exhibit 2
Allocation of Product Costs to Finished Goods and Inventory

ACCOUNT WORK IN PROCESS—POLISHING DEPARTMENT   ACCOUNT NO.

					Balance	
Date		Item	Debit	Credit	Debit	Credit
Mar.	1	Bal. 600 units, 1/3 completed			10,200	
	31	Sanding Dept. 10,000 units at $16	160,000		170,200	
	31	Direct labor	26,640		196,840	
	31	Factory overhead	18,000		214,840	
	31	Goods finished, 9,800 units		200,600		
	31	Bal., 800 units, 2/5 completed			14,240	

Goods Finished During March

600 units:	Inventory on March 1, 1/3 completed	$ 10,200	
	Conversion cost in March:		
	600 × 2/3, or 400 units at $4.50	1,800	
	Total		$ 12,000
	(Unit cost: $12,000 ÷ 600 = $20)		
9,200 units:	Materials cost in March, at $16 per unit	$147,200	
	Conversion cost in March:		
	9,200 at $4.50 per unit	41,400	
	Total		188,600
	(Unit cost: $188,600 ÷ 9,200 = $20.50)		
9,800 units:	Goods finished during March		$200,600

Polishing Department Inventory on March 31

800 units:	Materials cost in March, at $16 per unit	$ 12,800
	Conversion cost in March:	
	800 × 2/5, or 320 at $4.50	1,440
800 units:	Polishing Department inventory on March 31	$ 14,240

The conversion costs incurred in the Polishing Department during March total $44,640 ($26,640 + $18,000). The equivalent units of production for March, determined above, is 9,920. The conversion cost per equivalent unit is therefore $4.50 ($44,640 ÷ 9,920). Of the $214,840 debited to the Polishing Department work in process account, $200,600 was transferred to Finished Goods and $14,240 remained in the account as work in process inventory.

COST OF PRODUCTION REPORT

Objective 4
Prepare a cost of production report.

A cost of production report is normally prepared at periodic intervals for each processing department. This report summarizes the following production quantity and cost data for each department:

1. The *units* for which the department is accountable and the disposition of those units.
2. The *product costs* incurred by the department and the allocation of those costs.

The cost of production report may be used as the basis for allocating product costs between Work in Process and Finished Goods. The report is also used to control costs. Each department head is responsible for the units entering production and the costs incurred in the department. Any differences in unit product costs from one month to another are studied carefully, and any significant differences are investigated.

As a basis for illustration, the data for the Polishing Department of Bergen Manufacturing Inc., presented in the preceding section, are used. The cost of production report based on these data is presented in Exhibit 3.

Exhibit 3
Cost of Production Report

Bergen Manufacturing Inc.
Cost of Production Report—Polishing Department
For the Month Ended March 31, 1994

Quantities:		
Charged to production:		
In process, March 1, 1994		600
Received from Sanding Department		10,000
Total units to be accounted for		10,600
Units accounted for:		
Transferred to finished goods		9,800
In process, March 31, 1994		800
Total units accounted for		10,600
Costs:		
Charged to production:		
In process, March 1, 1994		$ 10,200
March costs:		
Direct materials from Sanding Department		
($16 per unit)		160,000
Conversion costs:		
Direct labor	$ 26,640	
Factory overhead	18,000	
Total conversion costs ($4.50 per unit)		44,640
Total costs to be accounted for		$214,840
Costs allocated as follows:		
Transferred to finished goods:		
600 units at $20	$ 12,000	
9,200 units at $20.50	188,600	
Total cost of finished goods		$200,600
In process, March 31, 1994:		
Direct materials (800 units at $16)	$ 12,800	
Conversion costs (800 units × 2/5 at $4.50)	1,440	
Total cost of inventory in process, March 31, 1994		14,240
Total costs accounted for		$214,840
Computations:		
Equivalent units of production:		
To process units in inventory on March 1, 1994:		
600 units × 2/3		400
To process units started and completed in March:		
9,800 units − 600 units		9,200
To process units in inventory on March 31, 1994:		
800 units × 2/5		320
Equivalent units of production		9,920
Unit conversion cost: $44,640 ÷ 9,920		$4.50

SERVICE DEPARTMENTS AND PROCESS COSTS

Objective 5
Allocate service department costs to producing departments.

In a factory with several manufacturing processes, there may be one or more service departments. A **service department** does not process materials directly, but renders services to other departments. Examples of service departments are the factory office, the power plant, and the maintenance and repair shop. These departments perform services for the benefit of other production departments. The costs that they incur, therefore, are part of the total manufacturing costs and must be allocated or assigned to the processing departments. This allocation is performed periodically in order to debit the factory overhead accounts of the processing departments with their share of the costs incurred by the service departments. The period usually chosen is a month, although a different period of time may be used.

To illustrate, assume that the Power Department of Bergen Manufacturing Inc. produced 600 000 kilowatt-hours (kwh) during the month. The total cost of producing the power was $30,000, or $.05 per kilowatt-hour ($30,000 ÷ 600 000). The factory overhead accounts of the manufacturing departments that used the power during the month are allocated power costs at a rate of $.05 per kwh. The following amounts of power were used during the month:

Assembly Department	100 000 kwh
Sanding Department	300 000 kwh
Polishing Department	200 000 kwh

The entry to allocate the Power Department costs is as follows:

Factory Overhead—Assembly Dept.	5,000	
Factory Overhead—Sanding Dept.	15,000	
Factory Overhead—Polishing Dept.	10,000	
Power Dept.		30,000

The allocation of the power costs to the accounts is shown in Exhibit 4.

Exhibit 4
Allocation of Power Department Costs

Power Department			
Fuel	12,000	To Factory Overhead—	
Wages	8,500	Assembly Dept.	5,000
Depreciation	3,000	To Factory Overhead—	
Maintenance	2,500	Sanding Dept.	15,000
Insurance	2,000	To Factory Overhead—	
Taxes	1,500	Polishing Dept.	10,000
Miscellaneous	500		
	30,000		30,000

Factory Overhead—Assembly Dept.	
Power	5,000

Factory Overhead—Sanding Dept.	
Power	15,000

Factory Overhead—Polishing Dept.	
Power	10,000

In the above illustration, there was only one service department. In some manufacturing companies, there may be several service departments. In addition, some service departments may render services to other service departments. For example, the Power Department may supply power for the factory office to operate data processing equipment. At the same time, the factory office provides general supervision for the Power Department, maintains its payroll records, buys its fuel, and so on. In such cases, the costs of the department rendering the greatest service to the other departments are allocated first, despite the fact that this department receives benefits from other service departments.

The costs of the department rendering the next largest amount of services are allocated next, and so on.[2]

JOINT PRODUCTS AND BY-PRODUCTS

Objective 6
Allocate product costs to joint products and by-products.

In some manufacturing processes, more than one product is produced. In processing cattle, for example, the meat packer produces dressed beef, hides, and other products. In processing logs, the lumber mill produces several grades of lumber in addition to scraps and sawdust. When the output of a manufacturing process consists of two or more different products, joint products or by-products may be produced.

When two or more goods of significant value are produced from a direct material, the products are called **joint products**. Likewise, the costs incurred in the manufacture of joint products are called **joint costs.** Common examples of joint products from the processing of crude oil are gasoline, naphtha, kerosene, paraffin, and benzine.

If one of the products of a manufacturing process has little value in relation to the main product or joint products, it is called a **by-product.** By-products are only incidental to the manufacture of the main product or joint products. By-products may be leftover materials, such as sawdust and scraps of wood in a lumber mill. By-products may be separated from the material at the beginning of production, as in the case of cottonseed from raw cotton.

Accounting for Joint Products

In deciding whether to produce and sell joint products, only the total revenue and total costs from the production and sale of the joint products as a group are relevant. Nothing is gained from allocating the joint costs to *each* product in making this decision. This is because one product cannot be produced without the others. A decision to produce a single joint product is in effect a decision to produce all of the joint products.

To value inventories of the various products and to determine the cost of goods sold, however, it is necessary to allocate joint costs among the joint products. Since joint products are processed from one material, costs cannot be traced to each separate product, based upon actual expenditures. Thus, a systematic, logical approach must be used to allocate joint costs to joint products.

One approach to allocating joint costs is the **market (sales) value method**. Under this method, joint costs are allocated on the basis of the relative sales values of the joint products. To illustrate, assume that 10,000 units of Product X and 50,000 units of Product Y were produced at a total cost of $63,000. The sales values of the two products and the allocation of the joint costs are shown in Exhibit 5.

Exhibit 5
Allocation of Joint Costs

Joint Costs	Joint Product	Units Produced	Sales Value per Unit	Total Sales Value
$63,000 {	X	10,000	$3.00	$30,000
	Y	50,000	1.20	60,000
	Total sales value			$90,000

Allocation of joint costs:

X: $\dfrac{\$30,000}{\$90,000} \times \$63,000$ **$21,000**

Y: $\dfrac{\$60,000}{\$90,000} \times \$63,000$ 42,000

Unit cost:

X: **$21,000** ÷ 10,000 units $2.10

Y: **$42,000** ÷ 50,000 units   .84

---

[2] Other approaches to service department cost allocations are discussed in advanced cost accounting texts.

Accounting for By-Products

The manufacturing cost allocated to a by-product is normally the sales value of the by-product less any additional costs necessary to complete and sell it. This cost is credited to the work in process account related to the manufacturing process that created the by-product. A finished goods inventory account is debited for the cost of the by-product.

To illustrate, assume that during April the Filtering Department incurred costs of $24,400 in processing the main product and also produced 1,000 gallons of by-product B. The estimated value of the by-product is $700, after estimated completion and selling costs have been deducted. The allocation of manufacturing costs to the by-product on April 30 is recorded by the following entry.

| Apr. 30 | Finished Goods—Product B | 700 | |
| | Work in Process—Filtering Dept. | | 700 |

ILLUSTRATION OF PROCESS COST ACCOUNTING

Objective 7
Illustrate the flow of costs, including journal entries, through a process cost accounting system.

The basic procedures and journal entries used in a process costing system are illustrated in this section, using a comprehensive illustration. As a basis for the illustration, assume that Montoya Inc. manufactures Product A. The manufacturing activity begins in Department 1, where all materials enter production. The materials are processed quickly in Department 1. As a result, there is usually no inventory of work in process in Department 1 at the end of the period. From Department 1, the materials are transferred to Department 2. In Department 2, there are usually inventories at the end of the accounting period. Separate factory overhead accounts are used for Departments 1 and 2. Factory overhead is applied at the rates of $.80 per machine hour for Department 1 and $.50 per machine hour for Department 2. There is one service department, Power. Power costs are allocated using a rate of $.05 per kwh. All inventories are costed by the first-in, first-out method.

The trial balance on January 1, the first day of the fiscal year for Montoya Inc., is as follows:

Montoya Inc.
Trial Balance
January 1, 1994

Cash	39,400	
Accounts Receivable	45,000	
Finished Goods—Product A (1,000 units at $36.50)	36,500	
Work in Process—Department 2 (800 units, 1/2 completed)	24,600	
Materials	32,000	
Prepaid Expenses	6,150	
Plant Assets	510,000	
Accumulated Depreciation—Plant Assets		295,000
Accounts Payable		51,180
Wages Payable		3,400
Common Stock		250,000
Retained Earnings		94,070
	693,650	693,650

Entries for the January transactions of Montoya Inc. are stated in summary form. In practice, the transactions would be recorded daily. The descriptions of the transactions and the entries are as follows:

(a) Materials purchased and prepaid expenses incurred	Materials	80,500	
	Prepaid Expenses	3,300	
	Accounts Payable		83,800

(b) Materials requisitioned for use	Power Department	6,300	
	Factory Overhead—Department 1	6,420	
	Factory Overhead—Department 2	5,700	
	Work in Process—Department 1	58,500	
	Materials		76,920

(c) Factory labor used	Power Department	4,500	
	Factory Overhead— Department 1	2,850	
	Factory Overhead— Department 2	2,100	
	Work in Process— Department 1	24,900	
	Work in Process— Department 2	37,800	
	Wages Payable		72,150

(d) Other costs incurred	Power Department	900	
	Factory Overhead—Department 1	1,800	
	Factory Overhead—Department 2	1,200	
	Selling Expenses	15,000	
	Administrative Expenses	13,500	
	Accounts Payable		32,400

(e) Expiration of prepaid expenses	Power Department	750	
	Factory Overhead—Department 1	1,350	
	Factory Overhead—Department 2	1,050	
	Selling Expenses	900	
	Administrative Expenses	600	
	Prepaid Expenses		4,650

(f) Depreciation	Power Department	1,050	
	Factory Overhead—Department 1	1,800	
	Factory Overhead—Department 2	2,700	
	Selling Expenses	600	
	Administrative Expenses	300	
	Accumulated Depreciation—Plant Assets		6,450

(g) Distribution of Power Department costs	Factory Overhead—Department 1	5,400	
	Factory Overhead—Department 2	8,100	
	Power Department		13,500

     Department 1 used 108 000 kwh and Department 2 used 162 000 kwh. Power is allocated at a rate of $.05 per kwh.

(h) Application of factory overhead costs to work in process	Work in Process—Department 1	19,920	
	Work in Process—Department 2	18,900	
	Factory Overhead—Department 1		19,920
	Factory Overhead—Department 2		18,900

     Factory overhead is applied at a rate of $.80 per machine hour in Department 1 and $.50 per machine hour in Department 2. The machine usage reports for January indicate that Department 1 used 24,900 machine hours and Department 2 used 37,800 machine hours.

| (i) Transfer of production costs from Department 1 to Department 2 | Work in Process—Department 2 | 103,320 | |
| | Work in Process—Department 1 | | 103,320 |

During January, 4,100 units were started in Department 1 and transferred to Department 2. There was no work in process in Department 1 at the beginning or at the end of January.

Total costs charged to Department 1:	
Direct materials	$ 58,500
Direct labor	24,900
Factory overhead	19,920
Total costs	$103,320
Unit cost of product transferred to Department 2:	
$103,320 ÷ 4,100	$ 25.20

(j) Transfer of production costs from Department 2 to Finished Goods

Finished Goods—Product A	153,840	
Work in Process—Department 2		153,840

During January, Department 2 completed 4,000 units, which were transferred to Finished Goods. On January 31, 900 units remain in process in Department 2. These units are 2/3 finished.

Equivalent units of production for Department 2:	
To process units in inventory on January 1:	
$800 \times 1/2$	400
To process units started and completed in January:	
$4,000 - 800$	3,200
To process units in inventory on January 31:	
$900 \times 2/3$	600
Equivalent units of production in January	4,200

Conversion costs:	
Direct labor [transaction (c)]:	$ 37,800
Factory overhead [transaction (h)]:	18,900
Total conversion costs	$ 56,700

Unit conversion cost:	
$56,700 ÷ 4,200	$ 13.50

Allocation of costs of Department 2:		
Units started in December, completed in January:		
Inventory on January 1, 800 units, 1/2 completed	$24,600	
Conversion costs in January, 400 at $13.50	5,400	
Total ($30,000 ÷ 800 = $37.50 unit cost)		$ 30,000
Units started and completed in January:		
From Department 1, 3,200 units at $25.20	$80,640	
Conversion costs, 3,200 at $13.50	43,200	
Total ($123,840 ÷ 3,200 = $38.70 unit cost)		123,840
Total transferred to Finished Goods—Product A		$153,840
Units started in January, 2/3 completed:		
From Department 1, 900 units at $25.20	$22,680	
Conversion costs, 600 at $13.50	8,100	
Total work in process—Department 2		30,780
Total costs charged to Department 2		$184,620

(k) Cost of goods sold

Cost of Goods Sold	143,900	
Finished Goods—Product A		143,900

Product A, 3,800 units:	
1,000 units at $36.50	$ 36,500
800 units at $37.50	30,000
2,000 units at $38.70	77,400
Total cost of goods sold	$143,900

		Debit	Credit
(l) Sales	Accounts Receivable	210,500	
	Sales		210,500
(m) Cash received	Cash	200,000	
	Accounts Receivable		200,000
(n) Cash paid	Accounts Payable	120,000	
	Wages Payable	72,500	
	Cash		192,500

A chart of the flow of costs from the service and processing department accounts into the finished goods account and then to the cost of goods sold account is shown in Exhibit 6. Entries in the accounts are identified by letters as an aid to tracing the flow of costs to the preceding journal entries.

Exhibit 6
Flow of Costs Through Process Cost Accounts

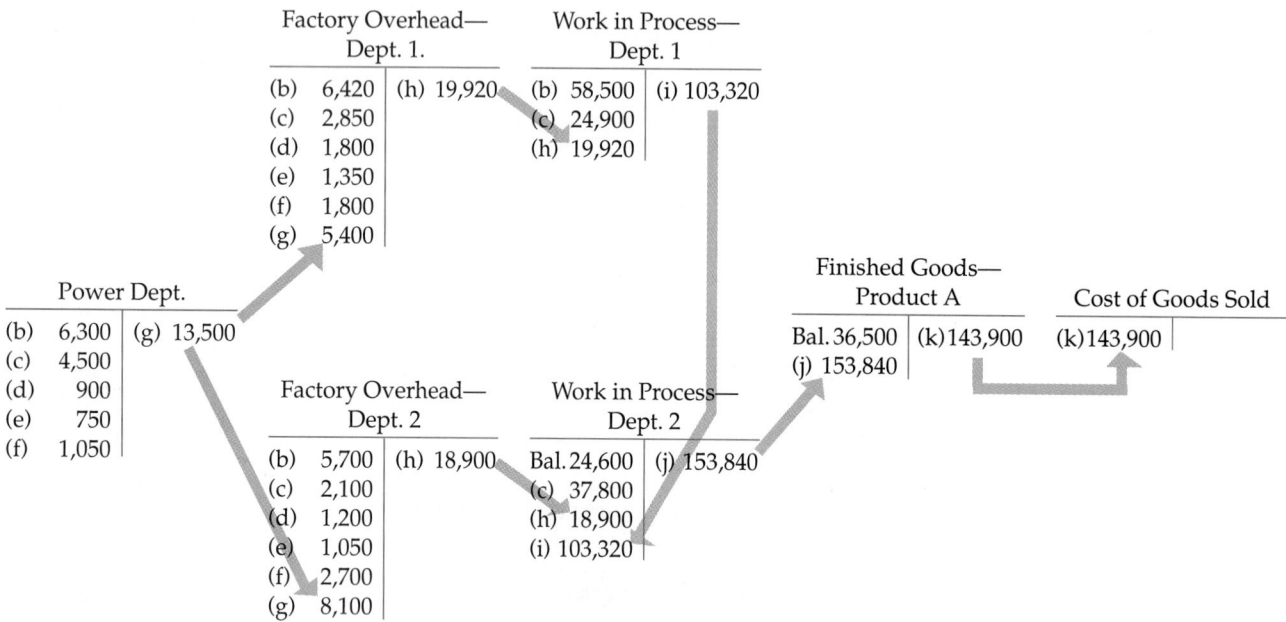

Cost of Production Reports

The cost of production reports for Departments 1 and 2 are presented in Exhibit 7.

Exhibit 7
Cost of Production Reports

Montoya Inc.
Cost of Production Report— Department 1
For the Month Ended January 31, 1994

Quantities:		
Units charged to production and to be accounted for		4,100
Units accounted for and transferred to Department 2		4,100
Costs:		
Costs charged to production in January:		
Direct materials		$ 58,500
Direct labor		24,900
Factory overhead		19,920
Total costs to be accounted for		$103,320
Total costs accounted for and transferred to Department 2		
(4,100 units × $25.20)		$103,320

Exhibit 7
Concluded

Montoya Inc.
Cost of Production Report—Department 2
For the Month Ended January 31, 1994

Quantities:
  Charged to production:
    In process, January 1, 1994 800
    Received from Department 1 4,100
    Total units to be accounted for 4,900
  Units accounted for:
    Transferred to finished goods 4,000
    To process, January 31, 1994 900
    Total units accounted for 4,900

Costs:
  Charged to production:
    In process, January 1, 1994 .... $ 24,600
    January costs:
      Direct materials from Department 1
        ($25.20 per unit) 103,320
      Conversion costs:
        Direct labor .... $ 37,800
        Factory overhead 18,900
        Total conversion cost ($13.50 per unit) 56,700
    Total costs to be accounted for $184,620
  Costs allocated as follows:
    Transferred to finished goods:
      800 units at $37.50 .... $ 30,000
      3,200 units at $38.70 123,840
      Total cost of finished goods $153,840
    In process, January 31, 1994:
      Direct materials (900 units at $25.20) .... $ 22,680
      Conversion costs (900 units × 2/3 × $13.50) 8,100
      Total cost of inventory in process, January 31, 1994 30,780
    Total costs accounted for $184,620

Computations:
  Equivalent units of production:
    To process units in inventory on January 1, 1994:
      800 units × 1/2 400
    To process units started and completed in January:
      4,000 units - 800 units 3,200
    To process units in inventory on January 31, 1994:
      900 units × 2/3 600
      Equivalent units of production 4,200
  Unit conversion cost:
    $56,700 ÷ 4,200 .... $13.50

Financial Statements

The financial statements for process cost systems are similar to those for job order cost systems. To illustrate, the January 31 trial balance and the condensed financial statements for Montoya Inc. are presented in Exhibit 8. Because the financial statements are interim statements for January, the net underapplied factory overhead of $1,650 ($1,950 – $300) is reported on the balance sheet as a deferred item.

Exhibit 8
Trial Balance and Financial Statements

Montoya Inc.
Trial Balance
January 31, 1994

Cash	46,900	
Accounts Receivable	55,500	
Finished Goods—Product A (1,200 units at $38.70)	46,440	
Work in Process—Department 2		
(900 units, 2/3 completed)	30,780	
Materials	35,580	
Prepaid Expenses	4,800	
Plant Assets	510,000	
Accumulated Depreciation—Plant Assets		301,450
Accounts Payable		47,380
Wages Payable		3,050
Common Stock		250,000
Retained Earnings		94,070
Sales		210,500
Cost of Goods Sold	143,900	
Factory Overhead—Department 1		300
Factory Overhead—Department 2	1,950	
Selling Expenses	16,500	
Administrative Expenses	14,400	
	906,750	906,750

Montoya Inc.
Income Statement
For Month Ended January 31, 1994

Sales		$210,500
Cost of goods sold		143,900
Gross profit		$ 66,600
Operating expenses:		
Selling expenses	$ 16,500	
Administrative expenses	14,400	
Total operating expenses		30,900
Income from operations		$ 35,700

Montoya Inc.
Retained Earnings Statement
For Month Ended January 31, 1994

Retained earnings, January 1, 1994	$ 94,070
Income for the month	35,700
Retained earnings, January 31, 1994	$129,770

Montoya Inc.
Balance Sheet
January 31, 1994

Assets				Liabilities		
Current assets:				Current liabilities:		
Cash		$ 46,900		Accounts payable	$ 47,380	
Accounts receivable		55,500		Wages payable	3,050	
Inventories:				Total liabilities		$ 50,430
Finished goods	$46,440					
Work in process	30,780					
Materials	35,580	112,800				
Prepaid expenses		4,800				
Total current assets			$220,000	**Stockholders' Equity**		
Plant assets		$510,000		Common stock	$250,000	
Less accumulated depreciation		301,450	208,550	Retained earnings	129,770	
Deferred debits:				Total stockholders' equity		379,770
Factory overhead underapplied			1,650	Total liabilities and		
Total assets			$430,200	stockholders' equity		$430,200

INVENTORY COSTING METHODS

Objective 8
Compute equivalent units of production, using the average cost method of inventory costing.

Throughout the preceding sections of this chapter, the first-in, first-out (fifo) cost method was used in determining product costs. The average cost method may also be used. Under the average cost method, all costs incurred in manufacturing the goods completed during a period are averaged. This average is then used in determining the unit product costs of the goods completed during the period and the work in process at the end of the period. Although the average cost method is not as accurate nor as useful to management in controlling costs as the fifo method, it is simpler to use and is therefore encountered in practice.

First-In, First-Out (Fifo) Cost Method

In most manufacturing processes, materials and products physically flow in a first-in, first-out manner. In other words, the first units entering the process are the first completed. In such processes, the work in process at the beginning of the period is completed before work is completed on new materials entering the process. The first-in, first-out cost method is consistent with this physical flow of products and is widely used.

When the fifo cost method is used, the beginning work in process product costs are kept separate from the costs incurred during the current period. As a result, the fifo cost method normally yields the following two unit costs for products completed during a period:

1. Unit cost of the units completed from the beginning work in process.
2. Unit cost of units started and completed during the current period.

These two unit costs are useful to management in controlling product costs. Management can compare the unit costs of the current period with the equivalent unit costs of the preceding periods. Any major differences can then be investigated on a timely basis and any necessary actions taken.

Although using two separate costs assists in the control of costs, it increases the complexity of determining unit costs. This complexity is increased even further when products completed by one process are used in subsequent processes. Primarily for these reasons, some enterprises prefer to use the average cost method.

Average Cost Method

The average cost method treats work in process (both units and costs) at the beginning of the current period as if the work in process was started and completed during the current period. In this way, the average cost method determines only one unit cost for products completed during a period. Although not as accurate as the fifo cost method, the average cost method avoids the problem of having two unit cost amounts for products completed during a period. When the average cost method is used, it is more difficult for management to evaluate and control current operations, since past costs and current costs are averaged.

To illustrate, assume the following data for the Cutting Department of Perrin Company for July of the current year. Assume also that all materials used in the Cutting Department are added at the beginning of the process.

Inventory in process, July 1, 500 units:		
Materials cost, 500 units	$24,550	
Conversion costs, 500 units, 70% completed	3,600	$28,150
Materials cost for July, 1,000 units		50,000
Conversion costs for July, 1000 units		9,660
Goods finished in July (includes units in process on July 1),		
1,100 units		—
Inventory in process, July 31, 400 units, 50% completed		—

To apply the average cost method, the average materials cost per unit and the average conversion cost per unit must be determined for July. These costs are computed in Exhibit 9.

Exhibit 9
Average Materials Cost per Unit
and Average Conversion Cost per
Unit

Materials cost for 500 units in process at July 1	$24,550
Materials cost for 1,000 units for July	50,000
Total materials cost (1,500 units)	$74,550
Average materials cost per unit ($74,550 ÷ 1,500)	$ 49.70
Conversion costs for units in process at July 1	$ 3,600
Conversion costs for July	9,660
Total conversion costs	$13,260
Equivalent units of production:	
To process units in inventory on July 1	500
To process units started and completed in July (1,100 units – 500 units)	600
To process units in inventory on July 31 (400 units × 50%)	200
Equivalent units of production in July	1,300
Average conversion cost per unit ($13,260 ÷ 1,300)	$10.20

In determining the average unit materials cost, the cost of materials in work in process on July 1 (the beginning inventory) is added to the materials cost for July. The total materials cost is then divided by the total units of materials in the cutting process during July. Likewise, in determining the average unit conversion cost, the conversion costs in work in process on July 1 (the beginning inventory) are added to the conversion costs for July. The total conversion cost is then divided by the equivalent units of production for July.

As discussed, the units in the beginning work in process are treated as if they were started and completed during the current period. In the above illustration, the beginning inventory of 500 units (70% complete) is treated as 500 units fully completed during the current period. To the 500 units is added the 600 equivalent units started and completed in the current period and the 200 equivalent units for work in process on July 31. The total equivalent units of production are thus 1,300 units, as shown in Exhibit 9. The total equivalent units may also be computed by adding the total of the units completed during the period, 1,100, and the equivalent units in the ending work in process, 200.

Using the average unit costs computed in Exhibit 9, the cost of finished goods during July and the cost of work in process on July 31 (ending inventory) can be determined as follows:

Goods finished during July:	
1,100 units: 1,100 units at $49.70 for materials costs	$54,670
1,100 units at $10.20 for conversion costs	11,220
Total (1,100 units at $59.90)	$65,890
Work in process, July 31:	
400 units: 400 units at $49.70 for materials costs	$19,880
400 units × 50% × $10.20 for conversion costs	2,040
Total	$21,920

When product costs do not change significantly from period to period, there is little difference between the unit costs for the average cost and the fifo cost methods. In these cases, the simpler average cost method is often used.

Inventory Costing Methods and Just-In-Time Manufacturing

As mentioned in an earlier chapter, more and more manufacturers are using just-in-time (JIT) manufacturing systems. In JIT manufacturing, materials are received *just in time* to enter production and the product is finished *just in time* to meet the demands of the next process or to meet customer orders. In a pure JIT system, little or no work in process will exist at the end of the period. Therefore, all product costs of the period can be traced to completed products. In such cases, product costs are applied to the units transferred to the Finished Goods when the products are completed. This transfer of costs is sometimes called **backflush costing** since production costs are said to be "flushed" out of the accounting system when products are completed.

HYBRID COST ACCOUNTING SYSTEMS

Objective 9
Explain the nature of hybrid cost accounting systems.

The two most commonly used cost systems—job order cost and process cost—have been described and illustrated. Some products have production characteristics that are common to both job order and process systems. For example, a manufacturer of men's sport shirts may mass-produce the shirts through a continuous-flow manufacturing process (cutting materials, sewing, etc.). Such a process is common for a process cost system. However, the shirts may then be customized by adding a customer's logo to a specific batch of shirts. Such a process is common for a job order cost system.

When continuous-flow processing is combined with custom-order processing, it is best to use a cost system that is specifically designed for the production process. Such a hybrid cost system would include characteristics of both process costing and job order costing.

One hybrid system, called an **operational cost system**, is used frequently in practice. Under an operational cost system, costs are accumulated for each batch of custom-ordered merchandise. For example, a shoe manufacturer may make shoes in batches. Each batch is unique, yet its manufacture shares common characteristics (processes) with other batches. For example, some batches of shoes are made using leather, and others are made using vinyl. In such cases, the materials costs (leather or vinyl) are accumulated for each batch, as in a job order cost system. However, all batches may be cut and sewed using the same basic processing procedures. The conversion costs—direct labor and factory overhead—are assigned to the product, as in a process cost system. Thus, operational costing is often used by manufacturers whose products are produced in batches that can vary from model to model or from style to style.

APPENDIX

ACTIVITY-BASED COSTING AND COST ALLOCATION

As discussed in this chapter and the job order cost chapter, factory overhead costs may be allocated by using predetermined rates. In the job order cost chapter, predetermined plant-wide overhead rates were used. In this chapter, departmental overhead rates were used.

The following paragraphs further discuss the use of plant-wide and departmental overhead rates. This appendix then discusses and illustrates how activity-based costing may provide more accurate and useful product cost data.

Plant-Wide and Departmental Overhead Rates

When a plant-wide factory overhead rate is used, the total factory overhead is applied to all products by that single rate. This rate is usually determined by using a volume-related activity driver, such as units produced, machine hours, direct labor hours, or direct labor dollars. The use of a plant-wide overhead rate assumes that the activities causing overhead costs are the same across all departments and products. If this is not the case, overhead costs could be misallocated and product costs could be distorted.

When production departments differ significantly in their manufacturing processes, overhead costs are likely to be incurred differently in each department. In such cases, overhead costs may be more accurately allocated by the use of departmental overhead rates than by a plant-wide rate. If the bases used to allocate factory overhead costs do not reflect the underlying causes of the overhead, however, misallocations may occur and product costs may be distorted. For example, Rockwell International conducted a special study after one of its best-selling axles had begun losing market share. The study found that incorrect factory overhead cost allocations had "overcosted" its highest-volume axle by roughly 20%, while underestimating the cost of low-volume axles by as much as 40%. Since sales prices were based on these estimated costs, Rockwell had underpriced its low-volume axles and overpriced its high-volume axle. As a result, competitors had begun to lure customers away from Rockwell's best-selling, high-volume axles.[3]

Activity-Based Costing (ABC)

Some overhead costs may not be directly related to volume-based activity drivers, such as units produced, machine hours, or direct labor hours. Thus, the use of such activity drivers for applying plant-wide or departmental overhead rates has the potential to distort product costs. Such distortions tend to allocate more overhead to the high-volume products and less overhead to the low-volume products, as in the preceding Rockwell International example.

When the use of plant-wide or departmental overhead rates distort product costs, companies may use activity-based costing. Activity-based costing (ABC) is a cost allocation method that initially traces or allocates costs to activities. In this first stage of product costing, overhead costs are traced to activities, such as machine usage, inspections, and production setups. In the second stage of product costing, costs are traced or allocated to the finished products. Overhead costs are allocated to products on the basis of the number of the activities, such as the number of production setups, involved in each product's manufacture.

To illustrate the application of ABC, assume that Weiss Inc. manufactures two products, X and Y. The production of these products requires four overhead activities—power, maintenance, quality control, and setup. The following expected overhead costs for these activities are to be allocated to Products X and Y:

---

[3] "Accounting Bores You? Wake Up," Ford S. Worthy, *Fortune*, October 12, 1987.

	Overhead Costs
Power	$360,000
Maintenance	105,000
Quality control	51,000
Setup	84,000
Total	$600,000

In applying ABC, the overhead activities must be analyzed to determine how the costs for these activities are incurred. That is, the activity drivers must be identified. For Weiss Inc., the appropriate activity drivers are as follows:

	Activity Driver
Power	Kilowatt-hours
Maintenance	Machine hours
Quality control	Number of inspections
Setup	Number of setups

The amounts of the activity drivers for each product are as follows:

	Kilowatt-Hours	Machine Hours	Number of Inspections	Number of Production Setups
Product X	800 000	10,000	400	48
Product Y	3 200 000	40,000	600	72
Total	4 000 000	50,000	1,000	120

Based upon the preceding data, the rates for each overhead activity are determined by dividing each overhead cost by its activity driver, as indicated below.

Power overhead rate = $360,000 ÷ 4 000 000 kilowatt-hours
Power overhead rate = $.09 per kilowatt-hour

Maintenance overhead rate = $105,000 ÷ 50,000 machine hours
Maintenance overhead rate = $2.10 per machine hour

Quality control overhead rate = $51,000 ÷ 1,000 inspections
Quality control overhead rate = $51 per inspection

Setup overhead rate = $84,000 ÷ 120 setups
Setup overhead rate = $700 per setup

Using the above rates, the overhead costs would be allocated to Products X and Y as shown below.

	Product X	Product Y
Overhead costs:		
Power:		
800,000 hours × $.09	$ 72,000	
3,200,000 hours × $.09		$288,000
Maintenance:		
10,000 hours × $2.10	21,000	
40,000 hours × $2.10		84,000
Quality control:		
400 inspections × $51	20,400	
600 inspections × $51		30,600
Setup:		
48 setups × $700	33,600	
72 setups × $700		50,400
Total	$147,000	$453,000

For Weiss Inc., a different activity driver was used for each overhead activity. In practice, many companies could identify a large number of overhead activities and it could become very costly to allocate each activity separately. For example, the preceding illustration assumed that kilowatt-hours could be traced directly to individual products. In practice, it would be very costly, if not impossible, to do so. In such cases, overhead activities may be grouped together in cost pools, and each cost pool would be allocated using a primary activity driver related to the costs within that pool. This reduces the cost of measuring a large number of activity drivers and simplifies the allocation process.

To illustrate, the percentage of each activity driver used by Product X and Product Y for Weiss Inc. is as follows:

	Kilowatt-Hours	Machine Hours	Number of Inspections	Number of Production Setups
Product X	20%*	20%**	40%***	40%****
Product Y	80*	80**	60***	60****
Total	100%	100%	100%	100%

*800 000 ÷ 4 000 000 (Product X) and 3 200 000 ÷ 4 000 000 (Product Y)
**10,000 ÷ 50,000 (Product X) and 40,000 ÷ 50,000 (Product Y)
***400 ÷ 1,000 (Product X) and 600 ÷ 1,000 (Product Y)
****48 ÷ 120 (Product X) and 72 ÷ 120 (Product Y)

Although each overhead cost could be allocated separately on the basis of the activity drivers identified, as illustrated previously, the expense of the allocation would be reduced by grouping activities into appropriate cost pools. These cost pools are identified in such a way that the costs within the pool are related to one primary activity driver.

As shown in the above table, Product X consumes or uses 20% of the power activity measure of kilowatt-hours and 20% of the maintenance activity measure of machine hours. Similarly, Product X uses 40% of the quality control and setups activity measures. Since power and maintenance have common kilowatt-hours and machine hours usage rates of 20% for Product X and 80% for Product Y, they can be pooled and applied to the two products, using either one of the activity measures. Similarly, the quality control and setup activities may be pooled and allocated, using either the number of inspections or the number of production setups. The activity measure selected should be the one that is the least costly to identify, since the primary purpose of using cost pools is to reduce the expense of allocating overhead.

To continue the illustration, assume that Weiss Inc. uses machine hours to allocate the power and maintenance cost pool and uses production setups to allocate the quality control and setup cost pool. The overhead rates for each of these cost pools would be as follows:

Power and Maintenance cost pool:
    Overhead costs:

Power	$360,000
Maintenance	105,000
Total	$465,000
Total machine hours	50,000 hours
Overhead rate	$9.30 per machine hour

Quality Control and Setup cost pool:
    Overhead costs:

Quality control	$ 51,000
Setup	84,000
Total	$135,000
Total number of production setups	120 setups
Overhead rate	$1,125 per setup

Using these rates, the overhead costs are allocated as follows. Note that the total overhead allocated to each product is the same amount that was allocated when four separate activity drivers were used.

	Product X	Product Y
Power and maintenance:		
10,000 hours × $9.30	$ 93,000	
40,000 hours × $9.30		$372,000
Quality control and setup:		
48 setups × $1,125	54,000	
72 setups × $1,125		81,000
Total	$147,000	$453,000

If a plant-wide rate of $12 per machine hour ($600,000 total overhead ÷ 50,000 machine hours) had been used in the preceding illustration, the overhead costs would be allocated to Products X and Y as follows:

	Product X	Product Y
Overhead costs:		
10,000 machine hrs. × $12	$120,000	
40,000 machine hrs. × $12		$480,000
Total	$120,000	$480,000

If 5,000 units of Product X and 7,500 units of Product Y are produced, the total overhead costs allocated to Product X and Y and the overhead costs per unit are as shown below, using ABC and the preceding plant-wide rate.

	Activity-Based Costing		Plant-Wide Overhead Rate	
	Total Overhead	Overhead Per Unit	Total Overhead	Overhead Per Unit
Product X	$147,000	$29.40	$120,000	$24.00
Product Y	453,000	60.40	480,000	64.00
	$600,000		$600,000	

Product Y is allocated more overhead costs using the plant-wide rate. As discussed previously, this is because a plant-wide overhead rate tends to allocate more overhead costs to high-volume products, such as Product Y, than to low-volume products, such as Product X. As a result, assuming that the ABC allocations better measure the causes of overhead, Product Y is overcosted and Product X is undercosted. If selling prices are based upon product costs, using a plant-wide overhead rate might lead management to overprice Product Y and underprice Product X. This was what happened in the Rockwell International example described previously.

The increased accuracy of ABC allows management to make better decisions in such matters as product pricing. In an environment where many companies manufacture a variety of products, accurate product costs are essential to long-term profitability.

An additional benefit of ABC is that it requires managers to focus their attention on activities that create overhead. As a result, management may often be able to identify activities that add value to the product, such as power supplied to automated equipment, as well as those activities that do not add value to the product. Managers can then focus their efforts on reducing or eliminating the non-value-adding activities. For example, the movement of materials among work stations is considered a non-value-adding activity. To reduce this movement of materials, a company could redesign its plant layout or reorganize the work stations.

A disadvantage of ABC is that it is usually more expensive to implement than plant-wide or departmental overhead rates. This is because more cost pools and activity drivers must be measured and accumulated. For many companies, however, the advantages of ABC outweigh these additional costs.

CHAPTER REVIEW

Key Points

Objective 1. Compare and contrast a job order cost system and a process cost system.

The main distinction between a job order cost system and a process cost system is the format in which the product costs are accumulated and reported. In a job order cost system, product costs are accumulated by individual jobs and are summarized on job order cost sheets. In a process cost system, costs are accumulated by department or process and are summarized in a cost of production report.

Objective 2. Explain the flow of costs in a process cost system.

In process cost accounting, product costs are accumulated in each department. In the processing departments, the costs incurred are accumulated in factory overhead and work in process accounts. The costs transferred from preceding departments and the costs of direct materials and direct labor incurred in each processing department are debited to the related work in process account. Each work in process account is also debited for the factory overhead applied. When the product is completed, the costs are transferred from Work in Process to Finished Goods.

Objective 3. Explain the accounting for inventories of partially processed units, including the computation of equivalent units.

Often, partially processed materials remain in a department at the end of a period. In such cases, manufacturing costs must be allocated between the units that have been completed and those that are only partially completed and remain within the department.

To allocate product costs between the output completed and the inventory of goods within the department, the number of equivalent units of production during the period are determined. The equivalent units of production are the number of units that could have been manufactured from start to finish during the period.

Objective 4. Prepare a cost of production report.

The cost of production report for each processing department summarizes (1) the units for which the department is accountable and the disposition of those units and (2) the costs charged to the department and the allocation of those costs. A cost of production report is illustrated in Exhibit 3.

Objective 5. Allocate service department costs to producing departments.

The costs of service departments, which do not process the materials directly, are allocated to the factory overhead accounts of the processing departments. The costs of the service department rendering the greatest service to other departments are allocated first, despite the fact that this department receives benefits from other service departments. The department rendering the next largest amount of services is allocated next, and so on.

Objective 6. Allocate product costs to joint products and by-products.

Joint costs are usually allocated among the joint products by using the market (sales) value method. The allocation is based upon the relative sales values of the joint products.

The product cost usually assigned to a by-product is the sales value of the by-product less any additional costs necessary to complete and sell it.

Objective 7. Illustrate the flow of costs, including journal entries, through a process cost accounting system.

The flow of costs through a process cost accounting system is illustrated in Exhibit 6.

Objective 8. Compute equivalent units of production, using the average cost method of inventory costing.

Using the average cost method to compute equivalent units, the units in the beginning work in process are treated as if they were started and completed during the current period. Thus, the total equivalent units for a period is computed by adding (1) the units in the beginning work in process, (2) the units *started and completed* during the period, and (3) the equivalent units in the ending work in process.

The total equivalent units may also be computed by adding (1) the total of the units *completed* during the period and (2) the equivalent units in the ending work in process.

Objective 9. Explain the nature of hybrid cost accounting systems.

Some production processes have characteristics common to both job order and process cost systems. In such cases, it is best to use a cost system that is specifically designed for the production process. An operational cost system is an example of a hybrid system that accumulates costs for each batch of custom-ordered products.

Glossary of Key Terms

Average cost method. The method of inventory costing that uses one unit cost for all products completed during the current period. **Objective 8**

Backflush costing. A cost accounting system in which product costs are applied to the units when the production process is complete; normally used in a just-in-time manufacturing environment. **Objective 8**

By-product. A product that has little value in relation to the other products resulting from a manufacturing process. **Objective 6**

Conversion cost. The combination of direct labor and factory overhead costs. **Objective 2**

Cost of production report. A report prepared periodically by a processing department, summarizing (1) the units for which the department is accountable and the disposition of those units and (2) the costs charged to the department and the allocation of those costs. **Objective 4**

Equivalent units of production. The number of units that could have been manufactured from start to finish during a period. **Objective 3**

First-in, first-out (fifo) method. A method of inventory costing based on the assumption that the unit product costs should be determined separately for each period in the order in which the costs were incurred. **Objective 8**

Joint costs. Costs common to the manufacture of two or more products (joint products). **Objective 6**

Joint products. Two or more products of significant value produced from a single principal direct material. **Objective 6**

Market (sales) value method. A method of allocating joint costs among products according to their relative sales values. **Objective 6**

Operational cost system. A cost accounting system that combines features of a job order cost system and a process cost system. **Objective 9**

Service department. A factory department that does not process materials directly but renders services for the benefit of production departments. **Objective 5**

Self-Examination Questions

Answers at end of chapter.

1. For which of the following businesses would the process cost system be most appropriate?
   A. Custom furniture manufacturer
   B. Commercial building contractor
   C. Crude oil refinery
   D. Automobile repair shop

2. The group of manufacturing costs referred to as conversion costs includes:
   A. direct materials and direct labor
   B. direct materials and factory overhead
   C. direct labor and factory overhead
   D. direct materials and indirect materials

3. Information relating to production in Department A for May is as follows:

May			
1	Balance, 1,000 units, 3/4 completed	$22,150
31	Direct materials, 5,000 units	75,000
31	Direct labor	32,500
31	Factory overhead	16,250

   If 500 units were 1/4 completed at May 31, 5,500 units were completed during May, and inventories are costed by the first-in, first-out method, what was the number of equivalent units of production for May?
   A. 4,500   C. 5,500
   B. 4,875   D. 6,000

4. Based on the data in Question 3, what is the unit conversion cost?
   A. $10   C. $25
   B. $15   D. $32

5. Which of the following departments is an example of a service department?
   A. Factory office   C. Maintenance
   B. Power plant   D. All of the above

ILLUSTRATIVE PROBLEM

Tate Company manufactures Product A by a series of four processes, all materials being introduced in Department 1. From Department 1, the materials pass through Departments 2, 3, and 4, emerging as finished Product A. All inventories are costed by the first-in, first-out method.

The balances in the accounts Work in Process—Department 4 and Finished Goods were as follows on May 1:

Work in Process—Department 4 (1,000 units, 1/4 completed)	$17,800
Finished Goods (1,800 units at $23.50 a unit)	42,300

The following costs were charged to Work in Process—Department 4 during May:

Direct materials transferred from Department 3: 4,700 units	
at $16 a unit	$75,200
Direct labor	25,500
Factory overhead	15,300

During May, 5,000 units of A were completed and 4,800 units were sold. Inventories on May 31 were as follows:

Work in Process—Department 4: 700 units, 1/2 completed	
Finished Goods: 2,000 units	

Instructions

Determine the following:

1. Equivalent units of production for Department 4 during May.
2. Unit conversion cost for Department 4 for May.
3. Total and unit cost of Product A started in a prior period and finished in May.
4. Total and unit cost of Product A started and finished in May.
5. Total cost of goods transferred to finished goods.
6. Work in process inventory for Department 4, May 31.
7. Cost of goods sold (indicate number of units and unit costs).
8. Finished goods inventory, May 31.

Solution

1. Equivalent units of production:

To process units in inventory on May 1:	
1,000 units × 3/4	750
To process units started and completed	
in May: 5,000 units − 1,000 units	4,000
To process units in inventory on May 31:	
700 units × 1/2	350
Equivalent units of production in May	5,100

2. Unit conversion cost: $\dfrac{\$25,500 + \$15,300}{5,100} = \$8$

3. Cost of Product A started in a prior period and finished in May:

1,000 units: Inventory on May 1, 1/4 completed	$17,800
Conversion cost in May, 750 × $8	6,000
Total	$23,800

   Unit cost: $23,800 ÷ 1,000 = $23.80

4. Cost of Product A started and finished in May:

4,000 units: Materials from Department 3, 4,000 × $16	$64,000
Conversion cost in May, 4,000 × $8	32,000
Total	$96,000

   Unit cost: $96,000 ÷ 4,000 = $24

5. Total cost of goods transferred to finished goods:

Cost of Product A started in a prior period	
and finished in May (1,000 units at $23.80)	$ 23,800
Cost of Product A started and finished in May	
(4,000 units at $24)	96,000
Total	$119,800

6. Work in process inventory, May 31:

700 units: Materials cost, 700 × $16	$11,200
Conversion costs in May, 350 × $8	2,800
Work in process inventory, May 31	$14,000

7. Cost of goods sold:

1,800 units at $23.50	$ 42,300
1,000 units at $23.80	23,800
2,000 units at $24.00	48,000
4,800 units	$114,100

8. Finished goods inventory, May 31:

2,000 units at $24	$ 48,000

DISCUSSION QUESTIONS

1. Which type of cost system, process or job order, would be best suited for each of the following: (a) oil refinery (b) custom jewelry manufacturer, (c) paper manufacturer, (d) automobile repair shop, (e) building contractor, (f) lumber mill? Give reasons for your answers.
2. Are perpetual inventory accounts for materials, work in process, and finished goods generally used for (a) job order cost systems and (b) process cost systems?
3. In job order cost accounting, the three elements of manufacturing cost are charged directly to job orders. Why is it not necessary to charge manufacturing costs in process cost accounting to job orders?
4. What two groups of manufacturing costs are referred to as conversion costs?
5. In the manufacture of 1,000 units of a product, direct materials cost incurred was $20,000, direct labor incurred was $7,500, and factory overhead applied was $4,500. (a) What is the total conversion cost? (b) What is the conversion cost per unit? (c) What is the total manufacturing cost? (d) What is the manufacturing cost per unit?
6. What is meant by the term *equivalent units?*
7. If Department 3 had no work in process at the beginning of the period, 5,000 units were completed during the period, and 1,000 units were 1/4 completed at the end of the period, what was the number of equivalent units of production for the period?
8. The following information concerns production in Department B for March. All direct materials are placed in process at the beginning of production. Determine the number of units in work in process inventory at the end of the month.

ACCOUNT WORK IN PROCESS—DEPARTMENT B   ACCOUNT NO.

Date		Item	Debit	Credit	Balance Debit	Balance Credit
Mar.	1	Bal. 6,000 units 3/4 completed			9,500	
	31	Direct materials, 15,000 units	7,500			
	31	Direct labor	14,450			
	31	Factory overhead	7,225			
	31	Goods finished, 13,500 units		28,550		
	31	Bal., ___ units, 1/2 completed			10,125	

9. For Question No. 8, determine the equivalent units of production for March, assuming that the first-in, first-out method is used to cost inventories.
10. What data are summarized in the two principal sections of the cost of production report?
11. What is the most important purpose of the cost of production report?
12. a. How does a service department differ from a processing department?
    b. Give three examples of a service department.
13. Lopez Company maintains a cafeteria for its employees at a cost of $9,750 per month. On what basis would the company most likely allocate the cost of the cafeteria among the production departments?
14. Muster Company has two processing departments: A and B. The power plant provides 100 000 kilowatt-hours of its total output of 300 000 kilowatt-hours to Department A. How much of the $45,000 of total power plant costs should be allocated to Department A?
15. Distinguish between a joint product and a by-product.
16. How is the amount of manufacturing cost usually assigned to a by-product determined?
17. The Cutting Department produces two products. How should the cost be allocated (a) if the products are joint products and (b) if one of the products is a by-product?
18. Where is net underapplied factory overhead reported on the interim balance sheet?
19. What are two common inventory costing methods used in process cost accounting?
20. What are the principal advantages of using the first-in, first-out method for costing inventories for process cost systems?
21. What is the principal advantage of using the average method for costing inventories for process cost systems?
22. What is an operational cost system?

REAL W RLD FOCUS   23. As production processes become more and more automated in what many see as the "age of robotics," materials may enter into and leave a production process without human intervention. For example, in the manufacture of automobiles, General Motors uses state-of-the-art paint systems, which are operated from an automated video control room. The control room supervisor monitors the preparation of the bare metal body of the automobile as it is submerged in a primer. Next, the body passes through nine pairs of robot painters teamed with other robot devices that open and close doors and paint inside surfaces. (a) In this type of production environment, would direct labor hours be an appropriate base for allocation of predetermined factory overhead? (b) Can you suggest other bases for allocating factory overhead?

ETHICS DISCUSSION CASE

Alex Perez, a cost accountant for Torrez Industries, has the responsibility of allocating service department costs. He allocates Power Department costs on a monthly basis to each of the producing departments, based on actual kilowatt usage. Roger Hayden, supervisor of the Assembly Department, recently complained to the vice-president of production that the allocations of Power Department costs were wrong and that they should be divided equally among all departments. He charges that because of the method of allocation used, his department receives a larger share and the Finishing Department receives a smaller share than is warranted. He also charges that the only reason for using the current method is that Perez's brother is the supervisor of the Finishing Department.

SHARPEN YOUR   ▶   Discuss the ethical issues of this case.
COMMUNICATION SKILLS

EXERCISES

EXERCISE 23-1
FLOWCHART OF
ACCOUNTS RELATED TO
SERVICE AND PROCESSING
DEPARTMENTS
Objective 2

Curry Co. manufactures two products. The entire output of Department A is transferred to Department B. Part of the fully processed goods from Department B are sold as Product P, and the remainder of the goods are transferred to Department C for further processing into Product Q. The service department, Factory Office, provides services for each of the processing departments.

Prepare a chart of the flow of costs from the service and processing department accounts into the finished goods accounts and then into the cost of goods sold account. The relevant accounts are as follows:

Cost of Goods Sold	Finished Goods—Product P
Factory Office	Finished Goods—Product Q
Factory Overhead—Department A	Work in Process—Department A
Factory Overhead—Department B	Work in Process—Department B
Factory Overhead—Department C	Work in Process—Department C

EXERCISE 23-2
ENTRIES FOR FLOW OF
FACTORY COSTS FOR
PROCESS COST SYSTEM
Objective 2

McCraken Company manufactures a single product by a continuous process, involving three production departments. The records indicate that direct materials, direct labor, and applied factory overhead for Department 1 were $90,000, $108,000, and $32,400, respectively. Also, work in process in the department at the beginning of the period totaled $45,000, and work in process at the end of the period totaled $52,000.

Journalize the entries to record (a) the flow of costs into Department 1 during the period for (1) direct materials, (2) direct labor, and (3) factory overhead, and (b) the transfer of production costs to Department 2.

EXERCISE 23-3
FACTORY OVERHEAD RATE,
ENTRY FOR APPLICATION
OF FACTORY OVERHEAD,
AND FACTORY OVERHEAD
ACCOUNT BALANCE
Objective 2

The chief cost accountant for H. L. Farrel Co. estimates total factory overhead cost for the Blending Department for the year at $20,000 and total direct labor costs at $50,000. During April, the actual direct labor cost totaled $4,000, and factory overhead cost incurred totaled $1,525.

a. What is the predetermined factory overhead rate based on direct labor cost?
b. Journalize the entry to apply factory overhead to production for April.
c. What is the April 30 balance of the account Factory Overhead—Blending Department?
d. Does the balance in (c) represent overapplied or underapplied factory overhead?

EXERCISE 23-4
EQUIVALENT UNITS OF
PRODUCTION
Objective 3

Units of production data for two departments for April of the current fiscal year are as follows:

	Stamping Department	*Polishing Department*
Work in process, April 1	10,000 units, 1/2 completed	9,000 units, 2/3 completed
Completed and transferred to next processing department during April	40,000 units	42,000 units
Work in process, April 30	8,000 units, 3/4 completed	10,000 units, 1/4 completed

If all direct materials are placed in process at the beginning of production, determine the equivalent units of production for April for (a) the Stamping Department and (b) the Polishing Department. Present your computations. Use the first-in, first-out method.

EXERCISE 23-5
EQUIVALENT UNITS OF
PRODUCTION AND
RELATED COSTS
Objective 3

The charges to Work in Process—Finishing Department for a period, together with information concerning production, are as follows. All direct materials are placed in process at the beginning of production, and the first-in, first-out method is used to cost inventories.

Work in Process—Finishing Department

2,000 units, 4/5 completed	49,100	To Finished Goods, 6,200 units	169,600
Direct materials, 4,200 at $15	63,000		
Direct labor	46,000		
Factory overhead	11,500		

SPREADSHEET
PROBLEM

Determine the following, presenting your computations: (a) equivalent units of production, (b) conversion cost per equivalent unit of production, (c) total and unit cost of product started in prior period and completed in the current period, and (d) total and unit cost of product started and completed in the current period.

EXERCISE 23-6
UNIT COSTS OF PRODUCT
Objective 3

The debits to Work in Process—Melting Department for a period, together with information concerning production, are as follows:

Work in process, beginning of period, 4,500 units, 3/5 completed	$272,260
Materials added during period, 18,200 units	382,200
Conversion costs during period	574,000
Work in process, end of period, 4,000 units, 1/10 completed	—
Goods finished during period, 18,700 units	—

All direct materials are placed in process at the beginning of the process, and the first-in, first-out method is used to cost inventories. Determine the following, presenting your computations: (a) equivalent units of production for the period, (b) conversion cost per equivalent unit for the period, (c) cost of goods finished during the period, and (d) cost of work in process at the end of the period.

EXERCISE 23-7
COST OF PRODUCTION
REPORT
Objective 4

Prepare a cost of production report for the Assembly Department of O'Brien Company for July of the current fiscal year, using the following data and assuming that the first-in, first-out method is used to cost inventories:

Inventory, July 1, 5,000 units, 2/5 completed	$120,000
Materials from the Sanding Department, 15,000 units	337,500
Direct labor for July	51,875
Factory overhead for July	31,125
Goods finished during July (includes units in process, July 1), 16,500 units	—
Inventory, July 31, 3,500 units, 3/5 completed	—

SPREADSHEET
PROBLEM

EXERCISE 23-8
ENTRY FOR ALLOCATION
OF SERVICE DEPARTMENT
COSTS
Objective 5

The Maintenance and Repair Department provides services to Processing Departments 1, 2, and 3. During May of the current year, the total cost incurred by the Maintenance and Repair Department was $80,000. During May, it was estimated that 60% of the services were provided to Department 1, 25% to Department 2, and 15% to Department 3.

Journalize the entry to record the allocation of the Maintenance and Repair Department cost for May to the Processing Departments.

EXERCISE 23-9
ALLOCATION OF COSTS
FOR BY-PRODUCT AND
JOINT PRODUCTS
Objective 6

The charges to Work in Process—Department 5, together with units of product completed during the period, are indicated in the following account:

Work in Process—Department 5

From Department 4	125,600	By-product B, 1,000 units
Direct labor	30,300	Joint product P, 4,000 units
Factory overhead	10,100	Joint product Q, 10,000 units

There is no inventory of goods in process at either the beginning or the end of the period. The value of B is $1 a unit; P sells at $25 a unit; Q sells at $15 a unit.

a. Allocate the costs to the three products and determine the unit cost of each, presenting your computations.

SHARPEN YOUR ▶
COMMUNICATION SKILLS

b. Explain the purpose of allocating joint costs among the joint products and the by-product.

EXERCISE 23-10
UNIT COSTS OF PRODUCT
BY AVERAGE COST
METHOD
Objective 8

The debits to Work in Process—Plating Department for a period, together with information concerning production, are as follows:

Work in process, beginning of period:

Materials costs, 4,500 units	$ 98,070
Conversion costs, 4,500 units, 3/5 completed	139,660
Materials added during period, 18,200 units	410,410
Conversion costs during period	586,140
Work in process, end of period, 4,000 units, 1/10 completed	—
Goods finished during period, 18,700 units	—

All direct materials are placed in process at the beginning of the process, and the average cost method is used to cost inventories.

a. Determine the following, presenting your computations:
   1. Average materials cost per unit for period.
   2. Equivalent units of production for period.
   3. Average conversion cost per unit for period.
   4. Cost of goods finished during period.
   5. Cost of work in process at end of period.

SHARPEN YOUR ▶
COMMUNICATION SKILLS

b. Discuss the main advantage of using the average cost method rather than the first-in, first-out method to cost inventories.

**APPENDIX EXERCISE
23-11**
ACTIVITY-BASED COSTING

Pita Inc. manufactures two products, R and S, which involves four overhead activities—factory supervision, maintenance, product engineering, and quality control. The expected costs for these activities are as follows:

Overhead costs:

Factory supervision	$150,000
Maintenance	200,000
Product engineering	120,000
Quality control	80,000
Total	$550,000

The appropriate activity drivers and the amounts of the activity drivers for each product are as follows:

Overhead Cost	Activity Driver
Factory supervision	Number of employees
Maintenance	Machine hours
Product engineering	Number of components
Quality control	Number of inspections

	Number of Employees	Machine Hours	Number of Components	Number of Inspections
Product R	45	12,000	36	180
Product S	30	8,000	44	220
Total	75	20,000	80	400

a. Develop an overhead rate for each overhead activity.
b. Allocate the overhead costs to each product, using the overhead rates from (a).

**APPENDIX EXERCISE
23-12
ACTIVITY-BASED COSTING**

Using the data from Exercise 23-11, (a) determine the percentage of each activity driver used by each product, (b) identify appropriate cost pools and determine an overhead rate for each pool (use machine hours and the number of inspections as the activity drivers), and (c) allocate the overhead costs to products R and S, using the overhead rates identified in (b).

**WhAT'S WRONG
WITH THIS?**

At May 1 of the current year, 3,500 units were 1/5 completed in Department 2. During May, 10,500 units entered the department from Department 1. During May, the units in process at the beginning of the month were completed. Of the 10,500 units entering the department, all were completed except 2,700 units that were 1/3 completed. The equivalent units of production for May for Department 2 were computed as follows:

Equivalent units of production in May:
   To process units in inventory on May 1:
      $3,500 \times 1/5$ 700
   To process units started and completed in May:
      $10,500 - 3,500$ 7,000
   To process units in inventory on May 31:
      $2,700 \times 1/3$ 900
   Equivalent units of production   8,600

How many errors can you find in the computation of equivalent units of production for Department 2 for May?

PROBLEMS

Series A

**PROBLEM 23-1A
WORK IN PROCESS
ACCOUNT DATA FOR TWO
MONTHS AND
DETERMINATION OF
DIFFERENCE IN UNIT
PRODUCT COST BETWEEN
MONTHS
Objectives 2, 3**

A process cost system is used to record the costs of manufacturing Product C5, which requires a series of five processes. All inventories are costed by the the first-in, first-out method. The inventory of Work in Process—Department 5 on July 1 and debits to the account during July were as follows:

Balance, 800 units, 1/4 completed	$13,040
From Department 4, 4,600 units	51,520
Direct labor	77,000
Factory overhead	19,250

During July, 800 units in process on July 1 were completed, and of the 4,600 units entering the department, all were completed except 1,100 units that were 1/4 completed.
Charges to Work in Process—Department 5 for August were as follows:

From Department 4, 4,125 units	$47,850
Direct labor	83,448
Factory overhead	20,862

During August, the units in process at the beginning of the month were completed, and of the 4,125 units entering the department, all were completed except 750 units that were 1/2 completed.

Instructions

1. Enter the balance as of July 1 in a 4-column account for Work in Process—Department 5. Record the debits and the credits in the account for July. Present computations for the determination of (a) equivalent units of production, (b) unit conversion cost, (c) cost of goods finished, differentiating between units started in the prior period and units started and finished in July, and (d) work in process inventory.
2. Record the transactions for August in the account. Present the computations listed in (1).
3. Determine the difference in unit cost between the product started and completed in July and the product started and completed in August. Determine also the amount of the difference attributable collectively to operations in Departments 1 through 4 and the amount attributable to operations in Department 5.

PROBLEM 23-2A
EQUIVALENT UNITS AND
RELATED COSTS; COST OF
PRODUCTION REPORT
Objectives 3, 4

Ramos Company manufactures Product A by a series of three processes, all materials being introduced in Department 1. From Department 1, the materials pass through Departments 2 and 3, emerging as finished Product A. All inventories are costed by the first-in, first-out method.

The balances in the accounts Work in Process—Department 3 and Finished Goods were as follows on March 1:

Work in Process—Department 3 (7,000 units, 1/2 completed)	$212,100
Finished Goods (12,000 units at $36.20 a unit)	434,400

The following costs were charged to Work in Process—Department 3 during March:

Direct materials transferred from Department 2:	
37,000 units at $24 a unit	$888,000
Direct labor	232,600
Factory overhead	140,000

During March, 35,000 units of A were completed and 37,200 units were sold. Inventories on March 31 were as follows:

Work in Process—Department 3: 9,000 units, 1/3 completed
Finished Goods: 9,800 units

Instructions

1. Determine the following:
   a. Equivalent units of production for Department 3 during March.
   b. Unit conversion cost for Department 3 for March.
   c. Total and unit cost of Product A started in a prior period and finished in March.
   d. Total and unit cost of Product A started and finished in March.
   e. Total cost of goods transferred to finished goods.
   f. Work in process inventory for Department 3, March 31.
   g. Cost of goods sold (indicate number of units and unit costs).
   h. Finished goods inventory, March 31.
2. Prepare a cost of production report for Department 3 for March.
3. Discuss the uses of the cost of production report.

PROBLEM 23-3A
ENTRIES FOR PROCESS COST
SYSTEM
Objectives 2, 3, 5, 7

Holman Company manufactures Product T. Material A is placed in process in Department 1, where it is ground and partially refined. The output of Department 1 is transferred to Department 2, where Material B is added at the beginning of the process and the refining is completed. On November 1, Holman Company had the following inventories:

Finished Goods (8,000 units)	$72,000
Work in process—Department 1	—
Work in process—Department 2 (12,000 units, 1/3 completed)	90,400
Materials	26,400

Departmental accounts are maintained for factory overhead, and there is one service department, Factory Office. The first-in, first-out method is used to cost inventories. Manufacturing operations for November are summarized as follows:

a. Materials purchased on account	$48,100
b. Materials requisitioned for use:	
Material A	$26,080
Material B	21,600
Indirect materials—Department 1	1,700
Indirect materials—Department 2	1,240
c. Labor used:	
Direct labor—Department 1	$53,900
Direct labor—Department 2	38,500
Indirect labor—Department 1	4,030
Indirect labor—Department 2	1,920
Factory Office	1,830
d. Miscellaneous costs incurred on account:	
Department 1	$ 7,000
Department 2	4,100
Factory Office	2,100

SPREADSHEET
PROBLEM

.SHARPEN YOUR
COMMUNICATION SKILLS

e. Expiration of prepaid expenses:

Department 1	$ 1,050
Department 2	700
Factory Office	300

f. Depreciation charged on plant assets:

Department 1	$14,350
Department 2	12,250
Factory Office	900

g. Distribution of Factory Office costs:

Department 1	80% of total Factory Office costs
Department 2	20% of total Factory Office costs

h. Application of factory overhead costs based on machine hours:

Department 1	$32,340
Department 2	21,175

i. Production costs transferred from Department 1 to Department 2: 21,600 units were fully processed, and there was no inventory of work in process in Department 1 at November 30.

j. Production costs transferred from Department 2 to finished goods: 22,140 units, including the inventory at November 1, were fully processed. 11,460 units were 1/2 completed at November 30.

k. Cost of goods sold during November: 25,200 units (Use the first-in, first-out method in crediting the finished goods account.)

Instructions

1. Journalize the entries to record the operations, identifying each entry by letter.
2. Compute the November 30 work in process inventory for Department 2.

PROBLEM 23-4A
COST OF PRODUCTION
REPORT
Objectives 4, 7

The data related to production during November of the current year for Department 2 of Holman Company are presented in Problem 23-3A.

Instructions

Prepare a cost of production report for Department 2 for November.

PROBLEM 23-5A
ENTRIES FOR PROCESS COST
SYSTEM
Objective 7

Irvin Manufacturing Inc. manufactures Product C. Materials are placed in production in Department 1, and after processing are transferred to Department 2, where more materials are added. The finished product emerges from Department 2. There is one service department: Maintenance and Repair.

There were no inventories of work in process at the beginning or at the end of July. Finished goods inventory at July 1 was 15,000 units of Product C at a total cost of $183,750.

Transactions related to manufacturing operations for July are summarized as follows:

a. Materials purchased on account, $119,750.
b. Materials requisitioned for use: Department 1, $76,100 ($67,700 entered directly into the product); Department 2, $36,700 ($28,400 entered directly into the product); Maintenance and Repair, $680.
c. Labor costs incurred: Department 1, $95,180 ($88,200 entered directly into the product); Department 2, $103,560 ($94,000 entered directly into the product); Maintenance and Repair, $3,960.
d. Miscellaneous costs and expenses incurred on account: Department 1, $14,150; Department 2, $12,340; Maintenance and Repair, $2,060.
e. Expiration of various prepaid expenses: Department 1, $1,260; Department 2, $920; Maintenance and Repair, $340.
f. Depreciation charged on plant assets: Department 1, $5,320; Department 2, $4,000; Maintenance and Repair, $1,760.

g. Maintenance and repair costs allocated on the basis of services rendered: Department 1, 60%; Department 2, 40%.

h. Factory overhead applied to production, based on machine hours: $44,100 and $37,600 for Departments 1 and 2, respectively.

i. Output of Department 1: 30,000 units.

j. Output of Department 2: 30,000 units of Product C.

k. Sales on account: 29,000 units of Product C at $20. Credits to the finished goods account are to be made according to the first-in, first-out method.

Instructions

Journalize the entries to record the transactions, identifying each by letter. Include as an explanation for entry (k) the number of units and the unit costs for the product sold.

Instructions for Solving Problem 23-5A Using Solutions Software

1. Load opening balances.
2. Save the opening balances file to your drive and directory.
3. Set the run date to July 31 of the current year and enter your name.
4. Select the General Journal Entries option and key the journal entries. Leave the reference field blank. Note: To review the chart of accounts, select F-1.
5. Display a journal entries report.
6. Display a trial balance.
7. Display an income statement, a retained earnings statement, and a balance sheet.
8. Save a backup copy of your data file.
9. Perform period-end closing.
10. Display a post-closing trial balance.
11. Save your data file to disk.
12. End the session.

PROBLEM 23-6A
FINANCIAL STATEMENTS
FOR PROCESS COST SYSTEM
Objective 7

The trial balance of Trier Products at July 31, the end of the first month of the current fiscal year, is shown on the next page.

Instructions

1. Prepare an income statement.
2. Prepare a retained earnings statement.
3. Prepare a balance sheet.

Instructions for Solving Problem 23-6A Using Solutions Software

1. Load opening balances.
2. Save the opening balances file to your drive and directory.
3. Set the run date to July 31 of the current year and enter your name.
4. Display an income statement, a retained earnings statement, and a balance sheet.
5. Save your data file to disk.
6. End the session.

Trier Products Inc.
Trial Balance
July 31, 19—

Cash	47,900	
Marketable Securities	30,000	
Accounts Receivable	322,500	
Allowance for Doubtful Accounts		25,000
Finished Goods—Product A	62,500	
Finished Goods—Product B	60,800	
Work in Process—Department 1	19,850	
Work in Process—Department 2	8,750	
Work in Process—Department 3	12,700	
Materials	30,250	
Prepaid Insurance	7,400	
Office Supplies	3,570	
Land	52,500	
Buildings	525,000	
Accumulated Depreciation—Buildings		344,500
Machinery and Equipment	391,000	
Accumulated Depreciation—Machinery and Equipment		280,600
Office Equipment	30,700	
Accumulated Depreciation—Office Equipment		12,780
Patents	40,000	
Accounts Payable		97,750
Wages Payable		12,100
Income Tax Payable		1,200
Mortgage Note Payable (due 2001)		75,000
Common Stock ($50 par)		500,000
Retained Earnings		276,190
Sales		415,000
Cost of Goods Sold	287,500	
Factory Overhead—Department 1	250	
Factory Overhead—Department 2		310
Factory Overhead—Department 3	160	
Selling Expenses	60,250	
Administrative Expenses	39,400	
Interest Income		200
Interest Expense	750	
Income Tax	6,900	
	2,040,630	2,040,630

PROBLEM 23-7A
UNIT COST OF FINISHED
PRODUCT BY AVERAGE
COST METHOD; COST OF
PRODUCTION REPORT
Objective 8

Waller Company manufactures Product Q by a series of four processes, all materials being introduced in Department 1. From Department 1, the materials pass through Departments 2, 3, and 4, emerging as finished Product Q. All inventories are costed by the average cost method.

The balance in the account Work in Process—Department 4 was as follows on May 1:

Materials cost (3,000 units)	$18,600
Conversion costs (3,000 units, 1/4 completed)	9,600

The following costs were charged to Work in Process—Department 4 during May:

Direct materials transferred from Department 3:	
27,000 units at $6 per unit	$162,000
Direct labor	210,000
Factory overhead	163,900

During May, 28,000 units of Product Q were completed and the work in process inventory on May 31 was 2,000 units, 3/4 completed.

Instructions

1. Determine the following for Department 4:
   a. Average materials cost per unit.
   b. Equivalent units of production in May.
   c. Average conversion cost per unit for May.
   d. Cost of goods finished during May.
   e. Cost of work in process at May 31.
2. Prepare a cost of production report for Department 4 for May.

APPENDIX PROBLEM 23-8A
ACTIVITY-BASED COSTING

Tosha Inc. manufactures two products, A and B, which involves four overhead activities—equipment maintenance and repairs, grounds, heating and lighting, and product engineering. The expected costs for these activities are as follows:

Overhead costs:

Equipment maintenance and repairs	$250,000
Grounds	80,000
Heating and lighting	320,000
Product engineering	150,000
Total	$800,000

The appropriate activity drivers and the amounts of the activity drivers for each product are as follows:

Overhead Cost	Activity Driver
Equipment maintenance and repairs	machine hours
Grounds	square feet
Heating and lighting	kilowatt-hours
Product engineering	number of components

	Machine Hours	Square Feet	Kilowatt-Hours	Number of Components
Product A	6,000	20,000	10 000	36
Product B	2,000	30,000	15 000	12
Total	8,000	50,000	25 000	48

Instructions

1. Determine an overhead rate for each overhead activity.
2. Allocate the overhead costs to each product, using the overhead rates from part (1).
3. Determine the percentage of each activity driver used by each product.
4. Using the percentages computed in (3), (a) identify appropriate cost pools and determine an overhead rate for each pool (use machine hours and the number of square feet as the activity drivers). (b) Allocate the overhead costs to products A and B, using the overhead rates identified in (a).

APPENDIX PROBLEM 23-9A
PLANT-WIDE OVERHEAD RATES AND ACTIVITY-BASED COSTING

Faris Inc. manufactures two products, E and F, which involves four overhead activities—maintenance, power, production setup, and quality control. Faris Inc. uses a plant-wide overhead rate, based upon units produced, to allocate overhead costs to Products E and F. The procedure for allocating overhead was initially established when only Product E was being produced.

Although management is pleased that sales of Product F are increasing, it is concerned because sales of the previously best-selling Product E are decreasing. Several former customers have indicated that Faris Inc.'s price for Product E is too high and that they can buy a competitor's product at significant savings. The president is concerned because the manufacture of Product E is costing too much, and perhaps the company should discontinue its production.

Faris Inc. has gathered the following data for use in analyzing the costs of manufacturing Products E and F:

Direct manufacturing costs (per unit):

	Product E	Product F
Direct materials	$12.00	$43.00
Direct labor	8.00	17.00
Expected production volume:	10,000 units	5,000 units

Overhead activities and costs:

Maintenance	$ 60,000
Power	40,000
Production setup	75,000
Quality control	65,000
Total	$240,000

Overhead activity drivers:

Maintenance	machine hours
Power	kilowatt-hours
Production setup	number of setups
Quality control	number of inspections

	Machine Hours	Kilowatt-Hours	Number of Setups	Number of Inspections
Product E	144,000	576 000	16	8
Product F	56,000	224 000	24	12
Total	200,000	800 000	40	20

Instructions

1. Determine the plant-wide overhead rate for Faris Inc., using expected production volume as the activity base.
2. a. Using the plant-wide overhead rate determined in (1), allocate overhead to Products E and F.
   b. Determine the per unit manufacturing cost for each product, based upon the direct materials and direct labor costs and the allocated overhead.
3. Determine the expected selling price of each product, based upon the per unit manufacturing cost determined in (2). Faris Inc. normally sets its prices at 20% above the manufacturing cost per unit.
4. a. Using activity-based costing, determine the percentage of each activity driver used by each product.
   b. Based upon your answer to (a), identify appropriate cost pools and determine an overhead rate for each cost pool (use machine hours and the number of setups as cost drivers).
   c. Allocate the overhead costs to Products E and F, using the overhead rates determined in (b).
   d. Determine the manufacturing overhead cost per unit for Products E and F.
   e. Determine the per unit manufacturing costs for each product, based upon the direct materials and direct labor costs and the allocated overhead.
5. Determine the expected selling price of each product, based upon the per unit manufacturing cost determined in (4). Faris Inc. normally sets its prices at 20% above the manufacturing cost per unit.
6. Based upon the preceding analysis, comment on possible reasons for the decreased sales of Product E and the increased sales of Product F.

SHARPEN YOUR COMMUNICATION SKILLS ▶

Series B

PROBLEM 23-1B
WORK IN PROCESS
ACCOUNT DATA FOR TWO
MONTHS AND
DETERMINATION OF
DIFFERENCE IN UNIT
PRODUCT COST BETWEEN
MONTHS
Objectives 2, 3

A process cost system is used to record the costs of manufacturing Product C, which requires a series of three processes. All inventories are costed by the first-in, first-out method. The inventory of Work in Process—Department 3 on July 1 and debits to the account during July were as follows:

Balance, 1,200 units, 2/3 completed	$11,640
From Department 2, 5,250 units	9,450
Direct labor	50,676
Factory overhead	12,669

During July, 1,200 units in process on July 1 were completed, and of the 5,250 units entering the department, all were completed except 2,000 units that were 3/4 completed.

Charges to Work in Process—Department 3 for August were as follows:

From Department 2, 6,100 units	$10,675
Direct labor	63,500
Factory overhead	15,875

During August, the units in process at the beginning of the month were completed, and of the 6,100 units entering the department, all were completed except 500 units that were 1/2 completed.

Instructions

1. Enter the balance as of July 1 in a 4-column account for Work in Process—Department 3. Record the debits and the credits in the account for July. Present computations for the determination of (a) equivalent units of production, (b) unit conversion cost, (c) cost of goods finished, differentiating between units started in the prior period and units started and finished in July, and (d) work in process inventory.
2. Record the transactions for August in the account. Present the computations listed in (1).
3. Determine the difference in unit cost between the product started and completed in July and the product started and completed in August. Determine also the amount of the difference attributable collectively to operations in Departments 1 through 2 and the amount attributable to operations in Department 3.

PROBLEM 23-2B
EQUIVALENT UNITS AND
RELATED COSTS; COST OF
PRODUCTION REPORT
Objectives 3, 4

Keene Company manufactures Product E3 by a series of four processes, all materials being introduced in Department 1. From Department 1, the materials pass through Departments 2, 3 and 4, emerging as finished Product E3. All inventories are costed by the first-in, first-out method.

The balances in the accounts Work in Process—Department 4 and Finished Goods were as follows on July 1:

Work in Process—Department 4 (6,000 units, 3/4 completed)	$ 66,300
Finished Goods (8,000 units at $13 a unit)	104,000

The following costs were charged to Work in Process—Department 4 during July:

Direct materials transferred from Department 3: 26,000 units	
at $5.20 a unit	$135,200
Direct labor	144,000
Factory overhead	72,000

During July, 25,000 units of E3 were completed and 26,800 units were sold. Inventories on July 31 were as follows:

Work in Process—Department 4: 7,000 units, 1/2 completed
Finished Goods: 6,200 units

**SPREADSHEET
P·R·O·B·L·E·M**

Instructions

1. Determine the following:
    a. Equivalent units of production for Department 4 during July.
    b. Unit conversion cost for Department 4 for July.
    c. Total and unit cost of Product E3 started in a prior period and finished in July.
    d. Total and unit cost of Product E3 started and finished in July.
    e. Total cost of goods transferred to finished goods.
    f. Work in process inventory for Department 4, July 31.
    g. Cost of goods sold (indicate number of units and unit costs).
    h. Finished goods inventory, July 31.
2. Prepare a cost of production report for Department 4 for July.
3. Discuss the uses of the cost of production report.

**▌SHARPEN YOUR   ▶
COMMUNICATION SKILLS**

PROBLEM 23-3B
ENTRIES FOR PROCESS COST
SYSTEM
Objectives 2, 3, 5, 7

Wallace Company manufactures Product Z. Material A is placed in process in Department 1, where it is ground and partially refined. The output of Department 1 is transferred to Department 2, where Material B is added at the beginning of the process and the refining is completed. On June 1, Wallace Company had the following inventories:

Finished Goods (6,150 units)	$107,625
Work in process—Department 1	—
Work in process—Department 2 (3,150 units, 2/3 completed)	51,345
Materials	61,470

Departmental accounts are maintained for factory overhead, and there is one service department, Factory Office. All inventories are costed by the first-in, first-out method. Manufacturing operations for June are summarized as follows:

a. Materials purchased on account $32,700

b. Materials requisitioned for use:

Material A	$51,705
Material B	9,840
Indirect materials—Department 1	2,160
Indirect materials—Department 2	540

c. Labor used:

Direct labor—Department 1	$73,050
Direct labor—Department 2	29,175
Indirect labor—Department 1	4,200
Indirect labor—Department 2	1,920
Factory Office	3,450

d. Depreciation charged on plant assets:

Department 1	$29,850
Department 2	14,400
Factory Office	1,650

e. Miscellaneous costs incurred on account:

Department 1	$ 5,535
Department 2	3,465
Factory Office	1,800

f. Expiration of prepaid expenses:

Department 1	$ 3,420
Department 2	735
Factory Office	1,125

g. Distribution of Factory Office costs:

Department 1	60% of total Factory Office costs
Department 2	40% of total Factory Office costs

h. Application of factory overhead costs:

Department 1	$51,135
Department 2	23,340

i. Production costs transferred from Department 1 to Department 2:
    12,300 units were fully processed, and there was no inventory of work in process in Department 1 at June 30.

j. Production costs transferred from Department 2 to finished goods:
    11,250 units, including the inventory at June 1, were fully processed. There were 4,200 units 3/5 completed at June 30.

k. Cost of goods sold during June:
    12,000 units (Use the first-in, first-out method in crediting the finished goods account.)

Instructions

1. Journalize the entries to record the operations, identifying each entry by letter.
2. Compute the June 30 work in process inventory for Department 2.

PROBLEM 23-4B
COST OF PRODUCTION
REPORT
Objectives 4, 7

The data related to production during June of the current year for Department 2 of Wallace Company are presented in Problem 23-3B.

**SPREADSHEET
PROBLEM**

Instructions
Prepare a cost of production report for Department 2 for June.

PROBLEM 23-5B
ENTRIES FOR PROCESS COST
SYSTEM
Objective 7

C. L. Yost Company manufactures Product A. Materials are placed in production in Department 1, and after processing, are transferred to Department 2, where more materials are added. The finished products emerge from Department 2. There is one service department: Maintenance and Repair.

There were no inventories of work in process at the beginning or at the end of March. Finished goods inventory at March 1 was 10,000 units of Product A at a total cost of $180,000.

Transactions related to manufacturing operations for March are summarized as follows:

a. Materials purchased on account, $256,900.
b. Materials requisitioned for use: Department 1, $100,540 ($92,140 entered directly into the product); Department 2, $65,210 ($56,500 entered directly into the product); Maintenance and Repair, $3,680.
c. Labor costs incurred: Department 1, $97,180 ($88,200 entered directly into the product); Department 2, $103,560 ($94,000 entered directly into the product); Maintenance and Repair, $6,910.
d. Miscellaneous costs and expenses incurred on account: Department 1, $25,150; Department 2, $23,140; Maintenance and Repair, $4,060.
e. Depreciation charged on plant assets: Department 1, $15,320; Department 2, $14,000; Maintenance and Repair, $2,760.
f. Expiration of various prepaid expenses: Department 1, $1,260; Department 2, $920; Maintenance and Repair, $340.
g. Maintenance and repair costs allocated on the basis of services rendered: Department 1, 70%; Department 2, 30%.
h. Factory overhead applied to production, based on machine hours: $70,560 and $61,100 for Departments 1 and 2, respectively.
i. Output of Department 1: 25,000 units.
j. Output of Department 2: 25,000 units of Product A.
k. Sales on account: 26,500 units of Product A at $30. Credits to the finished goods account are to be made according to the first-in, first-out method.

Instructions

Journalize the entries to record the transactions, identifying each by letter. Include as an explanation for entry (k) the number of units and the unit costs for the product sold.

Instructions for Solving Problem 23-5B Using Solutions Software

1. Load opening balances.
2. Save the opening balances file to your drive and directory.
3. Set the run date to March 31 of the current year and enter your name.
4. Select the General Journal Entries option and key the journal entries. Leave the reference field blank. Note: To review the chart of accounts, select F-1.
5. Display a journal entries report.
6. Display a trial balance.
7. Display an income statement, a retained earnings statement, and a balance sheet.
8. Save a backup copy of your data file.
9. Perform period-end closing.
10. Display a post-closing trial balance.
11. Save your data file to disk.
12. End the session.

PROBLEM 23-6B
FINANCIAL STATEMENTS
FOR PROCESS COST SYSTEM
Objective 7

The trial balance of F. L. Wilcox Co. at January 31, the end of the first month of the current fiscal year, is shown on the next page.

Instructions

1. Prepare an income statement.
2. Prepare a retained earnings statement.
3. Prepare a balance sheet.

Instructions for Solving Problem 23-6B Using Solutions Software

1. Load opening balances.
2. Save the opening balances file to your drive and directory.
3. Set the run date to January 31 of the current year and enter your name.
4. Display an income statement, a retained earnings statement, and a balance sheet.
5. Save your data file to disk.
6. End the session.

F. L. Wilcox Co.
Trial Balance
January 31, 19—

Cash	75,100	
Marketable Securities	65,500	
Accounts Receivable	245,000	
Allowance for Doubtful Accounts		9,900
Finished Goods—Product A1	95,600	
Finished Goods—Product A2	154,500	
Work in Process—Department 1	20,200	
Work in Process—Department 2	32,700	
Work in Process—Department 3	24,700	
Materials	59,700	
Prepaid Insurance	14,750	
Office Supplies	5,250	
Land	105,000	
Buildings	660,000	
Accumulated Depreciation—Buildings		319,200
Machinery and Equipment	342,000	
Accumulated Depreciation—Machinery and Equipment		216,600
Office Equipment	59,400	
Accumulated Depreciation—Office Equipment		25,560
Patents	66,000	
Accounts Payable		122,150
Wages Payable		19,750
Income Tax Payable		6,500
Mortgage Note Payable (due 2001)		120,000
Common Stock ($15 par)		600,000
Retained Earnings		518,220
Sales		755,500
Cost of Goods Sold	502,300	
Factory Overhead—Department 1	400	
Factory Overhead—Department 2	370	
Factory Overhead—Department 3		290
Selling Expenses	99,750	
Administrative Expenses	68,800	
Interest Income		350
Interest Expense	1,000	
Income Tax	16,000	
	2,714,020	2,714,020

PROBLEM 23-7B
UNIT COST OF FINISHED
PRODUCT BY AVERAGE
COST METHOD; COST OF
PRODUCTION REPORT
Objective 8

L. Short Inc. manufactures Product Q by a series of five processes, all materials being introduced in Department 1. From Department 1, the materials pass through Departments 2, 3, 4, and 5, emerging as finished Product Q. All inventories are costed by the average cost method.

The balance in the account Work in Process—Department 5 was as follows on May 1:

Materials cost (2,000 units)	$11,865
Conversion costs (2,000 units, 1/4 completed)	6,400

The following costs were charged to Work in Process—Department 5 during May:

Direct materials transferred from Department 4:	
17,500 units at $6.03 per unit	$105,525
Direct labor	167,300
Factory overhead	50,300

During May, 16,500 units of Product P were completed and the work in process inventory on May 31 was 3,000 units, 1/3 completed.

Instructions

1. Determine the following for Department 5:
   a. Average materials cost per unit.
   b. Equivalent units of production in May.
   c. Average conversion cost per unit for May.
   d. Cost of goods finished during May.
   e. Cost of work in process at May 31.
2. Prepare a cost of production report for Department 5 for May.

APPENDIX PROBLEM 23-8B
ACTIVITY-BASED COSTING

Straub Inc. manufactures two products, W and X, which involves four overhead activities—equipment maintenance and repairs, power, production setup, and quality control. The expected costs for these activities are as follows:

Overhead costs:

Equipment maintenance and repairs	$ 30,000
Power	24,000
Production setup	90,000
Quality control	70,000
Total	$214,000

The appropriate activity drivers and the amount of the activity drivers for each product are as follows:

Overhead Cost	Activity Driver
Equipment maintenance and repairs	machine hours
Power	kilowatt-hours
Production setup	number of setups
Quality control	number of inspections

	Machine Hours	Kilowatt-Hours	Number of Setups	Number of Inspections
Product W	11,000	330 000	5	8
Product X	9,000	270 000	20	32
Total	20,000	600 000	25	40

Instructions

1. Determine an overhead rate for each overhead activity.
2. Allocate the overhead costs to each product, using the overhead rates from part (1).
3. Determine the percentage of each activity driver used by each product.
4. Using the percentages computed in (3), (a) identify appropriate cost pools and determine an overhead rate for each pool (use machine hours and the number of setups as the activity drivers). (b) Allocate the overhead costs to products W and X, using the overhead rates identified in (a).

APPENDIX PROBLEM 23-9B
PLANT-WIDE OVERHEAD RATES AND ACTIVITY-BASED COSTING

Kirchoff Inc. manufactures two products, H and I, which involves four overhead activities—maintenance, power, production setup, and quality control. Kirchoff Inc. uses a plant-wide overhead rate, based upon units produced, to allocate overhead costs to Products H and I. The procedure for allocating overhead was initially established when only Product H was being produced.

Although management is pleased that sales of Product I are increasing, it is concerned because sales of the previously best-selling Product H are decreasing. Several former customers have indicated that Kirchoff Inc.'s price for Product H is too high and that they can buy a competitor's product at significant savings. The president is concerned because it is costing too much to manufacture Product H, and perhaps the company should discontinue its production.

Kirchoff Inc. has gathered the following data for use in analyzing the costs of manufacturing Products H and I:

Direct manufacturing costs (per unit):

	Product H	Product I
Direct materials	$15.00	$36.00
Direct labor	7.00	14.00
Expected production volume:	50,000 units	2,000 units

Overhead activities and costs:

Maintenance	$ 85,000
Power	65,000
Production setup	45,000
Quality control	65,000
Total	$260,000

Overhead activity drivers:

Maintenance	machine hours
Power	kilowatt-hours
Production setup	number of setups
Quality control	number of inspections

	Machine Hours	Kilowatt-Hours	Number of Setups	Number of Inspections
Product H	192,000	480 000	32	12
Product I	108,000	270 000	48	18
Total	300,000	750 000	80	30

Instructions

1. Determine the plant-wide overhead rate for Kirchoff Inc., using expected production volume as the activity base.
2. a. Using the plant-wide overhead rate determined in (1), allocate overhead to Products H and I.
   b. Determine the per unit manufacturing cost for each product, based upon the direct materials and direct labor costs and the allocated overhead.
3. Determine the expected selling price of each product, based upon the manufacturing cost per unit determined in (2). Kirchoff Inc. normally sets its prices at 25% above the manufacturing cost per unit.
4. a. Using activity-based costing, determine the percentage of each cost driver used by each product.
   b. Based upon your answer to (a), identify appropriate cost pools and determine an overhead rate for each cost pool (use machine hours and the number of setups as cost drivers).
   c. Allocate the overhead costs to Products H and I, using the overhead rates determined in (b).
   d. Determine the manufacturing overhead cost per unit for Products H and I.
   e. Determine the per unit manufacturing cost for each product, based upon the direct materials and direct labor costs and the allocated overhead.
5. Determine the expected selling price of each product, based upon the manufacturing cost per unit determined in (4). Kirchoff Inc. normally sets its prices at 25% above the manufacturing cost per unit.

SHARPEN YOUR COMMUNICATION SKILLS ▶ 6. Based upon the preceding analysis, comment on possible reasons for the decreased sales of Product H and the increased sales of Product I.

MINI-CASE 23 IPC INC.

IPC Inc. manufactures Product I-4 by a series of four processes. All materials are placed in production in the Die Casting Department and, after processing, are transferred to the Tooling, Assembly, and Polishing Departments, emerging as finished Product I-4.

On June 1, the balance in the account Work in Process—Polishing was $201,960, determined as shown below.

Direct materials: 12,000 units	$122,040
Direct labor: 12,000 units, 3/4 completed	64,530
Factory overhead: 12,000 units,	
3/4 completed	15,390
Total	$201,960

The following costs were charged to Work in Process—Polishing during June:

Direct materials transferred from	
Assembly Dept., 136,000 units	$1,428,000
Direct labor	988,920
Factory overhead	217,080

During June, 138,000 units of I-4 were completed and transferred to Finished Goods. On June 30, the inventory in the Polishing Department consisted of 10,000 units, one-half completed. All inventories are costed by the first-in, first-out method.

As a new cost accountant for IPC Inc., you have just received a phone call from Norma Sloan, the superintendent of the Polishing Department. She was extremely upset with the cost of production report, which she says does not balance. In addition, she commented:

"I give up! These reports are a waste of time. My department has always been the best department in the plant, so why should I bother with these reports? Just what purpose do they serve?"

The report to which Sloan referred is shown on the next page.

Instructions:

1. Based upon the data for June, prepare a revised cost of production report for the Polishing Department.
2. Assuming that all costs reported in the work in process account on June 1 were incurred in the preceding month, determine the unit direct materials cost and the unit conversion cost for May.
3. Based on (2), determine the change in the unit direct materials cost and unit conversion cost for June as compared to May.
4. ▮▮ ▸ Based on (3), what are some possible explanations for the changing unit costs?
5. ▮▮ ▸ Describe how you would explain to Sloan that cost of production reports are useful.

IPC Inc.
Cost of Production Report—Polishing Department
For Month Ended June 30, 19—

Quantities:
Charged to production:

In process, June 1		9,000
Received from Assembly Department		136,000
Total units to be accounted for		145,000

Units accounted for:

Transferred to finished goods		138,000
In process, June 30		5,000
Total units accounted for		143,000

Costs:
Charged to production:

In process, June 1		$ 201,960

June costs:

Direct materials from Assembly Department ($9.42 per unit)		1,428,000
Conversion costs:		
Direct labor	$988,920	
Factory overhead	217,080	
Total conversion costs ($8.04 per unit)		1,206,000
Total costs to be accounted for		$2,835,960

Costs allocated as follows:
Transferred to finished goods:

138,000 units at $17.46 ($9.42 + $8.04)		$2,409,480

In process, June 30:

Materials (5,000 units × $9.42)	$ 47,100	
Conversion costs (5,000 units × $8.04)	40,200	
Total cost of inventory in process		87,300
Total costs accounted for		$2,496,780

Computations:
Equivalent units of production:

To process units in inventory on June 1: 12,000 units × 3/4	9,000
To process units started and completed in June	136,000
To process units in inventory on June 30: 10,000 units × 1/2	5,000
Equivalent units of production	150,000
Unit conversion cost: $1,206,000 ÷ 150,000	$8.04

ANSWERS TO SELF-EXAMINATION QUESTIONS

1. **C** The process cost system is most appropriate for a business in which manufacturing is conducted by continuous operations and involves a series of uniform production processes, such as the processing of crude oil (answer C). The job order cost system is most appropriate for a business in which the product is made to a customer's specifications, such as custom furniture manufacturing (answer A), commercial building construction (answer B), and automobile repairing (answer D).

2. **C** The manufacturing costs that are necessary to convert direct materials into finished products are called conversion costs. The conversion costs include direct labor and factory overhead (answer C).

3. **B** The number of units that could have been produced from start to finish during a period is called the equivalent units. The 4,875 equivalent units (answer B) is determined as follows:

To process units in inventory on May 1: 1,000 × 1/4	250
To process units started and completed in May: 5,500 units – 1,000 units	4,500
To process units in inventory on May 31: 500 units × 1/4	125
Equivalent units of production in May	4,875

4. **A** The conversion costs (direct labor and factory overhead) totaling $48,750 are divided by the number of equivalent units (4,875) to determine the unit conversion cost of $10 (answer A).

5. **D** Service departments, such as factory office (answer A), power plant (answer B), and maintenance (answer C), perform services for the processing departments.

You and Accounting

What are the costs of operating your car?

The costs of operating a car include some costs that will not change on a day-to-day basis as you drive. For example, you will normally pay a license plate (tag) fee once a year. This cost does not change, regardless of the number of miles you drive. On the other hand, the total amount you spend on gasoline during the year changes on a day-to-day basis as you drive. The more you drive, the more you spend on gasoline.

How does such operating cost information affect you?

Information on how the costs of operating your car behave could be relevant in planning a summer vacation. For example, you might be trying to decide between taking an airline flight or driving your car to your vacation destination. In this case, your license plate fees and annual car insurance costs will not change, regardless of whether you drive your car or fly. Thus, these costs would not affect your decision. However, the estimated cost of gasoline and routine maintenance would affect your decision.

As in operating your car, all of the costs of operating a business do not behave in the same way. This chapter discusses commonly used methods for classifying costs according to how they change and how management uses such information in making decisions.

Chapter 24
Cost Behavior and Cost-Volume-Profit Analysis

LEARNING OBJECTIVES
After studying this chapter, you should be able to:

Objective 1
Classify costs by their behavior as:

Variable costs
Fixed costs
Mixed costs

Objective 2
Compute the contribution margin, the contribution margin ratio, and the unit contribution margin, and explain how they may be useful to managers.

Objective 3
Using the unit contribution margin, determine the break-even point and the volume necessary to achieve a target profit.

Objective 4
Using a cost-volume-profit chart and a profit-volume chart, determine the break-even point and the volume necessary to achieve a target profit.

Objective 5
Calculate the break-even point for an enterprise selling more than one product.

Objective 6
Compute the margin of safety and the operating leverage, and explain how managers use these concepts.

Objective 7
List the assumptions underlying cost-volume-profit analysis.

A variety of managerial cost terms, classifications, systems, and concepts have been described and illustrated in the preceding chapters. This chapter continues this discussion by focusing on how costs change or behave as the level of operations changes.

A thorough understanding of how costs behave is essential for planning and controlling operations. For example, classifying costs by their behavior allows management to establish standards for evaluating (controlling) the efficiency of current operations and for predicting (planning) the costs of future levels of operations.

An understanding of how costs behave is also essential in applying analyses such as cost-volume-profit analysis. Cost-volume-profit analysis is a commonly used tool that is discussed in this chapter. It provides management with useful information by relating the effects of changes in costs, revenues, and volume on profits.

COST BEHAVIOR

Cost behavior refers to the manner in which a cost changes as a related activity changes.[1] Knowledge of how costs behave is useful to management for a variety of purposes. For example, knowledge as to how costs behave allows managers to predict profits as sales and production volumes change. Knowledge of how costs behave is also useful for estimating costs. Estimated costs, in turn, affect a variety of management decisions, such as whether to use excess capacity to produce and sell a product at a reduced price.

To understand the behavior of a cost, two factors that are related to the cost must be considered. First, the activities that are thought to cause the incurrence of the cost must be identified. Such activities are called **activity bases (drivers)**. Second, the range of activity over which the changes in the cost are of interest to management must be specified. This range of activity is often called the **relevant range**.

To illustrate, hospital administrators must plan and control hospital food costs. To fully understand why food costs change, the activity that causes the incurrence of the cost must be identified. In the case of food costs, the feeding of patients is a major cause of these costs. The number of patients *treated* by the hospital would not be a good activity base, since some patients are outpatients who do not stay in the hospital. The number of patients who *stay* in the hospital, however, is an appropriate activity base for studying food costs. Once the proper activity base (driver) is identified, food costs can then be analyzed over the range of the number of patients who normally stay in the hospital (the relevant range).

Three of the most common ways in which costs are classified by behavior for management decision making include variable costs, fixed costs, and mixed costs. Each of these cost classifications is discussed below.

Variable Costs

Variable costs are costs that vary in total in proportion to changes in the level of activity. When the level of activity is measured in units produced, direct materials and direct labor costs are generally classified as variable costs. For example, assume that Jason Inc. produces stereo sound systems under the brand name of J-Sound. The parts for the stereo systems are purchased from outside suppliers for $10 per unit and are assembled in Jason Inc.'s Waterloo plant. The direct materials costs for Model JS-12 for the relevant range of 5,000 to 30,000 units of production are shown below.

Number of Units of Model JS-12 Produced	Direct Materials Cost per Unit	Total Direct Materials Cost
5,000 units	$10	$ 50,000
10,000	10	100,000
15,000	10	150,000
20,000	10	200,000
25,000	10	250,000
30,000	10	300,000

As illustrated above, the total direct materials cost varies in direct proportion to the number of units of Model JS-12 produced. That is, the direct materials cost for 10,000 units ($100,000) is 2 times the direct materials cost for 5,000 units ($50,000). The cost varies in proportion to the number of units produced because the cost per unit ($10) remains the same for all levels of production. Thus, producing 20,000 more units will increase the direct materials cost by $200,000 (20,000 units × $10), producing 25,000 more units will increase the materials cost by $250,000, and so on.

Exhibit 1 illustrates how the variable costs for direct materials for Model JS-12 behave in total and on a per unit basis as production changes.

[1] In this chapter, the term *costs* is often used as a convenience to represent both *costs* and *expenses*.

Exhibit 1
Total Variable Cost Graph and
Unit Variable Cost Graph

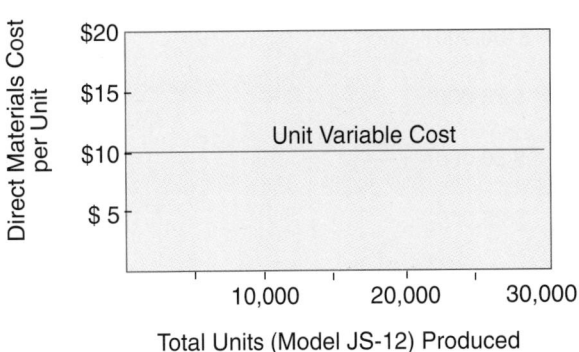

Fixed Costs

Fixed costs are costs that remain the same in total as the level of activity changes. When units produced is the measure of activity, examples of fixed manufacturing costs include straight-line depreciation of factory equipment, insurance on factory plant and equipment, and salaries of factory supervisory personnel.

To illustrate, assume that Minton Inc. manufactures, bottles, and distributes La Fleur Perfume at its Los Angeles plant. The production supervisor at the Los Angeles plant is Jane Sovissi, who is paid a salary of $75,000 per year. The relevant range of activity for a year is 50,000 to 300,000 bottles of perfume. Sovissi's salary is a fixed cost that does not vary with the number of units produced. Sovissi will receive a salary of $75,000, regardless of the number of bottles produced within the relevant range of 50,000 to 300,000 bottles.

Although the total fixed cost remains the same as the number of units (bottles) produced changes, the fixed cost per unit (bottle) changes. As more units (bottles) are produced, the total fixed costs are spread over a larger number of units (bottles), and thus the fixed cost per unit decreases. These attributes of the $75,000 total fixed cost and the fixed cost per unit are shown below.

Number of Bottles of Perfume Produced	Total Supervisory Salary	Supervisory Salary per Unit
50,000 bottles	$75,000	$1.500
100,000	75,000	.750
150,000	75,000	.500
200,000	75,000	.375
250,000	75,000	.300
300,000	75,000	.250

Exhibit 2 illustrates how the fixed cost of Jane Sovissi's salary behaves graphically in total and on a per unit basis as production changes.

Mixed Costs

A mixed cost has attributes of both a variable and a fixed cost. For example, over one range of activity, the total mixed cost may remain the same. It thus behaves as a fixed cost. Over another range of activity, the mixed cost may change in proportion to changes in the level of activity. It thus behaves as a variable cost. Mixed costs are sometimes called **semivariable** or **semifixed costs**.

To illustrate, assume that Simpson Inc. manufactures sails, using rented machinery. The rental charges are $15,000 per year plus $1 for each machine hour

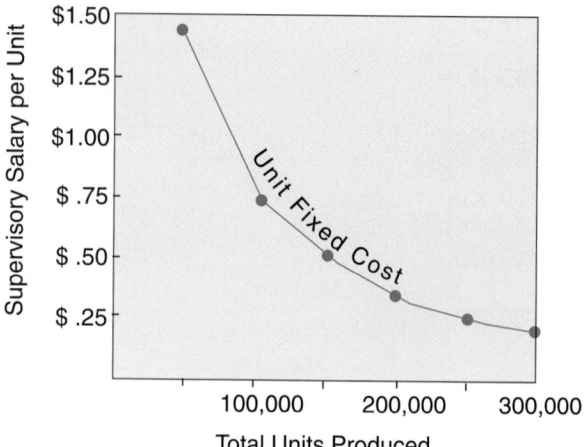

used over 10,000 hours. If the machinery is used 8,000 hours, the total rental charge is $15,000. If the machinery is used 20,000 hours, the total rental charge is $25,000 [$15,000 + (10,000 hours × $1)], and so on. Thus, if the level of activity is measured in machine hours and the relevant range is 0 to 40,000 hours, the rental charges are a fixed cost up to 10,000 hours and a variable cost thereafter. This mixed cost behavior is shown graphically in Exhibit 3.

Exhibit 3
Mixed Costs

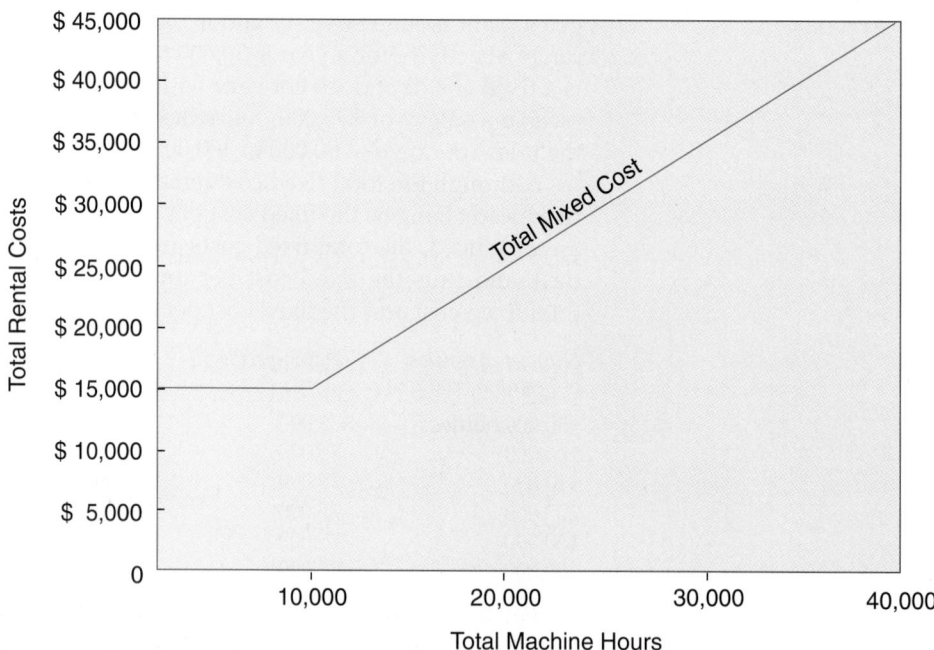

In practice, mixed costs are usually separated into their fixed and variable components for management analysis. The **high-low method** is a cost estimation technique that may be used for this purpose.[2] The high-low method uses the highest and lowest activity levels and their related costs to estimate the variable cost per unit and the fixed cost component of mixed costs.

[2] Other methods of estimating costs, such as the scattergraph method and the least squares method, are discussed in cost accounting textbooks.

To illustrate, assume that the Equipment Maintenance Department of Kason Inc. incurred the following costs during the past 5 months:

	Production	Total Cost
June	1,000 units	$45,550
July	1,500	52,500
August	2,100	61,500
September	1,800	57,000
October	750	41,250

The number of units produced is the measure of activity, and the number of units produced between June and October represents the relevant range of production. For Kason Inc., the difference between the number of units produced and the difference between the total cost at the highest and lowest levels of production are as follows:

	Production	Total Cost
Highest level	2,100 units	$61,500
Lowest level	750	41,250
Difference	1,350 units	$20,250

Since the total fixed cost does not change with changes in volume of production, the $20,250 difference in the total cost represents the change in the total variable cost. Hence, dividing the difference in the total cost by the difference in production provides an estimate of the variable cost per unit. For Kason Inc., the variable cost per unit is $15, as shown below.

$$\text{Variable Cost per Unit} = \frac{\text{Difference in Total Cost}}{\text{Difference in Production}}$$

$$\text{Variable Cost per Unit} = \frac{\$20,250}{1,350 \text{ units}} = \$15$$

The fixed cost will be the same at both the highest and the lowest levels of production. Thus, the fixed cost can be estimated at either of these levels. This is done by subtracting the estimated total variable cost from the total cost, using the following total cost equation:

Total Cost = (Variable Cost per Unit × Units of Production) + Fixed Cost

Highest level:
$61,500 = ($15 × 2,100 units) + Fixed Cost
$61,500 = $31,500 + Fixed Cost
$30,000 = Fixed Cost

Lowest level:
$41,250 = ($15 × 750 units) + Fixed Cost
$41,250 = $11,250 + Fixed Cost
$30,000 = Fixed Cost

The total equipment maintenance cost for Kason Inc. can thus be analyzed as a $30,000 fixed cost and a $15-per-unit variable cost. Using these amounts in the total cost equation above, the total equipment maintenance cost at other levels of production can be estimated.

Summary of Cost Behavior Concepts

As indicated in the preceding paragraphs, costs can be classified as variable costs, fixed costs, or mixed costs. For purposes of analysis, mixed costs are generally separated into their variable and fixed cost components. The following table summarizes the cost behavior attributes of variable costs and fixed costs:

Effect of Changing Activity Level

Cost	Total Amount	Per Unit Amount
Variable	Increases and decreases proportionately with activity level.	Remains the same regardless of activity level.
Fixed	Remains the same regardless of activity level.	Increases and decreases inversely with activity level.

Reporting Variable and Fixed Costs

Separating costs into their variable and fixed components and reporting them can be useful for management decision making. One method of reporting variable and fixed costs is called **variable costing** or **direct costing**. Under variable costing, only the variable manufacturing costs (direct materials, direct labor, and variable factory overhead) are included in the product cost. The fixed factory overhead is an expense of the period in which it is incurred.[3]

COST-VOLUME-PROFIT RELATIONSHIPS

Objective 2
Compute the contribution margin, the contribution margin ratio, and the unit contribution margin, and explain how they may be useful to managers.

After costs have been classified as fixed and variable, their effect on revenues, volume, and profits can be studied by using cost-volume-profit analysis. **Cost-volume-profit analysis** is the systematic examination of the relationships among selling prices, volume of sales and production, costs, expenses, and profits.

Cost-volume-profit analysis is a commonly used tool that provides management with information for decision making. For example, cost-volume-profit analysis may be used in setting selling prices, selecting the mix of products to sell, choosing among marketing strategies, and analyzing the effects of changes in costs on profits. In today's manufacturing and marketing environment, management must make such decisions quickly and accurately. As a result, the importance of cost-volume-profit analysis has increased in recent years.

Contribution Margin Concept

One relationship among cost, volume, and profit is the contribution margin. The **contribution margin** is the excess of sales revenues over variable costs. The contribution margin concept is especially useful in business planning because it gives insight into the profit potential of a firm. To illustrate, the income statement of Lambert Inc. in Exhibit 4 has been prepared in a contribution margin format.

Exhibit 4
Contribution Margin Income Statement

Sales	$1,000,000
Variable costs	600,000
Contribution margin	$ 400,000
Fixed costs	300,000
Operating income	$ 100,000

The contribution margin of $400,000 is available to cover the fixed costs of $300,000. Once the fixed costs are covered, any remaining contribution margin adds directly to the operating income of the company.

CONTRIBUTION MARGIN RATIO. The contribution margin can also be expressed as a percentage. The **contribution margin ratio** sometimes called the **profit-volume ratio**, indicates the percentage of each sales dollar available to cover the fixed costs and to provide operating income. For Lambert Inc., the contribution margin ratio is 40%, as computed below.

---

[3] The variable costing concept is discussed more fully in the appendix at the end of this chapter.

$$\text{Contribution Margin Ratio} = \frac{\text{Sales} - \text{Variable Costs}}{\text{Sales}}$$

$$\text{Contribution Margin Ratio} = \frac{\$1,000,000 - \$600,000}{\$1,000,000} = 40\%$$

The contribution margin ratio permits the quick determination of the effect on operating income of an increase or a decrease in sales volume. For example, assume that the management of Lambert Inc. is studying the effect of adding $80,000 in sales orders. Multiplying the contribution margin ratio (40%) by the change in sales volume ($80,000) indicates that operating income will increase $32,000 if the additional orders are obtained. The validity of this analysis is illustrated by the following contribution margin income statement of Lambert Inc.:

Sales	$1,080,000
Variable costs ($1,080,000 × 60%)	648,000
Contribution margin ($1,080,000 × 40%)	$ 432,000
Fixed costs	300,000
Operating income	$ 132,000

Variable costs as a percentage of sales are equal to 100% minus the contribution margin ratio. Thus, in the above income statement, the variable costs are 60% (100% − 40%) of sales, or $648,000 ($1,080,000 × 60%). The total contribution margin, $432,000, can also be computed directly by multiplying the sales by the contribution margin ratio ($1,080,000 × 40%).

In using the contribution margin ratio in an analysis, factors other than sales volume are assumed to remain constant. If such factors as the amount of fixed costs, the percentage of variable costs to sales, and the unit sales price are not constant, the effect of any change must be considered.

The contribution margin ratio is also useful in setting business policy. For example, if the contribution margin ratio of a firm is large and production is at a level below 100% capacity, a comparatively large increase in operating income can be expected from an increase in sales volume. A firm in such a position might decide to devote more effort to additional sales promotion because of the large change in operating income that will result from changes in sales volume. In contrast, a firm with a small contribution margin ratio will probably want to give more attention to reducing costs before attempting to promote sales.

UNIT CONTRIBUTION MARGIN. Similar to the contribution margin ratio, the unit contribution margin is also a useful relationship for analyzing the profit potential of proposed projects. The **unit contribution margin** is the dollars available from each unit of sales to cover fixed costs and provide operating profits. For example, if Lambert Inc.'s unit selling price is $20 and its unit variable cost is $12, the unit contribution margin is $8 ($20 − $12).

The contribution margin ratio is most useful when the increase or decrease in sales volume is measured in sales dollars. The unit contribution margin is most useful when the increase or decrease in sales volume is measured in sales units (quantities). To illustrate, assume that Lambert Inc. sold 50,000 units. Its operating income is $100,000, as shown in the following contribution margin income statement:

Sales (50,000 units × $20)	$1,000,000
Variable costs (50,000 × $12)	600,000
Contribution margin (50,000 units × $8)	$ 400,000
Fixed costs	300,000
Operating income	$ 100,000

If Lambert Inc.'s sales could be increased by 15,000 units, from 50,000 units to 65,000 units, its operating income would increase by $120,000 (15,000 units × $8), as shown below.

Sales (65,000 units × $20)	$1,300,000
Variable costs (65,000 × $12)	780,000
Contribution margin (65,000 units × $8)	$ 520,000
Fixed costs	300,000
Operating income	$ 220,000

Unit contribution margin analyses can provide useful information for managers. The preceding illustration indicates, for example, that Lambert could spend up to $120,000 to increase sales by 15,000 units. The additional expense might be incurred for special advertising or other product promotions.

MATHEMATICAL APPROACH TO COST-VOLUME-PROFIT ANALYSIS

Objective 3
Using the unit contribution margin, determine the break-even point and the volume necessary to achieve a target profit.

Accountants have proposed various approaches for expressing the effect of costs and expenses along with revenues and volume on profits (cost-volume-profit). The mathematical approach is one approach that is used frequently in practice.

The mathematical approach to cost-volume-profit analysis uses equations (1) to determine the units of sales necessary to achieve the break-even point in operations or (2) to determine the units of sales necessary to achieve a target or desired profit. These equations and their use by management in profit planning are described and illustrated in the paragraphs that follow.

Break-Even Point

The level of operations at which an enterprise's revenues and expired costs are exactly equal is called the **break-even point.** At this level of operations, an enterprise will neither realize an operating income nor incur an operating loss. The break-even point is useful as a guide to business planning, especially when either an expansion or a decline in operations is expected.

To illustrate the computation of the break-even point, assume that the fixed costs for Barker Corporation are estimated to be $90,000. The unit selling price, unit variable cost, and unit contribution margin for Barker Corporation are as follows:

Unit selling price	$25
Unit variable cost	15
Unit contribution margin	$10

The break-even point is 9,000 units, which can be computed by using the following equation:

$$\text{Break-Even Sales (Units)} = \frac{\text{Fixed Costs}}{\text{Unit Contribution Margin}}$$

$$\text{Break-Even Sales (Units)} = \frac{\$90,000}{\$10} = 9,000 \text{ units}$$

The validity of the preceding computation is shown by the following income statement:

Sales (9,000 units × $25)	$225,000
Variable costs (9,000 units × $15)	135,000
Contribution margin	$ 90,000
Fixed costs	90,000
Operating income	$ 0

The break-even point is affected by changes in the fixed costs, unit variable costs, and the unit selling price. The effect of each of these factors on the break-even point is discussed below.

EFFECT OF CHANGES IN FIXED COSTS. Although fixed costs do not change in total with changes in the level of activity, they may change because of such factors as changes in property tax rates or salary increases given to factory supervisors. Increases in fixed costs will raise the break-even point. Likewise, decreases in fixed costs will lower the break-even point.

To illustrate, assume that Bishop Co. is evaluating a proposal to budget an additional $100,000 for advertising. Fixed costs before the additional advertising are estimated at $600,000, and the unit contribution margin is $20. The break-even point before the additional expense is 30,000 units, computed as follows:

$$\text{Break-Even Sales (Units)} = \frac{\text{Fixed Costs}}{\text{Unit Contribution Margin}}$$

$$\text{Break-Even Sales (Units)} = \frac{\$600,000}{\$20} = 30,000 \text{ units}$$

If the additional amount is spent, the fixed costs will increase by $100,000 and the break-even point will increase to 35,000 units, computed as follows:

$$\text{Break-Even Sales (Units)} = \frac{\text{Fixed Costs}}{\text{Unit Contribution Margin}}$$

$$\text{Break-Even Sales (Units)} = \frac{\$700,000}{\$20} = 35,000 \text{ units}$$

The increased fixed cost of $100,000 increases the break-even point by 5,000 units of sales. The break-even point changes because, for each unit sold, the unit contribution margin of $20 is available to cover fixed costs. An increase in the fixed costs of $100,000 will require an additional 5,000 units ($100,000 ÷ $20) of sales to break even. In other words, an increase in sales of 5,000 units is required in order to generate an additional $100,000 of total contribution margin (5,000 units × $20) to cover the increased fixed costs.

EFFECT OF CHANGES IN UNIT VARIABLE COSTS. Although unit variable costs do not change with changes in volume of activity, they may change because of such factors as changes in the price of direct materials and increases in wages for factory workers providing direct labor. Increases in unit variable costs will raise the break-even point. Likewise, decreases in unit variable costs will lower the break-even point.

To illustrate, assume that Park Co. is evaluating a proposal to pay an additional 2% commission to its sales representatives as an incentive to increase sales. Fixed costs are estimated at $840,000, and the unit selling price, unit variable cost, and unit contribution margin before the additional 2% commission are as follows:

Unit selling price	$250
Unit variable cost	145
Unit contribution margin	$105

The break-even point is 8,000 units, computed as follows:

$$\text{Break-Even Sales (Units)} = \frac{\text{Fixed Costs}}{\text{Unit Contribution Margin}}$$

$$\text{Break-Even Sales (Units)} = \frac{\$840,000}{\$105} = 8,000 \text{ units}$$

If the sales commission proposal is adopted, variable costs will increase by $5 per unit ($250 × 2%). This increase in the variable costs will decrease the unit contribution margin by $5 (from $105 to $100). Thus, the break-even point is raised to 8,400 units, computed as follows:

$$\text{Break-Even Sales (Units)} = \frac{\text{Fixed Costs}}{\text{Unit Contribution Margin}}$$

$$\text{Break-Even Sales (Units)} = \frac{\$840,000}{\$100} = 8,400 \text{ units}$$

The additional 2% sales commission increases the break-even point by 400 units. The break-even point changes because, at the original break-even point of 8,000 units, the new unit contribution margin of $100 would only provide $800,000 to cover fixed costs of $840,000. Thus, an additional 400 units of sales will be required in order to provide the additional $40,000 (400 units × $100) contribution margin necessary to break even.

EFFECT OF CHANGES IN THE UNIT SELLING PRICE. Increases in the unit selling price will lower the break-even point, while decreases in the unit selling price will raise the break-even point. To illustrate, assume that Graham Co. is evaluating a proposal to increase the unit selling price of its product from $50 to $60. The following data have been gathered:

	Current	Proposed
Unit selling price	$50	$60
Unit variable cost	30	30
Unit contribution margin	$20	$30
Total fixed costs	$600,000	$600,000

The break-even point based on the current selling price is 30,000 units, computed as follows:

$$\text{Break-Even Sales (Units)} = \frac{\text{Fixed Costs}}{\text{Unit Contribution Margin}}$$

$$\text{Break-Even Sales (Units)} = \frac{\$600,000}{\$20} = 30,000 \text{ units}$$

If the selling price is increased by $10 per unit, the break-even point is decreased to 20,000 units, computed as follows:

$$\text{Break-Even Sales (Units)} = \frac{\text{Fixed Costs}}{\text{Unit Contribution Margin}}$$

$$\text{Break-Even Sales (Units)} = \frac{\$600,000}{\$30} = 20,000 \text{ units}$$

The increase of $10 per unit in the selling price increases the unit contribution margin by $10. Thus, the break-even point decreases by 10,000 units (from 30,000 units to 20,000 units).

Target Profit

At the break-even point, sales and costs are exactly equal. However, the break-even point is not the goal for the future operations of most enterprises. Rather, they seek to achieve the largest possible volume of sales above the break-even point. By modifying the break-even equation, the sales volume required to earn a target or desired amount of profit may be estimated. For this purpose, a factor for target profit is added to the standard break-even equation as shown below.

$$\text{Sales (Units)} = \frac{\text{Fixed Cost} + \text{Target Profit}}{\text{Unit Contribution Margin}}$$

To illustrate, assume that fixed costs are estimated at $200,000, and the desired profit is $100,000. The unit selling price, unit variable cost, and unit contribution margin are as follows:

Unit selling price	$75
Unit variable cost	45
Unit contribution margin	$30

The sales volume necessary to earn the target profit of $100,000 is 10,000 units, computed as follows:

$$\text{Sales (Units)} = \frac{\text{Fixed Costs} + \text{Target Profit}}{\text{Unit Contribution Margin}}$$

$$\text{Sales (Units)} = \frac{\$200,000 + \$100,000}{\$30} = 10,000 \text{ units}$$

The validity of this computation is shown in the following income statement:

Sales (10,000 units × $75)	$750,000
Variable costs (10,000 units × $45)	450,000
Contribution margin (10,000 units × $30)	$300,000
Fixed costs	200,000
Operating income	$100,000

GRAPHIC APPROACH TO COST-VOLUME-PROFIT ANALYSIS

Objective 4
Using a cost-volume-profit chart and a profit-volume chart, determine the break-even point and the volume necessary to achieve a target profit.

Cost-volume-profit analysis can be presented graphically as well as in equation form. Many managers prefer the graphic format because the operating profit or loss for any given level of sales can be visually determined. The following paragraphs describe two graphic approaches that managers find useful.

Cost-Volume-Profit (Break-Even) Chart

A **cost-volume-profit chart**, sometimes called a **break-even chart**, may assist management in understanding relationships among costs, sales, and operating profit or loss. To illustrate, the cost-volume-profit chart in Exhibit 5 is based on the following data.

Unit selling price	$50
Unit variable cost	30
Unit contribution margin	$20
Total fixed costs	$100,000

Exhibit 5
Cost-Volume-Profit Chart

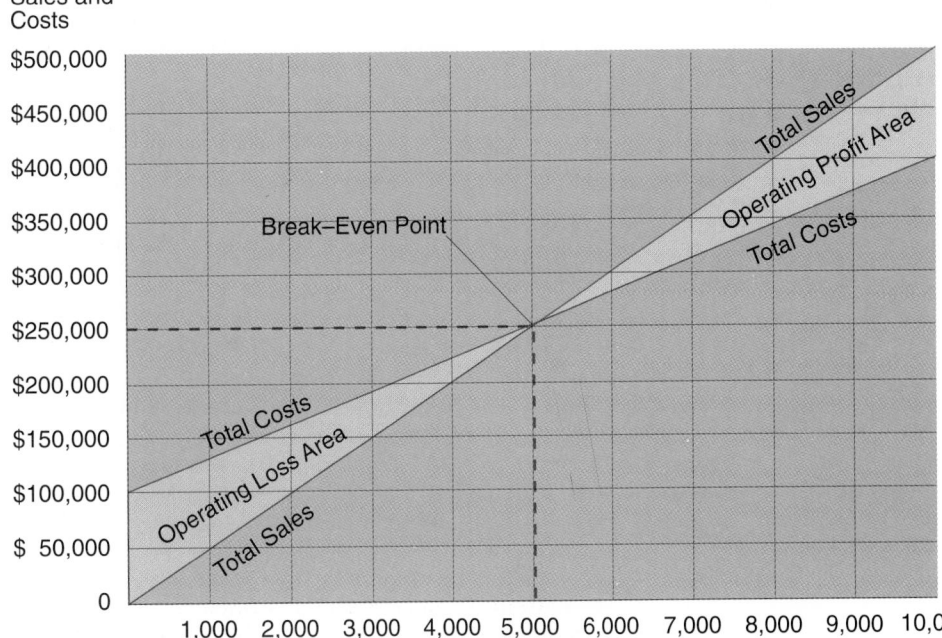

The cost-volume-profit chart in Exhibit 5 is constructed as follows:

1. Volume expressed in units of sales is indicated along the horizontal axis. The range of volume shown on the horizontal axis should reflect the relevant range in which the enterprise expects to operate. Dollar amounts representing total sales and costs are indicated along the vertical axis.
2. A sales line is plotted by beginning at zero on the left corner of the graph. A second point is determined by multiplying any units of sales on the horizontal axis by the unit sales price of $50. For example, for 10,000 units of sales, the total sales would be $500,000 (10,000 units × $50). The sales line is drawn upward to the right from zero through the $500,000 point.
3. A cost line is plotted by beginning with total fixed costs, $100,000, on the vertical axis. A second point is determined by multiplying any units of sales on the horizontal axis by the unit variable costs and adding the fixed costs. For example, for 10,000 units of sales, the total estimated costs would be $400,000 [(10,000 units × $30) + $100,000]. The cost line is drawn upward to the right from $100,000 on the vertical axis through the $400,000 point.
4. Horizontal and vertical lines are drawn at the point of intersection of the sales and cost lines, which is the break-even point, and the areas representing operating profit and operating loss are identified.

In Exhibit 5, the dotted lines drawn from the point of intersection of the total sales line and the total cost line identify the break-even point in total sales dollars and units. The break-even point is $250,000 of sales, which represents a sales volume of 5,000 units. Operating profits will be earned when sales levels are to the right of the break-even point (operating profit area). Operating losses will be incurred when sales levels are to the left of the break-even point (operating loss area).

Changes in the unit selling price, total fixed costs, and unit variable costs can be analyzed by using a cost-volume-profit chart. Using the data in Exhibit 5, assume that a proposal to reduce fixed costs by $20,000 is to be evaluated. In this case, the total fixed costs would be $80,000 ($100,000 − $20,000). As shown in Exhibit 6, the total cost line should be redrawn, starting at the $80,000 point (total fixed costs) on the vertical axis. A second point is determined by multiplying any units of sales on the horizontal axis by the unit variable costs and adding the fixed costs.

Exhibit 6
Revised Cost-Volume-Profit Chart

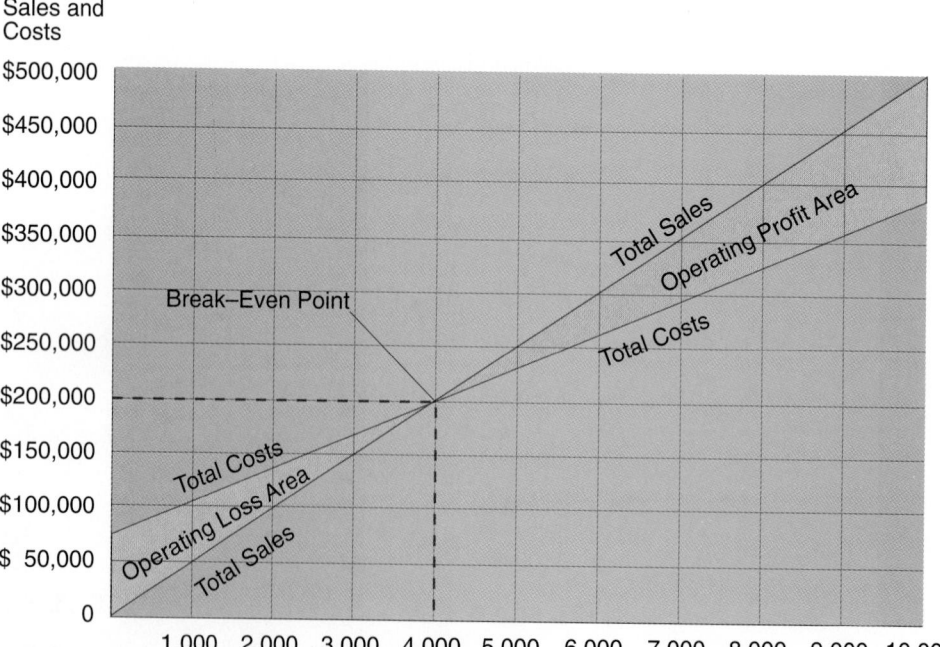

For example, for 10,000 units of sales, the total estimated costs would be $380,000 [(10,000 units × $30) + $80,000]. The cost line is drawn upward to the right from $80,000 on the vertical axis through the $380,000 point. The revised cost-volume-profit chart in Exhibit 6 indicates that the break-even point decreases to $200,000 or 4,000 units of sales.

Profit-Volume Chart

Another graphic approach to cost-volume-profit analysis, the **profit-volume chart**, focuses on profits. This is in contrast to the cost-volume-profit chart, which focuses on sales and costs. The profit-volume chart plots only the difference between total sales and total costs or profits. In this way, the profit-volume chart allows managers to determine the operating profit (or loss) for various levels of operations.

To illustrate, assume the profit-volume chart in Exhibit 7 is based on the same data as used in Exhibit 5. These data are as follows:

Unit selling price	$50
Unit variable cost	30
Unit contribution margin	$20
Total fixed costs	$100,000

The maximum operating loss is equal to the fixed costs of $100,000. Assuming that the maximum unit sales within the relevant range is 10,000 units, the maximum operating profit is $100,000, computed as follows:

Sales (10,000 units × $50)	$500,000
Variable costs (10,000 units × $30)	300,000
Contribution margin (10,000 units × $20)	$200,000
Fixed costs	100,000
Operating profit	$100,000

Exhibit 7
Profit-Volume Chart

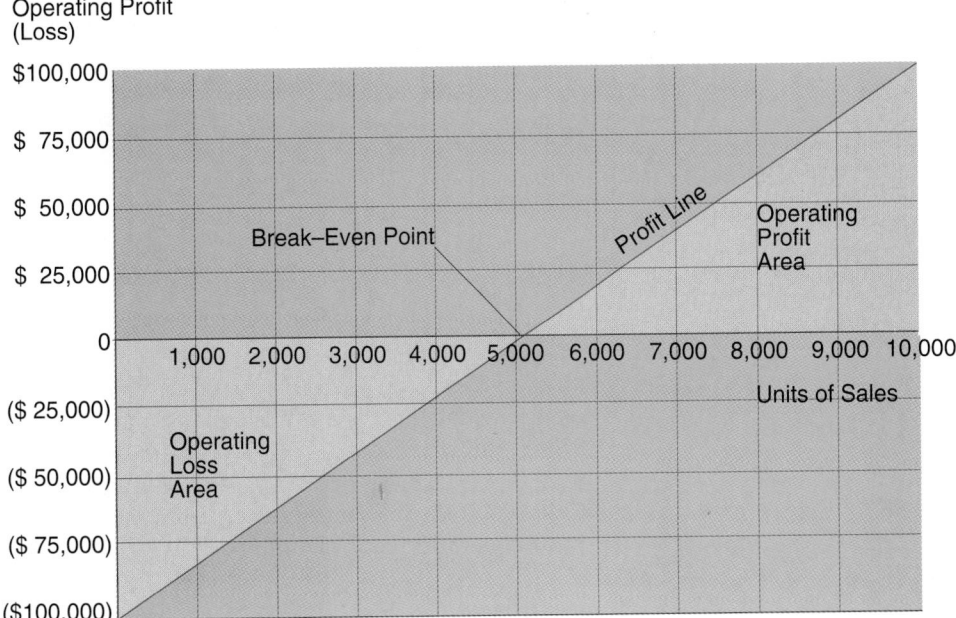

The profit-volume chart in Exhibit 7 is constructed as follows:

1. Volume expressed in units of sales is indicated along the horizontal axis. The range of volume shown on the horizontal axis should reflect the relevant range

in which the enterprise expects to operate. In this illustration, the maximum number of sales units within the relevant range is assumed to be 10,000 units. Dollar amounts indicating operating profits and losses are shown along the vertical axis.

2. A point representing the maximum operating loss is plotted on the vertical axis at the left. This loss is equal to the total fixed costs at the zero level of sales.

3. A point representing the maximum operating profit within the relevant range is plotted on the right.

4. A diagonal profit line is drawn connecting the maximum operating loss point with the maximum operating profit point.

5. The profit line intersects the horizontal axis at the break-even point expressed in units of sales, and the areas indicating operating profit and loss are identified.

In Exhibit 7, the break-even point is 5,000 units of sales, which is equal to total sales of $250,000 (5,000 units × $50). Operating profit will be earned when sales levels are to the right of the break-even point (operating profit area). Operating losses will be incurred when sales levels are to the left of the break-even point (operating loss area). For example, at sales of 8,000 units, an operating profit of $60,000 will be earned, as shown in Exhibit 8.

Exhibit 8
Operating Profit Plotted on
Profit-Volume Chart

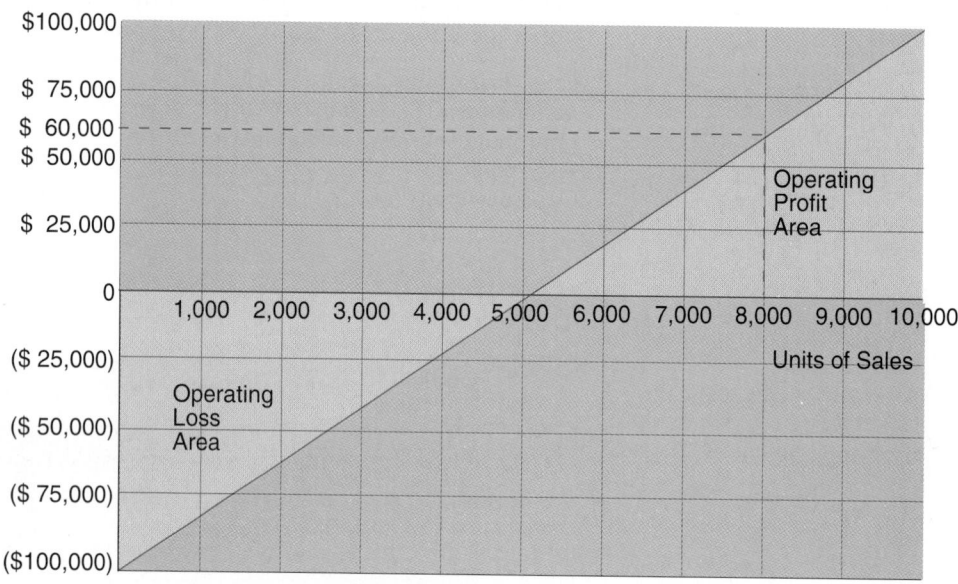

The effect of changes in the unit selling price, total fixed costs, and unit variable costs on profit can be analyzed using a profit-volume chart. To illustrate, using the data in Exhibits 7 and 8, assume that the effect on profit of an increase of $20,000 in fixed costs is to be evaluated. In this case, the total fixed costs would be $120,000 ($100,000 + $20,000), and the maximum operating loss would also be $120,000. If the maximum sales within the relevant range is 10,000 units, the maximum operating profit would be $80,000, computed as follows:

Sales (10,000 units × $50)	$500,000
Variable costs (10,000 units × $30)	300,000
Contribution margin (10,000 units × $20)	$200,000
Fixed costs	120,000
Operating profit	$ 80,000

A revised profit-volume chart is constructed by plotting the maximum operating loss and maximum operating profit points and drawing the revised profit line. The original and the revised profit-volume charts are shown in Exhibit 9.

Exhibit 9
Original Profit-Volume Chart and
Revised Profit-Volume Chart

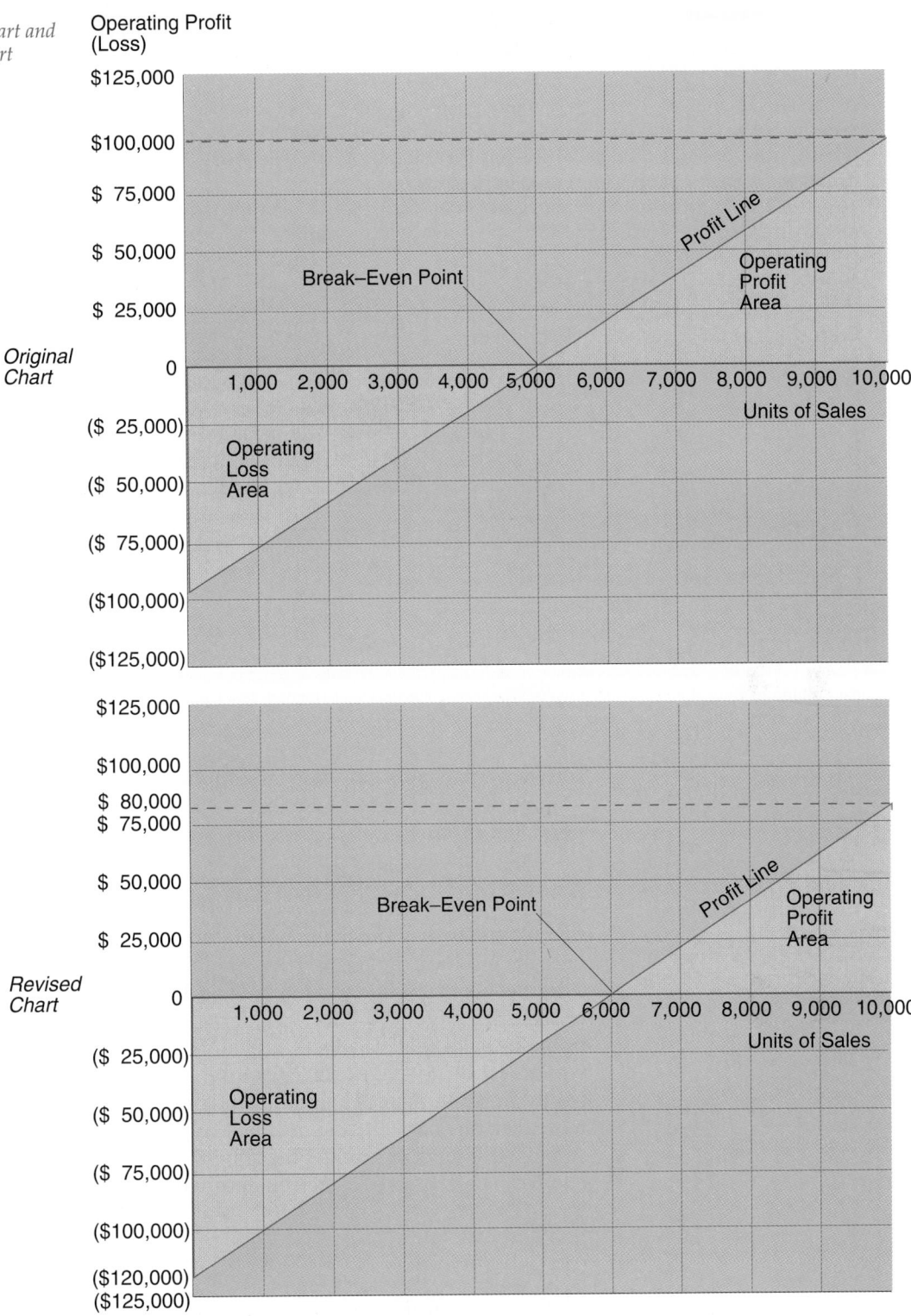

The revised profit-volume chart indicates that the break-even point is 6,000 units of sales. This is equal to total sales of $300,000 (6,000 units × $50). The operating loss area of the chart has increased, while the operating profit area has decreased under the proposed change in fixed costs.

Use of Computers in Cost-Volume-Profit Analysis

The graphic approach as well as the mathematical approach to cost-volume-profit analysis are becoming increasingly easy to use when managers have access to a computer terminal or a microcomputer. With the aid of computer

Break-Even Analysis—A Case Study

A break-even analysis based on a multidimensional approach, rather than the traditional two-dimensional approach, was described in an article in *The Journal of Accountancy*. Such an approach is used by The Motor Convoy Inc., a Georgia-based common carrier operating primarily in the southeastern U.S. The Motor Convoy Inc.'s

chief financial officer prepared the following break-even chart.

The chart illustrates a typical break-even analysis at The Motor Convoy for a normal load of 2,000 pounds over a relevant range of trips—from about 100 miles to 450 miles. The rate and cost per pound are plotted along the vertical axis, while the length of the trip (in miles) is plotted along the horizontal axis. The rate charged by The Motor Convoy's primary competitor is also graphed, so that the company can assess the effect of competition on developing its operating strategy.

In the above chart, the rate and cost curves are drawn only in the relevant range. The competitor's rate curve is parallel to The Motor Convoy's cost curve, and both rate curves cross at 110 miles. At this volume, The Motor Convoy's business should be concentrated on trips between 110 miles and 190 miles. On shorter trips, the competition is cheaper than The Motor Convoy, while on longer trips, The Motor Convoy is losing money.

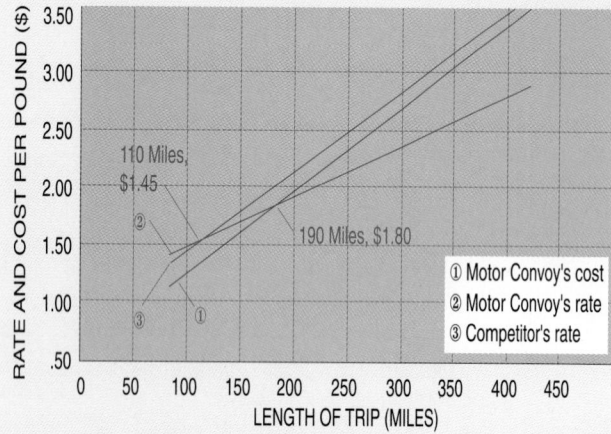

Source: "Multidimensional Break-Even Analysis," *The Journal of Accountancy* (January 1987), pp. 132–133.

software, managers can vary assumptions regarding selling prices, costs, and volume and can immediately see the effects of each change on the break-even point and profit.

SALES MIX CONSIDERATIONS

Objective 5
Calculate the break-even point for an enterprise selling more than one product.

In most business, more than one product is sold at varying selling prices. In addition, the products often have different unit variable costs, and each product makes a different contribution to profits. Thus, the sales volume necessary to break even or to earn a target profit for an enterprise selling two or more products depends upon the sales mix. The **sales mix** is the relative distribution of sales among the various products sold by an enterprise.

To illustrate the calculation of the break-even point for a company that sells more than one product, assume that Cascade Company sold 8,000 units of Product A and 2,000 units of Product B during the past year. The sales mix for products A and B can be expressed as percentages, as shown below, or as a ratio (80:20).

Product	Units Sold	Sales Mix
A	8,000	80%
B	2,000	20
	10,000	100%

Cascade Company's fixed costs are $200,000. The unit selling prices, unit variable costs, and unit contribution margins for products A and B are as follows:

Product	Unit Selling Price	Unit Variable Cost	Unit Contribution Margin
A	$ 90	$70	$20
B	140	95	45

To compute the break-even point, it is useful to think of the individual products as components of one overall enterprise product. For Cascade Company, this overall enterprise product is called E. The unit selling price of E can be thought of as equal to the total of the unit selling prices of products A and B, multiplied by their sales mix percentages. Likewise, the unit variable cost and unit contribution margin of E can be thought of as equal to the total of the unit variable costs and unit contribution margins of products A and B, multiplied by the sales mix percentages. These computations are as follows:

Unit selling price of E: $(\$90 \times .8) + (\$140 \times .2) = \$100$
Unit variable cost of E: $(\$70 \times .8) + (\$\ 95 \times .2) = \$\ 75$
Unit contribution margin of E: $(\$20 \times .8) + (\$\ 45 \times .2) = \$\ 25$

The break-even point of 8,000 units of E can be determined in the normal manner as follows:

$$\text{Break-Even Sales (Units)} = \frac{\text{Fixed Costs}}{\text{Unit Contribution Margin}}$$

$$\text{Break-Even Sales (Units)} = \frac{\$200,000}{\$25} = 8,000 \text{ units}$$

Since the sales mix for products A and B is 80% and 20%, the break-even quantity of A is 6,400 units (8,000 units × 80%) and B is 1,600 units (8,000 units × 20%). The validity of this analysis is shown in the following income statement:

	Product A	Product B	Total
Sales:			
6,400 units × $90	$576,000		$576,000
1,600 units × $140		$224,000	224,000
Total sales	$576,000	$224,000	$800,000
Variable costs:			
6,400 units × $70	$448,000		$448,000
1,600 units × $95		$152,000	152,000
Total variable costs	$448,000	$152,000	$600,000
Contribution margin	$128,000	$ 72,000	$200,000
Fixed costs			200,000
Operating profit			$ 0

The effects of changes in the sales mix on the break-even point can be determined by repeating the above analysis, assuming a different sales mix.

SPECIAL COST-VOLUME-PROFIT RELATIONSHIPS

Objective 6
Compute the margin of safety and the operating leverage, and explain how managers use these concepts.

Additional relationships can be developed from cost-volume-profit data. Two of these relationships that are especially useful to managers are the margin of safety and operating leverage.

Margin of Safety

The **margin of safety** is the difference between the current sales revenue and the sales at the break-even point. It indicates the possible decrease in sales that may occur before an operating loss results. For example, if the margin of safety is low, even a small decline in sales revenue will result in an operating loss.

The margin of safety, stated as a percentage of sales, is computed using the following formula:

$$\text{Margin of Safety} = \frac{\text{Sales} - \text{Sales at Break-Even Point}}{\text{Sales}}$$

If sales are $250,000, the unit selling price is $25, and sales at the break-even point are $200,000, the margin of safety is 20%, as computed below.

$$\text{Margin of Safety} = \frac{\$250,000 - \$200,000}{\$250,000} = 20\%$$

The margin of safety may also be stated in terms of units. In this illustration, for example, the margin of safety of 20% is equivalent to $50,000 ($250,000 × 20%). In units, the margin of safety is 2,000 units ($50,000 ÷ $25). Thus, the current sales of $250,000 may decline $50,000 or 2,000 units before an operating loss occurs.

Operating Leverage

Operating leverage is a measure of the relative mix of an enterprise's variable costs and fixed costs. It is computed as follows:

$$\text{Operating Leverage} = \frac{\text{Contribution Margin}}{\text{Operating Income}}$$

Since the difference between contribution margin and operating income is fixed costs, companies with large amounts of fixed costs will generally have a high operating leverage. Thus, companies in capital-intensive industries, such as the airline and automotive industries, will generally have a high operating leverage. A low operating leverage is normal for companies in industries that are labor-intensive, such as service industries.

Managers can use operating leverage to measure the impact of changes in sales on operating income. A high operating leverage indicates that a small increase in sales will yield a large percentage increase in operating income. In contrast, a low operating leverage indicates that a large increase in sales is necessary to significantly increase operating income. To illustrate, assume the following operating data for Jones Inc. and Wilson Inc.:

	Jones Inc.	Wilson Inc.
Sales	$400,000	$400,000
Variable costs	300,000	300,000
Contribution margin	$100,000	$100,000
Fixed costs	80,000	50,000
Operating income	$ 20,000	$ 50,000

Both companies have the same sales, the same variable costs, and the same contribution margin. Jones Inc. has larger fixed costs than Wilson Inc. and, as a result, a lower operating income and a higher operating leverage. The operating leverage for each company is computed as follows:

Jones Inc.

$$\text{Operating Leverage} = \frac{\$100,000}{\$20,000} = 5$$

Wilson Inc.

$$\text{Operating Leverage} = \frac{\$100,000}{\$50,000} = 2$$

Jones Inc.'s operating leverage indicates that, for a given percentage change in sales, operating income will increase 5 times that percentage. In contrast, a percentage change in sales for Wilson Inc. will have only 2 times that percentage impact on operating income. For example, if sales increased by 10% ($40,000) for each company, operating income will increase by 50% (10% × 5), or $10,000 (50% × $20,000), for Jones Inc. The sales increase of $40,000 will increase operating income by only 20% (10% × 2), or $10,000 (20% × $50,000), for Wilson Inc. The validity of this analysis is shown as follows:

	Jones Inc.	Wilson Inc.
Sales	$440,000	$440,000
Variable costs	330,000	330,000
Contribution margin	$110,000	$110,000
Fixed costs	80,000	50,000
Operating income	$ 30,000	$ 60,000

For Jones Inc., even a small increase in sales will generate a large percentage increase in operating income. Thus, managers may be motivated to think of ways to increase sales. In contrast, managers of Wilson Inc. might attempt to increase Wilson's operating leverage by reducing variable costs and, thereby, change the cost structure.

ASSUMPTIONS OF COST-VOLUME-PROFIT ANALYSIS

Objective 7
List the assumptions underlying cost-volume-profit analysis.

The reliability of cost-volume-profit analysis depends upon the validity of several assumptions. The primary assumptions are briefly described below.

1. Total sales and total costs can be represented by straight lines.
2. Within the relevant range of operating activity, the efficiency of operations does not change.
3. Costs can be accurately divided into fixed and variable components.
4. The sales mix is constant.
5. There is no change in the inventory quantities during the period.

The above assumptions simplify cost-volume-profit analysis. Since the assumptions are often valid for the relevant range of operations under consideration, cost-volume-profit analysis is often used by managers as an aid to decision making. The impact of violations of these assumptions are discussed in advanced accounting texts.

APPENDIX

VARIABLE COSTING

For financial reporting to external users, the cost of manufactured products normally consists of direct materials, direct labor, and factory overhead. The reporting of all these costs as product costs, called **absorption costing**, is required under generally accepted accounting principles. However, the **variable costing** or **direct costing** reporting format may be used for managerial decision making. This appendix further describes and illustrates this format.

In variable costing, the cost of goods manufactured is composed only of variable costs. When the level of activity is measured in units produced, variable costs normally include direct materials, direct labor, and variable factory overhead. Fixed factory overhead costs are related to the productive capacity of the manufacturing plant and are normally not affected by the number of units produced. Thus, in a variable costing income statement, fixed factory overhead costs do not become a part of the cost of goods manufactured. Instead, fixed factory overhead costs are treated as an expense of the period.

The difference between absorption costing and variable costing is highlighted in Exhibit 10. The difference between the two costing concepts is in the treatment of the fixed manufacturing costs, which consist of the fixed factory overhead costs.

To illustrate the preparation of a variable costing income statement, assume that 15,000 units were manufactured and sold at a price of $50 and the costs were as follows:

	Total Cost	Number of Units	Unit Cost
Manufacturing costs:			
Variable	$375,000	15,000	$25
Fixed	150,000	15,000	10
Total	$525,000		$35
Selling and administrative expenses:			
Variable ($5 per unit sold)	$ 75,000		
Fixed	50,000		
Total	$125,000		

Exhibit 10
Absorption Costing Compared to
Variable Costing

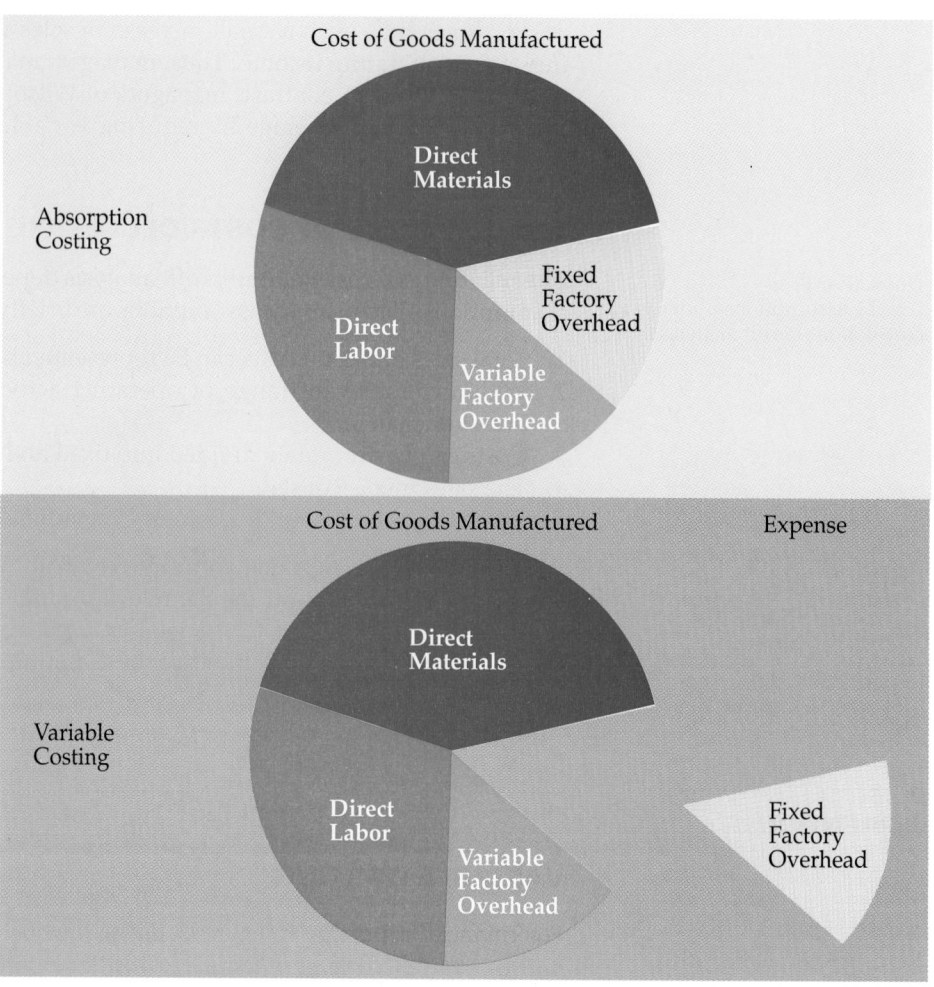

The variable costing income statement prepared from the preceding data is shown in Exhibit 11. The computations are shown in parentheses.

Exhibit 11
Variable Costing Income
Statement

Sales (15,000 × $50)		$750,000
Variable cost of goods sold (15,000 × $25)		375,000
Manufacturing margin		$375,000
Variable selling and administrative expenses		75,000
Contribution margin		$300,000
Fixed costs:		
Fixed manufacturing costs	$150,000	
Fixed selling and administrative expenses	50,000	200,000
Income from operations		$100,000

In a variable costing income statement, the **manufacturing margin** is the excess of sales over the variable cost of goods sold. In Exhibit 11, the manufacturing margin is $375,000 ($750,000 sales – $375,000 variable cost of goods sold). The variable selling and administrative expenses of $75,000 are deducted from the manufacturing margin to yield the contribution margin of $300,000. Income from operations of $100,000 is then determined by deducting fixed costs from the contribution margin.

The absorption costing income statement prepared from the same data is shown in Exhibit 12. The absorption costing income statement does not distinguish between variable and fixed costs. All manufacturing costs are included in the cost of goods sold. Deducting the cost of goods sold from sales yields the gross profit. Deducting the selling and administrative expenses from gross profit yields the income from operations.

Exhibit 12
Absorption Costing Income
Statement

Sales (15,000 × $50)	$750,000
Cost of goods sold (15,000 × $35)	525,000
Gross profit	$225,000
Selling and administrative expenses ($75,000 + $50,000)	125,000
Income from operations	$100,000

In the preceding illustration, 15,000 units were manufactured and sold. Both the absorption and the variable costing income statements reported the same income from operations of $100,000. Assuming no other changes, operating income will be the same under both methods when the number of units manufactured equals the number of units sold. When the number of units manufactured and the number of units sold are not equal, the operating incomes will differ as shown below.

Units manufactured:

Exceed units sold	Variable costing income is less than absorption costing income.
Less than units sold	Variable costing income is greater than absorption costing income.

As noted above, if the number of units manufactured exceeds the number of units sold, the operating income reported under variable costing will be less than the operating income reported under absorption costing. To illustrate, assume that in the preceding example only 12,000 units of the 15,000 units manufactured were sold. The two income statements that result are shown in Exhibit 13.

Exhibit 13
Units Manufactured Exceed Units
Sold

Variable Costing Income Statement

Sales (12,000 × $50)		$600,000
Variable cost of goods sold:		
Variable cost of goods manufactured (15,000 × $25)	$375,000	
Less ending inventory (3,000 × $25)	75,000	
Variable cost of goods sold		300,000
Manufacturing margin		$300,000
Variable selling and administrative expenses		60,000
Contribution margin		$240,000
Fixed costs:		
Fixed manufacturing costs	$150,000	
Fixed selling and administrative expenses	50,000	200,000
Income from operations		$ 40,000

Absorption Costing Income Statement

Sales (12,000 × $50)		$600,000
Cost of goods sold:		
Cost of goods manufactured (15,000 × $35)	$525,000	
Less ending inventory (3,000 × $35)	105,000	
Cost of goods sold		420,000
Gross profit		$180,000
Selling and administrative expenses [(12,000 × $5) + $50,000]		110,000
Income from operations		$ 70,000

The $30,000 difference in the amount of income from operations ($70,000 − $40,000) is due to the different treatment of the fixed manufacturing costs. The entire amount of the $150,000 of fixed manufacturing costs is included as an expense of the period in the variable costing statement. The ending inventory in the absorption costing statement includes $30,000 (3,000 × $10) of fixed manufacturing costs. This $30,000, by being included in inventory, is thus excluded from the current cost of goods sold and deferred to another period.

A similar analysis verifies that operating income under variable costing is greater than operating income under absorption costing when the units manufactured are less than the units sold. In both cases where sales and production differ, finished goods inventory will also be different under absorption costing and variable costing. As a result, increases or decreases in operating income due to changes in inventory levels could be misinterpreted by managers using absorption costing income statements as operating efficiencies or inefficiencies. This is one of the reasons that variable costing rather than absorption costing is used by managers for decision-making purposes.

Variable costing is especially useful to managers for cost control, product pricing, and production planning purposes. Such uses of variable costing are discussed in advanced accounting texts.

CHAPTER REVIEW

Key Points

Objective 1. Classify costs by their behavior as variable costs, fixed costs, or mixed costs.
Cost behavior refers to the manner in which a cost changes as a related activity changes. Variable costs are costs that vary in total in proportion to changes in the level of activity. Fixed costs are costs that remain the same in total dollar amount as the level of activity changes. A mixed cost has attributes of both a variable and a fixed cost.

Objective 2. Compute the contribution margin, the contribution margin ratio, and the unit contribution margin, and explain how they may be useful to managers in planning and controlling operations.
The contribution margin concept is useful in business planning because it gives insight into the profit potential of a firm. The contribution margin is the excess of sales revenues over variable costs. The contribution margin ratio is computed as follows:

$$\text{Contribution Margin Ratio} = \frac{\text{Sales} - \text{Variable Costs}}{\text{Sales}}$$

The unit contribution margin is the excess of the unit selling price over the unit variable cost.

Objective 3. Using the unit contribution margin, determine the break-even point and the volume necessary to achieve a target profit.
The mathematical approach to cost-volume-profit analysis uses the unit contribution margin concept and the following equations to determine the break-even point and the volume necessary to achieve a target profit for an enterprise:

$$\text{Break-Even Sales (Units)} = \frac{\text{Fixed Costs}}{\text{Unit Contribution Margin}}$$

$$\text{Sales (Units)} = \frac{\text{Fixed Costs} + \text{Target Profit}}{\text{Unit Contribution Margin}}$$

Objective 4. Using a cost-volume-profit chart and a profit-volume chart, determine the break-even point and the volume necessary to achieve a target profit.
A cost-volume-profit chart focuses on the relationships among costs, sales, and operating profit or loss. The preparation and use of a cost-volume-profit chart to determine the break-even point and the volume necessary to achieve a target profit are illustrated in this chapter.

The profit-volume chart focuses on profits rather than on revenues and costs. The preparation and use of a profit-volume chart to determine the break-even point and the volume necessary to achieve a target profit are illustrated in this chapter.

Objective 5. Calculate the break-even point for an enterprise selling more than one product.
The calculation of the break-even point for an enterprise selling two or more products is based upon a specified sales mix. Given the sales mix, the break-even point can be computed, using the methods illustrated for Cascade Company in this chapter.

Objective 6. Compute the margin of safety and the operating leverage, and explain how managers use these concepts.
The margin of safety as a percentage of current sales is computed as follows:

$$\text{Margin of Safety} = \frac{\text{Sales} - \text{Sales at Break-Even Point}}{\text{Sales}}$$

The margin of safety is useful in evaluating past operations and in planning future operations. For example, if the margin of safety is low, even a small decline in sales revenue will result in an operating loss.

Operating leverage is computed as follows:

$$\text{Operating Leverage} = \frac{\text{Contribution Margin}}{\text{Operating Income}}$$

Operating leverage is useful in measuring the impact of changes in sales on operating income without preparing formal income statements. For example, a high operating leverage indicates that a small increase in sales will yield a large percentage increase in operating income.

Objective 7. List the assumptions underlying cost-volume-profit analysis.
The primary assumptions underlying cost-volume-profit analysis are as follows:

1. Total sales and total costs can be represented by straight lines.
2. Within the relevant range of operating activity, the efficiency of operations does not change.

3. Costs can be accurately divided into fixed and variable components.

4. The sales mix is constant.

5. There is no change in the inventory quantities during the period.

Glossary of Key Terms

Activity bases (drivers). Activities thought to cause the incurrence of a cost. Used in analyzing and classifying the behavior of a cost. **Objective 1**

Break-even point. The level of enterprise operations at which revenues and expired costs are equal. **Objective 3**

Contribution margin. Sales less variable cost of goods sold and variable selling and administrative expenses. **Objective 2**

Contribution margin ratio. The percentage of each sales dollar that is available to cover the fixed costs and provide an operating income. **Objective 2**

Cost behavior. The manner in which a cost changes in relation to its activity base (driver). **Objective 1**

Cost-volume-profit analysis. The systematic examination of the relationships among selling prices, volume of sales and production, costs, expenses, and profits. **Objective 2**

Cost-volume-profit chart. A chart used to assist management in understanding the relationships among costs, expenses, sales, and operating profit or loss. **Objective 4**

Fixed costs. Costs that tend to remain the same in amount, regardless of variations in the level of activity. **Objective 1**

High-low method. A technique that uses the highest and lowest total costs as a basis for estimating the variable cost per unit and the fixed cost component of a mixed cost. **Objective 1**

Margin of safety. The difference between current sales revenue and the sales at the break-even point. **Objective 6**

Mixed cost. A cost with both variable and fixed characteristics, sometimes called a semivariable or semifixed cost. **Objective 1**

Operating leverage. A measure of the relative mix of an enterprise's variable costs and fixed costs computed as contribution margin divided by operating income. **Objective 6**

Profit-volume chart. A chart used to assist management in understanding the relationship between profit and volume. **Objective 4**

Relevant range. The range of activity over which changes in cost are of interest to management. **Objective 1**

Sales mix. The relative distribution of sales among the various products available for sale. **Objective 5**

Unit contribution margin. The dollars available from each unit of sales to cover fixed costs and provide operating profits. **Objective 2**

Variable costs. Costs that vary in total dollar amount as the level of activity changes. **Objective 1**

Variable costing. A method of reporting variable and fixed costs that includes only the variable manufacturing costs in the cost of the product. **Objective 1**

Self-Examination Questions
Answers at end of chapter.

1. Which of the following statements describes variable costs?
   A. Costs that vary on a per unit basis as the level of activity changes.
   B. Costs that vary in total in direct proportion to changes in the level of activity.
   C. Costs that remain the same in total dollar amount as the level of activity changes.
   D. Costs that vary on a per unit basis, but remain the same in total as the level of activity changes.

2. If sales are $500,000, variable costs are $200,000, and fixed costs are $240,000, what is the contribution margin ratio?
   A. 40%   C. 52%
   B. 48%   D. 60%

3. If the unit selling price is $16, the unit variable cost is $12, and fixed costs are $160,000, what are the break-even sales (units)?
   A. 5,714 units   C. 13,333 units
   B. 10,000 units   D. 40,000 units

4. Based on the data presented in Question 3, how many units of sales would be required to realize an operating profit of $20,000?
   A. 11,250 units   C. 20,000 units
   B. 15,000 units   D. 45,000 units

5. Based on the following operating data, what is the operating leverage?

Sales	$600,000
Variable costs	240,000
Contribution margin	$360,000
Fixed costs	160,000
Operating income	$200,000

   A. 0.8   C. 1.8
   B. 1.2   D. 4.0

ILLUSTRATIVE PROBLEM

Johnson Inc. expects to maintain the same inventories at the end of the year as at the beginning of the year. The estimated fixed costs for the year are $360,000, and the estimated variable costs per unit are $9. It is expected that 75,000 units will be sold at a price of $15 per unit. Maximum sales within the relevant range are 80,000 units.

Instructions

1. What is (a) the contribution margin ratio and (b) the unit contribution margin?
2. Determine the break-even point in units.
3. Construct a cost-volume-profit chart, indicating the break-even point.
4. Construct a profit-volume chart, indicating the break-even point.
5. What is the margin of safety?

Solution

1. a. $\text{Contribution Margin Ratio} = \dfrac{\text{Sales} - \text{Variable Costs}}{\text{Sales}}$

   $\text{Contribution Margin Ratio} = \dfrac{(75,000 \text{ units} \times \$15) - (75,000 \text{ units} \times \$9)}{(75,000 \text{ units} \times \$15)}$

   $\text{Contribution Margin Ratio} = \dfrac{\$1,125,000 - \$675,000}{\$1,125,000} = \dfrac{\$450,000}{\$1,125,000}$

   $\text{Contribution Margin Ratio} = 40\%$

   b. Unit Contribution Margin = Unit Selling Price - Unit Variable Costs
   Unit Contribution Margin = $15 - $9 = $6

2. $\text{Break-Even Sales (Units)} = \dfrac{\text{Fixed Costs}}{\text{Unit Contribution Margin}}$

   $\text{Break-Even Sales (Units)} = \dfrac{\$360,000}{\$6} = 60,000 \text{ units}$

3.

4.

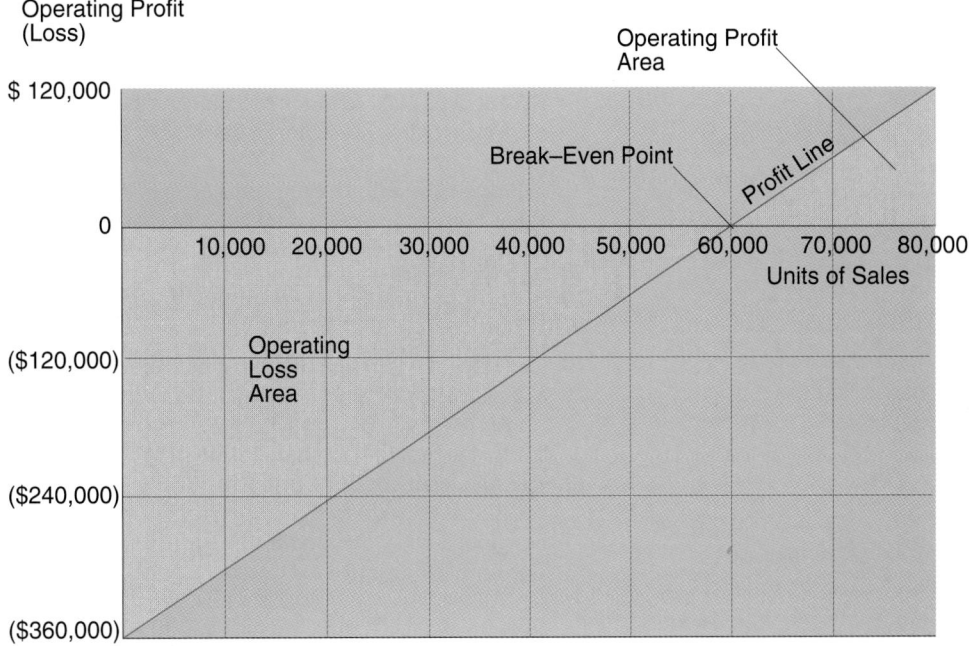

5. Margin of safety:
   Expected sales (75,000 units × $15) $1,125,000
   Break-even point (60,000 units × $15)   900,000
   Margin of safety $ 225,000

                          or

   $$\text{Margin of Safety} = \frac{\text{Sales} - \text{Sales at Break-Even Point}}{\text{Sales}}$$

   $$\text{Margin of Safety} = \frac{\$225,000}{\$1,125,000} = 20\%$$

DISCUSSION QUESTIONS

1. What are the three most common classifications used for classifying cost behavior?
2. Describe how total variable cost and unit variable costs behave with changes in the level of activity.
3. Which of the following costs would be classified as variable costs for units produced?
   a. Direct labor costs
   b. Straight-line depreciation
   c. Factory supervisor's salary
   d. Electricity costs of $.20 per kilowatt-hour
   e. Insurance premiums on factory plant and equipment of $3,000 per month
   f. Direct materials cost
   g. Oil used in operating factory equipment
   h. Rent of factory building
4. Describe the behavior of (a) total fixed costs and (b) unit fixed costs as the level of activity increases.

5. Which of the following costs are fixed costs for units produced?
   a. Oil and other lubricants used on factory equipment
   b. Straight-line depreciation of plant and equipment
   c. Direct materials
   d. Salary of factory supervisor, $80,000 per year
   e. Rent of $25,000 per month on factory building
   f. Electricity used in running machinery, $.08 per kilowatt-hour
   g. Direct labor
   h. Property insurance premiums of $5,000 per month on plant and equipment
6. What type of cost has both fixed and variable cost characteristics?
7. In applying the high-low method of cost estimation, how is the total fixed cost estimated?
8. What is contribution margin?
9. Schrad Inc. had sales of $650,000, variable costs of $390,000, fixed costs of $200,000, and operating income of $60,000. What is Schrad Inc.'s contribution margin?
10. Given the data for Schrad Inc. in Question 9, what is the contribution margin ratio?
11. a. If sales are $400,000 and variable costs are $272,000, what is the contribution margin ratio?
    b. What is the contribution margin ratio if variable costs are 55% of sales?
12. The management of Geurink Inc. is considering the effect on operating income of an additional $50,000 in sales orders. If Geurink Inc.'s contribution margin ratio is 30%, how much will operating income increase if the sales orders of $50,000 are obtained?
13. The unit selling price for Casad Inc.'s product is $25, and the unit variable cost is $16. (a) If Casad Inc. sold 40,000 units, what is the total contribution margin? (b) If fixed costs are $100,000, how much would operating income increase if Casad Inc. sells an additional 10,000 units? (c) What is the unit contribution margin for Casad Inc.?
14. a. What is the break-even point?
    b. What equation is used to determine the break-even point in sales units?
15. Fixed costs are $450,000, the unit selling price is $50, and the unit variable cost is $35. (a) What is the unit contribution margin? (b) What are the break-even sales units?
16. If the unit cost of direct materials is decreased, what effect will this change have on the break-even point?
17. If insurance rates are increased, what effect will this change in fixed costs have on the break-even point?
18. If the unit selling price is $250, the unit variable cost is $200, and the fixed costs are $700,000, what sales in units are required to realize an operating profit of $150,000?
19. Name the following chart and identify the items represented by the letters a through f.

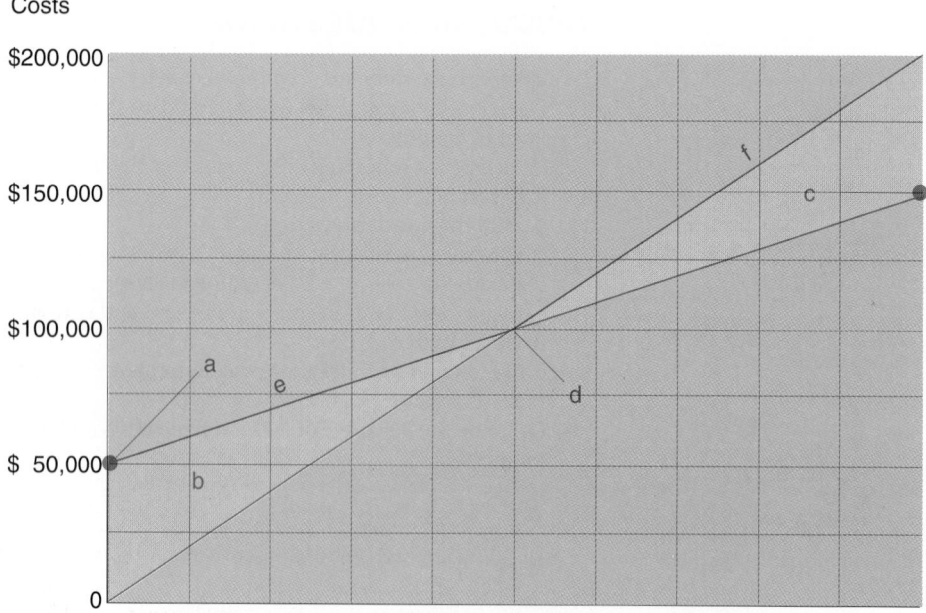

20. Name the following chart and identify the items represented by the letters a through f.

21. What is meant by sales mix?
22. a. What is meant by the margin of safety?
    b. If sales are $750,000, net income is $105,000, and sales at the break-even point are $525,000, what is the margin of safety expressed in sales dollars?
23. a. How is operating leverage computed?
    b. What does operating leverage measure?
24. Pratt Inc. has an operating leverage of 6 and operating income of $120,000. Sales are expected to increase by 5% next year. (a) What percentage will operating income increase? (b) What would be the expected operating income next year?

25. Dutch Pantry Inc. operates full-service family restaurants in the eastern states. To ensure consistent quality, many of the items served in the restaurants are prepared in a central food-processing plant. Classify each of the following costs and expenses of the food-processing plant as either variable or fixed:
    a. Garbage collection expense
    b. Salad dressing
    c. Office salaries
    d. Depreciation of equipment (straight-line method)
    e. Cooking oil
    f. Experimental costs
    g. Cleaning supplies
    h. Spices
    i. Water
    j. Property taxes
    k. Electricity

26. The 1991 annual report of The H. J. Heinz Company indicates that, compared to the previous year, sales were $561,431,000 higher and income from operations was $115,187,000 higher. The H. J. Heinz Company operated above the break-even point in 1991 and 1990. Assuming that fixed costs did not change significantly from the prior year, what is the estimated contribution margin ratio for The H. J. Heinz Company?

ETHICS DISCUSSION CASE

Samuel Klaus has been controller for Martin Enterprises for 12 years. Recently, Martin Enterprises purchased several microcomputers to be used for analyses such as cost-volume-profit analysis. Klaus does not know how to use a microcomputer, and he does not want to learn how to use one. He believes that he can fulfill his responsibilities as controller and adequately evaluate his staff's work without the microcomputer.

Discuss any ethical issues related to Klaus's refusal to use microcomputers.

EXERCISES

EXERCISE 24-1
CLASSIFICATION OF COSTS
Objective 1

Following is a list of various costs incurred in producing pencils. With respect to the manufacture and sale of pencils, classify each cost as either variable, fixed, or mixed.

a. Number 2½ lead.
b. Salary of the plant superintendent.
c. Straight-line depreciation of factory equipment.
d. Red paint for each pencil.
e. Erasers.
f. Property insurance premiums of $1,000 per month plus $.005 for each dollar of property over $2,000,000.
g. Property taxes on factory building and equipment.
h. Hourly wages of machine operators.
i. Pension cost of $.20 per employee hour on the job.
j. Wood costs per pencil.
k. Rent on warehouse of $3,000 per month plus $2 per square foot of storage used.
l. Metal to hold the eraser on the end of the pencil.
m. Electricity costs of $.025 per kilowatt-hour.
n. Janitorial costs of $2,000 per month.
o. Oils used to lubricate machinery.

EXERCISE 24-2
RELEVANT RANGE AND COMPUTATION OF FIXED AND VARIABLE COSTS
Objective 1

Fritz Inc. manufactures tool sets within a relevant range of 50,000 to 150,000 sets a year. Within this range, the following partially completed manufacturing cost schedule has been prepared:

| | Tool Sets Produced | | |
	50,000	100,000	150,000
Total costs:			
Total variable costs	$500,000	(d)	(j)
Total fixed costs	250,000	(e)	(k)
Total costs	$750,000	(f)	(l)
Cost per unit:			
Variable cost per unit	(a)	(g)	(m)
Fixed cost per unit	(b)	(h)	(n)
Total cost per unit	(c)	(i)	(o)

Complete the cost schedule, identifying each cost by the appropriate letter (a) through (o).

EXERCISE 24-3
COST ESTIMATION, USING THE HIGH-LOW METHOD
Objective 1

Dunn Industries has decided to use the high-low method to estimate the total cost and the fixed and variable cost components of the total cost. The data for the highest and lowest levels of production are as follows:

	Units Produced	Total Costs
Highest level	100,000	$370,000
Lowest level	50,000	220,000

a. Determine the variable cost per unit and the fixed cost.
b. Based on (a), estimate the total cost for 70,000 units of production.

EXERCISE 24-4
CONTRIBUTION MARGIN RATIO
Objective 2

(a) Hartman Company budgets sales of $1,100,000, fixed costs of $150,000, and variable costs of $748,000. What is the anticipated contribution margin ratio? (b) If the contribution margin ratio for White Company is 36%, sales were $750,000, and fixed costs were $125,000, what was the operating profit?

EXERCISE 24-5
**BREAK-EVEN SALES AND
SALES TO REALIZE
OPERATING PROFIT**
Objective 3

For the current year ending March 31, Andrews Company expects fixed costs of $264,000, a unit variable cost of $134, and a unit selling price of $200.

a. Compute the anticipated break-even sales (units).
b. Compute the sales (units) required to realize an operating profit of $49,500.

EXERCISE 24-6
BREAK-EVEN SALES
Objective 3

**SPREADSHEET
PROBLEM**

For the current year ending January 31, Packard Company expects fixed costs of $140,000 and a unit variable cost of $36. For the coming year, a new wage contract will increase the unit variable cost by $37.50. The selling price of $50 per unit is expected to remain the same.

a. Compute the break-even sales (units) for the current year.
b. Compute the anticipated break-even sales (units) for the coming year, assuming that the new wage contract is signed.

EXERCISE 24-7
BREAK-EVEN SALES
Objective 3

Currently, the unit selling price of a product is $25, the unit variable cost is $15, and the total fixed costs are $120,000. A proposal is being evaluated to increase the unit selling price to $27.

a. Compute the current break-even sales (units).
b. Compute the anticipated break-even sales (units), assuming that the unit selling price is increased and all costs remain constant.

EXERCISE 24-8
**COST-VOLUME-PROFIT
CHART**
Objective 4

For the coming year, Keller Inc. anticipates fixed costs of $400,000, a unit variable cost of $30, and a unit selling price of $50. The maximum sales within the relevant range are $2,000,000.

a. Construct a cost-volume-profit chart.
b. Estimate the break-even sales (dollars) by using the cost-volume-profit chart constructed in (a).
c. What is the main advantage of presenting the cost-volume-profit analysis in graphic form rather than equation form?

**SHARPEN YOUR
COMMUNICATION SKILLS**

EXERCISE 24-9
PROFIT-VOLUME CHART
Objective 4

Using the data for Keller Inc. in Exercise 24-8, (a) determine the maximum possible operating loss; (b) compute the maximum possible operating profit; (c) construct a profit-volume chart; (d) estimate the break-even sales (units) by using the profit-volume chart constructed in (c).

EXERCISE 24-10
**SALES MIX AND BREAK-
EVEN SALES**
Objective 6

Scholey Inc. manufacturers and sells two products, C and D. The fixed costs are $364,000, and the sales mix is 80% C and 20% D. The unit selling price and the unit variable cost for each product are as follows:

Product	Unit Selling Price	Unit Variable Cost
C	$ 50	$ 30
D	150	100

a. Compute the break-even sales (units) for the enterprise product, E.
b. How many units of each product, C and D, would be sold at the break-even point?

EXERCISE 24-11
MARGIN OF SAFETY
Objective 7

(a) If Brown Company, with a break-even point at $720,000 of sales, has actual sales of $900,000, what is the margin of safety expressed (1) in dollars and (2) as a percentage of sales? (b) If the margin of safety for Thomas Company was 20%, fixed costs were $350,000, and variable costs were 75% of sales, what was the amount of actual sales (dollars)?

EXERCISE 24-12
OPERATING LEVERAGE
Objective 7

Camlin Inc. and Waite Inc. have the following operating data:

	Camlin Inc.	Waite Inc.
Sales	$500,000	$300,000
Variable costs	250,000	180,000
Contribution margin	$250,000	$120,000
Fixed costs	150,000	80,000
Operating income	$100,000	$ 40,000

a. Compute the operating leverage for Camlin Inc. and Waite Inc.
b. How much would operating income increase for each company if the sales of each increased by 10%?

SHARPEN YOUR
COMMUNICATION SKILLS
c. Why is there a difference in the increase in operating income for the two companies? Explain.

APPENDIX
EXERCISE 24-13
ITEMS ON VARIABLE
COSTING INCOME
STATEMENT

In the following equations, based on the variable costing income statement, identify the items designated by X:

a. Net sales − X = Manufacturing margin
b. Manufacturing margin − X = Contribution margin
c. Contribution margin − X = Income from operations

APPENDIX
EXERCISE 24-14
VARIABLE COSTING
INCOME STATEMENT

On July 31, the end of the first month of operations, Nolan Company prepared the following income statement, based on the absorption costing concept:

Sales (4,400 units)		$66,000
Cost of goods sold:		
Cost of goods manufactured	$45,000	
Less ending inventory (600 units)	5,400	
Cost of goods sold		39,600
Gross profit		$26,400
Selling and administrative expenses		15,800
Income from operations		$10,600

Prepare a variable costing income statement assuming that the fixed manufacturing costs were $15,000 and the variable selling and administrative expenses were $7,700.

APPENDIX
EXERCISE 24-15
ABSORPTION COSTING
INCOME STATEMENT

On June 30, the end of the first month of operations, Fox Company prepared the following income statement, based on the variable costing concept:

Sales (18,000 units)		$360,000
Variable cost of goods sold:		
Variable cost of goods manufactured	$200,000	
Less ending inventory (2,000 units)	20,000	
Variable cost of goods sold		180,000
Manufacturing margin		$180,000
Variable selling and administrative expenses		36,000
Contribution margin		$144,000
Fixed costs and expenses:		
Fixed manufacturing costs	$ 50,000	
Fixed selling and administrative expenses	29,000	79,000
Income from operations		$ 65,000

Prepare an absorption costing income statement.

APPENDIX
EXERCISE 24-16
INCOME STATEMENTS
UNDER ABSORPTION
COSTING AND VARIABLE
COSTING

Bower Company began operations on July 1 and operated at 100% of capacity during the first month. The following data summarize the results for July:

Sales (12,000 units)		$600,000
Production costs (15,000 units):		
Direct materials	$150,000	
Direct labor	180,000	
Variable factory overhead	45,000	
Fixed factory overhead	30,000	405,000
Selling and administrative expenses:		
Variable selling and administrative expenses	$ 60,000	
Fixed selling and administrative expenses	18,000	78,000

a. Prepare an absorption costing income statement.
b. Prepare a variable costing income statement.

SHARPEN YOUR
COMMUNICATION SKILLS
c. What is the reason for the difference in the amount of operating income reported in (a) and (b)?

At a recent staff meeting, the question of the discontinuance of Product P from the product line was being discussed. The chief financial analyst reported the following current monthly data for Product P:

Units of sales	10,000
Break-even units	12,000
Margin of safety in units	2,000

For what reason would you question the validity of these data?

PROBLEMS

Series A

PROBLEM 24-1A
CLASSIFICATION OF COSTS
Objective 1

Helms Inc. manufactures blue jeans for distribution to several major retail chains. The following costs are incurred in the production and sale of blue jeans:

   a. Blue denim fabric.
   b. Salary of production vice-president.
   c. Rent on experimental equipment, $25,000 per year.
   d. Consulting fee of $50,000 paid to industry specialist for marketing advice.
   e. Janitorial supplies, $2,000 per month.
   f. Salesperson's salary, $12,000 plus 3% of the total sales.
   g. Thread.
   h. Brass buttons.
   i. Legal fees paid to attorneys in defense of the company in a patent infringement suit, $20,000 plus $100 per hour.
   j. Salary of designers.
   k. Insurance premiums on property, plant, and equipment, $10,000 per year plus $3 per $10,000 of insured value over $5,000,000.
   l. Hourly wages of sewing machine operators.
   m. Property taxes on property, plant, and equipment.
   n. Rental costs of warehouse, $2,000 per month plus $1 per square foot of storage used.
   o. Leather for patches identifying each jean style.
   p. Electricity costs of $.07 per kilowatt-hour.
   q. Sewing supplies.
   r. Shipping boxes used to ship orders.
   s. Blue dye.
   t. Straight-line depreciation of sewing machines.

Instructions
Classify the preceding costs for the production and sale of blue jeans as either fixed, variable, or mixed. Use the following headings, and place an X in the appropriate column.

Cost	Fixed Cost	Variable Cost	Mixed Cost

PROBLEM 24-2A
BREAK-EVEN SALES UNDER
PRESENT AND PROPOSED
CONDITIONS
Objectives 2, 3

McDermott Inc., operating at full capacity, sold 80,000 units at a price of $100 per unit during 1993. Its income statement for 1993 is as follows:

Sales		$8,000,000
Cost of goods sold		5,000,000
Gross profit		$3,000,000
Operating expenses:		
Selling expenses	$1,000,000	
Administrative expenses	400,000	
Total operating expenses		1,400,000
Operating profit		$1,600,000

The division of costs between fixed and variable is as follows:

	Fixed	Variable
Cost of sales	20%	80%
Selling expenses	30%	70%
Administrative expenses	75%	25%

Management is considering a plant expansion program that will permit an increase of $3,000,000 in yearly sales. The expansion will increase fixed costs by $500,000, but will not affect the relationship between sales and variable costs.

Instructions

1. Determine for 1993 the total fixed costs and the total variable costs.
2. Determine for 1993 (a) the unit variable cost and (b) the unit contribution margin.
3. Compute the break-even sales (units) for 1993.
4. Compute the break-even sales (units) under the proposed program.
5. Determine the amount of sales (units) that would be necessary under the proposed program to realize the $1,600,000 of operating profit that was earned in 1993.
6. Determine the maximum operating profit possible with the expanded plant.
7. If the proposal is accepted and sales remain at the 1993 level, what will the operating profit or loss be for 1994?

SHARPEN YOUR COMMUNICATION SKILLS

8. Based on the data given, would you recommend accepting the proposal? Explain.

PROBLEM 24-3A
BREAK-EVEN SALES AND COST-VOLUME-PROFIT CHART
Objectives 3, 4

For the coming year, Melvin Company anticipates a unit selling price of $80, a unit variable cost of $52, and fixed costs of $280,000.

Instructions

1. Compute the anticipated break-even sales (units).
2. Compute the sales (units) required to realize an operating profit of $112,000.
3. Construct a cost-volume-profit chart, assuming maximum sales of 25,000 units within the relevant range.
4. Determine the probable operating profit (loss) if sales total 8,750 units.

PROBLEM 24-4A
BREAK-EVEN SALES AND COST-VOLUME-PROFIT CHART
Objectives 3, 4

Last year, Purcell Company had sales of $900,000, based upon a unit selling price of $100. The variable cost per unit was $55, and fixed costs were $315,000. The maximum sales within Purcell Company's relevant range are 10,000 units. Purcell Company is considering a proposal to spend an additional $45,000 on billboard advertising during the current year in an attempt to increase sales and utilize unused capacity.

Instructions

1. Construct a cost-volume-profit chart indicating the break-even sales for last year.
2. Using the cost-volume-profit chart prepared in (1), determine (a) the operating profit for last year and (b) the maximum operating profit that could have been realized during the year.
3. Construct a cost-volume-profit chart indicating the break-even sales for the current year, assuming that a noncancellable contract is signed for the additional billboard advertising. No changes are expected in the unit selling price or other costs.
4. Using the cost-volume-profit chart prepared in (3), determine (a) the operating profit if sales total 9,000 units and (b) the maximum operating profit that could be realized during the year.

PROBLEM 24-5A
SALES MIX AND BREAK-EVEN SALES
Objective 6

Data related to the expected sales of products A and B for Finzel Inc. for the current year, which are typical of recent years, are as follows:

Product	Selling Price per Unit	Variable Cost per Unit	Sales Mix
A	$180	$80	25%
B	60	40	75

The estimated fixed costs for the current year are $300,000.

Instructions

1. Determine the estimated units of sales of the enterprise product necessary to reach the break-even point for the current year.
2. Based on the break-even sales (units) in (1), determine the unit sales of both A and B for the current year.

PROBLEM 24-6A
CONTRIBUTION MARGIN,
BREAK-EVEN SALES, COST-
VOLUME-PROFIT CHART,
MARGIN OF SAFETY, AND
OPERATING LEVERAGE
Objectives 2, 3, 4, 7

Linke Company expects to maintain the same inventories at the end of 1993 as at the beginning of the year. The total of all production costs for the year is therefore assumed to be equal to the cost of goods sold. With this in mind, the various department heads were asked to submit estimates of the costs for their departments during 1993. A summary report of these estimates is as follows:

	Estimated Fixed Cost	Estimated Variable Cost (per unit sold)
Production costs:		
Direct materials	—	$ 4.20
Direct labor	—	5.00
Factory overhead	$150,000	2.20
Selling expenses:		
Sales salaries and commissions	50,000	.30
Advertising	40,000	—
Travel	13,000	—
Miscellaneous selling expense	2,700	.12
Administrative expenses:		
Office and officers' salaries	40,000	—
Supplies	3,300	.15
Miscellaneous administrative expense	1,000	.03
Total	$300,000	$12.00

It is expected that 160,000 units will be sold at a price of $15 a unit. Maximum sales within the relevant range are 200,000 units.

**SPREADSHEET
PROBLEM**

Instructions

1. Prepare an estimated income statement for 1993.
2. What is the expected contribution margin ratio?
3. Determine the break-even sales (a) in units and (b) in dollars.
4. Construct a cost-volume-profit chart indicating the break-even sales.
5. What is the expected margin of safety?
6. Determine the operating leverage. Round to one decimal place.

Series B

PROBLEM 24-1B
CLASSIFICATION OF COSTS
Objective 1

Taylor and Taylor manufactures sofas for distribution to several major retail chains. The following costs are incurred in the production and sale of sofas:

    a. Fabric for sofa coverings.
    b. Springs.
    c. Hourly wages of sewing machine operators.
    d. Salary of designers.
    e. Salary of production vice-president.
    f. Rent on experimental equipment, $25 for every sofa produced.
    g. Cartons used to ship sofas.
    h. Rental costs of warehouse, $10,000 per month.
    i. Legal fees paid to attorneys in defense of the company in a patent infringement suit, $10,000 plus $75 per hour.
    j. Property taxes on property, plant, and equipment.
    k. Electricity costs of $.02 per kilowatt-hour.
    l. Consulting fee of $15,000 paid to efficiency specialists.
    m. Janitorial supplies, $10 for each sofa produced.
    n. Salesperson's salary, $12,000 plus 5% of the selling price of each sofa sold.
    o. Employer's FICA taxes on controller's salary of $75,000.
    p. Sewing supplies.
    q. Foam rubber for cushion fillings.
    r. Insurance premiums on property, plant, and equipment, $5,000 per year plus $20 per $10,000 of insured value over $8,000,000.
    s. Straight-line depreciation of factory equipment.
    t. Wood for framing the sofas.

Instructions

Classify the preceding costs for the production and sale of sofas as either fixed, variable, or mixed. Use the following headings, and place an X in the appropriate column:

Cost	Fixed Cost	Variable Cost	Mixed Cost

PROBLEM 24-2B
BREAK-EVEN SALES UNDER
PRESENT AND PROPOSED
CONDITIONS
Objectives 2, 3

Lane Company, operating at full capacity, sold 20,000 units at a price of $300 per unit during 1993. Its income statement for 1993 is as follows:

Sales		$6,000,000
Cost of goods sold		3,600,000
Gross profit		$2,400,000
Operating expenses:		
Selling expenses	$1,275,000	
Administrative expenses	375,000	
Total operating expenses		1,650,000
Operating profit		$ 750,000

The division of costs between fixed and variable is as follows:

	Fixed	Variable
Cost of sales	30%	70%
Selling expenses	20%	80%
Administrative expenses	84%	16%

Management is considering a plant expansion program that will permit an increase of $2,100,000 in yearly sales. The expansion will increase fixed costs by $300,000, but will not affect the relationship between sales and variable costs.

Instructions

1. Determine for 1993 the total fixed costs and the total variable costs.
2. Determine for 1993 (a) the unit variable cost and (b) the unit contribution margin.
3. Compute the break-even sales (units) for 1993.
4. Compute the break-even sales (units) under the proposed program.
5. Determine the amount of sales (units) that would be necessary under the proposed program to realize the $750,000 of operating profit that was earned in 1993.
6. Determine the maximum operating profit possible with the expanded plant.
7. If the proposal is accepted and sales remain at the 1993 level, what will the operating profit or loss be for 1994?
8. Based on the data given, would you recommend accepting the proposal? Explain.

SHARPEN YOUR COMMUNICATION SKILLS ►

PROBLEM 24-3B
BREAK-EVEN SALES AND
COST-VOLUME-PROFIT
CHART
Objectives 3, 4

For the coming year, Nolan Company anticipates a unit selling price of $100, a unit variable cost of $75, and fixed costs of $75,000.

Instructions

1. Compute the anticipated break-even sales (units).
2. Compute the sales (units) required to realize an operating profit of $30,000.
3. Construct a cost-volume-profit chart, assuming maximum sales of 5,000 units within the relevant range.
4. Determine the probable operating profit (loss) if sales total 4,500 units.

PROBLEM 24-4B
BREAK-EVEN POINT AND
COST-VOLUME-PROFIT
CHART
Objectives 3, 4

Last year, Grace Inc. had sales of $800,000, based upon a unit selling price of $200. The variable cost per unit was $120, and fixed costs were $240,000. The maximum sales within Grace Inc.'s relevant range of operations are 5,000 units. Grace Inc. is considering a proposal to spend an additional $40,000 on billboard advertising during the current year in an attempt to increase sales and utilize unused capacity.

Instructions

1. Construct a cost-volume-profit chart indicating the break-even sales for last year.
2. Using the cost-volume-profit chart prepared in (1), determine (a) the operating profit for last year and (b) the maximum operating profit that could have been realized during the year.
3. Construct a cost-volume-profit chart indicating the break-even sales for the current year, assuming that a noncancellable contract is signed for the additional billboard advertising. No changes are expected in the unit selling price or other costs.
4. Using the cost-volume-profit chart prepared in (3), determine (a) the operating profit if sales total $800,000 and (b) the maximum operating profit that could be realized during the year.

PROBLEM 24-5B
SALES MIX AND BREAK-EVEN SALES
Objective 6

Data related to the expected sales of products P and Q for Cox Company for the current year, which are typical of recent years, are as follows:

Product	Selling Price per Unit	Variable Cost per Unit	Sales Mix
P	$ 50	$30	80%
Q	125	75	20

The estimated fixed costs for the current year are $286,000.

Instructions

1. Determine the estimated units of sales of the enterprise product necessary to reach the break-even point for the current year.
2. Based on the break-even sales (units) in (1), determine the unit sales of both P and Q for the current year.

PROBLEM 24-6B
CONTRIBUTION MARGIN, BREAK-EVEN SALES, COST-VOLUME-PROFIT CHART, MARGIN OF SAFETY, AND OPERATING LEVERAGE
Objectives 2, 3, 4, 7

Collier Company expects to maintain the same inventories at the end of 1993 as at the beginning of the year. The total of all production costs for the year is therefore assumed to be equal to the cost of goods sold. With this in mind, the various department heads were asked to submit estimates of the costs for their departments during 1993. A summary report of these estimates is as follows:

	Estimated Fixed Cost	Estimated Variable Cost (per unit sold)
Production costs:		
Direct materials	—	$16.00
Direct labor	—	20.00
Factory overhead	$100,000	11.45
Selling expenses:		
Sales salaries and commissions	70,000	1.75
Advertising	35,000	—
Travel	22,000	—
Miscellaneous selling expense	7,000	.25
Administrative expenses:		
Office and officers' salaries	50,000	—
Supplies	11,500	.30
Miscellaneous administrative expense	4,500	.25
Total	$300,000	$50.00

It is expected that 8,000 units will be sold at a price of $100 a unit. Maximum sales within the relevant range are 15,000 units.

SPREADSHEET PROBLEM

Instructions

1. Prepare an estimated income statement for 1993.
2. What is the expected contribution margin ratio?
3. Determine the break-even sales (a) in units and (b) in dollars.
4. Construct a cost-volume-profit chart indicating the break-even sales.
5. What is the expected margin of safety?
6. Determine the operating leverage.

MINI-CASE 24 OLSON COMPANY

Olson Company manufactures Product P, which sold for $144 per unit in 1993. For the past several years, sales and operating profit have been declining. On sales of 7,000 units in 1993, the company operated near the break-even sales and used only 40% of its productive capacity. Ann Olson, your mother-in-law, is considering several proposals to reverse the trend of declining sales and operating profit, and to more fully use production facilities. One proposal under consideration is to reduce the unit selling price to $120.

Your mother-in-law has asked you to aid her in assessing the proposal to reduce the sales price by $24. For this purpose, she provided the following summary of the estimated fixed and variable costs for 1994, which are unchanged from 1993.

Variable costs:

Production costs	$50 per unit
Selling expenses	14 per unit
Administrative expenses	8 per unit

Fixed costs:

Production costs	$300,000
Selling expenses	80,000
Administrative expenses	70,000

Instructions:

1. Determine the break-even sales for 1994 in units, assuming (a) no change in sales price and (b) the proposed sales price.
2. How much additional sales are necessary for Olson Company to break even in 1994 under the proposal?
3. Determine the operating profit for 1994, assuming (a) no change in sales price and volume from 1993 and (b) the new sales price and no change in volume from 1993.
4. Determine the maximum operating profit for 1994, assuming the proposed sales price.
5. ▪▪▪ ‣ Briefly list factors that you would discuss with your mother-in-law in evaluating the proposal.

ANSWERS TO SELF-EXAMINATION QUESTIONS

1. **B** Variable costs vary in total in direct proportion to changes in the level of activity (answer B). Costs that vary on a per unit basis as the level of activity changes (answer A) or remain the same in total dollar amount as the level of activity changes (answer C), or both (answer D), are fixed costs.

2. **D** The contribution margin ratio indicates the percentage of each sales dollar available to cover the fixed costs and provide operating income and is determined as follows:

$$\text{Contribution Margin Ratio} = \frac{\text{Sales} - \text{Variable Costs}}{\text{Sales}}$$

$$\text{Contribution Margin Ratio} = \frac{\$500,000 - \$200,000}{\$500,000} = 60\%$$

3. **D** The break-even sales of 40,000 units (answer D) is computed as follows:

$$\text{Break-Even Sales (Units)} = \frac{\text{Fixed Costs}}{\text{Unit Contribution Margin}}$$

$$\text{Break-Even Sales (Units)} = \frac{\$160,000}{\$4} = 40,000 \text{ units}$$

4. **D** Sales of 45,000 units are required to realize an operating profit of $20,000, computed as follows:

$$\text{Sales (Units)} = \frac{\text{Fixed Costs} + \text{Targeted Profit}}{\text{Unit Contribution Margin}}$$

$$\text{Sales (Units)} = \frac{\$160,000 + \$20,000}{\$4} = 45,000 \text{ units}$$

5. **C** The operating leverage is 1.8, computed as follows:

$$\text{Operating Leverage} = \frac{\text{Contribution Margin}}{\text{Operating Income}}$$

$$\text{Operating Leverage} = \frac{\$360,000}{\$200,000} = 1.8$$

You and Accounting

Assume that you want to buy a new Ford Explorer but aren't sure you can afford it.

In deciding whether you can afford to buy the Explorer, you will first want to estimate the best price that you will be able to bargain for and what your initial down payment will be. You then will want to estimate what your payments will be on the amount borrowed, when the payments will be due (monthly, for example), and the amount of the payments. You might also estimate any increase in operating expenses associated with the Explorer, such as increased insurance premiums. By comparing the estimated costs of buying the Explorer with your financial resources, such as your checking account balance and estimated future income, you can determine whether you can afford the Explorer.

This financial planning process is similar to the planning that organizations of all types and sizes perform. This chapter discusses basic budgeting concepts used by business enterprises. You may also find these concepts useful in your own day-to-day life.

Chapter 25
Budgeting and Standard Cost Systems

Effective planning and control are necessary for the successful management of an enterprise's operations. Uses of accounting information by management in performing these functions have been described and illustrated in earlier chapters. For example, the role of cost accounting systems in planning production and controlling costs was described and illustrated. This chapter discusses budgeting and standard costs, two additional accounting tools that help managers plan and control the operations of a business.

LEARNING OBJECTIVES
After studying this chapter, you should be able to:

Objective 1
Describe budgeting and its objectives.

Objective 2
Prepare the basic budgets for a manufacturing enterprise.

Objective 3
Prepare a flexible budget.

Objective 4
Prepare a budget performance report.

Objective 5
Explain how the use of standard costs aids in planning and controlling operations.

Objective 6
Compute the basic variances for direct materials, direct labor, and factory overhead.

Objective 7
Journalize the entries for recording standards in the accounts.

Objective 8
Explain how standards may be used for nonmanufacturing expenses.

NATURE AND OBJECTIVES OF BUDGETING

A **budget** is a written statement of management's plans for the future, expressed in financial terms. It charts the course of future action for an enterprise and thus is useful for planning and control. A budget serves management in the same manner as an architect's blueprints aid a builder or a navigator's flight plan aids a pilot.

Although budgets are commonly associated with profit-making enterprises, they play an important role in operating most units of government. For example, budgets are important in managing rural school districts and small villages as well as agencies of the federal government. Budgets are also important for managing the operations of churches, hospitals, and other nonprofit institutions. Individuals and families also use budgeting techniques in managing their financial resources. In this chapter, the principles of budgeting are discussed in the context of a manufacturing enterprise organized for profit.

Budgeting involves (1) establishing specific goals for future operations and (2) periodically comparing actual results with the goals. These goals include both the overall goals of the business as well as the specific goals for individual units within the business. Establishing specific goals for future operations is part of the *planning* function of management. Periodically comparing actual results with these goals encompasses the *control* function of management.

It is important that all levels of management and all departments be involved in establishing the goals that they are expected to achieve. Such involvement encourages cooperation both within and among departments. It also heightens the awareness of each department's importance in the overall operations of the enterprise. Human behavior problems can develop if managers view the goals as unrealistic or unachievable. In such a case, managers may become discouraged as well as uncommitted to the achievement of the operating goals. As a result, the budget becomes less effective as a tool for planning operations. On the other hand, goals set within a range that managers consider realistic are likely to inspire managers to achieve the goals.

Human behavior problems may also arise when the budgeted and actual results are compared. These problems can be minimized if budgets are revised when major changes in expectations occur during a budget period. Otherwise, the budgets will be of little value as incentives and as aids for controlling costs and expenses.

BUDGETING SYSTEMS

The details of budgeting systems vary among business enterprises. They are affected by such factors as the type and complexity of operations, the organizational structure of the enterprise, and management's philosophy. A budgeting system used by an automobile manufacturer such as General Motors would obviously differ from the budgeting system used by a small paper products manufacturer. Differences among budgeting systems are even more significant among different types of businesses, such as manufacturers and service enterprises. The basic budgeting concepts illustrated in the following paragraphs, however, apply to all types of enterprises and organizations.

The budgetary period for operating activities normally includes the fiscal year of an enterprise. A year is short enough to make dependable estimates of future operations, yet long enough to view the future in a broad context. However, to achieve effective control, the annual budgets are usually subdivided into shorter time periods, such as quarters of the year, months, or weeks.

A variation of fiscal-year budgeting, called **continuous budgeting** maintains a twelve-month projection into the future. The twelve-month budget is continually revised by removing the data for the period just ended and adding estimated budget data for the same period next year.

The development of budgets for the next fiscal year usually begins several months prior to the end of the current year. The responsibility for initially developing the budget is normally assigned to a committee. Such a committee often consists of the budget director and such high-level executives as the controller, the treasurer, the production manager, and the sales manager.

There are several methods of developing budget estimates. One method requires all levels of management to start from zero and estimate sales, production, and other operating data as though operations are being started for the first time. Although this concept, called **zero-base budgeting** has been used often by governmental units, it can also be useful to commercial enterprises. A more common method of developing estimates is to start with last year's budget and revise its estimates for actual results and expected changes for the coming year.

The estimates received by the budget committee should be carefully studied, analyzed, revised, and finally integrated together in a **master budget.** The original estimates are normally not significantly revised by the committee without first giving the units submitting the estimates an opportunity to defend their original estimates. After the master budget is approved by the budget committee, it is distributed to the operating and administrative units. Periodic reports comparing actual results with the budget should likewise be distributed to all supervisory personnel.

In developing a master budget, many firms use computerized budgeting systems. Such systems can not only speed up the budgeting process, but they can also reduce the cost of budget preparation. This is especially true when large quantities of data need to be processed. Computers are particularly useful in continuous budgeting. Reports that compare actual results with amounts budgeted can also be prepared on a timely basis through the use of computerized systems.

By using computerized simulation models, which are mathematical representations of operating activities, the impact of various operating alternatives on the master budget can be assessed. For example, the impact of a proposed change in direct labor wage rates can be assessed and the master budget revised to reflect the new rates. Likewise, the effects on the master budget of a proposal to add a new product line can be quickly determined.

As a basis for illustrating a budgeting system, a small manufacturing enterprise, Sanchez Inc., is used. The major parts of Sanchez Inc.'s master budget are as follows:

Budgeted income statement
    Sales budget
    Cost of goods sold budget
        Production budget
        Direct materials purchases budget
        Direct labor cost budget
        Factory overhead cost budget
    Operating expenses budget

Budgeted balance sheet
    Capital expenditures budget
    Cash budget

Sales Budget

The first budget prepared is usually the sales budget. An estimate of the sales volume serves as the basis for the other budgets. Sales volume affects the factors entering into the determination of operating income.

The sales budget normally indicates for each product (1) the quantity of estimated sales and (2) the expected unit selling price. These data are often classified by regions and/or by sales representatives.

In estimating the quantity of sales for each product, past sales volumes are often used as a starting point. These amounts are revised for factors expected to affect future sales. Such factors include a backlog of unfilled sales orders, planned advertising and promotion, expected industry and general economic conditions, productive capacity, projected pricing policy, and findings of market research studies. Statistical analysis can be used in this process to evaluate the effect of these factors on past sales volume. Such analysis can provide a mathematical association between past sales and the several variables expected to affect future sales.

Once an estimate of sales volume is obtained, the expected sales revenue can then be determined by multiplying the volume by the expected unit sales price. The sales budget for Sanchez Inc. is shown in Exhibit 1.

Exhibit 1
Sales Budget

Sanchez Inc.
Sales Budget
For Year Ending December 31, 1994

Product and Area	Unit Sales Volume	Unit Selling Price	Total Sales
Product X:			
Region A	208,000	$ 9.90	$2,059,200
Region B	162,000	9.90	1,603,800
Region C	158,000	9.90	1,564,200
Total	528,000		$5,227,200
Product Y:			
Region A	111,600	$16.50	$1,841,400
Region B	78,800	16.50	1,300,200
Region C	89,600	16.50	1,478,400
Total	280,000		$4,620,000
Total revenue from sales			$9,847,200

Comparisons of actual sales with the budgeted volume, by product, region, and/or sales representative, can be used by management for control purposes. Any significant differences are investigated and any possible corrective actions taken.

Production Budget

Production should be carefully coordinated with the sales budget to ensure that production and sales are kept in balance during the period. The number of units of each product to be manufactured to meet budgeted sales and inventory needs is set forth in the production budget. The budgeted volume of production is determined as follows:

    Expected units of sales
+   Desired units in ending inventory
-   Estimated units in beginning inventory
    Total units to be produced

The production budget for Sanchez Inc. is shown in Exhibit 2.

Exhibit 2
Production Budget

Sanchez Inc.
Production Budget
For Year Ending December 31, 1994

	Units Product X	Product Y
Sales	528,000	280,000
Plus desired inventory, December 31, 1994	80,000	60,000
Total	608,000	340,000
Less estimated inventory, January 1, 1994	88,000	48,000
Total units to be produced	520,000	292,000

Direct Materials Purchases Budget

The production budget provides the starting point for determining the estimated quantities of direct materials to be purchased. These quantities, determined as shown below, are multiplied by the expected unit purchase price to determine the total cost of direct materials to be purchased.

Material needed for production
+   Desired ending material inventory
-   Estimated beginning material inventory
Direct material to be purchased

In Sanchez Inc.'s production operations, Materials A and C are required for Product X, and Materials A, B, and C are required for Product Y. The quantities of direct material expected to be used for each unit of product are as follows:

Product X:
   Material A: .75 pound per unit
   Material C: 1.00 pound per unit

Product Y:
   Material A: .50 pound per unit
   Material B: 1.00 pound per unit
   Material C: 1.10 pounds per unit

Based upon the above requirements and the production budget, the direct materials purchases budget is prepared. As shown in the budget in Exhibit 3, for Sanchez Inc. to produce 520,000 units of Product X, 390,000 pounds (520,000 units × .75 lb. per unit) of Material A are needed. Likewise, to produce 292,000 units of Product Y, 146,000 pounds (292,000 units × .50 lb. per unit) of Material A are needed. The requirements for Material B and Material C are computed in a similar manner. The desired ending inventory for each material is then added and the estimated beginning inventory deducted to arrive at the amount of each material to be purchased. These amounts are then multiplied by the estimated cost per pound to yield the total materials purchase cost.

Exhibit 3
Direct Materials
Purchases Budget

Sanchez Inc.
Direct Materials Purchases Budget
For Year Ending December 31, 1994

| | *Direct Materials* | | |
	Material A	*Material B*	*Material C*
Pounds required for production:			
Product X (Note A)	390,000	—	520,000
Product Y (Note B)	146,000	292,000	321,200
Plus desired inventory, Dec. 31, 1994	80,000	40,000	120,000
Total	616,000	332,000	961,200
Less estimated inventory, Jan. 1, 1994	103,000	44,000	141,200
Total pounds to be purchased	513,000	288,000	820,000
Price per pound	× $.60	× $1.70	× $1.00
Total direct materials purchases costs	$307,800	$489,600	$820,000	$1,617,400

Note A: Material A: 520,000 units × .75 lb. per unit = 390,000 lbs.
             Material C: 520,000 units × 1 lb. per unit = 520,000 lbs.

Note B: Material A: 292,000 units × .5 lb. per unit = 146,000 lbs.
             Material B: 292,000 units × 1 lb. per unit = 292,000 lbs.
             Material C: 292,000 units × 1.1 lbs. per unit = 321,200 lbs.

The direct materials purchases budget is useful for assisting management in maintaining inventory levels within reasonable limits. For this purpose, the timing of the direct materials purchases should be closely coordinated between the purchasing and production departments.

Direct Labor Cost Budget

The production budget also provides the starting point for preparing the direct labor cost budget. For Sanchez Inc., the labor requirements for each unit of product are as follows:

Product X:
   Department 1: .1 hour per unit
   Department 2: .08 hour per unit

Product Y:
   Department 1: .1 hour per unit
   Department 2: .16 hour per unit

Based upon the above labor requirements and the production budget, the direct labor budget is prepared. As shown in the budget in Exhibit 4, for Sanchez Inc. to produce 520,000 units of Product X, 52,000 hours (520,000 units × .1 hour per unit) of labor in Department 1 are required. Likewise, to produce 292,000 units of Product Y, 29,200 hours (292,000 units × .1 hour per unit) of labor in Department 1 are required. The direct labor hours needed in Department 2 to meet the budgeted production can be determined in a similar manner. The direct labor hours for each department are then multiplied by the estimated department hourly rate to yield the total direct labor cost for each department.

Exhibit 4
Direct Labor Cost Budget

Sanchez Inc.
Direct Labor Cost Budget
For Year Ending December 31, 1994

	Department 1	Department 2	
Hours required for production:			
Product X (Note A)	52,000	41,600	
Product Y (Note B)	29,200	46,720	
Total	81,200	88,320	
Hourly rate	× $15	× $20	
Total direct labor cost	$1,218,000	$1,766,400	$2,984,400

Note A: Department 1: 520,000 units × .1 hrs. per unit = 52,000 hours
           Department 2: 520,000 units × .08 hrs. per unit = 41,600 hours

Note B: Department 1: 292,000 units × .1 hrs. per unit = 29,200 hours
           Department 2: 292,000 units × .16 hrs. per unit = 46,720 hours

The direct labor requirements should be closely coordinated between the production and personnel departments. This ensures that there will be enough labor available to meet production needs. Efficient manufacturing operations minimize idle time and labor shortages.

Factory Overhead Cost Budget

The estimated factory overhead costs necessary to meet production needs make up the factory overhead cost budget. This budget usually includes the total estimated cost for each item of factory overhead, as shown in Exhibit 5.

Exhibit 5
Factory Overhead Cost Budget

Sanchez Inc.
Factory Overhead Cost Budget
For Year Ending December 31, 1994

Indirect factory wages	$ 732,800
Supervisory salaries	360,000
Power and light	306,000
Depreciation of plant and equipment	288,000
Indirect materials	182,800
Maintenance	140,280
Insurance and property taxes	79,200
Total factory overhead cost	$2,089,080

Supporting schedules that break down factory overhead costs by department are often prepared for distribution to the departments. Such schedules enable department supervisors to focus attention on those costs for which they are responsible. They also aid the production manager in evaluating performance in each department.

Cost of Goods Sold Budget

The direct materials purchases budget, direct labor cost budget, and factory overhead cost budget provide the starting point for preparing the cost of goods sold budget. The desired ending inventory and the estimated beginning inventory data are combined with these data to determine the budgeted cost of goods sold.

To illustrate, the cost of goods sold budget for Sanchez Inc., shown in Exhibit 6, is based on the following work in process and finished goods inventories:

Estimated inventories on January 1, 1994:
Finished goods	$1,095,600
Work in process	214,400

Desired inventories on December 31, 1994:
Finished goods	$1,195,000
Work in process	220,000

Exhibit 6
Cost of Goods Sold Budget

Sanchez Inc.
Cost of Goods Sold Budget
For Year Ending December 31, 1994

Finished goods inventory, January 1, 1994			$1,095,600
Work in process inventory, January 1, 1994		$ 214,400	
Direct materials:			
Direct materials inventory, January 1, 1994 (Note A)	$ 277,800		
Direct materials purchases (from Exhibit 3)	1,617,400		
Cost of direct materials available for use	$1,895,200		
Less direct materials inventory, December 31, 1994 (Note B)	236,000		
Cost of direct materials placed in production	$1,659,200		
Direct labor (from Exhibit 4)	2,984,400		
Factory overhead (from Exhibit 5)	2,089,080		
Total manufacturing costs		6,732,680	
Total work in process during period		$6,947,080	
Less work in process inventory, December 31, 1994		220,000	
Cost of goods manufactured			6,727,080
Cost of finished goods available for sale			$7,822,680
Less finished goods inventory, December 31, 1994			1,195,000
Cost of goods sold			$6,627,680

Note A: Material A: 103,000 units at $.60			$ 61,800
Material B: 44,000 units at $1.70			74,800
Material C: 141,200 units at $1.00			141,200
Direct materials inventory, January 1, 1994			$277,800

Note B: Material A: 80,000 units at $.60			$ 48,000
Material B: 40,000 units at $1.70			68,000
Material C: 120,000 units at $1.00			120,000
Direct materials inventory, December 31, 1994			$236,000

Operating Expenses Budget

The estimated selling and administrative expenses make up the operating expenses budget. This budget usually provides the expenses by nature or by type of expenditure, such as sales salaries, rent, insurance, and advertising. An operating expenses budget for Sanchez Inc. is shown in Exhibit 7.

Exhibit 7
Operating Expenses Budget

Sanchez Inc.
Operating Expenses Budget
For Year Ending December 31, 1994

Selling expenses:		
Sales salaries expense	$595,000	
Advertising expense	360,000	
Travel expense	115,000	
Telephone expense—selling	95,000	
Miscellaneous selling expenses	25,000	
Total selling expenses		$1,190,000
Administrative expenses:		
Officers' salaries expense	$360,000	
Office salaries expense	105,000	
Heating and lighting expense	75,000	
Taxes expense	60,000	
Depreciation expense—office equipment	27,000	
Telephone expense—administrative	18,000	
Insurance expense	17,500	
Office supplies expense	7,500	
Miscellaneous administrative expenses	25,000	
Total administrative expenses		695,000
Total operating expenses		$1,885,000

Detailed supporting schedules for each department are often prepared for major items in the operating expenses budget. For example, an advertising expense schedule for the Marketing Department should include the advertising media to be used (newspaper, direct mail, television), quantities (column inches, number of pieces, minutes), and the cost per unit. Careful attention to such details will result in realistic budgets. Effective control will result from the assignment of responsibility for achieving the budget to department supervisors.

Budgeted Income Statement

The budgets for sales, cost of goods sold, and operating expenses, combined with the data on other income, other expense, and income tax provide the basis for preparing the budgeted income statement. A budgeted income statement for Sanchez Inc. is shown in Exhibit 8.

The budgeted income statement condenses the estimates of all profit-making phases of operations. This allows management to assess the effects of the individual budgets on profits for the year. If the budgeted net income is too low, a review of operating plans could be undertaken in an attempt to improve income.

Capital Expenditures Budget

The capital expenditures budget summarizes plans for acquiring plant assets. Such expenditures are necessary as machinery and other plant assets wear out, become obsolete, or for other reasons fall below minimum standards of efficiency. In addition, an expansion of plant facilities may be necessary to meet an increasing demand for a company's product or to expand the company's product line.

The useful life of many plant assets extends over relatively long periods of time. In addition, the amount of the expenditures for such assets may change sig-

Exhibit 8
Budgeted Income Statement

Sanchez Inc.
Budgeted Income Statement
For Year Ending December 31, 1994

Revenue from sales		$9,847,200
Cost of goods sold		6,627,680
Gross profit		$3,219,520
Operating expenses:		
Selling expenses	$1,190,000	
Administrative expenses	695,000	
Total operating expenses		1,885,000
Income from operations		$1,334,520
Other income:		
Interest income	$ 98,000	
Other expense:		
Interest expense	90,000	8,000
Income before income tax		$1,342,520
Income tax		537,000
Net income		$ 805,520

nificantly from year to year. The normal practice, therefore, is to project the plans for a number of years into the future in preparing the capital expenditures budget. A five-year capital expenditures budget for Sanchez Inc. is shown in Exhibit 9.

Exhibit 9
Capital Expenditures Budget

Sanchez Inc.
Capital Expenditures Budget
For Five Years Ending December 31, 1998

Item	1994	1995	1996	1997	1998
Machinery—Department 1	$400,000			$280,000	$360,000
Machinery—Department 2	180,000	$260,000	$560,000	200,000	
Office equipment		90,000			60,000
Total	$580,000	$350,000	$560,000	$480,000	$420,000

The capital expenditures budget should be considered in preparing the other operating budgets. For example, the estimated depreciation of new equipment affects the factory overhead cost budget and the operating expenses budget. The plans for financing the capital expenditures may also affect the cash budget.

Cash Budget

The cash budget presents the expected inflow and outflow of cash for a day, a week, a month, or a longer period, as shown in the cash budget for Sanchez Inc. in Exhibit 10.

Data from the various operating budgets, such as the sales budget, the direct materials purchases budget, and the operating expenses budget, affect the cash budget. In addition, the capital expenditures budget, dividend policies, and plans for equity or long-term debt financing also affect the cash budget.

In the cash budget, receipts are classified by source and payments by purpose. The estimated cash balance at the end of the period is then compared with the minimum balance required by operations. Any expected excess or deficiency can thus be determined.

The minimum cash balance provides a safety buffer for variations in estimates and for unexpected emergencies. The amount stated as the minimum balance need not remain fixed. It could be larger during periods of "peak" business activity than during "slow" periods. In addition, for effective cash management, much of the minimum cash balance should be deposited in income-producing securities that can be readily converted to cash. U.S. Treasury Bills or Notes are examples of such securities.

Exhibit 10
Cash Budget

Sanchez Inc.
Cash Budget
For Three Months Ending March 31, 1994

	January	February	March
Estimated cash receipts from:			
Cash sales	$168,000	$185,000	$ 115,000
Collections of accounts receivable	699,000	712,800	572,000
Other sources (issuance of securities, interest, etc.)	—	—	27,000
Total cash receipts	$867,000	$897,800	$ 714,000
Estimated cash disbursements for:			
Manufacturing costs	$541,200	$557,000	$ 536,000
Operating expenses	150,200	151,200	140,800
Capital expenditures	—	144,000	80,000
Other purposes (notes, income tax, etc.)	47,000	20,000	160,000
Total cash disbursements	$738,400	$872,200	$ 916,800
Cash increase (decrease)	$128,600	$ 25,600	$(202,800)
Cash balance at beginning of month	280,000	408,600	434,200
Cash balance at end of month	$408,600	$434,200	$ 231,400
Minimum cash balance	300,000	300,000	300,000
Excess (deficiency)	$108,600	$134,200	$ (68,600)

In many cases, it is useful to prepare supporting schedules for amounts in the cash budget. For example, the schedule in Exhibit 11 supports Sanchez Inc.'s estimated cash receipts arising from collections of accounts receivable. For this schedule, it is assumed that the accounts receivable balance was $295,800 on January 1. The sales estimate for January is $840,000, for February, $925,000, and for March, $575,000. Sanchez Inc. expects to sell 20% of its merchandise for cash. Sixty percent of the sales on account are expected to be collected in the month of the sale and the remainder in the following month.

Exhibit 11
Schedule of Collections of Accounts Receivable

Sanchez Inc.
Schedule of Collections of Accounts Receivable
For Three Months Ending March 31, 1994

	January	February	March
January 1 balance of accounts receivable	$295,800		
January sales on account (80% × $840,000):			
Collected in January (60% × $672,000)	403,200		
Collected in February (40% × $672,000)		$268,800	
February sales on account (80% × $925,000):			
Collected in February (60% × $740,000)		444,000	
Collected in March (40% × $740,000)			$296,000
March sales on account (80% × $575,000):			
Collected in March (60% × $460,000)			276,000
Total	$699,000	$712,800	$572,000

Accurate cash budgeting is essential for successful operations. An unexpected shortage of cash can result in a loss of discounts, unfavorable borrowing terms on loans, and damage to the company's credit rating. On the other hand, excess cash can be used to reduce loans or purchase investments in income-producing securities. The Sanchez Inc. cash budget in Exhibit 10 indicates excess cash during January and February and a deficiency during March.

Getting the Most Out of Your Cash

Most businesses could reduce their interest expenses if they would improve their management of cash. The goal of cash management is to use the company's money to maximize earnings while paying all liabilities and maintaining adequate liquidity. Accelerating collections, delaying payments, and getting the needed information about the cash status are the foundation of effective cash management.

One of the most efficient cash management tools is the wire transfer, which is the safest and fastest way to move a large sum of money quickly. It is used by having your customers who monthly pay you large amounts wire the money directly to your bank.

Another efficient cash management tool is the lockbox, which is a system that has your customers mail their remittance checks directly to a post office box in the name of your company. You authorize your bank to collect the customers' payments, and each item is deposited directly to

the bank, according to your instructions. A lockbox greatly accelerates the transformation of your receivables into cash, and it eliminates delays from mail and processing.

If your company is borrowing from a bank and not using its cash as effectively as it can, your company is losing interest every day. If the money is not needed on a day-by-day basis, you should invest the excess money in overnight, one- or two-week or 30-day instruments. If you are required to keep a compensating balance, monitor the account so that you do not keep more than the required amount.

Every morning, through phone calls or through a third party, you can receive information on your previous night's bank balances, credits, and payments in order to determine what you have available for investments that day. You can arrange for your bank to transfer the money out of your account and into investments every day.

Source: Allen E. Fishman, "Getting the Most Out of Your Cash," *St. Louis Post-Dispatch* (May 5, 1986), p. 14A.

Budgeted Balance Sheet

The budgeted balance sheet provides estimates of the financial condition at the end of a budget period. The budgeted balance sheet assumes that all operating budgets and financing plans are met. It is similar to a balance sheet based on actual data in the accounts. Thus, a budgeted balance sheet is not illustrated for Sanchez Inc. If the budgeted balance sheet indicates a weakness in financial position, a revision of financing or other plans may be necessary. For example, an excessive amount of long-term debt in relation to stockholders' equity might require a revision of financing plans for capital expenditures. Such revisions might include issuing equity rather than debt.

FLEXIBLE BUDGETS

Objective 3
Prepare a flexible budget.

In the preceding discussion, it has been assumed that the sales volume and the level of manufacturing activity during a period approximate the goals set forth in the budgets. When expectations change during a period, the budgets should be revised to give effect to such changes. Otherwise, the budgets may not be of value as aids and incentives for controlling costs and expenses.

Possible changes in the level of activity can be "built in" to a budget system by the use of flexible budgets. A **flexible budget** contains budgeted amounts for varying levels of activity. It is, in effect, a series of budgets for different levels of activity. Such budgets are especially useful in estimating and controlling factory overhead costs and operating expenses.

When flexible budgets are used for factory overhead costs and operating expenses, the first step is normally to identify the fixed cost and variable cost components of the costs being budgeted. The costs can then be estimated (budgeted) using the variable and fixed categories. To illustrate, a flexible budget for the June factory overhead cost for Department 1 of Sanchez Inc. is shown in Exhibit 12. As noted previously, annual budgets are usually subdivided into shorter time periods, such as a month. Thus, the budget in Exhibit 12 is one of the supporting budgets for Sanchez's yearly factory overhead budget shown in Exhibit 5.

The flexible budget in Exhibit 12 classifies each factory overhead item by its variable and fixed cost components. For example, the variable cost component of the maintenance cost is $.02 per unit. For 80,000 units of production, the variable maintenance costs are $1,600; for 90,000 units, the costs are $1,800; and for 100,000

ILLUSTRATIVE PROBLEM

Wolfram Inc. manufactures Product S for distribution nationally. The standard costs and actual costs for direct materials, direct labor, and factory overhead incurred for the manufacture of 1,000 units of Product S were as follows:

	Standard Costs	Actual Costs
Direct materials	1,000 pounds at $75	980 pounds at $75.50
Direct labor	12,500 hours at $9	12,600 hours at $8.95
Factory overhead	Rates per machine hour, based on 100% of productive capacity of 15,000 machine hours:	
	Variable cost, $3.50	$44,150 variable cost
	Fixed cost, $1.00	$15,000 fixed cost

Twelve and one-half machine hours are required per unit.

Instructions

1. Determine the quantity variance, price variance, and total direct materials cost variance for Product S.
2. Determine the time variance, rate variance, and total direct labor cost variance for Product S.
3. Determine the volume variance, controllable variance, and total factory overhead cost variance for Product S.

Solution

1.   *Direct Materials Cost Variance*

Quantity variance:
Actual quantity	980 pounds	
Standard quantity	1,000 pounds	
Variance—favorable	–20 pounds × standard price, $75	$1,500

Price variance:
Actual price	$75.50 per pound	
Standard price	75.00 per pound	
Variance—unfavorable	$ .50 per pound × actual quantity, 980	490

Total direct materials cost variance—favorable $1,010

2.   *Direct Labor Cost Variance*

Time variance:
Actual time	12,600 hours	
Standard time	12,500 hours	
Variance—unfavorable	100 hours × standard rate, $9	$ 900

Rate variance:
Actual rate	$8.95	
Standard rate	9.00	
Variance—favorable	–$.05 per hour × actual time, 12,600	630

Total direct labor cost variance—unfavorable $ 270

3.   *Factory Overhead Cost Variance*

Volume variance:
Productive capacity of 100%	15,000 hours	
Standard for amount produced	12,500 hours	
Productive capacity not used	2,500 hours	
Standard fixed factory overhead cost rate	× $1	
Variance—unfavorable		$2,500

Controllable variance:
Actual factory overhead cost incurred	$59,150	
Budgeted factory overhead for 12,500 hours	58,750*	
Variance—unfavorable		400

Total factory overhead cost variance—unfavorable $2,900

* (12,500 hrs. × $3.50) + $15,000

Getting the Most Out of Your Cash

Most businesses could reduce their interest expenses if they would improve their management of cash. The goal of cash management is to use the company's money to maximize earnings while paying all liabilities and maintaining adequate liquidity. Accelerating collections, delaying payments, and getting the needed information about the cash status are the foundation of effective cash management.

One of the most efficient cash management tools is the wire transfer, which is the safest and fastest way to move a large sum of money quickly. It is used by having your customers who monthly pay you large amounts wire the money directly to your bank.

Another efficient cash management tool is the lockbox, which is a system that has your customers mail their remittance checks directly to a post office box in the name of your company. You authorize your bank to collect the customers' payments, and each item is deposited directly to

the bank, according to your instructions. A lockbox greatly accelerates the transformation of your receivables into cash, and it eliminates delays from mail and processing.

If your company is borrowing from a bank and not using its cash as effectively as it can, your company is losing interest every day. If the money is not needed on a day-by-day basis, you should invest the excess money in overnight, one- or two-week or 30-day instruments. If you are required to keep a compensating balance, monitor the account so that you do not keep more than the required amount.

Every morning, through phone calls or through a third party, you can receive information on your previous night's bank balances, credits, and payments in order to determine what you have available for investments that day. You can arrange for your bank to transfer the money out of your account and into investments every day.

Source: Allen E. Fishman, "Getting the Most Out of Your Cash," *St. Louis Post-Dispatch* (May 5, 1986), p. 14A.

Budgeted Balance Sheet

The budgeted balance sheet provides estimates of the financial condition at the end of a budget period. The budgeted balance sheet assumes that all operating budgets and financing plans are met. It is similar to a balance sheet based on actual data in the accounts. Thus, a budgeted balance sheet is not illustrated for Sanchez Inc. If the budgeted balance sheet indicates a weakness in financial position, a revision of financing or other plans may be necessary. For example, an excessive amount of long-term debt in relation to stockholders' equity might require a revision of financing plans for capital expenditures. Such revisions might include issuing equity rather than debt.

FLEXIBLE BUDGETS

Objective 3
Prepare a flexible budget.

In the preceding discussion, it has been assumed that the sales volume and the level of manufacturing activity during a period approximate the goals set forth in the budgets. When expectations change during a period, the budgets should be revised to give effect to such changes. Otherwise, the budgets may not be of value as aids and incentives for controlling costs and expenses.

Possible changes in the level of activity can be "built in" to a budget system by the use of flexible budgets. A **flexible budget** contains budgeted amounts for varying levels of activity. It is, in effect, a series of budgets for different levels of activity. Such budgets are especially useful in estimating and controlling factory overhead costs and operating expenses.

When flexible budgets are used for factory overhead costs and operating expenses, the first step is normally to identify the fixed cost and variable cost components of the costs being budgeted. The costs can then be estimated (budgeted) using the variable and fixed categories. To illustrate, a flexible budget for the June factory overhead cost for Department 1 of Sanchez Inc. is shown in Exhibit 12. As noted previously, annual budgets are usually subdivided into shorter time periods, such as a month. Thus, the budget in Exhibit 12 is one of the supporting budgets for Sanchez's yearly factory overhead budget shown in Exhibit 5.

The flexible budget in Exhibit 12 classifies each factory overhead item by its variable and fixed cost components. For example, the variable cost component of the maintenance cost is $.02 per unit. For 80,000 units of production, the variable maintenance costs are $1,600; for 90,000 units, the costs are $1,800; and for 100,000

Exhibit 12
Flexible Budget for Factory
Overhead Cost—Department 1

Sanchez Inc.			
Factory Overhead Cost Budget—Department 1			
For Month Ending June 30, 1994			
Units of product	80,000	90,000	100,000
Variable cost:			
Indirect factory wages	$16,000	$18,000	$20,000
Indirect materials	12,000	13,500	15,000
Maintenance	1,600	1,800	2,000
Total variable cost	$29,600	$33,300	$37,000
Fixed cost:			
Supervisory salaries	$15,000	$15,000	$15,000
Depreciation of plant and equipment	12,000	12,000	12,000
Insurance and property taxes	7,500	7,500	7,500
Power and light	6,000	6,000	6,000
Maintenance	3,000	3,000	3,000
Total fixed cost	$43,500	$43,500	$43,500
Total factory overhead cost	$73,100	$76,800	$80,500

units, the costs are $2,000. The fixed cost component of the maintenance cost is $3,000, which does not vary across the three levels of production.

In practice, the number of production levels and the interval between levels may vary with the range of production volume. For example, instead of budgeting for 80,000, 90,000, and 100,000 units, as in Exhibit 12, the flexible budget might be prepared for intervals of 5,000 units between 60,000 units and 120,000 units. Alternative volume measures, such as machine hours or direct labor hours, may also be used instead of units of product.

BUDGET PERFORMANCE REPORTS

Objective 4
Prepare a budget performance report.

A **budget performance report** compares actual results with the budgeted amounts for the level of operations achieved. Budget performance reports should be prepared periodically. This feedback enables management to investigate significant differences and to take corrective actions. If the differences are caused because of changes in conditions or underlying assumptions, the budget should be revised.

When a flexible budget is used, the budget performance report should be based on the budget figures for the level of operations achieved. Such a budget performance report for Sanchez Inc. is shown in Exhibit 13. The amounts reported in the Budget column were obtained from the 80,000 units column of Sanchez's flexible budget in Exhibit 12. The amounts in the Actual column are the costs actually incurred. The last two columns show the amounts by which actual costs are greater or lower than budgeted costs.

In Exhibit 13, the fixed costs do not differ from their budgeted amounts, which is typical. There will usually be differences, however, between the actual and budgeted amounts for some of the variable costs of factory overhead. For example, Exhibit 13 shows a difference in indirect materials cost. The cause of this difference should probably be investigated. If possible, corrective action should be taken. If the difference in indirect materials cost is caused by a marketwide increase in the price of materials, corrective action may not be possible. On the other hand, if the difference is caused by the inefficient use of materials, it may be possible to eliminate the inefficiency and save costs in the future.

THE NATURE AND OBJECTIVES OF STANDARDS

Objective 5
Explain how the use of standard costs aids in planning and controlling operations.

Standards are used to measure and evaluate performance in many areas of life. For example, colleges set standards for graduation, such as a C average. They may establish a B+ average for graduation with honors. Golfers use par as a standard in evaluating their play on the golf course. In each of these cases, the standard is

Exhibit 13
Budget Performance Report—
Department 1

Sanchez Inc.
Budget Performance Report—Factory Overhead Cost, Department 1
For Month Ended June 30, 1994

	Budget	Actual	Over Budget	Under Budget
Variable cost:				
Indirect factory wages	$16,000	$16,200	$200	
Indirect materials	12,000	12,650	650	
Maintenance	1,600	1,500		$100
Total variable cost	$29,600	$30,350	$850	$100
Fixed cost:				
Supervisory salaries	$15,000	$15,000		
Depreciation of plant and equipment	12,000	12,000		
Insurance and property taxes	7,500	7,500		
Power and light	6,000	6,000		
Maintenance	3,000	3,000		
Total fixed cost	$43,500	$43,500		
Total factory overhead cost	$73,100	$73,850	$850	$100

used to measure and evaluate an individual's performance. In a like manner, business enterprises may use standards to evaluate and control operations.

Service, merchandising, and manufacturing enterprises may all use standards. For example, an automobile repair shop may use a standard amount of time as a basis for computing labor charges for repairs and measuring the performance of mechanics. The driver of a delivery truck may be expected to make a standard number of deliveries each day. The widest use of standards is by manufacturing enterprises. Manufacturers normally establish standard costs for each of the three categories of manufacturing costs: direct materials, direct labor, and factory overhead.

Accounting systems that use standards for each element of manufacturing cost entering into the finished product are called **standard cost systems**. Such systems enable management to determine how much a product should cost (**standard cost**), how much it does cost (actual cost), and the causes of any difference (**variance from standard**) between the two. Standard costs thus serve as a device for measuring efficiency.

When actual costs are compared with standard costs, only the *exceptions* or variances are reported for cost control. This reporting by the *principle of exceptions* allows management to focus on the cause and correction of the variances. Thus, the use of standard costs assists management in controlling costs and in motivating employees to become more cost-conscious.

When manufacturing operations are automated, standard cost data can be integrated with the computerized system that directs operations. Variances can then be detected and reported automatically, and adjustments can be made to operations in progress.

Setting Standards

The setting of standards is both an art and a science. Although the standard-setting process varies among enterprises, it normally requires the joint efforts of accountants, engineers, and other management personnel. The managerial accountant plays an essential role by expressing the results of judgments and studies in dollars and cents. Engineers contribute to the standard-setting process by identifying the material, labor, and machine requirements needed to produce the product. For example, direct materials requirements can be determined by studying such factors as the materials specifications for the product and estimating normal spoilage in production. Time and motion studies may be used to determine the length of time required for each of the various manufacturing operations. Engineering studies may also be used to determine standards for some of the elements of factory overhead, such as the amount of power needed to operate machinery.

The setting of standards often begins with an analysis of past operations. However, standards are not just an extension of past costs and caution must be used in relying upon past cost data. For example, inefficiencies may be contained within past costs. In addition, changes in technology, machinery, or production methods may make past costs irrelevant for future operations.

Types of Standards

Implicit in the use of standards is the concept of an acceptable level of production efficiency. One of the major objectives in setting this performance level is to motivate workers to achieve the most efficient operations.

Like the budgets discussed earlier, standards that are too high, that is, standards that are unrealistic, may have a negative impact on performance. This is because workers may become frustrated with their inability to meet the standards and, therefore, may not be motivated to do their best. Such standards represent levels of performance that can be achieved only under perfect operating conditions, such as no idle time, no machine breakdowns, and no materials spoilage. These standards, often called **theoretical standards** or **ideal standards**, are not widely used.

Standards that are too low might not motivate employees to perform at their best. This is because the standard level of performance can be reached too easily. As a result, productivity may be lower than what could be achieved.

Most companies use **currently attainable standards** (sometimes called **normal standards**). These standards represent levels of operation that can be attained with reasonable effort. Such standards allow for reasonable production difficulties and mistakes, such as normal materials spoilage and machine breakdowns. When reasonable standards are used, employees become more cost-conscious. They often put forth their best efforts to achieve the best operating results at the lowest possible cost. Also, if employees are given bonuses for exceeding normal standards, the standards may be even more effective in motivating employees.

Review and Revision of Standards

Standard costs should be continuously reviewed, and when they no longer reflect operating conditions, they should be revised. Inaccurate standards may have a harmful effect on management decision making and may weaken management's ability to plan and control operations.

Standards should not be revised, however, just because they differ from actual costs. They should only be revised when they no longer reflect the operating conditions that they were intended to measure. For example, the direct labor standard would not be revised simply because workers were unable to meet properly determined standards. On the other hand, standards should be revised when prices, product designs, labor rates, or manufacturing methods change to such an extent that current standards are no longer a useful measure of performance.

VARIANCES FROM STANDARDS

Objective 6
Compute the basic variances for direct materials, direct labor, and factory overhead.

The total difference between actual costs and standard costs for a period is normally made up of several variances, some of which may be favorable and some unfavorable. There may be variances from standards in direct materials costs, in direct labor costs, and in factory overhead costs. Illustrations and analyses of these variances for Trilogy Company, a manufacturing enterprise, are presented in the following paragraphs. For illustrative purposes, it is assumed that only one type of direct material is used. There is a single processing department, and Product X is the only commodity manufactured. The standard costs for direct materials, direct labor, and factory overhead for a unit of Product X are as follows:

Direct materials:	
2 pounds at $1 per pound	$ 2.00
Direct labor:	
.4 hour at $16 per hour	6.40
Factory overhead:	
.4 hour at $8.40 per machine hour	3.36
Total per unit	$11.76

Direct Materials Cost Variance

Two major factors determine the standards for direct materials cost: (1) the quantity (usage) standard and (2) the price standard. If the actual quantity of direct materials used in producing a commodity differs from the standard quantity, there is a **quantity variance**. If the actual unit price of the materials differs from the standard price, there is a **price variance**.

To illustrate, assume that the actual and standard direct materials cost of producing 10,000 units of Product X during June were as follows:

Actual: 20,600 pounds at $1.04		$21,424
Standard: 20,000 pounds (10,000 units × 2 lbs. per unit) at $1.00		20,000
Total unfavorable direct materials cost variance		$ 1,424

The total unfavorable direct materials cost variance of **$1,424** results from an excess usage of 600 pounds of direct materials and from an excess cost of $.04 per pound. This analysis is shown in Exhibit 14.

Exhibit 14
Direct Materials Cost Variance

Quantity variance:		
Actual quantity	20,600 pounds	
Standard quantity	20,000 pounds	
Variance—unfavorable	600 pounds × standard price, $1	$ 600
Price variance:		
Actual price	$1.04 per pound	
Standard price	1.00 per pound	
Variance—unfavorable	$ .04 per pound × actual quantity, 20,600	824
Total direct materials cost variance—unfavorable		$1,424

DIRECT MATERIALS QUANTITY VARIANCE. The direct materials quantity variance is the difference between the actual quantity used and the standard quantity, multiplied by the standard price per unit. If the standard quantity exceeds the actual quantity used, the variance is favorable. If the actual quantity of materials used exceeds the standard quantity, the variance is unfavorable, as shown below for Trilogy Company.

Direct Materials	Actual Quantity Used –	Standard Price
Quantity Variance	= Standard Quantity	× per Unit
Quantity variance	= (20,600 pounds – 20,000 pounds)	× $1.00 per pound
Quantity variance	= 600 pounds	× $1.00 per pound
Quantity variance	= $600 unfavorable	

DIRECT MATERIALS PRICE VARIANCE. The direct materials price variance is the difference between the actual price per unit and the standard price per unit, multiplied by the actual quantity used. If the standard price per unit exceeds the actual price per unit, the variance is favorable. If the actual price per unit exceeds the standard price per unit, the variance is unfavorable, as shown below for Trilogy Company.

Direct Materials	Actual Price per Unit –	Actual Quantity
Price Variance	= Standard Price	× Used
Price variance	= ($1.04 per pound – $1.00 per pound)	× 20,600 pounds
Price variance	= $.04 per pound	× 20,600 pounds
Price variance	= $824 unfavorable	

REPORTING DIRECT MATERIALS COST VARIANCE. The direct materials quantity variance should be reported to the proper level of operating management for possible corrective action. For example, excessive amounts of direct materials might have been used because of the malfunction of equipment that has not been properly maintained or operated. However, an unfavorable direct materials quantity variance may not always be the responsibility of an operating department. For example, the excess usage of materials may be caused by the use of inferior raw materials. In this case, the Purchasing Department should be held responsible.

The direct materials price variance should normally be reported to the Purchasing Department, which may or may not be able to control this variance. If materials of the same quality could have been purchased from another supplier at the standard price, the variance was controllable. On the other hand, if the variance resulted from a marketwide price increase, the variance was not subject to control.

Direct Labor Cost Variance

As in the case of direct materials, two major factors determine the standards for direct labor cost: (1) the time (usage or efficiency) standard and (2) the rate (price or wage) standard. If the actual direct labor hours spent producing a product differ from the standard hours, there is a **time variance**. If the wage rate paid differs from the standard rate, there is a **rate variance**. For Trilogy Company, the actual and standard cost of direct labor in the production of 10,000 units of Product X during June are as follows:

Actual: 3,950 hours at $16.40	$64,780
Standard: 4,000 hours (10,000 units × .4 hr. per unit) at $16.00	64,000
Total unfavorable direct labor cost variance	$ 780

The total unfavorable direct labor cost variance of **$780** results from a favorable time variance of 50 hours and an unfavorable rate variance of $.40 per hour. This analysis is shown in Exhibit 15.

Exhibit 15
Direct Labor Cost Variance

Time variance:		
Actual time	3,950 hours	
Standard time	4,000 hours	
Variance—favorable	−50 hours × standard rate, $16	$ 800
Rate variance:		
Actual rate	$16.40 per hour	
Standard rate	16.00 per hour	
Variance—unfavorable $ .40 per hour × actual time, 3,950 hours		1,580
Total direct labor cost variance—unfavorable		$ 780

DIRECT LABOR TIME VARIANCE. The **direct labor time variance** is the difference between the actual hours worked and the standard hours, multiplied by the standard rate per hour. If the actual hours worked exceed the standard hours, the variance is unfavorable. If the actual hours worked are less than the standard hours, the variance is favorable, as shown below for Trilogy Company.

Direct Labor	Actual Hours Worked –	Standard Rate
Time Variance =	Standard Hours	× per Hour
Time variance =	(3,950 hours − 4,000 hours)	× $16 per hour
Time variance =	− 50 hours	× $16 per hour
Time variance =	− $800 favorable	

In the above illustration, when the standard hours (4,000) are subtracted from the actual hours worked (3,950), the difference is *−50 hours*. The minus sign indicates that the variance of 50 hours, or $800 (50 hours × $16), is favorable.

DIRECT LABOR RATE VARIANCE. The **direct labor rate variance** is the difference between the actual rate per hour and the standard rate per hour, multiplied by the actual hours worked. If the standard rate per hour exceeds the actual rate per hour, the variance is favorable. If the actual rate per hour exceeds the standard rate per hour, the variance is unfavorable, as shown below for Trilogy Company.

Direct Labor Rate Variance	=	Actual Rate per Hour – Standard Rate	×	Actual Hours Worked
Rate variance	=	($16.40 per hour – $16.00 per hour)	×	3,950 hours
Rate variance	=	$.40 per hour	×	3,950 hours
Rate variance	=	$1,580 unfavorable		

REPORTING DIRECT LABOR COST VARIANCE. The control of direct labor cost is often the responsibility of the production supervisors. To aid them, periodic reports analyzing the cause of any direct labor variance may be prepared. A comparison of standard direct labor hours and actual direct labor hours provides the basis for investigating any major time variances. For example, a major time variance may be incurred because of the shortage of skilled workers. Such variances may be uncontrollable unless they are related to unusually high turnover rates among employees, in which case the cause of the high turnover should be investigated.

A comparison of the rates paid for direct labor with the standard rates provides a basis for investigating any major rate variances. For example, unfavorable rate variances may be caused by the improper scheduling and use of workers. In such cases, skilled, highly paid workers may be used in jobs that are normally performed by unskilled, lower paid workers. If this is the case, the unfavorable rate variance should be reported for corrective action to the level of management responsible for scheduling work assignments.

Factory Overhead Cost Variance

Some of the difficulties of allocating factory overhead costs among products manufactured have been discussed in previous chapters. Some of these difficulties arise from the variety of costs that are included in factory overhead and their indirect nature. For these same reasons, determining standards and variances for factory overhead costs is more complex than for direct materials and direct labor costs.

A flexible budget may be used to establish a predetermined (standard) factory overhead rate. A flexible budget may also aid in reporting actual costs and variations from standards. The standard overhead rate is determined by dividing the standard factory overhead costs by the standard amount of productive capacity. The productive capacity is usually expressed in terms of an activity base, such as machine hours, direct labor hours, or direct labor cost. A flexible budget for Trilogy Company showing the standard factory overhead rate for June is shown in Exhibit 16.

In Exhibit 16, the standard factory overhead cost rate is determined on the basis of the projected factory overhead costs at 100% of productive capacity. This level of capacity represents the general expectation of business activity under normal operating conditions. The standard rate is **$8.40** per machine hour. This rate can be further broken down into variable factory overhead of **$6** per hour ($30,000 ÷ 5,000 hours) and fixed factory overhead of **$2.40** per hour ($12,000 ÷ 5,000 hours).

Variances from standard for factory overhead cost result from the following two factors:

1. Operating above or below 100% of productive capacity.
2. Incurring actual factory overhead costs greater or less than the budgeted (standard) overhead costs for the level of operations achieved.

The first factor results in a **volume variance**. This variance measures the cost of operating at less than 100% of productive capacity or the benefit from operating at

Trilogy Company
Factory Overhead Cost Budget
For Month Ending June 30, 1994

	80%	90%	100%	110%
Percent of productive capacity	80%	90%	100%	110%
Machine hours	4,000	4,500	5,000	5,500
Budgeted factory overhead:				
Variable costs:				
Indirect factory wages	$12,800	$14,400	$16,000	$17,600
Power and light	5,600	6,300	7,000	7,700
Indirect materials	3,200	3,600	4,000	4,400
Maintenance	2,400	2,700	3,000	3,300
Total variable cost	$24,000	$27,000	$30,000	$33,000
Fixed costs:				
Supervisory salaries	$ 5,500	$ 5,500	$ 5,500	$ 5,500
Depreciation of plant and equipment	4,500	4,500	4,500	4,500
Insurance and property taxes	2,000	2,000	2,000	2,000
Total fixed cost	$12,000	$12,000	$12,000	$12,000
Total factory overhead cost	$36,000	$39,000	$42,000	$45,000

Factory overhead rate per machine hour ($42,000 ÷ 5,000) $8.40

a level above 100% of productive capacity. The second factor results in a **controllable variance**. This variance measures the difference between the actual factory overhead costs incurred and the budgeted (standard) overhead costs for the standard product produced during the period.

To illustrate, assume that the actual cost and standard cost of factory overhead for Trilogy Company's production of 10,000 units of Product X during June were as follows:

Actual:	Variable factory overhead	$24,600	
	Fixed factory overhead	12,000	$36,600
Standard:	4,000 hours (10,000 units × .4) at $8.40		33,600
Total unfavorable factory overhead cost variance			$ 3,000

The total unfavorable overhead cost variance of **$3,000** is made up of an unfavorable volume variance and an unfavorable controllable variance. This analysis is shown in Exhibit 17.

Exhibit 17
Factory Overhead Cost Variance

Volume variance:

Productive capacity of 100%	5,000 hours	
Standard activity level for amount produced	4,000 hours	
Productive capacity not used	1,000 hours	
Standard fixed factory overhead cost rate	× $2.40	
Variance—unfavorable		$2,400
Controllable variance:		
Actual factory overhead cost incurred	$36,600	
Budgeted factory overhead for standard product produced	36,000	
Variance—unfavorable		600
Total factory overhead cost variance—unfavorable		$3,000

FACTORY OVERHEAD VOLUME VARIANCE. The factory overhead volume variance is the difference between the productive capacity and the standard activity level for the amount produced, multiplied by the standard fixed factory overhead rate. If the standard activity level for the amount produced exceeds the productive capacity, the variance is favorable. If the productive capacity exceeds the standard for the amount produced, the variance is unfavorable. The computation of the $2,400 unfavorable volume variance for Trilogy Company is shown below.

	Productive Capacity of 100% –	
Factory Overhead	Standard Activity for	Standard Fixed Factory
Volume Variance =	Amount Produced	× Overhead Rate
Volume variance =	(5,000 hours – 4,000 hours)	× $2.40 per hour
Volume variance =	1,000 hours	× $2.40 per hour
Volume variance =	**$2,400 unfavorable**	

In the above illustration, the unfavorable volume variance of $2,400 can be viewed as the cost of the available but unused productive capacity (1,000 hours). It should also be noted that the variable portion of the factory overhead cost rate was ignored in determining the volume variance. Variable factory overhead costs vary with the level of production. Thus, a reduction in production is accompanied by a related reduction in variable costs. On the other hand, fixed factory overhead costs are not affected by changes in the level of operations. The fixed factory overhead costs represent the costs of providing the capacity for production, and the volume variance measures the amount of the fixed factory overhead cost due to the variance between capacity used and 100% of productive capacity.

A volume variance may result from such factors as failure to maintain an even flow of work, machine breakdowns or repairs causing work stoppages, and failure to obtain enough sales orders to keep the factory operating at the expected level of operations. Large volume variances should be investigated for possible corrective actions. A volume variance caused by a failure of supervisors to maintain an even flow of work, for example, may be corrected. Volume variances caused by a lack of sales orders may be corrected through increased advertising or other sales efforts.

FACTORY OVERHEAD CONTROLLABLE VARIANCE. The **factory overhead controllable variance** is the difference between the actual factory overhead incurred and the budgeted (standard) factory overhead for the standard amount produced. If the budgeted factory overhead for the standard amount produced exceeds the actual factory overhead, the variance is favorable. If the actual factory overhead exceeds the budgeted factory overhead for the standard amount produced, the variance is unfavorable. For Trilogy Company, the standard machine hours for the amount produced during June was 4,000 (80% of capacity). The factory overhead budgeted at this level of activity is $36,000, as shown in Exhibit 16. When this budgeted factory overhead is compared with the actual factory overhead, as shown below, a $600 unfavorable controllable variance results.

Factory Overhead	Actual Factory	Budgeted Factory Overhead for
Controllable Variance =	Overhead	– Standard Amount Produced
Controllable variance =	$36,600	– $36,000
Controllable variance =	**$600 unfavorable**	

The controllable factory overhead variance indicates management's ability to keep the factory overhead cost within the limits set forth in the budget. Most of the controllable variance normally relates to the cost of the variable factory overhead items. This is because there is usually little or no variation in the fixed factory overhead costs. Since variable overhead costs are normally controllable at the departmental level, responsibility for controlling this variance usually rests with department supervisors.

REPORTING FACTORY OVERHEAD COST VARIANCE. The best means of reporting standard factory overhead cost variance data is through a **factory overhead cost variance report**. Such a report, shown in Exhibit 18, indicates both the controllable variance and the volume variance. This report can be used to highlight the causes of the variances for use in controlling costs.

Exhibit 18
Factory Overhead Cost Variance Report

Trilogy Company
Factory Overhead Cost Variance Report
For Month Ended June 30, 1994

| | | | Productive capacity for the month | 5,000 hours |
| | | | Actual production for the month | 4,000 hours |

	Budget	Actual	Variances Favorable	Variances Unfavorable
Variable costs:				
Indirect factory wages	$12,800	$13,020		$ 220
Power and light	5,600	5,550	$50	
Indirect materials	3,200	3,630		430
Maintenance	2,400	2,400		
Total variable cost	$24,000	$24,600		
Fixed costs:				
Supervisory salaries	$ 5,500	$ 5,500		
Depreciation of plant and equip.	4,500	4,500		
Insurance and property taxes	2,000	2,000		
Total fixed cost	$12,000	$12,000		
Total factory overhead cost	$36,000	$36,600		
Total controllable variances			$50	$ 650
Net controllable variances—unfavorable				$ 600
Volume variance—unfavorable:				
Idle hours at the standard rate for fixed factory overhead—1,000 × $2.40			2,400	
Total factory overhead cost variance—unfavorable				$3,000

It is possible to break down many of the individual factory overhead cost variances into quantity and price variances, similar to the analysis for direct materials and direct labor. For example, the indirect factory wages variance may include both time and rate variances. Likewise, the indirect materials variance may include both a quantity variance and a price variance.

STANDARDS IN THE ACCOUNTS

Objective 7
Journalize the entries for recording standards in the accounts.

Standard costs can be used solely as a management tool apart from the accounts in the general ledger. However, many companies include both standard costs and variances, in addition to actual costs, in their accounts. In doing so, one approach is to record the standard costs and variances at the same time the actual manufacturing costs are recorded in the accounts.

To illustrate, assume that Lee Corporation purchased, on account, 10,000 pounds of direct materials at $1 per pound. The standard price for direct materials is $.95 per pound. The entry to record the purchase and the unfavorable direct materials price variance is as follows:

Materials	9,500	
Direct Materials Price Variance	500	
Accounts Payable		10,000

The materials account is debited for the 10,000 pounds at the standard price of $.95 per pound. The unfavorable direct materials price variance is $500 [($1.00 actual price per pound − $.95 standard price per pound) × 10,000 pounds purchased]. The variance is recorded by debiting Direct Materials Price Variance for $500. Accounts Payable is credited for the actual cost, $10,000 (10,000 pounds × $1 per pound). If the variance had been favorable, Direct Materials Price Variance would have been credited for the amount of the variance.

The direct materials quantity variance is recorded in a similar manner. For example, assume that Lee Corporation used 4,900 pounds of direct materials to produce a product with a standard of 5,000 pounds. The entry to record the materials used is shown below.

Work in Process	4,750	
Materials		4,655
Direct Materials Quantity Variance		95

The work in process account is debited for the standard price of the standard amount of direct materials required, $4,750 (5,000 pounds × $.95). Materials is credited for the actual amount of materials used at the standard price, $4,655 (4,900 pounds × $.95). The favorable direct materials quantity variance of $95 [(5,000 standard pounds – 4,900 actual pounds) × $.95 standard price per pound] is credited to Direct Materials Quantity Variance. If the variance had been unfavorable, Direct Materials Quantity Variance would have been debited for the amount of the variance.

The entries for direct labor, factory overhead, and other variances are recorded in a manner similar to the entries for direct materials. The work in process account is debited for the standard costs of direct labor and factory overhead as well as direct materials. Likewise, the work in process account is credited for the standard cost of the product completed and transferred to the finished goods account.

In a given period, it is possible to have both favorable and unfavorable variances. At the end of the period, the balances of the variance accounts will indicate the net favorable or unfavorable variance for the period. Variances from standard costs are usually not reported to stockholders and others outside of management. If standards are recorded in the accounts, however, the variances are often reported in income statements prepared for use by management. An example of such an income statement prepared for Trilogy Company's internal use is shown in Exhibit 19.

Exhibit 19
Variances from Standards in Income Statement

Trilogy Company			
Income Statement			
For Month Ended June 30, 1994			
Sales			$190,000
Cost of goods sold—at standard			111,720
Gross profit—at standard			$ 78,280
	Favorable	*Unfavorable*	
Less variances from standard cost:			
Direct materials quantity		$ 600	
Direct materials price		824	
Direct labor time	$800		
Direct labor rate		1,580	
Factory overhead volume		2,400	
Factory overhead controllable	___	600	5,204
Gross profit			$ 73,076
Operating expenses:			
Selling expenses		$22,500	
Administrative expenses		19,225	41,725
Income before income tax			$ 31,351

At the end of the fiscal year, the variances from standard are usually transferred to the cost of goods sold account. However, if the variances are significant or if many of the products manufactured are still on hand, the variances should be allocated. The variances would be allocated to the work in process, finished goods, and cost of goods sold accounts. The result of such an allocation is to convert these account balances from standard cost to actual cost.

STANDARDS FOR NONMANUFACTURING EXPENSES

Objective 8
Explain how standards may be used for nonmanufacturing expenses.

The use of standards for nonmanufacturing expenses is not as common as the use of standards for manufacturing costs. A major reason for this is due in part to the fact that many nonmanufacturing expenses cannot be readily associated with a unit of product or a standard measure of performance. For example, the product costs associated with an Assembly Department can be measured and related to the product. On the other hand, the expenses associated with the work of the office manager are not easily related to any unit of output or standard measure of performance.

When nonmanufacturing activities are repetitive and generate a homogeneous product, the concept of standards can be applied. In these cases, the process of estimating and using standards is similar to that described for a manufactured product. For example, standards can be applied to the work of office personnel who process sales orders. A standard measure of performance and a standard unit expense for processing a sales order could be developed. The variance between the actual expense of processing a sales order and the standard expense could then be determined and used to control sales order expenses.

In practice, the use of standards for nonmanufacturing expenses is becoming more widely used. This is partially because managers have begun to direct more attention to controlling nonmanufacturing expenses. When standards are not used, such expenses are normally controlled by the use of budgets and budget performance reports of the type illustrated earlier in this chapter.

CHAPTER REVIEW

Key Points

Objective 1. Describe budgeting and its objectives.
Budgeting involves (1) establishing specific goals for future operations and (2) periodically comparing actual results with these goals. Budgeting helps managers in planning and controlling operations.

Human behavior problems can develop if managers view a budget as unrealistic or unachievable. Such problems can be minimized if managers are involved in setting budgets and if budgets are revised when major changes in expectations occur during a budget period.

Objective 2. Prepare the basic budgets for a manufacturing enterprise.
The basic budgets that are included in the master budget of a manufacturing enterprise are the sales budget, cost of goods sold budget, production budget, direct materials purchases budget, direct labor cost budget, factory overhead cost budget, operating expenses budget, capital expenditures budget, and cash budget. The preparation of these budgets is described and illustrated in this section. These budgets serve as the basis for preparing the budgeted income statement and budgeted balance sheet.

Objective 3. Prepare a flexible budget.
A flexible budget is prepared by budgeting amounts for varying levels of activity. The first step in preparing a flexible budget for factory overhead costs or operating expenses is normally to identify the variable and fixed components of the costs being budgeted. The costs can then be estimated (budgeted) for each level of activity, using the variable and fixed categories.

Objective 4. Prepare a budget performance report.
A budget performance report is prepared by listing budgeted costs, actual costs, and the differences. Major differences indicated in a budget performance report can be investigated by management and any possible corrective actions taken.

Objective 5. Explain how the use of standard costs aids in planning and controlling operations.
Standard costs enable managers to determine how much a product should cost (standard), how much it does cost (actual), and the causes of any difference (variance) between the two. Reporting differences by the principle of exceptions allows management to focus on the cause and correction of variances. Standard costs thus serve as a tool for controlling costs and motivating employees.

Objective 6. Compute the basic variances for direct materials, direct labor, and factory overhead.
The two basic variances for direct materials cost are the (1) direct materials quantity variance and (2) direct materials price variance. The two basic variances for direct labor costs are the (1) direct labor time variance and (2) direct labor rate variance. The two basic variances for factory overhead costs are the (1) factory overhead volume variance and (2) factory overhead controllable variance. The computation of each of these variances is described and illustrated in this chapter.

Objective 7. Journalize the entries for recording standards in the accounts.
Standard costs and variances can be recorded in the accounts at the same time the manufacturing costs are recorded in the accounts. For example, the purchase of direct materials on account is recorded as a debit to Materials for the standard cost of materials, and a credit to Accounts Payable for the actual cost. Any difference is debited or credited to the direct materials price variance account.

The entries for direct labor, factory overhead, and other variances are recorded in a manner similar to the entries for direct materials. The work in process account is debited for the standard costs of direct labor and factory overhead as well as direct materials. Likewise, the work in process account is credited for the standard cost of the product completed and transferred to the finished goods account.

Objective 8. Explain how standards may be used for nonmanufacturing expenses.
Standards may be used for nonmanufacturing expenses when nonmanufacturing activities are repetitive and generate a homogeneous product. Such standards may be useful to managers in planning and controlling nonmanufacturing expenses.

Glossary of Key Terms

Budget. A formal written statement of management's plans for the future, expressed in financial terms. **Objective 1**

Budget performance report. A report comparing actual results with budget figures. **Objective 4**

Continuous budgeting. A method of budgeting that provides for maintaining a twelve-month projection into the future. **Objective 2**

Currently attainable standards. Standards that represent levels of operation that can be attained with reasonable effort. **Objective 5**

Direct labor rate variance. The cost associated with the difference between the standard rate and the actual rate paid for direct labor used in producing a commodity. **Objective 6**

Direct labor time variance. The cost associated with the difference between the standard hours and the actual hours of direct labor spent producing a commodity. **Objective 6**

Direct materials price variance. The cost associated with the difference between the standard price and the actual price of direct materials used in producing a commodity. **Objective 6**

Direct materials quantity variance. The cost associated with the difference between the standard quantity and the actual quantity of direct materials used in producing a commodity. **Objective 6**

Factory overhead controllable variance. The difference between the actual amount of factory overhead cost incurred and the amount of factory overhead budgeted for the standard product produced. **Objective 6**

Factory overhead volume variance. The cost or benefit associated with operating at a level above or below 100% of productive capacity. **Objective 6**

Flexible budget. A series of budgets for varying rates of activity. **Objective 3**

Master budget. The comprehensive budget plan involving all the individual budgets related to sales, cost of goods sold, operating expenses, capital expenditures, cash, income statement, and balance sheet. **Objective 2**

Standard cost. A detailed estimate of what a product should cost. **Objective 5**

Standard cost systems. Accounting systems that use standards for each element of manufacturing costs entering into the finished product. **Objective 5**

Theoretical standards. Standards that represent levels of performance that can be achieved only under perfect operating conditions. **Objective 5**

Variance from standard. Difference between standard cost and actual cost. **Objective 5**

Zero-base budgeting. A concept of budgeting that requires all levels of management to start from zero and estimate budget data as if there had been no previous activities in their unit. **Objective 2**

SELF-EXAMINATION QUESTIONS
Answers at end of chapter.

1. The total estimated units of sales for the coming year is 250,000. The estimated inventory at the beginning of the year is 22,500 units, and the desired inventory at the end of the year is 30,000 units. The total production indicated in the production budget is:
   A. 242,500 units
   B. 257,500 units
   C. 280,000 units
   D. 302,500 units

2. A report comparing actual results with the budget amounts is called a:
   A. budget report
   B. budget performance report
   C. flexible budget report
   D. continuous budget report

3. The system that builds into the various budgets the effect of fluctuations in level of activity is called:
   A. budget performance reporting
   B. continuous budgeting
   C. flexible budgeting
   D. zero-base budgeting

4. The actual and standard direct materials costs for producing a specified quantity of product are as follows:

Actual:	51,000 pounds at $5.05	$257,550
Standard:	50,000 pounds at $5.00	250,000

   The direct materials price variance is:
   A. $50 unfavorable
   B. $2,500 unfavorable
   C. $2,550 unfavorable
   D. $7,550 unfavorable

5. The actual and standard factory overhead costs for producing a specified quantity of product are as follows:

Actual:	Variable factory overhead	$72,500	
	Fixed factory overhead	40,000	$112,500
Standard:	19,000 hours at $6		
	($4 variable and $2 fixed)		114,000

   If 1,000 hours were unused, the factory overhead volume variance would be:
   A. $1,500 favorable
   B. $2,000 unfavorable
   C. $4,000 unfavorable
   D. $6,000 unfavorable

ILLUSTRATIVE PROBLEM

Wolfram Inc. manufactures Product S for distribution nationally. The standard costs and actual costs for direct materials, direct labor, and factory overhead incurred for the manufacture of 1,000 units of Product S were as follows:

	Standard Costs	Actual Costs
Direct materials	1,000 pounds at $75	980 pounds at $75.50
Direct labor	12,500 hours at $9	12,600 hours at $8.95
Factory overhead	Rates per machine hour, based on 100% of productive capacity of 15,000 machine hours:	
	Variable cost, $3.50	$44,150 variable cost
	Fixed cost, $1.00	$15,000 fixed cost

Twelve and one-half machine hours are required per unit.

Instructions

1. Determine the quantity variance, price variance, and total direct materials cost variance for Product S.
2. Determine the time variance, rate variance, and total direct labor cost variance for Product S.
3. Determine the volume variance, controllable variance, and total factory overhead cost variance for Product S.

Solution

1.   *Direct Materials Cost Variance*

Quantity variance:

Actual quantity	980 pounds	
Standard quantity	1,000 pounds	
Variance—favorable	−20 pounds × standard price, $75	$1,500

Price variance:

Actual price	$75.50 per pound	
Standard price	75.00 per pound	
Variance—unfavorable	$ .50 per pound × actual quantity, 980	490
Total direct materials cost variance—favorable		$1,010

2.   *Direct Labor Cost Variance*

Time variance:

Actual time	12,600 hours	
Standard time	12,500 hours	
Variance—unfavorable	100 hours × standard rate, $9	$ 900

Rate variance:

Actual rate	$8.95	
Standard rate	9.00	
Variance—favorable	−$.05 per hour × actual time, 12,600	630
Total direct labor cost variance—unfavorable		$ 270

3.   *Factory Overhead Cost Variance*

Volume variance:

Productive capacity of 100%	15,000 hours	
Standard for amount produced	12,500 hours	
Productive capacity not used	2,500 hours	
Standard fixed factory overhead cost rate	× $1	
Variance—unfavorable		$2,500

Controllable variance:

Actual factory overhead cost incurred	$59,150	
Budgeted factory overhead for 12,500 hours	58,750*	
Variance—unfavorable		400
Total factory overhead cost variance—unfavorable		$2,900

* (12,500 hrs. × $3.50) + $15,000

DISCUSSION QUESTIONS

1. What is a budget?
2. a. Name the two basic functions of management in which accounting is involved.
   b. How does a budget aid management in the discharge of these basic functions?
3. Why should all levels of management and all departments participate in the preparation and submission of budget estimates?
4. Briefly discuss the type of human behavior problem(s) that might arise if goals used in developing budgets are unrealistic or unachievable.
5. What is meant by *continuous budgeting*?
6. How can computerized budgeting systems aid firms in the budgeting process?
7. Which budgetary concept requires all levels of management to start from zero and estimate sales, production, and other operating data as though the operations were being initiated for the first time?
8. Why should the production requirements as set forth in the production budget be carefully coordinated with the sales budget?
9. Why should the timing of direct materials purchases be closely coordinated with the production budget?
10. Zellner Inc., which estimates that 150,000 units will be sold during the current year, desires an ending inventory of 25,000 units. If 22,500 units are in the beginning inventory, what is the estimated production for the current year?
11. What are the three budgets from which data on relevant estimates of quantities and costs are combined with data on estimated inventories in preparing the budget for the cost of goods sold?
12. What is a capital expenditures budget?
13. a. Discuss the purpose of the cash budget.
    b. If the cash for the first quarter of the fiscal year indicates excess cash at the end of each of the first two months, how might the excess cash be used?
14. What is a flexible budget?
15. Sherman Corporation uses flexible budgets. For each of the following variable operating expenses, indicate whether there has been a saving or an excess of expenses, assuming that actual sales were $900,000.

Expense Item	Actual Amount	Budget Allowance Based on Sales
Supplies expense	$ 9,250	1%
Uncollectible accounts expense	26,500	3%

16. What is a budget performance report?
17. What are the basic objectives in the use of standard costs?
18. How can standards be used by management to help control costs?
19. What is a variance, as the term is used in reference to standard costs?
20. What is meant by reporting by the "principle of exceptions," as the term is used in reference to cost control?
21. How often should standards be revised?
22. a. What are the two variances between the actual cost and the standard cost for direct materials?
    b. Discuss some possible causes of these variances.
23. The materials cost variance report for Nickols Inc. indicates a large favorable materials price variance and a significant unfavorable materials quantity variance. What might have caused these offsetting variances?
24. a. What are the two variances between the actual cost and the standard cost for direct labor?
    b. Who generally has control over the direct labor cost?
25. A new assistant controller recently was heard to remark: "All the assembly workers in this plant are covered by union contracts, so there should be no labor variances." Was the controller's remark correct? Discuss.
26. a. Describe the two variances between the actual costs and the standards costs for factory overhead.
    b. What is a factory overhead cost variance report?
27. If variances are recorded in the accounts at the time the manufacturing costs are incurred, what does a debit balance in Direct Materials Price Variance represent?
28. If variances are recorded in the accounts at the time the manufacturing costs are incurred, what does a credit balance in Direct Materials Quantity Variance represent?

29. Are variances from standard costs usually reported in financial statements issued to stockholders and others outside the firm?
30. Assuming that the variances from standards are not significant at the end of the period, to what account are they transferred?

 REAL W RLD FOCUS

31. During the ten-year period, 1982–1991, the ratio of cost of products sold to sales for H. J. Heinz Company decreased from 61% to 66%. During this same period, the sales of H. J. Heinz Company increased by almost 86%. As sales increase, why would management normally expect the ratio of cost of products sold to sales to decrease?

ETHICS DISCUSSION CASE

Ann Santos, chief cost accountant for W. L. Weeks Company, has been assigned the task of reviewing the current standard costs. After studying the results of time and motion studies conducted by an independent engineering firm, she proposed changing the current standards. She explained that manufacturing methods recently had been changed and the current standards no longer represented a useful measure of performance. Frank Wilson, production supervisor, objected to the new standards because his workers would be held to a higher standard than the current standards.

 SHARPEN YOUR ► COMMUNICATION SKILLS

Discuss whether Ann Santos behaved in an ethical manner by proposing the new standards.

EXERCISES

EXERCISE 25-1
SALES AND PRODUCTION BUDGETS
Objective 2

Shuster Company manufactures two models of humidifiers, H4 and H6. Based on the following production and sales data for April of the current year, prepare (a) a sales budget and (b) a production budget.

	H4	H6
Estimated inventory (units), April 1	61,000	27,100
Desired inventory (units), April 30	70,000	23,500
Expected sales volume (units):		
East Region	81,500	40,800
West Region	66,200	24,800
Unit sales price	$14.50	$20.00

SPREADSHEET PROBLEM

EXERCISE 25-2
PROFESSIONAL FEES BUDGET
Objective 2

Thorne and Webb, CPAs, offer three types of services to clients: auditing, tax, and computer consulting. Based upon past experience and projected growth, the following billable hours have been estimated for the year ending December 31, 1994:

	Billable Hours
Audit Department:	
Staff	20,000
Partners	5,000
Tax Department:	
Staff	15,000
Partners	3,000
Computer Consulting Department:	
Staff	10,000
Partners	3,000

The average billing rate for staff is $40 per hour, and the average billing rate for partners is $80 per hour.

Prepare a professional fees budget for Thorne and Webb, CPAs, for the year ending December 31, 1994, using the following column headings and showing the estimated professional fees by type of service rendered:

Billable Hours	Hourly Rate	Total Revenue

EXERCISE 25-3
DIRECT LABOR COST
BUDGET
Objective 2

Based upon the data in Exercise 25-2 and assuming that the average compensation per hour for staff is $25 and for partners is $50, prepare a direct labor cost budget for Thorne and Webb, CPAs, for the year ending December 31, 1994. Use the following column headings:

Billable Hours Required

Staff   Partners

EXERCISE 25-4
SCHEDULE OF CASH
COLLECTIONS OF
ACCOUNTS RECEIVABLE
Objective 2

Ryan Company was organized on August 1 of the current year. Projected sales for each of the first three months of operations are as follows:

August	$160,000
September	200,000
October	300,000

SPREADSHEET
PROBLEM

The company expects to sell 25% of its merchandise for cash. Of sales on account, 60% are expected to be collected in the month of the sale, 30% in the month following the sale, and the remainder in the following month. Prepare a schedule indicating cash collections of accounts receivable for August, September, and October.

EXERCISE 25-5
SCHEDULE OF CASH
PAYMENTS
Objective 2

Vogel Company was organized on February 28 of the current year. Projected operating expenses for each of the first three months of operations are as follows:

March	$100,000
April	124,000
May	138,000

Depreciation, insurance, and property taxes represent $20,000 of the estimated monthly operating expenses. The annual insurance premium was paid on February 28, and property taxes for the year will be paid in December. Three-fourths of the remainder of the operating expenses are expected to be paid in the month in which they are incurred, with the balance to be paid in the following month.

Prepare a schedule indicating cash payments for operating expenses for March, April, and May.

EXERCISE 25-6
FLEXIBLE BUDGET FOR
OPERATING EXPENSES
Objective 3

Lane Company uses flexible budgets that are based on the following data:

Sales commissions	5% of sales
Advertising expense	6% of sales
Miscellaneous selling expense	$1,000 plus 1/2% of sales
Office salaries expense	$15,000 per month
Office supplies expense	1% of sales
Miscellaneous administrative expense	$500 per month plus 1/4% of sales

Prepare a flexible operating expenses budget for May of the current year for sales volumes of $200,000, $300,000, and $400,000. (Note: Use Exhibit 12 as a model for this budget.)

EXERCISE 25-7
BUDGET PERFORMANCE
REPORT
Objective 4

The operating expenses incurred during May of the current year by Lane Company were as follows:

Sales commissions	$20,000
Advertising expense	22,600
Miscellaneous selling expense	3,050
Office salaries expense	15,000
Office supplies expense	3,810
Miscellaneous administrative expense	1,620

Assuming that the total sales for May were $400,000, prepare a budget performance report for operating expenses on the basis of the data presented above and in Exercise 25-6.

EXERCISE 25-8
FLEXIBLE FACTORY
OVERHEAD COST BUDGET
Objective 3

Tudor Company prepared the following factory overhead cost budget for Department C for March of the current year, during which it expected to manufacture 20,000 units:

Variable cost:		
Indirect factory	$20,000	
Power and light	12,500	
Indirect materials	5,000	
Total variable cost		$37,500
Fixed cost:		
Supervisory salaries	$12,500	
Depreciation of plant and equipment	4,000	
Insurance and property taxes	2,000	
Total fixed cost		18,500
Total factory overhead cost		$56,000

Assuming that the estimated costs for April are the same as for March, prepare a flexible factory overhead cost budget for Department C for April for 18,000, 20,000, and 22,000 units of product.

EXERCISE 25-9
BUDGET PERFORMANCE
REPORT
Objective 3

During April, Tudor Company manufactured 22,000 units, and the factory overhead costs incurred in Department C were: indirect factory wages, $21,700; power and light, $14,000; indirect materials, $5,600; supervisory salaries, $12,500; depreciation of plant and equipment, $4,000; and insurance and property taxes, $2,000.

Prepare a budget performance report for Department C for April, using the appropriate amounts from the flexible budget prepared in Exercise 25-8.

EXERCISE 25-10
REAL WORLD FOCUS
Objective 5

Concrete Pipe & Products Co. Inc. manufactures concrete pipe in its operations in Richmond, Virginia. The primary materials used in producing concrete are cement, sand, and gravel. The costs for a batch of concrete weighing 13,250 pounds are as follows:

	Pounds per Batch	Price per Pound
Cement	2,350	$.03000
Sand	6,700	.00205
Gravel	4,200	.00270
	13,250	

Assuming 5% waste, compute the standard cost per pound for concrete. Use the following column headings for organizing the computations:

	Pounds per Batch	Price per Pound	Batch Cost	5% Waste	Total Batch Cost	Cost per Pound
Cement	2,350	$.03000				
Sand	6,700	.00205				
Gravel	4,200	.00270				
	13,250					

EXERCISE 25-11
DIRECT MATERIALS
VARIANCES
Objective 6

The following data relate to the direct materials cost for the production of 15,000 units of product:

Actual:	77,000 pounds at $1.82	$140,140
Standard:	75,000 pounds at $1.80	135,000

a. Determine the quantity variance, price variance, and total direct materials cost variance.

SHARPEN YOUR ▶ b. To whom should the unfavorable variances be reported for analysis and control? Discuss.
COMMUNICATION SKILLS

EXERCISE 25-12
STANDARD DIRECT
MATERIALS COST PER UNIT
FROM VARIANCE DATA
Objective 6

The following data relating to direct materials cost for August of the current year are taken from the records of K. C. Dugan Company:

Quantity of direct materials used	32,000 pounds
Unit cost of direct materials	$2.50 per pound
Units of finished product manufactured	41,250 units
Standard direct materials per unit of finished product	.8 pounds
Direct materials quantity variance—favorable	$2,400
Direct materials price variance—unfavorable	$3,200

Determine the standard direct materials cost per unit of finished product, assuming that there was no inventory of work in process at either the beginning or the end of the month.

EXERCISE 25-13
DIRECT LABOR VARIANCES
Objective 6

The following data relate to direct labor cost for the production of 5,000 units of product:

Actual:	42,500 hours at $19.75	$839,375
Standard:	42,000 hours at $20.00	840,000

a. Determine the time variance, rate variance, and total direct labor cost variance.

SHARPEN YOUR COMMUNICATION SKILLS

b. The time variance is unfavorable, and the rate variance is favorable. Discuss what might have caused these offsetting variances.

EXERCISE 25-14
FACTORY OVERHEAD COST VARIANCES
Objective 6

The following data relate to factory overhead cost for the production of 20,000 units of product:

Actual:	Variable factory overhead	$153,500
	Fixed factory overhead	120,000
Standard:	30,000 hours at $8	240,000

If productive capacity of 100% was 40,000 hours and the factory overhead cost budgeted at the level of 30,000 standards hours was $270,000, determine the volume variance, controllable variance, and total factory overhead cost variance. The fixed factory overhead rate was $3 per hour.

EXERCISE 25-15
ENTRIES FOR RECORDING STANDARDS IN ACCOUNTS
Objective 7

Appes Manufacturing Company incorporates standards in the accounts and identifies variances at the time the manufacturing costs are incurred. Journalize the entries to record the following transactions:

a. Purchased 500 units of direct material A at $25.20 per unit. The standard price is $25 per unit.
b. Used 190 units of direct material A in the process of manufacturing 50 units of finished product. Four units of material A are required, at standard, to produce a finished unit.

EXERCISE 25-16
INCOME STATEMENT INDICATING STANDARD COST VARIANCES
Objective 7

The following data were taken from the records of Delong Company for January of the current year:

Administrative expenses	$ 40,000
Cost of goods sold (at standard)	775,000
Direct materials quantity variance—favorable	3,100
Direct materials price variance—favorable	1,500
Direct labor time variance—unfavorable	4,000
Direct labor rate variance—unfavorable	2,200
Factory overhead volume variance—unfavorable	15,000
Factory overhead controllable variance—favorable	4,000
Interest expense	1,900
Sales	950,000
Selling expenses	71,500

Prepare an income statement for presentation to management.

WhAT'S WRONG WITH THIS?

The data related to factory overhead cost for the production of 75,000 units of product are as follows:

Actual:	Variable factory overhead	$127,500
	Fixed factory overhead	98,000
Standard:	30,000 hours at $7 (4.20 for variable factory overhead)	210,000

Productive capacity of 100% was 35,000 hours, and the factory overhead cost budgeted at the level of 30,000 standard hours was $224,000. Based upon these data, the chief cost accountant prepared the following variance analysis:

Volume variance:		
Productive capacity at 100%	35,000 hours	
Standard for amount produced	30,000 hours	
Productive capacity not used	5,000 hours	
Standard variable factory overhead rate	× $4.20	
Variance—unfavorable		$21,000
Controllable variance:		
Actual factory overhead cost incurred	$225,500	
Budgeted factory overhead for 30,000 hours	224,000	
Variance—unfavorable		1,500
Total factory overhead cost variance—unfavorable		$22,500

How many errors can you find in the factory overhead cost variance analysis?

PROBLEMS

Series A

PROBLEM 25-1A
FORECAST SALES VOLUME
AND SALES BUDGET
Objective 2

Rosa Company prepared the following sales budget for the current year:

Rosa Company
Sales Budget
For Year Ending December 31, 1993

Product and Area	Unit Sales Volume	Unit Selling Price	Total Sales
Product A:			
East	20,000	$25	$ 500,000
Central	15,000	25	375,000
West	30,000	25	750,000
Total	65,000		$1,625,000
Product B:			
East	15,000	$20	$ 300,000
Central	12,000	20	240,000
West	20,000	20	400,000
Total	47,000		$ 940,000
Total revenue from sales			$2,565,000

At the end of September 1993, the following unit sales data were reported for the first nine months of the year:

	Product A	Product B
East	14,100	11,475
Central	11,700	9,270
West	21,600	14,250

For the year ending December 31, 1994, unit sales are expected to follow the patterns established during the first nine months of the year ending December 31, 1993. The unit selling price for Product A is not expected to change, and the unit selling price for Product B is expected to be increased to $21, effective January 1, 1994.

Instructions

1. Compute the increase or decrease of actual unit sales for the nine months ended September 30, 1993, over expectations for this nine-month period. Since sales have historically occurred evenly throughout the year, budgeted sales for the first nine months of a year would be 75% of the year's budgeted sales. Comparison of this amount with actual sales will indicate the percentage increase or decrease of actual sales for the nine months over budgeted sales for the nine months. (Round percent changes to the nearest whole percent.) Place your answers in a table with the following format:

	Unit Budgeted Sales		Actual Sales for Nine Months	Increase (Decrease)	
	Year	Nine Months		Amount	Percent
Product A					
East					
Central					
West					
Product B					
East					
Central					
West					

2. Assuming that the trend of sales indicated in (1) is to continue in 1994, compute the unit sales volume to be used for preparing the sales budget for the year ending December 31, 1994. Place your answers in a columnar table with the following format:

	1993 Budgeted Units	Percentage Increase (Decrease)	1994 Budgeted Units
Product A			
East			
Central			
West			
Product B			
East			
Central			
West			

3. Prepare a sales budget for the year ending December 31, 1994.

PROBLEM 25-2A
SALES, PRODUCTION,
DIRECT MATERIALS, AND
DIRECT LABOR BUDGETS
Objective 2

The budget director of Fleming Company requests estimates of sales, production, and other operating data from the various administrative units every month. Selected information concerning sales and production for May of the current year are summarized as follows:

a. Estimated sales for May by sales territory:

Northeast:
    Product A: 6,000 units at $100 per unit
    Product B: 40,000 units at $40 per unit
Southeast:
    Product A: 7,200 units at $100 per unit
    Product B: 36,000 units at $40 per unit
Southwest:
    Product A: 3,600 units at $100 per unit
    Product B: 50,000 units at $40 per unit

b. Estimated inventories at May 1:

Direct materials:
    Material W: 18,200 lbs.   Material Y: 7,700 lbs.
    Material X: 6,000 lbs.   Material Z: 13,000 lbs.
Finished products:
    Product A: 1,800 units   Product B: 11,000 units

c. Desired inventories at May 31:

Direct materials:
    Material W: 20,000 lbs.   Material Y: 6,500 lbs.
    Material X: 4,000 lbs.   Material Z: 14,000 lbs.
Finished Products:
    Product A: 2,000 units   Product B: 12,000 units

d. Direct materials used in production:

In manufacture of Product A:
    Material X: 3.0 lbs. per unit of product
    Material Y: 1.2 lbs. per unit of product
    Material Z: .4 lb. per unit of product
In manufacture of Product B:
    Material W: 1.6 lbs. per unit of product
    Material Y: .4 lb. per unit of product
    Material Z: 1.0 lb. per unit of product

e. Anticipated purchase price for direct materials:

Material W: $10.00 per lb.   Material Y: $2.50 per lb.
Material X: $ .30 per lb.   Material Z: $ .90 per lb.

f. Direct labor requirements:

Product A:
    Department 20: 1.2 hours at $20 per hour
    Department 30: .3 hour at $15 per hour
Product B:
    Department 10: .2 hours at $12 per hour
    Department 20: .1 hour at $20 per hour

Instructions

1. Prepare a sales budget for May.
2. Prepare a production budget for May.
3. Prepare a direct materials purchases budget for May.
4. Prepare a direct labor cost budget for May.

PROBLEM 25-3A
BUDGETED INCOME
STATEMENT AND
SUPPORTING BUDGETS
Objective 2

The budget director of Baird Inc., with the assistance of the controller, treasurer, production manager, and sales manager, has gathered the following data for use in developing the budgeted income statement for June:

a. Estimated sales for June:

  Product X: 120,000 units at $40 per unit
  Product Y: 20,000 units at $15 per unit

b. Estimated inventories at June 1:

  Direct materials: Finished products:
    Material A: 14,300 lbs.   Product X: 16,000 units at $28 per unit
    Material B: 18,600 lbs.   Product Y: 3,000 units at $11 per unit

c. Desired inventories at June 30:

  Direct materials: Finished products:
    Material A: 20,000 lbs.   Product X: 11,000 units at $28 per unit
    Material B: 9,000 lbs.   Product Y: 1,500 units at $11 per unit

d. Direct materials used in production:

  In manufacture of Product X:
    Material A: 1.3 lbs. per unit of product
    Material B: .7 lb. per unit of product
  In manufacture of Product Y:
    Material B: .8 lb. per unit of product

e. Anticipated cost of purchases and beginning and ending inventory of direct materials:

  Material A: $7 per lb.
  Material B: $4 per lb.

f. Direct labor requirements:

  Product X:
    Department 100: .8 hour at $15 per hour
    Department 200: .1 hour at $12 per hour
  Product Y:
    Department 200: .2 hour at $12 per hour
    Department 300: .5 hour at $11 per hour

g. Estimated factory overhead costs for June:

Indirect factory wages	$125,000
Depreciation of plant and equipment	120,000
Supervisory salaries	100,000
Power and light	80,000
Indirect materials	40,000
Maintenance	25,000
Insurance and property taxes	20,000

h. Estimated operating expenses for June:

Sales salaries expense	$188,600
Officers salaries expense	150,000
Advertising expense	115,000
Office salaries expense	70,000
Depreciation expense—office equipment	39,000
Telephone expense—selling	27,000
Telephone expense—administrative	10,000
Travel expense—selling	7,500

Travel expense—administrative	$6,500
Office supplies expense	3,000
Miscellaneous selling expense	1,750
Miscellaneous administrative expense	1,250

i. Estimated other income and expense for June:

| Interest income | $25,000 |
| Interest expense | 19,550 |

j. Estimated tax rate: 35%.

Instructions

1. Prepare a sales budget for June.
2. Prepare a production budget for June.
3. Prepare a direct materials purchases budget for June.
4. Prepare a direct labor cost budget for June.
5. Prepare a factory overhead cost budget for June.
6. Prepare a cost of goods sold budget for June. Work in process at the beginning of June is estimated to be $28,500, and work in process at the end of June is estimated to be $29,000.
7. Prepare an operating expenses budget for June. Classify the expenses as either selling or administrative expenses.
8. Prepare a budgeted income statement for June.

PROBLEM 25-4A
CASH BUDGET
Objective 2

The treasurer of Minton Company instructs you to prepare a monthly cash budget for the next three months. You are presented with the following budget information:

	April	May	June
Sales	$240,000	$360,000	$410,000
Manufacturing costs	145,000	225,000	255,000
Operating expenses	37,000	53,000	61,000
Capital expenditures	—	85,000	—

The company expects to sell about 30% of its merchandise for cash. Of sales on account, 80% are expected to be collected in full in the month following the sale and the remainder the following month. Depreciation, insurance, and property taxes represent $25,000 of the estimated monthly manufacturing costs and $7,000 of the probable monthly operating expenses. The annual insurance premium is paid in March, and the annual property taxes are paid in August. Of the remainder of the manufacturing costs and operating expenses, 65% are expected to be paid in the month in which they are incurred and the balance in the following month.

Current assets as of April 1 are composed of cash of $29,000, marketable securities of $40,000, and accounts receivable of $176,400 ($140,000 from March sales and $36,400 from February sales). Current liabilities as of April 1 are composed of a $55,000, 12%, 60-day note payable due May 20, $42,500 of accounts payable incurred in March for manufacturing costs, and accrued liabilities of $10,200 incurred in March for operating expenses.

It is expected that $1,500 in dividends will be received in April. An estimated income tax payment of $15,000 will be made in May. Minton Company's regular quarterly dividend of $10,000 is expected to be declared in May and paid in June. Management desires to maintain a minimum cash balance of $25,000.

SPREADSHEET PROBLEM

Instructions

1. Prepare a monthly cash budget for April, May, and June.

2. On the basis of the cash budget prepared in (1), what recommendation should be made to the treasurer?

PROBLEM 25-5A
BUDGETED INCOME
STATEMENT AND BALANCE
SHEET
Objective 2

As a preliminary to requesting budget estimates of sales, costs, and expenses for the fiscal year beginning January 1, 1994, the following tentative trial balance as of December 31 of the preceding year is prepared by the Accounting Department of Mayberry Company:

Cash	39,000	
Accounts Receivable	60,000	
Finished Goods	90,000	
Work in Process	47,200	
Materials	31,300	
Prepaid Expenses	7,500	
Plant and Equipment	460,000	
Accumulated Depreciation—Plant and Equipment		300,000
Accounts Payable		75,000
Notes Payable		50,000
Common Stock, $20 par		200,000
Retained Earnings		110,000
	735,000	735,000

Factory output and sales for 1994 are expected to total 30,000 units of product, which are to be sold at $33 per unit. The quantities and costs of the inventories (lifo method) at December 31, 1994, are expected to remain unchanged from the balances at the beginning of the year.

Budget estimates of manufacturing costs and operating expenses for the year are summarized as follows:

	Estimated Costs and Expenses	
	Fixed (Total for Year)	Variable (Per Unit Sold)
Cost of goods manufactured and sold:		
Direct materials	—	$9.05
Direct labor	—	6.90
Factory overhead:		
Depreciation of plant and equipment	$15,000	—
Other factory overhead	10,000	2.85
Selling expenses:		
Sales salaries and commissions	40,000	1.00
Advertising	15,000	—
Miscellaneous selling expense	2,000	.30
Administrative expenses:		
Office and officers salaries	34,000	.20
Supplies	2,600	.03
Miscellaneous administrative expense	900	.02

Balances of accounts receivable, prepaid expenses, and accounts payable at the end of the year are expected to differ from the beginning balances by only insignificant amounts.

Federal income tax of $84,500 on 1994 taxable income will be paid during 1994. Regular quarterly cash dividends of $1.25 a share are expected to be declared and paid in March, June, September, and December. It is anticipated that plant and equipment will be purchased for $125,000 cash in May.

Instructions

1. Prepare a budgeted income statement for 1994.
2. Prepare a budgeted balance sheet as of December 31, 1994.

PROBLEM 25-6A
DIRECT MATERIALS, DIRECT
LABOR, AND FACTORY
OVERHEAD COST
VARIANCE ANALYSIS
Objective 6

Standard costs and actual costs for direct materials, direct labor, and factory overhead incurred for the manufacture of 1,500 units of product were as follows:

	Standard Costs	Actual Costs
Direct materials	1,500 pounds at $16	1,550 pounds at $16.40
Direct labor	6,000 hours at $12	5,800 hours at $13
Factory overhead	Rates per machine hour, based on 100% of productive capacity of 8,000 machine hours:	
	Variable cost, $1.20	$8,200 variable cost
	Fixed cost, $3.50	$28,000 fixed cost

Four machine hours are required per unit.

SPREADSHEET PROBLEM

PROBLEM 25-7A
STANDARD FACTORY
OVERHEAD VARIANCE
REPORT
Objective 6

Instructions
Determine (a) the quantity variance, price variance, and total direct materials cost variance, (b) the time variance, rate variance, and total direct labor cost variance, and (c) the volume variance, controllable variance, and total factory overhead cost variance.

Martino Inc. prepared the following factory overhead cost budget for Department A for May of the current year. The company expected to operate the department at 100% of capacity of 600 hours.

Variable costs:		
Indirect factory wages	$24,000	
Power and light	6,000	
Indirect materials	4,500	
Total variable cost		$34,500
Fixed costs:		
Supervisory salaries	$18,000	
Depreciation of plant and equipment	8,500	
Insurance and property taxes	3,500	
Total fixed cost		30,000
Total factory overhead cost		$64,500

During May, the department operated at 540 hours, and the factory overhead costs incurred were: indirect factory wages, $22,100; power and light, $4,990; indirect materials, $4,610; supervisory salaries, $18,000; depreciation of plant and equipment, $8,500; and insurance and property taxes, $3,500.

Instructions
Prepare a standard factory overhead cost variance report for May. To be useful for cost control, the budgeted amounts should be based on 540 hours.

PROBLEM 25-8A
FLEXIBLE FACTORY
OVERHEAD COST BUDGET
AND VARIANCE REPORT
Objective 6

North Inc. prepared the following factory overhead cost budget for the Shaping Department for May of the current year:

North Inc.
Factory Overhead Cost Budget—Shaping Department
For Month Ending May 31, 19—

Machine hours:		
Productive capacity of 100%		25,000
Hours budgeted		28,750
Variable cost:		
Indirect factory wages	$16,100	
Indirect materials	9,430	
Power and light	7,360	
Total variable cost		$32,890
Fixed cost:		
Supervisory salaries	$14,250	
Indirect factory wages	7,030	
Depreciation of plant and equipment	5,220	
Insurance	3,160	
Power and light	2,800	
Property taxes	1,940	
Total fixed cost		34,400
Total factory overhead cost		$67,290

During May, the Shaping Department was operated for 28,750 machine hours, and the following factory overhead costs were incurred:

Indirect factory wages	$25,430
Supervisory salaries	14,250
Indirect materials	9,700
Power and light	9,600
Depreciation of plant and equipment	5,220
Insurance	3,160
Property taxes	1,940
Total factory overhead cost incurred	$69,300

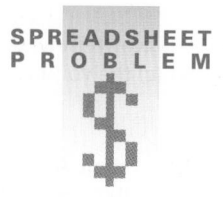

Instructions

1. Prepare a flexible budget for May, indicating capacities of 17,500, 21,250, 25,000, and 28,750 machine hours and the determination of a standard factory overhead rate per machine hour.
2. Prepare a standard factory overhead cost variance report for May.

Series B

PROBLEM 25-1B
FORECAST SALES VOLUME
AND SALES BUDGET
Objective 2

Morhaim Company prepared the following sales budget for the current year:

Morhaim Company
Sales Budget
For Year Ending December 31, 1993

Product and Area	Unit Sales Volume	Unit Selling Price	Total Sales
Product E:			
East	20,000	$28	$ 560,000
Central	30,000	28	840,000
West	40,000	28	1,120,000
Total	90,000		$2,520,000
Product F:			
East	50,000	$15	$ 750,000
Central	60,000	15	900,000
West	80,000	15	1,200,000
Total	190,000		$2,850,000
Total revenue from sales			$5,370,000

At the end of September 1993, the following unit sales data were reported for the first nine months of the year:

	Unit Sales	
	Product E	Product F
East	14,550	39,750
Central	22,950	44,100
West	28,800	64,800

For the year ending December 31, 1994, unit sales are expected to follow the patterns established during the first nine months of the year ending December 31, 1993. The unit selling price for Product E is expected to be increased to $30, effective January 1, 1994, and the unit selling price for Product F is expected to be increased to $17.

Instructions

1. Compute the increase or decrease of actual unit sales for the nine months ended September 30, 1993, over expectations for this nine-month period. Since sales have historically occurred evenly throughout the year, budgeted sales for the first nine months of a year would be 75% of the year's budgeted sales. Comparison of this amount with actual sales will indicate the percentage increase or decrease of actual sales for the nine months over budgeted sales for the nine months. (Round percent changes to the nearest whole percent.) Place your answers in a table with the following format:

	Unit Budgeted Sales		Actual Sales for Nine Months	Increase (Decrease)	
	Year	Nine Months		Amount	Percent
Product E					
East					
Central					
West					
Product F					
East					
Central					
West					

2. Assuming that the trend of sales indicated in (1) is to continue in 1994, compute the unit sales volume to be used for preparing the sales budget for the year ending December 31, 1994. Place your answers in a table with the following format:

	1993 Budgeted Units	Percentage Increase (Decrease)	1994 Budgeted Units
Product E			
East			
Central			
West			
Product F			
East			
Central			
West			

3. Prepare a sales budget for the year ending December 31, 1994.

PROBLEM 25-2B
SALES, PRODUCTION,
DIRECT MATERIALS, AND
DIRECT LABOR BUDGETS
Objective 2

The budget director of Winton Company requests estimates of sales, production, and other operating data from the various administrative units every month. Selected information concerning sales and production for May of the current year are summarized as follows:

a. Estimated sales for May by sales territory:
   East:
   Product A: 19,000 units at $45 per unit
   Product B: 20,000 units at $60 per unit
   Midwest:
   Product A: 23,000 units at $45 per unit
   Product B: 30,000 units at $60 per unit
   West:
   Product A: 29,000 units at $45 per unit
   Product B: 40,000 units at $60 per unit

b. Estimated inventories at May 1:
   Direct materials:
   Material W: 21,000 lbs.   Material Y: 21,500 lbs.
   Material X: 15,600 lbs.   Material Z: 27,600 lbs.
   Finished products:
   Product A: 10,000 units   Product B: 15,000 units

c. Desired inventories at May 31:
   Direct materials:
   Material W: 18,000 lbs.   Material Y: 28,000 lbs.
   Material X: 22,000 lbs.   Material Z: 20,000 lbs.
   Finished Products:
   Product A: 12,000 units   Product B: 25,000 units

d. Direct materials used in production:
   In manufacture of Product A:
   Material X: 1.2 lbs. per unit of product
   Material Y: .8 lb. per unit of product
   Material Z: 1.0 lb. per unit of product
   In manufacture of Product B:
   Material W: 1.5 lbs. per unit of product
   Material Y: .9 lb. per unit of product
   Material Z: 1.4 lbs. per unit of product

e. Anticipated purchase price for direct materials:
   Material W: $1.40 per lb.   Material Y: $2.00 per lb.
   Material X: $ .50 per lb.   Material Z: $1.75 per lb.

f. Direct labor requirements:
   Product A:
   Department 2: 1.0 hour at $14 per hour
   Department 3: .8 hour at $15 per hour
   Product B:
   Department 1: 1.4 hours at $16 per hour
   Department 2: .5 hour at $14 per hour

Instructions

1. Prepare a sales budget for May.
2. Prepare a production budget for May.
3. Prepare a direct materials purchases budget for May.
4. Prepare a direct labor cost budget for May.

PROBLEM 25-3B
BUDGETED INCOME
STATEMENT AND
SUPPORTING BUDGETS
Objective 2

The budget director of Reid Inc., with the assistance of the controller, treasurer, production manager, and sales manager, has gathered the following data for use in developing the budgeted income statement for March:

a. Estimated sales for March:

Product J: 50,000 units at $120 per unit
Product K: 30,000 units at $90 per unit

b. Estimated inventories at March 1:

Direct materials:
  Material A: 5,000 lbs.
  Material B: 40,000 lbs.
  Material C: 8,000 lbs.

Finished products:
  Product J: 10,000 units at $92 per unit
  Product K: 7,000 units at $75 per unit

c. Desired inventories at March 31:

Direct materials:
  Material A: 8,000 lbs.
  Material B: 35,000 lbs.
  Material C: 10,000 lbs.

Finished products:
  Product J: 15,000 units at $92 per unit
  Product K: 9,000 units at $75 per unit

d. Direct materials used in production:

In manufacture of Product J:
  Material A: .75 lb. per unit of product
  Material B: 1.5 lbs. per unit of product
In manufacture of Product K:
  Material B: 1.0 lb. per unit of product
  Material C: 1.2 lbs. per unit of product

e. Anticipated cost of purchases and beginning and ending inventory of direct materials:

Material A: $14.00 per lb.
Material B: $ .80 per lb.
Material C: $20.00 per lb.

f. Direct labor requirements:

Product J:
  Department 10: 2.5 hours at $18 per hour
  Department 11: 1.0 hour at $20 per hour
Product K:
  Department 11: .5 hour at $20 per hour
  Department 12: 2.4 hours at $15 per hour

g. Estimated factory overhead costs for March:

Indirect factory wages	$275,000
Depreciation of plant and equipment	195,000
Supervisory salaries	125,000
Power and light	115,700
Indirect materials	66,000
Maintenance	48,400
Insurance and property taxes	25,900

h. Estimated operating expenses for March:

Sales salaries expense	$450,000
Officers salaries expense	294,000
Advertising expense	286,000
Office salaries expense	125,000

Depreciation expense—office equipment	$84,500
Telephone expense—selling	47,900
Telephone expense—administrative	28,000
Travel expense—selling	26,500
Travel expense—administrative	8,300
Office supplies expense	4,000
Miscellaneous selling expense	11,200
Miscellaneous administrative expense	7,500

i. Estimated other income and expense for March:

Interest income	$90,000
Interest expense	75,000

j. Estimated tax rate: 35%.

Instructions

1. Prepare a sales budget for March.
2. Prepare a production budget for March.
3. Prepare a direct materials purchases budget for March.
4. Prepare a direct labor cost budget for March.
5. Prepare a factory overhead cost budget for March.
6. Prepare a cost of goods sold budget for March. Work in process at the beginning of March is estimated to be $140,000, and work in process at the end of March is estimated to be $150,000.
7. Prepare an operating expenses budget for March. Classify the expenses as either selling or administrative expenses.
8. Prepare a budgeted income statement for March.

PROBLEM 25-4B
CASH BUDGET
Objective 2

The treasurer of Gregory Company instructs you to prepare a monthly cash budget for the next three months. You are presented with the following budget information:

	April	May	June
Sales	$600,000	$550,000	$700,000
Manufacturing costs	400,000	370,000	460,000
Operating expenses	127,500	117,500	147,500
Capital expenditures	—	200,000	—

The company expects to sell about 25% of its merchandise for cash. Of sales on account, 60% are expected to be collected in full in the month following the sale and the remainder the following month. Depreciation, insurance, and property taxes represent $40,000 of the estimated monthly manufacturing costs and $7,500 of the probable monthly operating expenses. The annual insurance premium and the annual property taxes are paid in December. Of the remainder of the manufacturing costs and operating expenses, 70% are expected to be paid in the month in which they are incurred and the balance in the following month.

Current assets as of April 1 are composed of cash of $70,200, marketable securities of $80,000, and accounts receivable of $570,000 ($442,000 from March sales and $128,000 from February sales). Current liabilities as of April 1 are composed of a $100,000, 12%, 120-day note payable due June 20, $105,000 of accounts payable incurred in March for manufacturing costs, and accrued liabilities of $30,200 incurred in March for operating expenses.

It is expected that $4,000 in dividends will be received in May. An estimated income tax payment of $21,200 will be made in June. Gregory Company's regular quarterly dividend of $10,000 is expected to be declared in May and paid in June. Management desires to maintain a minimum cash balance of $60,000.

SPREADSHEET
PROBLEM

Instructions

1. Prepare a monthly cash budget for April, May, and June.

SHARPEN YOUR   ► 2. On the basis of the cash budget prepared in (1), what recommendation should be made
COMMUNICATION SKILLS   to the treasurer?

PROBLEM 25-5B
BUDGETED INCOME
STATEMENT AND BALANCE
SHEET
Objective 2

As a preliminary to requesting budget estimates of sales, costs, and expenses for the fiscal year beginning January 1, 1994, the following tentative trial balance as of December 31 of the preceding year is prepared by the Accounting Department of Bowen Company:

Cash	70,000	
Accounts Receivable	105,000	
Finished Goods	135,000	
Work in Process	87,800	
Materials	58,200	
Prepaid Expenses	9,000	
Plant and Equipment	800,000	
Accumulated Depreciation—Plant and Equipment		320,000
Accounts Payable		108,800
Notes Payable		50,000
Common Stock, $20 par		150,000
Retained Earnings		636,200
	1,265,000	1,265,000

Factory output and sales for 1994 are expected to total 60,000 units of product, which are to be sold at $20 per unit. The quantities and costs of the inventories (lifo method) at December 31, 1994, are expected to remain unchanged from the balances at the beginning of the year.

Budget estimates of manufacturing costs and operating expenses for the year are summarized as follows:

	Estimated Costs and Expenses	
	Fixed (Total for Year)	Variable (Per Unit Sold)
Cost of goods manufactured and sold:		
Direct materials	—	$3.25
Direct labor	—	5.25
Factory overhead:		
Depreciation of plant and equipment	$25,000	—
Other factory overhead	21,000	1.90
Selling expenses:		
Sales salaries and commissions	36,000	.50
Advertising	15,000	—
Miscellaneous selling expense	1,000	.05
Administrative expenses:		
Office and officers salaries	43,000	.25
Supplies	2,000	.10
Miscellaneous administrative expense	1,000	.04

Balances of accounts receivable, prepaid expenses, and accounts payable at the end of the year are expected to differ from the beginning balances by only insignificant amounts.

Federal income tax of $160,500 on 1994 taxable income will be paid during 1994. Regular quarterly cash dividends of $.30 a share are expected to be declared and paid in March, June, September, and December. It is anticipated that plant and equipment will be purchased for $200,000 cash in December.

Instructions

1. Prepare a budgeted income statement for 1994.
2. Prepare a budgeted balance sheet as of December 31, 1994.

PROBLEM 25-6B
DIRECT MATERIALS, DIRECT
LABOR, AND FACTORY
OVERHEAD COST
VARIANCE ANALYSIS
Objective 6

Standard costs and actual costs for direct materials, direct labor, and factory overhead incurred for the manufacture of 1,000 units of product were as follows:

	Standard Costs	Actual Costs
Direct materials	6,000 pounds at $12	6,200 pounds at $11.50
Direct labor	2,000 hours at $15	1,850 hours at $15.50
Factory overhead	Rates per machine hour, based on 100% of productive capacity of 2,500 machine hours:	
	Variable cost, $13	$28,000 variable cost
	Fixed cost, $5	$12,500 fixed cost

Two machine hours are required per unit.

**SPREADSHEET
P R O B L E M**

PROBLEM 25-7B
STANDARD FACTORY
OVERHEAD VARIANCE
REPORT
Objective 6

Instructions
Determine (a) the quantity variance, price variance, and total direct materials cost variance, (b) the time variance, rate variance, and total direct labor cost variance, and (c) the volume variance, controllable variance, and total factory overhead cost variance.

Conrad Company prepared the following factory overhead cost budget for Department C for June of the current year. The company expected to operate the department at 100% of capacity of 500 hours.

Variable costs:		
Indirect factory wages	$25,000	
Power and light	12,000	
Indirect materials	7,500	
Total variable cost		$44,500
Fixed costs:		
Supervisory salaries	$12,000	
Depreciation of plant and equipment	10,000	
Insurance and property taxes	3,500	
Total fixed cost		25,500
Total factory overhead cost		$70,000

During June, the department operated at 450 hours, and the factory overhead costs incurred were: indirect factory wages, $23,350; power and light, $10,000; indirect materials, $7,310; supervisory salaries, $12,000; depreciation of plant and equipment, $10,000; and insurance and property taxes, $3,500.

Instructions
Prepare a standard factory overhead variance report for June. To be useful for cost control, the budgeted amounts should be based on 450 hours.

PROBLEM 25-8B
FLEXIBLE FACTORY
OVERHEAD COST BUDGET
AND VARIANCE REPORT
Objective 6

Emery Inc. prepared the following factory overhead cost budget for the Polishing Department for July of the current year:

Emery Inc.
Factory Overhead Cost Budget—Polishing Department
For Month Ending July 31, 19—

Machine hours:		
Productive capacity of 100%		20,000
Hours budgeted		16,000
Variable cost:		
Indirect factory wages	$24,000	
Indirect materials	9,600	
Power and light	4,800	
Total variable cost		$38,400
Fixed cost:		
Supervisory salaries	$18,000	
Indirect factory wages	12,400	
Depreciation of plant and equipment	8,500	
Insurance	6,200	
Power and light	4,100	
Property taxes	2,800	
Total fixed cost		52,000
Total factory overhead cost		$90,400

During July, the Polishing Department was operated for 16,000 machine hours, and the following factory overhead costs were incurred:

Indirect factory wages	$37,500
Supervisory salaries	18,000
Power and light	9,600
Indirect materials	8,900
Depreciation of plant and equipment	8,500
Insurance	6,200
Property taxes	2,800
Total factory overhead cost incurred	$91,500

SPREADSHEET PROBLEM

Instructions

1. Prepare a flexible budget for July, indicating capacities of 14,000, 16,000, 18,000, and 20,000 machine hours and the determination of a standard factory overhead rate per machine hour.
2. Prepare a standard factory overhead cost variance report for July.

MINI-CASE 25 PALL COMPANY

Pall Company operates a plant in Decatur, Illinois, where you have been assigned as the new cost analyst. To familiarize yourself with your new responsibilities, you have gathered the following cost variance data for July. During July, 17,000 units of product were manufactured.

Factory Overhead Cost Variance Report

Productive capacity for the month	10,000 hours
Standard for amount produced during month	8,500 hours

			Variances	
	Budget	Actual	Favorable	Unfavorable
Variable costs:				
Indirect factory wages	$27,200	$27,700		$ 500
Power and light	17,850	18,200		350
Indirect materials	10,200	10,000	$200	
Maintenance	4,250	4,100	150	
Total variable cost	$59,500	$60,000		
Fixed costs:				
Supervisory salaries	$25,000	$25,000		
Depreciation of plant and equipment	10,000	10,000		
Insurance and property taxes	3,000	3,000		
Total fixed cost	$38,000	$38,000		
Total factory overhead cost	$97,500	$98,000		
Total controllable variances			$350	$ 850
Net controllable variance—unfavorable				$ 500
Volume variance—unfavorable:				
Idle hours at the standard rate for fixed factory overhead—1,500 × $3.80				5,700
Total factory overhead cost variance—unfavorable				$6,200

Direct Materials Cost Variance

Quantity variance:		
Actual quantity	20,500 pounds	
Standard quantity	20,400 pounds	
Variance—unfavorable	100 pounds × standard price, $4.50	$ 450
Price variance:		
Actual price	$4.80 per pound	
Standard price	4.50 per pound	
Variance—unfavorable	$ .30 per pound × actual quantity, 20,500	6,150
Total direct materials cost variance—unfavorable		$6,600

Direct Labor Cost Variance

Time variance:		
Actual time	8,750 hours	
Standard time	8,500 hours	
Variance—unfavorable	250 hours × standard rate, $24	$6,000
Rate variance:		
Actual rate	$23.50 per hour	
Standard rate	24.00 per hour	
Variance—favorable	$ (.50)per hour × actual hours, 8,750	4,375
Total direct labor cost—unfavorable		$1,625

After your review of the July cost variance data, you arranged a meeting with the factory superintendent to discuss manufacturing operations. During this meeting, the factory superintendent made the following comment:

"Why do you have to compute a factory overhead volume variance? I don't have any control over the level of operations. I can only control costs for the level of production at which I am told to operate. Why not just eliminate the volume variance from the factory overhead cost variance report?"

You next discussed the direct materials variance analyses with the Purchasing Department manager, who made the following comment:

"The materials price variance is computed incorrectly. The computations should be actual price minus standard price times the standard quantity of materials for the amount produced. By multiplying the difference in the actual and standard price by the actual quantity of materials used, my department is being penalized for the inefficiencies of the production department."

During August the standard costs were not changed, productive capacity was 10,000 hours, and the following data were taken from the records for the production of 18,000 units of product:

Quantity of direct materials used	21,800 pounds
Cost of direct materials	$4.84 per pound
Quantity of direct labor used	9,300 hours
Cost of direct labor	$23.20 per hour
Factory overhead costs:	
Indirect factory wages	$30,000
Supervisory salaries	25,000
Power and light	19,400
Indirect materials	10,600
Depreciation of plant and equipment	10,000
Maintenance	4,350
Insurance and property taxes	3,000

Instructions:

1. Prepare a factory overhead cost variance report for August.
2. Determine (a) the quantity variance, price variance, and total direct materials cost variance, and (b) the time variance, rate variance, and total direct labor cost variance for August.
3. ▬▬ ► Based upon the cost variances for July and August, what areas of operations would you investigate and why?
4. ▬▬ ► How would you respond to the comment by the factory superintendent?
5. ▬▬ ► How would you respond to the comment by the manager of the Purchasing Department?

ANSWERS TO SELF-EXAMINATION QUESTIONS

1. **B** The total production indicated in the production budget is 257,500 units (answer B), which is computed as follows:

Sales	250,000 units
Plus desired ending inventory	30,000 units
Total	280,000 units
Less estimated beginning inventory	22,500 units
Total production	257,500 units

2. **B** A budget performance report (answer B) compares actual results with budgeted figures.

3. **C** Flexible budgeting (answer C) provides a series of budgets for varying rates of activity and thereby builds into the budgeting system the effect of fluctuations in level of activity. Budget performance reporting (answer A) is a system of reports that compares actual results with budgeted figures. Continuous budgeting (answer B) is a variant of fiscal-year budgeting that provides for continuous twelve-month projections into the future. This is achieved by periodically deleting from the current budget the data

for the elapsed period and adding newly estimated budget data for the same period next year. Zero-base budgeting (answer D) requires managers to start from zero and assume operations are being started for the first time.

4. **C** The unfavorable direct materials price variance of $2,550 (answer C) is determined as follows:

Actual price	$5.05 per pound
Standard price	5.00 per pound
Price variance—unfavorable	$ .05 per pound

$.05 × 51,000 actual pounds = $2,550

5. **B** The unfavorable factory overhead volume variance of $2,000 (answer B) is determined as follows:

Productive capacity not used	1,000 hours
Standard fixed factory overhead cost rate	× $2
Factory overhead volume variance—unfavorable	$2,000

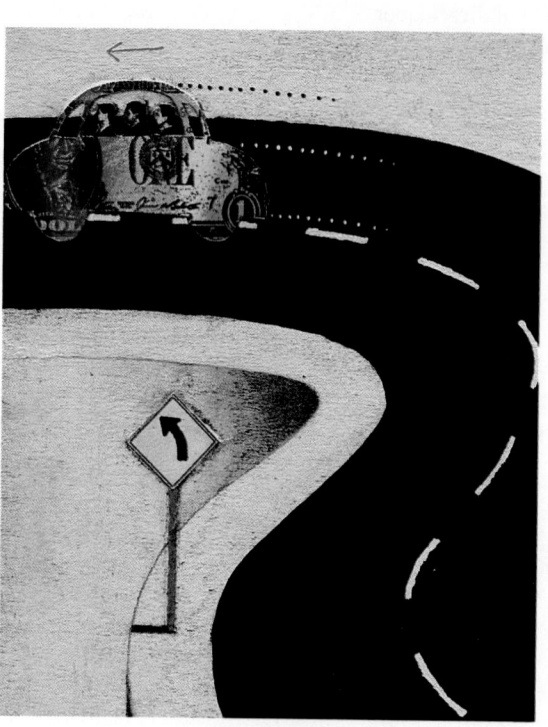

You and Accounting

Have you ever noticed how large retail stores, such as J.C. Penney and Sears, are divided into departments? Some typical departments are the Men's Department, Women's Department, Appliances Department, Home Entertainment Department, and Sporting Goods Department.

In many cases, each department is the responsibility of a department manager. The manager of the Sporting Goods Department, for example, is responsible for that department. The particular store may be one of several in a chain of stores, each of which is the responsibility of a store manager.

The separation of businesses into organizational units, such as departments and stores, and the role of accounting in assisting managers in planning and controlling such operations is the focus of this chapter.

Chapter 26
Accounting for Decentralized Operations; Transfer Pricing

LEARNING OBJECTIVES
After studying this chapter, you should be able to:

Objective 1
List the advantages and disadvantages of decentralized operations.

Objective 2
List the three types of responsibility centers and give an example of each type.

Objective 3
Prepare a responsibility accounting report for a cost center.

Objective 4
Prepare responsibility accounting reports for a profit center, using the following three income concepts:

Departmental margin
Gross profit
Income from operations

Objective 5
Compute operating income, rate of return on investment, and residual income for an investment center.

Objective 6
Explain how the following transfer pricing approaches may be used by decentralized segments of a business enterprise:

Market price approach
Negotiated price approach
Cost price approach

In a small business, almost all plans and decisions can be made by one individual. As a business grows or its operations become more diverse and complex, it is impossible or impractical for one individual to perform all these functions. For example, the responsibility for planning and controlling operations can be performed by the owner/manager in a one-person real estate agency. If the agency expands by opening an office in a distant city, some of the authority and responsibility for planning and decision making might be delegated to others. In other words, as an enterprise becomes more diverse and decentralized, more and more authority may be delegated from the owner/manager to others on the management team.

Various managerial accounting concepts that are useful in planning and controlling operations are discussed in other chapters. For example, a master budget, supported by departmental budgets and budget performance reports, is useful for these purposes. This chapter describes and illustrates additional managerial accounting concepts and tools that may be useful in planning and controlling decentralized operations. In addition, the pricing of products or services that are transferred between decentralized segments of a company is described and illustrated.

CENTRALIZED AND DECENTRALIZED OPERATIONS

The delegation of responsibility and the separation of the business into organizational and operating units for management purposes is termed **decentralization**. A completely **centralized** business is one in which all major planning and operating decisions are made by top management. For example, a one-person, owner/manager-operated business is centralized because all plans and decisions are made by one person. In a small owner/manager-operated business, centralization may be desirable. This is because the owner/manager's close supervision ensures that the business will be operated in the way the owner/manager wishes and desires.

In a decentralized business, responsibility for planning and controlling operations is delegated among managers. These managers have the authority to make decisions without first seeking the approval of higher management. The amount of decentralization varies significantly, and there is no one best level of decentralization for all businesses. In some companies, for example, division managers have authority over all plant operations, including plant asset acquisitions and retirements. In other companies, a division manager may only have authority for scheduling production and for controlling the costs of direct materials, direct labor, and factory overhead. The proper amount of decentralization for a company depends on the advantages and disadvantages of decentralization as they apply to a company's unique circumstances.

Advantages of Decentralization

As a business grows, it becomes more difficult for top management to maintain close daily contact with all operations. In such cases, delegating authority to managers closest to the operations usually results in better decisions. These managers often anticipate and react to operating data more quickly than could top management. In addition, as a company expands into a wide range of products and services, it becomes more difficult for top management to maintain operating expertise in all product lines and services. Decentralization allows managers to focus on acquiring expertise in their areas of responsibility. For example, in a company that maintains operations in insurance, banking, and health care, managers could become "experts" in the areas of their operations and responsibility.

When the responsibility for day-to-day operations is delegated from top management to middle management, top management is free to focus on strategic planning. **Strategic planning** is the process of setting long-term goals for an enterprise and developing plans to achieve these goals. For example, a goal to expand an enterprise's product line into new markets is a strategic goal. Plans to finance this expansion through the issuance of long-term debt rather than common stock is an example of a strategic-planning decision. In the current competitive business environment, strategic planning is receiving increased emphasis for its importance to the long-run success of a company.

Decentralized decision making also provides excellent training for managers. This may be a factor in enabling a company to retain quality managers. Since the art of management is best acquired through experience, this delegation of responsibility allows managers to acquire and develop managerial expertise early in their careers.

Decentralized operations are often located close to customers. This enables managers to respond quickly to customers' needs, which helps create good customer relations. In addition, because managers of decentralized operations tend to identify with customers and with operations, they are often more creative in suggesting operating and product improvements.

The delegation of responsibility also serves as a positive reinforcement for managers. Managers often view such delegation as an indication of top management's confidence in their abilities. This improves morale because managers feel that they have more control over factors affecting their careers and their performance evaluations.

Disadvantages of Decentralization

A primary disadvantage of decentralized operations is that decisions made by one manager may affect other managers in such a way that the profitability of the entire company may suffer. For example, two managers competing in a common product market may engage in price cutting to win customers. As a result, the overall company profit may be less than it might have been if the price cutting had not occurred.

Another potential disadvantage of decentralized operations is possible duplication of assets and costs in operating divisions. For example, each manager of a product line might have a separate sales force and administrative office staff. Centralization of these personnel could save money. Likewise, the costs of gathering and processing operating information in a decentralized operation might be greater than if such information were gathered and processed centrally.

Thinking Small

A focus on decentralization, which includes empowering managers to make a variety of decisions, is a major theme in today's business environment. One company that experienced positive results from decentralizing was NCR Corp., a multinational electronics and computer manufacturing corporation. At one time, NCR was a troubled company. Management began to examine NCR's problems and to reevaluate the company's structure, which appeared to be inhibiting NCR's ability to innovate and adapt. Additional background and the results of NCR's changes were reported in *Inc.*, as follows:

As part of this reevaluation process, NCR commissioned the McKinsey & Co. consulting group to study the attributes of a number of highly successful companies. The researchers looked at such corporations as Sperry, IBM, and Hewlett-Packard, to determine what they had done that might be applied to NCR.

Using this study as background, NCR developed a plan for restructuring itself. Analyzing the path of a product from idea to

implementation, it discovered some obvious impediments. The development, production, and marketing of a new product involved three separate divisions. This cumbersome system created opportunities for false starts and misinterpreting . . . the market. . . . It took a long time to get a product through this entire process, and sometimes products got lost in translation. . . .

So NCR proceeded to break up its product-management organization and move the parts to units that would develop, manufacture, and market products. In consulting jargon, this is called shifting from a "functional" to a "divisional" organization, and it has been done many times before in other industries. . . .

These changes transformed NCR Corp. from a highly centralized operation into a series of stand-alone (or decentralized) units. Today there is no requirement that one unit buy components from another NCR unit if it can find better or cheaper products outside the company. Moreover, based upon the nature of their products, the different divisions make their own decisions about how they want to structure themselves with regard to such activities as marketing.

Source: Eugene Linden, "Let a Thousand Flowers Bloom," *Inc.* (April 1984), pp. 64-76.

TYPES OF RESPONSIBILITY CENTERS

Objective 2
List the three types of responsibility centers and give an example of each type.

In a decentralized business, an important function of the managerial accountant is to assist individual managers in evaluating and controlling their areas of responsibility. These areas of responsibility are called **responsibility centers**. A term often used to describe the process of measuring and reporting operating data by responsibility centers is **responsibility accounting**.

Responsibility centers can be classified by the scope of responsibility assigned and the decision-making authority given to individual managers. Three common types of responsibility centers are cost centers, profit centers, and investment centers. Each of these types of responsibility centers is briefly described in the following paragraphs. Responsibility accounting for each type of center is then discussed and illustrated.

Cost Centers

In a **cost center**, the department or division manager has responsibility for the control of costs incurred and the authority to make decisions that affect these costs. For example, the controller has responsibility for the costs of the Accounting Department. Likewise, the supervisor of the Power Department has responsibility for the costs incurred in providing power. A cost center manager does not make decisions concerning sales or the amount of plant assets invested in the center.

Cost centers are the most widely used type of responsibility center. This is because areas where managers have responsibility for and authority over costs can be readily identified in most business organizations. Cost centers may vary in size from a small department with a few employees to an entire manufacturing plant. In addition, cost centers may exist within other cost centers. For example, an entire state university could be viewed as a cost center. The individual departments within the university could also be viewed as separate cost centers.

Profit Centers

In a **profit center**, the manager has the responsibility and the authority to make decisions that affect both costs and revenues (and thus profits). For example, a retail department store might decentralize its operations by product line. The manager of each product line could have responsibility for the cost of merchandise and decisions regarding revenues, such as the determination of sales prices. The manager of a profit center does not make decisions concerning the plant assets invested in the center. For example, the manager of the Sporting Goods Department of a department store normally could not make a decision to expand the available floor space for the department.

Profit centers are widely used in businesses in which individual departments or divisions sell products or services to those outside the company. A partial organization chart for a department store decentralized by retail departments as profit centers is shown in Exhibit 1.

Exhibit 1
Partial Organization Chart for Department Store Organized with Profit Centers

Sometimes, product or service is consumed entirely within the company. For example, a Repairs and Maintenance Department of a manufacturing plant could be treated as a profit center. In this case, the Repairs and Maintenance department manager bills other departments, such as the various production departments, for repair and maintenance services provided. Likewise, the manager of the Data Processing Department of a company might bill each of the company's administrative and operating units for computing services.

In a sense, a profit center may be viewed as a business within a business. While the major concern of a cost center manager is the control of costs, the profit center is concerned with both revenues and costs.

Profit centers are often viewed as an excellent training assignment for new managers. For example, Lester B. Korn, Chairman and Chief Executive Officer of

Korn/Ferry International, recently offered the following strategy for young executives en route to top management positions:

Get Profit-Center Responsibility—Obtain a position where you can prove yourself as both a specialist with particular expertise and a generalist who can exercise leadership, authority, and inspire enthusiasm among colleagues and subordinates.

Investment Centers

In an **investment center**, the manager has the responsibility and the authority to make decisions that affect not only costs and revenues, but also the plant assets invested in the center. For example, a divisional manager may have responsibility for setting selling prices of products and establishing controls over costs. In addition, the divisional manager could, within general constraints set by top management, expand production facilities through equipment acquisitions and retirements.

The manager of an investment center has more authority and responsibility than the manager of either a cost center or a profit center. The manager of an investment center occupies a position similar to that of a chief operating officer or president of a separate company. As such, an investment center manager is evaluated in much the same way as a manager of a separate company.

Investment centers are widely used in highly diversified companies. A partial organizational chart for a diversified company with divisions organized as investment centers is shown in Exhibit 2.

Exhibit 2
Partial Organization Chart for Diversified Company Organized with Investment Centers

RESPONSIBILITY ACCOUNTING FOR COST CENTERS

Objective 3
Prepare a responsibility accounting report for a cost center.

Since managers of cost centers have responsibility for and authority over costs, responsibility accounting for cost centers focuses on costs. The primary accounting tools used for controlling and reporting costs are budgets and standard costs, which are discussed in another chapter. Responsibility accounting for a cost center that uses budgeting to assist in the control of costs is illustrated in the following paragraphs. The basic concepts also apply to cost centers that use standard cost systems to control costs.

As a basis for illustrating responsibility accounting for cost centers, the organization chart for an enterprise's manufacturing operations is shown in Exhibit 3. This enterprise has three levels of cost centers. At the operating level, each department is a cost center, with the department supervisors responsible for controlling costs within their departments. At the next level of the organization, each plant is a cost center. Each plant manager is responsible for controlling plant administrative costs as well as supervising the control of costs in the departments. Finally, at the top level, the office of the vice-president of production is a cost center. The vice-president of production has responsibility for controlling the administrative costs of the office as well as supervising the control of costs in each plant.

Exhibit 3
Organization Chart—
Management Responsibility for
Production

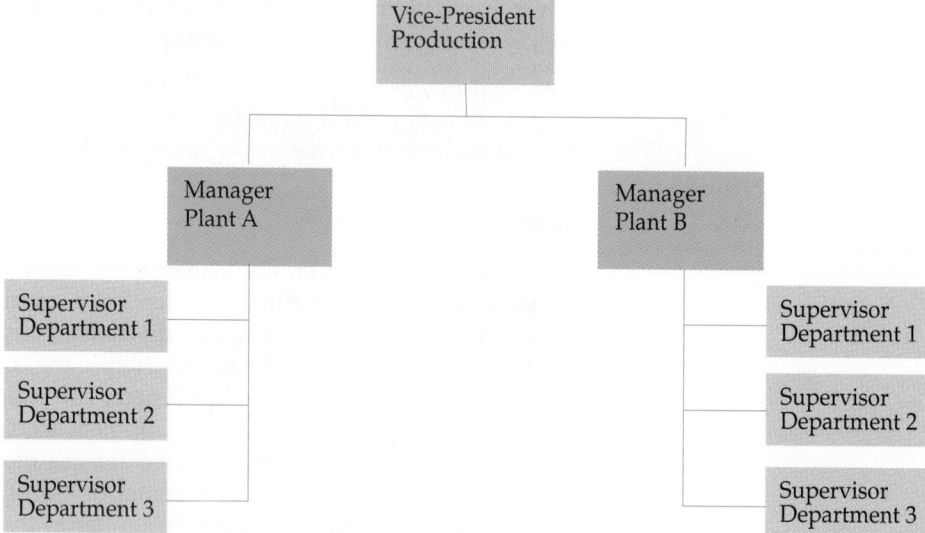

Managerial accounting reports can aid each level of management in carrying out its assigned responsibilities for the control of costs. To illustrate, the budget performance reports in Exhibit 4 are part of a responsibility accounting system for the enterprise shown in Exhibit 3.

Exhibit 4
Responsibility Accounting
Reports

Budget Performance Report
Vice-President, Production
For Month Ended October 31, 1994

	Budget	Actual	Over Budget	Under Budget
Administration	$ 19,500	$ 19,700	$ 200	
Plant A	467,475	470,330	2,855	
Plant B	395,225	394,300		$925
	$882,200	$884,330	$3,055	$925

Budget Performance Report
Manager, Plant A
For Month Ended October 31, 1994

	Budget	Actual	Over Budget	Under Budget
Administration	$ 17,500	$ 17,350		$150
Department 1	109,725	111,280	$1,555	
Department 2	190,500	192,600	2,100	
Department 3	149,750	149,100		650
	$467,475	$470,330	$3,655	$800

Budget Performance Report
Supervisor, Department 1—Plant A
For Month Ended October 31, 1994

	Budget	Actual	Over Budget	Under Budget
Factory wages	$ 58,100	$ 58,000		$100
Materials	32,500	34,225	$1,725	
Supervisory salaries	6,400	6,400		
Power and light	5,750	5,690		60
Depreciation of plant and equipment	4,000	4,000		
Maintenance	2,000	1,990		10
Insurance and property taxes	975	975		
	$109,725	$111,280	$1,725	$170

In Exhibit 4, the reports prepared for the department supervisors present details of the budgeted and actual manufacturing costs for their departments. Each supervisor can then focus on the items that created significant variations. In Exhibit 4, the budget performance report for Department 1—Plant A indicates a major variation between the budgeted and actual costs for materials. The supporting materials scrap report in Exhibit 5 indicates the cause of each major part of this variation. Such reports aid supervisors in deciding if corrective actions are necessary.

Exhibit 5
Scrap Report

Materials Scrap Report
Department 1—Plant A
For Month Ended October 31, 1994

Material No.	Units Spoiled	Unit Cost	Dollar Loss	Remarks
A392	125	$4.46	$ 557.50	Machine malfunction
C417	76	.80	60.80	Inexperienced employee
G118	5	1.10	5.50	
J510	120	8.25	990.00	Substandard materials
K277	2	1.50	3.00	
P719	7	2.10	14.70	
V112	22	4.25	93.50	Machine malfunction
			$1,725.00	

For higher levels of management, responsibility accounting reports are usually more summarized than for lower levels of management. In Exhibit 4, for example, the budget performance report for the plant manager summarizes budget and actual cost data for the departments under the manager's supervision. This report enables the plant manager to identify the department supervisors responsible for major variances. Likewise, the report for the vice-president of production summarizes the cost data for each plant. The plant managers can thus be held responsible for major differences in budgeted and actual costs in their plants.

RESPONSIBILITY ACCOUNTING FOR PROFIT CENTERS

Objective 4
Prepare responsibility accounting reports for a profit center, using the following three income concepts:

Departmental margin
Gross profit
Income from operations

Managers of profit centers have responsibility for and authority to make decisions regarding revenues and expenses. Therefore, responsibility accounting reports for profit centers are normally in the form of income statements. These income statements usually report revenues and expenses by the department responsible for their incurrence. The contribution of each department to overall company profit can thus be determined. Alternatively, some companies use traditional income statement formats that report gross profit or operating income by department.

Profit centers are widely used by merchandising enterprises, such as department stores. For this reason, a merchandising enterprise is used as the basis for the following discussion. Although the degree of use of profit centers varies, they are normally established for each major retail department of a merchandising enterprise. In the following illustrations, Tisch Company has established Departments X and Y as profit centers.

Departmental Margin

One approach to responsibility accounting for profit centers emphasizes the contribution of each department to overall company profit. This contribution to overall company profit is called **departmental margin.**

To prepare a responsibility accounting report using the departmental margin approach, it is necessary to classify operating expenses as direct and indirect expenses. Expenses or costs are classified as direct or indirect by identifying a cost object to which the expenses can (direct) or cannot (indirect) be traced. For Tisch Company, the cost objects are departments. **Direct expenses** traceable to or incurred for the benefit of a department (cost object) are usually subject to the control of the department manager. **Indirect expenses** are incurred for the benefit of the entire enterprise and are not usually subject to the control of department managers.

The departmental sales and cost of goods sold are presented on the departmental income statement in the normal manner. The direct expenses of each department are then deducted from the related departmental gross profit to determine the departmental margin. The remaining expenses, including the indirect expenses, are not reported by department. They are reported separately below the total departmental margin.

An income statement in the departmental margin format for Tisch Company is presented in Exhibit 6. A portion of the advertising expense is a direct expense, and a portion is an indirect expense. Newspaper advertising focuses on specific products from the departments and is a direct expense of each department. The billboard portion of advertising, which is for the benefit of the business as a whole, as well as officers' and office salaries, are reported as indirect expenses.

Exhibit 6
Income Statement—Departmental Margin

	Tisch Company Income Statement For Year Ended December 31, 1994		
	Department X	Department Y	Total
Net sales	$614,700	$262,900	$877,600
Cost of goods sold	323,350	180,750	504,100
Gross profit	$291,350	$ 82,150	$373,500
Direct departmental expenses:			
Sales salaries expense	$54,000	$30,900	$84,900
Advertising expense	9,100	4,900	14,000
Property tax expense	3,740	3,060	6,800
Uncollectible accounts expense	3,220	1,380	4,600
Depreciation expense—store equipment	2,640	1,760	4,400
Insurance expense	2,145	1,755	3,900
Total direct departmental expenses	74,845	43,755	118,600
Departmental margin	$216,505	$ 38,395	$254,900
Indirect expenses:			
Officers' salaries expense		$52,000	
Office salaries expense		17,600	
Rent expense		15,400	
Heating and lighting expense		5,100	
Advertising expense		5,000	
Miscellaneous selling expense		4,700	
Miscellaneous administrative expense		4,800	
Total indirect expenses			104,600
Income from operations			$150,300
Other expense:			
Interest expense			2,500
Income before income tax			$147,800
Income tax			64,444
Net income			$ 83,356

With departmental margin income statements, the manager of each department can be held responsible for the direct expenses of the department. A reduction in the direct expenses of a department will increase the department's contribution to the profit of the company.

The departmental margin income statement may also be useful to management in planning future operations. For example, the departmental margin income statement can be used in deciding whether to discontinue a department. If a department generates a departmental margin, it normally should be retained. This assumes that discontinuing the department would not cause any significant decrease in indirect expenses.

Gross Profit by Departments

The traditional income statement for a profit center may report revenues and expenses by departments through gross profit. An income statement showing gross profit by departments for Tisch Company is shown in Exhibit 7. To simplify, the operating expenses are shown in condensed form. Usually they would be listed in detail.

Exhibit 7
Income Statement—Departmental
Gross Profit

Tisch Company
Income Statement
For Year Ended December 31, 1994

	Department X		Department Y		Total	
Revenue from sales:						
Sales	$630,000		$270,000		$900,000	
Less sales returns and						
allowances	15,300		7,100		22,400	
Net sales		$614,700		$262,900		$877,600
Cost of goods sold:						
Inventories, Jan. 1, 1994	$ 80,150		$ 61,750		$141,900	
Purchases	$334,550		$200,350		$534,900	
Less purchases discounts	6,200	328,350	2,400	197,950	8,600	526,300
Goods available for sale		$408,500		$259,700		$668,200
Less inventories, Dec. 31, 1994		85,150		78,950		164,100
Cost of goods sold		323,350		180,750		504,100
Gross profit		$291,350		$ 82,150		$373,500
Operating expenses:						
Selling expenses					$113,000	
Administrative expenses					110,200	
Total operating expenses						223,200
Income from operations						$150,300
Other expense:						
Interest expense						2,500
Income before income tax						$147,800
Income tax						64,444
Net income						$ 83,356

For a merchandising enterprise, gross profit is one of the most significant amounts in the income statement. Since the sales and the cost of goods sold are both controlled by departmental management, the reporting of gross profit by departments is useful in cost analysis and control. In addition, such reports aid management in directing its efforts toward obtaining a mix of sales that maximizes profits. After studying the reports, for example, management may decide to change sales or purchases policies in order to achieve a higher gross profit for each department. However, care must be used to ensure that proposed changes affecting gross profit do not have an adverse effect on net income. A change that increases gross profit could result in an even greater increase in operating expenses and thereby decrease net income.

Departmental reporting may be extended to income from operations, or operating income. In such cases, the revenues and the cost of goods sold are reported for each department. In addition, the operating expenses are allocated to each department.

Some operating expenses may be easily identified and traced to the departments. For example, if each salesperson is assigned to a sales department, the sales salaries can be traced to separate departmental salary accounts each time the payroll is prepared. On the other hand, the salaries of company officers, executives, and office personnel usually cannot be traced to individual departments. Therefore, such expenses must be allocated to the departments in a logical manner.

Operating expenses should be allocated according to the cost of services rendered to the departments. Determining such allocations is not always a simple matter. First, they require the exercise of judgment, and accountants may differ in their opinions as to the proper basis for allocating operating expenses. Second, the cost of collecting data for use in allocating operating expenses must be kept within reasonable limits. Thus, data that are readily available may be used instead of more accurate information that would be more costly to collect.

To illustrate, assume that Tisch Company extends its departmental reporting through income from operations. The company's operating expenses for the year and the methods used in allocating them are discussed below.

Sales Salaries Expense is allocated to the two departments according to the distributions shown in the payroll records. Of the $84,900 total in the account, $54,000 relates to Department X and $30,900 relates to Department Y.

Advertising Expense, including billboard and newspaper advertising, is allocated according to the quantity of advertising incurred for each department. The billboard advertising totaling $5,000 emphasizes the name and the location of the company. This expense is allocated on the basis of gross sales. This assumes that the benefits from advertising the company name and location benefits each department in relationship to its gross sales. Analysis of the newspaper advertising of $14,000 indicates that 65% of the advertising was devoted to Department X and 35% to Department Y. The computations of the allocation of the total advertising expense are as follows:

	Total		Department X		Department Y	
Sales—dollars	$900,000		$630,000		$270,000	
Sales—percent	100%		70%		30%	
Billboard advertising		$ 5,000		$ 3,500		$1,500
Newspaper space—percent	100%		65%		35%	
Newspaper advertising		14,000		9,100		4,900
Advertising expense		$19,000		$12,600		$6,400

Depreciation Expense–Store Equipment is allocated according to the average cost of the equipment in each of the departments. The computations for the allocation are as follows:

	Total	Department X	Department Y
Cost of store equipment:			
January 1	$28,300	$16,400	$11,900
December 31	31,700	19,600	12,100
Total	$60,000	$36,000	$24,000
Average	$30,000	$18,000	$12,000
Percent	100%	60%	40%
Depreciation expense	$ 4,400	$ 2,640	$ 1,760

Officers' Salaries Expense and Office Salaries Expense are allocated according to the amount of time devoted to each department by the officers and office personnel. Obviously, this can be only an approximation. For Tisch Company, it is estimated that 60% of the officers' and office personnel's time relates to Department X.

Likewise, 40% of the time relates to Department Y. Thus, $31,200 ($52,000 × 60%) of the officers' salaries and $10,560 ($17,600 × 60%) of the office salaries are allocated to Department X. Likewise, $20,800 ($52,000 × 40%) of the officers' salaries and $7,040 ($17,600 × 40%) of the office salaries are allocated to Department Y.

Rent Expense and Heating and Lighting Expense are usually allocated according to the floor space devoted to each department. In allocating rent expense for a multistory building, differences in the value of the various floors and locations may be considered. For example, the space near the main entrance of a department store is more valuable than the same amount of floor space located far from the elevator on the sixth floor. For Tisch Company, rent expense is allocated on the basis of floor space used because there are no major differences in the values of the floor areas used by each department. In allocating heating and lighting expense, it is assumed that the number of lights, their wattage, and the extent of use are uniform throughout the sales departments. If there are major variations and the total lighting expense is material, further analysis and separate allocations may be necessary. The rent expense and the heating and lighting expense are allocated as follows:

	Total	Department X	Department Y
Floor space, square feet	160,000	104,000	56,000
Percent	100%	65%	35%
Rent expense	$15,400	$10,010	$5,390
Heating and lighting expense	$ 5,100	$ 3,315	$1,785

Property Tax Expense and Insurance Expense are related primarily to the cost of the inventories and the store equipment. The cost of these assets may differ from their assessed value for tax purposes and their value for insurance purposes. However, the cost of the assets is most readily available from the accounts in the general ledger and is often considered to be an acceptable basis for allocating these expenses. The computations for the allocations are as follows:

	Total	Department X	Department Y
Inventories:			
January 1	$141,900	$ 80,150	$ 61,750
December 31	164,100	85,150	78,950
Total	$306,000	$165,300	$140,700
Average	$153,000	$ 82,650	$ 70,350
Average cost of store equipment (computed previously)	30,000	18,000	12,000
Total	$183,000	$100,650	$ 82,350
Percent	100%	55%	45%
Property tax expense	$ 6,800	$ 3,740	$ 3,060
Insurance expense	$ 3,900	$ 2,145	$ 1,755

Uncollectible Accounts Expense, Miscellaneous Selling Expense, and Miscellaneous Administrative Expense are allocated according to gross sales. Uncollectible accounts expense may be allocated on the basis of an analysis of accounts receivable written off. For Tisch Company, however, it is assumed that uncollectible accounts expense is closely related to gross sales. The miscellaneous selling and administrative expenses are also allocated on the basis of gross sales. This assumes that gross sales are an approximate measure of the benefit each department receives from miscellaneous expenses. The computations for the allocations are as follows:

	Total	Department X	Department Y
Sales	$900,000	$630,000	$270,000
Percent	100%	70%	30%
Uncollectible accounts expense	$ 4,600	$ 3,220	$ 1,380
Miscellaneous selling expense	$ 4,700	$ 3,290	$ 1,410
Miscellaneous administrative expense	$ 4,800	$ 3,360	$ 1,440

An income statement reporting income from operations by departments for Tisch Company is shown in Exhibit 8. The amounts for sales and the cost of goods sold are reported in condensed form. Details could be reported, if desired, in the manner shown in Exhibit 7.

Exhibit 8
Income Statement—Departmental
Operating Income

Tisch Company
Income Statement
For Year Ended December 31, 1994

	Department X		Department Y		Total	
Net sales		$614,700		$262,900		$877,600
Cost of goods sold		323,350		180,750		504,100
Gross profit		$291,350		$ 82,150		$373,500
Operating expenses:						
Selling expenses:						
Sales salaries expense	$ 54,000		$ 30,900		$ 84,900	
Advertising expense	12,600		6,400		19,000	
Depreciation expense—store						
equipment	2,640		1,760		4,400	
Misc. selling expense	3,290		1,410		4,700	
Total selling expenses		$ 72,530		$ 40,470		$113,000
Administrative expenses:						
Officers' salaries expense	$ 31,200		$ 20,800		$ 52,000	
Office salaries expense	10,560		7,040		17,600	
Rent expense	10,010		5,390		15,400	
Property tax expense	3,740		3,060		6,800	
Heating and lighting exp.	3,315		1,785		5,100	
Uncollectible accounts exp.	3,220		1,380		4,600	
Insurance expense	2,145		1,755		3,900	
Misc. administrative exp.	3,360		1,440		4,800	
Total administrative exp.		67,550		42,650		110,200
Total operating expenses		140,080		83,120		223,200
Income (loss) from operations		$151,270		$ (970)		$150,300
Other expense:						
Interest expense						2,500
Income before income tax						$147,800
Income tax						64,444
Net income						$ 83,356

In a research study, 85% of the companies surveyed indicated that they allocate some operating expenses to profit centers (departments), using methods illustrated in the preceding paragraphs.[1] Managers should be careful, however, in using income statements departmentalized through income from operations. This is because the allocation of many operating expenses involves a high degree of judgment. In addition, the reporting of operating income by departments may be misleading, since the departments are not independent operating units. The departments are segments of a business enterprise, and no single department of a business can earn an income by itself. For Tisch Company, the departmental margin of $38,395 for Department Y in Exhibit 6 may be more reliable for management's use in making decisions than the $970 loss from operations shown in Exhibit 8.

[1] James M. Fremgen and Shu S. Liao, *The Allocation of Corporate Indirect Costs* (New York: National Association of Accountants, 1981), pp. 33-34.

RESPONSIBILITY ACCOUNTING FOR INVESTMENT CENTERS

Objective 5
Compute operating income, rate of return on investment, and residual income for an investment center.

Since investment center managers have responsibility for revenues and expenses, operating income is an essential part of investment center reporting. In addition, because the manager also has responsibility for the assets invested in the center, two additional measures of performance are often used. These additional measures are the rate of return on investment and residual income. In practice, most companies use a variety of performance measures. For example, a survey of manufacturers found that 70% of the respondents used operating income as a percent of sales, 62% used rate of return on investment, and 13% used residual income as performance measures in setting enterprise goals.[2] The following paragraphs focus on these performance measures for investment centers. Each of these performance measures is described and illustrated for Baldwin Company, a diversified company with three operating divisions, A, B, and C.

Operating Income

Because investment centers are evaluated as if they were separate companies, traditional financial statements are normally prepared for each center. For purposes of assessing profitability, operating income is the focal point of the analysis. Since determining operating income for responsibility reporting was discussed earlier in this chapter, only condensed divisional income statements are used in the following illustrations. Such statements for Baldwin Company are as follows:

	Division A	Division B	Division C
Sales	$560,000	$672,000	$750,000
Cost of goods sold	336,000	470,400	562,500
Gross profit	$224,000	$201,600	$187,500
Operating expenses	154,000	117,600	112,500
Operating income	$ 70,000	$ 84,000	$ 75,000

Based on the amount of divisional operating income, Division B is the most profitable of Baldwin Company's divisions. Division C is slightly more profitable than Division A.

Rate of Return on Investment

Although operating income is a useful measure of investment center performance, it does not reflect the amount of assets invested in each center. For example, if the amount of assets invested in Division B is twice that of the other divisions, then Division B is the least profitable of the divisions in terms of the rate of return on these assets. Since investment center managers also control the amount of assets invested in their centers, it is logical that they should also be held accountable for the use of these assets. One measure that considers the amount of assets invested is the **rate of return on investment (ROI)** or **rate of return on assets**. It is one of the most widely used measures of divisional performance for investment centers and is computed as follows:

$$\text{Rate of Return on Investment (ROI)} = \frac{\text{Operating Income}}{\text{Invested Assets}}$$

The rate of return on investment is useful because the three factors subject to control by divisional managers (revenues, expenses, and invested assets) are considered in its computation. By measuring profitability relative to the amount of assets invested in each division, the rate of return on investment can be used to compare divisions. The higher the rate of return on investment, the more

---

[2] Robert A. Howell, James D. Brown, Stephen R. Soucy, and Allen H. Seed, *Management Accounting in the New Manufacturing Environment* (Montvale, New Jersey: National Association of Accountants, 1987).

effectively the division is utilizing its assets to generate income. To illustrate, the rate of return on investment for each division of Baldwin Company, based on the book value of invested assets, is as follows:

	Operating Income	Invested Assets	Rate of Return on Investment
Division A	$70,000	$350,000	20%
Division B	84,000	700,000	12
Division C	75,000	500,000	15

Although Division B generated the largest operating income, its rate of return on investment (12%) is the lowest. Hence, relative to the assets invested, Division B is the least profitable division. In comparison, the rate of return on investment of Division A is 20% and Division C is 15%. These differences in the rates of return on investment can be analyzed, using an expanded form of the rate of return on investment formula. This expanded form is as follows:

$$\text{Rate of Return on Investment (ROI)} = \frac{\text{Operating Income}}{\text{Sales}} \times \frac{\text{Sales}}{\text{Invested Assets}}$$

In the expanded form, the rate of return on investment is the product of two factors. The first factor is the ratio of operating income to sales, often called the **profit margin**. The second factor is the ratio of sales to invested assets, often called the **investment turnover**. As shown below, the use of this expanded expression yields the same rate of return on investment for Division A, 20%, as computed previously.

$$\text{Rate of Return on Investment (ROI)} = \frac{\text{Operating Income}}{\text{Sales}} \times \frac{\text{Sales}}{\text{Invested Assets}}$$

$$\text{ROI} = \frac{\$70,000}{\$560,000} \times \frac{\$560,000}{\$350,000}$$

$$\text{ROI} = 12.5\% \times \$1.6$$

$$\text{ROI} = 20\%$$

The expanded expression for the rate of return on investment is useful in management's evaluation and control of decentralized operations. This is because the profit margin and the investment turnover focus on the underlying operating relationships of each division. The profit margin component focuses on profitability by indicating the rate of profit earned on each sales dollar. If a division's profit margin increases, and all other factors remain the same, the division's rate of return on investment will increase. For example, a division might add more profitable products to its sales mix and thereby increase its overall profit margin and rate of return on investment.

The investment turnover component focuses on efficiency in the use of assets and indicates the rate at which sales are generated for each dollar of invested assets. The more sales per dollar invested, the greater the efficiency in the use of the assets. If a division's investment turnover increases, and all other factors remain the same, the division's rate of return on investment will increase. For example, a division might attempt to increase sales through special sales promotions and thereby attempt to increase its investment turnover and rate of return on investment.

The rate of return on investment, using the expanded expression for each division of Baldwin Company, is summarized below.

$$\text{Rate of Return on Investment (ROI)} = \text{Profit Margin} \quad \times \quad \text{Investment Turnover}$$

$$\text{ROI} = \frac{\text{Operating Income}}{\text{Sales}} \times \frac{\text{Sales}}{\text{Invested Assets}}$$

Division A: $\text{ROI} = \dfrac{\$70,000}{\$560,000} \times \dfrac{\$560,000}{\$350,000}$

$\text{ROI} = 12.5\% \qquad\qquad \times\ 1.6$

$\text{ROI} = 20\%$

Division B: $\text{ROI} = \dfrac{\$84,000}{\$672,000} \times \dfrac{\$672,000}{\$700,000}$

$\text{ROI} = 12.5\% \qquad\qquad \times\ .96$

$\text{ROI} = 12\%$

Division C: $\text{ROI} = \dfrac{\$75,000}{\$750,000} \times \dfrac{\$750,000}{\$500,000}$

$\text{ROI} = 10\% \qquad\qquad \times\ 1.5$

$\text{ROI} = 15\%$

Although Divisions A and B have the same profit margins, Division A's investment turnover is larger than that of Division B (1.6 to .96). Thus, by more efficiently utilizing its invested assets, Division A's rate of return on investment is higher than Division B's. Division C's profit margin of 10% and investment turnover of 1.5 are lower than those of Division A. The product of these factors results in a return on investment of 15% for Division C, compared to 20% for Division A.

To determine possible ways of increasing the rate of return on investment, the profit margin and investment turnover for a division may be analyzed. For example, if Division A is in a highly competitive industry where the profit margin cannot be easily increased, the division manager might focus on increasing the investment turnover. To illustrate, assume that sales of Division A could be increased by $56,000 through increasing advertising expenditures. The cost of goods sold is expected to be 60% of sales, and operating expenses will increase to $169,400. If the advertising is increased, Division A's operating income would increase from $70,000 to $77,000, as shown below.

Sales ($560,000 + $56,000)	$616,000
Cost of goods sold ($616,000 × 60%)	369,600
Gross profit	$246,400
Operating expenses	169,400
Operating income	$ 77,000

The rate of return on investment for Division A, using the expanded expression, is recomputed as follows:

$$\text{Rate of Return on Investment (ROI)} = \frac{\text{Operating Income}}{\text{Sales}} \times \frac{\text{Sales}}{\text{Invested Assets}}$$

$$\text{ROI} = \frac{\$77,000}{\$616,000} \times \frac{\$616,000}{\$350,000}$$

$\text{ROI} = 12.5 \qquad\qquad \times\ 1.76$

$\text{ROI} = 22\%$

Although Division A's profit margin remains the same (12.5%), the investment turnover has increased from 1.6 to 1.76, an increase of 10% (.16 ÷ 1.6). The 10% increase in investment turnover also increases the rate of return on investment by 10% (from 20% to 22%).

The major advantage of the use of the rate of return on investment instead of operating income as a divisional performance measure is that the amount of divisional investment is directly considered. Thus, divisional performances can be compared, even though the sizes of the divisions may vary significantly.

In addition to its use as a performance measure, the rate of return on investment can assist management in other ways. For example, in considering a decision to expand the operations of Baldwin Company, management might consider giving priority to Division A because it earns the highest rate of return on investment. If the current rates of return on investment are maintained in the future, an investment in Division A will return 20 cents (20%) on each dollar invested. In contrast, investments in Division B will earn only 12 cents per dollar invested, and investments in Division C will return only 15 cents per dollar.

A disadvantage of the rate of return on investment as a performance measure is that it may lead divisional managers to reject new investments which could be profitable for the company as a whole. For example, assume that Division W of Struck Inc. has an overall rate of return on investment of 25%. The rate of return on investment for Struck Inc., with all divisions considered, is 15%. The manager of Division W has the opportunity of investing in a new project that is estimated will earn a 20% rate of return. If the manager of Division W invests in the project, however, Division W's overall rate of return will decrease from 25%. Thus, the division manager might decide to reject the project, even though the investment would increase Struck Inc.'s overall rate of return of 15%.

Residual Income

An additional measure of evaluating divisional performance—residual income—is useful in overcoming some of the disadvantages associated with the two measures in the preceding paragraphs. **Residual income** is the excess of divisional operating income over a minimum amount of desired operating income. The minimum amount of desired divisional operating income is set by top management, based upon such factors as the cost of financing the operations of the enterprise. It is normally computed by multiplying a minimum rate of return for the invested assets by the amount of divisional assets. To illustrate, assume that the top management of Baldwin Company has established 10% as the minimum rate of return on divisional assets. The residual incomes for Divisions A, B, and C are shown as follows:

	Division A	Division B	Division C
Divisional operating income	$70,000	$84,000	$75,000
Minimum amount of divisional operating income:			
$350,000 × 10%	35,000		
$700,000 × 10%		70,000	
$500,000 × 10%			50,000
Residual income	$35,000	$14,000	$25,000

The major advantage of residual income as a performance measure is that it considers both the minimum rate of return and the total amount of the operating income earned by each division. For example, Division A has more residual income than the other divisions of Baldwin Company, even though it has the least operating income. Also, Division C earns $11,000 more residual income than Division B, even though Division B generates more operating income than Division C. The reason for this difference is that Division B has $200,000 more assets than Division C. Hence, Division B's operating income is reduced by $20,000 ($200,000 x 10%) more than Division C's operating income in determining residual income.

TRANSFER PRICING

Objective 6
Explain how the following
transfer pricing approaches may
be used by decentralized
segments of a business
enterprise:

Market price approach
Negotiated price approach
Cost price approach

The use of responsibility accounting in measuring performance in decentralized companies can motivate managers to achieve profit goals. When decentralized divisions transfer products or render services to each other, a **transfer price** is used to charge for the products or services. The revenues and expenses of both the receiving division and the division providing the product or service are affected by the transfer price used. As a result, transfer prices affect the operating income for each division. Thus, setting transfer prices is a sensitive matter for division managers.

The objective of transfer pricing is to encourage each division manager to transfer goods and services between divisions if overall company income can be increased by doing so. As will be illustrated, however, transfer prices may be misused in such a way that overall company income suffers.

The following paragraphs discuss various approaches to setting transfer prices. The effect of transfer prices on the evaluation of decentralized performance and their potential impact on overall company income are also discussed. Three commonly used approaches to setting transfer prices are:[3]

1. Market price approach
2. Negotiated price approach
3. Cost price approach

Transfer prices may be used when decentralized units are organized as cost, profit, or investment centers. For purposes of illustration, a diversified company (Wilson Company) with two operating divisions (M and N) organized as investment centers will be used. Condensed income statements for Wilson Company's divisions, assuming no transfers between divisions, are shown in Exhibit 9.

Exhibit 9
Income Statement—No Transfers
Between Divisions

Wilson Company Divisional Income Statements For Year Ended December 31, 1994			
	Division M	*Division N*	*Total*
Sales:			
50,000 units x $20 per unit	$1,000,000		$1,000,000
20,000 units x $40 per unit		$800,000	800,000
			$1,800,000
Expenses:			
Variable:			
50,000 units x $10 per unit	$ 500,000		$ 500,000
20,000 units x $30* per unit		$600,000	600,000
Fixed	300,000	100,000	400,000
Total expenses	$ 800,000	$700,000	$1,500,000
Operating income	$ 200,000	$100,000	$ 300,000

*$20 of the $30 per unit represents materials costs, and the remaining $10 per unit represents other expenses incurred within Division N.

Market Price Approach

Under the **market price approach**, the transfer price is the price at which the product or service transferred could be sold to outside buyers. If an outside market ex-

---

[3] The discussion in this chapter highlights the essential concepts of transfer pricing. In-depth discussion of transfer pricing can be found in advanced texts.

ists for the product or service transferred, the current market price at which the purchasing division could buy the product or service may be an appropriate transfer price.

To illustrate, assume that materials used by Wilson Company in producing Division N's product are currently purchased from an outside supplier at $20 per unit. The same materials are produced by Division M. Division M is operating at full capacity of 50,000 units and can sell all it produces to either Division N or to outside buyers. A transfer price of $20 per unit (the market price) has no effect on the income of Division M or total company income. Division M will earn revenues of $20 per unit on all its production and sales, regardless of who buys its product. Likewise, Division N will pay $20 per unit for materials (the market price). Thus, the use of the market price as the transfer price has no effect on the income of Division M or total company income. In this situation, the use of the market price as the transfer price is appropriate. The condensed divisional income statements for Wilson Company under such circumstances would be as shown in Exhibit 9.

Negotiated Price Approach

If unused or excess capacity exists in the supplying division (Division M), and the transfer price is equal to the market price, total company profit may not be maximized. This is because the manager of Division N will be indifferent as to whether to purchase the materials from Division M or from outside suppliers. Thus, Division N may purchase the materials from outside suppliers. If, however, Division N purchases the materials from Division M, the difference between the market price of $20 and the variable costs of Division M can cover fixed costs and contribute to company profits. When the negotiated price approach is used in this situation, the manager of Division N is encouraged to purchase the materials from Division M.

The **negotiated price approach** allows the managers of decentralized units to agree (negotiate) among themselves as to the transfer price. The only constraint on the negotiations is that the transfer price be less than the market price but greater than the supplying division's variable costs per unit. If agreement cannot be reached between the division managers, the company's top management may intervene to set the transfer price.

To illustrate the use of the negotiated price approach, assume that instead of a capacity of 50,000 units, Division M's capacity is 70,000 units. In addition, assume that Division M can continue to sell only 50,000 units to outside buyers. A transfer price less than $20 would encourage the manager of Division N to purchase from Division M. This is because Division N's materials cost per unit would decrease, and its operating income would increase. At the same time, a transfer price above Division M's variable costs per unit of $10 (from Exhibit 9) would encourage the manager of Division M to use the excess capacity to supply materials to Division N. In doing so, Division M's operating profits would increase.

To continue the illustration, assume that Wilson Company's division managers agree to a transfer price of $15 for Division M's product. By purchasing from Division M, Division N's materials cost would be $5 per unit less. At the same time, Division M would increase its sales by $300,000 (20,000 units × $15 per unit) and increase its income by $100,000 ($300,000 sales − $200,000 variable costs). The effect of reducing Division N's materials cost by $100,000 (20,000 units × $5 per unit) is to increase its income by $100,000. Therefore, Wilson Company's income is increased by $200,000 ($100,000 reported by Division M and $100,000 reported by Division N), as shown in the condensed income statements in Exhibit 10.

In this illustration, any transfer price less than the market price of $20 but greater than Division M's unit variable costs of $10 would increase each division's income and would increase overall company profit by $200,000. By establishing a range of $20 to $10 for the transfer price, each division manager will have an incentive to negotiate the transfer of the materials.

Exhibit 10
Income Statements—Negotiated
Transfer Price

	Division M	Division N	Total
Wilson Company			
Divisional Income Statements			
For Year Ended December 31, 1994			
Sales:			
50,000 units × $20 per unit	$1,000,000		$1,000,000
20,000 units × $15 per unit	300,000		300,000
20,000 units × $40 per unit		$800,000	800,000
	$1,300,000	$800,000	$2,100,000
Expenses:			
Variable:			
70,000 units × $10 per unit	$ 700,000		$ 700,000
20,000 units × $25* per unit		$500,000	500,000
Fixed	300,000	100,000	400,000
Total expenses	$1,000,000	$600,000	$1,600,000
Operating income	$ 300,000	$200,000	$ 500,000

*$10 per unit of the $25 is incurred solely within Division N, and $15 per unit represents the transfer price per unit from Division M.

Cost Price Approach

Under the **cost price approach** cost is used as the basis for setting transfer prices. With this approach, a variety of cost concepts may be used. For example, cost may refer to either total product cost per unit or variable product cost per unit. If total product cost per unit is used, direct materials, direct labor, and factory overhead are included in the transfer price. If variable product cost per unit is used, the fixed factory overhead component of total product cost is excluded from the transfer price.

Either actual costs or standard (budgeted) costs may be used in applying the cost price approach. If actual costs are used, inefficiencies of the producing division are transferred to the purchasing division. Thus, there is little incentive for the producing division to control costs carefully. For this reason, most companies use standard costs in the cost price approach. In this way, differences between actual and standard costs are isolated in the producing divisions for cost control purposes.

When division managers have responsibility for cost centers, the cost price approach to transfer pricing is appropriate and is often used. The cost price approach may not be appropriate, however, for decentralized operations organized as profit or investment centers. In profit and investment centers, division managers have responsibility for both revenues and expenses. The use of cost as a transfer price ignores the supplying division manager's responsibility for revenues. When a supplying division's sales are all intracompany transfers, for example, the use of the cost price approach would prevent the supplying division from reporting any operating income. A cost-based transfer price may therefore not motivate the division manager to make intracompany transfers, even though they are in the best interests of the company.

CHAPTER REVIEW

Key Points

Objective 1. List the advantages and disadvantages of decentralized operations.
The advantages of decentralization may include better decisions by the managers closest to the operations, more time for top management to focus on strategic planning, training for managers, improved ability to serve customers and respond to their needs, and improved manager morale. The disadvantages of decentralization may include failure of the com-

pany to maximize profits because decisions made by one manager may affect other managers in such a way that the profitability of the entire company may suffer.

Objective 2. List the three types of responsibility centers, and give an example of each type.

Responsibility centers are classified as cost centers, profit centers, and investment centers. In a cost center, the manager has the responsibility for the control of costs incurred and the authority to make decisions that affect those costs. In a profit center, the manager has the responsibility and the authority to make decisions that affect both costs and revenues (and thus profits) for the department or division. In an investment center, the manager has the responsibility and the authority to make decisions that affect not only costs and revenues, but also the plant assets available to the center.

Objective 3. Prepare a responsibility accounting report for a cost center.

Since managers of cost centers have responsibility and authority to make decisions regarding costs, responsibility accounting for cost centers focuses on costs. The primary accounting tools for planning and controlling costs for a cost center are standards, budgets, and budget performance reports. An example of a budget performance report is shown in Exhibit 4.

Objective 4. Prepare responsibility accounting reports for a profit center, using the following three income concepts: departmental margin, gross profit, and income from operations.

In preparing a responsibility accounting report using the departmental margin approach, the departmental sales and cost of goods sold are presented on the departmental income statement in the normal manner. The direct expenses of each department are then deducted from the related departmental gross profit to determine departmental margin. The remaining expenses, including the indirect expenses, are not reported by department. They are reported separately below the total departmental margin. An example of this report format is shown in Exhibit 6.

In preparing a responsibility accounting report using the gross profit approach, each department's sales, cost of goods

sold, and gross profit are reported. Operating expenses are not reported separately by department. An example of this report format is shown in Exhibit 7.

In preparing a responsibility accounting report through income from operations, revenues and cost of goods sold are reported for each department. In addition, the operating expenses are allocated to each department on the basis of the cost of services rendered to each department. An example of this report format is shown in Exhibit 8.

Objective 5. Compute operating income, rate of return on investment, and residual income for an investment center.

Operating income for an investment center is the excess of sales over cost of goods sold and operating expenses. The rate of return on investment for an investment center is the operating income divided by invested assets. The rate of return on investment may also be computed as the product of (1) the profit margin and (2) the investment turnover. Residual income for an investment center is the excess of operating income over a minimum amount of desired operating income.

Objective 6. Explain how the following transfer pricing approaches may be used by decentralized segments of a business enterprise: market price approach, negotiated price approach, and cost price approach.

Under the market price approach, the transfer price is the price at which the product or service transferred could be sold to outside buyers.

Under the negotiated price approach, the managers of decentralized units agree (negotiate) among themselves as to the transfer price. The only constraint on the negotiations is that the transfer price be less than the market price but greater than the supplying division's variable costs per unit. If agreement cannot be reached between the division managers, the company's top management may intervene to set the transfer price.

Under the cost price approach, cost is used as the basis for setting transfer prices. A variety of cost concepts may be used, such as total product cost per unit or variable product cost per unit. In addition, actual costs or standard (budgeted) costs may be used.

Glossary of Key Terms

Cost center. A decentralized unit in which the department or division manager has responsibility for the control of costs incurred and the authority to make decisions that affect these costs. **Objective 2**

Cost price approach. An approach to transfer pricing that uses costs as the basis for setting the transfer price. **Objective 6**

Decentralization. The separation of a business into more manageable units. **Objective 1**

Departmental margin. Departmental gross profit less direct departmental expenses. **Objective 4**

Direct expenses. Expenses that can be traced directly to a unit within an enterprise or organization. **Objective 4**

Indirect expenses. Expenses that are incurred for an entire business enterprise as a unit and that are not subject to the control of individual department managers. **Objective 4**

Investment center. A decentralized unit in which the manager has the responsibility and authority to make decisions that affect not only costs and revenues but also the plant assets available to the center. **Objective 2**

Investment turnover. A component of the rate of return on investment, computed as the ratio of sales to invested assets. **Objective 5**

Market price approach. An approach to transfer pricing that uses the price at which the product or service transferred could be sold to outside buyers as the transfer price. **Objective 6**

Negotiated price approach. An approach to transfer pricing that allows managers of decentralized units to agree (negotiate) among themselves as to the transfer price. **Objective 6**

Profit center. A decentralized unit in which the manager has the responsibility and the authority to make decisions that affect both costs and revenues (and thus profits). **Objective 2**

Profit margin. A component of the rate of return on investment, computed as the ratio of operating income to sales. **Objective 5**

Rate of return on investment (ROI). A measure of managerial efficiency in the use of investments in assets, computed as operating income divided by invested assets. **Objective 5**

Residual income. The excess of divisional operating income over a "minimum" amount of desired operating income. **Objective 5**

Responsibility accounting. The process of measuring and reporting operating data by areas of responsibility. **Objective 2**

Strategic planning. The development of a long-range course of action to achieve enterprise goals. **Objective 1**

Transfer price. The price charged one decentralized unit by another for the goods or services provided. **Objective 6**

Self-Examination Questions
Answers at end of chapter.

1. When the manager has the responsibility and authority to make decisions that affect costs and revenues, but no responsibility for or authority over assets invested in the department, the department is called:
   A. a cost center
   B. a profit center
   C. an investment center
   D. a service center

2. The term used to describe the excess of departmental gross profit over direct departmental expenses is:
   A. income from operations
   B. net income
   C. departmental margin
   D. contribution margin

3. Division A of Kern Co. has sales of $350,000, cost of goods sold of $200,000, operating expenses of $30,000, and invested assets of $600,000. What is the rate of return on investment for Division A?
   A. 20%
   B. 25%
   C. 33%
   D. 40%

4. Division L of Liddy Co. has a rate of return on investment of 24% and an investment turnover of 1.6. What is the profit margin?
   A. 6%
   B. 15%
   C. 24%
   D. 38%

5. Which approach to transfer pricing uses the price at which the product or service transferred could be sold to outside buyers?
   A. Cost price approach
   B. Negotiated price approach
   C. Market price approach
   D. Standard cost approach

ILLUSTRATIVE PROBLEM

Reese Company has two divisions, A and B. Invested assets and condensed income statement data for each division for the past year ended December 31 are as follows:

	Division A	Division B
Sales	$3,125,000	$5,100,000
Cost of goods sold	2,500,000	4,000,000
Operating expenses	150,000	590,000
Invested assets	2,500,000	3,000,000

Instructions

1. Prepare condensed income statements for the past year for each division.
2. Using the expanded expression, determine the profit margin, investment turnover, and rate of return on investment for each division.
3. If management desires a minimum rate of return of 12%, determine the residual income for each division.

ETHICS DISCUSSION CASE

Jane Dillow, the assistant controller for Davis Enterprises, prepares responsibility accounting reports for the various divisions of the company. On December 18, a case of wine with a
card wishing "Happy Holidays" from Bob Barnes, manager of the beverage division, was
delivered to Dillow's home. Dillow accepted the wine and sent a note of thanks to Barnes.
Discuss whether Dillow behaved in an ethical manner.

SHARPEN YOUR COMMUNICATION SKILLS

EXERCISES

EXERCISE 26-1
BUDGET PERFORMANCE REPORT
Objective 3

The budget for Department 7 of Plant B for the current month ended July 31 is as follows:

Factory wages	$170,500
Materials	144,500
Power and light	51,000
Supervisory salaries	36,000
Depreciation of plant and equipment	21,300
Maintenance	19,300
Insurance and property taxes	12,000

During July, the costs incurred in Department 7 of Plant B were as follows:

Factory wages	$171,250
Materials	149,650
Power and light	50,400
Supervisory salaries	36,000
Depreciation of plant and equipment	21,300
Maintenance	19,180
Insurance and property taxes	12,000

a. Prepare a budget performance report for the supervisor of Department 7, Plant B, for the
 month of July.

SHARPEN YOUR COMMUNICATION SKILLS

b. For what significant variations in costs might the supervisor be expected to request supplemental reports?

EXERCISE 26-2
DEPARTMENTAL INCOME STATEMENT
Objective 4

The following data were summarized from the accounting records for Hahn Company for
the current year ended June 30:

Cost of goods sold:	
Department C	$170,500
Department D	237,000
Direct expenses:	
Department C	88,000
Department D	119,200
Income tax	37,000
Indirect expenses	76,400
Interest income	16,000
Net sales:	
Department C	332,100
Department D	466,200

SPREADSHEET PROBLEM

Prepare an income statement departmentalized through departmental margin.

EXERCISE 26-3
DECISION ON DISCONTINUANCE OF DEPARTMENT
Objective 4

A portion of an income statement in condensed form, departmentalized through loss from
operations for the year just ended, is as follows:

	Department G
Net sales	$226,600
Cost of goods sold	179,700
Gross profit	$ 46,900
Operating expenses	63,000
Loss from operations	$(16,100)

could be sold to outside buyers as the transfer price. **Objective 6**

Negotiated price approach. An approach to transfer pricing that allows managers of decentralized units to agree (negotiate) among themselves as to the transfer price. **Objective 6**

Profit center. A decentralized unit in which the manager has the responsibility and the authority to make decisions that affect both costs and revenues (and thus profits). **Objective 2**

Profit margin. A component of the rate of return on investment, computed as the ratio of operating income to sales. **Objective 5**

Rate of return on investment (ROI). A measure of managerial efficiency in the use of investments in assets, computed as operating income divided by invested assets. **Objective 5**

Residual income. The excess of divisional operating income over a "minimum" amount of desired operating income. **Objective 5**

Responsibility accounting. The process of measuring and reporting operating data by areas of responsibility. **Objective 2**

Strategic planning. The development of a long-range course of action to achieve enterprise goals. **Objective 1**

Transfer price. The price charged one decentralized unit by another for the goods or services provided. **Objective 6**

Self-Examination Questions
Answers at end of chapter.

1. When the manager has the responsibility and authority to make decisions that affect costs and revenues, but no responsibility for or authority over assets invested in the department, the department is called:
   A. a cost center
   B. a profit center
   C. an investment center
   D. a service center

2. The term used to describe the excess of departmental gross profit over direct departmental expenses is:
   A. income from operations
   B. net income
   C. departmental margin
   D. contribution margin

3. Division A of Kern Co. has sales of $350,000, cost of goods sold of $200,000, operating expenses of $30,000, and invested assets of $600,000. What is the rate of return on investment for Division A?
   A. 20%
   B. 25%
   C. 33%
   D. 40%

4. Division L of Liddy Co. has a rate of return on investment of 24% and an investment turnover of 1.6. What is the profit margin?
   A. 6%
   B. 15%
   C. 24%
   D. 38%

5. Which approach to transfer pricing uses the price at which the product or service transferred could be sold to outside buyers?
   A. Cost price approach
   B. Negotiated price approach
   C. Market price approach
   D. Standard cost approach

ILLUSTRATIVE PROBLEM

Reese Company has two divisions, A and B. Invested assets and condensed income statement data for each division for the past year ended December 31 are as follows:

	Division A	Division B
Sales	$3,125,000	$5,100,000
Cost of goods sold	2,500,000	4,000,000
Operating expenses	150,000	590,000
Invested assets	2,500,000	3,000,000

Instructions

1. Prepare condensed income statements for the past year for each division.
2. Using the expanded expression, determine the profit margin, investment turnover, and rate of return on investment for each division.
3. If management desires a minimum rate of return of 12%, determine the residual income for each division.

ILLUSTRATIVE PROBLEM ILLUSTRATIVE PROBLEM ILLUSTRATIVE PROBLEM

Solution

1.

Reese Company
Divisional Income Statements
For Year Ended December 31, 19—

	Division A	Division B
Sales	$3,125,000	$5,100,000
Cost of goods sold	2,500,000	4,000,000
Gross profit	$ 625,000	$1,100,000
Operating expenses	150,000	590,000
Operating income	$ 475,000	$ 510,000

2.

Rate of Return on Investment (ROI) = Profit Margin × Investment Turnover

$$ROI = \frac{\text{Operating Income}}{\text{Sales}} \times \frac{\text{Sales}}{\text{Invested Assets}}$$

$$\text{Division A: ROI} = \frac{\$475,000}{\$3,125,000} \times \frac{\$3,125,000}{\$2,500,000}$$

$$ROI = 15.2\% \qquad \times 1.25$$

$$ROI = 19\%$$

$$\text{Division B: ROI} = \frac{\$510,000}{\$5,100,000} \times \frac{\$5,100,000}{\$3,000,000}$$

$$ROI = 10\% \qquad \times 1.7$$

$$ROI = 17\%$$

3. Division A: $175,000 ($475,000 − $300,000)
   Division B: $150,000 ($510,000 − $360,000)

DISCUSSION QUESTIONS

1. What is responsibility accounting?
2. Name three common types of responsibility centers for decentralized operations.
3. Differentiate between a cost center and a profit center.
4. Differentiate between a profit center and an investment center.
5. In what major respect would budget performance reports prepared for the use of plant managers of a manufacturing enterprise with cost centers differ from those prepared for the use of the various department supervisors who report to the plant managers?
6. Indicate whether each of the following operating expenses incurred by an individual department within a merchandising enterprise is a direct or an indirect expense:

   a. Depreciation of store equipment
   b. Heating and lighting expense
   c. General manager's salary
   d. Insurance expense on building
   e. Uncollectible accounts expense
   f. Sales commissions

7. What term is applied to the dollar amount representing the excess of departmental gross profit over direct departmental expenses?
8. Recent income statements departmentalized through income from operations report operating losses for Department A, a relatively minor segment of the business. Management studies indicate that discontinuance of Department A would not affect sales of other departments or the volume of indirect expenses. Under what circumstances would the discontinuance of Department A result in a decrease in the net income of the enterprise?
9. The newly appointed manager of the Women's Shoes Department in a department store is studying the income statements presenting gross profit by departments. The manager wants to adjust operations to achieve the highest possible gross profit for the

department. (a) Suggest ways in which an income statement departmentalized through gross profit can be used in achieving this goal. (b) Suggest reasons why caution must be exercised in using such statements.

10. For each of the following types of expenses, select the allocation basis listed that is most appropriate for use in arriving at operating income by departments:

Expense:	Basis of allocation:
a. Rent expense	1. Cost of inventory and equipment
b. Advertising expense	
c. Sales salaries	2. Departmental sales
d. Property tax expense	3. Time devoted to departments
	4. Physical space occupied

11. Describe an appropriate basis for apportioning Officers' Salaries Expense among departments for purposes of the income statement departmentalized through income from operations.

12. Name three performance measures useful in evaluating investment centers.

13. What is the major shortcoming of using operating income as a performance measure for investment centers?

14. Why should the factors under the control of the investment center manager (revenues, expenses, and invested assets) be considered in the computation of the rate of return on investment?

15. Hubble Co. has $600,000 invested in Division D, which earned $108,000 of operating income. What is the rate of return on investment for Division D?

16. If Hubble Co. in Question 15 had sales of $1,800,000, what is (a) the profit margin and (b) the investment turnover for Division D?

17. What are two ways of expressing the rate of return on investment?

18. In evaluating investment centers, what does multiplying the profit margin by the investment turnover equal?

19. In a decentralized company in which the divisions are organized as investment centers, how could a division be considered the least profitable, even though it earned the largest amount of operating income?

20. Which component of the rate of return on investment (profit margin factor or investment turnover factor) focuses on efficiency in the use of assets and indicates the rate at which sales are generated for each dollar of invested assets?

21. Division C of Bailey Co. has a rate of return on investment of 8%. (a) If Division C increases its investment turnover by 25%, what would be the new rate of return on investment? (b) If Division C also increases its profit margin from 4% to 6%, what would be the new rate of return on investment?

22. How does the use of the rate of return on investment facilitate comparability of divisions of decentralized companies?

23. The rates of return on investment for Harmon Co.'s three divisions, A, B, and C, are 20%, 17%, and 15%, respectively. In expanding operations, which of Harmon Co.'s divisions should be given priority? Explain.

24. What term is used to describe the excess of divisional operating income over a minimum amount of desired operating income?

25. Division X of Gifford Co. reported operating income of $450,000, based on invested assets of $2,000,000. If the minimum rate of return on divisional investments is 20%, what is the residual income for Division X?

26. What is the objective of transfer pricing?

27. What approach uses as the transfer price the price at which the product or service transferred could be sold to outside buyers?

28. When is the negotiated price approach preferred over the market price approach in setting transfer prices?

29. If division managers cannot agree among themselves on a transfer price when using the negotiated price approach, how is the transfer price established?

30. When using the negotiated price approach to transfer pricing, within what range should the transfer price be established?

REAL W RLD FOCUS   31. Tandy Corporation's annual report for the year ended June 30, 1991, reports a profit margin of 4.3% and an investment turnover rate of 1.48. (a) What was the rate of return on investment for the year ended June 30, 1991? (b) If the investment turnover rate does not change for the year ended June 30, 1992, what must the profit margin be to earn a rate of return on investment of 8%? (Round to the nearest tenth of one percent.)

ETHICS DISCUSSION CASE

Jane Dillow, the assistant controller for Davis Enterprises, prepares responsibility accounting reports for the various divisions of the company. On December 18, a case of wine with a card wishing "Happy Holidays" from Bob Barnes, manager of the beverage division, was delivered to Dillow's home. Dillow accepted the wine and sent a note of thanks to Barnes. Discuss whether Dillow behaved in an ethical manner.

EXERCISES

EXERCISE 26-1
BUDGET PERFORMANCE
REPORT
Objective 3

The budget for Department 7 of Plant B for the current month ended July 31 is as follows:

Factory wages	$170,500
Materials	144,500
Power and light	51,000
Supervisory salaries	36,000
Depreciation of plant and equipment	21,300
Maintenance	19,300
Insurance and property taxes	12,000

During July, the costs incurred in Department 7 of Plant B were as follows:

Factory wages	$171,250
Materials	149,650
Power and light	50,400
Supervisory salaries	36,000
Depreciation of plant and equipment	21,300
Maintenance	19,180
Insurance and property taxes	12,000

a. Prepare a budget performance report for the supervisor of Department 7, Plant B, for the month of July.

b. For what significant variations in costs might the supervisor be expected to request supplemental reports?

EXERCISE 26-2
DEPARTMENTAL INCOME
STATEMENT
Objective 4

The following data were summarized from the accounting records for Hahn Company for the current year ended June 30:

Cost of goods sold:	
Department C	$170,500
Department D	237,000
Direct expenses:	
Department C	88,000
Department D	119,200
Income tax	37,000
Indirect expenses	76,400
Interest income	16,000
Net sales:	
Department C	332,100
Department D	466,200

Prepare an income statement departmentalized through departmental margin.

EXERCISE 26-3
DECISION ON
DISCONTINUANCE OF
DEPARTMENT
Objective 4

A portion of an income statement in condensed form, departmentalized through loss from operations for the year just ended, is as follows:

	Department G
Net sales	$226,600
Cost of goods sold	179,700
Gross profit	$ 46,900
Operating expenses	63,000
Loss from operations	$ (16,100)

The operating expenses of Department G include $30,000 for indirect expenses. It is believed that the discontinuance of Department G would not affect the sales of the other departments nor reduce the indirect expenses of the enterprise. Based on this information, determine the increase or decrease in income from operations of the enterprise if Department G had been discontinued prior to the year just ended.

EXERCISE 26-4
APPORTIONMENT OF
DEPRECIATION AND
PROPERTY TAX EXPENSE TO
DEPARTMENTS
Objective 4

In income statements prepared for Gibson Company, depreciation expense on equipment is allocated on the basis of the average cost of the equipment, and property tax expense is allocated on the basis of the combined total of the average cost of the equipment and the average cost of the inventories. Depreciation expense on equipment amounted to $150,000, and property tax expense amounted to $25,000 for the year. Determine the allocation of the depreciation expense and the property tax expense, based on the following data:

	Average Cost	
Departments	Equipment	Inventories
Service:		
A	$ 360,000	
B	240,000	
Sales:		
1	720,000	$360,000
2	480,000	120,000
3	600,000	120,000
Total	$2,400,000	$600,000

EXERCISE 26-5
RATE OF RETURN ON
INVESTMENT
Objective 5

The operating income and the amount of invested assets in each division of Kinney Company are as follows:

	Operating Income	Invested Assets
Division A	$210,000	$700,000
Division B	158,400	480,000
Division C	136,800	720,000

a. Compute the rate of return on investment for each division.
b. Which division is the most profitable per dollar invested?

EXERCISE 26-6
RESIDUAL INCOME
Objective 5

Based on the data in Exercise 26-5, assume that management has established a 15% minimum rate of return for invested assets.

a. Determine the residual income for each division.
b. Based on residual income, which of the divisions is the most profitable?

EXERCISE 26-7
DETERMINATION OF
MISSING ITEMS FOR
COMPUTATIONS OF RATE
OF RETURN ON
INVESTMENT
Objective 5

One item is omitted from each of the following computations of the rate of return on investment:

Rate of Return on Investment	=	Profit Margin	×	Investment Turnover
30%		20%		(a)
(b)		12%		1.5
36%		(c)		2.4
24%		15%		(d)
(e)		15%		1.2

Determine the missing items, identifying each by the appropriate letter.

EXERCISE 26-8
PROFIT MARGIN,
INVESTMENT TURNOVER,
AND RATE OF RETURN ON
INVESTMENT
Objective 5

The condensed income statement for Division D of Porter Company is as follows:

Sales	$600,000
Cost of goods sold	390,000
Gross profit	$210,000
Operating expenses	114,000
Operating income	$ 96,000

The manager of Division D is considering ways to increase the rate of return on investment.

a. Using the expanded expression for rate of return on investment, determine the profit margin, investment turnover, and rate of return on investment of Division D, assuming that $400,000 of assets have been invested in Division D.

▮ SHARPEN YOUR ◄
COMMUNICATION SKILLS

b. If expenses could be reduced by $24,000 without decreasing sales, what would be the impact on the profit margin, investment turnover, and rate of return on investment for Division D?

EXERCISE 26-9
DETERMINATION OF
MISSING ITEMS FOR COM-
PUTATIONS OF RATE OF
RETURN ON INVESTMENT
AND RESIDUAL INCOME
Objective 5

Data for Kotarsky Company is presented in the following table of rates of return on investment and residual incomes:

Invested Assets	Operating Income	Rate of Return on Investment	Minimum Rate of Return	Minimum Amount of Operating Income	Residual Income
$900,000	$180,000	(a)	15%	(b)	(c)
$420,000	(d)	15%	(e)	$42,000	$21,000
$600,000	(f)	(g)	(h)	$72,000	$36,000
$900,000	$216,000	(i)	20%	(j)	(k)

SPREADSHEET
PROBLEM

Determine the missing items, identifying each item by the appropriate letter.

EXERCISE 26-10
DECISION ON TRANSFER
PRICING
Objective 6

Materials used by Snead Company in producing Division R's product are currently purchased from outside suppliers at a cost of $40 per unit. However, the same materials are available from Division W. Division W has unused capacity and can produce the materials needed by Division R at a variable cost of $25 per unit.

a. If a transfer price of $32 per unit is established and 50,000 units of material are transferred, with no reduction in Division W's current sales, how much would Snead Company's total operating income increase?
b. How much would operating income of Division R increase?
c. How much would the operating income of Division W increase?

EXERCISE 26-11
DECISION ON TRANSFER
PRICING
Objective 6

Based on the Snead Company data in Exercise 26-10, assume that a transfer price of $30 has been established and 50,000 units of materials are transferred, with no reduction in Division W's current sales.

a. How much would Snead Company's total operating income increase?
b. How much would Division R's operating income increase?
c. How much would Division W's operating income increase?
d. If the negotiated price approach is used, what would be the range of acceptable transfer prices?

WhAT'S WRONG
WITH THiS?

What's wrong with the following analysis that was used for making a decision to discontinue Department T?

Lawson Corporation
Income Statement
For Year Ended October 31, 19—

	Department S	Department T	Total
Net sales	$1,250,000	$450,000	$1,700,000
Cost of goods sold	750,000	300,000	1,050,000
Gross profit	$ 500,000	$150,000	$ 650,000
Direct departmental expenses:			
Sales salaries and commissions expense	$155,000	$63,000	$218,000
Advertising expense	13,000	8,000	21,000
Depreciation expense—store equipment	12,600	5,400	18,000
Insurance expense	5,500	4,500	10,000
Uncollectible accounts expense	3,750	1,350	5,100
Officers' salaries expense	70,000	70,000	140,000
Total direct departmental expenses	259,850	152,250	412,100
Departmental margin	$ 240,150	$ (2,250)	$ 237,900

PROBLEMS

Series A

PROBLEM 26-1A
DECISION ON
DISCONTINUANCE OF
DEPARTMENT
Objective 4

E. E. Eden Company is considering discontinuance of one of its ten departments. If operations in Department J are discontinued, it is estimated that the indirect operating expenses and the level of operations in the other departments will not be affected.

Data from the income statement for the past year ended December 31, which is considered to be a typical year, are as follows:

	Department J		Other Departments	
Sales		$44,000		$765,000
Cost of goods sold		23,500		420,750
Gross profit		$20,500		$344,250
Operating expenses:				
Direct expenses	$16,500		$192,500	
Indirect expenses	9,000	25,500	99,000	291,500
Income (loss) before income tax		$(5,000)		$ 52,750

Instructions

1. Prepare an estimated income statement for the current year ending December 31, assuming the discontinuance of Department J.
2. On the basis of the data presented, would it be advisable to retain Department J? Explain.

SHARPEN YOUR
COMMUNICATION SKILLS

PROBLEM 26-2A
DEPARTMENTAL INCOME
STATEMENT THROUGH
DEPARTMENTAL MARGIN
Objective 4

Lakeshore Fashions has 20 departments. Department 10 and Department 16, which were established about twenty months ago on a trial basis, have the least sales volume. The board of directors believes that it is now time to consider the retention or the termination of these two departments. The following condensed trial balance was prepared as of August 31, the end of the first month of the current fiscal year. August is considered to be a typical month. The income tax accrual has no bearing on the decision and is excluded from consideration.

Current Assets	236,200	
Plant Assets	672,400	
Accumulated Depreciation—Plant Assets		168,100
Current Liabilities		118,100
Common Stock		200,000
Retained Earnings		403,304
Cash Dividends	30,000	
Sales—Department 10		32,500
Sales—Department 16		21,400
Sales—Other Departments		948,600
Cost of Goods Sold—Department 10	21,125	
Cost of Goods Sold—Department 16	14,980	
Cost of Goods Sold—Other Departments	569,160	
Direct Expenses—Department 10	8,125	
Direct Expenses—Department 16	7,490	
Direct Expenses—Other Departments	227,664	
Indirect Expenses	94,860	
Interest Expense	10,000	
	1,892,004	1,892,004

Instructions

1. Prepare an income statement for August, departmentalized through departmental margin.
2. State your recommendations for retaining or discontinuing of Departments 10 and 16, and give reasons for your answer.

SHARPEN YOUR
COMMUNICATION SKILLS

PROBLEM 26-3A
DEPARTMENTAL INCOME
STATEMENT THROUGH
DEPARTMENTAL MARGIN
Objective 4

Wilson Corporation consists of two departments, A and B. The bases to be used in allocating expenses between the two departments, together with other essential data, are as follows:

a. Sales salaries and commissions expense—basic salary plus 6% of sales. Basic salaries for Department A, $54,600; Department B, $26,520.
b. Advertising expense for brochures—usage within each department advertising specific products: Department A, $12,745; Department B, $6,090.

c. Depreciation expense—average cost of store equipment: Department A, $78,300; Department B, $56,700.

d. Insurance expense—average cost of store equipment plus average cost of inventories. Average cost of inventories was $58,100 for Department A and $26,900 for Department B.

e. Uncollectible accounts expense—3/8% of sales. Departmental managers are responsible for the granting of credit on the sales made by their respective departments.

The following data are obtained from the ledger on April 30, the end of the current fiscal year:

Sales—Department A		740,000
Sales—Department B		296,000
Cost of Goods Sold—Department A	495,800	
Cost of Goods Sold—Department B	192,400	
Sales Salaries and Commissions Expense	143,280	
Advertising Expense	18,835	
Depreciation Expense—Store Equipment	12,500	
Miscellaneous Selling Expense	2,020	
Administrative Salaries Expense	43,850	
Rent Expense	24,000	
Utilities Expense	14,620	
Insurance Expense	6,500	
Uncollectible Accounts Expense	3,885	
Miscellaneous Administrative Expense	710	
Interest Income		4,400
Income Tax	17,750	

Instructions

1. Prepare an income statement departmentalized through departmental margin.
2. Determine the rate of gross profit for each department.
3. Determine the rate of departmental margin to sales for each department.

PROBLEM 26-4A
DEPARTMENTAL INCOME
STATEMENT THROUGH
INCOME FROM
OPERATIONS
Objective 4

Walton Co. operates two sales departments—Department C for camping equipment and Department S for sporting goods. The following trial balance was prepared as of June 30, the end of the current fiscal year, after all adjustments, including those for inventories, were recorded and posted:

Cash	21,600	
Accounts Receivable	37,500	
Inventories—Department C	24,300	
Inventories—Department S	16,400	
Prepaid Insurance	1,750	
Store Supplies	1,600	
Store Equipment	83,200	
Accumulated Depreciation—Store Equipment		22,200
Accounts Payable		20,800
Income Tax Payable		2,900
Common Stock		50,000
Retained Earnings		63,400
Cash Dividends	11,000	
Income Summary	41,500	40,700
Sales—Department C		280,000
Sales—Department S		120,000
Sales Returns and Allowances—Department C	2,500	
Sales Returns and Allowances—Department S	1,700	
Purchases—Department C	131,600	
Purchases—Department S	70,400	
Sales Salaries Expense	70,000	
Advertising Expense	11,000	
Depreciation Expense—Store Equipment	5,500	
Store Supplies Expense	3,600	
Miscellaneous Selling Expense	3,000	
Office Salaries Expense	30,000	

Rent Expense	10,000
Heating and Lighting Expense	6,000
Property Tax Expense	3,200
Insurance Expense	2,800
Uncollectible Accounts Expense	2,200
Miscellaneous Administrative Expense	1,050
Interest Expense	600
Income Tax	6,000
	600,000 600,000

Inventories at the beginning of the year were as follows: Department C, $26,730; Department S, $14,770.

The bases to be used in apportioning expenses, together with other essential information, are as follows:

a. Sales salaries expense—payroll records: Department C, $45,000; Department S, $25,000.
b. Advertising expense—usage: Department C, $7,200; Department S, $3,800.
c. Depreciation expense—average cost of equipment. Equipment balances at beginning of year: Department C, $48,490; Department S, $26,110. Equipment balances at end of year: Department C, $54,080; Department S, $29,120.
d. Store supplies expense—requisitions: Department C, $2,420; Department S, $1,180.
e. Office salaries expense—Department C, 80%; Department S, 20%.
f. Rent expense and heating and lighting expense—floor space: Department C, 14,400 sq. ft.; Department S, 5,600 sq. ft.
g. Property tax expense and insurance expense—average cost of equipment plus average cost of inventories.
h. Uncollectible accounts expense, miscellaneous selling expense, and miscellaneous administrative expense—volume of gross sales.

SPREADSHEET PROBLEM

Instructions

Prepare an income statement departmentalized through income from operations.

PROBLEM 26-5A
DIVISIONAL INCOME
STATEMENTS AND RATE OF
RETURN ON INVESTMENT
ANALYSIS
Objective 5

Daley Company is a diversified company with three operating divisions organized as investment centers. Condensed data taken from the records of the three divisions for the year ended December 31 are as follows:

	Division G	Division H	Division I
Sales	$900,000	$1,875,000	$1,350,000
Cost of goods sold	595,000	1,200,000	810,000
Operating expenses	170,000	525,000	324,000
Invested assets	750,000	750,000	900,000

The management of Daley Company is evaluating each division as a basis for planning a future expansion of operations.

SPREADSHEET PROBLEM

Instructions

1. Prepare condensed divisional income statements for Divisions G, H, and I.
2. Using the expanded expression for rate of return on investment, compute the profit margin, investment turnover, and rate of return on investment for each division.

SHARPEN YOUR COMMUNICATION SKILLS ►

3. If available funds permit the expansion of operations of only one division, which of the divisions would you recommend for expansion, based on (1) and (2)? Explain.

PROBLEM 26-6A
EFFECT OF PROPOSALS ON
DIVISIONAL
PERFORMANCE
Objective 5

A condensed income statement for Division H of Searcy Company for the year ended October 31 is as follows:

Sales	$1,500,000
Cost of goods sold	1,050,000
Gross profit	$ 450,000
Operating expenses	270,000
Operating income	$ 180,000

The president of Searcy Company is concerned with Division H's rate of return on invested assets of $1,200,000, and has indicated that the division's rate of return on investment must be increased to at least 18% by the end of the next year if operations are to continue. The division manager is considering the following three proposals:

Proposal 1: Reduce invested assets by discontinuing a product line. This action would eliminate sales of $200,000, cost of goods sold of $140,000, and operating expenses of $49,000. Assets of $160,000 would be transferred to other divisions at no gain or loss.

Proposal 2: Purchase new and more efficient machinery and thereby reduce the cost of goods sold by $93,000. Sales would remain unchanged, and the old machinery, which has no remaining book value, would be scrapped at no gain or loss. The new machinery would increase invested assets by $300,000 for the year.

Proposal 3: Transfer equipment with a book value of $200,000 to other divisions at no gain or loss and lease similar equipment. The annual lease payments would exceed the amount of depreciation expense on the old equipment by $6,000. This increase in expense would be included as part of the cost of goods sold. Sales would remain unchanged.

Instructions

1. Using the expanded expression for rate of return on investment, determine the profit margin, investment turnover, and rate of return on investment for Division H for the past year.
2. Prepare condensed estimated income statements for Division H for each proposal.
3. Using the expanded expression for rate of return on investment, determine the profit margin, investment turnover, and rate of return on investment for Division H under each proposal.
4. Which of the three proposals would meet the required 18% rate of return on investment?
5. If Division H were in an industry where the profit margin could not be increased, how much would the investment turnover have to increase to meet the president's required 18% rate of return on investment?

PROBLEM 26-7A
DETERMINATION OF
MISSING ITEMS FROM
COMPUTATIONS
Objective 5

Data for Divisions A, B, C, D, and E of Mann Company are as follows:

	Sales	Operating Income	Invested Assets	Rate of Return on Investment	Profit Margin	Investment Turnover
Division A	$ 600,000	$ 60,000	$500,000	(a)	(b)	(c)
Division B	$1,080,000	(d)	$600,000	18%	(e)	(f)
Division C	(g)	$174,000	(h)	(i)	24%	1.25
Division D	$ 840,000	(j)	(k)	24%	20%	(l)
Division E	(m)	$ 75,600	$360,000	(n)	(o)	1.5

Instructions

1. Determine the missing items, identifying each by letters (a) through (o).
2. Determine the residual income for each division, assuming that the minimum rate of return established by management is 12%.
3. Which division is the most profitable?

PROBLEM 26-8A
DIVISIONAL
PERFORMANCE ANALYSIS
AND EVALUATION
Objective 5

SPREADSHEET
PROBLEM

The vice-president of operations of Guerra Company is evaluating the performance of two divisions organized as investment centers. Division Y has the highest rate of return on investment, but generates the smallest amount of operating income. Division A generates the largest operating income, but has the lowest rate of return on investment. Invested assets and condensed income statement data for the past year for each division are as follows:

	Division A	Division Y
Sales	$3,400,000	$3,840,000
Cost of goods sold	2,000,000	2,496,000
Operating expenses	801,600	768,000
Invested assets	2,720,000	2,400,000

Instructions

1. Prepare condensed divisional income statements for each division for the year ended July 31.
2. Using the expanded expression for rate of return on investment, determine the profit margin, investment turnover, and rate of return on investment for each division.

3. If management desires a minimum rate of return of 16%, determine the residual income for each division.

4. Discuss the evaluation of Divisions A and Y, using the performance measures determined in (1), (2), and (3).

PROBLEM 26-9A
DIVISIONAL
PERFORMANCE ANALYSIS
AND EVALUATION
Objective 5

The vice-president of operations of Swann Inc. recently resigned, and the president is considering which one of two division managers to promote to the vacated position. Both division managers have been with the company approximately ten years. Operating data for each division for the past three years are as follows:

	1994	1993	1992
Division A:			
Sales	$ 770,000	$ 650,000	$ 600,000
Cost of goods sold	462,000	390,000	360,000
Gross profit	$ 308,000	$ 260,000	$ 240,000
Operating expenses	200,200	175,500	163,200
Operating income	$ 107,800	$ 84,500	$ 76,800
Invested assets	$ 550,000	$ 500,000	$ 480,000
Total industry sales	$5,500,000	$5,200,000	$5,000,000
Division B:			
Sales	$ 966,000	$ 840,000	$ 750,000
Cost of goods sold	670,000	588,000	525,000
Gross profit	$ 296,000	$ 252,000	$ 225,000
Operating expenses	151,100	117,600	105,000
Operating income	$ 144,900	$ 134,400	$ 120,000
Invested assets	$ 700,000	$ 600,000	$ 500,000
Total industry sales	$6,440,000	$4,800,000	$3,750,000

Instructions

1. Using the expanded expression for rate of return on investment, determine the profit margin, investment turnover, and rate of return on investment for each division for each of the three years.
2. Assuming that 15% has been established as a minimum rate of return, determine the residual income for each division for each of the three years.
3. Determine each division's market share (division sales divided by total industry sales) for each of the three years.

4. Based on (1), (2), and (3), which division manager would you recommend for promotion to vice-president of operations?

5. What other factors should be considered in the promotion decision?

PROBLEM 26-10A
TRANSFER PRICING
Objective 6

Grant Company is diversified, with two operating divisions, F and G. Condensed divisional income statements, which involve no intracompany transfers and which include a breakdown of expenses into variable and fixed components, are as follows:

Grant Company
Divisional Income Statements
For Year Ended December 31, 19—

	Division F	Division G	Total
Sales:			
120,000 units × $40 per unit	$4,800,000		$4,800,000
40,000 units × $50 per unit		$2,000,000	2,000,000
			$6,800,000
Expenses:			
Variable:			
120,000 units × $24 per unit	$2,880,000		$2,880,000
40,000 units × $32* per unit		$1,280,000	1,280,000
Fixed	920,000	520,000	1,440,000
Total expenses	$3,800,000	$1,800,000	$5,600,000
Operating income	$1,000,000	$ 200,000	$1,200,000

*$28 of the $32 per unit represents materials costs, and the remaining $4 per unit represents other expenses incurred within Division G.

Division F is operating at two-thirds of capacity of 180,000 units. Materials used in producing Division G's product are currently purchased from outside suppliers at a price of $28 per unit. The materials used by Division G are produced by Division F. Except for the possible transfer of materials between divisions, no changes are expected in sales and expenses.

Instructions

1. Would the market price of $28 per unit be an appropriate transfer price for Grant Company? Explain.
2. If Division G purchases 40,000 units from Division F and a transfer price of $26 per unit is negotiated between the managers of Divisions F and G, how much would the operating income of each division and total company operating income increase?
3. Prepare condensed divisional income statements for Grant Company, based on the data in (2).
4. If a transfer price of $27 per unit is negotiated, how much would the operating income of each division and total company income increase?
5. a. What is the range of possible negotiated transfer prices that would be acceptable for Grant Company?
   b. Assuming that the division managers of F and G cannot agree on a transfer price, what price would you suggest as the transfer price?

Series B

PROBLEM 26-1B
DECISION ON
DISCONTINUANCE OF
DEPARTMENT
Objective 4

C. M. Lyle Company is considering discontinuance of one of its fourteen departments. If operations in Department 6 are discontinued, it is estimated that the indirect operating expenses and the level of operations in the other departments will not be affected.

Data from the income statement for the past year ended August 31, which is considered to be a typical year, are as follows:

	Department 6		Other Departments	
Sales		$68,000		$981,000
Cost of goods sold		44,200		588,600
Gross profit		$23,800		$392,400
Operating expenses:				
Direct expenses	$18,400		$208,000	
Indirect expenses	9,500	27,900	114,000	322,000
Income (loss) before income tax		$(4,100)		$ 70,400

Instructions

1. Prepare an estimated income statement for the current year ending August 31, assuming the discontinuance of Department 6.
2. On the basis of the data presented, would it be advisable to retain Department 6? Explain.

PROBLEM 26-2B
DEPARTMENTAL INCOME
STATEMENT THROUGH
DEPARTMENTAL MARGIN
Objective 4

Ross Department Store has 18 departments. Department 16 and Department 17, which were established about twenty months ago on a trial basis, have the least sales volume. The board of directors believes that it is now time to consider the retention or the termination of these two departments. The following condensed trial balance was prepared as of May 31, the end of the first month of the current fiscal year. May is considered to be a typical month. The income tax accrual has no bearing on the decision and is excluded from consideration.

Current Assets	333,200	
Plant Assets	642,700	
Accumulated Depreciation—Plant Assets		252,810
Current Liabilities		190,920
Common Stock		100,000
Retained Earnings		291,860
Cash Dividends	15,000	
Sales—Department 16		31,900
Sales—Department 17		24,200
Sales—Other Departments		861,500
Cost of Goods Sold—Department 16	22,330	
Cost of Goods Sold—Department 17	15,730	
Cost of Goods Sold—Other Departments	516,900	

Direct Expenses—Department 16	11,450	
Direct Expenses—Department 17	4,820	
Direct Expenses—Other Departments	126,760	
Indirect Expenses	58,300	
Interest Expense	6,000	
	1,753,190	1,753,190

Instructions

1. Prepare an income statement for May, departmentalized through departmental margin.
2. State your recommendations for retaining or discontinuing of Departments 16 and 17, and give reasons for your answer.

SHARPEN YOUR COMMUNICATION SKILLS

PROBLEM 26-3B
DEPARTMENTAL INCOME STATEMENT THROUGH DEPARTMENTAL MARGIN
Objective 4

Munoz Corporation consists of two departments, L and M. The bases to be used in apportioning expenses between the two departments, together with other essential data, are as follows:

a. Sales salaries and commissions expense—basic salary plus 5% of sales. Basic salaries for Department L, $40,800; Department M, $18,200.
b. Advertising expense for brochures—usage within each department advertising specific products: Department L, $9,685; Department M, $4,065.
c. Depreciation expense—average cost of store equipment: Department L, $60,500; Department M, $49,500.
d. Insurance expense—average cost of store equipment plus average cost of inventories. Average cost of inventories was $53,250 for Department L and $11,750 for Department M.
e. Uncollectible accounts expense—0.4% of sales. Departmental managers are responsible for the granting of credit on the sales made by their respective departments.

The following data are obtained from the ledger on December 31, the end of the current fiscal year:

Sales—Department L		550,000
Sales—Department M		220,000
Cost of Goods Sold—Department L	357,500	
Cost of Goods Sold—Department M	145,200	
Sales Salaries and Commissions Expense	97,500	
Advertising Expense	13,750	
Depreciation Expense—Store Equipment	9,500	
Miscellaneous Selling Expense	1,195	
Administrative Salaries Expense	32,000	
Rent Expense	18,300	
Utilities Expense	12,000	
Insurance Expense	4,800	
Uncollectible Accounts Expense	3,080	
Miscellaneous Administrative Expense	745	
Interest Income		5,000
Income Tax	23,800	

Instructions

1. Prepare an income statement departmentalized through departmental margin.
2. Determine the rate of gross profit for each department.
3. Determine the rate of departmental margin to sales for each department.

PROBLEM 26-4B
DEPARTMENTAL INCOME STATEMENT THROUGH INCOME FROM OPERATIONS
Objective 4

Mesa Co. operates two sales departments—Department A for small appliances such as radios and televisions, and Department L for large appliances, such as refrigerators and washing machines. The following trial balance was prepared as of October 31, the end of the current fiscal year, after all adjustments, including those for inventories, were recorded and posted:

Cash	26,880
Accounts Receivable	39,500
Inventories—Department A	12,240
Inventories—Department L	42,760
Prepaid Insurance	1,360

Store Supplies	1,330	
Store Equipment	55,320	
Accumulated Depreciation—Store Equipment		12,750
Accounts Payable		10,600
Income Tax Payable		3,310
Common Stock		40,000
Retained Earnings		28,340
Cash Dividends	16,000	
Income Summary	65,000	55,000
Sales—Department A		280,000
Sales—Department L		520,000
Sales Returns and Allowances—Department A	2,800	
Sales Returns and Allowances—Department L	4,200	
Purchases—Department A	168,000	
Purchases—Department L	338,000	
Sales Salaries Expense	33,900	
Advertising Expense	12,090	
Depreciation Expense—Store Equipment	6,200	
Store Supplies Expense	1,620	
Miscellaneous Selling Expense	2,600	
Office Salaries Expense	30,000	
Rent Expense	12,000	
Heating and Lighting Expense	10,200	
Property Tax Expense	3,800	
Insurance Expense	1,800	
Uncollectible Accounts Expense	1,500	
Miscellaneous Administrative Expense	1,700	
Interest Expense	1,250	
Income Tax	57,950	
	950,000	950,000

Inventories at the beginning of the year were as follows: Department A, $15,600; Department L, $49,400.

The bases to be used in apportioning expenses, together with other essential information, are as follows:

a. Sales salaries expense—payroll records: Department A, $11,800; Department L, $22,100.
b. Advertising expense—usage: Department A, $4,330; Department L, $7,760.
c. Depreciation expense—average cost of equipment. Equipment balances at beginning of year: Department A, $19,360; Department L, $29,320. Equipment balances at end of year: Department A, $22,240; Department L, $33,080.
d. Store supplies expense—requisitions: Department A, $500; Department L, $1,120.
e. Office salaries expense—Department A, 32%; Department L, 68%.
f. Rent expense and heating and lighting expense—floor space: Department A, 4,200 sq. ft.; Department L, 10,800 sq. ft.
g. Property tax expense and insurance expense—average cost of equipment plus average cost of inventories.
h. Uncollectible accounts expense, miscellaneous selling expense, and miscellaneous administrative expense—volume of gross sales.

SPREADSHEET PROBLEM

Instructions
Prepare an income statement departmentalized through income from operations.

PROBLEM 26-5B
DIVISIONAL INCOME
STATEMENTS AND RATE OF
RETURN ON INVESTMENT
ANALYSIS
Objective 5

Temple Company is a diversified company with three operating divisions organized as investment centers. Condensed data taken from the records of the three divisions for the year ended June 30 are as follows:

	Division 1	Division 2	Division 3
Sales	$1,100,000	$1,500,000	$1,800,000
Cost of goods sold	675,000	975,000	1,350,000
Operating expenses	293,000	345,000	252,000
Invested assets	880,000	1,000,000	1,200,000

The management of Temple Company is evaluating each division as a basis for planning a future expansion of operations.

SPREADSHEET
PROBLEM

SHARPEN YOUR
COMMUNICATION SKILLS

PROBLEM 26-6B
EFFECT OF PROPOSALS ON
DIVISIONAL
PERFORMANCE
Objective 5

Instructions

1. Prepare condensed divisional income statements for Divisions 1, 2, and 3.
2. Using the expanded expression for rate of return on investment, compute the profit margin, investment turnover, and rate of return on investment for each division.
3. If available funds permit the expansion of operations of only one division, which of the divisions would you recommend for expansion, based on (1) and (2)? Explain.

A condensed income statement for Division D of Mullins Company for the year ended May 31 is as follows:

Sales	$2,400,000
Cost of goods sold	1,480,000
Gross profit	$ 920,000
Operating expenses	620,000
Operating income	$ 300,000

The president of Mullins Company is concerned with Division D's rate of return on invested assets of $2,000,000, and has indicated that the division's rate of return on investment must be increased to at least 18% by the end of the next year if operations are to continue. The division manager is considering the following three proposals:

Proposal 1: Transfer equipment with a book value of $400,000 to other divisions at no gain or loss and lease similar equipment. The annual lease payments would exceed the amount of depreciation expense on the old equipment by $16,800. This increase in expense would be included as part of the cost of goods sold. Sales would remain unchanged.

Proposal 2: Reduce invested assets by discontinuing a product line. This action would eliminate sales of $150,000, cost of goods sold of $120,000, and operating expenses of $45,000. Assets of $200,000 would be transferred to other divisions at no gain or loss.

Proposal 3: Purchase new and more efficient machinery and thereby reduce the cost of goods sold by $134,400. Sales would remain unchanged, and the old machinery, which has no remaining book value, would be scrapped at no gain or loss. The new machinery would increase invested assets by $400,000 for the year.

Instructions

1. Using the expanded expression for rate of return on investment, determine the profit margin, investment turnover, and rate of return on investment for Division D for the past year.
2. Prepare condensed estimated income statements for Division D for each proposal.
3. Using the expanded expression for rate of return on investment, determine the profit margin, investment turnover, and rate of return on investment for Division D under each proposal.
4. Which of the three proposals would meet the required 18% rate of return on investment?
5. If Division D were in an industry where the profit margin could not be increased, how much would the investment turnover have to increase to meet the president's required 18% rate of return on investment?

PROBLEM 26-7B
DETERMINATION OF
MISSING ITEMS FROM
COMPUTATIONS
Objective 5

Data for Divisions A, B, C, D, and E of Sweeney Company are as follows:

	Sales	Operating Income	Invested Assets	Rate of Return on Investment	Profit Margin	Investment Turnover
Division A	$800,000	$120,000	$400,000	(a)	(b)	(c)
Division B	(d)	(e)	$600,000	12%	(f)	1.25
Division C	$420,000	(g)	(h)	(i)	15%	1.2
Division D	$375,000	(j)	(k)	(l)	16%	1.25
Division E	(m)	$ 88,000	(n)	22%	11%	(o)

Instructions

1. Determine the missing items, identifying each by letters (a) through (o).
2. Determine the residual income for each division, assuming that the minimum rate of return established by management is 10%.
3. Which division is the most profitable?

PROBLEM 26-8B
DIVISIONAL
PERFORMANCE ANALYSIS
AND EVALUATION
Objective 5

The vice-president of operations of Ramos Company is evaluating the performance of two divisions organized as investment centers. Division Y generates the largest amount of operating income but has the lowest rate of return on investment. Division X has the highest rate of return on investment but generates the smallest operating income. Invested assets and condensed income statement data for the past year for each division are as follows:

	Division X	Division Y
Sales	$4,500,000	$6,750,000
Cost of goods sold	2,700,000	4,320,000
Operating expenses	1,080,000	1,620,000
Invested assets	3,600,000	4,500,000

SPREADSHEET
PROBLEM

SHARPEN YOUR
COMMUNICATION SKILLS

Instructions

1. Prepare condensed divisional income statements for each division for the year ended December 31.
2. Using the expanded expression for rate of return on investment, determine the profit margin, investment turnover, and rate of return on investment for each division.
3. If management desires a minimum rate of return of 12%, determine the residual income for each division.
4. Discuss the evaluation of Divisions X and Y, using the performance measures determined in (1), (2), and (3).

PROBLEM 26-9B
DIVISIONAL
PERFORMANCE ANALYSIS
AND EVALUATION
Objective 5

The vice-president of operations of Hood Inc. recently resigned, and the president is considering which one of two division managers to promote to the vacated position. Both division managers have been with the company approximately ten years. Operating data for each division for the past three years are as follows:

	1994	1993	1992
Division B:			
Sales	$ 1,520,000	$ 1,360,000	$ 1,200,000
Cost of goods sold	900,000	800,000	720,000
Gross profit	$ 620,000	$ 560,000	$ 480,000
Operating expenses	460,400	410,400	345,600
Operating income	$ 159,600	$ 149,600	$ 134,400
Invested assets	$ 950,000	$ 800,000	$ 600,000
Total industry sales	$15,200,000	$10,880,000	$ 8,000,000
Division C:			
Sales	$ 900,000	$ 770,000	$ 500,000
Cost of goods sold	540,000	460,000	300,000
Gross profit	$ 360,000	$ 310,000	$ 200,000
Operating expenses	216,000	194,500	128,000
Operating income	$ 144,000	$ 115,500	$ 72,000
Invested assets	$ 600,000	$ 550,000	$ 400,000
Total industry sales	$11,250,000	$11,000,000	$10,000,000

Instructions

1. Using the expanded expression for rate of return on investment, determine the profit margin, investment turnover, and rate of return on investment for each division for each of the three years.
2. Assuming that 15% has been established as a minimum rate of return, determine the residual income for each division for each of the three years.
3. Determine each division's market share (division sales divided by total industry sales) for each of the three years.

SHARPEN YOUR
COMMUNICATION SKILLS
4. Based on (1), (2), and (3), which division manager would you recommend for promotion to vice-president of operations?
SHARPEN YOUR
COMMUNICATION SKILLS
5. What other factors should be considered in the promotion decision?

PROBLEM 26-10B
TRANSFER PRICING
Objective 6

Demars Company is diversified, with two operating divisions, X and Y. Condensed divisional income statements, which involve no intracompany transfers and which include a breakdown of expenses into variable and fixed components, are as follows:

Demars Company
Divisional Income Statements
For Year Ended December 31, 19—

	Division X	Division Y	Total
Sales:			
150,000 units x $60 per unit	$9,000,000		$ 9,000,000
50,000 units x $80 per unit		$4,000,000	4,000,000
			$13,000,000
Expenses:			
Variable:			
150,000 units x $30 per unit	$4,500,000		$ 4,500,000
50,000 units x $50* per unit		$2,500,000	2,500,000
Fixed	3,000,000	1,000,000	4,000,000
Total expenses	$7,500,000	$3,500,000	$11,000,000
Operating income	$1,500,000	$ 500,000	$ 2,000,000

*$40 of the $50 per unit represents materials costs, and the remaining $10 per unit represents other expenses incurred within Division Y.

Division X is operating at three-fourths of capacity of 200,000 units. Materials used in producing Division Y's product are currently purchased from outside suppliers at a price of $40 per unit. The materials used by Division Y are produced by Division X. Except for the possible transfer of materials between divisions, no changes are expected in sales and expenses.

Instructions

SHARPEN YOUR
COMMUNICATION SKILLS
1. Would the market price of $40 per unit be an appropriate transfer price for Demars Company? Explain.
SHARPEN YOUR
COMMUNICATION SKILLS
2. If Division Y purchases 50,000 units from Division X and a transfer price of $35 per unit is negotiated between the managers of Divisions X and Y, how much would the operating income of each division and total company operating income increase?
3. Prepare condensed divisional income statements for Demars Company, based on the data in (2).
SHARPEN YOUR
COMMUNICATION SKILLS
4. If a transfer price of $34 per unit is negotiated, how much would the operating income of each division and total company income increase?
SHARPEN YOUR
COMMUNICATION SKILLS
5. a. What is the range of possible negotiated transfer prices that would be acceptable for Demars Company?
   b. Assuming that the division managers of X and Y cannot agree on a transfer price, what price would you suggest as the transfer price?

MINI-CASE 26 VINCENT COMPANY

Your father is the president of Vincent Company, a privately held, diversified company with five separate divisions organized as investment centers. A condensed income statement for the Sporting Goods Division for the past year is as follows:

Vincent Company—Sporting Goods Division
Income Statement
For Year Ended December 31, 19—

Sales	$18,000,000
Cost of goods sold	12,500,000
Gross profit	$ 5,500,000
Operating expenses	1,900,000
Operating income	$ 3,600,000

The manager of the Sporting Goods Division was recently presented with the opportunity to add an additional product line, which would require invested assets of $5,000,000. A projected income statement for the new product line is as follows:

New Product Line
Projected Income Statement
For Year Ended December 31, 19—

Sales	$5,000,000
Cost of goods sold	3,500,000
Gross profit	$1,500,000
Operating expenses	600,000
Operating income	$ 900,000

The Sporting Goods Division currently has $15,000,000 in invested assets, and Vincent Company's overall rate of return on investment, including all divisions, is 15%. Each division manager is evaluated on the basis of divisional rate of return on investment, and a bonus equal to $5,000 for each percentage point by which the division's rate of return on investment exceeds the company average is awarded each year.

Your father is concerned that the manager of the Sporting Goods Division rejected the addition of the new product line, when all estimates indicated that the product line would be profitable and would increase overall company income. You have been asked to analyze the possible reasons why the Sporting Goods Division manager rejected the new product line.

Instructions:

1. Determine the rate of return on investment for the Sporting Goods Division for the past year.
2. Determine the Sporting Goods Division manager's bonus for the past year.
3. Determine the estimated rate of return on investment for the new product line.
4. ▪▪▪ ▸Why might the manager of the Sporting Goods Division decide to reject the new product line?
5. ▪▪▪ ▸Can you suggest an alternative performance measure for motivating division managers to accept new investment opportunities that would increase the overall company income and rate of return on investment?

ANSWERS TO SELF-EXAMINATION QUESTIONS

1. **B** The manager of a profit center (answer B) has responsibility for and authority over costs and revenues. If the manager has responsibility for only costs, the department is called a cost center (answer A). If the responsibility and authority extend to the investment in assets as well as costs and revenues, it is called an investment center (answer C). A service center (answer D) provides services to other departments. A service center could be a cost center, profit center, or investment center.
2. **C** When the departmental margin approach to income reporting is used, the direct departmental expenses for each department are deducted from the gross profit for each department to yield departmental margin (answer C). The indirect expenses are deducted from the total departmental margin to yield income from operations (answer A). The final total income is identified as net income (answer B). Contribution margin (answer D) is the sales less variable expenses.
3. **A** The rate of return on investment for Division A is 20% (answer A), computed as follows:

$$\text{Rate of Return on Investment (ROI)} = \frac{\text{Operating Income}}{\text{Invested Assets}}$$

$$\text{ROI} = \frac{\$350,000 - \$200,000 - \$30,000}{\$600,000}$$

$$\text{ROI} = \frac{\$120,000}{\$600,000} = 20\%$$

4. **B** The profit margin for Division L of Liddy Co. is 15% (answer B), computed as follows:

$$\text{Rate of Return on Investment (ROI)} = \text{Profit Margin} \times \text{Investment Turnover}$$

$$24\% = \text{Profit Margin} \times 1.6$$

$$15\% = \text{Profit Margin}$$

5. **C** The market price approach (answer C) to transfer pricing uses the price at which the product or service transferred could be sold to outside buyers. The cost price approach (answer A) uses cost as the basis for setting transfer prices. The negotiated price approach (answer B) allows managers of decentralized units to agree (negotiate) among themselves as to the proper transfer price. The standard cost approach (answer D) is a version of the cost price approach that uses standard costs in setting transfer prices.

Part 9

Decision Making

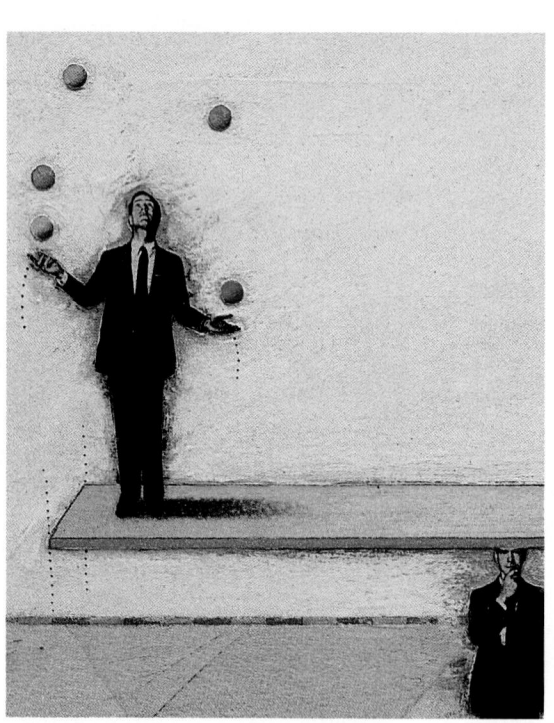

You and Accounting

Most of us will buy an automobile at some time. But rather than buying a car, would it be better to lease one?

To answer this question, you need to carefully consider the costs of owning the car versus the costs of leasing the car. For example, if you own the car, you will need to pay the license fees, insurance, and maintenance and repair costs. How many of these costs you need to pay to lease the car depends upon the specific lease contract. For example, the lease contract may require you to purchase a minimum amount of liability insurance. The lease contract will also require a monthly payment. In addition, if you drive the car more than a maximum number of miles (for example, 15,000 miles per year), you may be charged an additional cost per mile. Finally, whether you intend to keep the car or trade it in after three or four years may affect your decision.

The decision to buy or lease a car depends upon a comparison of the estimated costs of each alternative. Business enterprises make similar types of decisions. This chapter discusses the use of differential analysis in business decision making. This type of analysis may also be useful to you in making decisions that affect your everyday life.

Chapter 27
Differential Analysis and Product Pricing

A primary objective of accounting is to provide management with analyses and reports for planning and controlling operations. Depending upon the decisions to be made, the types of analyses and reports will differ. However, all decisions require managers to consider the effects of alternative decisions on the operating results of the enterprise.

This chapter discusses differential analysis, which provides reports on the effects of alternative decisions on total revenues and costs. The chapter also describes and illustrates practical approaches used by managers in setting product prices. The relationship of economic theory to these product pricing approaches is also discussed. Finally, the alternative price strategies used by management during a product's life cycle are discussed.

Objective 1
Prepare a differential analysis report for decisions involving:

Leasing or selling equipment
Discontinuing an unprofitable segment
Manufacturing or purchasing a needed part
Replacing usable plant assets
Processing further or selling an intermediate product
Accepting additional business at a special price.

DIFFERENTIAL ANALYSIS

Planning for future operations is chiefly decision making. For some decisions, revenue and cost data taken from the general ledger and other accounting records may be useful. However, the revenue and cost data needed to evaluate courses of future operations or to choose among competing alternatives are often not available in the basic records.

The relevant revenue and cost data used in analyzing alternatives focus on the differences between the alternatives being considered. The amounts of such differences are called **differentials**.

Differential revenue is the amount of increase or decrease in revenue expected from a course of action as compared with an alternative. To illustrate, assume that certain equipment is being used to manufacture Product M, which provides revenue of $150,000. If the equipment could be used to make Product T, which would provide revenue of $175,000, the differential revenue from making and selling Product T is $25,000.

Differential cost is the amount of increase or decrease in cost that is expected from a particular course of action as compared with an alternative. For example, if an increase in advertising expenditures from $100,000 to $150,000 is being considered, the differential cost of the action is $50,000.

Differential analysis focuses on the effect of alternative courses of action on the relevant revenues and costs. Differential analysis thus emphasizes the significant factors affecting a decision, clarifies the issues, and saves the time of the decision maker. It can aid management in making decisions on a variety of alternatives, including the following:

1. Leasing or selling equipment
2. Discontinuing an unprofitable segment
3. Manufacturing or purchasing a needed part
4. Replacing usable plant assets
5. Processing further or selling an intermediate product
6. Accepting additional business at a special price

The following paragraphs discuss the use of differential analysis in analyzing these alternatives.

Lease or Sell

Management may have a choice between leasing or selling a piece of equipment that is no longer needed in the business. In deciding which option is best, management may use differential analysis. To illustrate, assume that Marcus Company is considering disposing of equipment that cost $200,000 and has $120,000 of accumulated depreciation to date. Marcus Company can sell the equipment through a broker for $100,000 less a 6% commission. Alternatively, Potamkin Company (the lessee) has offered to lease the equipment for five years for a total of $160,000. At the end of the fifth year of the lease, the equipment is expected to have no residual value. During the period of the lease, Marcus Company (the lessor) will incur repair, insurance, and property tax expenses estimated at $35,000. Marcus Company's analysis of whether to lease or sell the equipment is shown in Exhibit 1.

In Exhibit 1, the $80,000 book value ($200,000 − $120,000) of the equipment was not considered. The $80,000 is a **sunk cost**; that is, it is a cost that will not be affected by later decisions. In other words, Marcus Company had already made the decision to acquire the equipment. The decision being considered now is between leasing or selling the equipment. The relevant factors to be considered are the differential revenues and differential costs associated with the lease or sell decision. The undepreciated cost of the equipment is irrelevant.

Exhibit 1
Differential Analysis Report—
Lease or Sell

Proposal To Lease or Sell Equipment June 22, 1994		
Differential revenue from alternatives:		
Revenue from lease	$160,000	
Revenue from sales	100,000	
Differential revenue from lease		$60,000
Differential cost of alternatives:		
Repair, insurance, and property tax expenses	$ 35,000	
Commission expense on sale	6,000	
Differential cost of lease		29,000
Net advantage of lease alternative		$31,000

    The validity of the report in Exhibit 1 is shown by the traditional analysis in Exhibit 2.

Exhibit 2
Traditional Analysis

Lease or Sell			
Lease alternative:			
Revenue from lease		$160,000	
Depreciation expense	$80,000		
Repair, insurance, and property tax expenses	35,000	115,000	
Net gain			$45,000
Sell alternative:			
Sales price		$100,000	
Book value of equipment	$80,000		
Commission expense	6,000	86,000	
Net gain			14,000
Net advantage of lease alternative			$31,000

    The alternatives presented in Exhibits 1 and 2 were relatively uncomplicated. Regardless of the complexity, the approach to differential analysis is essentially the same. Two additional factors that often need to be considered are (1) differential revenue from investing the funds generated by the alternatives and (2) any income tax differential. In Exhibit 1, there could be differential revenue related to the investment of the $94,000 net proceeds ($100,000 − $6,000) from the sale over the investment of the yearly net proceeds from the lease arrangement. Any income tax differential would be related to the differences in timing of the income from the alternatives and the differences in the amount of investment income.

Discontinue a Segment or Product

When a product or a department, branch, territory, or other segment of an enterprise is generating losses, management may consider eliminating the product or segment. It is often assumed, sometimes in error, that the total operating income of an enterprise would be increased if the operating loss could be eliminated. Discontinuing the product or segment usually eliminates all of the product or segment's variable costs (direct materials, direct labor, sales commissions, etc.). However, if the product or segment is a relatively small part of the enterprise, the fixed costs (depreciation, insurance, property taxes, etc.) may not be decreased by its discontinuance. It is possible in this case for the *total* operating income of a company to decrease rather than increase by eliminating the product or segment. To illustrate, the income statement for Mandel Inc. presented in Exhibit 3 is for a normal year ending August 31, 1994.

    Because Product A incurs annual losses, management is considering its discontinuance. An increase in annual operating income to $80,000 (Product B,

Exhibit 3
Income (Loss) by Product

Mandel Inc. Condensed Income Statement For Year Ended August 31, 1994				
	Product			
	A	B	C	Total
Sales	$100,000	$400,000	$500,000	$1,000,000
Cost of goods sold:				
Variable costs	$ 60,000	$200,000	$220,000	$ 480,000
Fixed costs	20,000	80,000	120,000	220,000
Total cost of goods sold	$ 80,000	$280,000	$340,000	$ 700,000
Gross profit	$ 20,000	$120,000	$160,000	$ 300,000
Less operating expenses:				
Variable expenses	$ 25,000	$ 60,000	$ 95,000	$ 180,000
Fixed expenses	6,000	20,000	25,000	51,000
Total operating expenses	$ 31,000	$ 80,000	$120,000	$ 231,000
Income (loss) from operations	$ (11,000)	$ 40,000	$ 40,000	$ 69,000

$40,000; Product C, $40,000) might seem to be indicated by the income statement in Exhibit 3 if Product A is discontinued.

Discontinuing Product A, however, would actually decrease operating income, by $15,000 to $54,000 ($69,000 – $15,000). This is shown by the differential analysis report in Exhibit 4, which assumes that discontinuing Product A would have no effect on fixed costs and expenses.

Exhibit 4
Differential Analysis Report—
Discontinue an Unprofitable
Segment

Proposal To Discontinue Product A September 29, 1994		
Differential revenue from annual sales of product:		
Revenue from sales		$100,000
Differential cost of annual sales of product:		
Variable cost of goods sold	$60,000	
Variable operating expenses	25,000	85,000
Annual differential income from sales of Product A		$ 15,000

The validity of the preceding differential analysis is shown by the traditional analysis in Exhibit 5.

Exhibit 5
Traditional Analysis

Proposal To Discontinue Product A September 29, 1994				
	Current Operations			
	Product A	Products B and C	Total	Discontinuance of Product A
Sales	$100,000	$900,000	$1,000,000	$900,000
Cost of goods sold:				
Variable costs	$ 60,000	$420,000	$ 480,000	$420,000
Fixed costs	20,000	200,000	220,000	220,000
Total cost of goods sold	$ 80,000	$620,000	$ 700,000	$640,000
Gross profit	$ 20,000	$280,000	$ 300,000	$260,000
Operating expenses:				
Variable expenses	$ 25,000	$155,000	$ 180,000	$155,000
Fixed expenses	6,000	45,000	51,000	51,000
Total operating expenses	$ 31,000	$200,000	$ 231,000	$206,000
Income (loss) from operations	$ (11,000)	$ 80,000	$ 69,000	$ 54,000

In Exhibit 5, only the short-term (one year) effects of discontinuing Product A were considered. In decisions involving the elimination of a product or segment, management should also consider the long-term effects. For example, the plant capacity made available by discontinuing Product A might be eliminated. This could reduce fixed costs. Some employees may have to be laid off, and others may have to be relocated and retrained. Also, there may be a related decrease in sales of more profitable products to those customers who were attracted by the discontinued product.

Make or Buy

The assembly of many parts is often a major element in manufacturing some products, such as automobiles. These parts may be made by the product's manufacturer, or they may be purchased. For example, some of the parts for an automobile, such as the motor, may be produced by the automobile manufacturer. Other parts, such as tires, may be purchased from other manufacturers. In addition, in manufacturing motors, such items as spark plugs and nuts and bolts may be acquired from suppliers.

Management uses differential costs to decide whether to make or buy a part or component. For example, if a part is purchased, management has concluded that it is less costly to buy the part than to manufacture it. Make or buy options often arise when a manufacturer has excess productive capacity in the form of unused equipment, space, and labor.

The differential analysis is similar, whether management is considering making a part that is currently being purchased or purchasing a part that is currently being made. To illustrate, assume that a manufacturer has been purchasing a component, Part X, for $5 a unit. The factory is currently operating at 80% of capacity, and no major increase in production is expected in the near future. The cost per unit of manufacturing Part X, including fixed costs, is estimated as follows:

Direct materials	$1
Direct labor	2
Factory overhead (150% of direct labor cost)	3
Total cost per unit	$6

If the *make* price of $6 is simply compared with the *buy* price of $5, the decision is to buy the part. However, if unused capacity could be used in manufacturing the part, there would be no increase in the total amount of fixed factory overhead costs. Thus, only the variable factory overhead costs need to be considered. Assume that variable factory overhead costs, such as power and maintenance, are estimated at $1.30 per unit. The relevant costs are summarized in the differential report in Exhibit 6.

Exhibit 6
Differential Analysis Report—
Make or Buy

Proposal To Manufacture Part X February 15, 1994		
Purchase price of part		$5.00
Differential cost to manufacture part:		
Direct materials	$1.00	
Direct labor	2.00	
Variable factory overhead	1.30	4.30
Cost reduction from manufacturing Part X		$ .70

Other possible effects of a decision to manufacture the part should also be considered. For example, one consideration is that an increase in production in the future might require the use of the currently idle capacity. The possible effect of decisions on employees and on future business relations with the supplier of Part X should also be considered. For example, the supplier of Part X may also provide other essential components that cannot be readily manufactured within the company. A decision to manufacture Part X might jeopardize the timely delivery of these other essential parts.

Replace Equipment

The usefulness of plant assets may be impaired long before they are considered to be worn out. Equipment may no longer be efficient for the purpose for which it is used. On the other hand, the equipment may not have reached the point of complete inadequacy. Decisions to replace usable plant assets should be based on studies of relevant costs. The relevant costs are the future costs of continued use of the equipment versus replacement. The book values of the plant assets being replaced are sunk costs and are irrelevant.

To illustrate, assume that an enterprise is considering the disposal of several identical machines having a total book value of $100,000 and an estimated remaining life of five years. The old machines can be sold for $25,000. They can be replaced by a single high-speed machine at a cost of $250,000. The new machine has an estimated useful life of five years and no residual value. Analyses indicate an estimated annual reduction in variable manufacturing costs from $225,000 to $150,000 with the new machine. No other changes in the manufacturing costs or the operating expenses are expected. The relevant costs are summarized in the differential report in Exhibit 7.

Exhibit 7
Differential Analysis Report—
Replace Equipment

Proposal To Replace Equipment November 28, 1994		
Annual variable costs—present equipment	$225,000	
Annual variable costs—new equipment	150,000	
Annual differential decrease in cost	$ 75,000	
Number of years applicable	× 5	
Total differential decrease in cost	$375,000	
Proceeds from sale of present equipment	25,000	$400,000
Cost of new equipment		250,000
Net differential decrease in cost, 5-year total		$150,000
Annual net differential decrease in cost—new equipment		$ 30,000

Additional factors are often involved in equipment replacement decisions. For example, differences between the remaining useful life of the old equipment and the estimated life of the new equipment could exist. In addition, the new equipment might improve the overall quality of the product, resulting in an increase in sales volume. Other factors that could be significant include the time value of money and other uses for the cash needed to purchase the new equipment.[1]

The amount of income that is forgone from an alternative use of cash is called **opportunity cost**. Although opportunity costs do not appear as a part of historical accounting data, they are useful in analyzing alternative courses of action. To illustrate, assume that the cash outlay of $250,000 for the new equipment, less the $25,000 proceeds from the sale of the present equipment, could be invested to yield a 10% return. Thus, the opportunity cost related to the purchase of the new equipment is $22,500 (10% × $225,000).

Process or Sell

When a product is manufactured, it progresses through various stages of production. Often a product can be sold at an intermediate stage of production, or it can

---

[1] The importance of the time value of money in equipment replacement decisions is discussed in another chapter.

be processed further and then sold. In deciding whether to sell a product at an intermediate stage or to process it further, differential analysis is useful. The differential revenues from further processing are compared to the differential costs of further processing. The costs of producing the intermediate product do not change, regardless of whether the intermediate product is sold or processed further. Thus, these costs are not differential costs and are irrelevant for the decision to process further.

To illustrate, assume that an enterprise produces Product Y in batches of 4,000 gallons. Standard quantities of 4,000 gallons of direct materials are processed, which cost $1.20 per gallon. Product Y can be sold without further processing for $2 per gallon. Product Y can be processed further to yield Product Z, which can be sold for $5 per gallon. Product Z requires additional processing costs of $5,760 per batch, and 20% of the gallons of Product Y will evaporate during production. The differential revenues and costs in deciding whether to process Product Y to produce Product Z are summarized in Exhibit 8.

Exhibit 8
Differential Analysis Report—
Process or Sell

Proposal To Process Product Y Further October 1, 1994		
Differential revenue from further processing per batch:		
Revenue from sale of Product Z [(4,000 gallons – 800 gallons evaporation) × $5]	$16,000	
Revenue from sale of Product Y (4,000 gallons × $2)	8,000	
Differential revenue		$8,000
Differential cost per batch:		
Additional cost of producing Product Z		5,760
Net advantage of further processing Product Y per batch		$2,240

The net advantage of further processing Product Y into Product Z is $2,240 per batch. The initial cost of producing the intermediate Product Y, $4,800 (4,000 gallons × $1.20), is not considered in deciding whether to process Product Y further. This initial cost will be incurred, regardless of whether Product Z is produced.

Accept Business at a Special Price

Differential analysis is also useful in deciding whether to accept additional business at a special price. The differential revenue that would be provided from the additional business is compared to the differential costs of producing and delivering the product to the customer. If the company is operating at full capacity, any additional production will increase both fixed and variable production costs. If, however, the normal production of the company is below full capacity, additional business may be undertaken without increasing fixed production costs. In this case, the differential costs of the additional production are the variable manufacturing costs. If operating expenses increase because of the additional business, these expenses should also be considered.

To illustrate, assume that the monthly capacity of an enterprise is 12,500 units of Product H. Current sales and production are averaging 10,000 units of Product H per month. The current manufacturing cost of $20 per unit consists of variable costs of $12.50 and fixed costs of $7.50. The normal selling price of the product in the domestic market is $30. The manufacturer receives an offer from an exporter for 5,000 units of the product at $18 each. Production can be spread over a three-month period without interfering with normal production or incurring overtime costs. Pricing policies in the domestic market will not be affected. A simple comparison of the sales price of $18 with the present unit manufacturing cost of $20 indicates that the offer should be rejected. However, by focusing only on the differential cost, which in this case is the variable cost, the decision is different. The differential analysis report for this decision is shown in Exhibit 9.

Proposal To Sell Product H to Exporter March 10, 1994	
Differential revenue from acceptance of offer:	
Revenue from sale of 5,000 additional units at $18	$90,000
Differential cost of acceptance of offer:	
Variable costs of 5,000 additional units at $12.50	62,500
Gain from acceptance of offer	$27,500

Proposals to sell a product in the domestic market at prices lower than the normal price may require additional considerations. For example, it may be unwise to increase sales volume in one territory by price reductions if sales volume is lost in other areas. Manufacturers must also conform to the Robinson-Patman Act, which prohibits price discrimination within the U.S., unless differences in prices can be justified by different costs of serving different customers.

SETTING NORMAL PRODUCT SELLING PRICES

Objective 2
Determine the selling price of a product, using the total cost, product cost, and variable cost concepts.

Differential analysis may be useful in deciding to lower selling prices for special short-run decisions, such as whether to accept business at a price lower than the normal price. In such cases, the minimum short-run price is set high enough to cover all variable costs. Any price above this minimum price will improve profits in the short run. In the long run, however, the normal selling price must be set high enough to cover all costs and expenses (both fixed and variable) and provide a reasonable profit. Otherwise, the enterprise may not survive.

The normal selling price can be viewed as the target selling price to be achieved in the long run. However, it may be deviated from in the short run because of such factors as competition and general market conditions. A practical approach to setting the normal price is the **cost-plus approach**. Using this approach, managers determine product prices by adding to a *cost* amount a *plus*, called a **markup**, so that all costs plus a profit are included in the selling price.

Three cost concepts often used in applying the cost-plus approach are: (1) total cost, (2) product cost, and (3) variable cost. Each of these cost concepts is described and illustrated in the following paragraphs.

Total Cost Concept

Using the **total cost concept**, all costs of manufacturing a product plus the selling and administrative expenses are included in the cost amount to which the markup is added. Since all costs and expenses are included in the cost amount, the dollar amount of the markup equals the desired profit.

The first step in applying the total cost concept is to determine the total cost of manufacturing the product. This cost, which includes the costs of direct materials, direct labor, and factory overhead, should be available from the accounting records that support the cost accounting system. The next step is to add the estimated selling and administrative expenses to the total cost of manufacturing the product. The cost amount per unit is then computed by dividing the total costs by the total units expected to be produced and sold.

After the cost amount per unit has been determined, the dollar amount of the markup is determined. For this purpose, the markup is expressed as a percentage of cost. This percentage is then multiplied by the cost amount per unit. The dollar amount of the markup is then added to the cost amount per unit to arrive at the selling price.

The markup percentage for the total cost concept is determined by applying the following formula:

$$\text{Markup Percentage} = \frac{\text{Desired Profit}}{\text{Total Costs}}$$

The numerator of the markup percentage formula includes only the desired profit. This is because all costs and expenses are included in the cost amount to which the markup is added. The denominator of the formula is the total costs.

To illustrate, assume that the costs for Product R of Pellit Co. are as follows:

Variable costs:
Direct materials	$ 3.00 per unit
Direct labor	10.00
Factory overhead	1.50
Selling and administrative expenses	1.50
Total	$16.00 per unit

Fixed costs:
Factory overhead	$50,000
Selling and administrative expenses	20,000

Pellit Co. desires a profit equal to a 20% rate of return on assets, $800,000 of assets are devoted to producing Product R, and 100,000 units are expected to be produced and sold. The cost amount for Product R is $1,670,000, or $16.70 per unit, computed as follows:

Variable costs ($16.00 × 100,000 units)		$1,600,000
Fixed costs:		
Factory overhead	$50,000	
Selling and administrative expenses	20,000	70,000
Total costs		$1,670,000
Cost amount per unit ($1,670,000 ÷ 100,000 units)		$16.70

The desired profit is $160,000 (20% x $800,000), and the markup percentage for Product R is 9.6%, computed as follows:

$$\text{Markup Percentage} = \frac{\text{Desired Profit}}{\text{Total Costs}}$$

$$\text{Markup Percentage} = \frac{\$160,000}{\$1,670,000} = 9.6\%$$

Based on the cost amount per unit and the markup percentage for Product R, Pellit Co. would price Product R at $18.30 per unit. The price computation is shown below.

Cost amount per unit	$16.70
Markup ($16.70 × 9.6%)	1.60
Selling price	$18.30

The ability of the selling price of $18.30 to generate the desired profit of $160,000 is verified by the following income statement:

Pellit Co.		
Income Statement		
For Year Ended December 31, 1994		
Sales (100,000 units × $18.30)		$1,830,000
Expenses:		
Variable (100,000 units × $16.00)	$1,600,000	
Fixed ($50,000 + $20,000)	70,000	1,670,000
Income from operations		$ 160,000

The total cost concept of applying the cost-plus approach to product pricing is often used by contractors who sell products to government agencies. In many cases, government contractors are required by law to be reimbursed for their products on a total-cost-plus-profit basis.

Product Cost Concept

Using the **product cost concept**, only the costs of manufacturing the product, termed the product cost, are included in the cost amount to which the markup is added. Estimated selling expenses, administrative expenses, and profit are included in the markup. The markup percentage is determined by applying the following formula:

$$\text{Markup Percentage} = \frac{\text{Desired Profit} + \text{Total Selling and Administrative Expenses}}{\text{Total Manufacturing Costs}}$$

The numerator of the markup percentage formula includes the desired profit plus the total selling and administrative expenses. Selling and administrative expenses must be included in the markup, since they are not included in the cost amount to which the markup is added. The denominator of the formula includes the costs of direct materials, direct labor, and factory overhead.

To illustrate, assume the same data used in the preceding illustration. The cost amount for Pellit Co.'s Product R is $1,500,000, or $15 per unit, computed as follows:

Direct materials ($3 × 100,000 units)		$ 300,000
Direct labor ($10 × 100,000 units)		1,000,000
Factory overhead:		
Variable ($1.50 × 100,000 units)	$150,000	
Fixed	50,000	200,000
Total manufacturing costs		$1,500,000
Cost amount per unit ($1,500,000 ÷ 100,000 units)		$15

The desired profit is $160,000 (20% × $800,000), and the total selling and administrative expenses are $170,000 [(100,000 units × $1.50 per unit) + $20,000]. The markup percentage for Product R is 22%, computed as follows:

$$\text{Markup Percentage} = \frac{\text{Desired Profit} + \text{Total Selling and Administrative Expenses}}{\text{Total Manufacturing Costs}}$$

$$\text{Markup Percentage} = \frac{\$160,000 + \$170,000}{\$1,500,000}$$

$$\text{Markup Percentage} = \frac{\$330,000}{\$1,500,000} = 22\%$$

Based on the cost amount per unit and the markup percentage for Product R, Pellit Co. would price Product R at $18.30 per unit. The price computation is shown below.

Cost amount per unit	$15.00
Markup ($15 × 22%)	3.30
Selling price	$18.30

Variable Cost Concept

Using the **variable cost concept**, only variable costs are included in the cost amount to which the markup is added. All variable manufacturing costs, as well as variable selling and administrative expenses, are included in the cost amount. Fixed manufacturing costs, fixed selling and administrative expenses, and profit are included in the markup.

The markup percentage is determined by applying the following formula:

$$\text{Markup Percentage} = \frac{\text{Desired Profit} + \text{Total Fixed Costs}}{\text{Total Variable Costs}}$$

The numerator of the markup percentage formula includes the desired profit plus the total fixed manufacturing costs and the total fixed selling and administrative expenses. Fixed manufacturing costs and fixed selling and administrative expenses must be included in the markup, since they are not included in the cost amount to which the markup is added. The denominator of the formula includes the total variable costs.

To illustrate, assume the same data used in the two preceding illustrations. The cost amount for Product R is $1,600,000, or $16.00 per unit, computed as follows:

Variable costs:	
Direct materials ($3 × 100,000 units)	$ 300,000
Direct labor ($10 × 100,000 units)	1,000,000
Factory overhead ($1.50 × 100,000 units)	150,000
Selling and administrative expenses ($1.50 × 100,000 units)	150,000
Total variable costs	$1,600,000
Cost amount per unit ($1,600,000 ÷ 100,000 units)	$16.00

The desired profit is $160,000 (20% × $800,000), the total fixed manufacturing costs are $50,000, and the total fixed selling and administrative expenses are $20,000. The markup percentage for Product R is 14.4%, computed as follows:

$$\text{Markup Percentage} = \frac{\text{Desired Profit} + \text{Total Fixed Costs}}{\text{Total Variable Costs}}$$

$$\text{Markup Percentage} = \frac{\$160,000 + \$50,000 + \$20,000}{\$1,600,000}$$

$$\text{Markup Percentage} = \frac{\$230,000}{\$1,600,000} = 14.4\%$$

Based on the cost amount per unit and the markup percentage for Product R, Pellit Co. would price Product R at $18.30 per unit. The price computation is shown below.

Cost amount per unit	$16.00
Markup ($16.00 × 14.4%)	2.30
Selling price	$18.30

The variable cost concept emphasizes the distinction between variable and fixed costs in product pricing.

Choosing a Cost-Plus Approach Cost Concept

The three cost concepts commonly used in applying the cost-plus approach to product pricing are summarized below.

Cost Concept	Covered in Cost Amount	Covered in Markup
Total cost	Total costs	Desired profit
Product cost	Total manufacturing costs	Desired profit + Total selling and administrative expenses
Variable cost	Total variable costs	Desired profit + Total fixed costs

All three cost concepts produced the same selling price ($18.30) for the Pellit Co. illustration. In practice, however, the three cost concepts are usually not viewed as alternatives. The following paragraphs discuss factors normally considered in choosing among the preceding cost concepts.

Each cost concept requires different estimates of costs and expenses. The complexity of the manufacturing operations and the difficulty of estimating costs and expenses should be considered in choosing a cost concept.

To reduce the costs of gathering data, estimated (standard) costs rather than actual costs may be used with any of the three cost concepts. However, management should exercise caution when using estimated costs in applying the cost-plus approach. The estimates should be based on normal (attainable) operating levels and not theoretical (ideal) levels of performance. In product pricing, the use of estimates based on ideal- or maximum-capacity operating levels might lead to setting product prices too low. In this case, the costs of such factors as normal spoilage or normal periods of idle time might not be considered.

The decision-making needs of management are also an important factor in selecting a cost concept for product pricing. For example, managers who often make special pricing decisions are more likely to use the variable cost concept. In contrast, a government defense contractor would be more likely to use the total cost concept.

A variation of the cost concepts discussed in the preceding paragraphs is the **target cost concept**. Under this concept, a product unit cost that will allow the company to compete effectively in the market and earn a normal profit is estimated. The product is then designed, manufactured, and sold to achieve this target cost. In effect, the target cost concept uses external market conditions as a basis for determining the acceptable level of costs, expenses, and prices. In contrast, the three cost concepts discussed rely primarily upon internal cost data in setting selling prices.

Activity-Based Costing

As illustrated in the preceding paragraphs, costs are an important consideration in setting product prices. To more accurately measure the costs of producing and selling products, some companies have implemented activity-based costing. **Activity-based costing** (ABC) focuses on identifying and measuring activities that cause the incurrence of costs and expenses, as discussed in other chapters. The related costs and expenses then are traced (allocated) to specific products, based upon the activities. These activities are often called **activity drivers**.

Activity-based costing may be useful in making product pricing decisions where diverse and complex manufacturing operations involve large amounts of factory overhead. In such cases, plant-wide or departmental overhead rates based upon volume-related activity drivers, such as units produced or machine hours, may yield inaccurate cost allocations. This, in turn, may result in distorted product costs and product prices.

To illustrate, plant-wide or departmental overhead rates normally allocate more overhead to high-volume products than low-volume products. However, some overhead activities such as design and engineering costs may not be related to the volume of production. A low-volume product might require more design and engineering time (costs) than a high-volume product. Likewise, the number of quality control inspections required for a product may depend more on the number of component parts rather than the number of units produced. Thus, by providing more accurate product cost allocations, activity-based costing aids in setting product prices that will cover costs and expenses.[2]

ECONOMIC THEORY OF PRODUCT PRICING

Objective 3
Summarize the economic theory of product pricing.

In addition to costs, other factors may influence the pricing decision. In considering these factors, which include the general economic conditions of the marketplace, a knowledge of the economic theory underlying product pricing is useful. Although the study of **price theory** is generally considered a separate discipline in the area of microeconomics, the following paragraphs present an overview of the economic concepts for explaining pricing behavior.

---

[2] Activity-based costing is further discussed and illustrated in an appendix at the end of the process cost systems chapter.

Maximization of Profits

In microeconomic theory, management's primary objective is assumed to be the maximization of profits. Profits will be maximized at the point at which the difference between total revenues and total costs is the greatest amount. Thus, microeconomic theory focuses on the behavior of total revenues as price and sales volume vary and the behavior of total costs as production varies.

Revenues

Generally, it is not possible to sell an unlimited number of units of product at the same price. At some point, price reductions will be necessary in order to sell more units. Total revenue may increase as the price is reduced, but there comes a point when further price decreases will reduce total revenue. To illustrate, the following **revenue schedule** indicates the effect on revenue when each $1 reduction in the unit selling price increases the number of units sold.

Revenue Schedule

Price	Units Sold	Total Revenue	Marginal Revenue
$11	1	$11	$11
10	2	20	9
9	3	27	7
8	4	32	5
7	5	35	3
6	6	36	1
5	7	35	−1

In the revenue schedule above, a price reduction from $11 to $10 increases total revenue by $9 (from $11 to $20). This increase (or decrease) in total revenue realized from the sale of an additional unit of product is called the **marginal revenue**. With each additional price reduction from $11 to $6, the total revenue increase is less. Finally, a price reduction from $6 to $5 decreases total revenue by $1.

Costs

As production and sales increase, the total cost increases. The amount of the increase in total cost varies, however, as more and more production and sales are squeezed from limited facilities. Economists assume that as the total number of units produced and sold increases from a relatively low level, the total cost increases but in decreasing amounts. This assumption is based on efficiencies created by **economies of scale**. Economies of scale generally imply that, for a given amount of facilities, it is more efficient to produce and sell large quantities than small quantities. At some point, however, the total cost will begin to increase by increasing amounts because of inefficiencies created by such factors as employees getting in each other's way and machine breakdowns caused by heavy use. The increase in total cost from producing and selling an additional unit of product is known as **marginal cost**. To illustrate, the following cost schedule indicates the effect on cost when one additional unit is produced and sold:

Cost Schedule

Units Produced and Sold	Total Cost	Marginal Cost
1	$ 9	$9
2	17	8
3	24	7
4	30	6
5	37	7
6	45	8
7	54	9

In the cost schedule above, the cost of producing 1 unit is $9, and for each additional unit the total cost per unit increases by $8, $7, $6, $7, $8, and $9. The marginal cost of producing and selling the second unit is $8, which is the difference between the total cost of producing and selling 2 units ($17) and the total cost of 1 unit ($9). As production and sales increase from 1 unit to 4 units, the marginal cost decreases from $9 to $6. After the production and sale of 4 units, however, the marginal cost increases from $6 for the fourth unit to $9 for producing and selling the seventh unit.

Product Price Determination

A price-cost combination that maximizes the total profit of an enterprise occurs when marginal revenues and marginal costs are equal. In the illustration, the marginal revenue equals the marginal cost for 3 units of sales and production, as shown below.

Maximization of Profits

Price	Units Produced and Sold	Total Revenue	Marginal Revenue	Total Cost	Marginal Cost
$11	1	$11	$11	$ 9	$9
10	2	20	9	17	8
9	3	27	7	24	7
8	4	32	5	30	6
7	5	35	3	37	7
6	6	36	1	45	8
5	7	35	-1	54	9

For the third unit of sales and production, marginal revenue and marginal cost equal $7. To sell 3 units, the revenue schedule indicates that the price should be set at $9 per unit. At this price, total revenue is $27. The cost schedule indicates that the total cost of the 3 units is $24. Thus, profit will be $3, as follows:

Total revenue (3 units × $9)	$27
Total cost (from cost schedule)	24
Profit	$ 3

The more theoretical economic approach is not widely used for product pricing. This is because the data required by the economic approach are often unavailable. For example, it is difficult to predict the amount that customers will buy over a range of prices without actually offering the product for sale at those prices. Since total cost data can be estimated reliably from accounting records, the cost-plus approach to product pricing illustrated earlier in this chapter is often used.

Pricing Strategies

Within the constraints of market conditions, managers must decide upon a pricing strategy for a company's various products. The pricing strategy chosen for a product depends upon the factors previously discussed. In addition, the stage in the product's life cycle at which the product is offered for sale has an important effect. The product life cycle concept is based on the idea that a product normally passes through various stages from the time that it is introduced until the time that it disappears from the market.

The normal life cycle for a product is divided into the following five stages:

1. Introductory stage
2. Rapid growth stage
3. Turbulent stage
4. Maturity stage
5. Terminating stage

The Art of Pricing Air Fares

One industry in which pricing plays a significant role is the airline industry. Fare wars and frequently changing fares are commonplace among the major airlines. The fine tuning involved in pricing fares is described in the following excerpt from an article in *The Wall Street Journal*:

The latest round of fare wars . . . has put a spotlight on how carriers use state-of-the-art computer software, complex forecasting techniques and a little intuition to [determine] how many seats at what prices they will offer on any given flight. . . .

Too many wrong projections can lead to huge losses of revenue, or even worse. The inability of People Express to manage its inventory of seats properly, for example, was one of the major causes of its demise.

"It's a sophisticated guessing game," said [the] vice president of pricing and product planning at American Airlines. . . . "You

don't want to sell a seat to a guy for $69 when he's willing to pay $400."

. . . American and the other airlines base their forecasts largely on historical profiles of each flight. Business travelers, for example, book heavily on many Friday afternoon flights, but often not until the day of departure. The airlines reserve blocks of seats for those frequent fliers. Few, if any, discounts are made available. . . .

For the bargain hunter, finding a discount will increasingly depend on the season, day and time of travel, destination and length of stay. . . .

The following table indicates the difference between the number of seats sold at each fare for a Wednesday and Friday flight of American Airlines:

How Two Flights Compare on Type of Seats Sold

Both examples are based on one-way fares for actual American Airlines flights from LaGuardia to Dallas/Fort Worth on a DC-10, which has coach capacity of 258 passengers.

Peak Flight   **Friday, Feb. 13, 5 p.m.**

Full coach ($230 or more)	89 seats
Intermediate discount ($80–$229)	146 seats
Deepest discount ($79 or less)	0 seats*
Empty	23 seats

Off-Peak Flight   **Wednesday, Feb. 11, 1 p.m.**

Full coach ($230 or more)	6 seats
Intermediate discount ($80–$229)	138 seats
Deepest discount ($79 or less)	40 seats
Empty	74 seats

*Such seats may have been available, with certain restrictions on sales, but none were sold.   Source: American Airlines

Source: Eric Schmitt, "The Art of Pricing Air Fares," *The Wall Street Journal*, March 4, 1987.

Graphically, the relationship of these stages to total dollar sales during a product's life cycle is shown in Exhibit 10.

Exhibit 10
Product Life Cycle

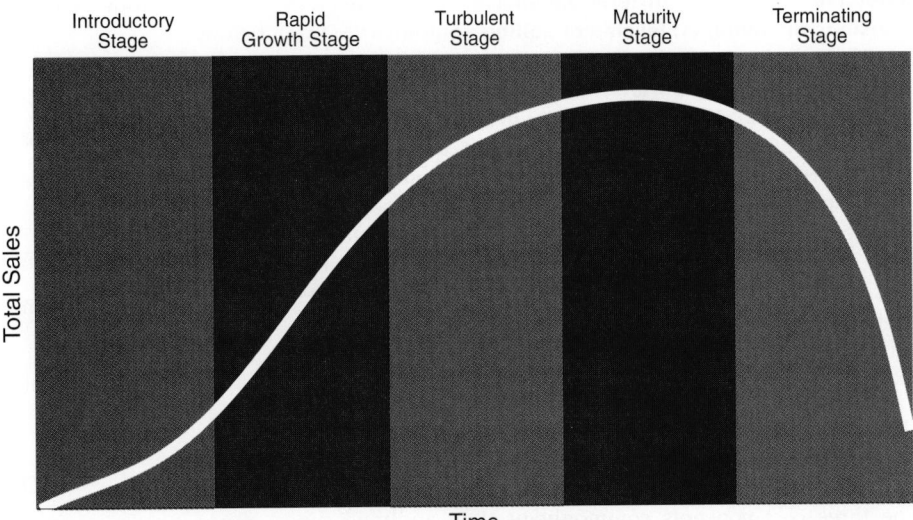

In the introductory stage, the product is new to the market and no direct competition exists. During this stage, management normally spends large amounts on promotional activities in order to develop a market for the product. Since no competition exists, prices are normally set to provide coverage of all costs and to provide high profit margins. Total sales begin low and expand rapidly as more consumers discover the product.

In the rapid growth stage, the product has caught on with consumers and competitors begin to enter the market. Total sales expand rapidly, since the industry cannot meet consumer demand for the product. Prices normally remain high during this stage but begin to decrease as competition increases. Management normally continues to set prices high enough to cover all costs and provide for a reasonable profit.

In the turbulent stage, competition increases significantly as more and more competitors enter the market. Although sales continue to be strong, increasing price competition causes total sales to increase at a decreasing rate. Management normally continues to set prices high enough to cover all costs, but profit margins are reduced to meet competition. For short periods of time, management may offer the product for sale at special prices that cover only variable costs. During this stage, one or two companies may achieve dominant positions in the market as less efficient competitors are driven out of the market.

In the maturity stage, competition stabilizes and few, if any, new competitors enter the market. Management normally sets prices at a relatively low level to cover all costs and to allow for a low profit margin. The consumer demand for the product levels off and may decline. Total sales reach a maximum and begin to decline.

In the terminating stage, the strategy of management is to reduce the chance of any losses and to get as much profit out of the remaining product demand as possible. Near the end of this stage, prices are often set to cover only product variable costs. This reduces the chance that the company will be left with excess inventories after consumer demand has disappeared.

One example of the product life cycle concept is the market for the IBM personal computer during the 1980s. During this period, the price of a standard IBM personal computer decreased from approximately $3,500 in 1980, when it was first introduced, to less than $1,000 in 1990. IBM attempted to prolong the computer's relatively brief life cycle by introducing new enhancements, such as hard disk drives, additional memory, and color monitors.

CHAPTER REVIEW

Key Points

Objective 1. Prepare a differential analysis report for decisions involving (1) leasing or selling equipment, (2) discontinuing an unprofitable segment, (3) manufacturing or purchasing a needed part, (4) replacing usable plant assets, (5) processing further or selling an intermediate product, and (6) accepting additional business at a special price.
Differential analysis reports for leasing or selling, discontinuing a segment or product, making or buying, replacing equipment, processing or selling, and accepting business at a special price are illustrated in the text. Each analysis focuses on the differential revenues and/or costs of the alternative courses of action.

Objective 2. Determine the selling price of a product, using the total cost, product cost, and variable cost concepts.
The three cost concepts commonly used in applying the

cost-plus approach to product pricing are summarized below.

Cost Concept	Covered in Cost Amount	Covered in Markup
Total cost	Total costs	Desired profit
Product cost	Total manufacturing costs	Desired profit + Total selling and administrative expenses
Variable cost	Total variable costs	Desired profit + Total fixed costs

The markup percentages used in applying each cost concept are as follows:

Total cost concept:

$$\text{Markup Percentage} = \frac{\text{Desired Profit}}{\text{Total Costs}}$$

Product cost concept:

$$\text{Markup Percentage} = \frac{\text{Desired Profit} + \text{Total Selling and Administrative Expenses}}{\text{Total Manufacturing Costs}}$$

Variable cost concept:

$$\text{Markup Percentage} = \frac{\text{Desired Profit} + \text{Total Fixed Costs}}{\text{Total Variable Costs}}$$

Objective 3. Summarize the economic theory of product pricing.
According to the economic theory of product pricing (price theory), the point where marginal revenue and marginal cost are equal is the level of sales and production at which profits are maximized. Most products experience a product life cycle. Each stage of the product life cycle affects the pricing strategy for the product.

Glossary of Key Terms

Activity-based costing. A cost allocation method that identifies activities causing the incurrence of costs and expenses and allocates these costs and expenses to products (or other cost objects) based upon activity drivers (bases). **Objective 2.**

Differential analysis. The area of accounting concerned with the effect of alternative courses of action on revenues and costs. **Objective 1**

Differential cost. The amount of increase or decrease in cost expected from a particular course of action compared with an alternative. **Objective 1**

Differential revenue. The amount of increase or decrease in revenue expected from a particular course of action as compared with an alternative. **Objective 1**

Economies of scale. An economic concept that implies that, for a given amount of facilities, it is more efficient to produce and sell large quantities than small quantities. **Objective 3**

Marginal cost. The increase in the total cost of producing and selling an additional unit of product. **Objective 3**

Marginal revenue. The increase in the total revenue realized from the sale of an additional unit of product. **Objective 3**

Markup. An amount that is added to a "cost" amount to determine product price. **Objective 2**

Opportunity cost. The amount of income forgone from an alternative to a proposed use of cash or its equivalent. **Objective 1**

Price theory. A separate discipline in the area of microeconomics which studies the setting of product prices. **Objective 3**

Product cost concept. A concept used in applying the cost-plus approach to product pricing in which only the costs of manufacturing the product, termed the product cost, are included in the cost amount to which the markup is added. **Objective 2**

Product life cycle concept. A concept that assumes that a product passes through various stages from the time that it is introduced until the time it disappears from the market. **Objective 3**

Sunk cost. A cost that is not affected by subsequent decisions. **Objective 1**

Total cost concept. A concept used in applying the cost-plus approach to product pricing in which all the costs of manufacturing the product plus the selling and administrative expenses are included in the cost amount to which the markup is added. **Objective 2**

Variable cost concept. A concept used in applying the cost-plus approach to product pricing in which only the variable costs and expenses are included in the cost amount to which the markup is added. **Objective 2**

Self-Examination Questions
Answers at end of chapter.

1. The amount of increase or decrease in cost that is expected from a particular course of action as compared with an alternative is called:
   A. differential cost   C. sunk cost
   B. replacement cost   D. opportunity cost

2. Victor Company is considering the disposal of equipment that was originally purchased for $200,000 and has $150,000 of accumulated depreciation to date. The same equipment would cost $310,000 to replace. What is the sunk cost?
   A. $50,000   C. $200,000
   B. $150,000   D. $310,000

3. The amount of income that would result from the best available alternative to a proposed use of cash or its equivalent is called:
   A. actual cost   C. opportunity cost
   B. historical cost   D. sunk cost

4. For which cost concept used in applying the cost-plus approach to product pricing are fixed manufacturing costs, fixed selling and administrative expenses, and desired profit allowed for in the determination of markup?
   A. Total cost   C. Variable cost
   B. Product cost   D. Standard cost

5. According to microeconomic theory, profits of a business enterprise will be maximized at the point where:
   A. marginal revenue equals marginal cost
   B. the change in total revenue is greater than the change in total cost
   C. the change in total cost is greater than the change in total revenue
   D. economies of scale are zero

ILLUSTRATIVE PROBLEM

Berry Company recently began production of a new product, M, which required the investment of $2,000,000 in assets. The costs of producing and selling 100,000 units of Product M are estimated as follows:

Variable costs:

Direct materials	$ 2.40 per unit
Direct labor	6.50
Factory overhead	.90
Selling and administrative expenses	.20
Total	$10.00 per unit

Fixed costs:

Factory overhead	$ 60,000
Selling and administrative expenses	140,000

Berry Company is currently considering the establishment of a selling price for Product M. The president of Berry Company has decided to use the cost-plus approach to product pricing and has indicated that Product M must earn an 18% rate of return on invested assets.

Instructions

1. Determine the amount of desired profit from the production and sale of Product M.
2. Assuming that the total cost concept is used, determine (a) the cost amount per unit, (b) the markup percentage, and (c) the selling price of Product M.
3. Assuming that the product cost concept is used, determine (a) the cost amount per unit, (b) the markup percentage, and (c) the selling price of Product M.
4. Assuming that the variable cost concept is used, determine (a) the cost amount per unit, (b) the markup percentage, and (c) the selling price of Product M.
5. Assume that for the current year, the selling price of Product M was $15.60 per unit. To date, 80,000 units have been produced and sold, and analysis of the domestic market indicates that 15,000 additional units are expected to be sold during the remainder of the year. Recently, Berry Company received an offer from Wong Inc. for 4,000 units of Product M at $11.50 each. Wong Inc. will market the units in Korea under its own brand name, and no additional selling and administrative expenses associated with the sale will be incurred by Berry Company. The additional business is not expected to affect the domestic sales of Product M, and the additional units could be produced during the current year, using existing capacity. (a) Prepare a differential analysis report of the proposed sale to Wong Inc. (b) Based upon the differential analysis report in (a), should the proposal be accepted?

Solution

1. $360,000 ($2,000,000 × 18%)
2. a. Total costs:

Variable ($10 × 100,000 units)	$1,000,000
Fixed ($60,000 + $140,000)	200,000
Total	$1,200,000

Cost amount per unit: $1,200,000 ÷ 100,000 units = $12

   b. $$\text{Markup Percentage} = \frac{\text{Desired Profit}}{\text{Total Costs}}$$

   $$\text{Markup Percentage} = \frac{\$360,000}{\$1,200,000} = 30\%$$

   c.

Cost amount per unit	$12.00
Markup ($12 × 30%)	3.60
Selling price	$15.60

3. a. Total manufacturing costs:

Variable ($9.80 × 100,000 units)	$ 980,000
Fixed factory overhead	60,000
Total	$1,040,000

Cost amount per unit: $1,040,000 ÷ 100,000 units = $10.40

b. Markup Percentage = $\dfrac{\text{Total Selling and} \\ \text{Desired Profit} + \text{Administrative Expenses}}{\text{Total Manufacturing Costs}}$

Markup Percentage = $\dfrac{\$360,000 + \$140,000 + (\$.20 \times 100,000 \text{ units})}{\$1,040,000}$

Markup Percentage = $\dfrac{\$360,000 + \$140,000 + \$20,000}{\$1,040,000}$

Markup Percentage = $\dfrac{\$520,000}{\$1,040,000} = 50\%$

c.
Cost amount per unit	$10.40
Markup ($10.40 × 50%)	5.20
Selling price	$15.60

4. a. Variable cost amount per unit: $10
   Total variable costs: $10 × 100,000 units = $1,000,000

b. Markup Percentage = $\dfrac{\text{Desired Profit} + \text{Total Fixed Costs}}{\text{Total Variable Costs}}$

Markup Percentage = $\dfrac{\$360,000 + \$60,000 + \$140,000}{\$1,000,000}$

Markup Percentage = $\dfrac{\$560,000}{\$1,000,000} = 56\%$

c.
Cost amount per unit	$10.00
Markup ($10 × 56%)	5.60
Selling price	$15.60

5. a.

Proposal To Sell to Wong Inc.

Differential revenue from acceptance of offer:	
Revenue from sale of 4,000 additional units at $11.50	$46,000
Differential cost of acceptance of offer:	
Variable costs of 4,000 additional units at $9.80	39,200
Gain from acceptance of offer	$ 6,800

b. The proposal should be accepted.

DISCUSSION QUESTIONS

1. What term is applied to the type of analysis that emphasizes the difference between the revenues and costs for proposed alternative courses of action?
2. Explain the meaning of (a) *differential revenue* and (b) *differential cost*.
3. Lakeside Lumber Company incurs a cost of $85 per thousand board feet in processing a certain "rough-cut" lumber, which it sells for $120 per thousand board feet. An alternative is to produce a "finished-cut" at a total processing cost of $115 per thousand board feet, which can be sold for $170 per thousand board feet. What is the amount of (a) the differential revenue and (b) the differential cost associated with the alternative?
4. a. What is meant by *sunk costs*?
   b. A company is contemplating replacing an old piece of machinery which cost $500,000 and has $420,000 of accumulated depreciation to date. A new machine costs $750,000. What is the sunk cost in this situation?
5. For many years, Paxton Company has been operating at 75% of capacity. It has been purchasing Part A for $10 per unit. Part A can be manufactured using idle machinery, with estimated costs per unit of $4.50 for direct materials and $2.50 for direct labor. The predetermined factory overhead rate is $4.00 ($2.50 for variable factory overhead and $1.50 for fixed factory overhead) per unit. Should Paxton Company continue to purchase Part A or should it manufacture the part? Explain.

6. The condensed income statement for Rossiter Company for the current year is as follows:

	Product			
	A	*B*	*C*	*Total*
Sales	$400,000	$120,000	$350,000	$870,000
Less variable costs	210,000	80,000	200,000	490,000
Contribution margin	$190,000	$ 40,000	$150,000	$380,000
Less fixed costs	120,000	65,000	110,000	295,000
Income (loss) from operations	$ 70,000	$(25,000)	$ 40,000	$ 85,000

Management decided to discontinue the manufacture and sale of Product B. Assuming that the discontinuance will have no effect on the total fixed costs or on the sales of Products A and C, has management made the correct decision? Explain.

7. a. What is meant by *opportunity cost*?
    b. Peters Company is currently earning 8% on $250,000 invested in marketable securities. It proposes to use the $250,000 to acquire plant facilities to manufacture a new product that is expected to add $30,000 annually to net income. What is the opportunity cost involved in the decision to manufacture the new product?

8. A company has idle capacity for the remainder of the month, which it can use to manufacture 1,000 units of Product C. The normal per unit cost to manufacture Product C is $15 for variable costs and $5 for fixed costs. A customer offers to purchase 1,000 units for use in a promotion campaign that will not interfere with the normal sales of Product C. What are the differential costs for this decision?

9. In the long run, the normal selling price must be set high enough to cover what factors?

10. What are three cost concepts commonly used in applying the cost-plus approach to product pricing?

11. In using the product cost concept of applying the cost-plus approach to product pricing, what factors are included in the markup?

12. The variable cost concept used in applying the cost-plus approach to product pricing includes what costs in the cost amount to which the markup is added?

13. In determining the markup percentage for the variable cost concept of applying the cost-plus approach, what is included in the denominator?

14. Why might the use of ideal standards in applying the cost-plus approach to product pricing lead to setting product prices that are too low?

15. Although the cost-plus approach to product pricing may be used by management as a general guideline, what are some examples of other factors that managers should also consider in setting product prices?

16. In microeconomic theory, what is assumed to be management's primary objective for a business enterprise?

17. As the terms are used in microeconomic theory, what is meant by (a) marginal revenue and (b) marginal cost?

18. If the total revenue for selling 8 units of Product P is $90 and the total revenue for selling 9 units is $100, what is the marginal revenue associated with selling the ninth unit?

19. What does the concept of economies of scale generally imply?

20. For a given amount of facilities, why will the total costs begin to increase by increasing amounts at some point?

21. According to microeconomic theory, at what point is profit maximized?

22. Why is the more theoretical economic approach to product pricing not used as often as the cost-plus approach?

23. The graph at the top of the next page shows total sales for a product. Identify each stage of the product's life cycle.

24. In the personal computer hardware market, at what stage in the product life cycle is the 5 1/4-inch disk drive and at what stage is the 3 1/2-inch disk drive?

25. In July 1986, *The Wall Street Journal* reported that the brakes that General Motors produces at its Delco Moraine division for its automobile assembly plants cost up to 15% more to make than they would cost to buy from an outside supplier. The same article reported that Ford Motor Co. and Chrysler Corp. buy almost all their brakes from outside suppliers as far away as Brazil, and these companies save money in the process. The decision of General Motors to produce its brakes internally is an example of what type of decision illustrated in this chapter?

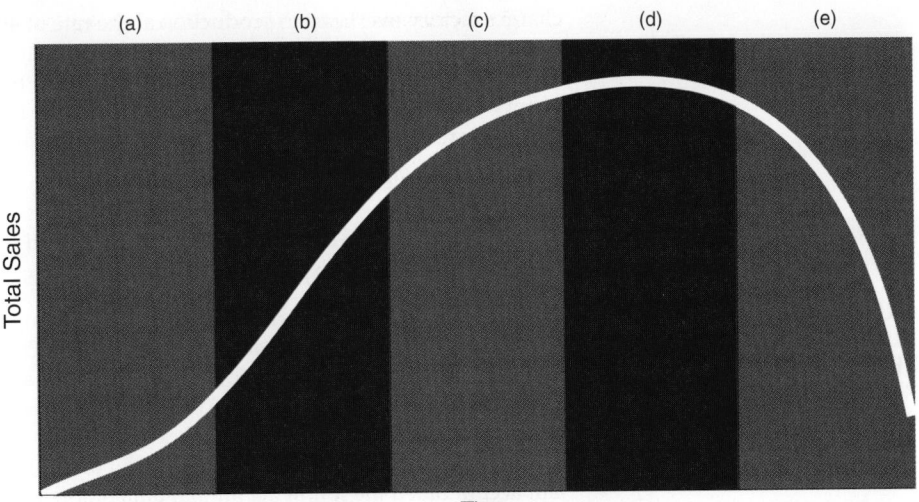

ETHICS DISCUSSION CASE

Lee Davis is a cost accountant for Morton Enterprises. Ann Yeager, vice-president of marketing, has asked Lee to meet with representatives of Morton's major competitor to discuss product cost data. Yeager indicates that the sharing of these data will enable Morton to determine a fair and equitable price for its products.

Would it be ethical for Davis to attend the meeting and share the relevant cost data?

EXERCISES

EXERCISE 27-1
LEASE OR SELL DECISION
Objective 1

Amaro Corporation is considering selling excess machinery with a book value of $200,000 (original cost of $325,000 less accumulated depreciation of $125,000) for $130,000 less a 10% brokerage commission. Alternatively, the machinery can be leased for a total of $155,000 for five years, after which it is expected to have no residual value. During the period of the lease, Amaro Corporation's costs of repairs, insurance, and property tax expenses are expected to be $30,000.

a. Prepare a differential analysis report, dated January 3 of the current year, for the lease or sell decision.

b. On the basis of the data presented, would it be advisable to lease or sell the machinery? Explain.

EXERCISE 27-2
DIFFERENTIAL ANALYSIS
REPORT FOR
DISCONTINUING A
PRODUCT
Objective 1

A condensed income statement by product line for Ellis Co. indicated the following for Product P for the past year:

Sales	$115,000
Cost of goods sold	70,000
Gross profit	$ 45,000
Operating expenses	60,000
Loss from operations	$(15,000)

It is estimated that 20% of the cost of goods sold represents fixed factory overhead costs and that 40% of the operating expenses are fixed. Since Product P is only one of many products, the fixed costs will not be materially affected if the product is discontinued.

a. Prepare a differential analysis report, dated January 3 of the current year, for the proposed discontinuance of Product P.

b. Should Product P be retained? Explain.

EXERCISE 27-3
MAKE OR BUY DECISION
Objective 1

Powell Company has been purchasing carrying cases for its portable typewriters at a delivered cost of $20 per unit. The company, which is currently operating below full capacity, charges factory overhead to production at the rate of 40% of direct materials cost. The costs to produce comparable carrying cases are expected to be $7 per unit for direct materials and $10 per unit for direct labor. If Powell Company manufactures the carrying cases, fixed factory overhead costs will not increase and variable factory overhead costs associated with the cases are expected to be 20% of the direct materials costs.

a. Prepare a differential analysis report, dated June 5 of the current year, for the make or buy decision.
b. On the basis of the data presented, would it be advisable to make or to continue buying the carrying cases? Explain.

SHARPEN YOUR COMMUNICATION SKILLS ▶

EXERCISE 27-4
DIFFERENTIAL ANALYSIS REPORT FOR MACHINE REPLACEMENT
Objective 1

SPREADSHEET PROBLEM

O'Brien Company produces a commodity by applying a machine and direct labor to the direct materials. The original cost of the machine is $300,000, the accumulated depreciation is $190,000, its remaining useful life is 10 years, and its salvage value is negligible. On January 20, a proposal was made to replace the present manufacturing procedure with a fully automatic machine that will cost $500,000. The automatic machine has an estimated useful life of 10 years and no significant salvage value. For use in evaluating the proposal, the accountant accumulated the following annual data on present and proposed operations:

	Present Operations	Proposed Operations
Sales	$595,000	$595,000
Direct materials	285,000	285,000
Direct labor	118,800	—
Power and maintenance	20,400	46,400
Taxes, insurance, etc.	13,200	20,000
Selling and administrative expenses	45,000	45,000

a. Prepare a differential analysis report for the proposal to replace the machine. Include in the analysis both the net differential decrease in costs anticipated over the 10 years and the net annual differential decrease in costs anticipated.
b. Based only on the data presented, should the proposal be accepted?
c. What are some of the other factors that should be considered before a final decision is made?

SHARPEN YOUR COMMUNICATION SKILLS ▶

EXERCISE 27-5
DECISION ON ACCEPTANCE OF ADDITIONAL BUSINESS
Objective 1

Osborn Company has a plant capacity of 60,000 units, and current production is 45,000 units. Monthly fixed costs are $130,000, and variable costs are $16 per unit. The present selling price is $25 per unit. On May 18, the company received an offer from FDI Company for 10,000 units of the product at $17 each. The FDI Company will market the units in a foreign country under its own brand name. The additional business is not expected to affect the regular selling price or quantity of sales of Osborn Company.

a. Prepare a differential analysis report for the proposed sale to FDI Company.
b. Briefly explain the reason why the acceptance of this additional business will increase operating income.
c. What is the minimum price per unit that would produce a contribution margin?

SHARPEN YOUR COMMUNICATION SKILLS ▶

EXERCISE 27-6
ACCEPTING BUSINESS AT A SPECIAL PRICE
Objective 1

Ballard Company expects to operate at 90% of productive capacity during May. The total manufacturing costs for May for the production of 18,000 grinders are budgeted as follows:

Direct materials	$117,000
Direct labor	36,000
Variable factory overhead	27,000
Fixed factory overhead	40,000
Total manufacturing costs	$220,000

The company has an opportunity to submit a bid for 1,500 grinders to be delivered by May 31 to a government agency. If the contract is obtained, it is anticipated that the additional activity will not interfere with normal production during May or increase the selling or administrative expenses. What is the unit cost below which Ballard Company should not go in bidding on the government contract?

EXERCISE 27-7
TOTAL COST CONCEPT OF PRODUCT PRICING
Objective 2

McFall Company uses the total cost concept of applying the cost-plus approach to product pricing. The costs of producing and selling 2,500 units of Product B are as follows:

Variable costs:		Fixed costs:	
Direct materials	$20.00 per unit	Factory overhead	$30,000
Direct labor	13.60	Selling and adm. exp.	15,000
Factory overhead	2.40		
Selling and adm. exp.	6.00		
Total	$42.00 per unit		

McFall Company desires a profit equal to an 18% rate of return on invested assets of $100,000.

a. Determine the amount of desired profit from the production and sale of Product B.
b. Determine the total costs and the cost amount per unit for the production and sale of 2,500 units of Product B.
c. Determine the markup percentage for Product B.
d. Determine the selling price of Product B.

EXERCISE 27-8
PRODUCT COST CONCEPT
OF PRODUCT PRICING
Objective 2

Based on the data presented in Exercise 27-7, assume that McFall Company uses the product cost concept of applying the cost-plus approach to product pricing.

a. Determine the total manufacturing costs and the cost amount per unit for the production and sale of 2,500 units of Product B.
b. Determine the markup percentage for Product B.
c. Determine the selling price of Product B.

EXERCISE 27-9
VARIABLE COST CONCEPT
OF PRODUCT PRICING
Objective 2

Based on the data presented in Exercise 27-7, assume that McFall Company uses the variable cost concept of applying the cost-plus approach to product pricing.

a. Determine the cost amount per unit for the production and sale of 2,500 units of Product B.
b. Determine the markup percentage for Product B.
c. Determine the selling price of Product B.

EXERCISE 27-10
ECONOMIC CONCEPT OF
PRICING
Objective 3

For the following revenue schedule and cost schedule for Product X, determine (a) the level of sales and production at which marginal cost is equal to marginal revenue, (b) the unit sales price at the level of sales determined in (a), and (c) the maximum profit for Product X at the level of sales determined in (a).

Revenue Schedule					Cost Schedule		
Price	Units Sold	Total Revenue	Marginal Revenue		Units Produced and Sold	Total Cost	Marginal Cost
$12	1	$12	$12		1	$ 9	$9
11	2	22	10		2	17	8
10	3	30	8		3	24	7
9	4	36	6		4	30	6
8	5	40	4		5	35	5
7	6	42	2		6	40	5
6	7	42	0		7	46	6

WhAT'S WRONG
WITH THiɞ?

On the basis of the following data, the general manager decided to discontinue Product X because it reduced income from operations by $17,000. Can you find the flaw in this decision?

Condensed Income Statement
For Year Ended August 31, 19—

	Product X	Product Y	Product Z	Total
Sales	$100,000	$300,000	$500,000	$900,000
Cost of goods sold:				
Variable costs	$ 65,000	$150,000	$220,000	$435,000
Fixed costs	20,000	60,000	120,000	200,000
Total cost of goods sold	$ 85,000	$210,000	$340,000	$635,000
Gross profit	$ 15,000	$ 90,000	$160,000	$265,000
Operating expenses:				
Variable expenses	$ 25,000	$ 45,000	$ 95,000	$165,000
Fixed expenses	7,000	20,000	25,000	52,000
Total operating expenses	$ 32,000	$ 65,000	$120,000	$217,000
Income (loss) from operations	$(17,000)	$ 25,000	$ 40,000	$ 48,000

PROBLEMS

Series A

PROBLEM 27-1A
DIFFERENTIAL ANALYSIS
REPORT INVOLVING
OPPORTUNITY COSTS
Objective 1

On December 1, Benton Company is considering leasing a building and buying the necessary equipment to operate a public warehouse. The project would be financed by selling $775,000 of 8% U.S. Treasury bonds that mature in 10 years. The bonds were purchased at face value and are currently selling at face value. The following data have been assembled:

Cost of equipment	$775,000
Life of equipment	10 years
Estimated residual value of equipment	$ 75,000
Yearly costs to operate the warehouse, in addition to depreciation of equipment	$ 74,000
Yearly expected revenues—first 5 years	$224,000
Yearly expected revenues—next 5 years	$200,000

**SPREADSHEET
PROBLEM**

Instructions

1. Prepare a report presenting the differential revenue and the differential cost associated with the proposed operation of the warehouse for the 10 years as compared with present conditions.
2. Based on the results disclosed by the differential analysis, should the proposal be accepted?
3. If the proposal is accepted, what is the total estimated income from operation of the warehouse for the 10 years?

PROBLEM 27-2A
DIFFERENTIAL ANALYSIS
REPORT FOR MACHINE
REPLACEMENT PROPOSAL
Objective 1

Fogarty Company is considering the replacement of a machine that has been used in its factory for four years. Relevant data associated with the operations of the old machine and the new machine, neither of which has any estimated residual value, are as follows:

Old Machine

Cost of machine, 9-year life	$630,000
Annual depreciation	70,000
Annual manufacturing costs, exclusive of depreciation	400,000
Related annual operating expenses	142,500
Associated annual revenue	965,000
Current estimated selling price	175,000

New Machine

Cost of machine, 5-year life	$700,000
Annual depreciation	140,000
Estimated annual manufacturing costs, exclusive of depreciation	245,000

Annual operating expenses and revenue are not expected to be affected by purchase of the new machine.

Instructions

1. Prepare a differential analysis report as of March 22 of the current year, comparing operations utilizing the new machine with operations using the present equipment. The analysis should indicate the total net differential decrease or increase in costs that would result over the 5-year period if the new machine is acquired.
2. List other factors that should be considered before a final decision is reached.

**SHARPEN YOUR
COMMUNICATION SKILLS**

PROBLEM 27-3A
DIFFERENTIAL ANALYSIS
REPORT FOR SALES
PROMOTION PROPOSAL
Objective 1

Higgins Company is planning a one-month campaign for April to promote sales of one of its two products. A total of $30,000 has been budgeted for advertising, contests, redeemable coupons, and other promotional activities. The data at the top of the next page have been assembled for their possible usefulness in deciding which of the products to select for the campaign.

No increase in facilities would be necessary to produce and sell the increased output. It is anticipated that 10,000 additional units of Product A or 6,000 additional units of Product B could be sold without changing the unit selling price of either product.

	Product A	Product B
Unit selling price	$50	$80
Unit production costs:		
Direct materials	$14	$24
Direct labor	10	19
Variable factory overhead	8	9
Fixed factory overhead	6	8
Total unit production costs	$38	$60
Unit variable operating expenses	5	7
Unit fixed operating expenses	3	5
Total unit costs	$46	$72
Operating income per unit	$ 4	$ 8

Instructions

1. Prepare a differential analysis report as of March 3 of the current year, presenting the additional revenue and additional costs anticipated from the promotion of Product A and Product B.

2. The sales manager had tentatively decided to promote Product B, estimating that operating income would be increased by $18,000 ($8 operating income per unit for 6,000 units, less promotion expenses of $30,000). It was also believed that the selection of Product A would increase operating income by only $10,000 ($4 operating income per unit for 10,000 units, less promotion expenses of $30,000). State briefly your reasons for supporting or opposing the tentative decision.

PROBLEM 27-4A
DIFFERENTIAL ANALYSIS
REPORT FOR FURTHER
PROCESSING
Objective 1

The management of Benton Company is considering whether to process further Product A into Product Y. Product Y can be sold for $90 per pound, and Product A can be sold without further processing for $20 per pound. Product A is produced in batches of 300 pounds by processing 400 pounds of raw material, which costs $9 per pound. Product Y will require additional processing costs of $5 per pound of Product A, and 3 pounds of Product A will produce 1 pound of Product Y.

Instructions

1. Prepare a report as of February 20, presenting the differential revenue and differential cost per batch associated with the further processing of Product A to produce Product Y.

2. Briefly report your recommendations.

PROBLEM 27-5A
DIFFERENTIAL ANALYSIS
REPORT FOR FURTHER
PROCESSING
Objective 1

Hester Refining Inc. refines Product R in batches of 100,000 gallons, which it sells for $5 per gallon. The associated unit costs are currently as follows:

Direct materials	$2.65
Direct labor	.87
Variable factory overhead	.33
Fixed factory overhead	.18
Sales commissions	.50
Fixed selling and administrative expenses	.12

    The company is presently considering a proposal to put Product R through several additional processes to yield Products R and W. Although the company had determined such further processing to be unwise, new processing methods have now been developed. Existing facilities can be used for the additional processing, but since the factory is operating at full 8-hour-day capacity, the processing would have to be performed at night. Additional costs of processing would be $12,500 per batch, and there would be an evaporation loss of 10%, with 65% of the processed material evolving as Product R and 25% as Product W. The selling price of Product W is $8 per gallon. Sales commissions are a uniform percentage based on the sales price.

Instructions

1. Prepare a report as of September 9, presenting the differential revenue and the differential cost per batch associated with the processing to produce Products R and W, compared with processing to produce Product R only.

2. Briefly report your recommendations.

PROBLEM 27-6A
PRODUCT PRICING USING
THE COST-PLUS APPROACH
CONCEPTS; DIFFERENTIAL
ANALYSIS REPORT FOR
ACCEPTANCE OF
ADDITIONAL BUSINESS
Objectives 1, 2

Rowan Company recently began production of a new product, C, which required the investment of $500,000 in assets. The costs of producing and selling 25,000 units of Product C are estimated as follows:

Variable costs per unit:

Direct materials	$ 5.00
Direct labor	3.25
Factory overhead	1.75
Selling and administrative expenses	2.00
Total	$12.00

Fixed costs:

Factory overhead	$70,000
Selling and administrative expenses	30,000

Rowan Company is currently considering the establishment of a selling price for Product C. The president of Rowan Company has decided to use the cost-plus approach to product pricing and has indicated that Product C must earn a 16% rate of return on invested assets.

Instructions

1. Determine the amount of desired profit from the production and sale of Product C.
2. Assuming that the total cost concept is used, determine (a) the cost amount per unit, (b) the markup percentage, and (c) the selling price of Product C.
3. Assuming that the product cost concept is used, determine (a) the cost amount per unit, (b) the markup percentage, and (c) the selling price of Product C. Round to the nearest cent.
4. Assuming that the variable cost concept is used, determine (a) the cost amount per unit, (b) the markup percentage, and (c) the selling price of Product C.

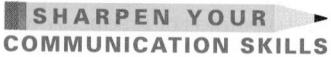

5. Comment on any additional considerations that could influence the establishment of the selling price for Product C.
6. Assume that as of May 1, 22,000 units of Product C have been produced and sold during the current year. Analysis of the domestic market indicates that 1,500 additional units of Product C are expected to be sold during the remainder of the year at the normal product price determined under the total cost concept. On May 5, Rowan Company received an offer from Yu Inc. for 1,000 units of Product C at $9.75 each. Yu Inc. will market the units in Japan under its own brand name, and no additional selling and administrative expenses associated with the sale will be incurred by Rowan Company. The additional business is not expected to affect the domestic sales of Product C, and the additional units could be produced using existing capacity.
   a. Prepare a differential analysis report of the proposed sale to Yu Inc.
   b. Based upon the differential analysis report in (a), should the proposal be accepted?

Series B

PROBLEM 27-1B
DIFFERENTIAL ANALYSIS
REPORT INVOLVING
OPPORTUNITY COSTS
Objective 1

On July 1, Adler Company is considering leasing a building and purchasing the necessary equipment to operate a public warehouse. The project would be financed by selling $800,000 of 9% U.S. Treasury bonds that mature in 20 years. The bonds were purchased at face value and are currently selling at face value. The following data have been assembled:

Cost of equipment	$800,000
Life of equipment	20 years
Estimated residual value of equipment	$150,000
Yearly costs to operate the warehouse, in addition to depreciation of equipment	$ 50,000
Yearly expected revenues—first 10 years	$175,000
Yearly expected revenues—next 10 years	$150,000

Instructions

1. Prepare a report presenting the differential revenue and the differential cost associated with the proposed operation of the warehouse for the 20 years as compared with present conditions.
2. Based on the results disclosed by the differential analysis, should the proposal be accepted?
3. If the proposal is accepted, what is the total estimated income from operation of the warehouse for the 20 years?

PROBLEM 27-2B
DIFFERENTIAL ANALYSIS
REPORT FOR MACHINE
REPLACEMENT PROPOSAL
Objective 1

Vernon Company is considering the replacement of a machine that has been used in its factory for three years. Relevant data associated with the operations of the old machine and the new machine, neither of which has any estimated residual value, are as follows:

Old Machine

Cost of machine, 9-year life	$ 300,000
Annual depreciation	33,333
Annual manufacturing costs, exclusive of depreciation	475,000
Related annual operating expenses	320,000
Associated annual revenue	1,120,000
Current estimated selling price	160,000

New Machine

Cost of machine, 6-year life	$600,000
Annual depreciation	105,000
Estimated annual manufacturing costs, exclusive of depreciation	345,000

Annual operating expenses and revenue are not expected to be affected by purchase of the new machine.

Instructions

1. Prepare a differential analysis report as of August 11 of the current year, comparing operations utilizing the new machine with operations using the present equipment. The analysis should indicate the total net differential decrease or increase in costs that would result over the 6-year period if the new machine is acquired.

▶ 2. List other factors that should be considered before a final decision is reached.

SHARPEN YOUR COMMUNICATION SKILLS

PROBLEM 27-3B
DIFFERENTIAL ANALYSIS
REPORT FOR SALES
PROMOTION PROPOSAL
Objective 1

Cross Company is planning a one-month campaign for May to promote sales of one of its two products. A total of $75,000 has been budgeted for advertising, contests, redeemable coupons, and other promotional activities. The following data have been assembled for their possible usefulness in deciding which of the products to select for the campaign:

	Product A	Product X
Unit selling price	$45	$125
Unit production costs:		
Direct materials	$17	$50
Direct labor	13	37
Variable factory overhead	3	7
Fixed factory overhead	2	2
Total unit production costs	$35	$ 96
Unit variable operating expenses	5	5
Unit fixed operating expenses	1	4
Total unit costs	$41	$105
Operating income per unit	$ 4	$ 20

No increase in facilities would be necessary to produce and sell the increased output. It is anticipated that 20,000 additional units of Product A or 5,000 additional units of Product X could be sold without changing the unit selling price of either product.

Instructions

1. Prepare a differential analysis report as of April 5 of the current year, presenting the additional revenue and additional costs anticipated from the promotion of Product A and Product X.

▶ 2. The sales manager had tentatively decided to promote Product X, estimating that operating income would be increased by $25,000 ($20 operating income per unit for 5,000 units, less promotion expenses of $75,000). It was also believed that the selection of Product A would increase operating income by only $5,000 ($4 operating income per unit for 20,000 units, less promotion expenses of $75,000). State briefly your reasons for supporting or opposing the tentative decision.

SHARPEN YOUR COMMUNICATION SKILLS

PROBLEM 27-4B
DIFFERENTIAL ANALYSIS
REPORT FOR FURTHER
PROCESSING
Objective 1

The management of Penn Company is considering whether to process further Product P into Product W. Product W can be sold for $150 per pound, and Product P can be sold without further processing for $85 per pound. Product P is produced in batches of 375 pounds by processing 500 pounds of raw material, which costs $30 per pound. Product W will require additional processing costs of $10 per pound of Product P, and 1.5 pounds of Product P will produce 1 pound of Product W.

Instructions

1. Prepare a report as of May 30, presenting the differential revenue and differential cost per batch associated with the further processing of Product P to produce Product W.
2. Briefly report your recommendations.

SHARPEN YOUR
COMMUNICATION SKILLS

PROBLEM 27-5B
DIFFERENTIAL ANALYSIS
REPORT FOR FURTHER
PROCESSING
Objective 1

Vance Refining Inc. refines Product C in batches of 50,000 gallons, which it sells for $5 per gallon. The associated unit costs are currently as follows:

Direct materials	$2.50
Direct labor	1.05
Variable factory overhead	.30
Fixed factory overhead	.15
Sales commissions	.25
Fixed selling and administrative expenses	.08

The company is presently considering a proposal to put Product C through several additional processes to yield Products C and D. Although the company had determined such further processing to be unwise, new processing methods have now been developed. Existing facilities can be used for the additional processing, but since the factory is operating at full 8-hour-day capacity, the processing would have to be performed at night. Additional costs of processing would be $22,125 per batch, and there would be an evaporation loss of 20%, with 45% of the processed material evolving as Product C and 35% as Product D. The selling price of Product D is $10 per gallon. Sales commissions are a uniform percentage based on the sales price.

Instructions

1. Prepare a report as of June 9, presenting the differential revenue and the differential cost per batch associated with the processing to produce Products C and D, compared with processing to produce Product C only.
2. Briefly report your recommendations.

SHARPEN YOUR
COMMUNICATION SKILLS

PROBLEM 27-6B
PRODUCT PRICING USING
THE COST-PLUS APPROACH
CONCEPTS; DIFFERENTIAL
ANALYSIS REPORT FOR
ACCEPTANCE OF
ADDITIONAL BUSINESS
Objectives 1, 2

TAC Inc. recently began production of a new product, L, which required the investment of $800,000 in assets. The costs of producing and selling 50,000 units of Product L are estimated as follows:

Variable costs per unit:		Fixed costs:	
Direct materials	$ 8.40	Factory overhead	$150,000
Direct labor	4.60	Selling and adm. exp.	50,000
Factory overhead	2.00		
Selling and adm. exp.	1.00		
Total	$16.00		

TAC Inc. is currently considering the establishment of a selling price for Product L. The president of TAC Inc. has decided to use the cost-plus approach to product pricing and has indicated that Product L must earn a 10% rate of return on invested assets.

Instructions

1. Determine the amount of desired profit from the production and sale of Product L.
2. Assuming that the total cost concept is used, determine (a) the cost amount per unit, (b) the markup percentage, and (c) the selling price of Product L.
3. Assuming that the product cost concept is used, determine (a) the cost amount per unit, (b) the markup percentage, and (c) the selling price of Product L.
4. Assuming that the variable cost concept is used, determine (a) the cost amount per unit, (b) the markup percentage, and (c) the selling price of Product L.

5. Comment on any additional considerations that could influence the establishment of the selling price for Product L.

6. Assume that as of September 1, 40,000 units of Product L have been produced and sold during the current year. Analysis of the domestic market indicates that 6,500 additional units are expected to be sold during the remainder of the year at the normal product price determined under the total cost concept. On September 3, TAC Inc. received an offer from DeVoe Company for 3,000 units of Product L at $15.50 each. DeVoe Company will market the units in Canada under its own brand name, and no additional selling and administrative expenses associated with the sale will be incurred by TAC Inc. The additional business is not expected to affect the domestic sales of Product L, and the additional units could be produced using existing capacity.

   a. Prepare a differential analysis report of the proposed sale to DeVoe Company.

   b. Based upon the differential analysis report in (a), should the proposal be accepted?

MINI-CASE 27 SCHOOLCRAFT MOTORS

Your father operates a family-owned automotive dealership. Recently, the city government has requested bids on the purchase of 8 sedans for use by the city police department. Although the city prefers to purchase from local dealerships, state law requires the acceptance of the lowest bid. The past several contracts for automotive purchases have been granted to dealerships from surrounding communities.

The following data were taken from the dealership records for the normal sale of the automobile for which current bids have been requested:

Retail list price of sedan	$18,000
Costs allocated to normal sale:	
Dealer cost from manufacturer	16,000
Fixed overhead	750
Shipping charges from manufacturer	400
Preparation charges	100
Sales commission based on selling price	6%

Your father has asked you to help him in arriving at a "winning" bid price for this contract. In the past, your father has always bid $300 above the total cost (including fixed overhead). No sales commissions will be paid if the bid is accepted, and your father has indicated that the bid price must contribute at least $300 per car to the profits of the dealership.

Instructions:

1. ▪▪▪▪ Do you think that your father has used good bidding procedures for prior contracts? Explain.

2. ▪▪▪▪ What should be the bid price, based upon your father's profit objectives?

3. ▪▪▪▪ Explain why the bid price determined in (2) would not be an acceptable price for normal customers.

ANSWERS TO SELF-EXAMINATION QUESTIONS

1. **A** Differential cost (answer A) is the amount of increase or decrease in cost that is expected from a particular course of action compared with an alternative. Replacement cost (answer B) is the cost of replacing an asset at current market prices. Sunk cost (answer C) is a past cost that will not be affected by subsequent decisions. Opportunity cost (answer D) is the amount of income that would result from the best available alternative to a proposed use of cash or its equivalent.

2. **A** A sunk cost is not affected by later decisions. For Victor Company, the sunk cost is the $50,000 (answer A) book value of the equipment, which is equal to the original cost of $200,000 (answer C) less the accumulated depreciation of $150,000 (answer B).

3. **C** The amount of income that could have been earned from the best available alternative to a proposed use of cash is called opportunity cost (answer C). Actual cost (answer A) or historical cost (answer B) is the cash or equivalent outlay for goods or services actually acquired. Sunk cost (answer D) is a cost that is not affected by later decisions.

4. **C** Under the variable cost concept of product pricing (answer C), fixed manufacturing costs, fixed administrative

and selling expenses, and desired profit are allowed for in the determination of the markup. Only desired profit is allowed for in the markup under the total cost concept (answer A). Under the product cost concept (answer B), total selling and administrative expenses and desired profit are allowed for in the determination of the markup. Standard cost (answer D) can be used under any of the cost-plus approaches to product pricing.

5. **A** Microeconomic theory indicates that profits of a business enterprise will be maximized at the point where marginal revenue equals marginal cost (answer A). At lower levels of production and sales, the change in total revenue is greater than the change in total cost (answer B); hence, more profit can be achieved by manufacturing and selling more units. At higher levels of production and sales, the change in total cost is greater than the change in total revenue (answer C); hence, less profit will be achieved by manufacturing and selling more units. Economies of scale (answer D) is an economic concept that recognizes that, for a given amount of facilities, it is more efficient to produce and sell large quantities rather than small quantities.

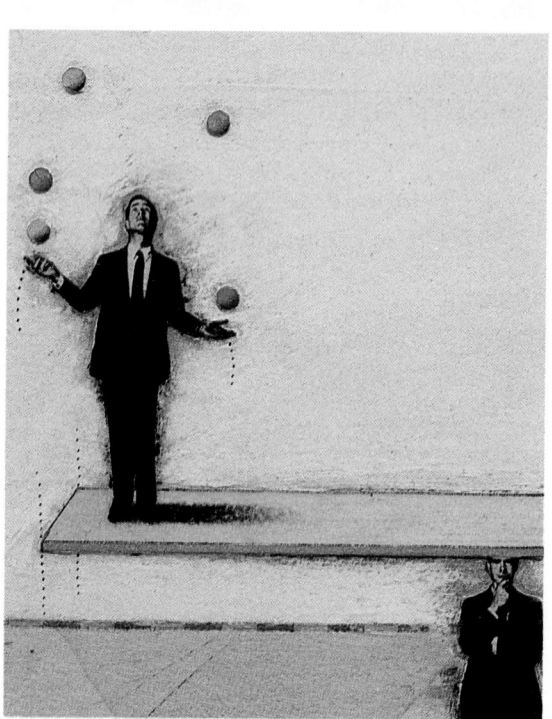

You and Accounting

Almost everyone would like to be a millionaire.

Question: If you invest $92,296 today at an interest rate of 10% compounded annually, would you be a millionaire in 25 years?

Answer: Yes. The amount of $92,296 invested today at 10% with interest compounded annually will accumulate to $1,000,000 in 25 years.

Question: If you win a state lottery totaling $2,000,000, payable at a rate of $80,000 per year for 25 years, and the average interest rate is 9% compounded annually, would you be a millionaire today?

Answer: No. The $2,000,000 lottery is worth $785,806 today.

The answers to the preceding questions can be easily determined by using the time value of money concepts discussed in this chapter. The management of a business enterprise often uses these concepts to evaluate the worth of alternative proposals for investments in plant assets. You may also find these concepts useful to you in your daily life.

Chapter 28
Capital Investment Analysis

LEARNING OBJECTIVES
After studying this chapter,
you should be able to:

Objective 1
Explain the nature and
importance of capital
investment analysis.

Objective 2
Evaluate capital investment
proposals, using the
following methods:

Average rate of return
Cash payback
Net present value
Internal rate of return

Objective 3
List examples of qualitative
considerations in capital
investment analysis,
especially as related to
today's manufacturing
environment.

Objective 4
List and describe factors that
complicate capital
investment analysis.

Objective 5
Diagram the capital
rationing process.

Objective 6
Summarize the basic
concepts for planning and
controlling capital
investment expenditures.

With the rapid growth of American industry, increasing attention has been given to long-term investment decisions involving plant assets. This chapter describes analyses useful for making such investment decisions, which may involve thousands, millions, or even billions of dollars. The similarities and differences among the most commonly used methods of evaluating investment proposals, as well as the uses of each method, are emphasized. Qualitative considerations affecting investment analyses are also discussed. Finally, considerations complicating investment analyses, the process of allocating available investment funds among competing proposals, and planning and controlling capital expenditures are briefly discussed.

NATURE OF CAPITAL INVESTMENT ANALYSIS

Objective 1
Explain the nature and importance of capital investment analysis.

The process by which management plans, evaluates, and controls investments in plant assets is called **capital investment analysis** or **capital budgeting.** Since capital investments involve a long-term commitment of funds, they affect operations for many years. These investments must earn a reasonable rate of return, so that the enterprise can meet its obligations to creditors and provide dividends to stockholders. Because capital investment decisions are some of the most important decisions that management makes, capital investment analysis must be carefully developed and implemented.

A capital investment program should include a plan for encouraging employees at all levels of an enterprise to submit proposals for capital investments. The plan should provide for communicating to employees the long-range goals of the enterprise, so that useful proposals are submitted. In addition, the plan may provide for rewarding employees whose proposals are implemented. All reasonable proposals should be given serious consideration, and the effects of the economic implications expected from these proposals should be identified.

METHODS OF EVALUATING CAPITAL INVESTMENT PROPOSALS

Objective 2
Evaluate capital investment proposals, using the following methods:

Average rate of return
Cash payback
Net present value
Internal rate of return

The methods of evaluating capital investment proposals can be grouped into the following two general categories:

1. Methods that do not use present values
2. Methods that use present values

Methods that use present values in the analyses consider the time value of money. The **time value of money concept** recognizes that an amount of cash invested today will earn income and therefore has value over time. For example, if $10,000 is invested to earn 10% per year, the $10,000 on hand today will accumulate to $11,000 ($10,000 plus $1,000 earnings) in one year. The **present value concept** recognizes that the cash to be received at some date in the future is not the equivalent of the same amount of cash received at an earlier date. For example, $10,000 on hand today is more valuable than $10,000 to be received a year from today. The $10,000 on hand today can be invested to earn income. Thus, the $10,000 on hand today, if invested to earn 10% per year, is the *present value* of the $11,000 to be received a year from today.

The two methods that do not use present values in evaluating capital investment proposals are (1) the average rate of return method and (2) the cash payback method. The two methods that use present values are (1) the net present value method and (2) the internal rate of return method.

Management often uses a combination of methods in evaluating capital investment proposals. A survey of business practices in a variety of industries reported the following use of capital investment analysis methods:[1]

Method	Percentage of Respondents Using the Method
Average rate of return method	46%
Cash payback method	71
Net present value method	64
Internal rate of return method	69

Each of the preceding methods has advantages and disadvantages. In addition, some of the computations can become complex. Computers, however, can perform the calculations quickly and easily. More importantly, computers can be used to develop models that indicate the effect of changes in key estimates on the evaluation of capital investment proposals.

---

[1] Robert A. Howell, James D. Brown, Stephen R. Soucy, and Allen H. Seed, *Management Accounting in the New Manufacturing Environment* (Montvale, New Jersey: National Association of Accountants and Computer Aided Manufacturing International, 1987).

Methods That Ignore Present Value

The average rate of return and the cash payback methods of evaluating capital investment proposals are easy to use. These methods are often used initially to screen proposals. Management normally sets minimum standards for acceptance, and proposals not meeting these minimum standards are dropped from further consideration. If a proposal meets the minimum standards, it is then subject to further analysis.

The methods that ignore present value are often useful in evaluating capital investment proposals that have relatively short useful lives. In such cases, the timing of the cash flows is less important. Management can thus focus attention on the amount of income expected to be earned from the investment and the total net cash flows to be received from the investment.

AVERAGE RATE OF RETURN METHOD. The expected **average rate of return,** sometimes called the **accounting rate of return,** measures the expected profitability of an investment in plant assets. The income expected to be earned from the investment is stated as an annual average over the number of years the asset is to be used. The amount of the investment may be considered to be the original cost of the plant asset, or recognition may be given to the effect of depreciation on the amount of the investment. According to the latter view, the investment gradually declines from the original cost to the estimated residual value at the end of its useful life. If straight-line depreciation and no residual value are assumed, the average investment is equal to one-half of the original cost.[2]

To illustrate, assume that management is considering the purchase of a machine at a cost of $500,000. The machine is expected to have a useful life of 4 years, with no residual value, and to yield total income of $200,000. The estimated average annual income is therefore $50,000 ($200,000 ÷ 4), and the average investment is $250,000 [($500,000 + $0 residual value) ÷ 2]. Thus, the expected average rate of return on the average investment is 20%, computed as follows:

$$\text{Average Rate of Return} = \frac{\text{Estimated Average Annual Income}}{\text{Average Investment}}$$

$$\text{Average Rate of Return} = \frac{\$200,000 \div 4}{(\$500,000 + \$0) \div 2} = \mathbf{20\%}$$

The expected average rate of return of **20%** should be compared with the rate set by management as the minimum rate for such investments. If the expected average rate of return equals or exceeds the minimum rate, the machine is desirable for investment purposes.

When several alternative capital investment proposals are considered, the proposals can be ranked by their average rates of return. The higher the average rate of return, the more desirable the proposal. For example, assume that management is considering the following alternative capital investment proposals and has computed the indicated average rates of return:

	Proposal A	Proposal B
Estimated average annual income	$ 30,000	$ 36,000
Average investment	$120,000	$180,000
Average rate of return:		
$30,000 ÷ $120,000	25%	
$36,000 ÷ $180,000		20%

If only the average rate of return is considered, Proposal A, with an average rate of return of 25%, would be preferred over Proposal B.

[2] The average investment is the midpoint of the depreciable cost of the asset. Since a plant asset is never depreciated below its residual value, this midpoint is determined by adding the original cost of the asset to the estimated residual value and dividing by 2.

In addition to its ease of computation, the average rate of return method has several advantages. One advantage is that it includes the amount of income earned over the entire life of the proposal. In addition, it emphasizes accounting income, which is commonly used by investors and creditors in evaluating management performance. Its main disadvantage is that it does not directly consider the expected cash flows from the proposal and the timing of these cash flows. Cash flows are important because cash coming from an investment can be reinvested in other income-producing activities. Therefore, the more funds and the sooner the funds become available, the more income that can be generated from their reinvestment.

CASH PAYBACK METHOD. The expected period of time that will pass between the date of an investment and the complete recovery in cash (or equivalent) of the amount invested is the **cash payback period.** To simplify the analysis, the revenues and operating expenses related to operating plant assets, other than depreciation, are assumed to be all in the form of cash. The excess of the cash flowing in from revenue over the cash flowing out for expenses is termed **net cash flow.** The time required for the net cash flow to equal the initial outlay for the plant asset is the payback period.

To illustrate, assume that the proposed investment in a plant asset with an 8-year life is $200,000 and that the annual net cash flow is expected to be $40,000. The estimated cash payback period for the investment is 5 years, computed as follows:

$$\frac{\$200,000}{\$40,000} = \text{5-year cash payback period}$$

In this illustration, the annual net cash flows are equal ($40,000 per year). If these annual net cash flows are not equal, the cash payback period is determined by adding the annual net cash flows until the cumulative sum equals the amount of the proposed investment. To illustrate, assume that for a proposed investment of $400,000, the annual net cash flows and the cumulative net cash flows over the proposal's 6-year life are as follows:

Year	Net Cash Flow	Cumulative Net Cash Flow
1	$ 60,000	$ 60,000
2	80,000	140,000
3	105,000	245,000
4	155,000	400,000
5	100,000	500,000
6	90,000	590,000

The cumulative net cash flow at the end of the fourth year equals the amount of the investment, $400,000. Thus, the payback period is 4 years. If the amount of the proposed investment had been $450,000, the cash payback period would occur during the fifth year. If the net cash flows are uniform throughout the period, the cash payback period in this case would be 4½ years.

The cash payback method is widely used in evaluating proposals for investments in new projects. A relatively short payback period is desirable, because the sooner the cash is recovered, the sooner it becomes available for reinvestment in other projects. In addition, there is less possibility of losses from changes in economic conditions, obsolescence, and other unavoidable risks when the payback period is short. The cash payback period is also important to bankers and other creditors who may be depending upon net cash flow for the repayment of debt related to the capital investment. The sooner the cash is recovered, the sooner the debt or other liabilities can be paid. Thus, the cash payback method is especially useful to managers whose primary concern is liquidity.

One of the disadvantages of the cash payback method is its failure to include the expected profitability of a proposal. For example, assume that Project A has a payback period of 3 years, while Project B has a payback period of 5 years. Project B, however, might be significantly more profitable than Project A over its entire useful life. In addition, any cash flows occurring after the payback period are ignored.

Present Value Methods

An investment in plant and equipment may be viewed as acquiring a series of future net cash flows composed of two elements: (1) the recovery of the initial investment and (2) income. The period of time over which these net cash flows will be received may be an important factor in determining the value of an investment.

NET PRESENT VALUE METHOD. The net present value method uses present value concepts to compute the net present value of the cash flows expected from a proposal. The net present value method is sometimes called the **discounted cash flow method.** To illustrate, if $1,000 is to be received in one year and if the current rate of earnings is 12%, the present value of the $1,000 is $892.86 ($1,000 ÷ 1.12). If the $1,000 is to be received one year later (two years in all), with the earnings compounded at the end of the first year, the present value amount would be $797.20 ($892.86 ÷ 1.12).

A present value of $1 table can be used to determine a present value amount. For example, the partial table in Exhibit 1 indicates that the present value of $1 to be received two years hence, with earnings at the rate of 12% a year, is .797. Multiplying .797 by $1,000 yields $797, which is the same amount determined in the preceding paragraph by two successive divisions. The small difference is due to rounding the present value factors in the table to three decimal places.[3]

Exhibit 1
Partial Present Value Table

Present Value of $1 at Compound Interest

Year	6%	10%	12%	15%	20%
1	.943	.909	.893	.870	.833
2	.890	.826	.797	.756	.694
3	.840	.751	.712	.658	.579
4	.792	.683	.636	.572	.482
5	.747	.621	.567	.497	.402
6	.705	.564	.507	.432	.335
7	.665	.513	.452	.376	.279
8	.627	.467	.404	.327	.233
9	.592	.424	.361	.284	.194
10	.558	.386	.322	.247	.162

The rate of return used in net present value analysis is determined by management. This rate is often based upon such factors as the nature of the business enterprise and its relative profitability, the purpose of the capital investment, the cost of securing funds for the investment, and the minimum desired rate of return. If the net present value of the net cash flow expected from a proposed investment at the selected rate equals or exceeds the amount of the investment, the proposal is desirable.

To illustrate, assume a proposal to acquire $200,000 of equipment with an expected useful life of 5 years and a minimum desired rate of return of 10%. The expected net cash flow for each of the 5 years and the analysis of the proposal are shown in Exhibit 2.

The present value of the net cash flow for each year is computed by multiplying the net cash flow for the year by the present value factor of $1 for that year. In the il-

---

[3] More complete tables of both present values and future values are in Appendix A.

Exhibit 2
Net Present Value Analysis

Year	Present Value of $1 at 10%	Net Cash Flow	Present Value of Net Cash Flow
1	.909	$70,000	$ 63,630
2	.826	60,000	49,560
3	.751	50,000	37,550
4	.683	40,000	27,320
5	.621	40,000	24,840
Total		$260,000	$202,900

Amount to be invested	200,000
Net present value	$ 2,900

lustration, the net cash flow of $70,000 to be received at the end of year 1 is multiplied by the present value of $1 for 1 year at 10% (.909). Thus, the present value of the $70,000 is $63,630. Likewise, the net cash flow at the end of the second year, $60,000, is multiplied by the present value of $1 for 2 years at 10% (.826) to yield $49,560, and so on. The amount to be invested, $200,000, is then subtracted from the total present value of the net cash flows, $202,900, to determine the net present value, $2,900. The net present value indicates that the proposal is expected to recover the investment and provide more than the minimum rate of return of 10%.

When capital investment funds are limited and several alternative investment proposals of the same amount are being considered, the one with the largest net present value is the most desirable. If the alternative proposals involve different amounts of investment, it is useful to prepare a relative ranking of the proposals by using a **present value index**. The present value index is computed by dividing the total present value of the net cash flow by the amount to be invested. The present value index for Exhibit 2 is computed as follows:

$$\text{Present Value Index} = \frac{\textbf{Total Present Value of Net Cash Flow}}{\textbf{Amount To Be Invested}}$$

$$\text{Present Value Index} = \frac{\$202,900}{\$200,000} = 1.01$$

To further illustrate, assume that the total present values of the net cash flow and the amounts to be invested for three alternative proposals are as follows:

	Proposal A	Proposal B	Proposal C
Total present value of net cash flow	$107,000	$86,400	$93,600
Amount to be invested	100,000	80,000	90,000
Net present value	$ 7,000	$ 6,400	$ 3,600

The present value index for each proposal is as follows:

	Present Value Index
Proposal A	1.07 ($107,000 ÷ $100,000)
Proposal B	1.08 ($ 86,400 ÷ $ 80,000)
Proposal C	1.04 ($ 93,600 ÷ $ 90,000)

Although Proposal A has the largest net present value, the present value indexes indicate that it is not as desirable as Proposal B. In other words, Proposal B returns 1.08 present value per dollar invested while Proposal A returns only 1.07. Proposal B requires an investment of $80,000, compared to an investment of $100,000 for Proposal A. The possible use of the $20,000 difference in investments should also be considered before a final decision is made.

An advantage of the net present value method is that it considers the time value of money. A disadvantage is that the computations are more complex than those for the methods that ignore present value. In addition, the net present value method assumes that the cash received from the proposal during its useful life can be reinvested at the rate of return used in computing the present value of the proposal. Because of changing economic conditions, this assumption may not always be reasonable.

INTERNAL RATE OF RETURN METHOD. The internal rate of return method uses present value concepts to compute the rate of return from the net cash flows expected from capital investment proposals. This method is sometimes called the **time-adjusted rate of return method.** It is similar to the net present value method, in that it focuses on the present value of the net cash flows. However, the internal rate of return method starts with the net cash flows and, in a sense, works backwards to determine the rate of return expected from the proposal.

To illustrate, assume that management is evaluating a proposal to acquire equipment costing $33,530, which is expected to provide annual net cash flows of $10,000 per year for 5 years. If a rate of return of 12% is assumed, the present value of the net cash flows can be computed using the present value of $1 table in Exhibit 1. These computations are shown in Exhibit 3.

Exhibit 3
Net Present Value Analysis

Year	Present Value of $1 at 12%	Net Cash Flow	Present Value of Net Cash Flow
1	.893	$10,000	$ 8,930
2	.797	10,000	7,970
3	.712	10,000	7,120
4	.636	10,000	6,360
5	.567	10,000	5,670
Total		$50,000	$36,050

In Exhibit 3, the $36,050 present value of the net cash flow, based on a 12% rate of return, is greater than the $33,530 to be invested. Therefore, the internal rate of return must be greater than 12%. Exhibit 4 indicates that 15% is the rate of return that equates the $33,530 cost of the investment with the present value of the net cash flows.

Exhibit 4
Net Present Value Analysis

Year	Present Value of $1 at 15%	Net Cash Flow	Present Value of Net Cash Flow
1	.870	$10,000	$ 8,700
2	.756	10,000	7,560
3	.658	10,000	6,580
4	.572	10,000	5,720
5	.497	10,000	4,970
Total		$50,000	$33,530

In the above illustration, a rate of 12% was assumed before the internal rate of return of 15% was identified. Such trial-and-error procedures are time-consuming. When equal annual net cash flows are expected from a proposal, as in the illustration, the computations are simplified by using a table of the present value of an annuity.[4]

An **annuity** is a series of equal cash flows at fixed intervals. The **present value of an annuity** is the sum of the present values of each cash flow. In other words,

---

[4] In Exhibits 3 and 4, equal annual net cash flows were assumed in order to simplify the illustration. If the annual net cash flows are not equal, the computations are more complex, but the basic concepts are the same.

the present value of an annuity is the amount of cash that is needed today to yield a series of equal cash flows at fixed intervals in the future. For example, the partial table of the present value of an annuity of $1 in Exhibit 5 indicates that the present value of cash flows at the end of each of five years, with a discounted internal rate of return of 15% per year, is 3.353. Multiplying $10,000 by 3.353 yields the same amount ($33,530) that was determined in the preceding illustration by five successive multiplications.

Exhibit 5
Partial Present Value of an
Annuity Table

Present Value of an Annuity of $1 at Compound Interest

Year	6%	10%	12%	15%	20%
1	.943	.909	.893	.870	.833
2	1.833	1.736	1.690	1.626	1.528
3	2.673	2.487	2.402	2.283	2.106
4	3.465	3.170	3.037	2.855	2.589
5	4.212	3.791	3.605	3.353	2.991
6	4.917	4.355	4.111	3.785	3.326
7	5.582	4.868	4.564	4.160	3.605
8	6.210	5.335	4.968	4.487	3.837
9	6.802	5.759	5.328	4.772	4.031
10	7.360	6.145	5.650	5.019	4.192

The procedures for using the present value of an annuity of $1 table to determine the internal rate of return are summarized below.

1. A present value factor for an annuity of $1 is determined by dividing the amount to be invested by the annual net cash flow. This computation is expressed by the following formula:

$$\text{Present Value Factor for an Annuity of \$1} = \frac{\text{Amount To Be Invested}}{\text{Annual Net Cash Flow}}$$

2. The present value factor determined in (1) is located in the present value of an annuity of $1 table. First locate the number of years of expected useful life of the investment in the Year column and then proceed horizontally across the table until the present value factor computed in (1) is found.
3. The internal rate of return is then identified by the heading of the column in which the present value factor in (2) is located.

To illustrate these procedures, assume that management is considering a proposal to acquire equipment costing $97,360. The equipment is expected to provide equal annual net cash flows of $20,000 for 7 years. The present value factor for an annuity of $1 is 4.868, computed as follows:

$$\text{Present Value Factor for an Annuity of \$1} = \frac{\text{Amount To Be Invested}}{\text{Annual Net Cash Flow}}$$

$$\text{Present Value Factor for an Annuity of \$1} = \frac{\$97,360}{\$20,000} = 4.868$$

For a period of 7 years, the partial present value of an annuity of $1 table indicates that the factor 4.868 is related to a percentage of 10%, as shown on the next page. Thus, 10% is the internal rate of return for this proposal.

If the minimum acceptable rate of return for similar proposals is 10% or less, then the proposed investment should be considered desirable. When several proposals are considered, management often ranks the proposals by their internal rates of return. The proposal with the highest rate is considered the most desirable.

Year	6%	10%	12%
1	.943	.909	.893
2	1.833	1.736	1.690
3	2.673	2.487	2.402
4	3.465	3.170	3.037
5	4.212	3.791	3.605
6	4.917	4.355	4.111
7	5.582	4.868	4.564
8	6.210	5.335	4.968
9	6.802	5.759	5.328
10	7.360	6.145	5.650

The primary advantage of the internal rate of return method is that the present values of the net cash flows over the entire useful life of the proposal are considered. An additional advantage of the method is that by determining a rate of return for each proposal, all proposals are placed on a common basis for comparison. The primary disadvantage of the internal rate of return method is that the computations are more complex than for some of the other methods. In addition, like the net present value method, this method assumes that the cash received from a proposal during its useful life will be reinvested at the internal rate of return. Because of changing economic conditions, this assumption may not always be reasonable.

The Internal Rate of Return Method—An Application Using the Microcomputer

The complexity of using the present value methods of evaluating capital investment proposals can be reduced by using a microcomputer. The following computer program, which was written in the BASIC programming language, computes the internal rate of return for an investment proposal with a series of equal net cash flows:

```
10   INPUT "periods":N: INPUT "investment":I: INPUT
     "annual net cash flow":C
20   INPUT "guess":G
30   X=(X+G)/100+1:S=I
40   FOR J=1 TO N:S=S+C/X^J:NEXT:X=(X–1)*100
50   IF ABS(Y–X)<= .001 THEN END
60   LPRINT X:Y=X:RESTORE:IF S>0 THEN 30
70   X=X–G:G=G/3:GOTO 30
```

To run this program, the user must have access to the BASIC programming system. The manual accompanying this system describes the procedures for calling up the system and entering, saving, loading, and running a program. When the program is run, the user will be required to input (1) the number of periods for which the proposed capital investment will yield annual cash inflows, (2) the cost of the investment expressed as a negative initial cash flow, (3) the annual net cash flows, and (4) an initial guess as to the approximate internal rate of return. The initial guess does not have to be close to the true value, since the computer will estimate the true value regardless of the accuracy of the initial guess. The initial guess only adds effi-

ciency to the estimation process. An example of the use of this computer program for the illustration presented on page 1062 is as follows:

```
periods? 7
investment? –97360
annual net cash flow? 20000
guess? 15
    15
    4.999995
    9.999991
    14.99999
    11.66666
    10.55554
    10.18517
    10.06172
    10.02057
    10.00685
    10.00227
    10.00456
    10.00303
```

The program will stop computing the estimated internal rate of return when successive estimates are reasonably close to one another and additional precision is not warranted. In the above example, the approximate internal rate of return is 10%. Note that the difference between the above estimate and the illustration in the text is due to rounding within the computer program.

Note: This program was written for the BASIC programming language using the IBM personal computer.

QUALITATIVE CONSIDERATIONS IN CAPITAL INVESTMENT ANALYSIS

Objective 3
List examples of qualitative considerations in capital investment analysis, especially as related to today's manufacturing environment.

The methods described and illustrated in the preceding paragraphs focus on the quantitative aspects of capital investment analysis. For example, in evaluating a proposal to purchase new equipment, the expected net cash inflows are compared with the amount of cash to be invested. However, some benefits of capital investments are qualitative in nature and cannot be readily estimated in dollar terms. If these qualitative considerations are not considered, the quantitative analyses may suggest the rejection of a worthy investment.

Qualitative considerations that may impact upon capital investment analysis include the impact of investment proposals on product quality, manufacturing flexibility, employee morale, manufacturing productivity, and manufacturing control. Many of these qualitative factors may be as important, if not more important, than the results of quantitative analysis in today's manufacturing environment. This environment is characterized by investments in automated equipment, redesign of the manufacturing process, and implementation of manufacturing systems such as just-in-time manufacturing and computer-integrated manufacturing. In this environment, qualitative factors may be especially important in capital investment analysis.

The importance of considering qualitative aspects of capital investments is best summarized by Patrick S. Parker, Chairman of Parker Hannifin Corporation, who stated, "In today's environment, we don't think the numbers really tell the story." Many investments, he indicates, are required just to stay ahead of the competition and to survive.[5]

Capital Investment in the New Manufacturing Environment

The importance of capital investment analysis in the new manufacturing environment is stressed in the following excerpts from an article in *Management Accounting*. Traditional capital investment methods should be reassessed in light of this new environment, especially when considering investments in manufacturing automation.

Automation is probably the most evident change in the new manufacturing environment. The objective of automation, besides adding capacity, is to produce high-quality goods consistently, quickly, and economically. Effective use of automation can leverage the success achieved through more fundamental efforts aimed at achieving higher quality, lower inventory, streamlined production flow lines, simplified processes, and other major trends in the factory. Thus, automation can enhance the overall competitiveness of a company.

In spite of the obvious advantages of investing in automation, issues central to the investment decision have changed dramatically over the past 20 years. The new manufacturing environment presents new issues of scope, timing, and uncertainty that require management accountants to reassess the whole capital budgeting process.

The investment decision evaluates whether an investment's returns exceed its costs. While the issue of returns versus costs is still the fundamental question, the nature and risks associated with those investments has changed dramatically in the new manufacturing environment.

. . . Investments are becoming more significant. Stand-alone pieces of equipment, such as robots and computerized numerical control machines, can sell for up to $1 million. Flexible manufacturing systems—a machine or group of machines linked together to perform a series of operations automatically for one or more product lines . . . can cost anywhere from $10 to $50 million. Investments in fully automated factories, such as the IBM Proprinter facility, can cost more than $100 million.

. . . The benefits associated with advanced automation are more indirect and intangible. Where emphasis . . . was previously on direct cost savings, today investments are designed to improve quality, delivery, and customer satisfaction. This new focus requires that management accountants devise new models and methodologies to capture these benefits to establish the value contributed by the investment.

Source: Robert A. Howell and Stephen R. Soucy, Capital Investment in the New Manufacturing Environment," *Management Accounting* (November 1987), pp. 26-32.

---

[5] John F. Towey, "How to Justify Investment in New Technology," *Management Accounting* (July, 1989), p. 55.

FACTORS THAT COMPLICATE CAPITAL INVESTMENT ANALYSIS

Objective 4
List and describe factors that complicate capital investment analysis.

In the preceding discussion, the basic concepts for four widely used methods of evaluating capital investment proposals were described and illustrated. In practice, additional factors may have an impact on the outcome of a capital investment decision. Some of the most important of these factors are discussed in the following paragraphs. These factors include the federal income tax, unequal lives of alternative proposals, leasing, uncertainty, and changes in price levels.

Income Tax

In many cases, the impact of the federal income tax on capital investment decisions can be material. One provision of the *Internal Revenue Code* (IRC) that should be considered is depreciation.

In determining depreciation for federal income tax purposes, useful lives that are much shorter than the actual useful lives can often be used. Also, depreciation can be calculated by methods that approximate the 200-percent declining-balance method. Thus, depreciation for tax purposes often exceeds the depreciation for financial statement purposes in the early years of an asset's use. The tax reduction in these early years is offset by higher taxes in the later years, so that accelerated depreciation does not result in a long-run saving in taxes. However, the timing of the cash outflows for income taxes can have a significant impact on capital investment analysis.[6]

Unequal Proposal Lives

In the preceding discussion, the illustrations of the methods of analyzing capital investment proposals were based on the assumption that alternative proposals had the same useful lives. In practice, however, alternative proposals may have unequal lives. To illustrate, assume that alternative proposals X and Y are being compared. Each proposal requires an initial investment of $100,000 and has the following expected cash flow and useful life:

	Net Cash Flows	
Year	*Proposal X*	*Proposal Y*
1	$30,000	$30,000
2	30,000	30,000
3	25,000	30,000
4	20,000	30,000
5	15,000	30,000
6	15,000	—
7	10,000	—
8	10,000	—

If the desired rate of return is 10%, each proposal's net present value could be determined as shown in Exhibit 6.

Because of the unequal useful lives of the two proposals, the net present values determined in Exhibit 6 are not comparable. To make them comparable for the analysis, the proposals can be adjusted to end at the same time. This can be done by assuming that Proposal X is to be terminated at the end of 5 years and the asset sold. This assumption requires that the residual value of Proposal X be estimated at the end of 5 years and that this value be included as a cash flow at that date. Both proposals will then cover 5 years, and net present value analysis can be used to compare the two proposals over the same 5-year period.

To illustrate, assume that Proposal X has an estimated residual value of $40,000 at the end of year 5. For Proposal X, the excess of the present value over the amount to be invested is $18,640 for a 5-year life, as shown in Exhibit 7.

---

[6] The impact of income taxes on capital investment analysis is described and illustrated in advanced textbooks.

Exhibit 6
Net Present Value Analysis

Proposal X

Year	Present Value of $1 at 10%	Net Cash Flow	Present Value of Net Cash Flow
1	.909	$ 30,000	$ 27,270
2	.826	30,000	24,780
3	.751	25,000	18,775
4	.683	20,000	13,660
5	.621	15,000	9,315
6	.564	15,000	8,460
7	.513	10,000	5,130
8	.467	10,000	4,670
Total		$155,000	$112,060
Amount to be invested			100,000
Net present value			$ 12,060

Proposal Y

Year	Present Value of $1 at 10%	Net Cash Flow	Present Value of Net Cash Flow
1	.909	$ 30,000	$ 27,270
2	.826	30,000	24,780
3	.751	30,000	22,530
4	.683	30,000	20,490
5	.621	30,000	18,630
Total		$150,000	$113,700
Amount to be invested			100,000
Net present value			$ 13,700

If a 5-year life is used for both proposals, the net present value for Proposal X (Exhibit 7) exceeds the net present value for Proposal Y (Exhibit 6) by $4,940 ($18,640 − $13,700). Therefore, Proposal X may be viewed as the more attractive of the two proposals.

Exhibit 7
Net Present Value Analysis

Year	Present Value of $1 at 10%	Net Cash Flow	Present Value of Net Cash Flow
1	.909	$ 30,000	$ 27,270
2	.826	30,000	24,780
3	.751	25,000	18,775
4	.683	20,000	13,660
5	.621	15,000	9,315
5 (Residual value)	.621	40,000	24,840
Total		$160,000	$118,640
Amount to be invested			100,000
Net present value			$ 18,640

Lease Versus Capital Investment

Leasing plant assets has become common in many industries. For example, hospitals often lease diagnostic and other medical equipment. Leasing allows an enterprise to acquire the use of plant assets without the use of large amounts of cash to purchase them. In addition, management may believe that a plant asset has a high degree of risk of becoming obsolete before the end of its useful life. In this case, the risk of obsolescence may be reduced by leasing rather than purchasing the asset. Finally, the *Internal Revenue Code* allows the lessor (the owner of the asset) to pass tax deductions on to the lessee (the party leasing the asset). These provisions of the tax law have made leasing assets more attractive. For example, a company that pays $50,000 per year for leasing for its use a $200,000 plant asset with a life of 8 years is permitted to deduct from taxable income the annual lease payments.

In many cases, before a final decision is made, management should consider the possibility of leasing assets instead of purchasing them. Normally, leasing assets is more costly than purchasing because the lessor must include in the rental price not only the costs associated with owning the assets but also a profit. Nevertheless, using the methods of evaluating capital investment proposals, management should consider whether it is more profitable to lease rather than purchase an asset.

Uncertainty

All capital investment analyses rely on factors that are uncertain. For example, the estimates related to revenues, expenses, and cash flows are uncertain. The long-term nature of capital investments suggests that some estimates are likely to involve uncertainty. Errors in one or more of the estimates could lead to incorrect decisions.

Changes in Price Levels

Periods of increasing price levels are described as periods of inflation. In recent years, the rates of inflation have varied widely, making the estimation of future revenues, expenses, and cash flows even more difficult. Management should, however, attempt to anticipate future price levels and consider their effects on the estimates used in capital investment analyses. Changes in anticipated price levels could significantly affect the analyses.

CAPITAL RATIONING

Objective 5
Diagram the capital rationing process.

Capital rationing is the process by which management allocates available investment funds among competing capital investment proposals. Normally, management uses various combinations of the evaluation methods described in this chapter in developing an effective approach to capital rationing.

In capital rationing, an initial screening of alternative proposals is usually performed by establishing minimum standards for the cash payback and the average rate of return methods. The proposals that survive this initial screening are further analyzed, using the net present value and internal rate of return methods. Throughout the capital rationing process, qualitative factors related to each proposal should also be considered. For example, the acquisition of new, more efficient equipment that eliminates several jobs could lower employee morale to a level that could decrease overall plant productivity. Alternatively, new equipment might improve the quality of the product and thus increase consumer satisfaction and sales.

The final step in the capital rationing process is to rank the proposals according to management's criteria, compare the proposals with the funds available, and select the proposals to be funded. The unfunded proposals may be reconsidered if funds later become available. The flowchart in Exhibit 8 portrays the capital rationing decision process.

PLANNING AND CONTROLLING CAPITAL INVESTMENT EXPENDITURES

Objective 6
Summarize the basic concepts for planning and controlling capital investment expenditures.

Proposals that are funded in the capital rationing process are included in the budget to aid the planning and financing of operations. A capital expenditures budget summarizes capital investments for a period usually ranging from one to five years. The capital expenditures budget, as discussed in another chapter, should be integrated with the master budget. The following capital expenditures budget was prepared for Latimer Company.

Latimer Company Capital Expenditures Budget For Five Years Ending December 31, 1998					
Item	*1994*	*1995*	*1996*	*1997*	*1998*
Machinery—Department A	$240,000	—	—	$168,000	$216,000
Machinery—Department B	108,000	$156,000	$336,000	120,000	—
Delivery equipment	—	54,000	—	—	36,000
Total	$348,000	$210,000	$336,000	$228,000	$252,000

Exhibit 8
Capital Rationing Decision
Process

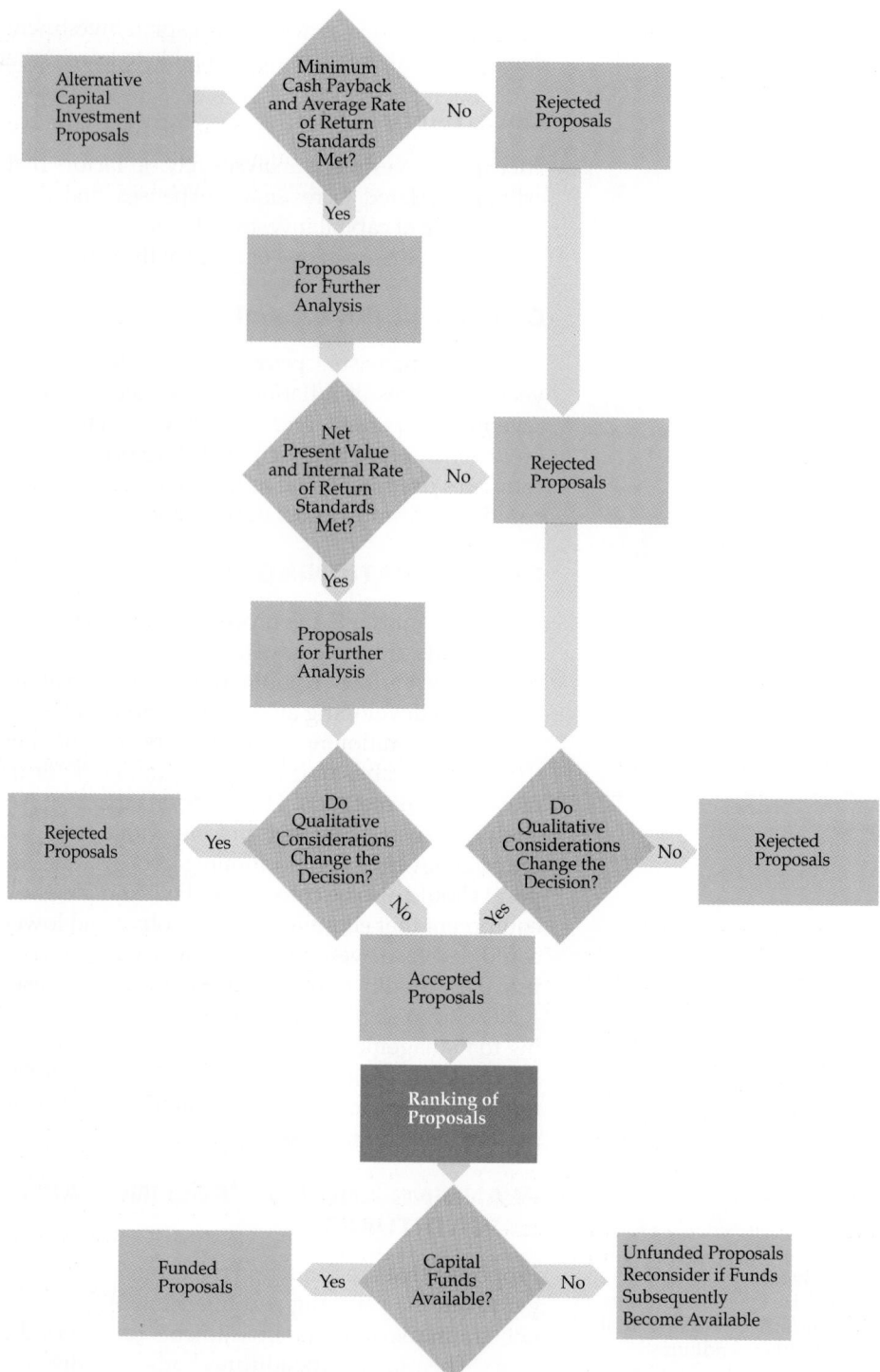

The capital expenditures budget does not authorize the purchase of plant assets. Rather, it serves as a planning tool to determine the effects of the capital expenditures on operations. Final authorization for capital expenditures must come
from the proper level of management. In some corporations, large capital expenditures must be approved by the board of directors.

Once the capital expenditures have been approved, control must be established over the costs of acquiring the assets. These costs include the costs of installation and testing before the assets are placed in service. Throughout this period
of acquiring the assets and readying them for use, actual costs should be
compared to planned (budgeted) costs. Timely reports should be prepared, so that

management can take any necessary corrective actions as quickly as possible. In this way, cost overruns and operating delays are minimized.

After the assets have been placed in service, actual operating expenses and budgeted operating expenses should be compared. Such comparisons provide opportunities for management to follow up on successful expenditures or to terminate or otherwise attempt to salvage failing expenditures.

CHAPTER REVIEW

Key Points

Objective 1. Explain the nature and importance of capital investment analysis.
Capital investment analysis is the process by which management plans, evaluates, and controls investments involving plant assets. Capital investment analysis is important to an enterprise because such investments affect an enterprise's profitability for a long period of time.

Objective 2. Evaluate capital investment proposals, using the following methods: average rate of return, cash payback, net present value, and internal rate of return.
The average rate of return method measures the expected profitability of an investment in plant assets. It is computed using the following formula:

$$\text{Average Rate of Return} = \frac{\text{Estimated Average Annual Income}}{\text{Average Investment}}$$

The expected period of time that will pass between the date of an investment and the complete recovery in cash (or equivalent) of the amount invested is the cash payback period. Investment proposals with the shortest cash payback are considered the most desirable.

The net present value method uses present values to compute the net present value of the cash flows expected from a proposal. The net present value of the cash flows are then compared across proposals. The present value of a cash flow is computed by looking up the present value of $1 from a table of present values and multiplying it by the amount of the future cash flow, as shown in the text.

The internal rate of return method uses present values to compute the rate of return from the net cash flows expected from capital investment proposals. When equal annual net cash flows are expected from a proposal, the computations are simplified by using a table of the present value of an annuity, as shown in the text.

Objective 3. List examples of qualitative considerations in capital investment analysis, especially as related to today's manufacturing environment.
Some benefits of capital investment analysis, which are especially important in today's manufacturing environment, cannot be readily estimated in dollar terms. Some examples of such considerations include improvements in product quality, manufacturing flexibility, employee morale, and manufacturing productivity and control.

Objective 4. List and describe factors that complicate capital investment analysis.
Factors that may complicate capital investment analysis include the impact of the federal income tax, unequal lives of alternative proposals, leasing, uncertainty, and changes in price levels. A brief description of the effect of each of these factors appears in the text.

Objective 5. Diagram the capital rationing process.
Capital rationing refers to the process by which management allocates available investment funds among competing capital investment proposals. A diagram of the capital rationing process appears in the text.

Objective 6. Summarize the basic concepts for planning and controlling capital investment expenditures.
Proposals that are funded in the capital rationing process should be included in the capital expenditures budget and integrated into the master budget. When plant assets are being acquired and readied for use, actual costs should be compared to planned costs, and timely reports should be prepared, so that management can minimize cost overruns and operating delays. After the assets have been placed in service, reports should also be prepared on a timely basis, comparing actual and budgeted revenues and expenses.

Glossary of Key Terms

Annuity. A series of equal cash flows at fixed intervals. **Objective 2**

Average rate of return. A method of evaluating capital investment proposals that focuses on the expected profitability of the investment. **Objective 2**

Capital expenditures budget. The budget summarizing future plans for acquisition of plant facilities and equipment. **Objective 6**

Capital investment analysis. The process by which management plans, evaluates, and controls long-term capital investments involving property, plant, and equipment. **Objective 1**

Capital rationing. The process by which management allocates available investment funds among competing capital investment proposals. **Objective 5**

Cash payback period. The expected period of time that will elapse between the date of a capital expenditure and the complete recovery in cash (or equivalent) of the amount invested. **Objective 2**

Inflation. A period when prices in general are rising and the purchasing power of money is declining. **Objective 4**

Internal rate of return method. A method of analysis of proposed capital investments that focuses on using present value concepts to compute the rate of return from the net cash flows expected from the investment. **Objective 2**

Net present value method. A method of analysis of proposed capital investments that focuses on the present value of the cash flows expected from the investments. **Objective 2**

Present value concept. Cash to be received (or paid) in the future is not the equivalent of the same amount of money to received at an earlier date. **Objective 2**

Present value index. An index computed by dividing the total present value of the net cash flow to be received from a proposed capital investment by the amount to be invested. **Objective 2**

Present value of an annuity. The sum of the present values of a series of equal cash flows to be received at fixed intervals. **Objective 2**

Time value of money concept. The concept that an amount of money invested today will earn income. **Objective 2**

Self-Examination Questions

Answers at end of chapter.

1. Methods of evaluating capital investment proposals that ignore present value include:
   A. average rate of return   C. both A and B
   B. cash payback   D. neither A nor B

2. Management is considering a $100,000 investment in a project with a 5-year life and no residual value. If the total income from the project is expected to be $60,000 and recognition is given to the effect of straight-line depreciation on the investment, the average rate of return is:
   A. 12%   C. 60%
   B. 24%   D. 75%

3. As used in the analysis of proposed capital investments, the expected period of time that will elapse between the date of a capital investment and the complete recovery of the amount of cash invested is called:
   A. the average rate of return period
   B. the cash payback period
   C. the net present value period
   D. the internal rate of return period

4. Which method of analyzing capital investment proposals determines the total present value of the cash flows expected from the investment and compares this value with the amount to be invested?
   A. Average rate of return   C. Net present value
   B. Cash payback   D. Internal rate of return

5. The process by which management allocates available investment funds among competing capital investment proposals is called:
   A. capital rationing
   B. capital expenditure budgeting
   C. leasing
   D. uncertainty

ILLUSTRATIVE PROBLEM

The capital investment committee of Bormann Company is currently considering two projects. The estimated operating income and net cash flows expected from each project are as follows:

	Project A		Project B	
Year	Operating Income	Net Cash Flow	Operating Income	Net Cash Flow
1	$ 9,000	$19,000	$ 5,000	$15,000
2	7,000	17,000	6,000	16,000
3	6,000	16,000	8,000	18,000
4	5,000	15,000	7,000	17,000
5	3,000	13,000	4,000	14,000
	$30,000	$80,000	$30,000	$80,000

Each project requires an investment of $50,000. Straight-line depreciation will be used, and no residual value is expected. The committee has selected a rate of 15% for purposes of the net present value analysis.

Instructions

1. Compute the following:
   a. The average rate of return for each project, giving effect to depreciation on the investment.
   b. The net present value for each project. Use the present value of $1 table appearing in this chapter.
2. Prepare a brief report for the capital investment committee, advising it on the relative merits of the two projects.

Solution

1.

   a. Average annual rate of return for both projects:

   $$\frac{\$30,000 \div 5}{(\$50,000 + \$0) \div 2} = 24\%$$

   b. Net present value analysis:

Year	Present Value of $1 at 15%	Net Cash Flow Project A	Net Cash Flow Project B	Present Value of Net Cash Flow Project A	Present Value of Net Cash Flow Project B
1	.870	$19,000	$15,000	$16,530	$13,050
2	.756	17,000	16,000	12,852	12,096
3	.658	16,000	18,000	10,528	11,844
4	.572	15,000	17,000	8,580	9,724
5	.497	13,000	14,000	6,461	6,958
Total		$80,000	$80,000	$54,951	$53,672
Amount to be invested				50,000	50,000
Net present value				$ 4,951	$ 3,672

2. a. Both projects offer the same average annual rate of return.
   b. Although both projects exceed the selected rate established for the net present value analysis, Project A offers a larger net present value. Thus, if only one of the two projects can be accepted, Project A would be the more attractive.

DISCUSSION QUESTIONS

1. Which two methods of capital investment analysis ignore present value?
2. Which two methods of capital investment analysis can be described as present value methods?
3. What is the time value of money concept?
4. a. How is the average rate of return computed for capital investment analysis, assuming that consideration is given to the effect of straight-line depreciation on the amount of the investment?
   b. If the amount of a 10-year investment is $500,000, the straight-line method of depreciation is used, there is no residual value, and the total income expected from the investment is $450,000, what is the average rate of return?
5. What are the principal objections to the use of the average rate of return method in evaluating capital investment proposals?
6. a. As used in analyses of proposed capital investments, what is the cash payback period?
   b. Discuss the principal limitations of the cash payback method for evaluating capital investment proposals.
7. What is the present value of $8,475 to be received one year from today, assuming an earnings rate of 13%.
8. Which method of evaluating capital investment proposals reduces their expected future net cash flows to present values and compares the total present values to the amount of the investment?

9. A net present value analysis used to evaluate a proposed equipment acquisition indicated a $9,750 net present value. What is the meaning of the $9,750 as it relates to the desirability of the proposal?
10. How is the present value index for a proposal determined?
11. What are the major disadvantages of the use of the net present value method of analyzing capital investment proposals?
12. What is an annuity?
13. What are the major disadvantages of the use of the internal rate of return method of analyzing capital investment proposals?
14. Give an example of a qualitative factor that should be considered in a capital investment analysis related to the acquisition of automated factory equipment.
15. What provision of the Internal Revenue Code is especially important for consideration in analyzing capital investment proposals?
16. What method can be used to place two capital investment proposals with unequal useful lives on a comparable basis?
17. What are the major advantages of leasing a plant asset rather than purchasing it?
18. What is capital rationing?
19. Which budget summarizes the capital expenditure decisions for a period?

REAL W●RLD FOCUS 20. Boston Metal Products, a small manufacturer in Medford, Mass., was considering the purchase of a robot. The company controller was asked to calculate whether the $200,000 investment made financial sense. Using traditional accounting techniques, the controller concluded that the investment did not meet the financial criteria that had been established. However, the company went ahead and made the investment. What qualitative considerations could Boston Metal Products have used to justify the capital investment in a robot?

ETHICS DISCUSSION CASE

Jan Carter, the controller of CGB Inc., has recently prepared the company's federal income tax return for the preceding year. In determining depreciation for federal income tax purposes, Carter used shorter useful lives for several assets than the estimated useful lives used in preparing the company's income statement. In addition, Carter deducted as expenses several expenditures which were related to depreciable assets acquired during the year. Carter believes it is highly unlikely that the company's tax return will be audited by the Internal Revenue Service.

 SHARPEN YOUR
COMMUNICATION SKILLS

    Discuss whether Carter behaved in an ethical manner.

EXERCISES

EXERCISE 28-1
AVERAGE RATE OF RETURN
Objective 2

The following data are accumulated by Baird Company in evaluating two competing capital investment proposals:

	Proposal C	Proposal D
Amount of investment	$450,000	$360,000
Useful life	6 years	8 years
Estimated residual value	-0-	-0-
Estimated total income	$243,000	$216,000

Determine the expected average rate of return for each proposal, giving effect to straight-line depreciation on each investment.

EXERCISE 28-2
CASH PAYBACK PERIOD
Objective 2

Bullard Company is evaluating two capital investment proposals, each requiring an investment of $300,000 and each with an 8-year life and expected total net cash flows of $480,000. Proposal 1 is expected to provide equal annual net cash flows of $60,000, and Proposal 2 is expected to have the following unequal annual net cash flows:

Year 1	$120,000	Year 5	40,000
Year 2	100,000	Year 6	40,000
Year 3	80,000	Year 7	40,000
Year 4	40,000	Year 8	20,000

Determine the cash payback period for both proposals.

EXERCISE 28-3
NET PRESENT VALUE
METHOD
Objective 2

The following data are accumulated by Bowen Company in evaluating the purchase of $120,000 of equipment having a 4-year useful life:

	Net Income	Net Cash Flow
Year 1	$25,000	$55,000
Year 2	10,000	40,000
Year 3	6,000	36,000
Year 4	5,000	35,000

a. Assuming that the desired rate of return is 12%, determine the net present value for the proposal. Use the table of the present value of $1 appearing in this chapter.

SHARPEN YOUR ▶
COMMUNICATION SKILLS

b. Would management be likely to look with favor on the proposal? Explain.

EXERCISE 28-4
PRESENT VALUE INDEX
Objective 2

Clary Company has computed the net present value for capital expenditure proposals A and B, using the net present value method. Relevant data related to the computation are as follows:

	Proposal A	Proposal B
Total present value of net cash flow	$318,000	$420,000
Amount to be invested	300,000	400,000
Net present value	$ 18,000	$ 20,000

Determine the present value index for each proposal.

EXERCISE 28-5
AVERAGE RATE OF RETURN,
CASH PAYBACK PERIOD,
NET PRESENT VALUE
METHOD
Objective 2

Elder Company is considering the acquisition of equipment at a cost of $400,000. The equipment has an estimated life of 5 years and no residual value. It is expected to provide yearly income of $40,000 and yearly net cash flows of $120,000. The company's minimum desired rate of return for net present value analysis is 10%. Compute the following:

SPREADSHEET
PROBLEM

a. The average rate of return, giving effect to straight-line depreciation on the investment.
b. The cash payback period.
c. The net present value. Use the table of the present value of $1 appearing in this chapter.

EXERCISE 28-6
INTERNAL RATE OF
RETURN METHOD
Objective 2

The internal rate of return method is used by Friedman Company in analyzing a capital expenditure proposal that involves an investment of $513,900 and annual net cash flows of $180,000 for each of the 4 years of useful life.

a. Determine a present value factor for an annuity of $1 which can be used in determining the internal rate of return.
b. Using the factor determined in (a) and the present value of an annuity of $1 table appearing in this chapter, determine the internal rate of return for the proposal.

EXERCISE 28-7
NET PRESENT VALUE
METHOD AND INTERNAL
RATE OF RETURN METHOD
Objective 2

Holmes Inc. is evaluating a proposed expenditure of $126,800 on a 4-year project whose estimated net cash flows are $40,000 for each of the four years.

SHARPEN YOUR ▶
COMMUNICATION SKILLS

a. Compute the net present value, using a rate of return of 15%.
b. Based on the analysis prepared in (a), is the rate of return (1) more than 15%, (2) 15%, or (3) less than 15%? Explain.
c. Determine the internal rate of return by computing a present value factor for an annuity of $1 and using the table of the present value of an annuity of $1 presented in the text.

WhAT'S WRONG
WITH THiS?

Rodgers Company is considering the purchase of automated machinery that is expected to have a useful life of 5 years and no residual value. The average rate of return on the average investment has been computed to be 20%, and the cash payback period was computed to be 5.2 years. Do you see any reason to question the validity of the data presented? Explain.

PROBLEMS

Series A

PROBLEM 28-1A
AVERAGE RATE OF RETURN
METHOD, NET PRESENT
VALUE METHOD, AND
ANALYSIS
Objective 2

The capital investment committee is considering two projects. The estimated operating income and net cash flows from each project are as follows:

	Project P		Project Q	
Year	Operating Income	Net Cash Flow	Operating Income	Net Cash Flow
1	$ 25,000	$ 75,000	$ 40,000	$ 90,000
2	25,000	75,000	30,000	80,000
3	25,000	75,000	20,000	70,000
4	15,000	65,000	6,000	56,000
5	10,000	60,000	4,000	54,000
	$100,000	$350,000	$100,000	$350,000

Each project requires an investment of $250,000. Straight-line depreciation will be used, and no residual value is expected. The committee has selected a rate of 12% for purposes of the net present value analysis.

SPREADSHEET
PROBLEM

Instructions

1. Compute the following:
   a. The average rate of return for each project, giving effect to depreciation on the investment.
   b. The net present value for each project. Use the present value of $1 table appearing in this chapter.

SHARPEN YOUR ►
COMMUNICATION SKILLS

2. Prepare a brief report for the capital investment committee, advising it on the relative merits of the two projects.

PROBLEM 28-2A
CASH PAYBACK PERIOD,
NET PRESENT VALUE
METHOD, AND ANALYSIS
Objective 2

Woburn Company is considering two projects. The estimated net cash flows from each project are as follows:

Year	Project G	Project R
1	$200,000	$190,000
2	175,000	185,000
3	50,000	90,000
4	50,000	30,000
5	50,000	30,000
Total	$525,000	$525,000

Each project requires an investment of $375,000, with no residual value expected. A rate of 15% has been selected for the net present value analysis.

Instructions

1. Compute the following for each project:
   a. Cash payback period.
   b. The net present value. Use the present value of $1 table appearing in this chapter.

SHARPEN YOUR ►
COMMUNICATION SKILLS

2. Prepare a brief report advising management on the relative merits of each of the two projects.

PROBLEM 28-3A
NET PRESENT VALUE
METHOD, PRESENT VALUE
INDEX, AND ANALYSIS
Objective 2

C. C. Kinney wishes to evaluate three capital investment projects by using the net present value method. Relevant data related to the projects are summarized as follows:

	Project C	Project D	Project E
Amount to be invested	$480,000	$240,000	$240,000
Annual net cash flows:			
Year 1	300,000	180,000	60,000
Year 2	240,000	120,000	120,000
Year 3	180,000	60,000	180,000

Instructions

1. Assuming that the desired rate of return is 20%, prepare a net present value analysis for each project. Use the present value of $1 table appearing in this chapter.
2. Determine a present value index for each project.

3. Which project offers the largest amount of present value per dollar of investment? Explain.

PROBLEM 28-4A
NET PRESENT VALUE
METHOD, INTERNAL RATE
OF RETURN METHOD, AND
ANALYSIS
Objective 2

Management is considering two capital investment projects. The estimated net cash flows from each project are as follows:

Year	Project I	Project II
1	$120,000	$30,000
2	120,000	30,000
3	120,000	30,000
4	120,000	30,000

Project I requires an investment of $364,440, while Project II requires an investment of $85,650. No residual value is expected from either project.

Instructions

1. Compute the following for each project:
    a. The net present value. Use a rate of 10% and the present value of $1 table appearing in this chapter.
    b. A present value index.
2. Determine the internal rate of return for each project by (a) computing a present value factor for an annuity of $1 and (b) using the present value of an annuity of $1 table appearing in this chapter.

3. What advantage does the internal rate of return method have over the net present value method in comparing projects?

PROBLEM 28-5A
EVALUATION OF
ALTERNATIVE CAPITAL
INVESTMENT DECISIONS
Objectives 2, 4

The investment committee of Marion Company is evaluating two projects. The projects have different useful lives, but each requires an investment of $150,000. The estimated net cash flows from each project are as follows:

Net Cash Flows

Year	Project A	Project B
1	$40,000	$55,000
2	40,000	55,000
3	40,000	55,000
4	40,000	55,000
5	40,000	
6	40,000	

The committee has selected a rate of 15% for purposes of net present value analysis. It also estimates that the residual value at the end of each project's useful life is $0, but at the end of the fourth year, Project A's residual value would be $80,000.

Instructions

1. For each project, compute the net present value. Use the present value of $1 table appearing in this chapter. (Ignore the unequal lives of the projects.)
2. For each project, compute the net present value, assuming that Project A is adjusted to a four-year life for purposes of analysis. Use the present value of $1 table appearing in this chapter.

3. In reporting to the investment committee, what advice would you give on the relative merits of the two projects?

PROBLEM 28-6A
CAPITAL RATIONING
DECISION INVOLVING SIX
PROPOSALS
Objectives 2, 5

Matthews Company is considering the allocation of a limited amount of capital investment funds among six proposals. The amount of proposed investment, estimated operating income, and net cash flow for each proposal are as follows:

	Investment	Year	Operating Income	Net Cash Flow
Proposal A:	$100,000	1	$20,000	$ 40,000
		2	10,000	30,000
		3	10,000	30,000
		4	5,000	25,000
		5	5,000	25,000
Proposal B:	$300,000	1	$25,000	$ 85,000
		2	15,000	75,000
		3	10,000	70,000
		4	10,000	70,000
		5	5,000	65,000
Proposal C:	$200,000	1	$50,000	$ 90,000
		2	20,000	60,000
		3	10,000	50,000
		4	5,000	45,000
		5	5,000	45,000
Proposal D:	$ 50,000	1	$ 2,500	$ 12,500
		2	2,500	12,500
		3	2,500	12,500
		4	2,500	12,500
		5	2,500	12,500
Proposal E:	$ 50,000	1	$20,000	$ 30,000
		2	10,000	20,000
		3	4,000	14,000
		4	2,500	12,500
		5	1,000	11,000
Proposal F:	$500,000	1	$40,000	$140,000
		2	25,000	125,000
		3	17,500	117,500
		4	17,500	117,500
		5	12,500	112,500

Matthews Company's capital rationing policy requires a minimum cash payback period of 4 years for projects of $100,000 and over and a minimum cash payback period of 3 years for projects under $100,000. In addition, a minimum average rate of return of 10% is required on all projects. If the preceding minimum standards are met, the net present value method and present value indexes are used to rank the remaining proposals.

Instructions

1. Compute the cash payback period for each of the six proposals.
2. Giving effect to straight-line depreciation on the investments and assuming no estimated residual value, compute the average rate of return for each of the six proposals.
3. Using the following format, summarize the results of your computations in (1) and (2). By placing a check mark in the appropriate column at the right, indicate which proposals should be accepted for further analysis and which should be rejected.

Proposal	Cash Payback Period	Average Rate of Return	Accept for Further Analysis	Reject
A				
B				
C				
D				
E				
F				

4. For the proposals accepted for further analysis in (3), compute the net present value. Use a rate of 10% and the present value of $1 table appearing in this chapter.
5. Compute the present value index for each of the proposals in (4).
6. Rank the proposals from most attractive to least attractive, based on the present values of net cash flows computed in (4).

7. Rank the proposals from most attractive to least attractive, based on the present value indexes computed in (5).

8. Based upon the analyses, comment on the relative attractiveness of the proposals ranked in (6) and (7).

Series B

PROBLEM 28-1B
AVERAGE RATE OF RETURN
METHOD, NET PRESENT
VALUE METHOD, AND
ANALYSIS
Objective 2

The capital investments committee is considering two projects. The estimated operating income and net cash flows from each project are as follows:

	Project A		Project X	
Year	Operating Income	Net Cash Flow	Operating Income	Net Cash Flow
1	$15,000	$ 39,000	$ 7,000	$ 31,000
2	10,000	34,000	9,000	33,000
3	8,000	32,000	10,000	34,000
4	6,000	30,000	10,000	34,000
5	6,000	30,000	9,000	33,000
	$45,000	$165,000	$45,000	$165,000

Each project requires an investment of $120,000. Straight-line depreciation will be used, and no residual value is expected. The committee has selected a rate of 10% for purposes of the net present value analysis.

SPREADSHEET
PROBLEM

Instructions

1. Compute the following:
   a. The average rate of return for each project, giving effect to depreciation on the investment.
   b. The net present value for each project. Use the present value of $1 table appearing in this chapter.

2. Prepare a brief report for the capital investments committee, advising it on the relative merits of the two projects.

PROBLEM 28-2B
CASH PAYBACK PERIOD,
NET PRESENT VALUE
METHOD, AND ANALYSIS
Objective 2

Harper Company is considering two projects. The estimated net cash flows from each project are as follows:

Year	Project E	Project F
1	$ 50,000	$150,000
2	250,000	150,000
3	100,000	100,000
4	50,000	60,000
5	50,000	40,000
Total	$500,000	$500,000

Each project requires an investment of $300,000, with no residual value expected. A rate of 20% has been selected for the net present value analysis.

Instructions

1. Compute the following for each project:
   a. Cash payback period.
   b. The net present value. Use the present value of $1 table appearing in this chapter.

2. Prepare a brief report advising management on the relative merits of each of the two projects.

PROBLEM 28-3B
NET PRESENT VALUE
METHOD, PRESENT VALUE
INDEX, AND ANALYSIS
Objective 2

Keane Company wishes to evaluate three capital investment proposals by using the net present value method. Relevant data related to the proposals are summarized as follows:

	Proposal X	Proposal Y	Proposal Z
Amount to be invested	$100,000	$100,000	$150,000
Annual net cash flows:			
Year 1	60,000	45,000	75,000
Year 2	45,000	40,000	70,000
Year 3	30,000	30,000	60,000

Instructions

1. Assuming that the desired rate of return is 15%, prepare a net present value analysis for each proposal. Use the present value of $1 table appearing in this chapter.
2. Determine a present value index for each proposal.
3. Which proposal offers the largest amount of present value per dollar of investment? Explain.

■ SHARPEN YOUR ►
COMMUNICATION SKILLS

PROBLEM 28-4B
NET PRESENT VALUE
METHOD, INTERNAL RATE
OF RETURN METHOD, AND
ANALYSIS
Objective 2

Management is considering two capital investment projects. The estimated net cash flows from each project are as follows:

Year	Project B	Project C
1	$50,000	$160,000
2	50,000	160,000
3	50,000	160,000
4	50,000	160,000

Project B requires an investment of $129,450, while Project C requires an investment of $456,800. No residual value is expected from either project.

Instructions

1. Compute the following for each project:
   a. The net present value. Use a rate of 12% and the present value of $1 table appearing in this chapter.
   b. A present value index.
2. Determine the internal rate of return for each project by (a) computing a present value factor for an annuity of $1 and (b) using the present value of an annuity of $1 table appearing in this chapter.
3. What advantage does the internal rate of return method have over the net present value method in comparing projects?

■ SHARPEN YOUR ►
COMMUNICATION SKILLS

PROBLEM 28-5B
EVALUATION OF
ALTERNATIVE CAPITAL
INVESTMENT DECISIONS
Objectives 2, 4

The investment committee of Conrad Company is evaluating two projects. The projects have different useful lives, but each requires an investment of $165,000. The estimated net cash flows from each project are as follows:

	Net Cash Flows	
Year	Project I	Project II
1	$45,000	$60,000
2	45,000	60,000
3	45,000	60,000
4	45,000	60,000
5	45,000	
6	45,000	

The committee has selected a rate of 15% for purposes of net present value analysis. It also estimates that the residual value at the end of each project's useful life is $0, but at the end of the fourth year, Project I's residual value would be $80,000.

Instructions

1. For each project, compute the net present value. Use the present value of $1 table appearing in this chapter. (Ignore the unequal lives of the projects.)
2. For each project, compute the net present value, assuming that Project I is adjusted to a four-year life for purposes of analysis. Use the present value of $1 table appearing in this chapter.
3. In reporting to the investment committee, what advice would you give on the relative merits of the two projects?

■ SHARPEN YOUR ►
COMMUNICATION SKILLS

PROBLEM 28-6B
CAPITAL RATIONING
DECISION INVOLVING SIX
PROPOSALS
Objectives 2, 5

Sharperson Company is considering the allocation of a limited amount of capital investment funds among six proposals. The amount of proposed investment, estimated operating income, and net cash flow for each proposal are as follows:

	Investment	Year	Operating Income	Net Cash Flow
Proposal A:	$100,000	1	$20,000	$ 40,000
		2	10,000	30,000
		3	10,000	30,000
		4	5,000	25,000
		5	5,000	25,000
Proposal B:	$ 75,000	1	$ 3,000	$ 18,000
		2	3,500	18,500
		3	4,000	19,000
		4	4,500	19,500
		5	3,750	18,750
Proposal C:	$200,000	1	$50,000	$ 90,000
		2	20,000	60,000
		3	10,000	50,000
		4	5,000	45,000
		5	5,000	45,000
Proposal D:	$500,000	1	$35,000	$135,000
		2	30,000	130,000
		3	22,500	122,500
		4	12,500	112,500
		5	12,500	112,500
Proposal E:	$ 50,000	1	$20,000	$ 30,000
		2	10,000	20,000
		3	4,000	14,000
		4	2,500	12,500
		5	1,000	11,000
Proposal F:	$300,000	1	$12,000	$ 72,000
		2	12,000	72,000
		3	12,000	72,000
		4	12,000	72,000
		5	12,000	72,000

The company's capital rationing policy requires a minimum cash payback period of 4 years for projects of $100,000 and over and a minimum cash payback period of 3 years for projects under $100,000. In addition, a minimum average rate of return of 10% is required on all projects. If the preceding minimum standards are met, the net present value method and present value indexes are used to rank the remaining proposals.

Instructions

1. Compute the cash payback period for each of the six proposals.
2. Giving effect to straight-line depreciation on the investments and assuming no estimated residual value, compute the average rate of return for each of the six proposals.
3. Using the following format, summarize the results of your computations in (1) and (2). By placing a check mark in the appropriate column at the right, indicate which proposals should be accepted for further analysis and which should be rejected.

Proposal	Cash Payback Period	Average Rate of Return	Accept for Further Analysis	Reject
A				
B				
C				
D				
E				
F				

4. For the proposals accepted for further analysis in (3), compute the net present value. Use a rate of 10% and the present value of $1 table appearing in this chapter.
5. Compute the present value index for each of the proposals in (4).
6. Rank the proposals from most attractive to least attractive, based on the present values of net cash flows computed in (4).

7. Rank the proposals from most attractive to least attractive, based on the present value indexes computed in (5).

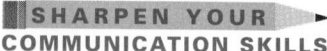
SHARPEN YOUR
COMMUNICATION SKILLS

8. Based upon the analyses, comment on the relative attractiveness of the proposals ranked in (6) and (7).

MINI-CASE 28 PLUNKETT INDUSTRIES INC.

Your mother is considering an investment of $400,000 in either Project G or Project H. In discussing the two projects with an advisor, it was decided that, for the risk involved, a return of 12% on the cash investment would be required. For this purpose, your mother estimated the following economic factors for the projects:

	Project G	Project H
Useful life	4 years	4 years
Residual value	-0-	-0-
Net income:		
Year 1	$ 20,000	$ 55,000
2	30,000	40,000
3	35,000	15,000
4	43,000	10,000
Net cash flows:		
Year 1	$120,000	$155,000
2	130,000	140,000
3	135,000	115,000
4	143,000	110,000

Although the average rate of return exceeded 12% on both projects, your mother has tentatively decided to invest in Project G because the rate was higher for Project G. Although she doesn't fully understand the importance of cash flow, she has heard others talk about its importance in evaluating investments. In this respect, she noted that the total net cash flow from Project G is $528,000, which exceeds that of Project H by $8,000.

Instructions:

1. Determine the average rate of return for both projects.
2. ▮▮▮▮ ▸ How would you explain the importance of net cash flows in the analysis of investment projects? Include a specific example to demonstrate the importance of net cash flows and their timing to these two projects.

ANSWERS TO SELF-EXAMINATION QUESTIONS

1. **C** Methods of evaluating capital investment proposals that ignore the time value of money are categorized as methods that ignore present value. This category includes the average rate of return method (answer A) and the cash payback method (answer B).
2. **B** The average rate of return is 24% (answer B), determined by dividing the expected average annual earnings by the average investment, as follows:

$$\frac{\$60,000 \div 5}{(\$100,000 + \$0) \div 2} = 24\%$$

3. **B** Of the four methods of analyzing proposals for capital investments, the cash payback period (answer B) refers to the expected period of time required to recover the amount of cash to be invested. The average rate of return (answer A) is a measure of the anticipated profitability of a proposal. The net present value method (answer C) reduces the expected future net cash flows originating from a proposal to their present values. The internal rate of return method (answer D) uses present value concepts to compute the rate of return from the net cash flows expected from the investment.

4. **C** The net present value method (answer C) uses the concept of present value to determine the total present value of the cash flows expected from a proposal and compares this value with the amount to be invested. The average rate of return method (answer A) and the cash payback method (answer B) ignore present value. The internal rate of return method (answer D) uses present value concepts to determine the internal rate of return expected from the proposal.

5. **A** Capital rationing (answer A) is the process by which management allocates available investment funds among competing capital investment proposals. Capital expenditure budgeting (answer B) is the process of summarizing the decisions that have been made for the acquisition of plant assets and preparing a capital expenditures budget to reflect these decisions. Leasing (answer C) is an alternative that management should consider before making a final decision on the acquisition of assets. Uncertainty (answer D) complicates capital investment analysis because of the need to rely upon estimates in evaluating alternative proposals.

INTEREST TABLES

The following present value and future value tables contain factors carried to six decimal places for interest rates of 5% to 14% for 50 periods.

Present Value of 1 at Compound Interest Due in n Periods: $p_{\overline{n}|i} = \dfrac{1}{(1+i)^n}$

n \\ i	5%	5.5%	6%	6.5%	7%	8%	9%	10%	11%	12%	13%	14%
1	0.952381	0.94787	0.943396	0.93897	0.934580	0.925926	0.917431	0.909091	0.90090	0.892857	0.88496	0.87719
2	0.907029	0.89845	0.889996	0.88166	0.873439	0.857339	0.841680	0.826446	0.81162	0.797194	0.78315	0.76947
3	0.863838	0.85161	0.839619	0.82785	0.816298	0.793832	0.772183	0.751315	0.73119	0.711780	0.69305	0.67497
4	0.822702	0.80722	0.792094	0.77732	0.762895	0.735030	0.708425	0.683013	0.65873	0.635518	0.61332	0.59208
5	0.783526	0.76513	0.747258	0.72988	0.712986	0.680583	0.649931	0.620921	0.59345	0.567427	0.54276	0.51937
6	0.746215	0.72525	0.704961	0.68533	0.666342	0.630170	0.596267	0.564474	0.53464	0.506631	0.48032	0.45559
7	0.710681	0.68744	0.665057	0.64351	0.622750	0.583490	0.547034	0.513158	0.48166	0.452349	0.42506	0.39964
8	0.676839	0.65160	0.627412	0.60423	0.582009	0.540269	0.501866	0.466507	0.43393	0.403883	0.37616	0.35056
9	0.644609	0.61763	0.591898	0.56735	0.543934	0.500249	0.460428	0.424098	0.39092	0.360610	0.33288	0.30751
10	0.613913	0.58543	0.558395	0.53273	0.508349	0.463193	0.422411	0.385543	0.35218	0.321973	0.29459	0.26974
11	0.584679	0.55491	0.526788	0.50021	0.475093	0.428883	0.387533	0.350494	0.31728	0.287476	0.26070	0.23662
12	0.556837	0.52598	0.496969	0.46968	0.444012	0.397114	0.355535	0.318631	0.28584	0.256675	0.23071	0.20756
13	0.530321	0.49856	0.468839	0.44102	0.414964	0.367698	0.326179	0.289664	0.25751	0.229174	0.20416	0.18207
14	0.505068	0.47257	0.442301	0.41410	0.387817	0.340461	0.299246	0.263331	0.23199	0.204620	0.18068	0.15971
15	0.481017	0.44793	0.417265	0.38883	0.362446	0.315242	0.274538	0.239392	0.20900	0.182696	0.15989	0.14010
16	0.458112	0.42458	0.393646	0.36510	0.338735	0.291890	0.251870	0.217629	0.18829	0.163122	0.14150	0.12289
17	0.436297	0.40245	0.371364	0.34281	0.316574	0.270269	0.231073	0.197845	0.16963	0.145644	0.12522	0.10780
18	0.415521	0.38147	0.350344	0.32189	0.295864	0.250249	0.211994	0.179859	0.15282	0.130040	0.11081	0.09456
19	0.395734	0.36158	0.330513	0.30224	0.276508	0.231712	0.194490	0.163508	0.13768	0.116107	0.09806	0.08295
20	0.376889	0.34273	0.311805	0.28380	0.258419	0.214548	0.178431	0.148644	0.12403	0.103667	0.08678	0.07276
21	0.358942	0.32486	0.294155	0.26648	0.241513	0.198656	0.163698	0.135131	0.11174	0.092560	0.07680	0.06383
22	0.341850	0.30793	0.277505	0.25021	0.225713	0.183941	0.150182	0.122846	0.10067	0.082643	0.06796	0.05599
23	0.325571	0.29187	0.261797	0.23494	0.210947	0.170315	0.137781	0.111678	0.09069	0.073788	0.06014	0.04911
24	0.310068	0.27666	0.246979	0.22060	0.197147	0.157699	0.126405	0.101526	0.08170	0.065882	0.05323	0.04308
25	0.295303	0.26223	0.232999	0.20714	0.184249	0.146018	0.115968	0.092296	0.07361	0.058823	0.04710	0.03779
26	0.281241	0.24856	0.219810	0.19450	0.172195	0.135202	0.106393	0.083905	0.06631	0.052521	0.04168	0.03315
27	0.267848	0.23560	0.207368	0.18263	0.160930	0.125187	0.097608	0.076278	0.05974	0.046894	0.03689	0.02908
28	0.255094	0.22332	0.195630	0.17148	0.150402	0.115914	0.089548	0.069343	0.05382	0.041869	0.03264	0.02551
29	0.242946	0.21168	0.184557	0.16101	0.140563	0.107328	0.082155	0.063039	0.04849	0.037383	0.02889	0.02237
30	0.231377	0.20064	0.174110	0.15119	0.131367	0.099377	0.075371	0.057309	0.04368	0.033378	0.02557	0.01963
31	0.220359	0.19018	0.164255	0.14196	0.122773	0.092016	0.069148	0.052099	0.03935	0.029802	0.02262	0.01722
32	0.209866	0.18027	0.154957	0.13329	0.114741	0.085200	0.063438	0.047362	0.03545	0.026609	0.02002	0.01510
33	0.199873	0.17087	0.146186	0.12516	0.107235	0.078889	0.058200	0.043057	0.03194	0.023758	0.01772	0.01325
34	0.190355	0.16196	0.137912	0.11752	0.100219	0.073045	0.053395	0.039143	0.02878	0.021212	0.01568	0.01162
35	0.181290	0.15352	0.130105	0.11035	0.093663	0.067635	0.048986	0.035584	0.02592	0.018940	0.01388	0.01019
40	0.142046	0.11746	0.097222	0.08054	0.066780	0.046031	0.031838	0.022095	0.01538	0.010747	0.00753	0.00529
45	0.111297	0.08988	0.072650	0.05879	0.047613	0.031328	0.020692	0.013719	0.00913	0.006098	0.00409	0.00275
50	0.087204	0.06877	0.054288	0.04291	0.033948	0.021321	0.013449	0.008519	0.00542	0.003460	0.00222	0.00143

Present Value of Ordinary Annuity of 1 per Period: $P_{\overline{n}|i} = \dfrac{1 - \dfrac{1}{(1+i)^n}}{i}$

n	5%	5.5%	6%	6.5%	7%	8%	9%	10%	11%	12%	13%	14%
1	0.952381	0.94787	0.943396	0.93897	0.934579	0.925926	0.917431	0.909091	0.90090	0.892857	0.88496	0.87719
2	1.859410	1.84632	1.833393	1.82063	1.808018	1.783265	1.759111	1.735537	1.71252	1.690051	1.66810	1.64666
3	2.723248	2.69793	2.673012	2.64848	2.624316	2.577097	2.531295	2.486852	2.44371	2.401831	2.36115	2.32163
4	3.545951	3.50515	3.465106	3.42580	3.387211	3.312127	3.239720	3.169865	3.10245	3.037349	2.97447	2.91371
5	4.329477	4.27028	4.212364	4.15568	4.100197	3.992710	3.889651	3.790787	3.69590	3.604776	3.51723	3.43308
6	5.075692	4.99553	4.917324	4.84101	4.766540	4.622880	4.485919	4.355261	4.23054	4.111407	3.99755	3.88867
7	5.786373	5.68297	5.582381	5.48452	5.389289	5.206370	5.032953	4.868419	4.71220	4.563757	4.42261	4.28830
8	6.463213	6.33457	6.209794	6.08875	5.971299	5.746639	5.534819	5.334926	5.14612	4.967640	4.79677	4.63886
9	7.107822	6.95220	6.801692	6.65610	6.515232	6.246888	5.995247	5.759024	5.53705	5.328250	5.13166	4.94637
10	7.721735	7.53763	7.360087	7.18883	7.023582	6.710081	6.417658	6.144567	5.88923	5.650223	5.42624	5.21612
11	8.306414	8.09254	7.886875	7.68904	7.498674	7.138964	6.805191	6.495061	6.20652	5.937699	5.68694	5.45273
12	8.863252	8.61852	8.383844	8.15873	7.942686	7.536078	7.160725	6.813692	6.49236	6.194374	5.91765	5.66029
13	9.393573	9.11708	8.852683	8.59974	8.357651	7.903776	7.486904	7.103356	6.74987	6.423548	6.12181	5.84236
14	9.898641	9.58965	9.294984	9.01384	8.745468	8.224237	7.786150	7.366687	6.96187	6.628168	6.30249	6.00207
15	10.379658	10.03758	9.712249	9.40267	9.107914	8.559479	8.060688	7.606080	7.19087	6.810864	6.46238	6.14217
16	10.837770	10.46216	10.105895	9.76776	9.446649	8.851369	8.312558	7.823709	7.37916	6.973986	6.60388	6.26506
17	11.274066	10.86461	10.477260	10.11058	9.763223	9.121638	8.543631	8.021553	7.54879	7.119630	6.72909	6.37286
18	11.689587	11.24607	10.827603	10.43247	10.059087	9.371887	8.755625	8.201412	7.70162	7.249670	6.83991	6.46742
19	12.085321	11.60765	11.158116	10.73471	10.335595	9.603599	8.950115	8.364920	7.83929	7.365777	6.93797	6.55037
20	12.462210	11.95038	11.469921	11.01851	10.594014	9.818147	9.128546	8.513564	7.96333	7.469444	7.02475	6.62313
21	12.821153	12.27524	11.764077	11.28498	10.835527	10.016803	9.292244	8.648694	8.07507	7.562003	7.10155	6.68696
22	13.163003	12.58317	12.041582	11.53520	11.061241	10.200744	9.442425	8.771540	8.17574	7.644646	7.16951	6.74294
23	13.488574	12.87504	12.303379	11.77014	11.272187	10.371059	9.580207	8.883218	8.26643	7.718434	7.22966	6.79206
24	13.798642	13.15170	12.550358	11.99074	11.469334	10.528758	9.706612	8.984744	8.34814	7.784316	7.28288	6.83514
25	14.093945	13.41393	12.783356	12.19788	11.653583	10.674776	9.822580	9.077040	8.42174	7.843139	7.32998	6.87293
26	14.375185	13.66250	13.003166	12.39237	11.825779	10.809978	9.928972	9.160945	8.48806	7.895660	7.37167	6.90608
27	14.643034	13.89810	13.210534	12.57500	11.986709	10.935165	10.026580	9.237223	8.54780	7.942554	7.40856	6.93515
28	14.898127	14.12142	13.406164	12.74648	12.137111	11.051078	10.116128	9.306567	8.60162	7.984423	7.44120	6.96066
29	15.141074	14.33310	13.590721	12.90749	12.277674	11.158406	10.198283	9.369606	8.65011	8.021806	7.47009	6.98304
30	15.372451	14.53375	13.764831	13.05868	12.409041	11.257783	10.273654	9.426914	8.69379	8.055184	7.49565	7.00266
31	15.592811	14.72393	13.929086	13.20063	12.531814	11.349799	10.342802	9.479013	8.73315	8.084986	7.51828	7.01988
32	15.802677	14.90420	14.084043	13.33393	12.646555	11.434999	10.406240	9.526376	8.76860	8.111594	7.53830	7.03498
33	16.002549	15.07507	14.230230	13.45909	12.753790	11.513888	10.464441	9.569432	8.80054	8.135352	7.55602	7.04823
34	16.192904	15.23703	14.368141	13.57661	12.854009	11.586934	10.517835	9.608575	8.82932	8.156564	7.57170	7.05985
35	16.374194	15.39055	14.498246	13.68696	12.947672	11.654568	10.566821	9.644159	8.85524	8.175504	7.58557	7.07005
40	17.159086	16.04612	15.046297	14.14553	13.331709	11.924613	10.757360	9.779051	8.95105	8.243777	7.63438	7.10504
45	17.774070	16.54773	15.455832	14.48023	13.605522	12.108402	10.881197	9.862808	9.00791	8.282516	7.66086	7.12322
50	18.255925	16.93152	15.761861	14.72452	13.800746	12.233485	10.961683	9.914814	9.04165	8.304498	7.67524	7.13266

Future Amount of 1 at Compound Interest Due in n Periods: $a_{\overline{n}|} = (1 + i)^n$

n	5%	5.5%	6%	6.5%	7%	8%	9%	10%	11%	12%	13%	14%
1	1.050000	1.05500	1.060000	1.06500	1.070000	1.080000	1.090000	1.100000	1.11000	1.120000	1.13000	1.14000
2	1.102500	1.11303	1.123600	1.13423	1.144900	1.166400	1.188100	1.210000	1.23210	1.254400	1.27690	1.29960
3	1.157625	1.17424	1.191016	1.20795	1.225043	1.259712	1.295029	1.331000	1.36763	1.404928	1.44290	1.48154
4	1.215506	1.23882	1.262477	1.28647	1.310796	1.360489	1.411582	1.464100	1.51807	1.573519	1.63047	1.68896
5	1.276282	1.30696	1.338226	1.37009	1.402552	1.469328	1.538624	1.610510	1.68506	1.762342	1.84244	1.92541
6	1.340096	1.37884	1.418519	1.45914	1.500730	1.586874	1.677100	1.771561	1.87041	1.973823	2.08195	2.19497
7	1.407100	1.45468	1.503630	1.55399	1.605781	1.713824	1.828039	1.948717	2.07616	2.210681	2.35261	2.50227
8	1.477455	1.53469	1.593848	1.65500	1.718186	1.850930	1.992563	2.143589	2.30454	2.475963	2.65844	2.85259
9	1.551328	1.61909	1.689479	1.76257	1.838459	1.999005	2.171893	2.357948	2.55804	2.773079	3.00404	3.25195
10	1.628895	1.70814	1.790848	1.87714	1.967151	2.158925	2.367364	2.593742	2.83942	3.105848	3.39457	3.70722
11	1.710339	1.80209	1.898299	1.99915	2.104852	2.331639	2.580426	2.853117	3.15176	3.478550	3.83586	4.22623
12	1.795856	1.90121	2.012196	2.12910	2.252192	2.518170	2.812665	3.138428	3.49845	3.895976	4.33452	4.81790
13	1.885649	2.00577	2.132928	2.26749	2.409845	2.719624	3.065805	3.452271	3.88328	4.363493	4.89801	5.49241
14	1.979932	2.11609	2.260904	2.41487	2.578534	2.937194	3.341727	3.797498	4.31044	4.887112	5.53475	6.26135
15	2.078928	2.23248	2.396558	2.57184	2.759032	3.172169	3.642482	4.177248	4.78459	5.473566	6.25427	7.13794
16	2.182875	2.35526	2.540352	2.73901	2.952164	3.425943	3.970306	4.594973	5.31089	6.130394	7.06733	8.13725
17	2.292018	2.48480	2.692773	2.91705	3.158815	3.700018	4.327633	5.054470	5.89509	6.866041	7.98608	9.27646
18	2.406619	2.62147	2.854339	3.10665	3.379932	3.996019	4.717120	5.559917	6.54355	7.689966	9.02427	10.57517
19	2.526950	2.76565	3.025600	3.30859	3.616528	4.315701	5.141661	6.115909	7.26334	8.612762	10.19742	12.05569
20	2.653298	2.91776	3.207135	3.52365	3.869684	4.660957	5.604411	6.727500	8.06231	9.646293	11.52309	13.74349
21	2.785963	3.07823	3.399564	3.75268	4.140562	5.033834	6.108808	7.400250	8.94917	10.803848	13.02109	15.66758
22	2.925261	3.24754	3.603537	3.99661	4.430402	5.436540	6.658600	8.140275	9.93357	12.100310	14.71383	17.86104
23	3.071524	3.42615	3.819750	4.25639	4.740530	5.871464	7.257874	8.954302	11.02627	13.552347	16.62663	20.36158
24	3.225100	3.61459	4.048935	4.53305	5.072367	6.341181	7.911083	9.849733	12.23916	15.178629	18.78809	23.21221
25	3.386355	3.81339	4.291871	4.82770	5.427433	6.848475	8.623081	10.834706	13.58546	17.000064	21.23054	26.46192
26	3.555673	4.02313	4.549383	5.14150	5.807353	7.396353	9.399158	11.918177	15.07986	19.040072	23.99051	30.16658
27	3.733456	4.24440	4.822346	5.47570	6.213868	7.988061	10.245082	13.109994	16.73865	21.324881	27.10928	34.38991
28	3.920129	4.47784	5.111687	5.83162	6.648838	8.627106	11.167140	14.420994	18.57990	23.883866	30.63349	39.20449
29	4.116136	4.72412	5.418388	6.21437	7.114257	9.317275	12.172182	15.863093	20.62369	26.749930	34.61584	44.69312
30	4.321942	4.98395	5.743491	6.61437	7.612255	10.062657	13.267678	17.449402	22.89230	29.959922	39.11590	50.95016
31	4.538039	5.25807	6.088101	7.04430	8.145113	10.867669	14.461770	19.194342	25.41045	33.555113	44.20096	58.08318
32	4.764941	5.54726	6.453387	7.50218	8.715271	11.737083	15.763329	21.113777	28.20560	37.581726	49.94709	66.21483
33	5.003189	5.85236	6.840590	7.98982	9.325340	12.676050	17.182028	23.225154	31.30821	42.091533	56.44021	75.48490
34	5.253348	6.17424	7.251025	8.50916	9.978114	13.690134	18.728411	25.547670	34.75212	47.142517	63.77744	86.05279
35	5.516015	6.51383	7.686087	9.06225	10.676581	14.785344	20.413968	28.102437	38.57485	52.799620	72.06851	98.10018
40	7.039989	8.51331	10.285718	12.41607	14.974458	21.724521	31.409420	45.259256	65.00087	93.050970	132.78155	188.88351
45	8.985008	11.12655	13.764611	17.01110	21.002452	31.920449	48.327286	72.890484	109.53024	163.987604	244.64140	363.67907
50	11.467400	14.54196	18.420154	23.30668	29.457025	46.901613	74.357520	117.390853	184.56483	289.002190	450.73593	700.23299

Future Amount of Ordinary Annuity of 1 per Period: $A_{\overline{n}|i} = \dfrac{(1+i)^n - 1}{i}$

n	5%	5.5%	6%	6.5%	7%	8%	9%	10%	11%	12%	13%	14%
1	1.000000	1.00000	1.000000	1.00000	1.000000	1.000000	1.000000	1.000000	1.00000	1.000000	1.00000	1.00000
2	2.050000	2.05500	2.060000	2.06500	2.070000	2.080000	2.090000	2.100000	2.11000	2.120000	2.13000	2.14000
3	3.152500	3.16802	3.183600	3.19922	3.214900	3.246400	3.278100	3.310000	3.34210	3.374400	3.40690	3.43960
4	4.310125	4.34227	4.374616	4.40717	4.439943	4.506112	4.573129	4.641000	4.70973	4.779328	4.84027	4.92114
5	5.525631	5.58109	5.637093	5.69364	5.750740	5.866601	5.984711	6.105100	6.22780	6.352847	6.48027	6.61010
6	6.801913	6.88805	6.975319	7.06373	7.153291	7.335929	7.523335	7.715610	7.91286	8.115189	8.32271	8.53552
7	8.142008	8.26689	8.393838	8.52287	8.654021	8.922803	9.200435	9.487171	9.78327	10.089012	10.40466	10.73049
8	9.549109	9.72157	9.897468	10.07686	10.259803	10.636628	11.028474	11.435888	11.85943	12.299693	12.75726	13.23276
9	11.026564	11.25626	11.491316	11.73185	11.977989	12.487558	13.021036	13.579477	14.16397	14.775656	15.41571	16.08535
10	12.577893	12.87535	13.180795	13.49442	13.816448	14.486562	15.192930	15.937425	16.72201	17.548735	18.41975	19.33730
11	14.206787	14.58350	14.971643	15.37156	15.783599	16.645487	17.560293	18.531167	19.56143	20.654583	21.81432	23.04452
12	15.917127	16.38559	16.869941	17.37071	17.888451	18.977126	20.140720	21.384284	22.71319	24.133133	25.65018	27.27075
13	17.712983	18.28680	18.882138	19.49981	20.140643	21.495297	22.953385	24.522712	26.21164	28.029109	29.98470	32.08865
14	19.598632	20.29257	21.015066	21.76730	22.550488	24.214920	26.019189	27.974983	30.09492	32.392602	34.88271	37.58107
15	21.578564	22.40866	23.275970	24.18217	25.129022	27.152114	29.360916	31.772482	34.40536	37.279715	40.41746	43.84241
16	23.657492	24.64114	25.672528	26.75401	27.888054	30.324283	33.003399	35.949730	39.18995	42.753280	46.67173	50.98035
17	25.840366	26.99640	28.212880	29.49302	30.840217	33.750226	36.973705	40.544703	44.50084	48.883674	53.73906	59.11760
18	28.132385	29.48120	30.905653	32.41007	33.999033	37.450244	41.301338	45.599173	50.39594	55.749715	61.72514	68.39407
19	30.539004	32.10267	33.759992	35.51672	37.378965	41.446263	46.018458	51.159090	56.93949	63.439681	70.74941	78.96923
20	33.065954	34.86832	36.785591	38.82531	40.995492	45.761964	51.160120	57.274999	64.20283	72.052442	80.94683	91.02493
21	35.719252	37.78608	39.992727	42.34895	44.865177	50.422921	56.764530	64.002499	72.26514	81.698736	92.46992	104.76842
22	38.505214	40.86431	43.392290	46.10164	49.005739	55.456755	62.873338	71.402749	81.21431	92.502584	105.49101	120.43600
23	41.430475	44.11185	46.995828	50.09824	53.436141	60.893296	69.531939	79.543024	91.14788	104.602894	120.20484	138.29704
24	44.501999	47.53800	50.815577	54.35463	58.176671	66.764759	76.789813	88.497327	102.17415	118.155241	136.83147	158.65862
25	47.727099	51.15259	54.864512	58.88768	63.249038	73.105940	84.700896	98.347059	114.41331	133.333870	155.61956	181.87083
26	51.113454	54.96598	59.156383	63.71538	68.676470	79.954415	93.323977	109.181765	127.99877	150.333934	176.85010	208.33274
27	54.669126	58.98911	63.705766	68.85688	74.483823	87.350768	102.723135	121.099942	143.07864	169.374007	200.84061	238.49933
28	58.402583	63.23351	68.528112	74.33257	80.697691	95.338830	112.968217	134.209936	159.81729	190.698887	227.94989	272.88923
29	62.322712	67.71135	73.629798	80.16419	87.346529	103.965936	124.135356	148.630930	178.39719	214.582754	258.58338	312.09373
30	66.438848	72.43548	79.058186	86.37486	94.460786	113.283211	136.307539	164.494023	199.02088	241.332684	293.19922	356.78685
31	70.760790	77.41943	84.801677	92.98923	102.073041	123.345868	149.575217	181.943425	221.91317	271.292606	332.31511	407.73701
32	75.298829	82.67750	90.889778	100.03353	110.218154	134.213537	164.036987	201.137767	247.32362	304.847719	376.51608	465.82019
33	80.063771	88.22476	97.343165	107.53571	118.933425	145.950620	179.800315	222.251544	275.52922	342.429446	426.46317	532.03501
34	85.066959	94.07712	104.183765	115.52553	128.258765	158.626670	196.982344	245.476699	306.83744	384.520979	482.90338	607.51991
35	90.320307	100.25136	111.434780	124.03469	138.236878	172.316804	215.710755	271.024368	341.58955	431.663496	546.68082	693.57270
40	120.799774	136.60561	154.761966	175.63192	199.635112	259.056519	337.882445	442.592556	581.82607	767.091420	1013.70424	1342.02510
45	159.700156	184.11917	212.743514	246.32459	285.749311	386.505617	525.858734	718.904837	986.63856	1358.230032	1874.16463	2590.56480
50	209.347996	246.21748	290.335905	343.17967	406.528929	573.770156	815.083556	1163.908529	1668.77115	2400.018249	3459.50712	4994.52135

CODES OF PROFESSIONAL ETHICS FOR ACCOUNTANTS

In recent years, governments, businesses, and the public have given increased attention to ethical conduct. They have insisted upon a level of human behavior that goes beyond that required by laws and regulations. Thus many businesses, as well as professional groups (such as accountants) and governmental organizations, have established standards of ethical conduct. This text emphasizes the ethical conduct of accountants, who serve various business interests as well as the public.

This appendix sets forth the standards of professional conduct expected of accountants in public accounting and private accounting. For accountants employed in public accounting, the American Institute of Certified Public Accountants' *Code of Professional Conduct* is presented.[1] For accountants employed in private accounting, the Institute of Management Accountants' *Standards of Ethical Conduct for Management Accountants* is presented as a guide to professional conduct.[2]

Supplementing the codes of professional ethics are ethics discussion cases that appear after the discussion questions in each chapter. These cases represent "real world" examples of ethical issues facing accountants. It should be noted that codes of professional ethics are general guides to good behavior and their application to specific situations often requires the exercise of professional judgment. In some cases, the line between right and wrong may be quite fine, and reasonable people may disagree. In addition, business is dynamic and everchanging, and what society considers to be acceptable behavior changes from time to time.

Code of Professional Conduct
as amended May 20, 1991

Composition, Applicability, and Compliance

The Code of Professional Conduct of the American Institute of Certified Public Accountants consists of two sections—(1) the Principles and (2) the Rules. The Principles provide the framework for the Rules, which govern the performance of professional services by members. The Council of the American Institute of Certified Public Accountants is authorized to designate bodies to promulgate technical standards under the Rules, and the bylaws require adherence to those Rules and standards.

The Code of Professional Conduct was adopted by the membership to provide guidance and rules to all members—those in public practice, in industry, in government, and in education—in the performance of their professional responsibilities.

Compliance with the Code of Professional Conduct, as with all standards in an open society, depends primarily on members' understanding and voluntary actions, secondarily on reinforcement by peers and public opinion, and ultimately on disciplinary proceedings, when necessary, against members who fail to comply with the Rules.

Other Guidance

The Principles and Rules as set forth herein are further amplified by interpretations and rulings contained in *AICPA Professional Standards* (volume 2).

Interpretations of Rules of Conduct consist of interpretations which have been adopted, after exposure to state societies, state boards, practice units and other interested parties, by the professional ethics division's executive committee to provide guidelines as to the scope and application of the Rules but are not intended to limit such scope or application. A member who departs from such guidelines shall have the burden of justifying such departure in any disciplinary hearing.

---

[1]*Code of Professional Conduct* (New York: American Institute of Certified Public Accountants, 1992), pp. 3–8.
[2]*Standards of Ethical Conduct for Management Accountants* (Montvale, New Jersey: Institute of Management Accountants, 1992), pp. 1–2.

Ethics Rulings consist of formal rulings made by the professional ethics division's executive committee after exposure to state societies, state boards, practice units and other interested parties. These rulings summarize the application of Rules of Conduct and interpretations to a particular set of factual circumstances. Members who depart from such rulings in similar circumstances will be requested to justify such departures.

Publication of an interpretation or ethics ruling in the *Journal of Accountancy* constitutes notice to members. Hence, the effective date of the pronouncement is the last day of the month in which the pronouncement is published in the *Journal of Accountancy*. The professional ethics division will take into consideration the time that would have been reasonable for the member to comply with the pronouncement.

Members should also consult, if applicable, the ethical standards of their state CPA society, state board of accountancy, the Securities and Exchange Commission, and any other governmental agency which may regulate their client's business or use their reports to evaluate the client's compliance with applicable laws and related regulations.

Section I—Principles

Preamble

Membership in the American Institute of Certified Public Accountants is voluntary. By accepting membership, a certified public accountant assumes an obligation of self-discipline above and beyond the requirements of laws and regulations.

These Principles of the Code of Professional Conduct of the American Institute of Certified Public Accountants express the profession's recognition of its responsibilities to the public, to clients, and to colleagues. They guide members in the performance of their professional responsibilities and express the basic tenets of ethical and professional conduct. The Principles call for an unswerving commitment to honorable behavior, even at the sacrifice of personal advantage.

Article I
Responsibilities

In carrying out their responsibilities as professionals, members should exercise sensitive professional and moral judgments in all their activities.

As professionals, certified public accountants perform an essential role in society. Consistent with that role, members of the American Institute of Certified Public Accountants have responsibilities to all those who use their professional services. Members also have a continuing responsibility to cooperate with each other to improve the art of accounting, maintain the public's confidence, and carry out the profession's special responsibilities for self-governance. The collective efforts of all members are required to maintain and enhance the traditions of the profession.

Article II
The Public Interest

Members should accept the obligation to act in a way that will serve the public interest, honor the public trust, and demonstrate commitment to professionalism.

A distinguishing mark of a profession is acceptance of its responsibility to the public. The accounting profession's public consists of clients, credit grantors, governments, employers, investors, the business and financial community, and others who rely on the objectivity and integrity of certified public accountants to maintain the orderly functioning of commerce. This reliance imposes a public interest responsibility on certified public accountants. The public interest is defined as the collective well-being of the community of people and institutions the profession serves.

In discharging their professional responsibilities, members may encounter conflicting pressures from among each of those groups. In resolving those conflicts, members should act with integrity, guided by the precept that when members fulfill their responsibility to the public, clients' and employers' interests are best served.

Those who rely on certified public accountants expect them to discharge their responsibilities with integrity, objectivity, due professional care, and a genuine interest in serving the public. They are expected to provide quality services, enter into fee arrangements, and offer a range of services—all in a manner that demonstrates a level of professionalism consistent with these Principles of the Code of Professional Conduct.

All who accept membership in the American Institute of Certified Public Accountants commit themselves to honor the public trust. In return for the faith that the public reposes in them, members should seek continually to demonstrate their dedication to professional excellence.

Article III
Integrity
To maintain and broaden public confidence, members should perform all professional responsibilities with the highest sense of integrity.
Integrity is an element of character fundamental to professional recognition. It is the quality from which the public trust derives and the benchmark against which a member must ultimately test all decisions.

Integrity requires a member to be, among other things, honest and candid within the constraints of client confidentiality. Service and the public trust should not be subordinated to personal gain and advantage. Integrity can accommodate the inadvertent error and the honest difference of opinion; it cannot accommodate deceit or subordination of principle.

Integrity is measured in terms of what is right and just. In the absence of specific rules, standards, or guidance, or in the face of conflicting opinions, a member should test decisions and deeds by asking: "Am I doing what a person of integrity would do? Have I retained my integrity?" Integrity requires a member to observe both the form and the spirit of technical and ethical standards; circumvention of those standards constitutes subordination of judgment.

Integrity also requires a member to observe the principles of objectivity and independence and of due care.

Article IV
Objectivity and Independence
A member should maintain objectivity and be free of conflicts of interest in discharging professional responsibilities. A member in public practice should be independent in fact and appearance when providing auditing and other attestation services.
Objectivity is a state of mind, a quality that lends value to a member's services. It is a distinguishing feature of the profession. The principle of objectivity imposes the obligation to be impartial, intellectually honest, and free of conflicts of interest. Independence precludes relationships that may appear to impair a member's objectivity in rendering attestation services.

Members often serve multiple interests in many different capacities and must demonstrate their objectivity in varying circumstances. Members in public practice render attest, tax, and management advisory services. Other members prepare financial statements in the employment of others, perform internal auditing services, and serve in financial and management capacities in industry, education, and government. They also educate and train those who aspire to admission into the profession. Regardless of service or capacity, members should protect the integrity of their work, maintain objectivity, and avoid any subordination of their judgment.

For a member in public practice, the maintenance of objectivity and independence requires a continuing assessment of client relationships and public responsibility. Such a member who provides auditing and other attestation services should be independent in fact and appearance. In providing all other services, a member should maintain objectivity and avoid conflicts of interest.

Although members not in public practice cannot maintain the appearance of independence, they nevertheless have the responsibility to maintain objectivity in rendering professional services. Members employed by others to prepare financial statements or to perform auditing, tax, or consulting services are charged with the same responsibility for objectivity as members in public practice and must be scrupulous in their application of generally accepted accounting principles and candid in all their dealings with members in public practice.

Activity V
Due Care

A member should observe the profession's technical and ethical standards, strive continually to improve competence and the quality of services, and discharge professional responsibility to the best of the member's ability.

The quest for excellence is the essence of due care. Due care requires a member to discharge professional responsibilities with competence and diligence. It imposes the obligation to perform professional services to the best of a member's ability with concern for the best interest of those for whom the services are performed and consistent with the profession's responsibility to the public.

Competence is derived from a synthesis of education and experience. It begins with a mastery of the common body of knowledge required for designation as a certified public accountant. The maintenance of competence requires a commitment to learning and professional improvement that must continue throughout a member's professional life. It is a member's individual responsibility. In all engagements and in all responsibilities, each member should undertake to achieve a level of competence that will assure that the quality of the member's services meets the high level of professionalism required by these Principles.

Competence represents the attainment and maintenance of a level of understanding and knowledge that enables a member to render services with facility and acumen. It also establishes the limitations of a member's capabilities by dictating that consultation or referral may be required when a professional engagement exceeds the personal competence of a member or a member's firm. Each member is responsible for assessing his or her own competence—of evaluating whether education, experience, and judgment are adequate for the responsibility to be assumed.

Members should be diligent in discharging responsibilities to clients, employers, and the public. Diligence imposes the responsibility to render services promptly and carefully, to be thorough, and to observe applicable technical and ethical standards.

Due care requires a member to plan and supervise adequately any professional activity for which he or she is responsible.

Article VI
Scope and Nature of Services

A member in public practice should observe the Principles of the Code of Professional Conduct in determining the scope and nature of services to be provided.

The public interest aspect of certified public accountants' services requires that such services be consistent with acceptable professional behavior for certified public accountants. Integrity requires that service and the public trust not be subordinated to personal gain and advantage. Objectivity and independence require that members be free from conflicts of interest in discharging professional responsibilities. Due care requires that services be provided with competence and diligence.

Each of these Principles should be considered by members in determining whether or not to provide specific services in individual circumstances. In some instances, they may represent an overall constraint on the nonaudit services that might be offered to a specific client. No hard-and-fast rules can be developed to help members reach these judgments, but they must be satisfied that they are meeting the spirit of the Principles in this regard.

In order to accomplish this, members should
- Practice in firms that have in place internal quality-control procedures to ensure that services are competently delivered and adequately supervised.
- Determine, in their individual judgments, whether the scope and nature of other services provided to an audit client would create a conflict of interest in the performance of the audit function for that client.
- Assess, in their individual judgments, whether an activity is consistent with their role as professionals (for example, Is such activity a reasonable extension or variation of existing services offered by the member or others in the profession?).

STANDARDS OF ETHICAL CONDUCT
FOR MANAGEMENT ACCOUNTANTS

Management accountants have an obligation to the organizations they serve, their profession, the public, and themselves to maintain the highest standards of ethical conduct. In recognition of this obligation, the Institute of Management Accountants has promulgated the following standards of ethical conduct for management accountants. Adherence to these standards is integral to achieving the *Objectives of Management Accounting.*[3] Management accountants shall not commit acts contrary to these standards nor shall they condone the commission of such acts by others within their organizations.

Competence

Management accountants have a responsibility to:
- Maintain an appropriate level of professional competence by ongoing development of their knowledge and skills.
- Perform their professional duties in accordance with relevant laws, regulations, and technical standards.
- Prepare complete and clear reports and recommendations after appropriate analyses of relevant and reliable information.

Confidentiality

Management accountants have a responsibility to:
- Refrain from disclosing confidential information acquired in the course of their work except when authorized, unless legally obligated to do so.
- Inform subordinates as appropriate regarding the confidentiality of information acquired in the course of their work and monitor their activities to assure the maintenance of that confidentiality.
- Refrain from using or appearing to use confidential information acquired in the course of their work for unethical or illegal advantage either personally or through third parties.

Integrity

Management accountants have a responsibility to:
- Avoid actual or apparent conflicts of interest and advise all appropriate parties of any potential conflict.
- Refrain from engaging in any activity that would prejudice their ability to carry out their duties ethically.
- Refuse any gift, favor, or hospitality that would influence or would appear to influence their actions.
- Refrain from either actively or passively subverting the attainment of the organization's legitimate and ethical objectives.
- Recognize and communicate professional limitations or other constraints that would preclude responsible judgment or successful performance of an activity.
- Communicate unfavorable as well as favorable information and professional judgments or opinions.
- Refrain from engaging in or supporting any activity that would discredit the profession.

Objectivity

Management accountants have a responsibility to:
- Communicate information fairly and objectively.
- Disclose fully all relevant information that could reasonably be expected to influence an intended user's understanding of the reports, comments, and recommendations presented.

---

[3]National Association of Accountants, *Statements on Management Accounting: Objectives of Management Accounting,* Statement No. 1B, New York, N.Y., June 17, 1982.

ALTERNATIVE METHODS OF RECORDING DEFERRALS

As discussed in Chapter 3, deferrals are created by recording a transaction in a way that delays or defers the recognition of an expense or a revenue. Deferrals may be either deferred expenses (prepaid expenses) or deferred revenues (unearned revenues).

In Chapter 2, deferred expenses (prepaid expenses) were debited to an *asset* account at the time of payment. As an alternative, deferred expenses may be debited to an *expense* account at the time of payment. In Chapter 2, deferred revenues (unearned revenues) were credited to a *liability* account at the time of receipt. As an alternative, deferred revenues may be credited to a *revenue* account at the time of receipt. This appendix describes and illustrates these alternative methods of recording deferred expenses and deferred revenues.

DEFERRED EXPENSES (PREPAID EXPENSES)

As a basis for illustrating the alternative methods of recording deferred expenses, the insurance premium paid by Computer King in Chapter 2 is used. The amounts related to this insurance are as follows:

Prepayment of insurance for 24 months, starting December 1	$2,400
Insurance premium expired during December	100
Unexpired insurance premium at the end of December	$2,300

Based on the above data, the entries to account for the deferred expense (prepaid insurance) recorded initially as an *asset* are shown in the journal and T accounts in Exhibit 1. The adjusting entry in Exhibit 1 was shown in Chapter 3. The entries to account for the prepaid insurance recorded initially as an *expense* are shown in the journal and T accounts in Exhibit 2.

Exhibit 1			*Exhibit 2*		
Prepaid Expense Recorded Initially as Asset			*Prepaid Expense Recorded Initially as Expense*		
Initial entry (to record initial payment):			Initial entry (to record initial payment):		
Dec. 1 Prepaid Insurance	2,400		Dec. 1 Insurance Expense	2,400	
Cash		2,400	Cash		2,400
Adjusting entry (to transfer amount **used** to proper expense account):			Adjusting entry (to transfer amount **unused** to the proper asset account):		
Dec. 31 Insurance Expense	100		Dec. 31 Prepaid Insurance	2,300	
Prepaid Insurance		100	Insurance Expense		2,300
Closing entry (to close income statement accounts with debit balances):			Closing entry (to close income statement accounts with debit balances):		
Income Summary	XXXX		Income Summary	XXXX	
Purchases		XXXX	Purchases		XXXX
Insurance Expense		100	Insurance Expense		100

Prepaid Insurance					Prepaid Insurance				
Dec. 1	2,400	Dec. 31 Adjusting	100		Dec. 31 Adjusting	2,300			
Insurance Expense					**Insurance Expense**				
Dec. 31 Adjusting	100	Dec. 31 Closing	100		Dec. 1	2,400	Dec. 31 Adjusting	2,300	
							31 Closing	100	

Either of the two methods of recording deferred expenses (prepaid expenses) may be used. As illustrated in Exhibits 1 and 2, both methods result in the same account balances after the adjusting entries have been recorded. Therefore, the amounts reported as expenses in the income statement and as assets on the balance sheet will not be affected by the method used. To avoid confusion, the method used by an enterprise for each kind of prepaid expense should be followed consistently from year to year.

Some enterprises record all deferred expenses using one method. Other enterprises use one method to record the prepayment of some expenses and the other method for other expenses. Initial debits to the asset account are logical for prepayments of insurance, which are usually for periods of one to three years. On the other hand, rent on a building may be prepaid on the first of each month. The prepaid rent will expire by the end of the month. In this case, it is logical to record the payment of rent by initially debiting an expense account rather than an asset account.

DEFERRED REVENUES (UNEARNED REVENUES)

As a basis for illustrating the alternative methods of recording deferred revenues, the rent received by Computer King in Chapter 2 is used. Computer King rented land on December 1 to a local retailer for use as a parking lot for three months, receiving $360 for the entire three months. On December 31, $120 ($1/3 \times \$360$) of the rent has been earned, and $240 ($2/3 \times \$360$) of the rent is still unearned.

Based on the above data, the entries to account for the deferred revenue (unearned rent) recorded initially as a liability are shown in the journal and ledger in Exhibit 3. The adjusting entry in Exhibit 3 was shown in Chapter 3. The entries to account for the unearned rent recorded initially as revenue are shown in the journal and ledger in Exhibit 4.

Exhibit 3				*Exhibit 4*		
Unearned Revenue Recorded Initially as Liability				*Unearned Revenue Recorded Initially as Revenue*		
Initial entry (to record initial receipt):				Initial entries (to record initial receipt):		
Dec. 1 Cash	360			Dec. 1 Cash	360	
Unearned Rent		360		Rent Income		360
Adjusting entry (to transfer amount **earned** to proper **revenue** account):				Adjusting entry (to transfer amount **unearned** to proper **liability** account):		
Dec. 31 Unearned Rent	120			Dec. 31 Rent Income	240	
Rent Income		120		Unearned Rent		240
Closing entry (to close income statement accounts with credit balances):				Closing entry (to close income statement accounts with credit balances):		
Dec. 31 Sales	XXXX			Dec. 31 Sales	XXXX	
Rent Income	120			Rent Income	120	
Income Summary		XXXX		Income Summary		XXXX

Exhibit 3 ledger:

Unearned Rent
| Dec. 31 Adjusting | 120 | Dec. 1 | 360 |

Rent Income
| Dec. 31 Closing | 120 | Dec. 31 Adjusting | 120 |

Exhibit 4 ledger:

Unearned Rent
| | | Dec. 31 Adjusting | 240 |

Rent Income
| Dec. 31 Adjusting | 240 | Dec. 1 | 360 |
| Dec. 31 Closing | 120 | | |

As illustrated in Exhibits 3 and 4, both methods result in the same account balances after the adjusting entries have been recorded. Therefore, the amounts reported as revenues in the income statement and as liabilities on the balance sheet will not be affected by the method used. Either of the methods may be used for all revenues received in advance. Alternatively, the first method may be used for advance receipts of some kinds of revenue and the second method for other kinds. To avoid confusion, the method used by an enterprise for each kind of unearned revenue should be followed consistently from year to year.

REVERSING ENTRIES FOR DEFERRALS

As discussed in the appendix at the end of Chapter 4, the use of reversing entries is optional. However, the use of reversing entries generally simplifies the analysis of transactions and reduces the likelihood of errors in the subsequent recording of transactions. Normally, reversing entries are prepared for deferrals in the following two cases:

1. When a deferred expense (prepaid expense) is initially recorded as an expense.
2. When a deferred revenue (unearned revenue) is initially recorded as a revenue.

The entry to reverse the adjustment to record the prepaid insurance in Exhibit 2 is as follows:

Jan. 1	Insurance Expense	2,300	
	Prepaid Insurance		2,300

The entry to reverse the adjustment to record the unearned rent in Exhibit 4 is as follows:

Jan. 1	Unearned Rent	240	
	Rent Income		240

EXERCISES

EXERCISE C-1
ADJUSTING ENTRIES FOR OFFICE SUPPLIES

The office supplies purchased during the year total $5,450, and the amount of office supplies on hand at the end of the year is $1,530.

a. Record the following transactions directly in T accounts for Office Supplies and Office Supplies Expense, using the system of initially recording supplies as an asset: (1) purchases for the period; (2) adjusting entry at the end of the period. Identify each entry by number.
b. Record the following transactions directly in T accounts for Office Supplies and Office Supplies Expense, using the system of initially recording supplies as an expense: (1) purchases for the period; (2) adjusting entry at the end of the period. Identify each entry by number.

EXERCISE C-2
ADJUSTING ENTRIES FOR PREPAID INSURANCE

During the first year of operations, insurance premiums of $4,500 were paid. At the end of the year, unexpired premiums totaled $2,000. Journalize the adjusting entry at the end of the year, assuming that (a) prepaid expenses were initially recorded as assets and (b) prepaid expenses were initially recorded as expenses.

EXERCISE C-3
ADJUSTING ENTRIES FOR ADVERTISING REVENUE

The advertising revenues received during the year totaled $280,000, and the unearned advertising revenue at the end of the year is $40,000.

a. Record the following transactions directly in T accounts for Unearned Advertising Revenue and Advertising Revenue, using the system of initially recording advertising fees as a liability: (1) revenues received during the period; (2) adjusting entry at the end of the period. Identify each entry by number.
b. Record the following transactions directly in T accounts for Unearned Advertising Revenue and Advertising Revenue, using the system of initially recording advertising fees as revenue: (1) revenues received during the period; (2) adjusting entry at the end of the period. Identify each entry by number.

EXERCISE C-4
YEAR-END ENTRIES FOR DEFERRED REVENUES

In their first year of operations, Snyder Publishing Co. received $400,000 from advertising contracts and $675,000 from magazine subscriptions, crediting the two amounts to Unearned Advertising Revenue and Circulation Revenue, respectively. At the end of the year, the unearned advertising revenue amounts to $60,000, and the unearned circulation revenue amounts to $150,000. Journalize the adjusting entries that should be made at the end of the year.

APPENDIX D

ALTERNATIVE METHOD OF RECORDING PERIODIC MERCHANDISE INVENTORIES

The recording of adjusting entries for merchandise inventory under the periodic inventory system is described and illustrated in Chapter 6. The alternative method presented in this appendix classifies the entries for the beginning and the ending merchandise inventories as closing entries instead of adjusting entries. Thus, this method is often called the **closing method.** The difference in procedure affects the work sheet, the sequence of entries in the journal, and the income summary account. It does not affect the financial statements in any way.

WORK SHEET

The merchandise inventory at the beginning of the period is reported on the income statement as a part of the cost of merchandise sold. On the work sheet, merchandise inventory at the beginning of the period is extended from the Trial Balance Debit column to the Adjusted Trial Balance Debit column and the Income Statement Debit column.

The merchandise inventory at the end of the period is reported on the balance sheet as an asset and on the income statement as a deduction from the cost of merchandise available for sale. The ending merchandise inventory is therefore entered on the worksheet as a debit in the Balance Sheet Debit column and as a credit in the Income Statement Credit column. Both the debit and credit amounts are placed on the same line as the beginning merchandise inventory.

The remainder of the work sheet is completed in the normal manner, as was illustrated in Exhibit 1 of Chapter 6, except that no entries are made in the Adjustments columns for merchandise inventory. A work sheet prepared under the closing method is illustrated in Exhibit 1 of this appendix.

Exhibit 1
Work Sheet for Merchandising
Enterprise—Closing Method

Computer King
Work Sheet
For Year Ended December 31, 1995

Account Title	Trial Balance Dr.	Trial Balance Cr.	Adjustments Dr.	Adjustments Cr.	Adjusted Trial Balance Dr.	Adjusted Trial Balance Cr.	Income Statement Dr.	Income Statement Cr.	Balance Sheet Dr.	Balance Sheet Cr.
Cash	52,950				52,950				52,950	
Notes Receivable	40,000				40,000				40,000	
Accounts Receivable	60,880				60,880				60,880	
Interest Receivable			(a) 200		200				200	
Merchandise Inventory	59,700				59,700		59,700	62,150	62,150	
Office Supplies	1,090			(b) 610	480				480	
Prepaid Insurance	4,560			(c) 1,910	2,650				2,650	
Land	10,000				10,000				10,000	
Store Equipment	27,100				27,100				27,100	
Accum. Depr.—Store Equip.		2,600		(d) 3,100		5,700				5,700
Office Equipment	15,570				15,570				15,570	
Accum. Depr.—Office Equipment		2,230		(e) 2,490		4,720				4,720
Accounts Payable		22,420				22,420				22,420
Salaries Payable				(f) 1,140		1,140				1,140
Unearned Rent		2,400	(g) 600			1,800				1,800
Notes Payable (final payment, 2000)		25,000				25,000				25,000
Jere King, Capital		153,800				153,800				153,800
Jere King, Drawing	18,000				18,000				18,000	
Sales		720,185				720,185		720,185		
Sales Returns and Allowances	6,140				6,140		6,140			
Sales Discounts	5,790				5,790		5,790			
Purchases	521,980				521,980		521,980			
Purchases Returns & Allowances		9,100				9,100		9,100		
Purchases Discounts		2,525				2,525		2,525		
Transportation In	17,400				17,400		17,400			
Sales Salaries Expense	59,250		(f) 780		60,030		60,030			
Advertising Expense	10,860				10,860		10,860			
Depr. Exp.—Store Equip.			(d) 3,100		3,100		3,100			
Miscellaneous Selling Expense	630				630		630			
Office Salaries Expense	20,660		(f) 360		21,020		21,020			
Rent Expense	8,100				8,100		8,100			
Depr. Exp.—Office Equip.			(e) 2,490		2,490		2,490			
Insurance Expense			(c) 1,910		1,910		1,910			
Office Supplies Expense			(b) 610		610		610			
Misc. Administrative Expense	760				760		760			
Rent Income				(g) 600		600		600		
Interest Income		3,600		(a) 200		3,800		3,800		
Interest Expense	2,440				2,440		2,440			
	943,860	943,860	10,050	10,050	950,790	950,790	722,960	798,360	289,980	214,580
Net Income							75,400			75,400
							798,360	798,360	289,980	289,980

(a) Interest earned but not received on notes receivable, $200.
(b) Office supplies used, $610 ($1,090–$480).
(c) Insurance expired, $1,910.
(d) Depreciation of store equipment, $3,100.
(e) Depreciation of office equipment, $2,490.
(f) Salaries accrued but not paid (sales salaries, $780; office salaries, $360), $1,140.
(g) Rent earned from amount received in advance, $600.

ADJUSTING ENTRIES

The adjusting entries journalized from the work sheet in Exhibit 1 are shown below. These entries are the same as those illustrated in Chapter 6, except that adjusting entries for merchandise inventory are not made.

	DATE		DESCRIPTION	POST. REF.	DEBIT	CREDIT	
1			Adjusting Entries				1
2	1995 Dec.	31	Interest Receivable	113	2 0 0 00		2
3			Interest Income	611		2 0 0 00	3
4							4
5		31	Office Supplies Expense	534	6 1 0 00		5
6			Office Supplies	116		6 1 0 00	6
7							7
8		31	Insurance Expense	533	1 9 1 0 00		8
9			Prepaid Insurance	117		1 9 1 0 00	9
10							10
11		31	Depreciation Expense—Store Equip.	522	3 1 0 0 00		11
12			Accumulated Depr.—Store Equip.	124		3 1 0 0 00	12
13							13
14		31	Depreciation Expense—Office Equip.	532	2 4 9 0 00		14
15			Accumulated Depr.—Office Equip.	126		2 4 9 0 00	15
16							16
17		31	Sales Salaries Expense	520	7 8 0 00		17
18			Office Salaries Expense	530	3 6 0 00		18
19			Salaries Payable	211		1 1 4 0 00	19
20							20
21		31	Unearned Rent	212	6 0 0 00		21
22			Rent Income	610		6 0 0 00	22

JOURNAL — PAGE 28

CLOSING ENTRIES

All accounts with balances in the Income Statement Credit column of the work sheet are closed in one compound journal entry by debiting each account and crediting Income Summary. All accounts with balances in the Income Statement Debit column are closed in one entry by debiting Income Summary and crediting each account. Income Summary and the owner's drawing account are then closed to the owner's capital account. All of the closing entries are a follows:

JOURNAL   PAGE 29

	DATE		DESCRIPTION	POST. REF.	DEBIT	CREDIT	
1			Closing Entries				1
2	1995 Dec.	31	Merchandise Inventory	115	62 1 5 0 00		2
3			Sales	410	720 1 8 5 00		3
4			Purchases Returns and Allowances	511	9 1 0 0 00		4
5			Purchases Discounts	512	2 5 2 5 00		5
6			Rent Income	610	6 0 0 00		6
7			Interest Income	611	3 8 0 0 00		7
8			Income Summary	312		798 3 6 0 00	8
9							9
10		31	Income Summary	312	722 9 6 0 00		10
11			Merchandise Inventory	115		59 7 0 0 00	11
12			Sales Returns and Allowances	411		6 1 4 0 00	12
13			Sales Discounts	412		5 7 9 0 00	13
14			Purchases	510		521 9 8 0 00	14
15			Transportation In	513		17 4 0 0 00	15
16			Sales Salaries Expense	520		60 0 3 0 00	16
17			Advertising Expense	521		10 8 6 0 00	17
18			Depreciation Exp.—Store Equip.	522		3 1 0 0 00	18
19			Miscellaneous Selling Expense	529		6 3 0 00	19
20			Office Salaries Expense	530		21 0 2 0 00	20
21			Rent Expense	531		8 1 0 0 00	21
22			Depreciation Exp.—Office Equip.	532		2 4 9 0 00	22
23			Insurance Expense	533		1 9 1 0 00	23
24			Office Supplies Expense	534		6 1 0 00	24
25			Miscellaneous Administrative Exp.	539		7 6 0 00	25
26			Interest Expense	710		2 4 4 0 00	26
27							27
28		31	Income Summary	312	75 4 0 0 00		28
29			Jere King, Capital	310		75 4 0 0 00	29
30							30
31		31	Jere King, Capital	310	18 0 0 0 00		31
32			Jere King, Drawing	311		18 0 0 0 00	32
33							33

The income summary account, as it will appear after the closing entries have been posted, is as follows:

ACCOUNT *Income Summary*   ACCOUNT NO. *312*

DATE		ITEM	POST. REF.	DEBIT	CREDIT	BALANCE	
						DEBIT	CREDIT
1995 Dec.	31	Revenue, etc.	29		798 3 6 0 00		798 3 6 0 00
	31	Expense, etc.	29	722 9 6 0 00			75 4 0 0 00
	31	Net income	29	75 4 0 0 00			

INCOME TAXES

The federal government and more than three-fourths of the states levy an income tax. In addition, some of the states permit municipalities or other political subdivisions to levy income taxes. In operating a business or determining one's personal income tax, it is good management to plan to keep these taxes to a minimum. This idea was expressed by Judge Learned Hand in *Newman* [35 AFTR 857], as follows:

Over and over again courts have said that there is nothing sinister in so arranging one's affairs as to keep taxes as low as possible. Everybody does so, rich or poor; and all do right, for nobody owes any public duty to pay more than the law demands; taxes are enforced exactions, not voluntary contributions. To demand more in the name of morals is mere cant.

An understanding of income taxes is almost impossible without some knowledge of accounting concepts. Such knowledge, combined with an understanding of the basic concepts of income taxes, serves as a basic foundation for minimizing income taxes. In many cases, this understanding leads one to seek the advice and assistance of professional accountants who specialize in determining the tax or developing plans to minimize the tax.

The discussion of the federal system in this appendix focuses on the basic nature of income taxes. The illustrations are brief and free of the many complexities encountered in actual practice. In addition, because the federal tax laws often change, the current tax law and tax rates should be examined before any tax-related decisions are made.[1] The tax law upon which this appendix is based is the Tax Reform Act of 1986 (as amended by the Revenue Act of 1987, the Technical and Miscellaneous Revenue Act of 1988, and the Omnibus Budget Reconciliation Act of 1990).

FEDERAL INCOME TAX SYSTEM

The present system of federal income tax began with the Revenue Act of 1913. This Act was enacted soon after the Sixteenth Amendment to the U.S. Constitution was ratified. All current income tax statutes, as well as other federal tax laws, are now codified in the *Internal Revenue Code (IRC)*.

The Treasury Department has administrative responsibility in federal tax matters. The division concerned specifically with enforcement and collection of the income tax is the Internal Revenue Service (IRS), headed by the Commissioner of Internal Revenue. Interpretations of the law and directives formulated according to express provisions of the IRC are issued in various forms. The most important and comprehensive are the "Regulations," which extend to more than two thousand pages.

A taxpayer is required to file income tax data on a timely basis, using official forms and supporting schedules, which are referred to collectively as a **tax return**. Failure to receive the forms from the IRS or failure to maintain adequate records does not relieve taxpayers of their legal obligations to file annual tax returns. Willful failure to comply with the income tax laws may result in severe civil and criminal penalties.

Through audits of tax returns, the IRS may allege that a taxpayer is deficient in reporting or paying tax. A taxpayer who disagrees with the IRS may appeal the case in informal conferences at district and regional levels. In some cases, unresolved disputes are taken to the federal courts for settlement. The taxpayer may seek relief in the Tax Court or may pay the disputed amount and sue to recover it.

---

[1] Major tax bills have been enacted on the average of every 18 months since the original tax law was passed in 1913.

The income tax is not levied on business units as such, but upon taxable entities. The primary taxable entities are individuals, corporations, estates, and trusts. Business enterprises organized as sole proprietorships are not taxable entities. The revenues and expenses of such business enterprises are reported in the individual tax returns of the owners. Partnerships are not taxable entities but are required to report on an informational return the details of their revenues, expenses, and allocations to partners. The partners then report on their individual tax returns the amount of net income and other special items allocated to them on the partnership return.

Corporations engaged in business for profit are normally treated as separate entities. However, it is possible for two or more corporations with common ownership to join in filing a consolidated return. Subchapter S of the IRC also permits a nonpublic corporation that conforms to specified requirements to elect to be treated in a manner similar to a partnership. The effect of the election is to tax the shareholders on their shares of the net income instead of taxing the corporation.

ACCOUNTING METHODS

Neither the IRC nor the Regulations provide uniform systems of accounting for use by all taxpayers. However, in some cases, detailed procedures are prescribed. In addition, the IRS has the authority to prescribe accounting methods if those used by a taxpayer fail to yield a fair determination of taxable income. In general, taxpayers have the option of using either the cash basis or the accrual basis of accounting.

Cash Basis

Because of its greater simplicity, the cash basis of determining taxable income is usually used by individuals whose sources of income are limited to salary, dividends, and interest. Professional and other service enterprises (such as physicians, attorneys, and insurance agencies) often use the cash basis in determining taxable income.

One of the advantages of the cash basis is that the fees charged to clients or customers are not considered to be earned until payment is received. Likewise, it is not necessary to accrue expenses incurred but not paid within the tax year. It is not allowable, however, to treat the entire cost of long-term assets as an expense of the period in which the cash payment is made.[2] Deductions for depreciation on equipment and buildings used for business purposes may be claimed in the same manner as under the accrual basis, regardless of when payment is made.

Under the cash basis, the recognition of revenue does not always depend upon the actual receipt of cash. In some cases, revenue is said to be *constructively received* at the time it becomes available to the taxpayer, regardless of when it is actually converted to cash. For example, a check for services rendered, received before the end of a taxable year, is income of that year. This is true, even though the check is not deposited or cashed until the following year. Other examples of constructive receipt are bond interest coupons due within the taxable year and interest credited to a savings account as of the last day of the taxable year.

Accrual Basis

For businesses in which production or trading in merchandise is an important factor, purchases and sales must be accounted for on the accrual basis. Thus, revenues from sales must be reported in the year in which the goods are sold,

---

[2] The current tax law allows small businesses to write off as an expense as much as $10,000 of annual equipment purchases.

regardless of when the cash is received. Likewise, the cost of goods purchased are reported in the year in which the liabilities are incurred, regardless of when payment is made. The usual adjustments must also be made for the beginning and ending inventories in order to determine the cost of goods sold and the gross profit. However, manufacturing and merchandising enterprises are not required to extend the accrual basis to all phases of their operations. A mixture of the cash and accrual methods of accounting is allowable, if it yields reasonable results and is used consistently from year to year.

INCOME TAX ON INDIVIDUALS

Methods of accounting in general, as well as many of the regulations affecting the determination of net business or professional income, are not affected by the legal form or organizational structure of the taxpayer. On the other hand, the tax base and the tax rate structure for individuals differ markedly from those that apply to corporations.

The individual's tax base, upon which the amount of income tax is determined, is called **taxable income**. Taxable income is gross income less certain deductions as specified by the IRC. It is determined as follows:

GROSS INCOME

minus

DEDUCTIONS FROM GROSS INCOME

equals

ADJUSTED GROSS INCOME

minus

ITEMIZED DEDUCTIONS AND EXEMPTIONS

equals

TAXABLE INCOME

The basic concepts underlying the determination of taxable income for individuals are discussed in the following paragraphs.

Items of gross income subject to tax are sometimes called **taxable gross income**. Some of the taxable and nontaxable items of gross income of individuals are shown in Exhibit 1.

Exhibit 1
Partial List of Taxable and Nontaxable Gross Income Items

Taxable Items	Nontaxable Items
Wages and other remuneration from employer.	All or portions of federal old-age pension benefits, depending on amounts of other income.
Tips and gratuities for services rendered.	Value of property received as a gift.
Cash dividends.	Value of property received by bequest, devise, or inheritance.
Rents and royalties.	
Income from a business or profession.	Life insurance proceeds received because of death of insured.
Gains from the sale of real estate, securities, and other property.	Interest on most obligations of a state or political subdivision.
Distributive share of partnership income.	Scholarships for tuition and fees.
Income from an estate or trust.	Compensation for injuries or for damages related to personal or family rights.
Prizes won in contests.	
Gambling winnings.	
Jury fees.	Worker's compensation insurance for sickness or injury.
Gains from illegal transactions.	
Unemployment compensation.	

Deductions from Gross Income

Business expenses and other expenses related to earning revenue are deductible in full or in part from gross income to yield adjusted gross income. For example, ordinary and necessary expenses incurred in the operations of a sole proprietorship are deductible from gross income. Also, expenses that are directly related to earning rent or royalty income are allowable as deductions from gross income.

A self-employed individual may establish a qualified retirement fund (called a Keogh plan) and deduct the annual contribution from gross income in determining adjusted gross income. Also, certain employees may deduct contributions to plans provided by employers (called 401K plans). The IRC and related regulations contain many limitations on the amount of such deductions from gross income.

Adjusted Gross Income

The expenses described in the preceding section are deducted from an amount of related gross income. The resulting amount is the adjusted gross income. The amount of adjusted gross income is used in determining the amount of some of the deductions described in the following section. For example, the medical deduction is limited to the portion of total medical expenses that exceed 7½% of adjusted gross income.

Itemized Deductions, the Standard Deduction, and Exemptions

Two categories of deductions are subtracted from adjusted gross income to yield taxable income. These deductions are (1) itemized deductions or the standard deduction and (2) exemptions. Each of these items is described in the following paragraphs.

ITEMIZED DEDUCTIONS. Certain specified expenditures and losses may be itemized and deducted from adjusted gross income. The deductions that are generally available to individuals who itemize deductions are described in the paragraphs that follow.[3]

CHARITABLE CONTRIBUTIONS. Contributions made by an individual to domestic organizations created exclusively for religious, charitable, scientific, literary, or educational purposes, or for the prevention of cruelty to children or animals are deductible. The organization must be nonprofit and cannot devote a substantial part of its activities to influencing legislation. Contributions to domestic governmental units and to organizations of war veterans are also deductible.

The amount of qualified contributions that may be deducted ranges from 20% of adjusted gross income for contributions to private foundations to 50% of adjusted gross income for contributions to public charities. There are also limitations related to contributions of various types of property other than cash.

INTEREST EXPENSE. Interest expense on indebtedness for the taxpayer's principal and second residences is deductible, subject to certain limits. Interest expense on indebtedness for investment purposes is fully deductible up to an amount equal to investment income.

TAXES. Most of the taxes levied by the federal government are not deductible from adjusted gross income. Some of the taxes of a nonbusiness or personal nature

---

[3] For certain high-income taxpayers, the itemized deductions (except for medical expenses) are limited.

levied by states or their political subdivisions are deductible from adjusted gross income. The common deductible state and local taxes are real estate, personal property, and income taxes.

MEDICAL EXPENSES. Amounts paid for prescription drugs and insulin and other medical expenses are normally deductible to the extent that they exceed 7½% of adjusted gross income. Other medical expenses deductible in total or in part include medical care insurance, doctors' fees, hospital expenses, etc.

STANDARD DEDUCTION. As an alternative to itemizing deductions, the taxpayer may take a standard deduction. The amount of the deduction depends upon whether the taxpayer is filing as a single taxpayer, as a head of household, or with a spouse (joint return). The deduction is adjusted annually for inflation.

EXEMPTIONS. In general, each taxpayer is entitled to a personal exemption.[4] An additional exemption is allowed for each dependent. The amount of the personal exemption is $2,300 in 1992 and is adjusted annually for inflation.

Taxable Income and Determination of Income Tax

After the taxable income is determined, the taxpayer uses various tax rate schedules to determine the amount of the income tax. For example, the individual tax rates for a single taxpayer are as follows for 1992:

Taxable Income	Tax Rate[5]
$0 – $21,450	15%
$21,450 – $51,900	28%
Over $51,900	31%

To illustrate the use of the tax rate schedules, assume that a single taxpayer has taxable income of $60,300. The tax is determined as follows:

Individual Tax Rates—Single Taxpayer

Tax on $21,450 at 15%	$ 3,218 (rounded)
Tax on 30,450 ($51,900 – $21,450) at 28%	8,526
Tax on 8,400 ($60,300 – $51,900) at 31%	2,604
Total on $60,300	$14,348

Credits Against the Tax

After the amount of the income tax has been determined, the tax may be reduced on a dollar-for-dollar basis by the amount of various credits. Such credits are quite different from deductions and exemptions, which are reductions of the income subject to tax. The most common credits are described in the following paragraphs.

CREDIT FOR THE ELDERLY. Some elderly taxpayers receive nontaxable retirement income, while others receive taxable retirement income. The credit for the elderly is an attempt to overcome this perceived inequity. The formula for determining the credit is complex, and the IRC should be consulted for the details.

CHILD AND DISABLED DEPENDENT CARE EXPENSES CREDIT. Taxpayers who maintain a household are allowed a tax credit for expenses, including house-

[4] For certain high-income taxpayers, the personal exemption is phased out.
[5] Capital gains are subject to a maximum tax rate of 28%. Such gains result from the sale of capital assets, most commonly stocks and bonds.

hold expenses, involved in the care of a dependent child under age 13. A credit is also allowed for a physically or mentally incapacitated dependent or spouse, provided the expenses were incurred to enable the taxpayer to be gainfully employed. The amount of the credit is on a sliding scale, depending on the amount of adjusted gross income and the number of dependents.

EARNED INCOME CREDIT. This credit against the tax is available to low-income workers who maintain a household for at least one of their dependent children and who have earned income (wages and self-employment income). The earned income is not like the other credits, which cannot exceed the amount of the tax before applying the credit. If the earned income credit reduces the tax liability below zero, the negative amount is paid to the taxpayer. For example, if a worker's tax liability before applying the credit is $150 and the earned income credit is $375, the taxpayer will receive a direct payment of $225. Direct payments of tax revenues to individuals who have no liability for federal income tax is a concept with important socioeconomic implications. The concept is often called a "negative income tax."

Filing Returns; Payment of Tax

The income tax withheld from an employee's earnings by an employer represents current payments on account. An individual whose income is not subject to withholding, or only partially so, or an individual whose income is fairly large must estimate the income tax in advance. The estimated tax for the year, after deducting the estimated amount to be withheld and any credit for overpayment from prior years, is paid usually in quarterly installments.

Annual income tax returns must be filed at the proper Internal Revenue Service office within 3½ months following the end of the taxpayer's taxable year. Any balance owed must accompany the return. If there has been an overpayment of the tax liability, the taxpayer may request that the overpayment be refunded or credited against the estimated tax for the following year.

INCOME TAX ON CORPORATIONS

The taxable income of a corporation is determined, in general, by deducting its ordinary business expenses from the total amount of its includable gross income. The corporate tax rates, in general, are as follows for 1992:

Taxable Income	Tax Rate[6]
$0 – $50,000	15%
$50,001 – $75,000	25%
Over $75,000	34%

TAX PLANNING TO MINIMIZE INCOME TAXES

There are various legal means of minimizing or reducing federal income taxes. Much depends upon the volume and the sources of a taxpayer's gross income, the nature of the expenses and other deductions, and the accounting methods used. Examples of means to minimize income taxes are presented in the following paragraphs.

Alternative Accounting Principles

There are many cases in which an enterprise may choose from among two or more optional accounting principles in determining the amount of its taxable

---

[6] The benefits of the initial 15% and 25% tax rates are phased out for companies whose income exceeds $100,000. For those companies, a 5% tax on income over $100,000 is added until the tax is equal to a flat rate of 34%.

income. The principle chosen may have an effect on the amount of income tax, not only in the year in which the choice is made but also in later years. To illustrate, the tax law generally permits an enterprise to choose its method of determining the cost of inventory. Two widely used methods are fifo (first-in, first-out) and lifo (last-in, first-out). The method chosen may have a significant effect on income and the tax on income in periods of changing price levels.

Under fifo, the first goods purchased during a year are assumed to be the first goods sold. During a period of rising prices, the first goods purchased are the least costly. If the least costly goods are sold, they are charged against revenue, and the most costly goods are included in inventory. Under lifo, however, the last goods purchased during a year are assumed to be the first goods sold. During a period of rising prices, the last goods purchased are the most costly. If the most costly goods are sold, they are charged against revenue, and the least costly goods are included in inventory. Thus, in periods of rising prices, lifo results in higher cost of goods sold, lower income, and lower taxes than fifo. During periods of declining prices, lifo results in lower cost of goods sold, higher income, and higher taxes than fifo.

In times of inflation, the use of lifo results in a lower annual income tax. Thus, during such periods, lifo permits the taxpayer to retain more cash, by lowering tax payments, to replace goods sold with higher-priced goods. This advantage is one of the most important reasons for lifo's popularity.

Use of Corporate Debt

When a corporation requires long-term financing for its operations, it generally considers borrowing money on a long-term basis or issuing stock. While interest on debt is a deductible expense in determining taxable income, dividends paid on stock are not. This difference in the treatment of interest and dividends is an important factor to consider in evaluating the two methods of financing.

To illustrate, assume that a corporation with an estimated tax rate of 34% is considering issuing (1) $1,000,000 of 10% bonds or (2) $1,000,000 of 10% cumulative preferred stock. If the bonds are issued, the deduction of the yearly $100,000 of interest in determining taxable income results in an annual net borrowing cost of $66,000 ($100,000 less tax savings of 34% of $100,000). If the preferred stock is issued, the dividends are not deductible in determining taxable income and the net annual outlay for this method of financing is $100,000. Thus, issuing bonds instead of preferred stock reduces the annual financing expenditures by $34,000 ($100,000 - $66,000).

Nontaxable Investment Income

Interest on bonds issued by a state or political subdivision is exempt from the federal income tax. To illustrate, the following table compares the income after tax on a $100,000 investment in a 10% industrial bond and a $100,000 investment in an 8% municipal bond for a corporation with a tax rate of 34%.

	Taxable 10% Industrial Bond	Nontaxable 8% Municipal Bond
Income	$10,000	$8,000
Tax (34% of $10,000)	3,400	—
Income after tax	$ 6,600	$8,000

Although the interest rate on the municipal bond (8%) is less than the rate on the industrial bond (10%), the aftertax income is larger from the investment in the municipal bond.

GENERAL IMPACT OF INCOME TAXES

The preceding discussion of the federal income tax system and tax minimization illustrates the importance of income taxes to individuals and to business enterprises. Many accountants, in both private and public practice, devote their entire attention to tax planning for their employers or their clients. The statutes and the administrative regulations, which are often changed, must be studied continuously by anyone who engages in the practice of tax accounting.

DISCUSSION QUESTIONS

1. a. Does the failure to receive the tax forms from the IRS qualify as a legitimate means of tax avoidance?
   b. Does the failure to maintain adequate records qualify as a legitimate means of tax avoidance?
2. a. What are the principal taxable entities subject to the federal income tax?
   b. How is the income of a sole proprietorship taxed?
3. Describe briefly the system used in subjecting the income of partnerships to the federal income tax.
4. The adjusted gross income of a sole proprietorship for the year was $88,000, of which the owner withdrew $60,000. What amount of income from the business enterprise must be reported on the owner's income tax return?
5. Do corporations electing partnership treatment (Subchapter S) pay federal income tax? Discuss.
6. Which of the two methods of accounting, cash or accrual, is more commonly used by individual taxpayers?
7. Describe constructive receipt of gross income as it applies to (a) a salary check received from an employer, (b) interest credited to a savings account, and (c) bond interest coupons.
8. Arrange the following items in their proper sequence for the determination of taxable income of an individual:
   (a) Itemized deductions and exemptions
   (b) Taxable income
   (c) Adjusted gross income
   (d) Expenses related to business or specified revenue
   (e) Gross income
9. Which inventory method (lifo or fifo) would result in the lower income tax during a period of rising prices? Explain.

EXERCISES

EXERCISE E-1
DETERMINATION OF
INCOME USING CASH
METHOD AND ACCRUAL
METHOD

John Montez, DDS, opened his dental office after graduation from medical school in early January of the current year. On December 30, the accounting records indicated the following for the current year to date:

	Total	Cash Received	Cash Paid
Fees earned	$119,000	$103,000	—
Lease of dental office and equipment	36,000	—	$33,000
Dental assistant salary	30,000	—	27,500
Dental supplies, utilities, etc.	9,500	—	8,700

a. Determine the amount of net income Montez would report from his practice for the current year under (a) the cash method and (b) the accrual method,
b. List the advantages of using the cash method rather than the accrual method in accounting for Montez's practice.

SHARPEN YOUR
COMMUNICATION SKILLS

c. What is the principal advantage of using the accrual method rather than the cash method in accounting for Montez's practice?

E–9

EXERCISE E-2
DETERMINATION OF
INCOME OF SOLE
PROPRIETOR FOR INCOME
TAX

In early January of the current year, Ann Garner opened a business that she operated as a sole proprietorship. On December 31, the accounting records indicated the following for the current year:

Administrative expenses	$ 20,200	Selling expenses	$31,600
Cost of merchandise sold	180,500	Withdrawals by owner	34,000
Sales	266,350		

Determine the amount of taxable income from the business that Garner should include in her tax return for the current year.

EXERCISE E-3
DETERMINATION OF
CORPORATION INCOME
TAX

During the current year, three corporations realized the following taxable incomes:

Corporation A	$70,000
Corporation B	5,000
Corporation C	90,000

Using the tax rates indicated in the appendix, determine the amount of income tax owed by each corporation.

EXERCISE E-4
EFFECTS OF USING FIFO
AND LIFO FOR INVENTORY
COSTING

Germaine Limousine Sales sold 30 limousines for $34,000 each during the first year of operations. Data related to purchases during the year are as follows:

	Quantity	Unit Cost
February 2	8	$29,000
April 22	7	29,500
June 30	6	29,750
October 15	9	29,800
November 30	5	30,000

Sales of limousines are the company's only source of income, and operating expenses for the current year are $60,100.

a. Determine the net income for the current year, using the fifo (first-in, first-out) inventory method.

b. Determine the net income for the current year, using the lifo (last-in, first-out) inventory method.

SHARPEN YOUR COMMUNICATION SKILLS ► c. Which method of inventory costing, fifo or lifo, would you recommend for tax purposes? Discuss.

EXERCISE E-5
EFFECTS OF CORPORATION
INCOME TAX ON TWO
FINANCING PLANS

The board of directors of C. D. Kluge Inc. is planning an expansion of plant facilities expected to cost $5,000,000. The board is undecided about the method of financing this expansion and is considering two plans:

Plan 1. Issue 100,000 shares of $50, 9% cumulative preferred stock at par.
Plan 2. Issue $5,000,000 of 20-year, 11% bonds at face amount.

The condensed balance sheet of the corporation at the end of the most recent fiscal year is as follows:

C. D. Kluge Inc.
Balance Sheet
December 31, 19—

Assets		Liabilities and Stockholders' Equity	
Current assets	$2,400,000	Current liabilities	$1,940,000
Plant assets	5,600,000	Common stock, $25 par	3,500,000
Total assets	$8,000,000	Paid-in capital in excess of par	1,000,000
		Retained earnings	1,560,000
		Total liabilities and stockholders' equity	$8,000,000

Net income has remained relatively constant over the past several years. As a result of the expansion program, yearly income after tax but before bond interest and related income tax is expected to increase to $725,000.

a. Prepare a table indicating the net annual outlay (dividends and interest after tax) for financing under each plan. (Use the 34% income tax rate indicated in the appendix.)

SHARPEN YOUR COMMUNICATION SKILLS ► b. Prepare a brief report listing factors other than the net cost of financing that the board should consider in evaluating the two plans.

APPENDIX F

MANUFACTURING WORK SHEET

Many accountants use a work sheet to assist them in preparing financial statements. The use of work sheets for merchandising enterprises was illustrated in Chapter 6. Work sheets may also be used for manufacturing enterprises. This appendix describes and illustrates the use of a work sheet for a manufacturing enterprise that uses a periodic inventory system. The illustration is based on the discussion of the general accounting system described in Chapter 22.

WORK SHEET PROCEDURES

A work sheet for a manufacturing enterprise using a periodic inventory system is shown in Exhibit 1. This work sheet expands upon the merchandise inventory work sheet by adding two columns—a debit column and a credit column—for the statement of cost of goods manufactured. All amounts that are included in determining the cost of goods manufactured are extended to these columns. After all these data have been extended, the Statement of Cost of Goods Manufactured columns are totaled, and the difference between the two column totals is determined. This difference is the "Cost of Goods Manufactured," and it is identified as such in the account title column. The amount of the cost of goods manufactured is transferred to the Income Statement columns by entries in the Statement of Cost of Goods Manufactured Credit column and the Income Statement Debit column. The remainder of the work sheet is completed in the same manner as for a merchandising enterprise.

Exhibit 1
Manufacturing Work Sheet

Burleson Manufacturing Company
Work Sheet
For Year Ended December 31,1994

Account Title	Trial Balance Dr.	Trial Balance Cr.	Adjustments Dr.	Adjustments Cr.	Statement of Cost of Goods Manufactured Dr.	Statement of Cost of Goods Manufactured Cr.	Income Statement Dr.	Income Statement Cr.	Balance Sheet Dr.	Balance Sheet Cr.
Cash	18,200								18,200	
Accounts Receivable	66,100								66,100	
Allowance for Doubtful Accounts		1,500								1,500
Finished Goods	78,500		(b) 91,000	(a) 78,500					91,000	
Work in Process	55,000		(d) 65,800	(c) 55,000					65,800	
Direct Materials	62,000		(f) 58,725	(e) 62,000					58,725	
Factory Supplies	4,700			(g) 2,900					1,800	
Prepaid Insurance	1,250								1,250	
Land	50,000								50,000	
Factory Buildings	240,000								240,000	
Accumulated Depreciation—Factory Buildings		30,000		(h) 6,000						36,000
Factory Equipment	446,000								446,000	
Accumulated Depreciation—Factory Equipment		111,500		(i) 22,300						133,800
Accounts Payable		58,800								58,800
Wages and Salaries Payable				(j) 5,450						5,450
Common Stock ($10 par)		200,000								200,000
Retained Earnings		515,325								515,325
Dividends	40,000								40,000	
Income Summary			(a) 78,500	(b) 91,000			78,500	91,000		
Manufacturing Summary			(c) 55,000 (e) 62,000	(d) 65,800 (f) 58,725	55,000 62,000	65,800 58,725				
Sales		915,800						915,800		
Direct Materials Purchases	220,800				220,800					
Direct Labor	214,250		(j) 4,500		218,750					
Indirect Factory Labor	48,350		(j) 950		49,300					
Depreciation—Factory Equipment			(i) 22,300		22,300					
Factory Heat, Light, and Power	21,800				21,800					
Factory Property Taxes	9,750				9,750					
Depreciation—Factory Buildings			(h) 6,000		6,000					
Insurance Expense—Factory	4,750				4,750					
Factory Supplies Expense			(g) 2,900		2,900					
Miscellaneous Factory Expense	2,050				2,050					
Selling Expenses	165,000						165,000			
Administrative Expenses	84,425						84,425			
	1,832,925	1,832,925	447,675	447,675	675,400	124,525				
Cost of Goods Manufactured						550,875	550,875			
					675,400	675,400	878,800	1,006,800	1,078,875	950,875
Net Income							128,000			128,000
							1,006,800	1,006,800	1,078,875	1,078,875

The manufacturing work sheet shown in Exhibit 1 is for Burleson Manufacturing Company, which uses a periodic inventory system. The unadjusted trial balance for Burleson Manufacturing Company on December 31, 1994, is shown in the first two columns. The data needed for the year-end adjustments are summarized below.

Inventories on December 31, 1994:
Finished goods	$91,000
Work in process	65,800
Direct materials	58,725
Factory supplies	1,800

Depreciation for the year:
Factory buildings	6,000
Factory equipment	22,300

Accrued wages and salaries on December 31, 1994:
Direct labor	4,500
Indirect labor	950

Adjusting Entries

The adjusting entries are recorded on the work sheet in the usual manner, except for the inventories of work in process and direct materials. As explained in Chapter 22, the work in process inventory account is adjusted through the manufacturing summary account. The inventory of work in process at the beginning of the period is transferred to the manufacturing summary account by debiting Manufacturing Summary and crediting Work in Process for $55,000 (entry (c) on the work sheet). The ending work in process inventory is recorded by debiting Work in Process and crediting Manufacturing Summary for $65,800 (entry (d) on the work sheet).

Like the work in process inventory, the direct materials inventory at the beginning of the fiscal period is transferred to the manufacturing summary account by debiting Manufacturing Summary and crediting Direct Materials for $62,000 (entry (e) on the work sheet). The direct materials inventory at the end of the period is recorded by debiting Direct Materials and crediting Manufacturing Summary for $58,725 (entry (f) on the work sheet).

The finished goods inventory account is adjusted by using the income summary account in the same manner as the merchandise inventory of a merchandising enterprise. The beginning finished goods inventory is transferred to the income summary account by debiting Income Summary and crediting Finished Goods for $78,500 (entry (a) on the work sheet). The ending finished goods inventory is recorded by debiting Finished Goods and crediting Income Summary for $91,000 (entry (b) on the work sheet).

Completing the Work Sheet

After all the adjustments have been entered on the work sheet, each account balance, as adjusted, is extended to the proper column. In Exhibit 1, the Adjusted Trial Balance columns, which appear in the work sheets illustrated in Chapter 6, have been eliminated. These columns are often omitted in practice.

In Exhibit 1, the adjusted account balances are entered directly into the proper financial statement columns. The accounts that appear in the statement of cost of goods manufactured are extended to the Statement of Cost of Goods Manufactured columns. The other accounts are extended to the Income Statement and Balance Sheet columns in the usual manner. The beginning and ending inventory amounts appearing opposite Income Summary and Manufacturing Summary in the Adjustments columns are extended individually rather than as the net amount. This is because both amounts are used in preparing the financial statements.

After all of the amounts have been extended to the proper columns, the work sheet is completed in the following manner:

1. The Statement of Cost of Goods Manufactured columns are totaled. In Exhibit 1, the total of the Dr. column is $675,400, and the total of the Cr. column is $124,525.
2. The difference between the two Statement of Cost of Goods Manufactured columns is determined and entered in the Statement of Cost of Goods Manufactured Cr. column and the Income Statement Dr. column. This difference ($550,875) is the cost of goods manufactured for the period.
3. The totals of the columns are entered. The Statement of Cost of Goods Manufactured columns should now be in balance.
4. The amount of net income is determined and is recorded in the Income Statement Dr. column and in the Balance Sheet Cr. column.
5. The totals of the last four columns, which should now be in balance, are entered.

Financial Statements

The completed work sheet summarizes the data necessary for preparing the income statement, statement of cost of goods manufactured, retained earnings statement, and balance sheet. For Burleson Manufacturing Company, these statements are shown in Exhibit 2.

Exhibit 2
Financial Statements for
Manufacturing Enterprise

Burleson Manufacturing Company Income Statement For Year Ended December 31, 1994		
Sales		$915,800
Cost of goods sold:		
Finished goods inventory, January 1, 1994	$ 78,500	
Cost of goods manufactured	550,875	
Cost of finished goods available for sale	$629,375	
Less finished goods inventory, December 31, 1994	91,000	
Cost of goods sold		538,375
Gross profit		$377,425
Operating expenses:		
Selling expenses	$165,000	
Administrative expenses	84,425	
Total operating expenses		249,425
Net income		$128,000

Exhibit 2 (continued)

Burleson Manufacturing Company
Statement of Cost of Goods Manufactured
For Year Ended December 31, 1994

Work in process inventory, January 1, 1994			$ 55,000
Direct materials:			
Inventory, January 1, 1994	$ 62,000		
Purchases	220,800		
Cost of materials available for use	$282,800		
Less inventory, December 31, 1994	58,725		
Cost of materials placed in production		$224,075	
Direct labor		218,750	
Factory overhead:			
Indirect labor	$ 49,300		
Depreciation of factory equipment	22,300		
Heat, light, and power	21,800		
Property taxes	9,750		
Depreciation of buildings	6,000		
Insurance expense	4,750		
Factory supplies expense	2,900		
Miscellaneous factory costs	2,050		
Total factory overhead		118,850	
Total manufacturing costs			561,675
Total work in process during period			$616,675
Less work in process inventory,			
December 31, 1994			65,800
Cost of goods manufactured			$550,875

Burleson Manufacturing Company
Retained Earnings Statement
For Year Ended December 31, 1994

Retained earnings, January 1, 1994		$515,325
Net income for year	$128,000	
Less dividends	40,000	
Increase in retained earnings		88,000
Retained earnings, December 31, 1994		$603,325

Exhibit 2 (concluded)

Burleson Manufacturing Company Balance Sheet December 31, 1994			
Assets			
Current assets:			
Cash			$ 18,200
Accounts receivable		$ 66,100	
Less allowance for doubtful accounts		1,500	64,600
Inventories:			
Finished goods		$ 91,000	
Work in process		65,800	
Direct materials		58,725	215,525
Factory supplies			1,800
Prepaid insurance			1,250
Total current assets			$301,375
Plant assets:			
Land			$ 50,000
Buildings		$240,000	
Less accumulated depreciation		36,000	204,000
Factory equipment		$446,000	
Less accumulated depreciation		133,800	312,200
Total plant assets			566,200
Total assets			$867,575
Liabilities			
Current liabilities:			
Accounts payable			$ 58,800
Wages and salaries payable			5,450
Total current liabilities			$ 64,250
Stockholders' Equity			
Common stock, $10 par			$200,000
Retained earnings			603,325
Total stockholders' equity			803,325
Total liabilities and stockholders' equity			$867,575

ADJUSTING ENTRIES

At the end of the accounting period, the adjusting entries in the work sheet are recorded in the journal and are posted to the ledger. This brings the ledger into agreement with the data reported in the financial statements. The adjusting entries for Burleson Manufacturing Company are as follows:

Adjusting Entries		
(a) Income Summary	78,500	
Finished Goods		78,500
(b) Finished Goods	91,000	
Income Summary		91,000
(c) Manufacturing Summary	55,000	
Work in Process		55,000
(d) Work in Process	65,800	
Manufacturing Summary		65,800
(e) Manufacturing Summary	62,000	
Direct Materials		62,000
(f) Direct Materials	58,725	
Manufacturing Summary		58,725
(g) Factory Supplies Expense	2,900	
Factory Supplies		2,900

(h) Depreciation—Factory Buildings	6,000	
Accumulated Depreciation—Factory Buildings		6,000
(i) Depreciation—Factory Equipment	22,300	
Accumulated Depreciation—Factory Equipment		22,300
(j) Direct Labor	4,500	
Indirect Factory Labor	950	
Wages and Salaries Payable		5,450

CLOSING ENTRIES

The closing entries are recorded in the journal immediately following the adjusting entries. The manufacturing accounts are closed to Manufacturing Summary. The balance in Manufacturing Summary ($550,875, the cost of goods manufactured), is closed to Income Summary, along with the other expense accounts. The remaining accounts are closed in the normal manner.

The closing entries for Burleson Manufacturing Company are as follows:

Closing Entries

Manufacturing Summary	558,400	
Direct Materials Purchases		220,800
Direct Labor		218,750
Indirect Factory Labor		49,300
Depreciation—Factory Equipment		22,300
Factory Heat, Light, and Power		21,800
Factory Property Taxes		9,750
Depreciation—Factory Buildings		6,000
Insurance Expense—Factory		4,750
Factory Supplies Expense		2,900
Miscellaneous Factory Expense		2,050
Sales	915,800	
Income Summary		915,800
Income Summary	800,300	
Selling Expenses		165,000
Administrative Expenses		84,425
Manufacturing Summary		550,875
Income Summary	128,000	
Retained Earnings		128,000
Retained Earnings	40,000	
Dividends		40,000

PROBLEMS

PROBLEM F-1
MANUFACTURING WORK SHEET AND FINANCIAL STATEMENTS

The accounts in the ledger of Gunn Manufacturing Inc., with unadjusted balances on December 31, the end of the current year, are as follows:

Cash	29,750	Accounts Payable	40,400
Accounts Receivable	48,250	Wages Payable	—
Allow. for Doubtful Accounts	900	Common Stock ($20 par)	300,000
Finished Goods	55,800	Retained Earnings	126,450
Work in Process	32,100	Dividends	20,000
Direct Materials	42,000	Income Summary	—
Prepaid Expenses (Controlling)	10,000	Manufacturing Summary	—
Land	50,000	Sales	668,500
Factory Buildings	260,000	Direct Materials Purchases	197,000
Accum. Depr.—Factory Bldgs.	90,000	Direct Labor	178,900
Factory Equipment	172,650	Factory Overhead (Controlling)	65,150
Accum. Depr.—Factory Equip.	97,950	Selling Expenses (Controlling)	70,275
Office Equipment	30,000	Adm. Expenses (Controlling)	68,825
Accum. Depr.—Office Equip.	10,000	Interest Expense	3,500

The data needed for the year-end adjustments on December 31 are as follows:

Inventories on December 31:

Finished goods	$60,000	
Work in process	35,600	
Direct materials	39,400	$135,000
Doubtful accounts at December 31 from analysis of accounts receivable		3,000
Prepaid insurance expired during year:		
Factory overhead	$ 4,200	
Administrative expenses	1,100	5,300
Accrued wages at December 31:		
Direct labor	$ 2,500	
Indirect labor	500	3,000
Depreciation expense for year:		
Factory buildings	$ 8,000	
Factory equipment	16,700	
Office equipment	2,600	27,300

Instructions

1. Prepare a manufacturing work sheet. (Leave one extra line after Manufacturing Summary and two extra lines after Factory Overhead and Administrative Expenses for use in recording the adjusting entries.)
2. Prepare a statement of cost of goods manufactured.
3. Prepare an income statement.
4. Prepare a retained earnings statement.
5. Prepare a balance sheet.

PROBLEM F-2
MANUFACTURING
FINANCIAL STATEMENTS

The chief accountant for Pyle Co. prepared the manufacturing work sheet shown on the following page for the current year.

Instructions

1. Prepare a statement of cost of goods manufactured.
2. Prepare an income statement.
3. Prepare a retained earnings statement.
4. Prepare a balance sheet.

PROBLEM F-3
ADJUSTING AND CLOSING
ENTRIES

The work sheet for Pyle Co. for the current year is presented in Problem F-2.

Instructions

1. Journalize the entries to adjust the accounts at the end of the year.
2. Journalize the entries to close the appropriate accounts at the end of the year.

PROBLEM F-4
STATEMENT OF COST OF
GOODS MANUFACTURED;
ADJUSTING ENTRIES AND
CLOSING ENTRIES

The following accounts related to manufacturing operations were selected from the pre-closing trial balance of Maye Co. at December 31, the end of the current fiscal year:

Depreciation of Factory Buildings	$ 19,500
Depreciation of Factory Equipment	30,500
Direct Labor	210,600
Direct Materials Inventory	60,000
Direct Materials Purchases	290,500
Factory Supplies Expense	6,150
Finished Goods Inventory	90,000
Heat, Light, and Power Expense	28,250
Indirect Labor	46,750
Insurance Expense	9,000
Miscellaneous Factory Costs	4,850
Property Taxes Expense	12,500
Work in Process Inventory	56,800

Inventories at December 31 were as follows:

Finished Goods	$102,300
Work in Process	66,500
Direct Materials	71,400

Instructions

1. Prepare a statement of cost of goods manufactured.
2. Journalize the entries to adjust the work in process and direct materials inventories.
3. Journalize the entries to close the appropriate accounts to Manufacturing Summary.
4. Journalize the entry to close Manufacturing Summary.

Pyle Co.
Work Sheet
For Year Ended December 31,19—

Account Title	Trial Balance Dr.	Cr.	Adjustments Dr.	Cr.	Statement of Cost of Goods Manufactured Dr.	Cr.	Income Statement Dr.	Cr.	Balance Sheet Dr.	Cr.
Cash	19,750								19,750	
Accounts Receivable	76,200								76,200	
Allowance for Doubtful Accounts		1,800								1,800
Finished Goods	90,000		(b) 95,000	(a) 90,000					95,000	
Work in Process	72,000		(d) 68,000	(c) 72,000					68,000	
Direct Materials	58,500		(f) 65,200	(e) 58,500					65,200	
Prepaid Insurance	8,700			(g) 5,900					2,800	
Factory Supplies	8,250			(h) 5,250					3,000	
Land	75,000								75,000	
Factory Buildings	290,000								290,000	
Accumulated Depreciation— Factory Buildings		170,000		(i) 16,000						186,000
Factory Equipment	446,000								446,000	
Accumulated Depreciation— Factory Equipment		211,500		(j) 22,300						233,800
Accounts Payable		64,100								64,100
Wages Payable				(k) 4,550						4,550
Common Stock ($20 par)		300,000								300,000
Retained Earnings		325,225								325,225
Dividends	60,000								60,000	
Income Summary			(a) 90,000	(b) 95,000			90,000	95,000		
Manufacturing Summary			(c) 72,000 (e) 58,500	(d) 68,000 (f) 65,200	72,000 58,500	68,000 65,200				
Sales		785,500						785,500		
Direct Materials Purchases	184,800				184,800					
Direct Labor	174,250		(k) 3,800		178,050					
Indirect Factory Labor	47,250		(k) 750		48,000					
Depreciation—Factory Equipment			(j) 22,300		22,300					
Factory Heat, Light, and Power	31,800				31,800					
Factory Property Taxes	12,750				12,750					
Depreciation—Factory Buildings			(i) 16,000		16,000					
Insurance Expense—Factory			(g) 5,900		5,900					
Factory Supplies Expense			(h) 5,250		5,250					
Miscellaneous Factory Expense	3,650				3,650					
Selling Expenses	100,500						100,500			
Administrative Expenses	98,725						98,725			
	1,858,125	1,858,125	502,700	502,700	639,000	133,200				
						505,800	505,800			
Cost of Goods Manufactured					639,000	639,000	795,025	880,500	1,200,950	1,115,475
Net Income							85,475			85,475
							880,500	880,500	1,200,950	1,200,950

SPECIMEN FINANCIAL STATEMENTS

This appendix contains selected statements and notes for real companies.

Pages G–3 through G–16 contain excerpts from financial statements for Hershey Foods Corporation.

Consolidated Statement of Income
(In Thousands, Except Per Share Amounts)

The Charles Schwab Corporation

Year Ended December 31,	1991	1990	1989
Revenues			
Commissions	$348,920	$244,419	$229,005
Interest	302,198	309,534	272,897
Principal transactions	63,421	3,614	1,708
Mutual fund service fees	54,152	45,555	29,360
Other	26,494	22,768	20,186
Total revenues	795,185	625,890	553,156
Interest expense	225,558	238,497	207,347
Net revenues	569,627	387,393	345,809
Expenses Excluding Interest			
Compensation and benefits	234,364	155,053	130,652
Communications	57,272	41,618	37,414
Depreciation and amortization	51,930	49,103	52,535
Occupancy and equipment	51,203	42,920	34,225
Advertising and market development	25,249	19,930	18,370
Commissions, clearance and floor brokerage	20,679	12,269	11,501
Professional services	12,037	15,904	10,426
Other	28,796	21,487	17,495
Total expenses excluding interest	481,530	358,284	312,618
Income before taxes on income	88,097	29,109	33,191
Taxes on income	38,629	12,328	14,272
Net Income	$ 49,468	$ 16,781	$ 18,919
Weighted average number of common and common equivalent shares	39,083	40,354	41,586
Earnings per Common Equivalent Share	$1.27	$.41	$.45
Dividends Declared per Common Share	$.127	$.087	$.060

See Notes to Consolidated Financial Statements.

THE HOME DEPOT, INC. AND SUBSIDIARIES

Amounts in thousands, except per share data

	Fiscal Year Ended		
	February 2, 1992 (52 weeks)	February 3, 1991 (53 weeks)	January 28, 1990 (52 weeks)
NET SALES	$5,136,674	$3,815,356	$2,758,535
COST OF MERCHANDISE SOLD	3,692,337	2,751,085	1,991,777
GROSS PROFIT	1,444,337	1,064,271	766,758
OPERATING EXPENSES:			
Selling and Store Operating	928,928	693,657	504,363
Pre-Opening	17,668	13,315	9,845
General and Administrative	116,063	91,664	67,901
TOTAL OPERATING EXPENSES	1,062,659	798,636	582,109
OPERATING INCOME	381,678	265,635	184,649
INTEREST INCOME (EXPENSE):			
Interest Income	26,790	17,579	13,320
Interest Expense (note 2)	(12,348)	(23,386)	(15,954)
INTEREST, NET	14,442	(5,807)	(2,634)
EARNINGS BEFORE INCOME TAXES	396,120	259,828	182,015
INCOME TAXES (note 3)	146,970	96,400	70,061
NET EARNINGS	$ 249,150	$ 163,428	$ 111,954
EARNINGS PER COMMON AND COMMON EQUIVALENT SHARE (note 4)	$ 1.20	$ .90	$ .63
WEIGHTED AVERAGE NUMBER OF COMMON AND COMMON EQUIVALENT SHARES	207,999	181,253	177,705

See accompanying notes to consolidated financial statements.

MANAGEMENT'S DISCUSSION AND ANALYSIS—
RESULTS OF OPERATIONS

Net Sales

Net sales rose $183.6 million or 7% in 1991 and $294.6 million or 12% in 1990. The increase in 1991 reflected growth from business acquisitions and confectionery selling price increases, and volume growth from the Corporation's pasta, international and refrigerated puddings businesses. The 1990 increase was due to unit volume growth from a combination of business acquisitions, new product introductions and existing brands.

Costs and Expenses

Cost of sales as a percent of net sales decreased to 58.4% in 1991 from 58.5% in 1990 and 60.1% in 1989. The resulting increase in gross margin in 1991 was primarily due to confectionery price increases almost entirely offset by a higher average cost per pound of peanuts and cocoa beans, as well as increases in overhead and employee benefits costs. The increase in gross margin in 1990 reflected declines in cocoa bean and durum wheat costs, partially offset by increases in the average cost per pound of sugar, milk and peanuts.

Selling, marketing and administrative costs increased in 1991 primarily as a result of business acquisitions and increased promotion expenses offset somewhat by lower advertising expenses. The increase in selling, marketing and administrative costs in 1990, as a percent of net sales, primarily reflected higher expenditures and incremental programs in support of acquired and existing brands, as well as new product introductions.

Gain on Business Restructuring, Net

The Corporation's financial results for 1990 included a net pre-tax gain from business restructuring activities totaling $35.5 million. This gain, which increased net income by $20.3 million resulted from two events.

In May 1990, the Corporation sold its equity interest in Marabou for $78.0 million. The sale resulted in a gain of $60.5 million and had the effect of increasing net income by $35.3 million.

In the fourth quarter of 1990, the Corporation recorded a manufacturing restructuring charge of $25.0 million associated with the modernization and relocation of certain manufacturing operations. The charge related to existing production facilities that will be impacted by the chocolate-processing facility under construction in Hershey, Pa., and other manufacturing strategies associated with the Corporation's confectionery and pasta operations. This charge reduced net income by $15.0 million.

Interest Expense, Net

Net interest expense was $2.2 million higher in 1991 than 1990, due to the additional debt required on an interim basis to finance capital additions, working capital requirements and business acquisitions, offset partially by higher capitalized interest. Net interest expense increased by $4.2 million in 1990 as a result of increased borrowings associated with the Ronzoni acquisition and investments in working capital.

Provision for Income Taxes

The Corporation's effective income tax rate on income from operations was 39.6%, 40.3% and 41.0% in 1991, 1990 and 1989, respectively. The principal factors causing differences in the effective income tax rates among the years were changes in the mix of the Corporation's income among various tax jurisdictions and an increase in non-taxable income. Such changes more than offset an increase in the Pennsylvania corporate income tax rate in 1991.

Net Income

Excluding the effect of a net gain on business restructuring in 1990, net income increased $23.9 million or 12% in 1991, following a $24.5 million or 14% increase in 1990. Net income as a percent of net sales was 7.6% in 1991, 7.2% in 1990 after excluding the net gain on business restructuring, and 7.1% in 1989.

THE HOME DEPOT, INC. AND SUBSIDIARIES

Amounts in thousands, except per share data

	Fiscal Year Ended		
	February 2, 1992 (52 weeks)	February 3, 1991 (53 weeks)	January 28, 1990 (52 weeks)
NET SALES	$5,136,674	$3,815,356	$2,758,535
COST OF MERCHANDISE SOLD	3,692,337	2,751,085	1,991,777
GROSS PROFIT	1,444,337	1,064,271	766,758
OPERATING EXPENSES:			
Selling and Store Operating	928,928	693,657	504,363
Pre-Opening	17,668	13,315	9,845
General and Administrative	116,063	91,664	67,901
TOTAL OPERATING EXPENSES	1,062,659	798,636	582,109
OPERATING INCOME	381,678	265,635	184,649
INTEREST INCOME (EXPENSE):			
Interest Income	26,790	17,579	13,320
Interest Expense (note 2)	(12,348)	(23,386)	(15,954)
INTEREST, NET	14,442	(5,807)	(2,634)
EARNINGS BEFORE INCOME TAXES	396,120	259,828	182,015
INCOME TAXES (note 3)	146,970	96,400	70,061
NET EARNINGS	$ 249,150	$ 163,428	$ 111,954
EARNINGS PER COMMON AND COMMON EQUIVALENT SHARE (note 4)	$ 1.20	$ .90	$ .63
WEIGHTED AVERAGE NUMBER OF COMMON AND COMMON EQUIVALENT SHARES	207,999	181,253	177,705

See accompanying notes to consolidated financial statements.

HERSHEY FOODS CORPORATION

CONSOLIDATED BALANCE SHEETS

(in thousands of dollars)

December 31,	1991	1990
ASSETS		
Current Assets:		
Cash and cash equivalents	$ 71,124	$ 26,626
Accounts receivable—trade	159,805	142,971
Inventories	436,917	379,108
Prepaid expenses and other	76,633	113,080
Total current assets	744,479	661,785
Property, Plant and Equipment, Net	1,145,666	952,094
Intangibles Resulting from Business Acquisitions	421,694	417,645
Other Assets	29,983	47,304
	$2,341,822	$2,078,828
LIABILITIES AND STOCKHOLDERS' EQUITY		
Current Liabilities:		
Accounts payable	$ 137,890	$ 127,572
Accrued liabilities	226,267	170,179
Accrued income taxes	22,000	19,126
Short-term debt and current portion of long-term debt	84,575	24,356
Total current liabilities	470,732	341,233
Long-term Debt	282,933	273,442
Other Long-term Liabilities	80,907	66,159
Deferred Income Taxes	171,999	154,457
Total liabilities	1,006,571	835,291
Stockholders' Equity:		
Preferred Stock, outstanding shares: none in 1991 and 1990	—	—
Common Stock, outstanding shares:		
74,921,282 in 1991 and 74,909,932 in 1990	74,921	74,910
Class B Common Stock, outstanding shares:		
15,265,054 in 1991 and 15,276,404 in 1990	15,265	15,276
Additional paid-in capital	52,509	49,249
Cumulative foreign currency translation adjustments	26,424	26,195
Unearned ESOP compensation	(47,902)	—
Retained earnings	1,214,034	1,077,907
Total stockholders' equity	1,335,251	1,243,537
	$2,341,822	$2,078,828

The notes to consolidated financial statements are an integral part of these balance sheets.

HERSHEY FOODS CORPORATION

CONSOLIDATED STATEMENTS OF INCOME

(in thousands of dollars except per share amounts)

For the years ended December 31,	1991	1990	1989
Net Sales	$2,899,165	$2,715,609	$2,420,988
Costs and Expenses:			
Cost of sales	1,694,404	1,588,360	1,455,612
Selling, marketing and administrative	814,459	776,668	655,040
Total costs and expenses	2,508,863	2,365,028	2,110,652
Gain on Business Restructuring, Net	—	35,540	—
Income before Interest and Income Taxes	390,302	386,121	310,336
Interest expense, net	26,845	24,603	20,414
Income before Income Taxes	363,457	361,518	289,922
Provision for income taxes	143,929	145,636	118,868
Net Income	$ 219,528	$ 215,882	$ 171,054
Net Income per Share	$ 2.43	$ 2.39	$ 1.90
Cash Dividends Paid per Share:			
Common Stock—Regular	$ .940	$ .840	$ .740
Common Stock—Special	—	.150	—
Class B Common Stock—Regular	.850	.755	.665
Class B Common Stock—Special	—	.135	—

The notes to consolidated financial statements are an integral part of these statements.

MANAGEMENT'S DISCUSSION AND ANALYSIS— RESULTS OF OPERATIONS

Net Sales

Net sales rose $183.6 million or 7% in 1991 and $294.6 million or 12% in 1990. The increase in 1991 reflected growth from business acquisitions and confectionery selling price increases, and volume growth from the Corporation's pasta, international and refrigerated puddings businesses. The 1990 increase was due to unit volume growth from a combination of business acquisitions, new product introductions and existing brands.

Costs and Expenses

Cost of sales as a percent of net sales decreased to 58.4% in 1991 from 58.5% in 1990 and 60.1% in 1989. The resulting increase in gross margin in 1991 was primarily due to confectionery price increases almost entirely offset by a higher average cost per pound of peanuts and cocoa beans, as well as increases in overhead and employee benefits costs. The increase in gross margin in 1990 reflected declines in cocoa bean and durum wheat costs, partially offset by increases in the average cost per pound of sugar, milk and peanuts.

Selling, marketing and administrative costs increased in 1991 primarily as a result of business acquisitions and increased promotion expenses offset somewhat by lower advertising expenses. The increase in selling, marketing and administrative costs in 1990, as a percent of net sales, primarily reflected higher expenditures and incremental programs in support of acquired and existing brands, as well as new product introductions.

Gain on Business Restructuring, Net

The Corporation's financial results for 1990 included a net pre-tax gain from business restructuring activities totaling $35.5 million. This gain, which increased net income by $20.3 million resulted from two events.

In May 1990, the Corporation sold its equity interest in Marabou for $78.0 million. The sale resulted in a gain of $60.5 million and had the effect of increasing net income by $35.3 million.

In the fourth quarter of 1990, the Corporation recorded a manufacturing restructuring charge of $25.0 million associated with the modernization and relocation of certain manufacturing operations. The charge related to existing production facilities that will be impacted by the chocolate-processing facility under construction in Hershey, Pa., and other manufacturing strategies associated with the Corporation's confectionery and pasta operations. This charge reduced net income by $15.0 million.

Interest Expense, Net

Net interest expense was $2.2 million higher in 1991 than 1990, due to the additional debt required on an interim basis to finance capital additions, working capital requirements and business acquisitions, offset partially by higher capitalized interest. Net interest expense increased by $4.2 million in 1990 as a result of increased borrowings associated with the Ronzoni acquisition and investments in working capital.

Provision for Income Taxes

The Corporation's effective income tax rate on income from operations was 39.6%, 40.3% and 41.0% in 1991, 1990 and 1989, respectively. The principal factors causing differences in the effective income tax rates among the years were changes in the mix of the Corporation's income among various tax jurisdictions and an increase in non-taxable income. Such changes more than offset an increase in the Pennsylvania corporate income tax rate in 1991.

Net Income

Excluding the effect of a net gain on business restructuring in 1990, net income increased $23.9 million or 12% in 1991, following a $24.5 million or 14% increase in 1990. Net income as a percent of net sales was 7.6% in 1991, 7.2% in 1990 after excluding the net gain on business restructuring, and 7.1% in 1989.

HERSHEY FOODS CORPORATION

CONSOLIDATED STATEMENTS OF CASH FLOWS

(in thousands of dollars)

For the years ended December 31,	1991	1990	1989
Cash Flows Provided from (Used by) Operating Activities			
Net income	$ 219,528	$ 215,882	$ 171,054
Adjustments to reconcile net income to net cash provided from operations:			
Depreciation and amortization	85,413	73,889	65,729
Deferred income taxes	20,654	(8,257)	3,369
Gain on business restructuring, net	—	(35,540)	—
Changes in assets and liabilities, net of effects from business acquisitions:			
Accounts receivable—trade	(6,404)	(21,028)	44,846
Inventories	(43,949)	(61,447)	(1,082)
Accounts payable	4,070	23,300	(26,546)
Other assets and liabilities	94,270	(5,398)	3,080
Other, net	(26,242)	5,105	5,195
Net Cash Provided from Operating Activities	347,340	186,506	265,645
Cash Flows Provided from (Used by) Investing Activities			
Capital additions	(226,071)	(179,408)	(162,032)
Business acquisitions	(44,108)	(78,153)	—
Sale of equity interest	—	78,041	—
Other, net	(1,510)	(4,501)	(2,316)
Net Cash (Used by) Investing Activities	(271,689)	(184,021)	(164,348)
Cash Flows Provided from (Used by) Financing Activities			
Net increase in short-term debt	56,489	1,131	—
Long-term borrowings	23,620	77,117	1,794
Repayment of long-term debt	(27,861)	(18,567)	(55,105)
Repayment of assumed debt	—	(250)	—
Loan to ESOP	(47,902)	—	—
Proceeds from sale of Common Stock to ESOP	47,902	—	—
Cash dividends paid	(83,401)	(87,757)	(65,592)
Net Cash (Used by) Financing Activities	(31,153)	(28,326)	(118,903)
Increase (Decrease) in Cash and Cash Equivalents	44,498	(25,841)	(17,606)
Cash and Cash Equivalents as of January 1	26,626	52,467	70,073
Cash and Cash Equivalents as of December 31	$ 71,124	$ 26,626	$ 52,467
Interest Paid	$ 24,468	$ 26,085	$ 21,329
Income Taxes Paid	$ 119,038	$ 147,099	$ 106,218

The notes to consolidated financial statements are an integral part of these statements.

HERSHEY FOODS CORPORATION

CONSOLIDATED STATEMENTS OF STOCKHOLDERS' EQUITY

(in thousands of dollars)

	Preferred Stock	Common Stock	Class B Common Stock	Additional Paid-in Capital	Cumulative Foreign Currency Translation Adjustments	Unearned ESOP Compensation	Retained Earnings	Total Stockholders' Equity
Balance as of January 1, 1989	$ —	$74,907	$15,279	$50,779	$20,581	$ —	$ 844,320	$1,005,866
Net income							171,054	171,054
Dividends—Common Stock and Class B Common Stock							(65,592)	(65,592)
Foreign currency translation adjustments					6,289			6,289
Incentive plan transactions				(567)				(567)
Balance as of December 31, 1989	—	74,907	15,279	50,212	26,870	—	949,782	1,117,050
Net income							215,882	215,882
Dividends—Common Stock and Class B Common Stock							(87,757)	(87,757)
Foreign currency translation adjustments					(675)			(675)
Conversion of Class B Common Stock into Common Stock		3	(3)					—
Incentive plan transactions				(963)				(963)
Balance as of December 31, 1990	—	74,910	15,276	49,249	26,195	—	1,077,907	1,243,537
Net income							**219,528**	**219,528**
Dividends—Common Stock and Class B Common Stock							**(83,401)**	**(83,401)**
Foreign currency translation adjustments					**229**			**229**
Conversion of Class B Common Stock into Common Stock		**11**	**(11)**					**—**
Incentive plan transactions				**(446)**				**(446)**
Employee stock ownership trust transactions				**3,706**		**(47,902)**		**(44,196)**
Balance as of December 31, 1991	$ —	$74,921	$15,265	$52,509	$26,424	$(47,902)	$1,214,034	$1,335,251

The notes to consolidated financial statements are an integral part of these statements.

HERSHEY FOODS CORPORATION

NOTES TO CONSOLIDATED FINANCIAL STATEMENTS

1. Summary of Significant Accounting Policies

Significant accounting policies employed by the Corporation are discussed below and in Notes 3, 8, 9, 12 and 13. Certain reclassifications have been made to prior year amounts to conform to the 1991 presentation.

Principles of Consolidation

The consolidated financial statements include the accounts of the Corporation and its subsidiaries after elimination of intercompany accounts and transactions. Investments in affiliated companies are accounted for using the equity method.

Cash Equivalents

All highly liquid debt instruments purchased with a maturity of three months or less are classified as cash equivalents.

Commodities Futures and Options Contracts

In connection with the purchasing of major commodities (principally cocoa and sugar) for anticipated manufacturing requirements, the Corporation enters into commodities futures and options contracts as deemed appropriate to reduce the risk of future price increases. These futures and options contracts are accounted for as hedges and, accordingly, gains and losses are deferred and recognized in cost of sales as part of the product cost.

Property, Plant and Equipment

Property, plant and equipment are stated at cost. Depreciation of buildings, machinery and equipment is computed using the straight-line method over the estimated useful lives.

Intangibles Resulting from Business Acquisitions

Intangible assets resulting from business acquisitions principally consist of the excess of the acquisition cost over the fair value of the net assets of businesses acquired (goodwill). Goodwill is amortized on a straight-line basis over 40 years. Other intangible assets are amortized on a straight-line basis over their estimated useful lives.

Accumulated amortization of intangible assets resulting from business acquisitions was $50.1 million and $37.6 million as of December 31, 1991 and 1990, respectively.

Foreign Currency Translation

Results of operations for international entities are translated using the average exchange rates during the period. For international entities operating in non-highly inflationary economies, assets and liabilities are translated to U.S. dollars using the exchange rates in effect at the balance sheet date. Resulting translation adjustments are recorded in a separate component of stockholders' equity, "Cumulative Foreign Currency Translation Adjustments."

Foreign Exchange Contracts

The Corporation enters into foreign exchange contracts to hedge transactions denominated in international currencies and to hedge payment of intercompany transactions with its non-domestic subsidiaries. Gains and losses are recognized as part of the underlying transactions.

License Agreements

The Corporation has entered into license agreements under which it has access to proprietary technology and manufactures and/or markets and distributes certain products. The Corporation's rights under these agreements are extendable on a long-term basis at the Corporation's option subject to certain conditions, including minimum sales levels. License fees and royalties, payable under the terms of the agreements, are expensed as incurred.

2. Gain on Business Restructuring, Net

The Corporation's financial results for 1990 included a net pre-tax gain from business restructuring activities totaling $35.5 million. This gain, which increased net income by $20.3 million, resulted from two events. In May 1990, the Corporation sold its equity interest in AB Marabou for $78.0 million. The sale resulted in a gain of $60.5 million and had the effect of increasing net income by $35.3 million. In the fourth quarter of 1990, the Corporation recorded a manufacturing restructuring charge of $25.0 million associated with the modernization and relocation of certain manufacturing operations. This charge reduced net income by $15.0 million.

3. Acquisitions

In October 1991, the Corporation purchased the shares of Nacional de Dulces, S.A. de C.V. (NDD) owned by its joint venture partner, Grupo Carso, S.A. de C.V., for $10.0 million. Prior to the acquisition, the Corporation owned 50% of the outstanding stock of NDD. NDD has its main offices and manufacturing plant in Guadalajara, Mexico. It produces, imports and markets chocolate products in the Mexican market under the *Hershey's* brand name.

In May 1991, the Corporation purchased certain assets of Dairymen, Inc.'s ultra-high temperature fluid milk-processing business, including a Savannah, Georgia manufacturing facility for $2.2 million, plus the assumption of $8.5 million in debt. The purchase price included a $.2 million adjustment based upon a final determination of inventory balances as of the acquisition date.

Also in May 1991, the Corporation completed the acquisition of the Gubor Schokoladen GmbH and Gubor Schokoladenfabrik GmbH (Gubor) chocolate business from H. Bahlsens Keksfabrik KG for

$31.9 million, plus the assumption of $9.0 million in debt. Gubor manufactures and markets high-quality assorted pralines and seasonal chocolates in Germany. The acquisition was effective as of January 1, 1991.

In February 1990, the Corporation purchased all of the outstanding voting securities of Ronzoni Foods Corporation (Ronzoni) from Kraft General Foods, Inc. for $78.2 million, plus the assumption of $3.7 million in debt. The purchase included Ronzoni's dry pasta, pasta sauces and cheese businesses.

In accordance with the purchase method of accounting, the purchase prices for the above acquisitions were allocated to the underlying assets and liabilities at the date of acquisition based on their estimated respective fair values, which may be revised at a later date. Results subsequent to the dates of acquisition are included in the consolidated financial statements. Had the results of these acquisitions been included in consolidated results for the entire length of each period presented, the effect would not have been material.

4. Capital Stock and Net Income Per Share

As of December 31, 1991, the Corporation had 530,000,000 authorized shares of capital stock. Of this total, 450,000,000 shares were designated as Common Stock, 75,000,000 shares as Class B Common Stock (Class B Stock), and 5,000,000 shares as Preferred Stock, each class having a par value of one dollar per share. As of December 31, 1991, there was a combined total of 90,186,336 shares of both classes of common stock outstanding. No shares of the Preferred Stock were issued or outstanding during the three-year period ended December 31, 1991.

The Common Stock and the Class B Stock generally vote together without regard to class on matters submitted to stockholders, including the election of directors, with the Common Stock having one vote per share and the Class B Stock having ten votes per share. However, the Common Stock, voting separately as a class, is entitled to elect one-sixth of the Board of Directors. With respect to dividend rights, the Common Stock is entitled to cash dividends 10% higher than those declared and paid on the Class B Stock.

Class B Stock can be converted into Common Stock on a share-for-share basis at any time. During 1991

and 1990, 11,350 and 2,900 shares, respectively, of Class B Stock were converted into Common Stock. There were no conversions of Class B Stock into Common Stock during 1989.

Hershey Trust Company, as Trustee for Milton Hershey School, as institutional fiduciary for estates and trusts unrelated to Milton Hershey School, and as direct owner of investment shares, held a total of 23,444,348 shares of the Common Stock, and, as Trustee for Milton Hershey School, held 15,153,003 shares of the Class B Stock as of December 31, 1991, and is entitled to cast approximately 77% of the total votes of both classes of the Corporation's common stock. Hershey Trust Company, as Trustee for Milton Hershey School, must approve the issuance of shares of Common Stock or any other action which would result in the Hershey Trust Company, as Trustee for Milton Hershey School, not continuing to have voting control of the Corporation.

Net income per share has been computed based on the 90,186,336 weighted average number of shares of the Common Stock and the Class B Stock outstanding during the year, for all years presented.

5. Interest Expense

Interest expense, net consisted of the following:

For the years ended December 31,	1991	1990	1989
(in thousands of dollars)			
Long-term debt and lease obligations	$ 32,252	$24,258	$27,492
Short-term debt	7,403	7,936	2,610
Capitalized interest	(10,386)	(5,875)	(6,594)
	29,269	26,319	23,508
Interest income	(2,424)	(1,716)	(3,094)
Interest expense, net	$ 26,845	$24,603	$20,414

6. Short-term Debt

Generally, the Corporation's short-term borrowings are in the form of commercial paper or bank loans with an original maturity of three months or less. The Corporation maintained lines of credit arrangements with commercial banks, under which it could borrow up to $168 million as of December 31, 1991 and $150 million as of December 31, 1990 at the lending banks' prime commercial interest rates or lower. These lines of credit, which may be used to support commercial paper borrowings, may be terminated at the option of the Corporation. The Corporation had outstanding domestic commercial paper borrowings and short-term international bank loans against these lines of credit of $53.5 million and $4.2 million, respectively, as of December 31, 1991 and $76.7 million and

$1.1 million, respectively, as of December 31, 1990. As described in Note 7, the outstanding commercial paper borrowings as of December 31, 1990, were classified as long-term debt.

Lines of credit were supported by commitment fee arrangements. The fees were generally ⅛% per annum of the commitment. There were no significant compensating balance agreements which legally restricted these funds.

As a result of maintaining a consolidated cash management system, the Corporation maintains overdraft positions at certain banks. Such overdrafts, which were included in accounts payable, were $23.5 million and $40.5 million as of December 31, 1991 and 1990, respectively.

7. Long-term Debt

Long-term debt consisted of the following:

December 31,	1991	1990
(in thousands of dollars)		
Medium-term Notes, 8.45% to 9.92%, due 1991-1998	$ 73,800	$ 88,800
Commercial Paper Borrowings	—	76,654
9.5% Sinking Fund Debentures due 2009	49,500	52,500
9.125% Sinking Fund Debentures due 2016	50,000	50,000
8.8% Debentures due 2021	100,000	—
Other obligations, net of unamortized debt discount	36,588	28,713
	309,888	296,667
Less — current portion	26,955	23,225
Total long-term debt	$282,933	$273,442

In February 1991, the Corporation issued $100 million of 8.8% Debentures due 2021 (Debentures) under its Form S-3 Registration Statement, which was declared effective in June 1990. A portion of the proceeds from issuance of the Debentures was used to repay $76.7 million of domestic commercial paper borrowings outstanding as of December 31, 1990 which were classified as long-term debt.

Aggregate annual maturities and sinking fund requirements during the next five years, net of repurchased debentures, are: 1992, $27.0 million; 1993, $9.7 million; 1994, $17.1 million; 1995, $10.4 million; and 1996, $5.0 million. Primarily all of the Corporation's debt is unsecured and is of equal priority. The Corporation is in compliance with all covenants included in the related debt agreements.

8. Income Taxes

The provision for income taxes is based on income before income taxes as reported in the consolidated statements of income. Tax credits are recognized as a reduction in the provision using the flow-through method.

Deferred income taxes are provided to reflect timing differences between reported results of operations for financial statement and income tax purposes. Timing differences related primarily to accelerated depreciation, employee benefits expenses, promotion expenses and, in 1990, the manufacturing restructuring charge. The provision for income taxes on income from operations was as follows:

For the years ended December 31,	1991	1990	1989
(in thousands of dollars)			
Current:			
Federal	$ 96,074	$121,924	$ 88,083
State	25,128	17,580	20,952
International	2,073	14,389	6,464
Current provision for income taxes	123,275	153,893	115,499
Deferred:			
Federal	12,618	(3,185)	2,110
State	6,111	6,726	(489)
International	1,925	(11,798)	1,748
Deferred provision (benefit) for income taxes	20,654	(8,257)	3,369
Total provision for income taxes	$143,929	$145,636	$118,868

The following table reconciles the Federal statutory income tax rate with the Corporation's effective income tax rate:

For the years ended December 31,	1991	1990	1989
Federal statutory tax rate	34.0%	34.0%	34.0%
Increase (reduction) resulting from:			
State income taxes, net of Federal income tax benefits	5.5	4.4	4.7
Non-deductible acquisition costs	1.0	1.0	1.1
Corporate owned life insurance	(1.1)	(0.5)	(0.1)
Other, net	0.2	1.4	1.3
Effective income tax rate	39.6%	40.3%	41.0%

The Financial Accounting Standards Board (FASB) has issued Statement of Financial Accounting Standards No. 109, "Accounting for Income Taxes" (FAS No. 109). FAS No. 109 accounting and disclosure rules must be adopted no later than 1993, although earlier implementation is permitted. The Corporation has not implemented the new standard. When the Corporation does adopt the new accounting rules, it may record the entire catch-up effect in the year of adoption or it may retroactively restate prior financial statements. The Corporation has not decided which option it will utilize nor in which year it will implement the change. However, management believes that based on the current Federal statutory corporate income tax rate, either method, when adopted, will have a favorable impact on net income.

11. Incentive Plan

The long-term portion of the 1987 Key Employee Incentive Plan (Plan) provides for grants or awards to senior executives and key employees of one or more of the following: performance stock units, non-qualified stock options (stock options), stock appreciation rights and restricted stock units.

As of December 31, 1991, 210,200 contingent performance stock units and restricted stock units had been granted for potential future distribution, primarily related to three-year cycles ending December 31, 1991, 1992 and 1993. The Plan provides for the deferral of performance stock unit awards by participants. Deferred performance stock units and accumulated dividend amounts totaled 236,448 shares as of December 31, 1991.

Stock options are granted at exercise prices of not less than 100% of the fair market value of a share of Common Stock at the time the option is granted and are exercisable for periods no longer than ten years from the date of grant. Each option may be used to purchase one share of Common Stock. No compensation expense is recognized under the stock options portion of the Plan.

The following table provides information regarding stock options:

	Shares under Options	
	Number of Shares	Option Price per Share
Outstanding — January 1, 1989	374,450	$23³/₄ to 28
Granted	55,000	$26 to 26³/₈
Exercised	(3,250)	$25³/₈ to 28
Cancelled	(10,500)	$25³/₈ to 28
Outstanding — December 31, 1989	415,700	$23³/₄ to 28
Granted	502,700	$35³/₈
Exercised	(77,840)	$25³/₈ to 28
Cancelled	(5,600)	$35³/₈
Outstanding — December 31, 1990	834,960	$23³/₄ to 35³/₈
Granted	59,800	$36¹/₄
Exercised	(30,135)	$23³/₄ to 28
Cancelled	(7,500)	$35³/₈
Outstanding — December 31, 1991	857,125	$23³/₄ to 36¹/₄

No stock appreciation rights had been granted or awarded as of December 31, 1991.

12. Supplemental Income Statement Information

Supplemental income statement information is provided in the table below. These costs were expensed in the year incurred.

For the years ended December 31, *(in thousands of dollars)*	1991	1990	1989
Promotion	$325,465	$315,242	$256,237
Advertising	117,049	146,297	121,182
Maintenance and repairs	72,192	66,203	58,842
Depreciation expense	72,735	61,725	54,543
Rent expense	23,288	20,758	20,033
Research and development	22,770	19,152	16,094

Rent expense pertains to all operating leases, which were principally related to certain administrative buildings, distribution facilities and transportation equipment. Future minimum rental payments under non-cancelable operating leases with a remaining term in excess of one year as of December 31, 1991, were: 1992, $9.5 million; 1993, $9.3 million; 1994, $11.4 million; 1995, $10.5 million; 1996, $10.5 million; 1997 and beyond, $123.1 million.

Amounts for taxes other than payroll and income taxes, amortization of intangibles resulting from business acquisitions, and royalties were less than 1% of net sales.

13. Supplemental Balance Sheet Information

Accounts Receivable—Trade

In the normal course of business, the Corporation extends credit to customers which satisfy pre-defined credit criteria. The Corporation believes that it has little concentration of credit risk due to the diversity of its customer base. Receivables, as shown on the consolidated balance sheets, were net of allowances of $9.5 million and $9.6 million as of December 31, 1991 and 1990, respectively.

Inventories

The majority of the Corporation's inventories are valued under the last-in, first-out (LIFO) method. The remaining inventories are stated at the lower of first-in, first-out (FIFO) cost or market. All inventories are stated at amounts that do not exceed realizable values. LIFO cost of inventories valued using the LIFO method was $334.5 million as of December 31, 1991 and $290.0 million as of December 31, 1990. Total inventories were as follows:

December 31, (in thousands of dollars)	1991	1990
Raw materials	$236,846	$200,030
Goods in process	30,039	35,020
Finished goods	227,405	199,724
Inventories at FIFO	494,290	434,774
Adjustment to LIFO	(57,373)	(55,666)
Total inventories	$436,917	$379,108

Property, Plant and Equipment

Property, plant and equipment balances included construction in progress of $170.5 million and $150.0 million as of December 31, 1991 and 1990, respectively.

Major classes of property, plant and equipment were as follows:

December 31, (in thousands of dollars)	1991	1990
Land	$ 37,911	$ 31,117
Buildings	384,117	280,897
Machinery and equipment	1,159,268	1,011,629
	1,581,296	1,323,643
Accumulated depreciation	435,630	371,549
Property, plant and equipment, net	$1,145,666	$ 952,094

Accrued Liabilities

Accrued liabilities were as follows:

December 31, (in thousands of dollars)	1991	1990
Payroll and other compensation	$ 55,346	$ 48,273
Advertising and promotion	63,344	58,758
Interest	24,366	3,486
Other	83,211	59,662
Total accrued liabilities	$226,267	$170,179

14. Segment Information

The Corporation operates in one line of business — consumer foods, involving the manufacture, distribution and sale of chocolate, confectionery, pasta and other food products.

The table below presents information about the Corporation's domestic and international operations. The international amounts presented represent primarily Canadian operations. Transfers of product between geographic areas were not significant.

For the years ended December 31.	1991	1990	1989
(in thousands of dollars)			
Net sales:			
Domestic	$2,566,448	$2,508,542	$2,235,728
International	332,717	207,067	185,260
Total	$2,899,165	$2,715,609	$2,420,988
Income before interest and income taxes:			
Domestic	$ 381,549	$ 344,303	$ 306,705
International	8,753	6,278	3,631
Gain on Business Restructuring, Net	—	35,540	—
Total	$ 390,302	$ 386,121	$ 310,336
Identifiable assets as of December 31:			
Domestic	$2,003,425	$1,820,434	$1,561,187
International	338,397	258,394	252,914
Total	$2,341,822	$2,078,828	$1,814,101

15. Quarterly Data (Unaudited)

Summary quarterly results were as follows:

(in thousands of dollars except per share amounts)

Year 1991	First	Second	Third	Fourth	Year
Net sales	$684,565	$585,166	$765,502	$863,932	$2,899,165
Gross profit	272,733	245,703	319,754	366,571	1,204,761
Net income	48,636	31,903	64,085	74,904	219,528
Net income per share[a]	.54	.35	.71	.83	2.43

Year 1990	First	Second	Third	Fourth	Year
Net sales	$681,244	$535,861	$735,438	$763,066	$2,715,609
Gross profit	281,924	221,699	302,004	321,622	1,127,249
Net income	47,090	65,844 [b]	56,557	46,391 [b]	215,882 [b]
Net income per share[a]	.52	.73 [b]	.63	.51 [b]	2.39 [b]

[a] The weighted average number of shares outstanding was 90.186.336 for all periods presented.

[b] Net income for the second quarter, fourth quarter and year 1990, included the after-tax impact of the Gain on Business Restructuring, Net of $35.3 million, $(15.0) million, and $20.3 million, respectively. Net income per share was similarly impacted.

RESPONSIBILITY FOR FINANCIAL STATEMENTS

Hershey Foods Corporation is responsible for the financial statements and other financial information contained in this report. The Corporation believes that the financial statements have been prepared in conformity with generally accepted accounting principles appropriate under the circumstances to reflect in all material respects the substance of applicable events and transactions. In preparing the financial statements, it is necessary that management make informed estimates and judgments. The other financial information in this annual report is consistent with the financial statements.

The Corporation maintains a system of internal accounting controls designed to provide reasonable assurance that financial records are reliable for purposes of preparing financial statements and that assets are properly accounted for and safeguarded. The concept of reasonable assurance is based on the recognition that the cost of the system must be related to the benefits to be derived. The Corporation believes its system provides an appropriate balance in this regard. The Corporation maintains an Internal Audit Department which reviews the adequacy and tests the application of internal accounting controls.

The financial statements have been audited by Arthur Andersen & Co., independent public accountants, whose appointment was ratified by stockholder vote at the stockholders' meeting held on April 29, 1991. Their report expresses an opinion that the Corporation's financial statements are fairly stated in conformity with generally accepted accounting principles, and they have indicated to us that their examination was performed in accordance with generally accepted auditing standards which are designed to obtain reasonable assurance about whether the financial statements are free of material misstatement.

The Audit Committee of the Board of Directors of the Corporation, consisting solely of outside directors, meets regularly with the independent public accountants, internal auditors and management to discuss, among other things, the audit scopes and results. Arthur Andersen & Co. and the internal auditors both have full and free access to the Audit Committee, with and without the presence of management.

REPORT OF INDEPENDENT PUBLIC ACCOUNTANTS

To the Stockholders and Board of Directors of Hershey Foods Corporation:

We have audited the accompanying consolidated balance sheets of Hershey Foods Corporation (a Delaware Corporation) and subsidiaries as of December 31, 1991 and 1990, and the related consolidated statements of income, stockholders' equity and cash flows for each of the three years in the period ended December 31, 1991, appearing on pages 22, 24, 26, 28 and 29 through 37. These financial statements are the responsibility of the Corporation's management. Our responsibility is to express an opinion on these financial statements based on our audits.

We conducted our audits in accordance with generally accepted auditing standards. Those standards require that we plan and perform the audit to obtain reasonable assurance about whether the financial statements are free of material misstatement.

An audit includes examining, on a test basis, evidence supporting the amounts and disclosures in the financial statements. An audit also includes assessing the accounting principles used and significant estimates made by management, as well as evaluating the overall financial statement presentation. We believe that our audits provide a reasonable basis for our opinion.

In our opinion, the financial statements referred to above present fairly, in all material respects, the financial position of Hershey Foods Corporation and subsidiaries as of December 31, 1991 and 1990, and the results of their operations and cash flows for each of the three years in the period ended December 31, 1991 in conformity with generally accepted accounting principles.

Arthur Andersen & Co.

New York, N.Y.
February 11, 1992

HERSHEY FOODS CORPORATION

SIX-YEAR CONSOLIDATED FINANCIAL SUMMARY

(all dollar and share amounts in thousands except market price and per share statistics)	1991	1990	1989	1988	1987	1986
Summary of Operations[a]						
Net Sales	$2,899,165	2,715,609	2,420,988	2,168,048	1,863,816	1,635,486
Cost of Sales	$1,694,404	1,588,360	1,455,612	1,326,458	1,149,663	1,032,061
Selling, Marketing and Administrative	$ 814,459	776,668	655,040	575,515	468,062	387,227
Gain on Business Restructuring, Net	$ —	35,540	—	—	—	—
Interest Expense, Net	$ 26,845	24,603	20,414	29,954	22,413	8,061
Income Taxes	$ 143,929	145,636	118,868	91,615	99,604	100,931
Income from Continuing Operations	$ 219,528	215,882	171,054	144,506	124,074	107,206
Discontinued Operations	$ —	—	—	69,443	24,097	25,558
Net Income	$ 219,528	215,882	171,054	213,949	148,171	132,764
Income Per Share from Continuing Operations	$ 2.43	2.39[f]	1.90	1.60	1.38	1.15
Net Income Per Share	$ 2.43	2.39[f]	1.90	2.37	1.64	1.42
Weighted Average Shares Outstanding	90,186	90,186	90,186	90,186	90,186	93,508
Dividends Paid on Common Stock	$ 70,426	74,161[c]	55,431	49,433	43,436	40,930
Per Share	$ .940	.990[c]	.740	.660	.580	.520
Dividends Paid on Class B Common Stock	$ 12,975	13,596[c]	10,161	9,097	8,031	7,216
Per Share	$ .850	.890[c]	.665	.595	.525	.472
Income from Continuing Operations before Interest and Income Taxes as a Percent of Net Sales	13.5%	12.9%[d]	12.8%	12.3%	13.2%	13.2%
Income from Continuing Operations as a Percent of Net Sales	7.6%	7.2%[d]	7.1%	6.7%	6.7%	6.6%
Depreciation	$ 72,735	61,725	54,543	43,721	35,397	31,254
Advertising	$ 117,049	146,297	121,182	99,082	97,033	83,600
Promotion	$ 325,465	315,242	256,237	230,187	171,162	122,508
Payroll	$ 398,661	372,780	340,129	298,483	263,529	238,742
Year-end Position and Statistics[a]						
Working Capital	$ 273,747	320,552	281,821	273,716	190,069[e]	174,147
Capital Additions	$ 226,071	179,408	162,032	101,682	68,504	74,452
Total Assets	$2,341,822	2,078,828	1,814,101	1,764,665	1,544,354	1,262,332
Long-term Debt	$ 282,933	273,442	216,108	233,025	280,900	185,676
Stockholders' Equity	$1,335,251	1,243,537	1,117,050	1,005,866	832,410	727,941
Current Ratio	1.6 : 1	1.9 : 1	2.0 : 1	1.8 : 1	1.7 : 1[e]	2.0 : 1
Capitalization Ratio	22%	19%	17%	22%	27%	21%
Net Book Value Per Share	$ 14.81	13.79	12.39	11.15	9.23	8.07
Operating Return on Average Stockholders' Equity	17.0%	16.6%	16.1%	17.5%	19.0%	18.2%
Operating Return on Average Invested Capital	13.8%	13.4%	13.2%	13.3%	13.5%	13.5%
Full-time Employees at Year-end	14,000	12,700	11,800	12,100	10,540	10,210
Stockholders' Data						
Outstanding Shares of Common Stock and Class B Common Stock at Year-end	90,186	90,186	90,186	90,186	90,186	90,186
Market Price of Common Stock at Year-end	$ 44³/₈	37¹/₂	35⁷/₈	26	24¹/₂	24⁵/₈
Range During Year	$44¹/₂-35¹/₈	39⁵/₈-28¹/₄	36⁷/₈-24³/₄	28⁵/₈-21⁷/₈	37³/₄-20³/₄	30-15¹/₂
Year-end Common Stock and Class B Common Stock Holders	31,029	30,052	29,998	30,430	29,151	23,502
Approximate Annual Composite Trading Volume[b]	27,975	31,024	41,220	46,693	48,145	22,838

Notes:

(a) All amounts for years prior to 1988 have been restated for discontinued operations, where applicable. Operating Return on Average Stockholders' Equity and Operating Return on Average Invested Capital have been computed using Net Income, excluding the gain on the sale of Friendly Ice Cream Corporation and the Gain on Business Restructuring, Net.

(b) Composite trading volume for 1986 has not been adjusted for the three-for-one stock split effective September 15, 1986.

(c) Amounts included a special dividend for 1990 of $11.2 million or $.15 per share on Common Stock and $2.1 million or $.135 per share on Class B Common Stock.

(d) Operating margin before interest and income taxes, and operating margin, exclude the Gain on Business Restructuring, Net. Including the gain, operating margin before interest and income taxes and operating margin were 14.2% and 7.9%, respectively.

(e) Amounts exclude net assets of discontinued operations.

(f) Income Per Share from Continuing Operations and Net Income Per Share for 1990 included a $.22 per share Gain on Business Restructuring, Net. Excluding the impact of this gain, Income Per Share from Continuing Operations and Net Income Per Share would have been $2.17.

GLOSSARY

A

Accelerated depreciation methods. Depreciation methods that provide for a high depreciation expense in the first year of use of an asset and a gradually declining expense thereafter. (385)

Account. The form used to record additions and deductions for each individual asset, liability, owner's equity, revenue, and expense. (38)

Account form of balance sheet. A form of balance sheet with assets on the left-hand side and liabilities and owner's equity on the right-hand side. (188)

Accounting. An information system that provides essential information about the economic activities of an entity to various individuals or groups. (8)

Accounting cycle. The sequence of basic accounting procedures during a fiscal period. (125)

Accounting equation. The expression of the relationship between assets, liabilities, and owner's equity; most commonly stated as Assets = Liabilities + Owner's Equity. (14)

Accounting system. The methods and procedures used by an enterprise to record and report financial data for use by management and external users. (230)

Account payable. A liability created by a purchase made on credit. (15)

Account receivable. A claim against a customer for services rendered or goods sold on credit. (16)

Accounts payable ledger. The subsidiary ledger containing the individual accounts with suppliers (creditors). (235)

Accounts receivable ledger. The subsidiary ledger containing the individual accounts with customers (debtors). (235)

Accounts receivable turnover. The relationship between credit sales and accounts receivable, computed by dividing net sales on account by the average net accounts receivable. (739)

Accrual basis. Revenues are recognized in the period earned and expenses are recognized in the period incurred in the process of generating revenues. (84)

Accruals. Expenses that have been incurred or revenues that have been earned, but have not been recorded. (85)

Accrued expenses. Expenses that have been incurred but not recorded in the accounts. Sometimes called accrued liabilities. (85)

Accrued revenues. Revenues that have been earned but not recorded in the accounts. Sometimes called accrued assets. (85)

Accumulated depreciation account. The contra asset account used to accumulate the depreciation recognized to date on plant assets. (91)

Acid-test ratio. The ratio of the sum of cash, receivables, and marketable securities to current liabilities. (739)

Activity bases (drivers). Activities thought to cause the incurrence of a cost. Used in analyzing and classifying the behavior of a cost. Activity bases used to assign overhead costs to jobs. (828, 904)

Activity-based costing (ABC). A cost allocation method that identifies activities causing the incurrence of costs and expenses and allocates these costs and expenses to products (or other cost objects) based upon activity drivers (bases). (838, 1036)

Adequate disclosure. The concept that financial statements and their accompanying footnotes should contain all of the pertinent data believed essential to the reader's understanding of an enterprise's financial status. (469)

Adjusting entries. Entries required at the end of an accounting period to bring the ledger up to date. (84)

Adjusting process. The process of updating the accounts at the end of a period. (84)

Administrative expenses. Expenses incurred in the administration or general operations of a business. (186)

Aging the receivables. The process of analyzing the accounts receivable and classifying them according to various age groupings, with the due date being the base point for determining age. (323)

Allowance method. A method of accounting for uncollectible receivables, whereby advance provision for the uncollectibles is made. (320)

Amortization. The periodic expense attributed to the decline in usefulness of an intangible asset. (396)

Annuity. A series of equal cash flows at fixed intervals. (601, 1061)

Appropriation. The amount of a corporation's retained earnings that has been restricted and therefore is not available for distribution to shareholders as dividends. (565)

Assets. Physical items (tangible) or rights (intangible) that have value and that are owned by the business entity. (14, 38)

Average cost method. The method of inventory costing that is based on the assumption that costs should be charged against revenue in accordance with the weighted average unit costs of the items sold. The method of inventory costing that uses one unit cost for all products completed during the current period. (353, 873)

Average rate of return. A method of evaluating capital investment proposals that focuses on the expected profitability of the investment. (1057)

B

Backflush costing. A cost accounting system in which product costs are applied to the units when the production process is complete; normally used in a just-in-time manufacturing environment. (875)

Balance of the account. The amount of difference between the debits and the credits that have been entered into an account. (39)

Balance sheet. A financial statement listing the assets, liabilities, and owner's equity of a business entity as of a specific date. (18)

Bank reconciliation. The method of analysis that details the items that are responsible for the difference between the cash balance reported in the bank statement and the balance of the cash account in the ledger. (281)

Betterment. An expenditure that increases operating efficiency or capacity for the remaining useful life of a plant asset. (390)

Bill of materials. A list of all materials required to manufacture a product. (825)

Bond. A form of interest-bearing note employed by corporations to borrow on a long-term basis. (598)

Bond indenture. The contract between a corporation issuing bonds and the bondholders. (599)

Book value of the asset. The difference between the balance of a plant asset account and its related accumulated depreciation account. (92)

Boot. The balance owed the supplier when an old asset is traded for a new asset. (393)

Break-even point. The level of enterprise operations at which revenues and expired costs are equal. (910)

Budget. A formal written statement of management's plans for the future, expressed in financial terms. (942)

Budget performance report. A report comparing actual results with budget figures. (952)

Business entity concept. The concept that accounting applies to individual economic units and that each unit is separate and distinct from the persons who supply its assets. (12, 462)

Business transaction. The occurrence of an exchange or an economic event that must be recorded in the accounting records. (14)

By-product. A product that has little value in relation to the other products resulting from a manufacturing process. (866)

C

Capital expenditures. Costs that add to the utility of assets for more than one accounting period. (389)

Capital expenditures budget. The budget summarizing future plans for acquisition of plant facilities and equipment. (1067)

Capital investment analysis. The process by which management plans, evaluates, and controls long-term capital investments involving property, plant, and equipment. (1056)

Capital leases. Leases that include one or more of four provisions that result in treating the leased assets as purchased assets in the accounts. (395)

Capital rationing. The process by which management allocates available investment funds among competing capital investment proposals. (1067)

Capital stock. Shares of ownership of a corporation. (528)

Carrying amount. The amount at which a temporary or a long-term investment or a long-term liability is reported on the balance sheet; also called basis or book value. (326, 605)

Cash basis. Revenue is recognized in the period cash is received, and expenses are recognized in the period cash is paid. (84)

Cash dividend. A cash distribution of earnings by a corporation to its shareholders. (569)

Cash equivalents. Highly liquid investments that are usually reported on the balance sheet with cash. (291)

Cash flows from financing activities. The section of the statement of cash flows which reports cash flows from transactions that affect the equity and debt of the entity. (681)

Cash flows from investing activities. The section of the statement of cash flows which reports cash flows from transactions that affect investments in noncurrent assets. (681)

Cash flows from operating activities. The section of the statement of cash flows which reports the cash transactions that affect the determination of net income. (680)

Cash payback period. The expected period of time that will elapse between the date of a capital expenditure and the complete recovery in cash (or equivalent) of the amount invested. (1058)

Cash payments journal. The journal in which all cash payments are recorded. (245)

Cash receipts journal. The journal in which all cash receipts are recorded. (239)

Chart of accounts. The system of accounts that make up the ledger for a business enterprise. (38)

Check register. A modified form of the cash payments journal used to record all transactions paid by check. (288)

Closing entries. Entries necessary to eliminate the balances of temporary accounts in preparation for the following accounting period. (118)

Common-size statement. A financial statement in which all items are expressed only in relative terms. (736)

Common stock. The basic ownership class of corporate capital stock. (528)

Completed-contract method. The method that recognizes revenue from long-term construction contracts when the project is completed. (468)

Composite-rate depreciation method. A method of depreciation based on the use of a single rate that applies to entire groups of assets. (389)

Computer-integrated manufacturing (CIM). The use of automated equipment to perform routine, repetitive tasks with a minimum of human involvement. (796)

Conservatism. The concept that dictates that in selecting among alternatives, the method or procedure that yields the lesser amount of net income or asset value should be selected. (475)

Consistency. The concept that assumes that the same generally accepted accounting principles have been applied in the preparation of successive financial statements. (473)

Consolidated statements. Financial statements resulting from combining parent and subsidiary company statements. (639)

Consolidation. The creation of a new corporation by the transfer of assets and liabilities from two or more existing corporations. (638)

Constant dollar. Historical costs that have been converted into dollars of constant value through the use of a price-level index. (465)

Contingent liabilities. Potential obligations that will materialize only if certain events occur in the future. (319)

Continuous budgeting. A method of budgeting that provides for maintaining a twelve-month projection into the future. (942)

Contra accounts. Accounts that are offset against other accounts. (91)

Contract rate. The interest rate specified on a bond; sometimes called the coupon rate of interest. (602)

Contribution margin. Sales less variable cost of goods sold and variable selling and administrative expenses. (908)

Contribution margin ratio. The percentage of each sales dollar that is available to cover the fixed costs and provide an operating income. (908)

Controllable costs. Costs that can be directly controlled by a specific level of management. (787)

Controller. The chief managerial accountant of a division or other segment of a business enterprise. (783)

Controlling. The process by which managers attempt to achieve the goals identified in an enterprise's strategic and operational plans. (781)

Controlling account. The account in the general ledger that summarizes the balances of the accounts in a subsidiary ledger. (235)

Conversion costs. The combination of direct labor and factory overhead costs. (790, 861)

Corporation. A separate legal entity that is organized in accordance with state or federal statutes and in which ownership is divided into shares of stock. (13)

Cost. A disbursement of cash (or a commitment to pay cash in the future) for the purpose of generating revenues. (786)

Cost accounting system. An accounting system that uses the perpetual system of inventory accounting for the three manufacturing inventories: direct materials, work in process, and finished goods. (822)

Cost behavior. The manner in which a cost changes in relation to its activity base (driver). (904)

Cost center. A decentralized unit in which the department or division manager has responsibility for the control of costs incurred and the authority to make decisions that affect these costs. (987)

Cost ledger. A subsidiary ledger used in a job order cost system. It contains an account for each job order. (830)

Cost method. A method of accounting for an investment in common stock, by which the investor recognizes as income its share of cash dividends of the investee. (634)

Cost object. The object or segment of operations to which costs are related for management's use, such as a product or department. (786)

Cost of goods sold. The cost of the manufactured product sold. (793)

Cost of merchandise sold. The cost of merchandise purchased by a merchandise enterprise and sold. (793)

Cost of production report. A report prepared periodically by a processing department, summarizing (1) the units for which the department is accountable and the disposition of those units and (2) the cost charged to the department and the allocation of those costs. (863)

Cost price approach. An approach to transfer pricing that uses costs as the basis for setting the transfer price. (1003)

Cost principle. The principle that the monetary record for properties and services purchased by a business should be maintained in terms of actual cost. (13)

Cost-volume-profit analysis. The systematic examination of the relationships among selling prices, volume of sales and production, costs, expenses, and profits. (908)

Cost-volume-profit chart. A chart used to assist management in understanding the relationships among costs, expenses, sales, and operating profit or loss. (913)

Credit. (1) The right side of an account; (2) the amount entered on the right side of an account; (3) to enter an amount on the right side of an account. (39)

Credit memorandum. The form issued by a seller to inform a buyer that a credit has been posted to the buyer's account receivable. (155)

Cumulative preferred stock. Preferred stock that is entitled to current and past dividends before dividends may be paid on common stock. (530)

Current assets. Cash or other assets that are expected to be converted to cash or sold or used up, usually within a year or less, through the normal operations of a business. (116)

Current cost. The amount of cash that would have to be paid currently to acquire assets of the same age and in the same condition as existing assets. (465)

Current liabilities. Liabilities that will be due within a short time (usually one year or less) and that are to be paid out of current assets. (116)

Currently attainable standards. Standards that represent levels of operation that can be attained with reasonable effort. (954)

Current ratio. The ratio of current assets to current liabilities. (738)

Cycle time. The time required to manufacture a product from receipt of an order until it is shipped to the customer. Sometimes referred to as throughput time. (796)

D

Debit. (1) The left side of an account; (2) the amount entered on the left side of an account; (3) to enter an amount on the left side of an account. (39)

Debit memorandum. The form issued by a buyer to inform a seller that a debit has been posted to the seller's account payable. (157)

Decentralization. The separation of a business into more manageable units. (986)

Decision making. The process by which managers select one course of action over another. (781)

Declining-balance depreciation method. A method of depreciation that provides declining periodic depreciation expense over the estimated life of an asset. (383)

Deferrals. Delays in the recognition of expenses that have been incurred or revenues that have been received. (84)

Deferred expenses. Items that are initially recorded as assets but are expected to become expenses over time or through the normal operations of the enterprise. Sometimes called prepaid expenses. (85)

Deferred revenues. Items that are initially recorded as liabilities but are expected to become revenues over time or through the normal operations of the enterprise. Sometimes called unearned revenues. (85)

Deficiency. The debit balance in an owner's equity account of a sole proprietorship or a partnership. (505)

Deficit. A debit balance in the retained earnings account. (527)

Departmental margin. Departmental gross profit less direct departmental expenses. (991)

Depletion. The cost of metal ores and other minerals removed from the earth. (396)

Depreciation. In a general sense, the decrease in usefulness of plant assets other than land. In accounting, refers to the systematic allocation of a plant asset's cost to expense. (91)

Depreciation. The periodic cost expiration for the use of all plant assets except land. (381)

Differential analysis. The area of accounting concerned with the effect of alternative courses of action on revenues and costs. (1026)

Differential cost. The amount of increase or decrease in cost expected from a particular course of action compared with an alternative. (787, 1026)

Differential revenue. The amount of increase or decrease in revenue expected from a particular course of action as compared with an alternative. (1026)

Direct costs. Costs that can be traced directly to a cost object. (786)

Direct expenses. Expenses that can be traced directly to a unit within an enterprise or organization. (991)

Directing. The process by which managers, given their assigned level of responsibilities, run day-to-day operations. (780)

Direct labor cost. Wages of factory workers who are directly involved in converting materials into a finished product. (790)

Direct labor rate variance. The cost associated with the difference between the standard rate and the actual rate paid for direct labor used in producing a commodity. (957)

Direct labor time variance. The cost associated with the difference between the standard hours and the actual hours of direct labor spent producing a commodity. (956)

Direct materials cost. The cost of materials that are an integral part of the finished product. (789)

Direct materials inventory. The cost of direct materials which have not yet entered into the manufacturing process. (793)

Direct materials price variance. The cost associated with the difference between the standard price and the actual price of direct materials used in producing a commodity. (955)

Direct materials quantity variance. The cost associated with the difference between the standard quantity and the actual quantity of direct materials used in producing a commodity. (955)

Direct method. A method of reporting the cash flows from operating activities as the difference between the operating cash receipts and the operating cash payments. (681)

Direct write-off method. A method of accounting for uncollectible receivables, whereby an expense is recognized only when specific accounts are judged to be uncollectible. (320)

Discontinued operations. The operations of a business segment that have been disposed of. (560)

Discount rate. The rate used in computing the interest to be deducted from the maturity value of a note. (436)

Discount. The interest deducted from the maturity value of a note. The excess of par value of stock over its sales price. (318, 436, 531, 602)

Discretionary cost. A cost that is not essential to short-term operations. (788)

Dishonored note receivable. A note that the maker fails to pay on its due date. (319)

Double-entry accounting. A system for recording transactions, based on recording increases and decreases in accounts so that debits always equal credits. (42)

Drawing. The amount of withdrawals made by a sole proprietor or partner. (38)

E

Earnings per share (EPS) on common stock. The profitability ratio of net income available to common shareholders to the number of common shares outstanding. (564, 745)

Economies of scale. An economic concept that implies that, for a given amount of facilities, it is more efficient to produce and sell large quantities than small quantities. (1037)

Effective rate. The market rate of interest at the time bonds are issued. (602)

Electronic funds transfer (EFT). A payment system that uses computerized electronic impulses rather than paper (money, checks, etc.) to effect a cash transaction. (292)

Employee's earnings record. A detailed record of each employee's earnings. (429)

Equities. The rights or claims to the properties of a business enterprise. (14)

Equity method. A method of accounting for investments in common stock, by which the investment account is adjusted for the investor's share of periodic net income and property dividends of the investee. (634)

Equity per share. The ratio of stockholders' equity to the related number of shares of stock outstanding. (536)

Equity securities. Preferred or common stock. (634)

Equivalent units of production. The number of units that could have been manufactured from start to finish during a period. (862)

Exchange rate. The rate at which one currency can be converted into another currency. (651)

Expenses. Assets used up or services consumed in the process of generating revenues. (16, 38)

Extraordinary items. Events or transactions that are unusual and infrequent. (561)

Extraordinary repair. An expenditure that increases the useful life of an asset beyond the original estimate. (390)

F

Factory overhead controllable variance. The difference between the actual amount of factory overhead cost incurred and the amount of factory overhead budgeted for the standard product produced. (959)

Factory overhead cost. All of the costs of operating the factory except for direct materials and direct labor. (790)

Factory overhead volume variance. The cost or benefit associated with operating at a level above or below 100% of productive capacity. (958)

FICA tax. Federal Insurance Contributions Act tax used to finance federal programs for old-age and disability benefits (social security) and health insurance for the aged (Medicare). (422)

Financial Accounting Standards Board (FASB). The current authoritative body for the development of accounting principles for all entities except state and municipal governments. (12, 460)

Financial accounting. The branch of accounting that is concerned with the recording of transactions using generally accepted accounting principles (GAAP) for a business enterprise or other economic unit and with a periodic preparation of various statements from such records. (778)

Finished goods inventory. The cost of finished products on hand that have not been sold. (793)

Finished goods ledger. The subsidiary ledger that contains the individual accounts for each kind of product. (832)

First-in, first-out (fifo) method. A method of inventory costing based on the assumption that the costs of merchandise sold should be charged against revenue in the order in which the costs were incurred. A method of inventory costing based on the assumption that the unit product costs should be determined separately for each period in the order in which the costs were incurred. (351, 873)

Fiscal year. The annual accounting period adopted by an enterprise. (124)

Fixed costs. Costs that tend to remain the same in amount, regardless of variations in the level of activity. (788, 905)

Flexible budget. A series of budgets for varying rates of activity. (951)

FOB destination. Terms of agreement between buyer and seller whereby ownership passes when merchandise is received by the buyer, and the seller pays the transportation costs. (159)

FOB shipping point. Terms of agreement between buyer and seller whereby ownership passes when merchandise is delivered to the freight carrier, and the buyer pays the transportation costs. (159)

Funded. An appropriation of retained earnings accompanied by a segregation of cash or marketable securities. (567)

Future value. The amount that will accumulate at some future date as a result of an investment or a series of investments. (608)

G

General accounting system. An accounting system that extends the periodic system of inventory accounting used by merchandising enterprises to the three manufacturing inventories: direct materials, work in process, and finished goods. (822)

General journal. The two-column form used for entries that do not "fit" in any of the special journals. (236)

General ledger. The primary ledger, when used in conjunction with subsidiary ledgers, that contains all of the balance sheet and income statement accounts. (235)

Generally accepted accounting principles (GAAP). Generally accepted guidelines for the preparation of financial statements. (11)

Going concern concept. The concept that assumes that a business entity has a reasonable expectation of continuing in business at a profit for an indefinite period of time. (463)

Goodwill. An intangible asset that attaches to a business as a result of such favorable factors as location, product superiority, reputation, and managerial skill. (398)

Gross pay. The total earnings of an employee for a payroll period. (421)

Gross profit. The excess of net sales over the cost of merchandise sold. (186)

Gross profit method. A means of estimating inventory on hand, based on the relationship of gross profit to sales. (360)

H

High-low method. A technique that uses the highest and lowest total costs as a basis for estimating the variable cost per unit and the fixed cost component of a mixed cost. (906)

Horizontal analysis. The percentage of increases and decreases in corresponding items in comparative financial statements. (732)

I

Income from operations. The excess of gross profit over total operating expenses. (186)

Income statement. A summary of the revenues and expenses of a business entity for a specific period of time. (18)

Income Summary. The account used in the closing process for summarizing the revenue and expense accounts. (118)

Indirect costs. Costs that cannot be traced directly to a cost object. (786)

Indirect expenses. Expenses that are incurred for an entire business enterprise as a unit and that are not subject to the control of individual department managers. (992)

Indirect method. A method of reporting the cash flows from operating activities as the net income from operations adjusted for all deferrals of past cash receipts and payments and all accruals of expected future cash receipts and payments. (681)

Inflation. A period when prices in general are rising and the purchasing power of money is declining. (1067)

Installment method. The method of recognizing revenue, whereby each receipt of cash from installment sales is considered to be part cost of merchandise sold and part gross profit. (467)

Intangible assets. Long-lived assets that are useful in the operations of an enterprise, are not held for sale, and are without physical qualities. (380)

Internal controls. The detailed policies and procedures used by an enterprise to direct operations and provide reasonable assurance that the enterprise objectives are achieved. (230)

Internal control structure. Consists of the following three elements: (1) the accounting system, (2) the control environment, and (3) the control procedures. (232)

Internal rate of return method. A method of analysis of proposed capital investments that focuses on using present value concepts to compute the rate of return from the net cash flows expected from the investment. (1061)

Inventory turnover. The relationship between the volume of goods sold and inventory, computed by dividing the cost of goods sold by the average inventory. (741)

Investment center. A decentralized unit in which the manager has the responsibility and authority to make decisions that affect not only costs and revenues but also the plant assets available to the center. (989)

Investment turnover. A component of the rate of return on investment, computed as the ratio of sales to invested assets. (998)

Invoice. The bill provided by the seller (who refers to it as a sales invoice) to a buyer (who refers to it as a purchase invoice) for items purchased. (153)

J

Job cost sheet. An account in the cost ledger in which the costs charged to a particular job order are recorded. (830)

Job order cost system. A type of cost system that provides a separate record of the cost of each particular quantity of product that passes through the factory. (824)

Joint costs. Costs common to the manufacture of two or more products (joint products). (866)

Joint products. Two or more products of significant value produced from a single principal direct material. (866)

Journal. The initial record in which the effects of a transaction on accounts are recorded. (40)

Journalizing. The process of recording a transaction in a journal. (40)

Just-in-time (JIT) manufacturing systems. Systems of manufacturing in which a primary emphasis is on the manufacture of products only as they are needed by the next stage of production or by the marketplace. (794)

L

Last-in, first-out (lifo) method. A method of inventory costing based on the assumption that the most recent merchandise costs incurred should be charged against revenue. (352)

Ledger. The group of accounts used by an enterprise. (38)

Leverage. The tendency of the rate earned on stockholders' equity to vary from the rate earned on total assets because the amount earned on assets acquired through the use of funds provided by creditors varies from the interest paid to these creditors. (744)

Liabilities. Debts of a business enterprise owed to outsiders (creditors). (14, 38)

Liquidating dividend. A distribution out of paid-in capital when a corporation permanently reduces its operations or winds up its affairs completely. (572)

Liquidation. The winding-up process when a partnership goes out of business. (503)

Long-term investments. Investments that are not intended to be a ready source of cash in the normal operations of a business and that are listed in the Investments section of the balance sheet. (613)

Long-term liabilities. Liabilities that are not due for a long time (usually more than one year). (116)

Lower-of-cost-or-market method. A method of valuing inventory that reports the inventory at the lower of its cost or current market value (replacement cost). (358)

M

Management by exception. The philosophy of managing which involves monitoring the operating results of implemented plans and comparing the expected results with the actual results. This feedback allows management to isolate significant variations for further investigation and possible remedial action. (781)

Managerial accounting. The branch of accounting that uses both historical and estimated data in providing information which management uses in conducting daily operations and in planning future operations and developing overall business strategies. (778)

Marginal cost. The increase in the total cost of producing and selling an additional unit of product. (1037)

Marginal revenue. The increase in the total revenue realized from the sale of an additional unit of product. (1037)

Margin of safety. The difference between current sales revenue and the sales at the break-even point. (919)

Market (sales) value method. A method of allocating joint costs among products according to their relative sales values. (866)

Market price approach. An approach to transfer pricing that uses the price at which the product or service transferred could be sold to outside buyers as the transfer price. (1001)

Marketable securities. Investments in securities that can be readily sold when cash is needed. (326)

Markup. An amount that is added to a "cost" amount to determine product price. (1032)

Master budget. The comprehensive budget plan involving all the individual budgets related to sales, cost of goods sold, operating expenses, capital expenditures, cash, income statement, and balance sheet. (943)

Matching. The concept that expenses incurred in generating revenue should be matched against the revenue in determining the net income or net loss for the period. (18, 466)

Matching concept. The concept that all expenses incurred should be matched with the revenue they generate during a period of time. (84)

Materiality. The concept that recognizes the practicality of ignoring small or insignificant deviations from generally accepted accounting principles. (473)

Materials ledger. The subsidiary ledger containing the individual accounts for each type of material. (825)

Materials requisitions. Forms used by the appropriate manufacturing department to authorize the issuance of materials from the storeroom. (826)

Maturity value. The amount due at the maturity or due date of a note. (316)

Merchandise inventory. Merchandise on hand and available for sale to customers. (152)

Merger. The combining of two corporations by the acquisition of the properties of one corporation by another, with the dissolution of one of the corporations. (638)

Minority interest. The portion of a subsidiary corporation's capital stock that is not owned by the parent corporation. (642)

Mixed costs. Costs with both variable and fixed characteristics, sometimes called semivariable or semifixed costs. (788, 905)

Multiple-step income statement. An income statement with several sections, subsections, and subtotals. (186)

N

Natural business year. A year that ends when a business's activities have reached the lowest point in its annual operating cycle. (124)

Negotiated price approach. An approach to transfer pricing that allows managers of decentralized units to agree (negotiate) among themselves as to the transfer price. (1002)

Net income. The final figure in the income statement when revenues exceed expenses. (18)

Net loss. The final figure in the income statement when expenses exceed revenues. (18)

Net pay. Gross pay less payroll deductions; the amount the employer is obligated to pay the employee. (421)

Net present value method. A method of analysis of proposed capital investments that focuses on the present value of the cash flows expected from the investments. (1059)

Net realizable value. The amount at which merchandise that can be sold only at prices below cost should be valued, determined as the estimated selling price less any direct costs of disposal. (359)

Nominal accounts. Revenue or expense accounts that are periodically closed to the income summary account; temporary owner's equity accounts. (117)

Noncontrollable costs. Costs that cannot be directly controlled by specific level of management. (787)

Nonparticipating preferred stock. Preferred stock where dividend preference is limited to a certain amount. (528)

Note receivable. A written promise to pay, representing an amount to be received by a business. (314)

Number of days' sales in inventory. The relationship between the volume of sales and inventory, computed by dividing the inventory at the end of the year by the average daily cost of goods sold. (741)

Number of days' sales in receivables. The relationship between credit sales and accounts receivable, computed by dividing the net accounts receivable at the end of the year by the average daily sales on account. (740)

O

Operating leases. Leases that do not meet the criteria for capital leases and thus are accounted for as operating expenses. (395)

Operating leverage. A measure of the relative mix of an enterprise's variable costs and fixed costs computed as contribution margin divided by operating income. (920)

Operational cost system. A cost accounting system that combines features of a job order cost system and a process cost system. (875)

Operational planning. The development of short-term plans to achieve goals identified in an enterprise's strategic plan. Sometimes referred to as tactical planning. (779)

Opportunity cost. The amount of income that would result from the best available alternative to a proposed use of cash or its equivalent. (789, 1030)

Organizing. The process by which management assigns responsibility to individuals for achieving enterprise goals. (780)

Other expense. An expense that cannot be traced directly to operations. (186)

Other income. Revenue from sources other than the primary operating activity of a business. (186)

Outstanding stock. The stock that has been issued to stockholders. (528)

Overapplied factory overhead. The amount of factory overhead applied in excess of the actual factory overhead costs incurred for production during a period. (828)

Owner's equity. The rights of the owners in a business enterprise. The claim of owners against the assets of the business after the total liabilities are deducted. (14, 38)

P

Paid-in capital. The capital acquired from stockholders. (527)

Par. The monetary amount printed on a stock certificate. (528)

Parent company. The company owning a majority of the voting stock of another corporation. (638)

Partnership. An unincorporated business of two or more persons to carry on as co-owners a business for profit. (13, 494)

Partnership agreement. The formal written contract creating a partnership. (494)

Payroll. The total amount paid to employees for a certain period. (420)

Payroll register. A multicolumn form used to assemble and summarize payroll data at the end of each payroll period. (425)

Percentage-of-completion method. The method of recognizing revenue from long-term contracts over the entire life of the contract. (468)

Period costs. Those costs that are used up in generating revenue during the current period and that are not involved in the manufacturing process. These costs are recognized as expenses on the current period's income statement. (791)

Periodic inventory system. A system of inventory accounting in which only the revenue from sales is recorded each time a sale is made. The cost of merchandise on hand at the end of a period is determined by a detailed listing (physical inventory) of the merchandise on hand. (161)

Perpetual inventory system. A system of inventory accounting in which both the revenue from sales and the cost of merchandise sold are recorded each time a sale is made, so that the records continually disclose the amount of the inventory on hand. (162)

Petty cash fund. A special cash fund used to pay relatively small amounts. (290)

Physical inventory. The detailed listing of merchandise on hand. (161, 348)

Planning. The process of setting goals for the use of an organization's resources and developing ways to achieve these goals. (779)

Plant assets. Tangible assets that are owned by a business enterprise, are permanent or have a long life, and are used in the business. (91, 380)

Point-of-sale method. The method of recognizing revenue, whereby the revenue is determined to be realized at the time that title passes to the buyer. (467)

Pooling-of-interests method. A method of accounting for an affiliation of two corporations resulting from an exchange of voting stock of one corporation for substantially all of the voting stock of the other corporation. (639)

Post-closing trial balance. A trial balance prepared after all of the temporary accounts have been closed. (123)

Posting. The process of transferring debits and credits from a journal to the accounts. (40)

Predetermined factory overhead rate. The rate used to apply factory overhead costs to the goods manufactured. (828)

Preemptive right. The right of each shareholder to maintain the same fractional interest in the corporation by purchasing shares of any additional issuances of stock. (528)

Preferred stock. A class of stock with preferential rights over common stock. (528)

Premium. The excess of the issue price of bonds over the face amount. The excess of the sales price of stock over its par amount. (531, 602)

Prepaid expenses. Purchased commodities or services that have not been used up at the end of an accounting period. (15)

Present value. The estimated present worth of an amount of cash to be received (or paid) in the future. (600)

Present value concept. Cash to be received (or paid) in the future is not the equivalent of the same amount of money received at an earlier date. (1056)

Present value index. An index computed by dividing the total present value of the net cash flow to be received from a proposed capital investment by the amount to be invested. (1060)

Present value of an annuity. The sum of the present values of a series of equal cash flows to be received at fixed intervals. (601, 1061)

Price theory. A separate discipline in the area of microeconomics which studies the setting of product prices. (1036)

Price-earnings (P/E) ratio. The ratio of the market price per share of common stock, at a specific date, to the annual earnings per share. (746)

Price-level index. The ratio of the total cost of a group of commodities prevailing at a particular time to the total cost of the same group of commodities at an earlier base time. (465)

Prime costs. The combination of direct materials and direct labor costs. (790)

Prior-period adjustments. Corrections of material errors related to a prior period or periods, excluded from the determination of net income. (563)

Private accounting. The profession whose members are accountants employed by a business firm or not-for-profit organization. (9)

Proceeds. The net amount available from discounting a note. (318, 436)

Process cost system. A type of cost system that accumulates costs for each of the various departments or processes within a factory. (824)

Product cost concept. A concept used in applying the cost-plus approach to product pricing in which only the costs of manufacturing the product, termed the product cost, are included in the cost amount to which the markup is added. (1034)

Product costs. The three components of manufacturing cost: direct materials, direct labor, and factory overhead costs. (790)

Product life cycle concept. A concept that assumes that a product passes through various stages from the time that it is introduced until the time it disappears from the market. (1038)

Profit center. A decentralized unit in which the manager has the responsibility and the authority to make decisions that affect both costs and revenues (and thus profits). (988)

Profit margin. A component of the rate of return on investment, computed as the ratio of operating income to sales. (998)

Profit-volume chart. A chart used to assist management in understanding the relationship between profit and volume. (915)

Profitability. The ability of a firm to earn income. (743)

Promissory note. A written promise to pay a sum in money on demand or at a definite time. (314)

Public accounting. The profession whose members render accounting services on a fee basis. (9)

Purchase method. The accounting method employed when a parent company acquires a controlling share of the voting stock of a subsidiary other than by the exchange of voting common stock. (638)

Purchase orders. Forms issued by the Purchasing Department to suppliers, requesting the delivery of materials. (825)

Purchase requisition. The form used to inform the Purchasing Department that items are needed by a business. (825)

Purchases discounts. An available discount taken by a buyer for early payment of an invoice; a contra account to Purchases. (156)

Purchases journal. The journal in which all items purchased on account are recorded. (243)

Purchases returns and allowances. Reductions in purchases, resulting from merchandise being returned to the seller or from the seller's reduction in the original purchase price; a contra account to Purchases. (157)

Q

Quick assets. The sum of cash, receivables, and marketable securities. (739)

R

Rate earned on common stockholders' equity. A measure of profitability computed by dividing net income, reduced by preferred dividend requirements, by common stockholders' equity. (744)

Rate earned on stockholders' equity. A measure of profitability computed by dividing net income by total stockholders' equity. (744)

Rate earned on total assets. A measure of the profitability of assets, without regard to the equity of creditors and stockholders in the assets. (743)

Rate of return on investment (ROI). A measure of managerial efficiency in the use of investments in assets, computed as operating income divided by invested assets. (997)

Real accounts. Balance sheet accounts. (117)

Realization. The sale of assets when a partnership is being liquidated. (503)

Receiving report. The form used by the Receiving Department to indicate that materials have been received and inspected. (825)

Relevant range. The range of activity over which changes in cost are of interest to management. (904)

Report form. The form of balance sheet with the liability and owner's equity sections presented below the asset section. (20)

Report form of balance sheet. A form of balance sheet with the liabilities and owner's equity sections below the asset section. (188)

Residual income. The excess of divisional operating income over a "minimum" amount of desired operating income. (1000)

Residual value. The estimated recoverable cost of a depreciable asset as of the time of its removal from service. (381)

Responsibility accounting. The process of measuring and reporting operating data by areas of responsibility. (987)

Retail inventory method. A method of inventory costing based on the relationship of the cost and the retail price of merchandise. (360)

Retained earnings. Net income retained in a corporation. (527)

Revenue expenditures. Expenditures that benefit only the current period. (389)

Revenues. Increases in owner's equity as a result of providing services or selling products to customers. (15, 38)

S

Sales discounts. An available discount granted by a seller for early payment of an invoice; a contra account to Sales. (154)

Sales journal. The journal in which all sales of merchandise on account are recorded. (236)

Sales mix. The relative distribution of sales among the various products available for sale. (918)

Sales returns and allowances. Reductions in sales, resulting from merchandise being returned by customers or from the seller's reduction in the original sales price; a contra account to Sales. (155)

Selling expenses. Expenses incurred directly in the sale of merchandise. (186)

Service department. A factory department that does not process materials directly but renders services for the benefit of production departments. (865)

Single-step income statement. An income statement in which the total of all expenses is deducted in one step from the total of all revenues. (188)

Sinking fund. Assets set aside in a special fund to be used for a specific purpose. (608)

Slide. The erroneous movement of all digits in a number, one or more spaces to the right or the left, such as writing $542 as $5,420. (56)

Sole proprietorship. An unincorporated business owned by one individual. (13)

Solvency. The ability of a firm to pay its debts as they come due. (738)

Special journals. Journals designed to be used for recording a single type of transaction. (236)

Standard cost. A detailed estimate of what a product should cost. (953)

Standard cost systems. Accounting systems that use standards for each element of manufacturing costs entering into the finished product. (953)

Stated value. A value approved by the board of directors of a corporation for no-par stock. Similar to par value. (528)

Statement of cash flows. A summary of the major cash receipts and cash payments for a period. (18, 680)

Statement of cost of goods manufactured. A separate statement for a manufacturer that reports the cost of goods manufactured during a period. (794)

Statement of owner's equity. A summary of the changes in the owner's equity of a business entity that have occurred during a specific period of time. (18)

Statement of stockholders' equity. A summary of the changes in the stockholders' equity of a corporation that have occurred during a specific period of time. (649)

Stock dividend. Distribution of a company's own stock to its shareholders. (570)

Stock split. A reduction in the par or stated value of a share of common stock and the issuance of a proportionate number of additional shares. (572)

Stockholders. The owners of a corporation. (526)

Stockholders' equity. The equity of the shareholders in a corporation. (527)

Straight-line depreciation method. A method of depreciation that provides for equal periodic depreciation expense over the estimated life of an asset. (383)

Strategic planning. The development of a long-range course of action to achieve enterprise goals. (779, 986)

Subsidiary company. The corporation that is controlled by a parent company. (638)

Subsidiary ledger. A ledger containing individual accounts with a common characteristic. (235)

Sum-of-the-years-digits depreciation method. A method of depreciation that provides for declining periodic depreciation over the estimated life of an asset. (384)

Sunk costs. Costs that are not affected by subsequent decisions. (787, 1026)

T

T account. A form of account resembling the letter T. (39)

Taxable income. The base on which the amount of income tax is determined. (558)

Temporary accounts. Revenue or expense accounts that are periodically closed to the income summary account; nominal accounts. (117)

Temporary differences. Differences between income before income tax and taxable income created by items that are recognized in one period for income statement purposes and in another period for tax purposes. Such differences reverse or turn around in later years. (558)

Temporary investments. Investments in securities that can be readily sold when cash is needed. (326)

Theoretical standards. Standards that represent levels of performance that can be achieved only under perfect operating conditions. (954)

Time tickets. The form on which the amount of time spent by each employee and the labor cost incurred for each individual job, or for factory overhead, are recorded. (827)

Time value of money concept. The concept that an amount of money invested today will earn income. (1056)

Total cost concept. A concept used in applying the cost-plus approach to product pricing in which all the costs of manufacturing the product plus the selling and administrative expenses are included in the cost amount to which the markup is added. (1032)

Total quality control (TQC). A quality control program that begins with product design and continues through production; it involves an ongoing commitment to improving product quality. (796)

Trade discounts. Special discounts from published list prices, offered by sellers to certain classes of buyers. (159)

Transfer price. The price charged one decentralized unit by another for the goods or services provided. (1001)

Transposition. The erroneous arrangement of digits in a number, such as writing $542 as $524. (56)

Treasury stock. A corporation's own outstanding stock that has been reacquired. (534)

Trial balance. A summary listing of the balances and the titles of the accounts in the ledger. (55)

U

Underapplied factory overhead. The amount of actual factory overhead in excess of the factory overhead applied to production during a period. (829)

Unit contribution margin. The dollars available from each unit of sales to cover fixed costs and provide operating profits. (909)

Units-of-production depreciation method. A method of depreciation that provides for depreciation expense based on the expected productive capacity of an asset. (383)

V

Variable cost concept. A concept used in applying the cost-plus approach to product pricing in which only the variable costs and expenses are included in the cost amount to which the markup is added. (1034)

Variable costing. A method of reporting variable and fixed costs that includes only the variable manufacturing costs in the cost of the product. (908)

Variable costs. Costs that vary in total dollar amount as the level of activity changes. (788, 904)

Variance from standard. Difference between standard cost and actual cost. (953)

Vertical analysis. The percentage analysis of component parts in relation to the total of the parts in a single financial statement. (734)

Voucher. A document that serves as evidence of authority to pay cash. (285)

Voucher register. The modified form of the purchases journal, in which all vouchers are recorded. (286)

Voucher system. Records, methods, and procedures employed in verifying and recording liabilities and paying and recording cash payments. (285)

W

Work in process inventory. The direct materials costs, the direct labor costs, and the factory overhead costs which have entered into the manufacturing process, but are associated with products that have not been finished. (793)

Work sheet. A working paper used to summarize adjusting entries and assist in the preparation of financial statements. (92)

Working capital. The excess of total current assets over total current liabilities at some point in time. (738)

Z

Zero-base budgeting. A concept of budgeting that requires all levels of management to start from zero and estimate budget data as if there had been no previous activities in their unit. (943)

*Pages numbers highlighted in color refer to real companies referenced in the annotations, which are found only in the Annotated Instructor's Edition.

CHECK FIGURES FOR SELECTED PROBLEMS

Prob.	Check Figure
1-1A	1. Apr. 30, Cash, $1,070
1-2A	1. Net income, $27,655
1-3A	1. Net income, $2,350
1-4A	2. Net income, $3,050
1-5A	3. Net income, $1,430
1-6A	1. Net income, $35,900
1-1B	1. Oct. 31, Cash, $1,595
1-2B	1. Net income, $18,300
1-3B	1. Net income, $2,470
1-4B	2. Net income, $2,675
1-5B	3. Net income, $2,105
1-6B	1. Net income, $93,375
2-1A	3. Total credits, $24,960
2-2A	3. Total debits, $36,350
2-3A	3. Total debits, $29,950
2-4A	4. Total credits, $100,040
2-5A	4. Total credits, $248,065
2-6A	7. Total debits, $33,338.10
2-7A	1. Total credits, $78,190
2-1B	3. Total debits, $27,100
2-2B	3. Total credits, $58,400
2-3B	3. Total debits, $20,125
2-4B	4. Total debits, $103,015
2-5B	4. Total credits, $304,950
2-6B	7. Total debits, $33,338.10
2-7B	1. Total debits, $103,090
3-3A	1. Adjusted trial balance totals, $66,980
3-6A	3. Adjusted trial balance totals, $468,720
3-3B	1. Adjusted trial balance totals, $66,980
3-6B	3. Adjusted trial balance totals, $470,500
4-2A	2. Net income, $9,710
4-3A	2. Net income, $3,561.11
4-4A	2. Net income, $42,870
4-5A	3. Net income, $22,424
4-2B	2. Net income, $25,490
4-3B	2. Net income, $3,692.71
4-4B	2. Net income, $44,830
4-5B	3. Net income, $22,590
Comp. Pb. 1	4. Net income, $5,235
5-5A	4. Trial balance totals, $200,590
5-6A	1. Cost of merchandise sold, $536,500
5-5B	4. Trial balance totals, $221,600
5-6B	1. Cost of merchandise sold, $480,000
6-1A	Net income, $47,750
6-2A	1. Net income, $70,000
6-3A	3. Total assets, $550,000
6-4A	1. Net income, $124,050
6-6A	1. Net income, $138,905
6-8A	Net income, $11,960
6-9A	1. Net income, $111,800
6-1B	Net income, $26,590
6-2B	1. Net income, $52,490
6-3B	3. Total assets, $390,200
6-4B	1. Net income, $124,050
6-6B	1. Net income, $139,805
6-8B	Net income, $50,420
6-9B	1. Net income, $106,050
Comp. Pb. 2	4. Net income, $49,100
7-1A	3. a. $14,720
7-2A	4. Total accounts receivable, $10,360
7-3A	6. Subsidiary ledger total, $9,775
7-4A	5. a. $42,177.05
7-5A	4. Total accounts payable, $9,460
7-6A	5. Total debits, $177,072
7-7A	3. $16,170
7-1B	3. a. $14,445
7-2B	4. Total accounts receivable, $10,360
7-3B	6. Subsidiary ledger total, $17,950
7-4B	5. a. $51,681.35
7-5B	4. Total accounts payable, $10,002
7-6B	5. Total credits, $172,415

Prob.	Check Figure
7-7B	3. a. $15,370
Comp. Pb. 3	7. Total debits, $151,334
8-1A	Adj. bal., $23,037.55
8-2A	1. Adj. bal., $9,898.02
8-3A	3. Total, $19,200
8-5A	4. Total, $23,500
8-6A	5. Total, $5,700
8-1B	1. Adj. bal., $17,629.90
8-2B	1. Adj. bal., $12,026.09
8-3B	4. Adj. bal., $17,615.50
8-5B	4. Total, $16,100
8-6B	5. Total, $17,650
9-2A	2. Note 3, (d) $6,352.83
9-4A	3. $662,300
9-5A	1. Bal. of Allow., Year 4, $11,850
9-6A	1. Net income, $99,500
9-2B	2. Note 1, (d) $15,130
9-4B	3. $320,300
9-5B	1. Bal. of Allow., Year 4, $8,750
9-6B	1. Net income, $99,700
10-1A	1. 1994 Net income, $60,000
10-2A	3. Net income, $98,000
10-3A	1. $11,256
10-4A	1. June 26 inv.: 3 at $235, 10 at $240
10-5A	LCM, $54,745
10-6A	2. a. Net income, $72,000
10-7A	1. $347,200
10-1B	1. 1994 Net income, $100,000
10-2B	3. Net income, $86,250
10-3B	1. $8,807
10-4B	1. Sep. 30 inv.: 25,000 at $6
10-5B	LCM, $54,605
10-6B	2. a. Net income, $77,000
10-7B	1. $207,200
11-6A	Accum. depr., June 30, 1996, $1,875
11-7A	Accum. depr., Sep. 30, 1994, $257,850
11-8A	1. Net income, $103,000
11-6B	Accum. depr., Dec. 31, 1995, $1,525
11-7B	Accum. depr., Mar. 31, 1994, $262,350
11-8B	1. Net income, $96,344
12-4A	2. d. $20,204.50
12-5A	1. Total employee earnings, $6,293.00
12-7A	4. $5,500
12-4B	2. d. $20,427.15
12-5B	1. Total employee earnings, $6,323.00
12-7B	4. $6,420
Comp. Pb. 4	5. Total assets, $997,390
13-1A	2. Third year net income, $58,650
13-2A	3. Loss, $30
13-3A	1995 income, $465,000
13-4A	Third year net income, $170,250
13-6A	3. Income from operations, $5,750
13-1B	2. Third year net income, $39,200
13-2B	3. Gain, $38
13-3B	1995 income, $275,000
13-4B	Third year net income, $66,130
13-6B	3. Income from operations, $15,850
14-1A	Total assets, $119,000
14-2A	2. f. Bode, $48,000
14-3A	2. Acosta Capital, 12/31, $87,500
14-4A	3. Total assets, $196,450
14-5A	2. Ark, $4,066.67
14-6A	1. Cash to Gray, $5,400
14-7A	2. Cash to Just, $60,000
14-1B	2. Total assets, $169,700
14-2B	2. f. Mair, $16,500
14-3B	2. Nall Capital, 12/31, $83,500
14-4B	3. Total assets, $231,450
14-5B	2. Fox, $3,733.33
14-6B	1. Cash to Gray, $400
14-7B	2. Cash to Anku, $10,000

Prob.	Check Figure	Prob.	Check Figure
15-1A	2. Preferred stock, $11	23-4A	Equivalent units, 23,870
15-2A	Total stockholders' equity, $1,625,375	23-5A	k. Cost of goods sold, $351,750
15-3A	2. Total stockholders' equity, $2,875,000	23-6A	3. Total assets, $982,640
15-4A	2. Total stockholders' equity, $1,506,500	23-7A	1. b. Equivalent units, 29,500 units
15-5A	2. Total stockholders' equity, $357,200	23-1B	1. Work in process, Aug. 31, $4,000
15-6A	3. Total assets, $524,700	23-2B	1. a. Equivalent units, 24,000
15-7A	D. Common stock, $28.50	23-3B	2. Work in process, June 30, $74,760
15-1B	2. Preferred stock, $7.50	23-4B	Equivalent units, 11,670
15-2B	Total stockholders' equity, $6,911,000	23-5B	k. Cost of goods sold, $485,250
15-3B	2. Total stockholders' equity, $3,131,000	23-6B	3. Total assets, $1,454,620
15-4B	2. Total stockholders' equity, $7,399,500	23-7B	1. b. Equivalent units, 17,500
15-5B	2. Total stockholders' equity, $381,450	24-2A	3. Present break-even point, 40,000 units
15-6B	3. Total assets, $560,100	24-3A	1. Anticipated break-even point, 10,000 units
15-7B	D. Common stock, $19.60	24-4A	Operating profit: 2. a. $90,000; 4. a. $45,000
16-1A	1. Year-end balances, 4th year, $40,500	24-5A	1. Break-even point, 7,500 units
16-2A	Net income, $69,000	24-6A	1. Income from operations, $180,000
16-3A	Retained earnings, 12/31, $940,000	24-2B	3. Present break-even point, 13,750 units
16-4A	3. Total stockholders' equity, $2,593,980	24-3B	1. Anticipated break-even point, 3,000 units
16-5A	4. Total retained earnings, $838,800	24-4B	Operating profit: 2. a. $80,000; 4. a. $40,000
16-7A	2. Net income, $105,600	24-5B	1. Break-even point, 11,000 units
16-1B	1. Year-end balance, 4th year, $13,500	24-6B	1. Income from operations, $100,000
16-2B	Net income, $120,000	25-1A	3. Total sales, $2,559,860
16-3B	Retained earnings, 12/31, $1,105,000	25-2A	1. Total sales, $6,720,000
16-4B	3. Total stockholders' equity, $1,633,250	25-3A	8. Net income, $473,200
16-5B	4. Total retained earnings, $1,253,940	25-4A	1. April excess, $75,700
16-7B	2. Net income, $105,600	25-5A	2. Total assets, $560,500
17-1A	1. Plan 2, $2.00 EPS	25-7A	Volume variance, $3,000 U
17-4A	2. 1995 Premium on Bonds, $371,850	25-8A	2. Volume variance, $5,160 F
17-5A	4. carrying amt. of bonds, Dec. 31, 1995, $4,436,355	25-1B	3. Total sales, $6,021,400
17-1B	1. Plan 3, $2.24 EPS	25-2B	1. Total sales, $8,595,000
17-4B	2. 1995 Discount on Bonds, $287,280	25-3B	8. Net income, $407,550
17-5B	4. carrying amt. of bonds, Dec. 31, 1995, $22,095,305	25-4B	1. April excess, $82,200
Comp. Pb. 5	2. a. Net income, $400,950	25-5B	2. Total assets, $1,151,100
18-2A	2. Total assets, $1,478,700	25-7B	Volume variance, $2,550 U
18-3A	2. b. Goodwill, $90,000	25-8B	2. Volume variance, $10,400 U
18-4A	4. Net income, $250,000	26-1A	1. Income before income taxes, $43,750
18-5A	2. Total assets, $3,242,490	26-2A	1. Departmental margin: 10, $3,250
18-6A	Total assets, $1,017,200	26-3A	1. Departmental margin: A, $118,400
18-7A	Total assets, $3,190,000	26-4A	Income from operations, Dept. C, $41,540
18-2B	2. Total assets, $978,050	26-5A	2. Division G: ROI, 18%
18-3B	2. b. Goodwill, $90,000	26-6A	1. ROI, 15%
18-4B	4. Net income, $367,800	26-8A	2. Division A: ROI, 22%
18-5B	2. Total assets, $2,024,080	26-9A	1. Division A: 1994 ROI, 19.6%
18-6B	Total assets, $1,007,820	26-1B	1. Income before income taxes, $60,900
18-7B	Total assets, $3,095,000	26-2B	1. Departmental margin: Dept. 17, $3,650
19-1A	Net cash flow from operating activities, $93,200	26-3B	1. Departmental margin: L, $103,970
19-2A	Net cash flow from operating activities, $202,900	26-4B	Income from operations, Dept. A, $67,148
19-3A	Net cash flow from operating activities, $73,100	26-5B	2. Division 1, ROI, 15%
19-4A	Net cash flow from operating activities, $700	26-6B	1. ROI, 15%
19-5A	Net cash flow from operating activities, $67,000		3. Proposal 2, ROI, 17.5%
19-6A	Net cash flow from operating activities, $93,200	26-8B	2. Division X: ROI, 20%
19-7A	Net cash flow from operating activities, $83,960	26-9B	1. Division B, 1994 ROI, 16.8%
19-1B	Net cash flow from operating activities, $101,200		2. Division B, 1994, $17,100
19-2B	Net cash flow from operating activities, $137,100		3. Division B, 1994, 10%
19-3B	Net cash flow from operating activities, $76,950	27-1A	1. Gain from warehouse, $60,000
19-4B	Net cash flow from operating activities, $61,600	27-2A	1. Net cost reduction, $250,000
19-5B	Net cash flow from operating activities, $84,300	27-3A	1. Gain: A, $100,000; B, $96,000
19-6B	Net cash flow from operating activities, $101,200	27-4A	1. Net advantage to process further, $1,500
19-7B	1. Net cash flow from operating activities, $82,460	27-5A	1. Net advantage of further processing per batch, $10,000
20-5A	4. Working capital, $199,500	27-6A	6. a. Loss from offer, $250
20-5B	4. Working capital, $187,875	27-1B	1. Gain from warehouse, $160,000
Comp. Pb. 6	1. Net cash flow from operating activities, $25,000	27-2B	1. Net cost reduction, $340,000
21-7A	1. Cost of goods manufactured, $1,768,800	27-3B	1. Gain: A, $70,000; X, $55,000
21-8A	1. Cost of goods manufactured, $978,000	27-4B	1. Net advantage from further processing, $1,875
21-7B	1. Cost of goods manufactured, $345,300	27-5B	1. Net advantage of further processing per batch, $13,500
21-8B	1. Cost of goods manufactured, $563,000	27-6B	6. a. Gain from offer, $1,500
22-2A	4. Balance in finished goods, $11,590	28-1A	1. b. Project P, $5,510
22-4A	5. Total assets, $815,225	28-2A	1. b. Project G, $17,650
22-5A	3. Total debits, $1,150,585	28-3A	1. Project C, $40,680
22-2B	4. Balance in finished goods, $22,825	28-4A	1. a. Project I, $15,840
22-4B	5. Total assets, $509,986	28-5A	2. Project A, $10,000
22-5B	3. Total debits, $2,017,680	28-1B	1. b. Project X, $4,686
23-1A	1. Work in process, Aug. 31, $17,250	28-2B	1. b. Project E, $17,250
23-2A	1. a. Equivalent units, 34,500	28-3B	1. Project X, $5,960
23-3A	2. Work in process, Nov. 30, $85,377	28-4B	1. a. Project B, $22,450
		28-5B	2. Project I, $9,280

Abbreviations and Acronyms Commonly Used in Business and Accounting

AAA	American Accounting Association
ABC	Activity-based costing
ACRS	Accelerated Cost Recovery System
AICPA	American Institute of Certified Public Accountants
CIA	Certified Internal Auditor
CIM	Computer-integrated manufacturing
CMA	Certified Management Accountant
CPA	Certified Public Accountant
Cr.	Credit
Dr.	Debit
EFT	Electronic funds transfer
EPS	Earnings per share
FAF	Financial Accounting Foundation
FASB	Financial Accounting Standards Board
FEI	Financial Executives Institute
FICA tax	Federal Insurance Contributions Act tax
FIFO	First-in, first-out
FOB	Free on board
GAAP	Generally accepted accounting principles
GASB	Governmental Accounting Standards Board
GNP	Gross National Product
IMA	Institute of Management Accountants
IRC	Internal Revenue Code
IRS	Internal Revenue Service
JIT	Just-in-time
LIFO	Last-in, first-out
Lower of C or M	Lower of cost or market
MACRS	Modified Accelerated Cost Recovery System
n/30	Net 30
n/eom	Net, end-of-month
P/E Ratio	Price-earnings ratio
POS	Point of sale
ROI	Return on investment
SEC	Securities and Exchange Commission
TQC	Total quality control

Classification of Accounts

Account Title	Account Classification	Normal Balance	Financial Statement
Accounts Payable	Current liability	Credit	Balance sheet
Accounts Receivable	Current asset	Debit	Balance sheet
Accumulated Depreciation	Plant asset	Credit	Balance sheet
Accumulated Depletion	Plant asset	Credit	Balance sheet
Advertising Expense	Operating expense	Debit	Income statement
Allowance for Doubtful Accounts	Current asset	Credit	Balance sheet
Amortization Expense	Operating expense	Debit	Income statement
Appropriation for _____	Stockholders' equity	Credit	Retained earnings statement/ Balance sheet
Bonds Payable	Long-term liability	Credit	Balance sheet
Building	Plant asset	Debit	Balance sheet
_____ Capital	Owners' equity	Credit	Statement of owner's equity/ Balance sheet
Capital Stock	Stockholders' equity	Credit	Balance sheet
Cash	Current asset	Debit	Balance sheet
Cash Dividends	Stockholders' equity	Debit	Retained earnings statement
Cash Dividends Payable	Current liability	Credit	Balance sheet
Common Stock	Stockholders' equity	Credit	Balance sheet
Cost of Merchandise (Goods) Sold	Cost of merchandise (goods sold)	Debit	Income statement
Deferred Income Tax	Current liability/Long-term liability	Credit	Balance sheet
Depletion Expense	Operating expense	Debit	Income statement
Discount on Bonds Payable	Long-term liability	Debit	Balance sheet
Discounts Lost	Other expense	Debit	Income statement
Dividend Income	Other income	Credit	Income statement
Dividends	Stockholders' equity	Debit	Retained earnings statement
Donated Capital	Stockholders' equity	Credit	Balance sheet
Employees Federal Income Tax Payable	Current liability	Credit	Balance sheet
Equipment	Plant asset	Debit	Balance sheet
Exchange Gain	Other income	Credit	Income statement
Exchange Loss	Other expense	Debit	Income statement
Factory Overhead (Overapplied)	Deferred credit	Credit	Balance sheet (interim)
Factory Overhead (Underapplied)	Deferred debit	Debit	Balance sheet (interim)
Federal Income Tax Payable	Current liability	Credit	Balance sheet
Federal Unemployment Tax Payable	Current liability	Credit	Balance sheet
FICA Tax Payable	Current liability	Credit	Balance sheet
Finished Goods	Current asset	Debit	Balance sheet
Gain on Disposal of Plant Assets	Other income	Credit	Income statement
Gain on Redemption of Bonds	Extraordinary item	Credit	Income statement
Gain on Sale of Investments	Other income	Credit	Income statement
Goodwill	Intangible asset	Debit	Balance sheet
Income Tax	Income tax	Debit	Income statement
Income Tax Payable	Current liability	Credit	Balance sheet
Insurance Expense	Operating expense	Debit	Income statement
Interest Expense	Other expense	Debit	Income statement
Interest Income	Other income	Credit	Income statement
Interest Receivable	Current asset	Debit	Balance sheet
Investment in Bonds	Investment	Debit	Balance sheet
Investment in Stocks	Investment	Debit	Balance sheet
Investment in Subsidiary	Investment	Debit	Balance sheet